ELECTRONIC AND ATOMIC COLLISIONS

XIth International Conference on the
Physics of Electronic and Atomic Collisions
29 August - 4 September, 1979
Kyoto International Conference Hall, Kyoto, Japan

Abstracts of Contributed Papers

Edited by

K. Takayanagi and N. Oda

1979

NORTH-HOLLAND PUBLISHING COMPANY - AMSTERDAM · NEW YORK · OXFORD

Local organizers of the Eleventh International Conference on the Physics of Electronic and Atomic Collisions are Science Council of Japan and The Society for Atomic Collision Research (Japan).

They are indebted to the following sponsors:
International Union of Pure and Applied Physics,
Japan World Exposition Commemorative Fund.

Generous donations from many companies and societies are greatly appreciated. A list of names of these companies and societies will be distributed with a participants list at the conference.

Published by:
The Society for Atomic Collision Research (Japan)

Sole distributors worldwide:
NORTH-HOLLAND PUBLISHING COMPANY
AMSTERDAM/NEW YORK/OXFORD

ISBN 0 444 85393 6

Printed in Japan 1979

PREFACE

This is the book of abstracts of contributed papers accepted by the Eleventh International Conference on the Physics of Electronic and Atomic Collisions. The conference is the eleventh in a series that started in 1958 at the New York University. The abbreviation ICPEAC is often used for this series of conferences. The sites of the previous ICPEAC meetings were: New York (1958), Boulder (1961), London (1963), Québec (1965), Leningrad (1967), Cambridge (USA) (1969), Amsterdam (1971), Beograd (1973), Seattle (1975), and Paris (1977).

This is the first ICPEAC held outside North America and Europe. The number of accepted contributed papers is 528, and that of invited papers is 72 including papers reported at symposia. A collection of these invited papers will be published after the conference.

All the contributed papers, other than those presented at the symposia, are reported at poster sessions. In the Paris ICPEAC (1977), we collected responses to questionaires on ICPEAC. It was found that the idea of "contributed papers in poster sessions" was supported by majority of the conference participants. We sincerely hope that this poster session formula will be successful. However, it has both merits and demerits. These must be carefully evaluated at the end of the conference.

Editors of this book wish to express their gratitude to the members of the International Program Committee and those of the Local Subcommittee for Scientific Programs for their dedicated efforts in the selection of papers, the arrangement of sessions in the program, and in the preparation of this Book of Abstracts.

July 1979

K. Takayanagi
N. Oda

INTERNATIONAL CONFERENCE ON THE PHYSICS OF ELECTRONIC AND ATOMIC COLLISIONS ORGANIZATION 1977–1979

OFFICERS

Chairman

J. Kistemaker
FOM Institute for Atomic and
Molecular Physics
Kruislaan 407
Amsterdam-Watergraafsmeer
THE NETHERLANDS

Vice Chairman

R. F. Stebbings
Department of Space Physics
and Astronomy
Rice University
Houston, Texas 77001
USA

Secretary

J. S. Risley
Department of Physics
North Carolina State University
Raleigh
North Carolina 27650
USA

Treasurer

F. J. de Heer
FOM Institute for Atomic and
Molecular Physics
Kruislaan 407
Amsterdam-Watergraafsmeer
THE NETHERLANDS

Treasurer-Elect

G. Watel
Service de Physique Atomique
CEN. Saclay B. P. n°2
91190 Gif-Sur-Yvette
FRANCE

EXECUTIVE COMMITTEE

Officers and

V. V. Afrosimov
A. F. Ioffe Physico-Technical
Institute, USSR Academy of
Sciences, Leningrad
USSR

M. Barat
Laboratoire des Collisions
Atomiques et Moléculaires
Université Paris-Sud, 91405 Orsay
FRANCE

I. V. Hertel
Fachbereich Physik
Freie Universität Berlin
Boltzmannstr. 20, 1000 Berlin
GERMANY

M. Inokuti
Argonne National Laboratory
9700 South Cass Av.
Argonne, Illinois 60439
USA

F. H. Read
Department of Physics
University of Manchester
Manchester M13 9PL
UK

F. T. Smith
SRI International
Menlo Park, California 94025
USA

K. Takayanagi
Institute of Space and Aeronautical
Science
University of Tokyo
Komaba 4-6-1, Meguro-ku, Tokyo 153
JAPAN

GENERAL COMMITTEE

AUSTRALIA — E. Weigold

BELGIUM — F. Brouillard

CANADA — G. W. F. Drake*
P. Marmet*

DENMARK — T. Andersen*

FRANCE — M. Barat*
J. Durup
R. I. Hall
H. Van Regemorter*
G. Watel

GERMANY — I. V. Hertel*
H. Hotop
P. H. Mokler
N. Stolterfoht*
J. P. Toennies*

INDIA — N. C. Sil*

ITALY — F. A. Gianturco

JAPAN — H. Suzuki*
K. Takayanagi
H. Tawara

NETHERLANDS — F. J. de Heer*
J. Kistemaker
M. J. van der Wiel*

UNITED KINGDOM — J. S. Briggs
K. T. Dolder*
B. Gilbody
F. H. Read*
M. J. Seaton*

USA — D. H. Crandall
A. Gallagher
M. Inokuti*
J. H. Macek*
J. T. Park*
D. Pritchard
J. S. Risley
A. Russek
F. T. Smith*
R. F. Stebbings
H. S. Taylor

USSR — V. V. Afrosimov*
R. Damburg
G. F. Drukarev*
L. P. Presnyakov*

YUGOSLAVIA — L. Vušković

(*term expiring in 1979)

PROGRAM COMMITTEE
Executive Committee and

A. E. de Vries
M. Gavrila
H. G. M. Heideman
C. J. Joachain
Y. Kaneko
J. Los

A. Niehaus
G. Nienhuis
F. W. Saris
I. Shimamura
M. J. van der Wiel

LOCAL COMMITTEE

K. Takayanagi, Chairman
H. Suzuki, Secretary
Y. Kaneko, Treasurer
T. Arikawa
K. Kodera
T. Makita
N. Oda

LOCAL SUBCOMMITTEE
FOR SCIENTIFIC PROGRAMS

N. Oda, Chairman
H. Inouye
K. Kuchitsu
M. Matsuzawa
F. Nishimura
S. Ohtani
I. Shimamura
H. Tawara
T. Watanabe

CONTENTS

3. Molecular (Dissociative) Photoionization

II Electron-Atom Collisions

8. Inelastic Scattering: Theory. I

13. Ionization of Ions and Dielectronic Recombination

14. Autoionization and Resonances

15. Inner-Shell Excitation and Ionization

III. Electron-Molecule Collisions

21. Electronic Excitation and Ionization

IV. Ion (Atom)-Atom Collisions

33. Electron Detachment

38. Inner-Shell Ionization: X-Ray Spectra and Auger Spectra

VI. Special Topics

I. Photon Impact

RESONANCE PHOTOABSORPTION BY THE TWO-ELECTRON SYSTEMS BETWEEN THE n = 2 AND n = 3 THRESHOLDS

V.S. Senashenko   and   A. Wagué

Institute of Nuclear Physics, Moscow State University;
Moscow 117234; USSR

The photoabsorption by the two-electron systems of photons with an energy close to the excitation energy of the autoionizing states converging to the n = 3 threshold of the H-like ion are of great interest[1,2] since the autoionising levels excited in this energy region can subsequently decay to both the ground state and excited states of the residual ion. In this case of simple atomic systems we are faced with the multichannel problem of photoionization. A qualitative analysis of photoabsorption of the He-atom in the vicinity of the $(3s3p)^1P$ autoionizing state was made by Fano and Cooper[3]. More detailed calculations of the resonance photoabsorption cross sections of He in this energy region are discussed in[4].

In the present report a further analysis is made of the resonance photoabsorption by two-electron systems between the n=2 and n=3 thresholds. Energies and eigenwidths of the $^1P^{(-)}$ autoionising le vels converging to the n=3 threshold as well as the branching ratios characterizing the ion yield in the ground and excited states formed in the decay of autoionizing levels are calculated on the basis of the diagonalization approximation[5] for the He atom and Li$^+$ ions. The asymptotic dependences of the resonance photoabsorption characteristics upon atomic number Z are obtained. It is shown that the effect of the coupling between the open channels on the resonance characteristics decreases with increasing Z which is in agreement with the conclusions of the paper[6].
The $(3s3p)^1P$ resonance is studied most comprehensively. Calculations are made of all parameters extracted from the experimental data. The photoabsorption cross section in the vicinity of this resonance is also obtained. It follows from a comparison of our calculations with the experimental data[2] and the close-coupling calculations[7] that the diagonalization approximation can be applied for describing the photoabsorption by two-electron systems in the considered energy region. It is shown that in the multichannel problem of photoionization the effect of the direct coupling between continua on the various characteristics of the photoionization process is different. Therefore, dissimilar requirements, in terms of their adequacy, must be imposed on theoretical methods used in calculations of the total photoabsorption cross sections, branching ratios and the angular and energy distributions of photoelectrons.

REFERENCES

1. R. P. Madden and K. Codling. Astrophys.J. 141, 364(1965)
2. P. Dhez and D.L. Ederer, J. Phys. 6B, L59 (1973).
3. U. Fano and J.W. Cooper, Phys.Rev. 137A, 1364 (1965)
4. A. Wagué and V.S. Senashenko. The VII All-Union Conference on Electron-Atom Collisions. Thesis. Petrozavodsk, p.31 (1978)
5. V.V. Balashov, S.G. Grishanova, I.M. Kruglova and V.S. Senashenko. Optica Spectrosc. 28, 859 (1970)
6. L.P. Presnyakov A.M. Urnov, JETP, 68, 61 (1975)
7. P.G. Burke and A.J. Taylor , J. Phys. 2B, 44 (1969).

PHOTOIONIZATION OF TWO-ELECTRON SYSTEMS ACCOMPANIED BY
EXCITATION OF THE RESIDUAL ION TO THE STATES WITH n = 2

U.I.Safronova [+],V.S.Senashenko [++], D.S.Victorov [+]

+ Institute of Spectroscopy, USSR Academy of Sciences
    Podol'sky district, Moscow, USSR

++Institute of Nuclear Physics, Moscow State University,
    Moscow 117234 USSR

New experimental studies of the photoionization of the helium atom with the excitation of the residual ion to the states
with n=2 have again drawn attention to the problem of photoionization of two-electron systems accompanied by excitation of the
residual ion. [1] A comparison between the experimental data [1]
and the results of theoretical studies [2,3] shows that neither the
close method coupling nor the simpler calculations are capable
of reproducing the observed dependence of the ratio of the cross
sections for helium ionization by photons with energies E from
65 to 110 ev when the helium ion is either in the ground state
or is excited to the states with n=2.

The direct photoionization of two-electron systems accompanied by the excitation of the residual ion to the states with
n=2 is of a purely correlative nature.In the single -particle
approximation, when the wave functions for the initial and final
state are the eigenfunctions for one and the same Hamiltonian
the probability of the process is zero. Taking into account
electron correlations is the necessary requirement for obtaining correct results.

In the present paper, the cross sections for the photoionization of helium and helium-like ions have been obtained taking
into account all possible transitions to the continuum adjacent
to the 2s and 2p states of the hydrogen-like ion. The calculations have been performed in first-order many-body perturbation
theory with the electron correlations in the initial and final
state taken into account [4], and also with the variational wave
functions [5]. We have studied in detail the influence of transitions to the various states of the continuum upon the relative
yield of ions in the excited states formed in photionization
of helium -like ions. The effect of electron correlations in the
initial and final states in the partial photoionization cross
sections is discussed. The obtained results are compared with

the experimental date [1] and the results of other calculations
2-5 .

1. F.Wuilleumier et.al. X‹ICPEAC, Abstracts of papers, Paris,
   p.1170, (1977)

2. V.L.Jacobs and P.G.Burke. J.Phys. 4B, L67, (1972).

3. E.E.Salpeter and M.H.Zaidi Phys. Rev. 125,248, (1962).

4. M.Chatterji and B.Talukdar Phys. Lett 55A, 143, (1975).

5. A.V.Awdeev et.al. The VII All-Union Conference on Electron-
   Atom Collisions, Thesis. Petrozavodsk, p.32, (1978).

RESONANCE PHOTOABSORPTION OF THREE-ELECTRON ATOMIC SYSTEMS

U.I.Safronova

Institute of Spectroscopy, USSR Academy of Sciences,
Podol'sky district, Moscow, USSR

V.S.Senashenko
Institute of Nuclear Physics, Moscow State University,
Moscow 117234,USSR

Not so long ago the experimental investigation of the resonance photoabsorption of three-electron systems was confined to
an examination of the absorption spectra of atoms in the ground
state [1]. The new experimental technique extended the range of
application of the photoabsorption method for studying the autoionising states. In recent years, the resonance photoabsorption
of the Li atoms in the lowest-lying excited state [2] and the photoabsorption spectra of other three-electron systems [3] have been
investigated.The excitation energies of a large number of the
autoionising levels and the intensities of the corresponding
resonance lines were obtained [2-3]. An analysis of the observed
spectra permitted one to determine the sign and to estimate the
order of magnitude of the Fano parameter q for some resonances.
In the present work, the excitation energies,autoionizing width,
the radiation transition probabilities and the Fano parameter of
autoionizing states belonging to the ($1s2s^2$), ($1s2s2p$) and
($1s2p^2$) configurations of three-electron atomic systems with
atomic number $Z \leq 30$ are obtained on the basis of the perturbation theory with respect to $1/Z$. The calculations of the excitation energy of autoionizing states were performed in the second order perturbation theory with respect to $1/Z$ and the
relativistic corrections accounted for by the Breit operator [4].
For the levels degenerate in the zero-order approximation,con-
figuration mixing effects were taken into account. The autoionization widths were obtained in the first order perturbation
theory.

The calculations show that for $Z \simeq 20$ the values of the
probabilities of autoionization and radiation decays of the
autoionization states we considered become close. In a number
of cases when in the LS coupling the direct transitions to the
continuum are prohibited by the selection rules the autoionization widths turn out to be non-zero due to relativistic effects
and increase with Z as $\alpha^4 Z^6$ (α is the fine structure cons-

tant) whereas the probabilities of the inter combinative transitions are increasing as $\alpha^7 z^{10}$.

In accordance with the papers [5-6] the Fano parameter is
equal to the relation between the real and imaginary part of
amplitude of the autoionization level photoexcitation and calculated with the wave functions of the initial and final states
which included the electron interaction in the first order per-
turbation theory. The calculations give $|q| \gg 1$ for the most
considered resonances which corresponds to the practically symmetrical profile of photoabsorption lines and agrees qualitatively with the experimental data [1-3]. For the resonances
corresponding to the 1s electron excitation in the nonrelativistic limit at $Z \to \infty$ the parameter q increases in proportion to Z . The calculations of the excitation energies, parameters q , probabilities of autoionization and radiation decays of the autoionization states of three-electron atomic
systems are discussed alongside with the experimental photoabsorption spectra [1-3].

1. D.L.Ederer et al.Phys. Rev. Lett.25,1537, (1970)

2. T.J.McIlrath et.al. Phys. Rev.Lett. 38,1390,(1977)

3. E.T.Kennedy et.al. Phys. Lett. 64A, 37,(1977)

4. U.I.Safronova and V.S.Senashenko J.Phys.11B, 2623,(1978)

5. S.V.Khristenko. Optica and Spectr. 39, 443, (1975)

6. U.I.Safronova, V.S.Senashenko and S.V.Khristenko. Optica
   and Spectr. 45, 833, (1978).

INTERACTION OF QUASI-STATIONARY STATES OF THE TYPE "PARTICLE-HOLE" AND "TWO PARTICLES-TWO HOLES" IN THE SPECTRA OF THE ATOMS OF HEAVY INERT GASES: NEON

S.I. Strakhova   and   V. A.   Shakirov

Institute ofNuclear Physics, Moscow State University;Moscow 117234;

U S S R

The present study is the continuation of a series of investigations carried out in Moscow State University and concerned with the excitation of autoionizing states of the atoms of inert gases by photons and electrons[1]. The present work deals with the influence of quasi-stationary states of the type "two particles-two holes" upon the characteristics of the autoionizing states of the type "particle-hole" excited by photons.

In order to determine the wave function of an atom at an excitation energy above the threshold of ionization, we have used the method of strong coupling of open and closed channels in the Bloch integral formulation[2]. When using this method, one does not have to struggle with the technical problem of searching for the closely located narrow resonances. In the presented work, the K-matrix determining, on the energy surface, the cross section for electron scattering by an ion explicitly enters into the set of integral equations; such an approach simplifies the sturcutre of a computational program.

We have calculated the characteristics of the lowest resonances in the spectrum of photoabsorption of neon, taking into account the strong coupling between the $2s^{-1}3p^1P$, $2p^{-2}3s3p^1P$, $2p^{-1}$ ϵs^1P and $2p^{-1}$ ϵd ^1P configurations. As the basis functions for the description of states in closed channels the Hartree-Fock functions are used. Two sets of basis functions are employed to describe open channels: functions in the Herman-Skillman potential and in the Hartree-Fock frozen-core approximation. Inlike the authors of ref.[3], we aim, along with a quantitative description of the resonance characteristics, at elucidating the effects of coupling between open channels, closed channel coupling through the continuum, effect of "prediagonalization" of the continua upon the K-matrix in open channel space, sensitivity of the resonance characteristics in photoelectron spectra to these effects, as well as to the basis functions and basis dimension.

1. V.V. Balashov et al., J.Phys.B: Atom.Molec.Phys.(to be published); Opt. spectrosc. (to be published), Phys.Lett.67A, 266(1978).
2. C. Bloch, "E. Fermi"-XXXVI Corso, C.E.N. de Saclay, 394(1966).
3. T.M. Lüke, J.Phys.B:Atom.Molec.Phys.11,14,2457(1978).

RESONANCE PARTIAL WIDTHS AND PARTIAL PHOTOIONIZATION RATES USING THE ROTATED
COORDINATE METHOD

T. Noro, H. Taylor, and R. Yaris

University of Southern California
Department of Chemistry
University Park
Los Angeles, CA 90007, U.S.A.

The Rotated Coordinate Method has long been known to give the energy and
total (not partial) width of resonances. In this paper we shall show how the
rotated wavefunction can yield partial width information. No other discrete basis
set diagonalization method has ever been able to accomplish this. Results of
calculations on a model problem shall be presented. The relation of this method
to the stabilization method shall be made quite precise and stabilization will
appear as the first step in the most simple and most physical way of carrying out,
for resonance properties, the RCM computations. It will also be shown how, when
RCM is combined with quantum electrodynamics, a single complex resonance eigenvalue obtained from a discrete set diagonalization will yield the photoionization
rate.

The associated eigenfunction will be shown to yield the partial, channel to
channel, photoionization rates. The method holds great promise for treating inner-
shell and regular photoionization problems.

EXCITATION OF CII LINES BY PHOTOIONIZATION OF NEUTRAL CARBON

H. Hofmann and E. Trefftz

Max-Planck-Institut für Physik und Astrophysik
Föhringer Ring 6, 8 Munich 40, FRG

In the cool dilute plasma of a cometary coma the observed visible spectra is excited by solar radiation. In the ultraviolet the fluorescence mechanism works only when a solar emission line of the correct frequency (taking account of Doppler shift according to the comets motion) enables the excitation. Otherwise another process must be found to explain the observed ultraviolet emission. We tried to explain the C^+ $2s2p^2$ ^2D - $2s^22p$ $^2P^o$ line at 1335 $\overset{o}{A}$ by inner shell photoionization of neutral carbon. Excitation of C^+ $2s2p^2$ ^2D by ionization from carbon ground state is a highly indirect process which requires careful treatment of electron correlation and coupling of the possible channels of the $(C^+ + e)$-system. Multi-configuration Hartree-Fock wave functions were used to describe the target C^+ [1]. The close coupling program of Eissner and Seaton [2] gave the wave functions for the additional electron before and after ionization. The five lowest terms of C^+: $2s^22p$ $^2P^o$, $2s2p^2$ ^4P, ^2D, ^2S, ^2P were taken into account. The scattering matrix of the $(C^+ + e)$ system as well as the photoionization cross section shows rich resonance structure corresponding to Rydberg series converging to the different $2s2p^2$ target terms. The resonance structure is being analyzed with Fano-Lu plots. Fig. 1 gives the total photoionization cross section into the C^+ $2s2p^2$ ^2D and ^4P state. ^4P can be reached directly by removing a 2s electron from neutral carbon ground state. The relative size of the two cross sections shows the strength of the coupling. To calculate the photoionization rates the ultraviolet radiation of the sun was taken from [3]. At a distance of 1 AU ($\sim 1.5 \times 10^8$ km) the rates are (in units of 10^{-9} sec^{-1}): 540 for $2s^22p$ $^2P^o$, 13.5 for $2s2p^2$ ^4P, 1.05 for $2s2p^2$ ^2D, 0.13 for $2s2p^2$ ^2S, and 1.87 for $2s2p^2$ ^2P.

1)   W. Dankwort, E. Trefftz, Astron. Astrophys. 65, 93 (1978)

2)   W. Eissner, M.J. Seaton, J. Phys. B: Atom. Molec. Phys. 5, 2187 (1972)

3)   J.C. Timothy, in "The Solar Output and Its Variation", ed. O.R. White, Colo. Ass. Univ. Press, Boulder 1977, p. 237, and J.E. Manson, ibid, p. 261.

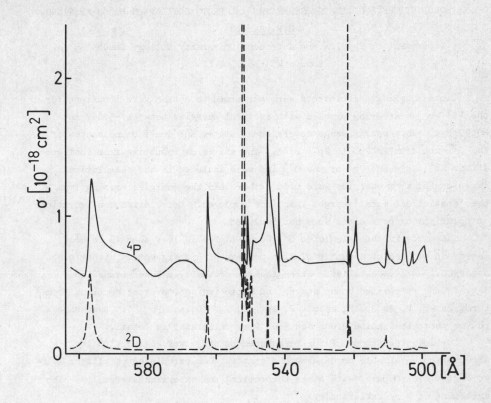

Fig. 1.

Photoionization cross section σ
of neutral carbon in its ground
state into excited states $2s2p^2\ ^4P$
and ^2D of C^+, as a function of
photon wave length.

O IV: BOUND STATES, OSCILLATOR STRENGTHS AND PHOTO IONIZATION CROSS SECTIONS.

H.E. Saraph

Department of Physics and Astronomy University College London

London WC1 E6BT, U.K.

Close coupling calculations were performed to obtain wave functions for the $(O^{4+} + e^-)$ scattering problem with incident energies between -5.667 and $+0.95$ Ryd. This energy range covers bound states and quasi bound states of the O^{3+} ion from $2s^2 2p^2$ to $2p^2(^3P)4d$. The six terms resulting from configurations $2s^2$, $2s2p$ and $2p^2$ of the O^{4+} ion were included in the calculations. Experimental term energies were used rather than the energies arising from the 'statistical model' target functions employed. Correlation configurations or polarization potentials were not included.

The error in the calculated O^{3+} bound states is less than 1% in most cases and we predict a number of high members of Rydberg series hitherto not observed. We give oscillator strengths for optically allowed transitions between the calculated bound states and photo ionization cross sections from terms $2s^2 2p\ ^2P$, $2s^2 3p\ ^2P$, $2s2p^2\ ^4P$, $2p^3\ ^4S$, $2p^3\ ^2D$, and $2p^3\ ^2P$. Resonances in the photo ionization cross sections were calculated in detail.

Our identifications of the resonances do not always agree with the few observations available on quasi bound states. Our calculated oscillator strengths are compared with other theoretical and experimental results. The agreement is very satisfactory.

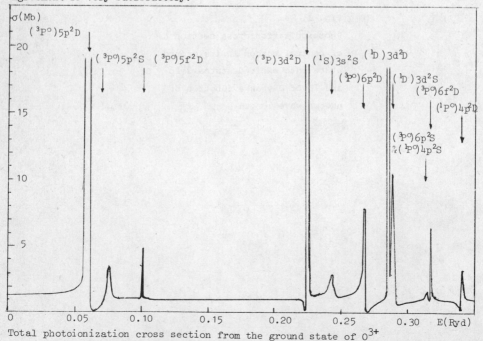

Total photoionization cross section from the ground state of O^{3+}

BOUND-BOUND AND BOUND-FREE TRANSITIONS INVOLVING HIGH RYDBERG STATES

Hoang Binh Dy and Henri Van Regemorter

Observatoire de Paris, 92190 Meudon, France

The interpretation of many recent studies of Rydberg states and of multiphoton processes requires the calculation of many bound-bound and bound-free matrix elemets between non hydrogenic wave functions. In a recent paper[1] we have proposed a very simple semi-analytical method for calculating the radial matrix elements between bound states in the Coulomb approximation. Contrary to previous method like the method of Bates and Damgaard, it can be applied very easily for transitions involving high Rydberg states and consequently for the calculation of the polarizabilities of these states. It avoids all numerical quadrature which become inefficient and lengthy for intermediate values of the effective quantum number ν and fail for high values.

The same principles are now applied to photoionization processes of excited atoms. In this case the method of Burgess and Seaton[2] can only be applied for the photoionization from low excited states, as shown by Peach[3] who has computed the radial integrals by numerical quadrature for $\nu \leqslant 12$. The proposed method is valid in the region close to threshold where the photoionization cross section can be obtained as an extrapolation of discrete oscillator strengths as well as in the case of larger values of the ejected electron energies. Results for bound-bound and for bound-free transitions will be presented.

1. H. Van Regemorter, Hoang Binh Dy and M. Prud'homme, J. Phys. B 12, 1053, (1979).

2. A. Burgess and M.J. Seaton, Mon. Not. R. Astron. Soc. 120, 121 (1960).

3. G. Peach, Mem. R. Astron. Soc. 71, 13 (1967).

ENERGY DEPENDENCE OF LOW ENERGY PHOTOELECTRON ANGULAR
DISTRIBUTIONS AND MATRIX ELEMENTS FOR HIGH Z ELEMENTS

Young Soon Kim, Akiva Ron, H. K. Tseng and R. H. Pratt

Department of Physics and Astronomy, University of Pittsburgh
Pittsburgh, Pennsylvania 15260, U. S. A.

It is known from experiment and theory that even at low energies there are
cases with big deviations from nonrelativistic (NR) dipole predictions for photoelectron angular distributions. We have now studied systematically both the matrix elements and the resulting angular distributions for photoelectrons ejected
from various shells of Uranium and Mercury, as a function of photoelectron energy,
from threshold and as high as 100 keV above threshold. We have used a partial-
wave single-electron-transition code (qualitatively useful in some cases below
100 eV, quantitatively accurate at higher energies) to calculate numerically relativistic, multipole and screening effects in a central potential (Dirac-Fock) approximation.

A photoelectron angular distribution is in general characterized by the co-
efficients B_k in the Lengendre polynomial expansion $d\sigma/d\Omega = (\sigma/4\pi) \sum_{k=0}^{\infty} B_k P_k(\cos\theta)$,
where $B_0=1$. In NR dipole approximation the only other nonvanishing B_k is
$B_2 \equiv \beta_{NL}/2$, where β_{NL} is the so called "asymmetry parameter". For s waves $\beta_{NO} \equiv 2$.

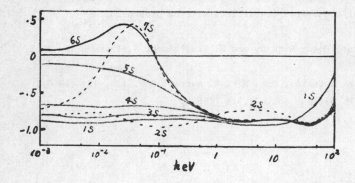

Fig. 1
Electron energy depen-
dence in keV of B_2 co-
efficients for photo-
electrons ejected from
1s-7s shells of
Uranium.

We show in Fig. 1, B_2 for the s states of U. We see major deviations from
the NR dipole prediction $B_2=-1$ for outer shell cases at low energy. We also
notice that for higher energies B_2 for most subshells has a similar energy dependence. This reflects the fact that well above threshold (photon energy several
times threshold energy) the matrix element for a given shell is determined at
rather small distances, where all s state wave functions have the same shape.
(For U the 1s wave function is still not well above threshold at the highest energies shown.) As we approach low energies, each given (inner) shell successively
ceases to be well above its threshold, its matrix element begins to be determined

at larger distances, and so the character of its B_2 begins to be determined at
larger distances, and so the character of its B_2 begins to deviate from the common character of those shells exterior to the given shell.

We have thus also confirmed the conclusions of our previous investigation
namely, (1) that for inner shells higher multipole effects persist to low energies
(B_1 and B_3 are in fact sizable all the way down to thresholds for 1s, 2s and 3s),
(2) for inner shells B_2 differs little from the nonrelativistic values, indicating that relativistic spin orbit splitting is unimportant, and (3) for outer
shells higher multipoles are unimportant (only B_0 and B_2 are sizable) but, as
Fig. 1 shows, relativistic splittings cause large deviations from the NR predictions.

We have also obtained expression for the B_k in terms of transition matrix
elements and phase shifts; in particular

$$B_2 = -[R_{3/2}^2 + 2\ R_{3/2}R_{1/2}\ \cos(\delta_{3/2} - \delta_{1/2})]/[R_{1/2}^2 + 2\ R_{3/2}^2],$$

where the R's are the transition matrices from an initial bound s state to final
continuum $p_{1/2}$ and $p_{3/2}$ states respectively, and δ's are the continuum phase
shifts for the two states. We have examined their energy dependence for all the
s states. We find (see Fig. 2) that the large deviation (see Fig. 1) of B_2 for
outer shells near threshold, from the NR prediction is due to the different
(shifted) positions of the zeros of $R_{1/2}$ and $R_{3/2}$, which would coincide in NR
dipole approximation.

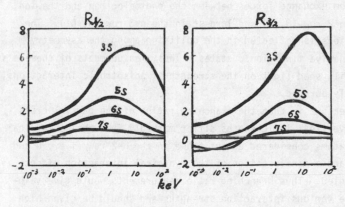

Fig. 2
Electron energy depen-
dence in keV of matrix
elements $R_{1/2}$ and $R_{3/2}$
for the transitions
from 3s, 5s, 6s and 7s
states to final contin-
uum $p_{1/2}$ and $p_{3/2}$ states
in arbitrary units.

Fig. 2 shows that for inner shells (as 3s) the matrix elements do not vanish
above threshold and so B_2 remains close to -1. This behavior persists until 5s,
where $R_{3/2}$ has nearly vanished by threshold, and so B_2 deviates substantially
from -1 (approaching 0) at threshold. For 6s $R_{3/2}$ has passed through 0 above
threshold, allowing B_2 = .4 at its maximum (rather than .5 which we would get if
$\delta_{3/2} = \delta_{1/2}$), but $R_{1/2}$ has not gone through 0 by threshold and so B_2 does not re-
turn to the -1 region. By 7s both R's have gone through 0 above threshold, so
that after the peak value of B_2=.4, B_2 has returned to -0.7 by threshold.

PHOTOIONIZATION OF CHALCOGEN AND HALOGEN ATOMS:
CROSS SECTIONS AND ANGULAR DISTRIBUTIONS

Steven T. Manson* and Alfred Msezane[†]

Department of Physics, Georgia State University, Atlanta, GA 30303 U.S.A.

and

Anthony F. Starace[‡] and Siamak Shahabi

Behlen Laboratory of Physics
The University of Nebraska, Lincoln, NE 68588 U.S.A.

We present extensive theoretical calculations of the photoionization cross sections and photoelectron angular distributions of the outer p-subshell of the chalcogen atoms O, S, Se, and Te and the halogen atoms F, Cl, Br, and I. Our purpose is to provide the same theoretical understanding for the outer shell photoabsorption spectrum of open-shell atoms having outer configurations p^4 and p^5 as has been provided in an earlier paper[1] for the closed shell atoms having outer configuration p^6. All our calculations employ Hartree-Fock continuum orbitals calculated in the field of a relaxed ionic core. Dynamical effects of atomic and ionic term level structure are thus explicitly taken into account and comparison is made with model potential calculations that ignore such term level effects.

The most striking feature of these calculations is that anisotropic interactions, which result from exchange forces between the photoelectron and the ion, are negligible in the n=2 row (O, F) and largest in the n=3 row (S, Cl). The size of these interactions is reflected in the splitting among the asymmetry parameters β for alternative final ionic states. Thus, measurements of these β's for open-shell atoms will shed light on the strength of anisotropic interactions, and should be vigorously pursued.

Another notable feature is that the branching ratios of the partial cross sections for alternative final ionic states differ markedly from the geometrical values for all of the atoms considered except those in the n=2 row (i.e., O and F). These deviations are a manifestation of the dynamical interaction effects within the systems studied. Thus branching ratio measurements would give valuable information on the various interaction strengths and should be given high priority. Note that even <u>relative</u> measurements are extremely valuable since they provide these branching ratios.

*Research supported by the U.S. National Science Foundation under Grant No. PHY76-80123.

[†]Present address: Department of Physics and Astronomy, Louisiana State University, Baton Rouge, Louisiana 70803.

[‡]Research supported by the U.S. Department of Energy under Contract No. EY-76-S-02-2892.A002 and by the Alfred P. Sloan Foundation.

Finally, note that these results were obtained neglecting correlation effects (i.e., neglecting those electron interaction effects not included within the HF approximation). It would be extremely useful to know how correlation affects these results. We are fairly certain that the qualitative nature of our results would not change, but the magnitude and systematics of any additional anisotropic interactions resulting from the inclusion of correlation would be of great interest.

[1]D.J. Kennedy and S.T. Manson, Phys. Rev. A 5, 227 (1972).

Ab Initio TREATMENT OF FINAL STATE SPIN ORBIT INTERACTION:
PHOTOIONIZATION OF THE 6s ELECTRON IN CESIUM[*]

Keh-Ning Huang[†] and Anthony F. Starace[‡]

Behlen Laboratory of Physics
The University of Nebraska, Lincoln, Nebraska 68588, U.S.A.

Ab initio theoretical calculations are presented for the cross section, photoelectron angular distribution, and photoelectron spin polarization resulting from photoionization of the 6s-electron of cesium. Starting from an initial basis of non-relativistic Hartree-Fock wavefunctions, the effect of final state spin-orbit interaction in the Breit-Pauli approximation is treated exactly. That is, in addition to the spin-orbit interaction of the photoelectron in the field of the nucleus, we have evaluated exactly the matrix elements of the mutual spin-orbit operator.[1] This mutual spin-orbit operator arises from the relativistic Breit-Pauli correction[2] to the non-relativistic Hartree-Fock Hamiltonian. The final state perturbation matrix elements were then used to obtain improved final state wavefunctions in the $J = 3/2$ and $J = 1/2$ photoelectron channels by means of the K-matrix method.[3,4]

Our calculations are carried out using both frozen and relaxed ionic core wavefunctions in order to demonstrate the effect of core relaxation, which is threefold: it reduces the 6s electron binding energy, it shifts the zero in the HF radial dipole matrix elements, and it reduces the magnitude of the spin-orbit matrix elements. A merit of the present approach is such disentangling of various effects on experimentally measurable quantities.

Our results ignoring intershell correlations are in qualitative agreement with previous Dirac-Fock calculations,[5,6] but agree more closely with experiment near threshold than all previous ab initio calculations. Extensive comparison of our results with experiment and with other theoretical calculations will be presented. Intershell correlation effects between the 5p and 6s subshells can easily be incorporated in our approach, and results including these additional effects will also be presented.

[1] K.-N. Huang and A.F. Starace, Phys. Rev. A 18, 354 (1978).
[2] H.A. Bethe and E.E. Salpeter, Quantum Mechanics of One- and Two-Electron Atoms (Springer-Verlag, Berlin, 1957), §38-39.
[3] U. Fano and J.W. Cooper, Rev. Mod. Phys. 40, 441 (1968), §6.
[4] A.F. Starace, Phys. Rev. A 2, 118 (1970).

[*] Work supported by the U.S. Department of Energy under Contract No. EY-76-S-02-2892.A002
[†] Present address: Department of Physics, University of Notre Dame, Notre Dame, Indiana 46556.
[‡] Work supported by the Alfred P. Sloan Foundation.

[5]J.J. Chang and H.P. Kelly, Phys. Rev. A <u>5</u>, 1713 (1972).
[6]W. Ong and S.T. Manson, Phys. Letters <u>66A</u>, 17 (1978).

APPARATUS FOR STUDYING PHOTOELECTRON POLARIZATION
BY MEANS OF CIRCULARLY POLARIZED SYNCHROTRON RADIATION

U. Heinzmann, F. Schäfers, K. Thimm, A. Wolcke and J. Kessler

Physikalisches Institut der Universität Münster, 4400 Münster, Germany

Synchrotron des Physikalischen Instituts der Universität Bonn

Photoelectrons emitted by unpolarized atoms exposed to circularly polarized light can be spin polarized (called Fano effect)[1,2]. Because only a few atoms and hardly any molecule have their photoionization threshold in the normal uv range, an apparatus using circular polarization of synchrotron radiation has been built at the 2.5 GeV Synchrotron in Bonn. The radiation, which is linearly polarized in the plane of the synchrotron, is elliptically polarized with a high fraction of left and right circular polarization in the directions above and below the plane, respectively.

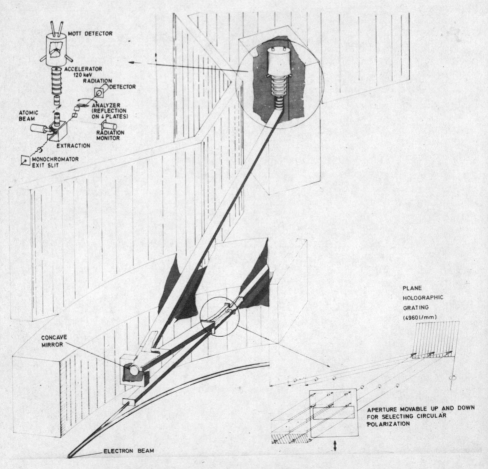

Fig. 1 schematic diagram of the apparatus

A schematic diagram of the apparatus is shown in Fig. 1. A 10 m normal-inci-
dence monochromator with a plane holographic grating (4960 1 mm^{-1}) and a concave
mirror, which produces an image of the electron beam (entrance slit) in the exit
slit, has been built. The radiation coming from the electron beam within an accepted horizontal angle of 20 mrad is cut off in vertical direction by an aperture
which is movable up and down for selecting circularly polarized radiation. The
size of the electron beam as entrance slit determines the resolution of the monochromator: the bandwidth of the radiation coming through the 1.5 mm exit slit has
been measured to be 0.05 nm using a second vuv monochromator for calibration. The
10m monochromator covers a wavelength range of 40 to 180 nm. The circularly polarized radiation, of which the intensity behind the exit slit has been estimated to
be more than 10^9 photons s^{-1} for wavelengths between 50 and 120 nm, passes the
atomic beam and is analyzed by a linear analyzer through reflection on four gold
mirrors with an angle of incidence of 60°. The ratio of the signals in the detector
and the monitor (open multipliers) as a function of the position of the rotated
analyzer determines the circular polarization. In order to be sure that no incoherent unpolarized radiation background falsifies this measurement and to test the
analyzing power of the analyzer, a MgF$_2$-quarter-wave plate (for 150 nm)[3] has been
placed in the radiation beam at 150 nm. Thus a total degree of polarization and an
analyzing power of the analyzer of better than 0.99 have been measured. The circular polarization of the synchrotron radiation emitted into vertical angles of more
than 1 mrad with respect to the plane has been determined to be 0.80±0.03 for
100 nm.

The photoelectrons produced are extracted by an electric field[4] and are focused by electron optical components before being accelerated to 120 keV. Their spin
polarization is then determined with a Mott detector[4]. The first results obtained
at Xenon atoms using this apparatus are published elsewhere[5].

1. U. Fano, Phys. Rev. 178, 131 (1969)
2. J. Kessler, Polarized Electrons (Springer Verlag, Berlin 1976)
3. U. Heinzmann, J. Phys. E 10, 1001 (1977)
4. U. Heinzmann, J. Phys. B 11, 399 (1978
5. U. Heinzmann, F. Schäfers, XI ICPEAC Kyoto 1979, book of abstracts

THE FANO EFFECT AT XENON ATOMS USING CIRCULARLY POLARIZED SYNCHROTRON RADIATION

U. Heinzmann and F. Schäfers

Physikalisches Institut der Universität Münster, 4400 Münster, Germany

Synchrotron des Physikalischen Instituts der Universität Bonn

Using the apparatus[1] at the 2.5 GeV synchrotron in Bonn it has been found that the photoelectrons emitted by unpolarized xenon atoms exposed to circularly polarized synchrotron radiation are highly spin polarized, after this has been predicted by Lee[2]. As the upper part of Fig. 1 shows, the photoionization cross section shows a very intensive resonance behavior due to autoionization processes between the first and the second ionization thresholds (102.2 nm and 92.2 nm) which correspond to the states $^2P_{3/2}$ and $^2P_{1/2}$ of the residual xenon ion, respectively. The solid curve in the upper part of Fig. 1 is the photoelectron intensity measured with our apperatus and thus not exactly the photoionization cross section, because light and atomic beam intensity were not constant with time. But nevertheless the positions of the peaks and the structures observed are in very good agreement with the well known cross section[3,4]. This indicates that the used bandwidth of 0.05 nm suffices to resolve partially also the narrow resonances.

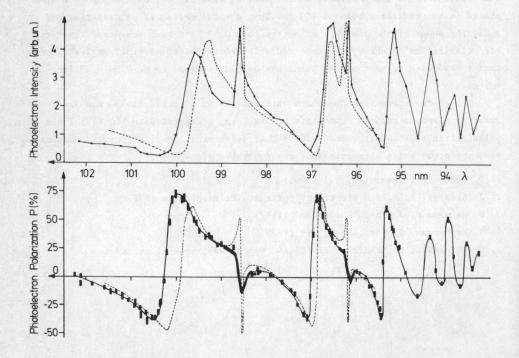

Fig. 1   solid line: experimental results, dashed line: theoretical prediction[2]
     upper part: cross section, lower part: spin polarization

In the lower part of Fig. 1 the measured polarizations are shown as black rectangles which are connected by the solid line. The base of each rectangle is the bandwidth of the radiation used and the height represents the error bar of the polarization result including the uncertainties of light polarization and spin polarization analysis (single statistical error). The measured spin polarization shows also a pronounced resonance structure as predicted by Lee[2] (dashed curve). But there are some interesting discrepancies between Lees prediction and our measured values in the positions of the broad resonances (which are also seen in the cross section and the angular distribution parameter β[5]) as well as in the shape of the narrow resonances, which are shown in Fig. 2 a. and b. using a broader wavelength scale.

In Fig. 3 one can see the measured spin polarizations of photoelectrons on the other side of the second threshold between 92 and 45 nm where the cross section drops monotonously[3]. These polarizations are average values for both kinds of photoelectrons (with polarizations of opposite sign[6]) corresponding to the two ionic states, because a resolving electron spectrometer could not used in the experiment. Although the fine structure of the ions is thus not resolved, the polarization measured does not vanish, which means, that the spin orbit interaction must also have an unnegligible influence on to the continuum states (origin of the Fano effect[7]).

1. U. Heinzmann, F. Schäfers, K. Thimm, A. Wolcke, J. Kessler, XI ICPEAC Kyoto
                    1979, book of abstracts
2. C.M. Lee, Phys. Rev. A 10, 1598 (1974)
3. R.E. Huffman, Y. Tanaka, J.C. Larrabee, J. Chem. Phys. 39, 902 (1963)
4. V. Saile, thesis, Universität München (1976)
5. J.A.R. Samson, J.L. Gardner, Phys. Rev. Lett. 31, 1327 (1973)
6. N.A. Cherepkov, JETP 38, 463 (1974)
7. U. Fano, Phys. Rev. 178, 131 (1969)

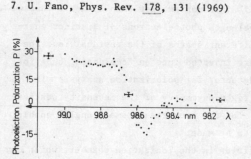

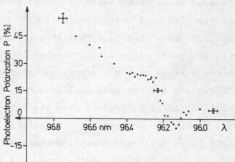

Fig. 2a. and b. measured spin polarization at the narrow resonances

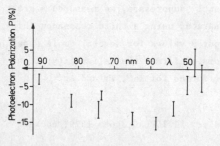

Fig. 3

measured spin polarization in the continuum

AN APPARATUS FOR THE MEASUREMENT OF SPIN POLARIZATION OF
PHOTOELECTRONS PRODUCED BY UNPOLARIZED RADIATION AT UNPOLARIZED ATOMS

U. Heinzmann and G. Schönhense

Physikalisches Institut der Universität Münster, 4400 Münster, Germany

The complication of such a polarization experiment is that it combines the intensity problem of photoelectron spin analysis with the difficulties of photoelectron angular distribution experiments. Therefore we used new windowless capillary
discharge tubes of high intensity as sources of vuv radiation. The tubes, shown in
Fig. 1, and the gas inlet systems are built using UHV components in order to have
very clean conditions for the d.c.discharge of the flowing He or Ne gas. The whole
lamp is placed in the vacuum, including the water cooling, in order to be as near
as possible with respect to the photoionization target. CuCoBe-alloy (87%,12.5%,.5%)
has been found as better material for the electrodes than very pure aluminum or
stainless steel. The anode and the light capillary are built into the discharge tube (Al_2O_3), which has a diameter of 2 mm and a length of 60 mm. The highest He I
intensity obtained at a He pressure of 750 Pa is constant with the discharge current
for values higher than 100 mA. Using a light capillary with a diameter of 1.75 mm
10^{13} and $5 \cdot 10^{12}$ photons s^{-1} have been measured at the target for He I (21.2eV) and
Ne I (16.8eV), respectively. With a light capillary of 0.8 mm diameter the intensity is a factor of 5 less.

The schematic diagramm of the whole apperatus is shown in Fig. 2. The angles
between the radiation emitted by the two sources and the direction of photoelectrons observed are $54^{\circ}44'$ (magic angle) and $180^{\circ}-54^{\circ}44'$. The photoelectrons are
produced in an atomic beam and enter an electron spectrometer (cylindrical mirror
analyzer) with an energy resolution of 0.7% (but not smaller than 35 meV). Thus we
take account of the fact that at each wavelength photoelectrons of distinct energies are produced, which correspond to different states of the residual ion. The
photoelectrons with the energy selected are injected into an accelerator tube for
120 keV and hit the gold foil of a Mott detector for polarization analysis. The
polarization is determined from the left-right asymmetry of the intensity scattered into the two counters at 120 degrees[1]. The two counters of small angles enable
corrections for instrumental asymmetries to be made.

In order to check whether residual fields in the ionization chamber, which may
deflect the photoelectrons, had been sufficiently suppressed, we measured a great
number of asymmetry parameters β with our apparatus using a third resonance lamp
placed at an angle of 16°. The agreement of our β values for several noble gases
and molecules with those found by other authors confirmed the reliability of the
polarization measurements, which have been performed for Xe[2], Kr and Ar.

1. U. Heinzmann, J. Phys. B **11**, 399 (1978)

2. U. Heinzmann, G. Schönhense, J. Kessler, XI ICPEAC Kyoto 1979, book of
    abstracts

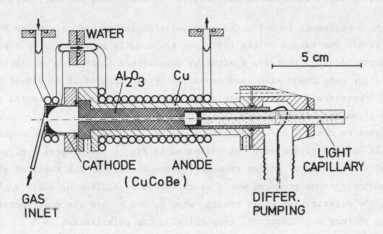

Fig. 1 Longitudiual section of the resonance lamp used

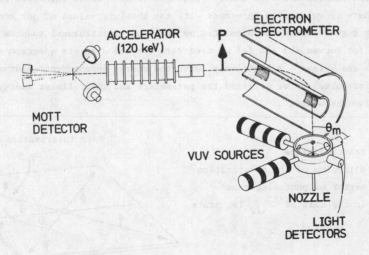

Fig. 2 Schematic diagram of the apparatus

POLARIZATION OF PHOTOELECTRONS EJECTED BY UNPOLARIZED LIGHT FROM XENON ATOMS

U. Heinzmann, G. Schönhense and J. Kessler

Physikalisches Institut der Universität Münster, 4400 Münster, Germany

In the experiments in which the spin polarization of photoelectrons has been studied, either the target or the radiation was usually polarized[1]. Spin polarization of photoelectrons that are ejected by unpolarized light from unpolarized targets has first been found with lead atoms last year[2] after such an effect had been predicted theoretically for rare gas atoms[3,4]. Here detailed experimental results for xenon atoms are reported.

In order to observe the polarization one has to detect photoelectrons emitted into a well defined direction θ. As indicated in Fig. 1 the direction of polarization is, for reasons of mirror symmetry, perpendicular to the reaction plane. If all the photoelectrons produced would be extracted regardless of their angle of emission, the polarization would vanish. When $\vec{k}_i$ and $\vec{k}_o$ are the unit vectors of the momenta of photons and electrons, respectively, the polarization is[3,4]

$$\vec{P}(\theta) = \frac{2\xi(\vec{k}_i \cdot \vec{k}_o)(\vec{k}_i \times \vec{k}_o)}{1 - \frac{\beta}{2}(\frac{3}{2}(\vec{k}_i \cdot \vec{k}_o)^2 - \frac{1}{2})} = \frac{2\xi\cos\theta\sin\theta}{1 - \frac{\beta}{2}(\frac{3}{2}\cos^2\theta - \frac{1}{2})} \cdot \vec{n}$$

where β is the asymmetry parameter determining the angular distribution of the cross section. Like β, ξ depends on the photon energy, photoelectron energy and the target atom. The apparatus used is described elsewhere[5].

Fig. 2 shows the measured polarizations and the values of ξ. For comparison theoretical results are also shown: curve (a) (RPAE[4]) shows the wrong sign, although there is reasonable agreement with the absolute values of our measurements. The other curves have been calculated by means of "multichannel quantum defect theory". For curves (b) and (c) we used data for the discrete spectrum given by Lee and Dill[6] and Geiger[7], respectively, with the energy independent quantum defects, whereas for curve (d) we utilized the parameters and their linear energy dependences given by Geiger[8].

Fig. 1 reaction plane
  direction of the polarization
  vector of photoelectrons
  in the case of $^2P_{1/2}$ ion state

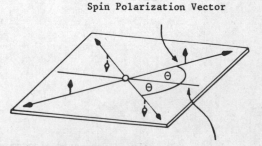

Spin Polarization Vector

Direction of Radiation

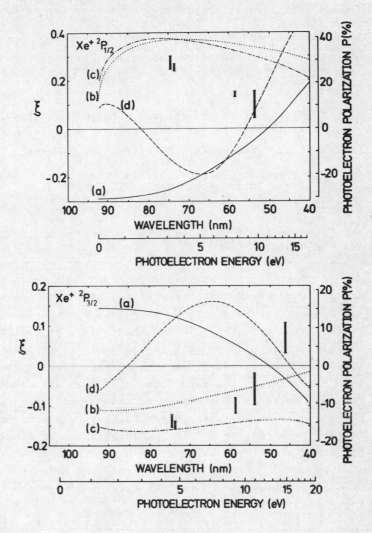

Fig. 2 Experimental
values with error
bars (one standard
deviation) and
theoretical curves.

1. J. Kessler, Polarized Electrons (Springer Verlag, Berlin, 1976)

2. U. Heinzmann, G. Schönhense, A. Wolcke, Abstr.Contr.Papers and Proc.Int.Work-
   shop on "Coherence and Correlation in Atomic Coll." 1978, Plenum press,inpress.

3. C.M. Lee, Phys. Rev. A 10, 1598 (1974)

4. N.A. Cherepkov, JETP 38, 463 (1974) and J. Phys. B 11, L 435 (1978)

5. U. Heinzmann, G. Schönhense, XI ICPEAC Kyoto 1979, book of abstracts

6. D. Dill, Phys. Rev. A 7, 1976 (1973)

7. J. Geiger, Z. Physik A 276, 219 (1976)

8. J. Geiger, Z. Physik A 282, 129 (1977)

POST-COLLISION INTERACTION IN PHOTOEXCITED ARGON LMM AUGER PROCESSES

H.Hanashiro, Y.Suzuki, A.Mikuni, and T.Sasaki

>   Synchrotron Radiation Laboratory, University of Tokyo,
>   Midoricho, Tanashi, Tokyo 188, Japan

S.Ohtani and T.Hino

>   Institute of Plasma Physics, Nagoya University,
>   Furocho, Chikusa-ku, Nagoya 464, Japan

A.Yagishita, T.Takayanagi, K.Wakiya, and H.Suzuki

>   Department of Physics, Sophia University,
>   Kioicho, Chiyoda-ku, Tokyo 102, Japan

Y.Danjo

>   Department of Physics, Niigata University,
>   Niigata 950-21, Japan

Studies on post-collision interaction between photoelectrons and Auger electrons following photoionization from Argon 2p sub-shell near threshold will be discussed in the present paper.   The effect manifests itself in the shift of Auger electron spectra to the higher energies as well as the modified profile of each Auger line which tails toward the high energy side.   The phenomena have been interpreted in terms of the different amount of screening of the core hole due to the more or less slowly outgoing photoelectron for photon energies near threshold, but much more experimental work will be required for a fuller understanding of the effect.   Only few experimental results have been so far reported, for instance, studies of PCI effects in Krypton MNN and Xenon NOO Auger processes by electron impact by Ohtani et al.,[1] and in photoexcited Xenon NOO Auger spectra by Schmidt et al.[2]

The present studies are carried out by using synchrotron radiation from the SOR-RING, a 400 MeV electron storage ring constructed as the dedicated light source.[3]   Monochromatic radiations of 1 eV resolution around 250 eV are supplied to a collision cell followed by an electron analyzer of 127° cylindrical type through a 2 m grazing-incidence monochromator of the modified Vodar geometry with 100 μm slits and a gold-coated grating with 2400 grooves per mm at 85° incidence.   A typical $L_{2,3}$MM Auger spectrum at 260 eV excitation is shown in the upper part of the Figure, and another obtained at 249 eV, just between L_2 and L_3 thresholds, in the lower part.   The latter shows a shift of

approximately 0.3 eV as determined with L_3MM ($^1D_2$) line to the
higher energy, and an obviously assymmetric profile for each $L_{2,3}MM$
line while the Auger lines for 260 eV excitation appear rather
symmetric.   Energy calibrations of the Auger spectrum have been
done by measuring the energy of the 3p photoelectrons at the same
photon energy.   It should be noted in this respect that the
Argon LMM Auger lines for electron impact at as high as 300 eV
reported by H. Suzuki et al.[4] show a characteristic assymmetric
profile of PCI effect.

1. S.Ohtani, H.Nishimura, H.Suzuki, and K.Wakiya, Phys. Rev.
   Lett. 36 863 (1976).
2. V.Schmidt, N.Sandner, W.Mehlhorn, M.Y.Adam, and F.Wuilleumier,
   Phys. Rev. Lett. 38 63 (1977).
3. T.Miyahara et al., Particle Accelerators 7 163 (1976).
4. H.Suzuki, M.Muto, T.Takayanagi, K.Wakiya, and S.Ohtani,
   Abstacts of papers of XI ICPEAC (Kyoto, 1979).

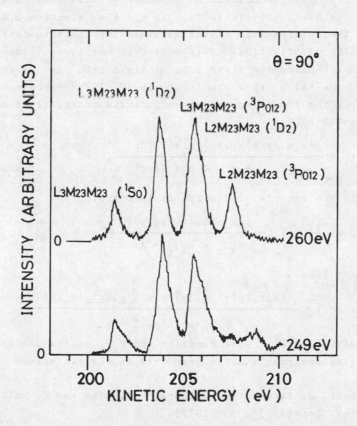

ELECTRON CORRELATION IN THE AUGER PROCESS FOLLOWING
PHOTOIONIZATION NEAR THE THRESHOLD

Junya Mizuno*, Takeshi Ishihara** and Tsutomu Watanabe***

  *Japan Business Automation Co. Ltd.
   4-2 Nihonbashi, Chuo-ku, Tokyo 103, Japan
 **Institute of Applied Physics, University of Tsukuba
   Ibaraki 300-31, Japan
***Department of Applied Physics, University of Tokyo
   Tokyo 113, Japan

In the xenon NOO Auger process following photoionization near
the threshold, a shift of the position of the peak maximum to higher
energies and a characteristic asymmetric intensity distribution of
the Auger line are observed by Schmidt et al.[1] Niehaus[2] has calculated the energy shift by modifying the classical model of Barker
and Berry.[3]

We calculate the energy shift of the argon LMM line using the
many-body perturbation theory. Argon is chosen for calculational
simplicity. The main contributing diagrams are shown in Fig.1,
where the expansion is in terms of $V^{N-2}(3p^{-2})$ basis set. The difference in the H. F. potentials felt by the slow electron k_1s in the
final and the intermediate states might be important in determining
the intensity distribution. This effect in the lowest order can be
included by changing the first term of Fig.1 into the one shown in
Fig.2.[4,5] The thick arrow stands for the $V^{N-1}(2p^{-1})$ propagator.
The t-matrix for Fig.1, summing over infinite order, is given in the
usual notation by

$$t_1 = \frac{(k_2p,2p|v|3p,3p)(k_1s|H_\gamma|2p)}{\omega - \varepsilon_{k_1s} + \varepsilon_{2p} - \Delta + \frac{i}{2}\Gamma} \, ,$$

where H_γ is the external radiation field operator and

$$\Delta - \frac{i}{2}\Gamma = \sum_{k'} \frac{|(k'p,2p|v|3p,3p)|^2}{\varepsilon_{k_2p} - \varepsilon_{k'p} + i\eta}$$

We have, for Fig.2,

$$t_2 = \sum_{k'} \frac{(k_2p,2p|v|3p,3p)(k_1s|\underline{k's})(\underline{k's}|H_\gamma|2p)}{\omega - \underline{\varepsilon}_{k's} + \varepsilon_{2p} + i\eta}$$

where $|\underline{k's})$ is the V^{N-1} wave function and $\underline{\varepsilon}_{k's}$ is its energy.
Detailed analysis will be presented in the conference.

1. V. Schmidt, N. Sander, W. Mehlhorn, M.Y. Adam and F. Wuilleumier,
   Phys. Rev. Letters 38, 63 (1977).

2. A. Niehaus, J. Phys. B10, 1845 (1977)

3. R.B. Barker and H.W. Berry, Phys. Rev. 151, 14 (1966)

4. T. Ishihara and R.T. Poe, Phys. Rev. A6, 111 (1972); Phys. Rev. A6, 117 (1972)

5. M.Ya. Amusia, M.Yu. Kuchiev, S.A. Sheinerman and S.I. Shestel, J. Phys. B10, 1535 (1977)

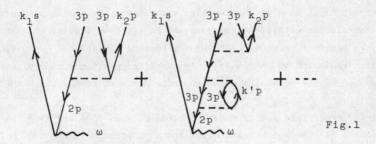

Fig.1

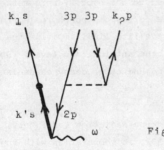

Fig.2

THE PHOTOELECTRON SPECTRA OF ATOMIC Ba

AT SELECTED AUTOIONIZING RESONANCES*

R. A. Rosenberg, M. G. White, G. Thornton, and D. A. Shirley

Materials and Molecular Research Division
Lawrence Berkeley Laboratory
and
Department of Chemistry
University of California
Berkeley, California 94720 USA

Using the light available at the Stanford Synchrotron Radiation Laboratory (SSRL) and a recently developed time-of-flight (TOF) electron energy analyzer,[1] situated at the "magic angle" (54°44'), we have recorded the photoelectron spectra of atomic Ba at several autoionizing resonances. Extensive population of electron correlation satellites is observed, in a manner similar to that seen previously in a spectrum recorded using He I resonance radiation.[2,3] By tuning the synchrotron radiation to autoionizing levels of a specific symmetry, we have been able to observe the mechanism by which these discrete states mix with the continuum.

A total electron yield spectrum of Ba, taken between 700Å and 490Å, is shown in Fig. 1. All the major features of the absorption spectrum of Connerade, et al.[4] are reproduced. Photoelectron spectra taken at the two resonances indicated in Fig. 1 are shown in Fig. 2. Based on the work of Connerade, et al.,[4] the two autoionizing levels involved are assigned to the same Rydberg series and correspond to excitation of an nd electron. The corresponding photoelectron spectrum shows extensive population of the nd satellite line, implying that Auger type decay is a dominant decay channel of the autoionizing level. Spectra taken at other wavelengths will also be presented and other decay channels will be discussed.

*This work was performed at the Stanford Synchrotron Radiation Laboratory, which is supported by the NSF Grant No. DMR 73-07692 A02, in cooperation with the Stanford Linear Accelerator Center and was done with support from the Division of Chemical Sciences, Office of Basic Energy Sciences, U. S. Department of Energy, under contract No. W-7405-Eng-48.

1. M. G. White, R. A. Rosenberg, G. Gabor, E. D. Poliakoff, G. Thornton, S. H. Southworth, and D. A. Shirley, submitted to Rev. Sci. Instr.

2. S.-T. Lee, S. Süzer, E. Matthias, R. A. Rosenberg, and D. A. Shirley, J. Chem. Phys. 66, 2496 (1977).

3. H. Hotop and D. Mahr, J. Phys. B 8, L301 (1975).

4. J. P. Connerade, M.W.D. Mansfield, G. H. Newsom, D. H. Tracy, M. A. Baig, and K. Thimm, Phil. Trans. R. Soc. Lond. A 290, 327 (1979).

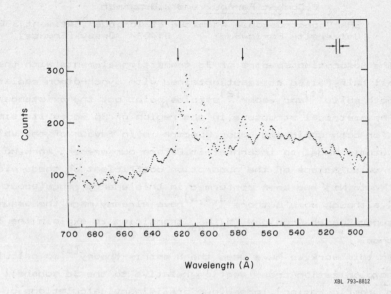

Wavelength (Å)

XBL 793-8812

Figure 1. Total electron yield spectra of Ba. Photoelectron spectra (Fig. 2) were taken at the two wavelengths indicated by the arrows. The bandpass of the excitation monochromator (2.5Å) is indicated in the upper right hand corner.

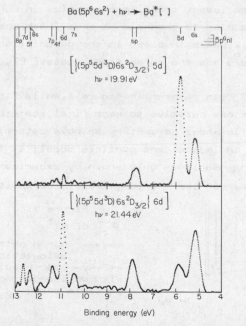

Figure 2. Photoelectron spectra of atomic Ba taken at two auto-ionizing resonances. The assignments are based on the work of Connerade, et al.[4]

XBL 792-610

THEORETICAL EVIDENCE OF SUPER-COSTER-KRONIG TRANSITIONS
IN NICKEL SPECTRA: AB INITIO CALCULATIONS.

F.Combet Farnoux and M.Ben Amar

ERA "Spectroscopie Atomique et Ionique",Bâtiment 350,
Université Paris-Sud;   91405   Orsay (France)

The absorption spectra of 3d transition elements(with the 3d
subshell half-filled at least)obtained with Synchrotron radiation
from both solid[1] and vapor[2] samples,point out the existence of a
large asymmetrical structure,in the region of 3p edges.Its similar
shape for both solid and vapor spectra is in favour of the validity
of an atomic model to interpret it.Before our présent work,no ab
initio calculations of the absorption coefficient of these elements
(from Mn to Ni) had been performed in this energy range(about 30-
90 eV),although some authors[3,4,5] have already made the assumption
of a super-Coster-Kronig $M_{23}M_{45}M_{45}$ transition to explain the large
resonance.

In this work,we have used the R matrix theory[6] to calculate
the photoionization cross section relative to the 3d subshell of Ni^+
($3p^6 3d^9$ configuration).Indeed,our preliminary calculations of the
same σ_{3d} for neutral Ni($3p^6 3d^8 4s^2$)and Ni^+ using an independent
particle model have shown that the two curves are different,close
to the 3d threshold but very similar beyond their maximum,i.e. in
the region which we are dealing with.Because we have introduced the
five 3d thresholds and only the lowest three 3p thresholds in our R
matrix calculations,we have coupled 12 channels at most (both open
and closed)to find the R matrix basis involved in the description
of the initial state $^2D^e (3p^6 3d^9)$ and the three final states($^2P^o$,
$^2D^o$ and $^2F^o$).

Our results for total σ_{3d} can be seen in figure 1,while figure
2 shows the partial cross sections relative to each final state;both
figures show a wide Fano profile(whose parameters we have determined)
which cannot be obtained with an independent particle model; it is
followed by many narrow and intense lines only shown by experimental
vapor spectra[2].In figure 1,we can see the large multiplet splitting

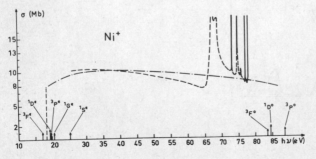

Figure 1:
σ_{3d} of Ni^+:
------ our R matrix
       calculations;
—.—.— our results
with an independent
particle model.

of the various 3d and 3p thresholds introduced in our calculations. These calculations support the hypothesis of a super-Coster-Kronig $M_{23}M_{45}M_{45}$ mechanism to explain the Fano type profile,as far as they introduce the interference of two processes:

1°] creation of an excited state $3p^5 3d^{10}$ which decays into the various continua $3p^6 3d^8 \,\mathcal{E}f$ and $3p^6 3d^8 \,\mathcal{E}p$;

2°] direct ionization: $3p^6 3d^9 + h\nu \longrightarrow 3p^6 3d^8 + \mathcal{E}p$ or $\mathcal{E}f$.

The other lines(relative to transitions from $3p^6 3d^9$ to $3p^5 3d^9 4s$ (5s,4d,5d...etc) are the first lines of series which converge on the various 3p thresholds.It is important to note that,while the position of the M_{23} edge is the same for a solid spectrum as that of the autoionizing $3p^5 3d^{10}$ level,the 3p ionization threshold for a vapor spectrum is located much beyond this level.In figure 2,we can see that the Fano type profile due to the autoionizing transition $3p^6 3d^9 \longrightarrow 3p^5 3d^{10}$ is concentrated in the partial cross section relative to the $^2P^o$ final state.The $3p^6 3d^9 \longrightarrow 3p^5 3d^9 4s$ transition is likely to account for the first line of both $^2D^o$ and $^2F^o$ partial cross sections.

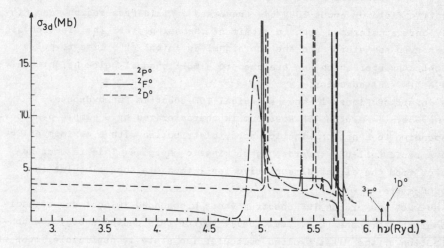

Figure 2: Partial cross sections relative to the 3 final states

[1] B.Sonntag,R.Haensel and C.Kunz   Sol.State Comm.7,597(1969)
[2] R.Bruhn,B.Sonntag and H.W.Wolff   DESY Report SR-78/14(1978)
    J.P.Connerade,M.W.D.Mansfield and M.A.P.Martin
                    Proc.Roy.Soc.Lond.A350,405 (1976)
[3] E.J.McGuire   J.Phys.Chem.Solids   33,577(1972)
[4] R.E.Dietz,E.G.McRae,Y.Yafet and C.W.Caldwell
                    Phys.Rev.Lett.33,1372 (1974)
[5] L.C.Davis and L.A.Feldkamp   Sol.State Comm.19,413 (1976)
[6] K.A.Berrington,P.G.Burke,M.Le Dourneuf,W.D.Robb,K.T.Taylor
    and Vo Ky Lan   Comp.Phys.Comm. 14,367 (1978)

DISSOCIATIVE AUTOIONIZATION OF HYDROGEN AND DEUTERIUM BY PHOTON
IMPACT

K. Köllmann[*], P.M. Guyon[+], K. Ito[+], I. Nenner[§], and L.F.A. Ferreira[+]

*) I. Institut für Experimentalphysik Univ. Hamburg
   Jungiusstr. 9 D 2000 Hamburg 36 W.-Germany
+) Laboratoire des collisions ioniques univ. Paris-Sud
   91405 Orsay France
§) C. E. A. Saclay France

Using the synchrotron radiation of Orsay's electron storage ring (ACO)
and a 1m normal incidence monochromator (McPherson) with a platin coated
holographic grating time-of-flight (TOF) spectra of ions from H_2 and D_2
were measured for photon energies between 21eV and 31eV. A delayed electron-ion coincidence technique was used.

Photoelectrons and photoions produced in the intersection region of crossed
photon and molecular beams were accelerated in opposite directions by an
electric field of about 200V/cm, traversed a field-free region, and finally were accelerated each to a pair of channel plates. The electron signal served as 'start' and the ion signal as 'stop' of a time-to-pulse
height converter which was branched to a multichannel pulse height analyser
and a TEK 4051 computer.

The insert of figure 1 shows a typical TOF spectrum for hydrogen.

At hv=25eV the proton TOF spectrum is characterized by a simple peak corresponding to a proton kinetic energy distribution with a maximum at 0eV
and a rapid fall-off towards higher kinetic energies. This is what we
expect from the direct dissociative ionization via the molecular ion
ground state.

At hv=28eV the proton TOF spectrum shows pronounced 'wings' due to additional fast protons (k.e. 2eV...5eV). As for this photon energy the contribution of the first excited molecular ion state is negligible, most of
these fast protons arise from autoionization of doubly excited states
(high-lying Rydberg states) to the vibrational continuum of the molecular
ion ground state[1,2].

Integrating the proton TOF spectra taken at various photon energies in a
time interval (T1,T2) corresponding to a kinetic energy range 1eV...8eV
and normalizing to constant photon flux for $\Delta\lambda$=1.5Å in this experiment
a diagram intensity of rapid protons against photon energy (see figure 1)
is obtained. As expected from theory[3] for the lowest optically accessible
doubly excited state $H_2^{**}(Q_1{}^1\Sigma_u^+)$ the onset is found to be near 26eV.
This result is in accordance with electron impact measurements[4].

for deuterium similar results have been obtained.

To deduce partial cross sections for the formation of rapid protons and
deuterons via autoionization of high-lying repulsive Rydberg states a
further treatment of the corresponding TOF data is in progress.

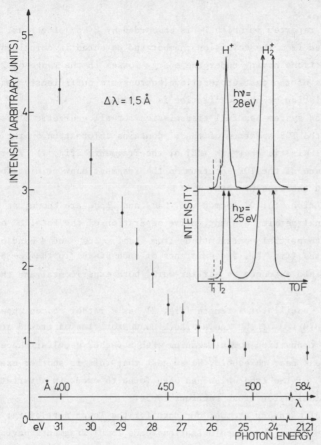

Figure 1: Intensity of fast protons versus photon energy.

Insert Fig. 1: TOF spectra of H^+ and H_2^+ from H_2 at $h\nu=25eV$ and $28eV$

1) S. Strathdee and R. Browning   J. Phys. B 9(1976) L 505

2) B. van Wingerden, Ph.E. van der Leeuw, F.J. de Heer and M.J. van der
   Wiel   to be published (1979)

3) K. Kirby, S. Guberman and A. Dalgarno   to be published (1979)

4) K. Köllmann   J. Phys. B 11(1978) 339

FORMATION OF ENERGETIC D$^+$ FRAGMENTS FROM D$_2$ BY PHOTOEXCITATION IN THE 25 - 40 eV RANGE

B. van Wingerden, Ph.E. van der Leeuw, F.J. de Heer and M.J. van der Wiel

FOM-Institute for Atomic and Molecular Physics
Kruislaan 407, Amsterdam, The Netherlands

An experiment is reported in which D$_2$ is bombarded by 8 keV electrons. D$^+$ fragments are extracted from the collision chamber and detected in coincidence with forward scattered electrons having undergone energy losses in the range of 25-40 eV. Momentum transfers of the fast projectile electrons are sufficiently small that an accurate simulation of photoexcitation is obtained.

The ion extraction system has full transmission for all energetic D$^+$ fragments; nevertheless, the TOF spectrum of the D$^+$ contains information on the distribution over initial kinetic energies (KE) of the fragments (fig. 1). There is also a slight dependence of the TOF spectrum on the fragment angular distribution, but this is ignored in the present work.

Since KE distributions for D$^+$ formed via $1s\sigma_g$ and $2p\sigma_u$ are known, an analysis of the D$^+$ TOF-signal permits a quantitative separation of the total D$^+$ oscillator strength [1] into partial contributions from $1s\sigma_g$, $2p\sigma_u$ and a band of autoionizing Rydberg states (fig. 2). The existence of such states in the 26-35 eV energy range was put into evidence by earlier work, both experimental and theoretical [2].

The $2p\sigma_u$ partial oscillator strength (fig. 2) has a rather common appearance. However, after deconvolution of the known Franck-Condon overlap of ground state and $2p\sigma_u$, an electronic transition moment remains with a rather peculiar shape, namely with a sharp peak near threshold. We suggest that this is another example of a "shape resonance" of the type which has been found to occur in a variety of other molecular photoionization cross sections [3-5].

As for the band of Rydberg states, our data for the lower part of the band, i.e. for 26-30 eV, indicates that autoionization leads to D$^+$ fragments having an average KE of 3 eV. Our interpretation is that we are dealing with doubly excited states with potential energy curves similar to that of the $2p\sigma_u$. Excitation to such states is followed by a rapid increase in internuclear distance and an autoionizing transition somewhere along the repulsive curve; the available excess energy is thus shared between the heavy particles and the ejected electron.

The expected result would be that both vibrationally excited D$_2^+$ and some D$^+$ were formed. However, it turns out that an isotope effect between H$_2$ and D$_2$ is totally absent, which implies that a competition between D$_2^+$ and D$^+$ formation does not occur for this particular mode of decay. Our conclusion is that the lifetime for autoionization is long in the ground-state FC region, but that it shortens drastically at larger internuclear distances.

The upper part of our Rydberg band, around 35 eV, gives rise to lower energy fragments, on the average only 1 eV. This is ascribed to a higher, and less repulsive, Rydberg state not connected with the $2\,p\sigma_u$, which autoionizes to the $1s\sigma_g$ ionic ground-state with only little gain in internal energy.

[1] C. Backx, G.R. Wight and M.J. van der Wiel, J. Phys. B. <u>9</u> (1976) 315

[2] for a review of earlier references see K. Köllmann, J. Phys. B. <u>11</u> (1978) 339

[3] J.L. Dehmer, J. Chem. Phys. <u>56</u> (1972) 4496

[4] R.B. Kay, Ph.E. van der Leeuw and M.J. van der Wiel, J. Phys. B. <u>10</u> (1977) 2513

[5] T. Gustaffson, Phys. Rev. A <u>18</u> (1978) 1481

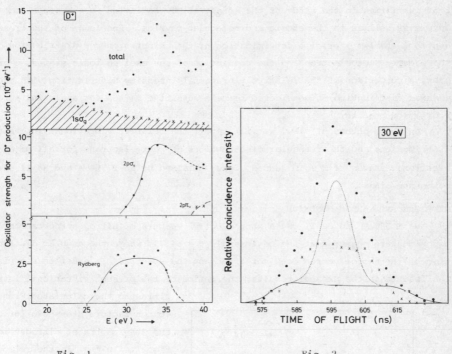

Fig. 1   Fig. 2

Fig. 1   TOF distribution of D^+ signal, coincident with 30 eV energy loss electrons.

   ● - measured signal; solid curve - computed distribution of $2\,p\sigma_u$ fragments, fitted to the tails of the measured signal; dotted curve - computed $1s\sigma_g$ contribution; crosses - remaining signal due to Rydberg states.

Fig. 2   Partial oscillator strengths for $1s\sigma_g$, $2\,p\sigma_u$ and Rydberg states to the total D^+. Absolute scale from ref [1].

PHOTOELECTRON SPECTROSCOPY OF SEVERAL GASES USING He RESONANCE LINES

Masatoshi Nakamura and Yoshihiro Iida

Institute of Physics, University of Tsukuba
Sakura-mura, Ibaraki 300-31, Japan

INTRODUCTION

Photoelectron spectroscopy is recognized and used as a useful tool for the study of atomic and molecular physics. For instance, knowledge of vibrational spacing and intensity distribution of a vibrational progression in the photoelectron spectrum of molecule is invaluable in the interpretation of the nature of the molecular orbital from which the photoelectron is ejected.

The partial and differential photoionization cross sections are also important quantities in the study of the effect of EUV radiation in the apper atmosphere as well as in the atomic and molecular physics. Knowledge of the cross sections enables a precise determination of the kinetic energy distribution of the ejected photoelectron and the population of the excited ionic states. Moreover, a comparison of the relative vibrational intensity distribution with the angular distribution is considered to be a sensitive method for analyzing autoionization process.

On these points of view, we will report the relative vibrational intensity distributions and their angular distributions of photoelectrons for all major electronic states of N_2^+, CO^+ and H_2^+ ions, obtained by He I 584 $\overset{\circ}{A}$ and He II 304 $\overset{\circ}{A}$ resonance lines.

NITROGEN AND CARBON MONOXIDE

He I 584 A and He II 304 A photoelectron spectra of nitrogen and carbon monoxide were measured at the magic angle, $\theta = 54.7°$, where the angular distribution of the photoelectron does not affect on the spectra. In order to see visually the feature of the present results, the ratios of the present vibrational intensities to the calculated Franck-Condon factors are shown for 584- and 304-spectra of nitrogen in Fig. 1. In Fig. 1, the ratios are normalized to unity at the most intense vibrational peak of each progression and the data of Franck-Condon factors are used from Lee and Rabalais[1] for nitrogen.

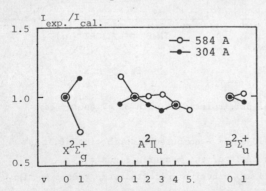

Fig. 1. Ratios of the observed vibrational intensities to the Franck-Condon factors for nitrogen.

Asymmetry parameter, β, of angular distribution in the photoelectron is defined by the well-known equation,

$$\frac{d\sigma}{d\Omega} = \frac{\sigma_t}{4\pi}\{1 - \frac{1}{2}\beta P_2(\cos\theta)\}$$

for unpolarized light, where θ is an angle between photon beam and the ejected electron. In order to symplify the procedure of least mean square method, the above equation is rewritten as

$$I(\theta) = I_0(1 - k\cos^2\theta)$$

where $I(\theta)=(d\sigma/d\Omega)_\theta$ and $I_0=(d\sigma/d\Omega)_{\theta=90°}$. Then, the β-value is obtained by

$$\beta = 4k/(k + 3)$$

The β values thus obtained are shown in Fig. 2 for 584- and 304-spectra of nitrogen.

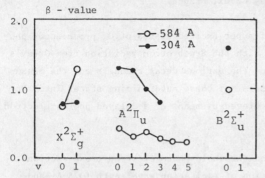

Fig. 2. Asymmetry parameter, β, of nitrogen.

The relative vibrational intensity distributions and their angular distributions obtained in the present will be discussed in the conference, in conjunction with the autoionization process and the other data obtained by Gardner and Samson[2], Carlson and Jonas[3].

HYDROGEN MOLECULE

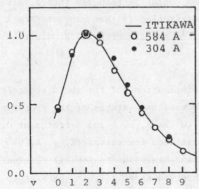

Fig. 3. Relative vibrational intensities of hydrogen.

The vibrational intensity distribution and the angular distribution were measured by 584 and 304 Å lines. In Fig. 3 are shown the obtained vibrational inten-intensity distributions at 584 and 304 Å and the calculated one by Itikawa[4].

The asymmetry parameter, β, of each vibrational peak is measured by 584 Å line and compared with the theoretical calculation by Itikawa[5]. The agreement is fairly good. Since signal intensity of photoelectron by 304 Å is so small, the asymmetry parameter is not measured for each vibrational peak and therefore only the averaged value is obtained in the present.

1. T. H. Lee and J. W. Rabalais, J. Chem. Phys. 61 2747 (1974)

2. J. L. Gardner and J. A. R. Samson, J. Chem. Phys. 61 5472 (1974)

3. T. A. Carlson and A. E. Jonas, J. Chem. Phys. 55 4713 (1971)

4. Y. Itikawa, J. Electron Spectrosc. 2 125 (1973)

5. Y. Itikawa, Chem. Phys. 28 461 (1978) *ibid.* 30 109 (1978)

RESONANT AND NON-RESONANT AUTOIONIZATION OF O_2 IN PHOTO-SELECTED SUPEREXCITED STATES USING SYNCHROTRON RADIATION.

I. Nenner[a], L.F.A. Ferreira[b], K. Köllmann[c], P. Morin[a], P.M. Guyon[b], K. Ito[b]

L.U.R.E., Laboratoire C.N.R.S., Université Paris-Sud, Bât. 209c,
91405 Orsay Cédex, France.

We are investigating the decay of super excited states of O_2 produced by photon excitation in the 12-26 eV range, with the Synchrotron radiation from Orsay's ACO storage ring. The identification of the various decay channels and the measurement of the associated branching ratios of these autoionizing states into the various accessible states of O_2^+ are achieved by means of a delayed photon-electron coincidence experiment.

1. EXPERIMENTAL TECHNIQUE

Firstly, total photoionization and threshold photo-electron cross sections are measured simultaneously as a function of excitation wavelength (0.5 Å band width) using a double time of flight spectrometer[1] where threshold electrons are energetically selected by their angular as well as temporal characteristics ; a 20 meV electron energy resolution is thus obtained.

Secondly, photoelectron spectra are measured at selected wavelengths, using a time of flight coincidence technique : the electron signal (angular discriminated only) starts a time-to-amplitude converter which is stopped by the ACO signal given by a pick up electrode mounted into the ring. The output is then fed into a pulse-height-analyzer. The electron time of flight distribution is then converted to a photo-electron spectrum using as apparatus function, the electron T.O.F. distribution, obtained with helium at various wavelengths.

2. RESULTS

Figure 1 shows only part of the total photoionization and threshold photoelectron (TPES) cross sections from 12 to 19 eV. The various features of the spectrum (I) are autoionizing Rydberg states converging to the A, a, b and B states of O_2^+, the other spectrum exhibits the known optically allowed ion states (X, a, A, b) formed by direct ionization but additions or enhancements due to (quasi) resonant autoionization, i. e. 0 to 200 meV, are often observed especially in the X state region where autoionization dominates.

On top of Fig. 1, four examples of photoelectron spectra are given at selected wavelengths and show some dramatic changes in the vibrational and electronic distribution. These results are interpreted in terms of electronic, spin orbit and even vibrational autoionization.

a) DRA-SRIRMA, C.E.N. Saclay, B.P. 2, 91190 gif-sur-Yvette, France.
b) Laboratoire des Collisions Atomiques et Moléculaires, Bât. 351, Université Paris-Sud, 91405 Orsay Cédex, France.
c) Institut für Experimentalphysik, Univ. Hamburg, 2 Hamburg 36, R.F.A.

1) T. Baer, P.M. Guyon, I. Nenner, A. Tabché-Fouhailhé, R. Botter, L.F. Ferreira and T.R. Govers, J. Chem. Phys., 70(04) (1979), 1585.

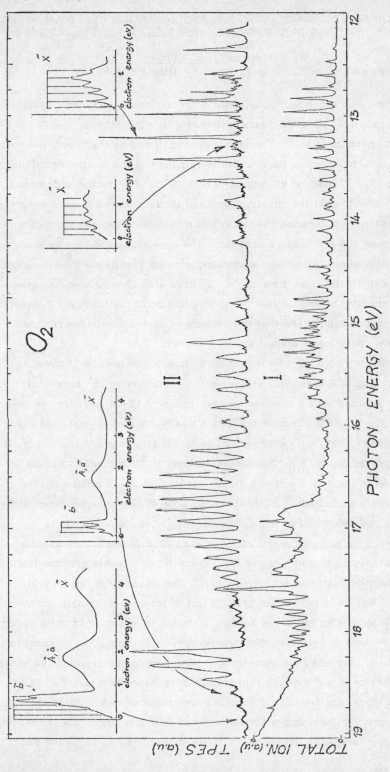

Figure 1 : Total ionization (I) and threshold photoelectron (II) cross sections of O_2, and photoelectron spectra taken at 16.70 eV ($X^2\Pi_g$, v=5), 16.75 eV (valley v=5,6 of $X^2\Pi_g$, v=3), 18.59 eV ($b^4\Sigma_g^-$, v=3) and 18.35 eV ($b^4\Sigma_g^-$, v=5)

PHOTOELECTRON SPECTROSCOPY USING A SUPERSONIC MOLECULAR BEAM SOURCE. RENNER-TELLER SPLITTING IN THE BENDING VIBRATION OF N_2O^+ $X^2\Pi$ AT 584 Å .*

P. M. Dehmer and J. L. Dehmer
Argonne National Laboratory, Argonne, Illinois 60439, USA

We have combined a compact supersonic molecular beam source with a high-resolution hemispherical photoelectron spectrometer to reinvestigate[1] the HeI 584 Å photoelectron spectrum of N_2O. This arrangement allowed us to observe previously unresolved vibronic structure (Renner-Teller splitting) in the nominally forbidden $(0,1,0)$ and the $(0,2,0)$ bending vibrations of N_2O^+ $X^2\Pi$. The drastic differences between the relative intensities observed here and those observed in zero-energy photoelectron spectra[2] underscore the dynamical differences between ionization in the open continuum and resonance ionization. The apparatus used for this study was described previously in connection with experiments that determined the photoelectron spectra of the rare gas dimers.[3,4] We have also showed how this same apparatus will simplify molecular spectra by reducing both rotational and Doppler broadening of the target gas, and that the benefits of such a source are realized for spectrometers operating at resolutions of < 20 meV.[5]

In the present work we have measured the photoelectron spectra of the N_2O^+ $X^2\Pi$, $A^2\Sigma$, $B^2\Pi$, and $C^2\Sigma$ electronic states, using both effusive and supersonic molecular beam sources with a spectrometer resolution of 12–14 meV. In the case of the effusive spectra, the effective resolution was worse due to rotational and Doppler broadening. Previously unreported vibrational structure is observed in all four of the electronic bands, but of particular interest is the vibronic structure of the bending mode in the $X^2\Pi$ electronic state. Figure 1 shows a portion of this spectrum taken with a supersonic molecular beam source; the spectrum taken with an effusive source is identical except for poorer resolution, which tends to obliterate the weak feature on the tail of the intense $(0,0,0)$ peak. The assignments of the vibronic components of the $(0,1,0)$ and $(0,2,0)$ levels are from the fluorescence study of Callomon and Creutzberg.[6] The intensity of the $(0,1,0)$ component at 12.945 eV is only about 1/2% of that of the $(0,0,0)$ transition; however, this is not surprising since the bending vibration is forbidden in units of odd quanta in linear-linear transitions. The present results are in marked contrast to relative intensities obtained from zero-energy photoelectron spectroscopy, in which the relative intensity of the same $(0,1,0)$ transition is larger by a factor of 30 or more.[2] Several other less dramatic differences are also observed, both in the $X^2\Pi$ and the $A^2\Sigma$ states. A likely interpretation of these intensity variations is that autoionizing states which are degenerate with the ionic state to which they decay

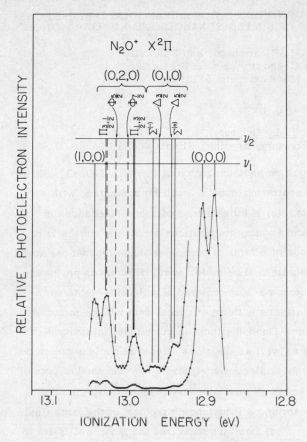

FIG. 1. HeI 584 Å photo-electron spectrum of N_2O^+ $X^2\Pi$, taken with a supersonic molecular beam source and a spectrometer resolution of 12-14 meV.

contribute in an irregular way in the resonance photoionization experiments. At present, the character of these states is not known.

*Work supported by the U.S. Department of Energy.

1. C. R. Brundle and D. W. Turner, J. Mass Spectry. Ion Phys. **2**, 195 (1969).

2. R. Frey, B. Gotchev, W. B. Peatment, H. Pollak, and E. W. Schlag, Chem. Phys. Lett. **54**, 411 (1978).

3. P. M. Dehmer and J. L. Dehmer, J. Chem. Phys. **68**, 3462 (1978).

4. P. M. Dehmer and J. L. Dehmer, J. Chem. Phys. **69**, 125 (1978).

5. P. M. Dehmer and J. L. Dehmer, J. Chem. Phys. (in press).

6. J. H. Callomon and F. Creutzberg, Phil. Trans. Roy. Soc. **277**, 157 (1974).

MOLECULAR PHOTOELECTRON BRANCHING RATIOS AND ANGULAR DISTRIBUTIONS FROM 0 TO 10 Ry. EFFECTS OF SHAPE RESONANCES AND NUCLEAR MOTION[*]

Scott Wallace,[†] J. R. Swanson, and Dan Dill
Department of Chemistry, Boston University
Boston, Massachusetts 02215 USA

and

J. L. Dehmer
Argonne National Laboratory, Argonne, Illinois 60439 USA

Results of recent calculations on photoionization of N_2, CO, NO, O_2, BF_3, and SF_6, utilizing the multiple-scattering model[1,2] will be presented, with emphasis on the following points: (a) Manifestations of shape resonances in photoelectron branching ratios and angular distributions for all the subshells of the above molecules. Comparison of effects of particular shape resonances accessed from alternative initial subshells will be made, e.g., differences produced when a resonance is populated from a sulfur-centered or a fluorine-centered molecular orbital in SF_6. Comparisons with experimental data will be included. (b) Prediction of strong non-Franck-Condon effects in vibrational intensity distributions near shape resonances, as well as the gross effects of nuclear motion on the whole vibrational band. (c) An analogous analysis of the combined effects of nuclear motion and shape resonances on photoelectron angular distributions of individual vibrational levels, resolving a longstanding problem of the large final-state v-dependence of β in N_2.[3-5] (d) Demonstration that the inner-well state in the t_{1u} channel in SF_6 falls within the Rydberg series of that channel. (e) Evolution from shape resonance structure to EXAFS structure in SF_6 photoionization. (f) A total dipole oscillator strength distribution for N_2 from the first dipole-allowed excitation to 100 Ry above the K-shell edge.

[*]Work supported by the U.S. Department of Energy, National Science Foundation Grant CHE78-08707, and American Chemical Society Petroleum Research Fund Grant 10785-AC6.

[†]Present address: Center for Materials Science and Engineering, Massachusetts Institute of Technology, Cambridge, Massachusetts 02139.

1. For treatment of continuum states, see D. Dill and J. L. Dehmer, J. Chem. Phys. 61, 692 (1974), and J. L. Dehmer and D. Dill, in Electron and Photon Molecule Collisions, V. McKoy, T. Rescigno, and B. Schneider, Eds. (Plenum Press, New York-London, 1979).

2. For treatment of bound states, see, e.g., K. H. Johnson, in Advances in Quantum Chemistry, P.-O. Löwdin, Ed. (Academic Press, New York, 1973) Vol. 7, p. 143.

3. T. A. Carlson, Chem. Phys. Lett. <u>9</u>, 23 (1971).

4. C. Duzy and R. S. Berry, J. Chem. Phys. <u>64</u>, 2421 (1976).

5. D. M. Mintz and A. Kuppermann, J. Chem. Phys. <u>69</u>, 3953 (1978).

6. See, e.g., J. L. Dehmer, J. Chem. Phys. <u>56</u>, 4496 (1972).

THE GAUSSIAN - PLANE WAVE FUNCTION FOR CALCULATION

OF MOLECULAR PHOTOIONIZATION CROSS SECTION

Suehiro IWATA

Institute of Physical and Chemical Research,

Wako, Saitama 351, Japan

Because of the recent development of the synchrotron radiation source and of
the electron energy loss technique, the dependence of the total and differential
ionization cross sections on the excitation energy becomes available for atoms
and some simple molecules. From the theoretical point of view, however, especially for molecules, the continuum wavefunction of the ejected electron is difficult to be calculated. To circumvent the difficulty, the methods are developed[1,2]
in which the discrete (square integrable) basis functions are used to describe
the continuum part of the wavefunction. The Stieltyes-Tchebycheff procedure
developed by Langhoff[3] has successfully been applied to several molecular total
photcionization cross sections. This method is particularly attractive since the
well-developed quantum chemical computer programs can be employed. One of the
difficulty in the Stieltyes imaging, in our own experience,[4] is choice of the
basis functions to be used; for example, there seem to be no systematic ways to
augment the basis functions for an ionization cross section.

In the present report, a new type of square integrable functions is proposed.
Recently most of molecular quantum chemical calculations are based on the gaussian
type function (GTF):

$$G(1,m,n,\alpha; \mathbf{r}) = x^1 y^m z^n \exp(-\alpha r^2) \qquad\qquad (1)$$

The new function is a simple modification of it as

$$GP(\alpha, \mathbf{k}; \mathbf{r}) = \exp(-\alpha r^2 + i\,\mathbf{k}\,\mathbf{r}) \qquad\qquad (2)$$

The exponent α can be chosen such that the size of the molecule or the atom is
smaller than $1/\sqrt{\alpha}$. The function (2) may be called the gaussian - plane wave (GP)
function. Because of the gaussian part, the function is confined within the
molecular region, but it oscillates, dependent on $|\mathbf{k}|$. The function (2) is prac-
tically discrete on " energy $k^2/2$ ", because two GP functions, $GP(\alpha, \mathbf{k})$ and
$GP(\alpha, \mathbf{k}')$, become nearly overcomplete if $(\mathbf{k}-\mathbf{k}')^2/2 \lesssim 2\alpha$. In addition to the
energy, the direction of the wave vector $\mathbf{k}$ has to be discrete. In the present
approximation, only a limited number of directions is chosen in the basis such as[5]

$$\mathbf{n} = \mathbf{k}_i/|\mathbf{k}| = (0,0,1),\ (\pm 1/\sqrt{2},\pm 1/\sqrt{2},\pm 1/\sqrt{2}),\ (\pm 1/\sqrt{3},\pm 1/\sqrt{3},\pm 1/\sqrt{3}),\dots \qquad (3)$$

In practice the real representation of (2),

$$CGP(\alpha,k,\mathbf{n}; \mathbf{r}) = \exp(-\alpha r^2)\cos(\mathbf{k}\,\mathbf{r})\quad,\ \text{and}$$

$$SGP(\alpha,k,\mathbf{n}; \mathbf{r}) = \exp(-\alpha r^2)\sin(\mathbf{k}\,\mathbf{r})\quad,\qquad (4)$$

is convenient. Thus, near the molecule, the continuum
wavefunction of the ejected electron with energy ε

may be approximated as

$$\psi(\varepsilon,\mathbf{r}) = \sum_i a_{i\varepsilon} G(1_i m_i n_i \alpha_i;\mathbf{r}) + \sum_{jl} \sum w_1 [b_{j1\varepsilon} CGP(\alpha_j k_j \mathbf{n}_1;\mathbf{r}) + c_{j1\varepsilon} SGP(\alpha_j k_j \mathbf{n}_1;\mathbf{r})], \quad (5)$$

where the weight w_1 is required because of the discreteness of the direction $\mathbf{n}_1$.[5]

The advantage of the present GP basis functions is that any types of many-center molecular integrals between GP functions and between GP and GT functions can be given in closed forms as in the case of GTF. All the necessary matrix elements of the one-electron operators except the core attraction operator can be written in terms of the auxiliary function:

$$S(n,k,\alpha) = \int_{-\infty}^{\infty} dx\, x^n \exp(-\alpha x^2 + ikx) = (-i)^n (\pi/\alpha)^{1/2} (4\alpha)^{-n/2} \exp(-k^2/4\alpha) Hn(-k/2\sqrt{\alpha})$$

where $Hn(t)$ is the Hermite polynominal function. To obtain the matrix elements of the core attraction and the electron repulsion, the Laplace transformation, $1/r = \int_{-\infty}^{\infty} du \exp\{-u^2(x^2+y^2+z^2)\}$, and the transformation of the variable, $u^2 + \alpha = \alpha/(1-t^2)$, are required.[6] After some manipulation, the final expressions are given in terms of another auxiliary function:

$$\begin{matrix} Ec(m,\beta,\gamma) \\ Es(m,\beta,\gamma) \end{matrix} \Big] = \int_0^1 dt\ (1-t^2)^m \exp\{-\beta(1-t^2)\} \Big[\begin{matrix} \cos\{\gamma(1-t^2)\} \\ \sin\{\gamma(1-t^2)\} \end{matrix}$$

For the atomic (one-center) problem, where γ is zero, $Ec(m,\beta,0)$ becomes the confluent hypergeometric function. Thus, the numerical integration is not necessary.

To determine the wavefunction (5), the static exchange approximation (equivalent to the IVO, or EHP method) is used. The configuration interaction is also applied. In both methods, the traditional quantum chemical program packages can be used with a minor change. One way to calculate the cross section is the Stieltyes-Tchebycheff procedure. If a large number of GP functions with broad range of $k^2/2$ values are taken as a basis set, the pseudo eigenvalues in the static exchange approximation are also found in the broad range of energy. Thus, the Stieltyes imaging can systematically be improved. In the alternative way, when the cross section at a particular energy range is needed, a set of GP functions with $\{k_j^2/2 = k_0^2/2 \pm j\Delta,\ j= 1,2,...\}$ can be taken, where Δ should be larger than 2α. Even in this case, a few GP functions with large and small $k^2/2$ may have to be added. Much numerical work is required to examine the applicability of the present basis function. The calculation for the one-center problem is under way.

1. P.G.Burke, J.Phys.(Paris), Colloq. C-4, 27 (1978).

2. P.W.Langhoff, C.T.Corcoran, and J.S.Sims, Phys.Rev.A, 16, 1513 (1977)

3. G.R.J.Williams and P.W.Langhoff, Chem.Phys.Letters, 60, 201 (1979) and the other references therein.

4. S.Iwata, N.Kosugi, and O.Nomura, Jpn.J.Appl.Phys., 17S, 109 (1978), and to be published.

5. M.Abramowitz and I.Stegun, 'Handbook of Mathematical Functions', Dover Publish.Inc., New York (1972).

6. J.C.Browne and R.D.Rochusta, J.Chem.Phys., 36, 1933 (1962).

DIPOLE OSCILLATOR STRENGTHS FOR IONIC FRAGMENTATION OF N_2O AND CO_2 (10-75 eV)

C.E. Brion and A.P. Hitchcock[+]

Department of Chemistry, University of British Columbia, Vancouver, Canada V6T 1W5

and

M.J. Van der Wiel

FOM Institute for Atomic and Molecular Physics,
407 Kruislaan, Amsterdam, The Netherlands

Quantitative dipole oscillator strengths for molecular photoionization and ionic fragmentation can be derived from inelasticly scattered fast electrons detected in coincidence with the respective ionization products (electrons or ions). A number of studies [1] have shown that the combination of electron-electron and electron-ion coincidence methods is well suited to studies of the fragmentation of the ground and excited states of molecular ions. Recently the partial photoionization oscillator strengths of N_2O and CO_2 up to 60 eV have been obtained from (e,2e) measurements performed at the Dept. of Chemistry, UBC, Vancouver [2]. We now report complementary measurements of the photofragmentation of N_2O and CO_2 up to 75 eV obtained with the (e,e+ion) apparatus at the FOM Institute, Amsterdam.

The photoabsorption spectrum, ionization efficiency and the fractional yields of the parent and fragment ions (see Fig. 1) were obtained using the methods outlined previously [3]. This data was then used to determine the dipole oscillator strength spectra for the production of each ionic species. The ion fragment

Fig. 1.   Ratio of fragment to parent ion
          formation in photoionization of
          N_2O and CO_2.

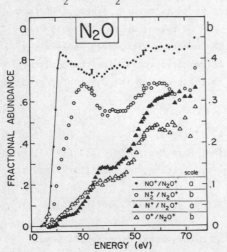

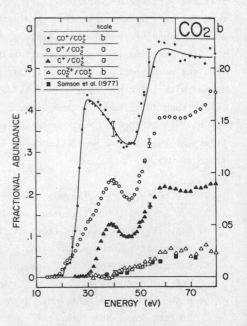

oscillator strengths have been combined with the previously reported ion state partial oscillator strengths [2] to study the fragmentation of the molecular ions. Fig. 2 illustrates the breakdown of the ion state oscillator strengths into molecular and dissociative components. For CO_2, the $\tilde{X}$, $\tilde{A}$ and $\tilde{B}$ states are stable against fragmentation while all higher energy states dissociate. For N_2O, the $\tilde{X}$ state and ca. 63% of the $\tilde{A}$ state are responsible for N_2O^+ production while all higher energy states and ca. 37% of the $\tilde{A}$ are dissociative. Further details of the fragmentation schemes of the dissociation ion states will be presented along with a discussion of double ionization in N_2O and CO_2.

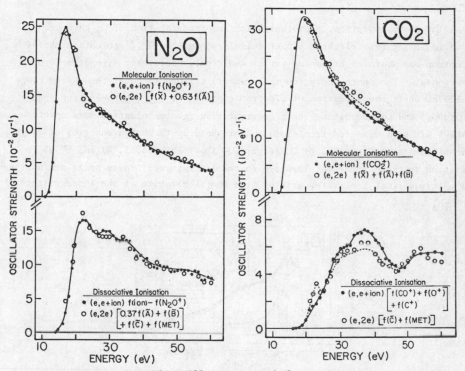

Fig. 2. Partition of total oscillator strength for ionization of N_2O and CO_2 over molecular and fragment ion formation.

Financial support for this work was provided by the National Research Council of Canada, the North Atlantic Treaty Organization and the Netherlands Organization for the Advancement of Pure Research (Z.W.O).

1. K.H. Tan, C.E. Brion, Ph.E. Van der Leeuw and M.J. Van der Wiel, Chem. Phys. 29 (1978) 299 and references therein.
2. C.E. Brion and K.H. Tan , Chem. Phys. 34 (1978) 141.
3. C. Backx, R.R. Tol, G.R. Wight and M.J. Van der Wiel, J. Phys. B 8 (1975) 2050, 3007.

[+] present address: Department of Chemistry, McMaster University, Hamilton, Canada.

DIPOLE OSCILLATOR STRENGTHS FOR THE PHOTOABSORPTION,
PHOTOIONIZATION AND FRAGMENTATION OF MOLECULAR OXYGEN

C.E. Brion and K.H. Tan,

Department of Chemistry, University of British Columbia,
Vancouver, Canada, V6T1W5.

and

M.J. Van der Wiel and Ph.E. Van der Leeuw,

FOM Institute for Atomic and Molecular Physics,
Amsterdam, The Netherlands.

The photoabsorption, photoionization and fragmentation of O_2 have been studied[1] using fast electron impact coincidence methods[2,3,4] to obtain photo-electron and photoion branching ratios and dipole oscillator strengths (cross-sections). The photoabsorption measurements (figure 1) cover the energy range 5-300 eV while the formation of electronic states of O_2^+ (photoelectron spectroscopy) and the resulting ionic fragmentation (photoionization mass spectrometry) are both measured from close to threshold up to photon energies of 75 eV. The binding energy spectra of O_2 (figure 2) show peaks at 33, 47 and 57 eV in addition to those reported elsewhere in the literature. These peaks are assigned to multiple final ion states arising from photoionization of the inner valence orbitals.

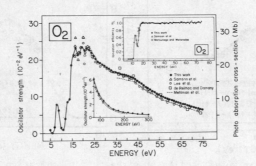

Figure 1

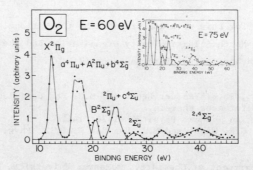

Figure 2

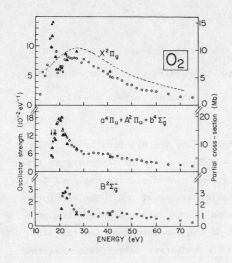

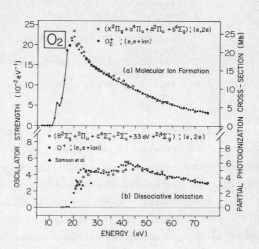

Figure 3

Figure 4

▲   Samson, PES

O   (e,2e) this work

---   Theory

Structure in the O_2^+ electronic state partial oscillator strength curves (figure 3) is in good agreement with recent theoretical work[5] which predicts the existence of several shape resonances. A quantitative picture (figure 4) of the dipole-induced breakdown of O_2 is obtained for the energy range 12-75 eV. The photoionization efficiency is found to be constant above 20 eV.

1. C.E. Brion, K.H. Tan, M.J. Van der Wiel and Ph.E. Van der Leeuw, J. Electron Spectrosc. 1979, in press.

2. C.E. Brion, A. Hamnett, G.R. Wight and M.J. Van der Wiel, J. Electron Spectrosc. 12 (1977) 323.

3. C. Backx and M.J. Van der Wiel, J. Phys. B 8 (1975) 3020.

4. C.E. Brion and A. Hamnett, "Continuum Optical Oscillator Strength Measurements by Electron Spectroscopy in the Gas Phase", Advances in Chemical Physics (J. Wiley, N.Y.) 1979, in press.

5. A. Gerwer, C. Asaro, B.V. McKoy and P.W. Langhoff, to be published.

PHOTOIONISATION OF SF_6 IN THE XUV REGION

M. Sasanuma*, E. Ishiguro*, T. Hayaishi**, H. Masuko[+], Y. Morioka[+],
T. Nakajima[+] and M. Nakamura[+]

*   Department of Applied Physics, Osaka City University, Osaka 558,
     Japan
**   Institute of Physical Technology, University of Tsukuba, Ibaraki
     300-31, Japan
+   Institute of Physics, University of Tsukuba, Ibaraki 300-31,
     Japan

Photoionisation spectra of SF_6 are obtained using the synchrotron radiation
and mass spectrometer in the region from 300 to 820 Å. A 50 cm Seya-Namioka type
monochromator equipped with a 1200 lines/mm platinum coated grating was used to
disperse the radiation. The wavelength resolution was about 2 Å. The resolution
of mass spectrometer was, $M/\Delta M = M$. A collision chamber was connected through a
differential pumping section to the exit slit of the monochromator and the mass
spectrometer was connected at right angles to the radiation beam. Mass analized
ions were detected by an electron multiplier with the use of counting method and
the output signal was fed to a multichannel analyzer. The spectral distribution
of each fragment ion was measured for every 0.5 Å division between 300 and 820 Å.

Fragment ions, SF_5^+, SF_4^+ and SF_3^+ are observed in the present experiment.
Appearance potentials (in eV) of these ions are determined as $15.3 \pm 0.2 (SF_5^+)$,
$19.1 \pm 0.5 (SF_4^+)$ and $19.4 \pm 0.5 (SF_3^+)$, respectively. The relative abundance of
these ions observed in the present experiment is shown in Fig. 1. The relative
abundance is proportional to the partial cross section σ_{mi} for the fragments SF_m^+ (
$m = 3,4,5$) and the total ionisation cross section σ_i is considered to be a sum of
these three, that is, $\sigma_i = \sum_{m=3}^{5} \sigma_{mi}$. On the other hand, σ_i is also obtainable from
the value of total absorption cross section σ and of ionisation efficiency γ, by
a relation $\sigma_i = \gamma \cdot \sigma$. Absolute values of the ordinate in Fig. 1 is obtained by
normalizing the present relative value at 23.2 eV(535 Å) peak to the previously
observed value[1], $\sigma_i = 86$ Mb($\sigma = 155$ Mb, $\gamma = 0.56$). Two curves of σ_i are compared
in the figure; curve B is obtained from the previous work[1] and the curve C is
from the present work. Though there are some 20 to 30 percent of discrepancies
between the two σ_i in some places, whole spectra have a trend of agreement with
each other. It may be considered that the discrepancy between the two σ_i above
30 eV, is probably caused by errors involved in the previous work, due to the
stray light in the shorter wavelength region. In Fig. 1, there is also given a
curve of total absorption cross section obtained in the previous work for comparison.

Several broad structures appear in each ion spectrum as can be seen in Fig.1.
Most of the structures in SF_5^+ spectrum correspond to those in the total absorption
of which structures are interpreted in the scheme of the electron transitions
between the molecular orbitals[1].   Broad structure c centered at ca. 18.8 eV is
peculiar to SF_5^+ and it can not be recognized in the absorption spectrum. We

consider its origin as a dissociative product of the excited state that corresponds to the Rydberg transition of $4t_{1u}$ electron, of which adiabatic ionisation limit is 22.08 eV[1]. Structure f is also the Rydberg series[2] caused by the transition of $5t_{1u}$ electron. It is noticiable that the two Rydberg states dissociate wholly to SF_5^+.

The appearance of SF_6^+ with unusually small relative abundance reported by Dibeler and Walker[3], who measured it using helium 584 Å, could not be observed in the present experiment.

1. M. Sasanuma, E. Ishiguro, H. Masuko, Y. Morioka and M. Nakamura, J. Phys. B, Atom. Molec. Phys. 11, 3655(1978).

2 K. Codling, Chem. Phys. 44, 4401(1966).

3. V. H. Dibeler and J. A. Walker, J. Chem. Phys. 44. 4405(1966).

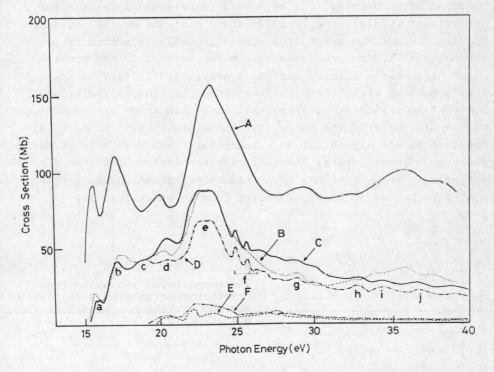

Fig. 1, Partial and total ionisation cross sections of the fragment ions. In the figure, curve A is the total absorption, σ, obtained in the previous work. Curve B is the total ionisation cross section which can be obtained by the relation, $\sigma_i = \gamma \cdot \sigma$ for each photon energy. Curve C is a sum of the values of curve D, E and F, and is normalized to a point of curve B at 23.2 eV. Curve D, E and F are for the spectra of SF_5^+, SF_4^+ and SF_3^+ ions.

RADIATIVE DISSOCIATION OF SELECTIVELY EXCITED VIBRATIONAL LEVELS
OF THE B STATE OF H_2

H. Schmoranzer and R. Zietz[*]

Fachbereich Physik, Universität Kaiserslautern
D 6750 Kaiserslautern, Germany

Vacuum ultraviolet continuous emission from selectively excited vibrational levels of the B $2p$ $^1\Sigma_u^+$ state of molecular hydrogen into the dissociation continuum of the electronic ground state
X $1s$ $^1\Sigma_g^+$ has been observed recently[1]. In the present work the
range of observation is extended towards higher vibrational levels
and a comparison of the results with the semi-classical difference
potential concept of Mulliken[2] is discussed.

Monochromatized synchrotron radiation from the storage ring
DORIS at DESY, Hamburg, has been used to selectively excite the
vibrational levels v'=0,...,13 of the B state of H_2. The emission
spectra recorded by means of a specially designed secondary monochromator at 1.5 nm resolution are shown in Fig. 1. The spectra
which have been corrected for the spectral sensitivity of the entire apparatus clearly exhibit structured continuous radiation
for $v \geqslant 7$ occurring at wavelengths longer than those corresponding
to transitions from the upper vibrational level B,v' under consideration to the highest bound vibrational level X,v" = 14 of the
electronic ground state. The radiative transitions into the dissociation continuum of the bound electronic ground state represent a mechanism of energy transfer from an electronically,

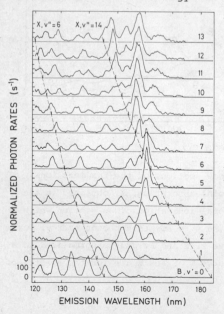

Fig. 1

Vuv bound-bound and bound-free
emission spectra from selectively
excited vibrational levels of the
B state of H_2.

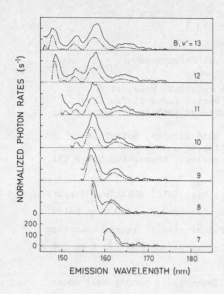

Fig. 2
Bound-free emission continua from
v'=7...13 of the B state of H_2

———————— experimental normalized
photon rates

··——··—·· quantum mechanical calculation[6]

vibrationally and rotationally excited state of a diatomic molecule into kinetic energy of the two atoms, the former constituents
of the dissociating molecule.

The H_2 B - X continuum represents a model situation, where
both potential curves involved as well as the dependence of the
electronic transition moment on internuclear distance have been
corroborated experimentally[3]. With regard to the use of the Mulliken concept for determining potential curves of a diatomic molecule[4] or an excimer[5] it is interesting to test the accuracy of the
semi-classical concept applying to the case of a lower bound electronic state for the first time. The construction of the difference potential for the H_2 B - X case predicts a maximum wavelength
of 162.3 nm for continuous radiation. This corresponds to transitions at constant internuclear distance from any v'-level to the
maxima of the respective difference potentials. As can be seen
from Fig. 1, about 80 % of the continuous radiation is measured
within the classically allowed wavelength region, whereas a small
discrepancy remains. Quantum mechanically calculated transition
probabilities[6] and relative experimental photon rates, as compared
in Fig. 2, are in good agreement for the individual v'-levels.

*)Present address: DESY, HASYLAB, D 2000 Hamburg 52

1   H. Schmoranzer and R. Zietz, Phys. Rev. A18, 1472 (1978)
2   R.S. Mulliken, J. Chem. Phys. 55, 309 (1971)
3   H. Schmoranzer, J. Phys. B 8, 1139 (1975)
4   J. Tellinghuisen, Phys. Rev. Lett. 34, 1134 (1975)
5   H. Schmoranzer, R. Wanik and H. Krüger, this conference
6   T.L. Stephens and A. Dalgarno, J.Q.S.R.T. 12, 569 (1972)

UPPER LIMIT OF THE CROSS SECTION FOR PHOTODISSOCIATION OF H_2
INTO EXCITED ATOMS IN THE RANGE 620 - 350 Å

M. Glass-Maujean[a], K. Köllmann[b] and K. ITO[c]

LURE, Laboratoire Commun C.N.R.S. et Université
Paris-Sud, 91405 Orsay, Cedex - France.

a)Also at Laboratoire de Spectroscopie Hertzienne de l'ENS, Université
  Pierre et Marie Curie, 4 place Jussieu - 75230 Paris, Cedex 05 France.
b)Also at Institut für Experimental Physik, Universität Hamburg, Jungiusstr.9,
  D 2000 Hamburg 36, West Germany.
c)Also at Laboratoire des Collision Atomiques et Moléculaires, Université
  Paris-Sud, Bâtiment 351, 91405 Orsay, Cedex - France, and on the leave from
  Department of Chemistry, Tokyo Institute of Technology, Meguro-ku, Tokyo 152,
  Japan.

Using synchrotron radiation of Orsay's strage ring (ACO) which was dispersed
by a 1-m normal incidence Mc-Pherson monochromator (Pt-coated, 3600 ℓ/mm holographic grating), the production of Lyman-α and Balmer atomic fluorescence from
the photodissociation of molecular hydrogen was investigated from 620 Å to 350 Å
with a 2.5 Å bandwidth.

The monochromatic light passed through a differentially pumped cell where
the pressure was maintained to a few 10^{-2} Torr (fig.1). Lyman-α fluorescence was
detected with a solarblind EMR photomultiplier (quantum efficiency:~20% for Ly-α)
through a MgF_2 window (transmission:~30%). An electric field of ~60 V/cm was
applied to induce the 2S $\longrightarrow$ 2P transition. Balmer fluorescence was detected
with 9658 R photomultiplier (quantum efficiency: ~5% for Balmer-α).

The ratio of the absorption cross section (σ_{abs}) to the Ly-α production
cross section ($\sigma_{Ly\alpha}$) is

$$\sigma_{Ly\alpha} / \sigma_{abs} = (n_{Ly\alpha} /n_{abs}) (\ell / \int \Delta\Omega d\ell),$$

where $n_{Ly\alpha}$ is the number of Ly-α photons reaching the detector defined by the
solid angle $\Delta\Omega$, and n_{abs} the number of incident photons absorbed by H_2 in the
cell of the effective length ℓ. The dark current was 16 $\pm$ 2 cps. We observed
that there was no variation in this count number over the entire region of 620 Å
- 350 Å when the H_2 gas was introduced. The absorption cross sections have already been measured several times and found to be 1.5 - 7.3 x 10^{-18} cm^2 in this
region [1]. From these values and our measurement we can deduce an upper limit for
the cross section of the photodissociation leading to H(n=2) atoms. It varies
from 1.7 x $10^{-20} cm^2$ at 350 Å to 1.2 x 10^{-20} cm^2 at 620 Å with a minimum 1 x 10^{-20}
cm^2 at 425 Å.

The same type of measurement on the Balmer emission led to :

$$\sigma_{Balmer -\alpha} < 2 \times 10^{-21} cm^2 .$$

These results differ greatly from those obtained by electron impact, where
the role of the triplet states and the singlet gerade states is important. They
also indicate that the optically accessible doubly excited repulsive states of H_2

predominantly decay via autoionization in this energy region.

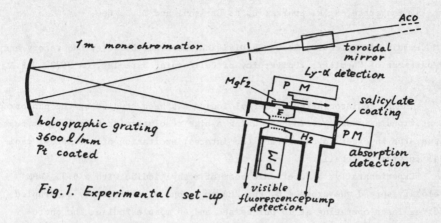

Fig.1. Experimental set-up

1. J.A.R. Samson and R.B. Cairns, J. Opt. Soc. Am., 55, 1035 (1965) ; L.C. Lee., R.W. Carlson and D.L. Judge., J. Quant. Spectrosc. Radiat. Transfer, 16, 873 (1976).

ENERGY DISPOSAL IN THE PHOTODISSOCIATION OF CH_3I AT 266 NM [†]

K. Shobatake[††], R. K. Sparks, L. R. Carlson, and Y. T. Lee

Materials and Molecular Research Division, Lawrence Berkeley Laboratory and
Department of Chemistry, University of California, Berkeley, CA 94720 U.S.A.

The photodissociation of methyl iodide has been studied by the photofragment translational spectroscopy using a high resolution cross molecular beam apparatus in order to understand the internal excitation of the methyl radical in greater detail.

Experimentally, a supersonic beam of methyl iodide with a 6.3% FWHM velocity spread was crossed by the 266 nm output of a frequency quadrupled Nd:Yag laser operating at 10 pulses/sec and 40 mJoules/pulse. The photofragments were observed in the plane of the two beams with an electron bombardment quadrupole mass spectrometer operated in the pulse counting mode. The flight length of the neutral fragments was 34.4 cm. The time-of-flight (TOF) spectrum was obtained at 1 μsec intervals by an on-line computer.

The experimental data for detection of $m/e=15(CH_3^+)$ are shown in Fig. 1. The corresponding c.m. translational energy distribution is shown in Fig.2. The two peaks arise from the two electronic states of iodine atoms produced:

$$CH_3I \xrightarrow{h\nu} CH_3 + I(5^2P_{3/2})(\equiv I) \quad \text{and} \quad CH_3 + I(5^2P_{1/2})(\equiv I^*).$$

Since convolution broadening was found to be small, the maximum c.m. translational energy of the photofragment production has been determined reasonably accurately. From the maximum c.m. translational energy of the pairs of products and the energy of the laser photons ($h\nu$ =107.5 kcal/mol) we have determined the CH_3—I dissociation energy to be 52.9 ±.5 kcal/mol, which is believed to be more accurate than the value adopted previously, 55 ±1[1]. From Fig. 2 we also find that at the peak of the I^* production only 11% of the total energy available, E_{avl}^* (32.9 kcal/mol), is partitioned in the internal excitation of the CH_3, and the FWHM of the c.m. recoil energy distribution is 9.3% of E_{avl}^*. The corresponding values for the I production are 12 and 13.7% of the maximum energy available, E_{avl}(54.6 kcal/mol).

† This work was supported by the Division of Chemical Sciences, Office of
    Basic Energy Sciences, U. S. Department of Energy.
†† IBM Postdoctral Fellow, 1977-78.

1.   S. J. Riley and K. R. Wilson, Discuss. Faraday Soc. __53__, 132 (1972).

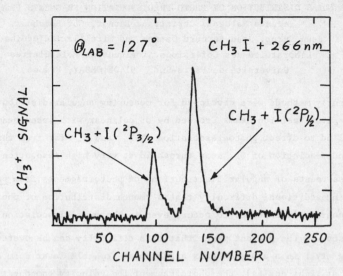

Fig. 1.   Observed time-of-flight spectrum for detected methyl
radicals at 127° laboratory angle relative to the incident
direction of the molecular beam. The time scale is 1 μsec/
channel. Background has been subtracted.

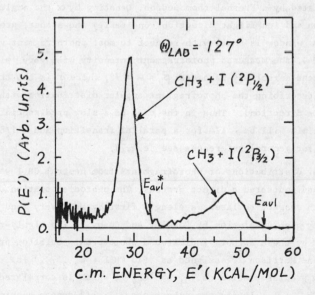

Fig. 2.   Single Newton-diagram inversion of the data of Fig. 1; the
c.m. translational energy distribution, $P(E')$, versus c.m.
translational energy, E'. E_{avl}^{*} (or E_{avl}) $-E'$ is the
internal energy of the methyl radical for the I^{*} (or I)
production.

ANGULAR DISTRIBUTION OF PHOTO-PREDISSOCIATION FRAGMENTS FROM CH_3I^+

Laurence Malegat, Christiane Pernot, Guy Bouchoux,
<u>Jean Durup</u>, Jean-Bernard Ozenne and Mireille Tadjeddine.
Laboratoire des Collisions Atomiques et Moléculaires [*],
Université de Paris-Sud, 91405 ORSAY, France.

Recently methods were developed for measuring angular distributions of photofragments from fast ion beams crossed by or colinear with laser beams, and they were applied to direct photodissociation of D_2^+ and O_2^+ far from threshold [1] and to photo-predissociation of O_2^+ near threshold at very high resolution [2].

Measurements of angular distributions of photofragments from <u>polyatomic</u> ions present the additional difficulty that a smooth distribution of photofragment kinetic energies is expected to occur, even in photo-predissociation.

We show in the present paper that this difficulty can be overcome in the following way : in a crossed-beams arrangement (tunable laser beam and parent ion beam at right angles), the photofragment ion velocity component parallel to ion flight direction is analyzed with a narrow window, set at the parent ion velocity, so that only fragments ejected at essentially 90° with respect to ion flight direction are collected ; further, a broad apparatus collection angle ensures that no angular discrimination takes place ; finally the laser polarization is rotated by a Fresnel rhomboedron. Denoting by α the angle between laser polarization and ion flight direction, one easily shows that, provided the velocity analysis window is small with respect to most photofragment velocities (in the c.o.m. frame), the measured photofragment intensity will vary with α according to an apparent anisotropy parameter $\beta' = -\beta/2$, where β is the true anisotropy parameter (describing the photofragment angular distribution with respect to laser polarization direction). Thus in the case of a slow predissociation β' in the classical limit will be - 1/4 for a parallel transition and + 1/8 for a perpendicular one (for general references see e.g. [3]).

Angular distributions of photofragments from neutral CH_3I were reported long ago [4,5], and indicated a direct process. The photodissociation of CH_3I^+ was studied with respect to laser wavelength first by McGilvery and Morrison [6] and then at very high resolution by Moseley and Cosby [7]. The highly-resolved structure observed by these authors indicated a photo-predissociation process, which McGilvery and Morrison [6] assigned as (1) $CH_3I^+(^2E_{3/2,1/2}) + h\nu \rightarrow CH_3I^+(^2A_1)$ followed by predissociation of $^2A_1$ by $^2E_{1/2}$, which is correlated to the observed fragments $CH_3^+ + I$. In (1) the subscripts 3/2, 1/2 denote quantum number Ω in a quasi-diatomic description ; $^2A_1$ has $\Omega = 1/2$. This assignment was based on previous work by photoelectron spectroscopy [8-11].

Using the above-described method we recorded the angular distribution of CH_3^+

* Associated to the C.N.R.S.

fragments from CH_3I^+ at a wavelength of 594 nm where according to McGilvery and Morrison [6] the lower level belongs to the $^2E_{1/2}$ state. In spite of the very low photofragment energies (5 meV at half-maximum of the velocity distribution), we observed nice oscillations of the photofragment ion intensity with respect to laser polarization direction, with minima at α =0 and π and a maximum at $\alpha = \pi/2$, clearly indicating a predissociation following a _parallel_ transition (see above). The observed oscillation amplitude (0.2, with respect to maxima) was less than the theoretical one (0.33) probably because of the finite velocity resolution.

Thus the $^2E_{1/2} \rightarrow {}^2A_1$ transition in CH_3I^+ has its dipole moment parallel to the C_3 axis. Therefore its direction is not controlled by the orbital symmetry (an $E \rightarrow A_1$ transition is perpendicular to the axis in the absence of spin-orbit coupling) , but by the variation in the projection Ω of the total angular momentum, here $\Delta\Omega = 0$.

These data will be used for deriving from the observed velocity distribution the c.o.m. photofragment energy distribution, which in turn has to be known to permit a quantitative determination of the anisotropy parameter with account of instrumental effects.

This work was partly performed on contract ATP 3753 with the C.N.R.S.

1. C. Pernot, J.-B. Ozenne, M. Pánczél and J. Durup, X ICPEAC, Abstr.Pap. v. 1 , 94 (1977).

2. C. Pernot, J. Durup, J.-B. Ozenne, J.A. Beswick, P.C. Cosby and J.T.Moseley, submitted to J. Chem. Phys.

3. J. Durup, Colloques Internat. CNRS 273, 107 (1977).

4. S.J. Riley and K.R. Wilson, Disc. Faraday Soc. 53, 133 (1972).

5. M. Dzvonik, S.Yang and R. Bersohn, J. Chem. Phys. 61, 4408 (1974).

6. D.C. McGilvery and J.D. Morrison, J. Chem.Phys. 67, 368 (1977) ; Int. J.Mass Spectrom. Ion Phys. 28, 81 (1978).

7. P.C. Cosby, private communication (1978).

8. J.L. Ragle, I.A. Stenhouse, D.C. Frost and C.A. McDowell, J.Chem.Phys. 53, 178 (1970).

9. J.H.D. Eland, R. Frey, A. Kuestler, H. Schulte and B.Brehm, Int. J. Mass Spectrom. Ion Phys. 22, 155 (1976).

10. D.M. Mintz and T. Baer, J. Chem. Phys. 65, 2407 (1976).

11. L. Karlsson, R. Jadrny, L. Mattsson, Foo Tim Chau and K. Siegbahn, Phys. Scripta 16, 225 (1977).

PHOTODISSOCIATION OF HEH++ BY ELECTRONIC TRANSITION

K.K.Datta, Samir Saha and A.K.Barua

Department of General Physics and X-rays
Indian Association for the Cultivation of Science
Calcutta 700032, India

Photodissociation cross sections of HeH++ by electronic transition from the weakly bound 2pσ state to the repulsive 3dσ state have been calculated over the accessible range of wavelength $\lambda\lambda$ 800-5800Å. The calculations are almost exact within the limits of Born-Oppenheimer separation and the dipole approximation. The expression for the partial photodissociation cross section is given by[1]

$$\sigma_{vj} = (4\pi)^2 (\frac{\mu^2 V}{3\hbar^3 \lambda}) |Q_{vj}^o|^2 \qquad \ldots(1)$$

where

$$Q_{vj}^o = \int \chi_{kl}^*(r) Q(r) \chi_{vj}(r) dr \qquad \ldots(2)$$

The present formulation differs only in the normalization of the continuum wavefunction χ_{kl} that had been carried out in the earlier work[2] by matching

$$\chi_{kl}(r) \longrightarrow \sin(kr - l\pi/2 + \delta_l) \qquad \ldots(3)$$

at asymptotic range, which is valid only if the asymptotic potential energy falls out faster than $1/r$. But HeH++ in the 3dσ state dissociates into He+ and H+ that interact asymptotically as $1/r$ which is of Coulomb type. To consider the effect of this (modified) Coulomb potential, χ_{kl} was normalized by matching

$$\chi_{kl}(r) \longrightarrow \sin[kr - \eta \ln(2kr) - l\pi/2 + \gamma_l + \delta_l] \qquad \ldots(4)$$

asymptotically, where $\eta = \mu Z_1 Z_2 e^2 / k\hbar^2$, Z_1 and Z_2 being the nuclear charges of the separating ions and γ_l the Coulomb phase shift.

The eigenenergies (E_{vj}) and the radial wavefunctions (χ_{vj} and χ_{kl}) were obtained for all the vibrational levels(v) and for rotational levels j=15 and 18 which are the most probable values at temperatures 20000 and 28000°K respectively. The radial Schrödinger equation was integrated numerically using the Numerov method.[2] The interaction potential energies and transition dipole moments, $Q(r)$, are those obtained by Lane and coworkers.[3,4]

The partial cross sections σ_{vj} are to be summed over v and j with an appropriate weighting factor to get the total cross section σ. In this calculation following Von Busch and Dunn,[5] we neglected the sum over j and used the relation

$$\sigma = \sum_{vj} p_{vj}\sigma_{vj} = \sum_{v} p'_{vj_{eff}}\sigma_{vj_{eff}} \quad \ldots(5)$$

where j_{eff} is an effective rotational quantum number which was
taken as the most probable value at the temperature of calculation.
Following Argyros,[6] the weighting factor $p'_{vj_{eff}}$ was taken as the
Boltzmann distribution factor. This seems to be most probable
under the conditions of thermodynamic equilibrium at high
temperatures of our calculations.

The cross sections σ_{vj} when plotted against λ show a peak at
$\lambda \sim 1475\text{Å}$ for v=0 and for v=1, there are two peaks at $\lambda \sim 1250$
and 1850Å with j=15 or 18. The plot of cross section σ against λ
exihibits a single peak at $\lambda \sim 2200\text{Å}$ for j=15 or 18. The $\sigma-\lambda$
curve shows small kinks as those observed by Argyros[6] for the
system H_2^+. The maximum order of σ is $10^{-18}cm^2$ which is one order
less than that for H_2^+ (or its isotopes)[1,7,8] and HeH^{+2}. The value
of σ is of considerable magnitude over the range of $\lambda\lambda$ 1000-4400Å
and gradually falls below $10^{-20}cm^2$ at λ below $\sim 800\text{Å}$ and above
$\sim 5800\text{Å}$.

1. G.H. Dunn, Phys. Rev. 172, 1 (1968).
2. S. Saha, K.K. Datta and A.K. Barua, J. Phys. B 11, 3349
   (1978).
3. T.G. Winter, M.D. Duncan and N.F. Lane, J. Phys. B 10, 285
   (1977).
4. T.G. Winter and N.F. Lane, unpublished (1978).
5. F. Von Busch and G.H. Dunn, Phys. Rev. A 5, 1726 (1972).
6. J.D. Argyros, J. Phys. B 7, 2025 (1974).
7. M. Tadjeddine and G. Parlant, Mol. Phys. 33, 1797 (1977).
8. K.K. Datta, S. Saha and A.K. Barua, Ind. J. Phys. A 51, 215
   (1977).

HYPERSPHERICAL ANALYSIS OF H⁻ ¹Pᵒ RESONANCES NEAR H(n=3)[*]

Chris H. Greene

Department of Physics, University of Chicago,
Chicago, Illinois 60637, U.S.A.

The hyperspherical method of studying two electron correlations was used by Lin[1] recently to classify H⁻ resonances near the n=2 level of hydrogen. The present study uses Lin's adiabatic approach to determine the properties of doubly-excited H⁻ states near the n=3 level. In this method the two-electron Schrödinger equation was first solved at fixed values of $R = (r_1^2 + r_2^2)^{\frac{1}{2}}$ to yield a set of adiabatic potential curves $U_\mu(R)$. Approximate energy levels and wavefunctions were then calculated by solving a one-dimensional Schrödinger equation in the hyper-radius R.

The five adiabatic potential curves which converge to the n=3 level of hydrogen at large R are plotted in the figure. Two of these curves are attractive at large R and support an

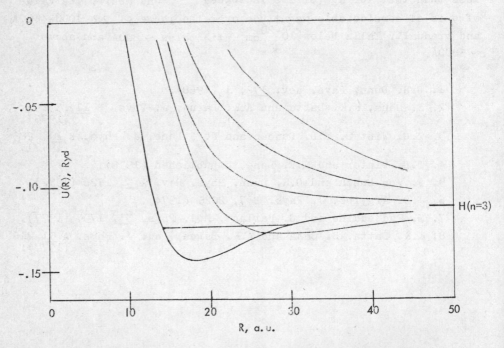

infinite number of bound levels (ignoring the spin-orbit interaction and the Lamb shift). The lowest energy level belongs to the state labelled "+", and its position in the adiabatic approximation is 0.0132 Ry below the n=3 threshold. Because the "+" states penetrate to much smaller R, they should autodetach faster than the "−" states by one or two orders of magnitude. We emphasize that this situation is rather different here than near the n=2 threshold, where the "+" channel is repulsive at large R and has no bound levels (though it does give rise to a strong shape resonance just above its threshold). Note also that there is no evidence in the figure for any $^1P^o$ shape resonance above the n=3 threshold. Recent experimental results appear to confirm these conclusions.[2] In addition to the above, we hope to have more quantitative results on the shapes and widths of the "+" and "−" resonances to present at the conference.

*Work supported by the Department of Energy, Office of Basic Energy Sciences.

1. C. D. Lin, Phys. Rev. Lett. 35, 1150 (1975).

2. M.E. Hamm, J. Donahue, P.A.M. Gram, J.C. Pratt, M.A. Yates-Williams, H.C. Bryant, D.A. Clark, C.A. Frost, H. Sharifian, H. Tootoonchi, and W.W. Smith, Bull. Am. Phys. Soc. 24, No. 4, 561 (1979).

LIFETIME OF He$^-$ FORMED THROUGH COLLISIONS OF He$^+$ AND Ca VAPOR*

R. N. Compton, G. D. Alton, A. D. Williamson, and A. E. Carter

Oak Ridge National Laboratory, Oak Ridge, Tennessee 37830, U.S.A.

The properties of metastable He$^-$ ions have been extensively studied both experimentally and theoretically. Until about 1975 it was generally assumed that long-lived He$^-$ ($\tau > 10^{-6}$ sec) existed only in the (1s 2s 2p) ^{4}P state. The $^4P_{3/2,1/2}$ submultiplets can decay through spin-orbit and spin-spin interaction via coupling with the doublet P states while $^4P_{5/2}$ He$^-$ can decay only through the considerably weaker spin-spin interaction.

Three groups[1-4] have presented experimental evidence that He$^-$ can also exist in a long-lived doublet state. Recent theoretical calculations,[5] however, could produce no long-lived even parity, doublet states of He$^-$.

We have measured the lifetime of He$^-$ ions produced in collisions between He$^+$ and Ca vapor. Provided that the Wigner spin rule is not violated and that double collisions are negligible, doublet He$^-$ states are expected[1] in such collisions. The experimental arrangement is shown in Fig. 1. In brief, the lifetime is

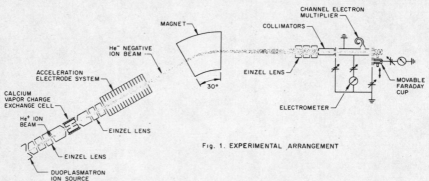

Fig. 1. EXPERIMENTAL ARRANGEMENT

determined by measuring the ratio of the electron current collected on a positively biased 26-cm-long plate of a parallel plate charge collector to the total He$^-$ ion beam current reaching the Faraday collector. The transit time (decay time) is varied by changing the ion beam energy from 40 to 100 keV. In order to remove the small effects of stripping due to background gas ($P_o \sim 2 \times 10^{-7}$ torr), we have measured the ratio of electron signal to ion beam signal for various N_2 gas pressures and extrapolated this ratio to zero pressure. This extrapolated ratio for various ion energies is used to determine the lifetime from the exponential decay of He$^-$. Our lifetime of He$^-$ is 10.5 $\pm$ 2 μsec and is compared with other data in Table I.

The present results do not resolve the controversy surrounding the existence of a long-lived doublet state of He$^-$ since we cannot be certain that spin "flip" collisions are not creating quartet He$^-$. However, these are the first measurements for He$^-$ lifetimes where a long-lived doublet state is logically expected. It is

Table I. Measured Lifetimes of He$^-$

Source of He$^-$	Lifetime (μsec)	Reference
He$^+$ + He	18.2	7
He$^+$ + N$_2$	9^{+5}_{-3}	8
He$^+$ + K	11.5 $\pm$ 5 and 345 $\pm$ 90	9
He ($2^{1,3}$s) + H$_2$	>1	4
He$^+$ + K	500 $\pm$ 200, 10 $\pm$ 2, 16 $\pm$ 4	10
He$^+$ + Ca	10.5 $\pm$ 2	Present

noteworthy that our lifetime matches the short-lived component lifetime for He$^-$ from other collision pairs (see Table I).

These studies are a prelude to experiments underway in our laboratory which will examine resonant laser photodetachment of long-lived He$^-$. A tunable dye laser is crossed with the He$^-$ beam and the photodetached electrons are counted with a channel electron multiplier (see Fig. 1.). If He$^-$ (^{2}P) exists in the beam, structure should occur at the wavelengths corresponding to transitions from (1s 2p^2) ^{2}P^e He$^-$ to higher doublet states which have been observed in electron collision experiments.[6] Also, breaks or "cusps" are expected at the wavelengths corresponding to the opening of inelastic channels at other thresholds [e.g., (1s 3s)^{3}S He + e$^-$]. Thus, laser resonance photodetachment could provide exact identification of the metastable states of He$^-$ as well as spectroscopic information on resonance levels and lifetimes.

*Research sponsored by the U.S. Department of Energy under contract W-7405-eng-26 with the Union Carbide Corporation.

1. R. A. Baragiola, abstracts of papers, VIII ICPEAC (Belgrade) 827 (1973).

2. E. H. Pedersen, F. R. Simpson, and P. Hvelplund, J. Phys. B 7, 1294 (1974); Phys. Rev. A 11, 516 (1975).

3. R. A. Baragiola and E. R. Salvatelli, J. Phys. B 8, 382 (1975).

4. K. F. Dunn, B. J. Gilmore, F. R. Simpson, and H. B. Gilbody, J. Phys. B 11, 1797 (1978).

5. C. F. Bunge and A. V. Bunge, Int. J. Quantum Chem. 12, 345 (1978); Phys. Rev. (in press).

6. J.N.H. Brunt, G. C. King, and F. H. Read, J. Phys. B 10, 433-448 (1977).

7. D. J. Nicholas, C. W. Trowbridge, and W. D. Allen, Phys. Rev. 167, 38 (1968).

8. F. R. Simpson, R. Browning, and H. B. Gilbody, J. Phys. B 4, 106 (1971).

9. L. M. Blau, R. Novick, and D. Weinflash, Phys. Rev. Lett. 24, 1268 (1970).

10. R. Novick and D. Weinflash, Proc. Int. Conf. Precision Measurements and Fundamental Constants, (Gaithersburg, MD), ed. D. N. Langenberg and B. N. Baylor, NBS Spec. Pub. 343, p. 403.

PHOTODETACHMENT OF K$^-$ TO THE $4^2S_{1/2}$, $4^2P_{1/2}$ AND $4^2P_{3/2}$ LEVELS OF K.*

R. A. Falk, D. Leep, R. Geballe

Physics Department, University of Washington
Seattle, Washington, U.S.A.

We have measured relative cross sections for the reaction $K^- + h\nu \rightarrow K^* + e$ where * denotes the $4^2S_{1/2}$, $4^2P_{1/2}$ and $4^2P_{3/2}$ levels of potassium. A 2.5 keV beam of K$^-$ crosses the beam of either a dye laser or an Ar ion laser so that photon energies are available in a continuous range near the P thresholds and at a few discrete energies up to about 1eV above threshold. At right angles to the crossed beams, a photometer with either a 7665 Å or 7699 Å interference filter detects the fluorescence due to the K(4^2P-4^2S) decay. Downstream of the inter-action region the K$^-$ beam is separated from the neutral K. The K$^-$ beam is collected in a Faraday cup. The neutrals are detected by secondary electron emission. Thus the total number of neutrals and the number of neutrals in the P channels are measured. As only the S and P channels are energetically accessible, the branching ratios can be determined.

The data obtained with the Ar$^+$ laser at photon energies of 19430, 20135, and 20486 cm^{-1} are as follows. The branching ratios at these three energies are the same within the 10% measurement uncertainty, namely 0.17 for the $P_{1/2}$ level and 0.33 for the $P_{3/2}$ level. These values are in accord with the 2:1 statistical-weight ratio of these levels, and their sum agrees well with the branching ratio measured for the combined ^{2}P levels by Kasdan and Lineberger.[1]

The results for the photon energies covered by the dye laser are shown in Figure 1. The behavior in the region from 17020 cm^{-1} to 17100 cm^{-1} is in good agreement with earlier work done by Slater et al. who detected the low-energy electrons.[2] The data above the $4^2P_{3/2}$ threshold shows structure which appears to be interference between the $4^2P_{1/2}$ and $4^2P_{3/2}$ channels.

*Work supported by National Science Foundation Grant PHY 78-00856.

1.   A. Kasdan, and W. C. Lineberger, Phys. Rev. A 10, 1658(1974).
2.   J. Slater, F. H. Read, S. E. Novick, and W. C. Lineberger, Phys. Rev.
       A 17, 201(1978).

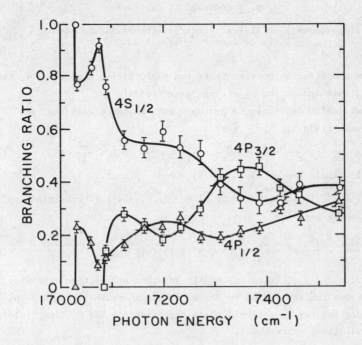

Figure 1.   Branching ratios for the reaction $K^- + h\nu \rightarrow K(4^2S_{1/2}, 4^2P_{1/2}, 4^2P_{3/2})$ near the $4^2P_{1/2}$ and $4^2P_{3/2}$ thresholds.

ATOMIC IONIZATION BY STRONG LASER FIELDS

H. S. Brandi and L. Davidovich

Departamento de Física, Pontifícia Universidade Católica
Rio de Janeiro - Brasil 20.000

We show the relation between three non perturbative approaches to the problem of atomic ionization by strong laser fields[1,2,3].

The Hamiltonian describing a hydrogen atom in the presence of an electromagnetic field is ($\hbar = c = 1$)

$$H = \frac{p^2}{2m} - \frac{e^2}{r} + H' = \frac{p^2}{2m} - \frac{e^2}{r} - \frac{e}{m}\ \vec{p}.\vec{A} + \frac{e^2}{2m}\ A^2, \qquad (1)$$

where, in the dipole approximation, $\vec{A}(t) = \dfrac{\vec{E}_0}{\omega}\ \sin \omega t$.

In ref. 1, H' is substituted by $\bar{H}' = - e\vec{r}.\vec{E}$, and the transition amplitude for ionization is given by

$$\tau_{q,o}^{(0)} = \int_0^t dt' < \bar{\Phi}_q\ (\vec{r},t'), \bar{H}'(t')\phi_0(\vec{r},t') > . \qquad (2)$$

In equation (2), $\bar{\phi}_q$ is an asymptotic solution of the time dependent Schrödinger equation associated to $\bar{H}'$; ϕ_0 is an unperturbed atomic bound state. Neglecting the logarithmic phase associated to the Coulomb field (which is done in all three approaches),

$$\bar{\phi}_q(\vec{r},t) = \frac{1}{(2\pi)^{3/2}}\ e^{i\left[\vec{q} - e\,\vec{A}(t)\right].\vec{r}}\ e^{i\int_0^t \frac{1}{2m}\ \left[\vec{q} - e\,\vec{A}(\tau)\right]^2 d\tau} . \qquad (3)$$

In the space translation approximation (STA)[2], ionization is also described by eq. (2), replacing $\bar{H}'$ by H'. In both cases we can use the identity

$$\bar{\phi}_q(\vec{r},t) = \phi_q(\vec{r},t) + \int_0^t dt' \int d^3r\ \ G^0(\vec{r},t;\vec{r},t')\ H'(t')\phi_q(\vec{r}',\vec{t}'), \qquad (4)$$

where $\phi_q(\vec{r},t)$ is a free-electron plane wave and G^0 is the retarded Green's function corresponding to $H_0 = \dfrac{p^2}{2m} + H'$. In (4), H' denotes either H or H'. Using eq. (4) we rewrite eq. (2) (symbolically) as

$$\tau_{q,o}^{(0)} = \int_{-\infty}^t dt'\ \ \left[\ <\phi_q,H'\phi_0> + <\phi_q, H'G^0H'\phi_0>\right]\ , \qquad (5)$$

where the lower limit of integration has been extended to $-\infty$ (which does not change the results). This expression coincides with the one given in ref. 3, except for the $A^2(t)$ term which is discarded in that reference. For weak fields, it reduces to the usual first-order perturbation theory result. However, it does not reproduce the second-order result, where instead of G^0 one has the Green's function corresponding to the unperturbed atomic Hamiltonian. In fact, as discussed in reference 3, $\tau_{q,o}^{(0)}$ is the first term in the expansion of the exact transition amplitude in powers of V. The next term is

$$\tau_{q,o}^{(1)} = <\phi_q, H'G^0 VG^0 H'\phi_0> .$$ (6)

The criterium for neglecting this and the following terms in the expansion with respect to the second term in expression (5) is:

$$\left| \frac{\tau_{q,o}^{(1)}}{<\phi_q, H'G^0 H' \phi_0>} \right| << 1 .$$ (7)

Calculation for the hydrogen atom shows that this is the case for

$$\gamma = \frac{\omega\sqrt{2mI_0}}{e\ E_0} << 1 .$$ (8)

The parameter γ defines the range of applicability of these methods. For typical values of ω, eq.7 implies that $E >> 10^7 V/cm$. For this range of γ, the contribution of the term $A^2(t)$ is important, and should be retained in the calculation.

1. L. V. Keldysh, Sov. Phys.- JETP 20, 1307 (1965)
2. F. H. M. Faisal, J. Phys. B 6, L89 (1973
3. J. Gersten and M. H. Mittleman, Phys. Rev. A 10, 74 (1974)

COMPLEX SCALING APPROACH FOR ATOMIC
PHOTOIONIZATION IN INTENSE RADIATION
AND MAGNETIC FIELDS*

Shih-I Chu

Department of Chemistry, University of Kansas
Lawrence, Kansas 66045

A nonperturbative method is presented for the treatment of the interaction of atoms with radiation in the presence of a magnetic field, based on the generalization of the quasienergy formalism for intense field multiphoton ionization.[1] Using the complex scaling transformation appropriate for the Stark-Zeeman operator[2], and L^2 discretization of the atomic continuum, the shifted and broadened quasienergy states can be located and photoionization or multiphoton ionization rates determined as a function of arbitrary radiation and magnetic field intensities. The theory will be illustrated by several examples.[3]

*Research supported in part by the University of Kansas General Research Fund 3721-20-0038.

1. S. I. Chu, Chem. Phys. Letters 54, 367 (1978).
2. S. I. Chu, Chem. Phys. Letters 58, 462 (1978).
3. S. I. Chu, Chem. Phys. Letters (in press 1979).

ATOMS INTERACTING WITH A QUANTIZED RADIATION MODE

A. Tip

FOM-Institute for Atomic- and Molecular Physics,
Kruislaan 407, Amsterdam, The Netherlands

We have investigated the properties of a model consisting of an atom interacting with a quantized radiation mode in dipole approximation. The model describes multiphoton processes (excitation and ionization), bremsstralung phenomena and free-free transitions. Scattering of photons is outside its scope, since it is not possible to construct photon wave-packets that disappear from localized regions in space for large times due to the circumstance that only a finite number of radiation modes is taken into account. For a hydrogen atom coupled to a single field mode the Hamiltonian is given by

$$H = [\underline{p}_1 - e\,\underline{A}\,(\underline{x}_1)]^2 \,/\, (2m) + V(\underline{x}_1) + H^f \tag{1}$$

where $\underline{p}_1$, $\underline{x}_1$ are the electron momentum and position vectors, $\underline{A}(\underline{x})$ the vector potential, $V(\underline{x})$ the Coulomb interaction, and H^f the field Hamiltonian. In dipole approximation $\underline{A}(\underline{x}_1)$ is replaced by $\underline{A}(o)$ and after expressing the field creation and annihilation operators in terms of coordinates and momenta $\underline{x}_2$ and $\underline{p}_2$ (two-dimensional, since there are two polarization directions) and performing a unitary transformation the Hamiltonian transforms into (γ is basically the fine structure constant)

$$\hat{H} = \underline{p}_1^2 \,/\, (2m) + V(\underline{x}_1 - \gamma\,\underline{x}_2) + \omega\,[\tfrac{1}{2}\,(\underline{x}_2^2 + \underline{p}_2^2) - 1] \tag{2}$$

We have shown that $\hat{H}$ has an infinite number of negative bound states. They accumulate at zero where the continuous spectrum starts. Other branches of the latter start at ω, 2ω,..... etc. We also demonstrated that the dilatation analytic (complex rotation) method[1,2] applies to this model. Thus after a change $x \to x\,\exp[\,i\psi]$, $p \to p\,\exp[\,-i\psi]$ of the dynamical variables $\hat{H}$ turns into $\hat{H}(\psi)$, a non-Hermitean operator with spectrum as given in figure 1.

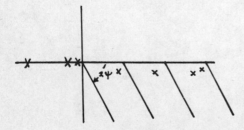

Fig. 1.
Spectrum of $H(\psi)$, crosses are eigenvalues, solid lines continuous spectrum.

Complex eigenvalues with positive real part now appear. (They reduce to
sums of atomic and oscillator eigenvalues for γ=o). Their imaginary parts
are connected with the probabilities for multi-photon ionization processes
and with the widts of resonances in elastic scattering. Thus there is a
strong analogy with the dilatation-analytic treatment of atomic auto-ionization processes[2]. As in that case the method has the advantage that only
square-integrable functions are needed in approximate calculations. Secondly
no expansion in powers of γ is involved, i.e. arbitrarily strong fields can
be handled. The method generalises easily to more complex atoms, including
spin-terms.

1. E. Balslev and J.M. Combes, Comm. Math. Phys. 22, 269 (1971).

2. B. Simon, Annals of Math. 97, 247 (1973).

TWO-PHOTON IONIZATION OF HELIUM FROM 2^3S STATE

R.K. Sharma and K.C. Mathur
Department of Physics, University of Roorkee,
Roorkee- 247672, India.

The generalized cross section for the two-photon ionization
from an initial state a_g to a final state a_f of an atom is given
by[1] (The notations used here are the same as in reference [2])

$$\hat{\sigma} = (2\pi\alpha\omega)^2 \ \frac{m}{\hbar} \ \frac{k}{(2\pi)^2} \int \left| K^{(2)}_{a_f, a_g} \right|^2 d\Omega_k,$$

The transition matrix $K^{(2)}_{a_f, a_g}$ involves an infinite summation over
intermediate states. Recently we[2] studied the two-photon ionization
of He from its metastable 2^1S state using truncated summation method
in the non-relativistic dipole approximation. Here we extend this
approach to the calculation of two-photon ionization of He from 2^3S
state for circularly and linearly polarized light. In these
calculations we include the contribution of the N states (2^3P, 3^3P,
4^3P and 5^3P) exactly and ignore the contribution of the remaining
states. Fig. 1. shows our results for the variation of the ratio of
the cross section for circularly polarized light to that of linearly
polarized light ($\hat{\sigma}_C/\hat{\sigma}_L$) with wavelength in the range 3180-4000 A^o.

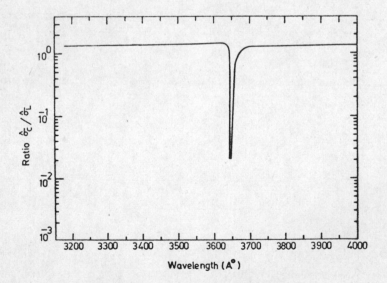

Fig.1.

The variation is in a manner similar to that of ionization of He from 2^1S state[2]. It shows a sharp minima nearly at 3650 A^o and the maximum value acquired is never greater than 1.5 satisfying the theory of Klarsfeld and Maquet[3].

Further we can account for the contribution of the states omitted in the truncated summation method through the use of the closure technique. The transition matrix is then given by

$$K^{(2)}_{a_f, a_g} = \sum_{a_j=1}^{N} \langle a_f|R|a_j\rangle \langle a_j|R|a_g\rangle \{(\omega_{a_j, a_g} -\omega + i\gamma/2)^{-1} - $$

$$(\omega_{N+1, a_g} -\omega + i\gamma/2)^{-1}\} + \langle a_f|R^2|a_g\rangle (\omega_{N+1, a_g} -\omega + i\gamma/2)^{-1}$$

where we have assumed an average intermediate state energy equal to $\hbar\omega_{N+1}$. We find that the states omitted in the truncated summation method give a significant contribution to the cross section in the off resonance region. The results for this will be presented at the time of the conference.

1. H.B.Bebb and A.Gold, Phys. Rev. 143,1 (1966)
2. R.K.Sharma and K.C.Mathur, IEEE J.Q.Electronics USA 14,771(1978)
3. S.Klarsfeld and A.Maquet, Phys.Rev.Lett.29,79(1972).

THREE–PHOTON, TWO–PHOTON IONIZATION OF METASTABLE 2^1S AND 2^3S HELIUM ATOMS

L.A. LOMPRE, B. MATHIEU, G.MAINFRAY and G. WATEL

Centre d'Etudes Nucléaires de Saclay, Service de Physique

Atomique, B.P. N° 2 – 91190 GIF-sur-Yvette (France)

A linearly polarized ruby laser beam, fundamental radiation (14396 cm^{-1}) or first harmonic radiation (28792 cm^{-1}), is focused by a spherical lens into a metastable helium atomic beam. The He 2^1S component of the beam can be quenched by optical pumping and the ratio of the singlet component to the triplet component is measured by a time-of-flight technique. The density of metastable atoms is typically $10^3 - 10^4$ atoms per cm^3 and the residual pressure in the apparatus is 10^{-9} Torr.

The He$^+$ ions, are collected with a weak transverse electric field, mass identified with a time-of-flight mass spectrometer and are detected by an electron multiplier. The multiplier output signal is recorded on an oscilloscope.

The variation of the number of ions per pulse N$^+$ as a function of the light energy W is shown in fig.1 in log-log coordinates. At low energy the slopes of the graphs are equal to three, which corresponds to the order of the process and decrease at higher values of photons flux : the singlet curve exhibits typical saturation effects due to the total ionization of all metastable atoms present in the interaction volume. At the slope change, the generalised cross-section $\hat{\sigma}_S^{(3)}$ for singlet is given by $\hat{\sigma}_S^3 = 1/\tau_3 I^3$ where τ_3 is the effective interaction time for a 3rd order process and I the laser intensity (photons.cm^{-2}.s^{-1}). The saturation is not observed on the triplet curve but the generalised cross section $\hat{\sigma}_T^{(3)}$ for triplet is given by $\hat{\sigma}_T^{(3)} = \hat{\sigma}_S^{(3)} \dfrac{N_T^+}{N_S^+} \dfrac{n_S}{n_T}$ where n_S and n_T are the densities of singlet and triplet in the beam.

Our first measurements give experimental three-photon ionization cross sections much smaller than those obtained by Bakos /1/. The comparison with the recent theoretical results of Olsen /3/ is shown in Table 1.

/1/ BAKOS J., KANTOR J. and KISS A. (1970) Sov. Phys. JETP Lett. 12, 555.

BAKOS J., DELONE N.B., KISS A., MANAKOV N.L. and NAGAEVA M.L. (1976)

Sov. Phys. JETP 44, 268.

/2/ OLSEN T. , LAMBROPOULOS P., WHEATLEY S.E. and ROUNTREE S.P., J. Phys.B

11, 4167 (1978).

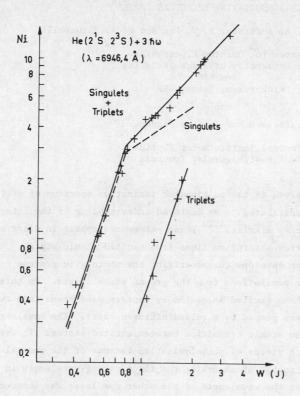

Fig.1.
Variation of the number of Helium ions He$^+$ as a function of the light energy.

TABLE 1

	Present results	Olsen et al
$\hat{\sigma}(3)$ $_S$ cm^{6}s^2 (14396 cm^{-1})	(2.4 ± 1.0) 10^{-81}	$9.2 \ 10^{-80}$
$\hat{\sigma}(3)$ $_T$ cm^{6}s^2 (14396 cm^{-1})	(1.6 ± 0.9) 10^{-82}	$3.4 \ 10^{-81}$
$\hat{\sigma}(3)_S / _T$ ^{1} ^{3} (14396 cm^{-1})	17 ± 4	27
$\hat{\sigma}(2)$ $_S$ cm^{4}s (28792 cm^{-1})	(1.3 ± 0.7) 10^{-50}	
$\hat{\sigma}(2)$ $_T$ cm^4 s (28792 cm^{-1})	(5.0 ± 3.6) 10^{-51}	

Three-photon ionization cross section $\hat{\sigma}^{(3)}$ Two-photon ionization cross section $\hat{\sigma}^{(2)}$.

MULTIPHOTON IONIZATION OF Cs_2 DIMERS
THROUGH DISSOCIATIVE MOLECULAR STATES*

C. B. Collins, J. A. Anderson, F. W. Lee and P. A. Vicharelli

Center for Quantum Electronics
The University of Texas at Dallas
Box 688
Richardson, Texas, USA

and

D. Popescu and Iovitzu Popescu

Central Institute for Physics
Bucharest/Magurele, Roumania

Hybrid resonances observed in the multiphoton ionization spectrum of cesium and rubiduim dimers have contributed to an improved understanding of the interatomic potentials of the heavy alkalis.[1,2] These resonances appear in dispersion curves of ion yields as narrow absorption lines from excited atomic states, modulated in intensity by an envelope characterizing the photolytic process producing the absorbing atomic populations from the ground state dimers. In this work such resonances have been excited in cesium by superimposed beams from two separately tunable dye lasers pumped by a pulsed nitrogen laser. The wavelength of one laser was fixed on an atomic transition between excited states. It was observed to give only modest yields of photoionization because of the general absence of excited states capable of absorbing the illuminating wavelength in the relatively cold vapor. When the wavelength of the other dye laser was scanned through the visible wavelengths increases in the ionization yield of better than an order of magnitude were encountered. These enhancements were resolved into several distinct absorption bands for the photolytic excitation of Cs_2 yielding specific atomic products. Significant differences were observed in the resulting bands leading individually to the production of appreciable populations of $6P_{1/2}$, $6P_{3/2}$, $5D_{3/2}$ and $5D_{5/2}$ cesium atoms.

*Conducted as part of the U.S.-Roumanian Cooperative Program in Science and Technology supported by NSF Grant INT 76-18982.

1. C. B. Collins, B. W. Johnson, M. Y. Mirza, D. Popescu, and I. Popescu, Phys. Rev. A10, 813 (1974).
2. C. B. Collins, S. M. Curry, B. W. Johnson, M. Y. Mirza, M. A. Chellehmalzadeh, J. A. Anderson, D. Popescu and I. Popescu, Phys. Rev. 14, 1662 (1976).

LIFETIMES AND ABSORPTION CROSS SECTION MEASUREMENTS
OF SELECTED ROTATIONAL STATES OF $NO_2(^2B_2)$*

C. H. Chen, S. D. Kramer, D. W. Clark[†], and M. G. Payne

Oak Ridge National Laboratory, Oak Ridge, Tennessee 37830, USA

A cooled NO_2 beam with a rotational temperature below 10°K was obtained by the expansion of a mixture of 1% NO_2 in Ar through a supersonic nozzle jet. A tunable, pulsed dye laser with a wavelength resolution of 0.6 cm^{-1} was used to promote the rotationally cooled NO_2 to selected excited rotational states of $NO_2(^2B_2)$. The decay of the excited NO_2 molecules was measured by means of time-resolved fluorescence spectra. The absolute value of the laser wavelength was determined to an accuracy of $\pm$ 2 $\overset{o}{A}$, while the laser power and the beam size were also accurately measured.

A high resolution fluorescence excitation spectrum of rotationally cooled NO_2 was obtained from 4500 $\overset{o}{A}$ to 6000 $\overset{o}{A}$. More than two hundred vibronic bands were observed. This high resolution fluorescence excitation spectrum was used to determine rotational constants for the lower and upper vibronic states.

Time-resolved fluorescence excitation spectra were used to measure the lifetimes of selected rotational states of $NO_2(^2B_2)$. The lifetimes of more than one dozen vibronic bands were studied. A simple exponential decay was observed for each individual vibronic band. This may imply that the multiexponential decay reported by Donnelly and Kaufman[1] is due to collisional conversion. The lifetimes found in our experiments are significantly shorter than those obtained from cell experiments.

The absorption cross sections of selected rotational states of $NO_2(^2B_2)$ can also be measured by varying the laser power. It was found that the cross sections for various rotational states in the same vibronic band can differ by a factor of two. The absorption cross sections for a 0.6 cm^{-1} excitation bandwidth are in the range of 10^{-18} cm^2 for $NO_2(^2B_2)$.

*Research sponsored by the Office of Health and Environmental Research, U.S. Department of Energy, under contract W-7405-eng-26 with the Union Carbide Corp.

[†]ORAU Summer Student Research Participant from The Pennsylvania State University.

1. V. M. Donnelly and F. Kaufman, J. Chem. Phys. **66**, 4100 (1977).

II.   Electron-Atom Collisions

SEPARABLE-FACTOR EXPANSION OF PERTURBATION HAMILTONIAN AND
ITS APPLICATION TO ELECTRON HYDROGEN-ATOM SCATTERING

Smio Tani

Department of Physics, Marquette University
Milwaukee, Wisconsin, 53233, U.S.A.

One can show that the method of Padé approximant in potential scattering is closely related with the method of approximating the perturbation Hamiltonian by using a sum of separable potentials (finite rank approximation) [1]. We recapitulate the essential formulas, starting from the Lippmann-Schwinger equation

$$\psi = \phi_f + \lambda \, G \, V \, \psi \;, \tag{1}$$

where ϕ_f is the free (unperturbed) state, which satisfies the Schroedinger equation for the unperturbed problem for energy E

$$(H_0 - E) \, \phi_f = 0 \;. \tag{2}$$

The standing-wave Green's function of H_0 is denoted by G, $G = (H_0 - E)^{-1}$, while λ is the variable for the magnitude of the perturbation V ; when λ is equal to unity, it corresponds to the physically realizable situation. Choose N trial wave functions $\{ \alpha_i , i = 1, 2, \cdots, N \}$ such that, when all channel coordinates are small, the state of close collision, ψ_c , may be approximated by a linear combination of $\{ \alpha_i \}$

$$\psi_c = G \, V \, \psi \simeq \sum_{i=1}^{N} c_i \, \alpha_i \;, \text{ (small channel coordinates).} \tag{3}$$

Next, carry out the Schmidt orthogonalization and normalization, considering V to be the metric of the functional space. The members of the new set $\{ \chi_i \}$ satisfy

$$< \chi_i^\dagger , V \chi_j > = \delta_{ij} \;, \tag{4}$$

where χ_i is a certain linear combination of $\{ \alpha_i \}$

$$\chi_i = \sum_{j=1}^{N} C_{ij} \, \alpha_j \;. \tag{5}$$

We then replace the perturbation Hamiltonian V by

$$V = \sum_{i=1}^{N} | V \chi_i > < \chi_i^\dagger V | + R^{[N]} \;. \tag{6}$$

The sum on the right-hand side defines the rank N approximation of V , whereas $R^{[N]}$ is the residual term. If we start with the set generated by iteration of the kernel introduced in Eq.(1), $\alpha_{i+1} = (G \, V)^i \, \phi_f$, in which the first member is $\alpha_1 = \phi_f$, and if we discard $R^{[N]}$, the [N,N] Padé approximant will be automatically reproduced [1].

Once the basis $\{ \chi_i \}$ is chosen, we may evaluate the matrix elements

$$M_{ij} = < \chi_i^\dagger , \quad V G V \chi_j > \quad , \tag{8}$$

and determine the T matrix in the rank N approximation

$$T^{[N]} = \lambda \sum_{i,j} |V \chi_i > (1 - \lambda M)_{ij} < \chi_j^\dagger V| \quad . \tag{9}$$

If necessary, one may improve the accuracy by performing a perturbation calculation, considering $R^{[N]}$ to be a small perturbation. The objective of the present work is to extend the above method, sketched for potential scattering, to
few body scattering problems. We must confront with a number of problems that
arise from the complex nature of few body systems: (i) First, Green's function
shows a complicated structure that depends on the variety of possibilities of
dividing the entire system into subsystems. (ii) Second, the choice of $\{ \chi_i \}$
may depend on energy E_γ , say, available in each channel γ [2]. In our study of
the electron hydrogen-atom collision, we employ the hyperspherical coordinates[3] .
The results obtained with moderate values of rank N in our approximation will
be compared with the results of the close-coupling and other methods.

1. S. Tani, Bull. Am. Phys. Soc. 24, 54 (1979); C.R. Garibotti and
    M. Villani, Nuovo Cimento 63A, 1367 (1969); G. Turchetti, Fortschr.
    Phys. 26, 1 (1978).

2. G.E. Brown and A.D. Jackson, The Nucleon-Nucleon Interaction, North-
    Holland, Amsterdam, (1976), Chap. V , Sec. C .

3. C.D. Lin, Phys. Rev. A 14, 40 (1976); D.L. Knirk, J. Chem. Phys. 60,
    66 (1974); W.G. Cooper and D.J. Kouri, J. Chem. Phys. 57, 2487 (1972);
    J. Macek, J. Phys. B (GB) 1 , 831 (1968).

NONSINGULAR VARIATIONAL PRINCIPLE FOR THE SCATTERING
LENGTH FOR THE TARGET WAVE FUNCTION IMPRECISELY KNOWN

Leonard Rosenberg[*] and Larry Spruch

Department of Physics, New York University
New York, New York 10003

Some time ago Demkov[1] showed that the variational principle for low-energy electron-atom scattering parameters could be preserved even when, as is usually the case, the target ground-state wave function ϕ is imprecisely known. However, the effectiveness of this approach is diminished by the appearance of singularities, with the consequence that even for trial functions of very reasonable form there can be values of the nonlinear variational parameters which lead to very poor estimates for the phase shift. It was pointed out recently[2] that in the case of zero-energy scattering a simple modification of the Demkov principle leads to a minimum principle, not for the true scattering length A, but for an auxiliary quantity $\tilde{A}$ which differs from A by terms of order $\phi - \phi_t$, where ϕ_t is the trial target ground-state wave function. The merit of this procedure (which has now been tested numerically[3]) lies in the fact that by virtue of the minimum principle the nonlinear parameters in the trial scattering wave function can be systematically improved without encountering numerical instabilities. Results are stationary with respect to variations in all parameters except those which appear in ϕ_t. In a recent attempt to obtain a result which is completely variational we have examined the integrals which appear in the functional representing $\tilde{A}$ in order to explicitly identify the first-order error.[4] While this attempt was not successful we believe that the approach is correct and that a simple expression for the first-order error can be obtained. By subtracting off this error term we will arrive at a true nonsingular variational expression, as we hope to demonstrate in detail.

[*]1978-79 JILA Visiting Fellow.

1. Yu. N. Demkov, Variational Principles in the Theory of Collisions (MacMillan, New York, 1963), p. 27.

2. R. Blau, L. Rosenberg, and L. Spruch, Phys. Rev. A 15, 1475 (1977).

3. I. Aronson, R. Blau, C. Kleinman, L. Rosenberg, and L. Spruch, Phys. Rev. A (to be published).

4. L. Spruch and L. Rosenberg, in Atomic Scattering Theory, Mathematical and Computational Aspects, edited by J. Nuttall (University of Western Ontario, 1978), p. 95.

LOW ENERGY ELECTRON-HYDROGEN SCATTERING

M.Dash Khan

Indian Association for the Cultivation of Science

Department of Theoretical Physics Calcutta 700032 - India

C.A. Falcon[*] and A.S. Ghosh[**]

Laboratoire d'Astrophysique[§], Université de Bordeaux I

33400 Talence - France

Temkin and Lamkin[1] and Sloan[2] have used the polarized orbital method (P.O.M.) to study the e⁻ - H scattering process. They have used the adiabatic dipole polarization potential. The choice is purely empirical. It has been argued that inclusion of other multipole terms may not be desirable because of the non-adiabatic condition in the atomic scattering processes. Callaway et al.[5] have used a potential which is the sum of the first three components ($\ell=0$, 1,2) of the adiabatic polarization and the first two components ($\ell=0,1$) of the non-adiabatic polarization potential. Their potential contains too much repulsion. Their singlet s-wave phase shifts are seriously lowered. The effect of the non-adiabatic polarization potential has been found to be important by Walters[3].

We have used the P.O.M. as suggested by Temkin and Lamkin[1] and Sloan[2]. Considering the importance of long range potentials we have included the adiabatic and non-adiabatic polarization potentials as used by Callaway et al. to study the e⁻ - H scattering problem.

In the table 1 we have tabulated the s-wave phase shifts along with those of Temkin and Lamkin[1], Callaway et al[5] and Schwartz[4].

Table 1. Elastic singlet and triplet s-wave phase shifts for e⁻ - H scattering

k	Singlet				Triplet			
	Present	Schwartz	Callaway	Temkin	Present	Schwartz	Callaway	Temkin
.1	2.4950	2.5530	2.4357	2.583	2.9311	2.9388	2.9477	2.945
.2	1.9906	2.0673	1.9099	2.114	2.7025	2.7171	2.7351	2.732
.3	1.6240	1.6964	1.5371	1.750	2.4778	2.4996	2.5254	2.519
.4	1.3485	1.4146	1.2586	1.469	2.2646	2.2938	2.3275	2.320
.5	1.1353	1.2020	1.0423	1.251	2.0677	2.1046	2.1454	2.133
1.	0.6297		0.5258	0.758			1.4854	1.460

The present results for the s-wave phase shifts are better than those of Callaway et al. when comparison is made with the variational results of Schwartz which are considered to be the most accurate. Our results lie always

below those of Schwartz. It is well known that the P.O.M. does not satisfy the
variation principle. Moreover we have not taken into account the non-static
condition of the system in the exchange kernel. This might be responsible for
the discrepancy between the present results with those of Schwartz.

Our p-wave phase shifts, that we have not given here, are in very
good accord with those of Armstead[6].

We conclude that it is reasonable to include the multiple components
of the adiabatic potential and also the distortion potential.

[*]On leave of absence from Instituto de Astronomia y Fisica del Espacio
1428 Buenos Aires - Argentina

[**]On leave of absence from Theoretical Physics, Indian Association for the
Cultivation of Science Calcutta 700032 - India

[§]Equipe de Recherche CNRS N° 137

1. A. Temkin and J.C. Lamkin, Phys. Rev. 121, 788 (1961)

2. I.H. Sloan Proc. Roy. Soc. (London) A281, 151 (1964)

3. H.R. Walters J. Phys. B. Atom. and Mol. Phys. 9, 227 (1976)

4. C. Schwartz Phys. Rev. 124, 1468 (1961)

5. J. Callaway, R.W. LaBahn, R.T. Pu and W.M. Duxler Phys. Rev. 168,
168 (1968)

6. R.L. Armstead, Phys. Rev. 171, 91 (1968)

*Elastic scattering of electron by hydrogen atoms in the adiabatic
approximation (electron - H scattering)*

Lee Mu-Tao, Ione Iga, J.C. Nogueira
Departamento de Química, Universidade Federal de São Carlos
São Carlos, S.P. (13560) - Brasil

The elastic scattering of electrons in the low and intermediate energy
range (8.7 - 30.0 eV) by atomic hydrogen was studied by the adiabatic
approximation, where the perturbed target wavefunction was expanded as a sum
of basis functions, $\emptyset$ $(1,2) = \Sigma C_i(2)\chi_i(1)$, where index $\underline{1}$ refer to the target
electron and index $\underline{2}$ to the scattered electron. The coeficients were
determined variationally, by minimization of the target energy (E_R) in each
scattered electron position. Six atomic hydrogen wavefunction $(1s, 2s, 2p_0,$
$3s, 3p_0$ and $3d_0)$ form the basis set, and the minimization was done between
$0-20$ a_0. The adiabatic scattering potential was obtained as:

$V = -\frac{1}{R} + E_R - E_0$, where E_0 is the ground state target energy.

The scattering wavefunction was expanded as partial wave series and the
radial differential equation was solved numerically. The local exchange
potential[1] was also included. The firsts four phase shifts for E = 8.7 eV
were compared with other theoretical results[2-5] and are shown in Table I.
In Table II, the calculated integrated elastic cross sections were compared
with the others[6]. The differential elastic cross sections were compared
with the absolute measurements of Williams[7]. The agreement is very good
over a wide angular range (Table III). The good agreement in the intermediate
energy range suggests that the adiabatic approximation could be extended to
higher energy ranges. Attempts to generalize the method for inelastic
scattering and for more complex atoms are in progress in this laboratory.

1- M.E. Riley and D.G. Truhlas, J. Chem. Phys. $\underline{63}$, 2182 (1975).

2- C. Schwortz, Phys. Rev. $\underline{124}$, 1468 (1961).

3- R.L. Armstead, Phys. Rev. $\underline{171}$, 91 (1968).

4- M.K. Gaitilis, Sov. Phys. - JETP, $\underline{20}$, 107 (1965).

5- P.G. Burke, D.F. Gallaher and S. Geltman, J. Phys. B: Atom and molec.
      Phys. $\underline{2}$, 1142 (1969).

6- J. Callaway and J.F. Williams, Phys. Rev. A, $\underline{12}$, 2312 (1975).

7- J.F. Williams, J. Phys. B: Atom. and Molec. Phys., $\underline{8}$, 1683 and 2191
      (1975).

Table I - Phase shifts for 8.7 eV electrons scattered by atomic hydrogen
(in radians).

		S = 0	S = 1
L = 0	a)	0.83066	1.5294
	b)	0.886	1.643
	c)	0.651	1.614
	d)	0.823	1.641
L = 1	a)	-0.006	0.544
	b)	-0.004	0.428
	c)	-0.116	0.321
	d)	-0.021	0.418
L = 2	a)	0.0384	0.065
	b)	0.073	0.068
	c)	-0.014	0.033
	d)	0.070	0.066
L = 3	a)	0.022	0.024
	c)	-0.002	0.004
	d)	0.025	0.026

a) Present results
b) s-wave from ref. 2, p-wave from ref. 3 and, d-wave from ref. 4
c) static-exchange approximation, ref. 5
d) pseudo-state approximation, ref. 5

Table II - Integrated elastic cross sections for electron-H scattering
(in πa_0^2).

Energy		12 eV	20 eV	30 eV
σ	a)	6.921	4.110	2.621
	b)	5.796	3.414	1.921
	c)	1.670	1.183	0.865

a) Present results
b) ref. 6
c) First Born Approximation

Table III - Differential elastic cross sections for electron-H scattering
(in $a_0^2 sr^{-1}$).

Energy angle	8.7 eV (a)	8.7 eV (b)	20 eV (a)	20 eV (b)	30 eV (a)	30 eV (b)
10^0	9.42	7.16±0.44	7.38	6.33±0.67	6.77	5.32±0.57
50^0	3.79	2.89±0.19	1.65	1.21±0.13	0.93	0.64±0.065
100^0	1.16	1.29±0.28	0.35	0.32±0.038	0.16	0.13±0.011
140^0	1.32	1.51±0.09	0.20	0.21±0.032	0.09	0.09±0.009

a) Present results   b) ref. 7

CALCULATION OF MOMENTUM-TRANSFER CROSS SECTION FOR SLOW ELECTRONS IN HELIUM

A.R.Tančić

Boris Kidrič Institute for Nuclear Sciences,Beograd
Yugoslavia

The momentum transfer cross section for electron helium collision at low energy range ($<$ 10 eV) has been calculated from an analysis of scattering phase shifts which are obtained in the framework of the random phase approximation with exchange (RPAE)[1,2].

An expression for a small phase shift in term of the self energy part could be found :

$$\Delta \hat{\delta_\ell}(E) = -\pi < \phi_{E\ell} | \Sigma | \phi_{E\ell} > \ ,$$

where $\phi_{E\ell}$ is the Hartree-Fock (HF) wave function of a scattered electron with energy E and angular momentum ℓ ,and Σ is the correction of the self energy part according to the HF potential in the range of RPAE.

Incident electron wave functions have been calculated in the field of a neutral atom,and for the virtual states-in the field of the corresponding single ionized ion.The scattering phase shifts for the first five partial waves for the energies from 0 to 30 eV have been calculated.The most important contribution to Σ is given by II-order diagrams.

Fig.1. show the momentum transfer cross section calculated for He (Fig.1. ―――― our results-RPAE, ----- [3],oooo [4]).

1. M.Ya.Amusia,N.K.Cherepkov and L.V.Chernisheva,JETP 60, 160 (1971) .

2. M.Ya.Amusia,A.R.Tančić and L.V.Chernisheva,Fizika (to be published) .

3. R.W.Crompton,M.T.Elford and A.G.Robertson,Aust.J.Phys. 23, 667 (1970) .

4. L.S.Frost and A.V.Phelps,Phys.Rev. A136, 1538 (1964) .

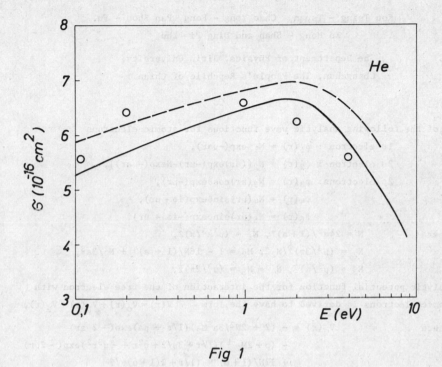

Fig 1

The Calculation of Total Cross Sections for The Scattering of
Slow Electrons by Nitrogen, Oxygen and Neon Atoms

Kou Tsing - Tsuan, Chao Yong - Fang, Pan Shou - Fu,
Xu Hong - Shan and Ding Pi - Zhu

The Department of Physics, Jirin University,
Changchun, The People's Republic of China

By use of the following analytic wave functions for atomic electrons

1s electron : $\psi_1(\underline{r}) = N_1 \exp(-\mu ar)$,

2s electron : $\psi_2(\underline{r}) = N_2((\mu r)\exp(-\mu r)-N\exp(-\mu ar))$,

2p electrons: $\psi_3(\underline{r}) = N_3(\mu r)\cos\theta\exp(-\mu r)$,

$\psi_4(\underline{r}) = N_4(\mu r)\sin\theta\exp(i\phi - \mu r)$,

$\psi_5(\underline{r}) = N_5(\mu r)\sin\theta\exp(-i\phi - \mu r)$.

where $\quad N = 24a^3/(1+a)^4$, $N_1 = (\mu^3 a^3/\pi)^{\frac{1}{2}}$,

$N_2 = (\mu^3/3\pi)^{\frac{1}{2}}/M_2^{\frac{1}{2}}$, $M_2 = 1 - 16N/(1 + a)^4 + N^2/3a^3$,

$N_3 = (\mu^3/\pi)^{\frac{1}{2}}$, $N_4 = N_5 = (\mu^3/2\pi)^{\frac{1}{2}}$,

the analytic potential function for the interaction of the free electron with
the atomic electrons is derived to have the form $\quad V(r) = V_o(r) + V_p(r) + V_e(r)$,

where
$$V_o(r) = - (2 + 2N^2/3a^3 M_2)(1/r + \mu a)\exp(-2\mu ar)$$
$$- (p + 2M_2^{-1})(1/r + 3\mu/2 + \mu^2 r + \tfrac{1}{3}\mu^3 r^2)\exp(-2\mu r)$$
$$+ 32N/(1+a)^4 M_2(1/r + 2(1+a)\mu/3$$
$$+ \tfrac{1}{6}(1+a)^2\mu^2 r)\exp(-(1+a)\mu r),$$
$$V_p(r) = - (1/2)(\alpha_1/(r_1^2 + r^2)^2 + \alpha_2/(r_2^2 + r^2)),$$

and
$$V_e(r) = - 3\gamma(3/4\pi)^{\frac{1}{3}}\{N_1^2 \exp(-2\mu ar)$$
$$+ N_2^2((\mu r)\exp(-\mu r) - N\exp(-\mu ar))$$
$$+ (p/2)N_3^2(\mu r)^2 \exp(-2\mu r)\}^{\frac{1}{3}}$$

are the static potential, polarization potential and exchange potential respectively. $\gamma = 0\cdot15$. The parameters

for N: $p = 3$, $a = 3.47$, $\mu = 1.925$, $r_1 = 0.225$, $r_2 = 1.29$, $\alpha_1 = 4.5 \times 10^{-3}$,
$\alpha_2 = 7.60$,

for O: $p = 4$, $a = 3.44$, $\mu = 2.23$, $r_1 = 0.197$, $r_2 = 1.10$,
$\alpha_1 = 2.64 \times 10^{-3}$, $\alpha_2 = 5.20$.

for Ne: $p = 6$, $a = 3.35$, $\mu = 2.88$, $r_1 = 0.157$, $r_2 = 0.87$,
$\alpha_1 = 1.06 \times 10^{-3}$, $\alpha_2 = 2.66$.

The distorted wave functions, phase shifts and scattering cross-sections are calculated using the partial wave method. The numerical results are in good agreement with experiment. See Figs. 1-3.

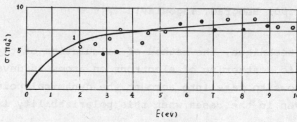

Fig. 1. Total cross-section for scattering by N

1. present work; o ∅ •, experimental points(1).

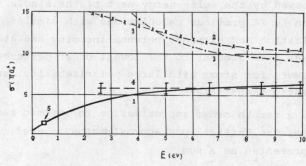

Fig. 2. Total cross-section for scattering by O

1. present work; 2. don't consider polarization; 3. don't consider polarization and exchange; 4. experiment(2); 5. experimental point(3).

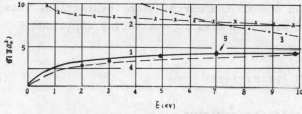

Fig. 3. Total cross-section for scattering by Ne

1. present work; 2. don't consider polarization; 3. don't consider polarization and exchange; 4. experiment(4); 5. •, experimental points(5).

(1) R.H.Neynaber et al., Phy. Rev. 129, 2069 (1963).

(2) A.Temkin, Phy. Rev. 107, 1004 (1957).

(3) S.C.Lin and Kivel, Phy. Rev. 114, 1026 (1959).

(4) A.Salop and H.H.Nakano, Phy. Rev. A2, 127 (1970).

(5) T.S.Stein et al., Phy. Rev. A17, 1600 (1978).

ELASTIC SCATTERING OF ELECTRONS BY ATOMS
WITH GREAT POLARIZABILITY

D. Davidović, M. Amusya,[*] N. Cherepkov[*] and V. Sosnivker[*]

Boris Kidrič Institute of Nuclear Sciences, POB 522,
11001 Beograd, Yugoslavia

Using many-body technique, the method of calculation of the cross section of elastic scattering of electrons on atoms is developed. This method allows to take into account the dynamical polarizability of atoms even in the cases when this polarizability is large.

As it is known[1], the elastic scattering amplitude of electrons by atoms, can be expressed by the self-energy part of the single particle Green function Σ. In previous calculations with similar technique,[2] the polarization and exchange between incoming and atomic electrons, was taken into account to the lowest order perturbation theory in Σ. However, for atoms with large polarizability, such approximation is evidently insufficient.

In this work, as a zeroth order approximation for atomic and incoming electrons also, the Hartree-Fock approximation is used. The phase shift is represented as a sum

$$\delta_\ell (E) = \delta_\ell{}^{HF}(E) + \Delta\delta_\ell (E) \tag{1}$$

where $\delta_\ell{}^{HF}$ is the phase shift of Hartree-Fock wave-functions and $\Delta\delta_\ell (E)$ is the correction due to the correlation interaction. This correction is connected with the elastic scattering amplitude F through

$$tg\Delta\delta_\ell (E) = -\Pi \; <E\ell|F(E)|E\ell> \tag{2}$$

where F is the solution of the equation

$$<E\ell|F(\omega)|E'\ell> = <E\ell|\Sigma(\omega)|E'\ell> +$$

$$+ P\!\int \frac{<E\ell|\Sigma(\omega)|E''\ell><E''\ell|F(\omega)|E'\ell>}{\omega - E''} \, dE'' \tag{3}$$

[*]Present address: Physico-technical Institute A.F. IOFFE,
Leningrad, USSR.

Here P is a symbol for the principal value; the integral over
E" includes also the summation over discrete states, including the
occupied ones.

For the energies of the incoming electron which are greater
than the threshold energy of the ionization of the atom, Σ becomes
complex and so does $\Delta\delta_\ell$.

Let

$$\delta_\ell(E) = \lambda_\ell(E) + i\mu_\ell(E)$$

where

$$\lambda_\ell(E) = \delta_\ell^{HF}(E) + \text{Re } \Delta\delta_\ell(E),$$

$$\mu_\ell(E) = \text{Im } \Delta\delta_\ell(E) \tag{4}$$

then the cross section for elastic scattering is given by[3]

$$\sigma_{e\ell} = \sum_{\ell=o}^{\infty} \frac{2\Pi}{k^2}(2\ell+1)(ch2\mu_\ell-cos2\lambda_\ell)e^{-2\mu_\ell} \tag{5}$$

and for inelastic scattering

$$\sigma_{ne} = \frac{\Pi}{k^2} \sum_{\ell=o}^{\infty} (2\ell+1)(1 - e^{-4\mu_\ell}).$$

The matrix elements for Σ were calculated in the second order
perturbation theory in the Coulomb interaction. This is equivalent
to the summation of infinite series of graphs in the RPAE "forward
in time", when for the intermediate states for incoming electron
the wave functions obtained in the single-ion field are used.[2]

The calculations were performed for Ar and Ca atoms. The corrections to the phase shifts were calculated for ℓ-o,1,2,3,4. The
main contribution comes from dipole excitations of atoms.

1. J. S. Bell and E. J. Squires, Phys.Rev.Lett. 3, 96 (1959).
2. M. Ya. Amusya and N. A. Cherepkov, Case Studies in Atomic
   Physics, 5, 47 (1975).
3. N. Mott and H. Massey, The Theory of Atomic Collisions,
   Oxford 1965.

ELASTIC DIFFERENTIAL ELECTRON SCATTERING FROM He, Ne, Ar, AND Kr

FOR INCIDENT ELECTRON ENERGIES FROM 7.5eV to 20eV

W.R. NEWELL, D.F.C. BREWER[*] AND A.C.H. SMITH

Department of Physics and Astronomy, University

College London

[*]Present Address : Scicon Consultancy Ltd., 49-57
Berners Street London W1P 4AQ

In this paper we will present high resolution elastic differential cross-sections for electron scattering from He, Ne, Ar, and Kr for incident electron energies of 7.5eV to 20eV. The only recent published experimental data for elastic scattering from the rare gases at energies less than 20eV has been con-fined to the helium atom[1,2]. Using a new type of co-axial electron spectrometer, which operates over an incident electron energy range of 5eV to 50eV and an angular scattering range of $\pm130^{\circ}$, we have measured the elastic electron scat-tering cross-sections at 7.5, 10, 12.5, 15, 17.5, and 20eV for He, Ne, Ar, and Kr over an angular range of $\Theta = 20^{\circ}$ to 130°.

Although the apparatus was used in a crossed beam mode each measurement was accompanied by a subsidiary measurement which provided the small, but finite, contribution to the scattered signal from the background gas and in addition the constancy of the product of the gas beam number density and electron beam current was monitored using a second, fixed angle, electron detector. Using the facili-ties of the on line PDP8 computer the scattered electron flux detected at $+\Theta^{\circ}$ was normalized, every scan   to the scattered electron flux detected at $+22^{\circ}$. The energy resolution of the apparatus was determined from observation of the helium resonance at 19.31eV and the angular resolution obtained from the measurement of the deep minimum in the Argon differential cross-section at 50eV[3].

Figure 1 shows the elastic differential cross-section at 20eV incident ener-gy in Argon. The present data which is normalized at small angles to the work of Andrick,and Williams and Willis is in good agreement with the Andrick data over the full angular range but diverges significantly from the data of Williams and Willis at larger scattering angles.

Data for the elastic differential cross-section for electron scattering from He, Ne, and Kr will be presented and comparisons with theory and experi-mental work made.

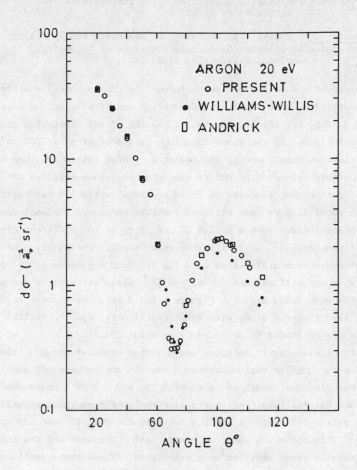

ARGON 20 eV
○ PRESENT
● WILLIAMS-WILLIS
□ ANDRICK

FIGURE (1)

1. Andrick D., and Bitsch A., 1975
          J. Phys. B: Atom. Molec. Phys. **8** 393-411
2. McConkey J.W. and Preston J.A. 1975
          J. Phys. B: Atom. Molec. Phys. 8 63-74

CROSS SECTIONS FOR ELASTIC SCATTERING OF INTERMEDIATE-ENERGY
ELECTRONS BY Ar AND Kr[*]

S. K. Srivastava, H. Tanaka[+], A. Chutjian, D. Register, and S. Trajmar
Jet Propulsion Laboratory, California Institute of Technology
Pasadena, California, 91103 USA

We have employed the relative-flow technique[1] to obtain absolute differential elastic scattering cross sections (DCS) for Ar and Kr at electron impact
energies of 3, 5, 7.5, 10, 15, 20, 30, 50, 75 and 100 eV and scattering angles
ranging from 15 to 130°. By the above technique ratios of Ar or Kr DCS to that
of He at each electron impact energy are measured. These ratios are then multiplied by the absolute values of He DCS to determine the cross sections for the
two gases. Our most recent absolute He cross sections[2] which are estimated to be
accurate within about 5% have been utilized for this purpose. The measurements
were repeated several times over a period of two years on two different electron
scattering spectrometers and under different experimental conditions. The final
results thus obtained show differences with the previous measurements of Williams
and Willis[3] for Ar and Williams and Crowe[4] for Kr. These differences are more
pronounced at low scattering angles. Figures 1 and 2 show the present results at
20 eV electron impact energy along with other experimental and theoretical results.
Present results are estimated to be accurate to about 20%.

In order to obtain elastic integral and momentum-transfer cross sections the
values of DCS in the angular region between 0 and 15° and between 130 and 180°
were needed. For electron impact energies of 3, 5, and 7.5 eV a phase-shift
fitting procedure was followed. At higher electron impact energies we still used
this method to obtain the shape of the DCS curve in the 0 to 15° and 130 to 180°
angular region. This shape was used for extrapolation purposes and the integral
and momentum-transfer cross sections were calculated. These cross sections are
compared with several previous measurements and will be presented in detail at the
meeting.

[*]Supported in part by NASA Contract No. NAS7-100.

[+]Permanent address: Sophia University, Faculty of Science and Technology 7, Kioicho
Chiyoda-Ku, Tokyo, 102, Japan.

1. S. K. Srivastava, A. Chutjian and S. Trajmar, J. Chem. Phys. 63, 2659 (1975).

2. D. Register, S. Trajmar and S. K. Srivastava, results will be presented at
    ICPEAC, Kyoto.

3. J. F. Williams and B. A. Willis, J. Phys. B: Atom. Molec. Phys. 8, 1670 (1975).

4. J. F. Williams and A. Crowe, J. Phys. B: Atom. Molec. Phys. 8, 2233 (1975).

5. R. D. DuBois and M. E. Rudd, J. Phys. B: Atom. Molec. Phys. 8, 1474 (1975).

    A correction of a factor of 1.4 as suggested by the authors was applied to
    their results at 20 eV impact energy.

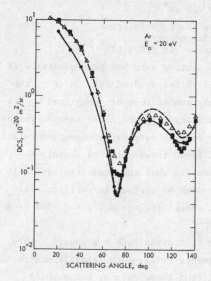

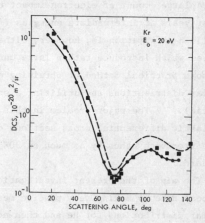

Fig. 1. Elastic DCS of Argon at electron impact energy of 20 eV. ■ Williams and Willis[3], △ DuBois and Rudd[5], --- Walker (theory)[6], ● Present joined by a best visual fit line.

Fig. 2. Elastic DCS of Kr at electron impact energy of 20 eV. ■ Williams and Crowe[4], -- Walker (theory)[6], ● Present joined by a best visual fit line.

ABSOLUTE ELASTIC DIFFERENTIAL ELECTRON SCATTERING
CROSS SECTIONS FOR He; A PROPOSED CALIBRATION
STANDARD FROM 5 TO 200 eV[*]

D. F. Register, S. Trajmar and S. K. Srivastava
California Institute of Technology, Jet
Propulsion Laboratory, Pasadena, CA 91103 USA

A large emount of electron impact cross section data has been generated in
recent years at intermediate energies (few eV to few hundred eV). Most of the
available information is, however, either only qualitative or normalized by procedures which introduce rather large uncertainties into the cross section values.
The most practical method of obtaining cross section data is by measuring relative
angular distributions and utilizing a set of known cross sections (mainly He
elastic).[1] The major problem in this respect is that the presently available
He elastic differential cross sections determined by various investigators deviate from each other by as much as 30% and, therefore, are not acceptable as a
standard.

The aim of the present investigation is to provide such a standard. This
has been done by making very precise measurements (±3%) of the elastic scattering
angular distributions for He and then normalizing these data by phase shift
analysis and/or by utilizing total cross section data. The differential cross
sections thus obtained are believed to be accurate to ±5% and can serve as a
standard for cross section measurements.

The experiments were carried out in such a way that no effective path length
corrections were needed to transform the measured scattered signal intensitites to
relative cross sections (small, well collimated nozzle beam target and appropriate
electron beam and detector geometry). The normalization to the absolute scale was
achieved by the method of phase shift analysis below 18 eV. Above this impact
energy the phase shift analysis method was used to parametrize the relative angular distributions and to extrapolate the measured distribution to 0° and 180°
scattering angles. The integral elastic cross sections were then normalized by
utilizing accurately known (±3%) total[2-4] and ionization cross sections.[5]
The only other quantity needed for this normalization is the total excitation
cross section at each impact energy. On the basis of critical examination of all
available experimental and theoretical data de Heer and Jansen[5] proposed a set
of semiempirical values for Q_{EXC}. The elastic integral and differential cross
sections obtained by this procedure are estimated to be accurate to within about
5%.

The cross sections have been determined at 5, 12, 18, 20, 25, 30, 40, 50, 60,
70, 75, 80, 90, 100, 150 and 200 eV impact energies. Some of the results are
shown in Figs. 1 and 2. In general the present results agree well with those of

[*]Work supported by the National Aeronautics and Space Administration, Contract
No. NAS7-100.

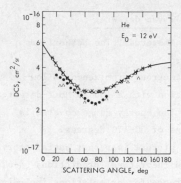

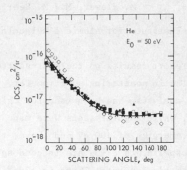

Fig. 1. Elastic differential cross sections at 12 eV impact energy. Gibson-Dolder, △ ; McConkey-Preston, ● ; Andrick-Bitsch, o; Present x, joined by line.

Fig. 2. Same as Fig. 1 except: Chamberlain et al., △; Srivastava-Trajmar, ▲; LeBah-Callaway, ▢ ; Winters, et al., ◇; Scott and Taylor, ■.

Andrick and Bitsch[6] below 20 eV. At the intermediate energies there is some deviation between the present results and other experimental and theoretical data but the agreement improves at the higher energies. Among the theoretical data, those of Scott and Taylor[7] are in best agreement with the present results. The momentum transfer cross sections obtained from the present analysis merge smoothly with the low energy results of Milloy and Crompton.[8]

1. S. K. Srivastava, A. Chutjian and S. Trajmar, J. Chem. Phys., 63, 2659 (1975).

2. R. E. Kennerly and R. A. Bonham, Phys. Rev., A17, 1866 (1978).

3. T. W. Stein, W. E. Kauppila, V. Poe, J. H. Smart, and G. Jesion, Phys. Rev., A17, 1600 (1978).

4. R. W. Wagenaar, Ph.D. Thesis, FOM Institute Amsterdam, The Netherlands, April, 1978, (FONNR. 43.948).

5. F. J. de Heer and R. J. J. Jansen, J. Phys. B: Atom. Molec. Phys., 10, 3741 (1977).

6. D. Andrick and H. Bitsch, J. Phys. B: Atom. Molec. Phys., 8, 393 (1975).

7. T. Scott and H. S. Taylor, (to be published).

8. H. B. Milloy and R. W. Crompton, Phys. Rev., A15, 1847 (1977).

9. J. R. Gibson and K. T. Dolder, J. Phys. B: Atom. Molec. Phys., 2, 1180 (1969).

10. J. W. McConkey and J. Preston, J. Phys. B: Atom. Molec. Phys., 8, 63 (1975).

11. G. E. Chamberlain, S. R. Mielczarek, and C. E. Kuyatt, Phys. Rev., A2, 1905 (1970).

12. S. K. Srivastava and S. Trajmar, J. Chem. Phys., 64, 3886 (1976).

13. R. W. LaBahn and J. Callaway, Phys. Rev. A2, 366 (1970).

14. K. H. Winters, C. D. Clark, B. H. Brandsen and J. P. Coleman, J. Phys. B: Atom. Molec. Phys. 1, 788 (1974) and private communication.

SPINPOLARISATION IN ELASTIC SCATTERING OF 5 - 300 eV ELECTRONS FROM XENON

M. Klewer, M.J.M. Beerlage and M.J. van der Wiel

FOM-Institute for Atomic & Molecular Physics, Amsterdam, The Netherlands

We report results on the Mott-scattering of electrons from xenon. A low-energy elastic scattering spectrometer, in combination with a 100 kV Mott-detector for spin analysis, has been used for this purpose. The energy range covered is 5-300 eV, while angular scans were made in the range of 30-120 degrees.

For energies of 100 eV and above, the general picture is rather satisfactory; several experiments [1-3] are in good agreement and theoretical predictions [4-6] are remarkably accurate. There is a definite preference for calculations including exchange with the projectile electron [5,6]. An interesting situation occurs at impact energies near 150 eV and scattering angles in the vicinity of 110 degrees. Here the more common types of calculations exhibit a strong positive polarization feature, whereas only the use of polarized orbitals or of an optical potential gives rise to a reversal of the sign, in accordance with the present work (fig.1) and earlier experiments by Kessler et al [2]. Our measurements at slightly lower and higher energies show that this polarization feature depends dramatically on impact energy, as was suggested before [2]; the inset of fig. 1 shows that at 140 eV the polarization has a clear positive maximum.

At 50 eV impact energy large differences exist between various experimental results, also for the differential cross sections [1,3,7]. Therefore no conclusion can be drawn as to the reliability of the various theoretical predictions (see fig. 2)

For still lower energies, no polarization data have been reported before. It turns out that two - and in some cases three - sets of experimental data for the differential cross section are in fair agreement; moreover, theory appears to give a good description of the angular behaviour. However, the same calculations for the polarization are in strong disagreement with our experimental results. This is demonstrated e.g. for 25 eV by the comparison of our data (fig. 3) with the calculation of Fink and Yates [4].

Down to the very lowest energies (7.5 eV), the spin polarization retains non-negligible values throughout the angular range (fig. 4).

Similar results for ceasium will be presented at the conference.

[1] K. Schackert, Z. Physik 213 (1968) 316

[2] J. Kessler, C.B. Lucas and L. Vušković, J. Phys. B.:Atom Molec. Phys. 10 (1977) 847

[3] M. Klewer, M.J.M. Beerlage and M.J. van der Wiel, J. Phys. B., to be published

[4] M. Fink and A.C. Yates, Electronic Research Center, University of Texas, Austin, Technical Rep. 88

[5] D.W. Walker, (as taken from C.B. Lucas and J.E. McCarthy, preprint 1977)

[6] I.E. McCarthy, C.I. Noble, B.A. Phillips and A.D. Turnbull, Phys. Rev. A
    15 (1977) 2173

[7] J. Mehr, Z. Physik 198 (1967) 345

[8] M.A. Coulthard, (as taken from K. Schackert, PhD Thesis, Uni.Mainz (1968)

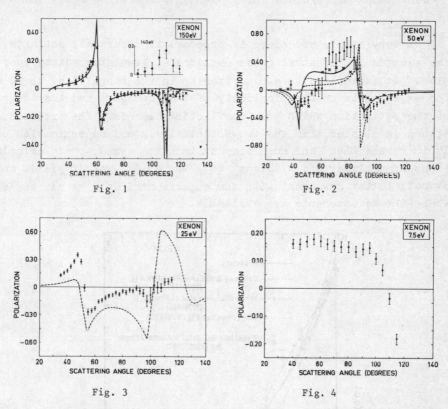

Fig. 1   Fig. 2

Fig. 3   Fig. 4

Figs. 1-4: Spin polarization of 150, 50, 25 and 7.5 eV electrons elastically
           scattered by xenon

⬤ — this work

Fig. 1: inset: this work at 140 eV
        x — experiment, Kessler et al [2]
        solid line — theory, Walker [5]
        dashed line — theory, McCarthy et al [6]

Fig. 2: x — experiment, Schackert [1]
        solid line — theory, McCarthy et al [6]
        dashed line — theory, Fink and Yates [4]
        dotted line — theory, Coulthard [8]

Fig. 3: dashed line — theory, Fink and Yates [4]

A TWO-POTENTIAL APPROACH FOR ELECTRON-ATOM ELASTIC SCATTERING AT LOW INTERMEDIATE ENERGIES

M.K. Srivastava

Department of Physics, University of Roorkee, Roorkee, India

A very simple procedure is proposed to accurately estimate the elastic differential cross sections at low intermediate energies. It is applied to e-H scattering in the range 15 eV to 30 eV. The emphasis is on the simplicity of the procedure and the accuracy of the estimation which pose conflicting demands. The proposed method is simpler than the two-potential eikonal approximation of Ishihara and Chen[1] and much simpler than the pseudo-state calculations of Callaway and Williams[2] and Fon et al[3] yet it yields an overall better agreement with the experimental data at all angles where the measurements are available.

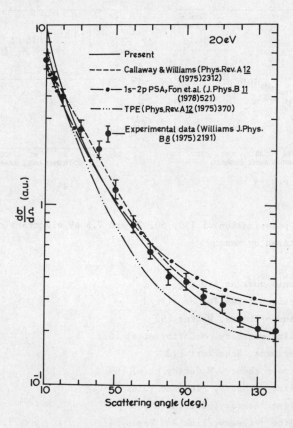

It essentially relies on the observation that in this energy
region the contribution of the static potential of ground state
hydrogen atom should be included exactly and the remaining multiple
scattering series should be summed with all the terms evaluated
on the same footing. The later is simply a manifestation of poor
convergence of the Born series. We have evaluated these terms in
the Glauber approximation. The scattering amplitude is given by

$$F = f \, (V_{st}) + f_G(V) - f_G(V_{st}) \; .$$

In order to maintain the over all simplicity of approach the
exchange contribution is evaluated in the Glauber-Bonham-Ochkur
approximation[4].

Figure 1 displays our results along with other theoretical
results at 20 eV. The agreement with the experimental data is
very good.

Main drawback of the method is that it completely ignores
the long range polarization contribution, suffers from the
logarithmic divergence in the forward direction and perhaps can
not be pushed to energies less than 1 Rydberg.

1.   T. Ishihara and J.C.Y. Chan, Phys. Rev. A12, 370 (1975).
2.   J. Callaway and J.F. Williams, Phys. Rev. A12, 2312 (1975).
3.   W.C. Fon, P.G. Burke and A.E. Kingston, J. Phys. B 11, 521
     (1978).
4.   C. Khayrallaha, Phys. Rev. A14 , 2064 (1976).

ELECTRON-ATOM ELASTIC SCATTERING AT INTERMEDIATE AND HIGH ENERGIES

M.K.Srivastava and M. Lal

Department of Physics, University of Roorkee, Roorkee-247672, India.

The eikonal-Born series (EBS) proposed by Byron and Joachain[1] for electron/positron scattering by atoms has been found to be quite successful at intermediate and high energies. This approach aims to obtain the scattering amplitude correct to $1/k^2$. It has been argued that the higher order Glauber terms (ignored in EBS) do make a significant contribution[2]. See Refs. 2 and 3 for the improvement in the results.

We have attempted to make a further improvement in the elastic scattering cross-sections by exactly including (rather than in the Glauber sense) the contribution of the static part of the interaction. This is known to improve the cross-sections in the large scattering angle region and can be obtained by solving the radial Schrödinger equation for (say) $\ell \leq 10$. The expressions

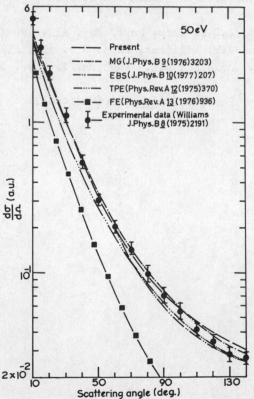

for the scattering amplitude in the EBS approximation, the modified
Glauber approximation (MG, Ref.2) and the present approach are
given by

$$F_{EBS} = f_{B1} + f_{B2} + f_{G3}$$

$$F_{MG} = f_G + f_{B2} - f_{G2}$$

$$F_P = f^{(st)} + (f_{B2} - f_{B2}^{(st)}) + (f_G - f_{G2} - f_G^{(st)} + f_{G2}^{(st)}).$$

The exchange contribution has been included in the Glauber-
Bonham-Ochkur approximation[4].

    Figure 1 shows our results along with other theoretical
results at 50 eV. The present results show a better agreement with
the experimental data through out the angular range. This feature
persists at higher energies though the different results tend to
merge into each other as the energy increases. The method is hardly
any more difficult than the MG approximation.

1. F.W. Byron, Jr. and C.J.Joachain,Phys.Rev.,A8,1267(1973).
2. T.T. Gien, J.Phys. B 9,3203 (1976).
3. T.T.Gien, Phys. Rev. A 16,123 (1977).
4. C.Khayrallah, Phys. Rev. A 14,2064 (1976).

ELASTIC e-H SCATTERING AT 50, 100, AND 200 eV IN A MODIFIED
APPROACH TO THE GLAUBER APPROXIMATION

A. Birman and S. Rosendorff

Department of Physics, Technion-Israel Institute of Technology,
Haifa, Israel

A modified Glauber theory was proposed by one of us[1] some time ago. This
theory is similar in many respects to the conventional Glauber theory, but there
is one important difference: all terms of order higher than one in the amplitude
are evaluated by keeping the average excitation energy of the atom in its intermediate states at a finite value. This fact eliminates many shortcomings from
which the conventional Glauber theory suffers. The modified Glauber amplitude
(MGA) for scattering from state σ_i to state σ_n is given by

$$f_{ni}^{(MG)}(\underline{k_n}, \underline{k_i}) = -i^{M_n+1}\sqrt{k_n k_i}\int_0^{\infty} b\, db\, J_{M_n}(bQ)$$

$$\times \langle \sigma_n e^{-iM_n\varphi}|\, i\Lambda_{k_n-k_i} + \alpha_{k_n-k_i}\left(e^{i\Lambda_0} - i\Lambda_0 + 1\right)|\sigma_i\rangle, \quad (1)$$

where $\underline{Q} = \underline{k_i} - \underline{k_n}$, and φ is the azimuthal angle of the impact parameter $\underline{b}$; M_n
is the magnetic quantum number of σ_n. The quantity $\alpha_{k_n-k_i}$ is defined by

$$\alpha_{k_n-k_i} = \frac{\Lambda_{k_n-\bar{k}} \cdot \Lambda_{\bar{k}-k_i}}{\Lambda_0^2} \quad (2)$$

where the modified Glauber phase function is given by

$$\Lambda_{\Delta k} = -\frac{\mu}{\hbar^2 \bar{k}}\int_{-\infty}^{\infty} V(\underline{b} + \hat{k}_i z, \underline{s})e^{-i\Delta k z}\, dz . \quad (3)$$

$\bar{k}$ is the average momentum related to the average excitation energy E_{exc} by

$$k_i^2 - \bar{k}^2 = 2\mu E_{exc} , \quad (4)$$

We have proved that the MGA satisfies the unitarity theorem (to all orders of the
coupling constant).

    In order to evaluate the amplitude numerically, we have determined E_{exc} via
the optical theorem where the three-term Bethe-Born expression of Kim and
Inokuti[2] for the total cross section has been used. We believe that E_{exc} obtained
in this way is reliable within the error limit of 10%. The surprising result is
that E_{exc} is essentially independent of energy (1 Ry) decreasing slightly with
increasing energy.

    The MGA has been examined by analyzing the experimental data[3] for elastic
e-H scattering at 50, 100, and 200 eV. Re $F_B^{(2)}$ and the exchange amplitude by
Forster and Williamson[4] have been included. The results fit the experimental data

well. Possible improvement of the MGA by including higher order terms in the phase function will be discussed.

1. S. Rosendorff, Proc. Roy. Soc. (London) A353, 11 (1977).

2. Y.K. Kim and M. Inokuti, Phys. Rev. A3, 665 (1971).

3. J.F. Williams, J. Phys. B8, 2191 (1975).

4. G. Forster and W. Williamson, Phys. Rev. A13, 2023 (1976).

ASYMMETRY IN SCATTERING OF ELECTRONS FROM HYDROGEN: EXCHANGE-CORRECTED-GLAUBER APPROXIMATION

George A. Khayrallah

Department of Physics, University of Arizona
Tucson, Arizona, 85721

The effect of the electron spin in the elastic scattering of polarized electron from polarized hydrogen atoms has been investigated in the exchange-corrected-Glauber approximation.[1] One can define an experimental asymmetry parameter

$$A = \frac{\frac{d\sigma \uparrow\downarrow}{d\Omega} - \frac{d\sigma \uparrow\uparrow}{d\Omega}}{\frac{d\sigma \uparrow\downarrow}{d\Omega} + \frac{d\sigma \uparrow\uparrow}{d\Omega}}$$

where $\sigma\uparrow\uparrow$ and $\sigma\uparrow\downarrow$ are the differential cross sections scattering when the spins of the electron and the electron on the hydrogen atom are parallel and anti-parallel respectively. Rewriting in terms of the direct and exchange amplitudes f and g:

$$A = \frac{|f+g|^2 - |f-g|^2}{|f+g|^2 + |f-g|^2}$$

For the Born approximation the asymmetry is independent of energy. However, the exchange-corrected Glauber approximation predicts a change with angle.

A comparison of the experimental data, and several more complex theoretical approximations[4,5,6] [at 90°] is shown in Fig. 1. It is seen that the present

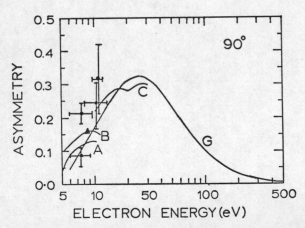

Fig. 1. The asymmetry in the differential cross section for elastic scattering of polarized electrons from polarized ground state hydrogen atoms at 90°; G-Glauber, A-pseudostate,[4] B-virtual 2S,[5] C-pseudostate,[6] ▲measurement,[3] ♣measurement.[2]

simple calculation agrees quite well with the experimental data, as well as with the previous more elaborate calculation, thus confirming that exchange is importnat in the understanding and calculation of the scattering cross section of electrons from hydrogen atoms.

1. G. A. Khayrallah, Phys. Rev. A 14, 2064 (1976).

2. M. A. Alguard, V. W. Hughes, M. S. Lubell, and P. F. Wainright, Xth ICPEAC, Abstracts of Papers, 506-507 (1977).

3. J. F. Williams, J. Phys. B8, 1683 (1975).

4. P. G. Burke, D. F. Gallagher, and S. Geltman, J. Phys. B2, 1142 (1969).

5. K. Smith, R. P. McEachran, and P. A. Fraser, Phys. Rev. 175, 553 (1962).

6. J. Callaway and J. F. Williams, Phys. Rev. A 12, 2312 (1975).

Acknowledgment is made to the Donors of the Petroleum Research Fund, administered by the American Chemical Society, for the support of this research under contract number PRF 10233-AC6

RELATIVISTIC GLAUBER AMPLITUDES FOR ELASTIC ELECTRON
SCATTERING BY HYDROGEN ATOMS AND HYDROGEN-LIKE IONS

Arne Reitan

Department of Physics, University of Trondheim
N-7055 Dragvoll, Norway

In recent years, a number of papers on the application of the Glauber approximation to electron-atom collisions have appeared in the literature. The reader is referred to the review articles by Gerjuoy and Thomas[1] and Byron and Joachain[2] for references to such calculations through 1976. Since that time, a major interest in this field has been the treatment of exchange effects[3], which become increasingly important as the energy decreases.

The present work is concerned with scattering at higher energies, where the relativistic corrections to the Coulomb scattering amplitude may become appreciable. To study the influence of these effects on the atomic scattering process we use a formulation of the Glauber theory where the amplitude for the scattering of the projectile on the individual scatterers in the target is used as input, rather than the potential between the projectile and the scatterers. In doing this, we use an approximate form of the relativistic Coulomb amplitude, including spin-flip terms. We limit ourselves to elastic electron or positron scattering by hydrogen atoms and hydrogen-like ions in the ground state, and target relativistic effects are not included.

In non-relativistic Glauber theory the exponential of the phase-shift function for Coulomb scattering of a projectile with charge $Z_1 e$ on a nucleus with charge $Z_2 e$ is $S_{nr}(\eta, b) = (kb)^{2i\eta}$, where $\vec{b}$ is the impact parameter, $k = |\vec{k}_i| = |\vec{k}_f|$ is the momentum of the projectile and $\eta = Z_1 Z_2 \alpha / \beta$, in which $\alpha = 1/137$ and β is the projectile velocity (units $\hbar = c = 1$). The z-axis (which is perpendicular to $\vec{b}$ and the momentum transfer $\vec{q} = \vec{k}_i - \vec{k}_f$) is chosen in the direction of $(\vec{k}_i + \vec{k}_f)/2$. The corresponding relativistic operator is

$$S(\eta, b) = S_o(\eta, b) + (\vec{\sigma} \times \vec{e}_z) \cdot \hat{b} \, S_1(\eta, b) \ ,$$

where $\vec{\sigma}$ is the spin operator for the projectile, and where $S_o \to S_{nr}$ and $S_1 \to 0$ in the non-relativistic limit.

For the composite target (nucleus plus one electron in the ground state) the scattering operator then takes the form

$$F(\vec{q}) = F(q) + iG(q)\vec{\sigma} \cdot \vec{n} \ ,$$

where $\vec{n} = (\vec{k}_f \times \vec{k}_i)/|\vec{k}_f \times \vec{k}_i|$. With $\eta_1 = Z_1 \alpha / \beta$ and $\lambda = 2/a$, in which a is the Bohr radius of the ion in question, we have

$$F(q) = F_o(q) + F_1(q), \qquad G(q) = G_o(q) + G_1(q) \ ,$$

$$F_j(q) = ik \int_o^\infty b\,db\,J_o(qb)P_{Fj}(b), \qquad G_j(q) = ik \int_o^\infty b\,db\,J_1(qb)P_{Gj}(b) \ ,$$

$$P_{\gamma j}(b) = (4\pi)^{-1}\lambda^3(\partial/\partial\lambda) \int_0^\infty sds K_o(\lambda s) \int_0^{2\pi} d\phi \ T_{\gamma j}(b,s,\cos\phi) \ ,$$

$$T_{FO} = S_o S_o' \ , \quad T_{F1} = S_1 S_1' \ \hat{b}'\cdot\hat{b} \ , \quad T_{GO} = S_1 S_o' \ , \quad T_{G1} = S_o S_1' \ \hat{b}'\cdot\hat{b} \ ,$$

$$S_i S_j' = S_i(\eta,b)S_j'(-\eta_1,b') \ ,$$

$$b'^2 = b^2 + s^2 - 2bs \cos\phi \ , \quad \hat{b}'\cdot\hat{b} = (b - s\cos\phi)/b' .$$

These amplitudes can be written in closed form in terms of hypergeometric functions.

Numerically, it is found that for low Z_2 the scattering process is well described either as non-relativistic scattering on the composite target or as relativistic point-charge scattering on the nucleus. For higher Z_2, however, it becomes important to consider the composite-target effects and relativistic effects at the same time.

1. E. Gerjuoy and B.K. Thomas, Rep. Prog. Phys. **37**, 1345 (1974).
2. F.W. Byron, Jr. and C.J. Joachain, Phys. Reports **34C**, 233 (1977).
3. W. Williamson, Jr., G. Foster and R. Kwong, Phys. Rev. **A17**, 1823 (1978).

FRESNEL AND RECOIL CORRECTIONS TO THE GLAUBER THEORY OF ELASTIC ELECTRON
SCATTERING BY HYDROGEN ATOMS AND HYDROGEN-LIKE IONS

Arne Reitan

Department of Physics, University of Trondheim
N-7055 Dragvoll, Norway

We consider the Fresnel and recoil corrections to the non-relativistic
Glauber amplitude for elastic electron or positron scattering by hydrogen atoms
and hydrogen-like ions, introducing these corrections by a method similar to that
employed by Fäldt[1] for the case of hadron scattering by deuterons. Recoil is considered only in the scattering of the projectile on the target electron, not in
the scattering on the nucleus.

When the Fresnel and recoil terms are included, the Glauber propagator
$P_G = (\pm q_{ez} + i\delta)^{-1}$ is replaced by

$$P = [\pm q_{ez} - (1/2)k^{-1}q_{en}^2 - k^{-1}\vec{P}_n \cdot \vec{q}_{en} + i\delta]^{-1} ,$$

$$\vec{q}_e = \vec{p}' - \vec{p}, \qquad \vec{P} = \frac{1}{2}(\vec{p}' + \vec{p}) ,$$

where $\vec{p}$ is the initial and $\vec{p}'$ the final momentum of the target electron. The index n indicates the component perpendicular to the z-axis, this being chosen along
$(\vec{k}_i + \vec{k}_f)/2$, with $k = |\vec{k}_i| = |\vec{k}_f|$. Above, the $\vec{q}_{en}$ term represents the recoil
correction and the one proportional to q_{en}^2 the Fresnel correction.

The resulting scattering amplitude can approximately be written in closed
form in terms of hypergeometric functions.

At intermediate energies the recoil correction is not very important from a
numerical point of view, whereas the Fresnel correction becomes quite pronounced
for energies below some 200 eV. The correction leads to a difference between the
cross sections for e^+ and e^- scattering, of the opposite sign of that arising from
the so-called modified Glauber approximation[2].

1. G. Fäldt, Nucl. Phys. B29, 16 (1971); ibid. B46, 460 (1972).
2. T.T. Gien, Phys. Rev. A16, 123 (1977); ibid. A16, 1736 (1977).

GLAUBER THEORY FOR ELASTIC ELECTRON SCATTERING FROM A THOMAS-FERMI ATOM

Arne Reitan

Department of Physics, University of Trondheim
N-7055 Dragvoll, Norway

The amplitude for elastic scattering of electrons or positrons by complex
atoms is calculated in a non-relativistic Glauber model where the electrons of the
target are taken to be in a common spherically symmetric state given by the
Thomas-Fermi density distribution. To facilitate the calculations, the Thomas-
Fermi potential is approximated by a sum of Yukawa functions, and the atomic
scattering amplitude can then be written as a one-dimensional integral over the
impact parameter.

The differential cross section for scattering on rare gases is compared with
experiments and with the results from various potential-scattering models.

ELASTIC SCATTERING OF ELECTRONS BY HELIUM IN TWO-POTENTIAL EIKONAL APPROXIMATION

S.S. Taylal,   A.N. Tripathi   and M.K.Srivastava

Department of Physics, University of Roorkee, Roorkee, India

Recent efforts in obtaining an accurate description of electron-atom scattering in the intermediate energy region centre on eikonal and eikonal related method, particularly the high energy straight line trajectory approach due to Glauber[1]. Various methods have been suggested to improve upon the Glauber approximation[2]. Among these the two-potential eikonal approximation (TPEA) proposed by Ishihara and Chen[3] has been found to be quite successful and easy to use. The basic idea underlying this approach is to properly treat the close encounter collisions where the electron-atom interaction is $-Z/r$ $(r \to 0)$ and the condition $V \ll E$ does not hold good even for high energies. The method essentially consists in pulling out a static potential V_{ST} incorporating the singularity of the total interaction V and evaluating its contribution by solving the radial Schrödinger equation. The rest of the interaction $V_O = V - V_{ST}$ which is smooth enough is treated in the Glauber approximation.

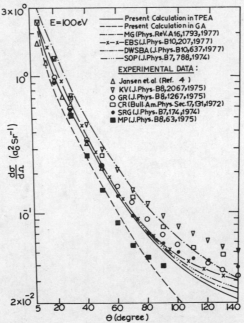

E=100eV

Present Calculation in TPEA
Present Calculation in GA
MG (Phys.Rev.A16,1793,1977)
x—x—EBS(J.Phys.B10,207,1977)
DWSBA (J.Phys.B10,637,1977)
SOP(J.Phys.B7,788,1974)

EXPERIMENTAL DATA:

△ Jansen et.al.(Ref. 4)
▽ KV(J.Phys.B8,2067,1975)
○ GR(J.Phys.B8,1267,1975)
□ CR(Bull.Am.Phys.Sec.17,131,1972)
● SRG(J.Phys.B7,174,1974)
■ MP(J.Phys.B8,63,1975)

$\frac{d\sigma}{d\Omega}$ $(a_0^2 \, sr^{-1})$

θ (degree)

We have calculated e-He elastic scattering differential cross-sections (DCS) at 100,200,400 and 700 eV. Figure 1 displays our results at 100 eV. They have been compared with those in the conventional Glauber approximation and many other theoretical calculations. Also shown are the measurements of various experimental research groups. It is seen that the present TPEA results reasonably improve the conventional Glauber results at all scattering angles and particular so at large angles. The reason is that (i) the singularity of the interaction contained in the V_{ST} is accurately taken into account by partial wave summation and (ii) the semiclassical condition necessary for the applicability of the Glauber is actually satisfied for the remaining interaction. The present results agree to within 5% with the absolute measurements of Jansen et al[4] in the angular range 10° to 50° of the scattering angles for which the data are available.

1. R.J.Glauber, Lectures in Theoretical Physics, ED. by W.E. Brittin et al (Interscience, New York, 1959), Vol.I, p.315.
2. B.H. Bransden and M.R.C. McDowell, Phys. Rep.30, 207 (1977).
3. T.Ishihara and J.C.Y. Chen, Phys. Rev. A12 , 370 (1975).
4. R.H.J.Jansen, F.J. de Heer, H.J. Luyken, B.Van Wingerden and H.J. Blaauw, J.Phys. B 9 , 185 (1976).

A TWO-POTENTIAL APPROXIMATION FOR ELASTIC SCATTERING OF ELECTRONS FROM COMPLEX ATOMS

B.B. SRIVASTAVA AND S.S. DHAL

Physics Department, Meerut University, Meerut-250001,INDIA

AND

R. SHINGAL

Physics Department, Meerut College, Meerut-250001, INDIA.

Recently the authors have developed an intermediate-energy approximation[1] for the calculation of the differential cross sections (DCS) for the elastic scattering of electrons from atoms and molecules. This approximation is based on a two-potential treatment of the first order static and the second order polarization-absorption parts of the optical model potential for the electron-target system. Under it the direct scattering amplitude, f_{TPE}, can be written as $f_{B1}+f_E-f_{EST}$, where f_{B1} is the first Born amplitude due to the static potential and f_E and f_{EST} are the eikonal amplitudes due to the optical potential and the static potential, respectively. The exchange is included through the Ochkur[1] approximation. This approximation yields with only a moderate amount of computation even for complex targets DCS in good agreement with experiment over the entire angular range at intermediate energies as seen from its applications to e-He and e-CH_4 systems.[1,2]

This approximation has now been improved by taking the contribution to the scattering amplitude from the static potential, V_{oo}, more accurately than in the first Born approximation by computing it from the phase shifts obtained from the differential equation corresponding to V_{oo}. This procedure has been used to calculate DCS for e-He elastic scattering at 100,200 and 500 eV and for e-Ne elastic scattering at 200,300 and 500 eV and the results are shown in Figs.1 and 2, respectively. along with the experimental data.[1,3,4] The wave function and polarization potential used for e-He case are the same as in reference 1 while for the Ne the wave function given by Sheorey[5] and the polarization potential given by Jhanwar and Khare[6] have been used. The absorption has not been considered. The calculated DCS are seen to be in almost as good agreement with

experiment over full angular range as are those from more
elaborate calculations.[1],[7]

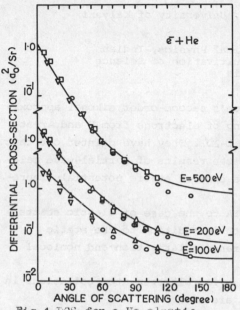

Fig.1.DCS for e-He elastic
scattering at 100,200 and
500 eV. The present results are
shown by solid lines. The
experimental data are due to
Sethuraman et al.(O)(Ref.1),
Crooks and Rudd(△)(Ref.1),
Jansen et al.(▽)(Ref.1),and
Bromberg (□)(Ref.1).

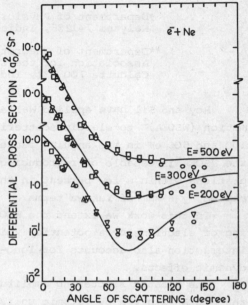

Fig.2.DCS for e-Ne elast-
ic scattering at 200,300
and 500 eV. The present
results are shown by
solid lines.The experim-
ential data are due to
Gupta and Rees(O)(Ref.3),
Jansen et al.(△)(Ref.1),
Bromberg (□)(Ref.1),and
Williams and Crowe(▽)
(Ref.4).

References

[1] R.Shingal and B.B.Srivastava,J.Phys.B$\underline{10}$,3725 (1977),and the
references therein.
[2] S.S.Dhal,B.B.Srivastava and R.Shingal,J.Phys.B(to be published).
[3] S.C.Gupta and J.A.Rees,J.Phys.B$\underline{8}$,1267 (1975b).
[4] J.F.Williams and A.Crowe,J.Phys.B$\underline{8}$,2238 (1975).
[5] V.B.Sheorey,J.Phys.B$\underline{2}$,442 (1969).
[6] B.L.Jhanwar and S.P.Khare,J.Phys.B$\underline{9}$,L527 (1976).
[7] B.L.Jhanwar,S.P.Khare and Ashok Kumar Jr.J.Phys.B $\underline{11}$,887(1978)
and the references therein.

ELASTIC SCATTERING OF ELECTRONS FROM HELIUM IN THE WALLACE'S SECOND ORDER EIKONAL APPROXIMATION

A. C. Roy* and N. C. Sil**

*Department of Physics, University of Kalyani
Kalyani 741235, India

**Department of Theoretical Physics, Indian
Association for the Cultivation of Science
Calcutta 700 032, India

Roy and Sil[1] have applied Wallace's second-order eikonal approximation (WSOEA)[2] to elastic scattering of electrons from H and Ar at 100 and 500 eV in the angular range 0-20°. They have pointed out that the WSOEA is capable of reproducing the results of partial-wave calculations within a few percent in the case of static potentials represented by a sum of Yukawa terms.

In this work we extend the WSOEA to the case of elastic scattering of electrons by a potential which in addition to the static interaction also accounts for long-range polarization and nonlocal dynamic effects.

The elastic scattering amplitude for electron-atom collisions in the WSOEA is given by (atomic units are used)

$$f(\theta) = \frac{k}{i} \int_0^\infty b \, db \, J_0(qb) \left\{ \exp\left[i \left(X(b) + \gamma(b) \right) \right] - 1 \right\} , \tag{1}$$

where

$$X(b) = -1/\kappa \int_{-\infty}^{\infty} dz \, V(b,z) , \tag{2}$$

$$\gamma(b) = -1/\kappa^3 \int_0^\infty dz \left(1 + b \frac{\partial}{\partial b} \right) V^2(b,z) , \tag{3}$$

and

$$q = 2k \sin\left(\tfrac{1}{2}\theta\right) .$$

Here, k is the wave number of the incident electron, J_0 is the zeroth-order Bessel function of the first kind, q is the magnitude of momentum transfer and V is the atomic potential. Glauber's first-order eikonal amplitude (FOEA)[4] is obtained by ignoring the second-order correction γ in Eq. (1). The potential V is chosen to be that proposed by Paikeday[3] :

$$V(r) = \sum_{i=1}^{4} \sum_{\rho=1}^{4} A_{i\rho} e^{-\lambda_i r} r^{\rho-2} + P \frac{1 + e^{-c_3 r}}{r^4 + d^4} .$$

Following the technique of Ref. 1 we have obtained differential cross sections (DCS) in the angular range 0-20°. TABLE I presents the DCS obtained in the WSOEA and the FOEA along with the predictions of PWC at an incident energy of 500 eV.

TABLE I. Comparisons of present WSOEA and FOEA cross sections with those of PWC at 500 eV.

θ (deg)	DCS (a_o^2 sr^{-1})		
	FOEA	WSOEA	PWC
2	1.23	1.28	1.41
10	0.494	0.525	0.555
20	0.205	0.222	0.218

It is evident from TABLE I that the WSOEA gives good agreement with the PWC and shows an improvement upon the FOEA. The details of the theory and the calculated cross sections at lower energies will be presented at the conference.

1.   A. C. Roy and N. C. Sil, J. Phys. B 11, 2729 (1978).
2.   S. J. Wallace, Ann. Phys. 78, 190 (1973).
3.   J. M. Paikeday, J. Chem. Phys. 65, 397 (1976).
4.   R. J. Glauber, in Lectures in Theoretical Physics, edited by
     W. E. Brittin and L. G. Dunham (Interscience, New York, 1959),
     Vol. I, p. 315.

ELASTIC ELECTRON-LITHIUM SCATTERING AT INTERMEDIATE
ENERGIES WITH THE INCLUSION OF GLAUBER EXCHANGE EFFECT*

T.T. Gien

Department of Physics, Memorial University of Newfoundland,
St. John's, Newfoundland, Canada A1C 5S7

Recently [1], experimental data of the differential cross
sections of elastic collision of lithium by electrons have been
made available at lower intermediate energies (20 and 60 eV). No
calculation within the conventional Glauber method especially with
the inclusion of the Glauber exchange effect has been done for
this process at these energies. Here, I wish to report the results of an analysis of the e-Li elastic scattering at intermediate energies, using the Glauber method and, without neglecting the
Glauber exchange effect.

The calculations are carried out within both the frozen-core
and full Glauber approximations. Note that the Glauber elastic
differential cross sections of lithium atoms have been evaluated
before [2], but not at these lower intermediate energies and, no inclusion of the Glauber exchange effect has been attempted. The
neglect of the Glauber exchange effect, as was done so far in the
literature, is probably due to the complexity of the exchange formula in this case. Here, the wave functions by Veselov et al. [3]
are also chosen for the ground state of lithium atom. The choice
of this wave function makes the calculation of the Glauber exchange effect manageable, while the direct scattering cross sections
calculated with this wave function have been checked, at least in
the frozen-core approximation, to yield values not drastically
different from those obtained with the more complex wave function
by Clementi et al. [4]. Similar to the case of e-H scatterings [5],
the Glauber exchange effects are evaluated with the two-dimensional integral form by Foster and Williamson [6].

The differential cross sections at 20, 60, 100, 200 and 400eV
have been obtained. The results at lower intermediate energies
(20 and 60 eV) are compared with experimental data. It is found
that the results of both the frozen-core and full Glauber approximations do not agree well with experimental data. At larger scattering angles, the frozen-core results stay much closer to experimental data than those given by the full Glauber method. The

inclusion of the Glauber exchange effect modifies significantly
the differential cross sections at 20 eV, but not very much at
60 eV and higher energies. It should also be noted that contrary
to a previous prediction [2], the results at lower intermediate
energies of the frozen-core and full Glauber approximations differ
drastically from each other at larger scattering angles. By comparing the two results obtained in the two approximations, one
finds that the two differ significantly at higher energies (200,
400 eV), less significantly at around 100 eV, but then drastically
again as the energy becomes lower.

In conclusion, the Glauber approximations (frozen-core and
full) with or without considering the Glauber exchange effects do
not work quite well at lower intermediate energies (60 and 20 eV)
for e-Li elastic scattering in so far as to compare with the unique
set of experimental data available at present [1]. Experimental
data at higher energies where the Glauber methods would more likely
be successful at small scattering angles are urgently needed for
comparison with the theoretical results obtained.

*Work supported in part by the Natural Sciences and Engineering
Research Council Canada (Operating Grant A-3962).

1. W. Williams, S. Trajmar and D. Bozinis, J. Phys. B: Atom.
   Molec. Phys. 9, 1529 (1976).
2. F.T. Chan and C.H. Chang, Phys. Rev. A 14, 189 (1976).
3. Veselov et.al., Opt. Spektrosk. 10, 693 (1961) (Opt.
   Spectrosc. 10, 367 (1961)).
4. E. Clementi et al., Atom. Data Nucl. Data Tables 14, 177
   (1974).
5. T.T. Gien, Books of Abstracts, Xth ICPEAC (CEA, Paris,
   1977), p. 398; Phys. Lett. 61A, 299 (1977); Phys. Rev. A
   16, 123 (1977); Phys. Lett. 64A, 369 (1978); Phys. Lett.
   65A, 201 (1978).
6. G. Foster and W. Williamson, Jr. Phys. Rev. A 13, 2023
   (1976).

GLAUBER CROSS SECTIONS FOR 1s-nlm EXCITATION OF HYDROGEN BY
ELECTRON IMPACT

N. C. SIL AND S. K. SUR

Department of Theoretical Physics, Indian Association for the
Cultivation of Science, Jadavpur, Calcutta 7oo o32, India

A simple and elegant method is proposed for evaluating the
Glauber scattering amplitude for arbitrary 1s-nlm excitation of
atomic hydrogen by charged particle impact. The customary polynomial
representation of the associated Laguerre function occuring in the
hydrogen wave functions is replaced, following Sil and coworkers,[1]
by a form involving a complex integration along a properly chosen
closed contour C.[2]

Following the works of Thomas and Gerjuoy[3] and of Toshima,[4]
and quantizing the atomic wave functions in the direction in the
centre of mass system along which the Glauber path-integration is
performed, we obtain the final form of the nonvanishing Glauber sca-
ttering amplitudes (for $l + |m| =$ an even integer) as

$$F(1s-nlm;\ \vec{q}) = e^{-im\Phi} n^{-3/2}\ K_i\ F_{nlm}(q),\qquad n>1,\qquad (1)$$

where $F_{nlm}(q)$ involves an integral along the contour C with Gauss
${}_2F_1$-hypergeometric functions occuring in the integrand.

Choosing the contour C as a circle centered at the origin and
having a radius proportional to n, the integral in $F_{nlm}(q)$ can be
evaluated without difficulty. Furthermore, as $(1/n^2) \to o$, $F_{nlm}(q)$ becomes independent of n, thereby revealing an explicit $n^{-3/2}$-depen-
dence of the scattering amplitude. The corresponding integral in
Eq.(1) takes a simpler form.

Whereas the available methods[3,4] become extremely laborious for
studying high excitations because of the occurrence of large number
of repeated parametric differentiations, the present procedure involves only a single integration and is especially useful for large-n
states.

A general computer program for the $\underline{n}$-cubed Glauber cross sections for arbitrary $\underline{s}$- and $\underline{p}$-excitations of hydrogen by electron
impact has been prepared, which reproduces the cross section results
of the earlier workers for low excitations ($\underline{n}=2$ and 3) and/$\overset{those}{\,}$converging
to the corresponding limiting asymptotic values for $\underline{n} \geq 0$.

Some of our results for electron impact Glauber cross sections
for $1\underline{s}$-$\underline{n}\underline{s}$ and $1\underline{s}$-$\underline{n}\underline{p}$ excitations of hydrogen are compared in TABLE I
with the corresponding Born results[1] at high energy for the states
$n=4$ and $n \to \infty$.

TABLE I. $\underline{n}$-cubed total cross sections in (πa_0^2).

| Energy eV | $1\underline{s} - \underline{n}\,\underline{s}$ | | | | $1\underline{s} - \underline{n}\,\underline{p}$ | | | |
| | $\underline{n} = 4$ | | $\underline{n} \to \infty$ | | $\underline{n} = 4$ | | $\underline{n} \to \infty$ | |
	Born	Glauber	Born	Glauber	Born	Glauber	Born	Glauber
15	–	.534–1*	–	.268–1	–	.856	–	.526
30	–	.342	–	.282	–	.3o4+1	–	.245+1
60	–	.332	–	.283	–	.317+1	–	.258+1
1oo	.273	.237	.234	.204	.290+1	.261+1	–	.212+1
2oo	.14o	.13o	.12o	.112	.184+1	.174+1	–	.141+1

* $x \pm y \equiv x \times 10^{\pm y}$

1. N. C. Sil, B. C. Saha, H. P. Saha, and P. Mandal, Phys. Rev. A
       (1978) (in press); C.Mitra, N. Roy, and N. C. Sil, J. Phys. B
       11, 18o7 (1978).
2. H. Margenau and G. M. Murphy, The Mathematics of Physics and Che-
       mistry (Van Nostrand Reinhold Company, New York, 1955), Vol.I,
       pp. 127, 129.
3. B. K. Thomas and E. Gerjuoy, J. Math. Phys. 12, 1567 (1971).
4. N. Toshima, J. Phys. Soc. (Japan) 43, 61o (1977).

AN UNITARIZED BORN TREATMENT OF ALIGNMENT AND ORIENTATION
PARAMETERS FOR 2^1P EXCITATION OF He ATOM BY ELECTRON IMPACT

W.C. Fon

Department of Mathematics, University of Malaya,
Pantai Valley, Kuala Lumpur, Malaysia.

The well known difficulties of absolute calibration in scattering
experiments suggest the desirability of other experiments that measure
features of the scattering processes free from normalization.   Recently,
Eminyan et al (1974) have measured the normalization-free alignment and
orientation parameters (λ,χ) for the 2^1P excitation from the ground state
of helium in the angular range $0 < \theta \leqslant 40^o$.   Their measurement has shown
that, in this angular range, the simple first Born approximation are more
successful in predicting the value of λ than those elaborate calculations
of Thomas et al (1974) which gives differential cross-section for 2^1P
excitation in closest agreement with the measurements (eg.Truhlar et al(1973).
At large angles (See Fig. 1) the measurements of Sutcliffe et al (1978)
and Hollywood et al (1979) have shown that the first Born approximation is
grossly in error at large angles and gives zero value for χ for all angles.
To date, there are no satisfactory theories except perhaps the R-matrix
method calculation of Berrington et al (1975), which gives all-round
consistant prediction for excitation of n = 2 states of helium in total
and differential cross sections,and (λ,χ) values for the P states.

    In this paper, we present 1^1S-2^3S-2^1S-2^3P-2^1P unitarized Born
approximation (originally proposed by Seaton 1961) which not only preserves
the unitarity condition but also allows (to the first order) for intermediate transitions between different atomic states, included in the
calculation.   The C.I. atomic wave functions used are exactly the same
as those employed by Berrington et al (1975).   Comparison between theoretical
calculations and experiments are made in Figures 1-3, the present calculation shows major improvement over the first Born approximation in the
prediction of λ and χ, and seems to be in closer agreement with experiments
than the calculations by DWPO method, Ten-channel eikonal approximation
and Many-body Green's Function method in the prediction of λ at small
angular range.

1. K. A. Berrington, P. G. Burke and A. L. Sinfailam. 1975,
     J. Phys. B. 8, 1459.
2. M. Eminyan, K. B. MacAdam, J. Selevin and H. Kleinpoppen,
     1974, J. Phy. B. 7, 1519.
3. M. R. Flannery and K. J. McCann, 1975, J. Phys. B. 8 , 1716.
4. M. T. Hollywood, A. Crowe and J. F. Williams, 1979,
     J. Phys. B. 12, 819.
5. Madison and Calhom (1978 quoted by Sutcliffe et al. 1978)
6. G. D. Meneses, N. T. Padial and G. Y. Csanak, 1978,
     J. Phys.B. 11, L237.
7. T. Scott and M.R.C. McDowell, 1976, J. Phys. B. 9, 2235.
8. M. J. Seaton, 1961, Proc. Phys. Soc. 77, 174.
9. D. H. Madison and W. N. Shelton, 1973, Phys. Rev.
     A7, 499.
10. K. H. Tan, J. Fryar, P. S. Farago and J. W. McConkey, 1977,
     J. Phys. B. 10, 1073.
11. L. D. Thomas, G. Y. Csanak, H. S. Taylor and B. S. Yarlagada,
     1974, J. Phys. B. 2, 1719.
12. Truhlar et al. 1973, Phys. Rev. A8, 2475.
13. V. C. Sutcliffe, G. N. Haddock, N. C. Steph and D. E. Golden,
     1978, Phys. Rev. A17, 100.

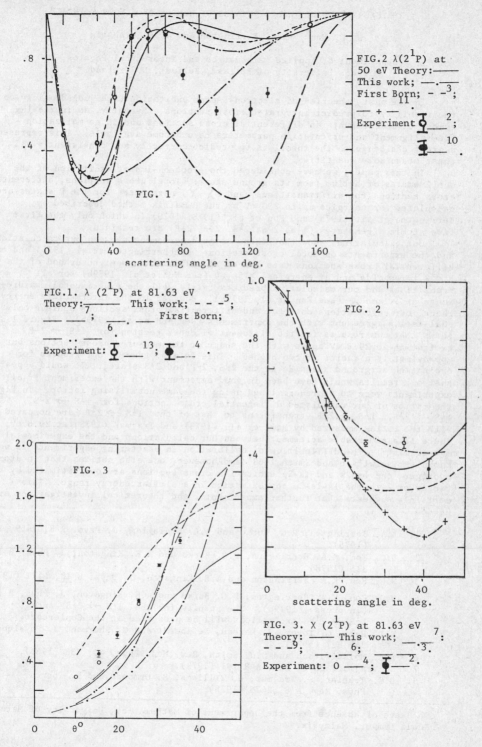

FIG.2 λ(2^{1}P) at 50 eV Theory:——— This work; —.— First Born; — —$\frac{3}{11}$; — + — Experiment ⊖ —$\frac{2}{}$; ● —$\frac{10}{}$.

FIG. 1

scattering angle in deg.

FIG.1. λ (2^{1}P) at 81.63 eV
Theory:$\frac{}{7}$——— This work; - - -$\frac{5}{}$;
— — —$\frac{}{6}$. ——— First Born;
— ·· — Experiment: ⊖ —$\frac{13}{}$; ● —$\frac{4}{}$.

FIG. 2

FIG. 3

scattering angle in deg.

FIG. 3. X (2^{1}P) at 81.63 eV
Theory: ——— This work; —$\frac{7}{}$:
- - -$\frac{9}{}$; —·—$\frac{6}{}$; —·—$\frac{3}{}$.
Experiment: ⊖ —$\frac{4}{}$; ● —$\frac{2}{}$.

THE EXCITATION OF n = 2 STATES OF HELIUM BY ELECTRON IMPACT

W. C. Fon[*], K. A. Berrington and A. E. Kingston

Department of Applied Mathematics and Theoretical Physics,
Queen's University of Belfast, Belfast, N. Ireland.

In the past, theories of electron-impact excitation were judged mainly on their ability to predict integrated cross sections. Recently, an increasing number of measurements in differential cross sections and in normalization - free alignment and orientation parameters have become available. This represents a great challenge to the theorists to predict correctly and consistently all these measurable quantities.

In this paper, we have considered the electron-impact excitation of the n = 2 states of helium from its ground state. Total cross sections, differential cross sections for all transitions, and (λ, χ) parameters for the P states are calculated for energies up to 200 eV by the R-matrix method described by Berrington et al. (1975) and Fon et al. (1978, 1979) in which only the first five atomic eigenstates (1^1S, 2^3S, 2^1S, 2^3P, 2^1P) are retained.

Our calculations show that there is good agreement between our calculations and the experiments on total cross sections (see Berrington et al. 1975) and on differential cross sections (see Fon et al. 1978) at the neighbourhood of the n = 2 thresholds and at energies $\geqslant$150 eV (see Fon et al. 1979b) for all transitions and our calculation predicts fairly well the experimental measurements of λ and χ (see Fon et al. 1979a). However in the intermediate energy range, our calculations on total and differential cross sections achieve only qualitative agreement with the experiments (see Fon et al. 1979b). Figure 1 shows that our results for the differential cross section for $1^1S \rightarrow 2^1P$ excitation at 29.6 eV agree with the shape of the measured cross sections but are approximately a factor of two higher. This is also true of our results for excitation of ground state He to the 2^3S, 2^3P and 2^1S states. It would appear that our results would have been in good agreement with the experiment if all the experiments were to be renormalised using the same normalising factor. In Fig. 2, the ratios of our calculated differential cross sections for $1^1S \rightarrow 2^3S$, $1^1S \rightarrow 2^1S$, $1^1S \rightarrow 2^3P$ transitions to that of the $1^1S \rightarrow 2^1P$ are compared with the ratios measured by Hall et al. (1973) and Trajmar (1973) at 29.6 eV. There is a remarkable agreement between our calculations and the experimental measurements. The difficulties of calibration in scattering experiments is well known (Moiseiwitsch and Smith 1968) and however, one also notices that in atomic hydrogen, the 1s-2s and 1s-2p excitation cross sections are overestimated by a factor of 2 in the 1s-2s-2p approximation in a similar energy range. This certainly suggests that further experimental and theoretical investigations are needed.

1. K.A. Berrington, P.G. Burke and A.L. Sinfailam, J. Phys. B $\underline{8}$, 1459 (1975).
2. W.C. Fon, K.A. Berrington, P.G. Burke and A.E. Kingston, J. Phys. B $\underline{11}$, 325 (1978).
3. W.C. Fon, K.A. Berrington and A.E. Kingston, J. Phys. B $\underline{12}$, L171 (1979a).
4. W.C. Fon, K.A. Berrington, P.G. Burke and A.E. Kingston, J. Phys. B $\underline{12}$ (in press) (1979b). The results for the $1^1S \rightarrow 2^1S$ and $1^1S \rightarrow 2^1P$ excitations will be presented at the Conference.
5. R.I. Hall, G. Joyez, J. Mazeau, Reinhardt and C. Sherman, J. Physique $\underline{34}$, 827 (1973).
6. B.L. Moiseiwitsch and S.J. Smith, Rev. Mod. Phys. $\underline{40}$, 238 (1968).
7. S. Trajmar, Phys. Rev. A $\underline{8}$ 191 (1973).
8. D.G. Truhlar, S. Trajmar, W. Williams, S. Ormonde and B. Torres, Phys. Rev. A $\underline{8}$, 2475 (1973).

---

[*] On leave of absence from the Department of Mathematics, University of Malaya, Kuala Lumpur, Malaysia.

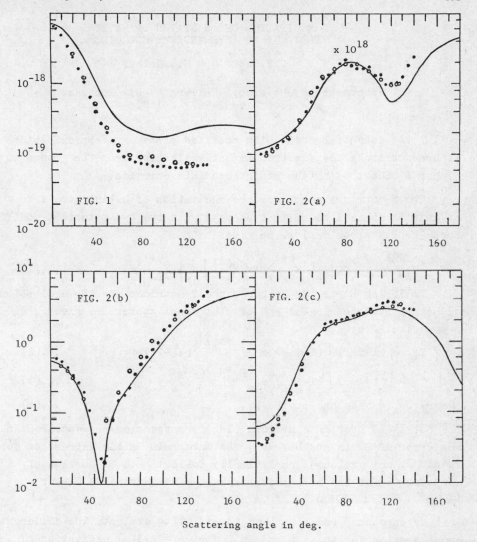

Scattering angle in deg.

Fig. 1   Differential cross section for $1^1S \rightarrow 2^1P$ at energy
          29.6 eV: ————— This work; o ————[5]; ● ————[8]
          (in units of cm^2/sr).

Fig. 2   Scattering intensity ratios (to 2^1P) at 29.6 eV
          (a) 2^3S,   (b) 2^1S,   (c) 2^3P:
          ————————— This work;   o ————[5]; ● —————————[7] .

EXCITATION OF S STATES OF HE BY ELECTRON AT INTERMEDIATE ENERGIES

G.P.Gupta and K.C.Mathur

Department of Physics, University of Roorkee,
Roorkee- 247672 , India

A two potential model with modified plane wave approximation is used to study the electron impact excitation from the ground to higher S states of helium at intermediate energies.

The T-matrix element for the excitation of helium atom from an initial state i to a final state f , in the two potential modified Born (TPMB) approximation, is given by[1]

$$T_{i \to f}^{TPMB} = \left\langle \phi_f \left| U_2 \right| \chi_{i2}^{(+)} \right\rangle + \left\langle \chi_{f2}^{(-)} \left| W_2 \right| \chi_{i2}^{(+)} \right\rangle \qquad \ldots(1)$$

Following Gupta and Mathur[2], the T-matrices for the excitation of helium atom to singlet and triplet final states are given, respectively, by

$$T_+ = \Gamma(1-ia_i)\,\Gamma(1-ia_f)\,e^{(a_i+a_f)/2}\,(I_D - I_E) \qquad \ldots(2)$$

and

$$T_- = \Gamma(1-ia_i)\,\Gamma(1-ia_f)\,e^{(a_i+a_f)/2}\,I_E \qquad \ldots(3)$$

where $a_i = \delta/K_i$ and $a_f = \delta/K_f$. $\qquad \ldots(4)$

The notations used in equations (1-4) are the same as described in the paper of Gupta and Mathur[2]. The integrals in the expression for I_D and I_E are evaluated analytically following the technique of Nordsieck[3]. For the evaluation of I_E, we have used the Ochkur-Rudge[4] approximation.

We have used the equations (3 and 4) to evaluate the differential cross section for the n^1S and n^3S for (n = 2,3,4) excitation of helium respectively. Here we present only results for the case of 2^3S excitation at an energy of 100 eV. From the figure 1, it is seen that the present results (curve P) show a considerable improvement over the Ochkur-Rudge approximation (curve OR). This improvement in our results is due to the following reasons.

(i)   Our expression for the amplitude comes out to be predominantly imaginary whereas the OR amplitudes are purely real.

(ii) The use of the coulomb waves instead of the plane waves (as in OR) leads to better results at larger angles.

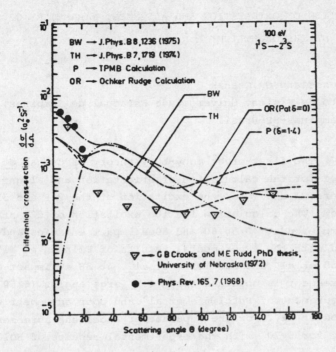

Fig.1.

1.   D.R. Junker, Phys. Rev. A11, 1552(1975)

2.   G.P.Gupta and K.C.Mathur, J.Phys.B, in press (1979)

3.   A.Nordsieck, Phys. Rev. 93, 785(1954)

4.   M.R.H.Rudge, Proc. Phys. Soc.(London) 85,607(1965)

THE APPLICATION OF THE FIRST ORDER MANY-BODY THEORY FOR THE
CALCULATION OF ORIENTATION AND ALIGNMENT PARAMETERS OF THE 2^1P
AND 3^1P STATES OF HELIUM*

G.D.Meneses and Gy.Csanak
Instituto de Física, Universidade Estadual de Campinas, CP.1170
13100 Campinas-SP-Brasil

The first-order many-body theory of Csanak et al[1] has
been used for the calculation of orientation and alignment
parameters: λ and χ for the excitation of the 2^1P and 3^1P states
of helium. The calculation for the excitation of 2^1P state has
been completed at 40,50,60 and 80eV impact energies and will be
compared with the experimental results of Eminyan et al[2],
Hollywood et al[3] and Sutcliffe et al[4]. At 80 eV impact energy
good agreement is obtained for λ for large angles ($\theta>50^\circ$) with
the measurement of Sutcliffe et al[4] and poor agreement with
Hollywood et al[3]. For the χ parameter excellent agreement is
obtained for $\theta>70^\circ$ with the experimental results of Hollywood
et al[3].

The results for the 3^1P excitation will be compared
with the experimental results of Eminyan et al[5] and Standage
and Kleinpoppen[6].

*Work supported in part by Conselho Nacional de Desen
volvimento Científico e Tecnológico (Brazil)

1. Gy.Csanak, H.S.Taylor, R.Yaris, Phys.Rev. A3, nº 4, 1322
   (1971)
2. M.Eminyan, K.B.Mac Adam, J.Slevin and H.Kleinpoppen, J.Phys.
   B7, 1519 (1974)
3. M.T.Hollywood, A.Crowe and J.F.Williams (private communication)
4. V.C.Sutcliffe, G.N.Haddad, N.C.Steph and D.E.Golden, Phys.
   Rev. A17, 100 (1978)
5. M.Eminyan, K.B.Mac Adam, J.Slevin, M.C.Standage and H.
   Kleinpoppen, J.Phy. B: Atom.Molec.Phys. 8, 2058 (1975)
6. M.Standage and H.Kleinpoppen, Phys.Rev.Lett. 36, 577 (1976)

THE APPLICATION OF THE FIRST ORDER MANY BODY THEORY
FOR THE CALCULATION OF THE DIFFERENTIAL CROSS SECTIONS
OF THE EXCITATION OF THE $3s\left[1\frac{1}{2}\right]^{\circ}$ (J=1,2) AND $3s'\left[\frac{1}{2}\right]^{\circ}$ (J=0,1)
STATES OF NEON*

Luiz Eugênio Machado, Emerson Pires Leal

Depto. de Física, Universidade Federal de São Carlos

13560 - São Carlos - SP - Brasil

and

Gy. Csanak

Instituto de Física, Universidade Estadual de

Campinas 13100 - Campinas - SP - Brasil

The first order many body theory of Csanak et al[1] has been used for
the calculation of the differential cross section for the lowest lying four
states of neon. The static-exchange orbitals have been calculated using an
extended version of a program written by Bates[2]. The excited states has been
calculated via the scheme of Cowan and Andrew[3] where spin-orbit interaction
has been taken into consideration semiempirically and the coupling
parameters have been provided by Cowan[4].

The excited states orbitals have been calculated in the fixed core
Hartree-Fock approximation using the program of Bates[2]. Calculations have
been completed at 20,30,40,50,80, 100 and 120 eV impact energies, and will
be compared with the experimental results of Roy ande Carette[5]. Orientation
and alignment parameters (λ and χ) have also been calculated and will be
compared with the experimental results of Ugbabe et al[6] at 80 eV and 120 eV
impact energies.

References

1. Gy. Csanak, H.S.Taylor, and R.Yaris, Phys. Rev. A3 1322 (1971)

2. G.N.Bates, Computer Phys. Commun. 8, 220 (1974)

3. R.D.Cowan and K.L.Andrew, J.Opt.Soc. Am. 55, 502 (1965)

4. R.D.Cowan, private communication

5. D.Roy and J.D.Carette, Can. J.Phys 52, 1178 (1974)

6. A.Ugbabe, P.J.O. Teubner, E.Weigold, and H.Arriola, J.Phys. B 10
   71 (1977)

(*)Work supported in part by Conselho Nacional de Desenvolvimento Cientí -
fico e Tecnológico (Brasil).

The application of the first order many-body theory to the calculation of
the differential cross section for the electron impact excitation of the
4s $[1 1/2]$ º (J=1,2), 4s' $[1/2]$ º   (J=0,1) states of argon*.

N.T.Padial, G.D.Meneses and Gy.Csanak

Instituto de Física, Universidade Estadual de Campinas, C.P. 1170,
13100 Campinas-SP-Brasil

        The first order many-body theory of Csanak et al[1] has been used
in a simplified form for the calculation of the differential cross section
for the four lowest lying states of argon. The static-exchange scattering
orbitals were calculated numerically using an extended and modified form
of a program of Bates[2]. The transition density matrix was calculated in the
fixed-core Hartree-Fock approximation and configuration mixing of singlet
and triplet states was considered semiempirically using the scheme of Cowan
and Andrew[3] and values provided by Cowan[4]. Calculation have been completed
at 16,20,30,50 and 80. 4eV impact anergies. The orientation and alignment
parameters λ and χ   have also been calculated for the optically allowed
(J=1) states. Results will be compared to the recent experimental data for
the differential cross section of Chutjian and Cartwright (5) and for the
λ and χ of Malcolm and McConkey(6) at 50eV.

1.   Gy.Csanak, H.S.Taylor, R.Yaris, Phys.Rev. A3, 1322 (1971)
2.   G.N.Bates, Computer Physics Comm. 8, 220 (1974)
3.   R.D.Cowan and K.L.Andrew, J. of Opt. Soc. of America 55 , 5 (1965)
4.   R.D.Cowan - private communication
5.   A.Chutjian and D.C.Cartwright - private communication
6.   I.C.Malcolm and J.W.McConkey - private communication

   * Work partially supported by Conselho Nacional de Desenvolvimento
     Científico e Tecnológico. (Brazil)

APPLICATION OF THE MANY BODY THEORY TO ELASTIC AND INELASTIC SCATTERING OF ELECTRONS OFF HELIUM AND OTHER RARE GAS ATOMS

T. Scott, H.S. Taylor, and P. Driessen

University of Southern California
Department of Chemistry
University Park
Los Angeles, Ca.   90007   U.S.A.

A simplified, non-selfconsistent version of the Many Body theory (MBT) is used to compute a second order optical potential for elastic scattering of electrons from Helium [1,2,3], and a comparison is made with the second order optical potential approach of Bransden and Coleman [4,5], and the polarized orbital method [6,7].

The infinite sum over target states appearing in the present theory is truncated using a single pseudostate of ^1P type symmetry. The functional form of this state is guided by consideration of the polarized orbital method, and the single parameter (effective charge) is chosen so as to reproduce the long range dipole polarization potential in $-\alpha/r^4$, where α is the static dipole polarizability of Helium. The choice of the static polarizability is justified by showing [2] that the response function of the target is probed only in the very low energy region ($\sim <_{10}$ev) where the dipole polarizability is nearly constant and equal to its static value.

The results are compared to other theories [5,8,9,10] and recent experiments [11]. The agreement with experiment is excellent over a large energy range in contrast to other theories which are usually designed for specific energy regions.

New applications of the first order MBT to inelastic scattering of electron from Helium [12,13] and Argon [14,15] will be surveyed.

[1] T. Scott and H.S. Taylor (1978) submitted to J. Phys. B.

[2] T. Scott and H.S. Taylor (1978) submitted to J. Phys. B.

[3] T. Scott (1978) submitted to J. Comp. Phys.

[4] B.H. Bransden and J.P. Coleman, J. Phys. B., 5, 537 (1972)

[5] K.H. Winters, C.D. Clark, B.H. Bransden and J.P. Coleman, J. Phys. B., 7,788(1974)

[6] R.J. Drachman and A. Temkin, "Case Studies in Atomic Collision Physics II", Edited by M.R.C. McDowell and E.W. McDaniel, Amsterdam, North Holland, 399, (1972)

[7] J. Callaway, R.W. LaBahn, R.T. Pu and W.M. Duxler, Phys. Rev., 168, 12 (1968)

[8] R.W. LaBahn and J. Callaway, Phys. Rev. A, 2, 366 (1970)

[9] B.D. Buckley and H.R.J. Walters, J. Phys. B., 7, 1380 (1974)

[10] F.W. Byron and C.J. Joachain, Phys. Rev. A, 15, 128 (1977)

[11] D. Register, S. Trajmar and S.K. Srivastava, (1978) preliminary results to be published.

[12] G.D. Meneses, PhD Thesis, Universidade Estadual de Campinas (1978)

13 G. Csanak and G.D. Meneses (1978) to be published

14 N.T. Padial, PhD Thesis, Universidade Estadual de Campinas (1978)

15 G. Csanak and N.T. Padial, (1979), to be published

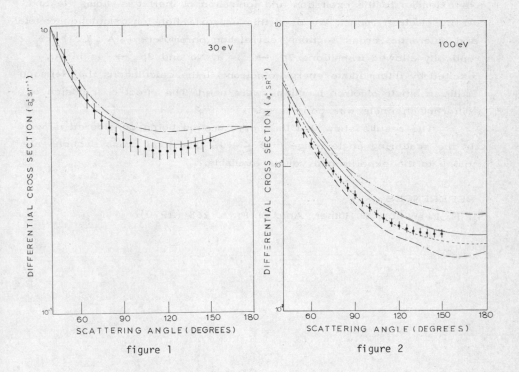

figure 1   figure 2

Figures: Elastic e⁻ - He differential cross section at 30ev (figure 1) and 100ev
        (figure 2). —— MBT (ref 2); —— —— Second order optical potential
        (ref 5); ——••—— Extended polarization calculation (ref 8); —— • ——
        Second Born (ref 9); - - - optical model (ref 10);• experiment (ref 11)

EXCITATION AND IONIZATION OF ATOMS BY
INTERMEDIATE ENERGY ELECTRON IMPACT

V.V. Balashov,   I.V. Kozhevnikov,   A.I. Magunov
Institute of Nuclear Physics, Moscow State University;
Moscow 117234; USSR

The multi-channel eikonal approximation proposed by Feshbach[1] is extended to the excitation and ionization of inert gas atoms Ne and Ar by electron impact. We used this approximation for calculation of total and differential cross sections, correlation parameters (λ , χ) for optically allowed transitions 2p $\rightarrow$ 3s in Ne and 3p $\rightarrow$ 4s in Ar, excited by intermediate energy electrons. Inthe calculations the Hermann-Skillman single-electron functions were used. The effect of inclusion of different channels was considered.

The results show that the approximation being considered is valid in the scattering angle range $\theta \leq 60°$. The total cross sections are close to the experimental values available.

REFERENCES

1. H. Feshbach, J. Hüfner, Ann. of Phys. **268** (1970).

EXCITATION OF RESONANCE TRANSITIONS IN ATOMS CALCULATED IN THE DWBA WITH OPTICAL POTENTIALS

V.V. Balashov, E.G. Berezhko, N.M. Kabachnik
and A.I. Magunov
Institute of Nuclear Physics, Moscow State University;
Moscow 117234; USSR

The use of the DWBA to calculate the total and differential cross sections for the excitation of optically allowed transitions in atoms by electrons and to determine the correlation parameters (λ and χ) has made it possible to improve significantly the agreement of theory with experiment. Most calculations have been restricted to the study of the simplest atoms, H and He. The present paper aims at studying further the potentialities of DWBA to describe inelastic electron scattering from atoms and, in particular, its use for describing the more complicated atomic systems. Special attention was paid to the study of the influence of the imaginary part of the optical potential.

We have calculated the differential and total excitation cross sections and the correlation parameters λ, χ for the 1s→2p transition in H and the 3p→4s transition in Ar. The DWBA was used with a centrally-symmetric local complex optical potential. The form of the potential and its parameters have been taken from studies of elastic electron scattering by the corresponding atoms.

REFERENCES

1. D.H. Madison and W.N. Shelton. Phys.Rev.A7, 499(1973).
2. R.V. Calhoun et al. Phys.Rev.A14,1380(1976).

GLAUBER GENERALIZED OSCILLATOR STRENGTH
FOR ALLOWED TRANSITIONS OF LITHIUM ATOM

S.S. Tayal   and   A.N. Tripathi

Department of Physics, University of Roorkee, Roorkee,U.P. India

Considerable theoretical interest has been shown in recent
years to the application of the Glauber approximation[1] to study
electron-atom scattering at lower and intermediate incident energies where first Born Approximation (FBA) compare poorly with
experiment. The principal success of the Glauber theory is the
inclusion of the incident particle and nucleus interaction. Recently Chan et al[2] have applied Glauber approximation (GA) to study
the minima and maxima of the generalized oscillator strength (GOS)
for the 2s-3p transition of atomic hydrogen. For a detailed discussion on the minima, reader is referred to the paper of Inokuti[3].
We have applied GA to investigate the dependence of the minima and
maxima of Glauber GOS on the incident energy for a few allowed
transitions in lithium atom. The Glauber GOS often referred as
apparent generalised oscillator strength (AGOS), is obtained from
the Glauber differential cross-section $(d\sigma/d\Omega)_{GA}$

$$f_{on}^{GA} (K) = \frac{\Delta E_{on}}{2} K^2 \frac{k_o}{k_n} (\frac{d\sigma}{d\Omega})_{GA} \qquad \cdots (1)$$

where $\vec{K}$ is the momentum transfer vector $\vec{K} = \vec{k}_o - \vec{k}_n$, k_o and k_n being
the incident electron momentum before and after the collision and
ΔE_{on} is the excitation energy. In the calculation of $(d\sigma/d\Omega)_{GA}$,
we have used the Hartree-Fock (HF) wave function of Weiss[4]. In
view of the one electron nature of the spectra involved, one may
expect that HF wave function would yield reasonably good results.
With the help of Eq.(1), we have computed the Glauber GOS for
2s-2p, 2s-3p and 3s-3p transition in lithium atom at several
energies. We are presenting only the results for 2s-3p transition
in Fig.1. We have also shown on the curve FBA GOS[5] calculated
in the length formulation. It is noticed that the Glauber GOS
has a marked energy dependence. From the Fig. 1 it is seen that
the position and magnitude of the minima in Glauber GOS shift
towards smaller K values as incident energy is decreased. This
feature is in accordance with the recently observed energy dependence of the experimental GOS in the case of rare gases and
mercury[6]. For high incident energies, the difference between

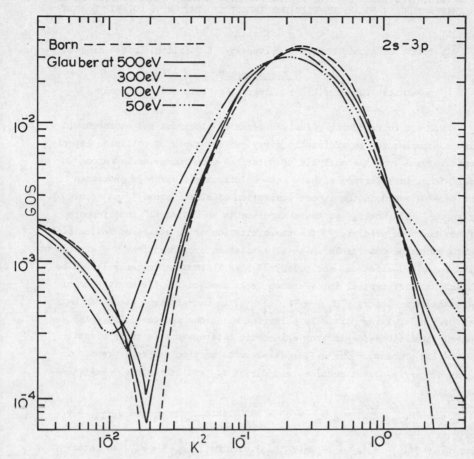

Glauber GOS curves is small and the Glauber GOS approaches to that of FBA GOS.

References

(1) E. Gerjucy and B.K. Thomas, Rep. Prog. Phys. 37, 1345 (1974).

(2) F.T. Chan, C.H. Chang, M. Lieber and Y.K. Kim, Phys. Rev. A 17, 1869 (1978)

(3) M. Inokuti, Rev. Mod. Phys. 43, 297 (1971)

(4) A.W. Weiss, Ap. J. 138, 1262 (1963)

(5) K.L. Bell, A.E. Kingston and A.N. Tripathi (unpublished)

(6) F. Hanne and J. Kessler, Phys. Rev. A 5, 2457 (1972)

DIFFERENTIAL CROSS SECTION OF INTERFERENCE BETWEEN DIRECT AND EXCHANGE INTERACTION IN POLARIZED ELECTRON IMPACT EXCITATION OF POLARIZED ATOMS

S Khalid

Institute of Atomic Physics, University of Stirling, United Kingdom

H Kleinpoppen*

Fakultät für Physik der Universität Bielefeld, W. Germany

Progress in producing polarized beams of electrons and atoms should enable experimental physicists to carry out new types of collision experiments. Based upon the analysis of polarized electron-polarized atom collisions, interference effects between direct and exchange processes could be detected in the impact ionization of alkali atoms[1] and atomic hydrogen[2]. In analogy to these experiments an "integral" interference effect has been predicted[3] for the excitation of ^2P states of sodium atoms which should be observable in total excitation cross sections for experiments with polarized electrons and polarized alkali atoms. Similarly it can be shown that differential interference cross section for the excitation of resonance transitions $(^2S_{1/2} \rightarrow {}^2P_{1/2,\,3/2})$ in one-electron atoms can be measured by applying partially polarized electrons and partially polarized one-electron atoms (neglecting spin-orbit interactions in the inelastic scattering process). The differential cross section can be expressed in terms of partial cross sections and direct f_{m_ℓ} and exchange g_{m_ℓ} amplitudes as follows[4]:

$$\sigma(^2S_{1/2} \rightarrow {}^2P_{1/2,\,3/2}) = \sum_{m_\ell} \sigma_{m_\ell} = \sigma_0 + 2\sigma_1 \text{ with } \sigma_{m_\ell=0} = \sigma_0 \text{ and } \sigma_{m_\ell=\pm1} = \sigma_1$$

and $\sigma_{m_\ell} = |f_{m_\ell}|^2 + |g_{m_\ell}|^2 - \mathrm{Re}(f_{m_\ell}g_{m_\ell}^*)$ with $\mathrm{Re}(f_{m_\ell}g_{m_\ell}^*) = \sigma_{m_\ell}^{int}$ as interference cross section.

It is interesting to demonstrate how total differential cross sections may vary rather smoothly with energy while the ratios of the interference cross sections to the total or partial differential cross sections may show dramatic structure in the angular dependence. This is indeed displayed in Fig. 1 and 2 where the total differential cross sections and the above ratios σ^{int}/σ, σ_0^{int}/σ_0 and σ_1^{int}/σ_1, are plotted for the excitation of the first resonance transition $3^2S_{1/2} \rightarrow 3^2P_{1/2,\,3/2}$ of sodium at 4eV. The predictions have been calculated by applying amplitudes from the four state exchange close coupling theory[5]. Further data for 3.3eV, 3.0eV and 5.0eV reveal additional structure in the interference cross sections. To our knowledge no experimental data exists for comparison. Furthermore anisotropy effects in the intensity or the polarization of the resonance line are expected if polarized electrons and polarized one-electron atoms are applied.

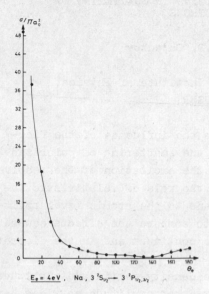

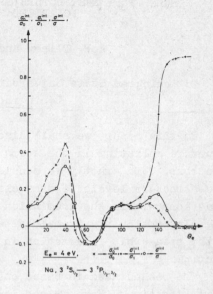

Fig.1

Differential cross section at
4eV for the first resonance line
of sodium calculated from four
state close coupling theory[5]

Fig.2

Ratios of interference cross
sections to the total or partial
differential cross sections at
4eV for the first resonance line
of sodium calculated from four
state close coupling theory[5].

*Permanent address: Institute of Atomic Physics, University of
Stirling, Stirling FK9 4LA, Scotland.

1. D. Hils, H. Kleinpoppen, J. Phys. $\underline{B11}$, L283 (1978).

2. M. J. Alguard, V.W. Hughes, M.S. Lubell and P.F. Wainwright,
   Phys. Rev. Lett. $\underline{39}$, 334-8 (1977).

3. H. Kleinpoppen, paper presented at the International Workshop
   on "Coherence and Correlation in Atomic Collisions", London
   18-19th September, 1978; to be published in the Workshop
   Proceedings dedicated to Sir Harrie Massey (Plenum Press, 1979)
   (Eds. H. Kleinpoppen and J.F. Williams).

4. H. Kleinpoppen, Phys. Rev. $\underline{A3}$, 2015 (1971).

5. D.L. Moores and D.W. Norcross, J. Phys. $\underline{B5}$, 1482 (1972).

ROLE OF FINE-STRUCTURE SPLITTING IN SCATTERING OF POLARIZED ELECTRONS

A.P. Blinov and V.D. Ob'edkov

Leningrad State University, Institute of Physics,
Leningrad, USSR

In this report we shall discuss the influence of the fine-structure splitting in the atoms on the scattering of polarized electrons. More exactly we consider the excitation of the resolved fine-structure levels to make clear the role of relativistic interactions within the atom which leads to the atomic level splitting. In particular it would allow to compare the effects caused by the spin-orbit interaction in the continuum and in the discrete spectrum.

The method used is based on the density-matrix and amplitude matrix technique. Here we can remark, that amplitude matrices have in general rectangular form because of the set of quantum numbers before the collision may differ from that after it.

Our main results are:

1. The differential cross section $\sigma(J)$ for each fine- structure level depends on the polarization vector $\vec{P}$ of the incident particle. This vector is included into $\sigma(J)$ in the scalar combination with some new vectors connected with the total angular momentum J of the atom. The cross section obtained by summation over all fine-structure components is independent on $\vec{P}$. So dependence of $\sigma(J)$ on $\vec{P}$ can be found if the fine-structure splitting is experimentally resolved.

2. The electrons which have excited the separate components of the fine structure acquire some degree of polarization even when they were unpolarized prior to the collision. The polarization induced in the initially unpolarized system due to excitation of fine-structure levels at some fixed energy depends on the scattering angle. It may be remarked here that polarization induced by the spin-orbit interaction in the continuum always has the direction of the normal to the scattering plane.

3. There is no left-right asymmetry in the scattering of polarized electrons after excitation of the fine-structure levels, although the differential cross section $\sigma(J)$ do depend on $\vec{P}$, as

it was mentioned above. This fact is next distinction of the discussed case from the case of well known Mott scattering.

We got the results for cross-sections and polarisation for the excitation of ^2P_j - states by electrons and unstructured spinless particles and ^3P_j - states by electrons.

The problem of $^1S_0$ $-^3P_j$ transition in mercury induced by transversally polarized incident electrons was first considered by Hanne (1976). Our results coincide with those given by Hanne if the same assumptions are made about initial transversal orientation of P and with the same connection between the amplitudes g_1 and g_{-1}. In general case when these assumptions are excluded we got the non zero polarization in any direction.

To conclude this report we give the results for the most simple case when a polarized $^2S_{1/2}$- state of the atom is excited into ^2P_j - state by a spinless particle. The cross-sections are:

$$\sigma(1/2) = \sigma_0 \left[1 + (\vec{P}\vec{P_0}) \right], \qquad \sigma(3/2) = \sigma_0 \left[2 - (\vec{P}\vec{P_0}) \right],$$

where $\sigma_0 = \frac{1}{3} \sum_M |f_M|^2$, f_M being the amplitude of transition, $\vec{P}$ - the initial polarization of the atom in $^2S_{1/2}$-state and $\vec{P_0}$- the new vector which arises in the collision and having components:

$$P_{0x} = - (\sqrt{2}/2) \left[f_0 (\bar{f_1} + \bar{f_{-1}}) + \bar{f_0} (f_1 + f_{-1}) \right] / 3\sigma_0$$

$$P_{0y} = i (\sqrt{2}/2) \left[f_0 (\bar{f_1} - \bar{f_{-1}}) - \bar{f_0} (f_1 - f_{-1}) \right] / 3\sigma_0$$

$$P_{0z} = \left(|f_{-1}|^2 - |f_1|^2 \right) / 3\sigma_0$$

It is interesting to emphasize that $\vec{P_0} = \langle \vec{J} \rangle$ for J=1/2, i.e. $\vec{P_0}$ is connected with the total angular momentum J of excited atom.

Undoubtedly the experimental discovery of discussed effects would be a new step in the physics of polarized particles.

1. G.F. Hanne, J. Phys. B 9, 805–815 (1976).

ABOUT THE EFFECTIVE POTENTIAL OF INTERACTION OF
SLOW ELECTRONS WITH ATOMS AND MOLECULES.

Yu.A.Kukharenko

All-Union Scientific Research of Metrology Service,

117337, Moscow, USSR

A method of calculation of elastic scattering cross section on any atoms and molecules based on the one-particle Schrödinger equation for an electron in effective external field was proposed in [1,2].

This paper reports a generalisation of this method for inelastic electron scattering. We have shown that the inelastic interaction of electrons with any atoms and molecules can be exactly described by the Schrödinger equation for two electrons, moving in the effective external field and interecting by effective two-particle potential. The results of calculation of this potential are given taking into account direct and exchange interactions of electrons and polarisation of the atomic shells. We have shown that as distinct from the usual approach [3] this method doesn't contain the fictitious exchange interaction of the electron with the nucleus in any approximation.

1. M.H.Mittleman, K.M.Watson, Phys. Rev., 113, 198, (1959).

2. B.A.Lippman, M.H.Mittleman, K.M.Watson, Phys. Rev., 116, 920 (1959).

3. M.L.Goldberger, K.M.Watson. Collision Theory. John Wiley, New-York-London-Sydney, 1964.

SEMICLASSICAL VERSION OF BORN–COULOMB APPROXIMATION
FOR THE SCATTERING OF ELECTRONS BY IONS. EXCITATION,
IONIZATION, DOUBLE SCATTERING

M.A. Braun and V.I. Ochkur

Institute of Physics, Leningrad State University,
Leningrad, USSR

In the previous papers by the authors[1,2] the semiclassical theory of electron-atom excitation and ionization, based on the first-order formulas of the perturbation theory has been developed. It added to better understending of the results of purely classical calculations of these processes as well as of those, made in the Born approximation.

In this report the same technique is used for the case of electron scattering by positive ions. We consider transitions for which both quantum numbers of initial and final states and their changes are large, as well as those for which the transferred angular momenta are small.

As an example for s - p transitions in a hydrogen-like ion we get:

$$\sigma_{s-p}(n,n') = \frac{\pi a_0^2}{Z^4} \frac{I(u,Z)}{1+u} F(n,n')$$

where $u = \varepsilon/\varepsilon - \varepsilon'$, ε and ε' being the kinetic energy of the colliding electron before and after collision, n and n' - the quantum numbers of initial and final states of the ion,

$$F(n,n') = \frac{16}{3} \frac{(nn')^5}{(n'^2-n^2)^{7/2}} \left\{ \frac{n^2}{4} - \frac{9}{4}n'^2 + 2nn'\sqrt{2(n'^2-n^2)} \right\}^{-1/2}$$

and $I(u,Z)$ - a smooth function of its arguments, which for ions is practically always close to unity. We suppose that the atomic electron moves in the field $U_1 = Ze^2/r$ and the incoming electron in the field $U_2 = (Z-1)e^2/r$.

Our calculations of this sort are compared with those made in the Born-Coulomb approximation and by other methods proposed for transitions between high levels and reviewed for instance in[3].

We consider also the effects of double scattering, which arise in the second order of perturbation theory. In this aproximation we have 36 terms in the expression for the cross-

section, 6 of which appear to give the main contribution in the
semiclassical limit.

First we consider the case when the transferred angular momenta are large. The same technique that was used previously gives
the final expressions of two types. The cross-sections of the first
type belong to the case when the incoming electron interacts with
an atomic one, which in its turn interacts with another atomic
electron. We will call these Auger-type processes. For such processes a rather simple formula is obtained, containing only one
numerical integration.

The processes of the second type (which we will call Gla-
uber-type) correspond to successive interactions of the incoming
electron with two atomic electrons. It is more difficult to calculate the corresponding cross-sections, although they greatly
simplify in the limit of high energies.

We consider also the case of small transferred angular momenta. For such processes it also proved possible to get comparatively simple final results.

1. M.A.Braun, V.I.Ochkur, in "Invited papers of the VI Inter-
          national Conf. on Atomic Physics, Riga,(1978)
2. M.A.Braun, V.I.Ochkur, X ICPEAC, 1074, Paris (1977)
3. I.C.Percival, D.Richards, in Adv. Atom. Molec. Phys. **11**,
                      1-88, (1975)

MICROSCOPIC OPTICAL POTENTIAL TREATMENT OF INELASTIC e-He$^+$ SCATTERING*

W. R. Garrett

Chemical Physics Section, Health and Safety Research Division,
Oak Ridge National Laboratory, Oak Ridge, Tennessee 37830, U.S.A.

Philip W. Coulter

Department of Physics and Astronomy, University of Alabama,
University, Alabama 35486, U.S.A.

Cross sections for electron scattering by atomic positive ions have recently gained significant importance in a number of basic and applied plasma physics studies. For example, in magnetically confined plasmas that are involved in various fusion energy studies, inelastic electron scattering by partially stripped plasma impurity ions contribute significantly to the total energy balance at early times in the evolution of the plasma discharge. In the context of plasma impurity ion studies, the physical parameters of interest include electron-ion cross sections for one or more discrete excitation channels, total ionization cross sections, the sum of cross sections for all discrete excitations, and the average energy loss per collision for electrons with energies of a few electron volts up to a few kilo-electron volts.

The microscopic optical potential formalism for describing multichannel electron scattering by atomic systems is especially well suited to theoretical treatment of plasma collisional processes, since the contributions to the total scattering interaction from real and virtual transitions to both discrete and continuum states of the target ion can be separated out in the formalism and investigated as to their importance in the description of scattering in various channels. Moreover, the relevant information for plasma applications can all be obtained conveniently and systematically. Using the method recently demonstrated by Coulter,[1] cross sections for scattering into individual channels can be extracted; the total ionization cross section and the sum of cross sections for all discrete excitations can be obtained readily;[2,3] and, as we shall demonstrate, the average energy loss per collision can be conveniently determined.

In order to assess the efficacy of the microscopic optical potential method for treating multichannel electron-ion scattering, we have employed the method of references 1 and 2 in a study of electron scattering by He$^+$ for incident energies from 45 to 300 eV. Here we have used a coulomb wave approximation in the Green's function that appears in the complex nonlocal optical potential.[2] The equations were treated, as before, in the distorted wave (diagonal) approximation with electron exchange ignored in all but the incident channel. Results for total ionization of He$^+$ and for the process He$^+$(1s) $\rightarrow$ He$^+$(2p) compare favorably with experiments by Dolder et al.[4] and by Dashchenko et al.,[5] respectively.

*Research sponsored by the U.S. Department of Energy under contract W-7405-eng-26 with the Union Carbide Corporation.

1. P. W. Coulter, Phys. Rev. A 18, 1908 (1978).

2. P. W. Coulter and W. R. Garrett, Phys. Rev. A 18, 1902 (1978).

3. G. D. Alton, W. R. Garrett, M. Reeves, and J. E. Turner, Phys. Rev. A 6, 2138 (1972).

4. K. T. Dolder, M.F.A. Harrison, and P. C. Thoneman, Proc. Roy. Soc. A 264, 367 (1961).

5. A. I. Dashchenko, I. P. Zapesochnyi, A. I. Imre, V. S. Bukstick, F. F. Danch, and V. A. Kel'man, Zh. Eksp. Teor. Fiz. 67, 503 (1978) [Sov. Phys.-JETP 40, 249 (1975)].

EXCITATION CROSS SECTION OF HELIUM-LIKE IONS AS INFERRED FROM RELATIVE
INTENSITIES OF CORONAL EMISSION LINES

Takashi Fujimoto

Department of Engineering Science, Kyoto University, Kyoto 606, Japan

and

Takako Kato

Institute of Plasma Physics, Nagoya University, Nagoya 464, Japan

Observed relative intensities of the helium-like-ion lines $1^1S - 2^1P$ (denoted
as R) , $1^1S - 2^3P$ (I) and $1^1S - 2^3S$ (F) from the solar corona are analyzed to give
information on excitation cross sections.

A set of rate equations for the population density is constructed for 61 discrete levels of helium-like ion, where the elementary processes considered are excitation - deexcitation and ionization - three-body recombination by electron collsions, radiative transition and recombination and dielectronic recombination.
For excitation cross sections we tentatively assume the Coulomb-Born-Oppenheimer
approximation,[1] which agrees with other calculations for $1^1S - 2^3P$, for example.
However, for some transitions disagreement with other data is substantial as shown

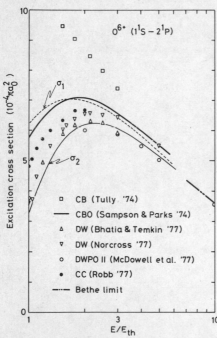

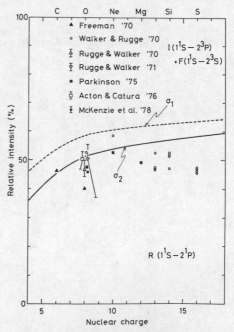

Fig. 1. Summary of the existing
cross section data for excitation
of $1^1S - 2^1P$ of O^{6+}. The cross sections σ_1 and σ_2 pose the upper and
lower bounds, respectively, of the
existing data except the Coulomb-
Born (CB) calculation.

Fig. 2. Percentage contributions
from (F+I) and from R to the total
vs nuclear charge. Calculated
results for o_1 and o_2 are shown.
Results of the observations are
compared.

in Fig. 1. The above set of equations is solved under the condition of the solar corona: the plasma is in ionization equilibrium with $n_e \longrightarrow 0$ and $T_e = T_m$, the temperature at which the emission intensities of the lines take their maxima.

Figure 2 gives the calculated percentage contributions from (I + F) and from R to the total for various nuclear charge z, where for the excitation cross section $1^1S - 2^1P$ the upper bound σ_1 or the lower bound σ_2 in Fig. 1 is assumed. Results

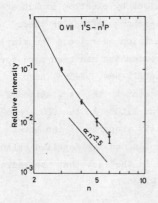

of several observations are also given. Comparison suggests that in order for the calculation to be consistent with the observation, especially that of Acton and Catura,[2] the cross section should be close to σ_2. The systematic deviation of the data by Walker and Rugge for high z elements is considered due to blend of lithium-like satellite lines into I or F; this effect is proportional to z^4 and can be pronounced for high z.

We apply the above-determined Gaunt factor of σ_2 to the excitation cross sections $1^1S - n^1P$ (n $\geqslant$ 3), then the calculated relative intensities of the resonance-series lines are in excellent agreement with the observation.[3] (Fig. 3)

Fig. 3. Relative intensities of the resonance-series lines normalized to R as observed by McKenzie[3]. Calculated values are connected by lines.

In conclusion, 1) for the excitation cross section $1^1S - 2^1P$ the most reasonable value is given by the distorted-wave[4] or by distorted-wave polarized-orbital[5] calculation. 2) The excitation cross sections $1^1S - n^1P$ share the same Gaunt factor.

1. D.H. Sampson and A.D. Parks, Ap. J.(Supplement) 263, 323 (1974).

2. L.W. Acton and R.C. Catura, Phil. Trans. R. Soc. London A 281, 383 (1976).

3. D.L. McKenzie et al., Ap. J. 221, 342 (1978).

4. D.W. Norcross, Informal Report LA-6691-MS (1977), A.K. Bhatia and A. Temkin, J. Phys. B 10, 2893 (1977).

5. M.R.C. McDowell et al., J. Phys. B 10, 2727 (1977).

ELECTRON IMPACT EXCITATION OF POSITIVE IONS
BY THE COULOMB-BORN-BELY APPROXIMATION

Shinobu Nakazaki and Tasuke Hashino

Department of Applied Physics, Faculty of Engineering,
Miyazaki University, Miyazaki 880, Japan

Cross sections for a lot of excitations in many ions by electron impact are required for astronomy and for fusion research. The exchange effect in these transitions is important even at relatively large collision energies. The simple approximation, the Coulomb-Born-Oppenheimer (CBO) approximation has been used for a large number of transitions by many theoreticians untill now. Bely[1] has extended the Ochkur approximation used in the neutral atom to the excitation of positive ions and simplified the exchange scattering amplitude in the CBO approximation. His approximation satisfies the orthogonality property of the total wave functions before and after the collision still holds and the detailed balance principle. The simplicity of this approximation lies in the fact that the radial integrals necessary in the exchange **R**-matrix can be given by

$$I(1_a 1, 1'_a 1') = \int_0^\infty P_{nl_a}(r) \, P_{n'l'_a}(r) \, F_{kl}(r) \, F_{k'l'}(r) \, r^{-2} \, dr$$

where the functions $P_{nl_a}(r)$ are the atomic radial wave functions and the functions $F_{kl}(r)$ are the regular Coulomb functions. This radial integrals have been expressed in terms of the Gauss hypergeometric functions[2] when the radial wave functions are represented analytically as a linear combination of Slater-type orbitals. Thus, computations using the Coulomb-Born-Bely (CBB) approximation are easier than the CBO approximation. There are very few papers about the CBB approximation.

Cross sections for various transitions of the hydrogen-, helium-, and beryllium-like ions ($Z = 2 \sim 10$) have been obtained using the CBB approximation and compared with the previous results of the CBO, DW, DWPO and CC approximations.

Results

1). Hydrogen-like ions

The present total cross sections for the $1s \rightarrow 2s$, $2p$, $3s$, $3p$ transitions in $Z = 2 \sim 10$ agree well with the CBO and DW results for $X \gtrsim 3$ in threshold unit. For $X < 3$, the CBB approximation for the $1s \rightarrow 2p$, $3p$ well improves the CB approximation. However, for the $1s \rightarrow 2s$, $3s$, present results lie far above those of the CB and DW approximations for $X < 2$ in even $Z \geq 6$.

2). Helium-like ions

The calculations for the $1s^2 \, ^1S \rightarrow 1s2s \, ^1S$, $1s2p \, ^1P$ transitions have been made using the target wave functions of Bhatia and Temkin[3] in order to compare with their results. For the $1s^2 \, ^1S \rightarrow 1s2s \, ^1S$ in O^{6+} ion, present results are in closer agreement with the DW of Bhatia and Temkin[3] for all value of X.(Fig.1)

For the $1s^2\ {}^1S \rightarrow 1s2p\ {}^1P$ in O^{6+} ion, it is seen that the CBB approximation well improves the CB approximation by taking into account the exchange effect and are larger than the DW approximation by about 15% for $X = 2$. (Fig.2)

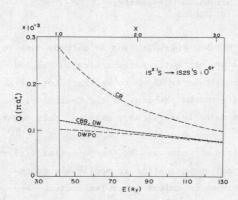

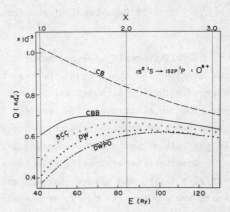

Fig. 1. Total cross sections for the $1s^2\ {}^1S \rightarrow 1s2s\ {}^1S$ transition in O^{6+}: CB and CBB, this work; DW, ref.3; DWPO, the distorted-wave polarized-orbital results (ref.4).

Fig. 2. As for Fig. 1 for the $1s^2\ {}^1S \rightarrow 1s2p\ {}^1P$ in O^{6+} and also 5CC; the five-states close coupling resuls (ref.5)

3). Beryllium-like ions

The wave functions for the initial and final states of the target are employed the configuration interaction wave functions. Present results for some transitions improve the CB approximation.

Thus, the CBB approximation is useful from the point of view that we can easily compute the cross sections for the excitation of ion by electron impact for $X \gtrsim 3$. The details of this work will be presented at the conference.

1. O. Bely, Nuovo Cimento 49, 66 (1967).

2. S. Nakazaki, J. Phys. Soc. Japan 45, 225 (1978).

3. A. K. Bhatia and A. Temkin, J. Phys. B. 10, 2893 (1977).

4. M. R. C. McDowell, L. A. Morgan, V. P. Myerscough and T. Scott, J. Phys. B. 10, 2727 (1977).

5. N. H. Magee, J. B. Mann, A. L. Merts and W. D. Robb, Los Alamos Scientific Laboratory Report LA-6691-MS (1977).

TREATMENT OF LONG RANGE COULOMB INTERACTION IN THE EIKONAL APPROXIMATION

Takeshi Ishihara and Hajime Narumi*

Institute of Applied Physics, University of Tsukuba,
Ibaraki 300-31, Japan

* Department of Physics, Hiroshima University,
Hiroshima 730, Japan

Straightforward application of the Glauber approximation is already made to the electron-ion scattering. The results are not quite satisfactory in the low energy region.[1-3] Although the Glauber amplitude is known to be exact for the pure Coulomb scattering, its applicability to the problems of the Coulomb plus short range interaction has not yet been made clear. We have examined this point in the case of potential scattering.

Consider the scattering of a particle of unit mass by the potential $V(r) = -(Z/r) + V_0(r)$, and assume that the eikonal approximation is applicable to the short range potential $V_0(r)$. We use atomic units unless otherwise stated. The phase shift for angular momentum ℓ is written $\Delta_\ell = \sigma_\ell + \delta_\ell$, where δ_ℓ is the Coulomb phase shift. The following expression for δ_ℓ is obtained if we evaluate it in the JWKB approximation to the first order in V_0:

$$\delta_\ell^c = -\int_{b_1}^\infty V_0(r)/\{2E + (2Z/r) - [(\ell + \tfrac{1}{2})^2/r^2]\}^{\frac{1}{2}} , \tag{1}$$

where b_1 is the apsidal distance for the Coulomb problem and E is the projectile energy. Eq.(1) can be interpreted as the integral of $-V_0(r)/v(r)$ along the classcal Coulomb trajectory, where $v(r) = \sqrt{2E + (2Z/r)}$ is the local velocity. If we neglect the Coulomb potential in the denominator of Eq.(1), it reduces to the usual Glauber phase shift for the short range potential

$$\delta_\ell^G = -\frac{1}{v} \int_0^\infty V_0(r)dz , \tag{2}$$

where $r^2 = b^2 + z^2$, $v = \sqrt{2E}$ and $b = (\ell + \tfrac{1}{2})/v$.

As an example, we compare in Table 1 exact δ_ℓ with δ_ℓ^c and δ_ℓ^G for the case of $V_0 = -e^{-r}$ and $Z = 1$ at $E = 20$ eV. We can see the importance of the Coulomb effects in the evaluation of δ_ℓ and they are well taken into account through the classical treatment of the Coulomb scattering. In order to go beyond the potential scattering, it is desirable to find the straight-line trajectory which containes much of the Coulomb effect. Such a choice may be that through the apse since the contribution to the integral of Eq.(1) comes mostly from the region of $r \sim b_1$. Therefore we replace the denominator of Eq.(1) by $v_1[1 - (b_1/r)^2]^{1/2}$ with $v_1 = [2E + (Z/b_1)]^{1/2}$. This velocity function agrees with that of Eq.(1) to the first derivative at $r = b_1$. Writing $r^2 = z^2 + b_1^2$, we obtain

$$\delta_\ell^s = \frac{1}{v_1} \int_0^\infty V_0(r)dz. \tag{3}$$

Numerical values of δ_ℓ^s are also shown in Table 1. They agree very well with δ_ℓ^c except for very small ℓ. At high energies, say $E \gtrsim 100$ eV, agreement between δ_ℓ^G and δ_ℓ^c becomes better. At any energies, as is expected, δ_ℓ^G gives overestimation of δ_ℓ for small ℓ values and underestimation for large ℓ values. For very large ℓ, δ_ℓ^G converges to δ_ℓ^c which is much smaller than δ_ℓ.

Further analysis along this line will be presented in the Conference.

Table 1

ℓ	δ_ℓ	δ_ℓ^c	δ_ℓ^G	δ_ℓ^s
0	0.48966	0.49542	0.71607	0.30812
1	0.45604	0.45915	0.41853	0.42785
2	0.30071	0.29345	0.21934	0.28636
3	0.16699	0.16203	0.10957	0.16009
4	0.08583	0.08358	0.05325	0.08299
5	0.04262	0.04150	0.02542	0.04131
10	0.00108	0.00098	0.00055	0.00098

1.   H. Narumi and A. Tsuji, Prog. Theor. Phys. **53**, 671 (1975).

2.   T. Ishihara and J.C.Y. Chen, J. Phys. **B8**, L417 (1975).

3.   B.K. Thomas and V. Franco, Phys. Rev. **A13**, 2004 (1976).

ORIENTATION AND ALIGNMENT PARAMETERS FOR THE ELECTRON IMPACT
EXCITATION OF THE RESONANT STATES OF SODIUM

P.J.O. Teubner, S.J. Buckman and J. Furst

Institute for Atomic Studies,
School of Physical Sciences,
The Flinders University of South Australia,
Bedford Park, South Australia, 5042

The electron impact excitation of the $3^2P_{1/2, 3/2}$ states of sodium has been
studied by observing the inelastically scattered electrons and the photons arising
from the excited state decay in delayed coincidence.   The polarisation of the
photons has been analysed by measuring the Stokes parameters P_1 and P_3.

A beam of electrons intersects a beam of sodium atoms.   The energy of the
inelastically scattered electrons is analysed by a cylindrical mirror spectrometer which views the interaction region.   Pulses from the channel electron
multiplier which detects the scattered electrons are amplified and act as start
pulses for a time to amplitude converter (TAC).   The photons which are emitted
normal to the scattering plane pass through a quarter wave plate and a linear
polariser and are detected in a fast, high gain, low noise photomultiplier tube.
Electrical signals from the PMT are amplified and delayed and act as the stop
pulses for the TAC.   The coincidence count rate is measured as a function of the
optic axis of the polariser and yields the linear Stokes parameter P_1. P_1 is
simply related to the alignment parameter[1].   The circular polarisation factor
P_3 is related to the orientation parameter and is measured by observing the
coincidence count rate as a function of the relative positions of the quarter
wave plate and polariser.   The data have been taken at sufficiently low neutral
beam densities that the problems of the resonant absorption of the 589 nm radiation are minimised.   In addition we find that by using the technique of Imhof
and Read[2] to fit the coincidence spectrum, we obtain a lifetime for the resonant
state of 16.0 nsecs which is in excellent agreement with that obtained by level
crossing measurements.

The orientation and alignment parameters have been measured at incident
electron energies of 54.4, 100 and 200eV and for electron scattering angles θ_e
such that $3° \leqslant \theta_e \leqslant 15°$.   The data are compared with those predicted by the
Born and DWPO[3] theories where we find that there is generally poor agreement
between theory and experiment.   This is interesting in view of the excellent
agreement between these theories and the observed differential cross sections
for inelastic scattering at forward angles.

1.   Morgan, L.A., McDowell, M.R.C., Comments Atom. Mol. Phys. **7**, 123 (1978).

2.   Imhof, R.E. and Read, F.H., J.Phys.B: Atom. Molec. Phys. **4**, 450 (1971).

3.   Kennedy, J.V., Myerscough, V.P. and McDowell, M.R.C., J.Phys.B:
      Atom. Molec. Phys. **10**, 3759 (1977).

ORIENTATION AND COHERENCE IN e^- + Na SCATTERING:
3^2P - 3^2S and 3^2P - 3^2D TRANSITIONS

H W Hermann, <u>I V Hertel</u>[*], and M H Kelley[**]

FB Physik, Universität Kaiserslautern, W Germany

Photon-electron coincidences[1] or scattering from optically
pumped atoms[2] allow to investigate magnitude and phase differences
of the amplitudes for collisional excitation of magnetic sublevels.
Therefore these quantities give finer details on the dynamics and
a more sensitive test for the theory than differential cross sections do. For the first time, collision induced transitions in Na
between the excited states 3^2P and 3^2D are reported. We compare
them to previous[3] 3^2P-3^2S results.

Using laser optical hyperfine pumping of a Na beam, the $3^2P_{3/2}$
state is prepared in the scattering center with a well known distribution of magnetic sublevels M relative to the $\mathbb{E}$ vector of the
exciting linear light. $\mathbb{E}$ may be rotated in the scattering plane by
an angle $\emptyset$ to the incoming electron direction $\mathbb{k}_{in}$. Using the
3x3 density matrix ρ of the collision-excited P-state with
$\rho_{MN} = \sum_{s,\overline{M}}(2s+1) \, f^s_{M\overline{M}} \, f^{s*}_{N\overline{M}}$, where the singlet (s=0) or triplet
(s=1) scattering amplitudes f^s_{MN} relate the initial state sublevel
M to a final N and $\overline{M} = 0$ ($\overline{M} = -2...2$) in the P-S (P-D) excitation,
the rate of electrons scattered into an angle ϑ_{col} reads

(1) $\quad I(\vartheta_{col},\emptyset) = \left[1+u_2/2\left(1-3\,\rho_{oo}+6\left|\rho_{-11}\right|\cos(2\emptyset+\arg\rho_{-11})\right)\right] \Big/ \left[1+u_2(1-3\rho_{oo})\right]$

This simple form is obtained only if the f^s_{MN} refer to a quantiza-
tion axis z = $\mathbb{k}_{in}$ x $\mathbb{k}_{out}$; then, to conserve parity, $f^s_{MN} = 0$ if
M-N is even, so that for P-S, $\rho_{oo} = 0$ and the optical pumping pa-
rameter u_2 can be determined. Similarly the left/right circular
asymmetry is written
$\quad (I^+-I^-)/(I^++I^-) = u_1(\rho_{11}-\rho_{-1-1})/(1+u_2(1-3\rho_{oo}))$
Thus all elements of the collisional density matrix ρ are measured;
we varied ϑ_{col} from $0°$ to $25°$ and E_{inc} from 3 to 20 eV for the
P-S transition; for P-D, E_{inc} was 6.5 eV.
The following observations will be commented:
- From the first Born approximation (FBA), $\arg(\rho_{-11}) = \measuredangle(\mathbb{k}_{in},\mathbb{k}_{in}-\mathbb{k}_{out})$
  which gives the correct tendency for the rotation of the aniso-
  tropy lobe eq. (1).

- The linear anisotropy $|\mathcal{S}_{-11}|$ is large for P-S, and low for P-D.
- In contrast, the orientation $\mathcal{S}_{11} - \mathcal{S}_{-1-1}$ is equally strong and positive in either case.
- For E_{inc} from 3 to 20 eV the dependence of the orientation on ϑ_{col} shifts from a decreasing to an increasing slope due to the increasing influence of higher partial waves.
- A coherent excitation of the M = +1 and M = -1 states gives $|\mathcal{S}_{-11}| / \sqrt{\mathcal{S}_{11} \cdot \mathcal{S}_{-1-1}} = 1$. In the P-S transition, only exchange scattering can destroy coherence, and in fact we find a strong indication of this (see figure). In contrast, in the P-D excitation, direct scattering, too, can lead to an incoherent population.

Degree of coherence
$$\frac{|\mathcal{S}_{11}|}{\sqrt{\mathcal{S}_{11} \cdot \mathcal{S}_{-1-1}}}$$
for the 2^2P-3^2S and the 3^2P-3^2D transitions in Na induced by electron impact. 4state close-coupling calculations[4] for the P-S underrate exchange scattering.

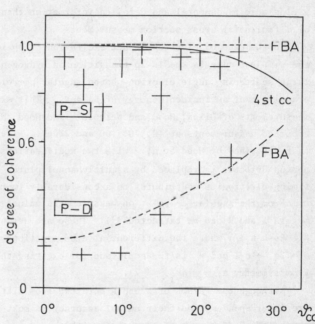

* Present address: FU Berlin, I f Molekülphysik, Boltzmannstr. 20
** Present address: Dept of Physics, Univ. of Texas, Austin,Tex,USA

1. see e.g. Kleinpoppen H, Comments Atom. Mol. Phys. **6** (1976) pp 35-47
2. Hertel I V & Stoll W in "Adv. Atom. Phys." vol **13** (1977)
3. Hermann H W, Hertel I V, and Kelley M H, submitted to J Phys B
4. Moores D L & Norcross D W, J Phys B **5** (1972) 1482

LARGE MOMENTUM TRANSFER ELECTRON-PHOTON CORRELATIONS

FOR THE 2p STATE OF ATOMIC HYDROGEN

E. Weigold, L. Frost and K.J. Nygaard*

Institute for Atomic Studies,
The Flinders University of South Australia,
Bedford Park, South Australia, 5042

It is well known that no exact solutions can be found for scattering problems involving more than two particles interacting via the electromagnetic interaction. A considerable number of approximation schemes have been developed, and these can best be tested by applying them to the simplest possible system.   Further, for the study of inelastic processes angular correlations of the reaction products yields more fundamental and detailed information than can be extracted from total or differential cross section measurements.

In the case of electron impact excitation of optically allowed transitions the simplest case is the 1s-2p transition in hydrogen.   We report here results of large scattering angle electron-photon angular correlation measurements for this transition at an incident energy of 54.4eV.   This extends the earlier small angle measurements of Dixon, Hood and Weigold[1], and Hood, Weigold and Dixon[2], who also reported measurements at 40, 70, 100 and 200eV.   The apparatus is the same as that described by Hood et al.[2] with two modifications.   The channeltron Ly-α photon detector is replaced by a multichannel plate.   This and improved fast timing electronics contributes to a considerably improved timing resolution.

From the angular correlation measurements values of the dimensionless parameters λ and R can be extracted[3,4].   These are defined by $\lambda = \sigma_0/\sigma$ and $R = Re\langle a_0 a_1 \rangle/\sigma$ where the differential cross sections $\sigma_0 = \langle a_0 a_0 \rangle$, $\sigma_1 = \langle a_1 a_1 \rangle$, $\sigma = 2\sigma_1 + \sigma_0$, and a_μ is the amplitude for exciting the $m = \mu$ magnetic substate. From symmetry $a_1 = -a_{-1}$.

Although the values of λ and R obtained from fitting each angular correlation are interdependent and their mutual accuracy is most properly reported as an error locus[2], for ease of comparison with theory we present them separately in figure 1.   The calculated values of λ and R in fig. 1 are obtained using the Born, distorted wave polarized orbital[5] (DWPO), distorted wave Born[6] (DWBA), unrestricted Glauber[7], classical path T-matrix[8], and hybrid close coupling[9] approximations.   The DWPO and UGA calculations are at 50eV.   Quite obviously no one theory adequately describes both λ and R over the entire range of angles. The predictions of the DWBA and hybrid close coupling calculations are in better agreement with the data than the other calculations.

* Permanent address: Department of Physics, University of Missouri, Rolla,
                 Missouri.

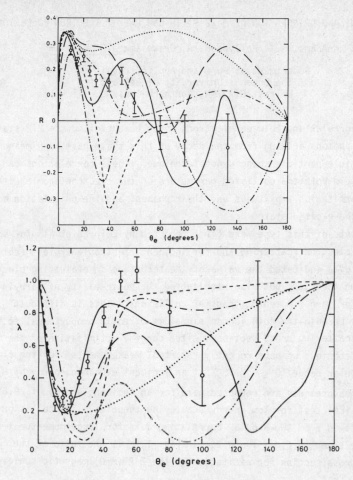

Fig. 1.   The parameters R and λ, measured at 54.4eV for the 1s-2p transition in
II as a function of the electron scattering angle θe, compared with
calculated values:- ⋯⋯ Born, —— —— DWPO[5], —— • —— DWBA[6],
- - - UGA[7], —— --- —— CPTM[8], —— hybrid CC[9].

1.   A.J. Dixon, S.T. Hood and E. Weigold, Phys. Rev. Lett. 40, 1262 (1978).

2.   S.T. Hood, E. Weigold and A.J. Dixon, J. Phys. B. 12, 631 (1979).

3.   U. Fano and J.H. Macek, Rev. Mod. Phys. 45, 553 (1973).

4.   L.A. Morgan and M.R.C. McDowell, Comm. Atom. Mol. Phys. 7, 123 (1978).

5.   L.A. Morgan and M.R.C. McDowell, J. Phys. B 8, 1073 (1975).

6.   R.V. Calhoun, D.H. Madison and W.N. Shelton, J. Phys. B. 10, 3523 (1977).

7.   J.N. Gau and J.H. Macek, Phys. Rev. A 12, 1760 (1975).

8.   M.J. Roberts, J. Phys. B. 9, 1293 (1976).

9.   J. Callaway, M.R.C. McDowell and L.A. Morgan, J. Phys. B. 9, 2043 (1976).

ALIGNMENT AND ORIENTATION OF He(2'P) IN LOW ENERGY ELECTRON COLLISIONS

R. McAdams, M.T. Hollywood, A. Crowe and J.F. Williams

Department of Pure and Applied Physics
The Queen's University of Belfast
Belfast BT7 1NN, Northern Ireland

Angular correlations between electrons which have excited the 2'P state of helium and photons arising from the decay of this state have been measured using the particle-particle coincidence technique. These correlations can be analysed to yield both the collision parameters of the electron atom excitation process i.e. excitation amplitudes and their phases, and the orientation and alignment of the excited state.

Measurements of this type were first reported by Eminyan et al[1] for small angle ($\leq 40^{\circ}$) electron scattering and for incident electron energies greater than 40 eV. These data indicated the value of the technique in evaluating electron atom excitation theories, but also highlighted the desirability of carrying out such studies for larger momentum transfer collisions. This is difficult experimentally because the coincidence signal is directly proportional to the differential scattering cross section. After careful optimisation of the experimental technique we have recently reported[2] measurements over the electron scattering angular range $10 \leq \theta \leq 130^{\circ}$ at an incident electron energy of 81.2 eV.

Similar measurements are reported here for an incident energy of 29.6 eV to provide a critical test for low energy scattering theories. The collision parameters derived from the angular correlation data for large momentum transfer collisions are shown in figs. 1 and 2. In Fig. 1, λ is the ratio of the differential cross section for excitation of the 2'P (M=0) magnetic sublevel to

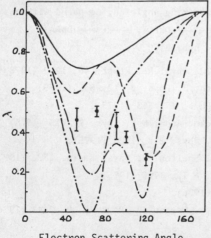

Electron Scattering Angle

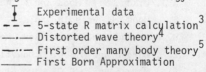

Fig. 1.

Variation of λ with electron scattering angle at 29.6 eV incident energy.

  Experimental data
- - - 5-state R matrix calculation[3]
—·— Distorted wave theory[4]
—··— First order many body theory[5]
——— First Born Approximation

the total 2'P differential cross section. The 5-state R matrix calculation of
Fon et al[3] and the distorted wave calculation of Scott[4] give reasonable
qualitative but poor quantitative agreement with the data. In Fig. 2, $|\chi|$ is
the relative phase between the scattering amplitudes for M=0 and M=±1 substates.
Agreement between the data and the only available theory[3] is good.

1. M. Eminyan, K.B. McAdam, J. Slevin and H. Kleinpoppen, Phys. Rev.
    Lett. 31, 576 (1973); J. Phys. B. 7, 1519 (1974).
2. M.T. Hollywood, A. Crowe and J.F. Williams, J. Phys. B12, 819 (1979).

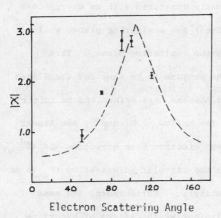

Fig. 2.

Variation of $|\chi|$ with electron
scattering angle at 29.6 eV incident
energy

    experimental data

— — 5-state R matrix calculation[3]

3. W.C. Fon, K.A. Berrington, A.E. Kingston and P.G. Burke (private
    communication).
4. T. Scott, PhD Thesis, University of London 1976 (unpublished).
5. L.D. Thomas, Gy. Csanak, H.A. Taylor and B.S. Yarlagadda, J. Phys. B 7,
    1719 (1974).

Vector Polarisation and Degree of Coherence from
Electron-Photon Coincidences of the 253.7 nm
Intercombination Line of Mercury

A Zaidi, I McGregor and H Kleinpoppen

Institute of Atomic Physics
University of Stirling, Stirling, Scotland

The electron-photon delayed coincidence rates have been measured for the

$6^1S_0 \rightarrow 6^3P_1 \rightarrow 6^1S_0$ transitions of mercury, by electron impact, in a crossed-

beam experiment. The electrons, inelastically scattered with an energy loss

of 4.9 eV, were detected in (and thus defined) the scattering plane, whilst

the photons were detected perpendicular to the scattering plane. This

allowed a full polarisation analysis of the photons to be made and the Stokes

parameters P_1, P_2 and P_3 of the coincident photons were determined as in the

experiment of Standage and Kleinpoppen[1] for helium. P_1 and P_2 are linear

polarisations with reference to the incident electron beam direction and 45°

to this direction, respectively, and P_3 is the circular polarisation (P_4 is an

intensity parameter and is normalised to unity). Furthermore, the same

technique as used by Zaidi et al.[2] for eliminating the effect of hyperfine

structure in the measured photon radiation has been applied. Accordingly, an

isotope cell, which absorbs the radiation from the odd mercury isotopes, was

placed between the photon detector and the interaction region.

As an example some preliminary data for these parameters at an excitation

energy of 5.5 eV and an electron scattering angle of 50° are given. The

vector polarisation, $\vec{|P|} = (P_1^2 + P_2^2 + P_3^2)^{1/2}$, and the degree of coherence,

$|\mu| = ((P_2^2 + P_3^2)/(1-P_1^2))^{1/2}$ are also given.

Hyperfine structure present: $P_1 = 0.31$, $\quad P_2 = {}^-0.21$, $\quad P_3 = {}^-0.14$
$\qquad\qquad\qquad\qquad\qquad\quad \pm 0.05 \qquad\qquad \pm 0.06 \qquad\qquad \pm 0.02$
$\qquad\qquad\qquad \vec{|P|} = 0.40 \pm 0.05, \quad |\mu| = 0.27 \pm 0.05$

Hyperfine structure eliminated: $P_1 = 0.57$, $P_2 = -0.33$, $\quad P_3 = -0.27$
$\qquad\qquad\qquad\qquad\qquad\qquad \pm 0.06 \qquad\qquad \pm 0.05 \qquad\qquad \pm 0.06$
$\qquad\qquad\qquad \vec{|P|} = 0.71 \pm 0.06, \quad |\mu| = 0.52 \pm 0.07$

It may be seen that this preliminary data indicates that the above process is

not completely coherent even when the hyperfine effects have been removed.

This contrasts with the measurement for the excitation of the helium 3^1P state and subsequent decay to the 2^1S state[1] which was found to be completely coherent.   This may be attributed to spin-orbit coupling on the excitation process and to the presence of a resonance at this excitation energy[2]. These effects will be further discussed.

References -

(1)   M C Standage and H Kleinpoppen, Phys. Rev. Letters <u>36</u>, 577, (1976)

(2)   A A Zaidi, I McGregor and H Kleinpoppen, J. Phys. B., <u>11</u>, L 151 (1978)

Differential Cross Section Measurements for Electron Impact Excitation
of He(3^3D) with Sub-meV Resolution using a Coincidence Technique

A Chutjian*, R Hippler†, I McGregor, H Kleinpoppen

Institute of Atomic Physics, University of Stirling, Scotland

A standard method for measuring the differential cross section for inelastic
electron scattering is to determine the scattered electron intensity for a
particular energy loss. For a given electron scattering angle Θ the intensity
$I(\Theta)$ is then directly related to the differential cross section $\sigma(\Theta)$ as

$$I(\Theta) = K_e \cdot V \cdot \sigma(\Theta) \tag{1}$$

where V relates to the scattering volume including atom density, electron
current etc., and K_e to the electron spectrometer acceptance angle, detection
efficiency etc. This method is limited to cases, where the spectrometer
resolution is sufficient to resolve electron scattering from individual states.
As an example, Fig. 1 gives a typical energy loss spectra of helium, obtained
with an energy resolution of 120 meV. Obviously, even with this relative low
resolution the individual n = 2 states can be resolved, however, it has not been
possible to separate all the individual n = 3 states. For instance, the energy
difference between the 3^1D and 3^3D states is as small as 0.4 meV.

A different approach to resolve the individual n = 3 states is to take
advantage of the higher optical resolution available. For instance, the 3^1D and
3^3D states decay within their lifetimes of a few nanoseconds to the 2^1P and 2^3P
states, respectively. The corresponding wavelengths of $\lambda(3^3$D$) = 587.6$ nm and
$\lambda(3^1$D$) = 667.8$ nm are well separated from each other and from other lines and
may easily be separated by use of interference filters. Observing the photons
perpendicular to the electron scattering plane in coincidence with the scattered
electrons, the coincidence count rate $\dot{N}_c$ is directly related to the differential
cross section $\sigma(\Theta)$

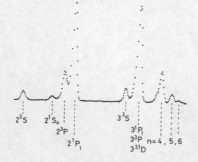

Fig. 1

Electron energy loss –
spectrum of helium

$$\overset{\circ}{N}_c(\Theta) = K_c \, . \, V \, . \, \sigma(\Theta) \qquad\qquad (2)$$

where K_c now contains the solid angles and the detection efficiencies of both the photon channel and the electron channel. To put the measured differential cross section on an absolute scale, it is necessary to determine K_c and V, which can be done, for instance, in a separate coincidence experiment on a resolved state whose differential and total cross sections are known. So far this method has been applied to measure differential cross sections for some singlet transitions in helium[1].

In Fig. 2 we give some preliminary results for the differential cross section of the 3^3D state excited by 39.7 eV electron impact, for electron scattering angles of 20° to 90°. The error bars represent only the statistical errors. So far, our data are normalised to the theoretical data of Chutjian and Thomas[2] at $\Theta_e = 45^O$. The shape of the experimental differential cross-section coincides with the theoretical differential cross-section, except at large angles, where the theory overestimates the experimental values.

It is intended to extend the measurements to other levels, for instance the 3^1D, and to other electron energies for which further calculations exist.[3]

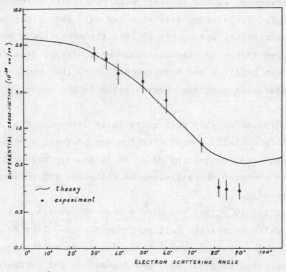

Fig. 2
Relative differential cross-section for electron excitation of He (3^3D) at 39.7 eV.

* Permanent address: Jet Propulsion Laboratory, Pasadena, California, U.S.A.

† Permanent address: Fakultät für Physik, Universität Bielefeld, W. Germany.

1. A Pochat, D Rozuel, J Peresse, J.Physique **34**, 701 (1973)

2. A Chutjian, L D Thomas, Phys. Rev. **A11**, 1583 (1975)

3. K H Winters, M Issa, B H Bransden, Can. J. Phys. **55**, 1074 (1977)

BENCHMARK CROSS SECTIONS FOR ELECTRON IMPACT EXCITATION OF n^1S LEVELS OF He

B. Van Zyl,[*] G. H. Dunn,[+] D. W. O. Heddle[‡] and G. E. Chamberlain[+]

Joint Institute for Laboratory Astrophysics
National Bureau of Standards and University of Colorado
Boulder, Colorado 80309 U.S.A.

Over the past half century there have been over 200 papers published dealing with experimental study of electron-impact excitation of the atoms, and most of these have been done during the 20 year history of the ICPEAC conference. Despite this, there are substantial differences between values obtained at different laboratories, and the assessment and discussion of uncertainties is so scant in the published material that it is difficult -- if not impossible -- to attach a meaningful uncertainty to any given measurement.

Since helium is such a convenient gas to use in most systems, it is nearly ideal for use as a standard or "benchmark" for excitation cross section measurements. With this in mind, we have measured the emission cross sections for electron impact excitation of ground state He to give the emissions 3^1S-2^1P at 728.1 nm, 4^1S-2^1P at 504.7 nm, 5^1S-2^1P at 443.8 nm, and 6^1S-2^1P at 416.9 nm at a limited number of energies between 50 eV and 2000 eV, with particular attention to the cross sections at 500 eV. Painstaking attention and care were given to determination of the basic experimental parameters so that the measurement puts one in direct touch with the procedures of absolute radiometry, target density determination, and electron beam handling and measurement. More than usual attention has been devoted to assessing possible uncertainties in the measured parameters.

The specific goals and purposes of this work quite fully determine the general configuration -- a differentially pumped electron gun produces a beam which passes through a collision cell containing He at an accurately measurable density, and light produced in electron-He collisions is collected and measured in a calibrated spectroradiometer.

The electron gun at about 6×10^{-6} Torr produced a beam of between 2 μA (at 50 eV) and 180 μA (at 2 keV) which enters the cell at about 8×10^{-4} Torr He pressure, and is collected in a deep Faraday cup. Light from e-He excitation is collected by a lens system apertured to about F/9, and focused on the entrance slit of an F/5.6 Czerny-Turner grating monochromator, after which it passes through an interference filter and onto the photocathode of a cooled photomultiplier. Multiplie pulses are counted by one of two scalers gated synchronously

---

[*]Presidential Intern at JILA, 1972-73. Permanent address: Physics Department, University of Denver, Denver, Colorado.
[+]Staff Member, Quantum Physics Division, National Bureau of Standards.
[‡]Visiting Fellow, JILA, 1968. Permanent address: Physics Department, Royal Holloway College, Egham, Surrey, England.

with a chopper wheel that periodically interrupts the light entering the monochromator. For calibration purposes, the monochromator can alternatively be
rotated such that the entrance slit is imaged into the cavity of a copper melting
point black body or onto the filament of a calibrated tungsten strip lamp.

Features of the measurements included: 1) radiometric calibration against
two separate standards of different types; 2) detailed mapping of the spatial
distribution of the electron beam and of the spatial dependence of sensitivity of
the spectroradiometer; 3) measurement of the electron beam both at the entrance
to and exit of the collision cell; 4) analysis and correction of the data to account for the finite lifetimes of the emitting states; 5) use of a doubly dispersive (spectrometer plus interference filters) spectroradiometer to eliminate the
effect of light far from line center contributing to the calibration when observing the continuum standard light sources; 6) detailed mapping of the instrument function of the spectroradiometer and numerical integration of this with the
radiances of the standards; 7) use of a specially devised and carefully evaluated
dynamic expansion technique for generating known helium densities; 8) measurement
of collision cell temperature at a number of locations and verification of the
modeled dependence of observed count rate as a function of temperature; 9) careful measurement and calibration of relevant slit heights, window transmissions,
and current meters; and 10) cross sections were measured as functions of electron
current and helium density.

Total uncertainties were assessed at "high confidence level" by combining
statistical and estimated systematic uncertainties in quadrature. Before combining, statistical uncertainties were computed at 98% confidence level (about
2.4 times standard deviation), and an attempt was made to estimate systematic
uncertainties at the same level. For the 504.7 nm line at 500 eV, the total HCL
uncertainty in the result is 3%. The worst total uncertainty is for the 728.1 nm
line at 100 eV, where the uncertainty is 11%.

The emission cross section for the 504.7 line at 500 eV is $2.05 \pm 0.06 \times 10^{-20}$
cm^2. Values will be given for all lines at 50 eV, 100 eV, 500 eV, 1000 eV, and
2000 eV. The measured emission cross sections have been "corrected" for branching and cascade to give excitation cross sections. These are compared with Born
and other calculations as well as with other measurements. For all four lines
the results are about 15% below Born results[1] at 500 eV, 5% below at 1000 eV,
and, on the average, 2.5% below at 2000 eV.

The measurements agreeing most closely with our values are those of Moussa
et al.,[2] where for 20 measurements the average difference is only 6%, and the
greatest difference is 18%.

1. Y. Kim and M. Inokuti, Phys. Rev. 175, 176 (1968); K. L. Bell, D. J. Kennedy
    and A. E. Kingston, J. Phys. B 2, 26 (1969).

2. H. R. Moustafa Moussa, F. J. Detteev and J. Schutten, Physica 40, 517 (1969).

DETERMINATION OF THE EFFECTIVE CROSS SECTION FOR DIRECT AND STEPWISE EXCITATION OF HELIUM

L.M.Volkova, A.M.Devyatov, E.A.Kralkina, A.S.Mechenov

Moscow State Univercity, USSR

The effective excitation cross sections (EECS) can be obtained both from the experiments with electron beams and discharge plasma. The production of the monokinetic electron beams is well known to be a complex experimental problem. If the beam electron energy distribution (EED) is far from monokinetic the intensities of spectral lines fit the equation

$$I(V_0) = c \, i \int_{eV_0}^{\infty} f(V_0, \varepsilon) \, q(\varepsilon) \, d\varepsilon \qquad (1)$$

Here V_0 is the potential of the electrode which gives the electron energy, i is the beam current, $f(V_0, \varepsilon)$ is EED, q is const which depends on the condition of the experiment. Solving equation (1) with the help of Tichonov's regularisation method[1] one can obtain $q(\varepsilon)$. To study the efficiency of the described method some model problems were solved[2]. The method was used for the investigation of He EECS fine structure. The conventional electron gun was used for the determination of $I(V_0)$. The measurements were carried out at He pressure 10^{-3} Torr. The beam currents did not exceed 50 μA. The distribution width in our experiment exceeded 3.5 eV. The results of 5876 A ($2^3P - 3^3D$) restoration are plotted at Fig.1.which shows that in contrast to the smooth shape of $I(V_0)$ the calculated EECS possesses sharp maximum at 23,5 eV. There is a reasonable agreement between our and experimentally measured EECS in[3]. The width of EED in [3] didn't exceed 0.02 eV. The described method can be also useful for the determination of EECS shape from the plasma glow measured under different conditions of experiment [4]. Fig.2 shows the 7065 A ($2^3P - 3^3S$) optical excitation function calculated from the values of the line intensity and EED measured in He hot-cathode arc discharge at pressures 0.025-0.3 Torr and discharge currents 6-100mA.

The calculated curve satisfactory agrees with the results of [5].
If the atom energy levels are populated both by direct and stepwise
excitation the intensities of spectral lines emitted by plasma fit
the equation

$$I_{\kappa i} = c \sum_{\ell < \kappa} \left\{ n_{\varepsilon} n \int_{V_{\kappa \ell}}^{\infty} q_{V \ell \kappa}(\varepsilon) f(\varepsilon) d\varepsilon \right\} q_{V \ell \kappa}^{max} \qquad (2)$$

If the shape of $q_{\ell \kappa}(\varepsilon)$ and $f(\varepsilon)$ are known equation (2) can be considered as a simple linear equation respectively the unknown peak va-
lues $q_{\ell \kappa}^{max}$. The necessary number of equations can be obtained by changing the conditions of the experiment. In our experiment $f(\varepsilon)$ were
obtained with the help of probe method. The shape of $q_{\ell \kappa}(\varepsilon)$ was
calculated using the results of [6]. $q_{\ell \kappa}^{max}$ for the transition
$2^{1}S-3^{1}S$ was found to be 13.2 $10^{-16} sm^2$.

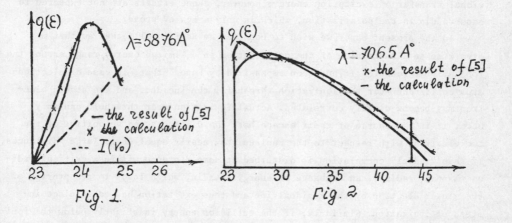

Fig. 1.

Fig. 2

References

1. А.Н.Тихонов, ДАН СССР, 151, 3, 1963.
2. К.В.Вавилин и др. в сб. :"Обработка и интерпретация физи-
   ческих экспериментов", ИЗД. МГУ, вып. 7, стр. 105, 1978.
3. D.W.O. Heddle et al. Proc. R. Soc. Lond. A337, 443, 1974.
4. А.М.Губанов и др. Кинетика и катализ, 13, вып. 1, 33, 1972.
5. И.П.Запесочный и др. Укр. физ. ж. 10, 1197, 1965.
6. M. Grizinski, Phys. Rev., A138, 305, 1965.

THE EFFECT OF ELECTRON CORRELATIONS ON THE POLARIZATION OF
ATOMIC LINE RADIATION EXCITED BY ELECTRON IMPACT

H.G.M. Heideman, W. van de Water, J. van Eck and L.J.M. van Moergestel

Fysisch Laboratorium van de Rijksuniversiteit, Utrecht, the Netherlands

The polarization of atomic spectral lines, excited by electrons, shows in some cases an anomalous behaviour near threshold. In the case of helium [1], for instance, the polarization of all spectral lines studied exhibits a large dip, which extends from threshold to about 5 eV above. In other instances, such as in the excitation of alkali resonance lines [2], this anomaly appears to be absent. There have been several attempts to explain the observed anomaly, none of which is able to satisfactorily deal with the whole effect. There is of course no doubt that negative-ion resonances will contribute to the depression of the polarization just above threshold, but they cannot account for that part of the dip which extends beyond the ionization energy, because in the case of helium no (discrete) negative-ion states are expected there. Other processes which tend to reduce the observed polarization are indirect excitation via cascade from higher levels or via collisional transfer of excitation energy; however, these effects are not expected to cause a dip in the polarization, which is only a few eV broad.

In the present paper we wish to consider an additional mechanism that may give rise to a depression of the polarization in a limited energy range around the ionization threshold. It has been amphasized by Fano [3] that, in case of electron-atom collisions near the ionization threshold, the incident and the atomic electron may become closely correlated. Actual ionization near threshold can only occur if in the course of their escape both the distances and velocities of the two electrons with respect to the nucleus stay nearly equal up to large distances. If this "radial" correlation is disturbed at some distance within a critical radius (Wannier radius), an exchange of energy sets in, which leads to recapturing of the slower electron by the residual ion and thus excitation has taken place instead of ionization. Similarly, if the collision energy is slightly below the ionization threshold, the excitation of states with excitation energies near the available energy is only possible if the motion of the two electrons remains correlated in the same way as required for near-threshold ionization. As argued by Fano [3] the Coulomb repulsion between the two electrons causes a (stable) angular correlation, as a result of which the two electrons may acquire significant orbital angular momenta (with opposite sign), even if their velocities are very small. Consequently the excitation of magnetic substates with $m \geq 1$ may become quite likely, resulting in a decrease in the polarization of the emitted radiation. Further one would expect the effect to become increasingly prominent for the excitation of states lying closer to the ionization threshold. Namely, for these states to be excited via the "correlation" mechanism it is necessary that the correlation persists up to larger distances, so that the angular momentum exchange can be more effective.

We have performed model calculations on the excitation of the n^1D states of helium which show that the above described mechanism may indeed cause a considerable drop in the polarization. In these calculations the relative population of the different magnetic substates is calculated under the assumption that the orbital angular momenta of the excited and scattered electron are equal in magnitude. According to the physical picture sketched this latter assumption, which considerably reduces the number of contributing partial waves, should become increasingly better for the excitation of states with smaller binding energies.

We have also performed experiments to test the proposed model. Fig. 1 shows our measured polarization curves for the $n^1D \rightarrow 2^1P$ (n = 4, 5, 6) transitions in helium. At the very threshold the polarization can be calculated exactly and should be 60% for all three transitions. Although the statistical spreading is large near the thresholds, the conclusion seems justified that the drop in the polarization increases with increase of the principal quantum number of the excited state concerned. This is in agreement with our expectation that the correlation effect should be more prominent for the excitation of states with smaller binding energies (larger radii). In this respect it is also understandable why the anomalous dip is not observed in the polarization curves of the alkali resonance lines [2]. The excitation of the alkali resonance levels does not involve a change in principal quantum number and therefore their radii are relatively small (comparable to those of the respective ground states). Their binding energies are 3 to 4 eV, whereas the binding energies of the helium levels, for which the polarization dip is observed are smaller than 1.5 eV. In the polarization of the $3^2D \rightarrow 2^2P$ transition in Li the dip is present again [2], as expected.

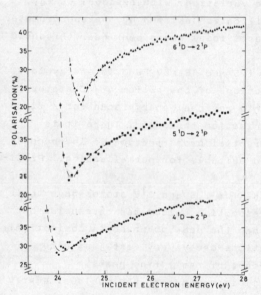

Fig. 1. Measured polarization curves of $n^1D \rightarrow 2^1P$ transitions in He. The dashed lines merely serve as guides to the eye.

1. R.H. McFarland and M.H. Mittleman, Phys. Rev. Lett. 20, 899 (1968)
2. H. Hafner and H. Kleinpoppen, Z. Phys. 198, 315 (1967)
3. U. Fano, J. Phys. B: Atom. Molec. Phys. 7, L401 (1974)

ANISOTROPIC THRESHOLD EXCITATION OF S STATES OF HELIUM
BY ELECTRON IMPACT

Gérard Joyez

Groupe de Spectroscopie Electronique et Ionique
L.P.O.C., Tour 12, E.5, 4,Place Jussieu
Université Pierre et Marie Curie
75230 Paris-Cédex 05 - France.

Using a microprocessor for monitoring a conventionnal electron-impact spectrometer, electron yields for excitation of various states and ionisation have been simultaneously measured with great accuracy for both incident and residual energies. The ratios between those various processes are almost free from the apparatus response which is critically energy dependant particularly at threshold. This effect is most likely due to the variation, with residual energy, of the electron beam image magnification skimmed by the spectrometer entrance slit, and produces an artificial sharp peak near threshold of any studied process.

With very good resolutions (25 and 18 meV FWHM in energy loss mode), the four excitations functions of the helium n = 2 states have been measured together with a residual energy scan for a fixed incident energy 0.8 eV above ionisation threshold. There it is known that the ionisation differential cross-section is independant of residual energy and angle and suitable for normalisation.[1] Preliminary results are as follows.

i) Apparatus generated peaks for 2^3S and 2^1S states have their maximum some 10 meV above the respective calibrated thresholds but about 10 meV nearer threshold than the peak observed in ionisation. This shows that their cross-sections decay very fast just after threshold, supporting the existence of real, fine peaks.

ii) The $2^1S/2^3S$ ratio (fig.1) is maximum at the residual energy of the peak and is strongly anisotropic. This ratio has a maximum at about 50-60 degrees and the value is drastically resolution dependant. This demontrates that at least one of these states does not have an isotropic angular distribution at threshold.

iii) The excitation to ionisation intensity ratios have a maximum for 0 residual energy and are also strongly anisotropic (fig.2 and 3)

These results are in contradiction with the generally accepted threshold behaviour as deduced from the Wigner laws[2]. This contradiction was already suspected indirectly from a study of the 2^1S cusp[3]. These phenomena suggest that long range electron correlations play an important role near threshold and should be investigated.

1. F. Pichou, A. Huetz, G. Joyez, M. Landau and J. Mazeau,
    J. Phys. B : Atom Mol Phys, 9, 933, (1976).

2. E.P. Wigner, Phys. Rev. 73, 1002, (1948)

3. A. Huetz, F. Gresteau, G. Joyez, J. Mazeau and F. Pichou,
    J. Phys.B : Atom. Molec. Phys., 9, 3023, (1976)

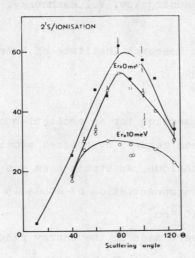

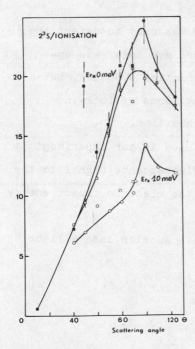

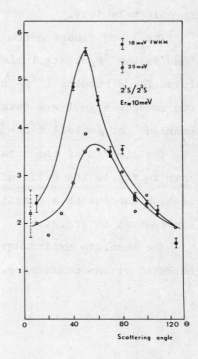

EXCITATION OF $^3P_1$ STATE OF CALCIUM BY ELECTRON
IMPACT.

V.E.Dobryshin. V.M.Shustrjakov. V.I.Rachovsky.

All-Union Scientific Research Institute of Metrological
Service, Moscow, USSR.

The relative cross section for an excitation of the $^3P_1$
state of calcium have been mesured by crossed atomic and modulated electron beams technique. An atomic beam was prodused
by effusion cell, with a concentration of atoms in the
collision region being $10^{11} cm^{-3}$.

These mesurements were made in the energy range from
5e.v to 20e.v. The energy spread of the electron beam was
approximately 1e.v.

The laser fluorescence method was used to detect the
atoms in the $^3P_1$ state.A single mode dye laser was employed for a pumping ($^3P_1 - ^3S_1$) transition $\lambda = 6122A$, but a
fluorescence signal was detected by means of lock-in
technique at $\lambda = 6162A$ ($^3S_1 - ^3P_2$) transition.

The diagram of the apparatus used in our experiment is
shown in fig.1. The ratio of the fluorescence signal to the
electron current as a function of the electron impact energy
is presented in fig.2.

The absolute excitation   cross section data will be
presented at the conference.

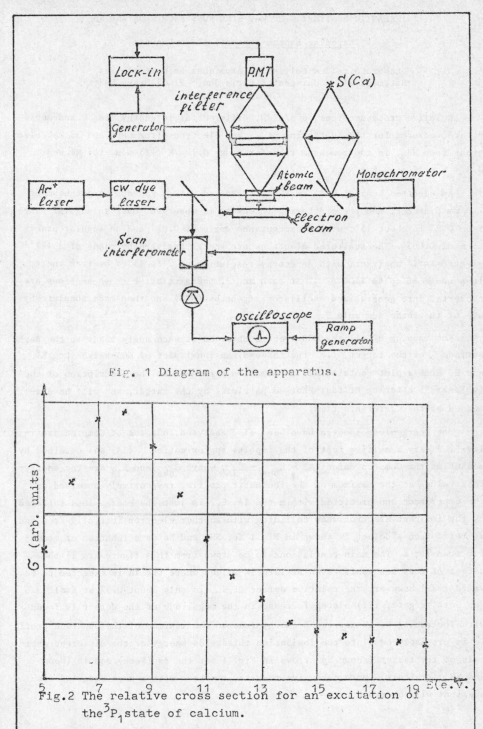

Fig. 1 Diagram of the apparatus.

Fig.2 The relative cross section for an excitation of
the $^3P_1$ state of calcium.

INELASTIC SCATTERING OF keV ELECTRONS FROM NEON AND NH_3

Azzedine Lahmam-Bennani, Alain Duguet

Laboratoire des Collisions Atomiques et Moléculaires
Bâtiment 210 - Université Paris-Sud - 91405 Orsay Cedex

Relative cross sections, $d^2\sigma/dEd\Omega$, differential in energy loss E and angle θ, are measured for the scattering of 25 keV electrons from neon and 35 keV electrons from NH_3, in the momentum transfer range $0.1 < K < 15$ a.u. for Ne and $0.3 < K < 12$ a.u. for NH_3.

An electron beam of 0.25 mm FWHM is crossed with a gaseous target beam of 1.0 mm diameter, and the scattering intensity is observed, over an angular range from 0.2° to about 15°, with an acceptance angle of 0.01° and an angular precision of 0.003°. The scattered electrons are energy analysed by means of a 127° electrostatic analyser, with an energy resolution of 2 to 15 eV over an energy loss range of up to 7500 eV [1]. At each angle, these relative cross sections are converted into generalized oscillator strengths (GOS) and then made absolute by use of the Bethe sum rule [2].

The mapping of all the GOS spectra obtained at each angle leads to the Bethe surface [2] of the target, i.e. the three-dimensional plot of GOS versus Log K^2 and E. Such a plot contains all information pertinent to the description of the inelastic scattering of fast charged particles by the target, and will be discussed at the Conference time.

The energy-loss spectra have been also analysed in terms of Compton profiles [3]. A very sensitive test of the impulse approximation [3] (IA) was obtained by measuring the Compton defect $\Delta E = E_{obs} - E_{IA}$, where E_{obs} and E_{IA} are the energy-loss values at the maximum of the inelastic profile, respectively observed in the experiment and predicted within the IA. E_{IA} is just the energy loss suffered by the incident electron when colliding with another electron initially free and at rest. Such a defect is shown in Fig.1 for NH_3 and Ne as a function of momentum transfer K. The main conclusions to be drawn from this figure are i) the defect ΔE does not vanish even at large K values where the IA is expected to be valid ; ii) however, the relative defect $\Delta E/E_{IA}$ is only about 0.3% at $K \approx 12$ a.u. for both targets, iii) a step increase in the magnitude of the defect is found with increasing K, whenever the energy-loss at the maximum of the observed profile is precisely equal to the ionisation thresholds energy of the different orbitals of the target (shown by arrows in Fig. 1 for the 2s (Neon) and 1s (Neon and NH_3) orbitals). More extensive results, together with a more detailed discussion, will be reported.

1. For a more detailed description of the apparatus and technique see :
   A. Lahmam Bennani, Thèse de Dostorat d'Etat, Université Paris Sud,
   Orsay 1978.

2. M. Inokuti, Rev. Mod. Phys., 43, 297, 1971.

3. R.A. Bonham, C. Tavard, J. Chem. Phys., 59, 4691, 1973.

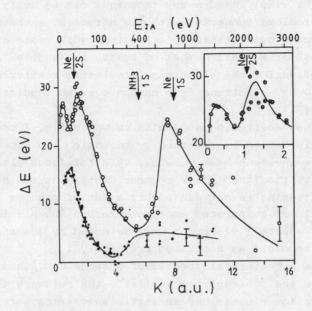

Fig. 1 : Compton defect ΔE versus momentum transfer K, for Ne(o)
and NH_3 (•) . The inset shows an enlarged plot of the
Ne small K values range.

MEASUREMENT OF ELECTRON EXCHANGE CONTRIBUTIONS TO THE LARGE ANGLE
SCATTERING CROSS SECTIONS OF 30 keV-ELECTRONS

H. Schmoranzer, H. Grabe and J. Imschweiler

Fachbereich Physik, Universität Kaiserslautern
D 6750 Kaiserslautern, Germany

In electron Compton scattering considerable advantages of the
method over the widely used x-ray technique can be fully realized
only if the problems connected with the effect of exchange scattering are overcome quantitatively[1]. Previous work restricted to
lower energies[2] or a small number of scattering angles[1,3] has been
extended by measuring the elastic and inelastic scattering cross
sections of 30 keV-electrons from carbon over an angular range
from 18° to 54°.

In the new scattering apparatus shown in Fig. 1 the scatte-
ring angle θ is varied by rotating by an angle γ the upper chamber
containing the incident beam produced by a telefocus electron gun[4]
with respect to the fixed lower chamber containing the scattered
beam. The scattering target was either a jet of gaseous butane
C_4H_{10} or a film of evaporated amorphous carbon 800 Å thick. Single
scattered (or ejected) electrons were detected by means of a silicon
detector and recorded as described previously[5].

From the experimental spectra of gaseous C_4H_{10} and solid C,
which resemble the one reported earlier[6], the relative differential
cross sections for elastic and inelastic scattering were determined.
The characterizing ratio of the differential inelastic over the differential elastic cross section is plotted as a function of scattering angle θ in Fig. 2. As an approximative theoretical ratio, assuming free target electrons, the expression

$$d\sigma_{inelast}/d\sigma_{elast} = (N/z^2)\,(\cos\theta/\cos^4\theta/2)\,(1-\tan^2\theta + \tan^4\theta) \quad (1)$$

discussed elsewhere[1] has been used for comparison and for normalizing the experimental ratios obtained for butane to those for carbon. The independent atom model applied to butane yields for the
number of electrons N = 34 and for the nuclear charge squared
z^2 = 154. Whereas the experimental carbon ratios are displayed directly together with the theoretical curve assuming N = 6 and
z^2 = 36, the experimental butane ratios have been multiplied by a
factor of $(N/z^2)_C/(N/z^2)_{C_4H_{10}}$ = 0.755 in order to be comparable
with the theoretical curve drawn for carbon.

The agreement between the measurements and the theoretical expression is rather good as far as the angular dependence is concerned. The tendency of the remaining discrepancy, similar for C
and C_4H_{10}, points towards a lower effective number of electrons.

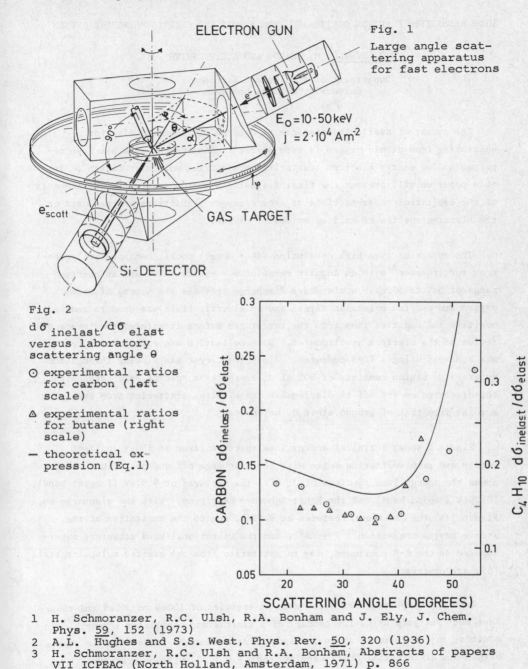

Fig. 1
Large angle scattering apparatus for fast electrons

ELECTRON GUN

$E_0 = 10\text{-}50\,keV$
$j = 2 \cdot 10^4\ Am^{-2}$

e^-_{scatt}

GAS TARGET

Si-DETECTOR

90°

Fig. 2

$d\sigma_{inelast}/d\sigma_{elast}$ versus laboratory scattering angle θ

⊙ experimental ratios for carbon (left scale)

△ experimental ratios for butane (right scale)

— theoretical expression (Eq.1)

SCATTERING ANGLE (DEGREES)

CARBON $d\sigma_{inelast}/d\sigma_{elast}$

C_4H_{10} $d\sigma_{inelast}/d\sigma_{elast}$

1 H. Schmoranzer, R.C. Ulsh, R.A. Bonham and J. Ely, J. Chem. Phys. 59, 152 (1973)
2 A.L. Hughes and S.S. West, Phys. Rev. 50, 320 (1936)
3 H. Schmoranzer, R.C. Ulsh and R.A. Bonham, Abstracts of papers VII ICPEAC (North Holland, Amsterdam, 1971) p. 866
4 B. Schiewe, H. Schmoranzer and P. Wollenweber, Rev. Sci. Instrum. 48, 893 (1977)
5 H. Schmoranzer, H. Grabe and B. Schiewe, Appl. Phys. Letters 26, 483 (1975)
6 H. Schmoranzer and H. Grabe, Abstracts of papers X ICPEAC (Commissariat a l'Energie Atomique, Paris, 1977), p. 444

HIGH RESOLUTION ELECTRON SCATTERING FROM ATOMIC AND EXCITED MOLECULAR OXYGEN

W.R. NEWELL, M. KHAKOO AND A.C.H. SMITH

Department of Physics and Astronomy,
University College London.

The amount of available experimental data on differential electron scattering from atomic oxygen is very sparse[1]. Some recent work has been reported on low energy electron scattering from excited molecular oxygen[2]. In this paper we will present the first inelastic electron scattering measurements of the excitation cross-sections of atomic oxygen transitions and new data on the electron spectra of excited molecular oxygen.

The apparatus is a high resolution ($\Delta E = 80meV$) double hemispherical electron spectrometer[3] with an angular range of $\theta = -5^{\circ}$ to $+ 30^{\circ}$ and an energy range of 5eV to 500eV. A microwave discharge provides the source of atomic oxygen and excited molecular oxygen and an electric field was used to remove all positive and negative ions from the target gas before it entered the interaction region of the electron spectrometer. Data collection and experimental control was achieved using a PDP8 computer. Since the target gas flowing through the interaction region consists of 90% of O_2 energy loss spectra were taken with the discharge on and off to distinguish the electron scattering from excited species from that of ground state O_2 molecules.

Figure 1 shows a typical energy loss spectrum taken at 150eV incident energy and zero scattering angle with the discharge off and on. Figure 1(a) shows the energy loss spectrum of O_2 with the features at 9.97eV (longest band), 10.29eV (second band) and the Runge-Schumman continuum. With the discharge on, Figure 1(b), the additional features at 9.51eV, due to the excitation of the atomic oxygen transition ($^3P \rightarrow {}^3S^0$), and the vibrational band structure superimposed on the R-S continuum, due to excitation from the excited molecular state $^1\Delta_g$, are observed.

Zero angle spectra have been taken at energies of 100eV to 500eV and these have been analysed using the concept of a generalized oscillator strength. In addition to the features shown in Figure 1 data on other transitions in atomic oxygen and differential cross-sections for $\theta = 0$ t 30° will be presented.

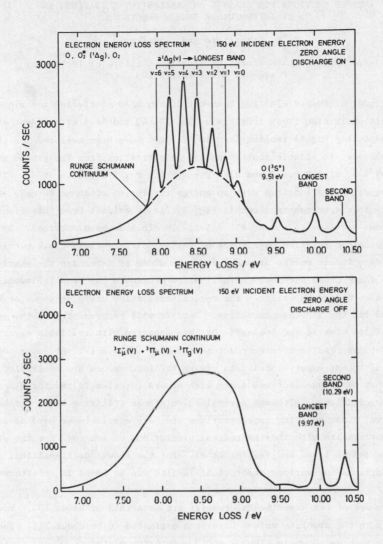

1. Dehmel R.C., Fineman M.A., and Miller D.R., 1976 Phys. Rev. A.13 115-121

2. Hall R.J., and Trajmar S., 1975 J. Phys. B: Atom. Molec. Phys. 8 293-6

3. Shuttleworth T., Newell W.R. and Smith A.C.H., 1977 J. Phys. B: Atom. Molec. Phys. 10 3307-21.

CROSS SECTIONS FOR ELASTIC AND INELASTIC EXCITATIONS IN
Na BY INTERMEDIATE ENERGY ELECTRONS[*]

S. K. Srivastava and L. Vušković[+]

Jet Propulsion Laboratory, California Institute of Technology
Pasadena, California 91103

Utilizing a crossed electron beam-metal atom beam scattering technique electron impact excitation cross sections at 10, 20, 40 and 54.4 eV incident energies and at scattering angles ranging from $10°$ to $120°$ have been measured for the following processes: 1) elastic scattering and 2) excitation from the ground state to a) 3^2P, b) 4^2S, c) $3^2D + 4^2P$ and d) $4^2D + 4^2F + 5^2P + 5^2S$ states of Na. The scattering data were acquired with an energy resolution of about 80 meV. A typical energy loss spectrum is shown in Fig. 1. As is evident from this figure excitation cross sections to almost all valence levels have been obtained. By the present technique relative magnitudes of various differentials cross sections (DCS) at each impact energy are measured. In order to determine the absolute values of these cross sections a normalization procedure has been followed. This normalization procedure utilizes the optical-excitation cross sections of Chen and Gallagher[1] for the 3^2P resonance line. Details will be presented at the meeting. The normalized elastic and inelastic DCS are compared with available experimental and theoretical results at electron impact energy of 54.4 eV. At lower impact energies no recent experimental data giving absolute values are available. Figures 3 and 4 show our cross sections along with others for elastic and for $3^2S_{\frac{1}{2}} \rightarrow$ $3^2P_{\frac{1}{2},3/2}$ excitations. Although several calculations utilizing Born, Glauber, distorted wave, close coupling approximations etc. are available we have chosen to compare our results with the theoretical predictions of Kennedy[2] for the elastic scattering and of Issa[3] and Teubner et al.[4] for the resonance transition. The intercomparisons for various theoretical results can be found in references 2 and 3.

The shape of our experimental results are uncertain by about 10%. However the errors in the absolute values have been estimated to be about 22%. The various DCS curves such as shown in Figs. 2 and 3 were extrapolated to $0°$ and to $180°$ using appropriate theoretical results. They were then utilized to calculate integral and momentum transfer cross sections for the elastic and inelastic transitions. The results will be presented in a tabular form.

[*]Research supported in part by NASA Contract No. NAS7-100 and partially by the California Institute of Technology through the Caltech President's Fund.

[+]Permanent address: Institute of Physics, P. O. Box 57, Belgrade, Yugoslavia.

1. S. T. Chen and A. C. Gallagher, Phys. Rev. A17, 551 (1978).

2. J. V. Kennedy, Valerie P. Myerscough and M. R. C. McDowell, J. Phys. B: Atom. Molec. Phys. 10, 3759 (1977).

3. M. R. Issa, Thesis Durham (1977).

4. P. J. O. Teubner, S. J. Buckman and C. J. Noble, J. Phys. B: Atom. Molec. Phys. 11, 2345 (1978).

5. T. Shuttleworth, W. R. Newell, and A. C. H. Smith, J. Phys. B: Atom. Molec. Phys. 10, 1641 (1977).

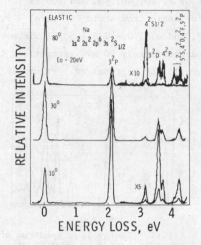

Fig. 1. Energy loss spectra of Na at 20 eV electron impact energy and scattering angles of 10, 30 and 80°.

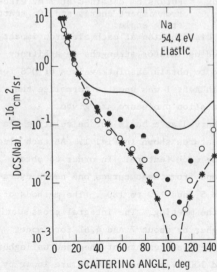

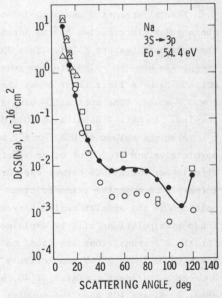

Fig. 2. DCS for elastic scattering of 54.4 eV electrons by Na. Teubner[4] (experiment) and --*-- Teubner[4] (optical model potential), — Issa[3], ● Present.

Fig. 3. DCS for the electron impact excitation of 3s→3p state in Na. The incident electron energy if 54.4 eV. ○ Buckman and Teubner[4], □ Kennedy[2], ▲ -Shuttleworth et al.[5], ● Present joined by a best visual fit solid line.

SCATTERING OF INTERMEDIATE ENERGY ELECTRONS BY POTASSIUM[*]

L. Vušković[+] and S. K. Srivastava

Jet Propulsion Laboratory, California Institute of Technology
Pasadena, California 91103

A crossed electron beam–atom beam collision technique has been used to study the electron scattering by Potassium atoms. Differential cross sections (DCS) have been measured at electron impact energies of 7, 20, 40, 60, and 100 eV for the following transitions: 1) elastic and 2) inelastic from state $^2S_{\frac{1}{2}}$ to a) 4^2P, b) $5^2S + 3^2D$, c) 5^2D, d) $4^2D + 6^2D + 4^2F + 6^2P$, and e) $5^2D + 7^2S + 5^2F$. Since the energy resolution of the spectrometer was approximately 80 mV, transitions to individual states indicated in b), d), and e) could not be resolved. Figure 1 represents a typical spectrum showing various features. Similar spectra were obtained at other scattering angles ranging from 5° to 120°. From each spectrum ratio of the intensity of a spectral feature to the intensity of the resonance transition ($^2S \rightarrow 4^2P$) was obtained. Uncertainty in these ratios has been estimated to be of the order of 10%.

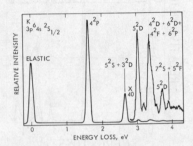

Fig. 1. Energy loss spectrum of Potassium obtained at 7 eV electron impact energy and 10° scattering angle.

Special attention was paid in obtaining the angular distribution of the intensity of the resonance feature (4^2P). This angular distribution at each electron impact energy was used to calculate the generalized oscillator strengths in arbitrary units. Bethe's limit theorem was then used to obtain absolute values of DCS for the 4^2P state. The optical f-value given in Ref. 1 was used to normalize the results. In Ref. 2 details of this normalization procedure are given.

Absolute values of DCS for 4^2P state served as a basis for calculating the absolute values of DCS of other spectral features shown in Fig. 1. At each electron impact energy DCS curves were drawn for each feature. In order to obtain integral and momentum transfer cross sections from these curves one needs extrapolation in the angular region between 0 to 5° and 120 to 180°. The methods of these extrapolations will be explained at the meeting. The integral cross sections for the 4^2P transitions are found to be higher by about 7 and 4.6% for impact energies of 7 and 20 eV respectively than the measurements of Chen and Gallagher[3]. However at incident energies of 40, 60, and 100 eV present results are lower by about 6, 8, and 10% than the results of Ref. 3.

[*]Research supported in part by NASA Contract No. NAS7-100 and partially by the California Institute of Technology through the Caltech President's Fund.

[+]Permanent address: Institute of Physics, P. O. Box 57, Belgrade, Yugoslavia.

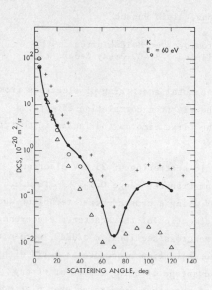

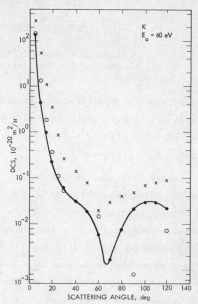

Fig. 2. Elastic DCS for 60 eV electron impact energy. × Williams and Trajmar[5], o Walters[4], △ Teubner (optical model)[6], ● present joined by a visual fit solid line.

Fig. 3. DCS for the resononce transitions ($^2S \rightarrow 4^2P$) obtained at 60 eV electron impact energy. + Williams and Trajmar[5], Kennedy et al.[7], ● present joined by a visual fit solid line.

Figures 2 and 3 show the DCS for elastic and 4^2P respectively for the electron impact energy of 60 eV. Other theoretical and experimental results are also shown in these figures for the sake of comparison. In general, the agreement with theoretical results has been found to be good at low scattering angles. Other results will be presented in the meeting.

1. A. Dalgarno and W. D. Davison, Mol. Phys. **13**, 479 (1967).

2. S. Trajmar, W. Williams, and S. K. Srivastava, J. Phys. B: Atom. Molec. Phys. **10**, 3323 (1977).

3. S. T. Chen and A. C. Gallagher, Phys. Rev. **17**, 551 (1978).

4. H. R. J. Walters, J. Phys. B: Atom. Molec. Phys. **6**, 1003 (1973).

5. W. Williams and S. Trajmar, J. Phys. B: Atom. Molec. Phys. **10**, 1955 (1977).

6. P. J. O. Teubner, private communication.

7. J. V. Kennedy, M. R. C. McDowell and V. I. Myerscough, J. Phys. B: Atom. Molec. Phys. **10**, 3795 (1977).

ELECTRON CORRELATION EFFECTS IN NEON

Azzedine Lahmam-Bennani, Alain Duguet

Laboratoire des Collisions Atomiques et Moléculaires
Bâtiment 210 - Université Paris-Sud - 91405 Orsay Cedex

Because the elastic contribution to the total scattering of electrons from an atomic target is quite insensitive to the electron correlation effects, a study of those effects was conducted for the first time on the inelastic contribution and is presented here.

Energy loss spectra due to the inelastic scattering of 25 keV electrons from Neon have been obtained in the momentum transfer range $0.5 < K < 10$ a.u. and the energy loss range $0 < E < \sim 7000$ eV using a crossed-beam technique and a simultaneous analysis of the energy and direction of the scattered electrons. The so obtained double differential relative cross sections, $d^2\sigma/dEd\Omega$, were normalised using the Bethe sum rule [1]. This normalisation procedure is valid within the first Born approximation and has the advantage of being inpendent of any other calculation or experiment. The spectra were then integrated over E at constant K value, leading to absolute values of the inelastic cross section $d\sigma/d\Omega$, differential with the scattering angle, and hence to the incoherent X ray scattering factor $S(K)$. The overall precision is estimated to be 1%.

The experimental scattering factors were compared to calculated ones using Hartree-Fock (HF) wavefunctions [2]. The difference curve $\Delta S_{exp} = S_{exp} - S_{HF}$, shown in Fig.1, reflects the influence of the electron correlation effects on the differential cross sections. Theoretical results [3] based on Nesbet correlated wave functions, (which reach 99% of the correlation energy), and on the Bethe-Goldstone approximation, are also shown as a difference curve $\Delta S_{cor} = S_{cor} - S_{HF}$. Altough the K position of the main extremum of ΔS_{exp} is correctly reproduced by ΔS_{cor}, a factor of about 2 is missing in its magnitude. Also a possible less defined experimental maximum at $K \sim 4.5$ a.u. is not present in the ΔS_{cor} curve. These deviations might be due to the approximations inherent to the theoretical results which become apparent when compared with high accuracy data.

1.   M. Inokuti, Rev. Mod. Phys., 43, 297, 1971.
2.   C. Tavard, D. Nicolas, M. Rouault, J. Chim. Phys., 64, 540, 1967.
3.   M. Naon, M. Cornille, J. Phys. B5, 1965, 1972.

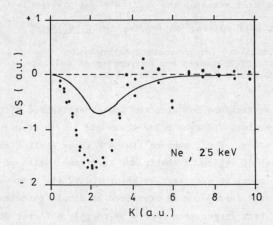

Fig. 1 : Difference curves, obtained by subtracting the HF
calcultaed scattering factor respectively from the
experimental one (•) and from the calculated one
using a correlated wave functions (——).

Electron Impact Excitation of the Zn II 4^2P and 5^2S Levels

W. T. Rogers, J. Ø. Olsen,[*] M. Reading and G. H. Dunn[+]

Joint Institute for Laboratory Astrophysics
National Bureau of Standards and University of Colorado
Boulder, Colorado 80309 U.S.A.

Absolute emission cross sections for electron impact excitation of the Zn II 4^2P and 5^2S levels have been measured from below threshold to 790 eV using the crossed-charged-beams technique. The resonance line 4^2P cross section exhibits structure in the near threshold region, probably due to a combination of cascade and resonance effects. At energies greater than about 100 eV the cross section approaches the E^{-1} ℓn E energy dependence as predicted by simple theories, but with a slope and magnitude both larger than theory by roughly a factor of two. The absolute radiometric calibration is currently under reexamination.

The 5^2S cross section is approximately 25 times smaller at threshold than the resonance line cross section, and drops more rapidly with increasing energy, approaching the E^{-1} behavior predicted for $\Delta\ell \neq 1$ cross sections by about 250 eV.

In addition to the cross section measurements, we measured the lifetime of the $3d^9 4s^2$ ^{2}D metastable state of Zn II by measuring the relative population of metastables at separated points along the beam as a function of transit time between those points. The result was $\tau_m = 15.3 \left(\begin{smallmatrix} +3.8 \\ -2.7 \end{smallmatrix} \right)$ μsec.

[*]On leave of absence from the Institute of Physics, University of Aarhus, DK-800 Aarhus, Denmark.

[+]Staff Member, Quantum Physics Division, National Bureau of Standards.

BINARY ENCOUNTER COLLISIONAL IONIZATION OF (nl) STATES OF HYDROGEN

Joseph A. Kunc

Physics Department and Space Sciences Institute
University of Southern California, University Park, Los Angeles, CA 90007

We consider electron collisional ionization of the hydrogen atom in the (nl) state (including ground state) on the basis of classical binary encounter theory. If we take $f(\nu_{nl}, nl)$ and $\sigma(\nu_e, \nu_{nl}, \Delta E)$ to denote the atomic electron velocity distribution function and the differential cross section for the exchange of the energy ΔE between the incident and atomic electron, respectively, then the electron ionization cross section of the excited state (nl) is as follows:

$$Q^{nl}(\nu_e, n, 1) = \iint \sigma(\nu_e, \nu_{nl}, \Delta E)\, f(\nu_{nl}, n, 1)\, d(\Delta E)\, d\nu_{nl}, \tag{1}$$

where ν_e is the velocity of the electron and ν_{nl} is the velocity of the atomic electron. In Eq. (1), $f(\nu_{nl}, n, 1)$ can be obtained from "naive" quantum mechanics and dynamics of Sommerfeld orbits.[1] Resolution of the Hamilton-Jacoby equation for the atomic electron with the above assumption gives for $1 \neq n-1$:

$$f(\nu_{nl}, n, 1)\, d\nu_{nl} = \frac{4}{\Pi}\, \frac{d\nu_{nl}}{(1+u_{nl}^2)^2 \left[1 - \frac{(1+U_{nl}^2)(1+1)}{2nU_{nl}}\right]^{1/2}}, \tag{2}$$

and σ-Dirac distribution for $1 = n-1$. In the above $u_{nl} = U_{nl}/\sqrt{2U_{nl}/m}$ and U_{nl} is ionization potential of the (nl) state.

B.E.A. differential cross section $\sigma(\nu_e, \nu_{nl}, \Delta E)$ (which takes also into account the change of energy of the incident electron in the atomic (field) has the form[2]

$$\sigma(\nu_e, \nu_{nl}, \Delta E) = \frac{\Pi e^4}{(\Delta E)^3}\, \frac{E_{nl}}{E_e + E_{nl} + U_{nl}}\, \left(\frac{4}{3} + \frac{\Delta E}{E_{nl}}\right). \tag{3}$$

After integrating Eq. (1) over ΔE we have:

a) for $1 \neq n-1$;

1) direct ionization:

$$Q_{dir}^{nl}(E_e, n, 1) = \frac{\Pi^4}{U_{nl}^2} \int F_{dir}(E_e, E_{nl})\, f(E_{nl}, n, 1)\, dE_{nl}, \tag{4}$$

2) exchange ionization:

$$Q_{exc}^{nl}(E_e, n, 1) = \frac{\Pi e^4}{U_{nl}^2} \int F_{exc}(E_e, E_{nl})\, f(E_{nl}, n, 1)\, dE_{nl}, \tag{5}$$

where

$$F_{dir}(E_e, E_{nl}) = \frac{E_{nl}}{E_e + E_{nl} + U_{nl}}\left\{\frac{2}{3}\left[1 - \left(\frac{U_{nl}}{E_e}\right)^2\right] + \frac{U_{nl}}{E_{nl}}\left(1 - \frac{U_{nl}}{E_e}\right)\right\}, \tag{6}$$

$$F_{exc}(E_e, E_{nl}) = \frac{E_{nl}}{E_e + E_{nl} + U_{nl}}\left\{\frac{2}{3}\left[\left(\frac{U_{nl}}{E_e}\right)^2 - \left(\frac{2U_{nl}}{E_e + U_{nl}}\right)^2\right] + \frac{1}{E_{nl}}\left(\frac{U_{nl}}{E_e} - \frac{2U_{nl}}{E_e + U_{nl}}\right)\right\}. \tag{7}$$

b)   for 1 = n-1

$$Q_{dir}^{nl} \ (E_e,n,1) = \frac{\Pi_e^{\,4}}{U_{nl}^{\,2}} \ \frac{U_{nl}}{E_e+2U_{nl}} \left\{ \frac{2}{3}\left[(\frac{U_{nl}}{E_e})^2 - (\frac{2U_{nl}}{E_e+U_{nl}})^2 \right] - \frac{2U_{nl}}{E_e+U_{nl}} + \frac{U_{nl}}{E_e} \right\} \qquad (8)$$

$$Q_{exc}^{nl} \ (E_e,n,1) = \frac{\Pi_e^{\,4}}{U_{nl}^{\,2}} \ \frac{U_{nl}}{E_e+2U_{nl}} \left\{ \frac{2}{3}\left[1 - (\frac{U_{nl}}{E_e})^2 \right] - \frac{U_{nl}}{E_e} + 1 \right\}. \qquad (9)$$

The total ionization cross section for that model of the electron-atom collision is given as:

$$Q_{tot}^{nl} \ (E_e,n,1) = Q_{dir}^{nl} \ (E_e,n,1) + Q_{exc}^{nl} \ (E_e,n,1), \qquad (10)$$

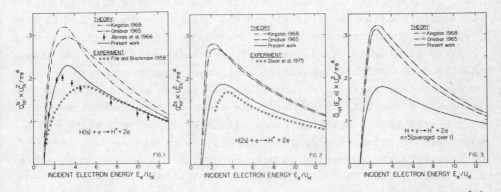

In figures 1,2 and 3 the present results have been compared with experiments and with theoretical calculations of Kingston[5] (who used the classical binary encounter approximation together with the quantum mechanical electron velocity distribution that was given by Fock[6]), Abrines et al.[7] (Monte Carlo method with microcanonical distribution) and Omidvar[8] (Coulomb-Born approximation).   In figure 3 the total cross section $\overline{Q}_{tot}$ (E_e,n) (averaged over all 1 sublevels) for n=5 is shown.   It is given by

$$\overline{Q}_{tot} \ (E_e,n) = \frac{1}{n^2} \ \sum_{1=0}^{n-1} \ (21 + 1) \ Q_{tot}^{nl} \ (E_e,n,1). \qquad (11)$$

The method can be adopted for some atoms and ions with one outer electron and for ionization by heavy ions (the results will soon be published).

1. E. V. Shpolski, Atomic Physics, Iliffe Books, London, 1969.

2. M. Gryzinski and J. Kunc, will soon be published in Journal of Physics B.

3. W. L. Fite and R. T. Brackmann, Phys. Rev. 112, 1141-51 (1958).

4. A. J. Dixon, A. Engel and M. F. A. Harrison, Proc. Roy. Soc. (London), A343, 33-349 (1975).

5. A. E. Kingston, Journ. Phys. B, 1, 559-66 (1968).

6. V. Fock, Z. Phys. 98, 145-54 (1935).

7. R. Abrines, I. C. Percival and N. A. Valentine, Proc. Phys. Soc. 89, 515-27 (1966).

8. K. Omidvar, Phys. Rev. 140A, 26-37 (1965).

ABSOLUTE PARTIAL ELECTRON IMPACT IONIZATION CROSS SECTION FUNCTIONS
FOR He, Ne, Ar AND Kr FROM THRESHOLD UP TO 180 eV

K. Stephan, H. Helm and T.D. Märk

Institut für Experimentalphysik, Abt.f. Kernphysik und Gaselektronik
Leopold Franzens Universität, A 6020 Innsbruck, Österreich (Austria)

The present paper is the last in a series from this laboratory
dealing with the upgrading of the quantitative knowledge of the
electron impact ionization of the rare gases in the low energy regime. The experimental setup consists of a Nier type electron impact
ion source (Varian MAT Intensitron M), a high resolution double focussing mass spectrometer (Varian MAT CH5) and a gas handling system.
Previous studies in our laboratory[1] with this instrument have shown,
that measured partial ionization efficiency curves are strongly dependent on the extraction conditions of the ion source, and that the
focussing potentials which guide the ion beam from the ion source
to the mass spectrometer entrance slit also effect the shape and
magnitude of measured efficiency curves. Meanwhile we have improved
considerably the operating conditions of the ion source, i.e. achieving complete ion extraction by means of a penetrating field extraction and achieving complete measurement and analysis of the extracted ion current by means of a new sweeping mass spectrometer technique[2]. Thus it became possible to measure accurate relative partial
ionization cross section functions and accurate cross section ratios.

Figures 1 to 4 give for He, Ne, Ar and Kr absolute partial ionization cross section functions, which have been obtained by normalizing our measured relative partial ionization cross sections with
help of the measured ion current ratios to the well established absolute total cross section curves[3]. In the upper part of each figure
the percentage deviation of our total cross section from those of
Ref.3 is shown. It can be seen that the total cross sections agree
in shape to within a few percent. The estimated maximum possible
errors for the reported absolute cross sections in their maximum
are: He^+: $\pm$ 3%, He^{++}: $\pm$ 15%, Ne^+: $\pm$ 3%, Ne^{++}: $\pm$ 7%, Ne^{+++}: $\pm$ 30%,
Ar^+: $\pm$ 3%, Ar^{++}: $\pm$ 7%, Ar^{+++}: $\pm$ 15%, Kr^+: $\pm$ 3%, Kr^{++}: $\pm$ 7%, Kr^{+++}:
$\pm$ 15%, Kr^{4+}: $\pm$ 30%.

Work partially supported by the Österreichischer Fonds zur Förderung der Wissenschaftlichen Forschung under Project S-18/08

1. K.Stephan, H.Helm and T.D.Märk, Proc. IXth SPIG,Dubrovnik (1978)7
2. H.Helm, K.Stephan and T.D.Märk,31st GEC, Buffalo (1978)98
3. D.Rapp and P.Englander-Golden, J.Chem.Phys., 43(1965) 1464

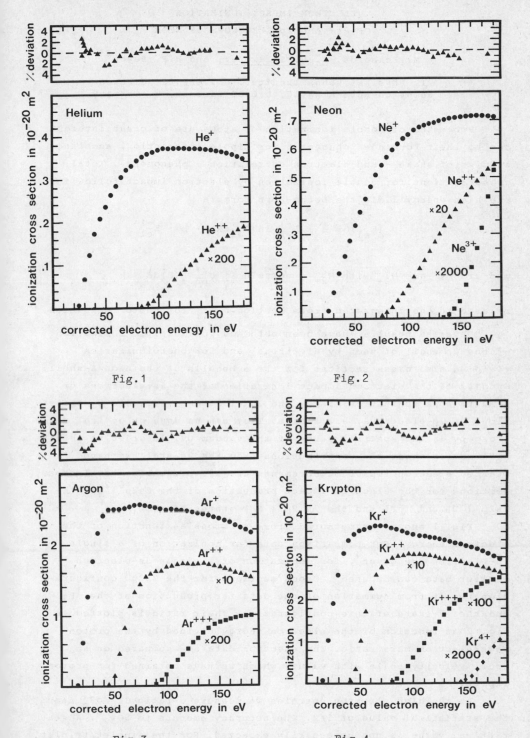

Fig.1

Fig.2

Fig.3

Fig.4

ELECTRON IMPACT IONIZATION
OF 2s- AND 2p-ELECTRONS OF NEON

M. Eckhardt, K.-H. Schartner, and H.F. Beyer[*]

I. Physikalisches Institut, Universität Giessen
Heinrich-Buff-Ring 16, D 6300 Giessen, W. Germany

Processes of double ionization of atoms are of great interest due to their forbidden character for dipole interaction, enabling studies of shake - and electron correlation - phenomena[1]. Total cross sections for double ionization by electron impact follow in the high energy limit the Bethe-Born formula

$$\sigma \ (E_{el}) = a \cdot E_{el}^{-1} \ \ln(E_{el}/R) + b \cdot E_{el}^{-1}$$

and are by $a = M_{2+}^2$ with $M_{2+}^2 = mc/\pi e^2 h \cdot \int_I^\infty \sigma_{ph.i}^{2+}(E)dE$

related to the integrated cross section $\sigma_{ph.i}$ for photo ionization.

Detailed results have been obtained for multiple ionization of the 2p shell of neon by electrons[2] and for photoionization[3] yielding also cross sections for the subshells of the neon L-shell. Studies of the electron impact ionization of the 2s-electrons or simultaneous ionization of 2s- and 2p-electrons, followed by transitions of 2p-electrons, are scarce. They can be done by optical spectroscopy in the spectral range of the vacuum UV. In order to obtain information about the contributions from the 2s-shell we have started electron impact measurements and are presenting total cross sections for the electron impact production of the $2s2p^6(^2S)$, the $2s2p^5(^1P)$ and (^3P) and the $2s^o2p^6(^1S_o)$ states of neon.

Fig. 1 shows the measured cross sections as function of the electron energy. For comparison data for ionization of a single 2p-electron are given[4], for ionization of a single 2s-electron earlier data can be used[5]. Cross sections for the $2s2p^5$ configuration result from summation of the data for production of the ^1P- and the ^3P-state of this configuration. Their ratio is plotted in fig. 2 as function of the electron energy divided by the proton mass/electron mass ratio. The electron data are compared on an equal velocity scale with values which we have obtained for proton impact.

At the high electron energies we measure a ratio $\sigma1_P/\sigma3_P$ near the statistical value of 1/3. The accuracy amounts to 50%[6]. A statistical value is not necessarily expected. For the singlet/triplet

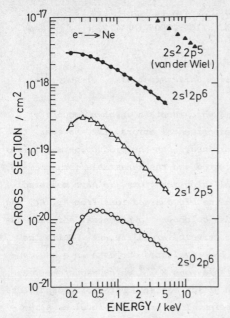

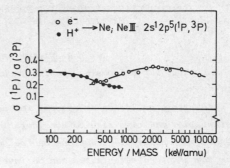

Fig. 1
Electron impact ionization cross sections
for the L-subshells of neon.

Fig. 2
Cross section ratio for the ^{1}P- and ^{3}P-
states of the 2s2p^5-configuration

o o o   electron data
● ● ●   proton data

ratio of the 1s2s^{2}2p^5-configuration strong deviations from 1/3 have
been measured which have been explained by configuration interaction
of continuum states[7]. More experimental efforts are needed to increase the accuracy of the singlet/triplet ratio also from the viewpoint of measurements with heavy ions for which the electron data
can serve as calibration standard.

An analysis of the Bethe-Fano plots of fig. 1 will be carried
out as well as a comparison of cross section ratios for single/
double ionization with shake off probabilities.

* Permanent address: Gesellschaft für Schwerionenforschung,
                      D-6100 Darmstadt, W. Germany

1. Th.A. Carlson and M.O. Krause, Phys. Rev. A 140, 1057 (1965)

2. M.J. van der Wiel and G. Wiebes, Physica 54, 411 (1971)

3. F. Wuilleumier and M.O. Krause, Phys. Rev. A 10, 242 (1974)

4. M.J. van der Wiel, Th.M. El-Sherbini, and L. Vriens,
    Physica 42, 411 (1969)

5. B.F.J. Luyken, F.J. de Heer, and R.Ch. Baas,
    Physica 61, 200 (1972)

6. H.F. Beyer, R. Hippler, K.-H. Schartner, and R. Albat,
    Z. Physik A 289, 239 (1979)

7. D. Chattarji, W. Mehlhorn, and V. Schmidt,
    Journal of Electron Spectroscopy and Related Phenomena
    13, 97 (1978)

APPARENT CROSS SECTIONS FOR PRODUCTION OF SINGLY AND DOUBLY CHARGED
METASTABLE NOBLE GAS IONS BY ELECTRON IMPACT

H. Winter and P. Varga

Institut für Allgemeine Physik, Technische Universität Wien, Vienna, Austria

In atomic collision processes, ion beams which contain unknown amounts of
metastables may give rise to considerable experimental errors. If , however, the
respective metastable fractions can be determined, both the production mechanisms
for the involved metastables can be investigated and the metastable ions themselves become available for well defined collision reactions. We have measured
metastable ion beam fractions for singly and doubly charged ions from Ar, Kr, and
Xe by utilizing the fact that electron yields belonging to potential emission due
to ground state ions and excited ions, respectively, are different[1]. While the
principle of this method is well known[2] we have evaluated our data in a new manner insofar that electron yields for metastable ions $X^{+z,m}$ which cannot be measured directly were determined from electron yields measured both for ground state
ions X^{+z} and $X^{+(z+1)}$ of the same atomic species. This procedure involves a semi-
empirical dependence between electron yields and metastable ion excitation energy.

Singly, doubly and trebly charged noble gas ions were produced in an electron
impact ion source with impact energy spread of 1 eV FWHM. As an example, fig. 1
shows for Ar^+ the course of metastable fraction with impact energy E_e. Because no
distinction is made between different metastable states of comparable excitation
energy, only apparent metastable fractions can be determined. These result from
direct excitation of several closely spaced metastable states as well as from population of the respective metastable levels by cascading from higher non-metasta-
ble levels. Additionally, long lived highly excited ions[3,4] can be produced. In
fig. 1 also data from other authors are given. One of these belong exclusively to
the admixture of a single metastable state[5] and, therefore, no influence due to
long lived highly excited states can be contained. The different data compared in
fig. 1 disagree markedly at higher impact energies. We note, however, that long
lived highly excited states can only be produced near and above the impact energy
threshold $IP(X^{+2})$ for production of doubly charged ions and their fraction may depend strongly on the specific apparative conditions because of possible quenching.

Apparent metastable fractions were determined also for beams from Kr^+ and Xe^+
as well as from doubly charged ions from Ar, Kr and Xe. For the latter results
no other data for comparison are available.

Absolute metastable fractions $f_{z,m}$ were determined as explained earlier. By
multiplying the respective $f_{z,m}$-values with absolute cross sections for production
of singly or doubly charged ions[6], absolute apparent cross sections $Q_{z,m}^{app}$ were obtained as shown e.g. for $Ar^{+,m}$ and $Ar^{+2,m}$ in fig. 2.

Overall experimental uncertainty for these data is 30 % for $Ar^{+,m}$ and 50 % for
$Ar^{+2,m}$, respectively.

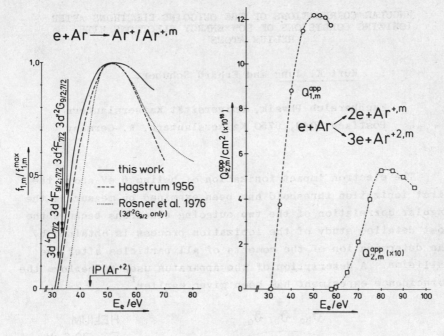

$$e + Ar \longrightarrow Ar^+ / Ar^{+,m}$$

fig. 1

Dependence of relative apparent
metastable fraction on electron
impact energy for Ar^+ ion beams

fig. 2

Apparent cross sections for
production of metastable $Ar^{+,m}$
and $Ar^{+2,m}$ by electron impact
on Ar

Our results suggest that ion beams produced at rather high electron impact
energy as e.g. in electron beam type ion sources ("EBIS", cf.[7]) may contain much
smaller metastable admixtures than ion beams produced at impact energies belonging to the respective ionization cross section maxima.

This work has been supported by the Austrian Fonds zur Förderung der wissenschaftlichen Forschung, Projekt Nr. 3283, and by GSI Darmstadt/FGR. We thank
Dr. T. D. Märk and colleagues for communicating their new ionization cross section data.

References

1. P. Varga and H. Winter, Phys.Rev. A 18,2453(1978)

2. H. D. Hagstrum, Phys.Rev. 104,309(1956)

3. J. Wm. McGowan and Larkin Kerwin, Can.J.Phys. 41,1535(1963)

4. S. E. Kupriyanov, Z.Z. Latypov and A.A. Perov, Sov.Phys.-JETP 20,14(1965)

5. S.D. Rosner, T.D. Gaily and R.A. Holt, J.Phys.B:Atom.Molec.Phys.9,L 489(1976)

6. K. Stephan, H. Helm and T. D. Märk, these proceedings

7. G. Clausnitzer, H. Klinger. A. Müller and E. Salzborn, Nucl.Instr.Meth.
   128, 1 (1975)

ANGULAR CORRELATIONS OF THE OUTGOING ELECTRONS AFTER IONIZING COLLISIONS OF LOW ENERGY ELECTRONS WITH HELIUM ATOMS

Kurt K. Jung and Erhard Schubert

Fachbereich Physik, Universität Kaiserslautern
Postfach 3049, 6750 Kaiserslautern, W.-Germany

The electron impact ionization of helium 6 eV above the first ionization threshold has been examined by measuring the angular correlation of the two outgoing electrons because the most detailed study of the ionization process is obtained by the determination of the momenta of all particles after the collision. A description of the apparatus used to perform the coincidence experiment has been given earlier[1].

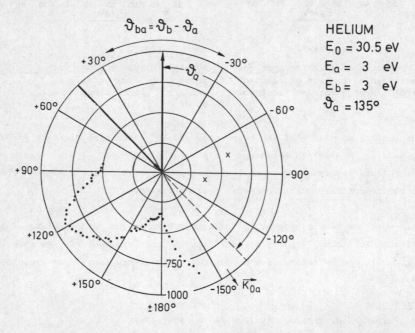

Fig.1. Polar plot of the angular dependence of the triple differential cross section as a function of the angle ϑ_{ba} between the momenta of both outgoing electrons. The distances of the dots from the centre of the polar diagram are proportional to the rate of true coincidences measured at the respective scattering angle ϑ_b.

At the collision energy of 30.5 eV some predictions of threshold theories[2,3,4,5] are confirmed, but a pure threshold behaviour of the ionization process cannot be seen. The triple differential cross section shows similar distributions as a function of the angle between the momenta of both emerging electrons for various scattering angles ϑ_a^b. But there exist deviations of the measured data from the angular correlation expected in the range of validity of the threshold law. All measurements show a peak at $\vartheta_{ba}^b = 120^\circ \pm 15^\circ$ with nearly constant intensity which reflects the influence of the mutual interaction of both electrons. Additionally there can be seen a second peak which seems to be coupled to the direction of the momentum transfer $\overrightarrow{K_{Oa}}$ similar to the behaviour of the cross section at higher collision energies. Moreover at this collision energy 6 eV above threshold the angular dependences of the coincidence cross section are independent of the ratio E_a/E_b, where E_a and E_b denote the energies of both secondary electrons.

The theories[6,7,8] for electron impact ionization which are able to reproduce in a satisfactory manner the measurements at collision energies higher than 100 eV differ very much from the experimental data in this low energy region.

1. K. Jung, E. Schubert, H. Ehrhardt and D.A.L. Paul, J. Phys. B: Atom. Molec. Phys. 9, 75-87 (1976)

2. G.H. Wannier, Phys. Rev. 90, 817 25 (1953)

3. A.R.P. Rau, Phys. Rev. A4, 207-201 (1976)

4. A.R.P. Rau, J. Phys. B: Atom. Molec. Phys. 9, L283-8 (1976)

5. R. Peterkop, J. Phys. B: Atom. Molec. Phys. 4, 513-21 (1971)

6. S. Geltman, J. Phys. B: Atom. Molec. Phys. 7, 1994 2002 (1974)

7. M. Schulz, J. Phys. B: Atom. Molec. Phys. 6, 2580-99 (1973)

8. E. Schubert, A. Schuck, K. Jung and S. Geltman, J. Phys. B: Atom. Molec. Phys. 12, 967-78 (1979)

ABSOLUTE TRIPLE DIFFERENTIAL CROSS SECTIONS FOR SCATTERING
200-2800 eV ELECTRONS INCIDENT ON HELIUM

B. van Wingerden, J.T. Kimman, B. Piraux[*], C.J. Joachain[*] and F.J. de Heer

FOM-Institute for Atomic and Molecular Physics, Amsterdam, The Netherlands

Absolute measurements of double and triple differential cross sections for
the ionization of helium by fast electrons have been performed and compared with
various theoretical approximations. In figure 1 we present a sketch of our
apparatus. The electrons are detected by means of electron energy analyzers, which
are provided with so called Heddle lenses [1] and which make both an angle of 45°
with respect to the incoming beam in one plane. Without coincidence technique
we measure the double differential cross section $d^2\sigma/d\Omega dE$. It serves as a check
for the reliability of the triple differential cross section $d^3\sigma/d\Omega_1 d\Omega_2 dE$, measured
by coincidence. The cross sections are made absolute by comparison with elastic
cross sections, which are measured in the same apparatus and normalized on previous results of Jansen et al. [2], (error 6%). We estimate the error in our $d^3\sigma$
data to be about 20%, which is a marked improvement over the previous experiments
of the Frascati group [3], which used a crossed beam technique. In our case we
use a collision chamber filled with gas, for which it is possible to determine
the gas pressure and the effective value of scattering length times solid angle
with great accuracy.

Because the present measurements are absolute, they are particularly suitable
for comparison with theoretical approaches. Our experimental results are shown in
figure 2, together with those of the Frascati group. They are compared with the
following theoretical calculations: first Born approximation, Coulomb Projected
Born with exchange [4], plane wave and distorted wave impulse approximations [5]
and a plane Coulomb waves impulse approximation [3], (* stands for this work). We
have also indicated the type of wave function used to describe the helium ground
state. Plane wave Born results agree to within 2% with the corresponding Born
values above 500 eV and hence have not been included in the figure. It is worth
noting that the particular kinematical conditions that we have used imply that
the first Born approximation should govern the scattering at sufficiently high
energies. From the examination of figure 2 it is seen that for energies above 1000 eV
our experimental data follow the energy dependence of the Born approximation. At
energies below 1000 eV the best agreement is obtained with CPB(E), PCWIA and PWIA
calculations.

Our experimental double differential cross sections at 45° contain an error of
about 10% and agree very well with our first Born results (both HF and screened).

* Université Catholique de Louvain, Belgium
* Université Libre de Bruxelles, Belgium

[1] D.W.O. Heddle, J. Phys. E: Scientific Instruments 4 (1971) 981

[2] R.H.J. Jansen, F.J. de Heer, H.J. Luyken, B. van Wingerden and H.J. Blaauw,
    J. Phys. B: Atom Molec. Phys. 9 (1976) 185

[3] G. Stefani, R. Camilloni and A. Giardini-Guidoni, Phys. Letters: 64 A (1978)
    364

[4] S. Geltman, J. Phys. B: Atom.Molec. Phys. 7 (1974) 1994

[5] I.E. McCarthy and E. Weigold, Phys.Reports, 27 C (1976)

Fig. 1 Experimental set up

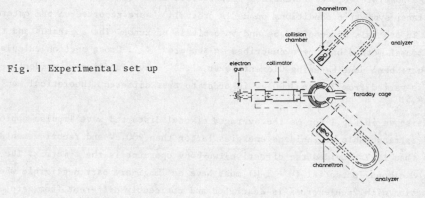

Fig. 2 Experimental and theore-
        tical results for d³σ

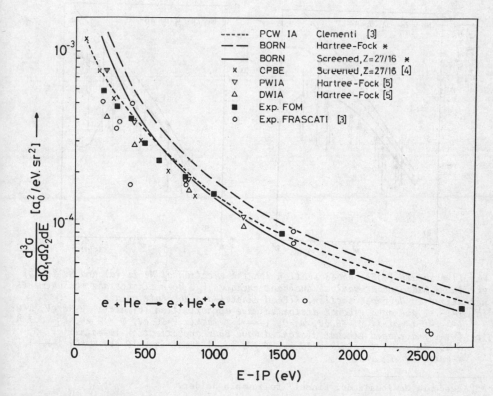

ABSOLUTE (e, 2e) COPLANAR SYMMETRIC CROSS SECTION MEASURED FOR VALENCE OR-
BITALS OF Ne AND Xe

A. Giardini-Guidoni, R. Fantoni[+], R. Tiribelli,

C.N.E.N., Divisione Nuove Attività, C.P. 65, 00044 FRASCATI (Rome), Italy

G. Stefani and R. Camilloni

C.N.R., Lab.Metod.Avanzate Inorganiche, Via Montorio Romano n.36, 00131 Rome, Italy

The absolute (e, 2e) five times differential cross sections already measured
in coplanar symmetric conditions on He 1s orbital [1] are reported on the outermost
2s and 2p orbitals of neon and 5s and 5p orbitals of xenon. The apparatus and the
experimental method have been described elsewhere [1,2]. Cross section calculations have been done by using Clementi's et al. [3] wave functions. Incident e-
nergy is varied from 200 to 3600 eV in order to test different theoretical models [4,5].

As shown in Fig.1 for Ne the averaged eikonal distorted wave impulse approximation is reasonable at incident energies larger than 200 eV and recoil momenta
q less than 1 eV provided the effective two-body operator is the t-matrix. The
averaged eikonal potential $(\bar{V} + i\ \bar{W})$ must have an imaginary part negligible when
interaction with 2p electrons is described and noticeably different from zero
for 2s electrons.

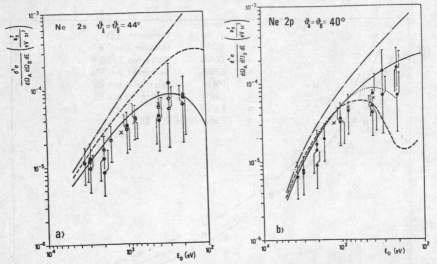

Fig.1: Absolute (e,2e) cross section for the ejection of Ne 2s (a) and Ne 2p (b)
electrons measured at various incident energies E_0. Open circles are measurements
normalized to He cross section, filled circles are absolute values.
(a) (-.-.-) averaged eikonal distorted wave approximation (v-matrix) $\bar{V}$=30 eV, W=0;
    (- - -) t-matrix $\bar{V}$ =30 eV, $\bar{W}$ =0; (———) t-matrix $\bar{V}$=30 eV, $\bar{W}$ =10 eV, R_d= 0.7 Å.
(b) (-.-.-) averaged eikonal distorted wave Born approximation (v-matrix) $\bar{V}$ =0,
    $\bar{W}$ =0; (- - -) t-matrix $\bar{V}$=20 eV, $\bar{W}$ =0; (...) t-matrix $\bar{V}$=10 eV, $\bar{W}$ =0; (———)
    t-matrix $\bar{V}$ =0, $\bar{W}$=0.

+ "Accademia Nazionale dei Lincei" fellowship holder.

Measurements for Xe are reported in Fig.2. For this atom measurements are normalized to the He cross section. The total cross section for the ejection of Xe 5s was reported by taking into account all its C.I. peaks. The averaged $\bar{V}$ potential which is needed to fit data is of the same order as the involved orbital binding energies. The imaginary part of the potential is small but not negligible for both the 5p and 5s states and a value $\bar{W} \cdot R_d \simeq 7$ eV.$\overset{\circ}{A}$ gives the best agreement with data.

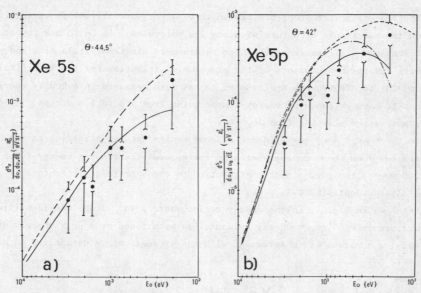

Fig.2: Absolute (e, 2e) cross section for the ejection of Xe 5s (a) and Xe 5p (b) electrons taken at various incident energies E_0.
(a) (- - -) averaged eikonal distorted wave (t-matrix) $\bar{V}=10$ eV, $\bar{W}=0$; (——) (t-matrix) $\bar{V}=10$ eV, $\bar{W}=10$ eV, $R_d=0.7$ Å.
(b) (- - -) averaged eikonal distorted wave (t-matrix) $\bar{V}=10$ eV, $\bar{W}=0$; (-.-.-)(t-matrix) $\bar{V}=0$, $\bar{W}=0$; (——)(t-matrix) $\bar{V}=10$ eV, $\bar{W}=10$ eV, $R_d=0.7$ Å.

1. G. Stefani, R. Camilloni and A. Giardini-Guidoni, Phys.Lett. 64A, 364 (1978)

2. R. Camilloni, A. Giardini-Guidoni, I.E. Mc Carthy and G. Stefani, Phys.Rev. A17, 1634 (1978)

3. E. Clementi and C. Roetti, "Atomic and Nuclear Data Tables", 14, 177 (1974)

4. I.E. Mc Carthy and E. Weigold, Phys.Rept. 27C, 275 (1976)

5. I. Fuss, I.E. Mc Carthy, C.J. Noble and E. Weigold, Phys.Rev. A17, 604 (1978).

INADEQUACY OF HARTREE FOCK SINGLE PARTICLE MODEL IN DESCRIBING INTERMEDIATE
STATE OF Xe

A. Giardini-Guidoni, R. Fantoni[+], R. Marconero

C.N.E.N., Divisione Nuove Attività, C.P. 65, 00044 FRASCATI (Rome), Italy

R. Camilloni and G. Stefani

C.N.R., Lab. Metod. Avanzate Inorganiche, Via Montorio Romano n.36, 00131 Rome, Italy

The (e, 2e) spectroscopy has proven to be a very useful tool in giving information on the electronic structure of atoms and molecules [1]. Up to now for atoms detailed momentum distributions have been obtained in single orbitals of s and p type. This work reports measurements of the momentum distribution for the 4d orbital in the Xe atom. The (e, 2e) energy spectrum of Xe has been measured in a 200 eV energy range in order to have evidence of energy losses going from 5 p to 4 s states. Incident energy was varied starting from 3600 eV.

In the energy spectrum evidence of some excited states belonging to the 5 s^{-1} symmetry has been found up to separation energy near the binding energy ε_λ of the 4d state. However, the predominant contribution to the spectroscopic factors is given by the alreay identified C.I. peaks [2].

As shown in Fig. 1, in the energy region where a $4d^{-1}$ state was identified by ESCA measurements [3] ($\varepsilon_\lambda \simeq 68$ eV) evidence has been found of a peak whose width at high and low q values is in agreement with the presence of an unresolved 4d doublet.

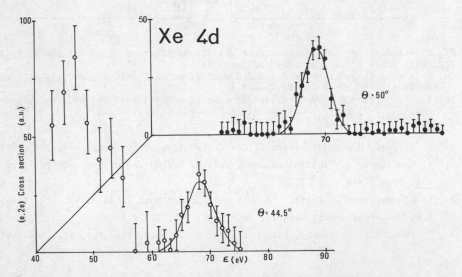

Fig. 1: (e, 2e) energy spectrum of Xe taken in symmetrical coplanar conditions
$I\vartheta_A = \vartheta_B = 44,5°$ and $\phi\vartheta_A = \vartheta_B = 50°$ at incident energy $E_o = 3600$ eV. In the abscissa the value $\varepsilon = E_o - E_A - E_B$ is reported. On the vertical axis coincidence counting rates are reported.

[+]"Accademia Nazionale dei Lincei" fellowship holder.

The angular distribution reported in Fig. 2 at high q values is in agreement with the distribution calculated from HF orbitals [4], while at q around zero an unexpected contribution to the momentum density appears. To best fit data the momentum distribution of the 5s orbital has been also reported.

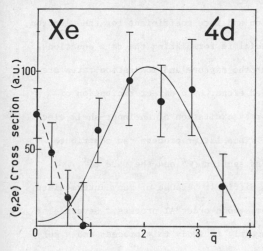

Fig. 2: Measured relative differential cross section of Xe 4d orbital taken at ε_λ = 68 eV, ϑ' = const and ϕ variable. Incident energy = 3668 eV. Full curve·is the momentum distribution of Xe 4d dashed curve is the momentum distribution of Xe 5s as calculated from Clement wave functions [4].

Due to present energy resolution (3,5 eV) the presence of a C.I. peak whose ε_λ is very near to the $4d^{-1}$ ε_λ and belonging to the $5s^{-1}$ state cannot be excluded with certainty. However, the width and position of peaks reported in Fig.1 tend to exclude the hypothesis of more than one contribution to this peak so that the most probable explanation appears to be a many electron correlation effect in the 4d orbital. This is supported also by unusually low measured cross sections for the 4s and 4p states which are inferred to be lower than 90% and 95% of the values calculated on the basis of Impulsive Approximation [1]. ESCA spectra[5] show only a peak, ascribed to the $4p_{3/2}^{-1}$, followed by a very broad structure, and a further peak ascribed to the $4s^{-1}$ state. Recently such data have been interpreted as a total failure of the SCF method [6] in describing these intermediate states within one electron model. Our results on the 4d momentum distribution and on the cross section value for the 4p and 4s orbitals strongly support this last interpretation. Further work is in progress to increase the energy of the incident beam in order to determine possible absorption effects and to avoid unadequate description of the reaction process.

1.   R. Camilloni et al.: Phys.Rev.Lett. 29, 618 (1972); I.E. Mc Carthy and E. Weigold, Phys.Rept. 27C, 275 (1976); R. Camilloni et al., Phys.Rev. 17A, 364 (1978).

2.   S.T. Hood, A. Hannett and C.E. Brion, J.Electron.Spectr. 11, 205 (1977)

3.   K. Siegbahn et al., E.S.C.A. Applied to Free Molecules, North-Holland, Amsterdam, 1969, p. 94

4.   E. Clementi and C. Roetti, Atomic Data and Nuclear Data Tables 14 (Academic Press, N.Y., 1974)

5.   V. Gelius, J. Electron.Spectr.Rel.Phen. 5, 985 (1974)

6.   G. Wendin and M. Ohno, Proc.II Int.Conf. Inner Shell Ionization Phenomena, Freiburg 1976 (ed.W. Mehlhorn and R. Brem) p. 166.

AUGER CONTRIBUTION TO ELECTRON IMPACT IONIZATION

Yukap Hahn

Department of Physics, University of Connecticut
Storrs, Connecticut 06238 U.S.A.

Reliable estimate of the cross section and rate coefficient for the electron impact ionization of positive ions is crucial in formulating the rate equations for high temperature plasma, in which both the capture and ionization rates are needed. The ionization is known to proceed either by a direct excitation of outer-shell electrons to continuum (DI) or by excitation of an inner-shell electron, followed by an Auger emission (AI). This latter process can contribute significantly to the total ionization cross section σ^I and the rate α^I. Theoretical estimate of σ^{AI} and α^{AI} is difficult because of many intermediate resonance states which are involved in the second-order AI process. Several theoretical attempts have been made[1,2] recently to study this process and a set of experiments has been carried out also for light ionic targets.[3] To ascertain the validity of the theoretical approximations introduced, we examine the four-electron systems $e + O^{5+}$, $e + Fe^{23+}$, and $e + Mo^{39+}$. For the oxygen case, comparison between the detailed calculation and the experimental cross section[3] can be made. Earlier empirical formulas[4] provide estimates, which will also be compared and improvements suggested for the other systems. Dependence of σ^I and α^I on the electron projectile energy, plasma temperature, and on the ionic core charge will be examined in detail, and a scaling law (and its breaking) will be developed. We will also report on an attempt to evaluate α^{AI} directly using an averaging procedure over the resonances and different angular momenta, along the line of ref. 1.

1. Y. Hahn, Phys. Rev. Lett. 39, 82 (1977) and Phys. Rev. A18, 1028 (1978).

2. R.D. Cowan and J.B. Mann, Los Alamos Report, LA-UR-79-104; L. Goldberg et al, Ann. d'Astrophys. 28 589 (1965).

3. D.H. Crandall et al, ORNL preprint; also D.H. Crandall et al, Phys. Rev. A18, 1911 (1978).

4. M.J. Seaton, Planet. Sp. Sci. 12, 55 (1964).

IONIZATION OF HYDROGENIC IONS BY CHARGED PARTICLES IN THE GLAUBER APPROXIMATION

Akio Tsuji, Hiroshi Kotegawa and Hajime Narumi

Department of Physics, Hiroshima University
Hiroshima 730, Japan

It is understood that the Glauber approximation provides reliable estimates of inelastic cross sections in the intermediate as well as high energy scattering of charged particles from neutral atoms.[1,2,3] Furthermore, by taking into account the asymptotic Coulomb potential, the excitation cross section of ion targets is reasonably predicted in the intermediate and high energy region.[4,5,6]

Now we apply the Glauber theory to the ionization process of ions by charged particle impact, while it is only discussed in the Coulomb-Born approximation or its variant.[7] In order to deal with exactly this break-up process, we consider an electron as the projectile and a hydrogenic ion with nuclear charge Z as the target. Let the incident electron momentum be $\vec{k}_i$, the momentum transfer $\vec{q} = \vec{k}_i - \vec{k}_f$ with the final momentum $\vec{k}_f$, and ejecting electron momentum $\vec{\kappa}$, then the Glauber amplitude is given by

$$f(\vec{k}_f, \vec{\kappa}) = \frac{ik_i}{2\pi} \int u_f^*(\vec{\kappa}, \vec{r})(1 - e^{i\chi(\vec{b}, \vec{r})})u_i(\vec{r})d\vec{r}d\vec{b}, \qquad (1)$$

where $u_i(\vec{r})$ and $u_f(\vec{\kappa}, \vec{r})$ are the initial bound and final continuum hydrogenic wave functions, respectively, and $\vec{b}$ denotes the impact parameter vector of the incident electron. The phase shift function in this equation can be written as[4]

$$\chi(\vec{b}, \vec{r}) = 2\eta\ln\frac{|\vec{b} - \vec{s}|}{b} - 2(Z-1)\eta\ln b + \chi_0 , \qquad (2)$$

where $\vec{s}$ is the projection of $\vec{r}$ onto the plane perpendicular to $\vec{k}_i$. The second and third terms of the right-hand side in Eq.(2) are respectively the phase function and the divergent constant resulting from the asymptotic Coulomb interaction screened by the ionic electron.

The Coulomb wave function $u_f^*(\vec{\kappa}, \vec{r})$ in power series representation diverges at large values of κ and the applicability of integral representation method to an ionic target is not always straightforward.[3] However, by using the relation for the confluent hypergeometric function of the radial part of the Coulomb wave function

$$F(\ell+1+i\alpha, 2\ell+2, 2i\kappa r) = \frac{2^{-2\ell-1}\Gamma(2\ell+2)e^{i\kappa r}}{\Gamma(\ell+1-i\alpha)\Gamma(\ell+1+i\alpha)} \int_{-1}^{1} e^{-i\kappa r\xi}(1+\xi)^{\ell-i\alpha}(1-\xi)^{\ell+i\alpha}d\xi , \qquad (3)$$

with $\alpha = Z/\kappa$, our previous method[2] is directly extended. Then we can reduce Eq.(1) to a one-dimensional integral including Meijer G functions[8] with complex arguments.

We assume that the faster electron is screened by the slower one between two electrons in the final state. Consequently the total cross section is obtained as follows in terms of the total energy E of the system:[9]

$$\sigma(E) = \int_0^{E/2} d(\kappa^2/2) \int d\hat{\kappa} d\hat{k}_f \kappa \frac{k_f}{k_i} \left| f(\vec{\kappa}, \vec{k}_f) \right|^2 . \qquad (4)$$

In Fig.1 the final result of the total ionization cross section of the hydrogenic helium ion by electron impact in comparison with the prediction in the Coulomb-Born approximation[7] and experimental results.[10] In addition to the target nuclear charge Z = 2, the result for Z = ∞ is also given for reference.

1.   E. Gerjuoy and B.K. Thomas, Rep. Prog. Phys. 37, 1345 (1974).

2.   H. Narumi, A. Tsuji and A. Miyamoto, Prog. Theor. Phys. 50, 338 (1973);
     54, 740 (1975).

3.   J.E. Golden and J.H. McGuire, Phys. Rev. Letters 32, 1218 (1974); Phys.
     Rev. A12, 80 (1975).

4.   H. Narumi and A. Tsuji, Prog. Theor. Phys. 53, 671 (1975).

5.   T. Ishihara and J.C.Y. Chen, J. Phys. B8, L417 (1975).

6.   B.K. Thomas, Phys. Rev. A18, 452 (1978).

7.   M.R.H. Rudge and S.B. Schwartz, Proc. Phys. Soc. 88, 563 (1966).

8.   B.K. Thomas and V. Franco, Phys. Rev. A13, 2004 (1976).

9.   M.R.H. Rudge and M.J. Seaton, Proc. Phys. Soc. 283, 262 (1965).

10.   B. Peart, D.S.Walton and T.K. Dolder, J. Phys. B2, 1347 (1969).

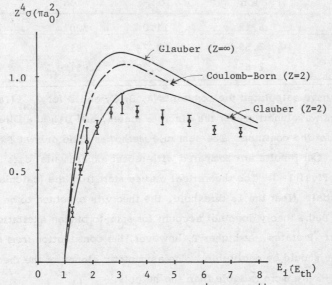

Fig.1.   Reduced ionization cross sections of He$^+$(e,2e)He^{++} versus the incident electron energy E_i(in the unit of the threshold energy E_{th}) in comparison with experimental results.[10]

BETHE CROSS SECTIONS FOR IONIZATION OF C^{3+}, N^{4+}, AND O^{5+} *

Yong-Ki Kim and Kwok-tsang Cheng

Argonne National Laboratory, Argonne, Illinois 60439 USA

A sum rule based on the Bethe theory,[1] leads to a cross section for the total inelastic scattering of electrons by an ion in the form

$$\sigma_{tot} = (A_{tot} \ln T + B_{tot} + C_{tot}/T)/T , \qquad (1)$$

where T is the incident electron energy and the constants A, B, and C depend on the properties of the ion. The Bethe cross section for ionization, σ_{ion}, is obtained by subtracting the sum of all (Bethe) cross sections for discrete transitions from σ_{tot}. An exchange correction based on the Mott formula[1] can also be expressed as an expansion in T^{-1}. The resulting Bethe cross section for ionization includes the ionization of the 1s electrons as well as the 2s electron by the nature of the sum rule, and is given by

$$\sigma_{ion} = (A_{ion} \ln T + B_{ion} + C_{ion}/T + D_{ion} \ln T/T)/T , \qquad (2)$$

where the constants A, B, C, and D are determined from the properties of the ion.

Table 1. Bethe parameters for σ_{ion}, Eq. (2). (T in eV and σ in $\overset{\circ}{A}{}^2$)

Ion	A_{ion}	B_{ion}	C_{ion}	D_{ion}
C^{3+}	5.12	-11.0	720	-1954
N^{4+}	3.59	-9.74	791	-1954
O^{5+}	2.65	-8.38	851	-1954

We have calculated the constants A, B, C, and D for σ_{ion} (Table 1) from the Dirac-Fock wavefunctions for the discrete states, and from the Dirac-Slater wavefunctions for the continua. The sum rule method is valid only at T > 1s ionization potential. Our results are compared with recent experimental data by Crandall et al.[2] in Figs. 1–3. The theoretical curves start from the (calculated) 1s ionization potential. Near the 1s threshold, the theory is expected to be too small because the Bethe theory does not account for spin-forbidden excitations, e.g., to the $1s2s\,n\ell\ ^4P$ states. At higher T, however, the contribution from spin-forbidden excitations should be negligible. The asymptotic slopes of the theoretical curves in Figs. 1–3 are more reliable than the heights.

We are grateful to Dr. D. H. Crandall for providing us with the experimental data prior to publication.

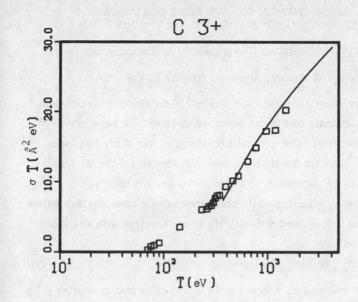

C 3+

FIG. 1--Fano plot for
the ionization of C^{3+}.
The squares represent
experimental data from
Ref. 2, and the solid
curve is the Bethe
cross section.

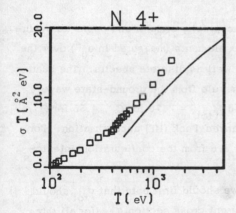

N 4+

O 5+

FIG. 2.--Fano plot for the ionization
of N^{4+}. See Fig. 1 caption for legends.

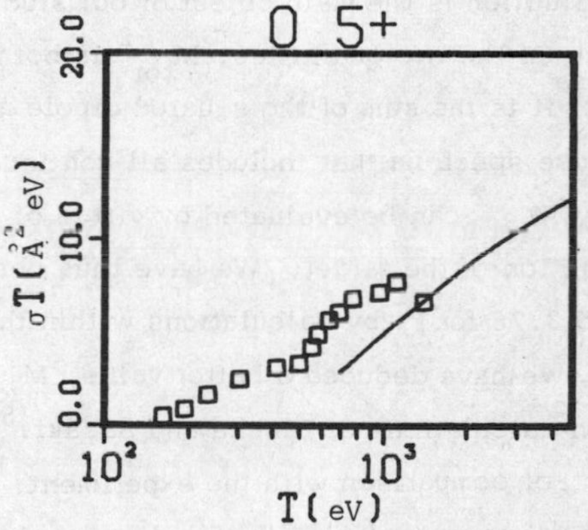

FIG. 3.--Fano plot for the ionization of O^{5+}. See Fig. 1 for
legends.

*Work performed under the auspices of the U.S. Department of Energy.

1. Y.-K. Kim and M. Inokuti, Phys. Rev. A **3**, 665 (1971).

2. D. H. Crandall, R. A. Phaneuf, B. E. Hasselquist, and D. C. Gregory,
Phys. Rev., in press.

THE BETHE TOTAL CROSS SECTION FOR INELASTIC COLLISIONS OF FAST CHARGED PARTICLES WITH C⁻, O⁻, and F⁻ IONS [*]

Mitio Inokuti, Kwok-tsang Cheng, and J. L. Dehmer

Argonne National Laboratory, Argonne, Illinois 60439 USA

Recent experiments by Peart, Forrest, and Dolder[1,2] on electron detachment from C⁻, O⁻, and F⁻ by electrons of kinetic energies up to 990 eV have prompted us to study the topic in the title. The general framework of our study has been fully described earlier,[3,4] and its merits have been illustrated for the H⁻ ion;[4] indeed, the present work is an extension of that work in many respects.

The total cross section σ_{tot} for inelastic collisions of any structureless particle of charge ze and speed v (assumed nonrelativistic for brevity) with any atomic or molecular target is given[3] by

$$\sigma_{tot} = 4\pi a_0^2 z^2 (R/T) M_{tot}^2 \ln(4c_{tot}T/R) , \qquad (1)$$

where $T = \frac{1}{2} mv^2$, R = 13.6 eV, and $a_0 = 0.529 \times 10^{-8}$ cm. The two quantities M_{tot}^2 and c_{tot} depend on the <u>target electronic structure only</u>, and their dependable evaluation is the main object of our study.

Of the two quantities, M_{tot}^2 is both conceptually simpler and easier to evaluate; it is the sum of the squared dipole matrix elements (measured in a_0^2) over the entire spectrum that includes all continua as well as discrete spectra. The quantity M_{tot}^2 can be evaluated by virtue of a sum rule from the ground-state wavefunction of the target. We have thus obtained $M_{tot}^2 = 7.76$ for C⁻, 4.55 for O⁻, and 3.78 for F⁻ by calculations within the Hartree-Fock (HF) approximation. For F⁻, we have deduced a better value, $M_{tot}^2 = 3.6$ from the configuration-interaction calculations of Tanaka and Sasaki.[5]

For comparison with the experiment,[1,2] we should first note that σ_{tot} should be a close upper bound to the electron-detachment cross section σ_{det} for all three negative ions because there appear to be no discrete bound states accessible by a dipole-allowed transition to the best of our knowledge.[6] Next, recall that a good way of analysis of any cross-section data for high incident speed is by the use of the Fano plot,[3,7] (as exemplified by Fig. 2 of Ref. 1 and by Fig. 3 of Ref. 2), in which one plots $T\sigma_{det}$ or $T\sigma_{tot}$ against $\ln T$. The slope of the linear asymptote, as suggested by Eq. (1), should be comparable to our theoretical values for M_{tot}^2.

With these ideas in mind, we have examined the experimental data,[1,2] and have come to a tentative conclusion that for F⁻ and O⁻ the slopes of the Fano plots of these data at highest energies are probably compatible with our theoretical results, within uncertainties of 10%.   For C⁻, the theoretical slope is much larger than the experimental.

A more detailed result is forthcoming. By several means we are evaluating c_{tot} (i.e., the second quantity in Eq. (1), which determines the intercept in the Fano plot).

We thank Professor Dolder for communicating the experimental results far in advance of publication.

*Work performed under the auspices of the U.S. Department of Energy.

1. B. Peart, R. Forrest, and K. T. Dolder, J. Phys. B 12, L115 (1979).

2. B. Peart, R. Forrest, and K. T. Dolder, J. Phys. B 12, 847 (1979).

3. M. Inokuti, Rev. Mod. Phys. 43, 297 (1971). See Sec. 4.3 in particular.

4. M. Inokuti and Y.-K. Kim, Phys. Rev. 173, 154 (1968).

5. K. Tanaka and F. Sasaki, Int. J. Quantum Chem. 5, 157 (1971).

6. H. Hotop and W. C. Lineberger, J. Phys. Chem. Ref. Data 4, 539 (1975).

7. U. Fano, Phys. Rev. 95, 1198 (1954).

MEASUREMENT OF CROSS SECTIONS FOR ELECTRON
IMPACT IONIZATION OF IONS UP TO 810 eV[*]

R. Becker, R. Frodl and H. Klein

Institut für Angewandte Physik, Universität Frankfurt,
Robert-Mayer-Str. 2-4, D-6000 Frankfurt, Germany

A. Müller and E. Salzborn

Institut für Kernphysik, Universität Giessen,
Leihgesterner Weg 217, D-6300 Giessen, Germany

H. Winter

Institut für Allgemeine Physik, Technische Universität Wien,
Karlsplatz 13, A-1040 Wien, Austria

A crossed (90 $^\circ$) beam experiment has been set up for the measurement of the cross sections for electron impact ionization of
ions. In the Giessen EBIS facility[1], which has been prooved to
yield beams of multiply charged ions with low metastable content,
a special computer designed ribbon beam electron gun[2] was interchanged with the gas charge exchange cell. This gun combines favour-
ably high electron current density (up to 0.145 A/cm^2 at 810 eV interaction energy), a long interaction path (6 cm), and - in spite of
the high electron current (300 mA at 1 kV anode voltage) - only a
small electron energy variation in the interaction region of less
than 1 %.

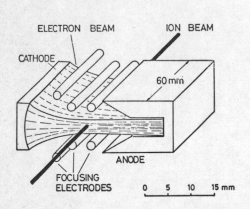

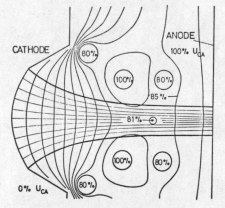

Fig. 1 Schematic sketch of the   Fig. 2 Electron trajectories
        penetration of electron   and equipotentials in
        and ion beam   the calculated gun

[*] Work supported bei the GSI, Darmstadt

Careful attention has been given to determine the possible
sources of error. The measured cross sections should be exact to
$\pm$ 9 % for energies above cross section maximum. For control of
accuracy, the ionization of Ne[+] ions has been studied, yielding
an agreement with measurements of Dolder et al.[3] within the experimental errors (fig. 3).

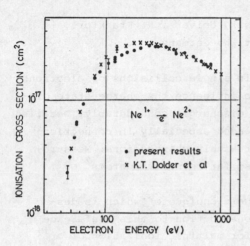

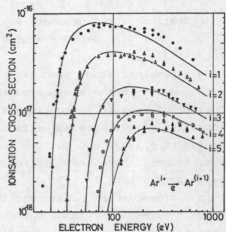

Fig. 3   Comparison of measured   Fig. 4   Comparison of measured
cross sections for Ne[1+] cross sections for Ar[+]
ions (•) with data obtai- - Ar[5+] with a simple fit-
ned by Dolder et al. (X) ting formula (see text)

The measured cross sections for the successive ionization of Ar[+]
- Ar[5+] ions are compared in fig. 4 with the formula

$$\sigma_{i \to i+1} = 1.6 \cdot 10^{-13} \cdot \frac{\ln E_e/E_i}{E_e E_i}$$

with E_e electron energy
     E_i ionization energy for $Ar^{i+} \to Ar^{(i+1)+}$.

[1] G. Clausnitzer, H. Klinger, A. Müller, and E. Salzborn, Nucl.
Instr. Meth. 128 (1975) 1 - 7
[2] R. Becker, R. Frodl, and H. Klein, GSI-Bericht GSI-P-33-77
(1977) 75
[3] K.T. Dolder, M.F.A. Harrison, and P.C. Thonemann, Proc. Roy.
Soc. A 274 (1963) 546

MULTIPLE IONIZATION OF ARGON IONS BY ELECTRON IMPACT[+]

A. Müller

Institut für Kernphysik, Universität Giessen, D-6300 Giessen,
W.-Germany

R. Frodl

Institut für Angewandte Physik, Universität Frankfurt,
D-600 Frankfurt, W.-Germany

Multiple ionization processes in single collisions of electrons
with atoms and ions are expected to influence the charge state distribution of ions in energetic gas discharges considerably. Detailed
information on such processes is needed especially in connection
with fusion plasmas and sources for highly charged ions. Measurements, however, have been limited so far to neutral atoms[2] or
singly charged ions[3,4].

In a crossed-beam experiment the technique of which is described in more detail in another contribution to this conference[5]
cross sections have been measured for multiple ionization of Ar^{i+}
ions (i = 1,2,3) by electron impact. The experimental electron
energies range from the respective thresholds up to about 800 eV.

As an example Fig. 1 shows measured cross sections $\sigma_{1,f}$ for
the removal of up to 4 electrons from Ar^{1+} by a single electron-
ion collision. With increasing final charge state f of the ions
the cross sections $\sigma_{1,f}$ decrease more rapidly than the cross sections $\sigma_{f-1,f}$ for single step ionization processes[5].

The threshold potentials for the production of Ar^{2+}, Ar^{3+} and
Ar^{4+} coincide with the combined ionization potentials of the respective number of outermost electrons removed from Ar^{1+}. In the
case of Ar^{4+} an additional ionization channel is opened above an
electron energy of about 250 eV indicated by a sudden increase of
the cross section $\sigma_{1,4}$. This leads to the assumption that besides
the removal of outer shell electrons also production of inner
shell vacancies is involved in the ionization process.

Further measurements with Ar^{2+} and Ar^{3+} ions confirm this
assumption. It is shown that for the production of L-shell va-

---

[+]Work supported by Gesellschaft für Schwerionenforschung (GSI),
D-6100 Darmstadt, W.-Germany

cancies in argon ions cross sections can be deduced which are
in good agreement with data for neutral Ar atoms obtained by
Auger electron spectroscopy[6].

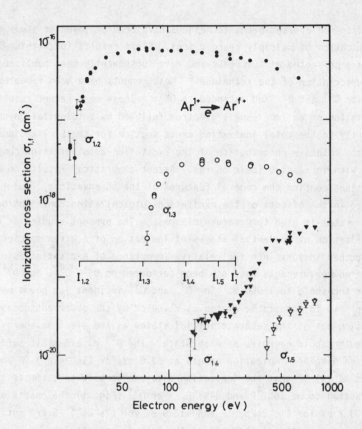

Fig. 1: Cross sections $\sigma_{1,f}$ for multiple ionization of Ar^{1+} ions.
The ionization thresholds $I_{1,f}$ of the f outermost electrons
and I_1^L of the $L_{2,3}$-shell of Ar^{1+} are indicated.

1.   R. Geller, Proc. XIIIth Int. Conf. Phenomena in Ionized Gases
             Berlin 1977, (Phys. Soc. of the GDR), p. 103
2.   B.L. Schram et al., Physica _32_ (1966) 197
3.   W.E. Sayle and R.K. Feeney, Xth ICPEAC, Paris 1977, Abstr. p.1084
4.   B. Peart and K.T. Dolder, J.Phys. _B2_ (1969) 1169
5.   R. Becker et al., this conference
6.   W. Mehlhorn, private communication

ELECTRON IMPACT IONIZATION OF OXYGEN IONS--O^{3+}, O^{4+}, O^{5+}*

D. H. Crandall and R. A. Phaneuf

Oak Ridge National Laboratory, Oak Ridge, Tennessee 37830, USA

Electron-ion crossed-beams techniques have been employed to study electron impact ionization of multiply charged ions. First results for lithium-like C^{3+} and N^{4+} were presented at X ICPEAC[1] and have subsequently been published with detailed description of the technique.[2] Measurements have been repeated and improved for C^{3+} and N^{4+} and extended to O^{5+}.[3] These most recent results revealed that excitation of an inner-shell electron followed by autoionization contributes significantly to the total ionization cross section for the Li-like ions studied and that the relative contribution of the excitation-autoionization component increases with increasing ionic charge. Recent theoretical results on excitation cross sections confirm the general features of the observations,[4] and interest has revived in the effects of the excitation-autoionization contribution to ionization rates in high temperature plasmas.[5] The present studies of electron impact ionization of sequential stages of ionization of a given species can provide further insight into the relative importance of excitation-autoionization.

Detailed measurements have now been performed on O^{3+}, O^{4+}, and O^{5+} from ionization threshold to 1500 eV. The O^{3+} and O^{4+} incident ion beams were found to contain ions in metastable states as revealed by the observed successive onsets of ionization out of the separate initial states as the electron energy was varied across the threshold energies of each state. The O^{3+} data exhibit sufficiently separate and distinct ionization onsets at 68.6 eV for $(1s^2 2s2p^2)$ ^4P and at 77.4 eV for $(1s^2 2s^2 2p)$ ^2P that the ionization data can be used to estimate the metastable fraction to be 16% ^4P and 84% ^2P. For O^{4+} (Fig. 1) the onsets of ionization at 103.7 eV for $(1s^2 2s2p)$ ^3P and 113.9 eV for $(1s^2 2s^2)$ ^1S are not distinct but allow a rough estimate that 50% of the beam is metastable.

For O^{3+} the observed ionization cross section of 7.0 x 10^{-18} cm^2 at 300 eV is 25% higher than predicted by the scaled Coulomb-Born values of Golden and Sampson[6] but is in good agreement with the semiempirical formula of Lotz.[7] For O^{4+}, Fig. 1 shows the measured cross section for the mixed state beam compared with the scaled Coulomb Born and Lotz predictions as calculated for a 50-50 mixture of initial beam states.

Excitation of an inner-shell electron followed by autoionization is observed in the O^{4+} data as a distinct increase in the total ionization cross section at 560 eV. Excitation of one of the 1s electrons can occur from the ground state through $(1s^2 2s^2) \rightarrow (1s2s^2 2p)$ and can occur from the metastable state through $(1s^2 2s2p) \rightarrow (1s2s^2 2p)$ or $(1s2s2p^2)$, all of which are expected to have threshold excitation energies near 560 eV. The magnitude of the increase in ionization cross section due to these inner-shell excitations is 1.5 x 10^{-19} cm^2 at 600 eV

in the O^{4+} case while for O^{5+} (Ref. 3) the excitation-autoionization contribution
is 2.5×10^{-19} cm^2 added to the direct ionization cross section of 6×10^{-19} cm^2.
For O^{3+} the excitation-autoionization process is not discernible in the present
data, but if the excitation contribution is smaller for O^{3+} than for O^{4+}, it
would contribute less than 2% to the total ionization and would not be detected.

For the oxygen ion sequence, the inner-shell excitation increases in proportion to the number of $n = 2$ orbital vacancies available for the $1s^2$ electron
excitation; that is, excitation of a 1s electron is smallest for O^{3+} and largest
for O^{5+}. Since the direct ionization cross section scales with the number of $n =$
2 electrons in the initial state, it is largest for O^{3+} and smallest for O^{5+}.
This qualitatively corresponds to the observation that for O^{3+} the excitation-
autoionization contribution to the ionization is not discernible in the ionization
cross section data while for O^{5+} it is a dominant feature.

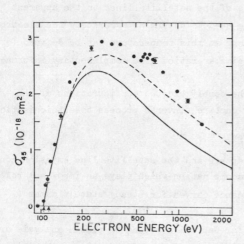

Fig. 1. Electron impact
ionization of O^{4+}. Points are
present data with 1 standard
deviation relative uncertainty
bars. Solid curve is scaled
Coulomb-Born (Ref. 6) and
dashed curve is Lotz formula
(Ref. 7), both calculated for
a 50% ^1S and 50% ^3P mixture of
initial ion states. Arrows
indicate threshold energies for
ionization out of the two
initial states.

*Research sponsored by the Office of Basic Energy Sciences, U. S. Department of
Energy, under contract W-7405-eng-26 with the Union Carbide Corporation.

1.   D. H. Crandall, P. O. Taylor, and R. A. Phaneuf, Abstracts of Papers of
     X ICPEAC (Paris), p. 1086, (1977).
2.   D. H. Crandall, R. A. Phaneuf, and P. O. Taylor, Phys. Rev. A 18, 1911
     (1978).
3.   D. H. Crandall, R. A. Phaneuf, B. E. Hasselquist, and D. C. Gregory, J.
     Phys. B Lett., accepted for publication (1979).
4.   R. J. W. Henry, J. Phys. B Lett., accepted for publication (1979).
5.   R. D. Cowan and J. B. Mann, Astrophys. J, accepted for publication (1979).
6.   L. B. Golden and D. H. Sampson, J. Phys. B 10, 2229 (1977).
7.   W. Lotz, Z. Phys. 216, 241 (1968).

DI-ELECTRONIC RECOMBINATION OF H -LIKE IONS

J. Dubau and L. Steenman-Clark

Observatoire de Paris, 92190-Meudon, France

Observatoire de Nice, BP 252 06007-Nice Cedex, France

In the last few years there has been considerable interest in the spectra of
H-like and He-like ions and the associated satellite lines which are due to transitions from doubly excited configurations. Resonance lines and Satellite lines
of elements ranging from Mg through Fe fall between $\sim$1.6 and 23 Å and these lines
are important features in Solar flares and Tokamak spectra in the X-ray region.
The satellite lines of H-like ions near to the resonance L_α arise from transitions
of the type, 1snl - 2pnl for n $\geqslant$ 2. For larger values of n for example n $>$ 4, these
lines are blended with L_α and therefore contribute to the L_α apparent intensity.
Gabriel (1972) has shown that the ratios of the satellite lines to the apparent
resonance line of the H-like ions can be used to determine accurately the electron
temperature of the emitting plasma as long as this temperature can be defined for
the evolving plasma. From He-like ions similar ratios give complementary information on the plasma parameters.

The main population mechanism of the doubly excited configurations of the
H-like satellite lines is di-electronic capture (inverse process to autoionisation)

$$1s + e \longrightarrow 2pnl$$

The complete process of di-electronic capture and the satellite line emission constitute what is known as di-electronic recombination which plays an important role
in the determination of ionisation abundance curves for steady state plasmas (
Summers, 1974, Jacobs et al., 1977).

The atomic physics data necessary for Gabriel's method of plasma analysis are,
for H-like ions, autoionisation probabilities for 2pnl and radiative probabilities
for 2pnl - 1snl and electron excitation cross sections rates for the 1s - 2p resonance line. Programs developed at University College London have been modified to
calculate such quantities. Other theoretical methods have been also used for comparison. Although the problem appears to be relatively simple, with one and two
electrons systems, major difficulties arise that necessitate a completely different approach for these cases : Firstly, the 2pnl configuration interacts very
strongly with the configuration 2snl' which do not decrease when n tends to infinity as the 2p and 2s ionisation limits are almost degenerate. This disturbing
feature has an effect both for determining the autoionisation probabilities and
the radiative probabilities. Some lines 1snl - 2snl are as intense as the dipole
transition 1snl - 2pnl. Secondly, another characteristic feature is that the more
tightly bound electron disturbes the " spectator " electron nl so much that " shake " processes are no longer negligible and give therefore rise to intense

1snl - 2pn'l where n' is slightly different from the n value. To extrapolate such results for higher values of n use was made of the " Quantum Defect Theory with long-range dipole interactions" developed by Dubau (1978).

So far data for more than 300 satellite lines have been obtained for Mg^{+11} and other calculations for Si^{+13} and Fe^{+25} are in progress.

Gabriel A.H., 1972, M. N. R. A. S., 160, 99

Summers H., 1974, M. N. R. A. S., 169, 663

Jacobs V.L., Davis J., Kepple P.C. and Blaha M., 1977, Astrophys. J., 211, 605

Dubau J., 1978, J. Phys. B., 11, 4095

DIELECTRONIC RECOMBINATION RATE FOR POSITIVE IONS

Y. Hahn, J. Gau, R. Luddy and J.A. Retter

Department of Physics, University of Connecticut
Storrs, Connecticut 06268 U.S.A.

Photocapture of electrons by ionic targets in a plasma proceeds either by a direct radiative recombination or by a dielectronic recombination (DR) involving initial excitation of inner-shell electrons followed by a radiative decay or cascade. Calculation of the DR rate α^{DR} for the Be-sequence has been carried out, extending the previous work[1] on Mo^{38+}, and also on the Ne-sequence. In particular, ionic targets Fe^{22+}, Ar^{14+}, and O^{4+} are studied using the general procedure developed earlier.[1] That is, a complete calculation of α^{DR} is first carried out using the simple angular-momentum-averaged (AMA) scheme, which is then followed by a more detailed calculation of a small number of dominant transitions selected from the AMA result using a specific coupling scheme. The AMA procedure tends to overestimate the rate, sometimes as much as a factor of two. We examine the errors involved in the AMA scheme and develop a systematic correction procedure. Unlike in the Ne-sequence, the Be-like ions are much more difficult to treat because of the near degeneracy among the L-shell electrons. The $\Delta n = 0$ transitions among the L-shell electrons are included using the quantum defect method, and its relative importance is studied as a function of the core charge Z_C. The scaling property and its breaking will be discussed, and the result compared with the phenomenological formulas of Burgess[2] and Merts.[3] A preliminary result on the relativistic corrections to α^{DR} will also be reported.

1. J. Gau, Y. Hahn, and J.A. Retter, to be published.

2. A. Burgess, Astro. J. 139, 776 (1964) and 141, 1588 (1965).

3. A.L. Merts, R.D. Cowan and N.H. Magee, Los Alamos Report, LA-6220-MS.

EXCITATION OF THE AUTOIONIZING STATES OF ALKALI ATOMS BY FAST ELECTRONS IN (e,2e) PROCESS

V.V.Balashov and A.N.Grum-Grzhimailo

Institute of Nuclear Physics, Moscow State University, Moscow
117234; USSR

The theory of excitation and decay of autoionizing states of
atoms in scattering of fast electrons which has been developed
for helium[1] is used to calculate the spectra of electrons detected
in coincidence during the ionization of sodium and lithium atoms
in the range of low-lying autoionizing states. Previously, the
excitation of such states in the (e,2e) process has been studied
experimentally[2-4] and theoretically[5-7] for inert gas atoms.

The dependence of the autoionizing resonance profiles on the
kinematics of process is studied. The angular correlation
functions between the scattered and ejected electrons in the
range of autoionizing states have been obtained.

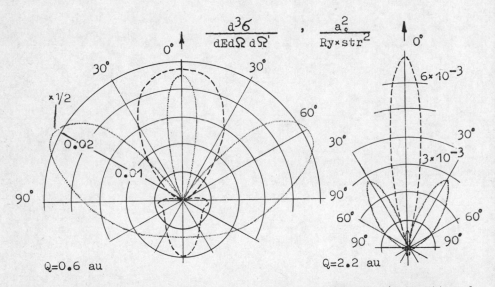

Fig.1. Function of the angular correlation between the scattered
       and ejected electrons for sodium. The ejected electron
       energy is 25.8 ev. Arrows indicate the direction of the
       momentum transfer Q. ---- calculation using the Hartree-
       Fock wave functions; ·········· plane-wave calculation

The calculations have been made in the Born approximation. The Hartree-Fock wave functions were used for the bound-state atomic electron and the continuum. Direct ionization in the range of autoionizing states was studied separately. The effect of distortions in the wave function for the ejected electron on the shape of the correlation function is discussed. To give an example, we show in fig.1 the angular correlation functions for the direct ionization of sodium by 1-keV electrons in the range of the $1s^2 2s^2 2p^5 3s^2$ state for two values of the momentum transfer Q.

A comparative characteristic of the correlation functions for the atoms of alkali metals and inert gases is given.

1. Balashov V.V.,Lipovetsky S.S. and Senashenko V.S., Sov.Phys. JETP, 36,858,1973
2. Weigold E.,Ugbabe A. and Teubner P.J.O., Phys.Rev.Lett.,35, 209,1975
3. Dillon A.M. and Lassetre E.N., J.Chem.Phys.,67,680,1977
4. Jung K.,Schubert E. and Ehrhardt E.,Abstracts of papers X ICPEAC, Paris,1977,p.670
5. Balashov V.V.,Lipovetsky S.S. and Senashenko V.S., Phys.Lett., 39A,103,1972
6. Balashov V.V. et al, Phys.Lett.,67A,266,1978
7. Balashov V.V. et al, J.Phys.B (in press)

ANGULAR CORRELATIONS BETWEEN SCATTERED AND EJECTED ELECTRONS
IN ELECTRON IMPACT AUTOIONISATION OF CADMIUM VAPOUR

N.L.S.Martin and K.J.Ross

Department of Physics, The University, Southampton, England

A new electron-electron coincidence spectrometer has been used to investigate the angular distributions of the ejected and scattered electrons arising in the autoionising process

$$Cd\,(4d^{10}5s^2) + e \rightarrow Cd(4d^9 5s^2 5p)\,^3P + e_{scattered}$$
$$\downarrow$$
$$Cd^+\,(4d^{10}5s) + e_{ejected}\,(3.82\ eV)$$

where the ionisation potential of cadmium is 8.99 eV.

Figure (1) shows the scattered electron intensity for an angular range of 10° about zero and an incident electron energy of 150 eV. Also shown is a theoretical curve which assumes the validity of the dipole approximation[1]. This predicts that the differential cross-section is proportional to the inverse square of the momentum transfer

$$d\sigma/d\theta_{sc} \propto 1/K^2. \qquad\qquad (1)$$

In figure (2) the preliminary results are presented of the angular correlation between the scattered electrons, over an angular range of 10° about zero, and electrons ejected from the cadmium atom at 90° with respect to the incident electron beam of 150 eV. The theoretical curve shown in the figure was obtained from the theory of Balashov[2]. Since the $Cd5\,^3P$

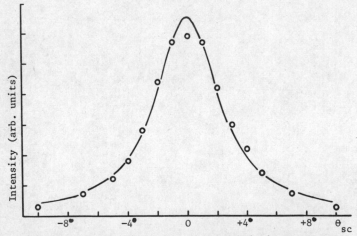

Fig.1. Scattered intensity for 150 eV incident electron energy. o experiment; ——— theory.

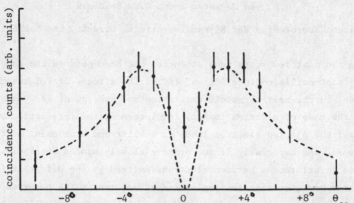

Fig. 2 Angular distribution of scattered electrons in θ_{sc} coincidence with ejected electrons at 90°. o experiment; - - - theory.

resonance is a very strong line in the autoionization spectrum of cadmium in a region of weak continuum[3], it is possible to neglect interference effects with the direct ionization process. The double differential cross section then takes the form[2]

$$d^2\sigma/d\theta_{sc}d\theta_{ej} \propto (d\sigma/d\theta_{sc}) \cos^2\theta_o \qquad (2)$$

where θ is the angle between the ejected electron and the momentum transfer vector $\underline{K}$. Assuming the dipole approximation[1] holds for the differential cross section $d\sigma/d\theta_{sc}$ this becomes

$$d^2\sigma/d\theta_{sc}d\theta_{ej} \sim (1/K^2) \cos^2\theta_o. \qquad (3)$$

This is the theoretical curve plotted in Fig. 2.

The experimental data in Fig. 2 have been normalised to the theoretical curve (Eq. 3) at $\theta_{sc} = +6^{\circ}$. The failure of the experimental curve to go to zero at $\theta_{sc} = 0^{\circ}$ reflects the finite angular resolution of the spectrometer.

1. M.Inokuti, Rev.Mod.Phys. 43, 297, (1971)
2. V.V.Balashov, S.S.Lipovetskii and V.S.Senashenko, Soviet Physics JETP 36, 858, (1973)
3. V.Pejcev, K.J.Ross, D.Rassi and T.W.Ottley, J.Phys.B: 10, 459, (1977)

TESTS OF SHAKE-DOWN AND SEMICLASSICAL MODEL FOR POST-COLLISION INTERACTION

W. van de Water and H.G.M. Heideman

Fysisch Laboratorium der Rijksuniversiteit, Utrecht, the Netherlands

During the past few years much attention has been paid to the so-called phenomenon of "post-collision interaction" (PCI). The effects of PCI become particularly evident in the near threshold excitation and subsequent decay of autoionizing
states. In the case of electron impact, for instance, the interaction between the
scattered and the ejected electron leads to a shift and broadening of the ejected
electron peaks; and especially if two or more closely spaced autoionizing states
are involved interferences between electrons emitted by the different (coherently)
excited states may give rise to complicated structures in the observed ejected
electron spectra. Recently two simple models, which greatly simplify the correlation between the two outgoing electrons and the residual ion, have been rather
succesful in reproducing the observed spectra. These are the "shake-down" model,
proposed by King et al[1] and the semiclassical model developed by Morgenstern et
al[2]. In the shake-down model the autoionization is viewed as an instantaneous
chance of the charge of the core and the probability for the scattered electron to
end up in a certain final state $\psi_f(\vec{k}_f)$ in the field of the ion is simply taken proportional to the square of the overlap of ψ_f with the initial state $\psi_i(\vec{k}_i)$ imme-
deately after the excitation of the autoionizing state. The semiclassical model
for PCI processes is based on a semiclassical description of the decay of an autoionizing state in the time-dependent field of the slowly receding scattered particle. The calculations based on the two models can be fitted to the experimental
data by adjusting a number of parameters involving various excitation (or ionization) amplitudes and their relative phases. For instance, in the case of the excitation of the (closely spaced) $(2s^2)^1S$ and $(2s2p)^3P$ autoionizing states of He by
electrons the cross section for production of ejected electrons with final momentum
$\vec{k}_f$ can be written as[3]: $\sigma \sim |a_s q_s + a_p q_p + b|^2 + |B|^2$, where a_s and a_p are proportional to the amplitudes for excitation of the ^1S and ^3P state, respectively, b
represents the coherent and B the incoherent component of the direct ionization
amplitude. The PCI amplitudes $q_{s,p}(\vec{k}_i \to \vec{k}_f)$ are provided by the model. It appears
that with both models very good fits to the measured spectra can be obtained by
adjusting the parameters a_s, a_p, b, B and their relative phases. There is no doubt
that the high quality of the fits is partly due to the large number of parameters
(6 in the above case).

In the present work we want to test the consistency of the models with the
measurements somewhat more thoroughly by measuring ejected electron spectra with
the electron spectrometer operating in three different modes. In mode 1 the incident electron energy E_o is kept constant while the ejected electron energy E_j is
scanned with the analyzer. In mode 2 the ejected electron energy is scanned with

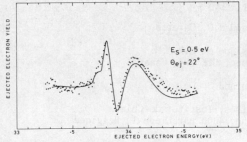

Fig. 1. Ejected electron spectrum of helium measured in mode 2 (see text). The full line represents a fit to the experimental data using the shake-down formula of ref. 3.

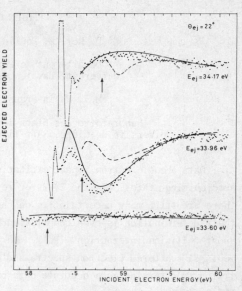

Fig. 2. Ejected electron spectra of helium measured in mode 3 at three ejected electron energies. The full and dashed lines represent calculations with the semiclassical and shake-down model, respectively and using parameters obtained from spectra taken in mode 2. The peaks at the left correspond to the excitation of singly excited states.

the incident energy varying at the same rate; in this mode the final energy E_s of the scattered electron is constant. Finally in mode 3 the analyzer is tuned so as to accept ejected electrons of a fixed energy while the incident energy is scanned. When now a set of parameters is found by fitting one of the models to a spectrum measured, say, in mode 1, it should be possible to reproduce with the same set of parameters the spectra measured in the other two modes (of course in corresponding energy ranges). Fig. 1 and 2 show the result of such a test for ejected electron spectra involving the $(2s^2)^1S$ and $(2s2p)^3P$ autoionizing states of helium. Fig. 1 shows a spectrum measured in mode 2; the ejection angle θ_{ej} was taken to be 22°. The full line represents a fit to the measurements using the shake-down formula of ref. 3; similar fits could be obtained when using the semiclassical model. With the parameters obtained from the fits we calculated for three ejected electron energies the spectra corresponding to mode 3. Fig. 2 shows the results together with the measurements. Apart from quantitative deviations in the 33.96 eV spectrum the semiclassical model appears to be consistent with the measurements. The shake-down calculations, however, exhibit some qualitative inconsistencies. This could be due to the fact that in the formula of ref. 3 asymptotic Coulomb wavefunctions were used.

1. G.C. King, F.H. Read and R.C. Bradford, J. Phys. B: Atom. Molec. Phys. **8**, 2210 (1975)

2. R. Morgenstern, A. Niehaus and U. Thielmann, J. Phys. B: Atom. Molec. Phys. **10**, 1039 (1977)

3. F.H. Read, J. Phys. B: Atom. Molec. Phys. **10**, L207 (1977)

ELECTRON IMPACT EXCITATION IN THE 24-29 eV

REGION OF ARGON*

D. Roy, A. Poulin and J.D. Carette

Département de Physique et C.R.A.M.
Université Laval, Québec, G1K 7P4, Canada

M.J. Hubin-Franskin and J. Delwiche

Laboratoire des Etats ionisés, Institut de Chimie
Université de Liège, Sart-Tilman, 4000 par Liège 1, Belgique

Data about electron impact excitation of argon are not very abundant for the autoionizing states. In the 24-29 eV region, where the $3s3p^6n\ell$ states are found, there are still many uncertainties on the energy positions of triplet terms and their determination is even complicated by the manifestations of the so-called "post-collision interaction" (PCI). We recently carried out a series of measurements of scattered electron spectra and ejected electron spectra in this region, trying to determine more accurate data on these states, in conditions where the PCI influence is weak.

The instrument used for these measurements is a high resolution electron spectrometer, involving cylindrical deflectors as monochromator and analyzer, and a static gas target[1]. The scattering angle was 2° and the energy resolution around 50 meV. Figure 1 presents an ejected spectrum and two energy loss (scattered electron) spectra. For the lower spectrum the incident electron energy was kept constant at 100 eV, while for the upper ones it was swept so as the residual (scattered) electron energy (E_r) was 10 eV for both. The energy calibration was carefully achieved by means of energy loss peaks caused by the excitation of the bound states $3p^54s(^1P)$ and $3p^53d$ through double collisions (features around 26 eV).

Since a series of spectra was measured for residual energies ranging from 2 to 70 eV, this makes possible to study the behaviour of the dominant features (shape, strength and position) as a function of the incident electron energy. Thus it is believed that the spectra measured for E_r = 10 eV (Fig. 1) are not influenced by the PCI, and that the dominant features therein are rather caused by triplet terms. The feature peaked at 26.56 eV is in agreement with the observation reported by Wilden *et al.*[2]. A curve fitting carried out on this feature by Marchand and Cardinal[3] places the energy of the state at 26.58 eV, with a width of about 80 meV (larger than the evaluation of 40 meV obtained by Wilden *et al.*[2]). Even though the position of the ^1P term determined by Madden *et al.*[4] at 26.61 eV is very near (it is observed at 26.62 eV in the lower spectrum of Fig. 1), we believe that the two features are distinct because of the behaviour observed as a function of the excitation energy.

*Work supported by the National Research Council of Canada, Ministère de l'Education du Québec and Coopération belgo-québécoise.

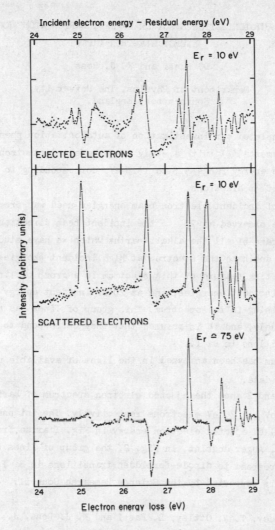

Fig. 1. Ejected electron and scattered electron spectra measured
in argon at a scattering angle of 2°. E_r is the residual
scattered electron energy. For the lower energy loss spectrum, the incident electron energy was kept constant at
100 eV, while it was properly swept for the two upper spectra.

References

1. D. Roy, A. Delâge and J.D. Carette, J. Phys. E **8**, 109 (1975).
2. D.G. Wilden, J. Comer and P.J. Hicks, Nature **273**, 651 (1978).
3. P. Marchand and J. Cardinal (to be published).
4. R.P. Madden, D.L. Ederer, and K. Codling, Phys. Rev. **177**, 136 (1969).

THE AUGER AND AUTOIONIZATION SPECTRUM OF FREE BARIUM ATOMS EXCITED BY LOW
ENERGY ELECTRON IMPACT

D. Rassi and K. J. Ross

Department of Physics, The University,
Southampton, England.

We have completed our investigation of autoionization phenomena in the
alkali-earth elements[1,2,3] with a study of the ejected electron spectrum
of barium in the energy range 5.5 to 15.5 eV, corresponding to the ionization
and excitation of 5p electrons.

The range of incident electron beam energies used was from 15 to 500 eV,
and spectra were observed at 75° to the incident beam direction.

As in the case of all the alkali-earths which we have studied previously
the Auger lines dominate the spectrum at high incident energies. Perhaps
the most interesting feature of this spectrum is a group of lines which
appears at low incident energies, and at 20 eV incident energy are the
only lines remaining in the spectrum. This group of lines has not been
observed previously, and it is assumed that they correspond to dipole-
forbidden transitions in Ba I.

The spectrum has been analyzed in the light of available ultraviolet
and theoretical data.

Figures I and 2 show the ejected electron spectrum of barium vapour
excited by 500 eV and 20 eV electrons respectively. The intense lines at
7.47 eV and 9.54 eV ejected electron energy in Fig. I arise from the
$5p^5 6s^2\ ^2P_{3/2,1/2}$ Auger doublet. In Fig. 2, the group of lines between 10 eV
and 10.5 eV correspond to dipole-forbidden transitions in Ba I.

This work is supported by the Science Research Council.

1. V. Pejcev, T. W. Ottley, D. Rassi and K. J. Ross, J. Phys. B:
    Atom. Molec. Phys. 10, 2389 (1977).

2. V. Pejcev, T. W. Ottley, D. Rassi and K. J. Ross, J. Phys. B:
    Atom. Molec. Phys. 11, 531 (1978).

3. M. D. White, D. Rassi and K. J. Ross, J. Phys. B:
    Atom. Molec. Phys. 12, 315 (1979).

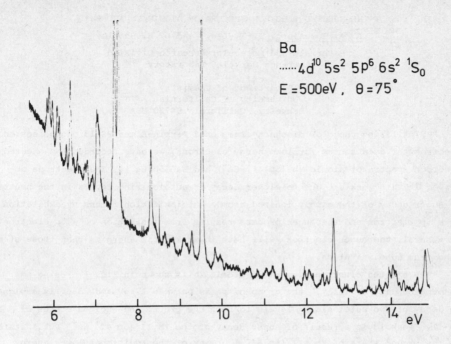

Ba
......$4d^{10}\,5s^2\,5p^6\,6s^2\ ^1S_0$
$E = 500\,eV,\quad \theta = 75°$

Fig. 1   Photograph of the spectrum of barium at 500 eV
incident electron energy

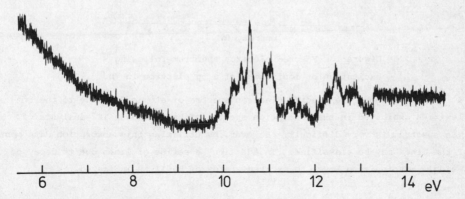

Ba
......$4d^{10}\,5s^2\,5p^6\,6s^2\ ^1S_0$
$E = 20\ eV,\quad \theta = 75°$

Fig. 2   Photograph of the spectrum of barium at 20 eV
incident electron energy

THE EJECTED ELECTRON SPECTRA OF ATOMIC Yb AND Ba*

R. A. Rosenberg, S.-T. Lee,[+] and D. A. Shirley

Materials and Molecular Research Division
Lawrence Berkeley Laboratory
and
Department of Chemistry
University of California
Berkeley, California 94720 USA

By utilizing the glow discharge lamp on a Perkin-Elmer PS-18 photoelectron spectrometer as a source for low energy electrons,[1] we have recorded the ejected electron spectra of atomic Yb ($5p^6 4f^{14} 6s^2$) and Ba ($5p^6 6s^2$). The electrons observed in this work are due to either decay of autoionizing levels in the neutral or Auger decay of the singly ionized atom. Autoionization occurs by excitation of a 5p electron and the Auger process results from ionization of a 5p electron. In general, the Auger electrons will have lower kinetic energies than those stemming from autoionization.

The ejected electron spectra of atomic Yb is shown in Fig. 1. Using the absorption data of Tracy,[2] the group of peaks between 17 eV and 23 eV is assigned to decay of two autoionizing levels to both the ground and excited states of Yb II. Peak 13 is a result of Auger decay of the Yb II ($5p^5 4f^{14} 6s^2\ ^2P_{3/2}$) state to the ground state of Yb III ($5p^6 4f^{14}$). Many of the additional lower energy peaks may be assigned to Auger decay to excited states of Yb III ($5p^6 4f^{13} n\ell$).

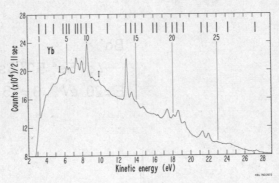

Figure 1. Ejected electron spectrum following
excitation or ionization of a 5p electron in Yb.

Figure 2 shows the ejected electron spectra of atomic Ba. Due to the complexities exhibited in the absorption spectra of Ba I[3] and Ba II[4] analysis of this spectrum is very difficult. However, by utilizing this absorption data most of the lines may be classified. In addition, a series of lines due to decay of a single autoionizing level to excited states of Ba II is indicated.

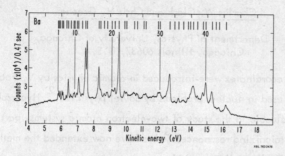

Figure 2. Ejected electron spectrum following
excitation or ionization of a 5p electron in Ba.

*This work was done with support from the Division of Chemical Sciences, Office of Basic Energy Sciences, U. S. Department of Energy, under contract No. W-7405-Eng-48.

†Permanent address: Eastman Kodak Research Labs., 1999 Lake Avenue, Rochester, New York 14615.

1. S.-T. Lee, R. A. Rosenberg, E. Matthias, and D. A. Shirley, J. Elec. Spec. and Rel. Phen. 10, 203 (1977).

2. D. H. Tracy, Proc. R. Soc. Lond. A 357, 485 (1977).

3. J. P. Connerade, M.W.D. Mansfield, G. H. Newsom, D. H. Tracy, M. A. Baig, and K. Thimm, Phil. Trans. R. Soc. Lond. A 290, 327 (1979).

4. R. A. Roig, J. Opt. Soc. Am. 66, 1400 (1976).

HYPERSPHERICAL APPROACH TO THREE ELECTRON DYNAMICS*

Charles W. Clark and Chris H. Greene

Department of Physics, University of Chicago,
Chicago, Illinois 60637, U.S.A.

Hyperspherical coordinates were introduced in atomic physics by V. Fock,[1] and have since been extensively used in nuclear problems by Soviet physicists.[2] Hyperspherical methods have proven valuable in the study of two-electron atomic systems, particularly in the classification of autoionizing resonances.[3] We have now extended the method to three-electron systems, specifically to He⁻ and Li I.

The hyperspherical coordinate system is chosen in analogy to that of Macek and Lin, by introducing the mock angles $\alpha_1 = \tan^{-1}(r_2/r_1)$, $\alpha_2 = \tan^{-1}[(r_1^2 + r_2^2)^{\frac{1}{2}}/r_3]$ and the hyper-radius $R = (r_1^2 + r_2^2 + r_3^2)^{\frac{1}{2}}$, where r_1, r_2, r_3 are the distances of the electrons from the nucleus. In this coordinate system the total kinetic energy operator (in a.u.) is separable:

$$T = -\tfrac{1}{2}\left\{\frac{d^2}{dR^2} + \frac{8}{R}\frac{d}{dR} - \frac{\Lambda^2}{R^2}\right\} \; .$$

Here Λ^2, the "grand angular momentum", operates on the two mock angles and the six angles describing the orientation of the three electrons in space. Its eigenvalues are $n(n+7)$ where $n \geq 0$ is an integer. Specification of the total electronic spin restricts the choice of n. For example, for quartet states the electronic spatial wavefunction must be completely anti-symmetric; so then for s waves $n = 6, 10, 12, 14, \cdots$, and the eigenfunctions are combinations of the spherical harmonics in the mock angles.

We have diagonalized the atomic Hamiltonian in this basis at fixed R, to obtain potential curves analogous to those calculated by Lin for two electron systems. Results for Li ^{4}S states are shown in the figure, and further work will be presented at the conference. These three curves correspond to the Rydberg series 1s2sns, 1s3sns, and 1s4sns. The Rydberg states associated with the upper two curves will autoionize to the continuum of the lowest curve. The narrowly avoided crossing at R ~ 6 a.u. suggests that the 1s3sns series members have "−" character,[3] and thus should autoionize more slowly than the 1s4sns series, in contrast to the usual case.

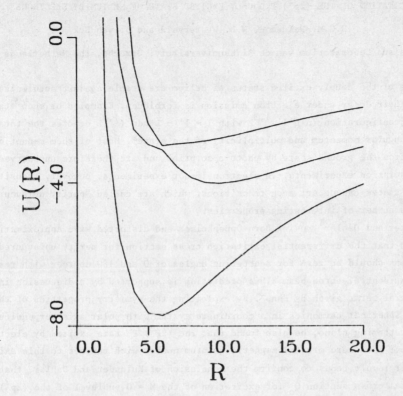

* Work supported by the Department of Energy, Office of Basic Energy Sciences.

1. V. Fock, Kgl. Norske Vidensk. Selsk. Forh. 31, 145 (1958).

2. Yu. F. Smirnov and K. V. Shitikova, Sov. J. Part. Nucl. 8, 344 (1977).

3. J. Macek, J. Phys. B 1, 831 (1968); C. D. Lin, Phys. Rev. A 10, 1986 (1974);
   C. D. Lin, Phys. Rev. Lett. 35, 1150 (1975); H. Klar and M. Klar, Phys. Rev.
   A 17, 1007 (1978).

EXCITATION OF THE $(2p^2)^3P$ DOUBLY EXCITED STATE OF HELIUM BY ELECTRONS

H.G.M. Heideman, W.B. Westerveld and J. van Eck

Fysisch Laboratorium van de Rijksuniversiteit, Utrecht, the Netherlands

Some of the doubly excited states of helium are stable against autoionization because their decay under electron emission is forbidden. Examples of such states have the configuration $(nln'l')^{1,3}L$ with $1 + 1' - L$ odd ($^{1,3}L$ denotes the total orbital angular momentum and multiplicity of the state). Most of them cannot be excited from the ground state by photo-absorption and are therefore unobserved in photo-absorption experiments. In electron impact experiments, however, transitions to these states can occur; such transitions, which are called "parity unfavoured", exhibit a number of interesting properties.

Becker and Dahler[1], using Born-Oppenheimer and distorted wave approximations, predicted that the differential excitation cross section for parity unfavoured transitions should be zero for scattering angles of 0 and 180 degrees with respect to the incident electron beam. This prediction is supported by a discussion in more general terms given by Fano[2]. By exploiting the symmetry properties of the relevant spherical harmonics in a coordinate system with polar axis perpendicular to the scattering plane, he also found that the $(2P^2)^3P$ state excited by electron impact must have zero orbital magnetic quantum number with respect to this axis. The latter result tends to confirm the conclusion of Kulander and Dahler[3] that the partial cross section Q_o for excitation of the $M = 0$ sublevel of the $(2p^2)^3P$ state should be zero (quantization axis along the electron beam). This would have the consequence that the polarization of the radiation emitted in the decay of the $(2p^2)^3P$ state is independent of the incident electron energy.

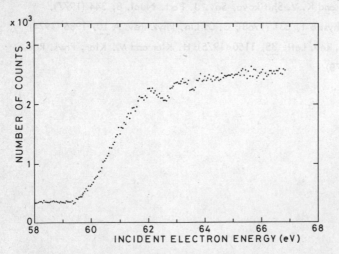

The aim of the present work is to obtain more detailed information on the impact excitation of parity unfavoured doubly excited states than is provided by the spectroscopic studies performed till now. We have studied the excitation of the $(2p^2)^3P$ state of helium in the energy range from threshold to 150 eV.

Fig. 1. Excitation of the doubly excited $(2p^2)^3P$ state of helium by electrons in the energy range near threshold.

This was done by observing with a VUV spectrometer the radiation at 32 nm emitted in the decay of that state to the $(1s2p)^3P$ singly excited state.

Fig. 1 shows our results in the threshold region. Just above 62 eV and below 64 eV clear resonance structures occur. They are most probably due to triply excited negative ion states having the configurations $(2s3s3p)^2P$ or $(2s3p)^2P$ (^2D). The $(2s3s^2)^2S$ and $(2s3p^2)^2S$ states must be ruled out since their decay to the $(2p^2)^3P$ state is parity forbidden. Ormonde et al[4] calculated energies of 62.95 and 63.45 eV for the $(2s3p^2)^2D$ and $(2s3s3p)^2P$ states, respectively.

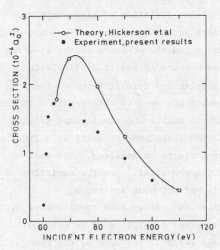

Fig. 2. Comparison of relative experimental cross sections for excitation of the $(2p^2)^3P$ state of He with Born-Oppenheimer calculations (ref. 5). The experimental data are normalized to the calculations at 110 eV.

In fig. 2 we compare the energy behaviour of our experimental $(2p^2)^3P$ cross section with recent calculations by Hickerson et al[5]. The relative measurements have been normalized to the theoretical cross section at 110 eV. The calculations were performed using the Born-Oppenheimer approximation. For the ground state of the helium atom a 20-term configuration interaction wave function was used and for the excited state a hydrogenic wave function. It is clear from the figure that the agreement between theory and experiment is rather poor. Further work is clearly needed.

More results (hopefully also on the polarization of the $(2p^2)^3P \rightarrow (1s2p)^3P$ radiation) and their interpretation will be presented at the conference.

This work is sponsored by FOM with financial support from Z.W.O.

1. P.M. Becker and J.S. Dahler, Phys. Rev. 136, A73 (1964)

2. U. Fano, Phys. Rev. 135, B863 (1964)

3. K.C. Kulander and J.S. Dahler, Phys. Rev. A6, 1436 (1972)

4. S. Ormonde, F. Kets and H.G.M. Heideman, Phys. Lett. 50A, 147 (1974)

5. D.L. Hickerson, L. Mlodinov and J.S. Dahler, J. Phys. B: Atom. Molec. Phys. 11, 2377 (1978)

ELECTRON ENERGY LOSS STUDIES OF THE EXCITATION OF AUTOIONIZING
STATES IN NEON AND ARGON

P. Mitchell,* J.A. Baxter and J. Comer

Physics Department, University of Manchester, Manchester
M139PL, England.

The studies reported here are concerned with the excitation by electron
impact of the autoionizing states $2s2p^6 3s$, $2s2p^6 3p$ in neon and $3s3p^6 4s$,
$3s3p^6 4p$ in argon. Several recent studies of the variation of line shape and
intensity of autoionizing states in the inert gases have been made by observing
the ejected electrons[1,2,3], but in neon and argon the presence in the ejection
spectrum of two closely spaced lines for each state makes it difficult to
resolve nearby energy levels such as the singlet and triplet terms of the
configurations listed above. In the present study spectra were recorded in the
energy loss mode with sufficient resolution to enable the singlet and triplet
terms to be resolved and the variation of line shape and intensity as a function
of incident electron energy and scattering angle to be measured. The only
previous energy loss results are those of Simpson et al.[4] on the variation of
intensity with energy for various states in helium, neon and argon.

The apparatus used is a conventional electron energy loss spectrometer with
energy selector and analyser providing a combined resolution of 50 meV and
variation of scattering angle over the range $0-110^0$. For each of the four
configurations studied spectra were recorded at a range of angles at 10 eV
above threshold and for a range of energies at 5^0 scattering angle. In
addition an angular scan at 20 eV above threshold was recorded for the neon 3s
configuration. Each spectrum was fitted to a pair of Beutler-Fano profiles
representing the singlet and triplet terms in order to extract the line shape
parameters and intensities.

Notable features of the results include (a) pronounced angular dependence of
the intensity, particularly in the s states where minima similar to those in the
differential cross-section for the excitation of bound states occur (b) quite
different angular variation of the singlet and triplet terms of a single
configuration eg in Ne 3p (c) rapid variation of line shape with angle for the
^{1}S terms near the regions of minimum intensity (d) an apparent inversion of the
^{1}S and ^{3}S terms in neon with the ^{3}S lying above the ^{1}S.

* Permanent address: School of Physics, University of New South Wales,
                    Kensington, NSW 2033, Australia.

1. F. Gelebart, R.J. Tweed and J. Peresse, J. Phys. B: Atomic Molec. Phys.
    9, 1739 (1976).

2. R.J. Tweed, F. Gelebart and J. Peresse, J. Phys. B: Atomic Molec. Phys.
    9,2643 (1976).

3. N. Oda, S. Tahira, F. Nishimura and F. Koike, Phys. Rev. 15A, 574 (1977).

4. J.A. Simpson, G.E. Chamberlain and S.R. Mielczarek, Phys. Rev. 139A, 1039 (1965).

CORRELATION STUDY OF "GIANT RESONANCE" IN La

V.V. Balashov, N.M. Kabachnik, I.P. Sazhina and A.N. Tkatchov
Institute of Nuclear Physics, Moscow State University;
Moscow 117234; USSR

Up to the present the nature of the "giant resonances" in photo-absorption spectra of La and nearby atoms in the soft X-ray region has been of a great interest. Discussed in this contribution are various possible correlation experiments which can yield additional information about such resonances. The experience gained with the autoionizing states shows[1] that most significant information may be obtained by studying the triple differential cross sections (TDCS) for inelastic scattering of fast electrons, i.e. by studying the excitation of the resonances in the experiments of the (e,2e) type. TDCS has been calculated for La ionization by electron impact near the $N_{IV,V}$ thresholds in terms of the Born approximation. The dependence of the resonance shape on momentum transfer and ejected electron emission angle is examined. The spectra of scattered and ejected electrons are also calculated . Angular distributions of photoelectron for photoionization of La are discussed. The anisotropy coefficient of photoelectrons has been shown to be sensitive to the model used in describing the giant resonance.

1. V.V. Balashov et al. Proc. of Coherence and Correlation Workshop (ed. Kleinpoppen), London, 1977.

A SINGLE PARTICLE PROJECTION OPERATOR-SADDLE POINT TECHNIQUE

FOR MULTIPLY EXCITED STATES

Kwong T. Chung

Department of Physics, North Carolina State University
Raleigh, North Carolina 27650 USA

The autoionizing states of a quantum system in a multiply excited state with vacancies in the inner shell have energies lying in the continuum.[1] To calculate this state a simple and accurate method is developed. Instead of making the closed channel wave function orthogonal to the open channels, the orbital vacancies in the excited state are directly built into the wave function. For example, if we represent a vacancy by a single particle wave function $\phi_o(\vec{r})$, then

$$\psi' = A(1-P_o(\vec{r}_j)) \, \psi(\vec{r}_1, \vec{r}_2, \ldots \vec{r}_j, \ldots \vec{r}_n) \tag{1}$$

where

$$P_o(\vec{r}) = |\phi_o(\vec{r})><\phi_o(\vec{r})|$$

is a wave function with this vacancy. A is the antisymmetrization operator. It is assumed that particle j has the same symmetry as ϕ_o and it is the only particle that may fill the vacancy.

If Eq. (1) is used with the Rayleigh-Ritz variation method, the lowest eigenvalue will correspond to the lowest state with that vacancy. The higher eigenvalues approximate the higher excited states in accordance with the MacDonald theorem.[2] To determine the vacancy orbital $\phi_o(\vec{r})$ we utilize the following theorem:

Let $H(\vec{r})$ be a Hermitian operator with normalized eigenfunctions $\psi_o(\vec{r})$, $\psi_1(\vec{r})$, $\ldots \psi_i(\vec{r}) \ldots$ and corresponding non-degenerate eigenvalues $E_o, E_1 \ldots E_i \ldots$. Define a normalized function

$$\phi_o(\vec{r}) = \sum_{j=0}^{N} t_j \psi_j(\vec{r})$$

for any $N \geq 1$. Let the eigenvalues of the secular equation of H in the subspace orthogonal to ϕ_o be $\lambda_1, \lambda_2 \ldots \lambda_i \ldots$, then $\underline{\lambda_i \text{ is an extremum and } \lambda_i = E_i \text{ when } t_i = 0}$.

It can be shown that if the lower state is what we wish to project out, then λ_i appears as a maximum. This theorem can be generalized to many electron systems as well as many vacancy systems.

In actual calculation, a certain functional form for $\phi_o(\vec{r})$ is assumed with one or more parameters q. By varying q we try to locate the maximum for each λ_i. To apply the Rayleigh-Ritz variation method, an unprojected trial function of linear combination of basis set with linear parameters c and non-linear parameter α is assumed. One can show that for attractive coulomb potential the energy is a minimum with respect to the variation of α and c. By minimizing the energy expression of the projected wave function with respect to the linear parameters a secular equation is obtained. The solution to this equation will be a function of α and q. The present theorem suggests that the true eigenvalue of the hamiltonian appears as a saddle point, which occurs for a minimum of α and a maximum of q.

We can make a theoretical test for this method using a two electron system. For example, the He(1s2s)^{1}S has a 1s vacancy. The energy of this state can be calculated with the saddle point technique. On the other hand, it can also be computed accurately with the MacDonald theorem.[2] Calculating with the same wave function the two results can be compared. The reliability of the saddle point technique can thus be assured. Calculation has been carried out for (1s2s)^{1}S for He, Li$^+$, Be^{++}, (1s3s)^{1}S and (1s3p)^{3}P for He. The disagreement between the results of the two methods all occur at the sixth or seventh digit.

For three electron systems, a multi-configuration interaction calculation is carried out. For example, for the single vacancy problem, the Li(1s2s2p)^{2}P state is calculated. The energy obtained is -5.3114 a.u. which is 58.954 eV above the ground state of Li. The experimental result is 58.91 ± 0.03 eV.[3] For double vacancy state, the He$^-$ (2s2s2p)^{2}P is calculated, the energy is 57.31 eV above the ground state of helium. The experimental result ranges from 57.1 to 57.2 eV.[4] We also found (2s2p2p)^{4}P of He$^-$ to be a closed channel resonance state. The energy for this state is -.79310 a.u. It is lower than the He(2s2p)^{3}P threshold energy by about 0.88 eV.

1. U. Fano, Phys. Rev. 124, 1866 (1961).
2. J.K.L. MacDonald, Phys. Rev. 43, 830 (1933).
3. D.J. Pegg, et al. Phys. Rev. A12, 1330 (1975); D.L. Ederer, et al. Phys. Rev. Lett. 25, 1537 (1970).
4. C.E. Kuyatt, et al., Phys. Rev. 138, A385 (1965); J.J. Quemener, et al., Phys. Rev. A4, 494 (1971).

A NEW VARIATIONAL TECHNIQUE FOR THE COMPLEX COORDINATE METHOD

B. R. Junker

ONR Code 421
800 N. Quincy St.
Arlington, VA., 22217

Doolen et al[1] suggested that one technique by which one could sort out
the approximate complex resonant energies (complex poles of the resolvent) from
the other eigenvalues obtained from a variational procedure based on the complex
coordinate method was to look for cusps or quasistationary behavior in the "θ-tra-
jectories". That is, although the resonant energies are suppose to be independent of θ, the basis (real functions of r) used by Doolen et al results in approximate resonant energies with a θ-dependence and they suggest that the best value is in the region of the complex energy plane where the dependence on θ is
minimized, particularly if several different wavefunctions produce this behavior
in the same region. We[2] have shown that the exact resonant wavefunction is, in
fact, a <u>complex</u> function of $r\,e^{i\theta}$, depending on r and θ only in this combination.
Thus in Doolen's basis this θ-dependence in the resonant wavefunction is forced
to be approximated in the complex linear coefficients. An alternate way of viewing their calculation is the following. They use a basis which is independent of
θ and spans a certain vector space. On the other hand, the resonant wavefunction
of the complex Hamiltonian, $H(\theta)$, is a function of θ. In general then their basis describes some θ-dependent component of the exact resonant wavefunction and
the quasistationary behavior arises when that component, i.e. the overlap, is
probably a maximum with respect to the exact resonant wavefunction.

If one uses a basis such as suggested by Doolen et al one can transform the
complex coordinate problem back to a real Hamiltonian, H, and a complex basis.
Since the basis functions vanish at infinity the same results are obtained on the
real r-axis, i. e., for $\theta = 0$. In fact recent calculations[3] have used Hermitian Hamiltonians with complex basis functions which contained a θ-parameter and
did not satisfy the asymptotic boundary condition for the resonant wavefunction
yet reproduced resonant eigenvalues with the above mentioned θ-behavior. The

role of θ can be interpreted in the following way. First it produces a complex basis which is <u>required</u> to represent the resonant wavefunction as mentioned above and second it serves as a <u>variational</u> parameter. In the region of θ where the basis best represents the exact resonant wavefunction one observes the quasistationary behavior.

Based on these interpretations of previous calculations, a more direct and faster converging calculational technique would be the following. Construct the variational wavefunction as we have previously suggested[2,4]. Then variation of the various nonlinear parameters in $\overset{\theta}{Q}$ should have little affect on the scatter-state energies while only those nonlinear parameters in the principal configurations characterizing the resonant should affect the resonant energies. For these parameters it is hoped that one would observe the same type of quasistationary behavior as observed in previous calcualtions. Variation of the parameter p in $\overset{\theta}{P}$ should cause the scattering energies to decrease when it is decreased and to increase when it is increased. The resonant energies should be relatively insensitive to this parameter if $\overset{\theta}{P}$ is sufficiently flexible. This behavior with respect to p has already been demonstrated[4]. Thus variation of the various nonlinear parameters and the observation of their effect on the eigenvalues of the secular equation should allow one to separate those eigenvalues approximating resonant states from those approximating scattering states and provide a means for selecting the optimum nonlinear parameters. Results from previous calculations[3] also indicate that this technique should work for $\theta = 0$. This is extremely important because this would eliminate the difficulties in applying the complex coordinate method to molecules.

These ideas are being tested with a model potential similar to that of Doolen[5] and on the $1s(2s)^2$ ^2S resonance in He^-.

1 G. D. Doolen, J. Nuttall, and R. W. Stagat, Phys. Rev. <u>A10</u>, 1612(1974).

2 B. R. Junker, Int. J. Quant. Chem. <u>XIV</u>, 371(1978).

3 C. W. McCurdy, Jr. and T. N. Rescigno, Phys. Rev. Lett. <u>41</u>, 1364(1978).

4 B. R. Junker and C. L. Huang, Phys. Rev. <u>A18</u>, 313(1978).

5 G. D. Doolen, Int. J. Quant. Chem. <u>XIV</u>, 523(1978).

RELATIONSHIP BETWEEN THE LIFETIMES OF THE $(1s2s2p)^4P_{3/2}$ AND $P_{1/2}$ AUTOIONIZATION STATES OF THREE-ELECTRON SYSTEMS

N.V. Orlova[+], U.I. Safonova[++], V.S. Senashenko[+] and G.A. Simonov[+]

+ Institute of Nuclear Physics, Moscow State University; Moscow 117234;

++Institute of Spectroscopy, USSR Academy of Sciences, Podol'sky district, Moscow, USSR

Long-lived autoionization states with different decay periods have been observed in three-electron atomic systems. The states are identified with the $(1s2s2p)^4P_j$ (j = 5/2, 3/2, 1/2) configuration levels[1-4]. The relationship between the lifetimes of the $^4P_{3/2}$ and $^4P_{1/2}$ states has been found to vary from Li atoms to lithium-like Ne ions. The available theoretical estimates[5,6] fail to agree with the experimental data[2,4] and, therefore, detailed theoretical calculations of the $^4P_{3/2}$ and $^4P_{1/2}$ state lifetimes have become necessary. Reported in this work are the results of the calculations of the probabilities of the radiative and non-radiative decay and the lifetime of the $(1s2s2p)^4P_{3/2}$ and $^4P_{1/2}$ antionization states of three-electron systems with atomic numbers Z = 3 - 30 including the direct transitions to continuum and the transitions induced by mixing the long-lived quarted and short-lived doublet states in spin-orbital interactions. The effects of the various decay channels on the lifetimes (τ_j) of the examined states have been studied. The 3/2 and 1/2 level lifetimes of the ions with Z > 20 have been shown to be determined in practice completely by the radiative transition rates, whereas the autoionization decay prevails for the ions with Z < 10. At 10 < Z < 20, the lifetime of metastable levels are significantly affected by both radiative and autoionization transitions. The calculations have shown that at Z > 10 $\tau_{3/2} < \tau_{1/2}$, at Z $\simeq$ 9 these life-times become comparable, and at Z < 9 their relationship reverses, i.e. $\tau_{3/2} > \tau_{1/2}$ In this case, the probability ratio of the direct autoionization decays of the $^4P_{3/2}$ and $^4P_{1/2}$ levels is practically unchained with varying Z, while the observable behaviour of the lifetimes depending on Z is determined by the probability ratio of induced autoionization transitions. Analysis of the structure of the eigenvectors of the $^4P_{3/2}$ and $^4P_{1/2}$ states obtained to the intermediate coupling has shown that the admixture of the $(1s2s2p)$ $^2P_-$ and $^2P_+$ states in the $^4P_{1/2}$ wave function varies little with Z, whereas the admixture of the $^2P_-$ state in the $^4P_{1/2}$ wave function increases by a factor of almost 2 from Z =3 to Z=12. It is this circumstance that results in a more rapid decrease of the $^4P_{3/2}$,lifetime

with increasing Z, thereby explaining the experimental relationship between the $^4P_{3/2,1/2}$ state lifetimes[2,4] .

REFERENCES

1. L.M. Blau, R. Novick and D. Weinflash. Phys.Rev.Lett.24,1268(1970)
2. M. Levitt, R. Novick and P.D. Feldman.Phys.Rev.3A,130(1971)
3. I.S. Dmitriev, Ya.A. Teplova, V.S.Nikolaev, JETP, 61,1359 (1971)
4. K.O. Groneveld, G. Nolte, S.Schuman. Jahresbericht,IKF-35,57(1975)
5. V.V. Balashov, V.S. Senashenko and B. Tekou.Phys.Lett.25A,417(1967)
6. S.T. Manson   Phys.Rev.3A, 147(1971).

AUGER-ELECTRON SPECTRA OF RARE-GAS ATOMS
BY ELECTRON IMPACT NEAR THRESHOLD

H. Suzuki, M. Muto, T. Takayanagi, and K. Wakiya

Department of Physics, Sophia University, Chiyoda-ku, Tokyo 102 Japan

and

S. Ohtani

Institute of Plasma Physics, Nagoya University, Nagoya 464 Japan

Influence of slowly receding electron(s) on Auger decay process, which is
an analogy with the post collision interaction effect in autoionization process,[1]
appeals to physical interests for several authors.[2-5] Auger-electron spectroscopy
revealed an occurence of the energy shift and the broadening in Auger peaks when
the impact energies of electrons or photons are lowered close to the threshold.[2,3]

In the Auger-electron peaks Xe $N_{4,5}OO$ induced by photoionization, on one hand,
Schmidt et al. observed an asymmetric profile and a shift of the peak position by
0.16 eV for photon energy of 68.3 eV, which is very close to the N_4-ionization
threshold.[3] In the Auger-electron peaks Xe $N_{4,5}OO$ and Kr $M_{4,5}NN$ induced by electron impact, on the other hand, noticeable asymmetry with a tailing toward higher
energy is observed on their profile, when the impact energy is lowered even within
30 eV above threshold. The shift of peak position amounts to nearly 0.2 eV for
the impact energy about 10 eV above the threshold.[2]

In this paper, we present results of a series of measurements on the spectral
profile and the energy shift in Auger-electron lines of the Ne KLL, Ar $L_{2,3}MM$,
Kr $M_{4,5}NN$, and Xe $N_{4,5}OO$ processes which are induced by electron impacts with
energies near the threshold of the respective inner-shell ionization.

A 127$°$ coaxial cylindrical analyzer, which has the mean radius of electron
trajectry of 50 mm, is used with an electron lens system. An energy resolution
of a 30 meV full width at half-maximum is steadily provided in the ejected electron spectrum.

Figure 1 shows an example of the Ar $L_{2,3}MM$ Auger-electron spectra, which reveals a drastic change in spectral shape for different impact energies. A remarkable tailing toward higher energy side and a large amount spread in each line are
observed for the impact energy of 270 eV, in spite of rather large amount of
excess energy above the threshold.

In Auger-decay process induced by electron impact near threshold, two sorts
of slow electrons must interact with an Auger-electron. One is the electron that
is inelastically scattered after the collision, the other is the electron ejected
from the inner-shell in the ionization stage. The two electrons may share the
excess energy with each other. Therefore, a decaying atom has always a certain
possibility to have a very slow electron in its vicinity, even if the amount of
excess energy is not so minute. This may be a main reason why the spectral shape

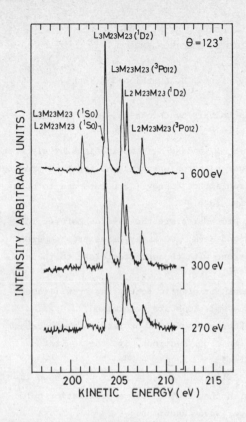

Fig. 1. Ar $L_{2,3}$MM Auger electron spectra induced by electron impacts of energies 600, 300, and ·270 eV. Observation angle is 123°. The length of vertical line drawn on the right-hand side of each spectrum indicates a half distance to the base line.

of Auger-peaks show a remarkable asymmetry even when the impact energy is not so close to the threshold of each inner-shell ionization.

   Results of measured Auger-electron spectra are compared with spectra deduced by a fitting calculation using a modified model of post collision interaction in Auger-process.

1. P.J. Hicks, S. Cvejanovic, J. Comer, F.H. Read, and J.M. Sharp, Vacuum 24 573 (1974).

2. S. Ohtani, H. Nishimura, H. Suzuki, and K. Wakiya, Phys. Rev. Lett. 36 863 (1976).

3. V. Schmidt, N. Sandner, W. Mehlhorn, F. Wuilleumier, and M.Y. Adam, Phys. Rev. Lett. 38 63 (1977); Abstracts of Papers X ICPEAC (Paris, 1977) p. 1062.

4. M.J.Van der Wiel, Proceedings of the Int. Conf. on Inner Shell Ionization Phenomena (Freiburg, 1976) p. 209.

5. G.R. Wight and M.J.Van der Wiel, J. Phys. B10 601 (1977).

CROSS SECTIONS FOR Ar-$L_{2,3}$ Kr-$M_{4,5}$ AND
Xe-$N_{4,5}$ IONIZATIONS BY ELECTRON IMPACT

T. Takayanagi, A. Nakashio, C. Hirota, H. Suzuki and K. Wakiya

Department of Physics, Sophia University Chioda-ku, Tokyo 102 Japan

Cross sections for Ar-$L_{2,3}$, Kr-$M_{4,5}$, and Xe-$N_{4,5}$ ionizations by electron
impact have been determined from Auger electron spectra, and reported previously.[1]
In this report, the ranges of electron impact energy   are extended to both
the threshold and the heigher energy sides.

The apparatus and experimental procedures are thè same as before. The
intensities of Ar-$L_{2,3}$MM, Kr-$M_{4,5}$NN and Xe-$N_{4,5}$OO Auger lines are compared
with the elastic scattering of electrons with the energies close to these
Auger lines.

Using differenrial cross sections for elastic scattering by Williams[2,3],
the cross sections for the Auger line emissions are determined.

Fluorescence yields are about the order of 10^{-3} or less in these cases,
so the sums of the Auger line emission cross sections give the ionization
cross sections for these inner shells.

The energy dependence of Kr-$M_{4,5}$ ionization cross section is shown in
fig.1, and our result is compared with that of the Born approximation calculated by Omidvar using Hartree Slater wave functions.

In fig.2, the energy dependence of measured Xe-$N_{4,5}$ ionization cross
section is shown. The cross section rises abruptly from the threshold and
has a first maximum at about 140 eV.

Such energy dependence of the cross sections has not been observed in
the other inner shell ionizations.

The second maximum at about 600 eV corresponds to the ordinary maximum
seen in other cases.

Comparision of our results with related experimental and theoretical
works are given.

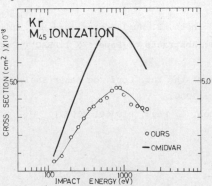

Fig.1
Energy dependence of
the cross section
for Kr $M_{4,5}$ ioniza-
tion.

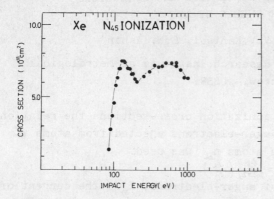

Fig.2
Energy dependence of
the cross section for
Xe-$N_{4,5}$ ionization.

Refferences

1) A. Nakashio, C. Hirota, T. Takayanagi, H. Suzuki and K. Wakiya:
   Abstracts of papers of Xth ICPEAC(Paris 1977) p.210
2) J.F Williams and B.A Wills: J. Phys. B **8** (1975) 1670
3) J.F. Williams and A. Crowe: J. Phys. B **8** (1975) 2233
4) K. Omidvar: J. Phys. B **10** (1977) L55.

MEASUREMENT OF IONIZATION CROSS SECTIONS
OF INNER SHELLS BY AES

V.I.Zaporozchenko, V.V.Kantsel, G.N.Kashin

All-Union Scientific Research Institute of Metrological
Service. Moscow. USSR.

For determination of ionization cross-sections the relation
between the current of auger-electrons ejected from atoms α
and the density of these atoms n_α was used.

$$\sigma_\alpha(E_p)\cdot(1+r_\alpha)=\frac{4\pi}{\Omega n_\alpha}\left(\frac{J_\alpha}{J_p}\right)$$

where I_α - the current of auger-electrons, I_p - the current of
primary electrons and r_α - the backscattering factor.

The total M-shell ionization cross-section of Ag and the total L-shell ionization cross-section of Si were measured and the
ratio of these quantities was calculated. The energy range of
primary electrons was from threshold to 2.4 kev. The absolute
value of Si L-shell ionization cross-section is $\sigma_N^{max}=4.9\times10^{-18}\text{ cm}^2$.

In the follows figures the ionization cross-sections as
functions of reduced energy are presented.

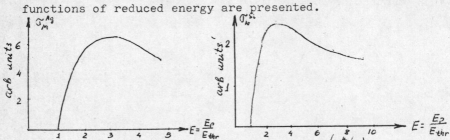

The error in the ratio of cross-sections $\left(\sigma_M^{Ag}/\sigma_N^{Si}\right)$was 5-7% and
consisted mainly of the error in determination of I_α and I_p.
The error in the absolute cross-sections was ~20%. This large
error was due to uncertainity in the density of Ag and Si.

DOUBLE DIFFERENTIAL IONIZATION CROSS SECTION
FOR NEON K-SHELL BY ELECTRON IMPACT

W. Sandner and C.E. Theodosiou

Fakultät für Physik der Universität Freiburg
Hermann-Herder-Str. 3, D-7800 Freiburg, W.-Germany

With the purpose of assessing the validity of various theoretical approaches in calculating cross sections we measured the double differential cross section (DDCS) for K-shell ionization in Ne by electron impact. The simple first Born approximation has some success in predicting total ionization cross sections, but increasingly fails to make correct predictions for the single, double, and triple differential cross sections. Experimental results on the DDCS for inner-shell ionization have been scarce.[1,2] We present measurements and calculations of the Ne K-shell DDCS for a variety of incident energies and detected electron energies and angles.

Experimentally, a rotatable parallel plate electrostatic analyzer (resolution 1.4%) was used to investigate the energy and angular distribution of the "scattered" and "ejected" electrons produced in the primary ionization process. To distinguish the K-shell from the L-shell ionization the subsequently emitted $K-L_{23}L_{23}$ Auger electrons were detected in coincidence by an electrostatic cylindrical mirror analyzer with an acceptance solid angle of about 10^{-2} of 4π.[3] The measured relative DDCS have been brought to an absolute scale using the previously measured[4] Auger emission cross sections for normalization. Figs. 1 a - c show our results for $E_{incident}$ = 2.4, 4 and 7 keV (2.7, 4.6, and 8 times the 1s binding energy) and detection angles θ from 20° - 90°, together with our theoretical results.

The theoretical results were obtained in a) plane-wave Born approximation and b) Born-Ochkur approximation, as detailed elsewhere.[3] Hartree-Slater wavefunctions were used to describe the bound and ionized atomic electron, whereas the incident and scattered electrons were treated as plane waves. For low detection energies and angles we see a reasonable agreement between theory and experiment, at least in shape. With increasing energies and angles an increasing discrepancy is observed. In this latter case none of the outgoing electrons can be adequately described by an "undistorted" plane wave. The magnitude of the discrepancy gives an indication of the expected distortion. A type of distorted-wave calculation (also for the incoming electron) is currently in progress.

1. C.A. Quarles and J.D. Faulk, Phys. Rev. Lett. <u>31</u>, 859 (1973)

2. W. Hink, G. Ulm, K. Brunner, and T. Ebding, Abstract of International X-XUV Conference, Sendai, Japan, 1978

3. W. Sandner and C.E. Theodosiou, to be published

4. G. Glupe, Ph.D. Thesis, Münster (1971)

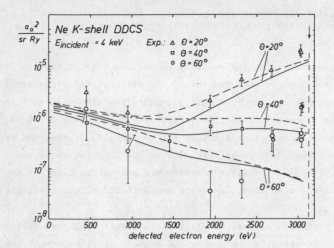

Fig. 1 a

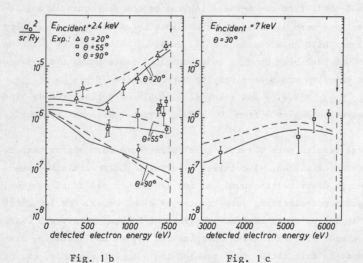

Fig. 1 b   Fig. 1 c

Fig. 1 a – c: Experimental and theoretical double differential ionization cross sections for Ne K-shell. (The arrows indicate the maximum energy for secondary electrons $E_{incident} - E_B(1s)$.)

Theoretical curves:

---------- Plane Wave Born Approximation without exchange

————— Plane Wave Born-Ochkur Approximation

EFFECTIVE CONTRIBUTION OF THE 1s ELECTRONS OF
Ar AND Ne TO THE BETHE SUM RULE [1]

Azzedine Lahmam-Bennani, Alain Duguet

Laboratoire des Collisions Atomiques et Moléculaires
Bâtiment 210 - Université Paris Sud - 91405 Orsay Cedex

During the last years, the Bethe sum rule [1] has been succesfully applied
for normalisation procedures of relative energy-loss spectra obtained in high
energy electron impact spectroscopy, and in particular in Compton profiles measurement [2]. This sum rule is written as :

$$\Sigma \int \frac{df(K,E)}{dE} \, dE = N \quad \text{at any fixed } K$$

where K is the momentum transfer under collision, E is the energy-loss suffered
by the incident electron, $df(K,E)/dE$ is the generalized oscillator strenght (GOS)
and N the number of electrons in the target. The summation is taken over all
allowed transitions, both discrete and continuous. Hence one has to experimentally
record GOS spectra over an energy-loss range extending from 0 to far beyond the
1s electrons binding energy, E_B. For light targets (e.g. up to Ne, $E_B \approx 870$ eV),
this is quite easily feasible, while the problem becomes serious for heavier
targets (e.g. Ar with $E_B \approx 3200$ eV). Some authors have tried to avoid this difficulty by measuring the GOS-spectra only up to E_B and using the Bethe sum rule
where N is replaced by N_v, N_v being the number of valence electrons in the target.

In this work, we present a measurement of the respective contributions of
the 1s electrons and the valence electrons in Ar and Ne to this sum rule. We
show that each of these contributions does not add up to the number of electrons
involved in the target but to a different "effective" number which will be discussed in detail at the Conference time.

1.   H. Bethe, Ann. Physik, 5, (1930), 325.
2.   R.A. Bonham, H.F. Wellenstein in "Compton Scattering" Chap.8, edit. by
      Williams, Mc Graw Hill, (1977).

Angular Distribution of X Radiation Following Electron Bombardment of Free Atoms

M Aydinol, <u>R Hippler</u>*, I McGregor and H Kleinpoppen

Institute of Atomic Physics, University of Stirling, Scotland

The angular distribution of x radiation following 2 keV to 15 keV electron bombardment of free atoms (argon, krypton, xenon) has been examined. The apparatus is a typical crossed beam experiment with an electron gun, which may be rotated through the angular range 30° to 150°, and the Si(Li) x-ray detector with an energy resolution of 205 eV which is fixed in position outside the vacuum chamber[1].

Fig.1 shows a typical x-ray spectrum obtained from 8 keV electron bombardment of xenon. It shows the Xe L diagram lines superimposed on a continuous bremsstrahlung spectrum having a high-energy cut-off at a photon energy equal to the incident electron energy, $h\nu_o = E_e$. The observed lines are identified as the $L\ell (2P_{3/2} \to 3S_{1/2})$, $L\alpha_{1,2}(2P_{3/2} \to 3D_{5/2, \ 3/2})$, $L\beta_1 \ (2P_{1/2} \to D_{3/2})$ and $L\beta_{3,4}(2S_{1/2} \to 3P_{3/2, \ 1/2})$, $L\beta_2 \ (2P_{3/2} \to 4D_{5/2})$ and $L\gamma_1 \ (2P_{1/2} \to 4D_{3/2})$ transitions. The $L\beta_{1,3,4}$ lines originate either from the $2P_{1/2}$ or the $2S_{1/2}$ states and hence can be used for normalisation since no anisotropy is expected for them.

From the angular distribution of the characteristic lines the degree of polarization can be obtained as

$$I(\Theta)/I(90^{\circ}) = 1 - P \cos^2\Theta. \tag{1}$$

$I(\Theta)$ is the intensity observed under a photon emission angle Θ and P the degree of polarization defined as $P = (I_{\|} - I_{\perp})/(I_{\|} + I_{\perp})$. $I_{\|}$ and $I_{\perp}$ are the intensities with the electric vector parallel and perpendicular, respectively, to the incoming electron beam direction. Fig.2 gives the degree of polarization for the combined $L\alpha_{1/2}$ line as function of the incident electron energy. It turns out that the degree of polarization is small, except near threshold where it amounts to +6.6%. In contradiction to measurements for the $L_3M_{2,3}M_{2,3}$ Auger decay in argon[2] our measurements tend to support $Q_o >> Q_1$ at threshold (Q_o, Q_1 the

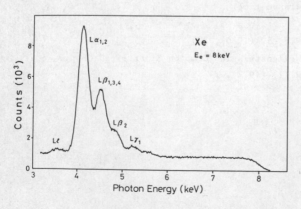

Fig. 1

partial cross sections for populating the $m_\ell = 0 \pm 1$ magnetic substates,
respectively), in agreement with x-ray polarization measurements on various
elements (Xe, Au, Ge, Cu) following proton bombardment[3,4].

Fig.3 gives the angular distribution of bremsstrahlung radiation following
6 keV electron impact on krypton. Now the intensity strongly varies with photon
emission angle, with minimum intensity in forward and backward directions. The
angle of maximum intensity is shifted from $90°$ to $\Theta_{max} = 80°$, which is due to
the retardation of the electromagnetic potentials. The angular distribution
can be represented by a modified Sommerfeld formula[5]

$$I(\Theta)/I(90°) = \left[(1-\beta\cos\Theta)^2 - P(\cos\Theta-\beta)^2\right]/\left[(1 - P\beta^2)(1-\beta\cos\Theta)^4\right] \qquad (2)$$

with $\beta = v/c$, v the average electron velocity, c the speed of light. For three
different photon energies E_{ph} the degree of polarization amounts to 65%, 75% and
85% corresponding to $E_{ph} = 2.4$ keV, 4.0 keV, 5.4 keV. The decrease of
polarization with decreasing photon energy is in qualitative agreement with
calculations of Kirkpatrick and Wiedmann.[6]

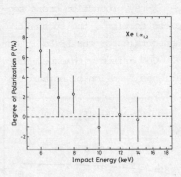

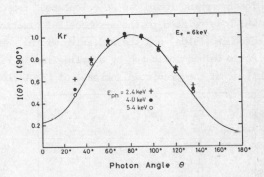

Fig. 2   Fig. 3

*Permanent address: Fakultät für Physik, Universität Bielefeld, W. Germany

1.   M Aydinol, R Hippler, I McGregor, H Kleinpoppen, Proc. Int. Workshop
      "Coherence and Correlation in Atomic Physics" (Plenum Press, 1979)

2.   W Sandner, W Schmitt, J Phys. B11, 1833 (1978)

3.   A Schöler, F Bell, Z Physik, A286, 163 (1978)

4.   W Jitschin, H Kleinpoppen, R Hippler, H O Lutz, to be published

5.   H Kulenkampff, M Scheer, E Zeitler, Z. Physik, 157, 275 (1959)

6.   P Kirkpatrick, L Wiedmann, Phys. Rev. 67, 321 (1945)

ENERGY DEPENDENCE OF THE Lβ/Lα BRANCHING RATIO AFTER
L-SHELL IONIZATION BY RELATIVISTIC ELECTRONS[+]

H. Genz, D.H.H. Hoffmann, W. Löw and A. Richter

Institut für Kernphysik, Technische Hochschule Darmstadt
6100 Darmstadt, Germany

L-shell ionization due to relativistic electron impact[1] can be investigated
by means of Si(Li) detectors. Figure 1 represents a typical L X-ray spectrum obtained by bombarding a thin Au foil with 40 MeV electrons from the Darmstadt electron linear accelerator. The very low and flat background of the spectrum enables
the determination of the Lβ/Lα intensity ratio with an accuracy of <3 %. The values measured for Au (Z=79), Pb (Z=82) and Bi (Z=83) at 20, 40 and 60 MeV electron
energy are plotted in Fig. 2 together with the experiments by other groups[2-4] for
energies between 0.5 and 900 MeV. It becomes apparent from Fig. 2 that the Lβ/Lα
branching ratio raises more than 14 % in this energy region.

The branching ratio can be calculated[5] from the L X-ray production cross section which is related to the L-subshell ionization cross section[6], the subshell
fluorescence yields[7] and the radiative width.[8] We then obtain for the Lβ/Lα intensity ratio values indicated by a solid line in Fig. 2. Comparison with experiment
exhibits that the predicted increase of the Lβ/Lα ratio as function of bombarding

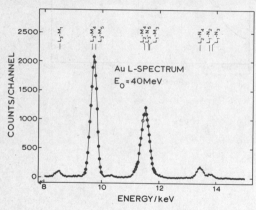

Fig. 1. Typical L X-ray spectrum
obtained by bombarding a
thin (200 μg/cm²) Au foil
with 40 MeV electrons.

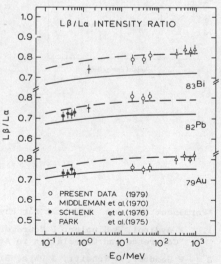

Fig. 2. The experimental Lβ/Lα
branching ratio and calculated
values based on the subshell
ionization cross sections by
Scofield[6] (solid line) and
assuming a complete suppression
of Coster-Kronig transitions
(dashed line).

[+]Work supported by
Deutsche Forschungsgemeinschaft

energy is much less pronounced than experimentally observed. If one, completely arbitrarily   neglects all Coster-Kronig transitions one obtains the dashed curve in Fig. 2. Both theoretical curves appear to yield upper and lower limits to the experimental results although it can hardly be decided in how far Coster-Kronig transitions may be suppressed nor its influence on ω_L .

A possible explanation for the not yet understood increase of the ratio could be the occurrence of multiple ionization. If for example with increasing energy electrons with larger spacial extensions (e.g. 3d compared to 3p) are stripped off preferably an energy dependence of the Lβ/Lα ratio might show up. Effects caused by the creation of multiple ionization in the initial state are currently under investigation by means of a high resolution crystal spectrometer.

Finally, it should be considered that perhaps the energy dependence of the calculated subshell ionization cross sections follows a different behaviour as predicted although the total L-shell cross section calculation by Scofield[6] is in good agreement with the experimental data.[1] If we for example try to deduce the L-subshell cross sections σ_{Li} from our experimental Lα and Lβ X-ray production cross sections we obtain in the case of Au the result shown in Fig. 3 together with the data of ref. 2. Unfortunately, the errors are relatively large (30-80 %) due to the fact that numbers of the same magnitude have to be subtracted from each other and due to the uncertainties in the L-subshell fluorescences yields. It becomes apparent that the experimental values of σ_L are in good agreement with theory while σ_{L1} - disregarding the large errors - is systematically too large and $\sigma_{L2,3}$ too small for the larger bombarding energies. A new calculation[9] might clear the situation.

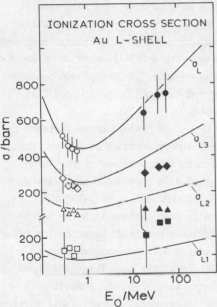

Fig. 3. Total L-shell ionization cross section for Au and the deduced subshell cross sections.

1. D.H.H. Hoffmann, C. Brendel, H. Genz, U. Kuhn, W. Löw and A. Richter, this conference and Z. Phys. to be published.
2. B. Schlenk, D. Berenyi, S. Ricz, A. Valek and G. Hock, J. Phys. B10, 1303 (1977).
3. Y.K. Park, M.T. Smith and W. Scholz, Phys. Rev. A12, 1358 (1975).
4. L.M. Middleman, R.L. Ford and R. Hofstadter, Phys. Rev. A2, 1429 (1970).
5. P. Richard in: Atomic Inner-Shell Process, ed. B. Crasemann (Academic Press, New York, 1975) p. 94.
6. J.H. Scofield, Phys. Rev. A18, 963 (1978).
7. W. Bambynek, B. Crasemann, R.W. Fink, H.-U. Freund, H. Mark, C.D. Swift, R.E. Price and P.V. Rao, Rev. Mod. Phys. 44, 716 (1972).
8. J.H. Scofield, Phys. Rev. 179, 9 (1969) and A10, 1507 (1974).
9. P. Eschwey, private communication.

K-, L- AND M-SHELL IONIZATION BY RELATIVISTIC ELECTRON IMPACT: CROSS SECTIONS AND SCALING BEHAVIOUR[+]

D.H.H. Hoffmann, C. Brendel, P. Eschwey, H. Genz, U. Kuhn, W. Löw and A. Richter

Institut für Kernphysik, Technische Hochschule Darmstadt
6100 Darmstadt, Germany

Investigations of inner-shell ionization by relativistic electron impact[1] have recently been extended to L and M shells.[2] Thus in the energy region between 20 and 60 MeV accurate total cross sections are now available for a detailed comparison with theoretical calculations.

In the present work we report about the final results of the Z and E dependence of the L- and M-shell ionization cross section and a general scaling behaviour including the data for the K-shell.[1] The measurements were performed at the DALINAC by bombarding thin selfsupporting solid or gaseous targets ($47 \leq Z \leq 92$ for L- and $79 \leq Z \leq 92$ for M-shell ionization) with electrons at relativistic energies ($20 \leq E_0 \leq 60$ MeV). The produced X-rays were detected with a Si(Li) detector of about 1 cm^3 active volume surrounded by about 10 cm of Pb-shielding and placed outside the scattering chamber. A typical L X-ray spectrum exhibiting the low and flat background is displayed in the accompanying paper.[3]

Figure 1 shows our results for the absolute L- and M-shell cross sections in a double logarithmic representation for electron impact energies of 40 MeV. The experimental error is of the order of 15 % which is mainly caused by the large uncertainty of the fluorescence yield. The L-shell data obey a $Z^{-\alpha}$ power law with $\alpha = 3.0$ compared to $\alpha = 2.45$ for the K-shell. A comparison with the calculations of Scofield[4] based on the relativistic Born approximation using Hartree-Slater wave functions shows that - similar to the K-shell data - the experimental L-shell cross sections lie systematically (11%) below the predicted values. Since no theoretical calculations exist for M-shell ionization cross sections we have extended the virtual photon method using theoretical photo ionization cross sections and Hartree-Slater wave functions and obtain the solid line shown in the right part of Fig. 1. The calculations again exceed the experimental data point by about 10 %.

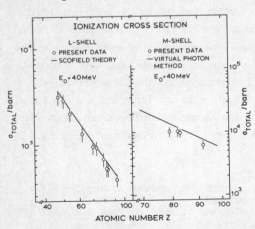

Fig. 1. Z dependence of the total L- and M-shell ionization cross section for 40 MeV electrons.

[+]Work supported by
Deutsche Forschungsgemeinschaft

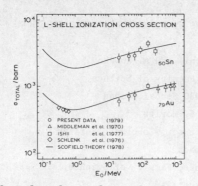

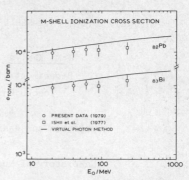

Fig. 2. E dependence of σ_L and calculations by Scofield.[4]

Fig. 3. E dependence of σ_M and calculations based on the virtual
photon method.

Figures 2 and 3, representative for two elements, show the energy dependence of the
L- and M-shell ionization cross section together with the data of other groups.[5-7]
The comparison with theory yields the same behaviour as stated above.

Finally, we have plotted all L- and M-shell data discussed here and the K-
shell measurements reported earlier[1] into a $\sigma I/N_i$ versus E_0/I representation (Fig.
4). Here $\sigma I/N_i$ represents a reduced cross section where I is the ionization energy
for the K-shell and the average binding energy for L and M shell respectively, and
N_i is the number of electrons per shell. From this representation we deduce that
the ionization cross sections for the inner shells obey a general scaling behaviour. The solid line in Fig. 4 is obtained from the K-shell data only. We thus

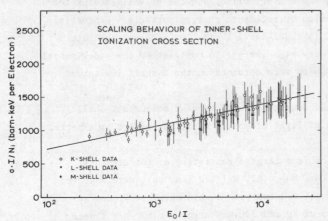

conclude that for large
impact energies the ioni-
zation cross section is
independent from the spe-
cific features of the
atomic cloud and that the
electrons can be described
by a model of independent
particles. The value of
the cross section per
electron depends only on
the binding energy.

Fig. 4. K-, L- and M-shell ionization cross section for
all data points in the investigated energy region.

1. D.H.H. Hoffmann, H. Genz, W. Löw and A. Richter, Phys. Lett. 65A, 304 (1978).
2. H. Genz, D.H.H. Hoffmann, W. Löw and A. Richter, Phys. Lett. A, submitted.
3. H. Genz, D.H.H. Hoffmann, W. Löw and A. Richter, this conference.
4. J.H. Scofield, Phys. Rev. A18, 963 (1978).
5. B. Schlenk, D. Berenyi, S. Ricz, A. Valek and G. Hock, J. Phys. B10, 1303 (1977).
6. K. Ishii, M. Kamiya, K. Sera, S. Morita, H. Tawara, M. Oyamada and T.C. Chu,
   Phys. Rev. A15, 906 (1977).
7. L.M. Middleman, R.L. Ford and R. Hofstadter, Phys. Rev. A2, 1429 (1970).

DENSITY EFFECT IN K-SHELL IONIZATIONS BY ULTRARELATIVISTIC ELECTRONS

M. Kamiya, Y. Kinefuchi, and A. Kuwako
Department of Physics, Faculty of Science,
Tohoku University, 980 Sendai, Japan
K. Ishii and S. Morita
Cyclotron and Radioisotope Center, Tohoku University
M. Oyamada
Laboratory of Nuclear Science, Faculty of Science,
Tohoku University

Cross sections of inner-shell ionization by ultrarelativistic electrons of first measured by Middleman et al.[1] for electrons of 150 — 900 MeV and then by ourselves[2] for electrons of 70 — 230 MeV. The results were well explained in terms of the PWBA by Davidovic and Moiseiwitch or the virtual photon theory by Kolbenstvedt. Futher, Scofield calculated the cross section by fully relativistic PWBA, giving nearly same results.

On the other hand, it has been well established that ionization energy loss of charged particles shows saturation at very high energy. This phenomenon is called the density effect and can be well interpreted by polarization of the medium by incident charged particle. Dangerfield[3] predicted the same effect in inner-shell ionization, showing the saturation of cross section at very high energy, in contrast to the experimental results mentioned above, which were obtained on the K-shell ionization of atoms heavier than Cu.

In order to detect the density effect, here we measured K-shell ionization cross sections of light elements, where the effect is expected to be sensitive.

X-ray intensity ratios from targets consisting of two elements, i.e., (F, Al), (Na, Cl), (Mg, Mn), (Al, Mn) and (Zn, Sn), were measured with a flow-type proportional counter with a thin entrance window at two incident electron energies of 70 and 230 MeV using the 300-MeV linear accelerator of Tohoku University. Cross sections for K-shell ionization of Na, Mg, Al and Cl and for L-shell ionization of Zn, and Sn were obtained.

In Fig. 1, ratios of the ionization cross sections at these two bombarding energies are compared with the theoretical value of 15 % for the increase in the cross section from 70 to 230 MeV, and the saturation is clearly seen in the experimental values. Differences in the rate of increase of the ionization cross section for the couple of elements are shown in Fig. 2, where we can see that the rate of increase is smaller for lighter elements than for heavier elements, showing that the density effect is much remarkable for lighter elements.

The results will be compared with theory including the density effect.

References

1. L. M. Middleman, R. L. Ford, and R. Hofstadter, Phys. Rev. A 2, 1429 (1970).
2. K. Ishii, M. Kamiya, K. Sera, S. Morita, H. Tawara, M. Oyamada, and T. C. Chu, Phys. Rev. A 15, 906 (1977).
3. G. R. Dangerfield, Phys. Lett. 46 A, 19 (1973).

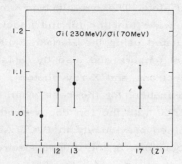

Fig. 1.
Ratios of K-shell ionization cross section at 70 MeV and 230 MeV as a function of target-atomic number.

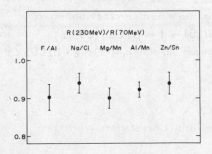

Fig. 2.
Ratios of x-ray intensity ratio of the two elements at 70 MeV and 230 MeV.

DWBA CALCULATIONS OF INNER-SHELL VACANCY ALIGNMENT

E.G. Berezhko and N.M. Kabachnik

Institute of Nuclear Physics, Moscow State University;

Moscow 117234; USSR .

Comparison of the calculated ionic alignment in the inner-shell ionization of atoms by electron impact with the experimental data[1] reveals that, at electron energies $E/E_B < 5$ (E_B being the electron binding energy in a given sub-shell), the latter systematically exceed the former. This discrepancy may be due to the invalidity in that energy region of the commonly used Born approximation (BA). To clarify this matter, we have calculated the statistical tensors which characterize the ionic state anisotropy in the distorted wave Born approximation (DWBA), i.e., we considered the distortion of the waves of the incident and scattered electrons by the atomic field. As the distorting potential, we have chosen an averaged atomic potential of the atomic ground state. The one-electron wave functions for bound states, as well as the wave function for the knocked--out electron in the continuum, were calculated using the Herman-Skillman potential. We have calculated the statistical tensors and also the anisotropy in the angular distribution of Auger electrons and X-ray photons, which are produced in electron-impact atomic ionization, for the case when the scattered electron is detected in coincidence with the ion decay product. The results are compared with those obtained previousely in BA[2]. As an example, fig. 1 shows BA and DWBA calculations of the Auger electron anisotropy coefficients $\beta_\perp$, $\beta_{\shortparallel}$ and the phase Υ for the $L_3M_{2,3}M_{2,3}(^1S_0)$ Auger transition in Ar as a function of the incident-electron scattering angle θ_e with an initial energy of 36.4 Ry and ejected electron energy 5Ry. The quantities determine the angular distribution of Auger electrons in the reaction plane $W(\theta) \sim 1 + \beta_{\shortparallel} \cos(2\theta - \Upsilon)$ and in the plane perpendicular to the primary beam direction, $W(\varphi) \sim 1 + \beta_\perp \cos 2\varphi$.

REFERENCES

1. W. Sandner et al. Proc. of Coherence and Correlation Workshop (ed. Kleinpoppen), London, 1977.
2. E.G. Berezhko et al. J.Phys. B11, 1819 (1978).
3. E.G. Berezhko and N.M. Kabachnik, J.Phys. B10, 2467(1977).

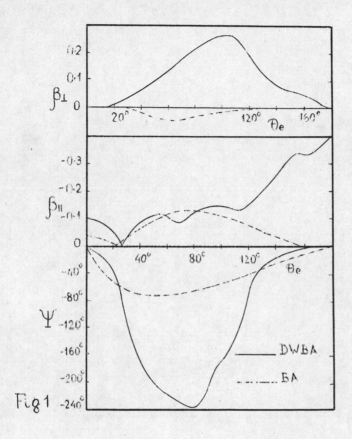

Fig 1

III.   *Electron-Molecule Collisions*

ELASTIC SCATTERING OF ELECTRONS FROM H_2^+ AND
STUDIES OF DYNAMIC PROCESSES IN THE $H_2^+ + e$ SYSTEM

H. Takagi[*], H. Nakamura[†] and Y. Itikawa[§]

[*] Physics Laboratory, School of Medicine, Kitasato University,
Sagamihara, Kanagawa 228, Japan

[†] Department of Applied Physics, Faculty of Engineering,
The University of Tokyo, Tokyo 113, Japan

[§] Institute of Plasma Physics, Nagoya University,
Nagoya 464, Japan

Variational calculations of the elastic scattering phasehsifts of s- and p-
waves are performed within the adiabatic approximation in the two-center spheroidal
coordinate system[1]. Quantum defects, and energies and widths of the two-electron
excited resonance states are obtained from the energy dependence of the phaseshifts. These are compared with the results of other calculations. By extending
the multi-channel quantum defect theory[2], the rate of autoionization of the
vibrationally excited Rydberg states is successfully expressed in an analytical
form in terms of the adiabatic quantum defects.

As long range basis wavefunctions in the variational calculation the two-
center Coulomb wavefunctions are employed, which are derived from the potential of
two one-half positive charges separated by the equilibrium internuclear distance
of H_2^+ ($R=2a_0$). The short range trial functions are assumed to have a form

$$\chi(r_1)\chi'(r_2) = \xi_1^n e^{-\alpha\xi_1} P_\ell(\eta_1)\xi_2^{n'} e^{-\alpha\xi_2}(\xi_2-1)^{|m|/2} P_{\ell'}^m(\eta_2) e^{im\psi},$$

where (ξ,η,ψ) are the prolate spheroidal coordinates, and $P_\ell^m(x)$ is the asociated
Legendre function. As an example, the results of the phaseshifts for the $p\sigma$-wave
are shown in figure 1, together with the results of the single-center expansion
calculation[3]. The ordinate of the figure is the phaseshift measured from the one-
center Coulomb phaseshift.

The rates of the vibrationally induced autoionization of the $p\sigma$ Rydberg states
of H_2 are shown in figure 2 as a function of the initial vibrational quantum number, together with the experimental results[4] and the results of other calculations[5].

A detailed study of photoionization of H_2 will be also discussed.

1. H. Takagi and H. Nakamura, J. Phys. B11, L675 (1978).

2. Ch. Jungen and O. Atabek, J. Chem. Phys. 66, 5584 (1977).

3. A. Temkin and K.V. Vasavada, Phys. Rev. 160, 109 (1967).

4. P.M. Dehmer and W.A. Chupka, J. Chem. Phys. 65, 2243 (1976).

5. R.S. Berry and S.E. Nielsen, Phys. Rev. A1, 395 (1970).

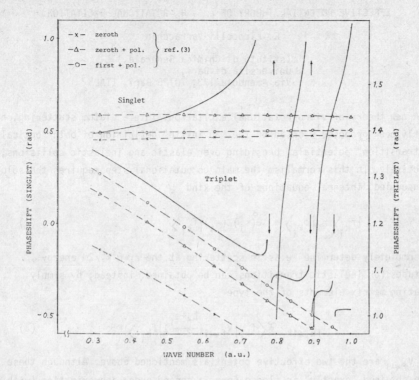

Fig.1 p(m=0)-wave phaseshifts. Arrows indicate
the positions of resonances.

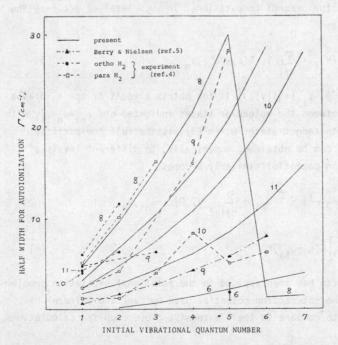

Fig.2 Autoionization
width. Figures
attached to the
lines indicate
the principal
quantum number.

EFFECTIVE POTENTIAL THEORY OF e^- - H_2 ROTATIONAL EXCITATION.

E. Ficocelli Varracchio

Istituto di Chimica Generale,
Università di Bari,
Via Amendola 173, 70126 Bari, ITALY

A new theory of vibro-rotational excitation, in e^- - diatom scattering, has recently been proposed[1], based on the "ab initio" definition of both "optical" and "transition" potentials, presiding over elastic and inelastic collisions, respectively. In this formalism the main computational step requires the solution of "uncoupled" integral equations of the kind

$$\left| f_{k_i} \right\rangle = \left| \Phi_{k_i} \right\rangle + \overset{\circ}{G}(\varepsilon_i)\Sigma(\varepsilon_i)\left| f_{k_i} \right\rangle \tag{1}$$

that completely determine elastic scattering at the $\varepsilon_i = \hbar^2 k_i^2 / 2m$ energy. Amplitudes for inelastic transitions can be obtained, instead, by simply evaluating matrix elements of the type

$$T_{fk_f;ik_i} \cong \left\langle f_{k_f} \left| V_{f \leftarrow i}(\frac{\varepsilon_f + \varepsilon_i}{2}) \right| f_{k_i} \right\rangle \tag{2}$$

Σ and $V_{f \leftarrow i}$ are the two effective potentials mentioned above. Although these can be obtained "exactly" in closed form, a second order approximation (with respect to the subsystems interaction potential,V) is most convenient numerically and has been adopted in the present computations. To such level of accuracy the optical potential becomes

$$\Sigma(\varepsilon_i) \cong \Sigma^{(1)}(\varepsilon_i) = \vec{1} \cdot V_{ii} + \sum_{n \neq i} V_{in}G(\varepsilon_i - \omega_{ni})V_{ni} \tag{3}$$

In (3), $\langle \vec{x} | \vec{1} | \vec{x}' \rangle = \delta(\vec{x} - \vec{x}')$, $V_{ij}(=\langle i | V | j \rangle)$ is the matrix element of the e^--diatom interaction potential between the molecular states indicated and $\omega_{ni} = \omega_n - \omega_i$, with ω_j the energy of the j-th target state. G, in (3), is the full one-particle Green's function, which can be obtained, numerically, to different levels of accuracy[2]. The transition potential similarly becomes

$$V_{f \leftarrow i}(\frac{\varepsilon_f + \varepsilon_i}{2}) \cong V_{f \leftarrow i}^{(1)}(\frac{\varepsilon_f + \varepsilon_i}{2}) = \vec{1} \cdot V_{fi} + \sum_{n \neq i,f} V_{fn}G(\varepsilon_i - \omega_{ni})V_{ni} \quad +$$

$$+ \left[V_{ff} - V_{ii} \right] G(\varepsilon_i - \omega_{fi})V_{fi} \tag{4}$$

The present formalism has been applied to the rotational excitation problem in e^- - H_2 collisions. The interaction potential used by Lane and Geltman[3] has been adopted, in order to compare to their extensive close coupling calculations.

Results for elastic processes have been obtained by solving (1), within the $\Sigma^{(1)}$ approximation to Σ. A partial wave expansion of this equation leads to $|f_{11'k}^{J}\rangle$ orbitals, in a conventional notation for the angular momentum coupling scheme [4]. Characteristic results for p-wave (1=1'=1) elastic scattering are shown in fig. 1. Total cross-sections for the $j_i=1\rightarrow j_f=3$ transition are given, as an illustration of the results obtained, in fig. 2. A more extensive collection of data will be presented at the Conference.

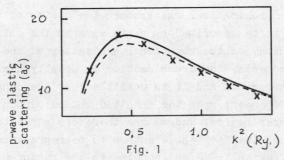

Fig. 1

Full and broken curves are solutions of eq. (1) with the first term, only, and both terms in the optical potential, respectively. Crosses are the exact close coupling results.

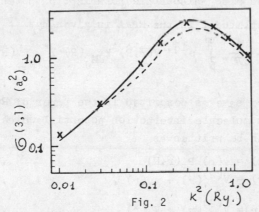

Fig. 2

Full and broken curves are the results of the present theory and of the distorted wave approximation, respectively. Crosses are close coupling values.

1. E. Ficocelli Varracchio, J. Phys. B 10, 503 (1977).
2. E. Ficocelli Varracchio, J. Phys. B (submitted).
3. N. F. Lane and S. Geltman, Phys. Rev. 160, 53 (1967).
4. A. M. Arthurs and A. Dalgarno, Proc. Roy. Soc. A256, 540 (1960).

ROTATIONAL EXCITATION OF H_2 MOLECULE BY ELECTRON IMPACT

G.P.Gupta and K.C.Mathur

Department of Physics, University of Roorkee,
Roorkee-247672, India.

The regional plane wave approximation (RPWA) is used in the study of the rotational excitation $(J=1\rightarrow3)$ of the H_2 molecule by electron impact.

In the Born approximation, one assumes the motion of the incident electron to be described by plane wave in the entire region of space. In the study of the rotational excitation of the molecules having permanent moments, the cross section is usually dominated by the long range interaction and it is possible that the cross sections are not strongly dependent upon the detailed nature of the wavefunction in the inner region. Rudge[1] has therefore suggested RPWA in which one assumes the incident electron to be represented by a plane wave in the region $r > \rho$ and nothing in the region $r < \rho$ where ρ is a cut off parameter. Rudge has used this procedure for the study of rotational excitation of molecules having permanent dipole moments. Here we extend the study to the case when the molecule has a quadrupole moment and also anisotropic polarization potential.

The scattering amplitude, in the RPWA is given by

$$f(JM_J;J'M_{J'}/K_iK_f) = -\frac{1}{2\pi} \int_\rho^\infty e^{i\vec{q}\cdot\vec{r}} V(\vec{r},\hat{R}) Y_{JM_J}(\hat{R}) Y_{J'M_{J'}}^*(\hat{R}) d\vec{r} d\hat{R}$$

$$...(1)$$

where the notations are same as described in the paper of Rudge[1]. $V(\vec{r},\hat{R})$ is the electron molecule interaction potential which for the case of H_2 molecule can be written as

$$V(\vec{r},\hat{R}) = v(r) P_2(\hat{r},\hat{R}) \qquad\qquad ...(2a)$$

where
$$v(r) = V_s^{(2)}(r) + v_1(r) , \qquad\qquad ...(2b)$$

$$v_1(r) = V_q^{(2)}(r) + V_p(r) \qquad\qquad ...(2c)$$

$V_s^{(2)}, V_q^{(2)}$ and V_p are defined in references [2,3].

The value of $\rho = 0$ in equation (1) gives the scattering amplitude in the Born approximation (BA). Following Takayanagi and Geltman[4], we have replaced $v_1(r)$ by $v_1(\rho)$ in the region $r < \rho$.

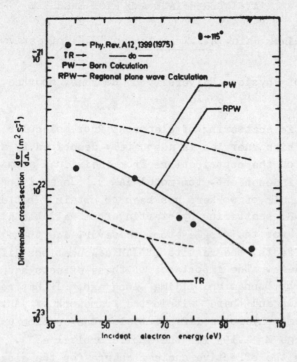

Fig.1.

We have used equation (1) to evaluate the J = 1→3 rotational excitation differential cross section for H_2 molecule. The cut off parameter P was chosen empirically to give the best results for the differential cross section. Figure 1 shows our results for the differential cross section at an angle of 115° for energies above 40 eV. A comparison is made with the other theoretical calculation and the experimental data. From the figure a reasonable agreement between the present calculation and the experiment is noted. Detailed results will be presented at the time of conference.

1.   M.R. H.Rudge, J.Phys. B7, 1323 (1974)
2.   P.K.Bhattacharyya and A.S.Ghosh, Phys. Rev. A12,408(1975)
3.   A.Dalgarno and R.J. Moffet, Proc. Natl.Inst.Sci.India A33, 511 (1963)
4.   K.Takayanagi and S.Geltman, Phys. Rev. 138A,1003 (1965)

ELASTIC SCATTERING OF ELECTRONS BY HYDROGEN MOLECULE
AT INTERMEDIATE AND HIGH ENERGIES

Ashok Jain, A.N.Tripathi and M.K.Srivastava

Department of Physics, University of Roorkee, Roorkee, India

The elastic scattering of electrons from molecular hydrogen at medium and high energies is adequately described by a coherent superposition of the contributions from individual atomic scattering centers (independent-atom-model IAM). In applying this model the main aim of workers has been to obtain a better description of the $e-H_2$ scattering by starting from reliable differential cross-sections for the single atom. However, due to neglect of the binding effects, the results of IAM calculations differ from the experimental data. The importance of these effects has in fact been observed by Bonham and Iijima[1] long ago. It has recently been analysed by Jain and Khare[2] within the framework of IAM. They have calculated atomic hydrogen differential cross-section using an effective charge $Z = 1.193$ for the atomic orbital e^{-Zr}. This choice of Z, which is the effective nuclear charge for the single hydrogenic orbital on each center, accounts for the effect of molecular binding (valence bond effects).

In view of very good eikonal-born series (EBS) results in the atomic case, we think it is worthwhile to use it along with molecular binding correction to investigate the $e-H_2$ elastic scattering within the IAM model. In IAM the differential cross-section for the $e-H_2$ scattering is given by[3]

$$(\frac{d\sigma}{d\Omega})_{eH_2} = 2 \{ (|f|^2 + |g|^2) + (|f|^2 - |g|^2) j_0(qR) \} \quad (1)$$

where j_0 is the spherical Bessel function of zeroth order, $\vec{q} = \vec{k_i} - \vec{k_f}$, is the momentum transfer and $\vec{k_i}$ and $\vec{k_f}$ are respectively the momenta of the incident and the scattered electrons. The scattering amplitudes f and g correspond to the direct and exchange scattering by the hydrogen atoms. The direct amplitude is evaluated in the EBS approximation[4] and the exchange amplitude in the Ochkur approximation.

We have calculated the elastic differential cross-sections (DCS) for $e-H_2$ scattering using equation (1) at 75 and 100 eV.

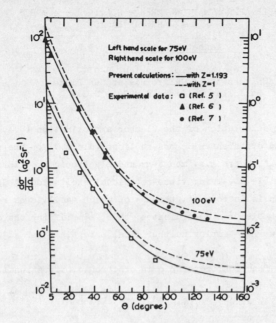

At 75 eV the comparison has been made with the measurements of
Srivastava et al[5]. The results obtained both by using $Z = 1$ and
$Z = 1.193$ have been displayed in Figure 1. It is clear that the
results with $Z = 1.193$ compare better with the measurements throughout the angular range. At 100 eV, we compare our results with the
recent absolute measurements of Wingerden et al[6] upto 50° and with
the measurements of Fink et al[7] (normalized to the measurements of
Wingerden et al) beyond 50°. It is clear from the figure that the
present results with $Z = 1.193$ agree on the average to within
about 5% of the experimental data throughout the angular range
considered.

1.   **R.A.** Bonham and T.Iijime, J.Phys. Chem. 67 , 2266 (1963).

2.   D.K.Jain and S.P.Khare, Phys. Lett. A 63 , 237 (1977).

3.   M.K.Srivastava, A.N.Tripathi and Mohan Lal, Phys. Rev. A 18 ,
     2377 (1978).

4.   F.W.Byron, Jr. and C.J.Joachain, Phys. Rev. A 8 , 1267 (1973).

5.   S.K.Srivastava, A.Chutjian and S.Trajmar,J. Chem. Phys. 63 ,
     2659 (1975).

6.   B.Van Wingerden, E.Weigold, F.J. deHeer and K.J.Nygaard,
     J.Phys. B 10 , 1345 (1977).

7.   M.Fink, K.Jost and D.Hermann, Phys. Rev. A 12 , 1374 (1975).

GLAUBER APPROXIMATION FOR $e^- + H_2(g.s.) \rightarrow e^- + H_2^*$
IN A GAUSSIAN BASIS

Kenneth J. LaGattuta

Department of Physics, B-019
University of California at San Diego
La Jolla, California 92093, U.S.A.

We describe our calculation of the Glauber approximation (G.A.) to the scattering amplitudes and differential cross-sections (d.c.s.) for the processes $e^- + H_2(g.s.) \rightarrow e^- + H_2^*$, where g.s. means ground electronic and vibrational state, and * denotes a possible low-lying vibro-rotational excitation. A Gaussian electronic basis function is introduced, the use of which facilitates reduction of integrals over target electron co-ordinates, thus, simplifying the computer arithmetic. In this work we employ neither model potentials nor adjustable parameters.

Our target wave-function, separable in electronic, vibrational, and rotational degrees of freedom is,

$$(1) \quad \Psi_{jm\nu}(\vec{r}_1,\vec{r}_2;\vec{R}) = \sqrt{(4a^3/\pi^3)}/(1+e^{-aR^2})\{e^{-a(|\vec{r}_1-\vec{R}/2|^2+|\vec{r}_2+\vec{R}/2|^2)}$$

$$+ e^{-a(|\vec{r}_1+\vec{R}/2|^2+|\vec{r}_2-\vec{R}/2|^2)}\}Y_{jm}(\hat{R})\phi_\nu(R),$$

where the parameter $a\equiv a(R)$ is chosen at each value of inter-nuclear separation, R, via minimization of the target electronic energy. Using (1), we proceed toward an explicit evaluation of the G.A. to the scattering amplitude, by performing the six-dimensional integral over target electron co-ordinates, exactly. The G.A. to the scattering amplitude reduces to the following five-dimensional integral:

$$(2) \quad f_{GA}^{(jm\nu,j'm'\nu')}(q;k) = (ik/2\pi)\int d\vec{R}\,\phi_{\nu'}^*(R)\phi_\nu(R)Y_{j'm'}^*(\hat{R})Y_{jm}(\hat{R})$$

$$\cdot\int d\vec{b}\,e^{i\vec{q}\cdot\vec{b}}\{ 1 - \Gamma^2(1+i/a_ok)(1/(1+e^{-aR^2}))(2ab_+b_-)^{-2i/a_ok}$$

$$\cdot[\Phi(-2ab_+^2)\Phi(-2ab_-^2) + e^{-aR^2}\cdot\Phi^2(-2ab^2)]\}.$$

In (2), $b_\pm \equiv |\vec{b}\pm\vec{R}_\perp/2|$, with $\vec{R}_\perp \equiv \vec{R} - \sqrt{R^2-\vec{R}\cdot\vec{1}}\cdot\hat{k}$; Γ is the ordinary Gamma-function, and $\Phi(x)\equiv\Phi(-i/a_ok;1;x)$ is the confluent hypergeometric-function.

Using (2), we calculate, numerically, d.c.s.'s for processes involving discrete vibro-rotational target transitions, as well as d.c.s.'s connecting the initial target state to all of the energetically accessible final rotational states; e.g., figures 1 and 2. Comparison is made between these results and the results obtained from a first Born approximation (F.B.A.) calculation. In calculating d.c.s.'s in F.B.A., we make use of the wave-function, equation (1).

In general, for the range of energies (intermediate and high) and scattering angles considered, the G.A. is found to compare with the F.B.A. and with the experimental data in a manner similar to that observed in e^- - atom systems (no electronic excitation). Something of an exception is the case of pure rotational excitation, figure 3, where the apparent dominance of polarization, at small scattering angles, causes a pronounced turning up of the experimentally determined d.c.s. Neither the G.A. nor the F.B.A. reproduce this effect, both predicting a d.c.s. which falls as the scattering angle goes to zero.(A part of the difficulty, here, may be traced to the fact that the wave-function, equation (1), leads to a target quadrupole moment which is too small by $\sim 35\%$)

Cross-sections (c.s.) integrated over angle are determined for the case of purely elastic scatter. The G.A. predicted c.s. is found to be superior to the F.B.A. for all energies considered; see figure 4.

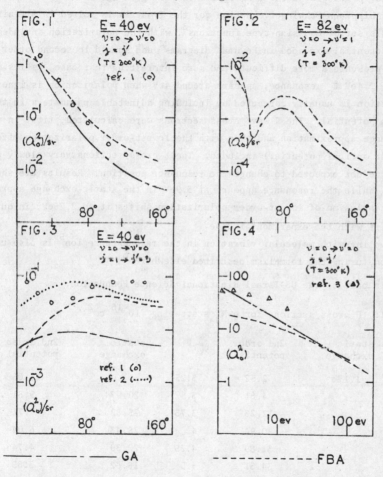

1.   S.K. Srivastava, P.I. Hall, S. Trajmar, and A. Chutjian, Phys. Rev. **124**, 1399 (1975).

2.   D.G. Truhlar and M.A. Brandt, J. Chem. Phys. **65**, 3092 (1976).

3.   F. Linder and H. Schmidt, Z. Naturforsch. **26a**, 1603 (1971).

AB INITIO CALCULATIONS OF LOW ENERGY
ELECTRON-MOLECULE SCATTERING WITH POLARIZATION[*]

Avner Klonover and Uzi Kaldor

Department of Chemistry, Tel-Aviv University, Tel Aviv, Israel

The method first proposed in ICPEAC X[1] for including polarization in low-energy electron-molecule scattering calculations without resort to any empirical parameters has in the meantime produced cross sections for elastic, vibrational and rotational processes in the e-H_2 system in very good agreement with experiment[2]. Briefly, the Lippmann-Schwinger equation for the T matrix is solved in a finite, discrete basis set of Gaussian-type functions[3], with the polarization included via an optical potential expanded in Feynman diagrams[4] and summed to second order. The e-N_2 system presents a more difficult and more interesting test case, as its major feature, the 2.4eV Π_g resonance, appears around 4eV when polarization is ignored, and its position is usually corrected by including adjustable parameters in the polarization potential. The Π wave cross sections were calculated, first in the static-exchange approximation and then with the lowest-order polarization effects (second-order optical potential) included. The Σ cross sections vary slowly with energy and are not expected to change the resonance position. Results are shown in table I. While the resonance appears at 3.9eV in the static-exchange approximation, the inclusion of lowest-order polarization shifts it to 2.75eV, in quite good agreement with the experimental 2.4eV.

The coupling with molecular vibration in the resonance region[5] is also under investigation, using the formalism described elsewhere.[6]

[*]Supported in part by the US-Israel Binational Science Foundation.

Table I: Π cross sections for e-N_2 scattering (10^{-16} cm^2)

E(eV)	static-exchange	2nd order potential	E	static exchange	2nd order potential
2	1.17	2.52	3.25		13.06
2.25		4.61	3.5	20.97	9.81
2.5		12.23	3.75	25.82	7.71
2.6		20.94	4	25.43	6.04
2.7		31.89	4.25	22.39	4.74
2.75		34.51	4.5	18.52	3.85
2.8		33.81	6	8.47	3.39
2.9		27.22	8	6.60	3.08
3	5.14	20.91			

1.   U. Kaldor and A. Klonover, Proc. ICPEAC X 488 (Paris, 1977).

2.   A. Klonover and U. Kaldor, J. Phys. B. 11, 1623 (1978); 12, 232 (1979); 12, L61 (1979).

3.   T.N. Rescigno, C.W. McCurdy and V. McKoy, Phys. Rev. A 10, 2240 (1974); 11, 825 (1975).

4.   J.S. Bell and E.J. Squires, Phys. Rev. Lett. 3, 96 (1959); R.T. Pu and E.S. Chang, Phys. Rev. 151, 31 (1966).

5.   N. Chandra and A. Temkin, Phys. Rev. A 13, 188 (1976).

6.   U. Kaldor, Phys. Rev. A 19, 105 (1979).

ROTATIONAL EXCITATION OF DIATOMIC POLAR MOLECULES BY SLOW ELECTRON IMPACT
PRACTICAL IMPLEMENTATION OF THE FRAME TRANSFORMATION THEORY

Vo Ky Lan, M. Le Dourneuf and B.I. Schneider

Observatoire de Paris, 92190 Meudon, France

The theory of electron molecule collisions is complicated at low energy by the competition between the long range (LR) electrostatic interactions and the dynamical coupling with the nuclear rotation, associated with the breakdown of the Born Oppenheimer (BO) approximation when the colliding electron departs slowly to infinity. The electrostatic interactions are easily described by mere extension of bound state techniques using the BO approximation in the molecular frame (MF). However, this formulation fails in the case of polar molecules, where the molecular permanent dipole interaction leads to infinite forward and total cross sections unless the averaging due to the rotation is explicitly included. The exact laboratory frame (LF) rotational close coupling (CC) which includes both electrostatic and rotational couplings becomes necessary at large distances. However, its use over all space is ruled out due to the convergence difficulties associated with the large number of coupled ℓj channels. Above all, physical intuition suggests that the different dynamical regimes which prevail at short range (BO approximation valid) and long range (ℓj dynamical coupling important) should be described by different representations. Our aim is to show that this important concept of frame transformation (FT) [1] can be implemented practically and successfully within the variable phase method (VPM) [2].

The main problem is to *delimit* the *largest* range of validity of the BO approximation, such that the simpler BO-MF equations could be solved for $r \leqslant r_t$ and the many channel LF rotational CC would converge quickly for $r_t \leqslant r$ with *no significant sacrifice in accuracy*. Let us outline the discussion on the simple case of a rigid $^1\Sigma^+$ molecule interacting with the colliding electron through local potentials. For each total angular momentum J and parity η, the exact MF equations can be written

$$\left[-\frac{d^2}{2dr^2} + \frac{\ell(\ell+1)}{2r^2} - \frac{k^2}{2} \right] G^{J\eta}_{\ell\lambda}(r) + \sum_{\lambda'} U^{J\eta\ell}_{\lambda\lambda'} G^{J\eta}_{\ell\lambda'}(r) + \sum_{\ell'} V^\lambda_{\ell\ell'}(r) G^{J\eta}_{\ell'\lambda}(r) = 0 \qquad (1)$$

with the electrostatic couplings $V^\lambda_{\ell\ell'}(r)$ diagonal in λ (projection of the colliding electron orbital momentum ℓ on the internuclear axis) and the rotational couplings $U^{J\eta\ell}_{\lambda\lambda'}$ diagonal in ℓ, but coupling different λ

$$U^{J\eta\ell}_{\lambda\lambda'} = B \sum_{j=|J-\ell|}^{J+\ell} {}^{J\eta}\Omega^\ell_{\lambda j} \; j(j+1) \, {}^{J\eta}\Omega^\ell_{j\lambda'} \qquad (2)$$

Ω= orthogonal angular transformation between LF and MF

At short distances, when the electrostatic interactions are dominant and a compound (N+1) electron system is formed , the BO adiabatic regime prevails. The colliding electron angular momentum ℓ becomes quantized along the internuclear axis (λ fixed) by the strong axial electrostatic field. The diagonal rotational term $U^{J\eta\ell}_{\lambda\lambda}$ accounts for the average change of relative kinetic energy of the colliding electron as it follows adiabatically the MF rotation. By contrast, the off diagonal rotational couplings describe the departure from the adiabatic BO regime and should be considered when they become comparable to the electrostatic couplings.

These simple remarks are the foundations of our generalized FT theory with no need of recoding existing programs. The most important features to be retained in our formulation of the FT are the following :

1. It still stay entirely within the confines of the BO approximation because we neglect the rotational couplings between λ which remains a good quantum number, but we *keep* the diagonal rotational term

$$k_{\ell J}^2 = k^2 - 2U_{\lambda\lambda}^{J\eta\ell} \tag{3}$$

which accounts for the change of relative kinetic energy of the colliding electron in the rotating MF.

2. This *non* degeneracy is the key generalization in our FT. It involves a negligible complication of the problem in the MF inner region (the energy dependent part of an R-matrix calculation is negligible), but is *essential* to retain the respective coherence of phase between separate channels when changing from the MF ($k_{\ell J}^2$) to the LF ($k_j^2 = k^2 - 2B(j+1)j$). While previous FT implementations neglected these diagonal terms, assuming the relative kinetic energy of the colliding electron unchanged by the nuclear motion or the nuclei pratically fixed during this fraction of the collision; therefore, the phase coherence is preserved only provided $(k - k_j)r_t \ll 1$. This unecessarily stringent condition must be reconciled with the opposite one, that r_t be large enough so that the calculation in LF beyond r_t converges as rapidly as possible. The compatibility of these two requirements makes all previous FT formulations [1,3,4] impracticable in electron polar molecule scattering at the low collision energies

3. On the contrary, the determination of r_t in our FT, including the dynamical effects, is easily implemented within the VPM approach which proceeds by direct outwards integration of the K-matrix

$$\underline{K}' = - (\underline{J} - \underline{N}\,\underline{K})\,2\underline{V}(\underline{J} - \underline{K}\,\underline{N}) \tag{4}$$

and allows to compare locally the rate of variation associated with each part of the potential. The value thus determined is, in many practical cases, larger than the value obtained by a rough estimation

$$r_t \simeq (D/2Bj_{max})^{1/2}$$

Moreover, the VPM + FT procedure is not only convenient but economical and physically clear.

Systematic illustration of the power of the VPM + FT procedure on electronic scattering by CO, HCL, HF, LiH, LiF using a single center close coupling expansion with different treatment of static exchange will be given at the meeting. Its necessity for an accurate predictions of cross sections in the low energy range (1 or 2 eV) of theoretical and technological interest [5] will be assessed. At higher energies, rotational excitation cross sections for polar systems can be reliably generated from standard MF T-matrix elements calculated in the fixed-nuclei approximation [6]. The conditions of validity of fixed nuclei calculations will be reexamined.

1. E.S. Chang and U. Fano, Phys. Rev. A6, 173 (1972)
2. M. Le Dourneuf and Vo Ky Lan, J. Phys. B10, L35 (1977); Proc. CECAM workshop on electron molecule scattering. Meudon (France) 1977; Electron and Photon Molecule Collisions, ed. by Rescigno, McKoy and Schneider (NY. Plenium Press 1979)
3. N. Chandra, Phys. Rev. A12, 2342 (1975)
4. C.W. Clark, to be published in Phys. Rev. 1979
5. K. Rohr, J. Phys. B10, L735 (1977)
6. L.A. Collins and D.W. Norcross, Phys. Rev. A18, 467 (1978)

RESONANT VIBRATIONAL EXCITATION OF DIATOMIC MOLECULES BY ELECTRON IMPACT
AN *ab initio* R-MATRIX CALCULATION FOR $e^- - N_2$

B.I. Schneider, M. Le Dourneuf and Vo Ky Lan

Observatoire de Paris, 92190 Meudon, France

In a recent paper, Schneider et al.[1] have generalized the R-matrix theory of electron molecule scattering to describe vibrational excitation and dissociative attachment. An important feature of the new theory is the claim that the dominant physics can be described within the confines of the Born Oppenheimer (BO) separation of electronic and nuclear motions for the compound system in the strong inter action, small distance range. In other words, no explicit account of dynamical coupling between electronic and nuclear motions [2], through a vibrational close coupling calculation [3], should be necessary to explain the structures observed in resonant vibrational excitation. We propose to assess these assumptions and illustrate the efficiency of the new theory on the widely studied $^2\Pi_g$ shape resonance in $e^- - N_2$ scattering in the 2-3 eV energy range.

The calculation proceeds in four major steps, each of which brings some physical insight into the understanding of the process :

1. The determination of the (N+1) electron R-matrix eigenstates at several internuclear distances, by diagonalizing the fixed nuclei electronic hamiltonian inside a spherical region $(r \leqslant a)$ containing the charge distribution of the target

$$\left[\mathcal{H}_e + \mathcal{L}_b - E_k(R) \right] | \Psi_k^{el}(R) \rangle = 0 \qquad (1)$$

provides a discrete set of R-matrix electronic energies $E_k(R)$ and scattering functions $F_k(r,R)$.[4]

2. The solution of the fixed nuclei $e^- - N_2(^2\Pi_g)$ scattering problem gives the electronic characteristics of the shape resonance. Only one partial wave $\ell = 2$ contributes outside the R-matrix sphere and only two R-matrix eigenstates contribute significantly to its description inside. The position $E_r(R)$ and width $\Gamma(R)$ agree closely with the semi empirical Boomerang model of Birtwistle and Herzenberg [5] in the single configuration approximation using core orbitals optimized in a separate $N_2^-(^2\Pi_g)$ SCF calculation. This simple *ab initio* procedure describes efficiently the strong correlations experienced by the trapped electron while the usual static exchange model (N_2 core orbitals) predicts too large resonance positions and widths.

3. The determination of the nuclear vibrational eigenstates for each R-matrix electronic state reduces to the trivial problem of solving a one dimension differential equation

$$\left[-\frac{1}{2\mu} \frac{d^2}{dR^2} + E_k(R) - E_{kq} \right] \Theta_{kq}(R) = 0 \qquad (2)$$

We have solved (2) using a variational R-matrix approach, in which the vibrational functions are expanded on an analytic basis of floating Gaussians and powers. From the comparison of the compound state vibrational spacings with the resonance width and from the strong off diagonal character of the Franck Condon factor between the N_2 (ground state) vibrational levels χ_{0v} and the two lowest compound R-matrix states Θ_{kq} , one expects significant probability of vibrational excitation, even before the dynamical calculation.

4. The final step of the calculation relies upon the construction of the vibrational R-matrix in the BO approximation

$$\mathcal{R}_{\ell v, \ell' v'}(a) = \sum_{k,q} \frac{\langle \chi_{0v} | F_{k\ell}(a,R) | \Theta_{kq} \rangle \langle \Theta_{kq} | F_{k\ell'}(a,R) | \chi_{0v'} \rangle}{E_{kq} - E} + \langle \chi_{0v} | \mathcal{R}_{\ell\ell'}^{NR} | \chi_{0v'} \rangle \qquad (3)$$

The first sum includes explicitly the contribution of the twelve lower vibrational levels of the first four R-matrix states and the second term gives the contribution of the remaining highly excited R-matrix states in the fixed nuclei approximation. The final $K_{\ell v, \ell' v'}$ matrix is obtained by matching to the outer region solutions (free waves in the present calculation neglecting any long range potentials outside a=8 a.u).

Our final results for vibrational excitation cross sections are compared with Schultz [6] and Wong [7] experiments on figure 1. We consider the systematic shape agreement to be remarkable. Moreover, our purely *ab initio* results support the latest normalization of Wong.

More details on the calculation will be presented at the meeting. However, it might be worthwhile to point out that, after the fixed nuclei electronic calculation was performed, we were able to calculate the vibrational cross sections at over 100 energies in 2 minutes of CDC 6600 time. This enabled us to study the details of individual transitions in a way which would be prohibitive even with the most efficient close coupling technique available.

Fig. 1. Vibrational excitation cross sections $\sigma_{o \to v}$ from the N_2 ground state

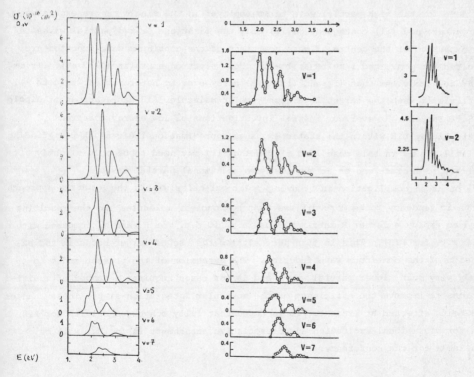

Present theory   Schultz's experiment   Wong's exp.

1. B.I. Schneider, M. Le Dourneuf and P.G. Burke, in press J. Phys. B (1979)
2. B.I. Schneider, Phys. Rev. A14, 1923 (1976)
3. N. Chandra and A. Temkin, 1976, Phys. Rev. A13, 188 and A14, 507
4. B.I. Schneider, 1975, Chem. Phys. Lett. 31, 237 ; Phys. Rev. A11, 1957
5. D.T. Birtwistle and A. Herzenberg, J. Phys. B4, 53 (1971)
6. G.J. Schultz, Phys. Rev. 135, A988 (1964)
7. S.F. Wong, unpublished display in fig. 4 of ref:"Principles of Laser Plasmas"
   G.J. Schultz, John Wiley and sons, 1976)

THE R-MATRIX THEORY FOR ELECTRON-MOLECULE COLLISIONS

B.D. Buckley, P.G. Burke* and L.A. Collins**

Science Research Council, Daresbury Laboratory,
Daresbury, Warrington WA4 4AD, U.K.

The multi-centre R-matrix theory of low energy electron-molecule scattering (Burke et al 1977), which has been applied successfully to the case of homonuclear targets (Buckley et al 1979), is being further tested and extended to the problems of a) scattering by a strongly polar molecule, LiH, and b) vibrational excitation and dissociative attachment in (e^-, H_2) via the $^2\Sigma_u^+$ shape resonance using the recently developed theory of Schneider et al (1979).

The calculations of Buckley et al on electron scattering by homonuclear targets within the static exchange approximation have shown (i) the explicit introduction of nuclear centred expressions for the continuum wave function obviates the need for the high partial wave terms employed in the single centre expansion approaches; and (ii) consequent on (i) only the first one or two partial waves in the expansion of the centre of mass component of the continuum wave function are required for converged results at low incident electron energies (0-13 eV). It is by no means obvious that (i) and (ii) will carry over to heteronuclear targets – particularly when the target is a highly polar molecule (LiH has a permanent dipole of 5.88 Debye). However our initial investigations of low energy electron scattering by LiH within the static exchange approximation indicate that a) finding (i) still holds in this case, and b) finding (ii) may need to be only slightly modified to include one or at the most two additional partial waves.

An added complication in studying polar molecules within the R-matrix approach is their tendency to be more diffuse than homonuclear molecules and the resulting need to employ a larger R-matrix radius (e.g. 10 a.u. for H_2 and N_2 compared with 15.0 a.u. for LiH). This in turn necessitates the use of larger bases in the expansion of the continuum wave function. The extension of the present codes to study very much higher partial waves and larger bases requires a number of modifications to improve the efficiency of the molecular integration step. These changes are being effected at present. It is hoped that fully converged results for LiH and for vibrational excitation and dissociative attachment in (e^-, H_2) will be available for the conference.

*   also: Department of Applied Mathematics and Theoretical Physics,
              The Queen's University, Belfast BT7 1NN, N. Ireland.

**   Theoretical Division (T-4), Los Alamos Scientific Laboratory, New Mexico 87545
       U.S.A.

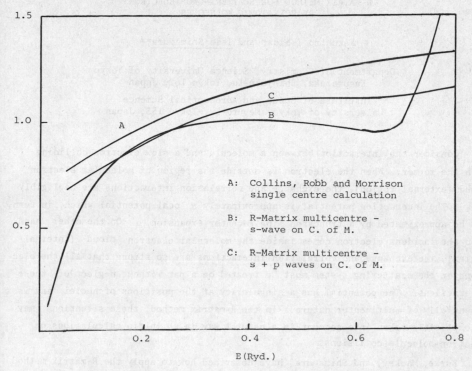

Static-exchange eigenphases for electron scattering by LiH in the $^2\Pi$ channel.

References

Buckley B.D., Burke P.G. and Vo Ky Lan (1979), submitted to Comp.Phys.Commun.

Burke P.G., Mackey I. and Shimamura I. (1977), J.Phys.B:Atom.Molec.Phys. 10, 2497.

Schneider B.I., Le Dourneuf M. and Burke P.G. (1979), submitted to J.Phys.B: Atom.Molec.Phys.

R-MATRIX METHOD FOR SCATTERING OF ELECTRONS
BY POLYATOMIC MOLECULES

Kazuhiro Ishida* and Isao Shimamura**

* Department of Chemistry, Science University of Tokyo
Kagurazaka, Shinjuku-Ku, Tokyo 162, Japan

** Institute of Space and Aeronautical Science
University of Tokyo, Meguro-Ku, Tokyo 153, Japan

Consider the interaction between a molecule and a slow electron colliding
with the former. When the electron is outside the region of molecular electron
cloud (external region), the exchange and correlation interactions are negligibly
weak. The interaction potential is approximately a local potential which, in tern,
may be approximated by a truncated single-center expansion. On the other hand,
when the incident electron comes inside the molecular electron cloud (internal
region), the exchange and correlation interactions are so strong that all the electrons in the scattering system must be treated on a par without neglect of these
interactions. The potential has a singularity at the positions of nuclei and is
essentially of multicenter nature. In the R-matrix method, these situations may
be explicitly taken into account in a natural way in ab initio calculations on
electron-molecule collisions.

Burke, Mackey, and Shimamura[1] have described how to apply the R-matrix method
to electron scattering by diatomic molecules. They have used Slater-type orbitals
as basis functions to form the internal-region wavefunction, and have applied the
variational R-matrix formulation discussed by Shimamura.[2,3] Schneider et al.[4,5]
have used Gaussian-type orbitals (GTO) in spheroidal coordinates to treat scattering by diatomic molecules. They have approximated the internal-region wavefunction,
which is sharply cut off to zero at the boundary $\mathcal{S}$ between the internal and external regions, by a linear combination of GTO which extend out to the external region.

In this paper, we extend the R-matrix method to electron scattering by polyatomic molecules. Single-center expansion of the internal-region wavefunction
destroys one of the main merits of the R-matrix method. Indeed, the importance of
multicenter treatment has been shown by Dehmer et al.[6] using the continuum multiple-scattering method. Although multicenter molecular integrals over a finite
integration-region are difficult to obtain, we have succeeded in devising a method
of computing them. We employ a spherical internal region as in a previous paper.[1]

To describe the wavefunctions of the target molecule, we start from a set of
primitive GTO in the polar coordinates (r, θ, ϕ). Contracted basis sets for atoms
composing the molecule are formed from the primitive GTO according to, for example,
Dunning.[7] In constructing molecular orbitals (MO), those contracted GTO (CGTO)
which decay rapidly are centered at nuclei as usual, but diffuse CGTO which reach
$\mathcal{S}$ are moved to the center of gravity G. These MO (which we call bound MO or BMO)
are used for variational determination of target states. Slightly changing the

exponents of the diffuse CGTO, we obtained no less accurate results than the usual LCAO MO calculations.

The additional electron in the total scattering system may, in the internal region, occupy a BMO which is not fully occupied by target electrons. We define continuum MO (CMO), which also may be occupied by the additional electron. For this purpose we first define continuum GTO which have a small exponent and which are centered at G. We construct a set of CMO by Schmidt-orthogonalizing the continuum GTO to BMO.

In the above choice of the basis set, all the primitive GTO centered at nuclei decay before they reach the boundary $\mathscr{S}$. Only those centered at G can reach $\mathscr{S}$. This fact greatly simplifies computations of multicenter integrals over the finite region, and hence of the Hamiltonian matrix defined over the internal region. Using this Hamiltonian matrix, we can obtain the R matrix on $\mathscr{S}$.

In the external region, we use a truncated single-center expansion of the nonspherical, local interaction potential about the center of gravity G. The external region is divided into subregions which are spherical shells, and in each of them a variational R-matrix formulation is applied.[8] In this formulation, the R matrix on the outer surface of a spherical shell is related variationally to the R matrix on the inner surface. Hence, the R matrix may be propagated from $\mathscr{S}$ out to the asymptotic region, where the R matrix is transformed into a K or S matrix.

Because the molecular frame of reference is appropriate in the internal region, and because the laboratory frame should be used in the asymptotic region, we employ a frame-transformation technique similar to the one described by Chang and Fano.[9] This may be done on $\mathscr{S}$, may be done at infinity, or may be done somewhere inside the external region.

A system of computer programs has been written to enable calculations of electronic states of polyatomic molecules and of electron scattering by polyatomic molecules. At the time of writing, this system is being tested on scattering by some diatomic molecules.

1. P. G. Burke, I. Mackey, and I. Shimamura, J. Phys. B10, 2497 (1977).

2. I. Shimamura, J. Phys. B10, 2597 (1977).

3. I. Shimamura, Electronic and Atomic Collisions, Invited Papers and Progress Reports, X ICPEAC, Paris, July 1977, ed. G. Watel (North-Holland, Amsterdam, 1978) pp.213-230.

4. B. I. Schneider, Phys. Rev. A11, 1957 (1975).

5. B. I. Schneider and P.J. Hay, Phys. Rev. A13, 2049 (1976).

6. J. L. Dehmer and D. Dill, Electron and Photon Molecule Collisions, V.McKoy, T. Rescigno, and B. Schneider, Eds. (Plenum Press, New York, 1979)

7. T. H. Dunning, Jr., J. Chem. Phys. 53, 2823 (1970).

8. I. Shimamura, Report of Workshop on Electron Molecule Collisions, CECAM, Orsay, August-September, 1977, pp.69-80.

9. E. S. Chang and U. Fano, Phys. Rev. A6, 173 (1972).

LOW-ENERGY ELECTRON-MOLECULE COLLISIONS: SINGLE-CENTER ITERATIVE CLOSE-COUPLING METHOD

L. A. Collins*, W. D. Robb* and M. A. Morrison[†]

* Theoretical Division
Los Alamos Scientific Laboratory
Los Alamos, New Mexico 87545

† Department of Physics
University of Oklahoma
Norman, Oklahoma 73069

We report the results of calculations of electron-molecule collisions performed by an iterative close-coupling (CC) method.[1] The dynamics are formulated in the body-frame within the adiabatic fixed-nuclei approximation. The continuum and bound orbitals are expanded in spherical harmonics about the center-of-mass of the molecule. By integrating over the angular variables, we obtain a set of coupled radial differential equations, which in turn are converted to a set of integral equations. When nonlocal exchange terms are present, the integral equations are solved iteratively by methods similar to those employed in electron-atom scattering.[2] At each iteration the exchange term is transformed to a local potential by dividing by the continuum wavefunction from the previous iteration.[3] This procedure places the integral equations in a form that is readily handled by the outward propagation schemes that we have developed for local potentials.[4] For total symmetries for which there is no corresponding bound orbital of the target molecule, the calculations converge quite rapidly, usually within four or five iterations. In cases where there are bound and continuum orbitals of the same symmetry, we find that forcing orthogonality speeds the convergence.

The single-center expansion is a natural and convenient formulation for treating a wide variety of molecular geometries and systems. The highly systematic convergence of the cross section in the various expansion parameters (e.g., number of channels) marks one major advantage of the single-center expansion. A possible drawback to the procedure may be slow convergence which leads to prohibitive computational costs; however, close-coupling calculations for molecular systems with thirty to forty channels have been efficiently performed.

As a first application, we have performed calculations in the static-exchange approximation for electron collisions with neutral and ionic molecules. For $e - H_2$ and N_2 our results are in good agreement with those of the L^2-methods[5] and noniterative close-coupling techniques[6] (except in the Π_g symmetry in N_2). For the resonance symmetry only, we find that the tightly bound 1σ orbitals of N_2 (which were neglected in earlier CC calculations) make a non-negligable contribution to the exchange component. We also report calculations for $e - CO$ and $e - LiH$ collisions. The Π resonance in CO at the static-exchange level is found at 3.8 eV; no resonances are observed in either the Π or Σ symmetries for the strongly polar system LiH. In addition, we describe a study of the behavior of the Π_g shape resonance in the $e - C_2$ system as a function of isoelectronic members (BN, BeO, LiF). Finally, we have performed calculations for electron collisions with the positive molecular ions, H_2^+ and CH^+. The results of these calculations are in reasonable agreement with earlier calculations.[7] We report results for electron collisions with the important atmospheric ion NO^+.

Another area of interest is electronic excitation. We have performed a two-state calculation for the electronic excitation of H_2^+. The closed-state results for the resonance symmetries show quite good agreement with the Steiltjes imaging method of Hazi[8] and away from resonance with the polarized orbital method.[9]

References

1. L. A. Collins, W. D. Robb and M. A. Morrison, J. Phys. B11, L777 (1978).

2. M. J. Seaton, Proc. Roy. Soc. A218, 400 (1973); T. L. John. Proc. Phys. Soc. (London) 76, 532 (1960).

3. J. C. Tully and R. S. Berry, J. Chem. Phys. 51, 2056 (1969).

4. M. A. Morrison and L. A. Collins, Phys. Rev. A18, 918 (1978); L. A. Collins and D. W. Norcross Phys. Rev. A18, 467 (1978).

5. B. I. Schneider, Phys. Rev. A11, 1957 (1975).
   M. A. Morrison and B. I. Schneider, Phys. Rev. A16, 1003 (1977).
   A. W. Fliflet et al, Phys. Rev. A17, 160 (1978).
   A. W. Fliflet and V. McKoy, Phys. Rev. A18, 2107 (1978).

6. B. D. Buckley and P. G. Burke, J. Phys. B. 10, 725 (1977).

7. A. Temkin and K. V. Vasavada, Phys. Rev. 160, 109 (1967).
   H. Lefebvre-Brion et al, J. Phys. B11, 2735 (1978).

8. A. Hazi, Proc. of the Workshop on Electron- and Photon-molecule Processes (Asilomar, 1978).

9. A. Temkin et al, Phys. Rev. 186, 57 (1969).

EFFECTS OF SHAPE RESONANCES, NUCLEAR MOTION, AND DIPOLE FIELDS ON ELECTRON-MOLECULE SCATTERING FROM 0-100 eV.[*]

Jon Siegel and J. L. Dehmer
Argonne National Laboratory, Argonne, Illinois 60439 USA

and

Dan Dill
Department of Chemistry, Boston University
Boston, Massachusetts 02215 USA

Using the continuum multiple-scattering model (CMSM)[1,2] with Hara exchange,[3,4] we have been surveying electron-molecule scattering processes in the range 0-100 eV, with special emphasis on shape resonances, effects of nuclear motion, and, most recently, scattering from polar molecules. Results to be presented here include: (a) Comprehensive electronically-elastic cross sections for e^--N_2 scattering between 0 and 50 eV. Momentum-transfer, and integrated and differential elastic, rotationally-inelastic, and vibrationally-inelastic cross sections will be used to characterize the π_g (2.4 eV) and σ_u (22 eV) shape resonances and will serve as input for future modeling of subexcitation electrons in N_2. (b) Electron scattering from polar molecules, as illustrated by e^--LiF scattering. A hybrid approach to this problem (similar in spirit to that of Collins and Norcross[5]) has been developed which combines a body-frame CMSM treatment for low-ℓ scattering, a semiclassical treatment[6] for intermediate to high-ℓ processes, and, finally, a first-Born extrapolation[7] to infinite ℓ. Our results are compared with experiment and recent results by Collins and Norcross.[5] (c) Comparison of our predictions of enhanced vibrational excitation via high-energy (10-30 eV) shape resonances in e^--N_2 and e^--CO_2 with experiment.[8] (d) Application of CMSM to electron scattering processes involving larger molecular systems, e.g., SF_6 and C_2H_4.

[*]Work supported by the U.S. Department of Energy, National Science Foundation Grant CHE78-08707, and American Chemical Society Petroleum Research Fund Grant 10785-AC6.

1. D. Dill and J. L. Dehmer, J. Chem. Phys. 61, 692 (1974).

2. J. L. Dehmer and D. Dill, in Electron and Photon Molecule Collisions, V. McKoy, T. Rescigno, and B. Schneider, Eds. (Plenum Press, New York-London, 1979).

3. S. Hara, J. Phys. Soc. Japan 22, 710 (1967).

4. J. Siegel, J. L. Dehmer, and Dan Dill, Phys. Rev. A, to be published.

5. L. A. Collins and D. W. Norcross, Phys. Rev. A $\underline{18}$, 467 (1978).

6. D. Mukherjee and F. T. Smith, Phys. Rev. A $\underline{17}$, 954 (1978).

7. O. H. Crawford and A. Dalgarno, J. Phys. B $\underline{4}$, 494 (1971).

8. For e-N_2, Z. Pavlovic, M. J. W. Boness, A. Herzenberg, and G. J. Schulz, Phys. Rev. A $\underline{6}$, 676 (1972); for e-CO_2, M. Tronc and co-workers, to be published.

VIBRATIONAL EXCITATION IN LOW ENERGY ELECTRON–CARBON MONOXIDE SCATTERING: A HYBRID THEORY CALCULATION*

B. H. CHOI AND ROBERT T. POE
Department of Physics, University of California
Riverside, California 92521 U.S.A.

Hybrid theory[1,2] was used to study the vibrational transitions in low energy e-CO scattering. In this theory, the condition of the fixed internuclear separation is relaxed and the vibrational states of the target molecule are coupled dynamically, while the adiabatic-nuclei approximations are made for the rotational motion. The static electron-molecule potential in the ground electronic state $^1\Sigma^+$ of CO was computed from the molecular wave functions obtained from the self-consistent field calculation[3] with an extended basis set of 17 Slater type atomic orbitals. The exchange effects were treated with the energy dependent local exchange approximation[4], but both spherical and non-spherical parts of the potential were included. The linear approximations were made around the equilibrium separation R_o for the polarizabilities of CO in the polarization potential. The values of $\alpha_0(R_o)$, $\alpha_0'(R_o)$, $\alpha_2(R_o)$ and $\alpha_2'(R_o)$ were partly obtained from the measurements[5,6] or partly computed from the molecular wave function.[3] The vibrational close-coupling calculations were made with the inclusion of seven vibrational states and five partial waves.

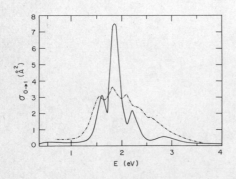

Figure 1. The $0\to1$ vibrational excitation cross section; —— present calculation; ·-·- experimental data taken from Ref. 7.

Reasonable agreements between experiment[7] and this ab initio theory were obtained for the cross sections and, in particular, for the substructures of $0 \to v$ ($v = 1,2,3,4..$) vibrational excitation cross sections around 1.7 eV $^2\Pi$ shape resonance. Furthermore, the present calculations predicted the strong resonance peak[8] at 1.4 eV in the $1 \to 2$ vibrational excitation. In general, the theoretical vibrational transition cross sections decrease in the present resonance region as $\Delta v = |v_f - v_i|$ increases.

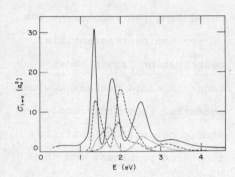

Figure 2. The $1 \to v$ vibrational excitation cross sections; ——— v=2; - - - - v=3; ···· v=4; —·—·— v=5.

*Work supported by NASA and AF/APL Contract No. F33615-77-C-2011.

1. N. Chandra and A. Temkin, Phys. Rev. A13, 188 (1976).

2. B. H. Choi and R. T. Poe, Phys. Rev. A16, 1831 (1977).

3. A. D. McLean and M. Yoshimine, IBM J. Res. Dev. Suppl. 12, 206 (1967).

4. S. Hara, J. Phys. Soc. Japan 22, 710 (1967).

5. N. J. Bridge and A. D. Buckingham, Proc. Roy. Soc. (London), Ser. A295, 334 (1966).

6. E. R. Lippincott and G. Nagarajan, Bull. Soc. Chim. Belges 74, 551 (1965).

7. H. Ehrhardt, L. Langhans, F. Linder and H. S. Taylor, Phys. Rev. 173, 222 (1968).

8. J. M. Phillips, J. A. Michejda and S. F. Wong, Bull. Am. Phys. Soc., Vol. 23, No. 9, 1081 (1978).

ELECTRON–CARBON DIOXIDE SCATTERING AT INTERMEDIATE AND HIGH ENERGIES; TWO-POTENTIAL APPROACH*

JAMES C. SUN, B. H. CHOI, AND ROBERT T. POE
Department of Physics, University of California
Riverside, California 92521 U.S.A.

A general and simple theoretical approach, the Two-Potential Approach[1], for electron-molecule scattering - elastic, vibrational and rotational excitations - was applied to e-CO_2 scatterings. In this approach, the scattering process is contributed from the incoherent sum of two dominant potentials; contribution from a short range shielded nuclear Coulomb potential from individual atomic centers and contribution from permanent and induced long range potential. The calculations were made on the cross sections for elastic scattering and the vibrational excitations from the ground state to the low lying excited states of, symmetric and asymmetric, stretching and bending modes.

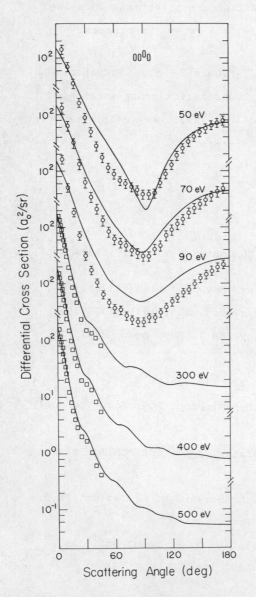

Figure 1. Vibrationally elastic differential cross sections. Experimental data were taken from Ref. 2.

The results for the elastic scattering from 50 ∿ 500 eV incident
electron energies yield excellent agreement with the absolutely
calibrated experimental data.[2] The present vibrational excitation cross sections are in agreement with available experimental
measurement.[3] The general feature of e-CO_2 scattering will also
be discussed.

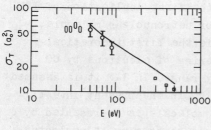

Figure 2. Vibrationally elastic
integral cross sections. Experimental data were taken from
Ref. 2.

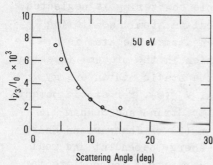

Figure 3. The ratio,
$\sigma(00^00) \rightarrow (00^01)/\sigma(00^00) \rightarrow (00^00)$,
for the differential cross sec-
tions. Experimental data from
Ref. 3.

*Work supported by NASA and Cal Tech President's Fund.

1. B. H. Choi, R. T. Poe, J. C. Sun and Y. Shan, Phys. Rev. A19,
    116 (1979).

2. T. W. Shyn, W. E. Sharp and G. R. Carignan, Phys. Rev. A17,
    1855 (1978); J. P. Bromberg, J. Chem. Phys. 60, 1717 (1974).

3. A. Skerbele, M. A. Dillon and E. N. Lassettre, J. Chem. Phys.
    49, 5042 (1968).

ELASTIC SCATTERING OF ELECTRONS BY CO MOLECULES

S.P.KHARE   AND DEO RAJ

Department of Physics, Meerut University,Meerut-250001,INDIA.

Independent atom model (IAM) has been utilised to investigate elastic scattering of electrons by carbon monoxide in the intermediate energy range. This is the first application of IAM in conjunction with partial waves for hetronuclear molecule, namely CO. As a matter of fact, it is the first theoretical investigation for the elastic scattering of electrons by CO molecules in the intermediate energy range. In IAM it is assumed that each atom scatters independently. In the present investigation the vibrational motion of the molecule is represented by a harmonic oscillator and the multiple scattering is neglected.

We employ partial waves to calculate atomic scattering amplitudes $f(\theta)$ for carbon and oxygen atoms. The atom is replaced by an optical potential, which in the present investigation has been taken as the sum of the static and an energy dependent real polarisation potential $V_{dp}(r)$. For static potential the analytical expression given by Strand and Bonham[1] is employed for both the atoms. Equation (2) of Jhanwar and Khare[2] is taken for spherically symmetric, energy dependent and real polarisation potential with various parameters appropriate for C and O atoms. Resultant differential equation is then numerically solved for phase shift δ_l of the lth partial wave.

After having thus obtained δ_l, $f(\theta)$ are calculated and finally the differential cross section (DCS) averaged over different orientations of the molecular axis for CO molecule is obtained. For comparison, we have also calculated DCS in first Born as well as in Khare and Shobha approximation (KSA) without exchange[3]. These results along with available experimental data[4] are displayed in figure 1 for 400 eV electrons.

It is evident that the shape of the present curve C is in good agreement with the experimental data. As a matter of fact all the small variations in the theoretical curve (due to oscillatory term) are supported by the experimental data. Quantitatively at low angles extremely good agreement between the theory and the experiment is obtained. Such an agreement at low angles indicates

the usefulness of the polarisation potential proposed by
Jhanwar and Khare[2], which also yielded fairly good results for
He,Ne and Ar targets[2,5,6]. For large angles ($\theta \geq 10°$) the present
results are slightly higher than the experimental data. However,
the difference is within about 25%.

We have obtained DCS for CO over a wide energy range of the
incident electrons (50-800 eV). Agreement between the theory
and the experiment is of the same nature as is shown in figure
1. Detailed results will be presented in the conference.The
investigations with the other homo and hetronuclear molecules
are in progress.

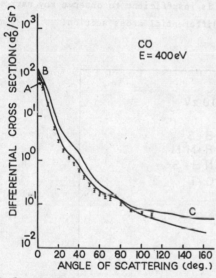

Fig.1 Elastic differential
cross section for electron-
carbon monoxide molecule at
400 eV.

Curve A-first Born approxi-
        mation.

Curve B-Khare and Shobha
        approximation
        (without exchange)

Curve C-partial wave method

ϕ - Bromberg (1970).

References

[1] T.G.Strand and R.A.Bonham,J.Chem.Phys.40, 1686 (1964).
[2] B.L.Jhanwar and S.P.Khare, J.Phys.B9,1527 (1976).
[3] S.P.Khare and P.Shobha,Phys.Lett.31A, 571 (1970).
[4] J.P.Bromberg, J.Chem.Phys.52, 1243 (1970).
[5] B.L.Jhanwar,S.P.Khare and A.Kumar Jr.J.Phys.B11,887 (1978).
[6] S.P.Khare and A.Kumar Jr., Pramana 10, 63 (1978).

Elastic differential electron scattering from the polyatomic molecules
CH_4, C_2H_2 and C_2H_4

W.R. NEWELL, D.F.C. BREWER[*] AND A.C.H. SMITH

Department of Physics and Astronomy, University
College London

[*]Present address : Scicon Consultancy Ltd.,
49-57 Berners Street London W1P 4AQ

In this paper we present new measurements for the elastic scattering of
monochromatic electrons from the polyatomic molecules methane, ethylene and
acetylene for incident electron energies of 7.5eV to 50eV and over an angular
range of $\Theta = 20^{\circ}$ to 130°. The previous work[1,2,3] was done using electron beams
of low monochromaticity ($\Delta E \sim 1eV$) which is insufficient to observe any narrow
width structure which may exist in the differential cross section.

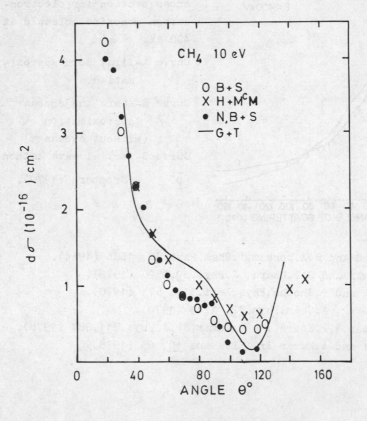

FIGURE (1)

O Bullard and Massey;   X   Hughes and McMillen

● Present Data; —— Gianturco and Thompson

The co-axial cone electron spectrometer used in these high resolution $(\Delta E = 90\text{meV})$ scattering experiments has been described in an accompanying paper. The apparatus is used in a crossed beam mode and the electron optics is so designed that the lens stack which detects the scattered electron flux has an acceptance angle which always views the total overlap of the electron and gas beams. Hence, no correction to the data is necessary for any change in scattering volume with scattering angle.

Figure 1 shows the elastic differential cross sections in CH_4 compared with the earlier work of Hughes and McMillen. Recent theoretical work by Thompson[4] on electron scattering of electrons from hydrides in which account is taken of the effects of exchange and polarization is in good agreement with the present measurements on CH_4. Experimental data will be presented for the molecules C_2H_2 and C_2H_4 and compared with current calculations.

1.   Hughes A.L. and McMillen J.H., 1933 Phys. Rev. <u>44</u> 876-82
2.   Childs E.C. and Woodcock A.H., 1934 Proc. Roy. Soc. A. <u>146</u> 199-205
3.   Bullard E.C. and Massey H.S.W., 1931 Proc. Roy. Soc. <u>133</u> 637-51
4.   Thompson A.G., Private Communication.

ELECTRON-IMPACT CROSS SECTIONS FOR v = 0 → 1 VIBRATIONAL EXCITATION IN
CO AT ELECTRON ENERGIES OF 3 TO 100 eV[*]

Hiroshi Tanaka[†] and Ara Chutjian[‡]

[†]Sophia University, Faculty of Science and Technology,
7 Kioi-chō, Chiyoda-ku, Tokyo 102, Japan

[‡]Jet Propulsion Laboratory, California Institute
of Technology, Pasadena, Calif. USA

Measurements have been carried out of normalized, absolute differential, integral and momentum-transfer cross sections of the v = 0 → 1 pure vibrational transition in CO. Incident electron energies were in the range 3-100 eV, and the range of scattering angles 10-135°. Comparison of the CO measurements is made to pure v = 0 → 1 vibrational cross sections in N_2,[1,2] as well as to a recent two-potential theory for electron scattering from diatomic molecules.[3,4]

Shown in Fig. 1 are experimental data for CO (crosses) at the higher energies of 50, 75 and 100 eV. Comparisons are made to earlier CO measurements[5] (triangles), N_2 data[2] (open circles), and theory[4] (solid line). Several points are evident in Fig. 1. First, the data for N_2 and CO are in remarkably good agreement with one another--to within combined experimental errors over most of the angular range. Similar agreement is also found in the energy range 3-30 eV. This result implies that the presence of the small dipole moment in CO (μ_e = 0.12D) has little effect on the scattering, and that vibrational excitation proceeds mainly via short-range forces in CO, rather than the long-range dipole potential. The two-potential theory[3,4] is in good agreement with the data, both in absolute magnitude and shape. In particular, the experimental dip at low angles ($\theta < 40^{\circ}$) is reproduced, and arises in the theory from the long-range polarization potential; while the dip at middle angles ($\theta \sim 80^{\circ}$, especially at 50 eV) arises from short-range atomic scattering amplitudes for C and O.

Results of integral and momentum-transfer cross sections are given in Fig. 2. The significant hump at 20 eV in both cross sections is further evidence of resonant-excitation processes in this energy region. This effect was seen earlier in data at only two scattering angles (40° and 80°).[5] It is more complete verification of resonance processes taking place in the energy range 15-30 eV, and results will be discussed in terms of many narrowly-spaced, doubly core-excited states in CO^-. Agreement with theory is satisfactory, especially for σ_I which weights more heavily the middle angles in Fig. 1, rather than for σ_M and higher angles.

[*]This work was supported by NASA under Contract No. NAS7-100 to the Jet
Propulsion Laboratory, California Institute of Technology.

1. D. G. Truhlar, M. A. Brandt, A. Chutjian, S. K. Srivastava and S. Trajmar,
    J. Chem. Phys. 65, 2962 (1976).

2. D. G. Truhlar, M. A. Brandt, S. K. Srivastava, S. Trajmar and A. Chutjian, J. Chem. Phys. 66, 655 (1977).

3. B. H. Choi, R. T. Poe, J. C. Sun and Y. Shan, Phys. Rev. A 19, 116 (1979).

4. J. C. Sun, B. H. Choi and R. T. Poe, Bull. Am. Phys. Soc. 23, 1083 (1978).

5. A. Chutjian, D. G. Truhlar, W. Williams and S. Trajmar, Phys. Rev. Lett. 29, 1580 (1972).

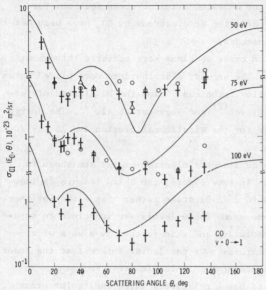

Figure 1. Differential cross sections for the v = 0 → 1 vibrational excitation in CO. Present measurements are given as crosses, earlier data[5] as triangles, and measurements for N_2[2] as open circles. Solid lines are results of the two-potential theory.[4]

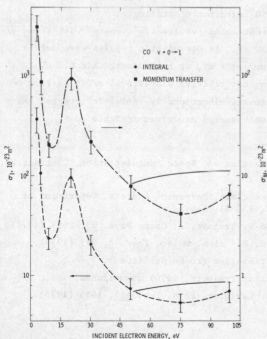

Figure 2. Integral and momentum-transfer cross sections for the v = 0 → 1 transition in CO. Solid lines are results for the two-potential theory[4] multiplied by a factor 0.5.

ELASTIC SCATTERING AND VIBRATIONAL EXCITATION
OF CO_2 BY 4, 10, 20 and 50 eV ELECTRONS[†]

Hiroyuki Nishimura[*], David F. Register and Sandor Trajmar

Jet Propulsion Laboratory, California Institute
of Technology, Pasadena, CA 91103

Absolute differential, integral and momentum transfer cross sections for elastic and vibrationally inelastic scattering of electrons by CO_2 have been measured at 4, 10, 20 and 50 eV impact energies.

Elastic and vibrational excitation cross sections were measured throughout a $10°$ to $140°$ angular scattering range. The angular distributions were placed on an absolute scale by using the relative flow technique[1] and the He elastic differential cross sections of Andrick and Bitsch[2] and Register et al.[3] The energy resolution of our apparatus was 70 meV for the elastic calibration and 25 meV for the vibrational excitation measurements.

Typical energy loss spectra at 4 eV incident electron energy are shown in Fig. 1 for several scattering angles. In this figure, the third feature is identified as the overlapping (1 0 0) and (0 $2^{0,2}$ 0) state rather than either of these single excitations. This has been done since these levels are too close to separate with the present instrumental resolution and this feature is always wider than either the elastic or (0 1^1 0) features. Of particular interest at the lower energies is the strong angular dependence of the inelastic cross sections. In Fig. 4, for instance, the (0 0 1) state has a relatively large excitation cross section at $30°$ but is very weak for $90°$ electron scattering.

In Fig. 2, the present elastic scattering results are compared with those of Danner[4] and Shyn[5] at 10, 20 and 50 eV. As our elastic results were not as extensively measured as those of Danner at 4 eV, we have adopted his 4.2 eV elastic cross sections for normalizing our relative vibrational cross section measurements at this energy. The elastic and vibrationally inelastic integral and momentum transfer cross sections at each energy are given in Table I.

[†]Work supported by the National Aeronautics and Space Administration, Contract No. NAS7-100.

[*]NRC-NASA Senior Resident Research Associate, Permanent Address, Department of Physics, Niigata University, Niigata 950-21, Japan.

1. S. K. Srivastava, A. Chutjian and S. Trajmar, J. Chem. Phys. 63, 2659 (1975).

2. D. Andrick and H. Bitsch, J. Phys. B: Atom. Molec. Phys. 8, 393 (1975).

3. D. Register, S. Trajmar and S. Srivastava (to be published).

4. D. Danner, Ph.D. Thesis (Universität Freiburg, 1970) unpublished.

5. T. W. Shyn, W. E. Sharp and G. R. Carignan, Phys. Rev. A17, 1855 (1978).

E_0	4	10	20	50
E1.	8.76	11.66	12.62	11.84
	6.21	10.19	7.89	5.38
(010	1.5	.202	.09	.102
	1.47	.162	.101	.106
(100-	1.20	.216	.134	.014
020)	.96	.219	.009	.020
(001)	–	.131	.08	.035
		.075	.035	.022

Table 1. Summary of Measured Cross Sections. Upper entry is integral cross section, lower entry is momentum transfer.

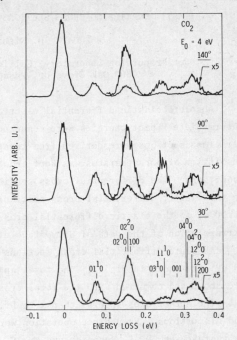

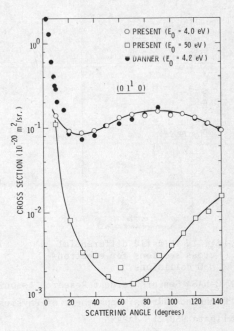

Fig. 1 4 eV Energy Loss Spectra

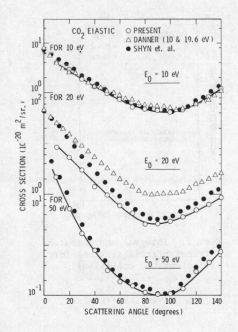

Fig. 2 CO_2 Elastic DCS

Fig. 3 CO_2 Inelastic $(01^1 0)$ DCS

ELASTIC SCATTERING CROSS SECTIONS OF H_2O BY LOW ENERGY ELECTRONS

H. Nishimura*

Jet Propulsion Laboratory, California Institute of Technology,
4800 Oak Grove Dr. Pasadena, California 91103

Absolute elastic differential electron scattering cross sections for H_2O at intermediate impact energies were measured. The integral and the momentum transfer cross sections were derived from these differential cross sections. The energy resolution of our apparatus was kept about 150 meV to achieve good signal to noise conditions. The differential cross sections at 30, 50 and 70 eV were normalized to the elastic differential cross sections of He measured by Register et al.[1] and at 90 eV to the elastic differential cross sections of N_2 which were obtained by extrapolation of the data of Srivastave et al.[2]

Absolute differential cross sections for H_2O at impact energy of 30 eV and 90 eV were shown in Fig. 1. The total and the momentum transfer cross sections are shown and compared with the total cross sections measured by Bruche[3] in Fig. 2.

The author owes special thanks to Dr. S. Trajmar for his helpful cooperations and discussions. Valuable cooperation were given us by Dr. A. Chutjian, Dr. S. K. Srivastave, Dr. D. F. Register and Mr. G. Stephensen.

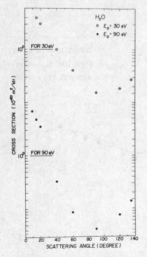

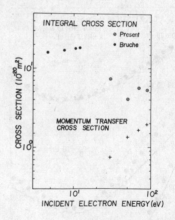

Fig. 1.   Elastic differential
cross sections for electron-
H_2O collisions.

Fig. 2.   Integral and momentum
transfer cross sections for
electron-H_2O collisions.

*   NRC-NASA Senior Resident Research Associate
    Permanent address: Department of Physics, Niigata University, Ikarashi,
    Niigata 950-21   JAPAN

1) D. F. Register, S. Trajmar and S. K. Srivastave (to be published)
2) S. K. Srivastava, A. Chutjian and S. Trajmar, J. Chem. Phys. 64, 1340 (1976)
3) E. Bruche, Ann. Physik, 1, 93 (1929)

Measurement of the Differential Cross Sections for Elastic Scattering of
Electrons (70–500 eV) by CCl_4 and As_4 Molecules

H. Daimon[*], T. Kondow and K. Kuchitsu

Department of Chemistry, Faculty of Science
The University of Tokyo, Bunkyo-ku, Tokyo, 113 Japan

Elastic differential cross sections (EDCS) of electrons in collision with
CCl_4 and As_4 were measured by a crossed beam method at scattering angles between
3° and 135° and at impact energies of 70, 300 and 500 eV for CCl_4 and 100 and
500 eV for As_4. A particular attention was paid to observing the effect of
intramolecular multiple scattering on the EDCS.
      A schematic diagram of the aparatus is shown in Fig. 1. The background pressure
was 1×10^{-6} Torr, and the effective pressure in the scattering region was estimated to be of the order of 10^{-4} Torr. Terrestrial magnetic field was less than
5 mG by a μ-metal shield and two pairs of Helmholtz coils. Primary electron beam
was about 5×10^{-7} A. Experimental uncertainties in the relative EDCS were estimated to be in the range from 3 to 10 % and angular resolution was about 2°.
Crystalline arsenic was heated to 400°C so as to obtain a sufficient vapor pressure of As_4 for the measurement of EDCS. The relative cross sections were normalized to those calculated on the basis of an independent-atom model (IAM) including
the effect of polarization and intramolecular multiple scattering.

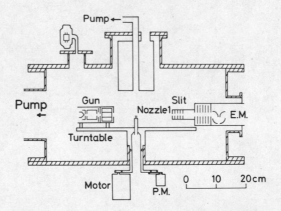

Fig. 1.

*Present address
      Institute for Solid State Physics, The University of Tokyo,
      Minato-ku, Tokyo, 106 Japan

The atomic potential, $V(r)$, of Green et al.[1] used in the present calculation has the form

$$V_{atom}(r) = -\frac{Z}{r} [DZ^{0.4} (e^{D/r} - 1) + 1]^{-1}$$

where Z is the atomic number and D is a constant. This potential gives the EDCS
of rare gases when D is chosen properly. The values of D for C, Cl and As were
taken as 0.880, 0.881 and 0.663 au. respectively. The effect of polarization was
also included by using a Buckingham type polarization potential,

$$V_{pol}(r) = -\alpha/(r^2 + d^2)^2$$

where α is the polarizability of a given molecule and d is a cut-off parameter.

The calculated cross sections of CCl_4 reproduced the observed ones within
the experimental uncertainty when the effect of intramolecular multiple scattering was included in the calculation (the solid curve in Fig. 2). The polarizability α was taken as 70.86 au. and the cut-off parameter d was set equal to
the bond distance between C and Cl atoms, 3.336 au.

The IAM cross sections of As_4 at 100 eV did not agree with the experimental
data. The disagreement was reduced considerably when the effect of intramolecular
multiple scattering was included in the calculation. The polarization potential
parameters α and d were ajusted by means of a least-squares method so as to make
these experimental cross sections agree with the calculated ones (Fig. 3).
The values of α and d thus obtained were 546 ± 175 and 5.88 ± 0.67 au., respectively.

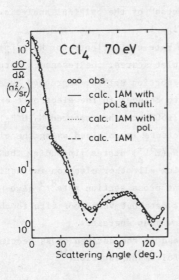

Fig. 2.

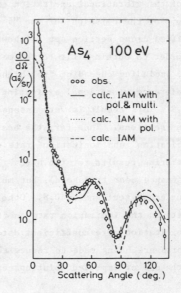

Fig. 3.

1) A. E. S. Green, D. L. Sellin and A. S. Zachor, Phys. Rev. **184**, 1 (1969)

A CONSISTENT SET OF ELECTRON COLLISION CROSS SECTIONS FOR N_2*

A. V. Phelps,** D. Levron+ and K. Tachibana‡

Joint Institute for Laboratory Astrophysics
University of Colorado and National Bureau of Standards, Boulder, CO 80309 USA

Electron collision cross sections for N_2 are determined from analyses of measured electron transport coefficients and collisional rate coefficients. In this analysis electron drift tube measurements[1] are expressed as the variation with characteristic electron energy[2] of effective collision frequencies or rate coefficients for momentum transfer collisions, for energy exchange, for excitation of the $N_2(A^3\Sigma_u^+)$ state[3] and the $N_2(C^3\Pi_u)$ state,[4] and for ionization.[5] Because of the low values of mean electron energy, i.e., 1 to 5 eV, the rate coefficients are used to test and to adjust the near threshold region of cross sections determined by electron beam techniques.

Previously determined[1] low energy momentum transfer and vibrational excitation cross sections plus recent electron beam determinations of cross sections for electron excitation[6] and the momentum transfer collisions[7] are the reference cross section set. The cross section set to be tested is used to calculate[2] the electron energy distribution and the electron collisional rate coefficients for comparison with experiment. As expected,[2] the fit to the momentum transfer collision frequency requires the inclusion of the inelastic contribution. A fit to the energy exchange collision frequency is obtained by increasing the resonance portion of the vibrational excitation cross sections by a factor of 1.5 in order to make up for the omission[8] of the "5 eV process" of the original analysis. This modified cross section set is shown in Fig. 1.

In order to obtain a fit to the measured rate coefficients for $N_2(A^3\Sigma_u^+)$ excitation, including cascading from higher triplet states, the resonance portion of the reference vibrational excitation cross section set[2] is increased by a factor of 1.9. This result is very insensitive to changes in the electronic excitation cross sections. Thus far, the best fit (±50%) to the measured $N_2(C^3\Pi_u)$ state excitation[4] and ionization[5] rate coefficients is obtained using the electron scattering results for the $N_2(C^3\Pi_u)$ and $N_2(E^3\Sigma_g^+)$ states (including the E state resonance near threshold), but multiplying all other electron inelastic scattering cross sections by 0.8. Other recent cross section sets[8,9] give better fits to the ionization rate coefficient data but very poor fits to the $N_2(A^3\Sigma)$ excitation rate coefficient data at low mean energies.

Efforts are being made to reduce the spread in the derived cross sections through the use of improved solutions of the Boltzmann equation.[10]

*Work supported in part by ARPA/ONR.
**Staff Member, Quantum Physics Division, National Bureau of Standards.
+Now at Nuclear Research Centre-Negev, Beer Sheva, Israel.
‡On leave from Kyoto Technical University, Kyoto, Japan.

1. J. J. Lowke, Australian J. Phys. 16, 115 (1963); R. W. Crompton and M. T. Elford, in Proc. VIth Int'l. Conf. on Ionization Phenomena in Gases, ed. by P. Hubert and E. Cremieu-Alcan (Serma, Paris, 1963), Vol. 1, p. 337; H. A. Blevin and M. Z. Hasan, Australian J. Phys. 20, 741 (1967); M. W. Naidu and A. N. Prasad, J. Phys. D 1, 763 (1968); N. Kontoleon, J. Lucas and L. E. Virr, J. Phys. D 6, 1237 (1973).

2. A. G. Engelhardt, A. V. Phelps and C. G. Risk, Phys. Rev. 135, A1566 (1964).

3. D. Levron and A. V. Phelps, Bull. Am. Phys. Soc. 24, 129 (1979).

4. K. Tachibana and A. V. Phelps (unpublished).

5. S. C. Haydon and O. M. Williams, J. Phys. D 9, 523 (1976).

6. D. C. Cartwright, S. Trajmar, A. Chutjian and W. Williams, Phys. Rev. A 16, 1041 (1977); A. Chutjian, D. C. Cartwright and S. Trajmar, Phys. Rev. A 16, 1052 (1977).

7. D. C. Cartwright, J. Appl. Phys. 49, 3855 (1978).

8. L. A. Newman and T. A. DeTemple, J. Appl. Phys. 47, 1912 (1976).

9. S. Pfau and R. Winkler, Beitr. Plasmaphys. 18, 113 (1978).

10. L. C. Pitchford (this meeting).

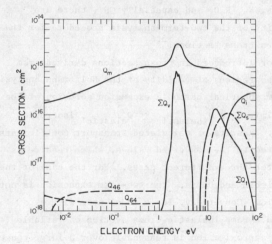

Fig. 1. Electron excitation cross sections adjusted to fit electron transport data. This figure shows the sums of the elastic and inelastic momentum transfer Q_m, vibrational excitation ΣQ_v, triplet excitation ΣQ_t, and singlet excitation ΣQ_s cross sections and representative rotational excitation Q_{46} and deexcitation Q_{64} cross sections.

ACCURACY OF CROSS SECTIONS DERIVED FROM SWARM EXPERIMENTS*

L. C. Pitchford

Joint Institute for Laboratory Astrophysics, University of Colorado
Boulder, Colorado 80309 U.S.A.

The determination of low energy electron scattering cross sections from the analysis of swarm experiments has proven itself in the case of helium where the cross sections so derived are probably the most accurate available.[1] Milloy and Watts[2] have shown that the usual analysis based on the two-term spherical harmonic expansion of the electron energy distribution function is valid for argon, and Milloy et al.[3] have inferred values for the depth and width of the Ramsauer minimum. Likewise, the validity of the determination of rotational and vibrational excitation cross sections in H_2 has been examined.[4] In these cases the average energy gain from the electric field per mean free path is small and $Q_{inelastic} \ll Q_{elastic}$. However in the cases of atoms or molecules with large inelastic cross sections, e.g., Cs, N_2, H_2O, and especially CH_4, there are serious questions as to the validity of the two-term analysis procedure for the determination of electron collision cross sections.[5,6]

In order to evaluate the error introduced in cross sections derived from swarm experiments and to extend the regions of validity of the Boltzmann analysis, we have developed a general n-term spherical harmonic expansion solution of the Boltzmann equation which is not limited to $Q_{inelastic} \ll Q_{elastic}$, isotropic scattering, or especially low E/N. Results of calculated transport coefficients from the two-term expansion compared to the converged values, which require as many as six terms, will be shown for three different cases. For the case of the model methane cross sections of Kleban and Davis,[5] the two-term expansion is not valid even for E/N as low as 1.2 Td. Conversely, for a model atom with a constant elastic cross section and a ramp inelastic cross section of variable threshold and slope, the two-term approximation is reasonable over a large range of E/N. A similar comparison is now in progress for N_2 at several values of E/N using recently derived cross sections.[6] Our converged Boltzmann results are consistent with Monte Carlo calculations.[7]

In the model atom for the case where the mean electron energy is about twice the inelastic threshold, ε_k, and where $Q_{inelastic}(2\varepsilon_k) \simeq 1/3 \ Q_{elastic} = 2 \times 10^{-16} \ cm^2$, the two-term approximation introduces errors of 3% and 20% compared to the converged values in the drift velocity and diffusion coefficient, respectively. For comparison, reducing the slope of the inelastic cross section by a factor of two produces changes of 6% and 31% in the drift velocity and diffusion coefficients, respectively. The potential for extremely accurate measurements of transport coefficients as seen in the experiments of the Australian group[3,4,8] warrants a careful examination of the Boltzmann analysis to reduce errors in the derived cross sections.

*Work supported by NSF; AFAPL, Wright-Patterson AFB, Ohio; and a computer grant from NCAR, Boulder, CO.

1. B. Bederson and L. J. Kieffer, Rev. Mod. Phys. 43, 601 (1971).

2. H. B. Milloy and R. O. Watts, Austr. J. Phys. 30, 73 (1977).

3. H. B. Milloy, R. W. Crompton, J. A. Rees, and A. G. Robertson, Aust. J. Phys. 30, 61 (1977).

4. R. W. Crompton, D. K. Gibson, and A. I. McIntosh, Aust. J. Phys. 22, 715 (1969).

5. P. Kleban and H. T. Davis, Phys. Rev. Lett. 39, 456 (1977).

6. A. V. Phelps, D. Levron and K. Tachibana, (this meeting).

7. Ivan Reid, thesis, Australian National University (1978).

8. R. W. Crompton, M. T. Elford and R. L. Jory, Aust. J. Phys. 20, 369 (1967).

SCATTERING OF ELECTRONS BY HALOCARBON MOLECULES CCl_3F AND CCL_2F_2 FOR COLLISION ENERGIES BELOW 10 eV

K. Rohr

FB Physik, Universität Kaiserslautern, 6750 Kaiserslautern
W.-Germany

Low energy electron scattering from CCl_3F and CCl_2F_2 molecules has been investigated using the crossed beam method. Differential cross sections in absolute units have been obtained for vibrationally elastic scattering and vibrational excitation. These cross sections are of practical interest in enviromental research (catalytic reactions in the atmosphere) and in laser applications.

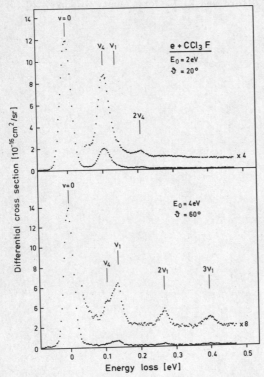

Fig 1: Energy loss spectra for e-CCl_3F scattering

Both molecules possess a weak permanent dipole moment (D_{CCl_3F} = 0.45 Debye , $D_{CCl_2F_2}$ = 0.51 Debye). Therefore besides resonance effects, dipole supported phenomena are influencing the scattering. For vibrational excitation in the case of CCl_3F (fig. 1) this leads to characteristical accentuations of the ν_1 and ν_4 modes.

The energy loss spectra show, that the excitation is highly selective, concerning the number of vibrational modes dominantly
excited (fig. 1,2). This result is coincident with recent investigations in benzene[1] and ethylene[2] and it is an effect generally
found in electron scattering from poliatomic molecules.

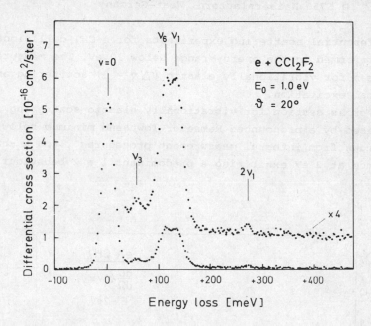

Fig. 2: Energy loss spectrum for e-CCl_2F_2 scattering

1. Wong S.F. and Schulz G.J., Phys. Rev. Lett. 35, 1429 (1975)
2. Walker I.C., Stamatovic A. and Wong S.F., J. Chem. Phys.
        69, 5532 (1978)

COLLISION PROCESSES IN e-CH$_4$ SCATTERING
AT LOW ENERGIES

Klaus Rohr

Fachbereich Physik, Universität Kaiserslautern
D 6750 Kaiserslautern, West-Germany

Differential scattering experiments for e-CH$_4$ collisions have been performed in the energy range below 10 eV. The measurements have been for vibrationally elastic ($\Delta v = 0$) scattering and vibrational excitation.

The cross section for vibrationally elastic scattering is characterized by a pronounced Ramsauer-Townsend minimum below 1 eV, well known from integral measurement procedures[1], and a shape resonance at 2 eV exhibiting a predominant l = 2 behaviour (fig. 1).

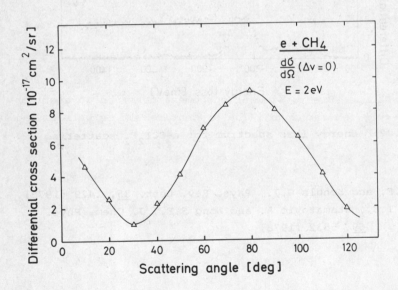

Fig. 1: Angular dependence for vibrationally elastic e-CH$_4$ scattering at a collision energy of 2 eV.

In the cross section for vibrational excitation of the v_2, v_4 modes (v_2 = 190 meV, v_4 = 162 meV), which are not resolved here, this resonance leads to a strong peak of about 0.5 eV width (fig. 2).

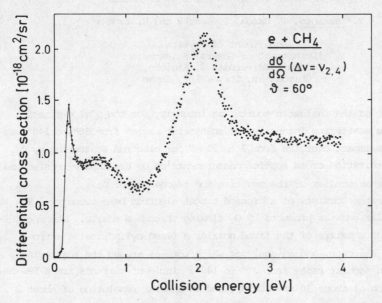

Fig. 2: Excitation function for v_2, v_4 excitation in e-CH_4
scattering at a scattering angle of $60°$.

At threshold the excitation function in addition shows a narrow
structure, comparable to similar phenomena observed in electron-
polar-molecule interactions[2]. The present result as well as recent
theoretical investigations[3,4] indicate, however, that such threshold structures are not limited to polar molecules. Instead it can
be expected, that they are a general phenomenon in electron-molecule scattering.

1. Brüche E., Ann. Phys., Lpz 83, 1065 (1927) and Lpz 4, 387 (1930)
   Duncan C.W. and Walker I.D., J. Chem. Soc. Faraday Trans.
        II 68, 1514 (1972)
   McCorkle D.L., Chrostophorou L.G., Maxey D.V. and Carter J.E.,
        J. Phys. B 11, 3067 (1978)
   Ramsauer C., and Kollath R., Ann. Phys. Lpz 4, 91 (1930)
2. Rohr K., J. Phys. B, 11, 1849 (1978)
3. Taylor H.S., to be published (1979)
4. Domcke W., Cederbaum L.S. and Kaspar F., J. Phys. B (1979)
        to be published

NEW FEATURES IN THE VIBRATIONAL EXCITATION IN O_2
BY ELECTRON IMPACT IN THE 2-20 eV REGION

T. Yamamoto, T. Okada, T. Suzuki and H. Tanaka*

Department of Physics
*Department of General Sciences
Sophia University 7, Kioicho,
Chiyoda-ku, Tokyo, 102, Japan

The ratio of the inelastic scattering intensity for the v"=1 excitation
to the elastic scattering intensity for scattering angles from 20° to 140° was
determined for impact energies from 2 to 20 eV for electron scattering by O_2.
Vibrational excitation cross section measurements[1] on O_2 are less extensive and
less precise than studies of the negative ion resonances of O_2.

Our apparatus consists of a crossed target electron beam geometry. The
target molecular beam is produced by O_2 flowing through a nozzle. The mechanical arrangement consists of the fixed nozzle, a fixed cylindrical electrostatic energy selector, and an analyzer which rotates around the scattering
volume over an angular range from 20° to 140°. Incident currents are a few nA
at a resolution of about 30 meV (FWHM), and an angular resolution of about 2°.

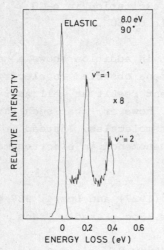

Fig. 1. Energy-loss spectrum of
O_2 at an impact energy of 8 eV and
scattering angles of 90°.

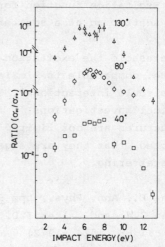

Fig. 2. Ratio of cross section
to the first vibrational states of O_2
to elastic cross section vs impact
energy.

Figure 2 shows the ratio of the first vibrational peak (v"=1) to the
elastic peak in the energy range 2-20 eV for three angles of observation.
Broad peaks, which have been mentioned in the literature (1), are clearly evident near 8 eV(nominal value) for all angles of observation. As the scattering
angle increases, an additional feature appears on top of the broad peaks.
Resonant structures in O_2 are particularly abundant and complex between 8-10 eV,[2]

and are responsible for the large cross sections of pure vibrational excitation.

In order to convert the vibrational inelastic spectra to an absolute cross section, we will separately measure the absolute elastic differential cross section of O_2 in the corresponding energy range with the help of a crossed electron beam molecular beam geometry and a relative gas flow technique developed by Trajmar et al.[3]

1. F. Gresteau, R. I. Hall, J. Mazeau and D. Vichon
   J. Phys. B10, L545 (1977).

2. S. Trajmar, D. C. Cartwright, R. I. Hall
   J. Chem. Phys. 65, 5275 (1976).

3. S. K. Srivastava, A. Chutjian, and S. Trajmar
   J. Chem. Phys. 63, 2659 (1975).

VIBRATIONAL EXCITATION OF CIS- AND TRANS-2-BUTENE BY LOW ENERGY ELECTRONS

Kurt K. Jung and Marion A.M. Kadisch

Fachbereich Physik, Universität Kaiserslautern
Postfach 3049, 6750 Kaiserslautern, W.-Germany

We have studied the vibrational excitation of cis- and trans-2-butene $CH_3-HC=CH-CH_3$ by electron impact in the energy range between 0.8 eV and 4.5 eV with an energy resolution of 25 meV. The apparatus used has been described by G. Seng and F. Linder[1].

Hints for the existence of a resonant state for olefines have been given by the trapped electron measurements of Bowman and Miller[2] and especially for cis- and trans 2 butene by Brongersma[3], Dance and Walker[4]. These authors have found anomalies in the trapped electron current for scattering energies about 2 eV.

We have directed our intention to the different behaviour of the two isomers, especially for excitation of vibrations due to a negative ion-state. Because of the large number of vibrations (3N-6=30) it was not possible to determine all cross sections of vibrations separately. The energy separation of two vibrational peaks is often in the order of 5 meV. With our resolution of 25 meV we had to determine the relative heights of the peaks by deconvolution of the energy loss spectra.

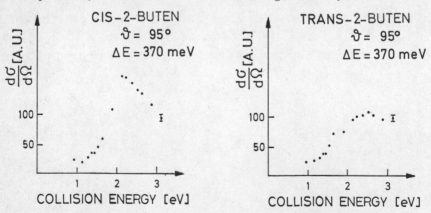

Fig.1. Excitation function of the C-H stretch vibration

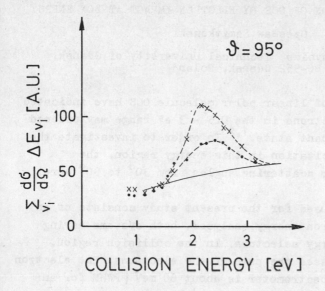

$\vartheta = 95°$

Fig.2.
Transfer of kinetic
energy into
vibrational energy
by electron impact
x cis-2-butene
• trans-2 butene

Figure 1 represents the cross section for the excitation of the
C-H stretch vibration as a function of the collision energy at
the scattering angle of $\vartheta = 95°$. It is obvious that the excitation
probability for cis 2-butene is much more stronger than for
trans-2 butene. The part of the direct scattering seems to be
equal in both cases whereas the resonance only seems strongly
to influence the cross-section of cis-2-butene.We have
investigated the energy dependence of the inelastic cross section
for 5 groups of vibrations.

To summarize all these results we have calculated the energy
transfer cross section which is shown in fig.2 for the same
scattering angle $\vartheta = 95°$. The crosses represent the results for
cis-2-butene, the dots for trans-2-butene. The results prove
certainly the existence of a resonant state for both isomers at
an energy of 2.3 eV. In the case of cis-2-butene the influence
of the ion-state to the excitation probability is twice as large
as in trans-2-butene. This difference can be explained by the
fact that the two molecules belong to different symmetry classes.

1. G. Seng and F. Linder, J. Phys. B, 9, 2539, (1976)
2. C.R. Bowman and W.D. Miller, J.Chem.Phys., 42,681 (1965)
3. H.H.Brongersma, J.A.V.d.Hart and L.J.Oosterhoff,
   Nobel Symposium, 5 , 211, (1967)
4. D.F. Dance and I.C. Walker, Proc.Roy.Soc., A334, 259
   (1973)

VIBRATIONAL EXCITATION OF OCS BY ELECTRON IMPACT AT LOW ENERGY

Czesław Szmytkowski

Institute of Physics, Technical University of Gdańsk,
80-952 Gdańsk, Poland

Previous studies of linear polar molecule OCS have indicated that scattering of electrons in the 0.5 - 3 eV range may proceed through the shape resonant state.[1,2] In order to investigate the role of vibrational excitation in this energy region, the energy-loss spectra for scattering angles from $30°$ to $90°$ were measured.

The spectrometer used for the present study consists of an electron gun and electron energy analyzer, both systems having $127°$ electrostatic energy selectors. In the collision region, the molecular beam crosses the path of the electrons. The electron energy resolution of spectrometer is about 60 meV (FWHM for an elastic peak in the energy-loss spectrum).

It has been observed that OCS influences the surface potentials of the electron optical system. Therefore frequent testing of the energy scale was required. The structure of the first excitation function of nitrogen (in mixture with OCS) around 2.3 eV was used for establishing the absolute energy scale. Noticeable broadening of the elastic peak in energy-loss spectra of OCS in comparison with the peak in N_2 was observed.

An energy-loss spectrum for OCS, obtained at the electron impact energy of 1.2 eV and a $30°$ scattering angle is presented in figure 1. The energy positions of some   energy-loss peaks can be attributed to the location of the 00n and n01 vibrational series. The data of Fig.1 also suggest that series of vibrational modes other than mentioned above can be populated.

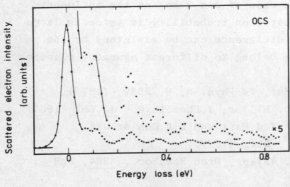

Fig.1. Energy-loss spectra for e-OCS scattering at energy 1.2 eV and an angle of observation of $30°$.

The results show that the vibrational excitation process in this energy region may be dominated by the resonance process which proceeds via short-lived shape resonance centered at 1.3 eV but a significant contribution of non-resonant processes is possible. Further experiments are in progress.

1. J.P. Ziesel, G.J. Schulz and J. Milhaud, J. Chem. Phys. <u>62</u>, 1936 (1975).
2. Cz. Szmytkowski and M. Zubek, Chem. Phys. Letters <u>57</u> 105 (1978).

HIGH ENERGY SHAPE RESONANCES IN MOLECULES :
RESONANT VIBRATIONAL EXCITATION IN CO_2 AND CO.

Michel Tronc and Roger Azria

Laboratoire de Collisions Atomiques et Moléculaires (associé au CNRS)
Université de Paris-Sud, Bât.351, 91405 ORSAY CEDEX (France)

Differential cross sections for vibrational excitation have been obtained in a crossed molecular-beam electron-beam apparatus for CO_2 and CO in the 1-35 eV energy range.

Figure 1 shows the excitation of the first symmetric stretch mode in CO_2 at 90°. Besides the well known π_u shape resonance at 3.8 eV[1], the two new broad and low intensity peaks centered at 10.8 and 30 eV are attributed to σ_g and σ_u shape resonances respectively[2] as predicted by multiple-scattering calculation by Dehmer and Dill[3].

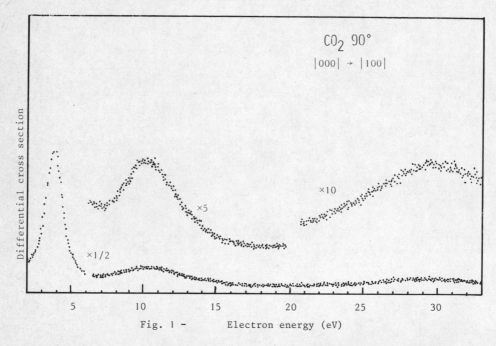

Fig. 1 -   Electron energy (eV)

Figure 2 shows the excitation of the v = 1 level in CO between 1 and 30 eV. Besides the well known π shape resonance at 1.8 eV[4], the broad peak centered at 19.5 eV is attributed to a σ shape resonance[5]. The angular distribution in the resonance energy region shows the contribution of the f wave ($\ell = 3$).

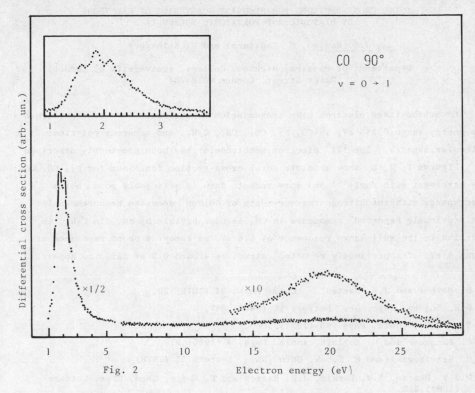

Fig. 2   Electron energy (eV)

Evidence for the existence of high energy shape resonances, observed in vibrational excitation channel, will be given for a series of molecules.

REFERENCES

1. CADEZ I., GRESTEAU F., TRONC M. and HALL R.I. ; J. Phys. B : Atom Molec. Phys. 10 3821 1977

2. TRONC M., AZRIA R. and PAINEAU R. ; J. Physique Lettres, 1979, in press

3. DEHMER J.L. and DILL D. ; Electron and Photon Molecules Collisions V. Mc Koy, T. Rescigno, B. Schneider eds. (Plenum Press, N.Y. 1979)

4. SCHULZ G.J. ; Phys. Rev. A 135 988 1964

5. TRONC M., AZRIA R. and LE COAT Y. ; J. Phys. B : Atom. Molec. Phys. 1979 submitted.

TOTAL CROSS-SECTIONS FOR RESONANT SCATTERING OF ELECTRONS
BY DIATOMIC AND POLYATOMIC MOLECULES

J.B. Hasted, S. Kadifachi and T. Solovyev*

Department of Physics, Birkbeck College, (University of London)
Malet Street, London WC1E 7HX

Monochromatized electron beam transmission measurements have been performed in the energy range 0.3-5 eV, in CO, N_2, CO_2, CH_4, C_2H_4, and numerous polyatomic molecular vapours. The 127° electron spectrometer has been previously described[1].

Figures 1, 2, 3, show absolute total cross-section functions for N_2, CO, CO_2; the agreement with early[3,4] and more recent[5] data is noticeably good, but a discrepancy with the nitrogen measurements of Golden[2] seems to be unremovable. The previously reported[6] resonance in CH_4 is unobservable by us. In C_2H_4, in addition to the well-known resonance at 1.6 eV, we report a broad resonance at about 8 eV. The previously reported[6] structure around 0.2 eV fails to appear.

1. D. Mathur and J.B. Hasted,   Chem. Phys. 34 (1978) 29.

2. D.E. Golden, Phys. Rev. Letters 17 (1966) 847.

3. E. Brüche, Annln. Phys. 83 (1927) 1065.

4. C. Ramsauer and R. Kollath, Annln. Phys. 4 (1930) 91.

5. C. Szmytkowski and M. Zubek, Chem. Phys. Letters 57 (1978)

6. M.J.W. Boness, I.W. Larkin, J.B. Hasted and L. Moore, Chem. Phys. Letters
   1 (1967) 292.

*Permanent address: Department of Radiophysics, Yakut State University, Yakutsk,
                                                                    USSR.

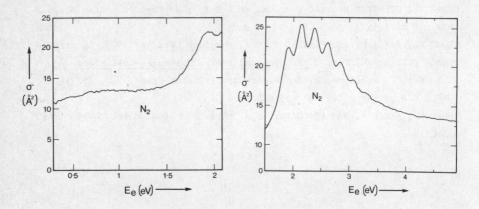

Figure 1

Total electron scattering cross-section for N_2.

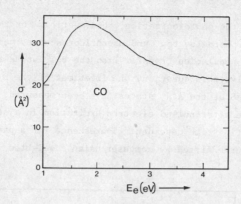

Figure 2

Total electron scattering cross-section for CO.

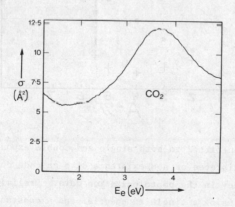

Figure 3

Total electron scattering cross-section for CO_2.

MEASURED LIFETIMES FOR THE B $^2\Sigma_u^+$ and the A $^2\Pi_u$ States in CO$_2^+$.*

Donal J. Burns, Ralph D. Hight and Charles R. Hummer

Department of Physics and Astronomy, Behlen Laboratory
University of Nebraska, Lincoln, Nebraska 68588

Comparison of the photoionization cross-sections for the A $^2\Pi_u$ and the B $^2\Sigma_u^+$ states obtained by photoelectron[1] and photofluorescence[2] measurements, has prompted speculation of population transfer from the B $^2\Sigma_u^+$ state to the A $^2\Pi_u$ state. In an attempt to resolve this question, the lifetimes of the B $^2\Sigma_u^+$ and the vibrational levels v=o to v=8 of the A $^2\Pi_u$ states have been measured. The method of time delayed coincidence after pulsed electron excitation in a static gas cell was employed. The resulting time dependent fluorescence for a particular transition was recorded and curve fitted by computer, using a weighted least squares minimization procedure.

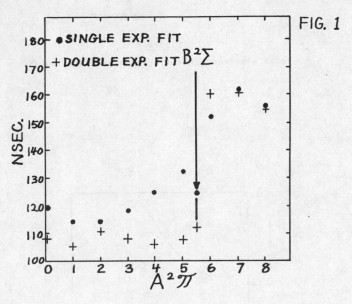

The data has been fitted to both single and double exponentials, in an attempt to prove the existence or non-existence of a cascade component which might explain the discrepancy in the photoionization data. Preliminary results for the A $^2\Pi_u$ and B $^2\Sigma_u^+$ states using a single exponential and a constant background term are shown in Fig. 1 by the solid circles. The vibrational lifetimes of the v=o to v=5 levels of the A state and of the B state agree well with measurements made by Hesser[3] who used the phase shift method and assumed no cascade.

The data has also been fitted to the sum of two exponentials producing chi-squared values of 20% to 30% lower than for a single exponential fit. The value of the lifetime of the fundamental component thus obtained are shown as crosses in Fig. 1 and agree well with the threshold-coincidence data of Schlag et al[4] for the v=o to v=3 levels of the A state and for the B state. Furthermore, we find a dramatic change in the value of the lifetime between v=5 and v=6 where the B state is located (indicated by the arrow in the diagram). The second component has a measured lifetime of $169^{+}_{-}34$ nsec and has a value close to that of the state at 17.93 eV which was noted by Schlag et al.

Additional data and discussion of this problem will be presented.

*Work supported by the National Science Foundation.

1. J. Samson and J. Gardner, J. Chem Phys. **58**, 3771 (1973).

2. L. Lee and D. Judge, J. Chem Phys. **57**, 4443 (1972).

3. J. E. Hesser, J. Chem Phys. **48**, 2518 (1968).

4. E. W. Schlag, R. Frey, B. Gotcher, W. B. Peatman and H. Pollak, Chem Phys Lett. **51**, 406 (1977).

A CLASSICAL TRAJECTORY STUDY OF THE CO_2^- $^2\Sigma_g^+$ DISSOCIATION

M. Sizun and S. Goursaud

Laboratoire de Collisions Atomiques et Moléculaires (associé au CNRS)
Université de Paris-Sud, Bât.351, 91405 ORSAY CEDEX (France)

The kinetic energy distribution of O^- ions formed by dissociative attachment from CO_2 in the electron energy range 7.8-9.3 eV exhibits two peaks, a sharp one close to zero energy and a second one, smaller and broader at approximately 0.6 eV[1]. When the electron energy E_{el} is varied from 7.8 to 9.3 eV the K.E. distribution remains nearly unchanged, spread from 0 to 1.2 eV. As it can be seen on table 1, the partitioning of the excess energy E greatly favors the internal energy and furthermore if the rotational energy is assumed to be negligible, there is a population inversion of the vibrational levels of the diatomic CO fragment

E_{el} (eV)	E (eV)	$E_{K_{max}}$ (eV)	Populated vibrational CO levels	
7.8	3.95	2.51	15>v>7	Table 1.
8.2	4.35	2.77	17>v>9	$(E_{K_{max}} = \dfrac{m_o + m_c}{2m_o + m_c} E)$
9.3	5.45	3.47	23>v>14	

The dissociation of CO_2^- $^2\Sigma_g^+$ has been studied on a Wall-Porter[2] potential energy surface with a classical trajectory method[3] in which the initial conditions are described by the Wigner probability density function. The competition between dissociation and autodetachment ($CO_2^- \to e + CO_2$) is represented with a survival probability $exp(\Gamma t_c / \hbar)$ which weakens the probability density function. The autodetachment width Γ is kept constant if r_1 and r_2 are smaller than a critical length r_c and is taken equal to zero if $r_1 > r_c$ or $r_2 > r_c$. The time spent by the representative point in the area $r_1 < r_c$ and $r_2 < r_c$ is the critical time t_c. Claydon et al.[4] and England et al.[5] have calculated some points of the CO_2^- $^2\Sigma_g^+$ potential energy surface ; the surface is repulsive with a minimum at 180° with respect to the variation of the angle of the two bonds. Since both the CO_2 target and the CO_2^- $^2\Sigma_g^+$ resonant ion have the same equilibrium angle (180°), the dissociation has been studied in the collinear approximation frame.

The influence of the autodetachment rate (fig.1) is very important. The KE distribution is spread from 0 to $E_{K_{max}}$ when $\Gamma = 0$; but, with $\Gamma > 0.2$ eV, the part of the distribution corresponding to $E_K > 1.2$ eV disappears and the maximum is located very close to zero energy. Such a result is surprising since, usually, trajectories with high E_K are fast and have a short dissociation time t_d. We have observed the contrary ;   trajectories (like T_1 on figure 2) have a long dissociation time because the numerous reflections on the potential walls and trajectories (like T_3 on figure 2) have a short dissociation time because they go directly in the valley with much vibrational energy. The reflections of trajectories like T_1 are found to be related to the mass ratio between O and C and to the subsequent inertial coupling. The influence of this mass ratio is more easily pictured if the potential surface is drawn in skewed coordinates (Fig.2). The angle of $55°$ (instead of $86.6°$ for H-O-H) explains the observed reflections.

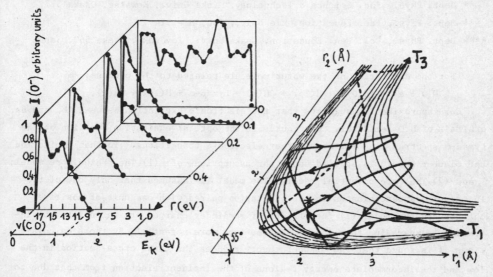

Fig.1 - KE distributions obtained with   Fig.2 - Surface and typical trajecto-
$E_{el}=8.2$ eV and $r_c=1.9$ Å as functions of Γ ries plotted in skewed coordinates.

The shape of the KE distribution between 0 and 1.2 eV is closely related to the shape of the potential energy surface. In order to obtain a sharp maximum close to zero energy and a second peak at about 0.6 eV (see fig.1), the surface must have a saddle point region flat ($V_s \lesssim 0.5$ eV) and located far from the Franck-Condon region ($r_s \simeq 1.6$ Å). With such a surface, $\Gamma=0.2$ eV and $r_c=1.9$ Å, we have also observed that the KE distribution is nearly independent of the amount of excess energy.

1.   P.J. Chantry, J. Chem. Phys. **57** 3180 (1972)

2.   F.T. Wall and R.N. Porter, J. Chem. Phys. **36** 3256 (1962)

3.   S. Goursaud, M. Sizun and F. Fiquet-Fayard, J. Chem. Phys. **65** 5453 (1976)
        "   "   "   **68** 4310 (1978)

4.   C.R. Claydon, G.A. Segal and H.S. Taylor, J. Chem. Phys. **52** 3387 (1970)

5.   W.B. England, J.B. Rosenberg, P.J. Fortune and A.C. Wahl, J. Chem. Phys. **65** 684 (1976)

DISSOCIATIVE EXCITATION OF WATER MOLECULE BY ELECTRON IMPACTS

T.Fujita, T.Iwai,* K.Ogura,** S.Watanabe*** and Y.Watanabe****

Dept. Mech. Eng., Fac. Engineering, Kansai Univ., Suita, Osaka 564

* Dept. Phys., Fac. Science, Osaka Univ., Toyonaka, Osaka 560

** Dept. Phys., Fac. Science & Technology, Kinki Univ., Kowakae, Osaka 577

*** Dept. Phys., Fac. Education, Mie Univ., Tsu, Mie 514

**** Dept. Phys., Col. Gen. Education, Osaka Univ., Toyonaka, Osaka 560, Japan

For the excitation of the water molecule related to the process:

$$H_2O + e^- \rightarrow (H_2O)^* \rightarrow H(2p) + OH(X) \rightarrow Lyman\text{-}\alpha + H(1s) + OH(X),$$

the Born approximation suggests that the electronic excitation between $1b_2$ and $6a_1$ orbitals of H_2O remarkably contributes to the optical excitation function of the Lyman-α spectral line far above other electronic transitions.[1] To that excitation the Glauber theory is applied under the assumptions of: (1) The frozen core model;[2] and (2) The core potential model.[3] The model (1) assumes that only one of two $1b_2$ electrons participates in the excitation paired with one unit of positive charges. In the model (2) the effects of remainder charges are taken into consideration by averaging them into a Hartree-type core potential. By those calculations it is found that the Glauber theory reduces the total cross-section in the low and the intermediate energy regions of the incident electron from that due to the BA. The adequacy of that model to the H_2O molecule is, however, not readily clear. It differs from the case of alkali atoms.[4] We can test that adequacy by the multiple scattering expansion of the Glauber profile function.

In the present work, we put the following simplifications as in our previous works: (1) The Lyman-α emission cross-section is uniquely represented by the excitation cross-section of one of the $1b_2$ electrons to the $6a_1(4sa_1)$ orbital; (2) Both of the orbitals of initial and final states are assigned by the members of a one-center basis set, namely of the simplest set of Lin and Duncan.[5] The profile function is expanded in terms of the multiplicity orders:

$$\prod_j \left(\frac{|\vec{b} - \vec{s}_j|}{b}\right)^{2i\eta} - 1 = \sum_j \Gamma(\vec{b};\vec{s}_j) + \sum_{j>\ell} \Gamma(\vec{b};\vec{s}_j)\Gamma(\vec{b};\vec{s}_\ell) + \ldots + \prod_j \Gamma(\vec{b};\vec{s}_j),$$

where $\Gamma(\vec{b};\vec{s}) = (|\vec{b} - \vec{s}|/b)^{2i\eta} - 1$, $\eta = 1/k_i$.

A tentative termination of the expansion up to the double scattering term yields the scattering amplitude

$$F(\vec{q}) = \frac{k_i}{2\pi i} \int d\vec{b}\, \exp(i\vec{q}\cdot\vec{b})\{<4sa_1|\Gamma|1b_2> + <4sa_1|2R\Gamma - \Gamma P\Gamma|1b_2>\},$$

where $R = \sum <j|\Gamma|j>$, $P = \sum |j><j|$ and the sum extends over all possible intermediate molecular orbitals.

Fig.1 illustrates our present result as compared with our previous ones and
with the experimental data of Tsurubuchi and Isaka normalized to our calculated
value at 500 eV.[6] The interference considered here further reduces the total
cross-section in the energy region higher than 40 eV. It is the most effective in
the region 50 < E < 200 eV. In spite of further reduction, theory predicts too
large cross-section in the region E < 100 eV. In this region, miscellaneous
processes may take place in the scattering such as the exchange of molecular and
incident electrons, two-electron excitation, the cascade transitions and so on.
The effect of exchange of electrons is estimated by using the simple Born-Ochkur
approximation.(Fig.2) The result tells us that the electron exchange process plays
minor role in the present problem.

There still remains considerable difference between the observed and the
theoretical data in the high energy extremity. It suggests that some other
processes may take a part, for example, the excitation of the $1b_2$ electron into
the 3d orbitals.

1. T.Fujita *et al.*, J. Phys. Soc. Japan 42, 1296 (1977).

2. T.Fujita *et al.*, J. Phys. Soc. Japan 42, 1305 (1977).

3. T.Fujita *et al.*, J. Phys. Soc. Japan 44, 286 (1978).

4. H.R.J.Walters, J. Phys. B (Atom. mol. Phys.) 6, 1003 (1973).

5. T.F.Lin and A.B.F.Duncan, J. chem. Phys. 48, 866 (1968).

6. S.Tsurubuchi and S.Isaka, J. Phys. Soc. Japan 38, 1224 (1975).

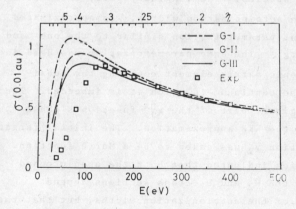

Fig.1. Comparison of the
cross-sections. Curves
G-I(ref.2), G-II(ref.3)
and G-III(present) are
theoretical results.
Squares are experimental
data(ref.6) normalized to
our calculated value at
500 eV.

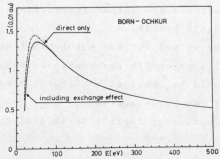

Fig.2. Effect of the electron
exchange collision estimated
by the Born-Ochkur approximation.

DISSOCIATIVE ATTACHMENT IN H_2 AND D_2 IN THE 10 eV REGION

George V. Nazaroff

Department of Chemistry, Indiana University at South Bend
South Bend, Indiana 46615 USA

The total dissociative attachment cross sections for H_2 and D_2 were evaluated numerically in the 8 – 12 eV energy region using the formalism of O'Malley and Taylor.[1] The calculations were carried out from first principles except for a parametrization of the molecular negative ion autoionization widths entering into the formulas.

The expression used to evaluate the cross sections was

$$\sigma_{DA} = \frac{4\pi^3}{k^2} \sum_J e^{-\rho_J} \sum_L C_{JL} |<\chi_J^{DA}|V_L|\chi_v>|^2 ,$$

where the summation indices J and L refer to the system's total and the incident electon's orbital angular momenta, respectively. The complex-valued continuum negative ion nuclear wavefunctions χ_J^{DA} were obtained numerically from a Schrödinger equation containing a complex-valued potential describing the scattering. The real part of the potential was taken to be the curve of Eliezer, et al.[2] for the $^2\Sigma_g^+$ molecular negative ion species. The imaginary part, which is related to the negative ion autoionization widths, was approximated by an internuclear-dependent parametrization similar to the one used by Birtwistle and Herzenberg.[3] The same parametrization was used in calculating V_L, the electronic matrix element coupling the quasi-bound molecular ion with the continuum in which it is imbedded. The factor ρ_J which is the imaginary part of the χ_J^{DA} function's phase shift was calculated using the WKB approximation. The initial target state vibrational wavefunction χ_v was taken to be a Morse function.

The computational studies indicated that both the absolute and the relative magnitudes of the H_2 and D_2 cross sections depend strongly on the magnitudes of the autoionization widths, but that the general shapes of the cross sections are rather insensitive to these parameters taken within reasonable bounds.

It was found that using the values for the autoionization widths suggested by Bardsley, et al.[4] a generally reasonable agreement between theory and experiment could be obtained both for the magnitudes and for the over-all shapes of the cross sections.

Use of Indiana University computing facilities is gratefully acknowledged.

1. T. F. O'Malley and H. S. Taylor, Phys. Rev. <u>176</u>, 207 (1968)

2. I. Eliezer, H. S. Taylor, and J. K. Williams, Jr., J. Chem. Phys. <u>47</u>, 2165 (1967)

3. D. T. Birtwistle and A. Herzenberg, J. Phys. B: Atom. Molec. Phys. <u>4</u>, 53 (1971)

4. J. N. Bardsley, A. Herzenberg, and F. Mandl, Proc. Phys. Soc. <u>89</u>, 321 (1966)

EFFECT OF VIBRATIONAL AND ROTATIONAL STATES ON
DISSOCIATION ATTACHMENT IN (e, H$_2$) COLLISIONS

Joseph C.Y. Chen

Department of Physics, University of California at San Diego
La Jolla, California 92093

Temperature dependence in dissociative attachment of electrons by molecules
arises from the initial population of molecular states with temperature and the
effects of these states on the cross section of dissociative attachment. The
effect of initial vibrational states can be readily appreciated with the help
of the Franck-Condon principle. The effect of rotational states on dissociative
attachment is however less apparent. It has been shown[1] that the effect comes
from the dependence of the dissociating radial wavefunction on the initial centrifugal stretching of the molecules and from the Kronig selection rule and symmetry requirements.

In the JWKB approximation, the dissociating radial wavefunction $\xi_J(R)$ at
the right-hand side of the turning point R_0 is[2]

$$\xi_J(R) = k_J(R)^{-\frac{1}{2}} \sin\left\{\tfrac{1}{4}\pi - D_J(R_0) + \int_{R_0}^{R} k_J(R')dR'\right\}$$

with

$$k_J(R) = \left\{2\mu[E - U_J(R) + i\tfrac{1}{2}\Gamma(R)]\right\}^{\frac{1}{2}}$$

$$U_J(R) = V(R) + (J + \tfrac{1}{2})^2/(2\mu R^2)$$

$$D_J(R_0) = D_J^{(+)}(R_0) - i\, D_J^{(-)}(R_0)$$

$$D_J^{(\pm)}(R_0) = -\frac{1}{6}\left[2\mu\Gamma(R_0)^3\right]^{\frac{1}{2}} \left[\frac{\dfrac{dU_J}{dR} \pm \tfrac{1}{2}\dfrac{d\Gamma}{dR}}{\left(\dfrac{dU_J}{dR}\right)^2 + \tfrac{1}{4}\left(\dfrac{d\Gamma}{dR}\right)^2}\right]_{R=R_0}$$

where $V(R)$ and $\tfrac{1}{2}\Gamma(R)$ are the complex potential for the dissociating molecular
ion and J is the total angular momentum.

An analysis of the J dependence of the phase shift in the dissociating radial
wave function reveals a strong rotational-state dependence for dissociative attachments if the breakup energy is comparable to the centrifugal barrier. This analysis is of particular interest for dissociative attachments in the (e, H$_2$)
system since it has been observed experimentally that H$^-$ ions first appear at
electron energies around 3.75 eV, near the theoretical threshold for the H$^-$ production. The dissociative-attachment cross section exhibits a vertical onset in
the first peak at around 3.75 eV, substantially lower than the second peak at
around 10 eV. One expects, therefore, a strong rotational-state dependence for
dissociative attachments at energies around 3.75 eV but not at energies around

10 eV. An estimation of the effect was made by Chen and Peacher based on the potentials of the intermediate H_2^- states calculated by Bardsley, Herzenberg and Mandl.[3]

The predicted effect was, however, not observed in a subsequent experimental attempt carried out by Spence and Schultz.[4] Not until very recently was this effect successfully observed by Allan and Wong.[5] The observed effect is, however, smaller than predicted. In view of the possible practical relationship between the H^- ions and the production of neutral beam for plasma heating in nuclear fusion, it is worthwhile to re-examine the effect of rotational states in dissociative attachment.

We found that the numerical predictions can be easily brought into agreement with the experimental data by simply modifying the interaction potentials of Bardsley, Herzenberg and Mandl adopted in the previous calculation. The rotational-state effect comes from the dependence of the dissociating radial wave function (hence the survival probabilities) on the initial centrifugal stretching of the molecule and from the Kronig selection rule. In their recent interpretation of the effects of rotational states, Wadehra and Bardsley[6] have also used a set of parametrized potentials for the intermediate H_2^- states. It would be desirable that independent theoretical calculation of the complex potentials for the H_2^- states be made.

1. J.C.Y. Chen and J.L. Peacher, Phys. Rev. _163_, 103 (1967).
2. J.C.Y. Chen, Phys. Rev. _156_, 12 (1967).
3. J.N. Bardsley, A. Herzenberg and E. Mandl, Proc. Phys. Soc. (London) _89_, 305 (1966).
4. D. Spence and G.J. Schultz, J. Chem. Phys. _54_, 5424 (1971).
5. M. Allan and S.F. Wong, Phys. Rev. Letter _41_, 1791 (1978).
6. J.W. Wadehra and J.N. Bardsley, Phys. Rev. Letter _41_, 1795 (1978).

CALCULATION OF DISSOCIATIVE ATTACHMENT CROSS SECTION TO F2, Cl2, AND I2 MOLECULES.

G.F.Drukarev and S.A.Pozdneev

Leningrad State University, Leningrad, USSR

The dissociative attachment is treated as a three-body rearrangment process: $e + AB \to (eA) + B$ by means of Faddeev eqeations [1,2].

The interaction of an electron with the halogen atom is represented by a separable potential

$$V(\kappa,\kappa') = g(\kappa)g(\kappa')(\lambda + \mu \cos(\theta)) \, , \qquad g(\kappa) = (\alpha^2 + \kappa^2)^{-1}$$

The term containing $\cos(\theta)$ is needed to account the p-state of the attached electron. The values of λ and μ were determined using the data of electron affinity and theoretical estimation of scattering length [3]. The remaining parameter in $g(\kappa)$ is adjusted to fit experimental data at certain energy.

For the numerical solution of Faddeev equations we used the technique developed in [4]. The results are shown on fig. I,2,3.

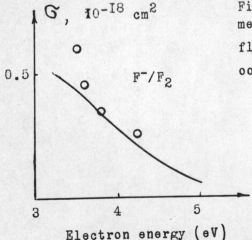

Fig.I. Total electron-attachment cross section of the fluorine molecule.

ooo-experimental results

P.J.Chantry

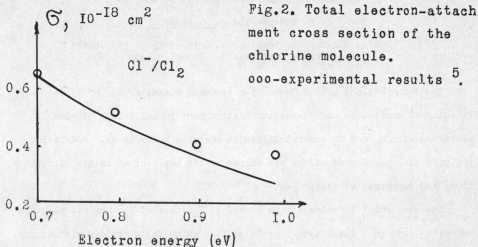

Fig.2. Total electron-attach ment cross section of the chlorine molecule. ooo-experimental results [5].

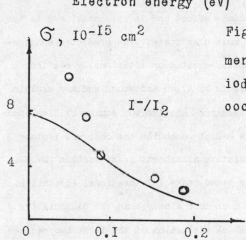

Fig.3. Total electron-attach-ment cross section of the iodine molecule. ooo-experimental results [6].

Electron energy (eV)

1. L.D.Faddeev JETP, $\underline{39}$, 1459, (1960).
2. G.F.Drukarev, S.A.Pozdneev JETP, $\underline{74}$, 2009, (1978).
3. Yu.N.Demkov, N.B.Berezina JETP, $\underline{68}$, 848, (1975).
4. N.M.Larson, J.H.Hehterington Phys.Rev., $\underline{C9}$, 699, (1974).
5. M.V.Kurepa, D.S.Belic J.Phys., $\underline{BII}$, 3719, (1978).
6. G.E.Caledonia Chem.Rev., $\underline{75}$, 333, (1975).

VIBRATIONAL EXCITATION AND DISSOCIATIVE EXCITATION IN ELECTRON COLLISIONS WITH H_2, D_2 and F_2.[*]

J. M. Wadehra and J. N. Bardsley

Physics & Astronomy Department, University of Pittsburgh
Pittsburgh, Pennsylvania 15260, U.S.A.

The contributions of the lowest two resonant states of H_2^- or D_2^- to vibrational excitation and dissociative attachment in collisions of slow electrons with H_2 and D_2 are calculated at energies below 12 eV. Models for the potential curves and widths are chosen on the basis of ab initio calculations and experimental data.

The very short lifetime of the ground X $^2\Sigma_u$ state of H_2^- against electron emission leads to a dissociative cross section which falls rapidly with energy above the threshold, shows a strong isotope effect and is very sensitive to the range of nuclear motion in the initial molecular state. The predicted enhancement of the cross section for vibrationally-excited or rotationally excited molecules agrees well with the measurements by Allan and Wong[1] and may explain the large H⁻ densities achieved in a discharge negative ion source by Nicolopoulou et al.[2] However these calculations cannot reconcile the observed isotope effect with the magnitude of the dissociative attachment cross section for H_2.

The X $^2\Sigma_u$ state also leads to very broad peaks in vibrational excitation. Above 4 eV the cross sections decrease much more slowly than the dissociative attachment cross sections. Even near 10 eV excitation of the first two excited vibrational levels is dominated by this state. However at such energies the excitation of higher vibrational levels and dissociative attachment proceed primarily through the B $^2\Sigma_g^+$ state of the negative ion. The differing roles of the two resonances explain the experimental results on vibrational excitation reported by Hall[3] at ICPEAC X. Our calculations suggest that for energies near 10 eV the angular distribution associated with vibrational excitation should be significantly different for high and low vibrational levels in the final state.

The analysis by Hall[4] of vibrational excitation and dissociative attachment in F_2 is being repeated in order to test the sensitivity of the results to the assumed resonance parameters and to take account of new experimental data by

Chantry[5]. Particular attention is being paid to the dependence of the dissociative attachment cross section upon the vibrational state of the F_2 molecule.

*This work has been supported by the National Science Foundation through Grant No. PHY76-21456.

1. M. Allan and S. F. Wong, Phys. Rev. Lett. 41, 1791 (1978).

2. E. Nicolopoulou, M. Bacal and H. J. Doucet, Journal de Physique 38, 1399 (1977).

3. R. Hall, Invited Papers and Progress Reports, ICPEAC X (North Holland, Amsterdam, 1978) p. 25.

4. R. J. Hall, J. Chem. Phys. 68, 1803 (1978).

5. P. J. Chantry, private communication.

DISSOCIATIVE RECOMBINATION OF ELECTRONS WITH H_2^+ IONS[*]

C. Derkits, J. M. Wadehra and J. N. Bardsley

Physics & Astronomy Department, University of Pittsburgh
Pittsburgh, Pennsylvania 15260, U.S.A.

In recent years it has been generally assumed[1] that at low energies dissociative recombination between electrons and H_2^+ ions proceeds primarily through the lowest doubly excited state of the H_2 molecule, $(1\sigma_u)^2\ {}^1\Sigma_g^+$. However quantitative agreement between theory and experiment[2] has not yet been obtained. Zhdanov and Chibisov[3] have suggested that the higher members of the Rydberg series $(1\sigma_u)\ (n\ell\lambda)$ may be more important because of their greater stability against auto-ionization. They showed that if electron emission is ignored the cross section for recombination through states with $n \gtrless 3$ exceeds the measured cross section.

In this paper the basic assumptions of Zhdanov and Chibisov[3] are examined. It is shown that their neglect of auto-ionization leads to a considerable over-estimation of the contribution from the Rydberg states. Preliminary results indicate that at low energies their contribution is significantly less than the observed cross sections. Hence the contribution from the $(1\sigma_u)^2\ {}^1\Sigma_u$ state is being reanalyzed.

When the usual resonant scattering theory, with a local width derived in terms of the Born-Oppenheimer approximation, is applied to electron-ion collisions the decay width changes discontinuously at the stabilization point. The effects of this change and the coupling with the infinite number of Rydberg states are being explored both through modifications of the standard theory and through the introduction of a non-local width.

[*]This work has been supported by the National Science Foundation through Grant No. PHY76-21456.

1. C. Bottcher, J. Phys. B 9, 2899 (1976).

2. D. Auerbach, R. Cacak, R. Caudano, T. D. Gaily, C. J. Keyser, J. W. McGowan, J.B.A. Mitchell and S.F.I. Wilk, J. Phys. B 10, 3797 (1977).

3. V. P. Zhdanov and M. I. Chibisov, Zh. Eksp. Teor. Fiz. 74, 75 (1978)

   (Sov. Phys. JETP 47, 38).

DISSOCIATIVE IONIZATION BY LOW ENERGY ELECTRON IMPACT. ION ENERGY
DISTRIBUTION OF N^{2+} FROM N_2 AND O^{2+} FROM O_2.

R. LOCHT, J. MOMIGNY

Institut de Chimie, Université de Liège, Sart-Tilman par
Liège I   Belgium

The formation of N^{2+} ions by electron and ion impact has been investigated
by several groups (1-4). The lowest threshold for the appearance energy is measured at around 61 eV (1, 2) and 54 eV (3). The N^{2+} ion energy distribution has
been examined as a function of the electron energy and the angle between ion
and electron beam (1-3). No thermal peak has been observed. The present contribution will report preliminary results on N^{2+} from N_2 and O^{2+} from O_2.

The experimental set-up is described elsewhere (5). Ion energy distributions are measured by recording the first differentiated retarding potential
curve. Fig. 1 shows the N^{2+}/N_2 kinetic energy distributions obtained for electron energies from 60-100 eV. Peak maxima
are measured at (1.2 $\pm$ 0.1) eV, (3.0 $\pm$ 0.1)
eV, (5.1 $\pm$ 0.1) eV and a shoulder around
7 eV, in agreement with CROWE (2). Furthermore, in the present work, a thermal peak of
low intensity is present at all electron
energies down to 65 eV.

A second feature in this experiment is
that no N^{2+} ion current is detected at 60 eV
(see fig. 1). The signals at 60 eV and 65 eV
are obtained both in the same experimental
conditions. This result un-ambiguously shows
that the appearance energy of the N^{2+} ions
lies below 65 eV and higher than 60 eV electron energy. These measurements agree with
those of VAN BRUNT (1) and CROWE (2) and
disagree drastically with the value of 54 eV
determined by DELEANU (3).

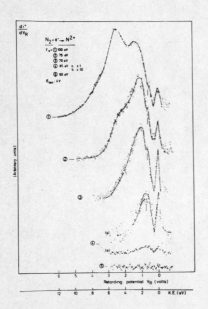

FIG. 1 - N^{2+}/N_2 ion energy
distribution at electron
energies 60-100 eV.

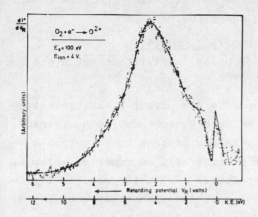

FIG. 2 - Ion energy distribution of O^{2+}/O_2 for 100 eV electrons.

For the first time the O^{2+} from O_2 ion energy distribution is examined. A distribution obtained for 100 eV electrons is shown in Fig. 2. Beneath the peak maxima at 4.4 eV and 1.6 eV ion energy a thermal peak is observed. Further experiments on both N^{2+}/N_2 and O^{2+}/O_2 are in progress for the determination of the appearance energy of each observed process.

(1) L.J. KIEFFER, R.J. VAN BRUNT, J. Chem. Phys. 46 (1967) 2728.

(2) A. CROWE, J.W. McCONKEY, J. Phys. B.8 (1975) 1765.

(3) L. DELEANU, J.A.D. STOCKDALE, J. Chem. Phys. 63 (1975) 3898.

(4) A.K. EDWARDS, R.M. WOOD, M.F. STEUER, Phys. Rev. A.15 (1977) 48.

(5) R. LOCHT, J. SCHOPMAN, Int. J. Mass. Spectr. Ion Phys. 15 (1974) 361.

DISSOCIATIVE IONIZATION OF CH_4 AND CD_4 BY LOW ENERGY ELECTRON IMPACT THE PROTON FORMATION.

J.L. OLIVIER, R. LOCHT, J. MOMIGNY

Institut de Chimie, Université de Liège, Sart-Tilman par Liège I
Belgium

The dissociative excitation and the dissociative electroionization of CH_4 giving rise to high Rydberg H atoms and to H^+ respectively have been published (1,2). In the present contribution a recent investigation of the last process will be reported which is in close agreement with the dissociative excitation result. It disagrees with the electroionization work (1) in both aspects : the lower part of the H^+ ion energy distribution and the lowest appearance energies measured for H^+.

The present dissociative ionization work on CH_4 (CD_4) producing H^+ (D^+) has been examined by electron impact using ion energy analysis. The instrument used in this work is fully described elsewhere (3). The kinetic energy distribution of H^+(D^+) has been recorded at electron energies from 22-75 eV. D^+ distributions obtained close to the threshold are shown in fig. 1. In agreement with previous results, <u>the peak at 2.3 eV has a constant FWHM over a wide electron energy range</u>. The features in the distribution at high ion energy for 30-75 eV electrons agree with those published earlier (1,2). APPELL (1) does not find a thermal peak, whereas it is detected in the present ion energy distribution from threshold up to 75 eV. Furthermore it has been verified that the peaks at 0 eV

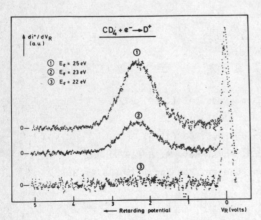

Fig.1 : D^+ ion energy distributions for 25 eV, 23 eV and 22 eV electrons.

and 2.3 eV are related to <u>first order processes</u> both with respect to the <u>pressure of CH_4</u> in the ion source and to the <u>electron beam intensity</u>. The intensity of about 0.5 eV ions appearing at higher electron energies is at least partially a second order process.

The first differentiated ionization efficiency curves of H^+ (D^+) have been recorded for different ion energies. For the ions of thermal and 2.3. eV energy the measured threshold is (21.3 $\pm$ 0.3)eV and (22.17 $\pm$ 0.1)eV respectively. The lowest threshold published by APPELL (1) is 24 eV, while the threshold for dissociative excitation of CH_4 in H (n = 4) atoms is measured at (22.0 $\pm$ 0.5)eV. A kinetic energy plot for the two first thresholds of H^+ (D^+) is shown in fig. 2. The processes at 21.3 eV and 22.17 eV are both interpreted by the excitation of CH_4 (CD_4) to a neutral Rydberg state. The subsequent dissociation can be described in the frame of the RICE-JORTNER model (4) where the dissociation takes place by interaction of a discrete state with a quasi continuum of vibronic levels interacting with the dissociation continuum. The results of the dissociation in high Rydberg H atoms (2) could be explained in the frame of the same model.

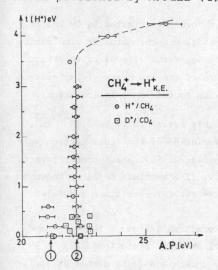

Fig.2 : Kinetic energy-versus - appearance energy plot for H^+/CH_4 and D^+/CD_4.

(1) J. APPELL, C. KUBACH, Chem. Phys. Letters 11 (1971) 486.

(2) J.A. SCHIAVONE, D.E. DENOHUE, R.S. FREUND, J. Chem. Phys. 67 (1977) 759.

(3) R. LOCHT, J. SCHOPMAN, Int. J. Mass. Spectr. Ion Phys. 15 (1974) 361.

(4) J. JORTNER, S.A. RICE, R.M. HOCHSTRASSER, Advances in Photo-chemistry, 7 (p. 256 ff) (1969) - Interscience Publishers.

PREDISSOCIATIONS IN THE DISSOCIATIVE ATTACHMENT PROCESSES
LEADING TO C^-/CO AND F^-/HF

R. Abouaf and D. Teillet-Billy

Laboratoire des Collisions Atomiques et Moléculaires (associé au CNRS)
Université de Paris-Sud, Bât.351, 91405 ORSAY CEDEX (France)

Dissociative attachment cross sections have been investigated in CO and HF using a mass spectrometer equipped with a trochoïdal monochromator as electron gun[1]. The good sensitivity and resolution of the apparatus allowed us to obtain convincing evidence of the predissociative nature of the processes giving rise to both C^-/CO (10 → 14 eV) and F^-/HF (from 12.5 eV up to the ion pair formation).

1. $\underline{C^-/CO}$. The C^-/CO cross section has been roughly estimated to be $7.10^{-23} cm^2$, in good agreement with previous results[2]. The variation of the cross section versus electron energy for C^-/CO is represented on fig. 1. Four peaks appear located respectively at 10.32, 10.58, 10.88 and 11.55 eV. (The absolute scale is known ± .05 eV). These results confirm -with more details- the interpretation suggested earlier by Sanche and Schulz[3].

The first two peaks are attributed to the predissociation of the v = 1 and v = 2 levels of the CO $^2\Sigma^+$ $(...(1\Pi)^4(5\sigma)^1(3s\sigma)^2)$ by a CO^- state (possibly $^2\Sigma^+$) correlated to $C^-(^4S) + O(^3P)$. The third peak is understood to be direct dissociative attachment through this state. The last peak would arise from dissociative attachment through another CO^- state correlated to $C^{-*}(^2D) + O(^3P)$.

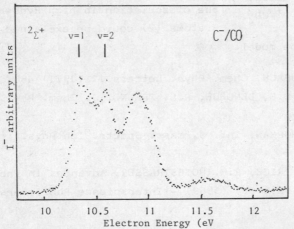

Fig.1 : C^-/CO current vs electron energy.

2. $\underline{F^-/HF}$. Recent investigation of the Feshbach resonances in hydrogen halides in a transmission experiment[4] has shown that HF behave quite differently than the others HX (X = Cl, Br, I). Particularly, only one well developed serie is observed, attributed to a $^2\Pi$ Feshbach resonance. This serie is perturbed around 12.8eV We found evidence in the dissociative attachment channel that this resonance is

strongly predissociated by another HF^- state correlated to $H^*(n=2 + F^-$ (5).
Our results are presented on fig.2. They show predissociation processes leading to
the formation of $F^- + H^*(n)$ up to n = 5. The steep rise around 16 eV represents
the ion pair formation. The relatively large cross section observed for the peak
at 12.8 eV (roughly estimated to $5.10^{-19} cm^2$) explains the strong perturbation observed in the transmission experiment[4].

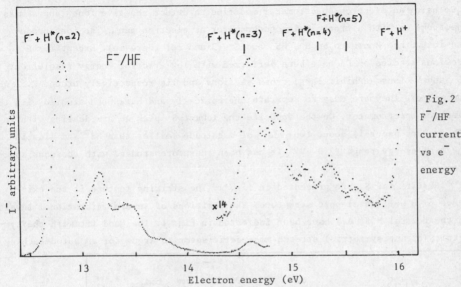

Fig.2
F^-/HF
current
vs e^-
energy

Good agreement with the results of Spence[4] is observed for the two first
peaks of the first serie although slight differences appear for the two others.
These differences are not clearly understood at the present time but we think that
the existence around 13 eV of the $B^1\Sigma$ neutral state opens up new exit channels for
the resonant state correlated to $F^- + H^*(n=2)$ which could modify strongly intensities and apparent positions of F^- peaks.

1.   R. Abouaf, R. Paineau, F. Fiquet-Fayard, J. Phys. B **9** 303 (1976)

2.   A. Stamatovic and G.J. Schulz, J. Chem. Phys. **53** 2663 (1970)

3.   L. Sanche and G.J. Schulz, Phys. Rev. A **6** 69 (1972)

4.   D. Spence and T. Noguchi, J. Chem. Phys. **63** 505 (1975)

5.   This work follows a sugggestion of R.N. Compton who had previously observed
      with low resolution F^- peaks in this energy region (unpublished results).

STRUCTURES IN DISSOCIATIVE ATTACHMENT CROSS SECTIONS OF H_2S and H_2Se

R. Abouaf, R. Azria, Y. Le Coat, D. Teillet-Billy, M. Tronc and D. Simon

Laboratoire de Collisions Atomiques et Moléculaires (associé au CNRS)
Université de Paris-Sud, Bât.351, 91405 ORSAY CEDEX (France)

Dissociative attachment   measurements have been carried out on H_2S and H_2Se using an electron spectrometer modified to detect negative ions[1] and a mass spectrometer with a trochoïdal monochromator as electron gun[2]. The ions produced in H_2S are known to be H^-, HS^- and S^- (3 and ref there in). Except for H^- [3] previous studies on DA have been performed with low electron energy resolution. HS^- and H^- ions exhibit large cross sections and lie respectively around 2.5 eV and 5-9 eV. They are easy to separate energetically and have been studied with the electron spectrometer. On the opposite the lowest S^- peak we are dealing with in the present paper is about two orders of magnitude smaller than HS^- and lies in the same energy range (2.5 eV). It has been therefore studied with the mass spectrometer.

Results for S^- are presented in fig. 1. The striking feature is the existence of a well developed structure. The positions of several vibrational levels of the neutral $H_2S(^1A_1)$ have been indicated in fig. 1. The good fit with the symmetric (or antisymmetric) stretch mode serie seems to argue for an autodetaching

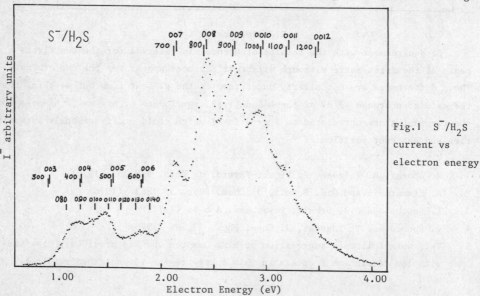

Fig.1 S^-/H_2S current vs electron energy

process from the resonance $^2A_1$ to the neutral $^1A_1$ state, the explanation in terms of opening of new exit channels being similar to what has been proposed for Cl^-/HCl [4]. Nevertheless the structure does not show the step-type structure which was observed for the hydrogen halides[4]. The peak type structure suggests more likely that a predissociation occurs between the $^2A_1$ surface and another resonant state the vibrational constants of which would be similar to those of the neutral $^1A_1$. Such a state has been already computed by Taylor for HCl [5] which has a dipole moment (1.08D) similar to H_2S (0.97D). Furthermore both vibrational excitation functions for HCl and H_2S exhibit a sharp peak at threshold attributed to "dipole" states[6]. Why the interference process seems dominant in H_2S although the autodetachment seems dominant in HCl is not understood at the present time but work is in progress for a better understanding of these results. Despite of some similarities we want to emphasize that the basically triatomic nature of the S^- formation may induce appreciable differences with the Cl^- process.

Figure 2 shows a constant ion energy spectrum for HS^- at a residual energy $E_R = 0$ and an angle of observation $\theta = 90°$. The positions of all the structures presented in this spectrum do not seem to correspond to the positions of vibrational series of the neutral $H_2S(^1A_1)$. We think that in that case the structures must be understood both in terms of opening of new exit vibrational channels for $H_2S(^1A_1)$ plus the predissociation of a "mimic" H_2S^- dipole state[5] by the $(^2A_1)$ H_2S^- state. Similar results have been observed for Se^- and HSe^- from H_2Se and will be presented at the conference.

The H^- ions yield spectrum from H_2S via the upper $^2A_1$ resonant state (in the 7.5 eV region) has been obtained, at an angle of observation $\theta = 90°$. Structures observed in this spectrum are assigned to the interaction of the $^2A_1$ repulsive state of H_2S^- with Feshbach resonances associated to Rydberg states of H_2S like in the case of H^-/HCl [7]. The spectrum will be presented at the conference.

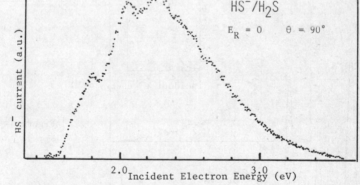

Figure 2

HS^-/H_2S

$E_R = 0 \qquad \theta = 90°$

HS^- current (a.u.)

2.0 Incident Electron Energy 3.0 (eV)

1. C. Scherman, I. Cadez, P. Delon, M. Tronc and R.I. Hall, J. Phys.E 11 746 (1978)
2. R. Abouaf, R. Paineau, F. Fiquet-Fayard, J. Phys. B 9 303 (1976)
3. R. Azria, Y. Le Coat, G. Lefèvre and D. Simon, J. Phys. B 12 679 (1979)
4. R. Abouaf and D. Teillet-Billy J. Phys. B 10 2261 (1977)
5. H.S. Taylor, E. Goldstein, G.A. Segal, J. Phys. B 10 2253 (1977)
6. K. Rohr and F. Linder J. Phys. B 9 2521 (1976) ; K. Rohr J. Phys. B
7. M. Tronc, R. Azria, Y. Le Coat and D. Simon J. Phys. B (1979) in press

DIFFERENTIAL CROSS SECTION FOR NEGATIVE ION FORMATION IN HCl

R. Azria, M. Tronc, Y. Le Coat and D. Simon

Lab. de Collisions Atomiques et Moléculaires (associé au CNRS)
Université de Paris-Sud, Bât.351, 91405 ORSAY CEDEX (France)

We have studied dissociative attachment in HCl by means of a crossed beam
electron impact spectrometer modified to detect negative ions by adjonction of a
momentum filter which separates electrons from ions after energy analysis[1]. Three
dissociative attachment processes exist in HCl [2] leading to Cl^- ions at .83 eV
and H^- ions at 7.1 and 9.2 eV. Figure 1 shows constant ion residual energy, spectrum for Cl^- ions (a) and for electrons (b) at a residual energy $E_R = 0$ and an
angle of observation of $\theta = 90°$.

Spectrum (a) is obtained with the same conditions as (b) but with the momentum filter operating.

The insert (c) is a constant ion energy spectrum for Cl^- ions at $E_R = 0$ and
$\theta = 90°$ obtained with 50 meV electron energy resolution. This spectrum exhibits
a structure at the maximum not reported before.

The sharp decreases (structures) presented in (a) and observed previously[3] [4]
seem essentially due to the opening of HCl vibrational exit channels[5] but the
small structure in (c) is more likely due to the $2\,^2\Sigma^+$ HCl "dipole state" [6].

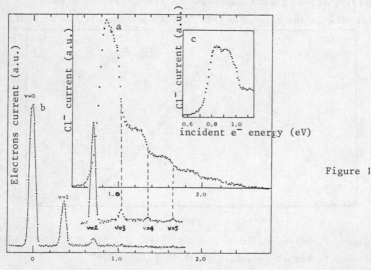

Figure 1

Incident electron energy (eV)

Figure 2 shows the H^- ions yield spectrum for an angle of observation of
120°.

This spectrum exhibits two peaks with a non vertical onset. The first structureless peak has an angular distribution characteristic of a pure dσ wave.

The second one at 9.2 eV shows structures superimposed on a broad peak. These structures are understood as interaction of the $^2\Pi$ state of HCl^-, responsible for the broad peak, with the series of Feshbach resonances associated with Rydberg states of HCl converging to the $X^2\Pi$ HCl^+ ground state[7]. This second peak has an angular distribution characteristic of a pure $d\Pi$ wave.

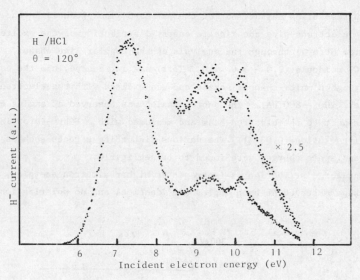

Figure 2

REFERENCES

1. C. Schermann, I. Cadez, P. Delon, M. Tronc and R. Hall, J. Phys. E : Sci. Instrum. 11 746 (1978)

2. R. Azria, L. Roussier, R. Paineau and M. Tronc, Rev. Phys. Appl. 9 469 (1974)

3. J.P. Ziesel, I. Nenner and G.J. Schulz, J. Chem. Phys. 63 1943 (1975)

4. R. Abouaf and D. Teillet-Billy, J. Phys. B : Atom. Mol. Phys. 10 2261 (1977)

5. F. Fiquet-Fayard, J. Phys. B : Atom. Mol. Phys. 7 810 (1974)

6. H.S. Taylor, E. Golstein and G.A. Segal, J. Phys. B : Atom. Mol. Phys. 10 2253 (1977)

7. D. Spence and T. Noguchi, J. Chem. Phys. 63 505 (1975)

KINETIC ENERGY DISTRIBUTION OF THE EXCITED HYDROGEN ATOM PRODUCED BY CONTROLLED ELECTRON IMPACT ON HCl

Morihide HIGO and Teiichiro OGAWA

Department of Molecular Science and Technology,
Kyushu University 86, Hakozaki, Fukuoka 812, Japan

A high resolution measurement of the Balmer-β line produced in the collision of HCl with electrons give the kinetic energy distribution of the excited hydrogen atom H*(n=4) through the analysis of the Doppler line shape.

The HCl molecule ($2.0 - 3.0 \times 10^{-4}$ Torr) was introduced into the collision chamber through a multi-channel nozzle and was excited with the electron-beam (25 - 300 eV, 100 - 800 µA). The photoemission was observed at angles of 90° and 55° with respect to the electron-beam and measured with a Fabry-Perot interferometer (resolution: 0.03 Å). The various disturbing effects such as secondary electrons and space charges were found to be negligible.

The angular distribution is isotropic at higher electron energies, since the line shape observed at both angles are identical and no polarization are observed.

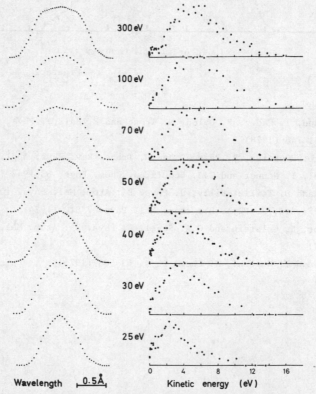

Fig.1.
Electron energy dependence of Balmer-β line shape and kinetic energy distribution of H*(n=4). Spectral resolution: 0.03 Å, Observation angle: 55°.

But at the electron energy of 25 eV, the line shape is anisotropic and polarization is observed. The kinetic energy distributions, $\Pi(E)$, of H*(n=4) are
calculated by the following relation[1] from the observed line shapes, $F(\lambda)$, at
angle of 55° and are shown in Fig.1.

$$\Pi(E) \quad \propto \quad dF(\lambda)/d\lambda$$

At the electron energy of 25 eV, the distribution has one component with its
maximum at about 3 eV. As the electron energy increases, the second component
appears and the slower component becomes weak. At higher electron energies (>70
eV), the distribution has one maximum at about 6 eV. The excitation function for
the Balmer-β line has been measured, having two onsets: 20.1 ± 0.6 and about 25
eV.

The potential curves for the formation of H$^+$ drawn with reference to the
photoelectron spectrum[2] are shown in Fig.2. Since the excited molecular states
converge to the ionic state, these curves can be carried over to the
investigation of the dissociative excitation. Thus the excited states involved
in the dissociative excitation process are the Rydberg states converging to HCl$^+$
states. The Rydberg states converging to the $^2\Sigma^+$ state are not dissociating.
The Rydberg states converging to $^4\Pi$ are triplet and produce the slower H*(n=4)
(~3 eV) by the interaction with those converging to $^2\Sigma^+$. This process is
important at lower electron energies. On the other hand, the Rydberg states
converging to $^2\Pi$ are singlet and important at higher electron energies; these
states produce the faster H*(n=4) (~6 eV). The transition to these states are
optically forbidden process due to two-electron excitation and are consistent
with the Fano-plot of Lyman-α line.[3]

Thus, the analysis of the kinetic
energy distribution of the fragment
species is useful to the elucidation on
the excited molecular states and thier
potential curves.

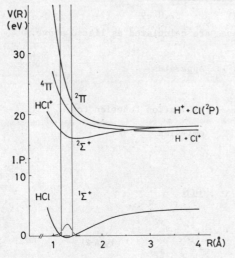

Fig.2.
Potential curves of HCl and HCl$^+$.

1. M.Higo and T.Ogawa, to be submitted.
2. H.J.Lempka, T.R.Passmore and W.C.Price, Proc. Roy. Soc. A304, 53 (1968).
3. G.R.Möhlmann, K.H.Shima and F.J.de Heer, Chem. Phys. 28, 331 (1978).

KINETIC ENERGY DISTRIBUTION OF H AND D ATOMS (n=4)
PRODUCED BY THE ELECTRON IMPACT ON HCN AND DCN

I. Nishiyama*, T. Kondow and K. Kuchitsu

Department of Chemistry, Faculty of Sience,
The University of Tokyo, Hongo, Bunkyo-ku, Tokyo 113, Japan

The line profile of the hydrogen and dueterium Balmer-β emissions produced
by the electron impact of hydrogen cyanide (HCN) and dueterium cyanide (DCN) were
measured with high resolution. The kinetic energy distributions of H(n=4) and
D(n=4) were obtained by the analyses of the Doppler profiles.

The apparatus is shown in Fig. 1. The electron beam of 10 - 1000 eV was
crossed with a gas beam in the vacuum chamber evacuated to 2×10^{-7} Torr. The
pressure of the sample gas was estimated to be about 10^{-3} Torr in the collision
region. The electron beam current was about 0.5 mA. The light emissions from
excited fragments were observed by a Spex 1704 monochromator and an HTV R585
photomultiplier. The optical resolution was about 0.01 - 0.02 nm with a slit
width of 10 - 20 μm. When the excitation function was measured, the optical band
pass was set at about 0.4 nm.

The excitation function of H_β emission is shown in Fig. 2. The threshold
energy was 17.8 ± 1.0 eV, and an additional onset was observed at 34 ± 2 eV. This
feature of the excitation function suggests that two dissociation processes
contribute to the formation of H(n=4) from HCN. The threshold energy of 17.8 eV
corresponds to the following dissociation process:

$$HCN \longrightarrow H(4) + CN(X) \qquad 18.0 \text{ eV} \qquad (1)$$

and the second onset at about 34 eV corresponds to

$$HCN \longrightarrow H(4) + CN^+(X) \qquad 32.0 \text{ eV} \qquad (2)$$

where the energies required for these processes are calculated as listed above.

← Fig. 1. Apparatus

Fig. 2. Excitation function for H_β

↓   emission

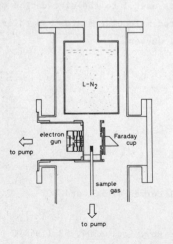

The Doppler profiles of H_β emission observed at several impact energies are shown in Fig. 3. The Doppler width becomes narrower as the impact energy is lowered. Accordingly, the average kinetic energy is smaller at lower impact energy. The kinetic energy distribution was obtained directly from an analysis of the Doppler profiles, as shown in Fig. 4. The angular distribution of H(n=4) produced from HCN was assumed to be isotropic. Two components, i.e., high- and low-energy components, were observed in the kinetic energy distribution obtained at 100 eV impact energy. The high-energy component corresponds to the H(4) atoms produced through process (2) found in the excitation function. The average kinetic energy, calculated from the kinetic energy distribution, was 7.2 ± 0.5 eV at 100 eV impact energy. Similar measurements were made for the D_β emission from DCN. However, no isotope effect was observed in the kinetic energy distribution; the average kinetic energy was 6.9 ± 0.8 eV at 100 eV impact energy.

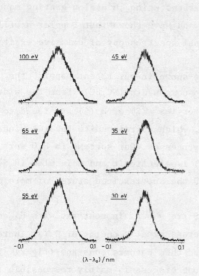

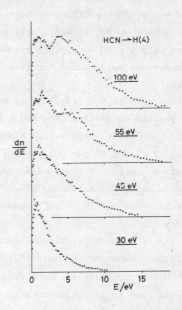

Fig. 3 Dependence of H_β emission   Fig. 4 Dependence of the kinetic
            profile on the impact   energy distribution of H(n=4)
            electron energy   on the impact electron energy

*Present address: Institute for Molecular Science, Okazaki 444, Japan

TRANSLATIONAL SPECTROSCOPY OF ELECTRON IMPACT DISSOCIATION OF
MOLECULES ISOELECTRONIC AND ISOSYMMETRIC WITH H_2O BY DOPPLER
PROFILE MEASUREMENTS OF BALMER-α EMISSION

N.KOUCHI, M.OHNO, K.ITO, N.ODA[*] and Y.HATANO

Department of Chemistry and Research Laboratory of Nuclear Reactors,[*]
Tokyo Institute of Technology, Meguro-ku, Tokyo 152, Japan.

Dissociation processes play a very important role in the decay of superexcited states. For better substantiation of superexcited states and their dissociation processes, it is certainly necessary to measure the kinetic energy of
fragments as well as the threshold energy of dissociation. Such measurements,
however, have been tried exclusively with charged particles, metastable atoms and
high Rydberg atoms, because it was not feasible to directly measure the kinetic
energy of the emissive excited atoms with short lifetimes. Recently, we have
observed the Doppler profiles of Balmer-α emission of $H^*(3)$ and $D^*(3)$ produced by
electron impact on H_2, D_2 and simple hydrocarbons using an etalon-grating monochromator with a high wavelength resolution and have shown that Doppler profile
measurements are very useful for translational spectroscopy of emissive excited
fragments.[1]

In the case of H_2O (fig.1a), as we have shown in our recent paper,[2] the
Doppler profile consists unexpectedly of two components (NC,BC). From the width of
the Doppler profiles, the average kinetic energies (KE) of $H^*(3)$ are found to be
0.4 eV and 4 eV for NC and BC, respectively, which correspond to the two kinds of
superexcited states and their dissociation processes. Our success in H_2O work
leads us to study the molecules (CH_4,NH_3,HF) isoelectronic and molecules (H_2S)
isosymmetric with H_2O in order to understand the superexcited states of more complicated molecules.

In fig.1b, some Doppler profiles of H_2S are shown. In contrast with H_2 and
H_2O, only one component is observed. The average kinetic energy of $H^*(3)$ increases
linearly with increasing impact energies, and then becomes constant (fig.2). These
two results lead to a conclusion that only one process is mainly responsible for
the formation of $H^*(3)$. We must note that the KE at 20 eV impact energy is already
large, 1.9 eV. Since the calculated minimum energies for the formation of $H^*(3)$
are 16.2 eV for

$$H_2S^{**} \longrightarrow H^*(3) \quad + \quad SH(X^2\pi) \qquad\qquad (1)$$

and $\geq$ 20 eV for the processes other than (1) and the electronic structure of H_2S
seemes to be rather similar to that of H_2O,[3] referring to the results of H_2O,[2] it
is concluded that the dissociation process observed here is ascribed to process
(1) where H_2S^{**} is core-excited or doubly excited and corresponds to the superexcited H_2O which is responsible for the BC. The Doppler profile at 20 eV impact
energy is very sharp, which indicates the existence of $H^*(3)$ with kinetic energy
nearly 0. This kind of $H^*(3)$ would be formed from the superexcited H_2S which corresponds to the core-excited H_2O contributing to the NC. These two superexcited

states of H_2S, however, would be considered to be much closer to each other in energy than corresponding superexcited states of H_2O. It is noticeable that the Doppler profiles change very much with the increase of impact energies (fig.1b). This result shows a good correspondence with our simulation of the Doppler profiles described in Ref.1a.

In fig.1c, some Doppler profiles of NH_3 are shown, and in fig.2 the results for CH_4 and NH_3 are shown together with those for H_2O and H_2S. The impact energy dependences of KE for CH_4 and NH_3 are rather different from that for H_2S.

We intend to discuss the results for CH_4, NH_3, H_2O, HF and H_2S systematically and to show their superexcited states and dissociation processes.

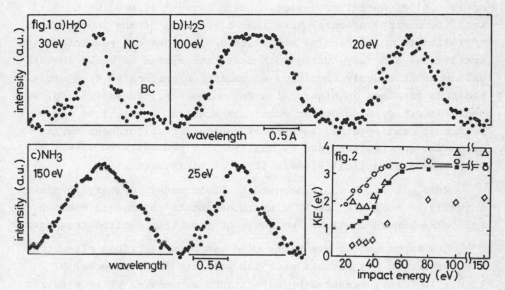

fig.1 The Doppler profiles of Balmer-α by electron impact on a) H_2O at 30 eV impact energy, b) H_2S at 100 eV and 20 eV and c) NH_3 at 150 eV and 25 eV.
fig.2 The impact energy dependence of the average kinetic energy (KE) of $H^*(3)$ ($\circ$-H_2S, $\triangle$-CH_4, $\blacksquare$-NH_3, $\diamond$-H_2O).

1) a. Ito, Oda, Hatano and Tsuboi, Chem.Phys.,17,35(1976); b. ibid.,21, 203(1977).
2) Kouchi, Ito, Hatano, Oda and Tsuboi, ibid.,36,239(1979).
3) Siegbahn et al., ESCA Applied to Free Molecules (North-Holland, Amsterdam, 1969).

ABSOLUTE EMISSION CROSS-SECTION OF NH($c^1\Pi \to b^1\Sigma^+$,O-O) VIBRATIONAL BAND OF AMMONIA

J.M.Kurepa and M.D.Tasić

Institute of Physics, Studentski trg 12/V,P.O.Box 57,
11001 Beograd,Yugoslavia

Our investigation of optical spectra which follow dissociative electron-molecular binary collision processes led us in such a type of experiments to substitute a standard single photon counting system as a quantitative optical detector by some more versatile automatic optical detection device. Such a device[1] allowed us to detect the desired spectral wave lenght interval of the investigated radiation in multiscanning mode with desired optical resolution and statistical accuracy. Using such detection system we could investigate more thoroughly the types of radiation originated from excited radicals obtained in binary electron-molecular interaction. So, we could investigate molecular continuum spectra, atomic line and vibrational band spectra, spectra of residual gases present during impacting interaction, and by multiscaling procedure to detect also very low-level optical signals if it is of interest.

This contribution is devoted to measurements of very low-level intesity of radiation of NH vibrational bands in ammonia embeded in molecular continuum of NH_3 molecule or its other excited fragments.

The experimental apparatus used has been described elsewhere[1,2]. The gas target was ammonia with the pressure in an interval of 10^{-4} - 10^{-3} torr measured by capacitance manometer, while electron impacting energy was from 50 to 500 eV. The chosen optical interval was 300-600 nm. Apart from detected Balmer lines[3] as the most prominent features in this spectral region, very low intensity vibrational bands radiation from NH fragments have been detected. They appear above the ammonium molecular or other heavy fragments continuum of the intensity of the same order of magnitude. The detected NH emissions were: NH($A^3\Pi_i \to X^3\Sigma^-$) band in interval 302-368 nm, and NH($c^1\Pi \to a^1\Delta$) band in interval 303-365 nm and NH($c^1\Pi \to b^1\Sigma^+$) band. The first two bands overlap each other on very large molecular contiuum and some of them are, due to their small emission cross-section values, disturbed by N_2 emission from residual gases ($1 \cdot 10^{-6}$ torr). So, with certainty only NH($c^1\Pi \to b^1\Sigma^+$,O-O) vibrational band at 452,3 nm could be investigated independent of molecular continuum contribution in this spectral region and independent also on the uncertainty of the width of vibrational band.

In Fig. 1 the emission cross-section for this band is presented by procedure already described[2], while in Fig. 2 the Fano plot of the obtained results is shown. From Fig. 2 it is obvious that the excited NH fragments are obtained by optically allowed transitions to superexcited states of ammonia.

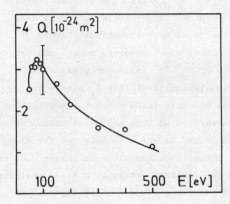

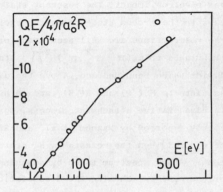

Fig. 1.
Absolute emission cross-section of $NH(c^1\Pi \rightarrow b^1\Sigma^+, 0-0)$ band of ammonia

Fig. 2.
Fano plot of emission cross-section of $NH(c^1\Pi \rightarrow b^1\Sigma^+, 0-0)$ band of ammonia

1. J.M.Kurepa, B.J.Levi, B.M.Panić, Spectrochem.Acta 32B, 413 (1977)

2. J.M.Kurepa, M.D.Tasić, Chem.Phys. (North Holland) in press

3. J.M.Kurepa, S.S.Manola, M.D.Tasić, Proc.V-th Int.Conf. of Atomic Physics, Berkeley, California, p. 392 (1976)

DISSOCIATIVE ATTACHMENT IN N_2

A. Huetz, F. Gresteau, R.I. Hall and J. Mazeau

Groupe de Spectroscopie par Impact Electronique et Ionique
L.P.O.C., Tour I2, E.5, 4,Place Jussieu
Université Pierre et Marie Curie
75230 Paris-Cédex 05 - France

Strong resonant structure has been previously observed in the cross-sections for excitation of the ($\pi_u^3 \sigma_g^2 \pi_g$) $A^3\Sigma_u^+$ state of molecular nitrogen under electron impact.[1] The resonant state responsible for these phenomena also decays to the ground state producing excitation of high vibrational levels[2,3]. These observations are well accounted for within the "boomerang model" and are attributable to a ($\pi_u^3 \sigma_g^2 \pi_g^2$) $^2\Pi_u$ state of N_2^- [3,4] whose potential curve and width have been deduced. Above the dissociation limit this N_2^- state can dissociate to $N^-(^3P)$ and $N(^4S)$, and we have now calculated the cross section for this dissociative attachment process. Observations of such a process have been recently reported by Mazeau et al[5] and Spence and Burrow[6] who detected the electron ejected when the metastable N^- state decays (ejected electron energy 0.07 eV) An energy-loss spectrum taken by scanning the incident energy at a fixed analysis energy of .07 eV, showing the dissociation process above 9.7 eV is represented in the figure. The normalized calculated cross section is seen to be in reasonable agreement and it can be assumed that the $^2\Pi_u$ state of N_2^- is also responsible for dissociative attachment.

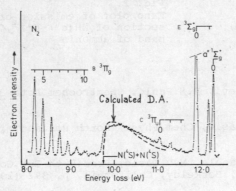

Energy-loss spectrum obtained in N_2 at a 135° scattering angle setting the analysis energy at 0·07 eV and sweeping the incident electron energy.

The absolute cross section has also been measured by normalization to the 2^3S cross section of He. The measured value is of the same order as the theoretical one and will be presented.

A puzzling feature of the observations is the onset of the structure below the dissociation limit. A possible explanation can be derived from the presence of rotationally excited target molecules. This has been invalidated by

a high-resolution study of the threshold at temperatures from 300°K to 900°K.
The observed rotational effect is insufficient to fully account for the onset
below the limit. A more feasible explanation is forthcoming from a survey of the
potential curves at large internuclear distance R. The N_2^- curve passes below the
A state curve into a stable zone as R increases. It must then re-intersect this
curve at large R as it goes to its limit 70 meV above that of neutral nitrogen
atoms. After the second   crossing the autoionising channel re-opens, and it is
the decay of the N_2^- (or N^- perturbed by N) near this crossing point which would
lead to the apparently precocious onset as well as to other phenomena observed
in electron scattering at incident energies near the dissociation limit[3,6].

Very strong enhancement of the dissociative attachment cross section has
been recently observed in H_2 as a function of the internal rotational and vibrational energy of the target molecules[7]. This has led us to look at this effect
in the case of N_2. Here the results are less spectacular. Rotational excitation
up to 900°K has almost no effect on the cross section. Furthermore, in a beam
containing vibrationally excited N_2, prepared in a micro-wave discharge, dissociation from v = 1 was found to have a cross section similar to that from v = 0.
This result was anticipated from the above mentioned calculations.

1. J. Mazeau, F. Gresteau, R.I. Hall, G. Joyez and J. Reinhardt
    J. Phys. B, 6, 862, 1973.
2. F. Gresteau, R.I. Hall, J. Mazeau and D. Vichon
    Abstracts X, ICPEAC, Paris, p 142, 1977.
3. A. Huetz, I. Čadež, F. Gresteau, R.I. Hall, D. Vichon and J. Mazeau
    to be published.
4. I. Čadež and F.F.Fayard, Abstracts VIII ICPEAC, Belgrade, p.454, 1973.
5. J. Mazeau, F. Gresteau, R.I. Hall and A. Huetz
    J. Phys. B : Atom. Molec. Phys. 11, L 557, 1978.
6. D. Spence and P.D. Burrow, J. Phys. B : Atom. Molec. Phys., 12,
    L 179, 1979.
7. M. Allan and S.F. Wong, Phys. Rev. Letters, 41, 1791, 1978

CROSS SECTION FOR RESONANT DISSOCIATION OF N_2 BY ELECTRON IMPACT[*]

David Spence

Argonne National Laboratory, Argonne, Illinois 60439 USA

and

P. D. Burrow

Behlen Laboratory, University of Nebraska, Lincoln Nebraska 68588 USA

The dissociative attachment process leading to the formation of negative ion and neutral fragments by electron impact on small molecules is well known. Such processes in diatomic molecules, for example, are initiated by the attachment of an incident electron to form a temporary negative molecular ion, or resonance. If attachment occurs above the ionic dissociation limit, the molecule may dissociate, yielding a neutral atom and a stable negative ion.

Strictly speaking, a proper dissociative attachment process cannot take place in molecules whose component atoms possess only unstable negative ions, since the electron must ultimately detach in the separated atom limit. Nevertheless, the analogous process may be envisioned in which the unstable atomic negative ion survives to large internuclear separation and ejects an electron having a kinetic energy equal to the magnitude of the atomic electron affinity. The process provides a mechanism for dissociation through the intermediate formation of a temporary negative ion, and hence could be classified as "resonant dissociation by electron impact."

In nitrogen the mechanism of resonant dissociation is

$$e + N_2 \rightarrow (N_2^{-x}) \rightarrow N(^4S) + N^-(^3P) \quad,$$

followed by $N^-(^3P) \rightarrow N(^4S) + e$.

The process is observed experimentally[2,3] by detection of a narrow band of slow electrons ejected from $N^-(^3P)$. The cross section for dissociation has a vertical onset just above the dissociation limit of N_2 and reaches a peak value of 2.5×10^{-18} cm^2 ± 50%, then decreases monotonically to zero at about 12.0 eV.

The resonant dissociation mechanism discussed here provides a source of superthermal N atoms from N_2 at the lowest possible impact energy; thus, it is likely to place a role of some importance in nitrogen plasmas (e.g., N_2 lasers and MHD plasmas) and in upper atmospheric phenomena such as auroras.

Finally, the reverse reaction, three-body recombination of N^4S atoms with an electron acting as the third body, should be greatly enhanced because of the resonance mechanism. This process may explain an observation by Brandt,[4] who reported that electrons were 10^7 or 10^8 times more efficient than ground state N_2 molecules in promoting recombination of N^4S atoms.

*Work performed under the auspices of the U.S. Department of Energy.

1. G. J. Schulz, Rev. Mod. Phys. <u>45</u>, 423 (1973).

2. J. Mazeau, F. Gresteau, R. I. Hall, and A. Huetz, J. Phys. B: Atom. Molec. Phys. <u>11</u>, L557 (1978).

3. D. Spence and P. D. Burrow, J. Phys. B: Atom. Molec. Phys. <u>12</u>, L179 (1979).

4. B. Brandt, Proceedings of the 6th Int. Conf. on Ionization Phenomena in Gases, Paris, Vol. 1, (North Holland Publ. Co., Amsterdam, 1963), p.43.

LINE SHAPES FOR ATTACHMENT OF THRESHOLD ELECTRONS TO SF$_6$ AND CFCℓ_3:
THRESHOLD PHOTOELECTRON (TPSA) STUDIES OF Xe, CO AND C$_2$H$_2$*

J. M. Ajello and A. Chutjian

Jet Propulsion Laboratory, California Institute
of Technology, Pasadena, CA 91103

Using the technique of threshold photoelectron spectroscopy by electron attachment (TPSA)[1], we are able, for the first time, to measure the shapes of electron attachment and dissociative attachment cross sections in molecules. The technique is quite general in that measured electron-capture peaks may be located not only at zero energy, but at higher electron energies as well.

The technique involves (1) direct photoionization to the $^2P_{1/2}$ level of Xe$^+$ to generate a narrow bandwidth of electrons of mean energy varying from 0-200 meV, (2) attachment of these photoelectrons to an admixed "trapping" molecule (here, SF$_6$ or CFCℓ_3), and (3) mass detection of the attachment product (SF$_6^-$ or Cℓ^-, respectively) as a function of photon energy. This technique differs considerably from swarm methods[2] in that (a) assumptions about a Maxwellian electron energy distribution are not made, (b) the electron energy range covered here is 0-200 meV while swarm rate measurements are restricted to energies greater than about 50 meV, and (c) only two-body collisions are involved.

The first direct measurement of the energy dependence of the attachment cross section in SF$_6$ is shown in Fig. 1.

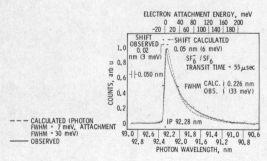

Fig. 1.
TPSA line profile (solid line) for the Xe$^+$ ($^2P_{\frac{1}{2}}$) level using SF$_6$ as the trapping gas. The measured FWHM and calculated transit time were for SF$_6^-$, 33 meV and 55μsec, respectively. The photon bandpass was 0.05 nm (7 meV). Theoretical (dashed line) fit of the SF$_6^-$ TPSA signal for the data. The FWHM's of the Lorentzian-shaped attachment cross section and the Gaussian-shaped photon bandpass are given. Also shown are the observed and calculated shifts of the peak of the signal.

The measured production, P, of SF$_6^-$ ions (solid line) at incident photon energy E$_o$ may be written symbolically as

$$P(E_o) = S \bigstar (\sigma_I \cdot \sigma_A) \tag{1}$$

where S is the incident photon bandwidth, σ_I and σ_A the Xe photoionization and SF$_6$ electron attachment cross sections, respectively, and where the star $\bigstar$ denotes convolution. The slit function S is taken to be Gaussian, with a width determined by the slit width for the spectrometer. The photoionization cross section σ_I has been measured to be nearly a step function at threshold,[3] and σ_A is assumed to be Lorentzian in shape. The dashed line in Fig. 1 represents a best fit using a Lorentzian profile for σ_A of 30 meV (FWHM). One sees good agreement between the measured and calculated curves. The most likely source of difference, especially at small electron energies (< 30 meV), lies in the assumption of a single, Lorentzian line shape for σ_A.[4] Measurements are currently underway to determine widths and thresholds of attachment peaks in other molecules.

The TPSA technique can also be used to measure threshold photoelectron spectra of atoms and molecules. A suitable trapping gas is admixed with the target species (which is substituted for Xe in step 1 above), and negative ion signal is monitored as a function of photon energy.[1] In Fig. 2 we show the photoionization

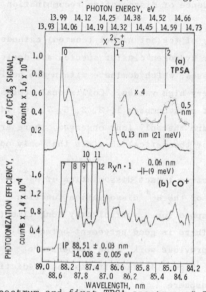

Fig. 2.
(a) TPSA spectrum ($Cl^-/CFCl_3$) of CO. Band origins of the levels $v' = 0 - 2$ of the X state are shown.
(b) Photoionization mass spectrum of CO, with one identified Rydberg series shown.

mass spectrum and first TPSA spectrum of CO. The latter spectrum clearly shows the first three vibrational levels of the X state. In addition, several spurious peaks are seen which are produced by more energetic electrons captured in the wings of the molecular threshold detector. Spectra will also be shown for the A and B states of CO^+. The importance of direct ionization and autoionization will be discussed in terms of TPSA line shapes (i.e., the shape of σ_I in Eq. (1)) and Franck-Condon factors.

*This work was supported by NASA under Contract NAS7-100 to the Jet Propulsion Laboratory, California Institute of Technology.

1. A. Chutjian and J. M. Ajello, J. Chem. Phys. 66, 4544 (1977).

2. R. N. Compton, L. G. Christophorou, G. S. Hurst and P. W. Reinhardt, J. Chem. Phys. 45, 4634 (1966).

3. J. A. R. Samson and R. B. Cairns, Phys. Rev. 173, 80 (1968).

4. R. W. Odom, D. L. Smith and J. H. Futrell, J. Phys. B: Atom. Molec. Phys. 8, 1349 (1975).

TRAP RECOMBINATION PROCESSES OF CLUSTER IONS

J.B. Hasted[+] D. Mathur[*] and S.U. Khan[+]

*Department of Physics, Birkbeck College, Malet Street, London WC1E 7HX.

[+]Department of Physics and Astronomy, University College London,
Gower Street, London WC1E 6BT

The hollow electron beam positive ion trap[1,2] (non-specific in mass) with concentric electron beam collision facility has previously found application for the study of ionization of atomic ions by electrons. We now apply it to molecular species, for which the temperature dependence of dissociative recombination processes can also be studied[3].

Advantage is taken of the capability of the hot nickel (coated) cathode to to emit the species H_5^+, from which other hydrogen cluster species are derived by electron-ion and ion-ion collision processes, which dominate within the hollow beam, which is collisionally pumped to very high vacuum. Collisional processes of electrons with hydrogenic trapped ions of mass numbers 1, 2, 3, 5, 7, 10, 14 and 20 have been investigated. Since these are the only ions observed, there are serious implications for the assumption by theoretical chemists that only odd number clusters exist[5].

Cross-section functions for the electron impact dissociation of H_2^+, H_3^+, H_5^+ are shown in Figures 1, 2, 3. The shape of the H_2^+ dissociation function indicates that the molecular ions are trapped for a sufficiently long time ($\sim$1 sec) for vibrational decay to v=0 to occur. There is good agreement between H_3^+ dissociation and recombination data and previous work. The temperature dependence of the H_5^+ recombination rate (Figure 4) facilitates the prediction of the recombination rate in the Jovian ionosphere.

1. J.B. Hasted and G.L. Awad, J. Phys. B 5 (1972) 1719.

2. M. Hamdan, K. Birkinshaw and J.B. Hasted, J. Phys. B 11 (1978) 331.

3. D. Mathur, S.U. Khan and J.B. Hasted, J. Phys. B 11 (1978) 3615.

4. D. Mathur, J.B. Hasted and S.U. Khan, J. Phys. B 12 (1979) 7921.

5. A.M. Sapse, M.T. Rayez-Meaume, J.C. Rayez, L.J. Massa Nature 278 (1979) 332.

6. D.F. Dance, M.F.A. Harrison, R.D. Rundel and A.C.H. Smith, Proc. Phys. Soc. 92 (1967) 577.

7. G.H. Dunn and B. van Zyl, Phys, Rev. 154 (1967) 40.

8. J.M. Peek, Phys. Rev. 154 (1967) 52.

9. B. Peart and K.T. Dolder, J. Phys. B 7 (1974a) 1567.
                                     J. Phys. B 7 (1974b) 236.

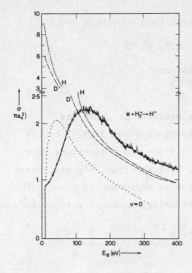

Figure 1

Electron impact cross-section for the dissociation of H_2^+. Pen tracing represents raw data, full line represents numerical smoothing. H, crossed beam data of Dance et al[6]; D, crossed beam data of Dunn and van Zyl[7]. Dotted curve, theory[8], using v=0 state of H_2^+.

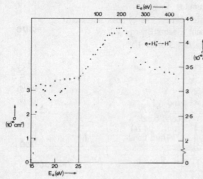

Figure 2

Cross-section functions for the electron impact dissociation of H_3^+. Squares and triangles, present data. Dots, data of Peart and Dolder[9].

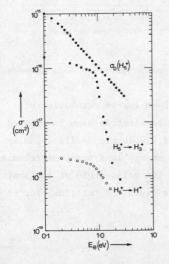

Figure 3

Electron impact cross-section functions for dissociation of H_5^+. Closed circles, totals; squares, H_3^+ product, open circles, H^+ product.

HIGH RESOLUTION INELASTIC ELECTRON SCATTERING FROM MOLECULAR OXYGEN

W.R. NEWELL, M. KHAKOO AND A.C.H. SMITH

Department of Physics and Astonomy,
University College London.

Interest in electron scattering from molecular atmospheric gases has recently been revised. There have been several experimental studies[1,2] on the electronic transitions in O_2 and new symmetries and state classifications have been assigned to well known features in the energy loss spectrum. In this paper we report high resolution inelastic electron scattering measurements from O_2 for incident electron energies of 5eV to 500eV and scattering angles of zero to $40°$.

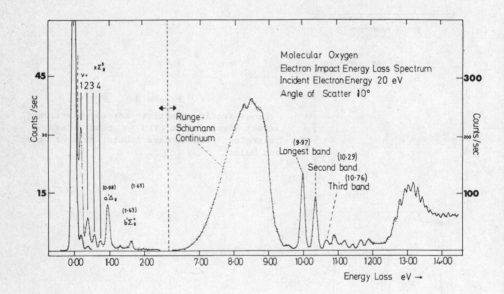

FIGURE 1

A double hemispherical electron spectrometer with an energy resolution of 80meV and an electron beam current of 5nA is used. The electron beam is crossed with a molecular gas beam derived from a demagnetised hypodermic needle which is positioned at 5mm from the electron beam. A typical energy loss spectrum taken at 20eV and $10°$ scattering angle is shown in Figure 1. The solid angle of the instrument is such that the analyser electron optics always views the total overlap of

the electron and gas beams hence removing the necessity of applying volume
corrections to the scattered signal obtained at different scattering angles.
Electron scattering from unwanted background gas, produced by the beam, is
determined by filling the experimental tank to the pressure observed when the
gas beam is present in the apparatus and repeating each measurement. This
signal is then subtracted from the original signal due to the combined effects
of beam and background gas.

Differential cross-sections for the excitation of the $^1\Delta_g$ $^1\Sigma_u^+$, Runge-Schumann
continuum, the longest band (9.97eV) and second band (10.29eV) have been obtained.
Where appropriate this has been analysed using the concept of a generalized oscillator strength as defined by Bethe[3] and optical oscillator strengths and matrix
elements for the transitions shown in Figure 1 will be given and comparisons made
with other experimental work, were appropriate, and current theory.

1. Trajmar S., Williams W. and Kuppermann A. 1972 J. Chem. Phys. 56 3759-65
2. Wakiya K. 1978 J. Phys. B: Atom. Molec. Phys. 11 3913-38
3. Bethe H.A. 1930 Ann. Phys. Lpz. 5 325-400.

ELECTRON ENERGY-LOSS SPECTRA IN MOLECULAR FLUORINE*

Hiroyuki Nishimura,[1]   David C. Cartwright[2] and Sandor Trajmar[3]

Theoretical Division
Los Alamos Scientific Laboratory, University of California
Los Alamos, New Mexico 87545 USA

Molecular fluorine has become the subject of a number of recent experimental and theoretical studies, in many cases motivated by its role in the hydrogen fluoride and rare gas fluoride laser systems. A detailed study of the absorption spectrum in the 78-102 nm region, and some emission characteristics of F_2, has recently been reported by Colbourn et al.[1] which resulted in the identification of many of the bound states of the molecule. A theoretical study has also been completed[2] that examines the valence electronic states and the $A^1\Pi_u \leftarrow X^1\Sigma_u^+$ continuum absorption in F_2. The purpose of this paper is to report electron energy-loss spectra in F_2, for incident electron energies of 30, 50 and 90 eV, selected scattering angles from 5 to 140°, and energy losses from 0 to 17.0 eV.

The measurements were carried out with a conventional apparatus utilizing a crossed electron-molecule beam geometry with differentially pumped electron gun and detector. Because of the reactive nature of F_2, a mixture of F_2 in Helium was used as the target gas.

Typical electron energy-loss spectra are shown in Figs. 1 and 2; Combined together, they illustrate the characteristics of the electron energy-loss spectrum of F_2 for energy losses from 0 to 15.3 eV. The upper trace in both Figs. 1 and 2 corresponds to an incident electron energy of 30 eV and a scattering angle of 90 degrees. The lower trace in Fig. 1 is for 90 eV and 5° and in Fig. 2 is 50 eV and 5°. In the upper portion of the figures, the best availabe information concerning the location of various electronic states is shown by horizontal or vertical lines and the appropriate term symbol. The indicated positions of the electronic states for energy-losses of 11 eV and below are based on ab initio configuration interaction calculations.[2] Those identifications above 11 eV are based on the analyses of optical data made by Colbourn, et al.[1]

As is evident by comparing the upper and lower spectra in Figs. 1 and 2, the spectra change significantly in moving from small (5°) to large (90°) scattering angles. The lower trace in Figs. 1 and 2 indicate that the strongest dipole exci-

*Research supported by NASA; Contract No. NAS7-100 and DOE, Contract No. EN-77-S-04-413.

[1]NRC/NASA Senior Resident Research Associate 1978; permanent address: Dept. of Physics, Faculty of Science, Niigata University, Ikarashi, Niigata 950/21, Japan.

[2]Theoretical Division, Los Alamos Scientific Laboratory, Los Alamos, NM 87545.

[3]California Institute of Technology, Jet Propulsion Laboratory, Pasadena, CA 91103.

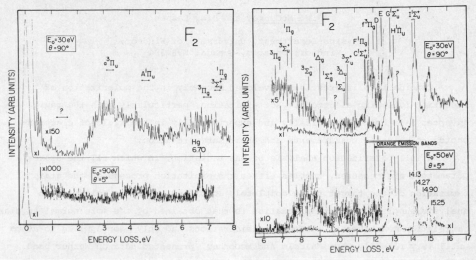

Fig. 1.   Fig. 2.

‌tation in F_2 is to the mixed valence-Rydberg-ionic states at 12.81 eV and the $1^1\Sigma_u^+$ state at 14.13 eV. This is somewhat unusual in that a valence state (the $A^1\Pi_u$ state at 4.6 eV) has a much smaller excitation cross section than the higher-lying mixed valence-Rydberg-ionic states.

At energy losses between 3.5 and 11.5 eV, a number of continuua appear in the spectra that are due to one or more of the eleven repulsive valence electronic states. Energy-loss spectra at a number of other angles and incident energies will be required to better identify which energy-loss features correlates with which excited states.

It is interesting to note that the broad features which reach maximum values at energy-losses 11.8 and 12.8 eV are produced by unresolved, overlapping, vibrational levels of two or more bound electronic states with equilibrium internuclear distances much larger[1] than the ground state. The spectra also show two well defined features, at 14.90 and 15.25 eV that are presently unidentified. Since they appear strong at the small scattering angles, they are probably dipole-allow and hence either $^1\Pi_u$ or $^1\Sigma_u^+$ states.

REFERENCES
1. E. A. Colbourn, M. Dagenais, A. E. Douglas and J. W. Raymonda, Can. J. Phys. 54, 1343 (1976).

2. D. C. Cartwright and P. J. Hay, J. Chem. Phys., (April 1979).

ELECTRON-IMPACT EXCITATION OF H_2 - INDIVIDUAL LINE POLARIZATIONS

J.W. McConkey and H.W. Dassen

Physics Department, University of Windsor,
Windsor, Ontario, Canada. N9B 3P4

Considerable interest has developed recently in the polarization of radiation following electron impact excitation, particularly with the rapid advances made both theoretically and experimentally in the field of electron-photon coincidence measurements and their interpretation.

A full polarization analysis of the radiation, in which all the Stokes' parameters are measured, enables either the excitation process or the state of excitation of the target to be completely specified. Such a polarization analysis supplies similar information to that obtained by the more normal angular correlation measurements. These considerations had only been applied to atoms until very recently when Malcolm and McConkey[1] presented data on Werner band excitation of H_2.

A necessary precursor to measurements of coincidence data, in which the scattering process is completely defined, is more straightforward measurement of linear polarization of all the emitted light, i.e. integrated over all scattered electron directions. The work reported here is mainly of this type.

The measurements are an extension of recent work by Malcolm et al.[2] where the polarization of selected Werner and Lyman bands of H_2 were measured as a function of incident electron energy. Because of intensity considerations, this earlier work was limited to measurements on the integrated band radiation but the experiment has now been modified to allow individual rotational lines to be studied. This allows more definitive comparison with theoretical predictions particularly in the threshold and high energy regions where some simplifying assumptions can be made.

P and R Lyman emissions and P, Q and R Werner emissions have been studied in the energy range up to 300 eV. The most strongly polarized lines are the Werner R lines where polarizations approaching 30 per cent are observed at 25 eV. The Q lines exhibit less polarization (25 per cent) at this energy, while the P lines are only weakly polarized (12 per cent). Complete data will be presented at the Conference, together with a full comparison with available theoretical predictions. It is also hoped to have "pseudo-threshold" data available obtained by a coincidence technique in another apparatus.

The authors are happy to acknowledge financial assistance from the Natural Sciences and Engineering Research Council of Canada and from N.A.T.O., Division of Scientific Affairs.

1. I.C. Malcolm and J.W. McConkey, J.Phys.B: Atom.Molec.Phys. 12, L 67, (1979).
2. I.C. Malcolm, H.W. Dassen and J.W. McConkey, J.Phys.B: Atom.Molec.Phys. 12, (1979). In press.

CROSS SECTIONS FOR ELECTRONIC EXCITATION OF MOLECULES BY ELECTRON IMPACT[*]

A. U. Hazi

Theoretical Atomic and Molecular Physics Group

Lawrence Livermore Laboratory, Livermore, California 94550

The impact parameter method of Seaton,[1] Stauffer and McDowell[2] has been extended to describe electronic excitation of molecules by electron impact. The Born-Oppenheimer separation of electronic and nuclear motions is employed. The internal target electrons are treated quantum mechanically, while the scattered electron is treated purely classically using straight-line trajectories. The method is applicable to spin-allowed ($\Delta S = 0$) transitions for which long range, electric multipole potentials dominate the electron-molecule interactions. Exchange between the target electrons and the projectile is ignored. It is assumed that energy and angular momentum are transfered between the target and the projectile at the point of closest approach. Requiring that energy and angular momentum be conserved during the collision leads to an expression for the integrated inelastic cross section which satisfies reciprocity. At high impact energies, where the initial and final velocities of the projectile are approximately the same, the formula for the cross section reduces to previous results.[1,2] Plane-wave approximations (e.g., the first Born) usually overestimate the partial cross sections for small impact parameters. To avoid this difficulty, a lower cut-off in impact parameter is employed. The value of this cut-off, which is chosen to produce the correct cross sections at high energies, appears to be a constant for a given molecule.

The method has been applied to several dipole allowed transitions in H_2, N_2 and F_2 with encouraging results. The method gives electronically inelastic cross sections which are significantly better than the corresponding Born cross sections for impact energies below 50 eV. Figure 1 shows the resulting cross sections for the case of $X^1\Sigma_g^+ \to B^1\Sigma_u^+$ in H_2 where accurate distorted-wave and close-coupling calculations are available for comparison. The impact parameter method gives surprisingly accurate cross sections as low as 15-20 eV. The method is very simple to use as the only input required consists of electric dipole, quadrupole, etc. transition moments which are available from electronic structure calculations.

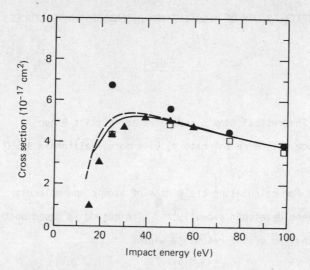

Fig. 1. Cross sections for $X^1\Sigma_g^+ \to B^1\Sigma_u^+$ excitation of H_2 by electron impact. Solid line: modified impact parameter method; dashed line: original[1,2] impact parameter method; ● Born approximation[3]; □ two-state close-coupling,[3] ▲distorted wave method.[4]

*Work performed under the auspices of the U. S. Department of Energy by the Lawrence Livermore Laboratory under contract No. W-7405-ENG-48.

1. M. J. Seaton, Proc. Phys. Soc. **79**, 1105 (1962).
2. A. D. Stauffer and M.R.C. McDowell, Proc. Phys. Soc. **89**, 289 (1966).
3. S. Chung and C. C. Lin, Phys. Rev. A**17**, 1874 (1978).
4. A. W. Fliflet and V. McKoy, Phys. Rev. A to be published.

THEORETICAL STUDY OF NEGATIVE ION RESONANCES IN MOLECULES

A. U. Hazi

Theoretical Atomic and Molecular Physics Group
Lawrence Livermore Laboratory, Livermore, California 94550

A new method for calculating the widths of atomic and molecular resonances has been developed recently[1,2]. The method is based on the golden-rule definition of the resonance width:

$$\Gamma(E) = 2\pi \left| <\phi_r \right| (H-E) \; \psi_E^+ > |^2$$

where ϕ_r is the localized, resonance wavefunction, and ψ_E^+ is the complementary, non-resonant scattering function. As usual, the resonance state is defined as the lowest solution of a projected Hamiltonian QHQ, where, in many electron targets, $P = 1 - Q$ projects onto approximate representations of the energetically open channels. The novel feature of the present method is that it uses only square-integrable (L^2) functions to approximate the non-resonant back-ground continuum.[3] In practice, PHP is diagonalized in a finite basis of L^2, many-electron wavefunctions to obtain a discrete representation of the continuum. Stieltjes-moment theory techniques[4] are employed to extract a continuous approximation for $\Gamma(E)$ from this discrete representation of the non-resonant continuum. If necessary, the energy shift can be computed from $\Gamma(E)$ by a straightforward evaluation of the required principal value integral.

Since the method utilizes L^2 functions exclusively, it has several advantages. Its implementation requires only existing atomic and molecular structure codes. Many electron effects, such as correlation and polarization, are easily incorporated into the calculation of the width via configuration interaction techniques.

The method has been applied to the $^1\Sigma_u$ and $^1\Pi_u$ doubly-excited, autoionizing states of H_2, the well-known $^2\Pi_g$ resonance of N_2^- and the proposed[5] $^2\Sigma$ and $^2\Pi$ shape-resonance of LiF. For the $(1\sigma_u\ 2\sigma_g)$ $^1\Sigma_u$ state of H_2, we confirm the conclusion of Kirby et al[6] that the width increases with increasing internuclear separation. In the case of the $^2\Pi_g$ resonance of N_2^-, the present resonance parameters calculated with the static-exchange model compare favorably with the values obained with other, more traditional methods.

*Work performed under the auspices of the U. S. Department of Energy by Lawrence Livermore Laboratory under contract No. W-7405-ENG-48.

1. A. U. Hazi, J. Phys. B $\underline{11}$, L259 (1978).

2. A. U. Hazi, "Stieltjes-Moment-Theory Technique for Calculating Resonance Widths," in <u>Electron- and Photon-Molecule Collisions</u>, eds. T. Rescigno, V. McKoy, B. Schneider (Plenum, New York, 1979).

3. P. W. Langhoff, Int. J. Quant. Chem. Symp. $\underline{8}$, 347 (1974).

4. A. P. Hickman, A. D. Isaacson, W. H. Miller, Chem. Phys. Lett. $\underline{37}$, 63 (1976).

5. L. A. Collins and D. W. Norcross, Phys. Rev. A $\underline{18}$, 467 (1978).

6. K. Kirby, S. Guberman, A. Dalgarno, J. Chem. Phys. to be published.

FESHBACH RESONANCES IN H_2^-, HD^- AND D_2^-

J.J. Jureta[*], J.N.H. Brunt[**], F.H. Read, G.C. King,
P. Hammond and S. Cvejanović[*]

Physics Department, University of Manchester,
Manchester M13 9PL, England.

The energies and symmetries of all the Feshbach resonances in H_2^- and its isotopic analogues, in the energy range from 11 to 13eV, have not yet been reliably established either experimentally[1,2,3,4] or theoretically[5,6,7,8]. To obtain more information, we have carried out high resolution measurements of the yields of metastable molecules produced by electron impact on H_2, HD and D_2, using the technique described by Brunt et al [9], and have determined the energies of the vibrational levels of two series of resonances. Further information has been obtained from high resolution threshold excitation, using the technique of Cvejanović and Read [10], and energy loss experiments.

The resonance energies of the two series appearing in the metastable excitation yields are different from those of the resonance series a and c observed previously in several different types of experiment [1,2,3]. The energies of the newly observed series are consistent for the three isotopic molecules, assuming that each series has the same potential function for the three molecules and that the lowest members of the two series are at 11.623 and 11.772eV respectively in H_2^-. One of the series lies consistently at approximately 20meV above the vibrational levels of the $c^3\Pi_u$ state of the neutral molecules. The two newly observed series have approximately the same energies as the series a and c in H_2^-, and hence can easily be confused with them, but this is not so in HD^- and D_2^-.

The energies of the resonance series, together with their suggested configurations and symmetries, will be presented.

1.   G.J. Schulz, Rev.Mod.Phys. 45, 423 (1973)

2.   G. Joyez, J. Comer and F.H. Read, J.Phys.B 6, 2427 (1973)

3.   A. Weingartshofer and M. Eyb, J.Phys.B 8, L278 (1975)

4.   A. Weingartshofer, E.M. Clarke, J.K. Holmes and J.W. McGowan,
         J.Phys.B 8, 1552 (1975)

5.   I. Eliezer, H.S. Taylor and J.K. Williams, J.Chem.Phys. 47, 2165 (1967)

6.   E.S. Chang, Phys.Rev. A 6, 2399 (1975)

7.   B.D. Buckley and C. Bottcher, J.Phys.B 10, 2635 (1977)

8.   J.N. Bardsley and J.S. Cohen, J.Phys.B 11, 3645 (1978)

9.   J.N.H. Brunt, G.C. King and F.H. Read, J.Phys. B 9, 2095 (1976)

10. S. Cvejanović and F.H. Read, J.Phys.B 7, 1180 (1974)

*   Permanent address : Institute of Physics, Belgrade, Yugoslavia

** Present address : Medical Biophysics Department, University of Manchester.

THEORETICAL STUDY OF ELECTRON IMPACT DEEXCITATION
OF KrF AND XeF EXCIMERS

T. N. Rescigno

Theoretical Atomic and Molecular Physics Group

Lawrence Livermore Laboratory, Livermore, California 94550

Electron quenching of electronically excited states have been identified
as an important process in the kinetics of electron-beam and discharge pumped
rare-gas halide lasers.[1] We have calculated cross sections and rate constants
for quenching of the excimer states of KrF and XeF by low energy electrons.
We have used a modified impact parameter method to obtain the required inelastic
cross sections.[2] This method relies on a quantum mechanical description of the
target electrons and a purely classical description of the scattered electron
based on straight line trajectories. This treatment involves one adjustable
parameter -- namely, the lower cut-off value for the impact parameter. This
parameter was fixed by normalizing the cross sections at high energy to the
first Born approximation. The latter were obtained from an ab-initio calculation
of the generalized oscillator strengths using large scale configuration-interaction
wavefunctions.[3]

For both KrF and XeF, we find that the B$\rightarrow$X transition dominates, with thermal
rate constants of 3×10^{-8} and 6×10^{-8} cm^3/sec respectively. The assumptions of
the method employed are most valid in situations where the molecular transitions
are dipole-dominated. Since these criteria are well met in the ionic-to-valence
rare-gas excimer transitions, we expect our theoretical results to be reasonably
accurate.

*Work performed under the auspices of the U. S. Department of Energy by the
Lawrence Livermore Laboratory under contract number W-7405-ENG-48.

1. A. E. Green and C. A. Brau, IEEE J. Quan. Elec. 14, 951 (1978).

2. M. J. Seaton, Proc. Phys. Soc. 79, 1105 (1962).

3. P. J. Hay and T. H. Dunning, J. Chem. Phys. 66, 1306 (1977);
    69, 2209 (1978).

HIGH RESOLUTION ELECTROIONIZATION DATA OF NH_3 AND ND_3 NEAR THRESHOLD

<u>Paul Marmet</u> and Michel Proulx

Département de physique, Université Laval
Québec, Qué. Canada G1K 7P4

The ionization threshold of ammonia has been determined by various methods such as the extrapolation of spectroscopic series[1], photoionization[2] and photoelectron spectroscopy[3]. No high resolution electron impact data has been published which could verify the ionization energy (10.17 eV) and show the short lived negative resonances which are inexistant in other methods.

In this experiment, electroionization data are obrained by counting the number of ions produced in a molecular beam which is crossed by a monoenergetic beam of electrons. The cross section is determined as a function of electron energy. The ions produced are mass analysed by a quadrupole mass filter before being registered in a computer memory.

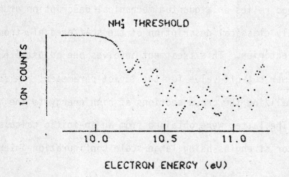

Fig. 1
Ionization efficiency
curve of ammonia as
usually presented.[6]

The ionization efficiency curves of many atoms and diatomic molecules such as O_2[4], CO[5] and N_2[6] had been obtained with monoenergetic electrons before it was realized that the threshold region of some more complex molecules was much more difficult to measure. It became evident recently that a small proportion of the electrons is scattered by the electrodes inside the electron selector. It is also observed in NH_3 and CH_4 that the power law near threshold is fairly large ($n \geq 3$). When such an ionization threshold is convolved with an electron beam containing some scattered electrons, it can be seen that the threshold may become undetectable.

Two electron selectors in series, coupled with suitable electron optics, made possible a spectacular improvement in our results as seen in Fig. 1.

There are numerous structures belonging to "autoionizing" NH_3* states or to resonant NH_3^{-*} and to NH_3^+(v=0,1) states. The caracteristic vibrational

energy spacing (120-130 meV) can be identified. Also the data shows some ions
apparently appearing below the ionization energy. Such ions are expected from
electron impact on thermally excited molecules. It is seen in Fig. 1 that
those structures have a comparatively much smaller amplitude than those above
threshold. By reducing the gaz temperature to a value much below room temperature it could be verified that those ions were indeed originating from thermal
excitation ($NH_{3\ v=1,2}$). Corresponding results were obtained from ND_3 and will
be presented at the meeting. More detailed results about the ionization
threshold and the contribution of the thermal vibrational excitation to the
ionization efficiency curves will be presented.

Finally we wish to point out that this experiment shows that it is possible
to detect vibrational energies excited at room temperature. Furthermore, the
sharp structures shown in Fig. 1 can be reproduced within an accuracy of ±10 meV.

We are indebted to the Natural Sciences an Engineering Research Council
Canada (A-3169) and to the Ministère de l'Education du Québec (F.C.A.C.) for
research grants.

1. K. Watanabe, S.P. Sood, Science of Light (Tokyo), 14, 36 (1965).
2. W.A. Chupka, M.E. Russel, J. Chem. Phys., 48, 1527 (1968).
3. M.J. Weiss, G.M. Lawrence, J. Chem. Phys., 53, 214 (1970).
4. R. Carbonneau and P. Marmet, Phys. Rev. A, 9, 1898 (1974).
5. R. Carbonneau and P. Marmet, Can. J. Phys, 51, 2202 (1973).
6. R. Carbonneau and P. Marmet, Int. J. Mass. Spectrom. and Ion Physics, 10, 143 (1972-73).

SINGLE AND DOUBLE ELECTRON IMPACT IONIZATION OF NO_2

H. Helm, Y.B. Kim, T.D. Märk, J. Ramler, G. Sejkora and K. Stephan

Institut für Experimentalphysik, Abt. f. Kernphysik und Gaselektronik
Leopold Franzens Universität,A 6020 Innsbruck, Österreich (Austria)

The present paper is one in a series from this laboratory
dealing with the upgrading of the quantitative knowledge of electron
impact ionization of free species. The current study is devoted to
the parent molecular ion of nitrogen dioxide. Very little work has
been reported previously on the electron impact ionization of this
stable free radical.

The experimental setup and technique used in the current study
are similar to those described in detail in Ref.1. In short, it consists of a Nier type electron impact ion source (Varian MAT Intensitron M), a high resolution double focussing mass spectrometer
(Varian MAT CH5) and a gas handling system. In the course of an
extensive recent study on the properties of this Nier type ion
source[1] it became possible to improve considerably the operating
conditions of this ion source, i.e. achieving complete ion extraction and complete measurement of the ion current by means of a new
"sweeping mass spectrometry" technique[1]. Normalization of the measured relative partial cross section functions has been made by a
modified molecular effusive flow method[2] using argon as reference
gas.

The absolute partial cross section values obtained for the
processes $NO_2 + e \rightarrow NO_2^+ + 2e$ and $NO_2 + e \rightarrow NO_2^{++} + 3e$ are shown as
a function of corrected electron energy in Fig.1 (the error bars
shown designate the estimated maximum possible error). It should be
noted, that in the present study it was for the first time possible
to substantiate the existence of NO_2^{++} produced via electron impact
(see Fig.2 which shows a mass spectrum of NO_2^{++} isotopes). Using
n.th root extrapolation, the following minimum ionization potentials have been derived from the cross section function near threshold (see also Fig.3) : $NO_2^+ = 10,4 \pm 0,3$ eV and $NO_2^{++} = 35,0 \pm 0,5$
eV.

Work partially supported by the Österreichischer Fonds zur Förderung der Wissenschaftlichen Forschung under Project S-18/08

1. K. Stephan, H. Helm and T.D. Märk, see same Conference
2. T.D. Märk, J.Chem. Phys., 63 (1975) 3731

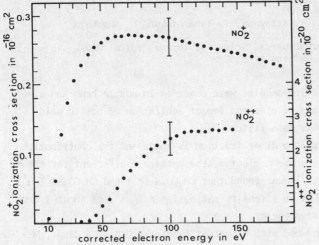

Fig.1 Absolute partial ionization cross section for the electron impact formation of NO_2^+ and NO_2^{++} as a function of corrected electron energy

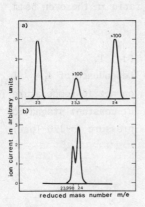

Fig.2 Mass spectra of NO_2^{++} isotopes.Upper part: m/e = 23 ($^{14}N^{16}O_2^{++}$), m/e = 23,5 ($^{15}N^{16}O_2^{++}$ and $^{14}N^{16}O^{17}O^{++}$) and m/e = 24 ($^{14}N^{16}O^{18}O^{++}$, $^{15}N^{16}O^{17}O^{++}$ and $^{12}C_2^+$).Lower part with high resolution shows NO_2^{++} and C_2^+ peak at reduced mass m/e = 24 resolved

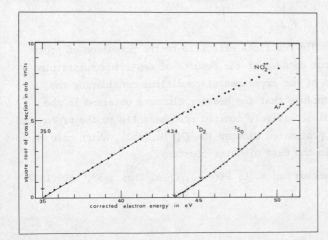

Fig.3 The square root of the double ionization cross section of NO_2^{++} and Ar^{++} as a function of corrected electron energy.

ELECTRON IMPACT IONIZATION OF ACETIC ACID ASSOCIATES

Y. Mori, T. Kitagawa, T. Yamamoto and S. Nagahara

Faculty of Pharmaceutical Sciences, Toyama Medical and
Pharmaceutical University

Several characteristic ion species were observed in nozzle beam and also
oven beam conditions by means of electron impact ionization of acetic acid
associates using a quadrupole mass filter.

In the oven beam, where the dimer fraction is known and the contribution
from the higher associates can be neglected, the pattern coefficient for the
dimer could be determined.   It was found that $CH_3CO_2H^+ (M^+)$ and $CH_3CO_2H_2^+ (MH^+)$
were dissociatively formed at an intensity ratio, I_M^+ / I_{MH}^+ , of about 1 from
the dimer at 60 eV of electron energy.

In the nozzle beam produced with a conical nozzle of 0.015 cm diam., MH^+ ion
were most predominantly formed.   The ratio of I_M^+ / I_{MH}^+ was found to be less
than 1 in these expansion conditions different from the ratio in the oven beam,
as shown in Fig. 1.

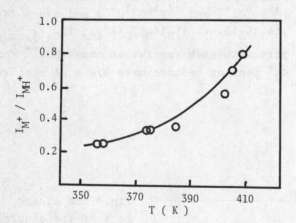

Fig. 1.
Dependence of I_M^+ / I_{MH}^+
on nozzle temperature T
at constant stagnation
pressure ($\sim$170 Torr)

In both beams, ion-molecule reactions effective to the formation of protonated ion MH^+ can be ruled out because of the results of deuterium substituted
acetic acid CH_3CO_2D beam and of our experimental conditions considering the
reaction rates.   Thus we conclude that the heavier clusters obtained in the
nozzle beam conditions are dissociatively ionized predominantly to the protonated
monomer ion MH^+, not to the protonated cluster ion $(M)_n H^+$ ($n \geq 2$), which have on
the contrary been observed in the case of water clusters.[1]

1.   J. Fricke, W. M. Jackson and W. L. Fite, J. Chem. Phys., 57, 580 (1972)

(e, 2e) SPECTROSCOPY ON ORIENTED MOLECULES: EFFECTS OF THE
ORIENTATION ON MOMENTUM DENSITY

A. Giardini-Guidoni, R. Fantoni[+],

C.N.E.N., Divisione Nuove Attività, C.P. 65, 00044 Frascati (Rome), Italy

R. Camilloni and G. Stefani

C.N.R., Lab. Metod.Avanzate Inorganiche, Via Montorio Romano n.36, 00131 Rome, Italy

The (e, 2e) spectroscopy allows to measure directly the electron momentum distribution of a given molecular orbital [1]. Provided kinematic conditions allow to use the Impulsive Approximation in describing the scattering process [2], the (e,2e) cross section is factorized as:

$$\frac{d^5\sigma}{d\Omega_1\,d\Omega_2\,dE_1} \propto (\frac{d^2\sigma}{d\Omega_1})_{ee}\;|\;F_\lambda\;(\bar{q})|^2; \quad F_\lambda\;(\bar{q}) = \; <\bar{q}\;\;\Psi_\lambda^I\;|\;\Psi^M> \tag{1}$$

$(d^2\sigma/d\Omega_1)_{ee}$ is the half off-shell (Mott) scattering cross section. λ refers to the energy level of the ion and $\bar{q}$ is the initial momentum of the bound electron.

Because of the random spatial orientation of the gaseous molecules in (e, 2e) experiments performed up to date, only the space averaged factor $|F_\lambda\;(q)|^2$ has been measured.

In the present work it is shown how by measuring the factor $|F_\lambda\;(\bar{q})|^2$, instead of the $|F_\lambda\;(q)\;|^2$, more detailed information on the electronic structure of molecular orbitals can be achieved. By representing the elctronic wave functions as antisymmetrized products of single particle orbitals $|\;\phi^M> = \;|\;\psi_j\;\phi_{(j)}^R\;>\;|F_\lambda\;(\bar{q})|^2$ becomes:

$$|F_\lambda\;(\bar{q})\;|^2 = \;|\;<q\;\phi_\lambda^I\;|\;\Psi_j\;\;\phi_{(j)-1}^R>\;|^2 = \rho_j\;(\bar{q})\;K_j^\lambda \tag{2}$$

$K_j^\lambda = \;|<\phi_\lambda^I\;|\;\phi_{(j)-1}^R>|^2$ is the spectroscopic factor, measuring the probability to populate the λ ionic state when the electron is ejected from the j-th orbital.

The form factor:

$$\rho_j\;(\bar{q}) = \;\left|\;<q\;|\;\Psi_j\;>\;\right|^2 = \frac{1}{(2\pi)^3}\left|\;\int e^{-i\bar{q}\cdot\vec{r}}\;\Psi_j\;(\vec{r})\;d\vec{r}\;\right|^2 \tag{3}$$

is given by the square modulus of the Fourier transform of the bound electron wave-function; it has the meaning of linear momentum density associated to the molecular orbital Ψ_j.

Although (e,2e) experiments on oriented molecules have not yet been performed calculations of $\rho\;(\bar{q}\;)$ for simple molecules (N_2, CO) have been done with the aim

---

[+] *"Accademia Nazionale dei Lincei" felloship holder.*

to show the powerful information that such measurements would supply. In fact up
to date by measuring only the shape of the averaged form factor it results difficult to identify the bonding or antibonding character of a π orbital when singly
examined and to distinguish it from a σ antibonding. This difficulty is immediately overcome when the directional form factor is considered for the molecule
oriented in space. This is clearly shown in the ρ_j $(\bar{q})$ maps reported in Fig.1.

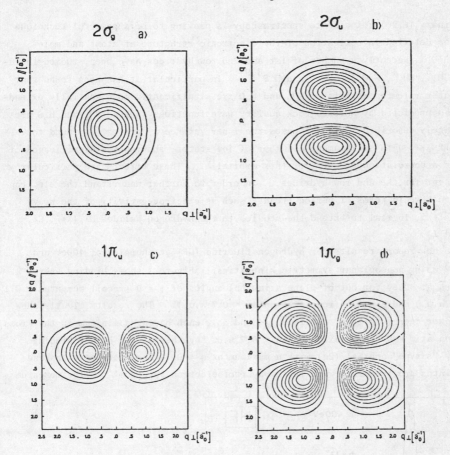

Fig. 1: *Contour maps of momentum density for some N_2 orbitals. Maps are drawn in a
plane containing the molecular axis. Cotinue curves j are ρ_j $(\bar{q})$ isovalues. Curves
are spaced of a tenth of the maximum value. For the $2\sigma_g$ orbital the innermost curve
is referred to $\rho(\bar{q}) = 2.93 \times 10^{-} a_o^3$; for the $2\sigma_u$ to $\rho(\bar{q}) = 2.44 \times 10^{-1} a_o^3$; for the
$1\pi_u$ to $\rho(\bar{q}) = 9.09 \times 10^{-2} a_o^3$; for the $1\pi_g$ to $\rho(\bar{q}) = 4.03 \times 10^{-2} a_o^3$.*

1. A. Giardini-Guidoni et al., J.Electr.Spectr. 12,405 (1977) and refs.therein.
2. J.E. Mc Carthy and E. Weigold, Phys.Rept. 27C, 275 (1976).

ELECTRONIC BINDING ENERGIES AND MOMENTUM DISTRIBUTIONS
FOR THE VALENCE ORBITALS OF HYDROGEN FLUORIDE

C.E. Brion[†], I.E. McCarthy, I. Suzuki* and E. Weigold

School of Physical Sciences,
The Flinders University of South Australia,
Bedford Park, S.A., 5042, Australia

Binary (e,2e) coincidence spectroscopy is proving to be a powerful technique for the detailed investigation of the electronic structure of atoms and molecules[1,2]. Recently a number of 1st and 2nd row hydrides have been studied including CH_4[3], NH_3[4], H_2O[5,6], PH_3[7] and H_2S[8,9]. In particular it has been found that the outer valence orbitals of NH_3 and H_2O are significantly more spatially extended than predicted by Hartree-Fock quality wave functions whereas PH_3 and H_2S are adequately described. In all cases the inner valence a_1 orbital is found to have its strength split among a number of ion states, showing the significance of electron correlation effects for this orbital[10]. These effects are particularly prominent for the 2nd row hydrides. In order to further understand the electronic structure in terms of period trends, such as electronegativity of the heavy atom, it is logical to extend the studies to the hydrogen halides HX (X=F, Cℓ, Br and I).

We now report results for hydrogen fluoride (HF) at energies of 400eV and 1200eV using noncoplanar symmetric kinematics. Figure 1 shows binding energy spectra at 400eV for out of plane azimuthal angles of $\phi = 0$ (recoil momentum ~ 0.1 - 0.3 a.u.) and $\phi = 13°$ (recoil momentum ~ 0.7 a.u.). The results clearly show two lower energy "p-type" orbitals (1π and 3σ), each having a minimum in the cross section at q = 0 and a maximum at q ~ 0.7 a.u. together with a higher binding energy "s type" orbital (2σ) with a maximum at q = 0. The peak positions and halfwidths are in accord with the X-ray photoelectron spectrum[11]. The momentum

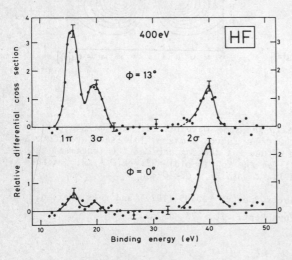

Fig. 1.   The binding energy
spectra at 400eV for
$\phi = 0°$ and 13°.

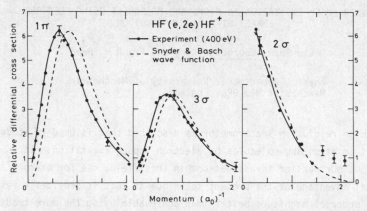

Fig. 2. The measured and calculated momentum distributions for electrons ejected from the indicated valence orbitals of HF.

distributions are shown in figure 2 in comparison with theoretical results obtained by the Plane Wave Impulse Approximation using the molecular orbital wave functions of Snyder & Basch[12] (essentially DZ quality). It is clear that the outer orbitals (1π and 3σ) are much more spatially extended (i.e. displaced to lower momenta) than is predicted. The fit for the 2σ orbital is quite good except in the region above $1.5\ a_o^{-1}$. Effects of absorption and distortion of the electron waves at 400eV are more significant for the deeper lying 2σ orbital. This is shown by comparison with studies made at 1200eV. Further work is in progress on the other hydrogen halides.

[†] Permanent address: Dept. of Chemistry, University of B.C., Vancouver, Canada.

[*] Permanent address: Electrotechnical Laboratory, Tanashi, Tokyo, Japan.

1. I.E. McCarthy and E. Weigold, Phys. Rep., 27C, 275 (1976).

2. I.E. McCarthy and E. Weigold, Endeavour, 2, 728 (1978).

3. S. Dey, A.J. Dixon, I.E. McCarthy, P.J.O. Teubner and E. Weigold, Chem. Phys. Lett. 41, 21 (1976).

4. S.T. Hood, A. Hamnett and C.E. Brion, Chem. Phys. Letters, 39, 252 (1976).

5. S.T. Hood, A. Hamnett and C.E. Brion, J. Electron Spectrosc., 11, 205 (1977).

6. A.J. Dixon, S. Dey, I.E. McCarthy, E. Weigold and G.R.J. Williams, Chem. Phys., 21, 81 (1977).

7. A. Hamnett, S.T. Hood and C.E. Brion, J. Electron Spectrosc., 11, 263 (1977).

8. C.E. Brion, J.P. Cook and K.H. Tan, Chem. Phys. Letters, 59, 241 (1978).

9. J.P.D. Cook, C.E. Brion and A. Hamnett, to be published.

10. W. Domcke, L.S. Cederbaum, J. Schermer, W. Von Niessen and J.P. Maier, J. Electron Spectrosc., 14, 59 (1978).

11. M.S. Banna and D.A. Shirley, Chem. Phys. Letters, 33, 441 (1975).

12. L.C. Snyder and H. Basch, Molecular Wave Functions and Properties, Wiley, New York, 1972.

INNER SHELL EXCITATION IN ATOMS AND MOLECULES USING ELECTRON IMPACT WITH HIGH RESOLUTION

David Shaw, George C. King and Frank H. Read

Physics Department, University of Manchester,
Manchester M13 9PL, England.

A new high resolution spectrometer is described that is used to study inner shell states in atoms and molecules by electron impact excitation. It is a development of our earlier investigations in this field, see for example[1,2,3]. The principal advantage of the present technique is that it provides a resolution which is an order of magnitude better than achievable using the more traditional methods of studying these states, for example by photon absorption. The spectrometer features high sensitivity and an energy resolution of 0.040-0.070 eV at excitation energies up to 500 eV. The incident electron energy is 1500 eV. It is also very stable and the energy loss scale can be maintained constant to within 0.010 eV over extended periods of operation. This performance enables the positions and widths of small structures to be accurately determined. For example, we have been able to measure the variation in natural width and hence lifetime in Rydberg series.

So far the spectrometer has been used to obtain energy loss spectra in Ar, CO, CO_2 and N_2 and an example of one of these is presented in figure 1. It corresponds to the region immediately below the K ionization edge in CO and shows previously unobserved Rydberg states. It is also hoped to show energy loss

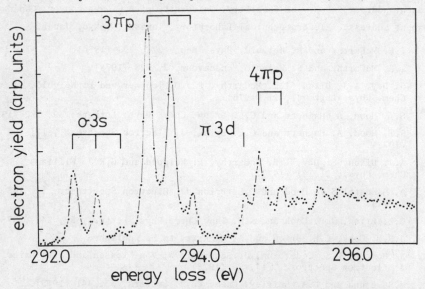

Figure 1. Energy loss spectrum of CO obtained at an incident energy of 1500 eV and with an energy resolution of 65 meV.

spectra in a number of other molecules including $C\ell_2$ which is particularly interesting because its "equivalent core" molecule is the rare gas halide $ArC\ell$.

1. G.C. King, M. Tronc, F.H. Read and R.C. Bradford, J.Phys.B: Atom Molec.
    Phys. <u>10</u>, 2479 (1977)
2. G.C. King, F.H. Read and M. Tronc, Chem.Phys.Letts. <u>52</u>, 50 (1977).
3. M. Tronc, G.C. King and F.H. Read, J.Phys.B: Atom Molec.Phys. <u>12</u>, 137
    (1979).

Negative ion resonances associated with inner shell excited states
of N_2, CO, CO_2, N_2O and NO

G.C. King, J.W. McConkey[*], F.H. Read and B. Dobson

Physics Department, University of Manchester,
Manchester M13 9PL, England.

Recently (King, McConkey and Read[1]), temporary negative ions (resonances)
were found that were associated with inner shell excited states of N_2 and CO.
These excited states consist of an inner shell electron of one of the constituent
atoms being promoted to an unfilled orbital of the molecule. It is to these
states that the incident electron is temporarily bound to form the resonance.
These authors used electron impact excitation and observed the resonances as
structure in the detected yield of positive ions. Such resonances have since
been observed by Ziesal et al[2] who used mass analysis of the reaction products
to investigate individual positive ion decay channels. We have now extended the
work of King et al and present further examples of this type of resonance.

The apparatus used for these measurements consists of an electron impact
spectrometer which produces an incident electron beam of energy close to the
excitation energy of the inner shell state, with an energy resolution of approximately 0.05eV. The electron beam is crossed at right angles with the target
gas beam which emanates from a hypodermic needle. A channel electron multiplier
placed in a direction at right angles to both the electron and gas beams is used
to detect positive ions which are produced. The resonances are observed as
structure in the yield of positive ions as the energy of the incident electron
beam is ramped about the excitation energy of the inner shell excited state.

The molecules studied were N_2, CO, CO_2, N_2O and NO and in all cases
resonance structure was observed. The structure was always a broad peak and was
typically 0.1-0.3% of the total positive ion signal. The positions of the
resonances were found by comparison with features in the metastable excitation
spectra of N_2 and Ar which are known accurately, Brunt et al [3,4]. Their
positions could then be compared with the excitation energies of the associated
inner shell excited states. In the interpretation of inner shell excited states
the equivalent core model, for example King et al[5], has been found to be very
useful. Here the atom with a hole in an inner shell resembles an atom with
nuclear charge greater by one unit. This means that in the present work the
resonance structure would be expected to be similar to resonance structure
associated with the outer shell excitation in the equivalent core molecule.

For example the inner shell resonance structure in NO would resemble outer shell resonance structure in O_2 and such comparisons are made in the present work. For N_2O, two resonance structures were observed and this is attributed to the non-equivalence of the central and terminal N atoms in the N-N-O molecule. In the case of N_2 structure was also observed in the detection channel corresponding to ejected electrons.

* Permanent address: Physics Department, University of Windsor, Ontario, Canada.

1. G.C. King, J.W. McConkey and F.H. Read, J.Phys.B: Atom.Molec.Phys. 10, L541 (1977)

2. J.P. Ziesal, D. Teillet-Billy, L. Bouby and R. Paineau, Chem.Phys. Letts, in press.

3. J.N.H. Brunt, G.C. King and F.H. Read, J.Phys.B: Atom.Molec.Phys. 11, 173 (1978).

4. J.N.H. Brunt, G.C. King and F.H. Read, J.Phys.B: Atom.Molec.Phys. 9, 2195 (1976).

5. G.C. King, F.H. Read and M. Tronc, Chem.Phys.Letts. 52, 50 (1977).

K–SHELL EXCITED NEGATIVE-ION RESONANCES IN CO AND N_2

D. <u>Teillet-Billy</u> and J.P. Ziesel

Laboratoire de Collisions Atomiques et Moléculaires (associé au CNRS)
Université de Paris-Sud, Bât. 351, 91405 ORSAY CEDEX (France)

The existence of resonant states associated with the inner-shell excited states $C^*O(C1s)^{-1}2p\pi$, $CO^*(O1s)^{-1}2p\pi$, $N_2^*(N1s)^{-1}2p\pi$ has been first pointed out[1] by the observation of an enhancement in the total positive ionization by electron impact, at incident electron energies close to the excitation energies C1s to $2p\pi$, O1s to $2p\pi$, N1s to $2p\pi$.

In a different experiment[2], with a target gas cell instead of a molecular beam and mass analysis of the parent and fragment ions, a resonant structure has been observed in the various ionization decay channels of the $(C1s)^{-1}(2p\pi)^2$ in CO. We have extended this work to the $(O1s)^{-1}(2p\pi)^2$ resonance in CO and to the $(N1s)^{-1}$ $(2p\pi)^2$ resonance in N_2.

<u>Nitrogen K-shell excited negative-ion resonance in N_2</u>

<u>Figure 1</u> shows the resonant structure (background subtracted) in the ionization-efficiency curve for the $(N^++N_2^{2+})$ formation. The energy positions of the resonant structure and of the parent state for the N_2 and CO (carbon K-shell excited) molecules are given in table I.

Table I :

	Resonant structure		Parent state
	Maximum	onset	v'=0 level
N_2	401.85 ± 0.15 eV	400.8 eV	400.86 eV
CO	287.3 ± 0.2 eV	286.3 eV	287.40 eV

The energy position of the resonant structure relative to the parent state is different in N_2 and CO. This behavior suggests some further comments : i) the shorter R_e of $N_2(X\ ^1\Sigma_g^+)$ relative to CO $(X\ ^1\Sigma^+)$ could account for a higher relative onset in N_2. Assuming that the spectroscopic constants of the resonant states are similar to that of the equivalent core $NO^-\ ^3\Sigma^-$ and $^1\Delta$ states[1,3] ($R_e'' = 2.39$ u.a., $\omega_e'' = 0.230$ eV, $\omega_e''x_e'' = 0.002$ eV), we observe that the computed Franck-Condon dis-

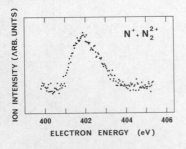

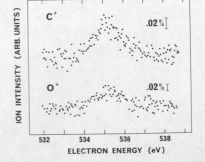

Fig.1   Fig.2

tribution maximum is shifted from v" = 4 (F.C. factor 0.14) in CO to v" = 8 (F.C. factor 0.09) in N_2. When mormalized to their maximum, we obtain 0.16, 0.47, 0.77 for the v" = 0,1,2 levels in CO and 0.02, 0.09, 0.22 in N_2. So the appearance of the N_2^{*-} state could be delayed by 0.4 eV at most. ii) The repulsive interaction between electrons is different for equivalent core states and for hole states since there is a single 1s electron in the core. Assuming that the antibonding valence $2p\pi$ orbital of the hole states is similar to that of the equivalent core molecule[4] NO and that this orbital is not modified when singly or doubly occupied (frozen orbitals approximation), we have related the vertical energy differences[*] $EA(AB^{+\ 1}\Pi \rightarrow AB^{*-\ 2}\Delta) = E(AB^{*\ 1}\Pi) - E(AB^{*-\ 2}\Delta)$ and $IP(AB^{*\ 1}\Pi) = E(AB^{*+\ 2}\Sigma^+) - E(AB^{*\ 1}\Pi)$ to the corresponding differences in the equivalent core states of NO. In the independent electron model, we obtain the relation (1) $EA(AB^{*\ 1}\Pi \rightarrow AB^{*-\ 2}\Delta) = IP(AB^{*\ 1}\Pi) + EA(NO^{\ 2}\Pi \rightarrow NO^{-\ 1}\Delta) - IP(NO^{\ 2}\Pi) + 3K_{1s\pi^+}$ where $K_{1s\pi^+}$ is the exchange integral between the singly occupied 1s atomic orbital and the molecular antibonding $2p\pi$ orbital. Relation (1) remains true when the vertical values are replaced by the adiabatic ones. When comparing N_2 and CO, the adiabatic ionization energies for the C1s hole state of CO and N1s hole state of N_2 are 8.65 and 9.04 eV respectively (9.26 eV in NO). The calculated exchange integral[5] is equal to 0.63 eV regarding the N center and 0.39 eV regarding the O center. If we replace the vertical $EA(NO^{\ 2}\Pi \rightarrow NO^{-\ 1}\Delta)$ by its adiabatic value[4] of -0.73 eV, we get, from (1), adiabatic energy differences $(AB^{*\ 1}\Pi \rightarrow AB^{*-\ 2}\Delta)$ of +0.55 eV in CO and +0.20 in N_2. The trends described by this rather crude model are then in agreement with experiment.

Oxygen K-shell excited negative-ion resonance in CO.

Figure 2 represents the ionization-efficiency curves for the formation of C^+ and O^+ (background subtracted). We observe the maximum of the structure at 535.3 eV, the energy position of the parent state being at 534.0 eV[1]. We can compare the decay of the O K-shell and C K-shell resonances in the C^+ and O^+ channels. The ratio O'/C' is 0.43 and 0.16 with the hole on the oxygen or carbon respectively. So there is some effect of the initial hole localization on the final fragmentation.

[*]Note that the $^2\Delta$, $^2\Sigma^{\pm}$ resonant states can be formed. The energetic separation between the $^2\Delta$ and $^2\Sigma^+$ is given by the exchange integral between the two π electrons, thus equal to the separation between the $NO^-\ ^3\Sigma^-$ and $^1\Delta$ shape resonances. but the lower state is the $^2\Delta$. The $^2\Sigma^-$ is at nearly the same energy as the $^2\Sigma^+$ in CO and the $^2\Delta$ in N_2.

1.   G.C. King, J.W. Mc Conkey, F.H. Read, J. Phys. B <u>10</u> L541 (1977)

2.   J.P. Ziesel, D. Teillet-Billy, L. Bouby, R. Paineau, Chem. Phys. Let. in press

3.   D. Teillet-Billy, F. Fiquet-Fayard, J. Phys. B <u>10</u> L111 (1977)

4.   G.C. King, F.H. Read, M. Tronc, Chem. Phys. Lett. <u>52</u> 50 (1977)

5.   M.E. Schwartz, Theoret. Chim. Acta (Berl.) <u>19</u> 396 (1970)

K-SHELL EXCITATION OF SMALL MOLECULES BY ELECTRON IMPACT

C.E. Brion and A.P. Hitchcock[+]

Department of Chemistry, University of British Columbia, Vancouver, Canada V6T 1W5

Inelastic electron scattering has been shown to be an effective technique for studying the excitation and ionization of the inner shell electrons of small gas phase molecules [1,2]. Under the experimental conditions employed (impact energy of 2.5 keV and small angle scattering, $\theta = 2 \times 10^{-2}$ rad), the inner shell electron energy loss (ISEELS) spectra are dominated by electric dipole transitions and thus the spectra are closely related to soft X-ray photoabsorption (PA) spectra. Previous studies [1,2] have demonstrated several advantages of electron scattering over photoabsorption for studies of inner shell excitation, including higher resolution above 200 eV, the absence of a structured instrumental response and experimental simplicity (as compared to synchrotron radiation studies). We now report the results of ISEELS studies of N_2, CO, O_2 and H_2CO.

Although the K-shell spectra of N_2, CO and O_2 have previously been studied by PA, ISEELS and by ab initio calculations, there are several discrepancies among the published data which we have attempted to resolve. For example, Fig. 1 shows the oxygen K-shell spectra of CO and O_2 recorded with 0.4 eV FWHM resolution. A weak peak at 531 eV reported in the PA spectrum of CO [3] has been shown to arise from impurity O_2. For all of these molecules except O_2 the K-shell continua exhibit prominent features which can be interpreted as shape resonances [4] or transitions to quasibound σ^* levels [5]. Fig. 1 compares the experimental results with ab initio calculations of the K-shell continuum shapes

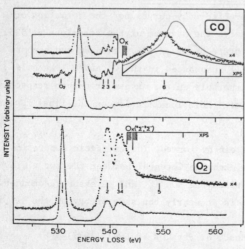

Fig. 1

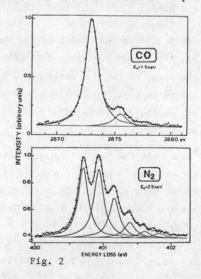

Fig. 2

(dashed line, Dehmer and Dill [4]; solid line, Padial et al [5]). The absence of a K-shell continuum maximum in O_2 is in agreement with the theoretical predictions.

Vibrational structure of the K→π* transitions of N_2 and CO (C 1s) has been observed in high resolution studies [Fig. 2]. These results are similar to those previously obtained with electron energy loss spectroscopy [2,6]. The values of natural linewidths, fundamental frequencies and anharmonicity derived from the two experiments are in agreement. These spectra demonstrate the superior resolution of electron impact as compared to photoabsorption at large excitation energies.

Fig. 3 shows the carbon and oxygen K-shell spectra of formaldehyde (0.5 eV FWHM). K-shell studies of H_2CO, either by PA or ISEELS, have not previously been reported to the best of our knowledge. A high resolution carbon 1s spectrum (0.12 eV FWHM) is shown in Fig. 4. The Rydberg structure (#'s 2-9) is well resolved while suggestions of vibrational structure can be seen in the K→π* transition. A discussion of the spectral assignments and a comparison of the K-shell spectra of CO and H_2CO will be presented.

This work was financially supported by the National Research Council of Canada.

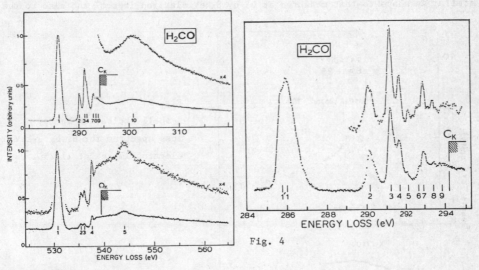

Fig. 3

Fig. 4

1. A.P. Hitchcock and C.E. Brion, J. Electron Spectry. 13 (1978) 345; 14 (1978) 417; 15 (1979) 201.
2. M. Tronc, G.C. King and F.H. Read, J. Phys. B 12 (1979) 137.
3. M. Nakamura, Y. Morioka, T. Hayaishi, E. Ishigura and M. Sasanuma, Proc. 3rd Int. Vac. UV Rad. Phys. Conf. (Tokyo, 1971) 1pA1-6.
4. J.L. Dehmer and D. Dill, J. Chem. Phys. 65 (1976) 5327.
5. N. Padial, G. Csanak, B.V. McKoy and P.W. Langhoff, J. Chem. Phys. 69 (1978) 2992.
6. G.C. King, F.H. Read and M. Tronc, Chem. Phys. Lett. 52 (1977) 50.

†Present address: Department of Chemistry, McMaster University, Hamilton, Canada.

GENERALIZED OSCILLATOR STRENGTHS FOR K-SHELL EXCITATION
AND IONIZATION OF N_2 BY ELECTRON IMPACT

N. Oda, F. Nishimura, and T. Osawa

Research Laboratory of Nuclear Reactors, Tokyo Institute
of Technology, Meguro-ku, Tokyo 152, Japan

The energy-loss spectra resulting from the K-shell excitation and ionization
of N_2 by 1- and 2-keV electron impact have been measured over the angular range
from 6° to 130°. The experimental apparatus is almost the same as that used
before.[1] Energy loss spectra have been measured by varying the retarding potential
applied on a retardation lens set in front of a 90° cylindrical electrostatic
energy analyzer which was operated at a constant electron energy of 90 eV. The
energy resolution was ~ 0.6 eV in full width at half maximum and the angular
resolution was $\sim 2^o$. The transmission efficiency of the analyzer as a function of
the retarding potential was determined by comparing the elastic peak intensities
with and without the retardation potential.

In Fig. 1 is shown the energy loss spectrum near the nitrogen K-edge measured
at 11° by 2-keV electron impact. While the spectrum at 11° shown in Fig. 1 is very
similar in shape to that measured at 0° by 8-keV electron impact[2] and also to the

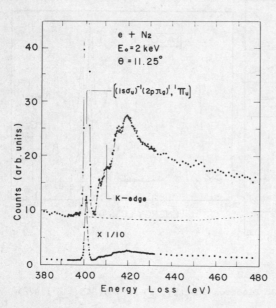

Fig. 1.
K-shell excitation energy
loss spectrum for N_2 by 2-keV
electron impact at 11.25^o.

photoabsorption spectrum,[3] the detailed structure of the spectrum changes with the
scattering angle, reflecting the difference in excitation modes between the photoabsorption (and also 0° electron scattering) and the electron impact. An intense
peak at 401.1 eV energy loss corresponds to the $(1s)^{-1}(2p\pi_g)^1\Pi$ inner shell excitation of N_2 and other peaks are tentatively identified by various investigators.[4,5]
The measured doubly differential cross sections for scattered electrons were put

on an absolute scale, by normalizing the elastic peaks which were measured along with the loss spectra with use of the absolute elastic scattering cross sections.[6]

Generalized oscillator strength as a function of the electron momentum transfer was derived from the absolute doubly differential cross section mentioned above, assuming the validity of the Born approximation. In Fig. 2 is shown the generalized oscillator strength as a function of $(Ka_0)^2$ for the $(1s)^{-1}(2p\pi_g)^1\Pi$ excitation, where are also included the pseudo-optical oscillator strengths measured by $0°$ electron scattering method[2] and by the photoabsorption method,[3] and the theoretical oscillator strengths calculated by the multiple scattering theory[5]

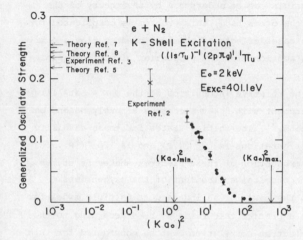

Fog. 2.
Generalized oscillator strength for $(1s)^{-1}(2p\pi_g)^1\Pi$ excitation of N_2 by electron impact and theoretical[5,7,8] and experimental[2,3] optical oscillator strengths.

and by the Stieltjes-Tchebycheff calculations.[7,8] From Fig. 2, it is seen that our generalized oscillator strengths smoothly approach to the optical oscillator strengths, passing through a pseudo-optical oscillator strength for the $0°$ electron scattering, when the $(Ka_0)^2$ decreases towards zero.

1. N. Oda, S. Tahira, F. Nishimura, and F. Koike, Phys. Rev. A 15, 574 (1977).
2. R.B. Kay, Ph.E. Van der Leeuw, and M.J. Van der Wiel, J. Phys. B 10, 2513 (1977).
3. A. Bianconi, H. Petersen, F.C. Brown, and R.Z. Bachrach, Phys. Rev. A 17, 1907 (1978).
4. G.R. Wight, C.E. Brion, and M.J. Van der Wiel, J. Electr. Spectr. Rel. Phen. 1, 457 (1972/3).
5. J.L. Dehmer and D. Dill, J. Chem. Phys. 65, 5327 (1976).
6. R.H. Jansen, F.J. de Heer, H.J. Luyken, B. van Wigerden, and H.J. Blaauw, J. Phys. B 9, 185 (1976).
7. T.N. Rescigno and P.W. Langhoff, Chem. Phys. Letters 51, 65 (1977).
8. S. Iwata, N. Kosugi, and O. Nomura, to be published in Proc. Intern. Conf. X-ray and XUV Spectroscopy (Sendai, 1978).

ELECTRON INDUCED X-RAY SATELLITES IN LIGHT ELEMENT ATOMS AND CHEMICAL BONDING

H.-U. Chun

Institute for Theoretical and Physical Chemistry,
University of Frankfurt, Frankfurt (Main), W.-Germany

The decay processes following the interaction of high-energy electrons with inner atomic shells do not only lead to the appearance of normal x-ray lines and Auger electrons. Due to multiple excitations and ionizations of inner shell electrons the appearance of x-ray satellites is also a prominent part of the decay processes. In principle, their origin can be understood by the theory of the sudden approximation.[1, 2, 3] On the other hand, this problem is complicated for light elements, because in these cases effects of chemical bonding play a dominant role in determing the cross sections for the production of multiple excitations and ionizations.

For oxygen in metal oxides the relative intensities of the O K - satellite lines α_3 and α_4 induced by bombardment with 5 kev electrons strongly depend on the nature of the metal-oxygen bond.[4,5] The initial states for these satellite lines are the double vacancy configurations $1s^{-1}2p^{-1}$ (^3P) and $1s^{-1}2p^{-1}$ (^1P). Thus, the cross section ratio for the production of these electron shake-off states seems to be very sensitive to the chemical environment of the oxygen ions.

This cannot be understood on the basis of an independent particle model for the shake-off process, which would predict this ratio to be 3 according to the statistical weights. Therefore electron correlation must be considered for this case. It has been shown that even for neon atoms, being isoelectronic with oxygen ions in crystals, this ratio deviates from the statistical value because of a configuration mixing between the continuum states belonging to the two channels.[6] The same considerations can be applied for an interpretation of the chemical effects on the $\sigma(^3P)$: $\sigma(^1P)$ ratio in the case of oxygen ions in crystals. Here this configuration mixing is more or less screened depending on the chemical environment of the oxygen ions.

1. T. Åberg, Phys. Rev. 156, 35 (1967).

2. T. Åberg, Phys. Lett. 26 A, 515 (1968).

3. T. Åberg, Ann. Acad. Sci. Fennicae, Ser. A VI, No. 308 (1969).

4. H.-U. Chun, Proc. Int. Symposium, X-ray Spectra and Electronic Structure of Matter I, ed. by A. Faessler and G. Wiech (München, 1973), p. 426.

5. H.-U. Chun, Phys. Fenn., 9 Suppl. S 1, 144 (1974).

6. D. Chattarji, W. Mehlhorn and V. Schmidt, J. Electr. Spectr. and Rel. Phenom. 13, 97 (1978).

IV. Ion (Atom)-Atom Collisions

CROSS SECTIONS FOR COLLISIONS OF O(^{3}P) ATOMS WITH PARTIAL ANALYSIS OF POPULATION

OF MAGNETIC SUBLEVELS[*]

V.Aquilanti, E.Luzzatti, F.Pirani and G.G.Volpi

Dipartimento di Chimica dell'Università, 06100 Perugia, Italy

Absolute integral cross sections for collisions of O(^{3}P) atoms with the rare gases at thermal energies were first reported from this laboratory a few years ago.[1] The observation of a partially quenched glory structure in the velocity dependence for the heavier rare gases indicated that the role of the full manifold of potential energy curves correlating with the separated atoms had to be taken into account in the interpretation of the results.

In this energy range, the cross sections are particularly sensitive to the well regions, whereby reliable recent calculations give only the behaviour of the short-range repulsive interactions[2] and estimates of the long-range attractive forces can be made with more accuracy than in the past.[3] Therefore, in order to assess the role of the manifold of potential energy curves on the scattering and to obtain sufficient data for the characterization of the relevant interactions in the well region, experiments are being performed using a Stern-Gerlach analysis for sampling collisions taking place with a specific population distribution of the magnetic sublevels of the oxygen atoms. Apart from the pioneer work by Berkling et al.[4] on gallium, no experiments of this kind have been reported for atoms, although measurements on magnetically oriented molecules have been recently performed.[5]

A schematic view of the apparatus is shown in the figure: as in previous work,[1] the oxygen atom beam is produced in a microwave discharge, is velocity selected by chopped wheels to within 3%, and is detected by a quadrupole mass spectrometer. The magnet, placed along the beam direction after the scattering chamber, provides a field strength of $\sim 5 \times 10^3$ G and the gradient in the direction perpendicular to the beam, which is of the order of 2×10^4 G cm^{-1}, eliminates all of the oxygen atoms having $m_j \neq 0$.

* Presented at the 11th ICPEAC, Kyoto, Japan, 1979. Work supported by Italian CNR and NATO Grants.

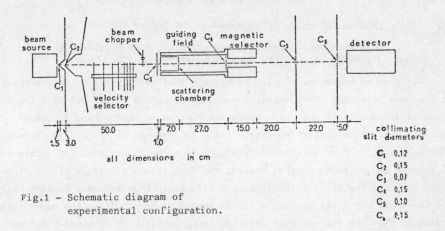

Fig.1 – Schematic diagram of
experimental configuration.

The effect on the integral cross sections of the altered m_j distribution resulting from the application of the magnetic field is small as expected, but nevertheless measurable. For example, for the O-Kr system, at a laboratory velocity of 1200 cm s^{-1}, where the effective collision cross section for the unselected beam is 230×10^{-16} cm^2, the ratio between cross sections with the magnet on and off is 1.051 ± 0.058; this velocity corresponds to a minimum in the glory pattern. At a velocity of 1560 cm s^{-1}, corresponding to an inflection in the glory pattern and an unselected cross section of 221×10^{16} cm^2, the same ratio is 1.089 ± 0.047.

1. V.Aquilanti, G.Liuti, F.Pirani, F.Vecchiocattivi, and G.G.Volpi,
   J.Chem.Phys. 65, 4751 (1976).

2. T.H.Dunning, Jr. and P.J.Hay, J.Chem.Phys. 66, 3767 (1977).

3. H.J.Werner and W.Meyer, Phys.Rev. A 13, 13 (1976).

4. K.Berkling, Ch.Schlier, and P.Toschek, Z.Phys. 168, 81 (1962).

5. J.Reuss, in "Electronic and Atomic Collisions", invited papers, X ICPEAC,
   North Holland, 1978.

POTENTIAL CURVES OF 1_u STATES OF RARE GAS DIMERS
FROM VUV EMISSION CONTINUA

Yoshio Matsuura, Osam Kanazaki, and Kuniya Fukuda

Department of Engineering Science, Faculty of Engineering
Kyoto University, Kyoto 606, Japan

Early works of Tanaka et al.[1] have shown that oscillatory structure appears in vacuum-ultraviolet (vuv) emission continua degrading to the red from the first atomic resonance lines when rare gases are excited by uncondensed discharge. These continua, called the "first continuum" (the 600 Å-bands for He_2), have been attributed to radiation from quasibound levels or from continuum levels of either or both of the two lowest bound excited states. The oscillatory structure of the first continua has been explained as interference effects in Franck-Condon factors between the lower and upper states, and a simple method of constructing the upper state potential from the structure of emission continua has been proposed.[2] But except for the He_2 $A^1\Sigma_u^+ - X^1\Sigma_g^+$ 600Å-bands, identification of the structure is very difficult because of complexity of the potentials of the lowest excited states.

We have observed new structures of Ne_2, Ar_2, and Kr_2 vuv emission continua which apparently start at the wavelengths of the atomic forbidden transitions from the $np^5(n+1)s$ $^3P_2$ states to the ground states, where n corresponds to 2, 3, and 4 for Ne, Ar and Kr, respectively. Glow discharge was made with varied currents at various gas pressures in a discharge tube of 8 mm i.d. and 11 cm length. Emission spectra in the vuv was photographed on SWR films with a Seya-Namioka SGV-50 spectrometer equipped with a Pt-coated grating of radius of curvature 50 cm and 1200 lines per mm. Figure 1 shows two spectra of Ne_2 continuum. The spectrum (a) is equivalent to the previously known emission structure or the Tanaka's first continuum, while the spectruum (b) is the new emission structure which clearly appeared when low discharge current ($I_d < 1$ mA) was sustained at low pressure ($p < 10$ Torr) in the discharge tube cooled by liquid nitrogen. The peak to peak spacings of intensity distribution of the new continuum are narrower than those of the Tanaka's continuum, and the peaks are more closely spaced towards the atomic line, 746.0 Å. The new continuum is considered as radiation from the $1_u(^3\Sigma_u^+)$ state ($3s^3P_2 + {}^1S_0$) in contrast to the Tanaka's continuum from the $0_u^+({}^1\Sigma_u^+)$ state ($3s^3P_1 + {}^1S_0$). In the cases of Ar and Kr discharges we also observed new structures which have narrower spacings converging on the atomic firbidden lines.

In the Ne_2 new continuum a very weak peak at 745.0 Å was definitely observed between the atomic first resonance and forbidden transitions on second order spectra as shown in Fig. 2. From the similarity to the He_2 600 Å-bands this peak indicates the existance of a quasibound state, hence of a hump of 0.02 - 0.03 eV in the 1_u potential. Assuming a relevant potential curve for the repulsive ground state, we can construct the attractive part of the 1_u state potentialof Ne_2 by a similar method used inthe analysis for the He_2 $A^1\Sigma_u^+$ state by Smith.[2] The calculated results are shown in Fig.3, where we adopted the two potential curves for the ground state[3,4], and for comparison the potential curve of Cohen's calculation[4] is also shown by the dashed curve. Both two potentials deduced from our experiment have deeper and wider wells than that of Cohen's. From the fact that the Cohen's l_u potential has only 11 vibrational states and consequently gives 11 intensity peaks in the continuum, while the observed continuum has 12 peaks up to 800 Å and more two or three peaks may exist in longer wavelength, it is also apparet that the Cohen's potential cannot reproduce the observed structure.

We will also present the results of the Ar_2 l_u state.

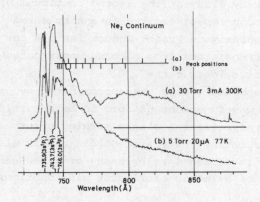

Fig. 1. Densitometer traces of the emission spectra of Ne_2. (a) the Tanaka's continuum. (b) new continuum.

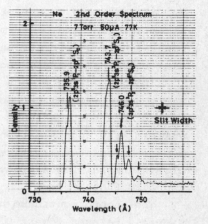

Fig. 2. Densitometertrace of second order spectrum of Ne_2 new continuum.

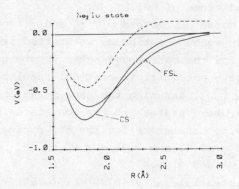

Fig. 3. Potential curves of Ne_2 l_u ($^3\Sigma_u^+$) state. The solid curve (FSL) is deduced using the ground state potential from ref.3, and CS from ref.4. The dashed curve is the ab initio calculation (ref.4).

1. Y. Tanaka, A. Jursa and P. LeBlanc, J. Opt. Soc. Am. **48**, 304 (1958).

2. A. L. Smith, J. Chem. Phys. **49**, 4813 (1968).

3. J. M. Farrar, T. P. Schafer and Y. T. Lee, Trasport Phenomina, AIP Conf. Proc. **11**, 279 (1973).

4. J. S. Cohen and B. Schneider, J. Chem. Phys. **61**, 3230 (1974).

DETERMINATION OF EXCIMER POTENTIAL CURVES FROM BOUND-FREE FLUO-RESCENCE INTENSITIES

H. Schmoranzer, R. Wanik and H. Krüger

Fachbereich Physik, Universität Kaiserslautern
D 6750 Kaiserslautern, Germany

The potential curves of excimers involved in the bound-free emission can be analyzed on the basis of precisely measured continuum intensity distributions and theoretical bound-free transition probabilities. An exemplary study of the second continuum of Kr will be based on keV-electron impact excited intensity normalized spectra[1] and uniform approximate Franck-Condon factors for bound-continuum vibrational transitions from a bound upper potential curve to a purely repulsive lower curve[2].

In these calculations the bound states are approximated by exactly normalized Miller-Good wavefunctions uniform in both turning points. For the continuum wavefunctions a single turning point uniform Airy approximation is taken. The Franck-Condon matrix element results approximatively in closed form by means of a new canonical integral for a product of harmonic oscillator wavefunctions and Airy functions.

The second continuum has been assumed to arise from the vibrationally relaxed lowest 0_u^+, $^1\Sigma_u^+$-state of Kr_2^*. (Taking the lowest 1_u, $^3\Sigma_u^+$-state as upper state of the second continuum would essentially result in a shift of the theoretical spectrum by about 15 Å towards longer wavelengths). Collisional mixing has been neglected in view of the excitation conditions of Ref. 1.

In order to estimate the Morse parameters D_e', r_e' and β' of the upper potential for the Kr second continuum, we started from semiempirical potential data for the corresponding Ar_2^* Rydberg states 0_u^+ [3] and 1_u [4] and density potential theoretical results[5] for the ion ground state Ar_2^+ A $^2\Sigma_{1/2u}^+$. Assuming the same relations between the parameters of the Rydberg states and the ion state for Kr as for Ar, we find the following parameters for the Kr_2^* excimer states 0_u^+, $^1\Sigma_u^+$ and 1_u, $^3\Sigma_u^+$: D_e' = 0.67 and 0.70 eV, r_e' = 2.63 and 2.64 Å, β' = 1.98 and 2.00 Å^{-1}.

For the repulsive lower potential, an $V''(r)=V_o'' \exp(-\alpha''r)$ was fitted to theoretical potentials for the Kr_2 dimer[6,7] which have been constructed to match spectroscopic data pertinent to the van-der-Waals potential well, and to the only elastic scattering data[8] in the relevant energy region. The potential extrapolation quoted by Docken and Schafer[6] yielded very good agreement with experiment[1] and was selected for calculating the spectra shown in Figs. 1 and 2.

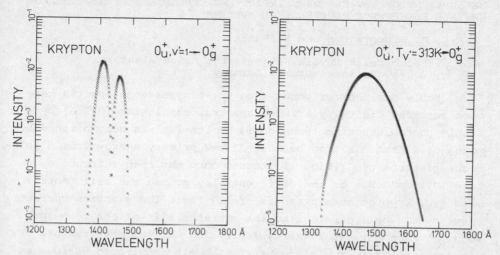

Figs.1,2 Calculated intensity distributions in 2nd Kr continuum
1: v' = 1 populated only   2: v' thermally populated at 313 K

The position of the intensity maximum calculated shifts towards shorter wavelengths by decreasing the dissociation energy D'_e, by increasing the equilibrium internuclear distance r'_e or by decreasing the potential energy V" in the region of overlap.

The calculated full width of the intensity distribution at half maximum intensity (FWHM) increases with increasing slope of the repulsive potential in the overlap region. This way the repulsive potential of Ref. 7 turned out too steep whereas the opposite is true for the experimental potential of Ref. 8.

A grant from the Deutsche Forschungsgemeinschaft is gratefully acknowledged.

1   H. Schmoranzer and R. Wanik, this conference
2   H. Krüger, Theoret. Chim. Acta (Berl.), to appear May 1979
3   R.C. Michaelson and A.L. Smith, J. Chem. Phys. 61,2566 (1974)
4   K.T. Gillen, R.P. Saxon, D.C. Lorents, G.E. Ice and R.E. Olson,
     J. Chem. Phys. 64, 1925 (1976)
5   H.H. Michels, R.H. Hobbs and L.A. Wright, J. Chem. Phys. 69,
     5151 (1978)
6   K.K. Docken and T.P. Schafer, J. Mol. Spectrosc. 46, 454 (1973)
7   J.A. Barker, R.O. Watts, Jong K. Lee, T.P. Schafer and Y.T.Lee,
     J. Chem. Phys. 61, 3081 (1974)
8   I. Amdur and E.A. Mason, J. Chem. Phys. 23, 2268 (1955)

MEASUREMENT OF keV-ELECTRON IMPACT EXCITED INTENSITY NORMALIZED
EXCIMER BOUND-FREE FLUORESCENCE SPECTRA

H. Schmoranzer and R. Wanik

Fachbereich Physik, Universität Kaiserslautern
D 6750 Kaiserslautern, Germany

Noble gas excimer bound-free vuv-fluorescence spectra have
been recorded digitally at high spectral resolution (0.3 Å) by
single photon counting techniques. Excitation was accomplished by
means of a fast electron beam of 22 keV primary energy from a telefocus electron gun[1] (Fig. 1) focused onto the open entrance aperture (0.1 mm I.D.) of the differentially pumped gas cell containing e.g. krypton at a pressure of 100 Torr. The electron current
entering the cell parallel to the entrance slit of the scanning
vacuum-uv-monochromator was typically 250 μA. The measurements
were controlled by a minicomputer which also monitored various experimental parameters with regard to the data analysis.

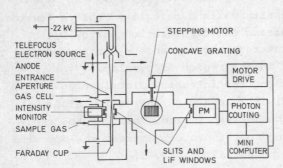

Fig. 1
keV-electron impact exci-
ted vuv fluorescence
spectrometer

The high resolution used allows for quantitative elimination
of the discrete spectrum (see Fig. 2), mostly due to impurities, so
that the intensity distribution of the continuous radiation can be
determined without falsification by unresolved lines. Furthermore,
the spectral sensitivity of the entire apparatus has been determined[2] by means of intensities of individual rotational lines of H_2
excited under single collision conditions by monoenergetic fast
electrons and calculated within the Born approximation in the limit
of small momentum transfer[3], including experimentally confirmed variations of the electronic transition moments[4].

Fig. 2 shows the intensity normalized fluorescence spectrum
of Kr at 100 Torr obtained as described under continuous 22 keV-
electron bombardment. The second continuum centered around 1460 Å
could be seen at pressures as low as 5 Torr which demonstrates the
sensitivity advantage of the continuous keV e-beam excitation over
pulsed e-beam[5] or synchrotron radiation[6] excitation for laboratory

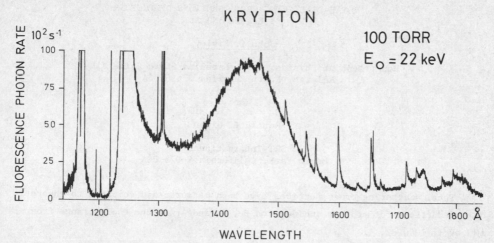

Fig. 2   Vuv fluorescence of Kr at 100 Torr excited by
         22 keV-electrons

studies of the type presented here. The intensity maximum of the
second continuum was observed at 1460 $\pm$ 5 Å for pressures from 5
to 100 Torr. The discrepancies between this work and earlier observations of other authors[5,6] (see Table 1) are probably due to
the fact that the spectral sensitivity of the apparatus could be
eliminated in this work. In order to compare the widths (FWHM) of
the second continuum observed (see Table 1) a smooth background
underlying the nearly Gaussian second continuum was interpolated
and subtracted.

Table 1   Position and width of second continuum of Kr

	Ref. 5	Ref. 6	This work
λ_{max} (Å)	1425	1470 $\pm$ 5	1460 $\pm$ 5
FWHM (Å)	95* (at 300 Torr)	100* (at 150 Torr)	120 $\pm$ 5 (at 100 Torr)

* estimated from spectra reproduced in Ref. 5 and 6.

A grant from the Deutsche Forschungsgemeinschaft is gratefully acknowledged.

1   B. Schiewe, H. Schmoranzer and P. Wollenweber, Rev. Sci.
    Instrum. 48, 893 (1977)
2   H. Schmoranzer, H. Teichmann and R. Wanik, to be published
3   M. Inokuti, Rev. Mod. Phys. 43, 297 (1971)
4   H. Schmoranzer, J. Phys. B 8, 1139 (1975)
5   P.K. Leichner and R.J. Ericson, Phys. Rev. A 9, 251 (1974)
6   R. Brodmann and G. Zimmerer, J. Phys. B 10, 3395 (1977)

TOTAL SCATTERING CROSS SECTIONS OF PROTONS
BY He, Ne AND Ar

John S. Risley

Department of Physics, North Carolina State University
Raleigh, North Carolina 27650 USA

and

Ronald E. Olson

SRI-International
Menlo Park, California 94025 USA

Total scattering cross sections have been measured and compared to theoretical predictions for protons incident on He, Ne and Ar in the energy range from 100 eV to 1000 eV.

A proton beam passing through two 0.05" diameter collimators spaced 4.4" apart entered a static gas cell which was 2.3" long. A Faraday cup was placed immediately in back of the gas cell. The scattering cross section was determined by measuring the exponential attenuation of a proton beam as a function of the gas pressure. The acceptance angle for the Faraday cup along the ion-beam path in the gas cell was defined by the radius of the exit aperture of the gas cell. Protons which were scattered through an angle larger than the acceptance angle contributed to the attenuation signal. In this experiment the acceptance angle varied from a few degrees at the entrance aperture of the gas cell to 90° at the end. For the He measurements two different diameters were used for the exit aperture of the gas cell; one diameter was 0.120", the other 0.250". For the Ne and Ar measurements only the 0.120" diameter exit aperture was used. The effective acceptance angle was 2° for the 0.210" exit aperture and 4° for the 0.250" aperture.

The experimental results for H$^+$ on He are shown in Fig. 1. The solid circles are data using the 0.120" aperture, the solid triangles are those for the

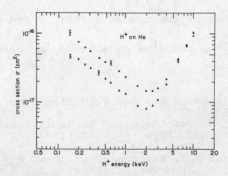

Fig. 1. Attenuation cross section for H$^+$ on He.

0.250" aperture. Above 2 keV the attenuation cross section is strongly influenced by the inelastic charge transfer cross section σ_{10}. The open circles are from previous measurements of σ_{10} using a different experimental arrangement.

Theoretical calculations have been made for the differential scattering cross sections for proton on He and Ar using *ab initio* potentials for the ground state ion-atom interaction. The differential cross sections have been integrated from a minimum scattering angle to 180° to obtain an effective total scattering cross section. A set of these cross sections for a range of minimum scattering angles has been folded into the experimental apparatus function to obtain an effective cross section for comparison with experiment. The apparatus function takes into account the finite interaction path length and diameter of the ion beam. In general good agreement is found.

This work has been supported in part by the Research Corporation, North Carolina Science and Technology Committee and the Atomic, Molecular and Plasma Physics Program and the Aeronomy Program of the U.S. National Science Foundation.

INTERATOMIC INTERACTION
IN THE ELECTRON EXCITED QUASIMOLECULES

G.K. Ivanov

(Institute of Chemical Physics, USSR Akademy of Science)

The interaction between an atom B and excited atom A^* is considered. We assume that the energy E of outer electron and the internuclear distance R satisfy the following conditions:

$$|E|\beta \ll 1 , \quad R^2 \gg 1 \tag{1}$$

where β is the polarizability of the particle B ($e = h = m_e = 1$).

The potential energy E(R) for the system A^* B is given by the equation

$$det | t_{ij} - (E(R)-E_i)\delta_{ij} | = 0 \tag{2}$$

Here $t_{ij} = \langle \varphi_{nem} | t | \varphi_{n'e'm'} \rangle$ are matrix elements, connecting unperturbed atomic states with various values of the energy E_i and orbital angular momentum l (m is a projection of l onto the vector $\vec{R}$ ', t is a local operator defined in ref.[1] :

For the case $m = m'$

$$\varphi^*_{nem}(\vec{\rho})\varphi_{n'e'm}(\vec{\rho}) = \sum_\nu \mathcal{D}_\nu(\rho)\left[\frac{\vec{R}\vec{\rho}}{R\rho}\right]^\nu$$

where $\vec{\rho}$ denotes the coordinate of the outer electron for the atom A^*. Approximating $\mathcal{D}_\nu(\rho)$ by the functions

$$\mathcal{D}_\nu(\rho) = \sum_{\kappa,\gamma} b_{\nu\kappa} \rho^\kappa e^{-\gamma_\kappa \rho}$$

we get analitic expressions for $t_{nem,n'e'm}$ (with $1,1' \le 3$):

$$t_{nem,n'e'm} = 2\pi L \varphi^*_{nem}(\vec{R})\varphi_{n'e'm}(\vec{R}) - \frac{\beta}{2R^4}\delta_{nn'}\delta_{ee'} - \beta\sum_{\nu,\kappa,\gamma} b_{\nu\kappa}(-1)^{\kappa-\nu}\frac{\partial^{\kappa-\gamma+1}}{\partial\gamma_\kappa^{\kappa-\gamma+1}} F_\nu(\gamma_\kappa,R) \tag{3}$$

$$F_1(\gamma,R) = \frac{\partial}{\gamma\partial\gamma}\left[F_0(\gamma,R+x)\right]'_x , \quad x \to 0 ;$$

$$F_2(\gamma,R) = -\frac{\partial}{\gamma\partial\gamma}F_0(\gamma,R) + \left(\frac{\partial}{\gamma\partial\gamma}\right)^2\left[F_0(\gamma,R+x)\right]''_{xx} ;$$

$$F_3(\gamma,R) = -3\frac{\partial}{\gamma\partial\gamma}F_1(\gamma,R) + \left(\frac{\partial}{\gamma\partial\gamma}\right)^3\left[F_0(\gamma,R+x)\right]'''_{xxx} \ ;$$

$$F_4(\gamma,R) = -3\left(\frac{\partial}{\gamma\partial\gamma}\right)^2 F_0(\gamma,R) - 6\frac{\partial}{\gamma\partial\gamma}F_2(\gamma,R) + \left(\frac{\partial}{\gamma\partial\gamma}\right)^4\left[F_0(\gamma,R+x)\right]^{iv}_{xxxx} \ ;$$

$$F_5(\gamma,R) = -15\left(\frac{\partial}{\gamma\partial\gamma}\right)^2 F_1(\gamma,R) - 10\frac{\partial}{\gamma\partial\gamma}F_3(\gamma,R) + \left(\frac{\partial}{\gamma\partial\gamma}\right)^5\left[F_0(\gamma,R+x)\right]^{v}_{xxxxx} \ ;$$

$$F_6(\gamma,R) = -15\left(\frac{\partial}{\gamma\partial\gamma}\right)^3 F_0(\gamma,R) - 45\left(\frac{\partial}{\gamma\partial\gamma}\right)^2 F_2(\gamma,R) - 15\frac{\partial}{\gamma\partial\gamma}F_4(\gamma,R) + \left(\frac{\partial}{\gamma\partial\gamma}\right)^6\left[F_0(\gamma,R+x)\right]^{vi}_{xxxxxx} \ ,$$

where $F_0(\gamma,R+x) = -\frac{1}{(R+x)^2}\frac{z}{8}\left[e^{-z}Ei(z) - e^z Ei(-z)\right] + \frac{1}{R^2}\left[\frac{1}{z^2} - \left(\frac{1}{z} + \frac{1}{z^2}\right)e^{-z}\right]$, $z = \gamma(R+x)$.

$F_0(\gamma,R)$ is the function describing the perturbation of the atom S-state [1], L is scattering length for the atom B.

At large distances $R \gg 1/|E|$

$$t_{nem,nem} = 2\pi L |\phi_{nem}(\vec{R})|^2 - \frac{C_{nem}}{R^6}$$

with $C_{nem} \sim \beta \langle \rho^2 \rangle$ in accordance with general results of the asymptotic theory. To examine the accuracy of the formulae (3) we applied them for the calculation of a set of potential curves for the quasimolecule Na^*-He (L = 1,1, β = 1,39). The comparison of our results to Bottcher s data [2] indicates on the high accuracy of the developed theory.

References

1. G.K.Ivanov. Teor. i exper. khimija. 14, 610 (1978).
2. C.Bottcher. Chem.Phys.Lett. 18, 367,(1973).

JWKB CALCULATION OF MOMENTUM-TRANSFER CROSS SECTIONS FOR A
SHIELDED COULOMB POTENTIAL: URANIUM IONS*

James S. Cohen and P. Jeffrey Hay

Theoretical Division, Los Alamos Scientific Laboratory,
University of California, Los Alamos, NM 87545, U.S.A.

Mometum transfer in collisions is an important characteristic of plasmas.
The momentum-transfer cross section for a Coulomb potential is, of course,
infinite so the Debye shielding of the plasma must be taken into account to
obtain a long-range potential of the form $(Z_1 Z_2/R) \exp (-R/\lambda_D)$ where λ_D is the
shielding length. Momentum transfer is dominated at low collision energies by the
long-range (though cut off) Coulomb potential and at relatively high energies by
the short-range repulsion. In the absence of detailed knowledge of the interactions the momentum-transfer cross section has often been approximated by arbitrarily neglecting the small-angle and large-angle scattering.

We have accurately decribed momentum transfer via U II - U I, U II - U II, and
U II - U III collisions in a U^+ plasma. We started by calculating numerical
relativistic Hartree-Fock charge densities for the ground and lowest excited
states of U I, U II, and U III. The potential curves for all pairs of these atoms
and ions were computed using the modified electron-gas model ignoring inversion
symmetry effects. The electron-gas model[1-2] is expected to be quite accurate for
the short-range repulsion important in fast collisions, and the intermediate-to-
long-range potential is dominated by either Coulomb repulsion or polarization
attraction.

The momentum-transfer (diffusion) and viscosity cross sections were calculated in the JWKB approximation utilizing the partial-wave expansion. The phase
integrals out to several times the classical turning point were performed by a
rapid and accurate method recently described[3] and the long-range shielded Coulomb
contributions were obtained by analytically expanding the integrand. The required
computer times are competitive with purely classical calculations. Results are
presented in Table I assuming a shielding length of about 5×10^{-4} cm. The momentum-
transfer cross section was found to be insensitive to the shielding length at
these energies.

Table I

E(eV)	$\sigma_D (10^{-16}$ cm$^2)$		
	U^+-U	U^+-U^+	U^+-U^{2+}
1	160	5500	20000
10	19	77	260
100	7.7	8.6	10.2
1000	2.9	2.9	2.9

*Work performed under the auspices of the U.S. Department of Energy.

1.   R. G. Gordon and Y. S. Kim, J. Chem. Phys. <u>56</u>, 3122 (1972);
     V. I. Gaydenko and V. K. Nikulin, Chem. Phys. Lett. <u>7</u>, 360(1970).

2.   A. I. M. Rae, Chem. Phys. Lett. <u>18</u>, 574(1973).

3.   J. S. Cohen, J. Chem. Phys. <u>68</u>, 1841(1978).

LOW-ENERGY COLLISIONS BETWEEN ALKALI AND RARE-GAS ATOMS

G. Peach

Department of Physics and Astronomy, University College
Gower Street, London WC1E 6BT, England

In the last few years a considerable amount of work has been carried out[1,2,3,4] on the development of semi-empirical model and pseudo-potential methods for the description of atom-atom interactions. These methods can prove quite economical in cases where an *ab initio* calculation of the molecular potentials would be extremely costly. Also both methods have the virtue that they certainly provide an accurate description of the long-range part of the interaction, which is an important feature for problems of atom-atom scattering at low energies. At the X ICPEAC meeting we reported on work[5] in which we applied our method[3] to the problem of alkali-rare gas scattering and obtained some encouraging results.

The original method has now been considerably improved and incorporates many new features. Both model and pseudo-potentials $V(r)$, have been developed for the electron-rare gas problem, and the method has also been extended to the electron-atomic ion system. The atom (or atomic ion) is treated as a core, and the general analytic form chosen for $V(r)$ is given by

$$V(r) = -\frac{z}{r} - N\left(\frac{1}{r} + \delta + \delta'r + \delta''r^2\right)\exp(-\gamma r) - \frac{\alpha_d}{2r^4}\omega_2(\beta r) - \frac{\alpha'}{2r^6}\omega_3(\beta r);$$

$$\alpha' = \alpha_q - 6\beta_1 - 24\gamma_1 E_e \tag{1}$$

where N is the number of electrons in the core, z is the residual charge on the core and δ, δ', δ'' and γ are empirical parameters. The dipole and quadrupole polarisabilities α_d and α_q, together with the coefficients β_1 and γ_1 are known, and β is taken to be $(\overline{r^2})^{-\frac{1}{2}}$ where $\overline{r^2}$ is the root-mean-square radius of the core. $\omega_2(\beta r)$ and $\omega_3(\beta r)$ are cut-off functions which tend to zero at small values of r, and E_e ryd is the energy of the electron. Seaton and Steenman-Clark[6] have shown that an energy-dependent term of order $1/r^6$ contributes to $V(r)$ and have defined γ_1. Using the basic form (1), empirical parameters are determined so that we obtain the following types of electron-atom (atomic ion) potentials. We only consider atoms (or ions) which have s and/or p electrons in the filled shells.

a) Model potentials for the electron-atom system ($z = 0$). The full s, p and d phaseshifts for elastic scattering derived from a solution of the radial wave equation in which $V(r)$ is given by (1), are fitted to the best data available for $0 \le E_e \le 1$.

b) Model potentials for the electron-atomic ion system ($z \ne 0$). The energies of the bound states nl as predicted using (1) with $l = 0,1$ or 2, are fitted to the known energies of the states nl.

c) Pseudo-potentials for the electron-atom system ($z = 0$).

For s-wave and/or p-wave scattering, we determine $V(r)$ such that the correct elastic scattering phaseshifts modulo π are reproduced. This is an l-dependent potential, but for scattering in which $l \geq 2$, the potential is identical to that described in a).

d) Pseudo-potentials for the electron-ion system ($z \neq 0$).
The energies of the bound states with $l = 0$ or 1 as calculated by using (1), are matched to known energies, so that the lowest s or p state supported by the pseudo-potential corresponds to the lowest real s or p state of the complex atom. This means that for $l = 0$ or 1 the principal quantum numbers of corresponding states are not the same, but for $l \geq 2$ the potential is identical with that described in b).

Various combinations of these potentials are then used to solve the atom-atom scattering problem. The model potentials contain virtual states, and when they are used, the atom-atom wave function is subject to the constraint that it must be orthogonal to the virtual states of the molecular core. Applications of these methods to alkali-rare gas systems will be presented at the conference. The molecular potentials obtained are used to calculate various types of scattering data, and also to study the closely associated problems of the broadening and shift of spectral lines of alkalis produced by the presence of rare gases.

1. J. Pascale and J. Vanderplanque, *J. Chem. Phys.* <u>60</u>, 2278 (1974).

2. C. Bottcher and A. Dalgarno, *Proc. Roy. Soc.* A <u>340</u>, 187 (1974).

3. G. Peach, *J. Phys. B: Atom. Molec. Phys.* <u>11</u>, 2107 (1978).

4. P. Valiron, R. Gayet, R. McCarroll, F. Masnou-Seeuws and M. Philippe, *J. Phys. B: Atom. Molec. Phys.* <u>12</u>, 53 (1979).

5. A.R. Malvern and G. Peach, *Proc. X ICPEAC* ed. G. Watel (Paris), p230 (1977).

6. M.J. Seaton and L. Steenman-Clark, *J. Phys. B: Atom. Molec. Phys.* <u>10</u> 2639 (1977).

CHARGE TRANSFER IN He^{2+} -H(1s) COLLISIONS

S C MUKHERJEE AND SHAYMAL DATTA

Indian Association for the Cultivation of Science
Jadavpur, Calcutta 700 032, India

The cross sections for the charge transfer from the ground state of atomic hydrogen, into the final 1s, 2s and 2p states of He$^+$ ion, by alpha particles are calculated in the high and intermediate energy region. This process represents an asymetric electron capture and has a special interest because of the possibility of accidental resonance, in the capture process due to the equality of energy in H(1s) and He$^+$(2s or 2p) states, neglecting the very small difference in the reduced masses. We have applied the Coulomb-Born approximation which takes into account the effect of the columb repulsive force between the proton and the positively charged He$^+$ ion left in the final state after the alpha particle has captured the electron from the target hydrogen atom.

The scattering amplitude in the coulomb-Born approximation is

$$F^{CB}(k_i \to k_f) = - \frac{\mu_f}{2\pi} \exp\left(-\frac{1}{2}\pi\alpha\right) \Gamma(1 + i\alpha) \int d\underline{r} d\underline{R}_f \exp\left(-i\underline{k}_f \cdot \underline{R}_f\right)$$

$$\Psi_f^*(\underline{r}) V \Psi_i(\underline{r}') \exp(i\underline{k}_i \cdot \underline{R}_i)\, {}_1F_1(-i\alpha; 1; ik_f R_f + i\underline{k}_f \cdot \underline{R}_f)$$

For the convenience of calculation we adopt for V the post form of interaction $V_{Post} = \frac{1}{R} - \frac{1}{r}$. The inter-nuclear separation $\underline{R}$, is approximated by $\underline{R}_f$, the distance between the proton and the Centre of mass of the He$^+$ion. This approximation amounts to the neglect of a small quantity of the order of 10^{-4}.

The final bound-state wave function is taken in the form

$$\Psi_f^*(\underline{r}) = C_f D(\mu, \underline{Y}) \exp(-\mu r - i\underline{Y} \cdot \underline{r}) \Big|\ \underline{Y} = 0,$$

where C_f is the normalization constant and $D(\mu, \underline{Y})$ is the appropriate differential operator which generates the required wave functions. Following a procedure similar to the coulomb-projected Born approximation of Geltman [1], we obtain the necessary amplitude as

$$F^{CB}(k_i \to k_f) = \frac{2\mu_f C_f \sqrt{\pi}}{m_p^6} \exp\left(-\frac{1}{2}\pi\alpha\right) \Gamma(1+i\alpha)\, D(\mu, \underline{Y}) \left[\mu \left\{ \int_0^1 dx \times \frac{1}{g^3 \lambda} \right.\right.$$

$$\left.\left. \frac{d}{d\lambda} \frac{1}{\lambda} \frac{d}{d\lambda} (\Phi(\lambda)) - \frac{1}{m_p^2} \int_0^1 dx\, x(1-x)\frac{1}{g^4 \lambda} \frac{d}{d\lambda} \frac{1}{\lambda} \frac{d}{d\lambda} \left(\frac{\Phi(\lambda)}{\lambda}\right) \right\} \right]_{\underline{Y}=0}$$

where , $C_1 = 1/m_p$, $C_2 = m_x (1/m_x - m_p)$,

$g = x + C_1^2(1-x)$, $\underline{\Delta} = \underline{Y} + C_2 \underline{k}_i$.

$$\underline{K}_o = C_1^2(1-x)\,\underline{\Lambda}\,/g,\qquad\qquad g\eta^2 = 1-x(1-\mu^2) + \Lambda^2 C_1^2(1-x) - K_o^2 g,$$

$$\lambda = C_1\eta,\qquad\qquad\qquad\qquad \underline{g} = C_1(-\underline{K}_o + \underline{K}_i + \underline{Y}) - \underline{K}_f,$$

$$\Phi(\lambda) = \left[\frac{q^2 + \lambda^2}{2}\right]^{-i\alpha-1}\left[\frac{q^2 + \lambda^2}{2} + K_f\cdot g - i\lambda K_f\right]^{i\alpha},$$

$m = M_{H^+} / (M_{H^+} + 1)$ and $m_p = M_{He^{2+}} / (M_{He^{2+}} + 1)$.

M_{H^+} and $M_{He^{2+}}$ being the masses of proton and alpha particle respectively. The integral for the scattering amplitude and finally the necessary integral for the total capture cross sections are performed numerically using Gauss–Legendre quadrature method. Using the values for capture cross sections Ω_{1s}, Ω_{2s} and Ω_{2p} obtained by the present calculation, we have made an estimate for the total capture cross section as done by Salin[2] and also by Belkic' and Janev[3]

$$\Omega\ (\text{total}) \simeq \Omega_{1s} + 1.616\ (\Omega_{2s} + \Omega_{2p})$$

some of the results of the present calculations are shown in the table below.

The theoretical values of capture cross sections

E(MeV)	$\Omega_{1s}(\pi a_o^2)$	$\Omega_{2s}(\pi a_o^2)$	$\Omega_{2p}(\pi a_o^2)$
0.1	0.306	0.111+1	0.512+1
0.5	0.573−1	0.152−1	0.894−1
1.0	0.967−2	0.216−2	0.490−2
10.0	0.399−6	0.567−7	0.796−8

Note :   The notation X $\pm$ n implies that the number
                X must be multiplied by $10^{\pm n}$

1. Geltman S J.Phys. B4 1288 (1971)

2. Salin A J.Phys. B3 937 (1970)

3. Belkic' Dž and Janev R K J.Phys. B6 1020 (1973)

GLAUBER SCATTERING AMPLITUDE FOR $1^1S \to n^1P$ EXCITATION OF HELIUM BY PROTON IMPACT

S.C.MUKHERJEE AND S.K.SUR

Department of Theoretical Physics, Indian Association for the
Cultivation of Science, Jadavpur, Calcutta 700 032, India

The Glauber scattering amplitude for $1^1S \to n^1P$ transitions in atomic helium under charged particle impact is reduced to a form which is computationally very advantageous. This is an extension of our earlier work[1] for proton impact $1^1S \to n^1S$ ($n = 2,3,4$) excitations of helium. As before, the single scattering part of the Glauber amplitude is separated for reduction along the lines of Thomas and Chan[2]. The remaining double scattering part of the amplitude can then be worked out by an extension of the procedure of Ref. 1.

We introduce a function $K_1(\lambda, \eta, b)$ given by

$$K_1(\lambda, \eta, b) = 2^{2i\eta} i \frac{\Gamma(i\eta)}{\Gamma(-i\eta)} \lambda^{-2} \int_0^\infty dt \left[t^{-2i\eta} J_1(t)/(t^2 + u^2) \right], \tag{1}$$

where $u = \lambda b$. $K_1(\lambda, \eta, b)$ is related to the modified Lommel function of Ref. 2 by

$$K_1(\lambda, \eta, b) = \lambda^{-3} b^{-1} (i\lambda b)^{-2i\eta} L_{2i\eta, 1}(i\lambda b). \tag{2}$$

The double scattering amplitude involves various derivatives of $K_1(\lambda, \eta, b)$. Evaluation of the integrals in $(\partial/\partial\lambda)^n K_1(\lambda, \eta, b)$ proceeds in a manner analogous to that of Sur, Mukherjee, and Sil[3]. The results for small as well as large values of u are checked against those obtained from Eq. (2) using the method of Ref. 2 (see TABLE I). In the intermediate range of values of u, where the computation of $L_{\mu,\nu}(i\lambda b)$ requires a very high precision work, the present method can be handled with normal computer precision.

The results for the total Glauber cross sections will be presented at the Symposium.

TABLE I . Values of $(\partial/\partial\lambda)^{\underline{n}} \underline{K}_1(\lambda,\eta,\underline{b})$ for $\lambda=2.0$.

η	$\underline{b}$	Method*		$\underline{n}=0$	$\underline{n}=1$	$\underline{n}=2$	$\underline{n}=3$
0.05	1.0	P	Re	-.2684-3**	.1309-3	.6377-3	-.4112-2
			Im	-.4491-1	.7564-1	-.1574	.3931
		D	Re	-.2707-3	.1301-3	.6388-3	-.4117-2
			Im	-.4495-1	.7567-1	-.1575	.3932
	10.0	P	Re	-.3191-6	.9646-6	-.3406-5	.1376-4
			Im	-.6250-3	.1250-2	-.3125-2	.9374-2
		A	Re	-.3191-6	.9646-6	-.3406-5	.1376-4
			Im	-.6250-3	.1250-2	-.3125-2	.9374-2
1.00	1.0	P	Re	.7256-3	-.5450-2	.2069-1	-.7312-1
			Im	-.2896-1	.4424-1	-.8363-1	.1879
		D	Re	.7023-3	-.5469-2	.2074-1	-.7326-1
			Im	-.2899-1	.4429-1	-.8367-1	.1879
	10.0	P	Re	-.6103-5	.1814-4	-.6274-4	.2473-3
			Im	-.6185-3	.1230-2	-.3055-2	.9089-2
		A	Re	-.6103-5	.1814-4	-.6274-4	.2473-3
			Im	-.6185-3	.1230-2	-.3055-2	.9089-2

*P-Present; D-Using direct series for $L_{\mu,\nu}$; A-Using asymptotic series for $L_{\mu,\nu}$. ** $x\pm y\equiv x\times10^{\pm y}$

1. S. K. Sur and S. C. Mukherjee, Phys. Rev. A (in press).
2. B. K. Thomas and F. T. Chan, Phys. Rev. A$\underline{8}$, 252 (1973).
3. S. K. Sur, S. C. Mukherjee, and N. C. Sil, Phys. Rev. A $\underline{18}$, 2384 (1978).

He$^+$(2S) FORMATION IN FAST He$^+$- H COLLISION

S.C. MUKHERJEE, SHYAMAL DUTTA and KANIKA ROY
Indian Association for the Cultivation of Science, Calcutta-32

The cross sections σ_{11}^* for the direct (1s - 2s) excitation of the projectile He$^+$ by the collision of atomic or molecular hydrogen have recently been measured by Shah and Gilbody[1] covering an energy region of 9-343 keV. Bell and Kingston[2] applied the first Born approximation to compute the cross sections for the formation of He$^+$ (2s or 2p) in He$^+$ (1s) + H (1s) collision upto an incident He$^+$ ion energy of 4000 keV. They also employed a coupled state calculation in the impact parameter treatment to calculate these cross sections. They have found that for both 2s and 2p formation, the single transition process (where the target remains unexcited) dominates the total cross section. Excepting for a very small low energy region of 10 to 40 keV, where the close coupling results are in good accord with the experiment, the observed results for the cross sections lie much above the calculated results in the entire energy region considered.

In the present paper we apply a procedure similar to the distortion approximation in the impact parameter treatment as suggested by Bates[3] to calculate the 2s- excitation cross section of the projectile He$^+$(1s) in the collision of He$^+$ and H atom in the high energy region, keeping the target unexcited.

Initially, the helium ion and the hydrogen atom are in their ground states represented by the wave function Ψ_{1s} :

$$\Psi_{1s} = 2^{-1/2} \; (\Psi_{1s}^{(1)} + \Psi_{1s}^{(2)}) \text{ where}$$

$$\Psi_{1s}^{(1)} = \Phi_{1s}(r_{A1}) \; U \; (r_{B2}) \; \exp\left[i \left\{ (E_{\Phi(1s)} + E_u)t - \tfrac{1}{2}\underline{v}\cdot(\underline{r}_1 - \underline{r}_2) - \frac{v^2 t}{4} \right\} \right]$$

and $\Psi_{1s}^{(2)} = \Phi_{1s}(r_{A2}) U(r_{B1}) \exp\left[i \left\{ \left(E_{\Phi(1s)} + E_u\right)t - \tfrac{1}{2}\underline{v}\cdot(\underline{r}_2 - \underline{r}_1) - \frac{v^2 t}{4} \right\} \right]$

Φ_{1s}, U and $E_{\Phi(1s)}$, E_U are respectively, the normalized wave functions and binding energies of He$^+$ (1s) and H (1s).

After the collision, the projectile He$^+$(1s) undergoes a transition to a final 2s state represented by the wave function Ψ_{2s}.

The distortion probability P_m^D in the final state is defined by

$$P_m^D = \left| A_m^D \right|^2 \text{ (Following the notation similar to Sur et al[4]).}$$

where

$$A_m^D = \frac{i}{v} \int_{-\infty}^{+\infty} \left[\exp \left\{ -\frac{i}{v} \int_{-\infty}^{s} \alpha \, ds' \right\} \beta \exp \left\{ -\frac{i}{v} \int_{-\infty}^{s} \gamma \, ds' \right\} \right] ds$$

and α, β, γ are the combinations of different overlap and interaction integrals.

The numerical computations are under progress and the results will be presented at the conference.

1. M. B. Shah and H. B. Gilbody J. Phys. B <u>11</u>, 121 (1978).

2. K. L. Bell and A. E. Kingston J. Phys. B <u>11</u>, 1259 (1978).

3. D. R. Bates, Proc. Phys. Soc A <u>73</u>, 227 (1959).

4. S. K. Sur, K. Roy, S. Roy and S. C. Mukherjee,
    Phys. Rev. A <u>16</u>, 1986 (1977).

EXCITATION OF HELIUM BY IMPACT OF HYDROGEN ATOMS

S. P. Ojha and P. Tiwari

Applied Physics Section
Institute of Technology
Banaras Hindu University
Varanasi-221005, INDIA

Scattering cross sections for the excitation of helium by impact of hydrogen atoms have been calculated employing Vainshtein, Presnyyakov and Sobelman (VPS) method under peaking approximation. Transitions from the ground state to n^1P and n^3P states have been included in the calculation. The results obtained have been compared with other theoretical and experimental data.

****

Theory For Collisions Between Arbitrary Ions or Atoms*

Victor Franco

Physics Department, Brooklyn College of the City University of New York,
Brooklyn, New York 11210, USA

We extend the applicability of the Glauber Theory to collisions between composite systems (ion or atoms). The phase shift function, χ, may be expressed entirely in terms of the known[1] proton-hydrogen (pH) and electron-hydrogen (eH) phase shift functions, χ_{pH} and χ_{eH}, and the known point Coulomb function $\overline{\chi}_c$. By expanding the profile function Γ_{fi} in terms of the known pH and eH profile functions, Γ_{pH} and Γ_{eH}, we obtain a first-order result linear in Γ_{pH} and Γ_{eH}. The contributions to the scattering amplitude from Γ_{pH} are obtained in closed form. The contributions from Γ_{eH} are obtained as a two-dimensional integral. If at least one of the atomic systems is neutral, the contributions from Γ_{eH} can also be reduced to closed form. Thus the scattering amplitude is reduced from an integral of dimension $3(M+N)+2$, where $M+N$ is the total number of electrons in the two atomic systems, to a two-dimensional integral for ion-ion collisions and to closed form for ion-atom and atom-atom collisions.[2] Applications[3] to reactions involving He^+ ions and H atoms will be presented and compared with other theories and with measurements.

* Work supported in part by the U. S. National Science Foundation and by a CUNY PSC - BHE Faculty Research Award.

1. V. Franco, Phys. Rev. Lett. **20**, 709 (1968).

2. V. Franco, Phys. Lett. **A** (to be published).

3. V. Franco, Phys. Rev. Lett. **42**, 759 (1979).

A Numerical Solution of the Schrödinger Equation for
Atomic Collisions

V. Maruhn-Rezvani, N. Grün, and W. Scheid

Institut für Theoretische Physik II
Universität Giessen, 6300 Giessen, W. Germany

The electronic wave functions in atomic collisions usually
are expanded in a set of basic functions, and this causes a number
of problems: (1) selection of an optimal basis providing adequate
flexibility with a minimum number of basis states, (2) electronic
translation factors, and (3) the representation of continuum wave
functions. To circumvent these problems we have solved the time-
dependent Schrödinger equation numerically on a spatial grid.

The feasibility of such numerical solutions has been demonstrated successfully for the time-dependent Hartree-Fock equations
applied to nuclear physics problems[1]. There are important differences to the atomic problem, however: (1) the singularities of the
Coulomb potential and its long range, and (2) the higher degree of
accuracy desired in comparison to the nuclear case.

As a first step, actual calculations were performed for the
H^+-H collision at impact parameters small compared to the Bohr
radius, so that one has to deal with the Schrödinger equation for
a single electron in an axially symmetric situation. The positions
of the protons, $\vec{r}_1(t)$ and $\vec{r}_2(t)$, enter as time-dependent parameters determined from the classical scattering orbits:

$$i\hbar \frac{\partial}{\partial t} \psi(\vec{r},t) = - \frac{\hbar^2}{2m} \psi(\vec{r},t)$$

$$+ \left\{ \frac{e^2}{|\vec{r}-\vec{r}_1(t)|} + \frac{e^2}{|\vec{r}-\vec{r}_2(t)|} \right\} \psi(\vec{r},t) .$$

For the initial condition we assumed the electron in the 1s-
orbital localized at one of the two protons approaching each other
with given energy of relative motion. The electronic wave function
was multiplied with the appropriate translation factor to match
the proton velocity. Translation factors are required only for the
initial condition. During the collision the wave function has almost unrestricted freedom and shows complicated excitations as
well as oscillations between the protons. The probability for
charge exchange may be computed easily from the final state wave
function and is found to be 0.88, 0.12, and 0.92 for E_{lab} = 20.1,
7.69, and 3.92 keV, respectively, in good agreement with experiment[2].

It is also possible to obtain theoretical values for excitation, ionisation, and charge exchange cross sections. To compare

these data with experiment, however, requires an extension of the
method to finite impact parameters.

+This work has been supported by the Gesellschaft für Schwerionenforschung (GSI).

1. K. T. R. Davies, V. Maruhn-Rezvani, et al., Phys. Rev.
Lett. 41, 632 (1978).
2. G. J. Lockwood and E. Everhart, Phys. Rev. 125, 567 (1962).

CHARGE EXCHANGE CROSS SECTION IN H$^+$-H COLLISIONS$^+$

N C SIL, P K ROY AND B C SAHA
Department of Theoretical Physics
Indian Association for the Cultivation of
Science, Jadavpur, Calcutta 700 032, INDIA.

A method has been presented for the evalution of the cross section of electron capture by proton from atomic hydrogen in the ground state into arbitrary excited state $(n\ell m)$ in the first Born approximation (FBA) with full interacting potential. To improve upon the FBA results by taking account of the lack of orthogonality of the initial and final states the method of Basel and Gerjuoy[1] (BG) and of Band[2] have been employed. The dependence of the asymptotic capture cross sections as $n \to \infty$ on ℓ and m has also been studied.

The charge-exchange amplitude in the FBA for transition between i and f is (notations are the same as used by Sil et al[3])

$$g_{if}(\hat{k}_i \cdot \hat{k}_f) = -\mu_f(I+J) \tag{1a}$$

where
$$I = -(2\pi)^{-1}\int (r)^{-1}\, F(\vec{r},\vec{r}\,',\vec{R}\,')d\vec{r}\, d\vec{R}\,' \tag{1b}$$

and
$$J = -(2\pi)^{-1}\int (|\vec{R}-\vec{r}|)^{-1}\, F(\vec{r},\vec{r}\,',\vec{R}\,')d\vec{r}\, d\vec{R}\,' \tag{1c}$$

with
$$F(\vec{r},\vec{r}\,',\vec{R}\,') = \exp\left[i(\vec{k}_i\cdot\vec{R}-\vec{k}_f\cdot\vec{R}\,')\right] \Phi_i(\vec{r})\, \Phi_f^*(\vec{r}\,')$$

and
$$\mu_f = M(M'+1)/(M+M'+1)$$

Atomic units are used. The evalution of I for the attractive potential (BK amplitude) is well-known. We consider the evalution of J which is rather complicated due to the presence of the ion-nucleus interaction. Performing the space integration over $\vec{r}$, the integral J takes the form

$$J= -\pi^{-5/2}\frac{\partial}{\partial \gamma_1}\int d\vec{Q}\; e^{i(\vec{Q}-\vec{C})\cdot\vec{r}\,'}\Phi_f^*(\vec{r}\,')d\vec{r}\,'/(Q^2[|\vec{B}-\vec{Q}|^2+\gamma_1^2]) \tag{2}$$

where
$$\vec{B}= \vec{k}_i[M/(M+1)]-\vec{k}_f \quad \text{and} \quad \vec{C}= \vec{k}_i-\vec{k}_f[M/(M+1)]$$

Employing Feynman technique, the integral J reduces to

$$J= -\pi^{-1/2}\frac{\partial}{\partial \gamma_1}\int_0^1 G\, \lambda^{-1}\, dx \tag{3a}$$

where
$$G= \int \exp(i\vec{K}\cdot\vec{r}-\lambda r)\Phi_f^*(\vec{r}\,')\, d\vec{r}\,' \tag{3b}$$

with
$$\vec{K}= \vec{B}(1-x)-\vec{C} \quad \text{and} \quad \lambda^2 = (1-x)(\gamma_1^2 + B^2 x)$$

Substituting the contour integral representation[3] of $\Phi_f^*(\vec{r}\,')$ in (3b) both the space and angular integration can be carried out

Thus one finally obtains

$$G = A \frac{\partial}{\partial \gamma_1} (2\pi i)^{-1} \oint_\Gamma dz \; z^{-n+\ell} \Big[K^2(1-z)^2 + \big\{ \gamma_1(1-z) + \gamma_n(1+z) \big\}^2 \Big]^{-(\ell+1)} \qquad (4)$$

with $A = 4\pi(i)^\ell N_{n\ell m} \; Y_{\ell m}(K) \; (2K)^\ell \ell!$

Γ is a closed contour encircling the origin. The contour integral in (4) may be evaluated easily by calculating the residues at z=0. Thus G becomes

$$G = -A(\pi)^{-1/2} \Big[\frac{\partial \delta}{\partial \lambda} \; C^{\ell+1}_{n-\ell-1}(\omega) + 2(\ell+1)\delta \; C^{\ell+2}_{n-\ell-2}(\omega) \frac{\partial \omega}{\partial \lambda} \Big]$$

where
$$\delta = \Big[K^2 + (\gamma_n - \gamma_1)^2 \Big]^{(n-\ell-1)/2} \cdot \Big[K^2 + (\gamma_n + \gamma_1)^2 \Big]^{-(n+\ell+1)/2}$$

$$\omega^2 = (K^2 + \gamma_1^2 - \gamma_n^2)^2 \Big[\big\{ K^2 + (\gamma_n + \gamma_1)^2 \big\} \big\{ K^2 + (\gamma_n - \gamma_1)^2 \big\} \Big]^{-1}$$

and $C_n^\rho(t)$ is the Gegenbauer Polynomial defined by

$$(1 - 2\alpha t + t^2)^{-\rho} = \sum_{n=0}^{\infty} C_n^\rho(t) \; \alpha^n$$

One can evaluate the scattering amplitude in the BG and Band approximation by knowing FBA. The transition amplitudes for the limitting case as $n \to \infty$ can be derived easily.

The cross sections — differential and total — have been computed by taking special care for large values of n and ℓ. Our results at E = 50keV along with those of Band have been displayed in Table I. In Table II we have tabulated our n^3 times the asymptotic results as $n \to \infty$ for 50 keV.

TABLE I: Total capture cross sections $[\sigma](a_o^2)$ for $1s \to 14\ell$ transition. $a(\pm b) = a.10^{\pm b}$

PRESENT RESULTS

	BK	FBA	BG	BAND	BAND[2]
0	5.458(-3)	7.725(-4)	1.018(-3)	9.189(-4)	9.30(-4)
1	8.491(-3)	1.039(-3)	9.411(-3)	1.202(-3)	1.19(-3)
2	2.030(-3)	2.644(-4)	1.998(-4)	2.991(-4)	--
3	1.906(-4)	2.490(-5)	1.954(-5)	2.819(-5)	--
4	9.377(-6)	1.183(-6)	1.010(-6)	1.355(-6)	--

TABLE II : $\Big[n^3 \sigma_{1s \to n\ell} \Big]_{n \to \infty}$ at 50 keV

	BK	FBA	BG	BAND
0	1.499(+1)	2.123	2.797	2.676
1	2.338(+1)	2.854	2.584	3.601
2	5.689	7.397(-1)	5.587(-1)	8.493(-1)
3	5.582(-1)	7.278(-2)	5.731(-2)	8.249(-2)
4	2.981(-2)	3.751(-3)	3.228(-3)	4.296(-3)

+ Work supported in part by the University Grants Commission, India.

[1] R H Bassel and E Gerjuoy, Phys. Rev. 117, 749 (1960)

[2] Y B Band, Phys. Rev. A 8, 243 (1973; ibid 8 2866 (1973)

[3] N C Sil, B C Saha, H P Saha and P Mandal, Phys. Rev.A (in press) 1979.

ELECTRON CAPTURE AT RELATIVISTIC ENERGIES

B.L. Moiseiwitsch and S.G. Stockman

Department of Applied Mathematics and Theoretical Physics
The Queen's University of Belfast,
Belfast BT7 1NN, Northern Ireland

The theory of electron capture from ground state H atoms by high energy incident protons has been generalised to allow for relativistic effects arising from the high velocity of relative motion of the particles and from the use of Dirac atomic wave functions for the electron. It has been shown that the impact parameter and wave treatments of the charge transfer collision are equivalent.

The Oppenheimer-Brinkman-Kramers approximation has been employed to obtain analytical formulae for the scattering amplitudes for capture into the ground state without and for capture with change of electron spin. The post and prior interaction forms of the capture cross sections are shown to be equal. By expanding in powers of the fine structure constant α we have derived simple analytical expressions for the OBK capture cross sections σ. For the case without electron spin change we obtain

$$\sigma^{(1)} = \frac{128}{5} \pi a_o^2 \alpha^{12} \frac{M_p c^2}{E_{kin}} \left\{ \frac{\chi^5}{(1+\alpha^2\chi)^5} + \chi^3(\chi + \frac{1}{4}) - \frac{5\pi\alpha}{11} \chi^{\frac{7}{2}} (\chi + \frac{1}{2}) \right\} \qquad (1)$$

and for the case with electron spin change

$$\sigma^{(2)} = \frac{8}{5} \pi a_o^2 \alpha^{12} \frac{M_p c^2}{E_{kin}} \left\{ \chi^3 + \frac{80\pi\alpha}{99} \chi^{\frac{7}{2}} \right\} \qquad (2)$$

where M_p is the proton mass, E_{kin} is the kinetic energy of the incident proton, and $\chi = 1 + 2 M_p c^2 E_{kin}^{-1}$. The simple formula (1) agrees with numerical integrations of our full analytical expression to better than 0.1% for $E_{kin} \geq 1$ MeV while formula (2) is very satisfactory for $E_{kin} \geq 100$ MeV although not as accurate as (1).

At extremely high energies the capture cross sections fall off as E_{kin}^{-1} in accordance with the result previously obtained by Mittleman[1].

For energies below about 10 MeV the last two terms in the { } brackets of formula (1), arising from the use of Dirac atomic wave functions for the electron, may be dropped, and in the limit where $E_{kin}/M_p c^2$ is small the cross section $\sigma^{(1)}$ tends to the non-relativistic OBK formula.

1. M.H. Mittleman, Proc. Phys. Soc. *84*, 453 (1964).

ELASTIC AND INELASTIC ATOM-ATOM CROSS SECTIONS
AT HIGH VELOCITIES FOR Z≤18

George H. Gillespie[†]

Physical Dynamics, Inc., P.O. Box 556, La Jolla, CA 92038, USA

and

Mitio Inokuti[*]

Argonne National Laboratory, Argonne, IL 60439, USA

When two complex atomic particles collide at high relative speeds a variety
of phenomena can occur. Bates and Griffing[1] initiated a study within the Born
approximation of the various possible processes for collisions between two hydrogen atoms. Subsequent work[2] has provided calculations for many different processes, although only the simpler atomic systems have been studied in detail. More
recently some work has been devoted toward the establishment of certain general
systematics of the relative importance of various phenomena relevant to fast collisions between complex atomic particles[3,4]. In extension of that work, we have
undertaken a systematic study of the asymptotic (high-velocity) Born cross sections for atom-atom collisions[5].

Because of the great number of possible final states of such collisions, it
is useful to simplify the problem by grouping the processes into a few broad classifications. In particular, we consider four types of collisions which can be
categorized according to whether each of the collision partners is scattered elastically or inelastically. For atoms A and B initially in their ground state (g),
these processes and their respective cross sections are the following:

$$A(g) + B(g) \rightarrow A(g) + B(g): \quad \sigma_{el,el} = 8\pi a_0^2 \left(\frac{v_0}{v}\right)^2 I_{el,el} \quad , \tag{1}$$

$$A(g) + B(g) \rightarrow A(g) + B(\Sigma): \quad \sigma_{el,in} = 8\pi a_0^2 \left(\frac{v_0}{v}\right)^2 I_{el,in} \quad , \tag{2}$$

$$A(g) + B(g) \rightarrow A(\Sigma) + B(g): \quad \sigma_{in,el} = 8\pi a_0^2 \left(\frac{v_0}{v}\right)^2 I_{in,el} \quad , \tag{3}$$

$$A(g) + B(g) \rightarrow A(\Sigma) + B(\Sigma): \quad \sigma_{in,in} = 8\pi a_0^2 \left(\frac{v_0}{v}\right)^2 I_{in,in} \quad , \tag{4}$$

where in (1)-(4) we indicate by Σ that all possible inelastic processes, either
excitation or ionization, have been included.

At high velocities the collision strengths ($I_{el,el}$, etc.) are independent of
v and may be expressed in terms of compact momentum transfer integrals over products of atomic form factors or incoherent scattering functions for the atoms involved[3-5]. We have numerically calculated the collision strengths appearing in
(1)-(4) for all possible combinations of atoms with Z≤18, using tabulations of
these functions given by Hubbell et al[6].

As a result, we now answer questions such as "what is the dominant collision process at high velocities?". In Fig. 1 we display the answer, as a function of $Z^{(A)}$ and $Z^{(B)}$. For atomic numbers of 3 or less the doubly inelastic collision process is dominant, as noted by Bates and Griffing for H-H collisions[1]. At higher atomic numbers, purely elastic collisions are dominant[3]. When one of the collision partners is H (and in select cases He) then singly inelastic collisions are dominant if the other collision partner has an atomic number greater than 3.

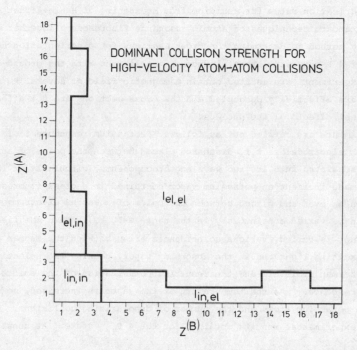

Fig. 1. Domains indicating the largest collision strength for the processes (1) - (4) as a function of the atomic numbers of the collision partners.

+Work supported by Physical Dynamics Independent Research and Development Fund.

*Work performed under the auspices of the U.S. Department of Energy.

1. D. R. Bates and G. W. Griffing, Proc. Phys. Soc. A 66, 961 (1953); 67, 663 (1954); 68, 90 (1955).
2. K. L. Bell and A. E. Kingston, Adv. Atom. Molec. Phys. 10, 53 (1974); and in Atomic Processes and Applications, ed. P. G. Burke and B. L. Moiseiwitsch (North-Holland, Amsterdam) 493 (1976).
3. M. Inokuti, Proc. XthICPEAC (Paris), 280 (1977).
4. G. H. Gillespie, Phys. Rev. A 18, 1967 (1978).
5. G. H. Gillespie and M. Inokuti, in preparation (1979).
6. J. H. Hubbell, Wm. J. Veigele, E. A. Briggs, R. T. Brown, D. T. Cromer, and R. J. Howerton, J. Phys. Chem. Ref. Data 4, 471 (1975); 6, 615 (1977).

DEPOLARIZATION OF 4^2P POTASSIUM ATOMS INDUCED IN RESONANT COLLISIONS

Piotr Skalinski and L. Krause

Department of Physics, University of Windsor
Windsor, Ontario, Canada. N9B 3P4

Most experimental and theoretical studies of collisional depolarization of excited atoms have dealt with the interactions between excited (and polarized) alkali atoms and noble (buffer) gas atoms,[1] though Gallagher and Lewis[2] obtained resonant depolarization rates for rubidium from broadening of Hanle-effect signals. We are using standard techniques of atomic resonance fluorescence together with a Zeeman scanning method to determine the cross sections for disorientation and disalignment of 4^2P potassium atoms, induced in collisions with the ground-state atoms. The experiments are carried out in a magnetic field of several kG in which J and I are effectively decoupled and the cross sections are not affected by the 'fly wheel effect' of the nucleus.[3]

The experiments are carried out as follows. Potassium resonance radiation emitted from an electrodeless r.f. discharge placed between the poles of an electromagnet, is separated into its two wavelength components, circularly or linearly polarized and made incident on potassium vapor contained in a glass fluorescence cell mounted in an oven and placed between the poles of a second electromagnet whose field can be varied continuously in the range 0-10 kG. When the field of the latter magnet is varied, various coincidences arise between the Zeeman components in the exciting light and in the absorbing vapor, causing the selective excitation of Zeeman sublevels and the resulting polarization of the emitted resonance fluorescence. As the temperature of the vapor is increased, so is the density of the potassium atoms and the number of depolarizing collisions. Fig.1 shows typical experimental results obtained for the $4^2P_{1/2}$ state. At densities

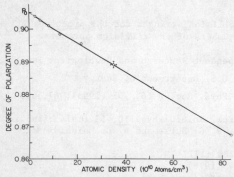

Fig. 1   A plot of the degree of circular polarization of the potassium resonance fluorescence (λ = 7699Å) against density of K atoms.

of the order of 10^{11} atoms/cm^3 the imprisonment of resonance radiation has virtually no effect on the experimental results.

The disorientation cross section for the $4^2P_{1/2}$ atom may be defined as:

$$\sigma_1 = 2\sigma(\tfrac{1}{2}, \tfrac{1}{2} \leftrightarrow \tfrac{1}{2}, -\tfrac{1}{2}) + \sigma_o , \tag{1}$$

where σ_o is the cross section for the collisional depopulation of the $^2P_{1/2}$ state and is much smaller than σ. Neglecting σ_o, we may write the following expression for Z, the number of disorienting collisions per excited atom per second:

$$Z = N\sigma_1 v_r = \big[(P_o/P) - 1\big]/\tau \tag{2}$$

where N is the atomic density of potassium, P is the corresponding degree of (circular) polarization of the fluorescence, v_r is the average relative speed of the colliding atoms, P_o is the degree of polarization at zero density and τ is the mean lifetime of the K $4^2P_{1/2}$ state.   Fig 2 shows a plot of the collision

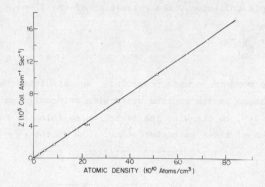

Fig. 2   A plot of collision numbers Z for disorientation of K $4^2P_{1/2}$ atoms against potassium vapor density.

numbers Z against the atomic density, whose slope directly yields the disorientation cross section $\sigma_1 = 3.2 \times 10^{-11} \text{ cm}^2$.

This cross section is three to four orders of magnitude larger than the typical cross section for disorientation by collisions with noble gas atoms[4] and is about one order larger than the cross section for disorientation of $5^2P_{1/2}$ Rb atoms determined in a Hanle effect experiment.[2]

1. W.E. Baylis in Progress in Atomic Spectroscopy, Part B, W. Hanle and H. Kleinpoppen, Eds., Plenum Publishing Corp. (1979).

2. A Gallagher and E.L. Lewis, Phys. Rev. A. 10, 231 (1974).

3. B.R. Bulos and W. Happer, Phys. Rev. A. 4, 849 (1971).

4. W. Berdowski and L. Krause, Phys. Rev. 165, 158 (1968).

COLLISIONAL TRANSFER BETWEEN ORIENTATION AND ALIGNMENT OF
ATOMS EXCITED BY A SINGLE MODE LASER BEAM

T. Yabuzaki, T. Manabe, and T. Ogawa

Ionosphere Research Laboratory, Kyoto University,
Uji, Kyoto, Japan

Collisional relaxation among Zeeman substates of excited atoms has been extensively studied for a long time. In most of these studies, collisions treated have been isotropic, so that each multipole component of the excited atoms relaxes independently. We report here the theoretical and experimental results on transfer between orientation (magnetic dipole moment) and alignment (electric quadrupole moment) by anisotropic collisions with ground state atoms. The anisotropy considered is due to the anisotropic velocity distribution of atoms excited by a single mode laser beam. By such anisotropic collisions, the relaxation of the 2^k-pole moment can generally be expressed as

$$d\rho_q^k / dt = - \sum_{k'q'} \Gamma_{qq'}^{kk'} \rho_{q'}^{k'}$$

so that the transfer among multipole moments becomes possible. We calculated the relaxation matrix element $\Gamma_{qq'}^{kk'}$ for atoms in the excited state with J=1 colliding with those in the ground state with J=0, by changing the laser tuning relative to the absorption line center and masses of these perturber atoms. As in the theories of isotropic collisions,[1-3] we assumed that the interaction between colliding atoms is van der Waals type interaction ($\propto 1/R^6$), and used the impact and linear-path approximations. We treated the case that the Doppler-broadened line width is much larger than the homogeneous width.

Typical theoretical results are shown in Fig. 1, which shows the values of $\Gamma_q^{kk'}$ ($\equiv \Gamma_{qq'}^{kk'}\delta_{qq'}$) as functions of axial velocity v_0 of excited atoms, determined by the detuning of laser frequency. (The quantization axis is taken to the direction of the laser beam.) The relaxation rates of alignment and orientation for isotropic collisions are shown by dotted lines. Figure 1 shows that, as one detunes the laser frequency from the line center, the relaxation rates of orientation and alignment become dependent

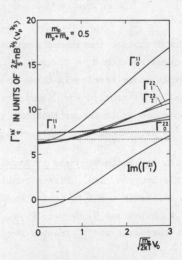

Fig. 1.
Relaxation matrix elements as functions of the axial velocity v_0 of excited atoms. m_e is the mass of an excited atom, and n, m_p and v_p are density, mass and velocity of perturber atoms, respectively. B is a constant defined in Ref. 3.

on the component q and their values increase monotonically. On the other hand, the transfer rate between alignment and orientation, which is pure imaginary, changes its sign as the detuning is increased. It should be noted that these results can be applied to the general cases of optical excitation by light with arbitrary spectral profile, by averaging $\Gamma_q^{kk'}$ with respect to v_0 over the corresponding axial velocity distribution of excited atoms.

An experiment was performed with respect to neon atoms in the $2p_4$ state colliding with ground state neon atoms in a discharge, to demonstrate the transfer from alignment to orientation. A linearly polarized single-mode laser beam from a cw dye laser was applied to a neon discharge tube, perpendicularly to the magnetic field. The frequency of the beam was stabilized by a neon Faraday filter,[4,5] to 594.5 nm for velocity-selective excitation of neon from the metastable state $1s_5$ to the $2p_4$ state. This excitation creates alignment in the $2p_4$ state. When the alignment is transferred to orientation by anisotropic collisions, the orientation signal should appear as the intensity difference of σ_+ polarized fluorescence from the $2p_4$ state (for example, the 609.6 nm line) propagated to the direction of the magnetic field. On the other hand, alignment can be observed as the intensity difference of fluorescence with linear polarizations parallel and perpendicular to the beam direction. Our theoretical calculation shows that orientation and alignment signals should have dispersion and Lorentzian shapes, respectively, as the magnetic field is swept through zero, and that the ratio of these signal intensities is approximately given by $\Gamma_1^{21}/(\Gamma_n+\Gamma_1^{11})$ where Γ_n is the natural decay rate of the $2p_4$ state. Figure 2 shows typical orientation and alignment signals as the magnetic field is swept, in the case that the laser frequency is tuned at about the center of the 594.5 nm line. In Fig. 2, the orientation signal is ten times magnified compared with the alignment signal. The ratio of signal intensities is $\sim$0.1, as expected roughly from our theory.

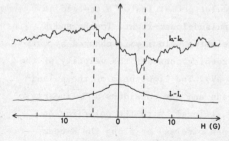

L+L

L-L

10   0   10   H (G)

Fig. 2.
Typical recorder traces showing the signals of orientation (upper trace) and alignment (lower trace) as the magnetic field is swept through zero.

1.   A. Omont, J. Phys. (Paris) 26, 26 (1965).
2.   M. I. D'yakonov and V. I. Perel', Sov. Phys. -JETP 21, 227 (1965).
3.   P. R. Berman and W. E. Lamb, Phys. Rev. 187, 221 (1969).
4.   T. Yabuzaki, T. Endo, M. Kitano, and T. Ogawa, Opt. Commun. 22, 181 (1977).
5.   T. Endo, T. Yabuzaki, M. Kitano, and T. Ogawa, IEEE J. Quantum Electron. QE-14, 977 (1978).

ENERGY DEPENDENCE OF THE TOTAL CROSS SECTIONS

FOR $K(4^2P_{j_1 m_1} \longrightarrow 4^2P_{j_2 m_2})$ + He COLLISIONS

J.PASCALE and M.Y. PERRIN

Service de Physique Atomique - CEN.SACLAY,

B.P. N° 2, 91190 GIF-SUR-YVETTE (France)

The energy dependent cross sections for the Zeeman transitions within the 4^2P level of K induced by collisions with ground state He have been calculated from 0.00716 eV up to 1eV using a quantum-mechanical theory[1] and two pseudo-potentials.[2,3] The cross sections $\sigma_o(j_1 m_1 \rightarrow j_2 m_2)$ and $\overline{\sigma}(j_1 m_1 \rightarrow j_2 m_2)$ which are relevant to crossed-atomic beam and cell-type experiments, respectively, have been determined. The energy dependence of σ_o and $\overline{\sigma}$ are generally very different. In particular it has been found that, for the two pseudo-potentials used in the calculations, the Zeeman cross sections which have the largest contributions to the value of the $4^2P_{1/2} \rightarrow 4^2P_{3/2}$ fine-structure cross section are $\sigma_o(\frac{1}{2}\frac{1}{2} \rightarrow \frac{3}{2} - \frac{1}{2})$ from threshold up to about 0.7 eV and $\sigma_o(\frac{1}{2}\frac{1}{2} \rightarrow \frac{3}{2} - \frac{3}{2})$ above 0.1 eV, these two cross sections having different energy dependence; in contrast all the Zeeman cross sections $\overline{\sigma}(\frac{1}{2} m \rightarrow \frac{3}{2} m')$ contribute to the fine-structure cross section and have a similar energy dependence. Therefore one lays emphasis on the great importance to consider carefully the optical preparation and the geometry of the system, and to refer to the $\sigma_o(j_1 m_1 \rightarrow j_2 m_2)$ cross sections when data of a crossed-atomic beam experiment have to be compared with theoretical results. This is clearly shown in figure 1 where very different energy dependences of the $4^2P_{3/2} \rightarrow 4^2P_{1/2}$ fine-structure cross section from that of the conventional one obtained by assuming that any ($j = \frac{3}{2}$, m_j) sublevel is equally populated by the exciting-light (crosses) are observed for two particular geometries of a crossed-atomic beam experiment and of linearly polarized pulsed-laser-light. The He and K beams are crossed at right-angle and the relative velocity is changed by varying the velocity of the rare gas beam and keeping constant the velocity of the K-beam (with a kinetic energy fixed to 0.2 eV). The light beam of the pulsed-laser is perpendicular to the collision plane and one considers a Π-linearly polarized broad-line excitation of the $4^2P_{3/2}$ level, with the polarization axis either along the relative velocity (open circles) or along the K-beam (full triangles). The duration of the laser pulse is assumed to be short enough so that the hyperfine structure can be ignored.

Full results of the calculations will be presented and discussed at the conference, with comparison to experimental data.

REFERENCES

1/ R.H.G. REID, J. Phys. B : Atom. Molec. Phys. 6, 2018 (1973).

2/ W.E. BAYLIS (private communication, 1973).

3/ J. PASCALE and J. VANDEPLANQUE, J. Chem. Phys. 60, 2278 (1974).

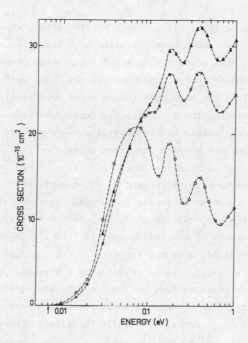

Figure 1. Conventional $4^2P_{3/2} \rightarrow 4^2P_{1/2}$ fine-structure cross section (crosses) for K-He collisions and those calculated for two particular geometries of a crossed-atomic beam experiment and of a pulsed-laser-light excitation (open circles and full triangles, see text).

CROSSED BEAM DETERMINATION OF ENERGY DEPENDENCE

OF FINE STRUCTURE TRANSITIONS IN K (4P) - He COLLISIONS

J.CUVELLIER, J. BERLANDE, C. BENOIT[+], M.Y. PERRIN, J.M. MESTDAGH, J.De MESMAY

C.E.N. SACLAY, Service de Physique Atomique, BP N° 2
91190 Gif-sur-Yvette (France).

+ Laboratoire de Collisions Atomiques et Moléculaires
Université de Paris XI Orsay.

Fine structure changing collisions of excited alkali atoms with unexcited atoms or molecules have been widely studied both experimentally and theoretically. It is clear that crossed beam experiments would check our understanding of these processes, often considered as the "simplest" inelastic atom-atom collisions. This has been done recently for some alkali-rare gas pairs[1-2-3]. For the K(4P)-He system, there exist a discrepancy between experimental data[3] and theoretical work [4]. This has stimulated a new experimental determination of the energy dependence of fine structure transition $K(4\,^2P_{1/2}) \rightarrow K(4\,^2P_{3/2})$ induced by collisions with helium atoms, in a wide energy range (0.07-0.4eV)[5].

A potassium nozzle beam is crossed at right angle with a helium oven-nozzle beam whose velocity is varied by varying the temperature of the oven[6]. The potassium beam has a velocity of 9.6×10^4 cm/s with a spread of 24%(FWHM); the velocity dispersion of the helium beam is 7 to 12% (FWHM). The atomic densities in the crossing zone are respectively 10^{12} at/cm^3 (He) and 10^9 at/cm^3 (K). The optical excitation is provided by a nitrogen pumped dye laser which illuminates the crossing zone perpendicularly to the collision plane. The intramultiplet mixing process is monitored by the sensitized fluorescence (SF) light ($4P_{3/2} - 4S_{1/2}$ transition) while the direct fluorescence (DF) light intensity is proportional to the excited $4P_{1/2}$ state population. A hight speed photon counting system allows to measure simultaneously DF and SF emissions , the latter being separated from the DF signal by two interference filters.

The polarisation and spatial anisotropy of the SF light due to partial aligment in the $P_{3/2}$ state after collision do not affect the data significantly (for our experimental geometry). The results are given on fig 1 in arbitrary units with their error bars. Very good agreement is found with previous work[3] in the range 0.07 - 0.12 eV but a discrepancy exists for $0.12 \leqslant E_r \leqslant 0.19$ eV. Furthermore we have observed that σ varies only slightly beyond 0.15 eV. These results are consistent with recent quantum mechanical calculations[4] of the process using different molecular potential (B69[8],B73[7] PV 74[9]) as reported on fig 1. The correspondance between molecular potentials and cross sections is complex. It has be shown however that the present work provides some test of the repulsive part of the available K(4P)-He molecular potentials in the range of   6-14 a.u. approximatively.

REFERENCES

1/   J.APT, D.A. PRITCHARD, Phys. Rev. Lett. 37, 91 (1976)

                          J. Phys. B 12, 83 (1979).

2/   W.D. PHILLIPS, C.L. GLASER, D. KLEPPNER, Phys. Rev. Lett. 38, 1018(1977).

3/   R.W. ANDERSON, T.P. GADDARD, C. PARRAVANO, J. WARNER, J. Chem. Phys. 64
     4037 (1976).

4/   R. OLSON, Chem. Phys. Lett. 33, 250 (1975).
     J.PASCALE (1975) Private communication.
     E. ROUEFF, J.M. LAUNAY, J. Phys. B 10 , L173 (1977).

5/   J. CUVELLIER et al. to be published.

6/   R. CAMPARGUE, M.A. GAVEAU, A. LEBEHOT, J.C. LEMONNIER, D. MARETTE (1979)
     Communication to the 7th Int. Symp. on molecular beams. Rival Del Garda
     (Unpublished).

7/   W.E. BAYLIS, J. Chem. Phys. 51, 2665 (1969).

8/   W.E. BAYLIS, (1973) Private communication.

9/   J.PASCALE, J. VANDEPLANQUE (1974) J. Chem. Phys. 60, 2278.

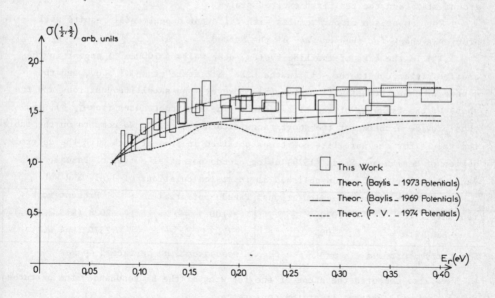

Fig.1. - Comparison between computed and measured
variations of $\sigma\left(\frac{1}{2}, \frac{3}{2}\right)$ versus collision energy.
All data are normalized to σ (0.072 eV).

MODEL POTENTIAL CALCULATIONS FOR LiNe, KNe AND KHe MOLECULAR SYSTEMS. OSCILLATIONS
IN VELOCITY DEPENDENT FINE STRUCTURE CHANGING CROSS SECTIONS

F. Masnou-Seeuws[+], C. Courbin-Gaussorgues[+] and M. Philippe[++]
[+]Laboratoire des Collisions Atomiques et Moléculaires, Bât.351
[++]Groupe d'Electronique dans les gaz. Institut d'Electronique Fondamentale,Bât.220
Université Paris-Sud, 91405 ORSAY FRANCE

The method developped by Valiron et al. (1979)[1] was used to compute the
molecular potential curves for the systems LiNe, KNe and KHe. The electron-alkali
ion interaction $V_a(r_a)$ was taken from Klapisch (1969)[2]. The electron-rare gas
interaction $V_g(r_g)$ was fitted to scattering data (Valiron et al., 1979[1], Philippe
et al., 1979)[3]. We took account of the three-body term V_3 introduced by Bottcher
and Dalgarno (1974)[4], and adopted the estimation of Sondergaard and Mason (1975)[5]
for the short-range core-core interaction $\mathcal{E}_c$. The one electron Schrödinger
equation :

$$\left(T + V_a(r_a) + V_g(r_g) + V_3(\underset{\sim}{r_a},\underset{\sim}{r_g},R)\right)\Psi = E(R)\Psi$$

was solved for each internuclear distance R using the computer code of Valiron
(1976)[6], and the potential energy $\mathcal{E}(R) = E(R) + \mathcal{E}_c(R)$ was determined for the
ground state and the ten first excited states.

The comparison of our results with different experimental results will
provide a check for the accuracy of the method.

1°) In the case of the LiNe system, deep wells ($>1000 cm^{-1}$) appear in the
excited states due to the well in the LiNe[+] $X^1\Sigma$ state at R=3.5 a.u., and thus
depending upon the estimation of $\mathcal{E}_c(R)$. However, the satellite positions and the
shape of the far wing of the Li resonance line are independant from $\mathcal{E}_c(R)$, and
thus provide a check for the short range accuracy of E(R). We compare on the table
the values for the satellite positions obtained in present work with the determination of Herman and Sando (1978)[7] using pseudo potential curves of Pascale and
Vandeplanque (1974)[8] and unpublished *ab initio* calculations of Janis and Wahl

	Ab initio calculations	Pseudo potential	Present work
red satellite	−2030	−2100	−2028 (R=3.2 a.u.)
blue satellite	5200	7703	2570 (R=4 a.)

Satellite positions (in cm⁻¹) for the Li resonance line perturbed by Ne.

We have also computed the shape of the far wing of the Li resonance line perturbed
by Ne, and will present it at the conference.

2°) In the case of the KHe system, we obtain a 200 cm^{-1} well in the $\Pi 4p$
state (see Fig. 1). The elastic total cross section for scattering by the $\Pi 4p$
state present glory oscillations which are sensitive to the estimation of the
short/range interaction $\mathcal{E}_c(R)$. The interpretation of the oscillations in the
velocity dependent fine-structure changing cross section :

$$K(4p^2P_{1/2}) + He \rightarrow K(4p^2P_{3/2}) + He$$

is in progress, will be presented at the conference and compared with the experimental results of Cuvelier et al.[9]

      3°) Structures appear in the Σ excited states for all the three systems, due to avoided crossings and very sensitive to the estimation of V_3. The most interesting case is the KNe case, where the $\sigma 5p$ and $\pi 5p$ curves (Fig.2) are tangent for $R \sim 8$ a.u. Oscillatory structures (Rosenthal-Bobashev effect) in the cross-section :

$$K(5p^2P_{1/2}) + Ne \rightarrow K(5p^2P_{3/2}) + Ne \qquad \text{are to be expected.}$$

References

1. P. Valiron, R. Gayet, R. McCarroll, F. Masnou-Seeuws, M. Philippe J.Phys.B 12 53 (1979)

2. M. Klapisch, Thesis, Université de Paris-Sud, unpublished (1969)

3. M. Philippe, F. Masnou-Seeuws, P. Valiron, J.Phys.B., in press (1979)

4. C. Bottcher and A. Dalgarno, Proc. Roy. Soc. A340, 187 (1974)

5. N.A. Sondergaard and E.A. Mason, J.Chem. Phys. 62, 1299 (1975)

6. P. Valiron Thèse de 3è cycle, Bordeaux, unpublished

7. P.S. Herman and K.M. Sando, J.Chem.Phys. 68, 1153 (1978)

8. J. Pascale and J. Vandeplanque, J. Chem.Phys. 60, 2278 (1974)

9. J. Cuvelier, J. Berlande, C. Benoit, M.Y. Perrin, J.M. Mestdagh, J. de Mesmay, XI ICPEAC, Abstracts of papers

Figure 1

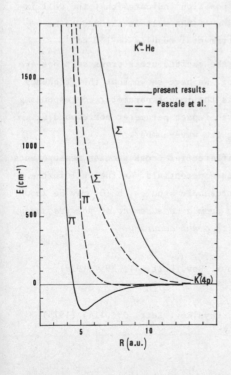

Figure 2

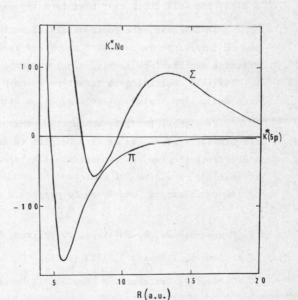

INTERFERENCE EFFECTS IN Na-Ne DIFFERENTIAL CROSS SECTIONS

F. Masnou-Seeuws[*], M. Philippe[**], E. Roueff[***] and A. Spielfiedel[***]

[*]   Laboratoire des Collisions Atomiques et Moléculaires, Bâtiment 351,
        Université de Paris-Sud, 91405 ORSAY Cedex, FRANCE

[**]   Groupe d'Electronique dans les gaz. Institut d'Electronique Fondamentale,
        Bâtiment 220, Université de Paris-Sud, 91405 ORSAY Cedex, FRANCE

[***]   Groupe de Recherches sur les Processus Atomiques et Moléculaires en Astro-
        physique, Département d'Astrophysique Fondamentale, Observatoire de Meudon,
        92190 MEUDON, FRANCE

We have computed the differential cross sections for Na(^{2}S and ^{2}P)-Ne
scattering, using the model potential results of Masnou-Seeuws et al. (1978)[1] for
the potential curves and the computer code of Launay (1976)[2] to solve the close
coupling equations.

The ground state cross sections σ_x reproduces well the experimental cross
section of Carter et al. (1975)[3] provided we assume a 8 mrd shift on the angle
scale (see fig. 1). The oscillations in the excited state cross section $\sigma^*_{3/2}$ are
then well reproduced (fig. 2). They are not affected by the ground state signal for
$\tau = E\theta > 510^{-4}$ a.u. Xrad.

We have interpreted the results in the framework of semi-classical scattering theory. The slow oscillation in the excited cross section is due to rainbow
scattering by the $A^2\Pi$ state. The experimental position indicates that the well is
deeper than the theoretical one. If the position of the well is assumed to be
5 a.u., the well depth that best fits the experimental results is 150 cm^{-1}.

In contrast, the rapid oscillations in the excited state cross sections are
due to interferences between Σ and Π scattering. We have shown that the frequency
of these oscillations is $k(b_\Sigma + b_\Pi)$ where b_Σ is the impact parameter corresponding
to classical scattering in direction θ and b_Π an impact parameter corresponding
to a deflection angle $-\theta$ (see fig. 3), k being the wave-number.

From these results, we conclude that differential cross section measurements
for similar systems can be very helpful to deduce potentials. As the well in the
$A^2\Pi$ potential curve can be determined by spectroscopic studies, $b_\Pi(\theta)$ may be known
so that *the repulsive $B^2\Sigma$ state can be deduced from a measurement of the frequency
of the oscillations, which can be performed with great accuracy.*

[1] F. Masnou-Seeuws, M. Philippe, P. Valiron, Phys. Rev. Lett. 41, 395 (1978).

[2] J.M. Launay, J.Phys.B 9, 1823 (1976).

[3] G. Carter, D. Pritchard, M. Kaplan, T. Ducas, Phys.Rev. Lett. 39, 1144 (1975)

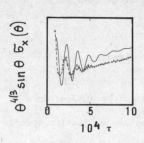

Fig. 1 – Ground state cross section σ_x; $\tau=E\theta$ in a.u. xrad. ; $E=5.10^{-3}$
—Theoretical results assuming a 10% velocity dispersion
---Experimental results shifted by $\Delta\tau=-4\times10^{-5}$ (arbitrary units)

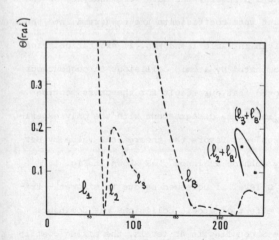

Fig.2 —— $\sigma^*_{3/2}-\sigma_x$ close coupling results.
---- $\sigma^*_{3/2}-\sigma_x$ close coupling results.
+++
o͞o͞o Experimental results of Carter et al. (1975) shifted by $\Delta\tau=-4\times10^{-5}$ (arbitrary units.) Circles and crosses correspond to different angular resolution .

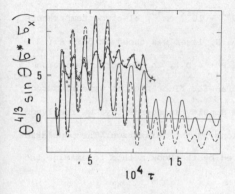

Fig. 3 – Classical scattering angle for elastic scattering by the $A^2\Pi$ and $B^2\Sigma$ potentials as a function of ℓ, relative angular momentum.

--- $\ell_1\ell_2\ell_3$ scattering by the $A^2\Pi$ potential
-·- ℓ_B scattering by the $B^2\Sigma$ potential
—— $\ell_2+\ell_B$ and $\ell_3+\ell_B$
■ Frequency of the rapid oscillations in the experimental cross section

Excitation Transfer between Excited Levels of He (n=3,4)
by Dye Laser Pumping

K. Fukuda , S. Oku and N. Yasumaru

Department of Engineering Physics, Faculty of Engineering,
Kyoto University, Kyoto 606, Japan

Collisional relaxation processes of excited states of He (n=3,4) in a He
glow discharge have been studied by time-resolved selective excitation spectroscopy with a short-pulse dye laser. The discharge conditions and plasma parameters are as follows: inner tube diameter 5 mm, pressure 2 - 8 Torr, discharge
current 20 - 80 mA, electron density $N_e = 10^{11} - 10^{12}$ cm^{-3}, electron temperature
$T_e = 3 - 5 \times 10^4$ K. The dye laser pumped by a N_2 laser was tuned at 5016 Å (2^1S
- 3^1P), 5876 Å ($2^3P - 3^3D$), or 4471 Å ($2^3P - 4^3D$). The temporal variation
and relative intensities of the direct and transfer fluorescences were measured
with a boxcar averager. By varying N_e and He density independently, we resolved
the effects of electronic and atomic collisions on the relaxation. The population
densities of pumped levels (n=2) were measured by the Hook method to examine the
radiation trapping of the fluorescences.

In the case of pumping to 3^1P and 3^3D levels, the data were analyzed on the
basis of the two-level model. Resultant rate coefficients are converted into the
averaged cross sections, which are given in Table 1 and Fig. 1; excitation transfer between 3^1P and 3^1D states was dominated by atomic collisions throughout our
discharge conditions. It should be noted that our result for the cross section
3^3D - 3^3P by electronic collision is in severe disagreement with the only experimental value by Wellenstein & Robertson[1] and favors the theoretical value by Herrick[2] and the semi-empirical value by Johnson & Hinnov[3], as shown in Fig. 1.

In the case of pumping to the 4^3D level, fluorescences due to singret - triplet transfer were observed, and the effect of atomic collisions was dominant.
On the assumption of breakdown of L - S coupling in 4F levels, the mixing coefficient[4] was utilized in the analysis. We also assumed only the $\Delta L = \pm 1$ transitions and the relationship of the detailed balance for them. The obtained cross
sections are presented in Table 1.

Table I. Excitation Transfer Cross Sections by Collision with Normal Atoms

	Transition	This exp.	Other exp.	Calc.
n = 3	$3^3D - 3^3P$	$1.0 ^+_- 0.8$	[a] $0.62 ^+_- 0.05$	[b] 0.95
$(\times 10^{-16} cm^2)$	$3^1P - 3^1D$	$22 ^+_- 10$	[a] $32 ^+_- 1$	
n = 4	$4^3D - 4^3P$	1.6	[c] 14	
$(\times 10^{-15} cm^2)$	$4^3D - 4^3F$	74	[c] 14	
	$4^3D - 4^1F$	14	[c] 5.1	

[a] H.F.Wellenstein and W.W.Robertson ('72)[1]

[b] J.S.Cohen ('76)[5]

[c] M.J.Shaw and M.J.Webster ('76)[6]

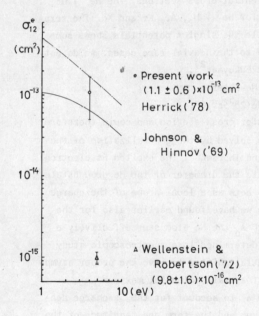

σ^e_{12}
(cm^2)

10^{-13}

• Present work
$(1.1 \pm 0.6) \times 10^{-13} cm^2$
Herrick('78)

Johnson &
Hinnov ('69)

10^{-14}

10^{-15}

▲ Wellenstein &
Robertson('72)
$(9.8 \pm 1.6) \times 10^{-16} cm^2$

1   10(eV)

Fig. 1

Excitation transfer cross section

($3^3D - 3^3P$) by collision

with electrons

1. H.F. Wellenstein and W.W. Robertson, J. Chem. Phys. 56, 1072 (1972).

2. D.R. Herrick, Molec. Phys. 35, 1211 (1978).

3. L.C. Johnson and E. Hinnov, Phys. Rev. 187, 143 (1969).

4. A.F.J. van Raan and H.G.M. Heideman, J. Phys. B. 7, L216 (1974).

5. J.S. Cohen, Phys. Rev. A. 13, 99 (1976).

6. M.J. Shaw and M.J. Webster, J. Phys. B. 9, 2893 (1976).

ENERGY TRANSFER BETWEEN METASTABLE HELIUM AND GROUNDSTATE NEON ATOMS

Hellmut Haberland and Peter Oesterlin

Fakultät für Physik der Universität Freiburg, Freiburg/Br., W. Germany

We have measured differential cross sections for collisions of $He(2^1S)$ and $He(2^3S)$ atoms with Ne atoms for several kinetic energies between 25 and 370 meV. Elastic and excitation transfer cross sections were obtained for both systems. An identification of the excited Neon configurations was possible via a kinematic analysis and TOF measurements, for those excited Neon states which are not too closely spaced. A detailed description of the apparatus is given in ref.[1].

Potentials for $He^* + Ne$ and $He + Ne^*$ were obtained from a simultaneous fit to the elastic and inelastic differential cross sections. The $He^* + Ne$ potentials show a similar behaviour as for $He^* + H_2$, Ar, Kr and Xe. The triplet potential is relatively smooth, while the singlet potentials shows some structure, but less pronounced compared to the heavier rare gases. We do not agree with the conclusions of Siska and Fukuyama[2].

The main pumping transition of HeNe-Laser

$$He(2^1S) + Ne \rightarrow He + Ne(2p^55s, {}^1P_1)$$

has by far the largest excitation transfer cross section and could therefore be treated as a 2-state problem. It was solved by the generalization of the Landau-Zener method proposed by Delos and Thorson[3]. The excited 5s electron of Neon has a mean radius of 20 a_o, while the diameter of the He groundstate atom is only 1.1 a_o. The small He atoms acts as a local probe of the charge density of the 5s electron, a behaviour we have found earlier also for the He^*-He potentials. Once inside of R ~ 20 a_o the He atom sees effectively a $He + Ne^+$ potential, which was recently determined in a spectroscopic study by Dabrowski and Herzberg[4]. This potential shifted to give the proper asymptotic energy gave only good agreement if a small potential maximum ($\Delta E = 10.8$ meV) was added around R = 20 a_o to account for the 5s charge density. The height and width of this maximum and the form and magnitude of the coupling matrix element between the $He^* + Ne$ and $He + Ne^*$ channels was treated as fitting parameters. A good agreement between the experimental and calculated differential cross sections is obtained. The total excitation transfer cross section calculated from this potential is given in Fig. 1. It agrees reasonably with flowing afterglow measurements of Arathoon. Note that the cross section in Fig. 1 is given in absolute units, although the differential cross section was not measured absolutely.

Excitation transfer to the higher Ne-states (4d, 4d', 4f, 4f' and 5p) was calculated by shifting the He + Ne$^+$ potentials appropriately and determining the coupling matrix elements by a fit to the elastic and inelastic cross sections.

[1] H. Haberland, K. Schmidt, J.Phys. B10, 695 (1977) and references cited therein.

[2] P.E. Siska, T. Fukuyama, X. ICPEAC, Paris 1977, Book of Abstracts, S. 552

[3] J.B. Delos, W.R. Thorson, Phys.Rev. A6, 728 (1972)

[4] I. Dabrowski, G. Herzberg, J.Mol.Spectr. 73, 183 (1978)

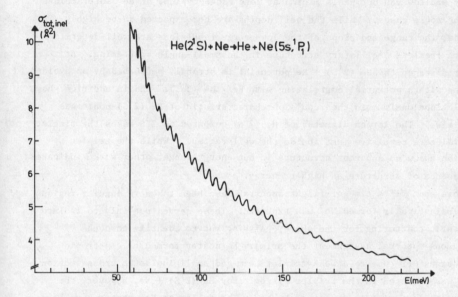

Fig. 1: Calculated excitation transfer cross section for the red line of the HeNe-Laser. The wavelength of the oscillations vary as the inverse of the velocity at the crossing point of the two potentials He* + Ne and He + Ne*.

$He^*(2^1S, 2^3S)$ + Ne DIFFERENTIAL SCATTERING:

ADIABATIC ENTRANCE CHANNEL POTENTIALS AND PRIMARY EXIT CHANNELS[**]

T. Fukuyama[***] and P. E. Siska

Department of Chemistry, University of Pittsburgh
Pittsburgh, Pennsylvania 15260, U.S.A.

Crossed atomic beam measurements of elastic and inelastic scattering angular distributions in the $He^*(2^1S, 2^3S)$ + Ne systems covering the energy range 0.02-0.12 eV have been used to extract entrance channel potentials in the adiabatic approximation. The resulting potentials are shown in Fig. 1. They display shallow van der Waals minima at long range typical of He^* interactions with the noble gases. While the well depths are not expected to be highly accurate, the range and slope of the low-energy repulsions are well-determined owing to resolved oscillatory structure in the small-angle scattering. At smaller distance the $He^*(2^1S)$ + Ne potential is strongly perturbed by an avoided crossing with a potential correlating with He + $Ne^*(3s_2)$,[1] and in addition shows a local slope maximum in the repulsion characteristic of $He^*(2^1S)$-noble gas potentials.[2] The larger diameter of $He^*(2^1S)$ compared to 2^3S makes the singlet potential more repulsive just inside the well region.[3] While the triplet repulsion shows no apparent structure in our energy range, other work[4] indicates the presence of structure at higher energy.

More than fifty time-of-flight spectra[5] have been taken in angular regions where inelastically formed Ne^* was expected. These served not only to isolate the elastic scattering for the above analysis, but to identify through unambiguous spectral assignment the primary Ne states formed by electronic energy transfer. Due to a weak triplet beam and small inelastic cross section, no Ne^* was detected in the triplet system. For $He^*(2^1S)$ + Ne, however, the wide-angle scattering is dominated by Ne^*. The following Ne^* states have been identified, with Q=E'-E (eV) values in parenthesis: $3s_2(-0.047)$, $3s_{4,5}(0.045, 0.056)$, $3s_1'^{-''''}(0.476$ to $0.479)$, $4d_{2-4}(-0.090$ to $-0.093)$. The endoergic states (Q<0) are not seen until above threshold. The exoergic states are not observed until the $3s_2$ channel opens, suggesting that they derive their intensity from $3s_2$. This might occur through crossings between these states at small distances. Formation of $3s_1'^{-''''}$ is surprising, since it is far off-resonance and requires a large electronic-to-translational energy conversion. Coupled channel analysis[1] is still in progress.

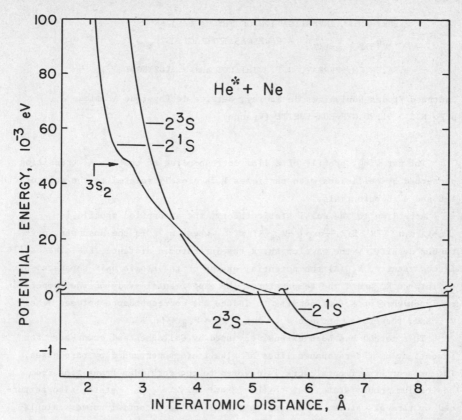

Fig. 1. Potentials for $He^*(2^1S, 2^3S) + Ne$. For 2^1S, $\epsilon = 0.00057$ eV and $r_m = 6.31$ Å; for 2^3S, $\epsilon = 0.00075$ eV and $r_m = 5.82$ Å. Note the change in scale at zero energy. The two curves are indistinguishable on this scale for $r > 6.8$ Å.

** Research supported by the U.S. National Science Foundation, the Petroleum Research Fund of the American Chemical Society, and the Alfred P. Sloan Foundation.

***Present address: Department of Chemistry, University of Tokyo, Tokyo, 113 Japan.

1. P. E. Siska and T. Fukuyama, X ICPEAC, Abstracts (Paris, 1977), p. 552.
2. D. W. Martin et. al., J. Chem. Phys. 69, 2833 (1978).
3. P. E. Siska, Chem. Phys. Lett. (1978), in press.
4. S. M. Trujillo, IX ICPEAC, Abstracts (Seattle, 1975), p. 437; G. Peach, J. Phys. B 11, 2107 (1978).
5. D. W. Martin et. al., J. Chem. Phys. 65, 3720 (1976).

EXPERIMENTAL INVESTIGATION OF THE Cs (7S) AND

Cs $(5D_{5/2}, _{m=1/2})$ - RARE GAS INTERACTION

B.SAYER, M. FERRAY, J.P. VISTICOT and J. LOZINGOT

Centre d'Etudes Nucléaires de Saclay, Service de Physique Atomique
B.P. N°2 - 91190 GIF-SUR-YVETTE (France).

The far wing profile of a line corresponding to the $A \rightarrow A^*$ transition perturbed by collisions with particles B is closely related to the molecular A-B and A^*-B potentials.

According to the quasi static theory, the absorption profile is

$K(\lambda) \sim n_A n_B \lambda^2 R^2 \, f(R) \frac{d\lambda}{dR} \exp \left[-V_{AB}(R)/kT \right]$ where $n_{A,B}$ is the absorber, perturber density, λ the wavelength, R the interatomic distance, f(R) the oscillator strength, $V_{AB}(R)$ the potential energy of the atomic pair separated by a distance R, and T the temperature. The experimental study of the temperature dependence of K (λ) permits to deduce the correspondance between λ and V_{AB} and, therefore, between V_{AB} and $V_{A^*B} = V_{AB} + hc/\lambda$.

This method has been extensively used by Gallagher and coworkers[1] for investigating the resonance lines of alkali atoms perturbed by rare gases. The present experimental work is devoted to the forbidden transition from the cesium ground state (6S) to the 7S and $5D_{5/2, m=1/2}$ state, also perturbed by rare gas atoms. According to the adiabatic potential curves calculated by a pseudo potential method, these two excited states are strongly coupled and their potential curves let appear a pronounced avoided crossing[2]. Consequently, the experimental determination of the relative positions of the two potential curves and their comparison with the theoretical predictions will be a very sensitive test of the calculations. The induced dipole moment is here a fast varying function of R, while it is not so for resonance lines. However, using the $V_{AB}(R)$ obtained by other methods (scattering experiments for example) we can determine $V_{A^*B}(R)$ and also f (R).

The absorption coefficient is determined by a sensitive laser fluorescence technique[3]. The experimental conditions are taken for avoiding the contribution onto the spectrum of both cesium dimers and cesium atoms interacting with two perturbers ($n_{Cs} \leqslant 10^{14}$ cm^{-3}, $n_{RG} \leqslant 2 \times 10^{19}$) . The explored temperature range is 180-410°C.

The results obtained show a progressive decrease of the repulsivity of the $Cs(5D_{5/2, m=1/2})$ -RG potential from Ne to Xe and in parallel an increase of the well depth of the Cs(7S) -RG potentials. Except for Ar, for which a relatively good agreement is found with the calculated curves, the 5D potentials appear less repulsive and the 7S more attractive than predicted. The proximity of these determined potential curves is found to be much larger than that calculated, in the investigated region (7-11 a.u.). Moreover the induced oscillator strengths of the 6S-7S and $6S-5D_{5/2, m=1/2}$ transitions have been determined and compared to the calculated values.

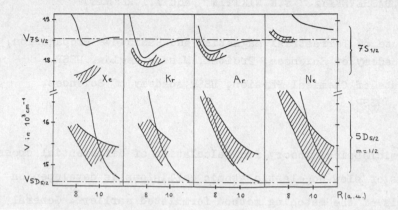

Fig.1. - Comparison of the present experimental results (hachured area) with the theoretical potential curves[2].

REFERENCES

1/   R. SCHEPS, Ch. OTTINGER, G. YORK and A. GALLAGHER, J. Chem. Phys. 63, 2581 (1975) and references therein.

2/   J. PASCALE and J. VANDEPLANQUE, J. Chem. Phys. 60, 2278 (1974).

3/   B. SAYER, M. FERRAY and J. LOZINGOT, J. Phys. B Atom. Molec. Phys. 12 227 (1979).

4/   J. PASCALE, J. Chem. Phys. 67, 204 (1977).

SEMICLASSICAL CALCULATION OF INTERFERENCE
EFFECTS IN SLOW NONELASTIC ATOMIC COLLISIONS

E.I.DASHEVSKAYA,[x] E.E.NIKITIN [≠] and A.I.REZNIKOV [≠]

[x]Institute of Terrestrial Magnetism and Radiowave Propagation,
USSR Academy of Sciences, Troitsk, Moscow Region, USSR
[≠]Institute of Chemical Physics, USSR Academy of Sciences,
Moscow, USSR

Semiclassical theory for calculation of differential cross
sections of slow nonelastic atomic collisions is developed on
the basis of the matching method formulated earlier[1]. General
formulas are specified for collisional processes in excited
alkali $M(^2P_j)$ - rare-gas $X(^1S_0)$ systems. In particular, the
following expression is obtained for the probability P of fine
structure mixing j=1/2-j=3/2 as a function of impact parameter b:

$$P_{1/2-3/2}(b)=2P_1(1-P_1)+(1-P_1)^2P_2-2P_1(1-P_1)(1-P_2)^{1/2}\cos\Delta\cos(\phi/2)$$

where P_1 and P_2 are the probabilities of mixing due to radial
and rotational motions of partners correspondingly, Δ is the
adiabatic action difference for the motion along the Π - and
Σ - terms of the quasimolecule $M(^2P_j)-X(^1S_0)$ ^{2}, ϕ is the angle
of the molecular axis rotation for the motion along the Σ -term[1].
In the figure shown are: the earlier quantum calculation[3] of
$P_{1/2-3/2}(b)$ for the system $Na(4^2P_j)$-He at the relative energy
0.04 ev with the pseudopotentials[4](full line) and our calculation
based on the obtained formula (crosses x). The probability P_1
is calculated using the exponential model[2] and the probability
P_2 is estimated taking account of terms up to the order $\Delta\epsilon^2$
where $\Delta\epsilon$ is the fine structure splitting.

It is seen from the figure that the semiclassical calculation
reproduces well the frequency of oscillations; the small difference
in amplitudes can be explained by the approximative treatment of
P_2 in our approach. The behaviour of $P_{1/2\rightarrow3/2}(b)$ at $b \geqslant R_1$, where
R_1 is the center of non-adiabaticity region for the radial
coupling[2], is not reproduced in our approach because the latter
neglects the transitions at $b \geqslant R_1$. In the same approximation we
have calculated $P_{1/2-3/2}(b)$ using the pseudopotentials[5](crosses +).
It is seen that in comparison with [4] the pseudopotentials [5]
lead to the smaller probability P_2 because the Π –terms[5] are
more repulsive and to the lower frequency of oscillations because
the Σ –term[5] is less repulsive than the corresponding terms[4].
Results of semiclassical calculations of differential cross
sections for $M(^2P_j)-X(^1S_o)$ systems are discussed.

1. E.I.Dashevskaya, E.E.Nikitin, Can.J.Phys.54, 789 (1976)

2. E.E.Nikitin, A.I.Reznikov, J.Phys.B:Atom.Mol.Phys.11,L659(1978)

3. R.H.G.Reid, J.Phys.B:Atom.Molec.Phys.6, 2018 (1973)

4. W.E.Baylis, J.Chem.Phys.51, 2665 (1969)

5. J.Pascale, J.Vandeplanque, J.Chem.Phys.60, 2278 (1974)

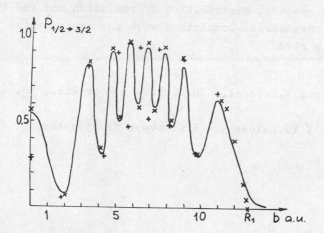

COLLISIONAL RELAXATION OF THE IODINE ATOM LEVELS
$5^2P_{1/2}$, $5^2P_{3/2}$

E.A.Yukov

P.N.Lebedev Physical Institute, Leninsky prospect 53, Moscow

Processes responsible for the relaxation of the sublevel of hyperfine structure of the ground term of atomic iodine (nuclear spin I=5/2) are considered. Collisional mixing of the sublevels of the ground state $5^2P_{3/2}$ differs substantially from the mixing of the sublevels of the excited state $5^2P_{1/2}$. Transitions between hyperfine sublevels of the ground state with electronic momentum J =3/2 are determined mainly by Van der Waals interaction [1]. Estimations show that in this case the cross-sections have only weak dependence on the kind of the perturbers and are of the order of 10^{-14} - $10^{-13} cm^2$. The cross-sections for transitions between the sublevels of the excited state $5^2P_{1/2}$ are, in contrast, strongly dependent on the perturbing particle. The most effective are the collisions with another iodine atom accompanied by a resonant transfer of the excitation energy. At thermal velocities the cross-section of such process is $\simeq 5.10^{-14} cm^2$. Estimation of the spin exchange cross-section in the case of collisions of the two excited iodine atoms gives the value $\simeq 5.10^{-15} cm^2$. In the case of collisions with spherically symmetric particles the cross-sections are smaller.

Collision induced radiative decay $5^2P_{1/2}$ - $5^2P_{3/2}$ is discussed. The spectral distribution of radiation and the total intensity are considered. Comparison with the experimental results [2] is given.

References
1. A.I.Okunevich, V.I.Perel, Zh.Eksper. i Teor.Fiz., 58, 666 (1970).
2. L.S.Ershov, V.Yu.Zalessky, Kvantovaya Elektronika, 5, 1139 (1978).

CLASSICAL MODEL FOR ELECTRONIC DEGREES OF FREEDOM IN
NON-ADIABATIC COLLISION PROCESSES

H. D. Meyer, C. W. McCurdy and W. H. Miller

Department of Chemistry, and Materials and Molecular Research Division
of the Lawrence Berkeley Laboratory, University of California
Berkeley, California 94720 U.S.A.

Theoretical models that describe some degrees of freedom quantum mechanically
(e.g., the electrons) and other degrees of freedom classically (e.g., translation,
vibration, rotation) can fail to describe certain features in the dynamics correctly because of this mixture of dynamical descriptions.[1] If one is to retain the
utility of describing the heavy particle motion classically, consistency then
demands that the electronic degrees of freedom also be described classically, and
we have recently[2] shown how this can be done.

It has been shown, for example, how a 2-state, 3-state, etc., quantum
mechanical system can be replaced by a classical system, i.e., by a classical
degree of freedom. In the two-state case, if $\{H_{i,j}\}$, i,j=0,1 is the diabatic
electronic Hamiltonian matrix, our model defines the classical electronic
Hamiltonian function as

$$H_{el}(n,q) = (1-n) H_{0,0} + n H_{1,1} + 2\sqrt{n(1-n)} \cos q\, H_{0,1} \quad ,$$

n and q being the classical action-angle variables for the electronic degrees of
freedom. Since the matrix elements depend parametrically on the nuclear positions
$\underset{\sim}{x}$, so does the classical electronic Hamiltonian, and the classical Hamiltonian
for the complete system, electronic and heavy particle degrees of freedom, then
has the form

$$H(\underset{\sim}{p},\underset{\sim}{x},n,q) = \frac{p^2}{2\mu} + H_{el}(n,q;\underset{\sim}{x}) \quad .$$

It is clear that in this approach the classical description need not refer to the
coordinates and momenta of individual electrons--although in the case of highly
excited Rydberg states this is the appropriate classical model--but in general to
a collective mode of the electronic degrees of freedom.

Applications have recently been completed for quenching of $F^*(^2P_{1/2})$ by
collision with H^+, Xe, and H_2, and the figure below shows the results for H^+.
The classical model in this case essentially corresponds to modeling $F(^2P)$ as
a rigid rotor, and the $^2P_{1/2} \rightarrow {}^2P_{3/2}$ transition is like a rotationally inelastic
process in an atom-diatom collision. In this case one sees that the results of
this completely classical model (points, with Monte Carlo error estimates) agree
quite well with the quantum mechanical results of Mies[3] (the solid curve).

This work was supported by the Division of Chemical Sciences, Office of
Basic Energy Sciences, U.S. Department of Energy under contract No. W-7405-Eng-48.

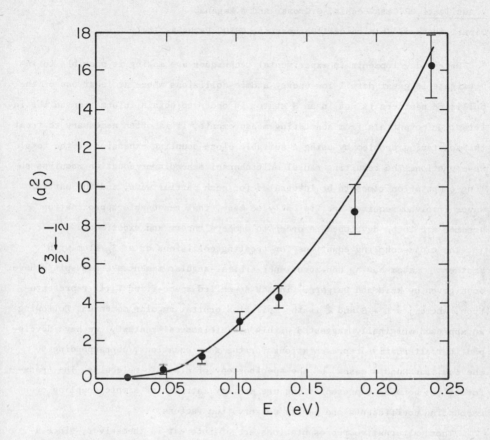

1. W. H. Miller, J. Chem. Phys. 68, 4431 (1978).
2. W. H. Miller and C. W. McCurdy, J. Chem. Phys. 69, 5163 (1978).
3. F. H. Mies, Phys. Rev. A 7, 957 (1973).

COUPLING SCHEMES AND DECOUPLING APPROXIMATIONS IN THE THEORY OF LOW ENERGY ATOMIC COLLISIONS[*]

V.Aquilanti, P.Casavecchia, G.Grossi and A.Laganà

Dipartimento di Chimica dell'Università, 06100 Perugia, Italy.

Recent developments in experimental techniques are making it possible to investigate in great detail low energy atomic collisions where at least one of the collision partners is not in an S state: in order to obtain information on the interaction potentials from scattering measurements, it is often necessary to treat the scattering problem by using a suitable close-coupling expansion of the total wavefunction. The resulting radial multichannel Schrödinger equation requires so long computation times to be integrated for each partial wave, and the partial waves involved required are tipically so many, that reasonable approximation schemes are to be developed in order to compare theory and experiment.

The close-coupling equations for treating collisions of a $^1S_0$ atom with another   atom having non-zero inner orbital angular momentum L and spin S have been given by Reid and Dalgarno[1] in the so-called space-fixed (j,ℓ) representation, where $\underset{\sim}{j} = \underset{\sim}{L} + \underset{\sim}{S}$ and ℓ is the collision orbital angular momentum. Following an approach originally suggested within a semiclassical context,[2] we have developed four alternative representations for the same equations, corresponding to the familiar Hund's cases of the spectroscopy of diatomic molecules. The transformations between representations are unitary matrices of simple coupling or recoupling coefficients and parity conservation factors.

These alternative representations are of interest in themselves, since a proper choice can lead to a simplification in the programming and/or in the saving of computer times. However, their main interest lies in the fact that a useful set of approximations can be developed by their means. We have explicitly considered two approximations which allow a partial decoupling of the equations: (i) Ω-conserving, obtained in the case c (j,Ω) representation, or in the case a (Ω,Λ) representation, assuming $\ell \approx J$. Here, Ω and Λ are the projections of j and L on the molecular axis, and J is the total angular momentum. This approximation is equivalent to the helicity-conserving decoupling schemes in the analo-

* Presented at the 11th ICPEAC, Kyoto, Japan, 1979. Work supported by Italian CNR and NATO Grants.

gous problem of collisional excitation of a rigid rotor; (ii) K-conserving, obtained in the case $\underset{\sim}{d}$ (ℓ, K) representation, or in the case b (K, Λ) representation, assuming $K \approx J$, where $\underset{\sim}{K} = \underset{\sim}{J} - \underset{\sim}{S}$. This approximation corresponds to spin-uncoupling[3] or, equivalently, to the assumption of degeneration of the atomic levels. A full decoupling is obtained by combining (i) and (ii), and leads to the so-called (iii) elastic approximation.[4]

Although the analysis itself allows an a-priori assessment of the validity of these approximations, we have developed computer programs which permit to carry out both the exact computations and the approximate ones in the various partial or full decoupling schemes. It is therefore possible to present a unified assessment of their reliability.

A further set of approximations which have been considered arises naturally by choosing the bests one of the five representations at each interatomic distance during the integration process. Since this choice can be unambiguously determined from the formalism, full decoupling approximations of a sudden type can be developed: however, more accurate results are obtained by allowing partial decoupling through a first-order Magnus method within the range of application of each representation. In these cases, it is possible to save drastically on computer time by using the JWKB method.

1. R.H.G.Reid and A.Dalgarno, Phys.Rev.Lett. 22, 1029 (1969).

   R.H.G.Reid, J.Phys. B 6, 2018 (1973).

   F.H.Mies, Phys.Rev. A 7, 942, 957 (1973).

   C.H.Becker, P.Casavecchia, J.T.Lee, R.E.Olson, and W.A.Lester, Jr. J.Chem.Phys., in press (1979).

2. E.I.Dashevskaya, F.Masnou-Seeuws, R.McCarroll, and E.E.Nikitin, Opt. Spektrosk. 37, 209 (1974). (Opt.Spectrosc. 37, 119 (1974).

   F.Masnou-Seeuws and R.McCarroll, J.Phys. B 7, 2230 (1974).

3. R.H.G.Reid and R.F.Franklin, J.Phys. B 11, 55 (1978).

4. C.Bottcher, T.C.Cravens, and A.Dalgarno, Proc.R.Soc. A 346, 157 (1975).

A MULTICHANNEL DISTORTED WAVE APPROXIMATION

Frederick H. Mies

Molecular Spectroscopy Division, National Bureau of Standards
Washington, D.C. 20234, U.S.A.

In formulating a molecular theory of atomic collisions using adiabatic electronic-rotational (AER) states[1] we have proposed a multichannel distorted wave approximation (MCDWA) which has proven very accurate[2]. This two state approximation incorporates the adiabatic effects of all other channels included in a close-coupling calculation, and is especially powerful in introducing essential perturbations caused by distant closed channels.

For example the inelastic, two channel coupling for the process $Hg(^3P_0)$ + $X(^1S_0) \rightarrow Hg(^3P_1) + X(^1S_0)$ can not be described, even below threshold, without including the molecular states associated with the $Hg(^3P_2)$ and the $Hg(^1P_1)$ asymptotes[3]. These states are essential in describing the strong spin-orbit interaction which dominates the collision process, and results in a calculation involving 6 channels for each parity. The matrix of radial functions $\{F_{ij}(R)\}$ are coupled by the symmetric 6x6 interaction matrix $\underline{U}(R)$ which includes the spin-orbit and the rotational coupling terms, i.e., $\underline{F}'' + \frac{2\mu}{\hbar^2}(E\underline{1}-\underline{U})\underline{F}=0$. Asymptotically the off-diagonal terms in $\underline{U}$ vanish and $U_{ii} \sim \ell_i(\ell_i+1)\hbar^2/2\mu R^2 + E_i^\infty$ where E_i^∞ are the channel state energies.

Using the MCDWA we can represent the coupling between channel i and j by the matrix element $r_{ij}(R)$ defined as follows

$$r_{ij}(R) = \int_o^R [f_i' \{\underline{M}'\underline{\tilde{M}}\}_{ij} f_j + f_i \{\underline{M}\,\underline{\tilde{M}}'\}_{ij} f_j']dR. \qquad (1)$$

$\underline{M}(R)$ is the orthogonal 6x6 matrix that diagonalizes $\underline{U}(R)$ at each interatomic distance R, $\underline{M}(R)\underline{U}(R)\underline{\tilde{M}}(R) = \underline{V}°(R)$, such that $\underline{M}(\infty)\sim\underline{1}$ and $\underline{V}°(\infty) \sim \underline{U}(\infty)$. The matrix $\underline{V}°(R)$ is diagonal and represents an adiabatic potential $V°_{ii}(R)$ for each channel. The functions $f_i(R)$ are solutions of the uncoupled equations, $f_i'' + \frac{2\mu}{\hbar^2}(E-V°_{ii})f_i=0$, and replace the usual distorted wavefunctions defined by $U_{ii}(R)$. f_i must vanish as $R\rightarrow 0$, and is required to approach $f_i \sim \cos\eta_i J_i + \sin\eta_i N_i$ as $R\rightarrow\infty$, where J_i and N_i are the conventional Bessel functions defined by the asymptotic wave number $k_i^2 = \frac{2\mu}{\hbar^2}(E-E_i^\infty)$, and the orbital angular momentum ℓ_i in channel i. All coupling effects have been transferred to $\underline{M}(R)$ which is required to be a continuous function of R such that the derivative M' exists. Note that the coupling between i and j in Eq. (1) involves a contraction over the entire set of channel states through the term $\{\underline{M}'M\}_{ij}$. It is in this sense that the approximation is multichannel.

If $k_i > 0$, then η_i is obviously the "elastic scattering" phase shift defined by the potential $V°_{ii}$. If both i and j are open channels the MCDWA predicts the following relationship between r_{ij} and the scattering matrix S_{ij},

$$|S_{ij}|^2 \overset{\sim}{=} 4|r_{ij}(\infty)|^{2ij} \quad i \neq j \tag{2}$$

$r_{ij}(\infty)$ is closely related to the reactance matrix element K_{ij}, and the R-dependence in Eq. (1) allows us to determine the explicit regions of inter-atomic distance where inelastic couplings are most dominant. The results of close-coupled calculations of the $^3P_0 \rightarrow ^3P_1$ cross-sections for Zn, Cd, and Hg have been compared to the MCDWA and indicate quantitative agreement for $|S_{ij}|^2 \leq 0.1$.

If $k_i < 0$, then channel i is closed and f_i is generally divergent, <u>except</u> when $(-1)^{\ell}i + \tan \eta_i = 0$. Since $\eta_i = \eta_i(E)$ this condition defines the eigenvalues $E = E_{i,\,n}$ which exist whenever V°_{ii} is attractive and sufficiently deep to support bound states. The MCDWA yields the following approximation for the partial width of state $E_{i,\,n}$ into the open channel j,

$$\Gamma_j(E_{i,n}) = -\frac{\partial E}{\partial \tan \eta_i} 4|r_{ij}(\infty)|^2 \tag{3}$$

These quantities are evaluated at $E = E_{i,\,n}$. Using the Levinson theorem for the potential V°_{ii} we find that $-\partial E/\partial \tan \eta_i$ may be approximated by the mean vibrational <u>spacing</u> $\overline{\Delta E}_{i,\,n}$ in the vicinity of the nth eigenvalue, and near threshold, we may relate the partial width to the inelastic matrix element S_{ij} just above threshold,

$$\Gamma_j(E_{i,\,n}) = \overline{\Delta E}_{i,\,n}|S_{ij}|^2 \tag{4}$$

Both Eq. (3) and the more speculation Eq. (4), have been compared to the close-coupled predissociation widths for the 1_u^- states of Hg_2, Cd_2, and Zn_2, and yield excellent results when $|S_{ij}|^2 < 0.1$.

The MCDWA was explicitly derived for use with molecular AER states which describe the adiabatic change in Hund's coupling in the course of collisions between atoms. However, it should be recognized that the MCDWA is closely related to the Gordon algorithm[4] for solving close-coupled equations and the theory may be of general use in many types of close-coupled calculations.

1. F. Mies, submitted to J. Molec. Spectrosc.

2. P. S. Julienne and F. Mies, submitted to Chem. Phys. Lett.

3. F. H. Mies, W. J. Stevens and M. Krauss, J. Molec. Spectrosc., <u>72</u>, 303 (1978).

4. R. Gordon, J. Chem. Phys. <u>51</u>, 14 (1969).

COLLISIONAL BROADENING OF OPTICAL
TRANSITIONS TO METASTABLE LEVELS*

E. N. Fortson

Department of Physics, University of
Washington, Seattle, Washington U.S.A.

In connection with optical-rotation experiments[1] designed to measure parity
non-conservation in atomic magnetic-dipole (M_1) transitions, we have begun studies
of the effect of atomic collisions on the line width and line shape of optical M_1
absorption to metastable levels. A major feature is the absence of resonance dispersion collisions[2], which normally through allowed E_1 emission dominate the line
shape at a high density of absorbing vapor. Instead, effects of electron-exchange
collisions become far more important than is usual in optical transitions.

We have devised a simple theory of collisional broadening for this case,
which predicts a number of potentially observable effects, some depending upon
the presence of nuclear spin and resolved hyperfine structure, and others having
to do with possible instances of collisional narrowing or merging of components
of a line.

Our experimental work thus far has been on the 8757 Å M_1 absorption line between the two lowest states of atomic bismuth. Our light source, a gallium-
arsenide tunable laser diode operating CW in a single-mode[3], readily resolves the
individual doppler-broadened hfs components of the line. Collisions are studied
in two ways, by their effects on the absorption profile and on the Faraday
Rotation[1] pattern associated with the absorption.

Introducing He buffer gas produces an increase in linewidth of about 8 MHz/
torr(He) at the 1100-1200 °C bismuth oven temperatures used. This size of
collisional broadening is reasonable for atoms such as bismuth with an unfilled
p shell. As the bismuth density is increased, some evidence appears of Bi-Bi
collisional broadening of about 10 MHz/torr(Bi). The interpretation is unclear,
however, because of the presence of Bi_2 molecules in addition to Bi atoms.

Clearer interpretation should be possible in studies now underway with M_1
(and E_2) transitions among the lower-lying levels of Pb and Tℓ. Both elements
have negligible numbers of molecules, and in the case of Pb, isotopes with and
without nuclear spin may be used.

*Work supported by NSF Grant No. PHY-7805897.

1. L. L. Lewis <u>et al</u>., Phys. Rev. Lett <u>39</u>, 795(1977). E. N. Fortson in Neutrinos-78 (Edited by E. C. Fowler) p. 417 Purdue University (1978).

2. S. Y. Ch'en and M. Takeo, Rev. Mod. Phys. <u>29</u>, 20(1957).

3. Lasers manusfactured by Mitsubishi Electronics and by Hitachi Ltd. See: H. Namizake, ITTT J. Quan. Elect. <u>11</u>, 427(1975); A. Aiki <u>et al</u>, Appl. Phys. Lett. <u>30</u>, 649(1977).

OBSERVATION OF THE INDUCED-DIPOLE TRANSITIONS FOR ALKALINE-EARTH ATOMS
COLLIDING WITH RARE GAS ATOMS

Kiyoshi Ueda, Takashi Fujimoto, and Kuniya Fukuda

Department of Engineering Science, Kyoto University
Kyoto 606, Japan

When a probing radiation field is applied during an atomic collision, information on the atomic state of the system and even on the interaction Hamiltonian
may be obtained from the absorption spectrum of the radiation.

For barium perturbed by collisions with rare gas atoms, we have observed the
induced-dipole transitions associated with $6s^2 {}^1S_0 - 6snd {}^1D_2$ (n=8, 9, and 10). An
example of the absorption spectrum is shown in Fig. 1. The typical experimental
conditions are as follows: a barium vapor is generated in a heat pipe oven containing rare gas atoms of $[X]=10^{17}-10^{18} cm^{-3}$, the product of barium density [Ba]
and the absorption length L were measured by the hook method and it was typically
$10^{17} cm^{-2}$ for temperatures of ~1200°K. Limited resolution of our monochromator
(~0.1Å) prevented us from measuring the detailed absorption profile $\exp\{-k(\nu)L\}$,
instead we measured the total absorption $A=\int_{line}[1-\exp\{-k(\nu)L\}]d\nu$. Figure 2 shows
that the absorption increases in propotion to [X] as well as to [Ba]. This implies
that the observed absorption is caused by two-body collisions between barium and
rare gas atoms. The effective oscillator strength per unit perturber density:

$$\frac{f_{CID}}{[X]} = \frac{mc}{\pi e^2} \int_{line} \frac{k(\nu)L}{[X][Ba]L} d\nu$$

has been deduced from Fig. 2, where the opacity effect of the absorption has been
corrected for to give the dashed lines. The result is summarized in Table 1.

Remarkable facts of the observation are as follows: 1) the transition is observed only for ${}^1D_2$ levels which have a closely lying ${}^1P_1$ level, resulting in the
satellite-like appearance of the absorption as shown in Fig. 1. 2) The absorption
begins at the wavelength corresponding to the unperturbed atomic transition and
increases toward the longer-wavelength side, to reach the maximum. The wavelength
difference is also given in Table 1 as "shift". 3) The dependence of $f_{CID}/[X]$ on
polarizability (α) of the perturbing gas is stronger than quadratic as seen in
Table 1.

The first point suggests that the observed induced-dipole transitions may be
interpreted from mixing of the closely-lying ${}^1P_1$ state into the ${}^1D_2$ state. This
mixing is the result of interaction in the barium-rare gas system. The interaction
is represented by the operators, for example, V_{dd} (dipole of barium and dipole of
rare gas atom) and V_{qd} (quadrupole-dipole) applied successively. This results in
the interaction of R^{-7} dependence, where R is the internuclear distance. The second point requires the interaction to be shorter-range than R^{-5} according to the
quasistatic approximation; the above interaction meets this requirement. The third

point, however, suggests that other interaction than assumed above may be operative.

A theory[1] has been proposed so far, in which the induced transition process is interpreted from a successive application of V_{qd} and V_r (radiation field). However, the result is inconsistent with our observation.

We will also present the result for calcium.

Table 1. Induced-dipole transitions from $6s^2\ {}^1S_0$

	$f_{CID}/[X]\ (10^{-23}cm^3)$			shift (cm^{-1})		
perturber $\alpha\ (\mathring{A}^3)$	Ar 1.63	Kr 2.465	Xe 4.01	Ar 1.63	Kr 2.465	Xe 4.01
$6s8d\ {}^1D_2$	0.205±0.010	1.84 ±0.11	6.63 ±0.30	- 4.3	- 8.3	-13.5
$6s9d\ {}^1D_2$	0.36 ±0.09	2.00 ±0.34	5.77 ±0.88	- 2.4	- 3.0	- 4.1
$6s10d\ {}^1D_2$	0.18 ±0.07	1.21 ±0.36	3.39 ±0.90	- 5.0	- 1.9	- 2.7

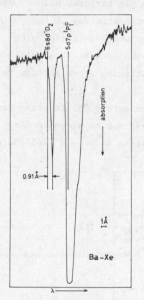

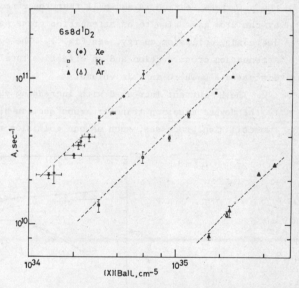

Fig. 1. Absorption for the induced-diple transition. [Xe] and [Ba]L are $1.03\times10^{18}cm^{-3}$ and $1.16\times10^{17}cm^{-2}$. Wavelengths corresponding to unperturbed atomic transitions are indicated by bars.

Fig. 2. The total absorption in frequency units. o, □, and △ refer to the temperature of ~1200°K or [Ba]L≈$1\times10^{17}cm^{-2}$, and ● and ▲ to ~1300°K or [Ba]L≈$3\times10^{17}cm^{-2}$.

1. A. Gallagher and T. Holstein, Phys. Rev. A 16, 2413 (1977)

SINGLE AND DOUBLE ELECTRON TRANSFER CROSS SECTIONS FOR PROTONS ON ATOMIC AND MOLECULAR TARGETS

John S. Risley and R.D. Britt[*]

Department of Physics, North Carolina State University
Raleigh, North Carolina   27650   USA

Absolute single and double electron transfer cross sections have been measured for protons on the rare gas atoms He, Ne, Ar, Kr and Xe and the diatomic molecules H_2, N_2 and O_2 for collision energies between 250 eV and 10 keV.

The ion beam was extracted from a duoplasmatron ion source, magnetically mass analyzed and passed through a static gas cell. An electrostatic deflector placed behind the gas cell separated the H^+ and H^- ion components. The ion beam was measured using long Faraday cups. The gas density was determined from measurements using a capacitance manometer.

The proton current was attenuated as the gas density was increased. For sufficiently low gas pressures, the attenuation signal yielded the single electron transfer cross sections σ_{10}. For He and Ne gas targets, below 2 keV, the σ_{10} cross section is so small that the effects of scattering of the protons by the atom gave rise to an attenuation cross section which increased with decreasing collision energy, see Fig. 1. The correspondence between this attenuation cross section and an effective total scattering cross section is discussed elsewhere in this volume.

The H^- current increased with increasing gas pressure. The increase was due to the double electron transfer cross section σ_{1-1} and due to second-order two-collision processes, such as one collision resulting in $H^+ \rightarrow H^0$ and the other

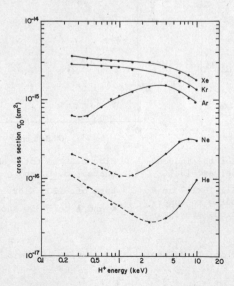

Fig. 1. Single electron transfer cross sections for protons on the rare gases.

in $H^o \to H^-$. If the σ_{1-1} cross section is sufficiently small, the second-order processes can significantly influence the pressure dependence of the H^- signal even for low gas densities. Since the H^- current depends linearly on the product of σ_{1-1} and the pressure and quadratically on the pressure and the product of a combination of charge charging cross sections, all data were used for a fit of a general polynomial of second degree in the pressure. The coefficient of the linear term gave the σ_{1-1} cross section.

The accuracy of the present measurements is estimated to be better than 10% for σ_{10} and better than 25% for σ_{1-1}. Comparison of the present results with previous measurements shows agreement between recent investigations but not with early studies.

This work was supported in part by the Research Corporation, the North Carolina Science and Technology Committee and the Atomic, Molecular and Plasma Physics Program of the National Science Foundation.

*Present address: Department of Physics, University of California, Berkeley, California.

CHARGE EXCHANGE AND EXCITATION IN He^{2+} - He COLLISIONS IN THE keV RANGE

C. Harel and A. Salin

Laboratoire d'Astrophysique, Université de Bordeaux I, 33400 Talence, France

We have studied the He^{2+} - He collisions in the keV energy range. We use the straight line impact parameter method. The electronic wave function is expressed as a time dependent linear combination of products of one-electron-diatomic-orbitals (OEDM) defined as the state of one electron in the field of two fixed nuclei.

The time dependent Schrödinger equation for the wave function Ψ describing the evolution of the system is :

$$(H_{e\ell} - i\frac{d}{dt}) \Psi (r_1, r_2, t) = \left| H(1) + H(2) + \frac{1}{r_{12}} - i\frac{d}{dt} \right| \Psi (r_1, r_2, t) = 0 \tag{1}$$

$$\text{where } H(i) = -\frac{1}{2}\nabla_{r_i}^2 - \frac{2}{r_{Ai}} - \frac{2}{r_{Bi}} \tag{2}$$

and r_{Ai} and r_{Bi} are the position vector of electron i with respect to the nuclei A and B. We expand the wave function Ψ as :

$$\Psi (r_1, r_2, t) = \sum_n a_n (t) \chi_n (r_1, r_2, t) \tag{3}$$

The functions χ_n are symetrized (singlet states) or antisymetrized (triplet states) combinations of the following basis states :

Gerade basis states	Ungerade basis states
$1s\sigma.1s\sigma \pm 2p\sigma.2p\sigma$	$1s\sigma.2p\sigma$
$1s\sigma.3d\pi \pm 2p\sigma.2p\pi$	$1s\sigma.2p\pi \pm 2p\sigma.3d\pi$
$(1s\sigma.3d\sigma-1s\sigma.2s\sigma) \pm (2p\sigma.4f\sigma-2p\sigma.3p\sigma)^{*}$	$(1s\sigma.4f\sigma-1s\sigma.3p\sigma) \pm(2p\sigma.3d\sigma-2p\sigma.2s\sigma)^{*}$
$2p\pi.2p\pi \quad (\Delta)$	

Each orbital is chosen as the eigen function of H(i). By introduction of (3) in (1), one obtains coupled equations whose diagonal matrix elements are of two different types.

-dynamic coupling (radial or rotational) : they can be expressed in terms of couplings between OEDM.

-electronic coupling : the matrix elements of $1/r_{12}$ between the basis states.

Both type of couplings have been calculated exactly. We give below our results for the total one electron and two electron charge exchange cross sections. Agreement with experiment is very good.

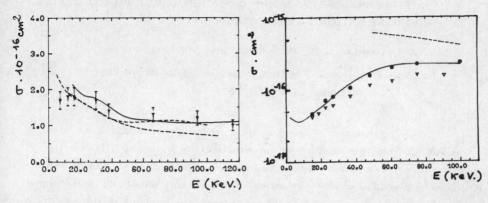

Figure 1

Figure 2

Two electrons charge exchange :

⥮ Experimental results of Berkner et al[4]

▬▬▬ Experimental results of Afrosimov et al[3]

▬▬▬ This work

▬▬▬This work (without inclusion of the basis states marked with a star in the table)

One electron charge exchange :

● this work

▽ this work (without inclusion of the basis states marked with a star in the table)

▬▬▬Experimental results of Afrosimov et al[3]

▬ ▬ ▬ Atomic calculations of Muckerjee et al[5]

The charge exchange probability as a function of energy for a fixed scattering angle is in excellent agreement with the results of a configuration interaction by Lopez et al[2]...

1. A. Salin, Computer Physics Comm. 14, 121 (1978)

2. V. Lopez, A. Macias, R.D. Piacentini, A. Riera and M. Yanez, J. Phys. B11, 2889 (1978)

3. V.V. Afrosimov, G.A. Leiko, Yu. A. Mamaev, M.N. Panov (1975) Sov. Phys. JETP 40, 661

4. K.H. Berkner, R.V. Pyle, J.W. Stearns, J.C. Warren,(1968) Phys. Rev. 166, 44

5. S.C. Muckerjee, K. Roy, N.C. Sil (1973). J. Phys. B6, 467

INNER-SHELL ALIGNMENT OF ATOMS DUE TO ELECTRON CAPTURE IN ION-ATOM COLLISIONS

E.G. Berezhko, N.M. Kabachnik and V.V. Sizov

Institute of Nuclear Physics, Moscow State University;
Moscow 117234; USSR

The alignment of the vacancy in the inner shell of an atom, resulting from the capture of an electron by incoming H^+ and He^+ ions has been examined. The calculations performed in the Brinkman-Kramers approximation for a number of atoms and subshells have shown that electron capture leads to a considerable alignment of the vacancy. The dependence of the degree of alignment upon the incident particle energy in the case of electron capture is significantly different from that due to the direct Coulomb ionization. It has been fow ned that the alignment resulting from electron capture can significantly contribute to the total alignment in the region of incident particle velocity V comparable with the atomic electron velocity V_{2p} . To investigate the sensitivity of the degree of alignment to the wave functions used, we have compared with results of the calculations using the hydrogen like wave functions with those involving the Herman–Skillman functions.

As an example, Fig. 1 gives the degree of alignment $(i+c)$ of the $Mg^+(2p^{-1}_{3/2})$ ion formed in a collision between the Mg atom and the proton, which has been calculated taking into account both direct ionization (i) and electron capture (c) . The calculation has been made using the Herman–Skillman wave functions. The degree of alignment due to the direct ionization was taken from ref.[1] . Fig. 1 shows that the consideration of the electron capture improves the agreement between theory and experiment [2] and makes it possible to account for the difference in the experimental data on ionization by protons and He^+ ions.

REFERENCES

1. E.G. Berezhko et al. J. Phys. **B11**, L421 (1978).
2. M. Rødbro et al.   J. Phys. **B11**, L551 (1978).

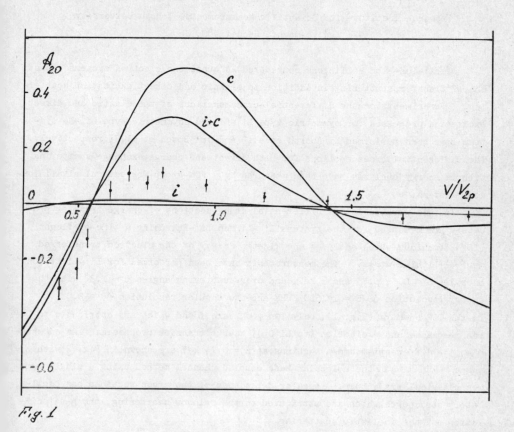

Fig. 1

TOF EXPERIMENT ON THE Li ATOM STATES PRODUCED IN CHARGE TRANSFER:
Li^+-Li AND Li^+-Na

N. Shimakura, S. Kita, T. Okamoto, Y. Sato, and H. Inouye

Research Institute for Scientific Measurements, Tohoku University

19-1 Sanjyo-machi, Sendai 980, Japan

Alkali ion-atom collisions considered as quasi-one electron systems cause charge transfer scattering in addition to elastic and direct excitation scattering.   Experiments on the differential cross sections of the elastic and direct excitation processes for symmetric type Li^+-Li and asymmetric type Li^+-Na systems have been performed by Aberth et al.[1] and von Busch et al.[2], respectively. The differential cross sections for both direct and charge exchange scattering without energy analyses have been measured by a FOM-group for several alkali ion-atom systems.[3]

In this work, relative differential cross sections of charge transfer processes are measured for the systems Li^+-Li and Li^+-Na, using a time-of-flight (TOF) technique which analyzes the kinetic energy of the electron transferred neutral Lithium atoms.   The measurements have been performed for Li^+-Li at ion energies E = 0.5, 0.75 and 1 keV, and over scattering angles θ = 1.3° with the energy resolution $\Delta E/E$ = 1/1500 FWHM and the angular resolution $\Delta\theta \simeq$ 0.03°. In the TOF spectra (Fig. 1), only two peaks are found which are attributed to the resonance and excitation (to Li(2p)) charge transfer processes.   As an example, the differential cross sections at E = 0.75 keV are shown in Fig. 2 with those calculated by the molecular base coupled channel method using a single common classical trajectory.   Angular dependence of the cross sections has oscillatory structures which are attributed to the rainbow scattering, the g-u oscillation and the inelastic scattering.

Similar experiments have been performed for Li^+-Na at ion energy E = 1 keV. The TOF spectra of this system indicate, in contrast to the case of Li^+-Li, that the intensity of Li(2p) exceeds that of Li(2s) for large scattering angles ($\geq$ 0.10°).   The measurement is extended to other energies with expectation that it will elucidate the mechanism of the Demkov transition.

Our calculated results for the Li^+-Li system have suggested that the excitation from Li(2s) to Li(2p) due to the rotational coupling occurs efficiently in a small range around the turning point.

The potential in calculating a single common trajectory for Li^+-Li was assumed to be the averages of the Σ_{gl} and Σ_{ul} states and of the Σ_{ul} and Π_{ul} states for the resonance and excitation charge transfer, respectively.   More elaborate calculations for Li^+-Li and Li^+-Na systems using semi-classical method will be presented at the Conference.

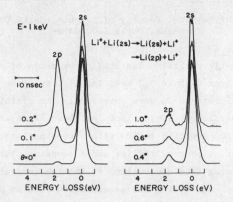

Fig. 1.
TOF spectra of fast Li atoms produced in charge exchange
reactions of fast Li$^+$ with stationary Li at ion energy
E = 1.0 KeV.

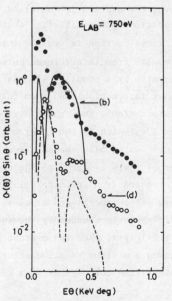

Fig. 2.
Reduced differential cross section as a
function of reduced scattering angle at ion
energy E = 1.0 KeV. Solid and open circles
are the experimental cross sections for the
resonance and excitation charge exchange
processes, respectively. Solid and dashed
curves are the calculated cross sections
for the resonance and excitation charge exchange, respectively.

References

1. W. Aberth et al., Phys. Rev. Lett., 24, 345 (1970).

2. F. von Busch et al., Chem. Phys. Lett., 35, 372 (1975).

3a. R. W. Wijnaendts van Resandt et al., Chem. Phys., 20, 107 (1977).

3b. R. W. Wijnaendts van Resandt et al., Chem. Phys., 26, 223 (1977) ; 29, 151 (1978).

INTERFERENCE BEHAVIOR OF OPTICAL EXCITATION FUNCTION IN Li$^+$- He COLLISION

Seiji Tsurubuchi, Tetsuya Masuda and Tsuruji Iwai

Department of Physics, Faculty of Science, Osaka University
Toyonaka, Osaka 560, Japan

The Li$^+$- He inelastic collision was studied by means of optical spectroscopy at the ionic energies from 0.45 to 4.2 keV. The Li I emission lines such as the transitions 2p→2s, 3d→2p and 4d→2p were observed in the visible region. Absolute measurements of the emission cross-sections for these lines were made by a synchronous-single-photon-counting method with a combination of a light chopper, a grating monochromator, a photomultiplier and a counting system. In order to eliminate an error arising from fluctuation of the ion current, a charge-integrator was used for controlling the accumulation time of photons.

Figure 1 represents the energy dependence of the emission cross-sections for Li I 2p→2s (6707.85 A) and 3d→2p (6103.5 A). An oscillatory structure is clearly observed for the transition 2p→2s, while no detectable oscillation is seen for the 3d→2p, which is in cascading relation to the 2p→2s. Another cascading transition 4d→2p is observed, but its emission cross-section is much smaller than those for the above two transitions. Therefore, the oscillation observed is considered to be due to the charge-exchange excitation to the Li($1s^2 2p$) state.

The oscillation phenomenon in the total cross-section is usually interpreted in terms of the Rosenthal-Foley model[1]; it results from interference between two inelastic channels, which are populated coherently by a coupling with an incoming channel at small internuclear separations(inner interaction) and then interact with each other at large separations(outer interaction). When the position of the peak in the cross-section was plotted against 1/v, which is the inverse of the relative velocity of the nuclei, the peak order was equally spaced, as shown by closed circles in Fig. 2. Here the peak order of 5 was assigned to the closed circle which first appears as the velocity decreases from infinite velocity; the straight line was obtained from a least-square fit to the closed circles. The slope gives the area between the two inelastic channels bounded by the two interaction regions. It is estimated at (57.43 ± 1.04) eV·A, when the average potential energy is assumed to be 30 eV; this energy gives a minimum relative error in the slope. An open circle deviated from the straight line corresponds to a broken arrow in Fig. 1.

Excitation of the Li($1s^2 2p$) state is well explained in terms of the rotational coupling between 2pσ and 2pπ molecular orbitals of the quasimolecule formed in the present collision[2]. At the energy range studied, the one-electron process, Li$^+$($1s^2$) + He($1s^2$) → Li($1s^2 2p$) + He$^+$($1s$), is a dominant process for excitation of Li($1s^2 2p$); the molecular state $(1s\sigma)^2 (2p\sigma)(2p\pi)$ $^1\Pi$ is populated by 2pσ→2pπ rotational coupling. This inelastic channel is strongly coupled with another channel terminating to Li$^+$($1s^2$) + He($1s2p$) because of an excitation sharing between the quasi-degenerate 2p-levels of Li and He. Under the radial coupling scheme, the two channels can be assigned as the $(1s\sigma)^2(2p\sigma)(2p\pi)$ $^1\Pi$ and the $(1s\sigma)^2(2p\sigma)(3d\pi)$ $^1\Pi$ states. Therefore, if the two $^1\Pi$ states are coherently populated by rotational couplings such as $2p\sigma{\rightarrow}2p\pi$, $2p\sigma{\rightarrow}3d\pi$ (inner interaction), the oscillatory structure observed is explained.

A similar oscillation for the He I $2p{\rightarrow}1s$ transition will be then expected to be in antiphase with the oscillation observed because of the sharing mentioned above. This was confirmed with a VUV spectroscopy. Detection of the He 584 A-line was made by use of a counting system with a vacuum monochromator and a channeltron multiplier. The optical excitation function for the transition $2p{\rightarrow}1s$ shows an oscillation indeed. The dip position of the corresponding structure is presented by triangle symbols in Fig. 2. The figure indicates that the two oscillations are in 180° out of phase with each other. The small amplitude of the oscillation observed suggests that the transition probability for $2p\sigma{\rightarrow}3d\pi$ is much small compared with that for $2p\sigma{\rightarrow}2p\pi$.

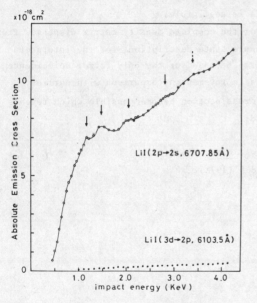

Fig. 1

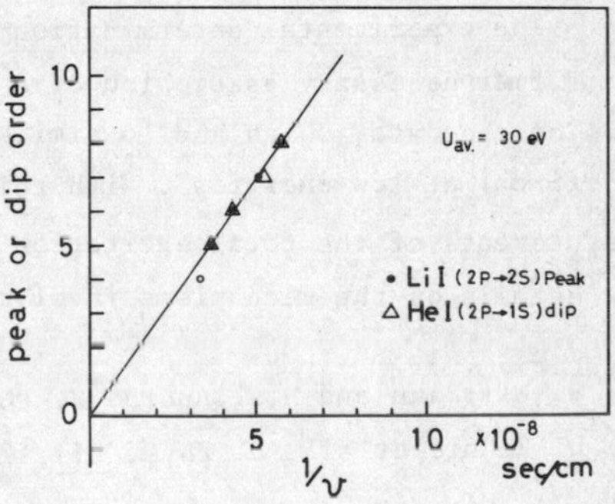

Fig. 2

1. H. Rosenthal and H.M. Foley, Phys. Rev. Lett. 23, 1480 (1969); H. Rosenthal, Phys. Rev. A4, 1030 (1971).

2. V. Sidis, N. Stolterfoht and M. Barat, J. Phys. B10, 2815 (1977).

He I 3^3P DENSITY MATRIX FROM MEDIUM ENERGY He$^+$-Ne COLLISSIONS WITH IMPACT PARAMETER SELECTION.

H.J. Andrä, H. Winter, R. Rauchfuß

Fachbereich Physik, Freie Universität Berlin, Berlin, Germany

A quasi coincidence method selective to impact parameters has been employed to determine the complete density matrix of the He I 3^3P excited term after He$^+$(1s) + Ne(2p^6) → He I (3^3P) + Ne$^+$ (?) collision processes for the He$^+$ energies from 5 to 355 keV.

Making use of the repulsive scattering potential at medium energies and of the lifetimes of the excited term to be observed one can select a certain impact parameter by observing the light emitted only from such atoms which are scattered into a certain solid angle off the central beam[1]. By measuring the complete state of polarization of this emitted light at two different angles with respect to the scattering plane the determination of all density matrix elements of the excited term becomes possible. For the particular term chosen here the influence of cascades and quantum beats on the results is negligible.

The experimental determination of the complete density matrix dispenses from the former necessary assumption of a pure state description[1] for the interpretation of the data, which had to similarly be used for the only former coincidence experiment at low energies[2]. With this improvement a comparison with earlier measurements of the total excitation cross section becomes possible which reveals new details on the mechanisms involved.

1   W. Wittmann and H.J. Andrä. Z. Phys. A288, 335 (1978).
2   L. Zehnle et al., J. Phys. B11, 2865 (1978).

SPECTROSCOPIC STUDIES OF COLLISIONS BETWEEN RARE-GAS ION OR LIGHT-ATOM ION AND
RARE GAS AT 1-10 keV ENERGY RANGE

Rei Okasaka and Kuniya Fukuda

Department of Engineering Science
Kyoto University, Kyoto, Japan

Electron temperature of helium plasma produced by a Z-pinch discharge, total
energy of which is less than 1 kJ, is about 5 eV. When a small amount of light-
atom molecular gas is mixed with the plasma as impurity, XUV radiation from the
multiply charged ions, such as CII-IV, NII-V, and OII-VI, is observed (ref.2).
It is difficult to interpret the mechanism of the generation of the multiply
charged ions only by collisions of such low energy electrons, and the charge transfer on atomic and ionic collisions are to be examined. The selective excitation
is inferred from the fact that the emission from the states including outer 2s-
vacancy are much stronger than the emission from the states of 2p-valence electron
(ref.1), and the charge exchange also plays important role in the process.

Energy of the particles is a few keV in the contracting current sheet of the
Z-pinch plasma. The atomic and ionic collisions in this energy range can be analysed by the quasimolecular model, and emission cross section of certain transitions have characteristic dependence on colliding energy.

In the present experiment, the ion beam extracted from "duodehcatron" ion
source is focused by two Einzel lenses and a set of deflector into a collision
chamber. The radiation from the collision chamber is observed with a visible-uv
and a VUV monochromator.

Figure 1 shows the emission cross sections of ArII at He^+-Ar collision as a
function of ion energy. The data are compared with the results by F. J. de Heer
et al. (ref.2). The cross section of $\lambda\,920A$ $3s^2 3p^5 - 3s3p^6$ line has a maximum at ion
energy of about 7 kV. The maximum can be explained by the adiabatic criterion of
Massey (ref.3) and, then, the channel of charge exchange to lead to the 3s-vacancy
production is seen for this transition. The cross section of other line from
upper level formed by two electron transitions increases, as ion energy decreases.
The maximum existing at energy of less than 1 kV can not be explained by the
adiabatic theory, and the effect of potential curve crossing for the states concerned should be taken into account.

The emission cross sections of NII and HeI at N^+-He collision are shown in
Fig.2. The maxima of the cross section predicted by the adiabatic criterion are
observed at about 5.5 kV for the $\lambda3437.2A$ line of NII and at about 7 kV for the
$\lambda5875.6A$ line of HeI.

In order to obtain the excitation function of the levels of the outer 2s-shell
electron excitation of NII, spectroscopic measurement in VUV region is in progress.
The observed results for CII and OII will be also presented.

References

1. K. Fukuda and H. Suemitsu, J. Phys. Soc. Japan <u>43</u>, 2109 (1977).

2. F. J. de Heer, B. F. J. Luyken, D. Jaecks, and L. Wolterbeek Muller, Physica <u>41</u>, 588 (1969).

3. H. S. W. Massey and E. H. S. Burhop, <u>Electronic and Ionic Impact Phenomena</u>, (Clarendon Press, Oxford, 1952), pp513-514.

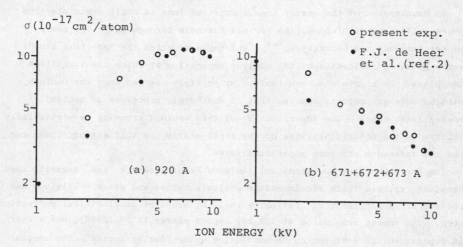

Fig. 1 The emission cross sections of ArII at He$^+$-Ar collision.
(a) λ919.8A $3p^5 {}^2P^0-3p^6 {}^2S$. (b) λ670.9A $3p^5 {}^2P^0-3d^2D$, $\lambda\lambda$671.9 and 672.9A $3p^5 {}^2P^0-4s^2D$. The data of present experiment are fitted to the results by de Heer et al. at 9 kV.

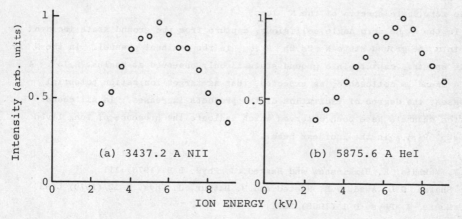

Fig. 2 The emission cross sections of NII and HeI at N$^+$-He collision.
(a) NII $2p3s\,{}^1P^0-2p3p\,{}^1S$. (b) HeI $1s2p\,{}^3P^0-1s3d\,{}^3D$.

COLLISION SPECTROSCOPY OF DOUBLY CHARGED NITROGEN IONS

J.B. Hasted[‡] S. Sharma[+], D. Mathur[‡] and T.N. Solovyev*

*Department of Physics, Birkbeck College, Malet Street, London WC1E 7HX
[+]Department of Physics and Astronomy, University College London,
Gower Street, London WC1E 6BT

By measurement of the energy loss spectra of ions in small angle electron capture collisions with atoms, the various channels through which the charge transfer proceeds can be analysed[1,2]. The angle at which the "spectral line" appears gives an indication of the nuclear separation at which the transition takes place. In single electron capture by multiply charged ions the Coulomb repulsion between products ensures that in exothermic processes an avoided crossing takes place. The separation R_x of this avoided crossing is particularly sensitive to the polarizabilities of the final states, so that its magnitude can allow the inference of these polarizabilities.

The curve-crossing spectrometer[1] includes Penning source, 180° magnetic mass separation, uniform field electrostatic analysis before and after collision, and selection and measurement of scattering angle by means of an electrical deflection system. The energy resolution at 1.7 keV impact energy is 2V (FWHM), but a four-fold improvement is achieved by deconvolution using Fourier series[3]. The angular resolution is 0.07^o FWHM and the accuracy 0.004^o.

Spectra have been taken at 0°, 0.008^o, $o.15^o$ and 0.26^o for N^{2+} ions in He, Ne, Ar, Kr, Xe, N_2, O_2, NO and the channels assigned. Figures 1, 2 illustrate the He and Ne zero angle spectra of the N^+ ions.

In the N^{2+}He zero angle collisions, capture from the ground state incident ions into the ground state N^+ $2s^2 2p^2 {}^3P_{0,,1,,2}$ is the dominant channel. In the N^+Ar and Kr spectra, capture into ground state is only observed at angles $\geqslant 0.15^o$. A marked trend is noticeable, as expected, that as target ionization potential decreases, the degree of excitation of the products increases. In all cases reaction channels have been observed which indicate the presence of long lived N^{2+} $2s2p^2 {}^4P_{\frac{1}{2},\frac{3}{2},\frac{5}{2}}$ in the incident beam.

1. Y.Y. Makhdis, K. Birkinshaw and Hasted, J. Phys. B 9 (1976) 111.
2. S. Sharma, G.L. Awad, J.B. Hasted and D. Mathur, J. Phys. B 12 (1979) L163.
3. L. Moore, J. Phys. D 1 (1968) 237.

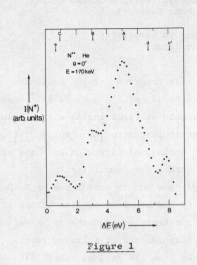

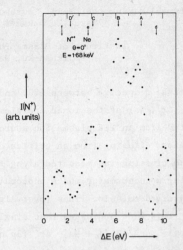

Figure 1   Figure 2

Figure 1

N^+ energy spectrum for N^+He collisions at $\theta=0^\circ$, 1.70 keV.

A $N^{2+}2s^22p\ ^2P^O_{\frac{1}{2},\frac{3}{2}}$ +He$^1S_0 \rightarrow N^+2s^22p^2\ ^3P_{0,1,2}$+He $1s^2S_{\frac{1}{2}}$ + 5.01 eV

B $\rightarrow N^+2s^22p^2\ ^1D_2$+He$^+1s\ ^2S_{\frac{1}{2}}$ + 3.12 eV

C $\rightarrow N^+2s^22p^2\ ^1S_0$+He$^+1s\ ^2S_{\frac{1}{2}}$ + 0.95 eV

c' $N^{2+}2s2p^2\ ^4P_{\frac{1}{2},\frac{3}{2},\frac{5}{2}}$+He$^1S_0\rightarrow N^+2s^22p^2\ ^1S_0$+He$^+1s\ ^2S_{\frac{1}{2}}$ + 8.05 eV

d $\rightarrow N^+2s2p^3\ ^5S^O_2$+He$^+1s\ ^2S_{\frac{1}{2}}$ + 6.24 eV

e $\rightarrow N^+2s2p^3\ ^3D^O_{3,2,1}$+He$^+1s^2S_{\frac{1}{2}}$+ 0.70 eV

Figure 2

N^+ energy spectrum for N^{2+}Ne collisions

A $N^{2+}2s^22p\ ^2P^O_{\frac{1}{2},\frac{3}{2}}$+Ne$^1S_0 \rightarrow N^+2s^22p^2\ ^3P_{0,1,2}$+Ne$^{+2}P^O$ + 8.05 eV

B $\rightarrow N^+2s^22p^2\ ^1D_2$ +Ne$^{+2}P^O$ + 6.15 eV

C $\rightarrow N^+2s^22p^2\ ^1S_0$+Ne$^{+2}P^O$ + 4.00 eV

D' $\rightarrow N^+2s2p^3\ ^5S_2$ +Ne$^{+2}P^O$ + 2.20 eV

e $N^{2+}2s2p^2\ ^4P^O_{\frac{1}{2},\frac{3}{2},\frac{5}{2}}$+Ne$^1S_0\rightarrow N^+2s2p^3\ ^3D^O_{3,2,1}$+Ne$^{+2}P^O$+ 3.74 eV

f $\rightarrow N^+2s2p^3\ ^3P^O_{0,1,2}$+Ne$^{+2}P^O$+ 1.60 eV

ELECTRON CAPTURE INTO ArII EXCITED STATE BY Ar^{2+} IMPACT ON Na (0.2-12 keV)

Atsushi Matsumoto*, Seiji Tsurubuchi*, Tsuruji Iwai*, Shunsuke Ohtani,
Kazuhiko Okuno** and Yozaburo Kaneko**

Institute of Plasma Physics, Nagoya University
Chikusa-ku, Nagoya 464, Japan

Emission spectra between 2800 and 6000 A were observed for the collision system (Ar^{2+}, Na) at the ionic energies from 0.2 to 12 keV. A beam of Ar^{2+} ions extracted from an ECR-plasma ion source was crossed at right angles with a beam of Na atoms effusing from an orifice of a temperature-controlled oven. Radiation from the crossing was measured along the third orthogonal direction by means of a grating monochromator and a photomultiplier with a d.c. amplifier.

Observed emission lines (over eighty lines) are due to ArII lines or Na D lines. This fact indicates that single-electron-capture into excited states of projectile, $Ar^{2+}(3p^4) + Na \rightarrow Ar^{+*}(3p^4nl) + Na^+$, takes place remarkably as well as direct excitation of target atoms. Absolute measurements of emission cross-sections were made for the emission lines coming from the ArII nl-states(nl = 4p, 4p', 4d, 5s). The spectral sensitivity of the detection system was determined by comparison with a tungsten ribbon lamp calibrated by NBS. The beam intensity of target atoms was obtained by use of a method of deposition and atomic absorption. The estimated accuracy was smaller than ±50 % for absolute measurements and ±15 % for relative ones.

The excitation cross-section for the j-th term of the nl-state $Q_j(nl)$ follows from the emission cross-sections observed. Values of the transition probability and the lifetime were referred to Wiese, Smith and Miles[1], and Fink, Bashkin and Bickel[2]. Corrections were made for cascade effects. The result obtained at 4 keV is as follows.

[exothermic reaction]: $Q(4p) = 3.20 \times 10^{-15} cm^2$, $Q(4p') = 1.51 \times 10^{-15} cm^2$;
[endothermic reaction]: $Q(4d) = 0.38 \times 10^{-15} cm^2$, $Q(5s) = 0.6 \times 10^{-17} cm^2$.

Here $Q(nl)$ means the sum of Q_j over all the terms of the nl-state. The total electron-capture cross-section was estimated from measurements of the ion-current attenuation to be $\lesssim 11 \times 10^{-15} cm^2$ at 4 keV within an error of ±50 %. It turns out that (i) cross-sections for the exothermic reactions are larger than those for the endothermic ones, and (ii) the sum of the cross-sections for electron-capture into the excited states observed is comparable with the total electron-capture cross-section.

*Permanent address: Department of Physics, Faculty of Science, Osaka University, Toyonaka, Osaka 560.

**Permanent address: Department of Physics, Faculty of Science, Tokyo Metropolitan University, Setagaya-ku, Tokyo 158.

Next we are concerned with the relative population distribution among the terms of the ArII 4p-state. Although there is some difference between the two distributions at 4 keV and 8 keV, the ^{4}D term is most populated and the ^{2}S term least, as seen in the column $\underline{a}$ of Table 1. Such a relative population observed can be interpreted in terms of statistics based on the building-up principle of the molecule. In Fig. 1, $(Ar,Na)_i^{2+}$ denotes possible molecular states arising from the initial atomic pair, $Ar^{2+}(^3P) + Na(^2S)$, and $(Ar,Na)_f^{2+}$ from the final one, $Ar^+(4p) + Na^+(^1S)$. Under the radial coupling scheme, the state $^2\Sigma^-$ correlates to the state $^2\Sigma^-$, $^2\Pi$ to $^2\Pi$, and so on. We assume that donor channels having the same number as that of sublevels of the initial molecular state (figure in parens. ()) are opened to the final state and are divided equally between the transition-allowed terms (arrows), and that the acceptable channel number (figure in parens. []) is proportional to the relative population among the product terms. This is the present statistics. The relative population estimated in this way is in agreement with the experimental one, as seen in Table 1. A similar statistical consideration is applied successfully to the case of the 4p'- and 4d-states.

The observed relative population among the fine-structure states, however, seems to be in proportion to the statistical weight (2J+1) for all the terms of the 4p-, 4p'- and 4d-states; it is governed by statistics for the product atomic system only. This fact suggests that redistribution of the population among the multiplets occurs during the collision time. The redistribution may be caused by another type of coupling, i.e., spin-orbit recoupling in the atomic region rather than in the molecular region.

Table 1. Excitation cross-section $Q_j(4p)$ in 10^{-16} cm^2 and relative population among the terms; $\underline{a}$:experimental, $\underline{b}$:statistics.

Term	(4keV)		(8keV)		
	Q_j	$\underline{a}(\%)$	Q_j	$\underline{a}(\%)$	$\underline{b}(\%)$
^{2}S	1.66	5	3.18	6	5.6
^{4}S	7.31	23	6.85	12	11.1
^{2}P	4.07	13	7.70	13	11.1
^{2}D	5.27	16	11.00	19	16.7
^{4}D	9.56	30	20.12	35	33.3
^{4}P	4.17	13	8.41	15	22.2

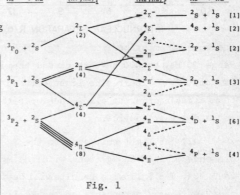

Fig. 1

1. W.L. Wiese, M.W. Smith and B.M. Miles, Atomic Transition Probabilities vol. 2, NSRDS-NBS 22 (1969).

2. U. Fink, S. Bashkin and W.S. Bickel, J. Q. S. R. T. <u>10</u>, 1241 (1970).

CHARGE TRANSFER IN Mg^{++}-Mg COLLISIONS

P. Bisgaard, T. Andersen, E. Horsdal Pedersen, and B.Vinther Sørensen
Institute of Physics, University of Aarhus
DK-8000 Aarhus C, Denmark

Recent studies[1] of single- and double-charge-transfer cross sections σ_{21} and σ_{20}, respectively, for the Mg^{++}-Mg system have revealed a pronounced interference structure in σ_{20} as a function of the projectile energy. A model[1] based upon interference at large internuclear distances $(R \simeq 9a_o)$ between the two amplitudes for resonant charge transfer originating from scattering in the two channels (i) Mg^{++}-Mg($3s^2$) and (ii) $Mg^+(3p)$-$Mg^+(3s)$ has been able to account for the observed structure in σ_{20}. The theoretical cross sections are, however, a factor of 2.5 smaller than the experimental ones.

Potential-energy curves for the $(Mg-Mg)^{++}$ system are shown in the figure[1]. At large R, states (1) and (2) separate into atomic configurations Mg^{++}-Mg($3s^2$) (E = 0.0) and $Mg^+(3p)$-$Mg^+(3s)$ (E = -2.97 eV), respectively. At smaller separations,

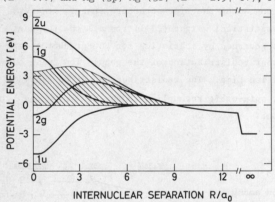

where the energy curve splits into two components corresponding to the formation of symmetric (g) and asymmetric (u) molecular states, the figure represents a rough estimate only. The hatched area indicates the mean-energy difference between the two channels.

We are at present performing a more detailed test of the phase-interference model by measuring the optical emission from the Mg^{++}-Mg collision. Mg^{++} ions with energies in the range 20 keV to 800 keV are passed through a Mg($3s^2$) vapour target at a pressure of about $2 \cdot 10^{-4}$ torr. The light emitted is observed at 54.7^o with respect to the beam axis in order to allow the separation of spectral lines belonging to the target and the projectile.

All the light emitted from the Mg^{++}-Mg collision can be attributed to the presence of excited Mg^+ ions with the Mg II($3p\rightarrow3s$) transition accounting for more than 90%. The following results will be presented at the conference: (A) The magnitude and energy dependence of the Mg II($3p\rightarrow3s$) emission cross section, which are predicted by the model to be equal to the σ_{21} cross section, (B) the ratio between the Mg II($3p\rightarrow3s$) emission cross sections for the projectile and target, respectively, which the model predicts to be $\sim$9 over the energy region studied, and (C) the polarization of the Mg II($3p\rightarrow3s$) transition. The model neglects the π states correlating with the $Mg^+(3p)$ state.

The preliminary data obtained for (B) and (C) require the model to be extended.

1. E. Horsdal Pedersen, J.V. Mikkelsen, J. Våben, and K. Taulbjerg,
   Phys.Rev.Lett. <u>41</u>, 1541 (1978)

STUDY OF THE OPTICAL EMISSION IN QUASI-TWO-ELECTRON SYSTEMS:
Mg(3s^2), Mg(3s3p^{3}P)-He, Ne, Ar AND Mg$^+$-Na, 1-80 keV

P. Bisgaard, T. Andersen, and B. Vinther Sørensen

Institute of Physics, University of Aarhus
DK-8000 Aarhus C, Denmark

We report measurements of total cross sections and polarizations for emission of the optical radiation from three types of systems, all characterized by the presence of two valence electrons outside closed shells: Mg(3s^2)-He, Ne, Ar, Mg(3s3p^{3}P)-He, Ne, Ar, and Mg$^+$-Na. The neutral Mg beams are generated through charge exchange of Mg$^+$ ions in Mg vapour for production of Mg(3s^2), in Na vapour for production of Mg(3s3p^{3}P). The content of Mg(3s3p^{3}P) in the applied beams is determined by means of an optical method based upon the validity of the Wigner-spin conversion rule for low-energy collisions.

Mg(3s^2)-He, Ne, Ar. These systems exhibit properties similar to those observed in the quasi-one-electron Mg$^+$ – rare-gas systems[1,2]. Figure 1 compares

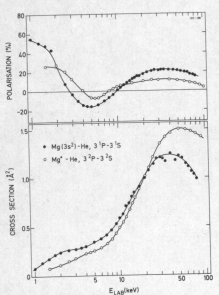

the dominant inelastic process in Mg-He and Mg$^+$-He collisions, the excitation of the resonance 3s3p^{1}P and 3p^{2}P levels, respectively. The energy defect is nearly the same in these two processes. The polarizations show close resemblance, taking the fine-structure effect for the ^{2}P$\rightarrow^2$S transition into account. For the quasi-symmetric Mg-Ne system, one-and two-electron excitations of the target are important. Only one-electron excitations have been seen for the projectile.

Mg(3s3p^{3}P)-He, Ne, Ar. Excitation of the Mg-3p electron to 3d or 4s is the dominating inelastic process at lower energies. At energies above ∿10 keV, excitation or ionization of the Mg-3s electron leading to Mg(3p^2 ^{3}P) or Mg$^+$(3p) also plays a significant role. The changes in the location of the cross-section maximum are in accordance with the Massey criterion. The total excitations for Mg(3s^2) and Mg(3s3p^{3}P) - rare-gas systems are comparable in the investigated energy range. For the Mg-Ne collision, the Mg(3s3p^{3}P) → Mg(3s3p^{1}P) excitation is observed.

Mg$^+$-Na. The dominant processes are the charge-exchange reactions leading to Mg(3s3p^{3}L) states. Charge exchange to singlet states and excitation of the Mg-3s and/or the Na-3s electron are observed too. Further results will be reported at the conference.

1. N. Andersen, T. Andersen, and K. Jensen, J.Phys.B:Atom.Molec.Phys. 9, 1373 (1976)

2. S.E. Nielsen and J.S. Dahler, J.Phys.B:Atom.Molec.Phys. 9, 1383 (1976); Phys.Rev. A 16, 563 (1977)

OUTER-SHELL EXCITATIONS OF Zn II LEVELS IN Zn$^+$-He, Ne, Ar, Kr COLLISIONS

B. Andresen and E. Veje

Physics Laboratory II, H. C. Ørsted Institute
Universitetsparken 5, DK-2100 Copenhagen Ø, Denmark

We have studied outer-shell excitations of Zn II levels (ground state configuration KLM 4s) in the collisions Zn$^+$-He, Ne, Ar, Kr, by means of optical spectrometry, in the projectile energy range 10 - 100 keV. For comparison excitation of Zn II levels by sputtering and beam-foil interaction are also being carried out.

In the gas collisions we observe that the relative cross section for different levels of the same Rydberg term series decreases faster than a power law as a function of the effective quantum number of the excited term, see Fig. 1. This is different from results of previous ion-atom collision studies[1], in which the relative cross sections were found to be proportional to $(n^*)^p$, where n* is the effective quantum number, and p is in the range $-5 < p < -3$, close to -3 at the highest collision energies[1]. The ion-atom results given in Fig. 1 differ from the beam-foil excitations[2], shown at the bottom of the figure. These follow the same power law seen previously in beam-foil excitations[3].

Relative cross sections are in Fig. 2 plotted versus the orbital angular momentum quantum number of the excited level, the data shown are all for levels with principal quantum number n = 5. We note that in the Zn$^+$-He, Ne collisions distinct maxima exist for p and d levels respectively, whereas the cross sections are almost equal for p, d, and f levels in the Zn$^+$-Ar collision, and the cross section increases with the orbital angular momentum quantum number in the Zn$^+$-Kr collision. This behavior is different from earlier studies[4] in which it was generally found that the cross section increases from s through d levels and decreases for f and g levels.

The monochromator used has been put at our disposal by the Danish Natural Research Science Foundation, which is gratefully acknowledged.

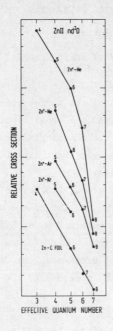

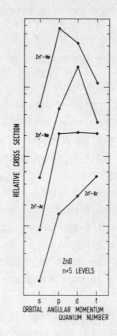

Fig. 1.
Relative cross sections for
Zn II d levels versus the
effective quantum number.

Fig. 2.
Relative cross sections for Zn II
levels with n = 5 versus the
orbital angular momentum quantum
number.

References
1.   B. Andresen, K. Jensen, N.B. Petersen, and E. Veje, Phys. Rev.
      A 15, 1469 (1977).
2.   S. Hultberg, L. Liljeby, A. Lindgård, S. Mannervik, S. E.
      Nielsen, and E. Veje, Phys. Lett. 69A, 185 (1978).
3.   B. Dynefors, I. Martinson, and E. Veje, Physica Scripta 13, 308
      (1976).
      E. Veje, in Proceedings from the Vth International Conference
      on Beam-Foil Spectroscopy, Lyon 1978.
4.   B. Andresen and E. Veje, Phys. Rev. A 16, 1980 (1977).

ADDITIVE RULE IN THE CHARGE-CHANGING PROCESS OF HE BEAM

Akio Itoh, Masatoshi Asari and Fumio Fukuzawa

Department of Nuclear Engineering, Faculty of Engineering,
Kyoto University, Yoshida, Kyoto 606, Japan

When the energy of incident particle is high enough, the target molecule is
assumed to appear as an assembly of individual atoms, and the cross sections for
the molecule are the simple sum of each cross section for the single atom.
This additive rule in the charge-changing process have been shown experimentally
to hold for hydrogen,[1,2] but not for iodine[3] projectiles.

We measured the growth curves of charge fractions of 0.7-2.0 MeV $He^{0,1+,2+}$
beams passing through various gases; H_2, He, N_2, O_2, CO_2, CH_4, C_2H_6 and C_3H_8
molecules. The charge-changing cross sections σ_{ij} were obtained by applying the
slope method to the curves in the single collision region.

I). When the additive rule is assumed to hold, the cross sections for
hydro-carbon molecules containing n carbon atoms can be expressed by the following
formula.

$$\sigma(C_nH_{2n+2}) = [\sigma(C) + 2\sigma(H)]n + 2\sigma(H),$$

where $\sigma(C)$ and $\sigma(H)$ are the cross sections for C and H atoms, respectively.

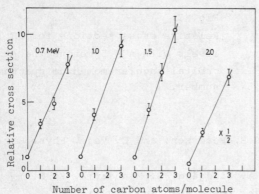

Fig. 1.
Relative electron loss cross
sections σ_{12} for hydro-carbon
molecules as a function of the
total number of carbon atoms
per target molecule.

All the measured cross sections $\sigma(C_nH_{2n+2})$ were found to have linear dependence
on n. An example of such a linear relation is shown for the case of σ_{12} in Fig. 1,
where the experimental cross sections for hydrogen molecule $\sigma(H_2)$ are used for
n=0. Therefore, the cross sections for carbon atom $\sigma(C)$ can be estimated by
applying the above formula.

II). The cross sections $\sigma(C)$ estimated in a similar manner with the measured
values of $\sigma(CO_2)$ and $\sigma(O_2)$ were in good agreement with those obtained in I.
Accordingly, the additive rule seems to be applicable for He projectile in this
energy region. Estimated cross sections $\sigma(C)$ are shown as a function of incident
energy in Fig. 2.

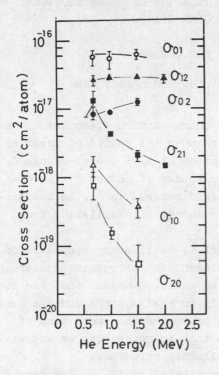

Fig. 2.
Charge-changing cross sections
for carbon atom estimated from
various combinations of target
molecules.

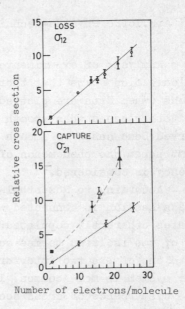

Fig. 3.
Relative electron loss and
capture cross sections of
1.5 MeV helium as a function
of the total number of electrons per molecule.

III). The cross sections for hydro-carbon molecules are plotted as a function of total number of electrons in a target molecule in Fig. 3. As is expected
from the validity of the additive rule mentioned above, these plots show the
linear relation. It is interesting to note that the electron loss cross sections
for other molecules are also on this straight line, while the capture cross
sections are on the different curve from the straight line of hydro-carbon cross
sections.

1. L.H. Toburen, M.Y. Nakai and R.A. Langley. Phys. Rev. 171, 114 (1968).
2. R. Dagnac, D. Blanc and D. Molina.   J. Phys. B 3, 1239 (1970).
3. A.B. Wittkower and H.D. Betz. J. Phys. B 4, 1173 (1971).

ON DISTURBANCE OF PERIODICITY IN OSCILLATION OF CROSS SECTIONS
IN INTERFERENCE OF QUASIMOLECULAR STATES.

V.M.Lavrov, Yu.F.Bydin, S.S.Godakov

A.F.Ioffe Physico-Technical Institute, Leningrad, USSR

Analysis of experimental data on charge-exchange,excitation,autoionization shows that there are cases when the period of oscillations (when data are plotted as a function of I/v) doesn't change [1], and other cases when smooth [2] or sharp change of period [2,3] is observed.Some cases of smooth change were discussed in [4] . In the present paper the phenomenon of the sharp change of oscillation frequency is considered.

According to Rosenthal-Foley model [5], oscillatory structure of cross section is connected with interference of two quasimolecular states coherently populated. It is reasonable to assume that the case of two isolated termes occurs rarely in real systems and the case when one of the two interfering terms approaches one more term of the system is more common. It is with this approach that we connect the disturbance of cross section oscillatory structure.

This situation is schematically presented in Fig.I. The term 2, which interferes with term I, approaches term 3 (in F region). When the system moves along the term 2 the scattering amplitude get an additional phase shift as a result of passing of pseudocrossing region. This shift is close to 0 when the collision velocity is small and is close to $\pi/4$ when the velocity is high. In some velocity range the probability of nonadiabatic transition in F region becomes so high that the population of state 2 is determined by pseudocrossing in D, but not in B region. In this case the area of the loop between the interfering terms as well as the oscillation frequency is increased, the scattering phase in the channel 2 is sharply changed and therefore the oscillation phase is changed also.

This model is realized,for example, in Na^+-Ne collisions and is proved by experimental observations.

I. There are some facts which show that excitation of Ne line 736 Å [3] is connected with σ-orbital interactions in slow collisions (E $\leqslant$ I kev). When discussing the oscillation mechanism of this line, the molecular orbital correlation diagram [6] may be used. It is seen that it is necessary to take into account the $4d\sigma$ as well as $4p\sigma$ and $3s\sigma$ orbitals. This $4d\sigma$ orbital approach $4p\sigma$ orbital at R $\approx$ 2,5 a.u. It is possible to show by using parameters for the additional

pseudocrossing region from correlation diagram [6] that the probability of nonadiabatic transition in this region becomes fairly high
at ion energy 0,3–0,4 kev. This value coincides with that at which
the disturbance of oscillatory structure is realy observed [3].
2. The population of $4p\sigma$ orbital gives rise to the excitation of
both $2s^2 2p^5 3s$ Ne state and of $2s2p^6 3s$ Ne autoionization state. It
is naturally to suppose that $2s2p^6 3s$ state excitation cross section will decrease in increasing probability of nonadiabatic transition in the additional pseudocrossing region. The excitation function for this state (Fig.2 [7]) falls down sharply after the cross
section maximum. This dependence realy takes plase in the same
energy range where oscillation structure is disturbed.

I.Yu.F.Bydin,S.S.Godakov,V.M.Lavrov, X ICPEAC,Abstracts of Papers,
                             966,(1977)
2.R.C.Isler, Phys.Rev.,A10,117,(1974)
3.S.V.Bobashev, JETP Lett.,11,260,(1970)
4.V.N.Ostrovsky,V.A.Kharchenko,Zh.Exp.Teor.Fiz.,48,664,(1978)
5.H.Rosenthal,H.M.Foley, Phys.Rev.Letters,23 ,1480,(1969)
   V.A.Ankudinov,S.V.Bobashev,V.I.Perel,Zh.Exp.Teor.Fiz.,60,906,1971
6.N.H.Tolk,C.W.White, Phys.Rev.Lett.,31,671,(1973)
7.Ju.F.Bydin,S.S.Godakov, Pisma Zh.Exp.Teor.Fiz.,23,566,(1976)

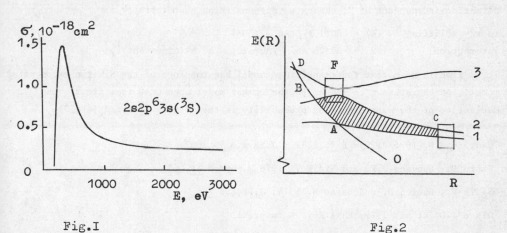

Fig.1   Fig.2

"INCORRECT DISSOCIATION" AND POPULATION SHARING

V. Sidis[+][*] and J.P. Gauyacq[+]

[+]*L.C.A.M. Bât. 351, Univ. Paris-Sud - 91405 ORSAY Cedex FRANCE*

[*]*C.M.O.A., 23 rue du Maroc, 75019 Paris, FRANCE*

The electron promotion model implicitly assumes that a collisional system can be described using single configuration wavefunctions built from MO. However, in some cases, even if excitation processes at small R are easily described in a single configuration basis set, there is no one to one correlation between MO configurations and definite atomic states. Notorious examples are : the ionic and covalent dissociations of $1s\sigma g^2$ and $2p\sigma u^2$ configurations in H_2 and similar situations in other symmetric systems (He+He[1], He[+]+He[2], Ar[+]+Ar[3]...) as well as the dissociation of Π^4 and/or $\Pi^2\sigma^2$ core configurations involved in two electron jumps at MO crossings (Na[+]-Ne)[4]. Other similar circumstances can be found in O[-]-rare gas[5] and C[+]-Ne[6].

The main characteristics of the above situation is the slow variation of the coupling h between the considered molecular states (ϕ_1,ϕ_2) in contrast to the rapid variation of their energy splitting ΔE (fig. 1). The suggested two state model assumes :

$$\Delta E(R) = \Delta\varepsilon + Ae^{-\lambda R}, \qquad h = constant$$

However as $R \to \infty$, the ϕ_1 and ϕ_2 states remain coupled. Actually, the question is what is the probability for producing the atomic states that diagonalize h at $R \to \infty$ once ϕ_1 or ϕ_2 has been primarily populated at small R. This problem can be handled in an equivalent basis set (ψ_1,ψ_2) obtained from the (ϕ_1,ϕ_2) set by a unitary transformation independant of R, chosen as diagonalizing h at infinity :

energy splitting $\Delta V (R) = \Delta U(1 + \Delta\varepsilon Ae^{-\lambda R}/\Delta U^2)$

interaction $\qquad\quad H = \Delta U(2h\ Ae^{-\lambda R}/\Delta U^2)/2, \qquad \Delta U = (\Delta\varepsilon^2 + 4h^2)^{1/2}$

It is readily seen that the transformed model has the form of the Nikitin exponential model[7], which is known to reduce to the Demkov model when $\Delta\varepsilon=0$ (see fig.2). The derivation of the wanted sharing probability is then straightforward (fig.3).

[1]Gauyacq J.P. 1976 J.Phys.B 9, 2289 ; J.Phys.B 9, 3067

[2]Stern B., Gauyacq J.P. and Sidis V. 1978 J.Phys.B 11, 653

[3]Sidis V., Dhuicq D. and Barat M. 1974, J.Phys.B 7

[4]Olsen J.O. et al. 1979, Phys.Rev. A in press

[5]Esaulov V., Gauyacq J.P. and Doverspike D. 1979 Submitted to J.Phys.B

[6]Dowek D., Fayeton J., Alamkan J. and Sidis V. 1977, X ICPEAC (Paris) p. 716

[7]Nikitin E.E. 1970 Adv. Quant. Chem. 5, 135

[8]Gauyacq J.P. 1977 These de Doctorat d'Etat (Université Paris XI)

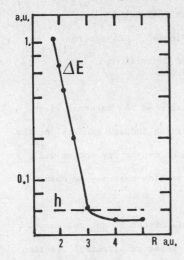

Fig. 1 : Energy difference and coupling in the ϕ_1, ϕ_2 basis set (π^4 and $\pi^2\sigma^2$ core configuration) in Na$^+$Ne^4

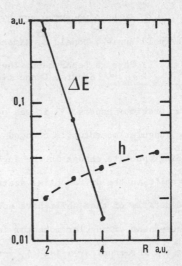

Fig. 2 : Energy difference and coupling in the ϕ_1, ϕ_2 basis set ($1\sigma_g^2 \, 1\sigma_u \, 2\sigma_u$ and $1\sigma_u^2 \, 1\sigma_g \, 2\sigma_g$ configurations) in He-He^1

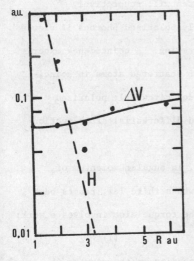

Fig. 3 : Energy difference and coupling in the ψ_1, ψ_2 basis set (same as Fig. 2)

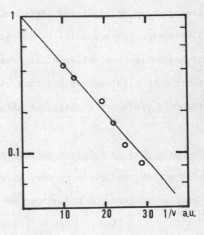

Fig. 4 : Probability ratio for the He-He case (——— : Demkov's model, o : exact calculation^8)

ANGULAR MOMENTUM EFFECTS IN ATOM-ATOM SCATTERING

Arnold Russek, Donald B. Kimball, Jr. and Michael J. Cavagnero

Physics Department, The University of Connecticut
Storrs, Connecticut 06268, U.S.A.

In two previous papers,[1,2] it was pointed out that when the internal (i.e.
electronic) angular momentum is changed during a collision induced excitation, the
corresponding opposite change in the angular momentum of trajectory motion will
produce a shift in the differential scattering cross section that may be observable. The details of that shift have now been worked out.

The component of angular momentum involved in this effect is <u>not</u> the component along the internuclear axis. A $\sigma \leftrightarrow \pi$ transition causes an azimuthal reaction
thrust which is not observable in any experiment which averages over all azimuthal
directions. Rather, the component of angular momentum under discussion is the
component <u>perpendicular</u> to the plane of collision. A radially induced transition
such as $s\sigma \leftrightarrow p\sigma$ will produce a superposition of states m = ± 1 about an axis perpendicular to the plane of collision. These two states will respectively
de-excite by means of right- and left-handed circularly polarized photons if viewed
along a direction perpendicular to the plane of scattering. A coincidence experiment which measures the differential cross section of scattered atoms in coincidence first with right-handed and then with left-handed circularly polarized
photons should yield two similar but slightly shifted differential cross section
curves.

The basic physics involved is that a change, ΔL, in angular momentum of
electronic motion requires a torque, T, which, by Newton's third law, reacts back
on the angular momentum of trajectory motion. But the torque also involves a work:

$$\Delta L = \int T dt = \int T d\theta / \dot{\theta} = \Delta W / \dot{\theta} . \qquad (1)$$

This work raises or lowers the electronic energy, depending on the sign of ΔL.
Thus, near minimum internuclear separation, when R is hardly changing, but θ is
changing most rapidly, the electronic energy can change from the elastic molecular
potential energy curve to the excited one, provided that the energy difference
between the two curves is exactly equal to $\Delta W = \dot{\theta} \Delta L$. As shown in the figure, this

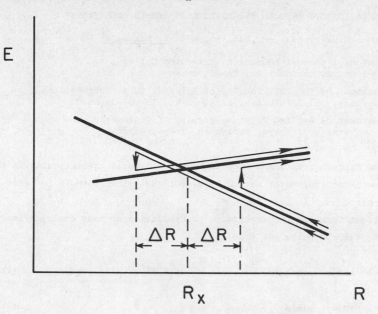

implies a different minimum internuclear separation (and hence impact parameter)
for the two different angular momenta. The shift $\Delta\tau$ in angle for the onset of
excitation for the two components of circular polarization has been derived:

$$\Delta\tau \simeq \frac{2P\Delta L}{mbD} \cdot \frac{d\tau}{db} \qquad\qquad (2)$$

where P is the relative momentum, m the reduced mass, b the impact parameter and
$D = d(E_2-E_1)/dR$ evaluated at the crossing. Equation 2 has been checked against
the exact solution of a model system. The 27% error between Eq. (2) and the
exact solution is solely due to the fact that the energy curves are not linear in
the crossing region.

For the case of Na^+ on Ne this shift is .41 keV·deg which can be resolved in
differential cross section measurements. Although the shift is proportional to
the square root of the collision energy, it is surprisingly best seen at lower
energies since the scattering angle increases as $1/E$.

1. Arnold Russek, Proceedings of the Tenth International Conference on the Physics
       of Electronic and Atomic Collisions, Abstracts of Papers p. 730.

2. Arnold Russek, Physical Review, June issue.

ROTATIONALLY INDUCED TRANSITIONS IN ATOMIC COLLISIONS

H. Yagisawa[*], M. Namiki[†], and <u>H. Nakamura</u>[§]

* Division of General Education, Takachiho College,
  2-19-1 Omiya, Suginami-ku, Tokyo, Japan

† Department of Physics, Faculty of Science, Tokyo Metropolitan
  University, 2-1-1 Fukazawa, Setagaya-ku, Tokyo, Japan

§ Department of Applied Physics, Faculty of Engineering,
  The University of Tokyo, Bunkyo-ku, Tokyo, Japan

Transitions through rotational coupling are investigated theoretically in the framework of the impact parameter method. A usuful analytical formula to treat the problem is proposed.

The analytical formulae for transition probabilities we have employed are given as follows (atomic units are used):

$$P(\rho,v,t) = 1 - \exp[-|\int_{-\infty}^{t} g(t_1) e^{-i\int_{-\infty}^{t_1}\delta(t_2)dt_2} dt_1|^2] \ , \tag{1}$$

$$g(t) = \frac{\rho v}{R^2} V_0 \ \exp[i\int_{0}^{t} \omega(R)dt] \ , \tag{2}$$

$$\text{and} \quad \delta(t) = Im[g(t)\int_{-\infty}^{t} g^*(t_1)dt_1] \ . \tag{3}$$

Here ρ, v, t, R are the impact parameter, collision velocity, time, and internuclear distance, respectively, and V_0 is the rotational coupling matrix element which is assumed to be constant, and $\omega(R)$ is the energy difference between the two adiabatic states. Eg.(1) is the formula proposed previously by one of the authors[1]. The method of deriving the formula can be related to other methods discussed by Langhoff et al.[2], and by Mehrotra and Boggs[3]. The phase factor $\delta(t)$ represents the level shift due to the coupling. This factor is shown to play an important role in the title transitions.

We have applied the following two simplifications of Eq.(1) to the same model system as that of Fritsch and Wille[4] which simulates the transition between the $2p\pi_u$ and $3p\sigma_u$ states in the Ne+Ne$^+$ system: (I) $\delta(t)$ is neglected, (II) $\delta(t)$ is replaced by $\delta(t=0)$. The results are shown in the figure (trajectory is assumed to be linear). The approximation II works very well over a wide range of velocity, indicating the validity of replacing the phase factor $\delta(t)$ by $\delta(t=0)$ as well as the importance of the factor. The transition mechanism pointed out by Russek[5] is confirmed. Namely, the transition at the turning point is dominant and the cross section is determined mainly by the region of the impact paremeter $\rho \sim R_x$. This is in accordance with the importance of the phase factor.

In order to make the formula more practical we have applied the uniform Airy approximation to the evaluation of the integral over t_1 in Eq.(1). In the case of the approximation II this results in

$$P_{UA}^{II} = 1-\exp\left[-4\pi^2 V_0^2\, g(\rho^2:\bar{R}_x)\, v^{2/3}\, A_i^2(v^{-2/3}\, f(\rho^2:\bar{R}_x))\right] ,\qquad(4)$$

where

$$f(\rho^2:\bar{R}_x) = \mp\left(\tfrac{3}{2}\right)^{2/3}\left|\left|\int_0^{\sqrt{\bar{R}_x^2-\rho^2}} \{\omega(vt,\rho^2) + \delta(t=0)\}d(vt)\right|\right|^{2/3} \quad \rho \lessgtr \bar{R}_x ,\qquad(5)$$

$$g(\rho^2:\bar{R}_x) = 2v^{2/3}\,\frac{1}{|(\frac{d\omega}{dR})_{\bar{R}_x}|\,\bar{R}_x^3}\,\frac{\rho^2}{|\bar{R}_x^2-\rho^2|^{1/2}}\,|f(\rho^2:\bar{R}_x)|^{1/2} ,\qquad(6)$$

$$\bar{R}_x = R_x - \delta(t=0)/\left[\tfrac{d\omega}{dR}\right]_{R_x} ,\qquad(7)$$

and $A_i(x)$ is the Airy function. The curve designated by UA in the figure is the result of this approximation. The agreement with the exact results is fairly good, indicating the usefulness of the formula.

In the case of the crossing at the united atom limit, Eq.(1) can also give essentially the same compact expression for the cross section as that derived by Demkov et al.[6] in the adiabatic limit $(v\to 0)$.

A method to treat analytically a three-state problem will also be discussed. This is important to deal with the two-electron excitation by a two-step rotational coupling at the united atom limit.

1. H. Yagisawa, J. Phys. B 9, 2757 (1976).

2. P.W. Langhoff, S.T. Epstein and M. Karplus, Rev. Mod. Phys. 44, 602 (1972).

3. S.C. Mehrotra and J.E. Boggs, J. Chem. Phys. 64, 2796 (1976).

4. W. Fritsch and U. Wille, J. Phys. B11, L43, (1978).

5. A. Russek, Phys. Rev. A4, 1918 (1971).

6. Y.N. Demkov, C.V. Kunasz and V.N. Ostrovskii, Phys. Rev. A18, 2097 (1978).

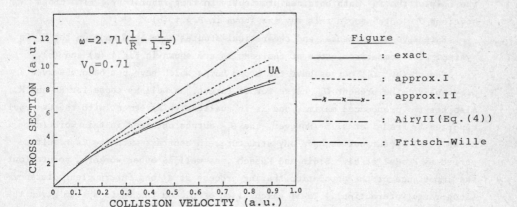

Figure

———————— : exact

- - - - - - - : approx.I

—x—x—x— : approx.II

—··—··— : AiryII(Eq.(4))

—·—·—·— : Fritsch-Wille

SINGLE-ELECTRON CAPTURE CROSS SECTIONS FOR H^+ IONS AND H(1s) ATOMS
INCIDENT UPON Cs, Rb AND K VAPORS

T. Nagata

Department of Science and Technology, Meisei University
Hodokubo, Hino-shi, Tokyo 191, Japan

Charge transfer processes of hydrogen ions and atoms in alkali vapors have
received practical and fundamental interests. In this study, the total cross
sections σ_{10} and σ_{0-1} for single-electron capture by H^+ ions and H(1s) atoms in
thin vapors of Cs, Rb and K have been determined experimentally in the projectile
energy range from 0.4 to 5.0 keV.

A momentum-analyzed, collimated beam of protons enters a collision cell containing alkali vapor. The charged and neutral components of the emerging beam are
separated by an electric field and then counted separately. When measurement is
made on H(1s) beam, the protons are neutralized in a gas cell before the collimation and the remaining ions are removed by a strong electric field applied immediately in front of the cell. From the counting rates of the primary ions (atoms)
and the collision products corrected for the background counts and the difference
in the counting efficiencies, the total cross sections have been determined. The
estimated errors are less than ±30 % at 5 keV and ±45 % around 0.5 keV.

Figure 1 (a) shows the total cross sections σ_{10} as a function of H^+ energy.
In low-energy charge exchange collisions between H^+ and heavy alkali atoms, the
electron capture into the n=2 excited states of H is thought to be dominant proc-
ess because of small energy defect. The σ_{10} is regarded as the sum of σ_{2s} and σ_{1s},
where σ_{2s} is the total cross section for the electron capture processes eventually
leading to formation of H(2s) atom and σ_{1s} is that of H(1s) atom. When a neutral
hydrogen H^o beam is produced under single-collision condition, the fraction of
H(2s) atoms in the H^o beam, f_{2s}, is given by the relation $f_{2s} = \sigma_{2s}/\sigma_{10}$. From
these relations, the partial cross sections σ_{2s} and σ_{1s} have been determined with
the help of the f_{2s} data obtained previously in this laboratory.[1] The cross
sections σ_{2s} obtained in this way are shown in Fig.1 (b).

Extensive experimental and theoretical studies have been made on the H^+-Cs
system. For comparison, some of the results are shown in Fig.1 (a) and (b).

The present σ_{10} curves have two broad humps which have not been observed
previously. The present σ_{2s} curve for Cs target, as well as those for Rb and K,
also has two pronounced maxima, and is in qualitative agreement with the Cs result
reported by Pradel et al.[3] However, the σ_{1s} curves obtained in this work (not
shown here) appear not to have any structure, in contrast with the Cs result reported by Pradel et al. Sidis and Kubach[7], as well as other workers, pointed out
the importance of the population sharing process at a long internuclear distance
(long-range interaction). Their calculation of σ_{10} on the H^+-Cs system gives the
result showing the structure similar to that in the observed curves. As for the
σ_{2s}, however, there are still considerable discrepancies between observation and

calculation.

Figure 1 (c) shows the obtained cross sections σ_{0-1} together with other reported experimental and theoretical results. Although the energy dependence of the present Cs curve is in good agreement with that of Cisneros and Alrarez[4], the absolute magnitude is about 2 times as large as their values. The Cs calculation of Olson et al.[6] is not in agreement with the sharply decreasing experimental cross section at the higher energies. The energy at which the cross section takes a maximum decreases as the energy defect E of the reactions decreases, in qualitative agreement with the prediction by Landau-Zener theory.

References

1. T.Nagata, J. Phys. Soc. Japan 46, 1622 (1979).
2. G.Spiess, A.Valance, and P. Pradel, Phys. Rev. A 6, 746 (1972).
3. P.Pradel, F.Roussel, A.S. Schlachter, G.Spiess, and A.Valance, Phys. Rev. A 10, 797 (1974).
4. C.Cisneros, I.Alvarez, C.F. Barnett and J.A.Ray, Phys. Rev. A 14, 76 (1976).
5. A.Valance and G.Spiess, J. Chem. Phys. 63, 1487 (1975).
6. R.E.Olson, E.J.Shipsey, and J.C.Browne, Phys. Rev. A 13, 180 (1976).
7. V.Sidis and C.Kubach, J. Phys. B 11, 2687 (1978).

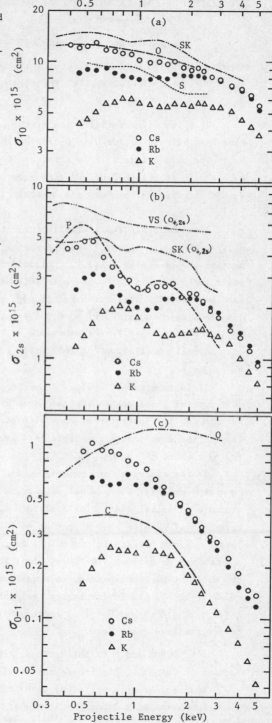

Fig.1 The experimental cross sections compared with other reported Cs data. $\sigma_{+,2s}$ indicates the cross section for direct electron capture into the 2s state of H. S: Spiess et al.(experiment); C: Cisneros et al.(experiment); P: Pradel et al.(Experiment); VS: Valance & Spiess(theory); O: Olson et al.(theory); SK: Sidis & Kubach (theory).

APPLICATION OF SEMICLASSICAL THEORY OF INELASTIC SCATTERING
TO H^+ + Cs $\longrightarrow$ H (2s) + Cs^+

A. VALANCE and M. El MADDARSI

Service de Physique Atomique, Centre d'Etudes Nucléaires de Saclay
BP N° 2 - 91190 GIF-SUR-YVETTE (France).

Relative differential cross section, for charge exchange scattering
have been calculated for H^+ + Cs via H (2s) + Cs^+ collisions at 25 eV.

For this analysis it is necessary to define a classical-trajectory /1/,
such a path is obtained by assuming a set of hybrid   potentials V_1(R) and
V_2 (R) (fig.1), which cross and smoothly join the relevant adiabatic potentials /2/.

Then there are two inelastic trajectories available: i) T_I following V_2
only to the first (inward) passage past R_X and switching to V_1 for all the
rest of the encounter. ii) T_{II} following V_2 all the way in to the turning
point and out again to R_X where it switches to V_1 for the rest of the outward passage. The deflection function Θ_I passes through a minimum corresponding to a rainbow value (Θ_r= -0.05517 rd. and β = 1.322). The deflection
Θ_{II} is always positive corresponding to a repulsive potential, we observe
also a small oscillation for low impact parameters (β between 0.4 - 0.7;
where β = b/R_e) /3/.

It is immediately obvious from the picture in the figure 2. that the
differential cross sections should display a rather complicated interference
pattern due to the fact that many reduced impact parameters (β_i; i = 1,4)
lead to the same scattering angle Θ (4 impact parameters for $\Theta \leqslant \Theta_r$ and 2 for
$\Theta > \Theta_r$, where $\Theta_r = |\Theta_r|$.

In the classical approximation, the inelastic cross section σ (Θ ,E)
formulation contains the product of a transition probability P_i (β_i) with an
ordinary classical scattering amplitude f_i (Θ , β_i) /3/. For 24.9 eV the
experimental results show a peak at 40 eV. deg, a minimum at 50 eV. deg, a
large maximum between 70 and 80 eV. deg, a deep minimum at 100 eV. deg and
a spread maxima between 110-130 eV. deg. The main peak is relative to a rainbow oscillation corresponding to a maximum value at 76 eV. deg. The minimum
value at 50 eV. deg is due to the fact that the probabilities P (β_1),
P (β_2), P (β_3) and P (β_4) corresponding to 50 eV. deg or to Θ = $\pm$ 0.034
rd are simultaneously zero.

/1/   R.E. OLSON and F.T. SMITH, Phys. Rev. A3 (1971) 1607.

/2/   R.L. CHAMPION, Electronic and Atomic Collisions, Invited papers and
       Progress Reports edited by G. WATEL (Service de Physique Atomique,
       Commissariat à l'Energie Atomique, Paris).

/3/   A. VALANCE and M. El MADDARSI, Chem. Phys. Letters (to be published).

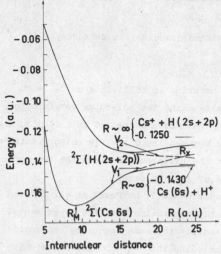

FIG. 1

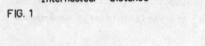

Internuclear distance

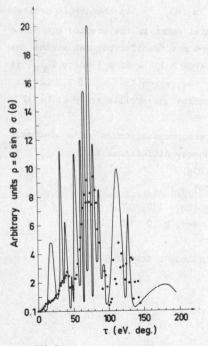

FIG. 3

Fig.1. - Adiabatic potential energy curves (solid line), hybrid potential energy curves V_1 and V_2 (dashed line).

Fig.2. -
a) Upper part. Deflection functions versus reduced impact parameter.

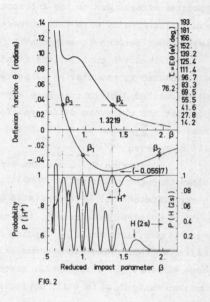

FIG. 2

Fig.2. -
b) Lower part. Probabilities to find H^+ and $H(2S)$ versus impact parameters calculated using perturbed stationary states method /2/.

Fig.3. -

Comparison between experimental data (points) and calculated (solid line) reduced cross-section of charge exchange via $H(2S)$ at 25 eV. versus reduced scattering angle.

Cs^+ + Rb and H^+ + Na CHARGE EXCHANGE CALCULATIONS

A. VALANCE, Q. NGUYEN-TUAN and K. TRINH DUC

Service de Physique Atomique, Centre d'Etudes Nucléaires de Saclay
BP n° 2 - 91190 GIF-sur-YVETTE (France).

The charge exchange processes occuring in collisions of Cs^+ + Rb
and H^+ + Na have been studied theoretically using the molecular wavefunction
approach. Our potential energy curves /1/ have been corrected in including the
repulsive effects due to the interaction between the cores, in using F.Koike's
result /2/. Finally with this correction the difference between the two potentials passes through a maximum at $R \simeq 6$ a.u. (Cs^++Rb case)

Then the oscillations found experimentally by Perel et al. /3/ can
be reproduced by calculation using two states approximation. The experimental
and calculated oscillations have approximately the same frequency and amplitude, but the phase are different. In including the $^2\Pi$ (Rb(5p)) state which
crosses the Σ states at R = 12.5 and 5.5 a_o the shift in energy dependence
will be removed /4/.

Observing $C_{\Sigma\Sigma}$ one might expect transitions between the adiabatic
states throughout the entire coupling region (R = 6 $\sim$ 25 a_o). However, the
energy difference ΔV between states grows   rapidly   as the atomic orbitals
begin to overlap. As a result, the exponential terms in the coupled equations
begin to oscillate rapidly, leading to a zero net transfer between states for
smaller R. Thus transitions occur only at large R (12 - 25 a_o) where $C_{\Sigma\Sigma}$ is
large while ΔV is still small. Moreover in the region (5-8 a_o) Δ V begins
constant while $C_{\Sigma\Sigma}$ is still appreciable leading an oscillating part in σ
/5/.

For the Na + H^+ system a two-states approximation is quite adequate
in the view of the coupling terms and the energy differences /6/.

/1/ A. Valance, J. Chem. Phys. 69, 355, (1978)

/2/ F. Koike, Chem. Phys. Letters 60, (1979), 271.

/3/ J. Perel, R.H. Vernon, H.L. Daley Phys. Rev. 138, 937, (1965)

/4/ C.F. Melius and W.A. Goddart III Phys. Rev. A 10 1541 (1974)

/5/ F.J. Smith Phys. Letters 20, 271 (1966)

/6/ R.W. McCullough, T.V. Goffe and H.B. Gilbody X ICPEAC (1977)
     and private communication.

Fig.1.

Difference potential energy $\Delta V_{\Sigma\Sigma}$ between Cs^+Rb (5s) and Rb^+Cs(6s) states with and without core-core correction. $C_{\Sigma\Sigma}$ radial coupling term versus internuclear distances.

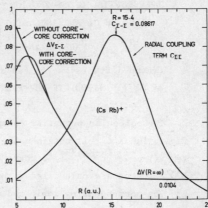

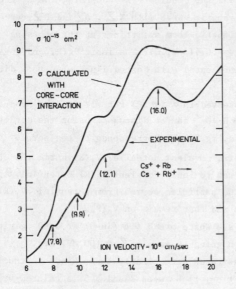

Fig.2.

Experimental and calculated charge exchange cross section for the reaction $Cs^+ + Rb \longrightarrow Cs + Rb^+$

Fig.3.

Differences potential energy and radial terms between states dissociating to:

i) Na+ H^+ and Na^+ + H(2s + 2p) solid line
ii) Na + H^+ and Na^++H(2s-2p) dotted line
ii) Na^++ H (2s + 2p) and Na^+ + H (2s − 2p) dashed line.

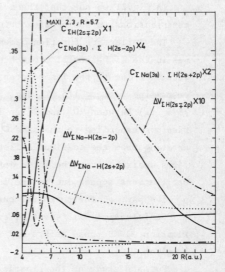

DIFFERENTIAL CROSS SECTION CALCULATION FOR ELASTIC SCATTERING OF
H(1S) ON Cs AND INELASTIC SCATTERING VIA H^-+Cs^+ at 50 eV

A. VALANCE and M. EL MADDARSI

Centre d'Etudes Nucléaires de Saclay – Service de Physique Atomique
BP N° 2 – 91190 GIF-SUR-YVETTE (France)

The molecular potential energy curves of CsH system are represented in
fig.1. The $X^1\Sigma^+$ is obtain using a Morse potential of the form
$V=D_e (1-e^{-2\beta(R-Re)/Re})^2$, where β, Re, De are given in ref /1/. The $A^1\Sigma^+$ and
$B^1\Sigma^+$ states are calculated with the help of the Klein-Rydberg method /1/.

The corresponding ionic and covalent diabatic curves can be constructed
using the above adiabatic curves and the results /2/ concerning the R_x crossing point values of the ionic diabatic curve with $X^1\Sigma$, $A^1\Sigma$ and $B^1\Sigma$ curves
and the results concerning the adiabatic-term splittings at the crossing
points (R_x=9.74, 15.9, 32.3 a_o, V = 0.51 eV...). The ionic $V_2(R)$ and covalent $V_1(R)$ diabatic curves are represented with dashed lines when they differ
from the relevant adiabatic curves.

The oscillatory structures observed in $\sigma(\theta,E)$ ref /3/ for the production
of H^- via the reaction $H(1S)+Cs \rightarrow H^-+Cs^+$ can be discussed using the deflection
functions θ_1 and θ_2 represented in fig.2. θ_1 corresponds to trajectory
where the particles follow diabatic covalent potential $V_1(R)$ until the outward passage where at R_x they switch to ionic covalent $V_2(R)$ potential. θ_2
corresponds to trajectory where the particles switch from potential $V_1(R)$ to
$V_2(R)$ at R_x on the inward passage and then remain on $V_2(R)$.

In fig.2. we see that there is a sharp break (dθ/db=0) at $b_x=R_x$ giving
contributions to the cross-section going to zero at $\mathcal{T}_x\approx$ 100 eV. deg.

The deflection function demonstrates very clearly three kind of structures in the differential cross-section. i) Between 2°and 3.5° a rainbow-type
structure due to the ionic potential curve. The rainbow angle $\theta_{2R}\approx 3.5°$ corresponding to $\mathcal{T}_r\approx$ 175 eV. deg. is in good agreement with experimental results
/3/. ii) Between 20' and 2° an interference structure due to four trajectories corresponding to the same θ, the contributions to the cross section
araising from the covalent deflection θ_1 being greather than the contributions araising from the ionic deflection θ_2. iii) Above 3.5° Stuekelberg
oscillations appear due to the interference due to trajectories from the repulsive part of the potential curves.

Semiclassical differential cross sections using stationary phase approximation, JWKB phase shifts and the Landau-Zener transition probability will
be given.

For the study of the elastic channel of the collision H(1S)+Cs fig.3.

shows the deflection function. The probability P_b for a diabatic transition at a single passage of the pseudo-crossing at Rx given by the Landau-Zener formula is large. So the structures araising from the repulsive covalent Θ_1 deflection function are important because weighted by P_b^2 while the structures araising from θ_2 which presents an attractive part are vanishing because weighted by $(1-P_b)^2$. This prediction is in agreement with experimental results /3/.

REFERENCES

1/   U. RINGSTROM, Jour. Spect. <u>36</u>, 232 (1970).

2/   R.K. JANEV, Jour. Chem. Phys. <u>64</u>, 1891 (1976).

    R.K. JANEV, Z.M. RADULOVIC, ICPEAC , Paris, 974 (1975).

3/   P. PRADEL and M. EL MADDARSI, Abstract at the present conference.

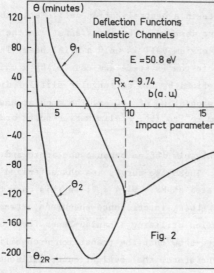

Fig. 2

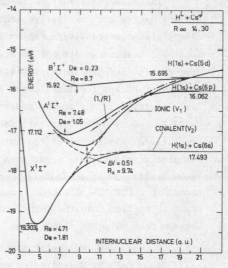

Fig.2.   Deflection functions for the inelastic scattering $H(1s) + Cs \longrightarrow H^- + Cs^+$

Fig.i. - Adiabatic potential energy curves for HCs system.

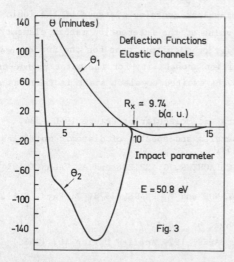

Fig. 3

Fig.3. Deflection functions for the elastic scattering H(1s) on Cs target

DIFFERENTIAL CROSS SECTIONS FOR ELASTIC SCATTERING
OF ATOMIC HYDROGEN FROM CESIUM VAPOUR

M. EL MADDARSI and P.PRADEL

Service de Physique Atomique, Centre d'Etudes Nucléaires de Saclay
BP N° 2 - 91190 GIF-SUR-YVETTE - France.

The differential cross section for elastic scattering of atomic hydrogen in the 1s state from cesium vapour has been measured at several incident
energies from 30 to 528 eV and over the angular range 40' to 7°. These measurements provide a direct test for the equilibrium values of potential curves
$H_{(1s)}Cs_{(6s)}$, which are known only from spectroscopy data [1,2].

Our ground state beam is obtained by near resonant charge transfer of
H^+ with cesium vapour via the 2p state in a neutralization cell. Metastable
atoms present in the outgoing beam are destroyed by Stark effet[3] so the beam
which is entering in the interaction cesium cell is only a H(1s) beam. The
elastically scattered hydrogen atoms in the 1s state are counted by a channeltron. The analysis direction Θ_L is defined by two rectangular slits of dimensions 0.4x3 mm and 0.6x3 mm, with a separation of 100 mm. The angular analysis
is possible for Θ_L angle varying from -5° to 15°. Preliminary results are
given in fig.1.

The observed structure is not clearly define because the ionic and covalent curves are competitive states. These two curves are characterized by
their diabatic transition region located at Rx = 9.74 a_o[5]; in this case the
observed structures are due to Stueckelberg interference phenomena between the
two curves. A rough and rapid estimation utilizing a Landau-Zener formula for
the two ionic and covalent lowest states show that the transition probability
are important in our energy range; therefore, the covalent curve influence
will be reduce by an important factor as it is confirmed by the experimental
results. An estimation of the internuclear crossing distance of the ionic and
excited covalent state leads to a value of the interaction matrix element H_{12}
much smaller by approximately 1 order of magnitude than for the former pseudo
crossing[6]. Then the diabatic transition probability for the outer pseudo-crossing is smaller than the unity, so the excited covalent state is taken as an
unimportant outgoing channel.

/1/   G. HERZBERG, Moleçular spectra and Moléçular structure 1950, 524.

/2/   A.G. GAYDON, Dissociation energies and spectra of diatomic molecules
       Chapman and Hall, London, 1947.

/3/   P.PRADEL, F. ROUSSEL, A.S. SCHLACHTER, G. SPIESS and A. VALANCE 1974,
       Phys. Rev. A10, 797.

/4/   H. SCHEIDT, G. SPIESS, A. VALANCE and P. PRADEL 1978, J. Phys. B 11,
       2665.

/5/   R.K. JANEV, 1976, J. Chem. Phys. 64, 1891.

/6/   R.E. OLSON, F.T.SMITH and E. BAUER, 1971 Applied Optics 10, 1848.

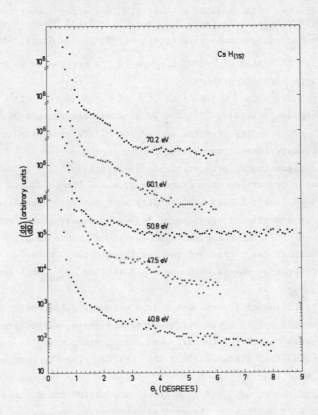

FIGURE 1 - Experimental differential cross-sections
for elastic scattering of atomic hydrogen from cesium
vapour plotted versus the lab-scattering angle θ_L.

DIFFERENTIAL CROSS SECTIONS FOR THE NEAR RESONANT

CHARGE   TRANSFER PROCESS H^++ Cs $\rightarrow$ H(2s)+ Cs^+ AT LOW ENERGY

P. PRADEL, G. SPIESS, V. SIDIS^{*+} and C. KUBACH*

Centre d'études Nucléaires de Saclay, Service de Physique Atomique, BP n°2
91190 - GIF sur YVETTE, France.

* Laboratoire des Collisions Atomiques et Moléculaires (Laboratoire associé au
CNRS (LA 281) Université de Paris Sud, Bat.351 - 91405 ORSAY, France.

$^+$ Centre de Mécanique ondulatoire Appliquée, 23 rue du Maroc, 75019 PARIS-France.

Formation of a beam of hydrogen atoms in the metastable 2s state by the near-
resonant charge exchange process

$$H^+ + Cs \rightarrow H (2s) + Cs^+ \qquad \Delta E = - 0.49 \text{ eV} \qquad (1)$$

has been extensively studied [1,2,3,4]. We present measurements of the inelastic
differential cross section for the production of H(2s) metastable atom from reaction (1). The experimental work is performed in the 20-100 eV lab. energy range,
and it is complemented by a theoretical investigation.

Briefly, a 500 eV ion beam extracted from a Colutron source (model 100), is
focused by a cylindrical lens and velocity analysed by a Wien filter. The H^+ beam
decelerated by a Menzinger retardation system undergoes charge exchange in a Cs
oven heated at 80°C. The scattered hydrogen atoms in the 2s state are quenched
inside a hemispherical mirror and the resulting Lyman α emission is detected. The
measured differential charge exchange cross section ($d\sigma_{+m}$ /$d\Omega$) for reaction (1)
are shown in Fig. 1.

The calculation of elastic and charge exchange differential cross sections
have been carried out in a two-state approximation. A coupled projected valence-
bond (PVB) basis[5] involving the $6s_{Cs}$ and the $\phi_H^+ =(2s_H + 2p_H)/\sqrt{2}$ orbitals is used
at large internuclear distances (R $\geqslant$ 15 a_o) to describe the charge exchange transition around $R_c \simeq 17.5$ a_o. The $\phi_H^- = (2s_H - 2p_H)/\sqrt{2}$ non bonding orbital that interacts negligibly with $6s_{Cs}$ and ϕ_H^+ has been neglected. For R $\leqslant$ 15 a_o the PVB
"atomic" basis is matched to the adiabatic uncoupled "molécular" basis (Fig.2)[6].
At the avoided crossing (R $\simeq$ 9 a_o) the system is found to behave diabatically and
the relevant energy curves used in the calculation are those shown in Fig. 2. The
calculated two-state quantum close-coupling[7] differential cross sections are found
to generally agree with experiment (Fig. 3). At large reduced angles $\tau > 100$ eV.
deg the two state approximation breaks down due to the opening of several other
excited channels.

1. Donnally B.L, Clapp T, Sawyer W and Schultz M - 1964. Phys. Rev. Lett 12, 502.
2. Cesati A, Cristofori F, Millazo Colli L and Sona P.G - 1966.Nucl.Energy 13,649.
3. Sellin I.A and Granoff L - 1967 Phys. Lett. 25 A.484.
4. Pradel P, Roussel F, Schlachter A.S, Spiess G and Valance A - 1974
                                                          Phys. Rev. A 10, 797.
5. C. Kubach and V. Sidis, Phys. Rev. A 14, 152 (1976).
6. C. Benoit et al, J. Phys. B 10, 1661 (1977).
7. R.G. Gordon, Meth. Comput. Phys. 10, 81 (1971).

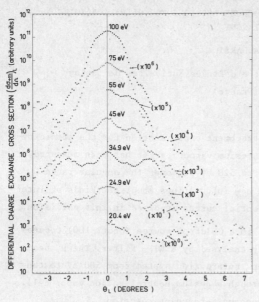

Figure 1 –

Figure 1 –

Experimental charge exchange cross sections for H (2s) from the H$^+$ + Cs collision.

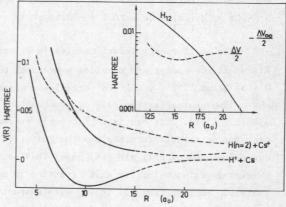

Figure 2 –

(—) Adiabatic potential energy curves used in the calculation for R $\leqslant$ 15 a$_o$. In the inset are shown the PVB charge exchange interaction H$_{12}$ and the energy difference (ΔV) used for R $\gtrsim$ 15 a$_o$.

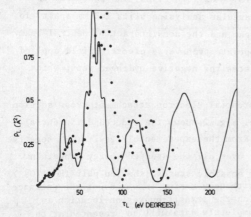

Figure 3 –

Sample of a comparison between experiment (. arbitrarily normalized) and theory (—) for reaction (1) at E = 24.9 eV.

The shift between experiment and theory is attributed to an overestimation of the experimental collision energy (due to plasma potential in the source and work function differences).

DIFFERENTIAL ELECTRON ATTACHMENT CROSS SECTIONS FOR H(1s) COLLIDING
WITH A CESIUM VAPOUR TARGET

P. PRADEL and M. EL MADDARSI

Service de Physique Atomique, Centre d'Etudes Nucléaires de Saclay
B.P. N° 2 - 91190 GIF-SUR-YVETTE (France)

The differential electron attachment cross section for the atomic hydrogen 1s state colliding with a cesium vapour target has been measured at
several incident energies from 30 to 528 eV and over the angular range 0
to 9°. These measurements provide new informations about the kinds of interactions and the nature of the potential curves involved in this collision.

A 500 eV ion beam is formed in a Colutron source (model 100) focused
by a cylindrical lens and velocity analysed by a Wien filter. The H^+ beam
is then decelerated by a Menzinger retardation system from 500 eV to the
desired energy, before passing through a cesium neutralization vapor cell.
This neutralization occurs from the quasi-resonant reaction
$$H^+ + Cs \rightarrow H\ (2s) + Cs^+ : \Delta E = - 0.49 \text{ eV.}$$
$$(2p)$$

The small energy defect results in a large cross section for this collision at low energy and provides a means of obtaining an intense H(2s) and
H (1s) beams[1,2,3,4] . Charged particles emerging with neutral particles from
the cesium neutralization cell are removed out off the beam by a transverse
electric field. This one is sufficiently strong to induce Stark mixing between the metastable 2s state and the radiative 2p state of hydrogen[4] : the
out-going beam is only a H (1s) beam. This neutral beam is then incident on
a central cesium cell; its exit aperture is made to permit an angular analysis θ_L varying from -5° to 15° with respect to the primary beam axis. The
H^- ions created from the reaction $H(1s) + Cs \rightarrow H^- + Cs^+$ and scattered in a
θ_L direction passe through two rectangular analysing slits 100 mm apart. In
order to separate the negative ion beam and the non-interacting neutral beam
scattered in a θ_L direction an appropriate transverse electric field applied
between two cyclindrical plates deviates the negative hydrogen ions, which
are detected by a channeltron.

The preliminary measured differential electron attachment cross section
are shown in Fig. 1 for two energies. Fig. 2 shows the reduced differential
cross section for $(H^- + Cs^+)$system. From the experimental results, H^- negative
ion formation mechanism is identical over all the studied energy range. In
spite of the existence of all cesium possible states, the ion pair $(H^- + Cs^+)$
formation process can be explained with only taking into account the entrance
and exit channels of the system, which the transition region location is
given by several authors.[5-6] More completely data will be presented at the
conference.

1. DONNALLY B.L, CLAPP T., SAWYER W and SCHULTZ M. - 1964. Phys. Rev. Lett 12, 502.

2. CESATI A., CRISTOFORI F., MILLAZO COLLI L. and SONA P.G. -1966 Nucl. Energy 13, 649.

3. SELLIN I.A. and GRANOFF L. - 1967 Phys. Lett. 25A. 484.

4. PRADEL P., ROUSSEL F., SCHLACHTER A.S., SPIESS G. and VALANCE A. -1974 Phys. Rev. A 10, 797.

5. JANEV R.K., 1976 J. Chem. Phys. 64, 1891.

6. VAN DEN BOS J. - 1970. J. Chem. Phys. 52, 3254.

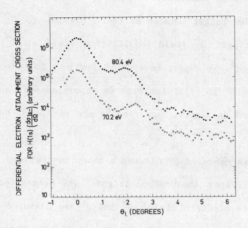

Fig.1 : Experimental differential electron attachment cross sections of H(1s)+Cs system plotted versus the lab-scattering angle Θ_L.

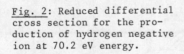

Fig. 2: Reduced differential cross section for the production of hydrogen negative ion at 70.2 eV energy.

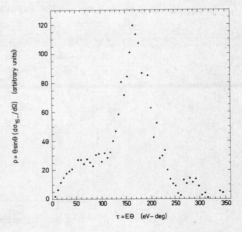

D⁻ FORMATION BY CHARGE-TRANSFER COLLISIONS OF 0.3 TO 10-keV DEUTERIUM IONS AND ATOMS IN CESIUM, RUBIDIUM, AND SODIUM VAPORS

A. S. Schlachter, K. R. Stalder, and J. W. Stearns

Lawrence Berkeley Laboratory
University of California
Berkeley, California 94720

D^- formation by charge-transfer collisions of D^+ in a metal-vapor target is interesting both as a basic atomic-collision study and as a promising means of providing intense D^o atom beams at high energies for plasma heating and fueling. Alkali metals are often used as the target because of their high D^+ to D^- conversion efficiencies.[1] The thick-target D^- yield (equilibrium yield or F_-^∞) for Cs vapor has been previously reported[2]. We report here cross sections for electron capture by D^o and electron loss from D^- in collision with Cs vapor, as well as the D^- equilibrium yield in Cs, Rb, and Na vapors. Our results are in the D energy range 0.3-10 keV.

The equilibrium yield, F_-^∞, was measured by passing a momentum-analyzed beam of D^+ through a recirculating metal-vapor (heat-pipe) target. The beam after the target is analyzed in a transverse electric field; D^+ and D^- are measured with magnetically suppressed Faraday cups, D^o is measured with a pyroelectric detector. Our results for F_-^∞ in Cs, Rb, and Na vapors are shown in Fig. 1. Also shown are our previous results for Mg and Sr vapors[1].

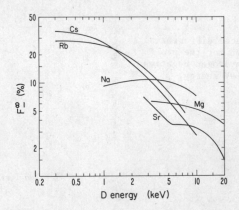

Fig. 1. Equilibrium yield F_-^∞ for deuterium after passage through thick targets of cesium, rubidium, sodium, magnesium, or strontium vapor. (All results are by the present authors.) Maximum uncertainties are ±10%.

29. *Metastable formation by charge transfer and related topics. I*

527

The cross sections σ_{0-} and σ_{-0} were measured in cesium vapor using the same apparatus. For σ_{-0} we used a D^- beam from a duoplasmatron source; for σ_{0-} we stripped D^- in Ar. Results are shown in Fig. 2. The ratio of σ_{0-} to the sum of σ_{0-} and σ_{-0} should give F_-^∞ in the 2-state approximation[1] (assuming ground-state D^0). Our results for σ_{0-} and σ_{-0} give a ratio which is consistent with our F_-^∞ measurements.

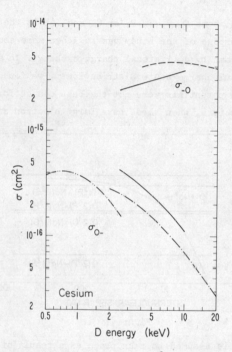

Fig. 2. Charge transfer cross sections for $D^0 \to D^-$ (σ_{0-}) and for $D^- \to D^0$ (σ_{-0}) in cesium vapor. Solid line, present results (absolute uncertainty 35%); dashed line, ref. 3 (renormalized upward by a factor of 2 from published values); dot-dashed line, ref. 4; 2-dot-dashed line, ref. 5.

This work was supported by the Fusion Energy Division of the U. S. Department of Energy under contract No. W-7405-ENG-48.

1. A. S. Schlachter, Proceedings of the Symposium on the Production and Neutraliza-tion of Negative Hydrogen Ions and Beams (Brookhaven National Laboratory, 1977, BNL 50727), p. 11, and references therein.
2. A. S. Schlachter, K. R. Stalder, and J. W. Stearns, Tenth ICPEAC (Paris, 1977), v. 2, p. 870.
3. T. E. Leslie, K. P. Sarver, and L. W. Anderson, Phys. Rev. A 4, 408 (1971).
4. A. S. Schlachter, P. J. Bjorkholm, D. H. Loyd, L. W. Anderson, and W. Haeberli, Phys. Rev. 177, 184 (1969).
5. C. Cisneros, I. Alvarez, C.F. Barnett, and J.A. Ray, Phys. Rev. A 14, 76(1976).

ELECTRON CAPTURE BY keV C, O, F, P, AND Cl ATOMS IN Na VAPOUR

P. Hvelplund and K. Tollund

Institute of Physics, University of Aarhus
DK-8000 Aarhus C, Denmark

The following process is investigated experimentally in the energy region from 10 to 500 keV,

$$X + Na \rightarrow X^- + Na^+ + \Delta E \quad ,$$

where X is one of the atoms C, O, F, P, or Cl and ΔE is the energy defect in the collision. The purpose of the study was to learn more about how to produce intensive negative beams by collisional charge exchange. In an earlier investigation of equilibrium charge-state distributions[1], we found that targets with small ionization potentials were not the best choice for producing large fractions of negative ions, when these have large electron affinities.

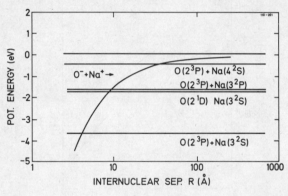

Figure 1

Charge transfer is assumed to take place as a result of interactions in the near vicinity of an avoided curve crossing between the Coulomb-potential curve and neutral-state curves (see Fig. 1). The total charge-exchange cross section found from the Landau-Zener theory can be given in the form[2]

$$\sigma_{0,-1} = 4\pi R_x^2 F_3(\lambda)$$

where

$$F_3(\lambda) = \int_1^\infty \exp(-\lambda x)\{1-\exp(-\lambda x)\}x^{-3}dx$$

in which

$$\lambda = \frac{\sqrt{2}\pi R_x^2 H_{if}^2(R_x)\mu^{\frac{1}{2}}}{E^{\frac{1}{2}}} \quad .$$

R_x is the crossing distance, μ the reduced mass, E the energy, and H_{if} the coupling element, all in atomic units. The coupling matrix elements are found in the approximate way described by Olson (see Ref. 2), and the cross section is multiplied by the high-energy LZ correction term derived by Dubrovskii[3],

$$F(k) = \{1 + \frac{k^2}{4}\}^{-1} \ ,$$

$$k = 0.34 \cdot \beta \cdot \sqrt{E} / \Delta E \cdot \sqrt{m} \ ,$$

where β is the electron affinity of the projectile (a.u.), E is the relative kinetic energy (eV), ΔE (eV) and m is projectile mass (a.m.u.).

The results obtained are shown in Fig. 2. For Cl and F interaction with Na, the experimental results agree very well with the calculated values. (In the case of F, a H_{if} value 30% smaller than the estimated value has been used.) The projectiles with smaller electron affinity present a very different picture, as shown in Fig. 2. It is not possible to bring the absolute values and the energy dependence found experimentally into accord with the calculated values. We do not believe that the primary beam contains an appreciable amount of metastables. The main difference between the two groups of systems is, in the present connection, that the crossing distance for F+Na and Cl+Na is around 10 Å, while it is ∿4 Å for C+Na, O+Na, and P+Na.

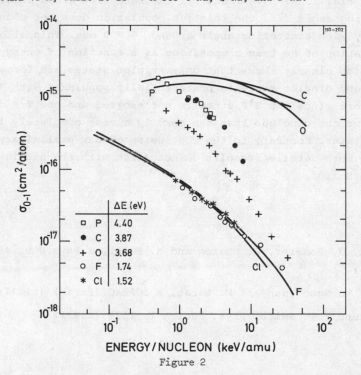

Figure 2

1. J. Heinemeier and P. Hvelplund, Nucl.Instrum.Methods 148, 65 (1978); ibid. 148, 425 (1978)

2. J.T. Moseley, R.E. Olson, and J.R. Peterson, Case Studies in Atomic Physics 5, 1 (1975); A.P.M. Baede, Adv.Chem.Phys. XXX, 463 (1975)

3. G.V. Dubrovskii, Sov.Phys. JETP 19, 591 (1964); 20, 429 (1965)

RELATIVE ABUNDANCE OF He(2³S) AND He(2¹S) FORMED BY CHARGE EXCHANGE ON ALKALI VAPOR.

C. Reynaud, J. Pommier, Vu Ngoc Tuan and M. Barat

L.C.A.M. Bât. 351 - Univ. Paris-Sud, 91405 ORSAY FRANCE

The charge exchange suffered by a He^+ beam with a alkali target leads to the selective excitation of He(n=2) states. This reaction is commonly used for the production of Helium metastable beams. The present work consists in a time of fligh (TOF) energy analysis[1] of the beam neutralyzed on Na, K, Rb and Cs targets in the 100-1500 eV energy range. The energy separations 0.8, 0.35, 0.25 eV between respectively the 2^3S, 2^1S, 2^3P, 2^1P required an energy resolution of about 0.25 eV which was achieved by improving the ion source conditions and increasing the fligh lenght. Typical energy loss spectra obtained at $\theta=0$deg. are given in fig. 1. We have found *(i)* the intensity drops drastically with scattering angle *(ii)* the relative population does not change significantly with scattering angle around $\theta = 0$ deg. This allows the determination of He beam composition as a function of energy (table I) which clearly shows that only triplet states are formed with sodium and singlet state is preferentially populated with Rb and Cs. Furthermore since the 2^1P state is not excited and the 2^3P decay on the 2^3S, we can conclude that the beam is almost completely in metastable states. Contrary to the conclusion of our preliminary work[2], these more detailed results do not agree with the prediction of Olson and Smith[3].

[1] J.C. Brenot, J. Pommier, D. Dhuicq and M. Barat, J.Phys.B 9, 448 (1975)

[2] J. Pommier, Vu Ngoc Tuan and M. Barat, X ICPEAC (Paris) (1977)

[3] R.E. Olson and F.T. Smith, Phys. Rev. A 7, 1529 (1973)

29. *Metastable formation by charge transfer and related topics. I*

531

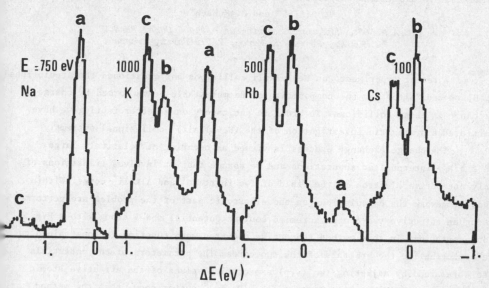

FIG. I : TYPICAL T.O.F. CHARGE EXCHANGE ENERGY LOSS SPECTRA FOR HE$^+$
HE$^+$-NA, K, RB AND CS COLLISIONS AT θ = 0°. PEAK A : HE(2^3S),
B : HE(2^1S) AND C : HE(2^3P)

	E(EV)	100	150	200	300	500	750	1000	1250	1500
N a	2^3S	–	99	98	97	95	94	90	80	80
	2^3P	–	1	2	3	5	6	7	10	10
	2^1S	–	0	0	0	0	0	3	10	10
K	2^3S	7	–	13	24	30	33	33	32	31
	2^3P	77	–	60	43	36	37	39	41	43
	2^1S	16	–	27	33	34	30	28	27	26
R b	2^3S	0	0	0	6	9	11	13		
	2^3P	41	37	38	38	44	50	49		
	2^1S	59	63	62	56	47	39	38		
C s	2^3P	43	49	–	64	65	60	58		
	2^1S	57	51	–	36	35	40	42		

BLE I : FRACTIONS OF HE EXCITED STATES PRESENT IN THE NEUTRAL
EMERGING BEAM.

SYSTEMATIC THEORETICAL INVESTIGATION OF CHARGE EXCHANGE IN He+/ALKALI-ATOM COLLISIONS

V. Sidis[+*] and C. Kubach[+]

[+]*L.C.A.M. Bât. 351, Univ. Paris-Sud - 91405 ORSAY FRANCE*
[*]*C.M.O.A., 23 rue du Maroc, 75019 Paris, France*

A recent experiment[1] on He+/alkali collisions has questioned the predictions of Olson and Smith[2] for the composition of He metastable beams formed by charge exchange in these collisions. In order to put theory on a better footing we have initiated a systematic investigation of the (He-Alkali)+ collisional systems.

The charge exchange process is viewed as occuring at relatively large ($R > 5\ a_0$) internuclear separations and we assume that it involves transitions of only one active electron in the field of two inert He+ and Alkali+ cores. Within this framework the calculations on the electronic part of the problem are performed using an effective two-center screened coulomb potential model along with a PVB[3] representation. In this method the active electron wave function is constrained to be orthogonal to the orbitals of the two cores. The parameters of the potentials are determined by adjusting two (s,p) expectation values of the effective atomic hamiltonians to SCF results. Tests on the (He-Na)+ system show that the method reproduces the results of all-electron calculations to better than 10^{-4} a.u. in the considered range of R.

Results obtained for He+/Cs are shown on Figs. 1,2,3. For these calculations the expansion basis sets have been carefully selected to adequatly account for exchange interactions and polarisation distortions. The successful comparison of the present theory with the experiments of Reynaud *et al.*[1] proceed from the correct treatment of essential points which were disregarded previously[2]. *(i)*As the system behaves adiabatically with respect to long range polarisation effects the relevant exchange interactions involve mixings of s,p,d orbitals of each partner. *(ii)* The $2s_{He}$-$2p_{He}$ interaction pushes the Alc+ + He (2p) Σ energy curve away from the entrance curve. Effects of the charge-quadrupole term and other $2p_{He}$-(3s, 3d)$_{He}$ interactions can hardly compensate this repulsion to yield the behaviour assumed by Olson and Smith for the $\Sigma(2p_{He})$ curve. *(iii)* Rotational coupling around the curve-crossing between the $\Sigma(6s)$ and the $\Pi(2p_{He})$ adiabatic energy curves strongly enhances the formation of He(2^3P). Inclusion of the $\Pi(6p_{Cs})$ and $\Pi(2p_{He})$ exchange interaction is essential for a correct description of this effect.

References

[1]C. Reynaud, J. Pommier, Vu Ngoc Tuan and M. Barat in this conference

[2]R.E. Olson and F.T. Smith, Phys.Rev.A 7, 1529 (1973)

[3]C. Kubach and V. Sidis, Phys.Rev. A 14, 152 (1976)

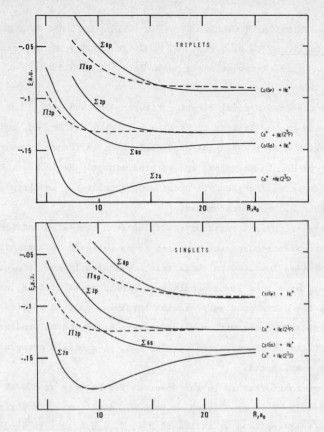

Fig. 1,2 : Adiabatic energy curves of (He–Cs)⁺ obtained by diagonalisation of the
PVB hamiltonian

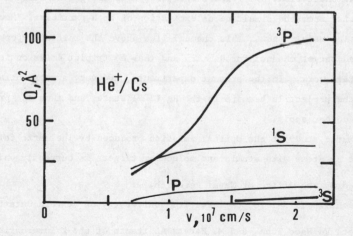

Fig. 3 : Total charge exchange cross sections for He⁺/Cs calculated in the impact
parameter approximation.

STUDY OF OPTICAL EMISSION IN COLLISIONS OF He[*] WITH ATOMIC AND MOLECULAR TARGETS

M. J. Coggiola, T. D. Gaily,[‡] K. T. Gillen, and J. R. Peterson

SRI International, Menlo Park, CA 94025 U.S.A.

Spectrally resolved optical emission between 3500 and 8000 Å has been observed for inelastic collisions of $He^*(2^1S, 2^3S)$ with He, Ne, Ar, and O_2 at laboratory energies near 1 keV. The projectile beam is formed by near-resonant charge transfer of He^+ in Na vapor, and is predominantly $He^*(2^3S)$.[1] Emission produced in a static gas target cell under single collision conditions is observed through a 0.5 m monochromator.

Measurements of optical emission resulting from atom-atom and ion-atom collisions of ground state species have led to an improved understanding of the excitation mechanisms involved in these two-body inelastic collisions. Detailed studies, however, have been limited mainly to ground state systems, and little is known regarding the corresponding processes involving excited species.[2] Collisions of metastable He atoms with various targets are found to produce excitations characteristic of the unpaired 2s electron. A specific example of this is given by the He^* + Ar system.

The most prominent feature in the spectrum for He^* + Ar at 800 eV collision energy is the $He(3^3D \to 2^3P)$ transition at 5876 Å. Additional transitions within the triplet manifold are seen at 4471 Å $(4^3D \to 2^3P)$ and 4713 Å $(4^3S \to 2^3P)$. This result is in marked contrast to ground state He + Ar collisions, which yield exclusively Ar excitation.[3,4] Triplet excitations in the ground state scattering could only arise from the simultaneous excitation of both particles. However, as the promotion model[4] shows, this channel lies above the initially populated doubly excited target channel for He + Ar, and thus no triplet emission is seen in the ground state work. In the present experiments, however, a substantial fraction of the projectile beam is in the $He^*(2^3S)$ state, and thus the previous restrictions do not apply.

A systematic study of the optical emission produced by inelastic collisions of metastable He atoms with atomic and molecular targets is currently under way.

Work supported by the Office of Naval Research.

[‡]Visiting scientist 1977-1978, on leave from University of Western Ontario.

1. J. Pommier, Vu Ngoc Tuan, and M. Barat, Abstracts of the X International Conference on the Physics of Electronic and Atomic Collisions, Paris, (Commissiariat A L'Energie Atomique, 1977) pp. 456-457.

2. M. Hollstein, A. Salop, J. R. Peterson, and D. C. Lorents, Phys. Letters 32A, 327 (1970).

3. V. Kempter, G. Riecke, F. Veith, and L. Zehnle, J. Phys. B 9, 3081 (1976).

4. J. C. Brenot, D. Dhuicq, J. P. Gauyacq, J. Pommier, V. Sidis, M. Barat, and E. Pollack, Phys. Rev. A 11, 1933 (1975).

STUDY OF LOW ENERGY CHARGE TRANSFER REACTIONS
BY THE TIME-OF-FLIGHT TECHNIQUE

T. Matsuo, N. Kobayashi and Y. Kaneko

Department of Physics, Tokyo Metropolitan University
Fukazawa, Tokyo 158, Japan

In the study of low energy charge transfer reactions, it is most important
to know accurately the amount of energy converted between the internal and the
translational energy. For this purpose, the time-of-flight (TOF) spectroscopy of
the product neutral atoms is expected to be powerful because a good resolution
can be achieved by TOF technique in low energy. Although the detection of low
energy neutral atoms is difficult when they are in the ground state, metastable
state atoms can be detected easily with a secondary electron multiplier even
below 10 eV.

Kadota and Kaneko found that metastable neutrals are often produecd from
metastable ions through a charge transfer reaction like

$$A^{+M} + X \longrightarrow A^M + X^+ + \Delta E \qquad\qquad (1)$$

in the 10 eV region.[1,2] The reaction (1) will be a good exercise for TOF study of
low energy charge transfer.

We have built a TOF spectrometer which consists of an ion source of electron
impact type, a 180° mass-analyzer made of a ferrite magnet, a flight tube and a
detector. The ions mass-analyzed pass through a effusive gas target. The flight
time of the product neutrals was measured with a conventional multi-channel
analyzer. The ion source and the mass-analyzer can be rotated around the
collision center. The detector is a secondary electron multiplier of 20-stage
Cu-Be dynodes. The flight length is 69 cm.

A typical time-of-flight spectra obtained for Ar^++ Ar collision are shown
in Fig. 1. They were taken with the scattering angle at 2°. Fig.1 (a) was taken
with the electron energy E_e= 50 eV, while (b) is taken with E_e= 30 eV. The
primary ion energy was kept at 46 eV throughout the experiment. Since the lowest
metastable state of argon ion lies 32.16 eV above the ground state argon atom,
no metastable state ion involved in the primary ion beam when E_e= 30 eV. The
peak appearing in Fig.1 (b) is due to the ground state Ar atoms produced through
symmetric resonance charge transfer process Ar^++ Ar $\rightarrow$ Ar + Ar^+. The product Ar
atom can be detected in spite of the extremely small detection efficiency because
the resonance charge transfer process has a large cross section. This peak gives
a standard of the energy. In Fig.1 (a), a broad peak appeares besides a sharp
peak corresponding to the resonance charge transfer. The broad peak must be due
to the metastable state atom Ar^M. As the detection efficiency of Ar^M is almost
unity, the peak height of Ar^M is comparable to that of Ar although the percentage

of Ar^{+M}in the primary beam is considered to be very small.

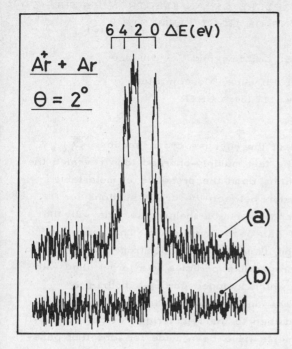

Fig. 1   The TOF spectra for Ar$^+$ + Ar collisions.
(a) E_e= 50 eV
(b) E_e= 30 eV

The Ar^M peak is shifted about 2.8 eV to the higher energy side from the Ar peak.   That means the reaction is exothermic in this case.   Several metastable states have been reported for argon atom and ion, but the exothermicity is calculated simply as $\Delta E > 4.68$ eV.   Therefore the Ar detected can not be considered due to the direct process like (1), but through a two-stage process like

$$Ar^{+M} + Ar \longrightarrow Ar^* + Ar^+ + \Delta E'$$
$$\searrow Ar^M + h\nu , \qquad (2)$$

where Ar* is radiative state higher than Ar^M.   The broadening of the Ar^M peak indicates that $\Delta E'$is 2∼4 eV and several states may be involved in the reaction. Similar results have been obtained for Ar$^+$ + Kr and Ar$^+$ + Ne collisions.

In this experiment, only forward scattering (0∼4°) was studied.   It should be noted that no endothermic reaction was observed in the experiment. Endothermic reactions seem to have smaller cross sections in this energy region.

1.   K. Kadota and Y. Kaneko,   Japan. J. appl. Phys. __13__, 1554 (1974)
2.   K. Kadota and Y. Kaneko,   J. Phys. Soc. Japan __38__, 524 (1975)

THE CROSS SECTION FOR CAPTURE OF AN ELECTRON BY THE HELIUM-LIKE METASTABLE IONS OF LIGHT ELEMENTS

Ya. A. Teplova, I.S. Dmitriev, and V.S. Nikolaev

Institute of Nuclear Physics, Moscow State University; Moscow 117234; USSR

An experimental research of the effective cross sections $\overline{\sigma}_{i,i-1}$ for capture of an electron by the fast multiply-charged ions revealed the dependence of these cross sections upon the presence of metastable ions in the beam[1]. The relationship between the cross sections for electron capture by unexcited and metastable helium-like ions with the nuclear charges Z from 3 to 8 has been investigated. The beams of the helium-like ions of lithium, berillium, carbon and nitrogen were formed by charge-exchange of fast hydrogen-like particles in a target filled with different gases. The ion beam, which included particles both in the ground and metastable states, was directed into the charge-exchange chamber filled with nitrogen and then to the registering device. To provide a check, similar measurements have been made for ions that passed through a solid film. The fraction α of metastable particles in the beam has been determined from the value. of the measured electron-loss cross section, using the previously found cross sections for electron loss by unexcited $\sigma^{o}_{i,i+1}$ and metastable $\sigma^{M}_{i,i+1}$ helium-like ions[2]. With increasing gas pressure in the target, the value of α varies smoothly from $\alpha_{max} \sim 0.6$ (at the target thickness $T \sim 10^{15}$ at/cm^2) to $\alpha_{min} \sim 0.07$ (at $T \sim 10^{17}$ at/cm^2) which correspond to equilibrium charge state of ions in the beam.

The values of the cross sections for electron capture by metastable ions $\sigma^{M}_{i,i-1}$ were determined from the relation

$$\sigma^{M}_{i,i-1} = \frac{1}{\alpha}\overline{\sigma}_{i,i-1} - \frac{(1-\alpha)}{\alpha}\sigma^{o}_{i,i-1} \tag{1}$$

where $\sigma^{o}_{i,i-1}$ is the cross section for electron capture by unexcited ions. The present results indicate that at ion velocity $V = 8.10^8$ cm/s the ratio $\sigma^{M}_{i,i-1} / \sigma^{o}_{i,i-1}$ decreases from 2.5 for Z=3 to 0.07 for Z=8 (fig.1). The ratio $\sigma^{M}_{i,i-1}/\sigma^{o}_{i,i-1}$ for a fixed ion decreases with decreasing ion velocity which corresponds to the increased probability for electron capture to the states with the principle quantum number $n \geq 2$ with a subsequent autoionization[2] .

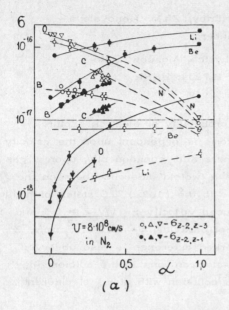

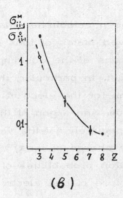

(a)

(b)

Fig.1.(a) The cross sections for capture and loss of electrons by helium-like ions as function of the metastable fraction α .

(b) The Z-dependence of the ratio $\sigma^{M}_{i,i-1} / \sigma^{o}_{i,i-1}$ for different ions at $V = 8.10^{8}$ cm/s — ($\bullet$) and $V = 4.10^{8}$ cm/s — ($\circ$)

REFERENCES

1. I.S. Dmitriev, V.S. Nikolaev, Yu.A. Tashaev, Ya.A. Teplova, JETP 67, 2047 (1974)

2. V.S. Nikolaev, I.S. Dmitriev, Yu.A. Tashaev, Ya.A. Teplova, Yu.A. Fainberg. J. Phys. B: Atom. Molec.Phys. 8 L58(1975).

FORMATION OF METASTABLE IONS WITH TWO
AND THREE ELECTRONS IN DIFFERENT GASES

Ya.A. Teplova, I.S. Dmitriev, Zh.M. Konovalova
and Yu.A. Fainberg

Institute of Nuclear Physics, Moscow State
University; Moscow 117234; USSR

It has been established that the probability of electron capture
to the long-lived states of ions and atoms is dependent upon the velocity
ratio of electrons of the colliding partners and, consequently, upon a gas
filling the target. In particular, there is a twofold difference between the
cross sections for the electron capture to the $(1s2s)^{1,3}S$ states of helium
atoms in helium and argon at the reduced velocity $S = V/V_o Z \simeq 0.5$ and
$S \simeq 0.6$, respectively (V-the velocity of particles, $V_o = 2.19 \cdot 10^8$ cm/s, Z
is the nuclear charge of ions)[1]. A marked difference is also observed
in the production probabilities of three-electron ions in the autoionizing
states in capture of one electron in a collision with atoms of different
gases[2].

Measurements are made of the number of metastable particles in the
beams of helium-like ions Li^+, B^{+3} and N^{+5} and lithium-like ions B^{+2},
N^{+4} at $V = 4$ and 8.10^8 cm/s, which are produced by the capture of one
electron by hydrogen- and helium-like ions, respectively, in collisions
with the molecules of hydrogen, helium, nitrogen, neon, and argon (See,
Fig.1).

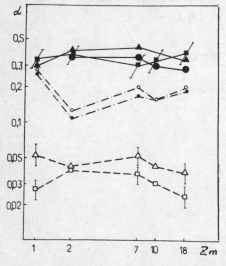

Fig.1. Dependence of the number of
excited particles α in the beams of
Li, B, N ions and He atoms on Z_m (Z_m -
the nuclear charge of the atoms
of the medium)

—●— Li^+ at $S = V/V_o Z \simeq 0.6$,

—▲— B^{+3} at $S \simeq 0.7$

—■— N^{+5} at $S \simeq 0.5$

--□-- N^{+4} at $S \simeq 0.5$

--○-- B^{+2} at $S \simeq 0.4$

--○--·   and   --·●--· He^o

from ref.[1] at $S \simeq 0.5$ and
$S \simeq 0.6$ respectively.

The experimental setup has been described earlier in ref.[3].

The data on the relative number of metastable atoms of helium produced in the capture of one electron in the same gases[1] at $S \sim 0.5$ and 0.6, respectively, are presented for comparison. A relative difference in α , depending upon Z_m - the nuclear charge of the medium atoms, for the lithium-like ions B^{+2} and N^{+4} does not exceed 30%. For helium-like ions the values of α exceed the values for the lithium-like ions by nearly 5-6 times and vary from 0.3 for the Li^+-ions in Ar to $\alpha \sim 0.45$ for the B^{+3} ions in N_2.

According to the conditions of the present experiment, the beam of hydrogen-like ions incident upon a gaseous target has no excited component. Therefore, on the basis of the α -data and of the values of the experimental capture cross section $\overline{\sigma}$ the cross section σ^M for the electron capture to the $(1s2s)^{1,3}S$ state is calculated in the single-collision conditions using the equations $\alpha /(1-\alpha) \sim \sigma^M/\sigma^o$, $\sigma^M + \sigma^o = \overline{\sigma}$ where σ^o is the cross section for electron capture to the ground state of an ion. In the considered cases, the electron capture cross section σ^M is smaller than that for capture to the ground state σ^o by 1.4-2.5 times.

REFERENCES

1. H.B. Gilbody, K.F. Dunn, R. Browning, C.J. Latimer
   J. Phys. B: Atom. Molec. Phys. 4, 800(1971)
2. P. Hvelplund   J. Phys.B. Atom.Molec.Phys. 9,1555(1976)
3. I.S. Dmitriev, V.S. Nikolaev, Yu.A. Tashaev, Ya.A. Teplova
   ZhETF, 67, 2047 (1974).

σ_{21} CROSS SECTIONS FOR NITROGEN IONS IN RARE GAS TARGETS

B. Hird, S. P. Ali and H. C. Suk*

University of Ottawa, Ottawa, K1N 6N5 Canada

Charge exchange measurements in thin targets of the rare gases have been measured between 20 keV and 200 keV. Theoretically only a few final states of the singly charged ions are expected to be significant because of atomic structure effects or large energy defects. It is possible that the ^4P state of N^{2+} may have a long enough lifetime to reach the target if it is produced in the RF type ion source.

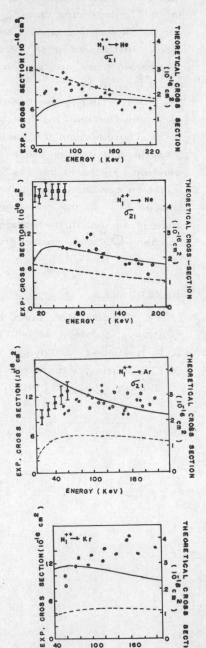

The continuous line shows Rapp and Francis type[1] theoretical predictions which include Coulomb and polarization corrections to the energy defect[2], assuming that the N^{2+} beam is entirely in the ground state. The possible states included for N^+ are the ^3P ground state, the $^1D_2$ state at 1.9 eV and the $^1S_0$ state at 4.05 eV. The target ion states were the ^2P states and the $^2S_{\frac{1}{2}}$ state in the heavier rare gas. In helium, only the ground state was assumed to be produced. The cross sections were combined with a relative weighting for the p-hole states three times that for the s-hole states.

The dashed line assumes that the beam was entirely in the ^4P metastable state and that instead of the $^1D_2$ and $^1S_0$ excitations, the $^5S^0$ excited state of N^+ is produced.

The spread in experimental cross sections which is larger than statistical variations, may be due to varying amounts of the ^4P metastable state in the beam, but it could not be correlated with any parameter of the ion source. The theoretical cross sections have about the correct magnitude for the He target, but are too small by factors which increase from 4 in neon to about 10 for the heavier targets.

*Present address: Kyung Pook National
University, Korea (R.O.K.)

1. D. Rapp and W. E. Francis, J. Chem.
   Phys. 37, 2631 (1962).
2. J. B. Hasted and A. R. Lee,
   Proc. Phys. Soc. (London) 79,
   702 (1962).

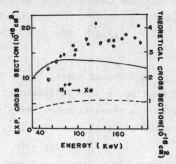

‡ N.V.Fedorenko, J.Tech.Phys.USSR,24, 769 (1954)

ELECTRON CAPTURE IN N⁺-Ne COLLISIONS – INFLUENCE OF METASTABLE IONS

U. Thielman[*], J. Krutein[+] and M. Barat

L.C.A.M. Bât. 351 – Univ. Paris-Sud 91405 ORSAY Cedex FRANCE

In a recent paper, Sidis and Matic[1] suggested that the large charge exchange cross-section in N⁺Ne collision at low keV energies[2] could only be explained by the presence of a sizeable amount of $N^+(^5S)$ metastable ions in the primary beam. Having undertaken a detail investigations of various direct and exchange processes occuring in N⁺Ne collision[3], we have then carefully looked at the presence of metastable ions in the beam. In a first experiment we have analyzed the energy losses suffered by the scattered ion beam (direct process). A small amount of (^1D) and (^1S) metastable states has been detected[3] but no evidence of (^5S) was found. On the other hand, using a time of flight (TOF) method we were able to analyze the various electron capture processes. Typical TOF spectra are given in Fig. 1. It is readily seen that *(i)* at very small angle the $N^+(^5S) \rightarrow N(^4S)$ strongly dominates. *(ii)* For E.θ⩾0.5 keV deg. electron capture from the ground state $N^+(^3D)$ to the $N(^2D)$ et $N(^2P)$ states becomes the most important process   *(iii)* Neither electron capture into the $N(^4S)$ from the N⁺ ground state nor capture from the metastable $N^+(^1D)$ and $N^+(^1S)$ states were actually seen.

Fig. 2 shows relative differential cross sections (DCS) for both processes *(i)* and *(ii)*. The $N^+(^5S) \rightarrow N(^4S)$ DCS is peaked at zero degrees in agreement with the suggested[1] quasi-resonant character of this process. In contrast, at all energies the $N^+(^3P) \rightarrow N(^2D)$, $N(^2P)$ DCS shows LZS behaviour characteristic of a population mechanism occuring at a curve crossing located at E.θ ≃ 1 keV deg. In conclusion these results confirm the suggestions of Sidis and Matic that the total cross section for N⁺Ne charge exchange is largely dominated at low keV energy by the contribution coming from the (^5S) metastable ion present in the beam.

[1] V. Sidis and M. Matic (1977) Abstract X ICPEAC Paris p. 720

[2] M. VuJovic *et al.* (1977) J.Phys.B, <u>10</u>, 3699

[3] U. Thielman, J. Krutein and M. Barat, to be publish

[*] On leave from Universität of Freiburg, Germany

[+] On leave from University of Kaiserslautern, Germany.

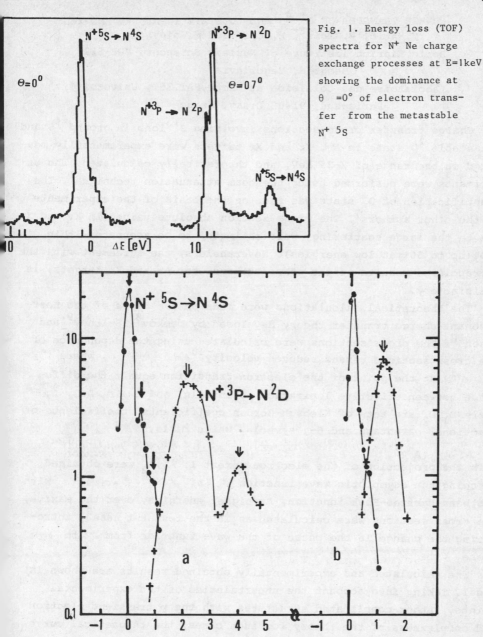

Fig. 1. Energy loss (TOF) spectra for N^+ Ne charge exchange processes at E=1keV showing the dominance at θ =0° of electron transfer from the metastable N^+ ^5S

Fig. 2. Differential cross section (in arbitrary unit) $\sigma(\theta)$ at (a) 500 eV and (b) 1 keV for the two dominant charge transfer processes. Heavy arrows indicate the maxima of the "Demkov-Stueckelberg" interference pattern occuring in the quasi resonant $N^+ {}^5S \rightarrow N^4S$. The double arrows show for the N^+ $^3P \rightarrow N^2D$ charge transfer maxima of the "LZS" interference pattern characteristic of a population occurrence at a curve crossing.

CHARGE TRANSFER OF O^+ ^4S AND ^2D STATE IN Ar, Kr AND Xe

M.Matić, V.Sidis[*+], B.Čobić and M.Vujović

Boris Kidrich Institute of Nuclear Sciences, POB 522,

Beograd, Yugoslavia

[*]Laboratoire des collision atomique,BAT.351, Université

Paris-sud, 91405 Orsay, France

Charge transfer cross sections involving O^+ ions in ground ^4S and metastable ^2D state in Ar, Kr and Xe targets were experimentally measured in the range of 2-25 keV, and theoretically calculated. The experiments were performed using the beam attenuation technique[1]. The identification of O^+ state was made on the basis of the experiments of the other authors[7]. The cross section absolute values in Kr and Xe due to the large scattering, were estimated to be accurate within ±20%(up to 30% at low energies). Nevertheless, the agreement with the extrapolated results of the other authors, for Ar and Kr targets, is satisfactory.

The theoretical calculations were made on the basis of the near-resonant charge transfer theory developed by Demkov[8], Smirnov[9] and Olson[10]. The cross sections were calculated using the dependence of the cross sections versus reduced velocity[10]: $\partial = \frac{\bar{\mu} \, \Delta(R_c)}{2 \, \gamma \, \nu}$, where $\frac{\gamma^2}{2}=I$ and $\Delta(R_c)$ at the point of the electron transition equals the difference between effective ionization potentials, and $\Delta = \sum_{\mu} \Delta_{\mu} \, D_1 D_2$ [9], where D_1, D_2 are sets of Klebsch-Gordan coefficients, coefficients of fractional parentage and 6-j symbols, while Δ_{μ} is,

$$\Delta_{\mu} = \partial_{\mu_1 \mu_2} \, A_1 A_2 \; R^{\left(\frac{1}{\gamma_1}+\frac{1}{\gamma_2}-1-|\mu|\right)} e^{-\left[\frac{R}{2}(\gamma_1+\gamma_2)+\frac{1}{2\gamma_1}+\frac{1}{2\gamma_2}\right]} \left[1 - \frac{a_1 a_2}{R}\right] \left[\frac{(2\ell_1+1)(2\ell_2+1)(\ell_1+|\mu|)!(\ell_2+|\mu|)!}{(\ell_1-|\mu|)!(\ell_2-|\mu|)! \, 3^{1/2} \, (\gamma_1+\gamma_2)^{|\mu|}}\right]^{1/2}$$

μ is the projection of the electron moment 1, A_1, A_2 were obtained matching the asymptotic wave function $R = A \, z^{\frac{1}{z}-1} e^{-\gamma z} \left[1 - \frac{a}{z} + O(z^2)\right]$ with Roothaan-Hartree-Fock function. At higher energies, over the maxima, the cross sections were calculated as in the resonant case[9], introducing the change in the phase of the wave function from $-\gamma z$ to $-\varkappa(\nu)z$, where $\varkappa(\nu) = \left[\frac{(\gamma_1^2 - \gamma_2^2)^2}{4 \, \nu^2} + \frac{(\gamma_1^2 + \gamma_2^2)}{2} + \frac{\nu^2}{4}\right]^{1/2}$.

The calculated and experimentally obtained results are shown in Fig.1. Taking into account the uncertainties of the experimental points, rather complicated structures with the p transient electron and complexness of the theory for such cases, the theoretical curve appreciably deviate from the experimental points only in the case of Ar targets, what indicates probably the unapplicability of the present theoretical approach to the electron transition mechanism in that particular case at low and medium energy.

[+]Also at C.M.O.A., 23 Rue du Maroc - 75019 Paris, France

30. Metastable formation by charge transfer and related topics. II

547

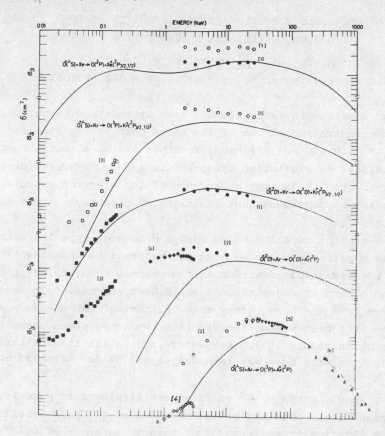

Fig. 1. Experimental points labelled as [1] and theoretical curves are the present results. Points labelled [2] - [6] correspond to the references of the same number. Open points - $O^+(^4S)$; black points - $O^+(^2D)$ state.

1. M.Vujović,M.Matić,B.Čobić,Yu.S.Gordeev, J.Phys.B **5**,2085(1972)

2. M.Matić,B.Čobić,M.Vujović, Proc.X ICPEAC,Paris,1977,p.882

3. B.M.Hughes,T.O.Tiernan, J.Chem.Phys.**55**,3419(1971)

4. T.F.Moran,J.B.Wilcox, J.Chem.Phys. **69**,1397(1978)

5. J.H.Ormrod,W.L.Mitchel, Can.J.Phys. **49**,606(1971)

6. H.H.Lo,W.L.Fite, Atomic Data **1**,305(1970)

7. J.A.Rutherford,D.A.Vroom, J.Chem.Phys. **55**,5622(1971)

8. Yu.N.Demkov,V.N.Ostrovskiy, ZHETF **69**,1582(1975)

9. B.M.Smirnov, "Asymptotic Methods in the Theory of Atomic Collisions"(in Russian) Moscow, 1972

10. R.E.Olson, Phys.Rev.A **6**,1822(1972)

ENERGY LOSS IDENTIFICATION OF $N^+(^5S)$ STATE
THROUGH COLLISIONAL DE-EXCITATION

M. Vujović, M. Matić and B. Čobić

Boris Kidrich Institute, Beograd 11001, POB 522, Yugoslavia

In our previous investigations[1], beam attenuation techniques enabled the separation of one of the three possible metastable states of N^+ (^1D, ^1S and ^5S), and, for that state, electron capture and collisional de-excitation cross-sections were measured for inert gas targets. From the energy dependence of the electron capture cross-section we concluded that the observed metastable state is the highest one, ^5S.

In the present experiment, we used a discharge type ion source with N_2 as a parent gas. As well as in the previous experiments[1], to increase the metastable fraction in the primary beam, f, Krypton was used as an attenuation gas target, while Neon was used to remove the metastables from the beam. After this "filtering" and energy monochromation, the beam was collimated into the interaction chamber. The interaction occurs at 3.5 keV energy,and, after the scattering angle selection, the beam was retarded to 550 eV for mass and energy analysis.

Energy loss spectra of N^+ on Argon are displayed in Fig. 1., a) for ground state beam and b) for mixed beam. The peak labelled A represents elastically scattered ions through an angle of 0.75°. For peak B, located between 11 eV and 12 eV, several transitions can be assigned as possible contributors. Those are: i) excitation of the ground state $N^+(^3P \rightarrow {}^3D)$, requiring 11.43 eV and ii) excitation of Argon target to the levels of 11.62 eV and 11.82 eV above the ground state.

Spectrum b), corresponding to the N^+ beam containing about 15% of metastables (measured by attenuation techniques), shows quite different picture comparing with the spectrum a). The most intense peak, C, at 5.8 eV can arise only as a consequence of the collisional de-excitation of $N^+(^5S)$ state, which, in accordance to the Wigner spin-conservation rule, can proceed through the process of electron exchange

$$N^+(^5S) + Ar(^1S) \longrightarrow N^+(^3P) + Ar(3p^54s)$$

requiring 5.74 eV and 5.92 eV (for two values of the quantum number K, respectively). The peak labelled D corresponds to the same process, involving the higher Argon states (probably $3p^55s$).

Present results are in full accordance with our earlier experiments where the large cross-section (of the order of $10^{-16} cm^2$) for collisionally induced de-excitation of the metastable state involved, was found. Also, the identification of this metastable state, ^5S, is verified.

The fraction of $N^+(^5S)$ state in the beam from the discharge type ion source does not exceed a few percents. However, it is interesting to note that, in a separate experiment[2], using the Nier-type ion source with very low working pressure of N_2 and electron energy higher than 120 eV, we obtained the N^+ ion beam containing about 50% metastables, here identified as the ^5S state.

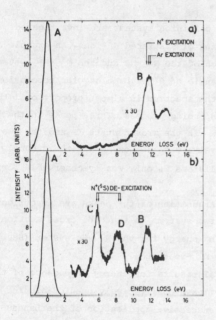

Fig. 1.
Energy loss spectra of the 3.5 keV N^+ ions scattered on Argon. Angle of scattering 0.75^o
a) ground state beam ($f \simeq 0$)
b) mixed beam ($f \simeq 15$%)
Arrows indicate transitions discussed in the text.

1. M. Vujović, M. Matić, B. Čobić and P. Hvelplund,
   J. Phys.B: Atom. Molec. Phys., 10, 3699-713 (1977)
2. B. Čobić, R. Petrović, M. Vujović and M. Matić,
   Proc. VIII SPIG (ed. B. Navinšek, J. Stefan Institute,
   Ljubljana, Yugoslavia) p.p. 97-100 (1976)

ELECTRON CAPTURE IN N^{++}-He AND N^{++}-Ne COLLISIONS*

Yukinori Sato** and John H. Moore

Chemistry Department, University of Maryland
College Park, Maryland   20742

Electron captures by N^{++} projectiles in collisions with He and Ne atoms,

$$N^{++} + He \rightarrow N^+ + He^+, \text{ and } N^{++} + Ne \rightarrow N^+ + Ne^+,$$

are studied in the moderate energy range 0.2 - 2.4 keV.

This type of charge exchange has been recognized as a process which proceeds through well separated curve-crossings located at relatively large internuclear distances[1].

The final states accessible to these collision systems are investigated using an electrostatic analysis[2] of energies of scattered N^+ ions. An example of energy spectrum is shown in Fig. 1 for each of the N^{++}-Ne and the N^{++}-He systems. The spectra are obtained at a scattering angle of 0° with an angular resolution of 1.2^o FWHM. The intensity of a peak in the spectrum is almost proportional to the integrated cross section of the corresponding process. Three peaks in the spectrum correspond to the production of N^+ in the ground state ^3P and the two lowest excited states ^1D and ^1S, respectively, with He^+ or Ne^+ in the ground state. Production of $N^+(^1S)$ in N^{++}-He collisions is only weakly observable for energies higher than 1 keV.

Energy dependences of the relative intensities of the peaks are investigated. The most striking difference between the two systems is that the cross section ratio $Q(^3P)/Q(^1D)$ decreases with increasing energy for the N^{++}-He system (See Fig. 3) and increases with energy for the N^{++}-Ne system.

In the N^{++}-Ne system, the experimental results for energy dependence of the ratios $Q(^3P)/Q(^1D)$ and $Q(^1S)/Q(^1D)$ are at least qualitatively predictable in terms of the curve-crossing mechanism by successive application of the Landau-Zener probability at each of crossing points encountered on a path along the potential curves which are approximated by the Coulomb repulsion and the dipole polarization. In the N^{++}-He system, energy dependence of the ratio $Q(^3P)/Q(^1D)$ cannot be interpreted by the curve-crossing mechanism alone. Crossings located at internuclear distances larger than 8 a_o are quite ineffective while those at around 5 a_o are mostly effective in inducing a transition. A combination of a transition at the 5.4 a_o crossing and a Demkov-type transition around 4.2 a_o (See Fig. 2) predicts well the energy dependence of the ratio as is shown in Fig. 3.

*Research supported by a grant from the National Science Foundation.

**Research Institute for Scientific Measurements, Tohoku University, Sanjyo-Machi, Sendai, Japan.

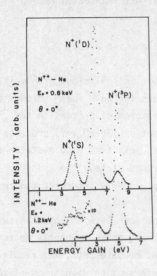

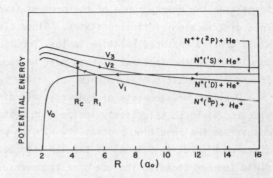

Fig. 1. Energy spectra of the foward scattered N^+ produced in N^{++}-Ne and N^{++}-He collisions.

Fig. 2. Scattering path for the production of $N^+(^1D)$ in the N^{++}-He system.

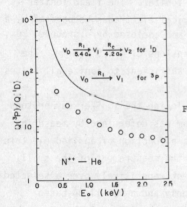

Fig. 3. Energy dependence of the cross section ratio $Q(^3P)/Q(^1D)$ in the N^{++}-He system. The solid line is a calculation based on the indicated paths for production of $N^+(^1D)$ and $N^+(^3P)$. The circles are the experimental results.

1. J. B. Hasted, S. M. Igbal and M. M. Yousaf, J. Phys. B **4**, 343 (1971)

2. J. H. Moore, Jr., J. Chem. Phys. **55**, 2760 (1971)

MEASUREMENT OF H ATOM RYDBERG-STATE POPULATION BY A TRANSMISSION METHOD*

F. W. Meyer and H. J. Kim

Oak Ridge National Laboratory, Oak Ridge, Tennessee 37830, USA

In our study of electron loss from fast H^o atoms in collisions with multi-charged ions,[1] the neutral H^o beam is obtained by passing an H^+ beam through a thick ($\sim 5 \times 10^{14}$ cm^{-2}) H_2O vapor target. Neutralization of protons in gas targets in the energy range of the present investigation (30-60 keV) produces H^o in a distribution of final n-states. Since electron loss from high n-states of H^o is greatly enhanced relative to loss from the ground state,[2] the Rydberg population in the incident H^o beam must be known to properly interpret the results of the electron loss measurements.

Previous measurements of Rydberg-state distributions have employed an axial electric field to selectively ionize high n-states, and to subsequently detect downstream the resulting protons.[3,4] In the present measurements, the requirement of large H^o flux (~ 0.1 μA) at the ion-atom beam intersection downstream of the field ionizer dictated the use of a transverse electric field, which permitted the use of larger beam-limiting apertures in the ionizer. The field ionizer consisted of two parallel 1.3 cm diameter cylindrical electrodes, separated by a gap of 0.28 cm through which the H^o beam passed, and enclosed by a grounded box, with beam entrance and exit apertures having dimensions of $\sim 1.5 \times 3$ mm. The maximum electric field attainable was 107 kV/cm, sufficient to ionize all states down to $n \approx 9$.

Since the transverse electric field trapped inside the ionizer any protons produced, the excited-state content of the H^o beam was determined by measuring its attenuation in passage through the ionizer as a function of applied electric field. To eliminate beam fluctuation effects in the measurement of the small attenuations expected, the electric field was swept repetitively over a selected range using a programmable high voltage power supply and a PDP-11/34-based multichannel analyzer. Nonlinearities in the data acquisition electronics were eliminated by dividing the raw spectrum of H^o current vs. electric field by a similar spectrum obtained by sampling a "dummy" constant current source of comparable magnitude (~ 0.1 μA), instead of the current from the H^o secondary electron emission detector.

Figure 1 shows a sample attenuation curve obtained in the manner outlined above. The linear dependence[4] of the H^o dependence vs. $\sqrt{\mathcal{E}}$ displayed in Fig. 1 indicates an excited-state population distribution of the form c/n^3, and was observed at all the energies investigated, as well as for all the ranges of electric field (i.e., n-states) measured. Table I summarizes the energy dependence of the population coefficient, c, obtained by a linear least-squares analysis of plots similar to Fig. 1. As can be seen from Table I, the excited-state population for $n > 9$ is a strong function of H^o energy, increasing by more than a factor of 2 in the energy interval 30-60 keV. Excited-state fractions calculated from the above population distributions are in good agreement with previous experimental results.[4]

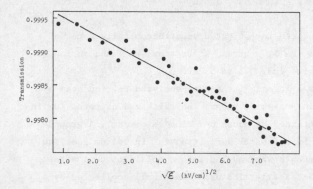

Fig. 1.   Fraction of 40-keV H^O beam transmitted through field ionizer vs. $\sqrt{\mathcal{E}}$.

Table I.   The population coefficient, c, obtained from least-squares fits of H^O field ionizer transmission data assuming c/n^3 excited-state distribution.

n-range	H^O Energy (keV)				Electric Field Range (10^3 kV/cm)
	30	40	50	60	
11-34	0.31	0.41	0.54	--	0.5-44
10-16	--	--	--	0.56	10-64
11-13	--	--	--	0.63	22-44
9-11	--	0.41	0.55	0.64	44-100

*Research sponsored by the Office of Fusion Energy, U. S. Department of Energy, under contract W-7405-eng-26 with the Union Carbide Corporation.

1. H. J. Kim and F. W. Meyer, Bull. Am. Phys. Soc. 23, 1095 (1978).

2. H. J. Kim and F. W. Meyer, "N-Scaling of Electron-Loss Cross Sections for Fast $H(n)^O + N^{3+}$ Collisions," abstract submitted to this Conference.

3. A. C. Riviere and D. R. Sweetman, in Atomic Collision Processes, edited by M. R. C. McDowell (North-Holland, Amsterdam, 1964), pp. 734-42.

4. R. N. Il'in, B. I. Kikiani, V. A. Oparin, E. S. Solov'ev, and N. V. Fedorenko, Sov. Phys. JETP 20, 835 (1965).

He I-EXCITATION IN COLLISONS OF He^m, He^g AND He^+ WITH He

Masahiro Kimura, Takami Egawa and Tsuruji Iwai

Faculty of Science, Osaka University
Toyonaka, Osaka 560, Japan

The excitation of He I has been investigated spectroscopically for the collisions of a metastable atom (He^m), a ground-state atom (He^g) and an ion (He^+) with He at the laboratory energies from 0.5 to 5 keV.

A metastable atomic beam was formed from a mass-analyzed He^+ ion beam by near-resonant charge transfer in potassium vapor; the thickness of potassium in a charge transfer oven was maintained at about 6-7 x10^{13} atoms/cm^2. A ground-state atomic beam was produced by resonant charge transfer in helium gas. The neutral atomic beam formed in such a way was led into a collision cell after removing ions from the beam electrically. The beam was finally collected by a Faraday cup. The neutral atomic beam intensity was determined from measurements of the secondary electron current, provided that the secondary-emission coefficient of neutral atom is the same as that of ion. The collision cell (30 mm in length, 40 mm in dia.) has two windows (8 mm in dia.) at its center-position; radiation through one of the windows (quartz) was observed along the direction perpendicular to the beam by means of a grating monochromator combined with a photomultiplier (A) and a photon counting system. Another photomultiplier (B) was attached just behind the other glass window and monitored the light transmitted. Pressures in the collision cell was usually maintained to be smaller than 2×10^{-3} Torr ; in this range the photon counting rate was confirmed to be linearly dependent on pressures. The period of the photon counting was set by the accumulation time of monitored photons in order to eliminate errors arising from fluctuations in both the beam intensity and the target pressure.

Emission cross sections were measured for such lines of He I as 3^3P-2^3S (3889 Å), 4^3D-2^3P(4471 Å), 4^3S-2^3P(4713 Å), 4^1D-2^1P(4922 Å), 3^1P-2^1S(5016 Å), 4^1S-2^1P(5048 Å) and 3^3D-2^3P(5876 Å). The results obtained are presented in Fig.1 for three typical lines. The values of the cross sections observed are normalized at 4 keV to the excitation cross sections measured by Wolterbeek Muller and de Heer[1] in He^++He collision. McCullough et al[2] measured $4\,^3S$ and $4\,^3D$ excitation in He^m+He and He^g+He collisions at higher energies. Their results are also shown in Fig.1 in different scale of collision energy. The metastable atomic beam consists of two components He^m and He^g. However, $He^m(2^3S)$ is the main component (>50 %) under the present experimental condition.[3] (He in 2^3P decays to 2^3S before entering the collision cell.) No correction was made for contamination of a metastable atomic beam with ground-state atoms.

Generally speaking, collisions of metastable atoms give largest excitation cross sections and the ones of ions smallest as seen in Fig.1. In particular, the

cross section for triplet excitation in $He^m + He$ collision (σ_m) is considerably
larger than that in $He^g + He$ collision (σ_g). For triplet excitation in $He^g + He$
collision, the spin-conservation rule requires to excite both the projectile and
target atoms into triplet states simultaneously. Since the endothermicity of this
process is more than 40 eV, the cross section σ_g should be small at this energy
range. On the other hand, the collision $He^m + He \rightarrow He^*$ ($n \geq 3$) is less endothermic
(a few eV) to produce the triplet state and such a small energy defect accounts
for the significantly increased cross section.

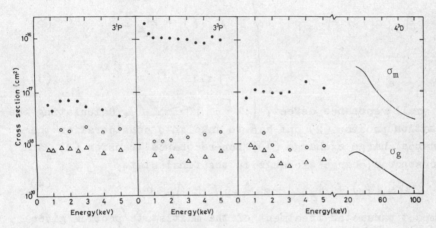

Fig.1.

Excitation cross section for the collision of metastable atoms (solid
circles), ground-state atoms (open circles) and ions (triangles) with He.
Solid curves after McCullough et al; upper one for metastable-atom collisions;
lower one for ground-state-atom collisions.

1. L. Wolterbeek Muller and F.J. de Heer, Physica **48**, 345 (1970).
2. R.W. McCullough, F.R. Simpson and H.B. Gilbody, J. Phys. B **6**, L322 (1973).
3. R.E. Olson and F.T. Smith, Phys. Rev. A **7**, 1529 (1973).

EXCITATION AND CHARGE EXCHANGE AT IONIC COLLISIONS.

L.A.BUREYEVA and L.P.PRESNYAKOV

P.N.Lebedev Physical Institute, Academy of Sciences of
the USSR, Moscow, USSR

We consider collisions between ions with identical nuclei

$$A_Z(a) + A_{Z+1} \longrightarrow \begin{cases} A_{Z+1} + A_Z(a) & (1) \\[2mm] A_Z(b) + A_{Z+1} & (2) \\[2mm] A_{Z+1} + A_Z(b) & (3) \end{cases}$$

with small resonance defect, $|\Delta E_{ab}| \ll Z^2 Ry$. Calculating the
excitation process (2) one has to take into consideration the
resonance charge exchange (1), non-resonance transfer (3), and
the resonance charge exchange in the final state,

$$A_Z(b) + A_{Z+1} \longrightarrow A_{Z+1} + A_Z(b) \qquad (4)$$

An impact parameter treatment of the multistate problem gives
the following results for transition probabilities

$$W_{00} = \frac{\cos^2\varphi}{1 + P_{02} + P_{03}} , \qquad W_{01} = \frac{\sin^2\varphi}{1 + P_{02} + P_{03}} , \qquad (5)$$

$$W_{02} = \frac{P_{02}\cos^2\chi + P_{03}\cdot\sin^2\chi}{1 + P_{02} + P_{03}} \qquad (6)$$

$$W_{03} = \frac{P_{03}\cdot\cos^2\chi + P_{02}\cdot\sin^2\chi}{1 + P_{02} + P_{03}} \qquad (7)$$

Here $\sin^2\varphi$ and $\sin^2\chi$ coincide with the transition probabilites
for the resonance charge exchange processes (1) and (4) respectively calculated without close coupling with the excitation
channel (see, for example, Ref.[1]). P_{02} and P_{03} coincide with
the transition probabilities for excitation $0 \rightarrow 2$ and charge
exchange $0 \rightarrow 3$ obtained on a base of the "two-level" close
coupling.

$$P_{02} = \exp\{-2\beta\} \, P_{ab}^{CB} \qquad (8)$$

where P_{ab}^{CB} is the Coulomb-Born excitation probability $[2,3]$, and in a case of multipole interactions ($V_{02} = V_{ab} \backsim \frac{\lambda n}{R^n}$) the Massey parameter β is defined by $[4]$

$$\beta = \frac{2^{1/n} \lambda^{1/n} |\Delta E_{ab}|^{(n-1)/n}}{\sqrt{}} \cdot \sin \frac{\pi}{2n} \tag{9}$$

Numerical calculations have been done for the $2S_{1/2} - 2P_{1/2}$ transitions in H-like ions and for transitions between fine structure components with the principal quantum number n = 2.

1. B.M.Smirnov. Asymptotic method in theory of atomic collisions. "Nauka", Moscow, 1973.

2. K.Alder et al. Rev. Mod. Phys. 28, 432 (1956).

3. V.P.Shevelko, I.Yu.Skobelev, A.M.Vinogradov. Phys.Scripta. 16, 123, 1977.

4. L.P.Presnyakov. Trudy (Proceedings) of the P.N.Lebedev Physical Institute 30, 236, 1964.

ONE-ELECTRON CHARGE EXCHANGE OF MULTIPLY CHARGED IONS WITH ATOMS AT INTERMEDIATE AND LARGE RELATIVE VELOCITIES.

L.P.PRESNYAKOV and V.P.SHEVELKO

P.N.Lebedev Physical Institute, Academy of Sciences of the
USSR, Moscow, USSR.

The charge exchange problem at low velocities $v \ll v_0$ may be treated using modifications of the Landau-Zener model. In the opposite case $v \gg v_0$ good results are given by the first order perturbation theory. In this case for multi-electron atomic targets the contribution of electron capture from inner shells is predominant [1,2]. In the intermediate region the calculations of cross sections are performed mainly by numerical methods [3-5].

In the present paper the analysis and calculations of one-electron capture cross sections are made at the relative energies 1 keV/a.m.u. $<$ E $<$ 10 Mev/a.m.u. in the framework of close-coupling of many states using the orthogonalized atomic basis [6]. Partial transition probability, corresponding to close coupling between the initial 0 and one of the final state n of the system, is obtained in the form:

$$P_{on} = \exp(-\pi \omega_{eff}/\gamma v) \sin^2 \int_{-\infty}^{+\infty} \left[\sum_{\ell m} \left| V(o \to n\ell m) \exp(i\omega_{eff} t) \right|^2 \right]^{\frac{1}{2}}$$

$$\gamma = \left(\sqrt{\frac{Z^2}{n^2} + \frac{v^2}{4}} + \sqrt{1 + \frac{v^2}{4}} \right)/2$$

where $n\ell m$ are quantum numbers of the final state and ω_{eff} is the effective energy difference between the atomic and ionic levels including the Stark shift.

Results of calculations of the total capture cross sections of ions with H-atoms are shown in Fig.1 together with experimental data given in papers [5,7,8].

1. L.P.Presnyakov and V.P.Shevelko. Sov. Phys. - JTP, 18, 1079 (1974)

2. V.P.Shevelko. Z.Physik A287, 19 (1978)

3. L.P.Presnyakov and A.D.Ulantsev. Sov. J.Quant. Electronics 4, 1320 (1975)

4. R.E.Olson and A.Salop.Phys.Rev.A16, 592 (1977)

5. H.Ryufuku and T.Watanabe. Phys. Rev. A 18, 2005(1978); Preprint JAERI-memo N 7895 (1978)

6. L.P.Presnyakov. X ICPEAC. Invited papers, p.407. North-Holland, 1977

7. D.P.Dewangan. J.Phys. B, 10,1083 (1977)

8. R.A.Phaneuf et al. X ICPEAC, Abstracts, p.p.872, 524, Paris, 1977.

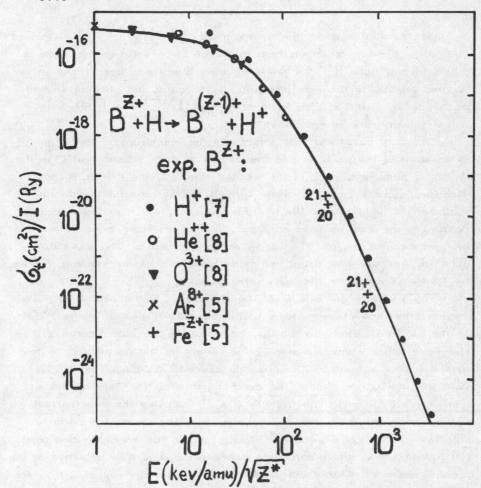

Fig.1. Solid line-present work, points-experiment; $Z^* = n\sqrt{I(Ry)}$, where I, n are the ionization potential and the principal quantum number of the ion $B^{(Z-1)+}$ in the ground state.

THE ANGULAR DISTRIBUTION AND POLARIZATION
OF X-RAYS EMITTED BY AN INCOMING PARTICLE IN ION–ATOM
CHARGE-TRANSFER COLLISIONS

E.G. Berezhko and N.M. Kabachnik

Institute of Nuclear Physics, Moscow State University;

Moscow 117234; USSR

The excited state of the hydrogen–like ion $I^{+(Z-1)}$ formed due to the capture of an electron in the collision between the beam of fully "stripped" ions I^{+Z} , and the target atoms has been found to be aligned relative to the beam direction. As a result, the photons emitted in the decay of the excited state of the ion $I^{+(Z-1)}$ are distributed anisotropically and are polarized[1,2].

The only parameter that determines the anisotropy in the angular distribution of the photons and the degree of their polarization P is the degree of alignment, A_{20}, of the excited state[3]. Using the Brinkman-Kramers approximation, we have derived expressions for the degree of alignment of any state of the hydrogen–like ion, which arises from the capture of an electron from an atom. Calculations have been made for electron capture by the F^{+9} ion in argon and helium. The wave functions for Ar were calculated using the Herman–Skillman potential; for He, the Hartree–Fock wave functions were used.

Fig. 1 shows the results of the calculation of the degree of polarization of the line corresponding to the 2p → 1s transition in the F^{+8} ion for the electron capture to the 2p state from the Ar atom (curve 1). The same figure shows (curve 2) the results of the calculation of polarization taking account of the possible cascade occupation of the 2p state from the upper states (the contributions from the 3s, 3d, and 4s states were included). The triangle (▲) indicates the experimental value taken from ref.[1]. As can be seen from the figure, the predicted polarization strongly depends on energy and in the energy region from 100 keV to 1 MeV the polarization changes its sign. The influence of the cascade occupation turns out significant in the energy region E ≳ 1 MeV. Similar results for the F^{+9} + He collisions are shown in fig.2, where the effect of cascade transitions is seen to be more significant.

REFERENCES

1. E.H. Pedersen et al., Phys.Rev. A11, 1267(1975)
2. Z.J. Gzuchlewski et al. Phys.Lett.A51,309(1975).
3. E.G.Berezhko, N.M. Kabachnik, J.Phys.B10, 2467(1977).

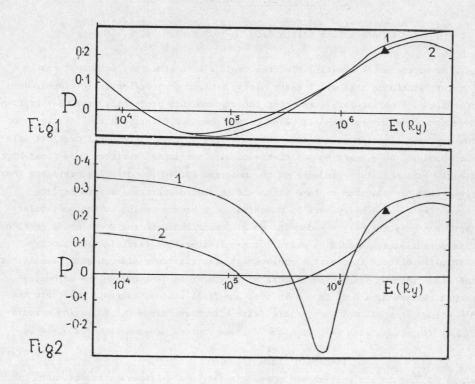

Fig1

Fig2

APPROACH TO ELECTRON CAPTURE INTO ARBITRARY PRINCIPAL SHELLS OF FAST PROJECTILES

J. Eichler and F.T. Chan[+]

Bereich Kern- und Strahlenphysik, Hahn-Meitner-Institut
für Kernforschung Berlin GmbH, D-1000 Berlin 39, W.-Germany

An approach for treating electron capture into arbitrary principal shells n (or into continuum states) of fast, highly ionized projectiles is developed. Such processes are particularly important for capture into projectile ions heavier than the target atoms. The approach[1] is based on the momentum density matrix[2] $\rho(\vec{q},\vec{q}')$ of the captured electron, summed over all substates l,m (or integrated over all emission angles). As a starting point, the density matrix is rewritten in a form which clearly exhibits its dependence on the momentum spread $|\vec{q}-\vec{q}'|$. Arguments are then given that for electron capture it should be a good approximation to replace $\rho(\vec{q},\vec{q}')$ by $\rho(\vec{q},\vec{q})$ everywhere in momentum space because owing to the particular capture kinematics only the domain $\vec{q} \approx \vec{q}'$ contributes to the total cross section. This approximation should be valid for any treatment of fast electron capture. Within the eikonal theory, the replacement prescription yields an *exact* result for the cross section describing capture of 1s electrons (subject to the effective target charges Z_t and Z_t' in the initial and final states, respectively) into the nth principal shell of a projectile (with effective charge Z_p) following a rectilinear trajectory with velocity $v \equiv 1/\eta$. The capture cross section is given by

$$\sigma_{1s-n} = \alpha_n \, \sigma_{1s-n}^{OBK} \tag{1a}$$

where σ_{1s-n}^{OBK} is the well-known[3] Oppenheimer-Brinkman-Kramers cross section

$$\sigma_{1s-n}^{OBK} = \frac{2^8 \, \pi \, z_p^5 \, z_t^5}{5n^3 \, v^2 \, [\, z_t^2 + (\frac{v}{2} - \epsilon\eta)^2 \,]^5} \tag{1b}$$

and the scaling factor is

$$\alpha_n = \frac{\pi\eta \, z_t'}{\sinh(\pi\eta z_t')} \, \exp\{-2\eta z_t' \, \tan^{-1}[(\frac{v}{2} - \epsilon\eta)/z_t]\}$$

$$\cdot \{1 - \frac{5}{8}\frac{z_t'}{z_t} + \frac{5}{48}\frac{z_t'^2}{z_t^2} + (\frac{1}{6}z_t'^2 + \frac{5}{4}\frac{z_t'}{z_t}\epsilon - \frac{5}{12}\frac{z_t'^2}{z_t^2}\epsilon)\eta^2 + \frac{5}{12}\frac{z_t'^2}{z_t^2}\epsilon^2\eta^4\} \tag{1c}$$

with the energy difference $\epsilon = -\frac{1}{2}(\frac{z_p^2}{n^2} - z_t^2)$.

It turns out that for not too high projectile energies a great number of principal shells contribute with a maximum in the vicinity of the resonant transition $\epsilon = 0$ or $n \approx Z_p/Z_t$. Only for very high energies (when the cross section is already quite small) the higher momentum tails of the lower shells rather than the resonance condition dominate the cross section. In order to account for contributions from all principal shells it is convenient to introduce a theoretical *over-all scaling factor* α through the relation

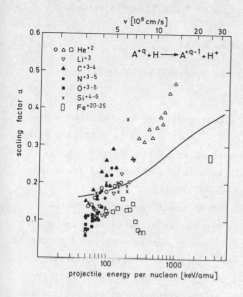

Fig. 1: Experimental and theoretical scaling factors for hydrogen targets

Fig. 2: Experimental and theoretical scaling factors for helium targets ($Z_t = Z_t' = 1.6875$)

$$\sigma^{capt} = \sum_n \sigma_{1s-n} = \alpha(v) \sum_n \sigma_{1s-n}^{OBK} \tag{2}$$

The numerical calculations show that $\alpha(v)$ varies between 0.1 and 0.4 and that it is a function of v/v_K (v_K is the target K-shell velocity) but is approximately independent of the target and projectile charges. Figs. 1 and 2 show a comparison between the theoretical scaling factor and experimental points calculated by dividing the experimental capture cross section by $\sum_n \sigma_{1s-n}^{OBK}$. It is seen that for hydrogen and helium targets good agreement is obtained with a large body of experimental data. We conclude that in view of its simplicity and better foundation our formula Eq. (1) should replace the OBK expression[3] as a reference formula.

[+]On leave from the Physics Department, University of Arkansas

1. F.T. Chan and J. Eichler, Phys. Rev. Lett. **42**, 58 (1979) and submitted to Phys. Rev.

2. V. Fock, Z. Physik **98**, 145 (1935)

3. M.R.C. McDowell and J.P. Coleman, Introduction to the Theory of Ion-Atom Collisions (North Holland, Amsterdam 1970)

ELECTRON CAPTURE BY Ar[6+] IONS FROM He IN THE KeV ENERGY RANGE

L. Opradolce[*], P. Valiron and R. McCarroll

Laboratoire d'Astrophysique, Université de Bordeaux I, 33400 Talence
France

Measurements of total cross sections of electron capture into excited states have been carried out by Afrosimov et al[1] for Ar^{3+} - Ar^{7+} ions in collision with He. Of particular interest is the Ar^{6+} - He system, where the charge exchange process involves only one active electron. In this case a theoretical treatment of the collision can be developed without undue difficulty.

In the experimental energy range (5 - 15 keV Ar beams) we may expect the molecular model of the collision to be valid, the charge exchange reaction occurring via the avoided crossings of the potential energy curves correlated to the initial $\left[Ar^{6+} + He\ (1s^2)\right]$ and final states $\left[Ar^{5+}\ (n\ell) + He^+\ (1s)\right]$. The first step of the work is to compute the potential energy curves of Ar He^{6+}. Here we adopt a model potential method[2,3,4] developed in our group for other applications. For this we require model potentials to describe the Ar^{6+} and He^+ cases. For He^+ we use the model potential of Bottcher[5] while for Ar^{6+} we use the method of Valiron[6]. The accuracy of our Ar^{6+} model potential may be ascertained from the following table.

Table Comparison of calculated and observed energy levels (in atomic units) of $Ar^{5+}\ (1s^2\ 2s^2\ 2p^6\ 3s^2\ n\ell)$.

$n\ell$	Model potential	Observed
3p	− 3.332	− 3.357
3d	− 2.395	− 2.361
4s	− 1.782	− 1.797
4p	− 1.589	−
4d	− 1.286	− 1.284

The results of the molecular calculations (fig. 1) show clearly the three avoided crossings responsible for the charge exchange process.

To compute the collision cross sections, a diabatic representation is used, an estimate of the non diagonal matrix elements being obtained using the procedure of McCarroll and Valiron[3]. Calculations of electron capture to the 4s and 4p states of Ar^{5+} have been carried out using the impact parameter method with straight line trajectories. Capture into the 3d state has been treated by the multi-state Landau-Zener formula.

The results are shown in figure 2. The agreement with experiment is satisfactory.

[*]On leave of absence from Instituto de Astronomia y Fisica del Espacio
1428 Buenos Aires, Argentin

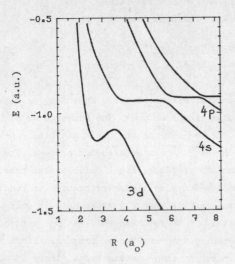

Figure 1 - Potential energy (in atomic units) of the Σ states of the system Ar He^{6+}. Charge exchange takes place via the avoided crossings, leading to the formation of Ar^{5+} in the 3d, 4s or 4p states.

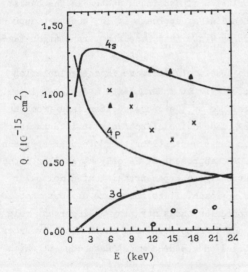

Figure 2 - Calculated cross sections (solid curves) for capture into the 3d, 4s and 4p states of Ar^{5+}. The experimental points[1] are as follows :

○ ⊘ capture into the 3d states,

✗ ✗ capture into the 4p state,

▲ ▲ capture into the 4s state

1. Afrosimov VV, Basalaev AA, Panov MN and Leiko GA 1977 JETP Lett. <u>26</u>, 699
2. McCarroll R and Valiron P 1975 Astron. Astrophys. <u>44</u>, 465
3. McCarroll R and Valiron P 1976 Astron. Astrophys. <u>53</u>, 83
4. Valiron R, Gayet R, McCarroll R, Masnou-Seeuws F and Philippe M 1979
   J. Phys. B : Atom. Molec. Phys. <u>12</u>, 53
5. Bottcher C 1973 J. Phys. B : Atom. Molec. Phys. <u>6</u>, 2368
6. Valiron P 1976 Thèse de 3e cycle, Université de Bordeaux I, N° 1279

CONNECTION BETWEEN CHOICE OF TRANSLATION FACTORS
AND SIZE OF MO BASIS IN CHARGE-TRANSFER CALCULATIONS

J. Vaaben[†] and K. Taulbjerg
Institute of Physics, University of Aarhus, Denmark

It is common to expand the time-dependent electronic wave function for slow ion-atom collisions in a basis of molecular eigenfunctions. The convergence of cross-section calculations as a function of the size of the basis has been examined by Winter and Lane[1] for the $He^{++} - H \rightarrow He^+ - H^+$ charge exchange process. The charge-exchange cross section was obtained by coupled-channel calculations based on 3, 10, and 20 state expansions. For the lowest velocities convergence was readily achieved. But for $v \gtrsim 0.1 v_o$ ($v_o = e^2/\hbar$), the results change just as much in going from 10 to 20 states as from 3 to 10 states. It therefore seems that one must add even further basis vectors in order to examine the convergence properly. Since rather highly-excited MO were already included in the 20-state basis, there is no reason to believe that one can avoid inclusion of continuum states in the basis. Rather than persuing this very cumbersome line of approach it is, however, appropriate to test the basic assumption made by Winter and Lane that translation factors may be neglected.

Translation factors are known to be absolutely decisive in the calculation of charge-transfer processes in an atomic basis at intermediate and higher impact velocities. It is apparent from the magnitude of the cross section (and from the $P(b)$ curves[1]) that charge-exchange takes place quite effectively at internuclear separations as large as $R \sim 6a_o$. For such large separations the molecular approach is no more relevant than the atomic (LCAO) approach. It is only at smaller impact parameters, where atomic orbitals may strongly interpenetrate, that a molecular expansion may be superior to the atomic approach. It is therefore obvious that inclusion of translation factors in the molecular basis may play an important role in the present case. The argumentation due to Piacentini and Salin[2] in favour of neglecting the translation factors is based on a *near-completeness* concept which is entirely unphysical.

In order to test the significance of translation factors we have calculated the cross section for charge transfer in $He^{++} - H$ collisions using a basis of *travelling* MO

$$\chi_n(\underline{r},\underline{R}) = \phi_n(\underline{r},\underline{R}) \exp \{if(\underline{r},\underline{R})\underline{v} \cdot \underline{r}\} \quad ,$$

where $\{\phi_n\}$ are eigenstates for the $(He-H)^{++}$ molecular ion. We choose translation factors of Schneiderman-Russek[3] type, i.e., the switching function $f(\underline{r},\underline{R})$ is taken to be common to all basis functions of the considered set. The dynamical equations corresponding to this basis have been developed in Ref. 4.

In the present calculations we employ the following form for the switching function

$$f(r,R) = \frac{1}{2} \frac{r_A^3 Z_B - r_B^3 Z_A}{r_A^3 Z_B + r_B^3 Z_A} + \frac{1}{2} \frac{Z_A - Z_B}{Z_A + Z_B} \ ,$$

where Z_A, Z_B are the nuclear charge numbers and $\underline{r}_A$, $\underline{r}_B$, and $\underline{r}$ are position vectors of the electron relative to the two nuclei and the centre of charge, respectively. This choice ensures correct dissociation at large separations and satisfies *reasonable* physical conditions[3] at small R values. Note that there is no orbital-dependent parameters in the expression for $f(\underline{r},\underline{R})$.

Our calculated cross sections are tabulated below. The '20'-state results were obtained by ignoring the six 4s, 4p, and 4d states which by Winter and Lane were found to influence the cross section by less than 5 percent. It is seen that the translation factors are essential for the convergence of the molecular multi-channel calculations. Conversely, it may be concluded that most of the MO in Winter and Lane's 20-state calculation were spuriously populated in order to compensate for the lack of inherent translational motion after electron transfer to the helium ion.

n-state v/v_0	Winter and Lane				This work	
	3*	3	10	20	3*	'20'*
.032		.297			$< 10^{-5}$	
.071	.127	.543			.004	
.100	.792	.850	.882		.477	.482
.174	3.64	3.55	3.68	4.32	4.45	4.49
.284	11.74	11.68	13.53	16.64	19.28	18.55
.449		19.07	25.7	33.5	37.0	34.4

Total charge-transfer cross section in units of a_0^2 for a selection of impact velocities v. A 2pσ trajectory[1] was used in columns marked with *. Other results were based on rectilinear trajectories.

† Present address: H.C. Ørsted Institute, DK-2100 Copenhagen Ø., Denmark.

1. T.G. Winter and N.F. Lane, Phys.Rev. A17, 66 (1979).

2. R.D. Piacentini and A. Salin, J.Phys. B7, 1666 (1974); B9, 563 (1976); B10, 1515 (1977).

3. S.B. Schneiderman and A. Russek, Phys.Rev. A181, 311 (1969).

4. K. Taulbjerg, J. Vaaben, and B. Fastrup, Phys.Rev. A12, 2325 (1975).

THEORY OF ELECTRON TRANSFER IN ION-ATOM COLLISIONS[*]

C. D. Lin

Department of Physics, Kansas State University
Manhattan, Kansas 66506 U.S.A.

Electron transfer has been recognized experimentally as an important process in the production of target K-shell vacancies in ion-atom collisions, particularly when the projectile charge is comparable to the target nuclear charge and the projectiles carrying K-shell vacancies into the collision. Recently we have generalized the two-center atomic eigenfunction expansion method, originally proposed by Bates,[1] to investigate theoretically the electron transfer cross sections in multielectron ion-atom collisions. This method is expected to be valid in the energy region where the projectile velocity is nearly identical to the orbital velocity of the electron.

This theory has been applied to a number of situations: (1) By applying the two-state, two-center atomic expansion and assuming small capture probability, a proper form of first order perturbation theory has been derived[2] and the theory is shown to predict accurate charge transfer cross sections for very asymmetric collisions; (2) By solving the two-state coupled equations non-perturbatively, the method is shown to account for the K-K charge transfer cross sections for near symmetric collisions;[3] (3) The differential cross sections[4] and double K-K capture cross sections[5] are also well-accounted for by the theory.

Current development of the theory includes: (1) Improvement of the atomic model for the multielectron atom —— the Hartree-Fock-Slater potential for the target atom has been implemented into the model; (2) Inclusion of certain intermediate states into the model to investigate the importance of intermediate coupling at lower energies; (3) Generalization to the outer-shell electron capture. Preliminary results indicate that K-K capture cross sections at lower energies are sensitive to the proper treatment of atomic model. We also have shown that electron capture from outer shells of multielectron atoms can be calculated using the present method, in conjunction with simple independent electron model.

Some recent K-K capture results, both theoretically and experimentally, are summarized in Table I.

TABLE I: K–K Capture Cross Sections Per Atom

	E(MeV/amu)	σ_{theory}	σ_{exp}	Reference
F^{9+} - Si	2.2	3.0×10^{-18}	1.9×10^{-18}	6
	1.6	3.2×10^{-18}	2.5×10^{-18}	
	1.2	2.7×10^{-18}	2.0×10^{-18}	
	0.8	1.7×10^{-18}	1.3×10^{-18}	
	0.4	6.0×10^{-19}	3.0×10^{-19}	
$C\ell^{17+}$ - Cu	1.71	4.2×10^{-20}	4.3×10^{-20}	7
S^{16+} - Cu	1.71	3.2×10^{-20}	2.4×10^{-20}	7
Si^{14+} - Cu	1.71	1.7×10^{-20}	9.0×10^{-21}	
Si^{14+} - Sc	1.93	7.8×10^{-19}	1.0×10^{-18}	8
Si^{14+} - Ti	1.93	4.7×10^{-19}	7.0×10^{-19}	
Si^{14+} - Cu	1.93	2.1×10^{-20}	8.0×10^{-21}	

*Research supported in part by the U. S. Department of Energy, Division of Basic Energy Sciences.

1. D. R. Bates, Proc. R. Soc. A 224, 294 (1958).

2. C. D. Lin, S. C. Soong and L. N. Tunnell, Phys. Rev. A 17, 1646 (1978).

3. C. D. Lin, J. Phys. B 11, L185 (1978).

4. C. D. Lin and S. C. Soong, Phys. Rev. A 18, 499 (1978).

5. C. D. Lin, Phys. Rev. 17 (to be published).

6. H. Tawara, P. Richard, T. Gray, J. Newcomb, K. A. Jamison, C. Schmiedekamp and J. M. Hall, Phys. Rev. A 18, 1373 (1978).

7. R. K. Gardner, T. Gray, P. Richard, C. Schmiedekamp, K. A. Jamison and J. M. Hall, Phys. Rev. A 15, 2202 (1977).

8. F. D. McDaniel, L. J. Duggan, G. Basbas, P. D. Miller and G. Lapicki, Phys. Rev. 16, 1375 (1977).

APPROXIMATE EVALUATION OF THE SECOND BORN CROSS-SECTION FOR CHARGE EXCHANGE

J.S. Briggs[+] and L. Dubé

Theoretical Physics Division, A.E.R.E. Harwell, Didcot, England

The second Born approximation for the transfer of an electron from any hydrogenic state n'l'm' of a target nucleus of charge Z_2 to any hydrogenic state nlm of a projectile nucleus of charge Z_1 has been reduced to an approximate form which requires a single numerical integration for its evaluation. In the limit of high but non-relativistic velocities v, the formula gives the exact asymptotic v^{-11} behaviour of the double-scattering process which is the dominant mechnism for forward charge transfer at high velocity[1]. In the particular case of 1 s → nlm charge transfer the asymptotic form of the cross-section has been evaluated analytically and shown to have the form

$$\sigma = \sigma_{B1} \ (a_o v^o + a_1 v^1 + a_3 v^3 + \ldots a_{2l+1} v^{2l+1})$$

where σ_{B1} is the asymptotic first Born cross-section and the coefficients a_1 depend only upon Z_1, Z_2 and n.

[+] Present address, Fakultät für Physik, Universität Freiburg, 7800 Freiburg, Germany

[1] L. Spruch and R. Shakeshaft Revs. Mod. Phys. 1979 (to be published).

CHARGE TRANSFER BY A DOUBLE-SCATTERING MECHANISM INVOLVING TARGET ELECTRONS

J.S. Briggs[†] and K. Taulbjerg[††]

† Fakultät für Physik, Universität Freiburg, Germany
†† Institute of Physics, University of Aarhus, Denmark

In 1927 Thomas suggested a classical mechanism of charge transfer whereby the attachment of a target electron to an incident ion is facilitated by the recoil of a second target electron. This second electron recoils with the speed of the incident ion in a direction perpendicular to the ion direction.

In a quantum-mechanical description this process may be identified by a particular contribution to the charge-exchange amplitude which is of second Born nature. In order to evaluate this double-scattering amplitude we have introduced a series of high-velocity approximations. Here we present a formula which becomes approximately valid in the region of classical Thomas scattering, i.e., when $u \sim v$ and $\underline{u} \cdot \underline{v} \sim 0$, where $\underline{v}$ is the velocity of the incident projectile and $\underline{u}$ is the velocity of the ejected recoil electron. In this region the cross sections for charge transfer, differential in the electron recoil velocity, may be expressed (in atomic units) as

$$\frac{d\sigma}{d\underline{u}} \simeq \frac{2^{13} Z_1^5 Z_2^8}{3\pi v^2 u^4 |\underline{u} + \underline{v}|^4 [(\underline{u} \cdot \underline{v})^2 + (Z_1 u + Z_2 |\underline{u} + \underline{v}|)^2][p^2 + 4Z_2^2]^3}$$

where

$$p = (\underline{u} \cdot \underline{v} + \tfrac{1}{2} v^2 + \varepsilon_i - \varepsilon_f)/v ,$$

ε_i and ε_f are initial and final electron energies and Z_1 and Z_2 refer to the nuclear charges of the projectile and the target, respectively. The validity of this analytic result has been substantiated by a more accurate numerical evaluation of the differential cross section. It is seen that the spectrum of recoil electrons peaks when the classical Thomas scattering conditions are satisfied, but the δ-function distribution of recoil electrons, which is predicted classically, is broadened by the initial momentum distribution of the target electrons.

The total cross section for charge exchange via this double-scattering mechanism may be evaluated in the limit of asymptotically high collision velocities v. We find

$$\sigma = 2^4 \pi^2 Z_1^5 Z_2^3 / [(Z_1 + \sqrt{2} Z_2) v^{11}] \quad \text{a.u.} ,$$

which exhibits the same v^{-11} descrease as the classical cross section of Thomas.

L.H. Thomas, Proc.Roy.Soc. (London) 114, 561 (1927).

THE HYDROGEN ATOM DESTRUCTION IN COLLISIONS WITH MULTICHARGE ION

E.L.Duman,L.G.Menshykov,B.M.Smirnov

I.V.Kurchatov Institute of Atomic Energy, Moscow, USSR

The aim of this article is to determine the total cross-section of the processes:

$$H + A^{+Z} \longrightarrow p + \begin{cases} A^{+(Z-1)} & \text{(Ia)} \\ A^{+Z} + e & \text{(Ib)} \end{cases}$$

The value of ion charge obeys the condition $Z \gg 1$ and we suggest that the electron transfer takes place at large distances R between nuclei:

$$\sqrt{Z} \ll R \ll Z \qquad (2)$$

(we use the system of atomic units). The condition (2) allows to change the ionic action by the electric field:

$$\mathcal{E} = Z/R^2 \qquad (3)$$

Let's consider some limiting cases. If the impact velocity V is rather small ($1 \ll V \ll \sqrt{Z}$), then the main chanal is (Ia). The probability per second of the electron tunneling into the ionic potential pit is equal to:

$$w(R) = \frac{4}{\mathcal{E}} exp\left(-\frac{b}{3\mathcal{E}}\right) \qquad (4a)$$

The charge exchange probability for the straight trajectory is

$$W(\rho) = 4\sqrt{\frac{3\pi}{2}}\left(\rho^2/\upsilon\sqrt{z}\right)exp\left(-\frac{2}{3}\frac{\rho^2}{z}\right) , \qquad (4b)$$

with ρ being the impact parameter. The main chanal for large impact velocities is the ionisation (Ib). According to the first order perturbation theory the ionisation probability equals:

$$W(\rho) = 1.14\left(\frac{z}{\rho\upsilon}\right)^2 exp\left(-\frac{\rho}{\upsilon}\right) \qquad (5)$$

We can obtain the expression for the destruction probability at the intermediate velocities, noting the fact, that electron leaves out the atom from the "tale" of the wave function, where the quasiclassical treatment is correct. This problem is quite analogous to that of Keldysh, having concerned the atomic ionisation by harmonic electric field. Since in our case there is other field, the exponential factor at intermediate velocities equals:

$$W(\rho) \backsim exp\left\{-\frac{2}{3}\frac{\rho^2}{z}g\left(\frac{\rho\upsilon}{z}\right)\right\} \qquad (6)$$

Values of g(x) are given in table I. The limiting cases (4),(5) are generalized by the eq. (6).

Table I

x	.3	.5	.7	I.0	I.5	2.0	2.5	5.0	I0
g(x)	.97	.94	.89	.8I	.69	.58	.50	.28	.I5

Using eqs. (4)-(6) we obtain the following expression for the destruction cross-section:

$$\sigma = z F\left(\frac{v}{\sqrt{z}}\right) \tag{7}$$

The universal function F(x) is given in table 2.

Table 2

x	.002	.008	.02	.08	.I	.2	.4	.8	2.0	4.0	I0
F(x)	55.7	48.5	43.7	37	36	35	I9.4	6.6	2.I	I.I	.36

The dependence (7) is correct in the limit of $z \rightarrow \infty$.

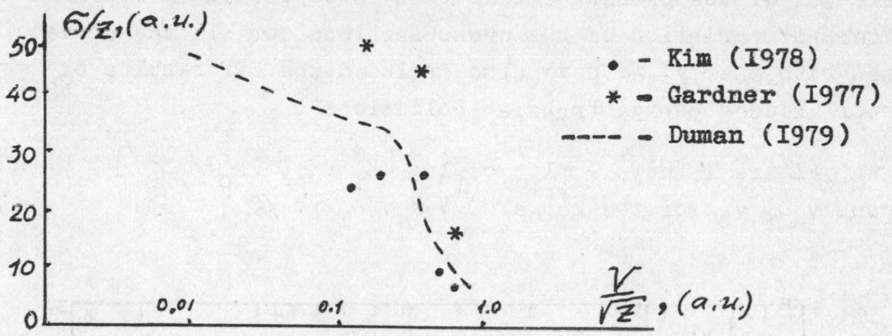

Fig.I. The comparison of these results with experiments.

[1] M.J.Tchibisov,JETP Lett. 24,56(1976).

[2] L.V.Keldysh, JETP 47 , I945 (I964).

[3] E.L.Duman,L.G.Menshykov,B.M.Smirnov,JETP 76 , 56I (I979).

[4] H.I.Kim et al.,Phys.Rev.Lett. AI7 , 854 (I978).

[5] L.D.Gardner et al.,Phys.Rev. AI6 , I4I5 (I977).

CHARGE TRANSFER CROSS SECTIONS FOR α - PARTICLES
COLLIDING WITH HYDROGENIC IONS

M.Lal, M.K.Srivastava and A.N. Tripathi

Department of Physics, University of Roorkee, Roorkee, India

The Coulomb projected Born approximation (CPB) has been
used to calculate the charge transfer cross-sections for α-
particles colliding with hydrogen and hydrogenic systems such
as $He^{1+}, Li^{2+}, Be^{3+}, B^{4+}, N^{6+}, O^{7+}$ and Fe^{25+} at medium and high
energies. The details of the method are given in Ref. 1. The
basic aim of the present calculation is to obtain an overall
pattern of variation of the cross-sections for all the above
cases with energy. We have also included the CPB results of
proton induced charge transfer collisions[1].

Figure 1 shows a plot of log $\left[Z_T^6 \; F \; \sigma(a_o^2)/ Z_P^5 \right]$
versus $v/Z_T \; v_o$ for the range $0.4 \ll v/Z_T \; vo \ll 4$ and

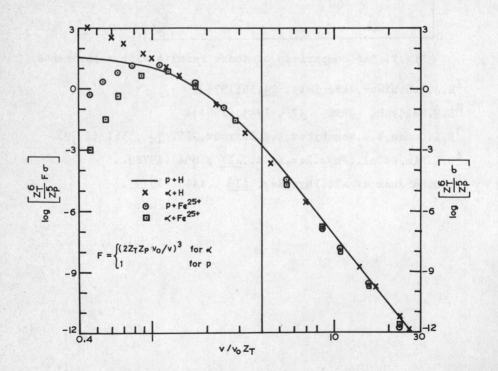

$\log \left[Z_T^6 \ \sigma(a_0^2)/Z_p^5 \right]$ versus $v/Z_T \ v_0$ for the range $4 < v/Z_T \ v_0 < 30$ for (p,H), (p,Fe^{25+}), (α, H) and (α, Fe^{25+}) charge transfer reactions to the 1s-state. Symbols have the usual meaning and the factor F is defined in the figure. We find that the CPB results quite accurately follow the scaling formulae[2].

$$\sigma(p, X_{Z_T}^{(Z_T-1)+}) = \sigma(p,H)/Z_T^6$$

$$\sigma(\alpha,H) = Z_p^5 \ \sigma(p,H)$$

in the range $v/Z_T \ v_0 > 2 \ Z_p$. For smaller values of the incident velocity, $v/Z_T \ v_0 < 2 \ Z_p$, the results are found to roughly follow the scalling formula[2]

$$\sigma(\alpha,H) = Z_p^2 \ (v/2Z_T Z_p v_0)^3 \ \sigma(p,H) .$$

All the cross-sections in the above are calculated at the same common $v/Z_T \ v_0$.

1. M.Lal, A.N.Tripathi and M.K.Srivastava, J.Phys. B **11**, 4249(1978).
2. V.S.Nikolaev, Sov. Phys. Usp.**8**, 269 (1975).

ION–ION CAPTURE COLLISIONS IN THE CONTINUUM DISTORTED WAVE APPROXIMATION

D. Basu & S. Mukherjee

Indian Association for the Cultivation of Science
Jadavpur, Calcutta - 700 032.

The continuum distorted wave approximation of Cheshire[1] is applied to the case in which a nucleus of charge z' captures an electron attached to another nucleus of charge z.

The process is described by the time-dependent Schrödinger equation (in atomic units)

$$\left(-\tfrac{1}{2}\nabla_r^2 - \frac{z'}{s} - \frac{z}{x} + \frac{zz'}{R} - i\frac{\partial}{\partial t} \right)\psi(r,t) = 0 \tag{1}$$

where $\bar{s}$, $\bar{x}$ and $\bar{r}$ are the position vectors of the electron relative to the projectile nucleus X, the target nucleus B and the mid-point of XB respectively. $\bar{R}$ is the position vector of X relative to B.

The transition amplitude is given by

$$a_{if} = \lim_{t \to -\infty} \langle \psi_f^- \mid \Phi_i \rangle \tag{2}$$

Φ_i and Φ_f are the asymptotic initial and final states satisfying the equations

$$\left(-\tfrac{1}{2}\nabla_r^2 - \frac{z}{x} + \frac{(z-1)z'}{R} - i\frac{\partial}{\partial t} \right)\Phi_i = 0 \tag{3}$$

$$\left(-\tfrac{1}{2}\nabla_r^2 - \frac{z'}{s} + \frac{z(z'-1)}{R} - i\frac{\partial}{\partial t} \right)\Phi_f = 0 \tag{4}$$

and having solutions

$$\Phi_i = \phi_{is}(x)\exp i\left\{ -\frac{\bar{v}\cdot\bar{r}}{2} - 1/8\ v^2 t - \epsilon_i t \right\} \exp\left\{ \frac{z'(z-1)}{v}\ i\ \ln(vR - v^2 t) \right\} \tag{5}$$

$$\Phi_f = \phi_{nlm}(s)\exp i\left\{ \frac{\bar{v}\cdot\bar{r}}{2} - 1/8\ v^2 t - \epsilon_f t \right\} \exp\left\{ \frac{-z(z'-1)}{v}i\ \ln(vR + v^2 t) \right\} \tag{6}$$

where ϕ_{is} and ϕ_{nlm} are the initial and final bound state eigen functions with corresponding eigen energies ϵ_i and ϵ_f. $\bar{v}$ is the velocity of X relative to B. Following Cheshire we introduce the distorted waves $X_{i,f}^{\pm}$ where

$$X_i^+ = \phi_i L_i ; \qquad\qquad X_i^+ = \lim_{t \to -\infty} \Phi_i \tag{7}$$

$$X_f^- = \phi_f L_f ; \qquad\qquad X_f^- = \lim_{t \to +\infty} \Phi_f \tag{8}$$

Substituting these in (1), equations are obtained for L_i and L_f and their approximate solutions are given by

$$L_i = e^{\frac{\pi z'}{2v}}\ \Gamma(1 - iz'/v)\ {}_1F_1\left\{ \frac{z'i}{v},\ 1,\ i(vs + \bar{v}\cdot\bar{s}) \right\} \exp\left\{ \frac{z'i}{v}\ \ln(vR - v^2 t) \right\} \tag{9}$$

$$L_f = e^{\frac{\pi z}{2v}}\ \Gamma(1 + iz/v)\ {}_1F_1\left\{ -\frac{zi}{v},\ 1,\ -i(vx + \bar{v}\cdot\bar{x}) \right\} \exp\left\{ -\frac{zi}{v}\ \ln(vR + v^2 t) \right\} \tag{10}$$

a_{if} now takes the form

$$a_{if} = -i\int_{-\infty}^{\infty} dt \langle \psi_f^- \mid H - i\frac{\partial}{\partial t} \mid X_i^+ \rangle \tag{11}$$

In evaluating a_{if}, X_f^- is substituted for ψ_f^-. For the ${}_1F_1$ functions[2] occurring in

L_i and L_f we use the integral representation

$$_1F_1 \ (i/v, \ 1, \ iq) = \frac{1}{2\pi i} \oint_\Gamma \frac{dw}{w} \ (1+1/w)^{-i/v} \ e^{-iwq} \tag{12}$$

where the contour Γ encloses the points 0 and -1. The total capture cross section is given by

$$Q_{if} = 2\pi \int_0^\infty b|a_{if}|^2 \ db \tag{13}$$

For the particular process

$$H^+ + He^+ \ (1s) \rightarrow H(1s) + He^{++} \tag{14}$$

we obtain

$$a_{if} = \int_0^\infty \eta d\eta J_0(\eta b) \ R(\eta,x) \tag{15}$$

where

$$R(\eta,x) = C'\left(\frac{B-C}{B}\right)^{-i/v}\left(\frac{A-F}{A}\right)^{-zi/v} \frac{1}{A^2B(B-C)}\left[2A-2z^2-v^2-2\epsilon_{if}-i\ (v+2\epsilon_{if}/v) + \right.$$

$$+\frac{1}{v(A-F)}\left\{iF(-zv^2-2z\epsilon_{if}-2z^3)+F\beta z(v+2\epsilon_{if}/v)\right.$$

$$\left.\left. + i3zAv^2 - 4z^2Av - 2z\beta Av + i2zA\epsilon_{if}\right\}\right] \tag{16}$$

Here $\beta = 1$

$$\left.\begin{array}{l} \epsilon_{if} = \ \epsilon_i - \epsilon_f \\ A = \eta^2 + v^2/4 + \epsilon_{if}^2/v^2 + \epsilon_{if} + z^2 \\ B = \eta^2 + v^2/4 + \epsilon_{if}^2/v^2 - \epsilon_{if} + \beta^2 \\ C = v^2 + i2\beta v - 2\epsilon_{if} \\ F = v^2 + i2zv + 2\epsilon_{if}. \end{array}\right\} \tag{17}$$

C' is a constant. Following Cheshire $Q_{(1s,1s)}$ takes the simple form

$$Q_{(1s,1s)} = 2\pi \int_0^\infty \eta d\eta |R(\eta,x)|^2 \tag{18}$$

which is evaluated numerically. In Table 1 we present a few of our cross section values obtained for the process(14).

TABLE 1 :- Capture cross sections (in πa_0^2) for the process (14)

Energy in KeV	$Q_{(1s,1s)}$
100	.125
200	.187(-1)
400	.145(-2)

1. Cheshire I.M. 1964, Proc. Phys. Soc. 84, 89.
2. Borowitz S.and Klein M.M. 1956, Phys. Rev. 103, 612.

CHARGE TRANSFER IN ION-ATOM COLLISIONS

D M BHATTACHARYYA AND PUSPAJIT MANDAL

Indian Association for the Cultivation of Science
Jadavpur, Calcutta 700 032, India

Of the charge-transfer reactions in atomic collision physics,
the symmetric process in proton-hydrogen atom collisions has been
investigated extensively using a wide variety of approximations by
different authors. This is mainly because of the relative simplicity
in the calculation in comparison with other symmetric and asymmetric
charge-transfer processes. In recent years, however, the problem of
asymmetric charge-transfer during scattering of alpha-particles from
atomic H has drawn attention of many workers due to the availability
of the observed data on the cross section. For the proton - H charge
-transfer, an expansion in Sturmian basis has yielded remarkably
good results, while for the alpha particle - H case, Basu et al[1], Malaviya[2] and Rapp[3] have obtained satisfactory results by using the impact parameter method where they have considered quite a few of the
low-lying excited states in their coupling scheme. When, on the other
hand, a calculation is attempted for many-electron target systems,
this method becomes rather difficult to handle and a coupled-state
study seems to be practically intractable. In the present work we
however follow a much simpler approach and use the Coulomb-projected
Born approximation (CPBA) of Geltman[4] to investigate the charge transfer from the multielectron targets to the incident ions. We consider here the K-shell electron capture from the many electron atoms C,
N, O, Ne and Ar by incident protons, from the atoms Ne and Ar by
fully stripped ions N^{7+}, and from Ne, Ar and Kr by incident F^{9+} ions
at moderately high energies of impact. The form of the CPBA scattering amplitude for these cases may be obtained from the two-state
approximation by treating the projectile-nucleus coordinate as part
of the unperturbed problem. The integrals in the amplitude expression may be finally reduced to an one-dimensional form from 0 to 1
which is then evaluated numerically using the Gauss-Legendre quadrature method with sufficient number of mesh points. The differential
and total cross sections thus obtained will be compared with the available theoretical and measured values. Numerical results are
under way.

1. D. Basu, D.M.Bhattacharyya and G.Chatterjee Phys Rev.163 8 (1967)
2. V. Malaviya J. Phys. B2 8473 (1969)
3. D. Rapp J. Chem. Phys. 58 2043 (1973)
4. S. Geltman J. Phys B4 1288 (1971)

ELECTRON STATES OF PARTICLES FORMED
IN He^{+2}-NOBLE GAS ATOM COLLISIONS

V.V. Afrosimov, A.A. Basalaev, G.A. Leiko, M.N. Panov

A.F.Ioffe Physico-Technical Institute,USSR Academy of Sciences
Leningrad,USSR

In He^{+2}-A collisions (A is a nouble gas atom) autoionisation states of quasimolecular system $(HeA)^{+2}$ are created because electron potential energy of this system is higher than the ionization potential.In this case processes of charge state change can occure due to the change both in kinetic energy of the fast particle and in electron potential energy of the system.

In this work we have measured cross sections for elementary processes of charge states change of colliding particles:
$$He^{+2} + A -- He^{+n} + A^{+k} + (n+k-2)e^-, \quad n=0,I,2, \quad k=I,2,3.$$
The initial kinetic energy of fast ions,E,was varied from 2 to I00 kev.

An elementary process was revealed using a simultaneous charge state analysis of both ions formed after collision and registration of these ions by coincidence technique.

Measurements of kinetic energy changes E and scattering angles of He^+ ions made it possible to identify electronic states of He^+ and A^{+k} ions after collision.

The experiment showed that in one electron capture process
$$He^{+2} + A -- He^+(n,l) + A^+ ,$$
where A-are Ar,Kr,Xe-atoms, fast He^+-ions were preferentially produced in excited n=2 states.Comparison of this cross section of capture on n=2 level with the data[2] for capture on 2s-level shows that the contribution of 2s-state is small and mainly 2p-state of He^+-ions is populated.In the case of Ar,Kr,Xe electron is captured by He^{+2}-ion from p-outer shells of target atoms and this process can be described by Demkov-model[3,4].

Theoretical results are in good agreement with experimental values of cross section (fig.I,Kr,Xe).In the case of He^{+2}-Ne collisions electron capture takes place from 2s-shell of Ne to Is-shell of He^+.This process can be described by Landau-Zener model.

In the case of capture with ionization
$$He^{+2} + A -- He^+(n,l) + A^{+2} + e^-$$

energy dependence of cross section of capture to the ground state
and exited states of He^+-ion is similar for all targets.At small
energies E (fig.2a) capture occurs due to exothermal channels and
it is accompanied by excitation of the target and transition of a
part of potential energy into kinetic energy of the fast particle
($\triangle E>0$,fig.2a).The increase in energy of He^+-ions by 8-I6 ev can
not be connected with the production of excited states of Xe^{+2}
ion.It indicates the important role of production of autoionizing
states of Xe^+ ions in capture with ionization.The autoionization
takes place in quasimolecule and can be described by Kishinevsky-
Parilis model[I].

At E > 20 kev (fig. 2b) endothermal channels of capture with
ionization become predominant.Different dependence of the probability of these channels on the incident particle kinetic energy
causes the minimuma on curves of the total cross section of the
elementary process (fig.I Xe).

I. L.M.Kishinevsky,E.S.Parilis,JETP 55,I932 (I968).
2. H.B.Shah,H.B.Gilbody, J.Phys.B. 7,256 (I974).
3. Yu.N.Demkov,JETP 45,I95 (I964).
4. R.E.Olson, Phys.Rev. A6 I822 (I972).

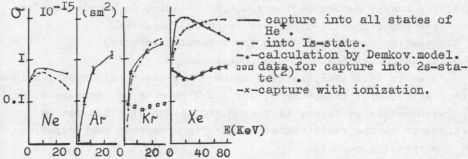

Fig.I.Cross section of capture and capture with ionization.

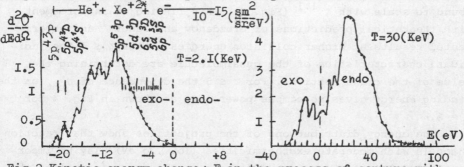

Fig.2.Kinetic energy change $\triangle$ E in the process of capture with
ionization.Values of $\triangle$ E corresponding to definite electron states
of He^+ and Xe^{+2} ions are indicated by arrows.

CHARGE TRANSFER COLLISIONS OF MULTIPLY CHARGED IONS

B.A.Huber, H.J.Kahlert, H.Schrey, K.Wiesemann

Institut für Experimentalphysik AG II
Ruhr-Universität, D-463o Bochum, West Germany

A mass selected ion beam of energy below 1o keV is shot into a collision chamber containing the target gas. The secondary ions are analysed with respect to emmission angle, kinetic energy and the charge to mass ratio. The projectiles have been Ar, Kr, Xe and Cs ions with charge numbers $\zeta = 1 \ldots 8$, as targets we used the different rare gases and hydrogen.

We report on the measurements of total and differential cross sections for charge transfer, especially the following four aspects have been studied:

1. Size and energy dependence of the total charge transfer cross section σ_{tot}.
2. Its dependence on the charge number ζ and the binding energy I_B of the electrons to be transferred.
3. The energy defect of the reaction (leading to a criterion for the importance of different reaction channels).
4. Dynamics of the collision for molecular targets.

The following results have been obtained:

Down to collision energies below 1 keV the total cross sections are nearly energy independent. For $\zeta \leq 3$ however an increase of σ_{tot} with collision energy is found (Fig. 1 and 2). This can be attributed to the small number of reaction channels participating in the transfer reaction.

For single electron transfer and $\zeta \geq 4$ the cross sections are found to scale with $\zeta^{1.1}$ (Fig. 3). This finding is in agreement with theoretical predictions of Grozdanov and Janev [1] and experimental results at higher collision energies [2]. For $\zeta \leq 4$ the individual characteristics of the quasimolecule are determining the value of the cross sections. For $\zeta \leq 5$ the dependence of σ_{tot} on the binding energy gives no simple power law, as shown in Fig. 4 for $\zeta = 5$.

The energy distributions of the projectiles show that reaction channels with moderate exothermicities (1o...2o eV) play an important role. The reactions occur at potential curve crossings of the quasimolecule at nuclear distances between 1.5 Å and 5 Å in accordance with assumptions of Winter et.al. [3] The number of crossings within this region allows a qualitative understanding of the size and the energy dependence of the total cross section. If more than one electron is transferred in the collision the important crossing region seems to be shiftet to smaller nuclear distances.

For the H_2 target the spectroscopy of the slow target ions shows that mainly H_2^+ ions are formed by single electron capture if ζ is large. For $\zeta \leq 2$ an appreciable amount of H^+ ions results from close collisions accompanied by maximum momentum transfer leading to vibrational dissociation.

1. T.P. Grozdanov, R.K. Janev, Phys. Rev. A 17, 880 (1978)
2. A. Müller, E. Salzborn, Phys. Lett. 62A, 391 (1977)
3. H. Winter, E. Bloemen, F.J. de Heer, J. Phys. B 10, L 599 (1977)

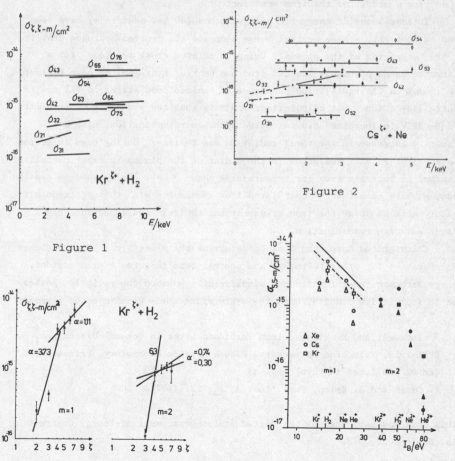

Figure 1

Figure 2

Figure 3

Figure 4

CHARGE EXCHANGE RECOMBINATION FOR HIGHLY IONIZED IRON*

D. E. Post, R. A. Hulse, E. Hinnov, and S. Suckewer

Princeton University, Plasma Physics Laboratory
Princeton, New Jersey 08655 USA

Tokamak experiments, such as the Princeton Large Tokamak (PLT), have achieved electron temperatures in excess of three kilovolts and electron densities of $10^{13} - 10^{14}/cm^3$. At such temperatures, iron exists in ionized states through Fe XXV. The coronal equilibrium distribution of ionized iron states has been calculated by balancing collisional ionization, and radiative and dielectronic recombination. The measured iron distribution is found to differ from the coronal calculation. The difference may be due to transport of the iron ions, and transport calculations have been performed to develop a model for the iron transport.

Intense beams of energetic neutral atoms (40 keV deuterons) have been used to heat PLT. These neutral beams increase the neutral hydrogen density in the hot region of the plasma. Using calculated cross sections[2] for charge exchange of highly ionized iron and neutral hydrogen, we have estimated the change in the equilibrium abundance of ionized iron states in PLT due to neutral injection. Our calculations indicate that the abundance of Fe XXIII and Fe XXIV is increased due to charge exchange recombination, with a resulting increase in the total radiation due to iron. During beam injection the level of Fe XXIV radiation in the center of the plasma is experimentally observed to increase even for temperatures above 3 keV. Using an iron transport code, we have compared the calculated iron abundances with the spectroscopic measurements to infer the iron transport and the relative importance of charge exchange recombination.

Calculations have been done to determine the effects of charge exchange recombination for other tokamaks, and neutral beam injected fusion devices. Charge exchange recombination can significantly enhance the radiative losses due to iron in low density, high temperature, intensely beam injected plasmas.

1. S. Suckewer and E. Hinnov, Iron Forbidden Lives in Tokamak Discharges, PPPL-1524, Princeton University, Plasma Physics Laboratory, Princeton, NJ (to be published in Phys. Rev. A)
2. R. Olson and A. Salop, Phys. Rev. A, 16, 531 (A77)

*This work was supported by the United States Department of Energy Contract No. EY-76-C-02-3073.

ELECTRON CAPTURE BY FAST He++ IONS IN ATOMIC AND MOLECULAR HYDROGEN

A. Andersen and P. Hvelplund

Institute of Physics, University of Aarhus
DK-8000 Aarhus C, Denmark

Single electron-capture cross sections for He++ with energies between 0.3 and 1 MeV have been measured in atomic and molecular hydrogen.

The experimental setup in the present investigation is essentially the same as that used in earlier cross-section measurements in molecular and noble-gas targets[1]. The target cell consists of a directly heated (2350 K) tungsten tube, through which hydrogen is flowing. The dissociation fraction is measured by the double-capture technique (300-keV He++) and is determined to be 0.80. The target thickness is determined by normalizing to cross sections for single-electron capture by 300-keV He++ measured by Shah and Gilbody[2]. Cross sections in molecular hydrogen are measured at room temperature.

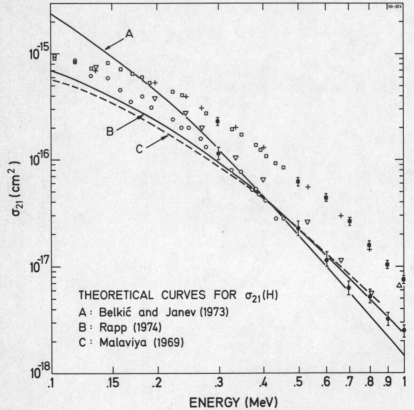

THEORETICAL CURVES FOR σ_{21}(H)
A : Belkić and Janev (1973)
B : Rapp (1974)
C : Malaviya (1969)

Fig. 1. Total electron-capture cross sections σ_{21} for ^{4}He++ incident on molecular end atomic H as a function of energy.

The results of the present measurements are shown in Fig. 1 together with previously reported measurements[1-3]. The consistency of existing measurements is better than 20%, but here it is worth bearing in mind that they are all coupled together in one way or another.

Curve A shows total-capture cross sections for electron capture in He^{++}-H collisions calculated by Belkić and Janev[4], and curves B and C show the (1s+2s+2p) capture cross sections calculated by Rapp[5] and Malaviya[6], respectively.

Within the experimental error, the measured values agree with curves B and C, while curve A is ∿30% lower. A similar trend was found[1] when comparing results for electron capture in He^{++}-He collisions with calculated values of Belkić and Janev[4].

Finally, it should be noted that in the high-energy region, the cross sections in molecular hydrogen are approximately three times those in atomic hydrogen.

Measurements at higher energies are in progress and will hopefully be presented at this meeting.

1. P. Hvelplund, J. Heinemeier, E. Horsdal Pedersen, and F.F. Simpson, J.Phys.B:Atom.Molec.Phys. 9, 491 (1976)

2. M.B. Shah and H.B. Gilbody, J.Phys.B:Atom.Molec.Phys. 11, 121 (1978)

3. R.E. Olson, A. Salop, R.A. Phaneuf, and F.W. Meyer, Phys.Rev. A 16, 1867 (1977)

4. Dz.S. Belkić and R.K. Janev, J.Phys.B:Atom.Molec.Phys. 6, 1020 (1973)

5. D. Rapp, J.Chem.Phys. 61, 3777 (1974)

6. V. Malaviya, J.Phys.B:Atom.Molec.Phys. 2, 843 (1969)

HIGHLY CHARGED Au^{q+} $(v \gtrsim v_o)$ ION INTERACTION WITH STATIC GASES.
ELECTRON CAPTURE, IONIZATION, AND EXCITATION

H.K. Haugen, P. Hvelplund, and H. Knudsen

Institute of Physics, University of Aarhus
DK-8000 Aarhus C, Denmark

In order to further the understanding of the interaction of highly charged
ions with matter, we have recently initiated a series of measurements on electron
capture, target ionization, and target excitation on gaseous targets.

Heavy ions from the Aarhus 6-MV tandem accelerator are poststripped (5<q<25)
in a carbon foil and charge-state analyzed before entering a differentially
pumped target cell.

A.   Electron capture by highly charged ions is known to take place to high Rydberg states[1], and we have therefore begun our investigation of capture by observations of projectile light emission during penetration of a molecular hydrogen
target. Via such spectroscopic information, we hope to acquire knowledge of into
which states the target electrons are captured. A spectrum of the emitted light
observed when a 20-MeV Au^{16+} beam penetrates a H_2 gas is shown in Fig. 1. Four
lines are attributed to the Au(XVI) spectrum, corresponding to transitions with
$\Delta n = 1$ for n values from 15 to 12, where n is the principal quantum number.
The other lines observed can be attributed to transitions in ions of lower q
resulting from electron capture in the beam line, an effect we are going to eliminate in the near future. According to Chibisov[1], the n value for the most
populated level should be $n = 8$, and we are planning to use other spectrometers
in order to investigate the lower wavelength region. In this connection it should
be noted that so far, no calibration of the relative line intensities has been
performed.

B.   Ionization has been investigated by a time-of-flight technique for
$Au^{(5-25)+}$-He collisions. A pulsed beam from the tandem accelerator provides a time
scale, and the target ions are extracted and analyzed. Until now, only relative
values have been obtained, but the charge-state dependence is similar to that
calculated by Olson[2], and the single-ionization cross section is approximately
three times the double-ionization cross section at high q values.

C.   Target excitation has been investigated only for Au^{q+}-N_2, where we measured
the relative intensity of the N_2^+ ($\lambda = 3914$) band. It was found that the cross
section for excitation of this band varies roughly as $q^{4/3}$, but a cleaner beam
has to be used in order to establish the exact dependence. In this connection, it
would be interesting to see whether the oscillations as a function of q found
by Kim et al.[3] also can be found in excitation or ionization.

Measurements with cleaner beams with respect to charge state are in progress, and results will be presented at this meeting.

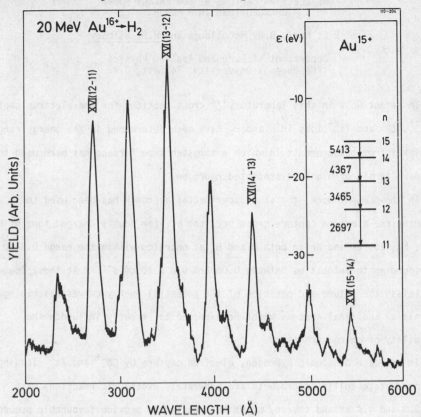

1. M.I. Chibisov, JETP Lett. 24, 46 (1976)
2. R.E. Olson, Phys.Rev. A 18, 2464 (1978)
3. H.J. Kim, P. Hvelplund, F.W. Meyer, R.A. Phaneuf, P.H. Stelson, and C. Bottcher, Phys.Rev.Lett. 40, 1635 (1978)

ONE-ELECTRON CAPTURE BY LOW ENERGY DOUBLY
CHARGED IONS IN H AND H_2

W.L. Nutt, R.W. McCullough and H.B. Gilbody

Department of Pure and Applied Physics
The Queen's University, Belfast, U.K.

In recent work in this laboratory[1,2] cross sections for one-electron capture by He^{2+}, C^{2+} and Ti^{2+} ions in H and H_2 have been determined in the energy range 0.5-14 keV from measurements in which a tungsten tube furnace has been used to provide a target of highly dissociated hydrogen.

In the present work, the same experimental approach has been used to determine one-electron capture cross sections σ_{21} for doubly charged ions of Ba, B, Ti, Mg, Cd, Zn and Kr in both H and H_2 at energies within the range 0.8-40 keV corresponding to velocities between 0.05 and 0.8 x 10^8cm.s^{-1}. At these low velocities, the nature and position of the potential energy curves describing the initial and final systems might be expected to greatly influence the probability of charge transfer.

In the case of atomic hydrogen, electron capture by Cd^{2+} and Zn^{2+} leading to ground state collision products are moderately exothermic reactions with ΔE = 3.3 and 4.4 eV and thereby might be expected to provide favourable pseudo-crossings between potential energy curves at about 8 a.u. and 6 a.u. respectively. Measured cross sections (Fig 1) are seen to be very large attaining peak values at low velocities. In contrast, the corresponding process with Mg^{2+} where ΔE = 1.4 eV provides a crossing at a comparatively large internuclear separation of 19 a.u.   In this case, the measured cross section is very small at low velocities.   In the same way, the processes with Kr^{2+} and B^{2+} for which ΔE = 11.0 and 11.6 eV and involve pseudo-crossings at the comparatively small internuclear separations of about 2.5 and 2.3 a.u. respectively are also small at low impact energies.   Similar cross sections are also observed for Ti^{2+} and Ba^{2+} in H which are endothermic for ground state products with energy defects ΔE = -0.03 and -3.6 eV respectively.

Our measured cross sections σ_{21} for Mg^{2+} - H are in good agreement with theoretical estimates[3] based on a semi-classical two state model and with

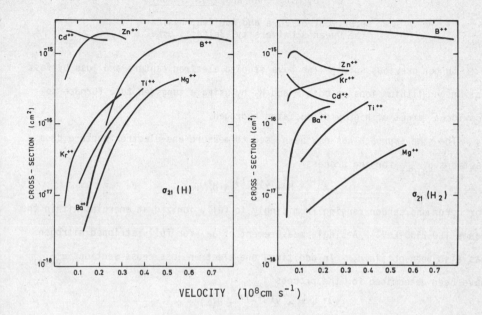

VELOCITY (10^8cm s^{-1})

Fig 1.   Cross sections for one-electron capture
by doubly charged ions in H and H_2

experimental cross sections[4] for the inverse H^+ - Mg^+ process at the same centre
of mass energies.   Recent theoretical estimates[5] of σ_{21} for Cd^{2+}, Zn^{2+} but not
B^{2+} based on a two-state exponential model are also in reasonable general accord
with the present data.

1.   W.L. Nutt, R.W. McCullough, K. Brady, M.B. Shah and H.B. Gilbody,
          J. Phys. B 11, 1457 (1978).

2.   W.L. Nutt, R.W. McCullough and H.B. Gilbody, J. Phys. B 11, L121 (1978).

3.   D.R. Bates, H.C. Johnston and I. Stewart, Proc. Phys. Soc. 84, 517
          (1964).

4.   B. Peart, D.M. Gee and K.T. Dolder, J. Phys. B 10, 2683 (1977).

5.   D.S.F. Crothers and N.R. Todd - Private communication.

ONE-ELECTRON CAPTURE AND LOSS BY FAST MULTIPLY
CHARGED BORON AND CARBON IONS IN H AND H_2

T.V. Goffe, M.B. Shah and H.B. Gilbody

Department of Pure and Applied Physics
The Queen's University, Belfast, U.K.

In our previous work[1,2], we have studied electron capture and loss by fast helium and lithium ions in both H and H_2 by using a tungsten tube furnace to provide a target of highly dissociated hydrogen.

The same approach has now been used to measure one-electron capture cross sections $\sigma_{q,q-1}$ for the process

$$X^{q+} + H \rightarrow X^{(q-1)} + H^+$$

for boron and carbon ranging from singly to fully ionized at energies within the range 100-2500 keV. A single measurement of σ_{76} for fully stripped nitrogen has also been obtained. In addition, one-electron loss cross sections $\sigma_{q,q+1}$ have been determined for the process

$$X^{q+} + H \rightarrow X^{(q+1)+} + H(\Sigma) + e$$

for boron ions with q=1 and 2 and for carbon ions with q=1, 2 and 3. The corresponding capture and loss cross sections in H_2 have also been determined.

Our capture cross sections decrease with increasing energy and increase with q. In atomic hydrogen, capture cross sections for different initial charge states q≥2 scale according to $\sigma_{q,q-1} = \sigma_0 q^n$ where n increases with velocity but attains roughly constant values of 2.4 and 2.5 for boron and carbon ions respectively at our highest velocities. Cross sections for carbon ions previously measured by Phaneuf et al[3] with q=1-4 are in good agreement with the present results. Our measured loss cross sections $\sigma_{q,q+1}$ attain maximum values at energies which increase with q and, at the higher impact energies, exceed the corresponding capture cross sections.

Cross sections in H_2 are comparable in magnitude with those in H. At our highest velocities, the ratios $\sigma_{q,q-1}(H)/\sigma_{q,q-1}(H_2)$ become significantly less than $\frac{1}{2}$.

Classical calculations[4] of $\sigma_{q,q-1}$ for completely and partially stripped boron and carbon ions are in rough general accord with our measured values. For completely stripped boron and carbon, capture cross sections σ_{54} and σ_{65} in H calculated[5] using a distorted-wave Born approximation exhibit a similar energy dependence but are rather larger than our measured values. The low energy trend of our capture cross sections is consistent with calculations based on a molecular description which is expected to be valid at energies somewhat below our low energy limit.

At high velocities, our present and previous capture cross sections for completely stripped ions of He, Li, B, C and N (but not H) appear to conform to the relation

$$\frac{\sigma}{Z^3} = 10^{-10}E^{-3.65}cm^2$$

where the atomic number $Z = q$ in these cases and E is the energy in keV a.m.u.$^{-1}$.

1. M.B. Shah and H.B. Gilbody, J. Phys. B **7**, 630 (1974); **9**, 1933 (1976); **11**, 121 (1978).

2. M.B. Shah, T.V. Goffe and H.B. Gilbody, J. Phys. B **11**, L233 (1978).

3. R.A. Phaneuf, F.W. Meyer and R.H. McKnight, Phys. Rev. A **17**, 534(1978).

4. R.E. Olson and A. Salop, Phys. Rev. A **16**, 531 (1977).

5. H. Ryufuku and T. Watanabe, Japan Atomic Energy Institute Memo 7895

(1978).

SYMMETRIC RESONANCE MULTIPLE-CHARGE-TRANSFER OF Ar^{++}, Kr^{++}, Xe^{++} AND Kr^{+++} IN THEIR OWN GASES FROM 0.04 eV TO 3.8 keV

K. Okuno,   T. Koizumi   and   Y. Kaneko

Department of Physics, Faculty of Science, Tokyo Metropolitan
University, Setagaya-ku, Tokyo 158, Japan

The cross sections of symmetric resonance multiple-charge-transfer processes

$$Ar^{++} + Ar \longrightarrow Ar + Ar^{++}, \tag{1}$$

$$Kr^{++} + Kr \longrightarrow Kr + Kr^{++}, \tag{2}$$

$$Xe^{++} + Xe \longrightarrow Xe + Xe^{++} \tag{3}$$

and

$$Kr^{+++} + Kr \longrightarrow Kr + Kr^{+++} \tag{4}$$

are measured in the wide energy range from 0.04 eV to 3.8 keV in the center-of-mass systems. The measurements are performed by the injected-ion drift-tube technique[1,2] for the reactions (2) and (3) in the energy range from 0.04 to 20 eV, by the tandem mass spectrometer technique[3,4] for (1) and (2) from 0.4 to 2.5 keV, and by the time-of-flight technique for (1), (2), (3) and (4) from 0.05 to 3.8 keV. In the time-of-flight experiment, the neutral products of multiple-charge-transfer are directly counted with a beam detector attached to the tandem mass spectrometer.

In Fig.1, the cross sections obtained are summarized together with those of the ordinary symmetric resonance single-charge-transfer measured. The results by the time-of-flight experiment agree well with those by the tandem mass spectrometer experiment, and they are distributed on the extrapolation of that in the low energy region by the injected-ion drift-tube experiment.

Below about 1 eV, the double-charge-transfer cross sections have energy dependence as $E^{-1/2}$, and they are very closed to the orbiting cross sections taking account of the charge-transfer probability as 1/2. The orbiting effect makes the double-charge-transfer cross sections exceed those of the single-charge-transfer even at the room temperature. The triple-charge transfer cross section for Kr^{+++} has no evidence of the orbiting effect within the energy region measured and is parallel to those of single- and double-charge-transfer as shown in Fig.1(b).

It has been well known that the cross section of the symmetric resonance single-charge-transfer is approximately given as $\sigma^{1/2} = a - b \ln v$, where v is velocity and a and b are constant. The relation $\sigma^{1/2} = a - b \ln v$ seems to be hold for the double- and triple-charge-transfer, also. It is noted that all the cross sections for the single-, double- and triple-charged ions is approximately scaled by means of the total binding energy of the electrons transfered.

In the collision system ($A^{q+} + A$), an attractive force due to polarization becomes stronger for larger q. If the multiple-charge-transfer for large q takes place with a large probability, the orbiting mechanism will make its cross section very large in the low energy region. Bisides its fundamental interest, the study of the symmetric resonance multiple-charge-transfer is of paticular importance for reseach on the behaviour of ions in hot plasma, electric discharge and heavy ion source, etc..

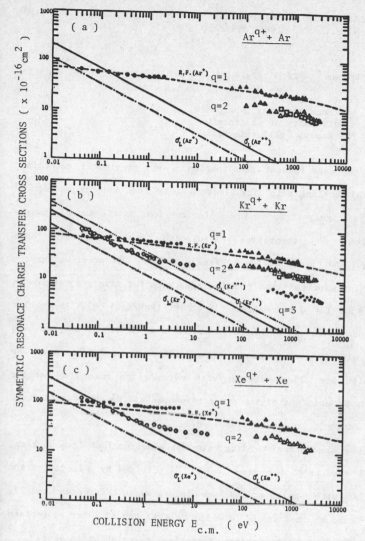

Fig.1.
Symmetric resonance
multiple-charge=
transfer cross sec-
tions versus colli-
sion energy.

● and ○ for Kr^{q+}+Kr
and Xr^{q+}+Xe: this
work by the injected-
ion drift-tube tech-
nique,
● for Ar^{+}+Ar: Ref.5,
□ : this work by the
tandem mass spectro-
meter technique,
▲,△ and ●: this work
by the time-of-flight
technique,
RF: theory for q=1 in
Ref.6,
σ_L: the orbiting
cross sections taking
account of probabili-
ty as 1/2.

This work was partly supported by the Grant-of-Aid for Scientific Reseach
from Ministry of Education.

1.   Y. Kaneko, N. Kobayashi and I. Kanomata, J. Phys.Soc. Japan, 27, 992 (1969).

2.   K. Okuno, T. Koizumi and Y. Kaneko, Phys. Rev. Lett., 40, 1708 (1978).

3.   K. Okuno and Y. Kaneko, Proc. 8th ICPEAC (Beograd), 2, 788 (1973).

4.   K. Okuno, Mass Spectroscopy, 24, 107 (1976).

5.   N. Kobayashi, J. Phys. Soc. Japan, 38, 519 (1975).

6.   Donald Rapp and W. E. Francis, J. Chem. Phys., 37, 2631 (1962).

CHARGE-STATE DEPENDENCE OF ELECTRON LOSS FROM H BY COLLISIONS
WITH HEAVY, HIGHLY STRIPPED IONS[*]

K. H. Berkner, W. G. Graham[**], R. V. Pyle, A. S. Schlachter and J. W. Stearns

Lawrence Berkeley Laboratory
University of California
Berkeley, California 94720

We have extended the experimental confirmation of our previously determined theoretical/experimental scaling rule[1] for electron loss from a hydrogen atom in collision with a heavy, highly stripped ion. Electron loss is the sum of charge exchange and ionization. The theoretical calculations covered the energy range E = 50 to 5000 keV/amu, and charge states q from 1 to 50. Our previous experimental cross sections for electron loss from hydrogen were for iron projectiles in charge states q = 3 to 22 (E ÷ q in the range 10 to 100 (keV/amu) ÷ q). The results we report here are for carbon ions in charge states 4 to 6 at 310 keV/amu and 1.1 MeV/amu, and for niobium ions in charge states 23 to 36 at 3.5 MeV/amu. We find that these results are all consistent with our scaling rule and that the scaled cross section is independent of the projectile species. The new experimental results cover the E/q range 50 to 280 (keV/amu) ÷ q.

Figure 1 shows the theoretical scaling rule for electron loss from H, along with our experimental results[1,2] for iron ions in H_2 (divided by a factor of the order of 2 for comparison with H calculations, see discussion in references 1 and 2), and our results for C and Nb ions in H_2 (divided by a factor of 2 for comparison with H calculations). The agreement with the theoretical calculation is good.

---

[*]This work was supported by the Fusion Energy Division of the U. S. Department of Energy under contract No. W-7405-ENG-48.
[**]Present address: New University of Ulster, Coleraine, Northern Ireland.

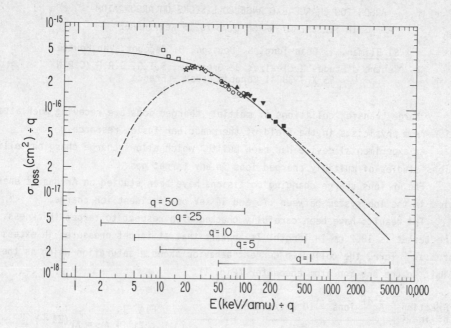

Fig. 1.   Cross section σ_{loss} for electron loss by atomic hydrogen
in collision with an ion in charge state q.   Solid line: calculation;
this curve is valid for $1 \leq q \leq 50$ and for energies in the range 50 to 5000
keV/amu. The range of E/q values for which the curve is valid is indicated by the bars drawn in the lower portion of the figure. The uncertainty in the calculated cross sections is ±25%. Dashed line: Plane-wave
Born-approximation cross section for ionization only (Refs. 3, 4). Closed Symbols: Present experimental results for $C^{+q} + H_2$ and $Nb^{+q} + H_2$,
divided by a factor of 2 to allow comparision with the calculations.
The uncertainty is 30%. Triangles, 0.31 MeV/amu carbon ions, q = 4–6;
squares, 1.1 MeV/amu carbon ions, q = 4–6; inverted triangles, 3.5 MeV/amu
niobium ions, q = 23–36. Open symbols: Previous experimental results by
the present authors (refs. 1 and 2) for $Fe^{+q} + H_2$ divided by a number
between 1.5 and 2.0 to allow comparison with the calculations. Squares,
108 keV/amu, q = 7–11; triangle, 110 keV/amu, q = 3; diamond, 282 keV/amu,
q = 9; stars, 290 keV/amu, q = 10–15; circles, 1140 keV/amu, q = 11–22.

1. R. E. Olson, K. H. Berkner, W. G. Graham, R. V. Pyle, A. S. Schlachter, and
    J. W. Stearns, Physical Review Letters 41, 163 (1978).
2. K. H. Berkner, W. G. Graham, R. V. Pyle, A. S. Schlachter, J. W. Stearns, and
    R. E. Olson, J. Phys. B. 11, 875 (1978).
3. D. R. Bates and G. Griffing, Proc. Phys. Soc., London (Sect. A) 66, 961(1953).
4. E. Merzbacher and H. W. Lewis, in Encyclopedia of Physics, edited by S. Flugge
    (Springer-Verlag, Berlin, 1958), Vol. 34, p. 166.

ARGON ION CHARGE EXCHANGE COLLISIONS ON ARGON ATOM
IN THE ENERGY RANGE 0.75 to 15 KeV/CHARGE

S. Bliman, N. Chan-Tung, S. Dousson, B. Jacquot, Van Houtte

Centre d'Etudes Nucléaires de Grenoble, S.I.G, D.R.F./C.P.N
85 X - 38041 Genoble Cedex - France

Charge transfer collisions of multiply charged ions are receving much attention from physicists in the field of thermonuclear fusion research.

An experimental device has been built [1] which allows charge changing collisions studies of multiply charged ions in any target gas.

The Ar ions charge changing collisions have been studied on Ar gas at energies in the lab system between .75 and 14 keV per incident ion charge.

The results have been carefully checked with respect to target thickness. The target is 18.2 cm in length. It appears that at target pressures in excess of 2.10^{-4} Torr, the collected current behavior shows a saturation which is the limit to the one ion atom encounter (Fig. 1).

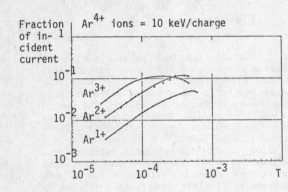

Fig. 1.

$$Ar^{Zi+} + Ar \rightarrow Ar^{(Zi-k)} + Ar^{n+} + (n-k)e + \Delta E$$

$$F = \frac{I(Ar^{(Zi-k)^+})}{I[Ar^{Zi+}(o)]} \times \frac{Zi}{(Zi-k)}$$

Target pressure (Torr).

The usual pressure condition in the target is of order 5.10^{-5} Torr. In these conditions solving in the linear approximation the set of evolution equation.

The partial cross sections in cm^2/atom are obtained for the different charge states originating from Ar^{+4}, from Ar^{3+} and Ar^{2+} (Fig. 2). In the high energy limit, it shows a reasonably good agreement with measured values by E. Salzborn[2].

It seems that for collisions starting from charge 4 or 3 to lower-charge state in this energy range the cross sections is quasi constant.

As to collision from Ar^{2+} to give charge 1 it seems that at the lowest energy there is a slight increase in measured cross sections which could be interpreted along the theoretical trends outlined by L.P. Presniakov[3,4].

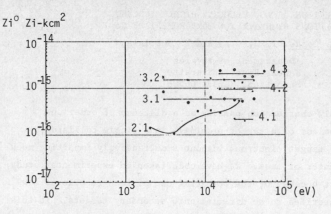

Zi^o $Zi-kcm^2$

Fig. 2.

Charge exchange cross
sections : Ar ions/
Argon atoms

1. S. Bliman, "Etude experimentale de la production de deuterons negatifs par double echange de charges dans le Xenon", submitted for publication to Journal de Physique.

2. E. Salzborn and A. Müller, Xth ICPEAC, p.530, Paris (1977).

3. L.P. Presniakov and al., Sov. J. Quant. Electron. 4, 1320, (1975).

4. L.P. Presniakov, Electronic and Atomic Collisions. Invited paper and progress reports, North Holland, pub. Comp. (1978), p. 407.

PRODUCTION OF LOW-VELOCITY HIGHLY-IONIZED
RECOIL IONS BY HEAVY ION BOMBARDMENT OF Ne$^+$

C. L. Cocke, T. J. Gray and E. Justiniano

Department of Physics
Kansas State University
Manhattan, Kansas 66506

A Fast-moving highly-charged ion passing at a distance of order one
atomic unit from the nucleus of a target atom may, in a single collision,
eject a large number of target electrons without simultaneously imparting much
energy to the target center of mass. We have undertaken an experimental study
of this process, in part because of the potential use of such recoils as low-
energy high-charge projectiles to be directed onto secondary targets. In this
paper we report recoil charge state spectra and production cross sections for
Ne recoils generated in bombardment of thin neon gas targets by 1 MeV/amu C,
N, O, F and Cl beams in various incident charge states.

The technique used is to extract the recoil ions with an electric field
directed at right angles to the beam and direct them into a distant channeltron
detector. The recoil in charge state q is detected in delayed coincidence
with the projectile ion, whose incident charge state Q is also measured. The
flight-time of the recoil to the channeltron provides a measure of q. Typical
time-of-flight q-spectra are shown in Fig. 1 for bare 1 MeV/amu F nuclei

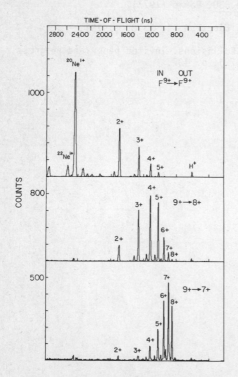

Fig. 1. Time-of-flight spectra showing
q-spectra of recoils from bombardment
by bare F projectiles, in coincidence
with exiting F in charge states $^+9$, $^+8$
and $^+7$.

incident upon neon. The final F charge states correspond to the capture of
zero, one, or two target electrons from the target. There is a strong correlation between recoil and projectile charge states. Collisions which are accompanied by projectile charge change ionize the target much more heavily than
those which do not.

We have measured cross sections $\sigma_q^{Q'Q}$ for the production of recoils in
charge state q by projectiles whose incident and exit charge states are Q' and
Q, respectively. Typical results are shown in Table 1.

TABLE 1. Cross sections $\sigma_q^{Q'Q}$ for F on Ne in units of 10^{-18} cm^2

q=	1	2	3	4	5	6	7	8
σ^{99}	1300	420	195	93	31	2.7	–	–
σ^{98}	–	8.8	22	29	23	9.5	3.4	.65
σ^{97}	–	–	–	.95	1.9	2.3	4.2	2.7

A model which describes the electron removal as an energy transfer by the projectile to the target electrons followed by a statistically weighted electron
ejection has been developed and accounts for many features of these cross sections. We summarize our major conclusions as:
1. For q ≤ 5, the major electron loss mechanism is ionization at sufficiently
large impact parameter that electron capture by the projectile is improbable.
2. For larger q, the characteristic impact parameters are sufficiently small
that capture (loss) to (from) the projectile becomes probable. A model-
dependent interpretation of this result leads to the conclusion that, for the
case of oxygen, single electron capture and loss takes place at surprisingly
large b ($\sim$ .5Å).
3. The recoil energies associated with q ≤ 7 are too small for us to detect,
but are expected from the size of the cross section to be ≤ 10eV. Further,
these ions are produced with sufficiently large $\sigma_q^{Q'Q}$ that the production of a
secondary high-q beam appears feasible.

[†]Supported in part by Division of Chemical Science, D.O.E.

SELECTIVE ELECTRON CAPTURE BY HIGHLY CHARGED VERY SLOW IONS: I. METHOD

H.F. Beyer, R. Mann, F. Folkmann and K.-H. Schartner[+]

Gesellschaft für Schwerionenforschung mbH, D-6100 Darmstadt, W-Germany
[+]I. Physikalisches Institut der Justus Liebig-Universität, D-6300 Gießen, West
Germany

Measured Auger-electron[1] and x-ray spectra[2] have shown that very heavy projectiles of specific energy 1.4 MeV/amu are likely to remove more than six electrons from light (Z$\sim$10) target atoms in a single collision, whenever the target
K shell gets ionized (see also preceding contribution). The produced few electron
recoil ions gain only very low recoil energies of $\leq$ 10 eV. This is concluded from
the kinematic line broadening[3] of the emitted Auger electrons and is in agreement
with the mean impact parameter estimated from both theoretical study[4] and measured total x-ray cross section[5].

Because of the very low velocities the recoil ions stay for a long time
($\sim$ 300 nsec) after creation in the viewing range of the spectrometers. Thereby
information is received not only from promptly decaying states produced in the
primary heavy ion collision but also processes are detected which occur after
some time delay and give rise to the emission of x rays or Auger electrons. One
such process is electron capture from surrounding neutral target atoms into outer
shells of metastable highly charged recoil ions what will be discussed below. By
application of gas targets containing more than one atomic (molecular) species it
is also possible to study reactions between highly ionized states of one and
ground states of another species. The great advantages of this sort of recoil ion
spectroscopy are the defined conditions under which highly charged very slow ions
are brought into a cold gaseous environment, where the distribution of highly excited states may be measured.

Concerning the electron capture process some indications to potential electron collectors are given by the core excited states being observed in the x-ray
and Auger-electron spectra emitted by neon gas targets. The observed initial
electronic configurations are:

$$(1s2_s^p)\ nl$$
$$(1s)\ nl$$
$$nl\qquad ,\ n \gtrsim 2.$$

All these configurations are observable in the x-ray decay channel with l=1
whereas the Auger-electron spectra almost exclusively arise from the lithium-like
configurations $(1s2_s^p)$ nl without strong limitation in the angular momentum l. The
core configurations within the brackets including bare nuclei have lifetimes
large enough to undergo a charge changing collision. Even the $1s2p\ ^3P_{0,2}$ states
with lifetimes of roughly 10^{-8} sec will act as such electron collectors.

As in the present state of experiment no extensive use has been made of a time delayed measurement using the pulsed structure of the heavy ion beam only the sum intensity of directly populated core excited states and the same states arising from electron capture into outer shells of these cores is measured. However, a discrimination between both mechanisms is possible because the electrons are transfered selectively into distinct outer shells leading to an enhancement of one line within line series as can be seen from Fig. 1.

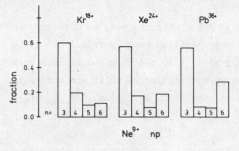
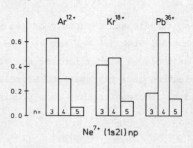

Fig. 1.
Ne x-ray intensity distribution within the H-like and Li-like series.

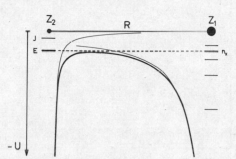

Fig. 2.
Electron capture discussed in the frame work of a one electron molecule.

In a simple one electron model (see Fig. 2) the electron transfer from a hydrogen atom with ionization potential J to a principal shell n_x around nucleus Z_1 is considered. By the strong field of nucleus Z_1 the electronic energy is lowered from J to E. At large internuclear distances R the broad Coulomb potential barrier which is higher than E keeps the electron centered around nucleus Z_2. But when the nuclei get closer the binding Energy E will exceed the maximum of the barrier and there will be a high probability of producing a hydrogen-like product state with nucleus Z_1. The values n_x and R for which the transfer occurs are compared with the detailed spectroscopic results in the next contribution.

1. N. Stolterfoht, D. Schneider, R. Mann and F. Folkmann, J.Phys. B10,L281 (1977)

2. H.F. Beyer, K.-H. Schartner, F. Folkmann and P.H. Mokler, J.Phys. B11, L363 (1978)

3. R. Mann, F. Folkmann, R.S. Peterson, Gy. Szabó and K.-O. Groeneveld, J.Phys. B11, 3045 (1978)

4. C. Bottcher, J.Phys. B10, L445 (1977)

5. J.A. Mowat, I.A. Sellin, P.M. Griffin, D.J. Pegg and R.S. Peterson, Phys. Rev. A9, 644 (1974)

SELECTIVE ELECTRON CAPTURE BY HIGHLY CHARGED VERY SLOW IONS:

II. SPECTROSCOPIC RESULTS

R. Mann, H.F. Beyer, K.-H. Schartner[+] and F. Folkmann

Gesellschaft für Schwerionenforschung mbH, D-6100 Darmstadt, W-Germany

[+]I. Physikalisches Institut der Justus Liebig-Universität, D-6300 Gießen, West
Germany

Pure neon targets and a variety of gas mixtures containing neon as one component
were bombarded with 1.4 MeV/amu very heavy projectiles ranging from Ar^{12+} up to
U^{40+}. The produced highly ionized and very slow ($\leq$ 10 eV) neon recoil ions emit
Auger-electron or x-ray spectra the relative intensities of which are strongly
affected by electron capture as a prominent population mechanism.

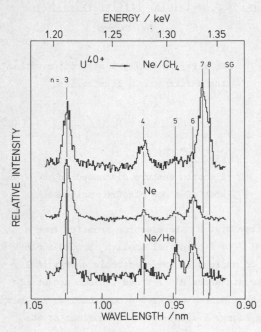

Fig. 1.
X-ray spectra of hydrogen-like neon
excited by 1.4 MeV/amu U^{40+}. The
vertical lines indicate calculated
energies for the transitions np → 1s.
Target gases are Ne/He, Ne and Ne/
CH_4 respectively.

In Fig. 1 selective electron capture by bare neon nuclei is demonstrated. Electrons are captured into hydrogen-like states with principal quantum number n_o
which is systematically raised from $n_o=5$ over 6 to $n_o=7$ as with the admixtured
species the ionization potential J is lowered thus giving rise to a strong enhancement of the corresponding x-ray line. Concerning the lithium-like line series a completely analogue observation is made in both x-ray and Auger-electron
spectra. In Fig. 2 are shown the Auger-electron spectra induced by Xe^{24+} impact
on pure neon and a Ne/CH_4 mixture respectively. In the first case helium-like
cores collect electrons into shells with $n_o=4$ whereas the methane admixture leads
to an occupation of the shells with $n_o=5$ and $n_o=6$.

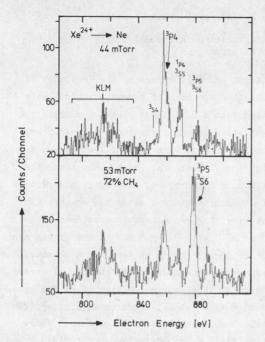

Fig. 2.
Auger-electron spectra of lithium-like neon. The configurations $(1s2^p_s, {}^{2S+1}L)nl$ are denoted as ${}^{2S+1}Ln$, l is not specified.

In the table the experimental observations n_o are summarized and compared to the values n_x predicted by the simple model of the preceeding contribution. From this model also the internuclear distance R_o (corresponding to n_o) is obtained at which the electron transfer takes place. More refined theoretical investigations[1,2] on electron capture by bare nuclei from atomic hydrogen yield values of n_x and R_o which are very close to the values predicted by the model.

The corresponding geometrical cross sections πR_o^2 are in good agreement with the experimentally determined capture cross sections which are in the range of 500 a_o^2.

Gas B	J_B/au	Ne^{10+} + B			Ne^{8+} + B		
		n_o	n_x	R_o/au	n_o	n_x	R_o/au
He	0.90	5	4.9	9.1	4	4.0	7.3
Ne	0.79	6(5)	5.2	16.8	4	4.3	6.6
Ar	0.58	6	6.0	12.3	–	5.0	
H_2	0.57	6	6.1	12.1	5	5.1	11.2
CH_4	0.46	7	6.8	17.9	5(6)	5.6	9.8

1. H. Ryufuku and T. Watanabe, Phys. Rev. A18, 2005 (1978)
2. A. Salop and R.E. Olson, Phys. Rev. A13, 1312 (1976)

CHARGE SPECTRA OF TARGET ATOMS EXCITED BY ENERGETIC IONS

M. Sakisaka, N. Maeda[*], N. Kobayashi[**] and T. Kusakabe[***]

Department of Nuclear Engineering, Kyoto University
Kyoto 606, Japan

When inner-shell ionization of target atoms is caused by the incidence of
heavy projectiles, one obtains a complicated spectrum of characteristic X-rays[1,2]
or Auger electrons,[3,4] which are resolved into normal lines plus a number of the
satellite lines. This means that target atoms are multiply ionized by a strong
Coulombic interaction of projectile nuclear charge with the shell electrons of
target atoms, and the fractions of high ionicity are far larger than those induced by electron- or photon-excitation.[5] In this report, we present a direct
measurement for the charge spectra of ion-excited target atoms and compare the
results with the statistical treatment[6] for single-electron ionizations.

A well-collimated ion beam (p, α or N^{2+}) with 0.5-2.5 MeV in energy was made
to collide with a stream of target gas (He, Ne or Ar) in an ionization chamber,
and the ionized target atoms were drawn out from a hole of the chamber electrode.
Then the ionized atoms (mass M and charge q) were charge-analyzed in an $E{\times}B$ spectrometer called "Wien filter"[7] and counted by a channel electron multiplier (CEM).
The vacuum pressure in the experimental chamber was kept at below $1{\times}10^{-6}$ Torr.
By applying a linearly sweeping electric field E, a constant magnetic field B and
other electronic devices, each specific charge spectrum (q/M) was displayed on a
multichannel pulse height analyzer. (See Fig. 1.)

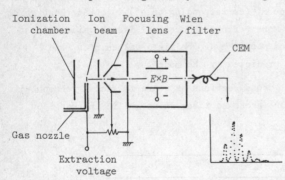

Fig. 1.
Outline of the experimental
arrangement for analyzing
the charge states of ion-
excited target atoms in a
counting mode.

The observed charge spectrum can be related to the multiple ionization cross
section[6] which combines statistically the single K-, L-, $\cdots$ electron ionization
probabilities $P_K(b)$, $P_L(b)$, $\cdots$, as

$$\sigma_{mKnL\cdots} = \int 2\pi b \ db \ {}_2C_m \ P_K(b)^m \left(1 - P_K(b)\right)^{2-m}$$
$$\times \ {}_8C_n \ P_L(b)^n \left(1 - P_L(b)\right)^{8-n}$$
$$\times \ \cdots$$

where b is the impact parameter. Of course ionicity change due to Auger process
should be taken into account in comparing the cross sections with the charge frac-

tions. When the gaussian-like $P(b)$'s after the BEA theory are used for the Ne+p,α
and Ar+p,α collisions, some deviations are found at higher charge states. (See
Fig. 2.) The step-like $P(b)$'s after the MO model theory are applied to the charge
spectra for the Ne+N^{2+} and Ar+N^{2+} collisions. Various data are presented and discussed.

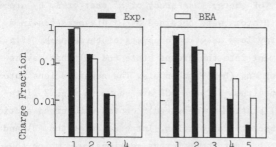

Fig. 2.
Charge state spectra for neon
bombarded with protons and
alpha particles.

Black bar: experimental,
White bar: theoretical (BEA).

This is also a device to produce and use highly stripped atoms with slow
velocities, although the metastable states having the lives of more than a few
tens microseconds may be contained. The preliminary charge-transfer experiment
for A+A^{i+} collisions at keV energy region is in progress.

*Present address: Fukui Technical College, Sabae, Fukui 910.
**Present address: Electrotechnical Laboratory, Tanashi, Tokyo 188.
***Present address: Kinki University, Higashi-Osaka, Osaka 577.

1. R.L. Watson, F.E. Jenson and T. Chiao, Phys. Rev. A10, 1230 (1974).

2. R.L. Kauffman, C.W. Woods, K.A. Jamison and P. Richard, Phys. Rev. A11,
    872 (1975).

3. N. Stolterfoht, F.J. de Heer and J. van Eck, Phys. Rev. Letters 30, 1159
    (1973).

4. N. Maeda, N. Kobayashi, H. Hori and M. Sakisaka, J. Phys. Soc. Japan 40,
    1430 (1976).

5. V. Schmidt, N. Sandner and H. Kunzemüller, Phys. Rev. A13, 1743 (1976).

6. W. Wien, Ann. Phys. 65, 440 (1898).

7. J.H. McGuire and P. Richard, Phys. Rev. A8, 1374 (1973).

H⁻ SCATTERING BY H

V.A. Esaulov

Laboratoire des Collisions Atomiques et Moléculaires - Bât. 351, Univ. Paris-Sud,
91405 ORSAY CEDEX - FRANCE

Results of a differential TOF energy loss study of H⁻ scattering by atomic
hydrogen are presented. The target H atoms were obtained by H_2 dissociation in a
R.F. discharge[1]. The neutral energy loss spectrum consists of three peaks (fig.1):
(C.E.) charge exchange, (D) detachment into the ground state and (E) that may be
the sum of peaks due to the (H+H*+e) and (H+H⁻*) channels. The negative ions autodetach and appear in the neutral spectrum. Reduced DCS are shown in fig. 2. Integration of the C.E.-DCS and its calibration to measured[2] total C.E. cross sections
(at the same velocity) yields an absolute calibration. Integration of the (D) and
(E) cross sections then yields a total detachment cross sections $Q_{T.D}$ which thus
appears to be energy *independent* from about 100 eV to 5 keV (fig.3) (the excitation
cross section Q_E is less than 10 % of Q_D at 300 eV).

Detachment in this system may occur via both the $^2\Sigma_g$($1s\sigma_g$ $2p\sigma_u^2$) and $^2\Sigma_u$
($1s\sigma_g^2$ $2p\sigma_u$) states. The $^2\Sigma_u$ state decays into the parent $^1\Sigma_g$($1s\sigma_g^2$) state. $^2\Sigma_g$
can decay both into the $^3\Sigma_u$ and $^1\Sigma_g$ continua, the former being more probable
theoretically[3]. The rapid decrease of the CE DCS indicates that both the $^2\Sigma_u$
and $^2\Sigma_g$ channels are strongly absorbed by detachment and excitation, though the
latter is small (fig. 2). If $^2\Sigma_g$ decays mainly into $^1\Sigma_g$ one can expect a broad
ejected electron spectrum and hence a broad neutral detachment peak (D), which is
not the case.

The basic excitation mechanism in H⁻H and HH collisions should be the
same i.e. $2p\sigma_u$-$2p\pi_u$ rotational coupling leading to H(2p) excitation. One can then
expect the same order of magnitude for the excitation cross section (once the
statistical ratio of the population of the incoming channels is taken into account)
if $^2\Sigma_g$ decays mainly into $^3\Sigma_u$. Results of this comparison will be presented and
discussed.

[1] J.C. Houver, J. Fayeton and M. Barat 1974, J.Phys. B7, 1358

[2] D.G. Hummer, R.F. Stebbings, W.L. Fite and L.M. Branscomb 1960, Phys.Rev. 119,
       668

[3] Yu.N. Demkov and V.N. Ostrovskii "Zero Radius Potential Method in Atomic Physics"
       (in Russian), Leningrad State University Press 1975.

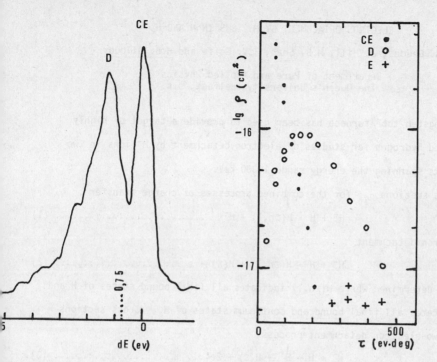

Fig.1. Neutral energy loss sepctrum
(210 eV, D⁻H)

Fig. 2. Reduced differential
cross section versus reduced
scattering angle for a 310 eV
H⁻D collision

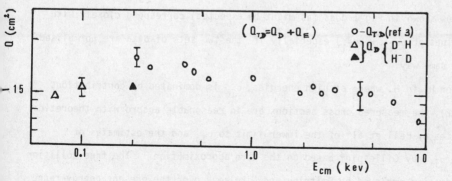

Fig. 3. Total detachment cross section.

ELECTRON DETACHMENT BY H⁻ IONS IN H AND H_2

J. Geddes, J. Hill, M.B. Shah, T.V. Goffe and H.B. Gilbody

Department of Pure and Applied Physics
The Queen's University, Belfast, U.K.

A tungsten tube furnace has been used to provide a target of highly dissociated hydrogen for studies of electron detachment by H⁻ ions in two experiments spanning the energy range 1-300 keV.

Cross sections $\sigma_{\bar{1}0}$ for the combined processes of charge transfer

$$H^- + H \rightarrow H(\Sigma n, 1) + H^- \quad \dots\dots\dots\dots\dots\dots\dots\dots (1)$$

and electron detachment

$$H^- + H \rightarrow H(\Sigma n, 1) + H(\Sigma) + e \quad \dots\dots\dots\dots\dots\dots (2)$$

have been determined where $H(\Sigma n, 1)$ indicates all final bound states of H and $H(\Sigma)$ indicates all final bound and continuum states of H. Cross sections for the two-electron detachment process

$$H^- + H \rightarrow H^+ + H(\Sigma) + 2e \quad \dots\dots\dots\dots\dots\dots\dots (3)$$

have also been determined. The corresponding cross sections for H⁻ in H_2 have been measured within the same energy range.

Our cross sections $\sigma_{\bar{1}0}$ and $\sigma_{\bar{1}1}$ for H⁻ in H are shown in Fig 1. Previous studies by Hummer et al[1] based on the modulated crossed beam technique provided charge transfer cross sections for (1) and total cross sections for electron production in the energy range 0.1-40 keV. The sum of these cross sections shown in Fig 1 does (as might be expected) correspond closely with our values of $(\sigma_{\bar{1}0} + 2\sigma_{\bar{1}1})$ especially if the two sets of data are normalised in the same way.

For H⁻ in H, where at high energies, $\sigma_{\bar{1}0}$ is dominated by contributions from (2), the measured cross sections are in reasonable accord with theoretical estimates by Bell et al[2] of the lower limit to $\sigma_{\bar{1}0}$ and the estimates of $(\sigma_{\bar{1}0} + \sigma_{\bar{1}1})$ by Gillespie[3] based on the Born approximation. The free collision approximation employed by Dmitriev and Nikolaev[4] over the present energy range and the classical impulse approximation used by Bates and Walker[5] in the range 10-40 keV provide values of $\sigma_{\bar{1}0}$ which are in generally poor accord with the present measurements.   At the lower impact energies, a lower limit theoretical

estimate of $\sigma_{\bar{1}0}$ by Bardsley[6] is in reasonable accord with experiment.

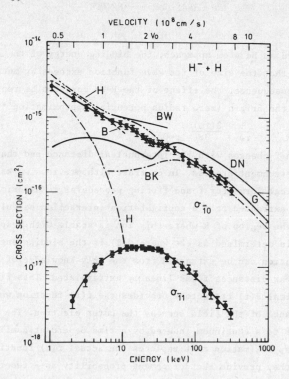

Fig 1.   Cross sections $\sigma_{\bar{1}0}$ and $\sigma_{\bar{1}1}$ for H⁻ in H.

●   - Present data.

H   - Hummer et al (1960); —·— cross section for (1); —··— sum of
         cross sections for electron production and charge transfer.

B.W. - Bates and Walker (1967); theory, $\sigma_{\bar{1}0}$.

D.N. - Dmitriev and Nikolaev (1963); theory, $\sigma_{\bar{1}0}$.

G   - Gillespie (1977), theory; $\sigma_{\bar{1}0} + \sigma_{\bar{1}1}$.

B.K. - Bell et al (1978), theory; lower limit to $\sigma_{\bar{1}0}$.

B   - Bardsley (1967), theory; lower limit to $\sigma_{\bar{1}0}$.

1. D.G. Hummer, R.F. Stebbings, W.L. Fite and L.M. Branscomb, Phys. Rev.
    119, 668 (1960).

2. K.L. Bell, A.E. Kingston, P.J. Madden, J. Phys. B 11, 3357 (1978).

3. G.H. Gillespie, Phys. Rev. A 15, 563 (1977).

4. I.S. Dmitriev abd V.S. Nikolaev, Soviet Physics, J.E.T.P.17, 447 (1963).

5. D.R. Bates and J.C.G. Walker, Proc. Phys. Soc. 90, 333 (1967).

6. J.N. Bardsley, Proc. Phys. Soc. 91, 300 (1967).

AB INITIO STUDY OF DETACHMENT PROCESS IN LOW ENERGY H⁻-He COLLISIONS

J.P. Gauyacq

*Laboratoire des Collisions Atomiques et Moléculaires - Université Paris-Sud, Bât 351
91405 ORSAY Cedex - FRANCE*

As a H⁻ ion and an He atom approach, the binding energy of the outer electron becomes so small that the size of its wave function exceeds by much the size of
the H-He core. As a consequence, the effect of the H-He core can be replaced by a
boundary condition at the origin (zero radius potential approximation[1,2]) :

$$\frac{1}{r\psi} \frac{\partial(r\psi)}{\partial r}\bigg|_{r=0} = f$$

The boundary condition f changes with the internuclear distance and that change is
responsible for the detachment process. In contrast with previous works[1,2] which
used arbitrary analytical forms for f and fitting procedures to experimental data,
the f(R) function was extracted from a configuration interaction calculation on the
(H-He)⁻ molecule. In the region of R where this ion is stable with respect to autodetachment (R>R_C), f is determined as $\sqrt{2\varepsilon}$ where ε(R) is the binding energy of the
electron. Much information can be extracted from the only knowledge of f for R>R_C ;
for smaller internuclear distances f was linearly extrapolated. This f(R) function
together with a classical R(t) trajectory provides the f(t) function which represents the time dependance of the field seen by the outer electron. The collision
equations (transitions to a continuum induced by a time dependant hamiltonian) are
solved in the sudden approximation that replaces the actual f(t) function by a step
function[3] (Fig. 1) ; they provide the detachment probability as a function of
impact parameter and energy. The image of this process is as follows : the wave
function of the initially bound electron is projected onto the continuum where it
forms a spreading wave packet ; at the end of the collision, a part of the wave
packet is recaptured into the bound state. The main interest of this method as
compared with a complex potential description lies in its ability to include all
dynamical effects which are important for detachment processes (isotope effects,
undercrossing transitions). For low energy (E<<100 eV) the elastic cross section is
obtained as the product of a classical cross section by the survival probability
and compared with experimental data[4] (Fig. 2). For higher energy, H⁻He scattering
is described as the independant scattering of the outer electron and of the H atom
by the He target[5] ; comparison with experimental data[5] for a 440 eV H⁻He collision
is presented on figure 3.

[1] Demkov Yu.N (1964) Sov.Phys. JETP 39, 410

[2] Devdariani A.Z. (1973) Sov.Phys. Tech.Phys. 18, 255

[3] Gauyacq J.P (1979) Submitted to J.Phys.B

[4] Lam S.K., Delos J.B., Champion R.L. and Doverspike L.D (1974) Phys.Rev. A 9, 1828

[5] Esaulov V., Dhuicq D. and Gauyacq J.P (1978) J.Phys.B 11, 1049

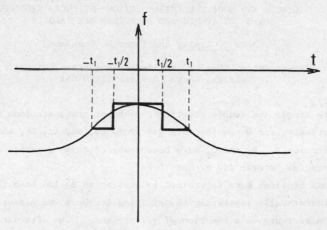

Fig. 1. Step function replacing the actual f(t) function in the calculation

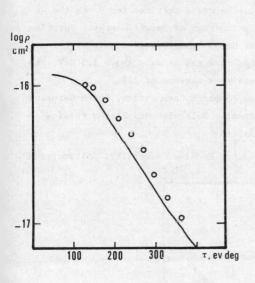

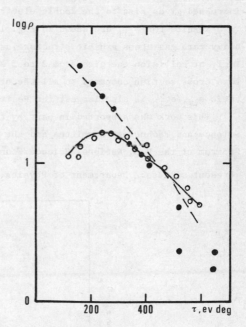

ig. 2. Elastic differential cross section
or D⁻-He collision (20 eV C.M.)

    —— : Theory,   ○   experiment

Fig. 3. Elastic and detachment
differential cross sections for
H⁻-He collision (440 eV Lab)

    ---, ● : elastic
    ——, ○ : detachment

SINGLE AND DOUBLE ELECTRON DETACHMENT CROSS SECTIONS
FOR H⁻ ON ATOMIC AND MOLECULAR GAS TARGETS

John S. Risley and Peter D. Tennyson[*]

Department of Physics, North Carolina State University
Raleigh, North Carolina 27650 USA

Absolute single and double electron detachment cross sections σ_{-10} and σ_{-11}, respectively, for H⁻ on the rare gas atoms He, Ne, Ar, Kr, and Xe and the diatomic molecules H_2, N_2 and O_2 have been measured to an accuracy of 10% for collision energies between 250 eV and 10 keV.

The cross sections were determined by passing an H⁻ ion beam through a gas cell, electrostatically separating the exciting ion beam and measuring the H⁻ and H⁺ ion currents as a function of gas pressure. The attenuation of the H⁻ current as the gas pressure is increased gives rise to the single electron detachment cross section σ_{-10} and the growth of the H⁺ current as the pressure is increased gives rise to the double electron detachment cross section σ_{-11}.

Results for σ_{-11} are shown in Fig. 1. The cross sections for H⁻ on the heavy rare gas atoms exhibit structure as a function of impact energy. Surprisingly at collision energies from 2 to 5 keV He has the largest double electron loss cross section compared to all the other rare gas atoms. Above 1.5 keV, the ratio $\sigma_{-11}/\sigma_{-10}$ is also largest for He reaching a maximum of 10%.

This work was supported in part by the Research Corporation, North Carolina Science and Technology Committee and the Atomic, Molecular and Plasma Physics Program of the U.S. National Science Foundation.

[*]Present address: Department of Physics, Johns Hopkins University, Baltimore, MD.

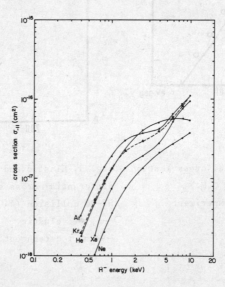

Fig. 1. Double electron detachment cross sections for H⁻ on the rare gas atoms.

H^- SCATTERING BY Na

V.A. Esaulov and Vu Ngoc Tuan

L.C.A.M. Bât. 351 - Univ. Paris-Sud 91405 ORSAY Cedex FRANCE

H^- scattering by Na has been studied for laboratory energies below 1 keV, using the time of flight method[1]. A typical neutral energy loss spectrum is shown in fig. 1. It consists of three peaks due to : (A) charge exchange (B) detachment into the ground state (H+Na+e) and (C) detachment and excitation (H+Na*+e and/or H+Na$^-$*).

The excitation mechanism in H^-Na collisions should be the same as in the parent HNa collisions[2]. Excitations occur due to the promotion of the *outermost Na orbital*[3] leading to the population of the Na(3p) levels. No H atom excitation is expected in agreement with experiment. Population of the Na$^-$*(^{3}P) level then appears improbable, and peak B should indeed be due to detachment into the ground state.

Differential cross section are shown in Fig. 2. Equal detector efficiencies were assumed for neutral to ion cross section calibrations. The detachment tail on peak B makes an accurate measurement of the detachment and excitation cross sections impossible. Estimated cross sections are obtained by integration of the peaks within the limits shown. The excitation cross section is thus only an upper limit. Both the charge exchange and elastic cross sections appear to be absorbed by detachment. The detachment peak B reproduces the superposition of detached electron spectra in both channels and the hump at about 1 eV is probably due to this.

Integration of our differential cross sections shows that unlike in the H^-H system[4] in H^-Na collisions charge exchange represents about 80 % of the detachment cross section at 300 eV, while in H^- scattering by D, Q(C.E) ~ 3Q(D) at the same laboratory energy.

[1] Brenot J.C., Pommier J., Dhuicq D. and Barat M. (1975), J.Phys.B **8**, 448

[2] Esaulov V., Dhuicq D. and Gauyacq J.P. (1978), J.Phys.B **11**, 1049

[3] Brenot J.C., Dhuicq D., Gauyacq J.P., Pommier J., Sidis V., Barat M. and Pollack E. (1975), Phys.Rev. A**11**, 1973.

[4] Esaulov V.A. In this conference.

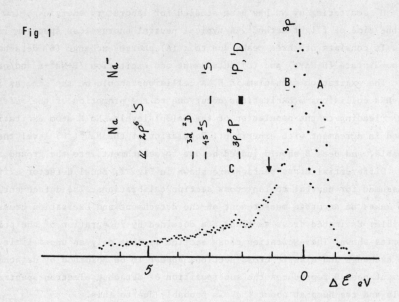

Fig 1

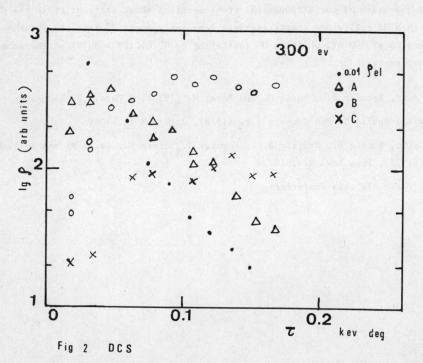

Fig 2   DCS

ELECTRON DETACHMENT IN COLLISIONS OF NEGATIVE HALOGEN IONS AND NOBLE GASES

C. de Vreugd, R.W. Wijnaendts van Resandt and J. Los

FOM-Institute for Atomic and Molecular Physics
Amsterdam, The Netherlands

Recently a considerable amount of experimental and theoretical work has been
carried out concerning the process of collisionally induced electron detachment
[1], [2], [3]. In order to study this process more closely, especially its
energy dependence, differential cross sections were measured for collisions of
F^-, Cl^-, Br^-, I^- and the noble gases. The cross sections were measured both for
the scattered ions and the neutrals in an angular range of 0-3 degrees and in an
energy range of 500-3000 eV. The experimental results indicate that the detachment
process cannot be described by means of an energy independent complex-potential
model. This is shown most clearly in the cross sections for I^- + Ne where the
electron detachment increases as the collisional energy increases. Such energy
dependence suggests that the dominant process leading to electron detachment is a
rotational coupling of the incoming I^- + Ne groundstate and the continuum.
Furthermore a remarkably small detachment probability was found in the case of
I^- + Ne. Calculations made by Olson [4] for Cl^- + Ar show that the Cl^- + Ar ground-
state crosses the continuum twice. The detachment probability of Cl^- + Ar appears
to be much larger than that of I^- + Ne. Therefore the suggestion is made that in
the case of I^- + Ne one is dealing with a groundstate that does not cross the
continuum boundary.

[1] J. Mizuno and J.C.Y. Chen, Phys. Rev. A $\underline{4}$ (1971) 1500
[2] J. Fayeton, D. Phuicq and M. Barat, J. Phys. B $\underline{11}$ (1978) 1267
[3] R.L. Champion and L.D. Doverspike, Phys. Rev. A $\underline{13}$ (1976) 609
[4] R.E. Olson and B. Liu, Phys. Rev. A $\underline{17}$ (1978) 1568

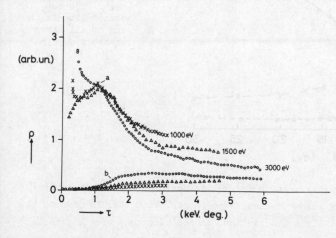

I^- +Ne cross sections
for (a) the scattered
ions and (b) the
neutrals

THE COLLISIONAL INDUCED DISSOCIATION AND ELECTRON DETACHMENT
CROSS SECTIONS FOR THE UF_6^--RARE GAS SYSTEMS[*]

R. L. Champion, L. D. Doverspike, E. Herbst and S. Haywood

Department of Physics, College of William and Mary
Williamsburg, Virginia 23185, USA

and

B. K. Annis and S. Datz

Chemistry Division, Oak Ridge National Laboratory
Oak Ridge, Tennessee 37830, USA

We report the results of recent total cross section measurements for the
endoergic reactions:

$$UF_6^- + X \begin{cases} UF_6 + e + X & (1) \\ UF_5 + F^- + X & (2) \\ UF_5^- + F + X & (3) \end{cases}$$

where X represents a rare gas atom. In addition, a study of the kinematics of
(2) has been performed using time-of-flight techniques. The energy range of
the experiments is from below threshold up to a (laboratory) energy of 500 eV.

The total cross sections for (1-3) have been measured on an apparatus
slightly modified from that used previously for collisional detachment studies.[1]
The results for X = Argon are shown below in Figure 1.

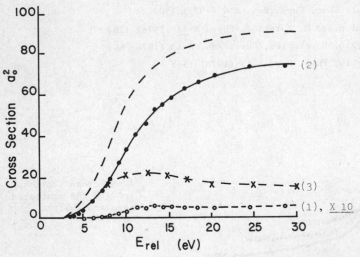

Fig. 1- Absolute total cross sections for collisions of UF_6^- with argon. The numbers refer to the channels defined in the text. The top dashed line is the sum of all three channels.

It is clear that the cross section for collisional detachment (1) remains
quite small over the energy range of these experiments, with the CID channel (2)
being the dominant process. This observation in addition to other kinematic

considerations has allowed us to measure the velocity spectra of the neutral
dissociation product, UF_5. The latter experiments have been performed on a
time-of-flight apparatus which was used previously in studies of collisional
detachment.[2] The data are consistent with the hypothesis that the reactions
proceed by a two-step process where the negative ion is first collisionally
excited and then decays by way of channels (1-3). The branching ratio, σ_3/σ_2,
does not depend upon the target species, X, but depends only upon the relative
collision energy, as may be seen in Figure 2.

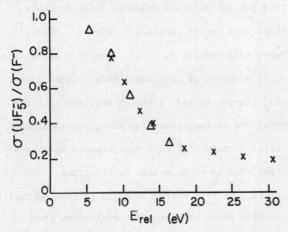

Fig. 2- Ratio of the cross
sections for collision-induced
dissociation, σ_3/σ_2, as a
function of the relative collision energy. The crosses
are for an argon target and
the triangles are for neon.

The experimental results will be analyzed in terms of a statistical model.

Research supported in part by the Division of Basic Energy Sciences, Department
of Energy, Contract ER10371 (William and Mary) and under contract with Union
Carbide Corp. (Oak Ridge National Laboratory).

1.   B. T. Smith, W. R. Edwards, L. D. Doverspike and R. L. Champion,
     Phys. Rev. 18, 945 (1978).
2.   J. T. Cheung and S. Datz, J. Chem. Phys. XX, XXXX (1979).

DOUBLY DIFFERENTIAL CROSS SECTIONS OF ELECTRON EJECTED
FROM ARGON BY 5-20KeV H^+, H_2^+ AND He^+

M.Sataka[*], K.Okuno[*], J.Urakawa and N.Oda

Research Laboratory for Nuclear Reactors,Tokyo Institute of
Technology, Meguroku, Tokyo, Japan
*Also at Tokai Research Establ., Japan Atomic Energy Research
Institute,Ibaragi,Japan

Total ionization cross sections for ion-atom and molecule collision have

been measured for the various systems over energy ranges of 100eV to 40KeV.[1]

However, the absolute cross sections, differential in ejected electron energy and

angle, have been only investigated in a series of work for 5KeV to 2.0MeV ions

by Rudd et al.[2] and Toburen et al..[3] In particular, although collisions in the

low energy range between 1 and 50 KeV are of importance for the understanding of

the physics of hot plasmas and stellar atomospheres,such measurements have been

so far very scarce and not sufficient, due to experimental difficulties.

Therefore, the purpose of our study in this energy range is to systematically

measure the absolute doubly differential cross sections of the electron ejected

from atom and molecule in more detail. In this work, absolute values of electron

production cross sections, differential in angle and energy of ejected electrons,

have been measured for electron energies of 1-26 eV and ejection angles from $30°$

to $140°$.

The measurement have been performed utilizing the crossed beam method. The

secondary electrons produced in single collisions were energy analyzed by a $30°$

electrostatic parallel-plate analyzer. The electrostatic analyzes has an energy

resolution of 1.7% and anguler range between $30°$ and $140°$ with respect to the beam

direction. Since our doubly differential cross sections by 20 KeV proton impact

on argon fairly well agree with the absolute doubly differential cross sections

by Criswell and Toburen[3] in general shape, our cross sections were put on a

absolute scale for angular range from $30°$ to $140°$.

Figs.1 and 2 shows double differential cross sections for collisions of H_2^+, He^+

on argon. The spectra are composed of discrete peaks arising from autoionizations

and a continuous part. In spectra of He^+ impact the discrete peak ratios are

considerably different from those by Gerber et al.[4] for the lower energy impacts.

Furthermore, marked differences have been observed for spectra between the collisions with H_2^+ and with He^+.

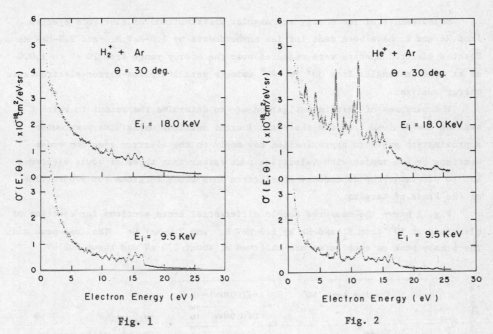

Fig. 1   Fig. 2

Doubly differential cross sections of electron ejected at $30°$ by 9.5 and 18.0 KeV H_2^+ on Ar and He^+ on Ar.

References

1) H.B.Gilbody and J.B.Hasted,Proc.Roy.Soc.A240,382(1955)

2) M.E.Rudd and J.H.Macek,Case Stud.At.Phys.3,47(1972)

3) T.L.Criswell, L.H.Toburen and M.E.Rudd,Phys.Rev.A16,508(1977)

4) G.Gerber, R.Morgenstern and A.Niehaus,J.Phys.B:Atom.Molec.Phys.5,1396(1972)

ENERGY AND ANGULAR DISTRIBUTIONS OF ELECTRONS EJECTED FROM
He AND H_2 BOMBARDED BY EQUAL VELOCITY H_2^+ AND He^+ IONS

N. Oda and F. Nishimura

Research Laboratory of Nuclear Reactors, Tokyo Institute
of Technology, Meguro-ku, Tokyo 152, Japan

Measurements of the energy and angular distributions of electrons ejected
from He and H_2 have been made for ion bombardments by 1.0-MeV H_2^+ and 2.0-MeV He^+.
Ejected electron spectra were measured over the energy range from 20 eV to 1,000
eV at ejection angles from 30° to 140° using a parallel-plate-mirror electrostatic
energy analyzer.

The purposes of this investigation are to determine the extent to which Z^2-
scaling law derived from the theoretical cross sections using binary encouter
approximation and Born approximation may apply to the electron ejection cross
sections by ion impact with velocities much faster than those of bound electrons
and to determine the dependency of electron loss cross sections for projectiles
on the kinds of targets.

Fig. 1 shows the measured double differential cross sections for ejection of
electrons at 30° from H_2 and He by 1.0-MeV H_2^+ and 2.0-MeV He^+. The loss peak and
the binary peak on each curve are observed at about 270 eV and about 800 eV,

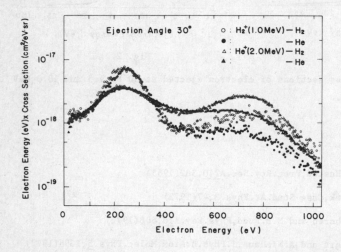

Fig. 1.
Doubly differential
cross sections times
electron energy at 30°.

respectively, for both kinds of projectiles. These features are qualitatively
understood by the kinematical theory of Drepper and Briggs.[1] Furthermore, for
both cases of H_2^+ and He^+ impacts, the shapes and the cross sections for the loss
peak on H_2 target are about the same to those on He target. This seems to imply
that the screened Coulomb potential felt by an electron bound to projectiles is
same for both H_2 and He targets.

In Figs. 2a and b, ratios of cross sections by He^+ impact to those by H_2^+

are shown as a function of the electron energy for H_2 and He targets, respectively. In the cases where the target is He, the cross sections by He^+ impact are seen to be twice those by H_2^+ impact over the electron energies higher than about 400 eV. Assuming that the cross sections by 1.0-MeV H_2^+ impact are twice those by 0.5-MeV H^+ impact,[2] one can get ratios of the cross sections by He^+ impact to those by H^+ impact are 4. As a result, the Z^2-scaling law for the electron ejection with higher energies seems to hold for the same velocity of the projectiles. In the case of H_2 target, the binary peaks are much more pronounced than those for He target (Fig. 1) and also the Z^2-scaling seems to hold over the electron energies between 500 eV and 800 eV.

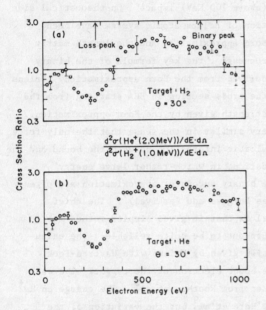

Figs. 2a and b.
Ratios of cross sections by He^+ to those by H_2^+ at electron ejection angle of $30°$. a) for H_2 target, b) for He target.

The cross sections for the energy range between 100 eV and 400 eV are not discussed here, because electrons ejected from the target and from the projectiles overlap each other and can not be simply understood. At energies below 100 eV, the cross section ratios for both H_2 and He targets are about unity at 100 eV and decrease to 0.7 as the energies of electrons decrease to 20 eV. These results indicate the screening effect of a bound electron is greater for the He^+ projectile than for the H_2^+ projectile.

Results for H^+ and H_3^+ impacts will be also discussed.

1. F. Drepper and J.S. Briggs, J. Phys. B 9, 2063 (1976).
2. W.E. Wilson and L.H. Toburen, Phys. Rev. A 7, 1535 (1973).

IONIZATION OF He BY He[+] ION IMPACT

S.N. TIWARY**

International Center for Theoretical Physics,
P.O. Box 586, Miramare
34100 Trieste, Italy

The exact treatment for ion-atom collision processes are the most complicated from both conceptually and computationally. Use of the independent particle model of the target and the ion projectile as a structureless particle makes the problem tractable. Martin et al.[1] and Pivovar et al.[2] measured the ionization cross section of He due to the high energy He[+] ion (above 100 KeV) impact. On theoretical side, calculation for He[+] ion impact ionization of helium atomic system have been carried out by Bell et al.[3] using the Born approximation and the length matrix element. As discussed by Bates and McDonough[4], the key formula of the binary encounter approximation (BEA) can be derived from the Born approximation. Vriens[5] has also obtained the expression for the cross section in BEA starting from the expression of generalized oscillator strength given by the Born approximation. Basically these two expressions are very similar in the sense that the only force which is taken into account is the Coulombic interaction between the bound and the free electrons (Kingston)[6]. For ionization, in which rather large energy transfers are involved, results of the binary encounter approximation are often superior to the Born approximation (see Burgess and Percival)[7]. The chief advantage of the binary encounter model is that it gives simpler method for estimating the cross sections which turn out to be quite reliable. The calculation has been done using the expression given by Vriens with Hartree-Fock velocity distribution function for the bound electron of the target. The wave function for the bound electron is taken from Roothan et al[8]. The charge on He[+] is not taken as 1.22 as suggested by O'Hare et al.[9] but the variation of the charge[10] with the velocity is taken into account.

The calculated cross section for the ionization of He by He[+] impact has been shown in the figure 1. For the sake of comparison, we have plotted other experimental and theoretical results available in the literature. It is evident from the figure that the present result is in much better agreement with the experimental as well as the Born results compared to the results reported by Tripathi and Rai[11] using the Gryzinski model. The BEA results are lower than the experimental data throughout the impact energy range. It shows that this model does not take into account of the more physical effects. Recently, McKnight and Rains[12], Tiwary and Rai[13], and Tiwary[14] have calculated the total ionization cross section for the atoms and molecules by proton and helium ion impact. They have shown that the BEA formalism yields better results by proton

** Permanent address: L.S. College, Bihar University, Muzaffarpur, Bihar, India.

bombardment but underestimate the cross section by helium ion impact. Our present
results indicate the same conclusion and indicate the smaller cross section for
the collision under consideration.

Fig. 1

Ionization of He by He$^+$ ion impact
Experimental data: O Martin et al.
(Ref. 1), X Pivovar et al.(Ref. 2)
Theoretical results: -.-.-.- Tripathi
and Rai (Ref. 11), ——
Present work, - - - - Bell et al.
(Ref. 3).

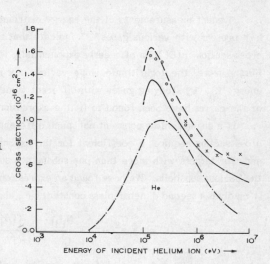

1. D.W. Martin, R.A. Langley, D.S. Harmer, J.W. Hooper and E.W. McDanniel,
    Phys. Rev. A 136, 385 (1964).
2. L.I. Pivovar, Yu. Z. Levchenko and A.N. Grigover, Sov. Phys. JETP 27
    669 (1968).
3. K.L. Bell, V. Does and A.E. Kingston, J. Phys. B: Atom.Molec. Phys. 3,
    183 (1970).
4. D.R. Bates and W.R. McDonough, J. Phys. B: 5, 1107 (1972).
5. L. Vriens, Case Studies in Atomic Collision Physics (1969) P. 335.
6. A.E. Kingston, Phys. Soc. 87, 193 (1966).
7. A. Burgess and I.C. Percival, Adv. in Atom. and Molec. Phys. 4, 109 (1968).
8. C.C.J. Roothan, I.M. Sachs and A.W. Weiss, Rev. Mod. Phys. 32, 186 (1960).
9. B.G. O'Hare, R.W. McCullough and H.B. Gilbody, J. Phys. B: Atom. Molec.
    Phys. 8, 2968 (1975).
10. I.K. Dmitrieva, G.I. Plindov and T.V. Sokolskaya, Sixth International
    Conference on Atomic Physics, Riga, USSR, Aug. 1978, P. 308.
11. D.N. Tripathi and D.K. Rai, J. Phys. Soc. Japan 29, 403 (1970).
12. R.H. McKnight and R.G. Rains, Phys. Rev. A 14, 1388 (1976).
13. S.N. Tiwary and D.K. Rai, J. Chem. Phys. 68, 2427 (1978).
14. S.N. Tiwary, Ind. J. Pure and Appl. Phys. —— in Press. (1978).

A NEW DESCRIPTION OF ELECTRON EJECTION BY LOW ENERGY PROTONS*

M. Eugene Rudd and J. Macek

Behlen Laboratory of Physics, University of Nebraska
Lincoln, Nebraska 68588

Recent measurements of the energy distributions of electrons from collisions of 5-100 keV protons with various gases[1,2,3] indicate that below about 50 keV the singly differential cross section $\sigma(E)$ falls off nearly exponentially with the energy E of the ejected electrons. Furthermore, the logarithmic slope varies in a regular manner with the incident proton energy E_p. By studying gases with different values of the ionization potential I, the shapes of the curves have been found to fit the expression $\exp - \alpha \, E/(IT)^{\frac{1}{2}}$ where $T = E_p/1836$ and α is a dimensionless constant not much different from unity. A complete equation for the cross section requires a coefficient for the exponential expression that depends on T and I and, for targets with more than one subshell, a summation of the partial cross sections for the various subshells. We have found an expression which works well for all six gases tested. It involves a second dimensionless constant β, also near unity. The equation is

$$\sigma(E) = 5\pi \, a_o^2 \, \alpha^3 \, \sum_i \frac{N_i I_H^2}{I_i^3} \, \frac{(T/I_i)^{\beta - \frac{1}{2}}}{4+(T/I_i)^{2\beta}} \, \exp - \alpha \, E/(I_i/T)^{\frac{1}{2}} \tag{1}$$

where $\alpha = 1.28$ and $\beta = 1.0$ for H_2 and He, while $\alpha = 0.91$ and $\beta = 0.75$ for N_2, O_2, Ne, and Ar. N_i is the number of electrons of binding energy I_i and a_o is the radius of the first Bohr orbit. Figure 1 shows the degree of agreement of the equation with experimental data for argon.

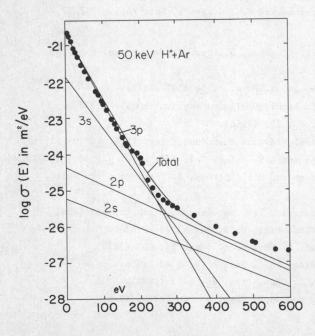

Fig. 1. Comparison of the energy distribution of electrons ejected by 50 keV protons in argon with calculations from Eq. 1. Dots are experimental data of Crooks and Rudd.[4]

This expression can be integrated over E to obtain

$$\sigma_e = 5\pi \, (a_o \, \alpha)^2 \; \sum_i \; \frac{N_i I_H^2}{I_i^2} \; \frac{(T/I_i)^\beta}{4+(T/I_i)^{2\beta}} \tag{2}$$

the total cross section for electron production. The dependence of this expression on T is similar to one suggested by Green and McNeal.[5]

The exponential form of Eq. (1) at low proton energies can be derived from Meyerhof's expression[6] for K-shell transition probabilities. As the proton approaches the target, a charge transfer involving an energy difference ΔE_1 takes place followed by a rotational coupling at the point of closest approach. This promotes the system to an excited state close to the ionization threshold from which it can make a transition of energy $\Delta E_2 + E$ into the continuum. The cross section for this process is

$$\sigma(E) \propto \frac{1}{1+e^{2x_1}} \; \sigma_{rot} \; \frac{1}{1+e^{2x_2}}$$

where $x_1 = \Delta E_1 \, \ell_1/2 \, \hbar v_p$ and $x_2 = (\Delta E_2 + E) \, \ell_2/2 \, \hbar v_p$. The characteristic lengths are given by $\ell_1 = \ell_2 = 2\alpha \, a_o (I_H/I)^{\frac{1}{2}}$ where α is a dimensionless length parameter which we identify with the constant α in Eq. 1. If v_o is the velocity in the first Bohr orbit, then $v_o = v_p(T/I_H)^{\frac{1}{2}}$ and since $2 a_o I_H = \hbar v_o$, we have $2 x_2 = \alpha (E + \Delta E_2)/(IT)^{\frac{1}{2}}$. If T is small and E is not too small we can make the approximation

$$1/(1+e^{2x_2}) \simeq \exp - 2x_2 = \exp - \alpha \Delta E_2/(IT)^{\frac{1}{2}} \; \exp - \alpha E/(IT)^{\frac{1}{2}}$$

which gives us the same exponential dependence on E as Eq. 1.

*Work supported by the National Science Foundation.

1. M. E. Rudd and D. H. Madison, Phys. Rev. A 14, 128 (1976).
2. T. L. Criswell, L. H. Toburen, and M. E. Rudd, Phys. Rev. A 16, 508 (1977).
3. M. E. Rudd, Phys. Rev. A (to be published).
4. J. B. Crooks and M. E. Rudd, Phys. Rev. A 3, 1628 (1971).
5. A. E. S. Green and R. J. McNeal, J. Geophys. Res. 76, 133 (1971).
6. W. E. Meyerhof, Phys. Rev. Letters 31, 1341 (1973).

DIFFERENTIAL CROSS SECTIONS FOR IONIZATION OF KRYPTON BY FAST PROTONS:
THEORY* AND EXPERIMENT**

L. H. Toburen
Battelle, Pacific Northwest Laboratory
Richland, Washington 99352 U.S.A.

and

Steven T. Manson
Georgia State University
Atlanta, Georgia 30303 U.S.A.

In a previous paper, we compared measured and calculated cross sections, differential in ejected electron energy and angle, for ionization of krypton by 1 MeV
protons.[1] In that work, we reported sizable discrepancies between theory and measurement for ejection of electrons into small emission angles with energies in the
range of 100 to 500 eV. These discrepancies were attributed to continuum-charge-
transfer (CCT) which, for 1 MeV protons, should maximize near 544 eV.[2] To provide
further insight into the ionization process contributing to this difference, we
have extended the energy range of these measurements to 4.2 MeV proton impact and
have investigated the theoretical subshell contributions to the differential cross
sections. If the discrepancies observed at 1 MeV were indeed due to CCT, agreement should improve at higher proton energies since this process is expected to
decrease rapidly with increasing proton energy.[2]

Measured cross sections for ejection of 136 eV electrons at 30° are shown in
Fig. 1 along with the theoretical cross sections for both the total yield and that
for individual subshells. The calculations were performed using the Born approximation and Hartree-Slater wave functions
for initial discrete and final continuum
electronic states except for the 4p-εd and
3d-εf channels. In these channels, a full
Hartree-Fock calculation was performed.
Note that the ratio of theoretical to experimental cross sections remains constant
at approximately 0.6 and agreement does
not improve as the proton energy increases.
We also observe that over 60% of the theoretical cross section arises from ionization of the 3d shell of krypton. Since
agreement does not improve with increasing
proton energy, it does not seem likely
that the differences between theory and
experiment in these high energy collisions

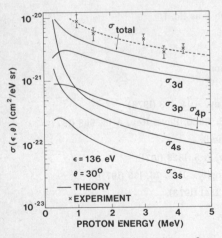

FIG. 1 Proton energy dependence for
ejection of 30 eV electrons with an
emission angle of 20°.

_____

*Supported by National Science Foundation.
**This paper is based on work performed under United States Department of Energy
   Contract EY-76-C-06-1830.

can be attributed entirely to CCT. A more probable cause for these discrepancies is for the calculation to underestimate the contribution from one or more of the subshells.

To provide some guidance to which subshell may be underestimated by the calculation, it is useful to consider the angular distribution of ejected electrons. The angular distribution of 136 eV electrons ejected by 3.67 MeV protons is shown in Fig. 2 along with contributions calculated for each of the subshells; 3s, 3p, 3d, 4s, and 4p. From the shape and magnitude of the subshell contributions, it would appear that an increase in the 3d cross sections by about 60% would provide good agreement between theoretical and experimental cross sections at all angles. If a 60% increase were made in the 4p contribution, agreement between measured and calculated cross sections could be achieved for only angles near 90° with little change for large or small emission angles. We note that the shape of the 3p and 3d angular distributions is similar, however, a very large change in the 3p contribution would be required to have any influence on the total ejected electron yield. We are presently exploring possibilities for why this calculation might underestimate the 3d subshell contribution and for other processes which may effect the cross sections. Data will be presented for proton energies from 1 to 4.2 MeV and for a broad range of ejected electron energies and emission angles.

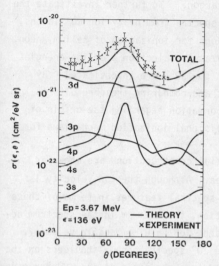

FIG. 2 Angular distribution of 30 eV electrons ejected from Kr by 3.67 MeV protons.

REFERENCES

1. S. T. Manson and L. H. Toburen, X ICPEAC Abstracts of Papers (Commissariat A L'Energie, Paris, 1977), p. 990.

2. S. T. Manson, L. H. Toburen, D. H. Madison, and N. Stolterfoht, Phys. Rev. A 12, 60 (1975).

SECONDARY ELECTROM EMISSION IN COLLISIONS OF
1.2 MeV C$^+$ IONS WITH He, Ne, Ar, and CH$_4$*

L. H. Toburen

Battelle, Pacific Northwest Laboratory
Richland, Washington 99352 U.S.A.

Electron production in sufficiently high energy (MeV/amu) collisions of heavy ions with atomic and molecular targets can be understood in terms of coulomb ionization processes.[1,2] For low energy collisions, mechanisms related to the molecular nature of the collision have been employed to interpret electron yields.[3] Recently, structure of unresolved origin has been identified in continuum electron spectra in low energy N$^+$ and O$^+$ ionization of argon.[4] To further investigate the systematics and spectral features of electron spectra from heavy ion collisions, we have measured electron emission cross sections for ionization of helium, neon, argon, and methane by 1.2 MeV C$^+$ ions (0.1 MeV/amu). Electron ejection energies from 10 to 800 eV and emission angles from 15° to 130° were investigated. By choosing targets with varying shell structures and comparing these results to ionization by proton impact, we can derive information regarding the origin of spectral features and obtain insight into collisional ionization mechanisms for heavy ion collisions.

Examples of the measured double differential cross sections are shown in Fig. 1 for both large and small emission angles. Although the ion velocity is relatively low, we are able to identify basic spectral features in terms of those observed for fast ions. In the forward direction, the maximum in the spectrum occurs near where the ejected electron and incident ion have comparable velocity, $v_e = v_i$. The maxima observed at $v_e = v_i$ in the 20° spectra become shoulders on the 130° spectra and arise from electrons stripped from the incident ion. Underlying the stripped electron peak and forming the major contribution to the low energy

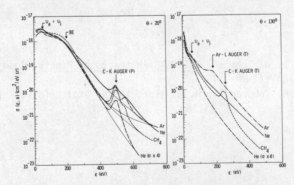

FIG. 1 Ionization of argon, neon, helium, and methane by 1.2 MeV C$^+$ ions. The designation P indicates features originating from projectile ionization and T indicates features arising from the target atom or molecule.

---

*This paper is based on work performed under United States Department of Energy Contract EY-76-C-06-1830.

portion of the spectra at large emission angles are electrons ejected in soft, large impact parameter collisions. Evidence of a broad binary encounter peak (BE) due to ionization in small impact parameter collisions is evident in the 20° spectra for electron energies near 200 eV and Auger spectra arising from the projectile (P) and target (T) are observed.

The yield of electrons near the binary encounter peak depends primarily on the number and binding energy of the outermost target electrons. For electron energies above the binary encounter peak in the 20° spectra and above about 100 eV in the 130° spectra, the electron cross sections are strongly dependent on the target structure. This dependence on target structure is similar to spectral shapes that have been observed for equal velocity proton impact in the work of Crooks and Rudd;[5] these similarities are illustrated in Fig. 2. Low energy proton data have recently been analyzed by Rudd[6] in terms of a model in which the exponential decrease in emission cross section with increasing electron energy is proportional to $I^{-\frac{1}{2}}$, where I is the electron binding energy. Such a model explains the change in slope observed in the carbon ion spectra at higher electron energies as resulting from the contribution of electrons ejected from inner shells of the target. The slower decrease in the neon cross sections is attributed to the influence of the 2s electrons, while inflection points at about 400 eV in the 20° spectra of argon and methane represent the increasing contribution to the spectra from the 2p and 1s electrons, respectively. For ejection of fast electrons into large emission angles, the target dependence appears to be somewhat larger than would be expected based on data for equal velocity protons.

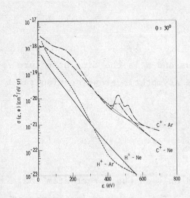

FIG. 2 Ionization of argon and neon by 1.2 MeV C[+] and equal velocity (0.1 MeV) H[+] impact. The proton data are from Ref. 5.

REFERENCES

1. N. Stolterfoht in Topics in Current Physics, Vol. 5 (Springer-Verlap, Berlin, 1978), pp. 155-199.

2. L. H. Toburen, in Proceedings of the 1978 Conference on the Application of Small Accelerators, IEEE Transactions on Nuclear Science, Vol. NS-26, pp. 1056-1061.

3. V. V. Afrosimov, Yu. S. Gordeev, A. N. Zinoviev, A. A. Korotkov, and A. P. Shergin, in Abstracts of Papers, X ICPEAC (Commissariat A L'Energie Atomique, Paris, 1977), p. 924.

4. N. Stolterfoht and D. Schneider in Proceedings of the 1978 Conference on the Application of Small Accelerators, *op.cit.*, pp. 1130-1132.

5. J. B. Crooks and M. E. Rudd, Phys. Rev. A 3, 1628 (1971).

6. M. E. Rudd, Phys. Rev. A (IN PRESS).

BORN CROSS SECTIONS FOR THE IMPACT IONIZATION OF HELIUM
BY FAST LITHIUM ATOMS AND IONS

George H. Gillespie[†]

Physical Dynamics, Inc., P. O. Box 556, La Jolla, CA 92038, USA

At high impact velocities the cross section for the ionization of an atom
assumes one of two asymptotic forms depending on whether the incident particle is
an ion or a neutral atom. For collisions with an ion of net charge q, the ionization cross section has the same velocity (v) dependence as in the Bethe theory[1]
and may be written as [2,3]

$$\sigma_{ion} = 4\pi a_o^2 \frac{\alpha^2}{\beta^2} \left\{ q^2 M_{ion}^2 \left[\ln\left(\frac{4\beta^2\gamma^2}{\alpha^2} \right) - \beta^2 \right] - 2q^2 L(-1)_{ion} \right.$$

$$\left. + [I_1 - I_2]_{ion} + 2 I_{in,ion} + \Gamma \frac{\alpha^2}{\beta^2} \right\}, \tag{1}$$

where $\beta = v/c$, $\gamma^2 = (1-\beta^2)^{-1}$, a_o is the Bohr radius and α is the fine structure
constant. For the case of neutral atom impact the asymptotic cross section takes
the form:

$$\sigma_{ion} = 4\pi a_o^2 \frac{\alpha^2}{\beta^2} \{ 2[I_{el,ion} + I_{in,ion}] + \Gamma \frac{\alpha^2}{\beta^2} \}. \tag{2}$$

The parameters M_{ion}^2 and $L(-1)_{ion}$ in Eq. (1) depend only on the target atom and
have values of .489 and .51, respectively, for He.[4] The constants in the second
line of Eq. (1) and those appearing in Eq. (2) involve atomic properties of both
the target atom and the incident ion. Calculations of these parameters have been
carried out for all charge states of Li colliding with He and the results are
summarized in Table I.

Table I. Cross section parameters appearing in Eqs. (1)-(2) for the collisional
ionization of He by fast Li atoms and ions.

Incident Particle	$[I_1 - I_2]_{ion}$	$2I_{el,ion}$	$2I_{in,ion}$	Γ
Li^0	----	3.32	3.16	-22.2
Li^+	2.91	----	1.01	-11.3
Li^{2+}	5.43	----	0.443	-10.7
Li^{3+}	9x(1.05)	----	----	9x(-1.21)

The method utilized to obtain the parameters in Table I is similar to that of Ref. 4, the total inelastic scattering parameters are evaluated first and then the contributions arising from discrete excited final states are subtracted out. The resulting cross sections thus include both single and double ionization processes for He. For Li^{3+} impact the results in Table I are simply 9 times the corresponding parameters for incident structureless charged particles.[4]

The theoretical cross sections of this work, the cross sections for structureless charged particle impact (Bethe cross sections)[4], and available experimental data[5] for two different energies are shown in Fig. 1 as a function of q^2. For highly stripped ions the asymptotic cross section is very close to q^2 times the Bethe cross section (the two are identical for fully stripped ions). In this case the ion behaves essentially as a point particle with only a long-range Coulomb field proportional to q. When q^2 is reduced as electrons are added, then the atomic structure of the ion becomes increasingly important. For example, at q=1 the structure effects are roughly as important as the long-range Coulomb contributions in the sense that the cross section is approximately a factor of two greater than the Bethe cross section. Finally at $q^2=0$ there is no long-range force contribution and an accurate description of the electronic structure of the Li atom is essential for determining the cross section.

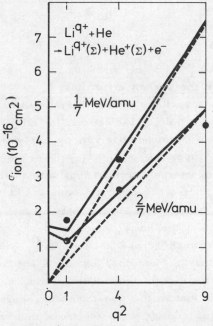

Fig. 1. Cross sections for the impact ionization of He by fast Li^{q+} projectiles as a function of q^2. Results are shown for ^7Li energies of 1 and 2 MeV: solid lines based on the results of this work, broken lines from the Bethe theory for structureless charged particles (Ref. 4), solid circles from the experimental data of Pivovar et al (Ref. 5). Departures from the Bethe cross sections reflect the importance of the electronic structure of the incident particle.

†Work supported by Physical Dynamics Independent Research and Development Fund.

1. M. Inokuti, Rev. Mod. Phys. 43, 297 (1971).
2. G. H. Gillespie, Y.-K. Kim and K. T. Cheng, Phys. Rev. A 17, 1284 (1978).
3. G. H. Gillespie, to be published.
4. M. Inokuti and Y.-K. Kim, Phys. Rev. 186, 100 (1969).
5. L. I. Pivovar, Yu. Z. Levchenko, and G. A. Krivonosov, Zh. Eksp. Teor. Fiz. 59, 19 (1970) [Soviet Physics - JETP 32, 11 (1971)].

THE CROSS SECTIONS FOR LOSS OF A PAIR
OF ELECTRONS FROM THE OUTER K- AND L-SHELLS OF FAST IONS

I.S. Dmitriev, V.S. Nikolaev, Ya.A. Teplova

and   Yu.A. Fainberg

Institute of Nuclear Physics, Moscow State University;

Moscow 117234; USSR

In order to study the dependence of the cross sections for outer electron loss on the quantum numbers n and l of their initial state the experimental data are obtained on the cross sections for the simultaneous loss of two or more electrons by a number of ions of light elements in their passing through helium and nitrogen at velocities V= 2.6 .10^8, 4. 10^8 and 8 .10^8 cm/s.

The obtained electron loss cross sections $\sigma_{i,i+m} \ (m \geqslant 2)$ have been used to determine the cross sections for loss of a pair of electrons from the outer K- and L-shells of ions[1].

$$\sigma_L^{(2)} = \binom{2}{q_L} \sum_{m=2} \binom{2}{m} \sigma_{i,i+m}\ , \qquad\qquad \text{at } q_L \geqslant 2$$

$$\sigma_{KL}^{(2)} = \frac{1}{2}\left(\sigma_{i,i+2} + 2\sigma_{i,i+3} \right), \qquad\qquad \text{at }\ q_L = 1 \qquad\qquad (1)$$

$$\sigma_K^{(2)} = \sigma_{i,i+2}\ , \qquad\qquad\qquad \text{at } q_L = 0$$

where q_L is the number of electrons in the L-shell of an ion.

An analysis of the obtained cross sections shows that at V=8.10^8 cm/s cross sections $\sigma_L^{(2)}$ for loss of a pair of L-electrons for all ions with q_L from 2 to 7 fall, within the experimental error, on one curve representing the dependence of $\sigma_L^{(2)}$ upon $I^{(2)} = I_i + I_{i+1}$ where I_i and I_{i+1} is the binding energy of an outer electron in ions with charges i and i + 1, respectively. And at $V \leqslant 4.10^8$ cm/s the values of $\sigma_L^{(2)}$ for ions with q_L = 2 and 3 and $I^{(2)} \sim$ 100–200 eV are 2–3 times smaller than those for ions with $q_L \geqslant 4$ at the same values of $I^{(2)}$ (Fig. 1). The revealed difference between the cross sections $\sigma_{2p}^{(2)}$ and $\sigma_{2s}^{(2)}$ for the loss of a pair of 2p and 2s electrons, just as a similar difference between the cross sections for loss of individual 2p and 2s electrons[2], is apparently due to the fact that in the quasiadiabatic approach of the colliding particles the binding energy of 2p electrons decreases whereas the binding energy of 2s electrons increases.

The cross sections $\sigma_K^{(2)}$ for loss of a pair of 1s electrons from the unexcited helium-like ions (q_L = 0) in the region of $I^{(2)} \sim$ 100–300 eV are 1.5–2 times the cross sections $\sigma_{2s}^{(2)}$ for the same values of $I^{(2)}$. For the lithium-like ions with q_L = 1 the cross sections $\sigma_{KL}^{(2)}$ for loss of a pair of electrons in different shells (K and L) are 1.5 times smaller than $\sigma_{2S}^{(2)}$ or $\sigma_{1S}^{(2)}$ at the same values of $I^{(2)}$.

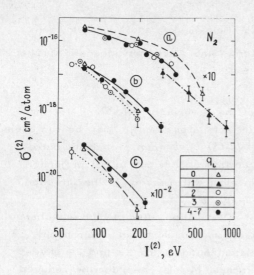

Fig. 1. Cross sections $\sigma^{(2)}$ for loss of a pair of electrons for ions with a different number of q_L electrons versus $I^{(2)}$ at $V = 8.10^8(a)$; $4.10^8(b)$ and $2.6 .10^8$ cm/s (c).

REFERENCES

1. I.S. Dmitriev, V.S. Nikolaev, L.N. Fateeva, and Ya.A. Teplova
JETP, 43, 361 (1962).

2. Yu.A. Tashaev, I.S. Dmitriev, V.S. Nikolaev, Ya.A. Teplova
J. Phys. B11, 223(1978).

ROLE OF TRANSITIONS WITH DIFFERENT CHANGES
OF THE ELECTRON ORBITAL ANGULAR MOMENTUM PROJECTION
IN THE PROTON IONIZATION OF THE 1s AND 2s STATES OF
HYDROGEN-LIKE IONS

V.A. Sidorovich, V.S. Nikolaev, V.V. Beloshitsky, and V.V. Goloviznin

Institute of Nuclear Physics, Moscow State University; Moscow 117234;
U S S R

It has been shown in ref.[1] that the probability $W(\varsigma)$ for inelastic atomic scattering at a fixed impact parameter ς may be represented as a sum of the probabilities $W_m(\varsigma)$, each probability corresponding to the transitions with a certain change m in the projection of the orbital angular momentum of an atom with respect to the direction of the colliding-particle relative velocity $\vec{v}$.

In the present paper the role of transitions with a different change in the projection of the orbital angular momentum of an electron has been considered, taking the proton ionization of the 1s and 2s states of the hydrogen-like ions as an example. In this case, for the reduced probability of ionization $w_m(\varsigma) = \left(\frac{Z v}{n}\right)^2 W_m(\varsigma)$ we have

$$w_m(\varsigma) = \frac{1}{\pi^2} \int d^3 x \left| \int \frac{d^2 q_\perp}{q^2} M_{if}(\vec{q}) J_m(q_\perp \varsigma) e^{-im\varphi} \right|^2 \tag{1}$$

where Z is the nuclear charge of an ion, n the principal quantum number of an electron in the initial state; $\vec{x}$ the electron momentum in the continuum; $\vec{q} = \vec{K}_f - \vec{K}_i$; $\vec{K}_i$ and $\vec{K}_f$ are the momenta of the relative motion of colliding particles before and after collision; $\vec{q}_\perp$ is the $\vec{q}$-vector component perpendicular to $\vec{v}$; $M_{if}(\vec{q})$ the matrix element of the electron transition to the continuum; J_m the Bessel function of the order of m ; φ the azimuthal angle of vector $\vec{q}$. All variables are taken in the Coulomb units multiplied or divided by n for the variables proportional to the length or velocity, respectively.

Calculations of $w_m(\varsigma)$ at ς varying from 0 to 3 for the values of v from the range between 1/9 and 10 were made by formula (1) in the first Born approximation.

It follows from the calculations that, at small impact parameters ς in the case of ionization of the 1s and 2s states for all velocities v , the main contribution to $w(\varsigma)$ is provided by the transitions with m=0 (figs.1 and 2). At $v \lesssim 1/2$ the values of $w_0(\varsigma)$ are dominant in the region of $\varsigma \lesssim 3$ (fig.2), and the total cross sections for ionization $\sigma = 2\pi \int w(\varsigma) \varsigma d\varsigma$ slightly differ from the value of $\sigma_0 = 2\pi \int w_0(\varsigma) \varsigma d\varsigma$. At $v \gtrsim 1$, the region of impact parameters $\S$, where the values of $\mathcal{W}(\S)$ are mainly determined by the value of $\mathcal{W}_o(\S)$, is narrowed with increasing velocity $\mathcal{V}$. At $\S \sim 1$, the values of $\mathcal{W}(\S)$ are determined by the values of $\mathcal{W}_o(\S)$ and $\mathcal{W}_{\mp 1}(\S)$ and at $\S \sim 2 \div 3$ $\mathcal{W}_{\mp 1}(\S)$ is dominant (fig.2). At $\S \leq 3$, the contribution from $\mathcal{W}_{\mp 2}(\S)$ to the total ionization probability $\mathcal{W}(\S)$ does not exceed 20% and 30% and the contribution from $\mathcal{W}_{\mp 3}(\S)$ is not higher than 5% and 20% in the case of the 1s and 2s states ionization, respectively (fig.2); the contribution from the terms with $|m| \geqslant 4$ does not exceed 5.%.

Thus, in the calculations of the proton ionization probabilities for the hydrogen–like ions at $\S \leq 3$ we may restrict ourselves to the inclusion of the transitions with $|m| \leqslant 3$ only. The cases are pointed out when at $\S \gtrsim 1$ the most probable values of $|m|$ are smaller than half of the most probable value of the orbital angular momentum of an electron in the final state[2,3].

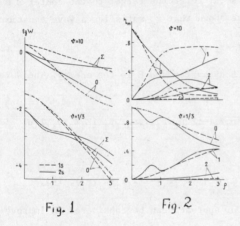

Fig.1.

Fig.2.

Fig.1. Reduced probabilities $\mathcal{W}(\S)$ and $\mathcal{W}_o(\S)$ of the proton ionization of the 1s and 2s states of hydrogen–like ions versus the impact parameter $\S$ at $\mathcal{V} = 1/3$ and 10. The signs Σ and 0 denote $\mathcal{W}(\S)$ and $\mathcal{W}_o(\S)$ respectively.

Fig.2. Ratios $\zeta_o = \dfrac{\mathcal{W}_o(\S)}{\mathcal{W}(\S)}$ and $\zeta_m = \dfrac{\mathcal{W}_{-m}(\S) + \mathcal{W}_m(\S)}{\mathcal{W}(\S)}$ for $|m| = 1, 2$ and 3 versus $\S$ at $\mathcal{V} = 1/3$ and 10. Numbers 0,1,2, and 3 indicate the values of $|m|$.

1. K. Taulbjerg, J. Phys. B10, 341 (1977)
2. G. Peach, Proc.Phys.Soc.,85, 709 (1965)
3. I.M. Kruglova, V.S. Nikolaev and V.I. Shulga. J.Phys.BII,2971(1977).

IONIZATION OF HYDROGENLIKE ATOMS BY FAST STRIPPED IONS

C.R.Garibotti and J.E.Miraglia

Consejo Nacional de Investigación Científica y Tecnologica and
Centro Atómico Bariloche*-Instituto Balseiro**
8400 S.C. de Bariloche, R.N. - Argentina

From a multiple scattering expansion of the T-matrix for the single ionization process we have obtained an expression for the final state of the colliding system. This wave is distorted by the electron-target $(V_1=-Z_1/r_1)$ and the electron-projectile $(V_2=-Z_2/r_2)$ interactions[1], and can be written[2]:

$$\chi_f^- = e^{-i\vec{k}_1 \cdot \vec{r}_1} \psi_{\vec{k}_1}^- (\vec{r}_1) \psi_{\vec{k}_2}^- (\vec{r}_2) \psi_{\vec{k}_1}^- (\vec{R}_1) \tag{1}$$

The $\psi_{\vec{k}}^- (\vec{r})$ are ingoing Coulomb waves. The variables $\mu_1, \vec{r}_1, \vec{k}_1$ are the reduced mass, the position and the momentum vectors of the electron relative to the target; $\mu_2, \vec{r}_2$, $\vec{k}_2$ refer the electron to the projectile, $\vec{R}_1, \vec{K}_1$ refer the target to the center of mass of the system electron-projectile. We have shown that χ_f^- satisfies a wave equation:

$$(H-E)\chi_f^- =-W\chi_f^- , \tag{2}$$

where H is the hamiltonian for the three body system and E is the energy. The W is a residual potential given by:

$$W= \frac{1}{\mu_1} \vec{\nabla}_{r_1} \ln {}_1F_1(-iZ_1\mu_1/k_1,1,u_1) \cdot \vec{\nabla}_{r_1} \ln {}_1F_1(-iZ_2\mu_2/k_2,1,u_2) {}_1F_1(iZ_1Z_2/v_i,1,u) \tag{3}$$

where:

$$u=-i(K_1R_1+\vec{K}_1 \cdot \vec{R}_1) \qquad\qquad u_i=-i(k_ir_i+\vec{k}_i \cdot \vec{r}_i), \quad i=1,2$$

v_i is the velocity of the incident ion. Our approach can be considered an improvement of the VPS method[3].

The first perturbative order for the scattering amplitude is evaluate with a no distorted initial state and the final state given by the Eq.(1). Integrating over the final directions of the projectile we obtain the cross section doubly differential in the energy and the angle of the electron. The calculation has been performed for the $H + H^+ \to H^+ + H^+ + e^-$ process for $v_i>1$ (atomic units).

The formalism developed gives an unified description of the capture to the continuum and the direct ionization processes. However, as shown in fig.1 the angular distributions are somewhat smaller than the experimental data at small angles[4].The interaction W, which can be included in a second order perturbative calculation, gives a qualitative account for that deviation. From Eq.3 we can show that

$$W_{r_1,r_2\to\infty} a_1 a_2 \frac{\hat{k}_1 \cdot \hat{k}_2}{r_1 r_2} (1-e^{i\phi}1)(1-e^{i\phi}2) \tag{4}$$

where ϕ_1 and ϕ_2 are real functions. When $r_1, r_2 \to \infty$ this potential goes to zero faster than the Coulomb interactions and χ_f^- has the correct asymtotic behaviour. For finite distances, the influence of W depends on the momentum of the ejected electron. Let us consider the velocity space of the electron (fig.2). If $k_1 \cdot k_2 < 0$ the W is atractive and should increase the cross section (region I at the fig.2). At the region II, $k_1 \cdot k_2 > 0$, the potential W is repulsive and should decrease the cross section. The W goes quickly to zero for large values of the $\vec{k}_1$ and $\vec{k}_2$. Furthermore, the different behaviour of W at the sides of the CTC peak explains the asymmetry of this peak[5].

* Comisión Nacional de Energía Atómica

** Universidad Nacional de Cuyo

1. K.Dettmann, K.G.Harrison and N.W.Lucas, J.Phys. B 7, 269 (1974)

2. C.R.Garibotti and J.E.Miraglia, Submitted for publication

3. L.Vainstein, L.Presnyakov, I.Sobelman, Sov.Phys.JETP 18, 1383 (1964)

4. L.H.Toburen and W.E.Wilson, Phys.Rev. A 5, 247 (1972)

5. R.Shakeshaft and L.Spruch, Phys.Rev.Lett. 41, 1037 (1978)

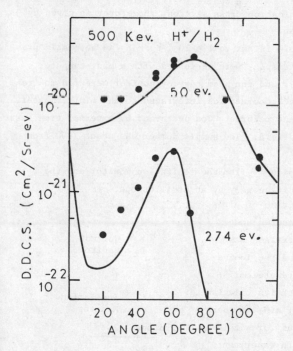

Fig.1 Comparison between theoretical and
experimental values[4].

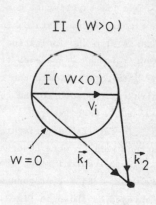

Fig.2 Velocity space of the
electron.

MEASUREMENT OF IONIZATION CROSS SECTION OF GASEOUS MOLECULE
FOR 0.02 - 385 GeV PROTONS

Hajime Ishimaru, K. Muto, Z. Igarashi, S. Hiramatsu and S. Shibata
National Laboratory for High Energy Physics, Oho, Tsukuba, Ibaraki, Japan

J.E. Griffin
Fermi National Accelerator Laboratory, Batavia, Illinois, U.S.A.*

M. Inokuti+
Institute of Space and Aeronautical Science, University of Tokyo
and Argonne National Laboratory, Argonne, Illinois, U. S. A.*

Primary ionization cross sections for high energy protons are of importance
in the design of ionization detectors. But very few values and only the calculated value for air are available in the literature. To measure the energy dependence of the ionization cross section, a "gas ionization monitor"[1] is inserted in a
high energy proton beam in an accelerator.

Experiments were carried out in the KEK 500 MeV booster, KEK 12 GeV main ring
and Fermilab 500 GeV main ring as shown in Fig.1. Assuming the ion collection efficiency and the gas pressure to be constant, the ion current of the ionization
monitor is proportional to $I_p \sigma(E)$, where I_p is the beam current, and $\sigma(E)$ is the
ionization cross section. The ionization cross section, therefore, is given by
$\sigma(E) \propto S/I_p$, where S is ion current.

In KEK experiment, gas pressure is set to 1×10^{-5} torr by an automatic pressure controller. Data taking and display were performed with a mini-computer.
Signals from the ionization monitor and the beam current monitor were fed to transient recorders, and each transient recorder was interfaced to the mini-computer.
The data acquisition to the transient recorders was performed by external time base
which corresponded to the guiding field. The sample number was about 2000 from
0.02 to 12 GeV.[2]

In Fermilab experiment, the signals from the ionization monitor and the
current monitor were observed simultaneously by an oscilloscope.

Relative ionization cross section of air
for 0.02 - 385 GeV protons was measured and
displayed as shown in Fig.2. Comparison was
made between the measured value and the ionization loss for air calculated by Sternheimer.[3]
Relative measured value agreed with its calculated value within 5 % for protons of kinetic energy
0.02 - 100 GeV. It is advantageous for simple
and clear comparison of theory with experiment
to plot $\beta^2 \sigma$ versus $\ln[\beta^2/(1-\beta^2)] - \beta^2$, as first
suggested by U. Fano.[4] The result is shown in

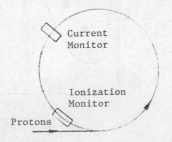

Fig.1 Experimental layout for
measurement of the gas ionization cross section in a
synchrotron.

* Work performed under the auspices of the U. S. Department of Energy.
+ Visiting Fellow, Japan Society for the Promotion of Science, Winter 1978-1979.

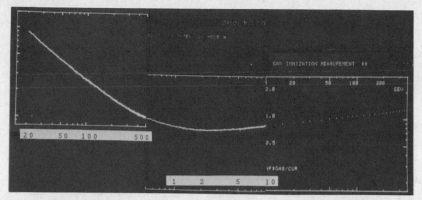

Fig.2   Relative ionization cross section of air for 0.02 - 385 GeV protons.

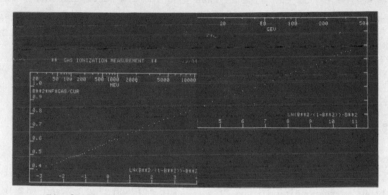

Fig.3   The data for air displayed on the Fano plot.

Fig.3.   Theory gives the universal straight line for any charged particle.

This experimental method is very simple and non-destructive for an accelerator beam. Single acceleration is enough for data taking and display. Measurements for the variety of gases are undergoing. The experiment was performed in real-time data acquisition, calculation, display and printout. Five minutes were enough to get the final results.

The authors would like to thank Professors T. Nishikawa and T. Kamei for their encouragements. We also wish to thank Drs. S. Ohnuma and T. Kasuga for their cooperation in Fermilab.

1.   H. Ishimaru, Z. Igarashi, K. Muto and S. Shibata, 1977 Particle Accelerator
     Conf. IEEE Trans. NS-24, No.3, 1977.

2.   H. Ishimaru, K. Muto, Z. Igarashi, S. Hiramatsu and S. Shibata, 6th Inter-
     national Congress of Radiation Research, May 1979, Tokyo.

3.   R. Sternheimer, Phys. Rev. 115, 137, 1966.

4.   U. Fano, Phys. Rev. 95, 1198, 1954.

ELECTRON SPECTRA EMITTED FROM CORE EXCITED Na AND K ATOMS
IN Na$^+$ + He AND K$^+$ + He COLLISIONS

T. Takayanagi, A. Yagishita[*] , A. Wada, K. Wakiya, and H. Suzuki

Department of Physics, Sophia University Kioicho, Chiyoda-ku, Tokyo 1o2 Japan

We measure the energy spectra of ejected electrons from L-shell excited Na
Atoms in Na$^+$ + He collisions and those from M-shell excited K atoms in K$^+$ + He
collisions.

Measurements are performed in the collision energy range bellow 10 keV, and
the observation angle are from 10° to 130° .

The incident ion beams are obtained by thermionic emission,and the ejected
electron spectrometer is the same as that used in Li$^+$+ He experiments.[1] In fig.1,
two typical electron spectra for Na$^+$ + He collisions are shown. The collision
energies are (a) 8 keV and (b) 2 keV, and the observation angle is 20° in both
case.

Electron energy is calibrated against Na 2s^{2}2p^{5}3s^2 ^{2}P$_{3/2}$ peak (25.63eV).
Absolute energy of this peak is deduced from the photo absorption measurements
of Walff et al.[2] and the Na$^+$ 2p^6 ^{1}s final-state energy of 5.138 eV.

Pegg et al.[3] have reported the energy spectra at collision energy of 70 KeV.
In Fig.1 (a) we show the positions of peaks detected by Pegg et al.

From the photo absorption measurements of Wolff et al.[2], it has been expected that there are many emitted electron lines in the energy region between
30 and 33 eV corresponding to the Na 2p^{5}3sns(n$\geq$4) and the 2p^{5}3snd (n$\gtrsim$3)
states.

Breûkmann et al.[4] identified some of the lines with the energies below 30 eV
as 2p^{5}3s3p states which were observed in their electron impact experiment. But
many other unidentified lines have been observed in both energy regions from 30
to 33 eV and below 30 eV by electron impact.[4,5] Figure 1 shows that several
states which have been unobserved in heigh energy ion-atom collisions are excited
in the slow collisions.

We impact He gas target with ions and electrons at the same time, and compare the emitted electrons with the elastically scattered ones. Using e + He
elastic cross sections, we determine the cross sections for the production of the
core excited alkali atoms in Na$^+$ + He and K$^+$ + He collisions.

* Tokai Establishment, Japan Atomic Energy Res. Inst., Tokai-mura,
  Ibaragi. 319-11

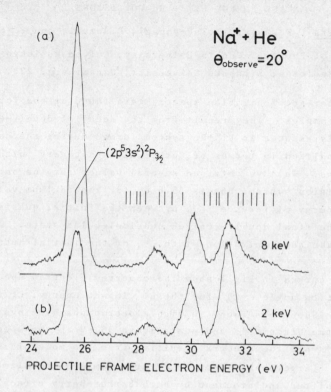

Fig.1   Emitted electron spectra from L-shell excited
Na atoms in Na$^+$ + He collisions. Vertical lines
show the peak positions detected by Pegg et al.
at the collision energy of 70 keV.

Refferences

1) A. Yagishita, H. Oomoto, K. Wakiya, H. Suzuki and F. Koike : J. Phys.
   B $\underline{11}$ (1978) L 111

2) H.W. Wolff, K. Radler, B. Sonntag and R. Haensel: Z. Phys. $\underline{257}$
   (1972) 353

3) D.J Pegg, H.H. Haselton, R.S. Thoe, P.M. Griffin, M.D. Brown, and
   I.A. Sellin: Phys. Rev. A $\underline{12}$, (1975) 1330

4) E. Breuckmann, B. Breuckmann, W. Mehlhorn and W. Schmitz: J. Phys.
   B $\underline{10}$ (1977) 3135

5) K.J. Ross, T.W. Ottley, V. PejceV and D. Rassi: J. Phys. B $\underline{9}$ (1976)
   3237

ELECTRON SPECTRA RESULTING FROM MOLECULAR AUTOIONIZATION
IN LOW ENERGY Li+ + He COLLISIONS

A.Yagishita*, K.Wakiya, T.Takayanagi, H.Suzuki, and F.Koike+

Department of Physics, Sophia University, Chiyodaku,Tokyo 102,Japan
+School of Medicine, Kitasato University, Sagamihara, 228, Japan

Molecular-autoionization spectra were found at the forward
observation-angles. They result from the decay of doubly-excited
quasimolecular-states in Li++He system formed during the collisions.
They were analized in termes of Gerber-Niehaus theory[1] with
modifications. We have obtained several values for the parameters
of the collision system. One is 35.8 eV for the maximum value of the
potential energy difference, ε_*, between the initial quasimolecular-
state and the final doubly-ionized quasimolecular-state. Another is
1.8 eV for the autoionization width, Γ, of the initial autoionizing
state.

Dotted curves in Fig.1 show the observed electron spectra at
the observation angle θ=20° for the Li+ impact energy, E, from 0.8
to 3.2 keV. Shoulders found in high electron energy wings of the
curves for the higher E's and peaks above 35 eV in the spectra for
the lower E's are the spectra resulting from the molecular-autoionization. Large peaks below 35 eV are atomic autoionization peaks,
which are shifted and broadend by both Barker-Berry effect[2] and the
Doppler effect[3].

According to the assumptions employed in the Gerber-Niehaus
theory, internuclear distance, R, is a product of the internuclear-
velocity, v, and the time, t, and the potential energy difference
between the initial quasimolecular-state and the final one is
expressed by ε_* and the second R derivative of the potential energy
difference at the maximum difference point, ε_*'', as $\varepsilon_* - \frac{1}{2}\varepsilon_*''R^2$.
We have made another assumption that the probability amplitude of the
initial autoionizing state decreases exponentially as $\exp(-\Gamma t/2)$.
Intensity,P, of the molecular-autoionization at an ejection energy,
ε, are expressed as

$$P(\varepsilon) \propto 4\pi^2 (\frac{2}{\varepsilon_*''v})^{1/3} |Ai([\frac{2}{\varepsilon_*''v}]^{1/3}[\varepsilon-(\varepsilon_*+i\Gamma/2)])|^2. \qquad (1)$$

Because the quasimolecule runs at a velocity of the center of
mass of the collision system during the autoionization, the ejected
electrons suffer a Doppler effect. The observed electron energy, ε_ℓ,
is higher than its ejection energy, ε, at the forward angles.

We made a least square fitting of eq.(1) to the experimental
data taking into account the Doppler effect. We have obtained the
aforementioned values for ε_* and Γ. The solid lines in Fig.1 show

the fitted curves. Agreement
between the theory and experiment
is fairly good. We conclude that
we have observed the molecular-
autoionization spectra. The
fitted value 1.8 eV for Γ suggests
that the autoionization width of
the quasimolecular state is
fairly large compared with the
corresponding ones of the atomic
autoionization states, which are
0.07 eV for $2p^2\ ^1D$ state of He
and 0.04 eV for $2s2p\ ^1P$ state of
He. Because the collision
duration time, τ, is roughly
estimated to be 10 atomic unit
at E=1keV, and , therefore,
$\Gamma\tau$ equals to about 1, the
largeness of Γ is consistent with
the fact that we observed the
molecular autoionization near
E = 1 keV. Slight discrepancies
can be found between the fitted
curves and the experimental data
in the spectra for the lower E's.
Detailed account of the
discussion on this point will be
given later.

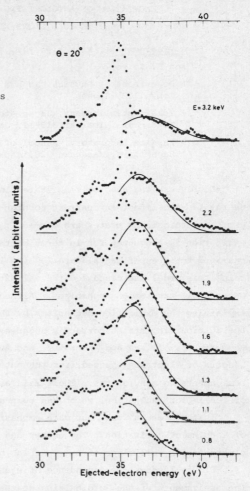

Fig. 1

Ejected-electron spectra at
the observation angle θ = 20°.
Dotted curves are the experimental
results for the Li$^+$ impact energies
E=3.2,2.2,1.9,1.6,1.3,1.1,0.8 keV.
Solid curves are the fitted results.

*Present adress: Tokai Research
Establ., Japan Atomic Energy
Research Institute,
Tokai-mura, Ibaraki, 319-11,
Japan

References
1. G.Gerber and A.Niehaus, J. Phys. B9, 123 (1976)
2. R.B.Barker and H.W.Berry, Phys. Rev. 151, 14 (1966)
3. A.Gleizes, P.Benoit-Cattin, A.Bordenave-Montesquieu, and H.Merchez,
   J. Phys. B9, 473 (1976)

EXCITATION OF AUTOIONIZING STATES OF INERT-GAS ATOMS

IN COLLISIONS WITH Li$^+$- IONS

A. Yagishita[*+], K. Wakiya[*], T. Takayanagi[*], H. Suzuki[*], and F. Koike[‡].

* Depertment of Physics, Sophia University, Chiyoda-ku, Tokyo 102, Japan

+ Tokai Establishment, Japan Atomic Energy Research Institute, Tokai-mura, Ibaraki 319-11, Japan

‡ Physics Laboratory, School of Medicine, Kitasato University, Sagamihara, Kanagawa 228, Japan

Doubly-excited autoionizing states in Ne are selectively excited by low-energy Li$^+$-ion impact in contrast to high-energy ion impact, where subshell-excited autoionizing states are formed.[1] In the low-energy regions, the excitation is accounted for in terms of the quasimolecular model. Barat et al.[2] examined their experimental data (by the inelastic energy-loss measurements) using this model and discussed the validity of electron "promotion" model for outer-shell excitation mechanisms. Although Barat et al.[2] succeeded in explaining the excitation mechanisms by the MO model, they could not identify the autoionizing states correctly because of poor energy-resolution in the measurements. Olsen and Andersen,[3] and Andersen and Olsen[4] measured energy spectra of electrons ejected from the autoionizing states in Ne, and gave assignments to many states. Their main aim was put on a "spectroscopic" aspect of ion-impact excitation, which had been seldomly investigated.

In the present work, our main emphasis is put on a "collisional" aspect of ion-impact excitation. The energy and angular distribution of the ejected electrons for collisions of Li$^+$ + Ne was measured extensively.

Figure 1 shows the dependence of ejected-electron spectra on impact energy. The assignments of the autoionizing states in Ne induced by Li$^+$-ion impact was given as follows by Andersen and Olsen[4]; the peak I is corresponding to the $(^1D)3s^2$ ^1D state, J to $(^3P)[3s4s(^3S)]$ ^1P, K to $(^3P)[3s3d(^3D)]$ ^1D, ^1F, ^1P, L to $(^3P)[3p^2(^3P)]$ ^1D, ^1P, (^1S) and $(^1S)3s^2$ ^1S, and N to $(^1D)[3s3d(^1D)]$. The peak O is not identified yet. The peak intensity scales are normalized so that the heights of the peak I's are equal in all spectra. Intensity ratios among the peaks depend on strongly the impact energy.

Figure 2 shows the dependence of ejected-electron spectra on observation angle. The normalization of the peak intensity is the same as in Fig. 1. Intensity ratios among the peaks depend on the observation angle. Cross sections for autoionization was measured in the energy range of 1.1 - 4.3 keV by the electron-ion simultaneous-collision technique. The details of the technique have been described in Ref. 5.

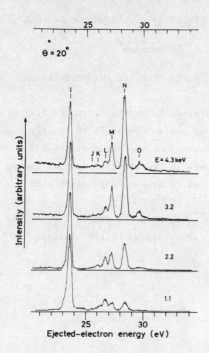

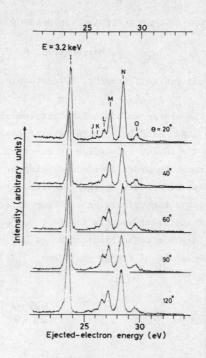

Fig. 1. Ejected-electron spectra at the observation angle θ = 20°. Inpact energies of Li⁺-ion are 4.3, 3.2, 2.2, and 1.1 keV (in laboratory system), as indicated on the right side of each spectrum.

Fig. 2. Ejected-electron spectra for the impact energy 3.3 keV of Li⁺-ion. Observation angles are 20, 40, 60, 90, and 120°, as indicated on the right side of each spectrum.

Similar measurements in the Li⁺ + Ar, Li⁺ + Kr, and Li⁺ + Xe collisions have been also performed, their results will be presented at the conference in detail.

1. A.K. Edwards and M.E. Rudd, Phys. Rev. 170, 140 (1968).

2. M. Barat, D. Dhuicq, R. François, and V. Sidis, J. Phys. B 6, 2072 (1973).

3. J. Østgaard Olsen and N. Andersen, J. Phys. B 10, 101 (1977).

4. N. Andersen and J. Østgaard Olsen, J. Phys. B 10, L 719 (1977).

5. A. Yagishita, K. Wakiya, T. Takayanagi, H. Suzuki, S. Ohtani, and F. Koike, to be submitted to Phys. Rev. A.

STUDY OF CHARGE EXCHANGE INTO AUTOIONIZING STATES IN COLLISIONS OF Ne-IONS

R. Morgenstern, A. Niehaus, G. Zimmermann[*]

Rijksuniversiteit Utrecht, Princetonplein 5, 3508 TA Utrecht, The Netherlands

The charge exchange into autoionizing states of Ne and Ne^+, in collisions of Ne^+, Ne^{++} and Ne^{+++} with several target atoms and molecules in the energy range 1 - 10 keV is studied by electron spectroscopy of the autoionization electrons. In order to avoid masking of structure in the electron spectra due to the Doppler broadening the electrons are detected in backward direction with respect to the primary Ne-ion beam direction.

Examples of spectra for Ne^+, Ne^{++}, and Ne^{+++} on He are shown in Fig. 1. The peaks are due to autoionization of Ne^+ or Ne^{++} as evidenced by the observed Doppler shift of energy positions.

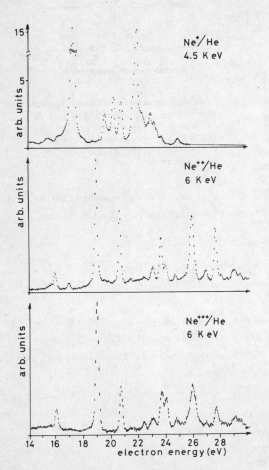

Fig. 1

Electron-energy-spectra arising from Ne^+, Ne^{++} and Ne^{+++} collisions on He at the indicated energies. Spectra are measured at an electron emission angle of $\theta = 180^\circ$ with respect to the beam direction to minimize the Doppler-broadening of the peaks.

The charge exchange processes leading to the observed spectra will be discussed at the conference. It is remarkable that all peaks observed for Ne^{+++}/He correspond to double electron capture into Ne^{+**}-autoionizing states. The same is true for Ne^{+++}/H_2-collisions. A spectrum for this system is shown in Fig. 2.

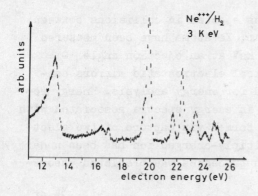

Ne^{+++}/H_2
3 K eV

Fig. 2

Electron energy spectrum arising from 3 keV collisions of Ne^{+++} on H_2. Again the spectrum is measured at an electron emission angle of $\theta = 180°$.

The very broad prominent feature at 13 eV is due to the process:

$$Ne^{+++} + H_2 \rightarrow Ne^{+**}(2s2p^5 \, nl) + H_2^{++}$$
$$\hookrightarrow Ne^{++}(2s^2 2p^4)^3P.$$

The broadening is due to post collision interaction of the autoionizing atom with the (dissociating) H_2^{++}. Post collision interaction is also the cause of the oscillations observed below the dominant peak of the Ne^+/He-spectrum of Fig. 1. More detailed analyses of these phenomena will be discussed.

* University of Freiburg, H. Herderstrasse 3, 78 Freiburg, West Germany

AUTOIONIZATION IN MULTIPLY CHARGED ION-ATOM COLLISIONS

G.N. OGURTSOV, V.M. MIKOUSHKIN, I.P. FLAKS

A.F.Ioffe Physico-Technical Institute, USSR Academy of Sciences,
Leningrad, K-21, USSR

Energy spectra of electrons ejected in collisions between $^3He^{2+}$, Ne^{2+} and Ne^{3+} ions and Ar, Xe atoms have been measured in ion energy range $E_o = 4 - 50$ keV at an ejection angle $\Theta = 54.5°$. A system of two cylindrical electrostatic mirrors connected in series have been used for energy analysis. Energy resolution was 0.6%. A structure in energy spectra associated with decay of autoionization states formed via capture of two electrons on excited levels of a multiply-charged ion has been under study. High probability of such processes was predicted theoretically in [1].

Fig. 1 shows energy spectra of electrons ejected in $^3He^{2+}$-Ar, Xe collisions at $E_o = 10$ keV. A distinct structure of the spectrum is associated with autoionization transitions $He^{**}(nl\ n'l') - He^+(1s) + e$. Identification of lines reveals excitation of the states $2s^2\ ^1S$, $2s2p\ ^3P$ (the first peak), $2p^2\ ^3P$, $2p^2\ ^1S$ (the second peak) and of the states with higher quantum numbers (the third peak). When varying ion energy the lines are shifted by Doppler effect. Cross sections for excitation of the autoionization states estimated by integration of the structure over electron energy and ejection angle reach the values of $\sim 1.10^{-16}$ cm^2. At $E_o > 30$ keV, they make considerable contribution to cross sections for capture with ionization, 2012, measured in [2].

Fig. 2 shows energy spectra of electrons ejected in Ne^{2+} - Xe, Ne^{3+} - Xe collisions at $E_o = 30$ keV. In contrast with the He^{2+}- Xe case, cross sections for excitation of autoionization states $Ne^{**}(2p^4nl\ n'l')$ via two-electron capture are very small. In the Ne^{3+}- Xe case, a distinct structure is associated with decay of the states $Ne^{+**}(2p^3nl\ n'l')$. Decay of these states can occur both to the ground state of Ne^{2+} ion (spectral lines at $E_e > 20$ eV) and to the excited state $Ne^{2+*}(2p^3 3s)$ (spectral lines at $E_e < 12$ eV). Cross section for excitation of the autoionization states is $\sim 6.10^{-16} cm^2$ at Ne^{3+} ion energy $E_o = 30$ keV.

The data obtained seem to confirm the suggestion that formation of autoionization states in He^{2+}- Ar, Xe collisions occurs via successive (but not simultaneous) capture of two electrons.

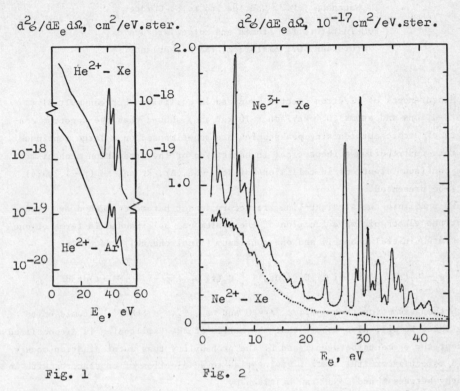

Fig. 1   Fig. 2

Fig. 1. Energy spectra of electrons ejected in He^{2+}- Ar, Xe collisions at incident ion energy E_0= 10 keV. Spectral lines are shifted due to Doppler effect by ΔE_D = 14.8 - 16.9 eV in electron energy range E_e= 45 - 55 eV.

Fig.2. Energy spectra of electrons ejected in Ne^{2+}, Ne^{3+} - Xe collisions at incident ion energy E_0= 30 keV. Spectral lines are shifted by ΔE_D= 2.1 - 6.2 eV in electron energy range E_e= 5 - 35 eV.

1. L.M.Kishinevsky, E.S.Parilis, Zh. Eksp. Teor. Fiz., 55, 1932, (1968)

2. M.N.Panov, VIII Intern. Summer School Phys. Ion. Gases, Inv. Lectures, p. 165, Dubrovnic, (1976)

THE ENERGY DISTRIBUTION OF EJECTED ELECTRONS DUE
TO MOLECULAR ORBITAL IONISATION

T. Watanabe[*], P.H. Woerlee and Yu.S. Gordeev[**]

FOM-Institute for Atomic and Molecular Physics
Kruislaan 407, Amsterdam, The Netherlands.

Measurements of electron spectra produced in collisions between multiply charged ions and atoms (0.1 keV/amu ~ 10 keV/amu) showed that the spectrum consists of atomic autoionising peaks which are superimposed on a large continuum[1]. In this contribution a theoretical investigation of the production mechanism of the continuum electrons in collisions of Ne^{n+} - Ne, Ar, Kr and Xe (n = 1,2,3,4) will be presented.

We shall use the straight-line trajectory impact parameter method and assume that the electronic wave function of the system can be expanded in terms of one discrete (initial channel) and one continuum (final channel) state i.e.

$$\psi = C_i(t)\ \psi_i\ \exp[-i \int_{-\infty}^{t} E_i(t)dt] + \int C_E(t)\ \psi_E\ \exp[-i \int_{-\infty}^{t} E(t)dt]dE$$

with the assumption that $< \psi_i, \psi_E > = 0$ and $<\psi_E, \psi_{E'}> = \delta(E-E')$. Atomic units are used. We will also assume that the matrix of the Hamiltonian is diagonalized except the elements between i and E. The probability that autoionisation occurs in a molecular orbital state i giving rise to an ejection of an electron with an energy between E and E + dE can be given by

$$|C_E(\infty)|^2\ dE = |\int_{-\infty}^{\infty} V_{Ei}(t)\ C_i(t)\ \exp[i \int_{-\infty}^{t} (E - E_i)dt']dt|^2\ dE$$

where $C_i(t) = \exp[-\pi \int_{-\infty}^{t} |V_{iE}(t')|^2 dt']$ and $V_{iE}(t)$ is the electronic coupling matrix element between i and E. Then the cross section for ejection of electrons with energies between E and E + dE is given by:

$$d\sigma = 2\pi \int |C_E(\infty)|^2\ b\ db\ dE$$

If the impact velocity is low, i.e. the main interaction time is much larger than 1 a.u., the integral

$$\int_{-\infty}^{\infty} f(t)\ \exp[i \int_{-\infty}^{t} (E(t') - E_i(t'))\ dt']dt$$

[*]   On leave from Dept. of Appl.Phys., Univ. of Tokyo, Bunkyo-Ku, Tokyo 113 Japan

[**] On leave from A.F. Ioffe Physical Technical Institute, Leningrad K-21, USSR

can be approximated by $\pi \, f(t_o) \, \delta \, (E - E_i)$, where t_o is the time where $E(t_o) = E_i(t_o)$ is satisfied. The final result we obtained is similar to the case of Penning ionisation, we shall call it the "static approximation". If the interaction time is comparable to 1 a.u., the static approximation cannot be applied anymore and dynamic effects which will also broaden the continuum electron spectrum have to be taken into account. This dynamic interaction may play an important role even if the system has no resonance condition for all internuclear distances.

We have made parametric calculations for molecular orbital Auger transitions using the static approximation for collisions of Ne^{4+} on Ar, Kr and Xe assuming that $|V_{iE}|^2 = \Gamma_o \, e^{-\alpha R}$ for $R \geq R_c$ (R_c is the crossing internuclear distance) and $|V_{iE}|^2 = 0$ for $R < R_c$, were α is taken as the sum of the exponents of the Slater type of orbitals for the $Ne^{4+}2p$, Ar 3p, Kr 4p and Xe 5p orbitals. We compared this calculation with experimental data for 100 keV Ne^{4+} - Ar. The absolute ionisation cross section becomes of the same order as the experiment when values of Γ_o are used such that $\Gamma_o \, e^{-\alpha R} \sim 10^{-3}$ a.u. at $R = 5$ a.u.. This result indicates that at least for this collision system, a static molecular orbital Auger ionisation may be one of the dominant processes.

For collisions where distances of closest approach less then 3 a.u. are reached the dynamic contribution to the molecular orbital ionisation was found to become dominant. This dynamic ionisation was studied by Woerlee et al[2] who explained their experimental data on the electron energy spectra for high energy Ne^{n+} - Ne collisions assuming radial coupling between the molecular orbitals and the continuum. Physically the dynamic ionisation is close to the Rozen-Zener transition probability. We shall estimate the cross sections for the dynamic interaction in the case of Ne^{n+} + Ne, Ar, Kr and Xe where n = 1,2,3. The electron energy distribution for the dynamic ionisation can be written as

$$\frac{d\sigma}{dE} = 4\pi \, |V_{iE}|^2 \, b_o^{\,2} (E - E_i)^{-2} \, \sin^2((E-E_i) \, \frac{b_o}{2v})$$

where v is the relative velocity and b_o is the impact parameter where the dynamic ionisation is dominant. In our case b_o is approximately equal to 3 a.u. More detailed results and comparison with the experiment will be reported at this conference.

1) P.H. Woerlee, T.M. El-Sherbini, F.J. de Heer and F.W. Saris
   Submitted to J.Phys.B. Atom. and Molec.Phys.
2) P.H. Woerlee, Yu.S. Gordeev, H.W. de Waard and F.W. Saris, this conference.
3) R. Rozen and C. Zener, Phys.Rev., 40 502 (1932).

THEORETICAL STUDY OF ELECTRON SPECTRA EJECTED BY MOLECULAR AUTOIONIZATION

S. Hara[*] and H. Sato[#]

* Institute of Physics, University of Tsukuba, Ibaraki 300, Japan

Department of Physics, Faculty of Science, Ochanomizu University

Otsuka, Bunkyo-ku, Tokyo 112, Japan

There has recently been considerable interest in the measurements of electron produced by the autoionization of quasi-molecular states during slow ion-atom collisions (molecular autoionization).[1,2] Gerber and Niehaus[2] analyzed their experimental results by approximate formulae. Here we derive a formula for the energy distribution of autoionized electrons, taking account of configuration mixing between discrete and continuous states.[3] For simplicity, we assume that the relative motion of two nuclei can be treated by classical mechanics and we consider one discrete and one continuous states only. Atomic units are used throughout this paper.

The wave function of the system can be written as follows;

$$\Psi(r,R,t) = [a(t)\phi(r,R) + \int d\epsilon\, b_\epsilon(t)\psi_\epsilon(r,R)]\exp[-i\int E(R)dt], \qquad (1)$$

where ϕ and ψ_ϵ are the wave functions of discrete and continuous states, respectively. E is the energy of the autoionizing state and ϵ the kinetic energy of the continuum electron. The differential equations for the coefficients $a(t)$ and $b_\epsilon(t)$ are given by

$$i\frac{da}{dt} = (E_0 - E)a + \int d\epsilon\, V_\epsilon^* b_\epsilon, \qquad (2)$$

$$i\frac{db_\epsilon}{dt} = \{\epsilon - (E - E_{ion})\}b_\epsilon + V_\epsilon a, \qquad (3)$$

where

$$\langle\phi|H|\phi\rangle = E_0, \qquad \langle\psi_\epsilon|H|\psi_{\epsilon'}\rangle = (\epsilon + E_{ion})\delta(\epsilon - \epsilon'), \qquad (4)$$

and

$$\langle\psi_\epsilon|H|\phi\rangle = V_\epsilon. \qquad (5)$$

The energy E and the width Γ of the autoionizing state are defined by

$$E = E_0 + \Delta, \qquad \Delta = P\int\frac{|V_\epsilon|^2}{(E - E_{ion}) - \epsilon}\,d\epsilon, \qquad (6)$$

and

$$\Gamma = 2\pi|V_\epsilon|^2, \qquad (\epsilon = E_0 - E_{ion}). \qquad (7)$$

At first we express b_ϵ in terms of a by neglecting $\frac{db_\epsilon}{dt}$ in eq. (3). Using that relation in eq. (2), we obtain

$$a(t) = a(0)\exp[-\int_0^t \frac{\Gamma}{2}\,dt]. \qquad (8)$$

Substitution of eq. (8) into eq. (3) gives

$$b_\varepsilon(t) = -ia(0)\exp[i\int^t \{(E - E_{ion}) - \varepsilon\}dt']$$

$$\times \int^t V_\varepsilon \exp[\int^{t'} \{-\frac{\Gamma}{2} - i((E - E_{ion}) - \varepsilon)\}dt'']dt'. \tag{9}$$

Therefore the energy distribution $P(\varepsilon)$ of the ejected electrons is

$$P(\varepsilon) = |a(0)|^2 |\int_0^\infty V_\varepsilon \exp[\int_0^t \{-\frac{\Gamma}{2} - i((E - E_{ion}) - \varepsilon)\}dt']dt|^2. \tag{10}$$

It is possible to extend eq. (10) to the case of several discrete states. We have calculated $E_0(R)^4$ and $\Gamma(R)$ for He + He^{2+} system from internuclear distance R = 0.0 to 0.5(a.u.). Figs. 1 and 2 show the results for Γ. We are now computing these values for larger R. With these results, we will calculate the electron spectra ejected by the molecular autoionization in He + He^{+2} collision.

1. G. Gerber, R. Morgenstern and A. Nichaus, J. Phys. B: Atom. Molec. Phys. **6**, 493 (1973).

2. G. Gerber and A. Niehaus, J. Phys. B: Atom. Molec. Phys. **9**, 123 (1976).

3. U. Fano, Phys. Rev. **124**, 1866 (1961).

4. S. Hara and H. Sato, J. Phys. B: Atom. Molec. Phys. **11**, 955 (1978).

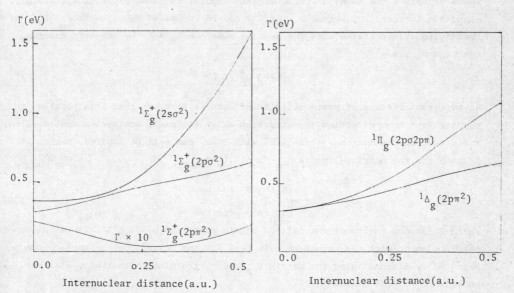

Fig. 1. Widths of He$_2^{2+}$.   Fig. 2. Widths of He$_2^{2+}$.

ANGULAR DISTRIBUTION OF AUTOIONIZATION ELECTRONS FROM POST-COLLISIONLLY
MIXED STATES

N. Stolterfoht

Hahn-Meitner-Institut für Kernforschung GmbH Berlin
Bereich Kern-und Strahlenphysik, D-1000 Berlin-39

Recently, in our laboratory electron emission has been measured from the
autoionization states $2s2p$ [1]P and $2p^2$ [1]D of He excited by slow Li^+ impact[1]. The
data has been interpreted by means of Stark mixing of the autoionization states in
the field of the receding projectile. This specific post-collision interaction
removes the M degeneracy of the autoionization states and, thus, produces additional
peak structures[1]. Moreover, the Stark mixing destroys the parity of the autoionization states. In the present contribution it will be shown that the loss of
parity as a good quantum number has important consequences for the angular distribution of the ejected autoionization electrons.

In the analysis an adiabatic approach is made. The electronic Hamiltonian is
$H=H_o+V$ where H_o is attibuted to the isolated target atom and $V=-\sum_i q/|\vec{R}-\vec{r}_i|$ accounts
for the interaction between the projectile and the target electrons. $\vec{R}$ and $\vec{r}_i$
denote the corresponding coordinates. q is the post-collision charge of the projectile. As the target nucleus is located at the coordinate origin, $\vec{R}$ is also the
internuclear vector. The eigenstates of H are (quasi)molecular states $|a>$ where the
index a implies the label $\alpha=1,2...$ and the angular momentum projection $\Lambda=\Sigma,\Pi,\Delta...$
along the internuclear vector $\vec{R}$. The $|a>$ can be expressed by eigenstates $|L_n\Lambda>$ of H_o
specifying atomic states with the angular momentum L_n and the magnetic quantum
number $M=\Lambda$, i.e.

$$|a>=\sum_n c_n^a |L_n\Lambda> \tag{1}$$

An important feature of post-collision effects is $R>>r_i$ so that $\vec{R}$ is parallel to
the incident beam direction (quantization axis) for small scattering angles. Also,
the dipole approximation $V=-q/R+qZ/R^2$ with $Z=\sum_i z_i$ can well be applied. Hence, it
follows for the matrix elements $H_{nm}=<L_n\Lambda|H|L_m\Lambda>$:

$$H_{nm} = \begin{cases} E_n - q/R & \text{for } n=m \\ qD_\Lambda/R^2 & \text{for } n\neq m \end{cases} \tag{2}$$

where E_n is the energy of the related atomic state and $D_\Lambda=<L_n\Lambda|Z|L_m\Lambda>$ is the dipole
matrix element with the selection rule $L_n=L_m\pm1$. The mixing coefficients c_n^a can be
obtained by diagonalizing the matrix H_{nm}. Also, the diagonalization yields the
energies E_a of the states $|a>$.

The calculation of the electron angular distribution is analogous to those
given in Refs. 2 and 3. For the transition rate $\dot{W}(\Theta)$ from the autoionization state

$|a\rangle$ to a final atomic state $|f\rangle$ resulting in electron ejection at angle Θ it follows that[4]

$$\dot{W}_a(\Theta) = Q_a \sum_{\nu} A_{\nu}^a \, P_{\nu}(\cos\Theta)$$

with

$$A_{\nu}^a = (-)^{\Lambda} [\nu] \sum_{nm} c_{nm}^a \, ([L_n] \, [L_m])^{1/2} \begin{pmatrix} L_n & L_m & \nu \\ \Lambda & -\Lambda & 0 \end{pmatrix} \begin{pmatrix} L_n & L_m & \nu \\ 0 & 0 & 0 \end{pmatrix} \qquad (3)$$

where $[J]=2J+1$, Q_a is the excitation probability[5] for the state $|a\rangle$, $P_{\nu}(\cos\Theta)$ are Legendre polynomials, and $c_{nm}^a = c_n^{a*} \, M_n^* \, c_m^a \, M_m$ with $M_n = \langle f_n | |V_c| | L_n \rangle$ being reduced matrix elements[3]. It is noted that the Stark mixing produces the 'off-diagonal' coefficients $c_{n \neq m}^a$ which, in turn, allow for odd ν values. Hence, $\dot{W}(\Theta)$ is not necessarily symmetric to $\Theta=90^{\circ}$. This is the essential result from the loss of parity as a good quantum number for the Stark mixed states.

Within the adiabatic model $\dot{W}_a(\Theta)$ depends parametrically on R through c_{nm}^a. By adopting $t=R/v$ (v projectile velocity) and taking the decay of the autoionization states properly into account, the total electron intensity $W_a(\Theta)$ can be obtained by time integration. Then, the coefficients c_{nm}^a have to be replaced in Eq.(3) by their 'mean values':

$$\bar{c}_{nm}^a = \int_0^{\infty} c_{nm}^a(t) \exp(-\int_0^t \Gamma_a(t') \, dt') \, dt \qquad (4)$$

where $\Gamma_a(t)=\int \dot{W}(\Theta) d\Omega = \sum_n \Gamma_n |c_n^a|^2$ and $\Gamma_n=|M_n|^2$. It is seen that $\Gamma_a(t)$ is a mean value of the atomic widths Γ_n weighted by $|c_n^a(t)|^2$. The $\Gamma_a(t)$ can be interpreted as the time-dependent decay width of the molecular state $|a\rangle$.

The present formalism may be applied to the recent Li^++He experiments[1]. It is noted that for a two-state system the problem of diagonalizing H_{nm} can be solved analytically. For 10-keV Li^+ impact the off-diagonal coefficients $\bar{C}_{PD}^a$ were calculated to be about 0.2 which indicates a significant Stark mixing. Accordingly the deviation of $W(\Theta)$ from symmetry around 90° is strong. For the Σ states it is found that the intensities at 30° and 150° differ by more than a factor of 3. Indeed, the experimental data[1] confirm this result.

1) D. Brandt, M. Prost, and N. Stolterfoht, XIth ICPEAC, this issue (1979)
2) B. Cleff and W. Mehlhorn, J. Phys. B 7, 593 (1974)
3) J. Eichler and W. Fritsch, J. Phys. B 9, 1477 (1976)
4) The Eq. 3 refers to a specific case where $|a\rangle$ is a singlet state and $|f\rangle$ implies an ionic S state. However, Eq. 3 can readily be extended to more general cases.
5) Because of the (partial) removal of the M degeneracy Eq. 3 does not imply a M(=Λ) summation as performed in Refs. 3 and 4. The remaining M degeneracy is accounted for in Q_a which refers to excitation for both Λ and $-\Lambda$.

THE EXCITATION OF LI 1s2snl TERMS BY PROTON IMPACT

P. Ziem, W.H.E. Schwarz[+], R. Schilling, N. Stolterfoht

Hahn-Meitner-Institut für Kernforschung GmbH,
Glienicker Straße 100, D-1000 Berlin-39, Germany

[+] Lehrstuhl für Theoretische Chemie der Universität
Bonn, Wegeler Straße 12, D-5300 Bonn, Germany

The analysis of electron spectra resulting from heavy ion impact excitation of autoionizing atomic states reveals information about the population probability of atomic states not accessible by optical excitation. Lithium is the first atom in the periodic system for which autoionizing states can be excited by single electron transitions. Although Lithium from that viewpoint should be ideally suited for atomic structure investigations, the interpretation of the data is impeded by strong correlation effects characteristic for few electron systems.

In this contribution we report on the excitation cross section of the Lithium $1s2s^2\,^2S$, $1s(2s2p\,^3P)\,^2P$, $1s(2s2p\,^1P)\,^2P$, $1s2p^2\,^2D$, $(1s2s\,^3S)3s\,^2S$, and $1s(2s3p\,^3P)\,^2P$ terms by 22.5- to 500-keV proton impact. Inside a scattering chamber a Lithium vapour target was crossed by a proton beam. At observation angles of 30°, 90° and 150° the electron emission was analyzed simultaneously by three electrostatic spectrometers[1]. In this manner the angular dependence of the line intensities due to the alignment[2] could be accounted for in the determination of the cross sections.

In case of the $1s2s^2\,^2S$ and $1s(2s2p\,^{3,1}P)\,^2P$ terms, the excitation cross section was calculated using first Born approximation (PWBA). To include electron correlation effects the target wave functions were built from multiconfiguration calculations with the generalized Brillouin theorem technique[3].

The experimental and calculated excitation cross sections are shown in Fig. 1. For clarity the optical forbidden transitions are separated from the dipole transitions. Whereas the agreement between experiment and theory is good for the ^2S term, the experimental ^2P cross sections approach only at high proton energies asymptotically the theoretical curve. As Fig. 1 indicates, the deviations have a distinct energy dependence for the two ^2P terms. The $1s(2s2p\,^3P)\,^2P$ cross section decreases more strongly at lower energies than predicted by the theory. These deviations indicate the increasing necessity of "kinematic" corrections to the PWBA. On the contrary, the enhancement of the $1s(2s2p\,^1P)\,^2P$ cross section cannot be understood within the framework of first order Born approximation. A two-step excitation mechanism like $1s^2\,2s \rightarrow 1s2s^2 \rightarrow 1s(2s2p\,^1P)$ might become significant[1]. This assumption is supported by the similar enhancement of the $1s2p^2\,^2D$ cross section which can be populated only by a double electron transition process. (see Fig. 1.)

Apart from these kinematic effects which exhibit the limits of a first order approximation, the data clearly show the influence of configuration interaction. E. g. the cross section ratio of the two $1s(2s2p\,^{3,1}P)\,^2P$ terms should be 3:1 in a single configuration treatment. But in contradiction to earlier suggestions[4]

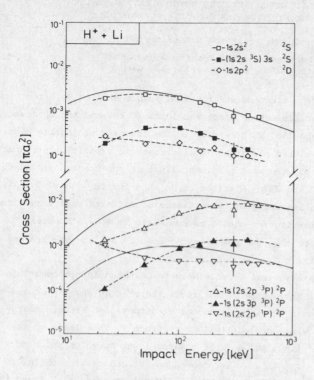

Fig. 1.

The excitation cross section of the Li terms for proton impact. The solid lines result from CI-calculations for the $1s2s^2\ ^2S$ and $1s(2s2p\ ^{3,1}P)^2P$ terms. The data points are connected by dashed lines.

the ratio is increased for high proton energies to 18:1 as indicated in Fig. 1 by the data as well as by the calculation. An analysis of our multiconfiguration calculations shows that the enhancement of the excitation ratio is predominantly caused by the strong interaction between the $1s^2 2p\ ^2P$ and the $1s(2s2p\ ^3P)^2_a P$ terms. Further details of our calculation will be discussed at the conference.

1. P. Ziem, R. Schilling, T.C. Chang, M. Meinhart, W.H.E. Schwarz, to be published

2. P. Ziem, W.H.E. Schwarz, D. Ridder, R. Schilling, in Abstracts of the VII. Int. Conf. X-Ray and XUV Spectra, (Sendai, Japan, 1978), p. 147

3. T.C. Chang, W.H.E. Schwarz, Theoret. Chim. Acta 44, 45 (1977)

4. A.D. Parks, D.H. Sampson, J. Phys. B8 774 (1975)

DECAY OF COLLISIONALLY EXCITED AUTOIONIZATION STATES
OF HE IN THE FIELD OF THE SLOW LI$^+$ - PROJECTILE

D. Brandt, M. Prost, and N. Stolterfoht

Hahn-Meitner-Institut für Kernforschung GmbH
Glienicker Straße 100, D-1000 Berlin-39, Germany

We measured autoionization electron spectra from doubly excited He after slow Li$^+$+He collisions. The projectile energy range was 10 to 40 keV and the observation angle θ varied between 20° and 150° with respect to the incoming projectile beam. For energy analysis of the emitted electrons an electrostatic parallel plate spectrometer (FWHM= 100 meV) was used. The most prominent lines in the spectra are expected from the decay of the 2p^2 ^{1}D and 2s2p ^{1}P states of He** to the 1s^{2}S ground state of He$^+$. If we assume excitation and decay of these states of definite parity as a two-step process, the angular distribution should be symmetric to 90°[1]. However, experimentally we observe more than two peaks in the spectra and the spectra are not symmetric to 90° (see Fig. 1).

For interpretation of the data several effects have to be taken into account. In addition to the instrumental broadening of the lines there is an angular dependent Doppler broadening proportional to sin θ. Also the electrons lose kinetic energy in the Coulomb field of the slow Li$^+$ projectile (Berry-effect[2]). This leads to an asymmetric broadening of the lines and a shift towards lower energies which does not depend on the observation angle. Furthermore, Morgenstern et al.[3] found that electrons from the decay of energetic close lying states may interfere in the Coulomb field of the projectile ion. This can produce additional peaks in the spectra. These well-known effects are not able to fully explain the experimental data. We suggest that Stark mixing of the autoionizing states has to be taken into account for a more satisfying interpretation. For this we obtain an indication from the following aspect of the measured data.

The position of the peaks denoted a,b,c and d in Fig. 1 were plotted for different projectile velocities v in Fig.2. The electron energy was calibrated with respect to the 2p^2 ^{1}S line[4] (not shown in Fig. 1). Its position was corrected for the Berry shift[2] $1/(2v\tau)$ using a theoretical lifetime τ[5]. The calculated peak positions of the 2p^2 ^{1}D and 2s2p ^{1}P line are shown

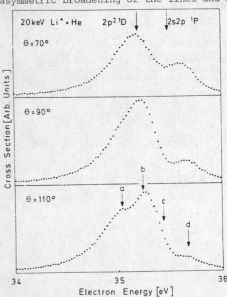

Fig.1: Electron energy distributions for 20 keV Li$^+$+He collisions. Observation angles are 70°, 90° and 110° with respect to the incoming projectile beam. The arrows indicate the expected line energies for the decay of the 2p^2 ^{1}D and 2s2p ^{1}P states of He**.

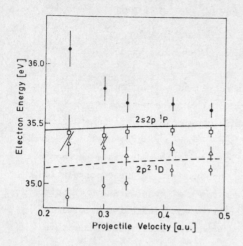

Fig. 2: Peak energy versus projectile velocity for 10 to 40 keV Li$^+$+He collisions. Open circles, open triangles, open squares and full circles denote the position of peak a,b,c and d in Fig. 1 respectively. Calculated values for the 2s2p ^{1}P line and 2p^2 ^{1}D line are shown for comparison.

for comparison. For this calculation energies and lifetimes given by Hicks[6] were used. For decreasing projectile velocity a significant shift of peak a and d to lower and higher energy is seen whereas peak b and c are relativly unaffected.

To explain this shift we assume that the electric field of the Li$^+$ ion produces a Stark mixing of the 2s2p ^{1}P and 2p^2 ^{1}D states which results in an energetic splitting of the mixed states depending on their magnetic quantum number. This splitting increases with decreasing internuclear distance. Most decays take place within the lifetime τ, which is correlated to a certain internuclear separation $R_\tau = v \cdot \tau$ and a Stark splitting ΔE_τ. For decreasing projectile velocity v R_τ decreases and ΔE_τ increases. The velocity dependence of the line shifts in Fig. 2 may be understood in this way. Stark mixing may also explain asymmetric angular distributions because for the mixed states parity is no longer a good quantum number[7].

1) B. Cleff and W. Mehlhorn; J. Phys. B: Atom. Molec. Phys. **7**, 593 (1974)

2) R.B. Barker and H.W. Berry; Phys. Rev. **151**, 14 (1966)

3) R. Morgenstern, A. Niehaus and U. Thielmann; J. Phys. B: Atom. Molec. Phys. **10**, 1039 (1977)

4) N. Oda, S. Tahira, F. Nishimura and F. Koike; Phys. Rev. A **15**, 574 (1977)

5) P.G. Burke and D.D. McVicar; Proc. Phys. Soc. **86**, 989 (1965)

6) P.J. Hicks and J. Comer; J. Phys. B: Atom. Molec. Phys. **8**, 1866 (1975)

7) N. Stolterfoht; Abstracts of Papers XIth ICPEAC, Kyoto, 1979 (this issue)

VELOCITY DEPENDENCE OF Ne(2s, 2p) $\leftrightarrow$ 3dσ SUBSHELL

CORRELATION FOR 15-60 keV Li$^+$-Ne COLLISIONS

P. Bisgaard, J. Østgaard Olsen and N. Andersen[+]

Institute of Physics, University of Aarhus, DK-8000 Aarhus C

The Molecular Orbital (MO) model has served as a starting point for the interpretation of a huge number of experimental and theoretical studies of electronic excitation processes in binary collisions for which the internuclear velocity is smaller than the velocity of the (inner- or outer-shell) electrons under consideration. In this model diabatic correlations are made between the limits of united and separated atoms. The construction of these correlations are guided by semi-empirical rules derived from e.g. consideration of adiabatic correlation diagrams. The analysis of Eichler et al.[1] indicated a possible alternative to the Barat-Lichten rules[2] concerning the correlations within a given subshell.

We have selected the Li$^+$-Ne collision, a simple K-L closed-shell system, for an experimental study of the Ne(2s, 2p) subshell correlation. Figure 1 shows schematically the correlations constructed from the rules of Barat-Lichten (full-drawn curves) and Eichler et al. (dotted curves), respectively. We have measured electron spectra from autoionizing levels in neon, giving rise to ejection of electrons with kinetic energies in the 15-35 eV range. Spectra

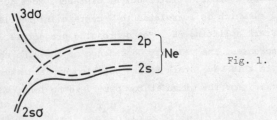

Fig. 1.

obtained with Li$^+$ impact energies ranging from 15 to 60 keV are presented in Figure 2. At 15 keV (v $\simeq$ 0.3 v_o) the configurations 2s^2 2p^4 (^{1}D) 3s nl (nl = 3s, 3p, 3d) dominate the spectra completely, while almost no 2s-vacancies are produced. This observation, which also holds at even lower energies[3], is readily interpreted using the full-drawn curves of Fig. 1. However, increasing the velocity by only a factor of two rapidly changes the spectral pattern. At 60 keV (v $\simeq$ 0.6 v_o) production of 2s^2 2p^4 (^{1}D) 3s nl levels is negligible, and the spectrum is dominated by strong features corresponding to various excited levels in Ne and Ne$^+$, like 2s 2p^6 nl and 2s 2p^5 nl (nl = 3s, 3p, 3d), all having a 2s vacancy. At this velocity there is therefore a large probability for a vacancy, created in the 3dσ orbital by crossings with higher lying empty orbitals, to end up in the 2s subshell, i.e. the dotted path.

Increasing the velocity further has no dramatic influence on the spectra, but we are here approaching velocities comparable to the orbital velocity of the

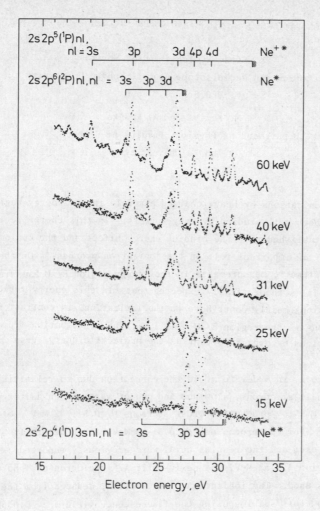

Fig. 2.

2p electrons $(v_{2p} \simeq 1.3\ v_o)$ where application of the MO picture is certainly questionable.

Permanent address:

[+] Physics Laboratory II, H.C. Ørsted Institute, DK-2100 Copenhagen Ø, Denmark.

1. J. Eichler, U. Wille, B. Fastrup and K. Taulbjerg, Phys.Rev. A14, 707 (1976).

2. M. Barat and W. Lichten, Phys.Rev. A6, 211 (1972).

3. J. Østgaard Olsen and N. Andersen, J.Phys. B10, 101 (1977); N. Andersen and J. Østgaard Olsen, J.Phys. B10, L719 (1977).

K-SHELL IONIZATIONS OF ALMINUM AND COPPER BY 0.5 — 32 MEV PROTONS

K. Sera, K. Ishii and S. Morita

Cyclotron and Radioisotope Center, Tohoku University,

980 Sendai, Japan

M. Kamiya and A. Kuwako

Department of Physics, Faculty of Science,

Tohoku University

K-shell ionizations by heavy charged particle in the energy region $E/\lambda U < 1$ have been well studied by many workers. In this energy region, it has been established that the binding energy effect and the Coulomb deflection play an important role in the ionization process.[1] On the other hand, systematic measurements in the energy region $E/\lambda U \geq 1$ are very few.[2-5] It is theoretically expected that, in this energy region, distant collisions mainly contribute to the ionization, in contrast with close collisions in the region $E/\lambda U < 1$, i.e., the contribution from distant collisions becomes important as the projectile energy gets higher.

In this work, in order to avoid the correction due to relativistic effect of K-shell electrons, aluminum and copper were chosen as target atoms and the K x-ray production cross sections by 0.5 — 32 MeV protons were measured. For the proton energy 0.5 — 3 MeV, a Van de Graaff generator was used and the results on Al were previously reported.[6] For the energy region 3 — 32 MeV, the newly-built AVF cyclotron of Tohoku University was used. The ionization cross section, deduced from the x-ray production cross section using the fluorescence yield $\omega_k = 0.0333$ and 0.445 for Al and Cu respectively, are shown in Figs. 1 and 2 as a function of the projectile energy.

The experimental errors of the cross sections are about 12 %. In these figures, theoretical predictions calculated from PWBA and BEA are also represented. The PWBA theory takes into account both distant and close collisions, whereas the BEA does only close collisions. Thus, it is expected that the contribution from distant collisions can be estimated by comparing the theoretical predictions and the experimental results in the higher energy region. In Fig. 1, the experimental results generally agree well with the PWBA calculation, but they increase and decrease more rapidly than the calculation in the lower and higher energy region, respectively. Concerning the projectile energy corresponding to the

maximum cross section, both of the theories give good agreement with the
experimental. It is seen that close collisions still have main contribution to the ionization in the energy region $1 < E/\lambda U < 10$, since the
BEA calculation is in agreement with the experiment within 20 %. Detailed
results and discussion will be reported in the conference.

References

1. G. Basbas, W. Brandt, and R. Laubert, Phys. Rev. A 7, 983 (1973).

2. G. Bissinger, J. M. Joyce, E. J. Ludwig, W. S. McEver, and S. M. Shafroth,
   Phys. Rev. A 1, 841 (1970).

3. G. Bissinger and J. M Joyce, Phys. Rev. A 16, 443 (1977).

4. T. L. Hardt and R. L. Watson, Physl Rev. A 7, 1917 (1973).

5. W. D. Ramsay, M. S. A. L. Al-Ghazi, J. Birshall, and J. S. C. McKee, Phys.
   Lett. 69A, 258 (1978).

6. H. Tawara, Y. Hachiya, K. Ishii, and S. Morita, Phys. Rev. A 13, 572
   (1976).

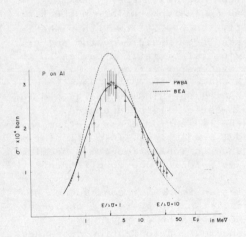

Fig. 1.
Excitation curve of the K-shell
ionization of Al by protons.

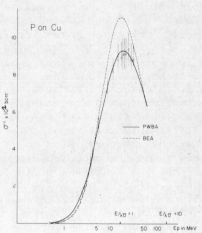

Fig. 2.
Excitation curve of the
K-shell ionization of
Cu by protons.

EFFECT OF COULOMB REPULSION IN THE INNER SHELL IONI=
ZATION CROSS SECTION BY PROTONS, DEUTERONS AND ALPHA
PARTICLES.

Mario Milazzo

Institute of Physics, University of Milan

Gaetano Riccobono

J.R.C. - C.E.E. Ispra Establishment

Atomic ionization of inner shells by collision processes has
been investigated by measuring the intensity of the characteristic
X lines emitted from thin targets in the electron rearrangement
following the ionization. Ionization cross section for Rb,Sr,Zr,
Cd, In, Sb, W by protons in the energy range from 500 Kev to 3 Mev
have been measured. Also measurements of ionization cross sections
by deuterons in the energy range from 800 Kev to 2.6 Mev on Rb,Sr,
Zr,Cd,Sb,and by He-ions in the energy range from 1.4 Mev to 2.8 Mev
on Cd and Sb have been performed.
A new method for correcting the predictions of binary encoun=
ter approximation (B.E.A.) model is introduced which is based on
the calculation of the "effective" ion collision energy taking in=
to account the effect of the coulomb nuclear potential on the Kine=
tic energy of the ion. This effective energy is lower than the i=
nitial energy and it can be calculated from basic momentum and e=
nergy conservation rules and employing relativistic dynamics in the
ion-electron collision. The "effective energy corrected" B.E.A.(E.
E.C.B.E.A.) calculations agree with those of the plane wave born
approximation (P.W.B.A.) model corrected for binding energy and for
Coulomb deflection except for the lowest collision energies.
All experimental results for the ionization cross section show
quite a good agreement with the model predictions. In particular it
has been found the expected difference in ionization cross section
for protons and deuterons of the same velocity due to different
slowing down effect.
At the lowest collision energies an important consequence of
the correction for the effective collision energy is the occurence
of an ionization "threshold" for the collision energy.
Only a discontinuity in the behaviour of ionization cross sec=
tion was found at the threshold values. An explanation for that
could be found assuming double (or, in priciple, multiple)collision
mechanism. In fact the threshold in the ionization energy occurs
only in single collision ionization processes. On the other hand,
at the lowest collision energies near the threshold the velocity
of the projectile becomes much lower than the (classical) atomic
electron velocity as a consequence, multiple collision ionization
processes are in principle possible.

REFERENCES

1. E. Merzbacher, H. Lewis, Handbuch der Physik,34 (1958),166
2. M. Gryzinski, Phys. Rev., 138 (1965), A 322
3. M. Gryzinski, Phys. Rev., 138 (1965), A 336
4. E. Gerjuoy, Phys. Rev., 148 (1966), 54
5. J.D. Garcia, E.Gerjuoy, J.E. Welker, Phys. Rev.,165(1968),66
6. B.K. Thomas, G.D. Garcia, Phys. Rev.,179 (1969),94
7. J.D. Garcia, Phys. Rev., A1 (1970),280
8. G. Basbas, W. Brandt, R.H. Ritchie, Phys. Rev., A7(1973),1971
9. G. Basbas, W. Brandt, R. Laubert, Phys. Rev.,A7 (1973),983
10. J.S. Hansen, Phys. Rev. A8 (1973), 822
11. J.H. McGuire, P. Richard, Phys. Rev., A8 (1973), 1374
12. J.D. Garcia, R.J. Fortner, T.M.Kavanagh, Rev. of Mod. Phys.,
    45 (1973), 111
13. R. Anholt,Phys. Rev., A17 (1978), 976
14. R. Anholt, Phys. Rev., AL7 (1978), 983

POLARIZATION OF L-SHELL X-RAYS OF Ag
PRODUCED BY PROTON IMPACT

V.P. Petukhov,   E.A. Romanovsky,   N.M. Kabachnik
V.V. Sizov and S.V. Ermakov

Institute of Nuclear Physics, Moscow State University;
Moscow 117234; USSR

The ions produced when the inner shells of the atoms with total angular momentum j $>$ 1/2 are ionized by a particle beam prove to be aligned with respect to the beam as a result of the difference between the ionization cross sections for the states with different projections of the angular momentum on the particle beam direction[1]. Therefore, the X-rays accompanying the filling of the vacancies in subshells with quantum number j $>$ 1/2 should be polarized.

A grating spectrometer-polarimeter with graphite crystal-analyzer[2] (2d = 6.76 Å) has been used to measure the polarization degree P of the $L\ell$, $L\alpha_{1,2}$ and $L\beta_{2,15}$ lines from an Ag atom excited by 150-500 keV protons. The target is 300 mcg/cm^2 thick foil mounted at 45° to the proton beam; the X-rays are detected at 90° to the beam. The angular divergence of the proton beam incident onto the target foils to exceed 1°. The systematic errors in measuring the polarization, which are due to calibration error, are excluded by normalizing the $L\ell$, $L\alpha_{1,2}$ and $L\beta_{2,15}$ intensities to the intensity of the $L\beta_1$ line which is not polarized. The statistical error in measuring the polarization degree does not exceed 2%.

Within the measurement errors, in the total range of proton energies E_p, the experimental values of the polarization degree of the $L\ell$, $L\alpha_{1,2}$ and $L\beta_{2,15}$ lines are close to the values calculated using the Born approximation with the Hartree-Slater wave functions (HS) and screened hydrogen-like wave functions of electron (θ = 0.54)[3]. The experimental values of the polarization degree of the $L\ell$ -line in the range 250 keV $<$ E_p $\leq$ 500 keV are two times as small as the values calculated disregarding the external screening (θ =1), see fig. 1. The calculations have been carried out including the contribution from the Coster-Kronig transitions to the formation of the L$_3$ subshell vacancies.

REFERENCES:
1. W. Mehlhorn , Phys.Lett. 26A, 166, (1968)
2. V.P. Petukhov, E.A. Romanovsky, A.M. Borisov, Proc. VII-th
   All-Union Conf. on Physics of Electronic and Atomic Collisions

(Abstracts), Petrozavodsk, (1978), p. 151.

3. E.G. Berezhko, N.M. Kabachnik, V.V. Sizov,   J.Phys. BII, L421(1978).

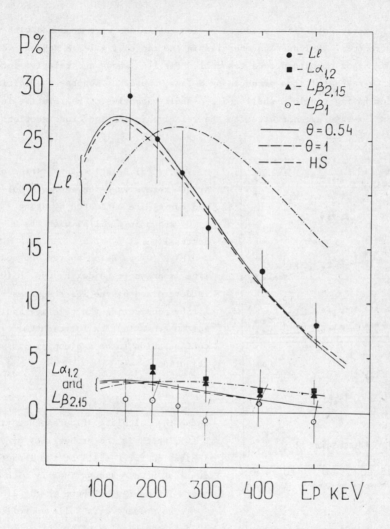

Fig. 1. The polarization degree of L-shell X-rays from
        Ag atom versus proton energy. The lines are the
        results of the Born approximation calculations.

ARGON Kα X-RAY SATELLITES BY IMPACT OF NITROGEN
ION IN THE 4.7-7.8 MEV/AMU ENERGY RANGE

T. Tonuma, Y. Awaya, T. Kambara, H. Kumagai, I. Kohno and S. Özkök*

The Institute of Physical and Chemical Research,
Wako, Saitama 351, Japan

Ar Kα x-ray satellites produced by ion collisions were measured with a crystal spectrometer. N-ions with energies in the range of 4.7-7.8 MeV/amu were used to bombard argon contained in a gas cell. Fig.1(a) shows the relative intensities of Ar KL^{ℓ} x-ray satellites produced by N-ions, where KL^{ℓ} denotes the initial configuration having single K-shell and ℓ L-shell vacancies. The relative intensities of KL^{ℓ} x-rays are converted to the relative ionization cross sections by

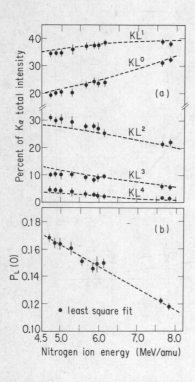

Fig.1. (a) Relative intensities of Ar KL^{ℓ} x-rays vs N-ion energy. Dotted curves are estimated by using $P_L(0)$ shown in fig.1(b) with the dotted line.

(b) $P_L(0)$ vs N-ion energy. Dotted line is drawn to guide the eye. $P_L(0)$ is determined by the least squares fit by considering the relative ionization cross section for each KL^{ℓ} configuration to be a binomial distribution.

using the calculated flourescence yield.[1] $P_L(0)$, which is the probability of single ionization for L-shell at the impact parameter of 0, decreases linearly with increasing N-ion energy as shown in fig.1(b).

The present data followed well the scaling law obtained on the basis of an increased binding effect by Schmiedekamp et al.[2]

* Present address: University of Istanbul Nuclear Physics Dept., Istanbul, Turkey.

1. F.P. Larkins, J. Phys. B4, L29(1971).

2. Carl Schmiedekamp, B.L. Doyle, Tom J. Gray, R.K. Gardner, K.A. Jamison and P. Richard, Phy. Rev. A18, 1892(1978).

ELECTRONIC RELATIVISTIC EFFECTS IN L-SHELL IONIZATION
BY CHARGED-PARTICLE IMPACT

T. Mukoyama

Institute for Chemical Research, Kyoto University, Kyoto, Japan

and

L. Sarkadi

Institute of Nuclear Research of the Hungarian Academy of Sciences (ATOMKI),
H-4001 Debrecen, Hungary

The L-shell ionization cross sections have usually been treated on the basis of the plane-wave Born approximation (PWBA),[1] and the nonrelativistic PWBA theory[2] has successfully been used to interpretate the experimental data. For slow projectiles, the effects of binding-energy increase and Coulomb deflection become important. The nonrelativistic PWBA theory with corrections for these effects (PWBA-BC)[3] predicts the L-shell ionization cross sections in good agreement with the experiment. However, at low incident energies for high-Z targets, comparison between theory and experiment has shown that the PWBA-BC underpredicts the L-shell ionization cross sections.[4]

In the case of high-Z targets, it is necessary to use relativistic wave functions both for the initial bound and final continuum electrons. This kind of calculations for L shells have been performed by Choi in the PWBA scheme.[5,6] However, the relativistic PWBA (RPWBA) considerably overpredicts the ionization cross sections because of neglection of binding-energy and Coulomb-deflection effects. Recently we have shown that for K-shell ionization the RPWBA theory modified with binding-energy and Coulomb-deflection effects (RPWBA-BC) gives the results in satisfactory agreement with the experimental data.[8]

In the present work, we have extended the RPWBA-BC theory to the case of L-shell ionization. The calculations have been made in the similar manner to

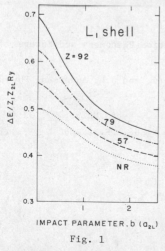

Fig. 1

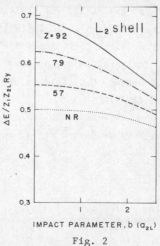

Fig. 2

Choi,[5] and the effects of binding-energy increase and Coulomb deflection have been taken into account by the method of Brandt and Lapicki.[3] The change in the binding energy

$$\Delta E = \int \psi^\star(\vec{r}) \; \frac{Z_i e^2}{|\vec{R} - \vec{r}|} \; \psi(\vec{r}) \; d\vec{r} \qquad (1)$$

has been estimated by the use of relativistic hydrogenic wave functions. The ΔE values thus obtained for L_1 and L_2 shells are shown in Figs. 1 and 2 as a function of impact parameter for different target atomic numbers and compared with the nonrelativistic values. In the case of L_3 shell deviation from the nonrelativistic values and also difference between different Z values are small.

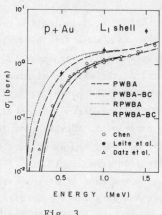

By the use of these results, the corrections for binding-energy and Coulomb-deflection effects have been estimated. Figure 3 shows comparison of the various theoretical calculations with the experimental data[4,7,9] in the case of L_1-shell ionization cross sections for protons on Au. It is clear from the figure that the prediction of the present model (RPWBA-BC) is in good agreement with the experimental data even in the region of low projectile energy.

Fig. 3

1. E. Merzbacher and H.W. Lewis, Handbuch der Physik (Springer, Berlin, 1958), Vol. 34, p. 166.

2. B.-H. Choi, E. Merzbacher, and G.S. Khandelwal, At. Data 5, 291 (1973).

3. W. Brandt and G. Lapicki, Phys. Rev. A 10, 474 (1974); G. Lapicki and W. Losonsky, Phys. Rev. A 15, 896 (1977).

4. J.R. Chen, Phys. Rev. A 15, 487 (1977).

5. B.-H. Choi, Phys. Rev. A 4, 1002 (1971).

6. B.-H. Choi, Proc. Int. Conf. Inner Shell Ionization Phenomena and Future Applications (Atlanta, 1972), p. 1093.

7. S. Datz, J.L. Duggan, L.C. Feldman, E. Laegsgaard, and J.U. Andersen, Phys. Rev. A 9, 192 (1974).

8. T. Mukoyama and L. Sarkadi, Bull. Inst. Chem. Res., Kyoto Univ., 57, 33 (1979).

9. C.V.B. Leite, N.V. de Castro Faria, and A.G. de Pinho, Phys. Rev. A 15, 943 (1977).

K SHELL IONIZATION OF Z=11-29 ATOMS BY 40-100 MeV OXYGEN ION BOMBARDMENTS

K.Shima, T.Mikumo, Y.Tagishi, Y.Iguchi, T.Arai, H.Kano and M.Takasaki*

Tandem Accelerator Center, University of Tsukuba, Ibaraki 300-31, Japan

In the ion-atom collision of $z_1 \ll z_2$, inner shell ionization of target atom z_2 is well established by the Coulomb excitation process.[1] In the low energy collision, corrections by the Coulomb deflection effect and the additive binding energy effect of the shell electron play an important role as well as the relativistic correction to the ionization of higher z_2 atoms. On the other hand, at high energy collision of up to $v_1 \sim v_{K \text{ or } L}$, experimental cross sections are in good agreement with BEA or PWBA when light ions are used as projectiles. However, in this swift collision region where the cross sections show a broad maximum behavior, only few experiments have been done with the use of incident ions with $z_1 \gtrsim 6$.

In order to test the z_1 dependence in K shell ionization around at the resonant velocities, oxygen induced Na, Al, Cl, K, Ca, Mn, Fe, Ni and Cu K-shell ionization cross sections have been measured from the observation of X-ray production cross sections. Thin targets of 18-80 $\mu g/cm^2$ thickness were bombarded by $O^{+5 \sim 8}$ ions which were provided by the 12 UD tandem accelerator at the University of Tsukuba. Emitted characteristic X-rays were detected by the Si(Li) semiconductor detector which was placed 135° with respect to the beam direction and was mounted within the vacuum chamber. Observed K X-ray energy shifts led to the estimation of the atomic fluorescence yields which ranged between 1.05 ω_o and 1.2 ω_o with respect to the normal value ω_o.

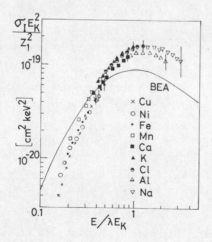

Fig. 1.
Universal plot of K-shell ionization cross sections bombarded by 40-100 MeV oxygen ions.

Fig.1 shows the universal plot of resulting K-shell ionization cross sections σ_I. Here, E_K denotes the K shell ionization potential, λ the ratio of projectile mass to electron mass, and E indicates the collision energy. Experimental error in the plotted values is estimated to be less than 25 % with the exception of sodium target. On account of large uncertainty in the value of fluorescence yield, the error in sodium data may amount to about 35 %. The deviation of experimental cross sections from the BEA prediction in the lower collision energy is attributed to the binding effect and the Coulomb deflection effect. The enhancement of the experimental behavior around at the broad maximum   is different from the universal plot of light ion induced cross sections. Present result is to be analyzed in the light of Basbas theory which predicts the existence of polarization effect.[2]

*National Laboratory for High Energy Physics, Ibaraki 300-32, Japan

1. G. Basbas, W. Brandt and R. Laubert, Phys. Rev. A 7, 983 (1973).
2. G. Basbas, W. Brandt and R. Laubert, Phys. Rev. A 17, 1655 (1978).

ALIGNMENT OF THE L3-SUBSHELL BY PROTON IMPACT IONIZATION

W. Jitschin, H. Kleinpoppen, R. Hippler and H.O. Lutz

Fakultät für Physik, Universität Bielefeld, West Germany

The different ionization cross-sections for electronic substates
with different magnetic quantum number result in a collisionally induced alignment, provided the substate angular momentum $j > 1/2$.
This alignment offers a sensitive tool to test theoretical approximations and atomic wavefunctions used in the description of impact
ionization. In the case of structureless ion projectiles large
alignment effects are predicted by theory at low impact velocities,
whereas at high velocities only small alignment is expected.[1,2] We
performed alignment measurements of the L3-subshell with heavy target atoms over a wide projectile energy range. The alignment was
experimentally determined from the anisotropic emission of collisionally induced x-ray lines or Auger electrons. Figure 1 displays as
an example the proton-induced alignment A_2 for Mg,[3] Xe and Au targets. The results show only qualitative agreement with theory.

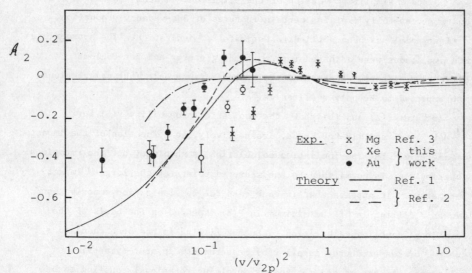

Figure 1: Proton induced alignment A_2 as a function of the projectile velocity v in units of the L3-electron velocity v_{2p}.

1. A. Schöler and F. Bell, Z. Physik A286, 163 (1978)
2. E.G. Berezhko, N.M. Kabachnik and V.V. Sizov, J. Phys. B10,
    L 421 (1978)
3. M. Rødbro, R. DuBois and V. Schmidt, J. Phys. B11, L 551 (1978)

IONIZATION OF THE 2pσ MOLECULAR ORBITAL IN HEAVY-ION COLLISIONS[*]

W. E. Meyerhof

Department of Physics, Stanford University, California 94305, USA

One of the outstanding problems in inner-shell ionization is the production of K-shell vacancies in near symmetric collisions in which all the incoming L orbitals are filled. Various mechanisms of K-vacancy production have been suggested: (1) a multiple-collision process (in solid targets), opening the 2pπ molecular orbital (MO), followed by 2pσ-2pπ electron promotion, (2) a single-collision process opening the 2pπ MO by coupling to empty MOs, followed by 2pσ-2pπ electron promotion, (3) one-step ionization of the 2pσ MO, (4) ionization of the 2pσ MO by a statistical vacancy diffusion process in a single collision.[1,2] In each case, sharing of the 2pσ vacancies between the K levels of the collision partners is assumed.

Since a simplified version of the Briggs united-atom ionization model[3] quite successfully explains certain features of 3dσ-vacancy production,[4] a similar model has been applied to estimate 2pσ ionization. The appropriate SCA amplitudes were adjusted for 2pσ binding energy and for Coulomb deflection effects. Because of the approximations made, the calculations are expected to be only qualitative.

Figures 1(a) and (b) show the ionization probability P(b) for 45-MeV Ni+Mn[5] and 118-MeV Kr+Ge,[6] respectively, as a function of the impact parameter b. The 2pσ-ionization calculation is absolute, but the rotational contribution[7] is normalized to the measured points at the large impact parameters. It appears that in each case the 2pσ ionization contribution causes a filling in of the minimum in P(b) expected on the basis of the rotational coupling calculation.[7] Such a filling in has been found to a greater or lesser degree in all P(b) measurements in near-symmetric collisions and has caused mechanisms involving rotational coupling to be rejected in favor of the statistical diffusion model.[5,8] The present work indicates that in a full explanation of K-vacancy production in near-symmetric collisions one-step ionization of the 2pσ MO may have to be included and that mechanisms involving 2pσ-2pπ rotational coupling may, after all, play an important role.

*Supported in part by the National Science Foundation.

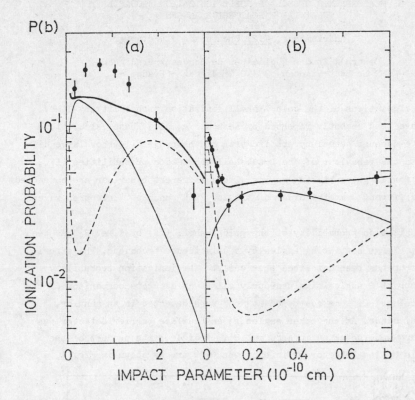

Fig. 1. Ionization probability as a function of impact parameter (a) for 45-MeV Ni+Mn (Ref. 5), (b) for 118-MeV Kr+Ge (Ref. 6). Thin solid line: present calculation of 2pσ ionization; dashed line: 2pσ–2pπ rotational coupling contribution; thick solid line: sum.

[1] W. E. Meyerhof, R. Anholt, and T. K. Saylor, Phys. Rev. A 16, 169 (1977).

[2] W. Brandt and K. W. Jones, Phys. Lett. 57A, 35 (1976).

[3] J. S. Briggs, J. Phys. B 8, L485 (1975).

[4] W. E. Meyerhof, Phys. Rev. A 18, 414 (1978).

[5] B. M. Johnson et al, Phys. Rev. A 19, 81 (1979).

[6] D. Liesen et al, Phys. Rev. A 17, 897 (1978).

[7] K. Taulbjerg, J. S. Briggs, and J. Vaaben, J. Phys. B 9, 1351 (1976).

[8] I. Tserruya, H. Schmidt-Böcking, and R. Schuch, Phys. Rev. A 18, 2482 (1978).

MEASUREMENTS OF GOLD L-SHELL IONIZATION PROBABILITY
AT LARGE SCATTERING ANGLES

S. Andriamonje, J.F. Chemin and J. Roturier

Centre d'Etudes Nucléaires de Bordeaux-Gradignan
Le Haut-Vigneau 33170 Gradignan - France -

Full calculations of the gold L-shell ionization probability by 1 MeV
protons have been recently reported by Aashamar et al.[1] These calculations
taking into account actual hyperbolic path of the projectile show large differences in the behaviour of the L-subshell ionization probabilities (I_{L_1},
I_{L_2}, I_{L_3}) for large scattering angles. These different behaviour are connected
with the different symmetry order of the 2s, $2p^{1/2}$ and $2p^{3/2}$ electron wavefunctions.

The ionization probability of the gold L-shell (I_L) by 1 MeV H^+ has been
measured at large scattering angles by a coincidence technique. The experimental set-up has been described previously.[2] The ionization probability
measurements at 2 angles simultaneously allows an accurate comparison of the
relative values. Protons scattered at 166° were detected in an annular,
300 mm^2, Si diode. At the other angles, 1 cm^2 surface barrier detector was
used. X-rays were detected in a 80 mm^2 Si(Li) diode : the product of the
solid angle by the detector efficiency was 0.12 sr. As shown in Fig. 1, a

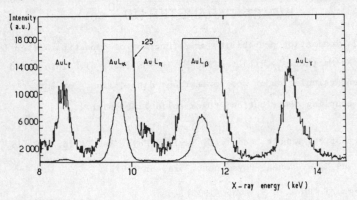

Fig. 1 : Typical L X ray spectrum of gold

clean separation of the L_α, L_β, L_γ, L_γ components was achieved but the resolution of the detector was not good enough to discriminate between the struc-
ture of these lines.

(I_L) was obtained at a given angle from the number of true coincidence
events between scattered H^+ and the total L X-ray transitions. A mean
fluorescence yield $\overline{\omega_L}$ = 0.35 has been used. The results are shown in Fig. 2

(•). They are in agreement with previous data by Laegsgaard et al at $30°$.[3] (■) The full line are the results of theoretical calculations.[1] The increase of the ionization probability at large scattering angle appears well reproduced. Analysis of the ionization probability subshells as developped for total cross section is not possible due to poor statistics in the coincidence experiment.[5] Nevertheless, since the sum of L_α and L_l transitions accounts for about 80 % of the electromagnetic deexcitation of the L_{III} subshell (see Fig. 1 and ref.[4]), the behaviour of the $L_\alpha + L_l$ X ray yield versus scattering angle should in first approximation reproduce the variation of the L_{III} ionization probability. The results are shown in Fig. 2 (▲). Experimental results have been normalized on the theoretical ionization probability value at $30°$.

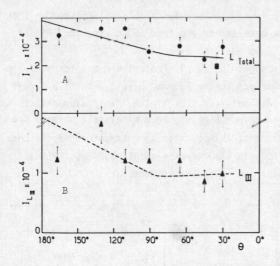

Fig. 2
L-shell ionization probability
versus scattering angle
a) total L-shell
b) L_{III} subshell

1. O. Aashamar, P. Amundsen, L. Kocbach, Phys. Lett. <u>67 A</u> (1978) 349
2. J.F. Chemin et al, Phys. Lett. <u>67 A</u> (1978) 116
3. Laegsgaard et al, Phys. Fenn. <u>9</u> suppl. <u>1</u> (1974) 49
4. S.I. Salem et al, Atom. Nucl. data tables <u>2</u> (1974) 91
5. S. Datz et al, Phys. Rev. <u>A 9</u> (1974) 192

Z-DEPENDENCE OF K-SHELL IONIZATION PROBABILITY IN
CENTRAL COLLISIONS OF 7 MEV PROTONS

M. Dost, S. Hoppenau, J. Kising and S. Röhl

Institut für Kernphysik, Universität zu Köln, D 5000 Köln, Germany

The understanding of Coulomb ionization has at present reached a high degree of refinement[1,2]. Recent steps were the realistic treatment of screening[3,4] and of the higher angular momenta of the electron in the continuum[5,6] possibly modified by projectile deflection[7] and nuclear recoil[8]. The semiclassical treatment of the ionization process has been very successful in most of these developments.

We have measured the K-shell ionization probability P_K of atoms with Z = 24 to 42 in central collisions with 7 MeV protons. Scattering of the protons by 21° defines impact parameters below 20 fm with quantum mechanical uncertainty[9] of similar size. The results are displayed in Fig. 1 as a function of atomic number Z or reduced velocity[2] ξ_K. The Fe and Mo data points are from 15° scattering. Fig. 2 shows the K-shell cross sections σ_K from the same experiment.

The experimental arrangement is shown in Fig. 3. Protons are scattered by $\theta_p = 21^O \pm 6^O$ into a 0.16 sr annular detector. The 200 mm^2 Si(Li) detects K X-rays in coincidence with protons by conventional fast-slow timing. Two proton detectors (DET 1 and 2) monitor the random coincidence time spectrum of elastic protons from a secondary target (Au) in order to detect any possible time structure of the beam. Only by use of an RF ion source could such structure be safely avoided. True-to-random ratios between 0.2 and 0.7 made such precautions necessary.

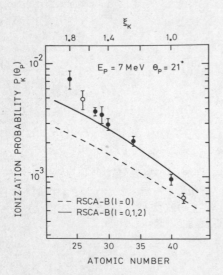

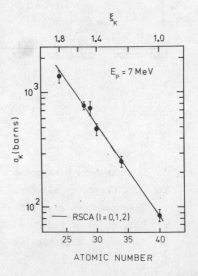

Fig.1: K-shell ionization probability P_K in central collisions of 7 MeV protons as a function of atomic number

Fig. 2: K-shell ionization cross sections σ_K for 7 MeV protons versus atomic number

Measured corrections for proton scattering by C and O contaminants were applied. They remained below 5%. The corrections for ionization in double scattering, calculated from the measured target thicknesses, are given in Table 1.

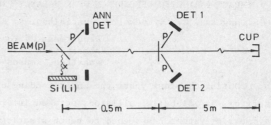

Fig. 3: Experimental set-up

The solid curve (RSCA-B) in Fig. 1 is a relativistic semiclassical calculation[6] including final electrons up to angular momentum $\ell=2$ and corrected by less than 10% for transiently modified electron binding[2]. Dirac wave functions for the bound electron are used. The dashed curve shows the same

target	24^{Cr}	26^{Fe}	28^{Ni}	29^{Cu}	30^{Zn}	34^{Se}	40^{Zr}	42^{Mo}
thickness ($\mu g/cm^2$)	67	80	28	97	182	152	601	331
correction (%)	12	9	4	18	23	14	30	17

Table 1: Target thicknesses and corrections for ionization in double scattering

calculation but for $\ell=0$ only. The experimental ionization probabilities for low Z are underestimated by a factor 1.8 , those for higher Z are somewhat overestimated. No such discrepancies are seen in the cross sections of Fig. 2. The solid curve in Fig. 2 is from the same RSCA calculation[6] as in Fig. 1 but without the less than 6% binding correction[2].

The deviations in P_K thus show that sudden, central collisions really test sensitively the semiclassical picture of ionization. The direction of improvement is possibly the correct treatment of nuclear recoil although the published numerical examples[8] rather indicate that theoretical predictions would come even lower.

Measurements to extend the data range up to Z=83 are in progress.

REFERENCES:

/1/ J. Bang and J. M. Hansteen, Kgl. Dan. Vid. Selsk. Mat.Fys.Med. 31(1959)no.13

/2/ G. Basbas, W. Brandt, and R. Laubert, Phys. Rev. A17(1978)1655

/3/ M. Pauli, F. Rösel, and D. Trautmann, Phys. Letters 67A(1978)28

/4/ O. Aashamar and L. Kocbach, J. Phys. B10(1977)869

/5/ O. Aashamar and L. Kocbach, Z. Physik A279(1976)237

/6/ M. Pauli, F. Rösel, and D. Trautmann, J. Phys. B11(1978)2511

/7/ J. U. Andersen, L. Kocbach, E. Laegsgaard, M. Lund, and C. D. Moak,
    J. Phys. B9(1976)3247

/8/ P. A. Amundsen, J. Phys. B11(1978)3197, see especially fig. 2

/9/ N. Bohr, Kgl. Dan. Vid. Selsk. Mat. Fys. Med. 18(1948)no. 8

IMPACT PARAMETER DEPENDENCE OF K VACANCY PRODUCTION IN Cu^{q+}-Kr COLLISIONS[†]

S. Hagmann, C. L. Cocke, E. Justiniano, J. R. Macdonald, H. Schmidt-Böcking[*]

Department of Physics
Kansas State University
Manhattan, Kansas 66506

During the last years the understanding of K vacancy production cross sections in adiabatic collisions between intermediate $Z(20 \leq Z \leq 40)$, nearly symmetric systems has seemed to reach a satisfactory stage: the differential measurement of Liesen et al.[1] for the Kr-Ge system and the projectile q-dependence of the total cross section[2-4] supported the viewpoint that $2p\pi-2p\sigma$ rotational coupling is the dominant mechanism for creating K-vacancies in the collision partners. The assumption has been made that the number of vacancies in the $2p\pi$ orbital is proportional to the number of incoming L-vacancies, in either collision partner. For no initial L-vacancies an unknown direct excitation mechanism has been proposed. We have subjected the hypothesis to experimental test by measuring the impact parameter dependence of the K-vacancy production probability in collisions of 0.86 MeV/u Cu^{+q} with Kr for impact parameters between 250 and 7000 fm and incident projectile charge states q between 9 and 21, i.e. up to two vacancies in the projectile L-shell. We find:

a) the shape of the probability distribution is not q-dependent and is not in agreement with that predicted by the rotational coupling model (see Fig. 1).

b) the absolute scale of the excitation probability increases sharply for $q \geq 19$ giving the q-dependence of the total cross section in agreement with that reported by Lennard et. al.[4] Excitations of the $2p\sigma$ to others bound states via the radial couplings will be discusssed.

[*] permanent address: Institut für Kernphysik, Universität Frankfurt, West Germany; and partially supported by Bundesministerium für Forschung und Technologie.

[†] partially supported by the Division of Basic Energy Sciences, U.S. Dept. of Energy.

1) Liesen, D., Macdonald, J. R., Mokler, P. and Warczak, A., 1978, Phys. Rev. A 17, 897.

2) Schiebel, U., Doyle, B., 1978, Zeitsch. f. Phys. A285, 241.

3) Warczak, A., Liesen, D., Macdonald, J. R., Mokler, P., 1978, Zeitsch. f. Phys. A285, 235.

4) Lennard, W. N., Mitchell, I. V., Foster, J. S., 1978, Phys. Rev. A18, 1949.

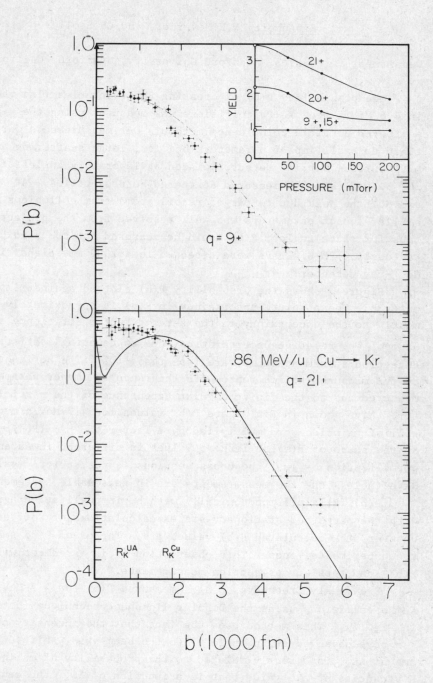

IMPACT PARAMETER DEPENDENCE OF $1s\sigma$ VACANCY PRODUCTION
IN 4.6-MeV/a.m.u. Xe+Pb COLLISIONS[*]

R. Anholt, W.E.Meyerhof, and Ch.Stoller[**]

Department of Physics, Stanford University, Stanford, California 94305

The probability $P(b)$ of creating Pb K vacancies ($1s\sigma$ vacancies)
in 4.6-MeV/a.m.u. Xe+Pb collisions was measured using the x-ray-
scattered particle coincidence method. Our measurements were confined to small impact parameters b, i.e., large scattering angles.
A Si surface barrier detector placed at laboratory angles of 10°, 15°,
20°, 30°, 40°, and 50° measured scattered Xe projectiles. At 30°, 40°,
and 50° the peak due to target recoil atoms from collisions with
smaller impact parameters was well resolved from the projectile peak,
thus for these angles, $P(b)$ could be measured for two b values simultaneously. Pb K x rays were detected in a 1000 mm^2 planar intrinsic
Ge γ-ray detector.

Figure 1 shows the probability $P(b)$ plotted against impact parameter b. The absolute uncertainty in $P(b)$ is approximately $\pm 20\%$, due
mostly to the uncertainty in the x-ray detector efficiency and solid
angle. The relative uncertainties, due to counting statistics and
detection system deadtime, are less than $\pm 10\%$. The horizontal bar
on the measured points represents the range of impact parameters
measured due to the finite angular acceptance of the particle detector. Also shown in Fig. 1 are $P(b)$ values for 4.7-MeV/a.m.u. Xe+Au
collisions which were multiplied by a factor of ^{2} $\sigma_K(Pb)/\sigma_K(Au)=0.8$.
As the shape of $P(b)$ at large b values is different in Au and Pb,[1]
normalization by just the cross sections is not strictly valid.
Nevertheless the two measurements are in reasonable agreement.

$P(b)$ falls off monotonically with b, in qualitative agreement
with the perturbed-stationary-states calculations of Soff et.al.[1]
However, the calculated $P(b)$ values are a factor of 0.33 smaller than
the experimental ones. This observation is in agreement with other
$P(b)$[2] and total-cross-section measurements.[3]

Previously Greenberg et al.[4] measured $P(b)$ for 4.7-MeV/a.m.u.
Xe+Pb collisions using the Doppler lineshape technique (dotted lines
in Fig. 1). This method uses the fact that the intensity of target
K x rays observed at an angle 0° to the beam axis, shifted by an
amount ΔE_x, is directly related to the probability of making target
K vacancies at a b value that is a function of ΔE_x, the center of
mass velocity, and the distance of closest approach in a head-on

collision.   The main problem with this method is to measure the
lineshape at large ΔE_x (small b values) where background due to the
Kβ x-ray line-tail, γ-rays, and 2pσ molecular orbital x-ray continua[5]
must be subtracted.   Also one must unfold the detector response-func-
tion, assuming a Gaussian distribution with a width determined by the
detector resolution, and take into account line broadening due to
unresolved satellite lines.

[*]Supported in part by the National Science Foundation.
[**]Supported by the Swiss National Science Foundation.

1.   G. Soff, private communication. Calculations based on W.
     Betz, G. Soff, B. Müller, W. Greiner, Phys. Rev. Lett. <u>37</u>,
     1046, (1976).
2.   D. Liessen, P. Armbruster, H.-H. Behncke, S. Hagmann,
     Z. Physik <u>A288</u>, 417 (1978).
3.   R. Anholt, *et al*, Z. Physik <u>A289</u>, 349 (1979).
4.   J. S. Greenberg, H. Bokemeyer, H. Emling, E. Grosse, D.
     Schwalm, F. Bosch, Phys. Rev. Lett. <u>39</u>, 1404 (1977).
5.   R. Anholt, W. E. Meyerhof, Phys. Rev. <u>A16</u>, 913 (1977).

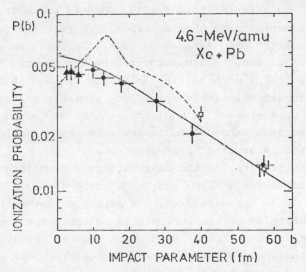

Fig. 1.   P(b) versus b for 1sσ vacancy production in 4.6-MeV/a.m.u.
Xe+Pb collisions.   Points: experiment from measurements of scattered
projectiles (•) and target recoils (▲)   and from 4.7-MeV/a.m.u. Xe+
Au collisions[1] (□), normalized as described in text.   Solid curve:
calculations of Soff et.al.[1] multiplied by 3.   Dashed line: Doppler
lineshape measurements of Greenberg et.al.[4]

IMPACT PARAMETER DEPENDENCE OF K AND L VACANCY PRODUCTION IN SLOW ION-ATOM COLLISIONS.

J. Bossler, R. Hippler, R. Shanker, H.O. Lutz

Fakultät für Physik, Universität Bielefeld,
D-4800 Bielefeld 1, West Germany

The impact parameter dependence of K and L vacancy creation in slow ion-atom collisions has been studied at impact energies between about 350 and 1400 keV. In particular, we investigated the K vacancy production in Ne^{++}-N_2, N^{++}-N_2, Ne^{++}-Ne, and the L vacancy production in Ar^{n+}-Ar (n = 1...4) and N^{m+}-Ar (m = 1,2) collisions.

Auger electrons following the decay of the K or L vacancies, respectively, have been detected in coincidence with ions scattered through given scattering angles θ. As described previously,[1,2] the impact parameter dependent excitation probability is then directly related to the coincidence rate.

The K excitation has been compared to the prediction of the $2p\sigma$ - $2p\pi$ rotational coupling theory.[3] Even though the collision velocities are rather high (between 0.12 and 0.22 r.u.), agreement between theory and experiment is fairly good. As known from previous work, the experimental data show a tendency to fill the valley between the "adiabatic" and "kinematic" peak. The position of the "adiabatic" peak is about where predicted by the theory. This is in contrast to studies of much heavier collision systems at about the same relative impact velocities which show a distinct shift to smaller impact parameters.[4] In addition, in the Ne^{++}-N_2 system the experiments have been extended to impact parameters smaller than that at which the "kinematic" peak appears.

Preliminary results for the Ar-L vacancy production in Ar - Ar collisions for a fixed scattered angle (θ = 2.7°) are presented in Fig. 1. In these studies, the impact parameter has been altered by a variation of the incident ion energy. For the Ar-Ar collision system, the L vacancy production changes slowly in the region of impact parameters investigated, whereas for N-Ar collisions it remains almost constant. Our data show a marked difference when compared with measurements of Thomson[5] for the same collision system and comparable impact parameters, though a larger scattering angle (θ = 14°). Thomson found a steep increase of the L vacancy production probability in Ar-Ar collisions for distances of closest approach $r_o \lesssim 0.25$ a.u., which was interpreted by the $3d\pi$ - $3d\delta$ rotational

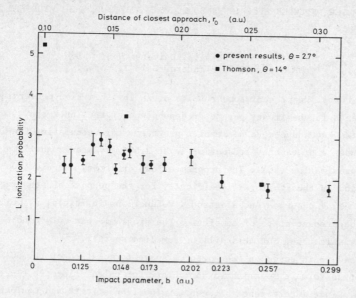

Fig. 1: Impact parameter dependence of Ar-L vacancy production in Ar-Ar collisions for fixed scattering angles θ.

coupling working at small impact parameters. The coupling of the 4fσ
orbital to higher unoccupied orbitals is expected to give an almost
constant probability for $r_o \lesssim 0.5$ a.u. Since in our experiment the
angular deflection is smaller, it may be expected that the 3dπ - 3dδ
rotational coupling has a lower probability, whereas the probability
due to coupling of the 4fσ to higher orbitals remains constant over
that impact parameter range.

1.   S. Sackmann, H.O. Lutz, J.S. Briggs, Phys. Rev. Lett.
      32, 805 (1974).

2.   N. Luz, S. Sackmann, H.O. Lutz, to be published in J.
      Phys. B: Atom. Mol. Phys.

3.   K. Taulbjerg, J.S. Briggs, J. Vaaben, J. Phys. B:
      Atom. Mol. Phys. 9, 1351 (1976).

4.   C.H. Annett, B. Curnutte, C.L. Cocke, to be published.

5.   G.M. Thomson, Phys. Rev. A 15, 865 (1977).

IMPACT PARAMETER DEPENDENCE OF INNER-SHELL IONIZATION OF LIGHT ATOMS BY PROTONS*

Kjell Aashamar and Per A. Amundsen

Institute of Physics, University of Oslo
P.O. Box 1048, Blindern, Oslo 3, Norway

In this report we present some results of an investigation concerning wavefunction effects in the impact parameter dependence of the inner-shell ionization
probability. We have developed a computer programme for calculating the impact parameter dependence of vacancy production in an arbitrary atomic shell in the semiclassical approximation (SCA). The program allows arbitrary one-electron central
potentials, and is thus tailored specifically for the purpose of studying the significance of using accurate one-electron wavefunctions in initial as well as final
states. In the present state of completion the programme can only handle the purely nonrelativistic case, but this will be remedied shortly.

The procedure is based on the momentum space formulation of the SCA[1], using a
fast Hankel transform in logarithmic variables[2] for calculating the electronic
form factors. Since interference between wavefunction effects and Coulomb deflection effects is negligible at high projectile energies, a straight line projectile
path is adequate for the purpose of the present discussion, and the corresponding
classical path factors can then be generated efficiently using a recursive computation scheme.

In the preliminary calculations reported here, we have considered two different one-electron potentials: First, the ordinary hydrogenic potential, and second,
a variationally optimized effective potential available in tabular form.[3] The latter has been determined in such a way that the total energy of the target state in
question, calculated with respect to the proper one-electron orbitals supported by
the potential, is minimized with respect to variations in the potential. The resulting total energy is within a few ppm from the corresponding true Hartree-Fock
value, and the differences in the one-electron bound-state wavefunctions are bare-
ly noticeable. Such potentials are now available for the ground states or near
ground states of all elements from Li through Rn.[3]

To make sure that the differences obtained are indeed due to different wavefunctions alone, we have used the same value for the electron binding energy for
both potentials. This ensures that we pick up contributions from the same range in
momentum space, and also that the path factors are the same.

Figures 1 and 2 show our results for the K-shell ionization probability I_b
(left-hand scale) in Ne for 1.5 MeV and 3 MeV proton projectiles, respectively.
The curve labeled 1 represents the hydrogenic case, and curve 2 the optimized potential case. Both calculations include multipoles up to L=3. Curve 3 shows the
ratio r (right-hand scale) of curves 2 and 1, and gives what might properly be
called the wavefunction correction factor with respect to the hydrogenic results.

The wavefunction effects are seen to be generally large for both energies considered, and they furthermore show a strong impact parameter dependence, a dependence which is just opposite to the findings at low energies.[4] A closer examination of the individual multipole contributions shows that different multipoles dominate at different impact parameters. We thus apparently have a tool for probing the individual multipole contributions to the oscillator strengths, and thereby also the spatial distribution of atomic wavefunctions.

We have received information to the effect that preliminary measurements for 1.5 MeV protons on Ne at small impact parameters[5] seem to indicate that using optimized effective central potentials instead of hydrogenic ones cuts the discrepancy between theory and experiment by some 50%.

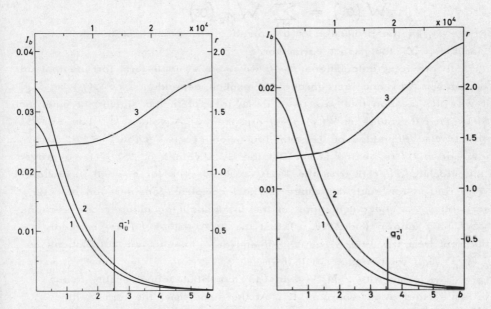

Figs. 1 and 2. Ionization probability I_b (left-hand scale) for 1.5 MeV protons (left) and 3 MeV protons (right) on Ne as a function of impact parameter b (bottom scale: K-shell radii; top scale: fm). Curve 1: hydrogenic case; curve 2: optimized potential case; curve 3: ratio r (right-hand scale) of curves 2 and 1.

We are grateful to E. Horsdal Pedersen and his coworkers for informing us of their results prior to publication.

*Supported in part by the Norwegian Research Council for Science and the Humanities.

1. L. Kocbach, Z. Phys. A279, 233-6 (1976).

2. J.D. Talman, J. Comp. Phys. 29, 35 (1978).

3. K. Aashamar, T.M. Luke and J.D. Talman, At. Data and Nucl. Data Tables (in press).

4. O. Aashamar and L. Kocbach, J. Phys. B10, 869-78 (1977).

5. E. Horsdal Pedersen, P. Bisgaard, F. Folkmann and N.H. Pedersen (private communication).

IMPACT PARAMETER DEPENDENCE
OF THE PROBABILITIES OF ATOMIC IONIZATION BY NUCLEI

A.K. Kaminsky   and   M.I. Popova

Institute of Nuclear Physics, Moscow State University;

Moscow 117234; USSR

The probability $W(x)$ for atomic inner shell ionization by nuclei has been expressed in /1/ as the sum

$$W(x) = \sum_{M_L} W_{M_L}(x) \qquad (1)$$

where M_L is the projection of the angular momentum L of the colliding particles, x the impact parameter.

In previous calculations /2-4/, we used a single-term formula instead of the sum (1) and disregarded the explicit dependence of $W(x)$ on M_L. It was this reason that was used in /1/ to explain the significant difference between our values of $W(x)$ /2-4/ and the SCA values /5/. The SCA /5/ and PWBA /6/ values of the total ionization cross section σ were assumed in /1/ to be the same. But the SCA values of σ have proved significantly different from the PWBA values even for K-shell ionization /7/. The reason for such difference is the incomplete consideration of outer screening /7/. The calculations of the L-subshell ionization cross sections σ have shown (see Fig. 1) that the SCA values /5/ are markedly different from the PWBA results /6/ and are close to our calculations of σ /3,4/ including a single term.

The terms with $M_L \neq 0$ in (1) contribute considerably to the cross section at all energies E. At the same time, the terms with $M_L \neq 0$ will significantly change the form of the dependence $W(x)$ only at large x (Fig. 2). The additional terms of the sum fail to alter the difference between our values of $W(x)$ /3,4/ and the SCA ones /5/ at small x. Our values of $W(x)$ are higher than SCA ones due to the more comprehensive consideration of the conservation laws. The measured values of $W(x)$ for Ag L-shell ionization by α particles are considerably higher that SCA values at small x /8/.

Thus our method of calculation of $W(x)$ including summation over M_L /1/ has significant advantages over SCA calculations /5/. Our method is more convenient for computing since the final expression for $W(x)$ implies summation over a single index M_L (instead of two indices ℓ and m in SCA) so the convergence of series (1) is more rapid.

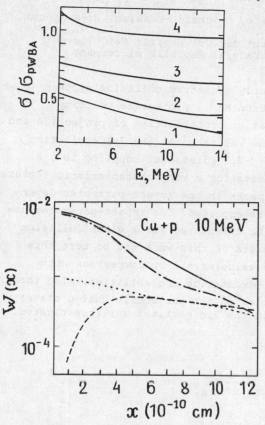

Fig. 1. Ratio σ/σ_{PWBA} of the different cross sections σ for Cu 2S ionization to the PWBA cross sections from /6/ as a function of proton energy E. We use the notations: 1-SCA values of σ /5/, 2 - the values of σ, obtained with our previous W(x), 3- the σ obtained with the only term W_o of (1), 4 - the σ calculated with the two terms W_o and W_1 of (1).

Fig.2. Ionization probability per electron for Cu 2S-ionization by 10 MeV protons Solid curve the term W_o of (1). Dot-dash curve -our previous calculations /3, 4/. The dashed curve is the term of (1) with M_L=1,the dotted curve -SCA values from /5/.

REFERENCES

1. K. Taulbjerg, J.Phys. B10, L341 (1977).

2. A.K. Kaminsky, V.S. Nikolaev, M.I. Popova, Phys.Lett. A53, 419(1975).

3. A.K. Kaminsky, S.V. Lovtsov, M.I. Popova, X ICPEAC, Abstracts of Papers, p. 56, Paris, 1977.

4. A.K. Kaminsky, S.V. Lovtsov, M.I. Popova, Phys.Lett.A61, 308(1977).

5. J.M. Hansteen, O.M. Johnsen, L. Kocbach, Atom. data nucl. data tables, 15, 305(1975).

6. B.H. Choi, E. Merzbacher, I.S. Khandelwal, Atomic data, 5, 291(1973).

7. E. Laegsgaard, J.U. Andersen, M. Lund, Electronic and atomic colli- sions. Proc. 10th ICPEAC, ed. by G Watel, p. 353 (1978).

8. K.G. Bauer, Q. Fazly, H. Mommsen, P. Schürkes, J.Phys.B11, 4227 (1978).

Impact-parameter dependence of K-shell excitation in near symmetric heavy ion collisions.*

R.Schuch, W.Lichtenberg†, G.Nolte, H.Schmidt-Böcking†, H.-J.Specht

Physikalisches Institut der Universität Heidelberg
D-6900 Heidelberg, Federal Republik of Germany

For a large variety of nearly symmetric collision systems (S on Ar, Ni on Ni, Ge and Rb, and Nb on Mo⁹ , projectile velocity $\geq$ 1 MeV/amu) the K-shell excitation probabilities of projectile and target were measured and the sum was taken as the $2p\sigma$ excitation probability $P_{2p\sigma}$(b). If the $2p\pi$ -$2p\sigma$ rotational coupling is the dominant process in the $2p\sigma$ excitation a very characteristic feature -kinematic peak and adiabatic peak- in the impact-parameter dependence of this $2p\sigma$ -excitation is expected. The impact-parameter dependence for this process can be calculated for a given collision system by a scaling law[1]. The aim of this work was to test this scaling law and also ab initio calculations by comparison with measured impact-dependent $2p\sigma$ -excitation probabilities. Also the dependence of these probabilities on the projectile charge states i.e. the number of vacancies in the $2p\sigma$ -orbital was investigated.

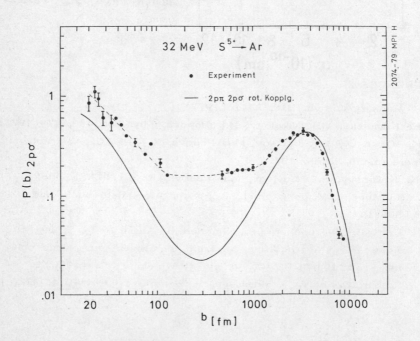

In fig.1 the impact-parameter dependence of the $2p\sigma$ excitation probability measured with 32 MeV S on Ar in comparison with the prediction of the $2p\pi$ -$2p\sigma$ rotational coupling model is presented. There is a clear indication of the kinematik peak below 2o fm and the adiabatic peak at about 3ooo fm but the valley between both is filled up. For heavier collision systems a more significant deviation from the theory has been found and will be discussed.

* Supported by BMFT

§ In cooperation with K.W. Jones a.B. Johnson, Brookhaven National Lab. U.S.A.

+ Present address: Institut f. Kernphysik, Universität Frankfurt, D-6ooo Frankfurt, Federal Republik of Germany

1) K. Taulberg, J.S. Briggs and J. Vaaben
J.Phys. B9, 1351, 1976

Interference effects in 2pς - 1sς vacancy sharing[§]

R. Schuch, G. Nolte, W. Lichtenberg[+] and H. Schmidt-Böcking[+]

Physikalisches Institut der Universität Heidelberg
D-6900 Heidelberg, Federal Republic of Germany

[+]Institut für Kernphysik, Universität Frankfurt
D-6000 Frankfurt/Main, Federal Republic of Germany

The K-shell excitation of the heavier collision partner is in
near symmetric heavy ion-atom collisions determined by the 2pς - 1sς
vacancy-sharing process. The ratio of K-shell excitation probabilities of heavy- and light collision partners is the so called vacancy-sharing ratio. A semi-empirical formula[1] for the impact-parameter dependence of this vacancy-sharing ratio has been derived and
was found in agreement with measured probabilities[2].

A strong interference effect in the impact-parameter dependence
of the vacancy-sharing ratio was predicted[1] by these calculations
for the case where a K-vacancy is already present on the incoming
part of the collision. This effect was found in the impact-parameter
dependence of the vacancy-sharing ratio measured with H-like sulphur
projectiles (charge state 15+) on an Ar gaseous target. This effect
and also quasi-molecular effects will be discussed as possible reasons for the structure in the vacancy-sharing ratio measured with
54 MeV and 90 MeV(8+) on Ge and Rb (fig.1).

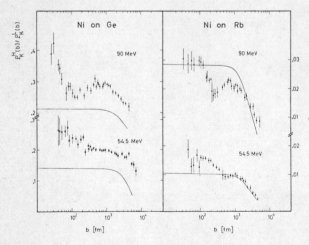

Fig. 1.
Measured vacancy-
sharing ratio in
comparison with the
prediction of the
semi-empirical for-
mula.

[§]Supported by Bundesminister für Forschung und Technologie

1. J.S. Briggs, Harwell T.P. 594
2. R. Schuch, H. Schmidt-Böcking, R. Schulé and I. Tserruya,
    Phys. Rev. Lett. 39, 79 (1977)

MULTIPLE COULOMB EXCITATION OF ELECTRON CONFIGURATIONS
IN SUPERHEAVY QUASIMOLECULES[*].

G. Soff

Gesellschaft für Schwerionenforschung (GSI), Darmstadt, West Germany

and

J. Reinhardt, W. Betz, J. Kirsch, K.-H. Wietschorke, V. Oberacker,
B. Müller and W. Greiner

Institut für Theoretische Physik, Universität Frankfurt, West Germany

In connection with positron emission in overcritial fields and a possible spectroscopy of electronic states in superheavy quasimolecules[1], we investigated various excitation processes leading to inner-shell vacancies in collisions of very heavy ions with $(Z_2+Z_2)\alpha \stackrel{>}{\sim} 1$. We also evaluated the influence of super strong magnetic fields on ionization and the δ-electron distribution[2], the emitted quasimolecular photon spectrum in comparison with background radiation phenomena and the internal conversion induced by nuclear Coulomb excitation[3].

We calculated inner-shell ionization by expanding the time-dependent electronic wave function in terms of the quasimolecular adiabatic basis states which are solutions of the stationary two-centre Dirac equation. The resulting set of coupled channel equations for the occupation amplitudes of bound and continuum states has been solved numerically by taking explicitly into account the continuum-continuum rearrangement, which leads to a shift of the δ-electron spectrum towards higher kinetic energies. The many particle problem has been treated by expanding the configuration states in terms of the fully time-dependent single particle states.

As example of such a configuration calculation we show in fig. 1 the number of created $1s\sigma$-vacancies per collision for the Xe-Au system as function of impact parameter b. Enhanced by strong relativistic effects we obtained several percent ionization probability for central collisions and a steep fall-off for increasing b. The dependence of $P_{1s\sigma}$(b) on kinetic projectile energy is displayed in fig. 2 for various selected impact parameters.

A steep dependence is found for relatively small ion energies whereas all curves flatten off for projectile energies close to the Coulomb barrier.

[*]Work supported by the Bundesministerium für Forschung und Technologie

1. G. Soff, B. Müller, W. Greiner, Phys. Rev. Lett. 40 (1978) 540
2. W. Greiner, B. Müller, G. Soff, Phys. Lett. 69A (1978) 27
3. G. Soff, V. Oberacker, W. Greiner, Phys. Rev. Lett. 41 (1978) 1167

4. J.S. Greenberg, H. Bokemeyer, H. Emling, E. Grosse, D. Schwalm, F. Bosch, Phys. Rev. Lett. 39 (1977) 1404

5. D. Liesen, P. Armbruster, H.-H. Behncke, S. Hagmann, Z. Physik A 288 (1978) 417

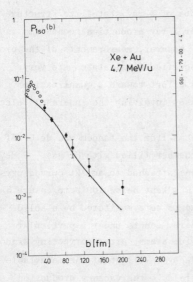

Fig. 1.
Number of created 1sσ-vacancies per collision as function of impact parameter b in comparison with experimental data[4],[5] from GSI.

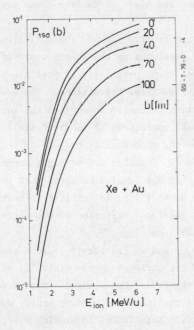

Fig. 2.
$P_{1s\sigma}(b)$ as function of bombarding energy for various impact parameters.

Fluorine K X-ray production by electron excitation, ionization
and capture processes in F^{q+} (q=1-9)+He collisions

H. Tawara*, P. Richard, K.A. Jamison. T.J. Gray, J. Newcomb and C. Schmiedekamp

Department of Physics, Kansas State University,
Manhattan, Kansas 66506, U.S.A.

Introduction :   From high resolution measurements of X-ray statellite structure
of projectile, some qualitative understanding for X-ray production mechanisms in
heavy ion-atom collisions has been obtained[1-2].   However, measurements of the projectile K vacancy production cross section to specified final states are very
limited so far. The present investigation is an effort toward a quantitative
understanding of heavy ion-atom collision processes involving the innershell electrons as well as the outer shell electrons.

Experimental procedures :   15 MeV F^{q+} (q=2-9) beams from the tandem van de Graff
at Kansas State University entered a collision chamber filled with He gas. 5 MeV
beams wereused for q=1. The collision chamber was attached to an ARL curved crystal (RAP) X-ray spectrometer. The gas pressure was kept below 100 μ to ensure a
single collision condition. The target constituents were monitored by a solid
state detector placed inside the chamber. The X-ray counts under a particular
peak were normalized to the number of recoil helium atoms, after correcting window
transmission, crystal reflectivity and partial decay-in-flight of the metastable
state ions. By using theoretical fluorescence yields[3], the vacancy production
cross sections have been determined from the observed X-ray production cross sections.

Results and discussions :   The observed F-K X-ray spectra from F^{q+}+He collision
are shown in Fig.1 and are found to be strongly dependent on the charge state of
the incident F ions. From these high resolution X-ray spectra, it is possible to
uniquely assign production mechanism to the observed X-ray transitions. The assignment of a transition to a particular production mechanism depends on the incident charge state of projectile. The shaded peaks correspond to single K-shell
electron ionization process and peaks just below the shaded peaks are due to K-
shell electron excitation. It is found that the $^3P/^1P$ ratios are strongly dependent on the incident charge state of projectile. It should also be noted that the
$^3P/^1P$ ratios are independent of He gas pressure up to 120 μ, in contrast to measurement by Fortner and Matthews[2] who reported significant variation of the ratio
with gas pressure of Ne and Ar due to collisional quenching.

The observed K-shell electron excitation (σ_{ee}) and ionization (σ_i) cross sections are shown in Fig.2 and 3 as a function of the incident charge state (q) of
projectile. σ_{ee} increases almost one order of magnitude when q changes from 2 to
6, whereas σ_i decreases with q mainly because of the increased binding energy due
to (high) ionization. The PWBA-CB calculation with this increased binding energy
* Present address : Nuclear Engineering Department, Kyushu University, Fukuoka.

correction is shown in Fig.3.

The energy dependence of the excitation and ionization cross sections for F^{6+} and of the excitation and capture cross sections for F^{8+} ions has been reported elsewhere.[4-5]

1. F. Hopkins, R.L. Kauffman, C.W. Woods and P. Richard, Phys. Rev. A9, 2413 (1974)

2. R.J. Fortner and D.L. Matthews, Phys. Rev. A16, 144 (1977)

3. T. Tunnel and C.P. Bhalla, private communication (1978)

4. H. Tawara, P. Richard, K.A. Jaimson and T.J. Gray, J. Phys. B11, L615 (1978)

5. H. Tawara, P. Richard, P. Pepmiller, T.J. Gray, J. Hall and J. Newcomb, Abstract of this meeting.

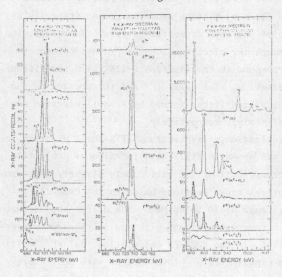

Fig.1

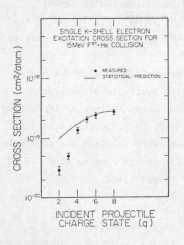

Fig.2

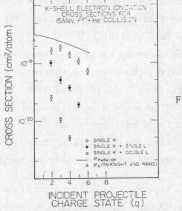

Fig.3

Excitation and ionization of K-shell electron in F^{6+} ions

in collision with He gas target

H. Tawara*, P. Richard, P. Pepmiller, T.J. Gray, J. Hall and J. Newcomb

Department of Physics, Kansas State University,

Manhattan, Kansas 66506, U.S.A.

In the present work, we have measured the cross sections for excitation and ionization of K-shell electron in F^{6+} ions incident on He gas as a function of the projectile energy. The experimental procedures are almost the same as those described previously[1]. A typical example of the observed F-K X-ray spectra from F^{6+} ions at 10 MeV is shown in Fig.1. The peak (A) is due to the $(1s2s2p)^4P \rightarrow (1s^2 2s)^2S$ transition. The excitation to the $(1s2s2p)^4P$ state from the ground state $(1s^2 2s)$ ^2S, however, is prohibited because of the spin conservation rule. Therefore, the observed ^4P peak may be formed through the electron exchange process between F^{6+} ion and He atom. The peak (B) correspond to the $(1s2s2p)^2P \rightarrow (1s^2 2s)^2S$ transition formed by the K-shell electron excitation. The peaks (C) and (D) are due to the $(1s2p)^3P \rightarrow (1s^2)^1S$ and $(1s2p)^1P \rightarrow (1s^2)^1S$ transitions formed by K-shell electron ionization accompanying the 2s-2p level mixing, respectively.

The measured excitation and ionization cross sections of K-shell electron in F^{6+} ions in collision with He gas are shown in Fig.2 as a function of projectile energy. The measured ionization cross sections are varied only slightly with projectile energy, whereas the theoretical cross sections based on the PWBA-CB[2] increase a factor of 5 in the energy range of 10 to 40 MeV. The discrepancy between the PWBA-CB and the observed data becomes significant with the increase of projectile energy. It should be noted that, in the PWBA-CB calculation, $He^{2+} + F^{6+}$ collisions are assumed, whereas, in the experiment, F^{6+} ions collide with He. Therefore, this discrepancy is believed to be due to the screening of nucleus (He) by two K-shell electrons. This arguement is supported by discussion of Basbas[3]. Similar observation of ionization cross sections of He by He^{2+} and He^0 has already been reported by Puckett et al.[4] The ionization of He by H^+ and H^0 ions seems to be very much similar.[5]

The observed excitation cross sections change very slightly with the projectile energy. However, no theoretical calculations are available on excitation cross sections. It is found that ratios of excitation cross section to ionization cross sections are almost constant in the present energy range investigated. It is also found that ratios of ^3P to ^1P transition peaks from F^{7+} ions due to single K-shell electron ionization change with the projectile energy ranging from 0.5 at lower energies to about unity at the highest energy investigated.

1.   H. Tawara et al., to be published in Phys. Rev. A (1979)

2.   G. Basbas, W. Brandt and R. Laubert, Phys. Rev. A7, 983 (1973)

* Present address : Nuclear Engineering Department, Kyushu University, Fukuoka.

3. G. Basbas, Abstract Book of Seattle ICPEAC-IX, p.501(1975)

4. L.J. Puckett,G.O. Taylor and D.W. Martin, Phys. Rev. 178,271)1969)

5. E.S. Solovev,R.N. Ilin,V.A.Opain and N.V.Fedorenko, Soviet Phys.-JETP 15,459
    (1962)

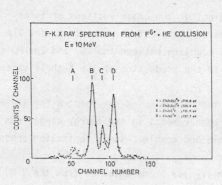

Fig. 1

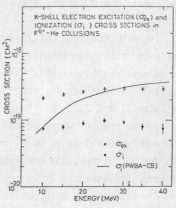

Fig. 2

SINGLE AND DOUBLE K-SHELL IONIZATION IN ASYMMETRIC
ION-ATOM COLLISIONS FOR Z_1, $Z_2 \leq 10$

K. Kawatsura, K. Ozawa, F. Fujimoto[*], K. Komaki[*] and M. Terasawa[**]

Japan Atomic Energy Research Institute, Tokai, Ibaraki 319-11, Japan
* College of General Education, University of Tokyo, Komaba, Tokyo 153, Japan
** Toshiba R & D Center, Tokyo Shibaura Electric Co., Ltd., Kawasaki 210, Japan

In heavy ion-atom collisions at low velocity, the cross sections of inner-shell ionization can be interpreted in terms of the electron promotion model via the molecular orbital (MO). The rotational coupling between the $2p\sigma$ and $2p\pi$ MO's at small internuclear distances gives rise to the production of the K-shell vacancies when Z_1 and $Z_2 \leq 10$.[1,2]

In the present work, we have measured the $K\alpha$ and $K\alpha^h$ X-ray spectra for the Be, B, O and F atoms induced by N^+ and Ne^+ ion bombardments in the energy range from 0.25 MeV to 1.1 MeV, and presented the single and double K-shell ionization cross sections (σ_{1K} and σ_{2K}).

The experiments were performed using heavy ion beams obtained from the 2 MV Van de Graaff accelerator of JAERI at Tokai. Thick solid targets of Be, B, BeO and LiF were used for the measurements. The X-ray spectra were observed by a flat crystal spectrometer and projectile energy dependence of X-ray yields was measured with a gas-flow proportional counter.

Fig. 1 shows an example of the $K\alpha$ and $K\alpha^h$ X-ray spectra from B atoms induced by 1.1 MeV N^+ ion bombardment. The similar spectra are also observed for Be, O and F atoms. The absolute cross sections for the single and double K-shell ionization (σ_{1K} and σ_{2K}) were obtained from the observed X-ray spectra and non-dispersive X-ray yields. Here, we assume that the fluorescence yield for the double K-shell ionization, ω_{2K}, is same as that for the single one, ω_{1K}.[3]

Fig. 2 shows the experimental results of σ_{1K} and σ_{2K} for the $N^+ \rightarrow B$ collision system. Taulbjerg et al have derived the scaling relation which allows the universal curve to be given for the σ_{1K} and σ_{2K} of the K-shell ionization via the $2p\sigma - 2p\pi$ rotational coupling in the asymmetric ion-atom collisions.[4] In this figure, the full and the dotted curves give the theoretical values of σ_{1K} and σ_{2K},

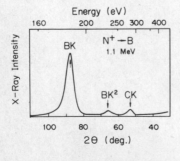

Fig. 1.
$K\alpha$ and $K\alpha^h$ X-ray spectra of B obtained by 1.1 MeV N^+ ion impact.

respectively, calculated by Taulbjerg et al, using the MO model. In the evaluation of the absolute K-shell ionization cross sections, the average number of vacancies in the $2p\pi_x$ MO in a particular many-electron collision system is necessary. This quantity has been assumed to be equal to one for the comparison shown in Fig. 2. The theoretical predictions by the MO model considering the rotational coupling give a good agreement with the experimental K-shell ionization cross sections, σ_{1K} and σ_{2K} for the $N^+ \to B$ collision system. The similar results are also obtained for the other collision systems such as $N^+ \to Be$ and $Ne^+ \to O$, F collision systems.

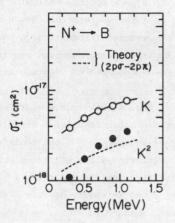

Fig. 2.
The single and double K-shell ionization cross sections for B in N^+ ion impact. Curves show the results of the MO calculations by Taulbjerg et al.

1.   U. Fano and W. Lichten, Phys. Rev. Lett. 14, 627 (1965).

2.   M. Barat and W. Lichten, Phys. Rev. A6, 211 (1972).

3.   C. P, Bhalla and M. Hein, Phys. Rev. Lett. 30, 39 (1973).

4.   K. Taulbjerg, J. S. Briggs and J. Vaaben, J. Phys. B9, 1351 (1976).

AUGER-SPECTRA OF 100- TO 500-keV P$^+$-PROJECTILES
EXCITED BY CARBON FOILS

D. Ridder and D. Schneider

Freie Universität Berlin, 1000 Berlin-33, W.-Germany
and
Hahn-Meitner-Institut für Kernforschung GmbH,
1000 Berlin-39, W.-Germany

Phosphorus projectiles of 100 to 500 keV are excited by 10 μg/cm^2 carbon foils.
Emitted Auger-electrons are observed at an emission angle of 9°. Widths of observed
lines are mainly due to kinematic effects and could be minimized at this small
angle and 500 keV impact energy to be $\Delta W \approx 2eV$. Thus, our spectra following high-
energy impact are used to study spectroscopic features whereas the change of the
spectral shape with decreasing energy is used to extract information on complete
Auger-groups and their excitation modes. The apparatus used has been described
previously[1]. Hartree-Fock calculations[2] have been performed to identify structures
in the low energy portion of the spectrum.

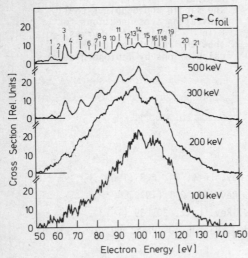

Fig. 1: Phosphorus-projectile Auger-
spectra corrected for kinematic shifts
and continuous background. Spectra are
normalized to equal intensity of line 3.

Fig. 1 shows our spectra corrected
for kinematic (Doppler-) effects and
after subtraction of the contribution
of electrons with continuous energy
distribution. The spectra are normalized
to equal intensity of line 3 which has
been assigned[3] as the transition $2p^5 3s^2$ -
$2p^6$. A total number of 21 discrete
features is observed. Most of these
structures are superpositions of lines
resulting from many individual transitions. Fig. 1 demonstrates the increase
of the relative intensity of the high-
energy Auger-structure with decreasing
projectile velocity. Also the increase
of resolution with increasing energy due
to kinematic effects is obvious. Using
absolute yield values[1] our data could

be put on an absolute scale.

Calculated energies for the Auger-transitions $L_{23}^i M^j - L_{23}^{i-1} M^{j+2}$ (i=1-2, j=0-3) show
that the high intensity above 100 eV can only be produced by double L_{23}-vacancy
states with a nearly complete M-shell or by transitions of the type $L_{23}^i M^i$ nl-M^{i+1}
with an active spectator electron. In the latter case very low intensity below
100 eV is expected. However, the decays of the double-vacancy states result in
single vacancy states with additional M-shell vacancies. Decays of the latter
can explain the intensity below 100 eV. In analogy to an earlier analysis of P$^+$-

projectile spectra excited by Ar-gas^3, we conclude that at low impact energies mainly vacancy-states $L^2_{23}M^i$ (i=0,1) are produced by a 3dó-promotion mechanism.

With increasing projectile energy, the low energy portion of the spectrum is favoured. This indicates an increased production of single L_{23}-vacancy states with a highly ionized M-shell. The growth of discrete lines 3,5,6 and 9-11 in our absolute cross-sections with increasing projectile velocity can only be explained by direct excitation of $L_{23}M^3$-states. Also double-vacancy production together with increased outer-shell ionization will shift the spectral intensity towards lower energies. Calculated energies indicate that at energies above 70 eV contributions from $L^2_{23} M^i$-decays are expected. In this region, our absolute data show some lines with very strongly increasing intensity at high impact energy, especially lines 6 and 8. Additional measurements are in progress to examine this dependence clearly.

Apart from the most prominent line 3, all the other lines are superpositions due to many transitions from different terms or even different charge states. The electrostatic and spin-orbit splitting of initial terms in the $2p^53s3p-2p^6$ transition has been calculated. We found that the terms $2p^5(3s3p^3P)^{4,2}S,P,D$ might account for structure near lines 5 and 6, and $^2S,P,D$-terms of $2p^5(3s3p^1P)$ may contribute to lines 7 and 8. The transitions from initial states $2p^53p^2$ are spread over the region of lines 9 through 11.

The first two lines in the spectrum are energetically lower than the $2p^53s^2-2p^6$ Auger-transition. Such lines of lower energy might in principle be caused by final-state configuration-interaction. However, CI-effects should not be present for a closed-shell. So, there is only the possibility of Coster-Kronig transitions of the type $2s2p^63s^23p^3nl-2s^22p^53s^23p^3$ (nl=3d,4s,4p) with calculated energies of 56.74 eV, 56.18 eV and 55.28 eV.

1. D. Schneider, Proc. of the V. Conf. on the Application of Small Accelerators, Denton 178, Texas, USA

2. C. Froese-Fischer, Comp. Phys. Comm. _4_, (1972) 107

3. P. Dahl, M. Rødbro, B. Fastrup, M.E. Rudd, J. Phys. B _9_, 1581 (1976)

ELECTRON SPECTRA PRODUCED IN HIGH ENERGY NE ON NE COLLISIONS

D. Schneider, M. Prost, R. DuBois, D. Ridder, N. Stolterfoht

Hahn-Meitner-Institut für Kernforschung GmbH,
1000 Berlin-39, West-Germany

In this contribution first measurements in the field of atomic physics at the
new high energy accelerator for heavy ions, VICKSI in Berlin, are reported.
Collisions of 120-MeV Ne^{5+} on Ne have been examined where secondary electrons up
to 6 keV were detected. The observed structures are due to Ne K-Auger electrons
from the target as well as from the projectile. A further structure is caused by
elastically scattered electrons from the projectile.

The experimental set-up is similar to that described in detail previously[1].
Within a scattering chamber of 50 cm in diameter the heavy ion beam crossed a gas
target produced by a jet. The ejected electrons were detected by two electrostatic
45°-parallel-plate analyzers whose position with respect to the beam direction
could be varied from 17° to 160°. The basic resolution of the spectrometers was
7.8% FWHM. The resolution could be improved up to 1% FWHM by decelerating the
electrons before entering the analysing field. The gas pressure in the scattering
region was about $3 \cdot 10^{-3}$ Torr whereas the basic pressure was $5 \cdot 10^{-6}$ Torr.

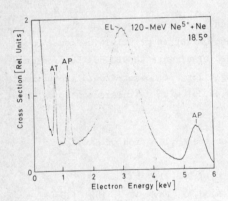

Fig. 1:

Total electron spectrum. The structures are the target Auger peak (AT),
the projectile Auger peaks (AP) and
the electron loss peak (EL), as
indicated.

Fig. 1 shows a total spectrum up to 6 keV
electron energy. It contains the target
K-Auger peak (AT), two projectile K-Auger
peaks (AP) and the electron-loss peak (EL).
The electron loss peak is due to outer-shell
projectile electrons which are elastically
scattered by the target. Simple arguments
indicate that the mean energy E of these
electrons corresponds to the velocity equal
to that of the projectile. The base width
of the peak ΔE is related to the binding
energy I_b of the scattered electrons via
the following formula[2]

$$\Delta E = 4 \ (E \cdot I_b)^{1/2} .$$

The base width ΔE could be determined to be
about 2600 eV resulting in a binding energy
of about 132 eV. Hartree-Fock calculations[3]
give binding energies of 158 eV and 172 eV for the 2p- and the 2s-electrons,
respectively. Thus, despite the uncertainties in the experimentel determination of
I_b the data show that the electron loss peak should mainly consist of scattered
2p-electrons.

Two projectile K-Auger peaks are observed because the projectile velocity
is higher than the velocity of the emitted electrons. The Doppler-broadening of

these peaks is about 100 eV and 250 eV, respectively. The low energy projectile
peak was also measured with higher resolution and two groups could be distinguished.
The low energy group consists mainly of intensities due to Li- and Be-like states.
This arrises from the fact that the incoming projectile has only three L-shell
electrons and no further or only one further outer-shell ionization is needed to
create these states. Intensity due to states with more than three L-shell electrons is also observed indicating that capture occurs. The second group, slightly
less intense, is observed at about 770 eV. This structure is attributed to hypersatellite Auger electrons[4].

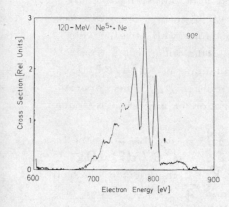

Fig. 2 shows a highly resolved target
K-Auger spectrum. The three higher energy
peaks can be assigned to KL^0-, KL^1- and
KL^2-Auger peaks, respectively. For the
other peaks such an assignment cannot be
given as in this range many lines overlap
from states with different target charge
states. However, an estimation of the
probability for L-shell excitation could
be performed. The analysis shows that a
statistical excitation of L-shell electrons
is rather probable. Measurements with
higher resolution should confirm this

Fig. 2:
Highly resolved target Auger spectrum. result. The mean value of outer-shell holes
after the collision was found to be 1.8. The
structure at higher energies than that of the KL^0-peak is due to states with a
higher degree of excitation.

1) N. Stolterfoht, Z. Phys. **248**, 81 (1971)

2) D. Burch, H. Wieman, W.B. Ingalls; Phys. Rev. Lett. **30**, 823 (1973)

3) C. Froese-Fischer; Comp. Phys. Comm. **4**, 107 (1972)

4) C.W. Woods, R.L. Kauffman, K.A. Jamison, N. Stolterfoht, and P. Richard;
   Phys. Rev. A **12**, 1393 (1975)

DOUBLY DIFFERENTIAL CROSS SECTIONS FOR
ATOMIC L-SUBSHELL IONIZATION

A.K. Kaminsky,   N.G. Myakishev and M.I. Popova
Institute of Nuclear Physics, Moscow State University;
Moscow 117234; USSR

The cross sections $d^2\sigma/dE_e\,d\Omega_e$, differential in electron energy E_e and spatial angle Ω_e for electron ejection from the L-subshell in collisions with atomic nuclei and light atoms, have been calculated in the first Born approximation with hydrogen-like wave functions. The sum rule has been used for collisions with atoms. The calculations have been carried out for the collision energies from 25 keV/amu to 600 MeV/amu. Similar calculations of $d^2\sigma/dE_e\,d\Omega_e$ for K-shell ionization by nuclei were made earlier /1,2/. The general scheme of $d^2\sigma/dE_e\,d\Omega_e$ calculation for ionization of any state by nuclei is presented in /3/.

The matrix elements $M_{Li}(q, K, \gamma)$ for the L-subshell ionization /4/ have been used in calculating $d^2\sigma/dE_e\,d\Omega_e$ Here, $\vec{q}$ is the momentum transfer, $\vec{K}$ the ejected electron momentum, γ the angle between $\vec{K}$ and $\vec{q}$. The values of the squared matrix elements $\varepsilon_{Li}(q, K)$ /5/ cannot be used in calculating $d^2\sigma/dE_e\,d\Omega_e$, being integrated over γ

The cross section $d^2\sigma/dE_e\,d\Omega_e$ for L-ionization by light atoms have been calculated using the formfactors from /6/. At sufficiently high energies, the energy spectra of electrons ejected from the projectile and target atom at small angles are separated in energy. Therefore one may use the sum rule to calculate the electron energy spectra in ion-atomic collisions. The doubly differential cross sections have been calculated in the coordinate systems related to both projectiles and target atoms. The relativistic effects at $E/A > 10$ MeV/amu have been included, whose magnitudes were estimated for light atom ionization in /6/.

Fig. 1a presents the values of $d^2\sigma/dE_e\,d\Omega_e$ for ionization of several hydrogenic states by protons. The curve obtained by scaling 1s-values according to /2/ is shown for comparison and differs ignificantly from the L-electron calculations. Comparison between the values of $d^2\sigma/dE_e\,d\Omega_e$ for H(nlm) ionization by nuclei (fig. 1a) and C atom (fig. 1b) has shown that at low E_e screening sharply decreases the $d^2\sigma/dE_e\,d\Omega_e$ values, but in the binary maxima region it is negligible. The calculated $d^2\sigma/dE_e\,d\Omega_e$ for N ionization by protons (fig. 2) are compared with experiment.

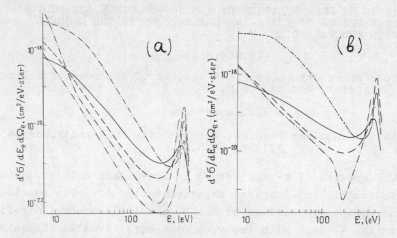

Fig.1. The values of $d^2\sigma/dE_e d\Omega_e$ for H(nlm) ionization by a proton (a) and C atom (b) at E/A= 250 keV/amu. The electron ejection angle $\chi_e =$ 1°. The solid curve is for 1s-ionization, the dotted curve for 2s , the curves (— ·· —) and (— · —) for $2p_0$ and $2p_1$. The curve (— ···· —) corresponds to the scaled 1s-values[2].

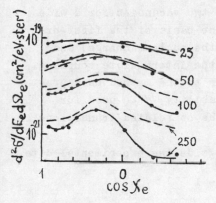

Fig.2.   The angular distributions of electrons ejected from nitrogen atom under 1.7 MeV proton bombardment. Electron energies E_e(eV) are indicated near the curves. Solid curve are experimental data from[7], dotted curves show our calculation for N atom, summed up over L-subshells and divided by 2.5.

REFERENCES

1. C.E. Kuyatt, T. Jorgensen, Phys.Rev. 130, 1444(1963).

2. G.N. Ogurtsov, Rev.Mod.Phys., 44, 1(1972).

3. S.T. Manson, L.H. Toburen, D.H. Madison, N. Stolterfoht,
   Phys. Rev. A12, 60(1975).

4. A.K. Kaminsky, S.V. Lovtsov, M.I.Popova, Phys.Lett.A61,308(1977).

5. B.H. Choi, E. Merzbacher, G.S. Khandelwall. Atomic Data,5,291(1973).

6. A.K. Kaminsky, R.A. Meshcherov, V.S. Nikolaev. Trans.Radiotechn.
   Inst. No.16, 330(1973).

7. J.B. Crooks, M.E. Rudd, Phys.Rev.A3, 1628(1971).

RATIO OF PROBABILITIES OF THE TWO-ELECTRON ONE-PHOTON
TRANSITIONS OF THE L-AND M-ELECTRONS TO THE K-SHELL
WITH TWO VACANCIES

U.I.Safronova

Institute of Spectroscopy, USSR Academy of Sciences, Podol'sky
district, Moscow, USSR.

V.S.Senashenko

Institute of Nuclear Physics, Moscow State University,Moscow
117234, USSR.

The spectra of x-rays formed in ion-atomic collisions have
been thoroughly investigated experimentally [1,2]. The twoelect-
ron one-photon transitions of the M- and L-electrons ($K_{\alpha\beta}$-li-
nes) to the K-shell with two vacancies were revealed alongside
the correlated transitions of two L-electrons ($K_{\alpha\alpha}$-lines). The
presently known calculations have been made, in fact, for the
two-electron systems with the variation wave functions [3] and
also on the basis of the many-body perturbation theory [4].

In the present paper, the calculations of the ratio of probabilities of the two-electron one-photon transitions of the
L-and M-electrons to the K-shell with two vacancies for a wide
region of Z have been performed on the basis of the first-order perturbation theory in $1/Z$ (Z is the nucleus charge) and
included the configuration mixing in the intermediate coupling.
The method of calculation is analogous to the method used previously in the papers [4,5]. The probability $W(K_{\alpha\alpha})$ used for
obtaining the probability ratios of the correlated transitions
was taken from [5].

Table 1. presents our results alongside the experimental data
and results of other authors.

Table I

Z	$W(K_{\alpha\beta})/W(K_{\alpha\alpha})$			3	4	Experiment 1,2
	present calculation					
	$1s^{-2}$	$1s^{-2}2s^{-1}$	$1s^{-2}2s^{-1}2p^{-1}$			
26	0.269	0.190	0.156	0.183	0.46	0.160±0.05 0.195±0.05
27	0.270	0.190	0.156	0.188	0.46	0.146±0.03
28	0.271	0.191	0.157	0.195	0.46	0.197±0.11
29	0.273	0.192	0.158	0.206	0.46	0.193±0.03
30	0.274	0.193	0.159	0.224	0.46	0.136±0.03

As one should expect, from the qualitative considerations, the value of $W(K_{\lambda\beta})/W(K_{\lambda\lambda})$ proved to be smaller than unit and in the accepted approximation, is increasing with Z which agrees with the results [3]. It is seen from the table that the ratio $W(K_{\lambda\beta})/W(K_{\lambda\lambda})$ is very sensitive to the structure of the considered atomic systems and dependent upon the number of additional vacancies in the electron shell.

The values of $W(K_{\lambda\beta})/W(K_{\lambda\lambda})$ obtained for the closed L-shell are somewhat larger than the experimental ones but their values can decrease with increasing number of vacancies. The inclusion of the configuration mixing and also the relativistic effects in the model with the same number of L vacancies doesn't effect the monotonous character of the Z-dependence at all Z we considered and cannot account for the available experimental data. At the same time, the assumption of a different number of vacancies in the L-shell of ions with different Z implies the nonmonotonous dependence of the ratio $W(K_{\lambda\beta})/W(K_{\lambda\lambda})$ upon which qualitatively agrees with the dependence observed experimentally.

1. C.Stoller et.al. Phys. Rev. 15A, 990, (1977)

2. W.N.Lennard et.al. J.Phys. 11B, 1283, (1978)

3. N.Moiseyev and J.Katriel Phys. Lett. 58A,303, (1976)

4. S.V.Khristenko Phys. Lett.59A, 202, (1976)

5. U.I.Safronova and V.S.Senashenko J.Phys.10B,L271,(1977)

TWO-ELECTRON, ONE-PHOTON, INNER-SHELL TRANSITIONS
IN NITROGEN IONS*

J. Richard Mowat and Erich Ormand

Department of Physics, North Carolina State University
Raleigh, North Carolina, USA

Atomic double K-vacancy states occasionally relax by a correlated transition whereby two L-shell electrons simultaneously jump to fill the two vacancies, and a single, monochromatic, x ray (designated $K\alpha\alpha$) is emitted. Previous experiments, summarized in Ref. 1, have concentrated on symmetric and nearly symmetric collisions between ions and either solid ($12 \leq Z \leq 28$) or gaseous[2,3] ($7 \leq Z \leq 10$) targets. We here present spectra obtained when N^+ ions collide with either a gaseous or a solid target.

N^+ ions from a 2MV Van de Graaff accelerator were magnetically analyzed and steered through a 1/16" diameter aperture into a windowless target region and were viewed at 90° by a Si(Li) detector. The target chamber, which could be flooded with gas, contained a ladder for solid targets. The 1/2 mil Be detector window severely attenuated projectile characteristic ($K\alpha$) and hypersatellite ($K\alpha^h$) x rays relative to $K\alpha\alpha$. X-ray energy calibration was performed with the detector in place and with 1 MeV protons incident of thick targets of Teflon, NaCl, MgO and Al.

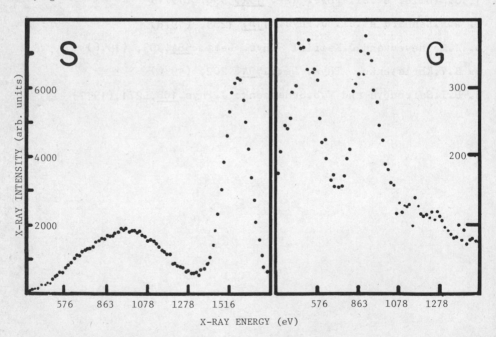

Some preliminary results obtained with 1 MeV N^+ ions are shown in the figure. Spectrum G was emitted from a ~ 400 milliTorr N_2 target. (The most probable charge state of 1 MeV nitrogen projectiles in N_2 gas[4] is N^{++}.) The two clearly resolved peaks are identified as nitrogen $K\alpha$ and $K\alpha\alpha$. Spectrum G is similar to one published in Ref. 2 for 0.2 MeV N^+ incident on NH_3, but exhibits better counting statistics. The $K\alpha\alpha$ energy is in reasonable agreement with the calculated value of Ref. 5.

Spectrum S was emitted from a solid aluminum target. The $A\ell$ $K\alpha$ line is evident, and a weaker, broader feature appears at a lower energy. (Neither spectrum has been corrected for detector window absorption.) This broad feature is tentatively interpreted as a quasi-molecular effect where a monotonically decreasing continuum is distorted into an apparent peak by the monotonically increasing detector window transmission.[6] There is no sign of N $K\alpha\alpha$ in spectrum S.

Work is in progress with other low Z ions.

*Supported by the Research Corporation and by the NSF (PHY 77-27526).

1. Ch. Stoller, W. Wolfli, G. Bonani, M. Stockli, and M. Suter, Phys. Rev. A15, 990 (1977).

2. Th. P. Hoogkamer, P. Woerlee, F.W. Saris, and M. Gavrila, J. Phys. B9, L145 (1976).

3. I.V. Mitchell, W.N. Lennard, and D. Phillips, Phys. Rev. A16, 1723 (1977).

4. H.D. Betz, Revs. Mod. Phys. 44, 465 (1972).

5. Bill Hodge, Phys. Rev. A16, 1543 (1977).

6. James R. Macdonald, Matt D. Brown, and Tang Chiao, Phys. Rev. Lett. 30, 471 (1973).

CHEMICAL EFFECT REFLECTED IN FLUORINE K^1L^n, K^2L^n AND RAE
SATELLITES INDUCED BY PHOTON AND ELECTRON IMPACTS

K. Maeda, H. Endo, M. Uda and Y. Sasa

The Institute of Physical and Chemical Research, Wako-shi, Saitama 351, Japan

Recently the L-shell vacancy refilling process prior to X-ray emission has been proposed to account for the bonding effect on the intensity distribution of F K^1L^n satellites produced by N^{4+} ions.[1] In heavy ion impact both Coulomb excitation and shake-off play an important role for producing multiple vacancy states, whereas on photon and electron impacts shake-off process is dominant for the multiple ionization of a light element such as F. Since relaxiation mechanism is independent of excitation modes, the same electron rearrangement should occur in photon and electron impacts. In this paper we employ the L-shell vacancy rearrangement process to explain the chemical effect reflected in the electron- and photon-excited F K^1L^n spectra. We also report the fluorine RAE (radiative Auger effect) satellites and K^2L^n hypersatellites.

Fig.1 shows the F K^1L^n peaks from several fluorides induced by photons and electrons. The spectra obtained by both the excitation modes are quite similar. For NaF the X-ray yield ratio of the K^1L^1 satellite to the diagram line K^1L^0, y_1^x/y_0^x, was independent of the impact electron energy of 3 - 9 keV. These facts support that the L-shell electron shake-off is dominant in K^1L^1 double ionization under such an experimental condition. As can be seen from Fig.1, the X-ray yield

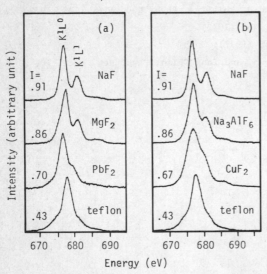

Fig.1. F K^1L^n spectra induced by (a) photons from X-ray tube (Rh-anode) and (b) electrons of 9 keV.

ratio y_1^x/y_0^x increased with the ionicity I of the fluoride. In the same way as in heavy ion impact, we assume that the primary vacancy distribution of F K^1L^n state, y_n, is not affected by the change in chemical bonding and the L-shell vacancy is filled by a ligand valence electron prior to X-ray emission. Then y_1^x/y_0^x is expressed as

$$\frac{y_1^x}{y_0^x} = \frac{\omega_1 \; (1 - f) \; y_1}{\omega_0 \; (f \, y_1 + y_0)} \qquad (1)$$

where ω_1 and ω_0 are fluorescence yields of K^1L^1 and K^1L^0 states, and f is the L-shell rearrangement probability defined as f = $\Gamma_L/(\Gamma_L + \Gamma_K)$, in which Γ_K and Γ_L

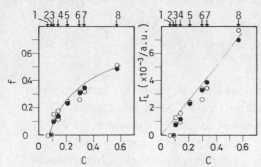

Fig.2. f and Γ_L plotted as functions of the covalency $C = 1 - I$, where I is the ionicity. o:photon-, ●:electron- and ——:N^{4+}-impacts. 1 CsF, 2 NaF, 3 LiF and CaF_2, 4 Na_3AlF_6 and MgF_2, 5 AlF_3, 6 NiF_2 and PbF_2 , 7 CuF_2 and 8 teflon.

are K- and L-shell widths. By means of Eq.(1), we calculated f and Γ_L values from the observed X-ray yield ratios. Here we assume f = 0 only for NaF, but not zero for the other fluorides, and also assume ω_1/ω_0 = 1.055 for all the fluorides. As shown in Fig.2, f and Γ_L increase with the covalency. f and Γ_L obtained by photon and electron impacts are in good agreement with those obtained by N^{4+} ion impact. This confirms that the L-shell vacancy refilling process is independent of the excitation modes.

Fig.3 (lower part) shows the low-energy side of the F K^1L^n lines from NaF and teflon. Asymmetric peaks A, B, C, D and E were observed in NaF. The energies of the peaks are close to the F KLL Auger electron energies (in Fig.3, upper part) and such asymmetric ones are characteristic of the satellites due to RAE. Hence these peaks are caused by RAE. Chemical effect could also be seen in RAE satellites. Teflon has a similar structure with that of NaF, but the peaks are much broader and the components B, C, D and E are not evident. Influence of chemical bonding to the hypersatellites due to K^2L^n states will be discussed.

Fig.3. The low-energy side of F K^1L^n induced by electron impact (lower part) compared with F KLL Auger electron spectra excited by Al $K\alpha_{1,2}$ (upper part).

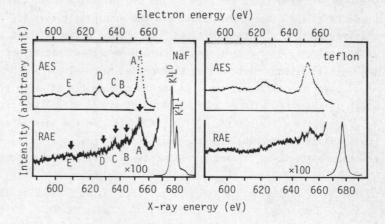

(1) M. Uda, H. Endo, K. Maeda, Y. Awaya, M. Kobayashi, Y. Sasa, H. Kumagai and T. Tonuma : to be published.

CHEMICAL EFFECTS THROUGH ELECTRON REARRANGEMENT PRIOR TO X-RAY EMISSION

M. Uda, H. Endo, K. Maeda, Y. Sasa and M. Kobayashi

The Institute of Physical and Chemical Research,
Wako-shi, Saitama 351, Japan

The use of enhanced $K\alpha$ satellites produced by ion impact has received much attention in recent years. Several investigations of change in intensity distributions of satellites have been performed on chemical compounds of F, Al, Si, S and Cl[1-5]. To explain chemical effects, an L shell vacancy refilling process is postulated in this paper. For quantitative and detailed understanding of the process a study of the satellites emitted from a wide range of target atomic number Z_2 is indispensable.

We have investigated the L shell vacancy rearrangement process in $K\alpha$ satellites produced by 6 MeV/amu N^{4+}, C^{4+}, α and p impacts. Chemical compounds composed of Z_2 = 9 - 35 were used for the comparison of their $K\alpha$ x-ray spectra which are expected to show chemical effects in their intensity distributions.

Assuming one-by-one cascading process of vacancy configurations and neglecting simultaneous multi-electron transfer to the L shell holes, the relaxed n^{th} satellite intensity y_n^X of the $K\alpha$ x-rays can be expressed by simultaneous equations,

$$y_n^X = \frac{\omega_n}{\bar{\omega}} (1 - f)(y_n + f_{n+1,n} \cdot y_{n+1} + f_{n+2,n+1} \cdot f_{n+1,n} \cdot y_{n+2} +$$
$$+ \ ----- \ + f_{8,7} \cdot f_{7,6} \cdot \ --- \ \cdot f_{n+1,n} \cdot y_8) \qquad --- \ (1)$$

where $\bar{\omega}$, ω_n, y_n and $f_{n,n-1}$ are the average fluorescence yield, a fluorescence yield of nth satellite, the term giving the initial L shell vacancy distribution produced at the time of collision, and the probability that $K^1 L^n$ configuration is transferred to $K^1 L^{n-1}$ through L shell refilling, prior to the K vacancy decay. If the velocity of incident ions is much higher than that of orbital electrons, the initial vacancy distribution is expected to be almost independent of the outer shell electron configurations. In such a case we can solve Eq.(1) to get $f_{n,n-1}$ which is connected with K- and L-shell widths, $\Gamma_K(K^1 L^n)$ and $\Gamma_L(K^1 L^n)$ as $f_{n,n-1} = \Gamma_L(K^1 L^n)/(\Gamma_K(K^1 L^n) + \Gamma_L(K^1 L^n))$. In the special case of small L shell ionization probability, the quantities $f_{n,n-1}$, $\Gamma_K(K^1 L^n)$ and $\Gamma_L(K^1 L^n)$ can now be replaced by $\tilde{f}$, $\tilde{\Gamma}_K$ and $\tilde{\Gamma}_L$ respectively which are independent of the L vacancy configurations. We deduced $\tilde{f}$ from the observed $K\alpha$ satellite intensities of F (NaF, Na_3AlF_6, AlF_3, NiF_2, CuF_2, $(CF_2)_n$), Na (NaF, Na_3AlF_6, Na_2SO_4, NaSCN, $Na_2S_2O_6$), Mg (MgO), Al (Al, Al_2O_3), S (Cu_2S, Na_2SO_4), Cl (KCl, NaCl), K (KCl), Ca (CaF_2), Fe (Fe, FeO, Fe_2O_3), and Ni (Ni, NiO), as shown in Fig.1. The solid line is for calculated $\tilde{f}$ values. Except F and Na, all the observed values of $\tilde{f}$ are smaller than the theoretical $\tilde{f}$ values.

Then we made a thorough investigation of F $K\alpha$ spectra. A dramatic change in intensity distributions depending upon the covalency of these fluorides can be seen in Fig.2. If we assume that ω_1/ω_0 is less sensitive to the change in the chemical environment than ω_2/ω_0, $\tilde{f}$, $\tilde{\Gamma}_L$ and ω_2/ω_0 can be estimated as shown in Fig.3. These values relate closely to the covalency of the fluorides. This means that the ion-excited x-ray spectroscopy is powerful tool to study chemical environments of the atoms whose x-ray transitions concern to their valence bands.

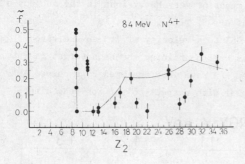

Fig.1. Z_2 dependence of an L shell refilling probability $\tilde{f}$, prior to $K\alpha$ x-ray emission.

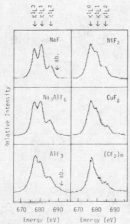

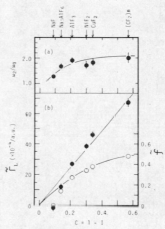

Fig.2. F $K\alpha$ satellite spectra of several fluorides induced by N^{4+}

Fig.3. $\tilde{\Gamma}_L$, $\tilde{f}$ and ω_2/ω_0 of F as a function of the covalency of the fluorides.

1) M.Uda, H.Endo, K.Maeda, Y.Awaya, M.Kobayashi, Y.Sasa, H.Kumagai, and T.Tonuma, Phys. Rev. Lett. (Submitted)

2) R.L.Watson, A.K.Leeper, B.I.Sonobe, T.Chiao, and F.E.Jenson, Phys. Rev.A15, 914 (1977)

3) R.L.Kauffman, K.A.Jamison, T.J.Gray, and P.Richard, Phys. Rev. Lett.36, 1074 (1976)

4) C.F.Moare, D.L.Matthews, and H.H.Wolter, Phys. Rev. Lett. 54A, 405 (1975)

5) J.A.Demarest and R.L.Watson, Phys. Rev. A17, 1302 (1978)

X-RAY SPECTROSCOPY OF HIGHLY EXCITED RECOIL IONS

H.F. Beyer, K.-H. Schartner[+] and F. Folkmann

Gesellschaft für Schwerionenforschung mbH, D-6100 Darmstadt, West Germany

[+]I. Physikalisches Institut der Justus Liebig-Universität, D-6300 Gießen, West
Germany

The ionization of neon atoms by impact of very heavy ions is the subject of the present investigation. The heavy ions Ar^{12+}, Ti^{14+}, Ni^{16+}, Kr^{18+}, Xe^{24+} and Pb^{36+} were accelerated by the UNILAC at GSI to a velocity of 7.5 au and were focussed into a differentially pumped gas cell containing the neon target gas at a constant pressure of 0.2 mbar. The neon K x rays were analyzed by a curved RbAP crystal spectrometer oriented perpendicular with respect to the ion beam direction.

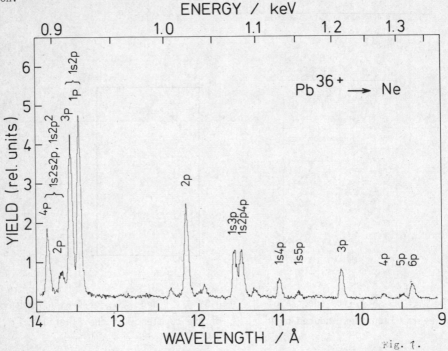

Fig. 1.

For line identification transition energies were calculated using a multi-configurational Dirac-Fock program[1]. The lines could be attributed to three, two and one-electron configurations[2]. Contributions from four electron configurations are very weak and get nearly lost for the impact of the heavier projectiles, where the degree of ionization is increased. In Fig. 1 the neon x-ray spectrum is displayed for the case of Pb^{36+} impact showing the high degree of ionization. The satellite spectrum is dominated by the helium-like configuration 1s2p, whereas in the high energy part of the spectrum a considerably high intensity from the

hydrogen-like series np → 1s is observed. The x rays are emitted by highly
ionized recoil ions, which have very small recoil energies of ≤ 10 eV thus making
possible the spectroscopic investigation of secondary collision processes like
electron capture discussed in detail in the subsequent contributions. Here consideration is given to these effects only with respect to seperating primary from
secondary population mechanisms. One consequence of electron capture is the strong
enhancement of the $^4P/^2P$ intensity ratio of the lithium-like satellites. The
1s2l2p ^4P states are nearly completely populated by cascading transitions from the
1s2lnl' ^4P states which themselves arise from the capture process 1s2l + e⁻ →
1s2lnl'.

The cascades have been subtracted and the extracted relative cross sections
$\sigma(KL^i)$ for producing one K-shell and i L-shell vacancies were compared with a binomial distribution (see Fig. 2). This yields L-shell ionization probabilities at
zero impact parameter ranging from 73% to 94% for the projectiles used in the
present experiment.

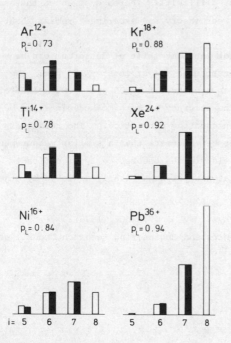

■ MEASURED RELATIVE CROSS SECTION $\sigma(KL^i)$

☐ BINOMIAL DISTRIBUTION

Fig. 2.
Relative cross sections for production of neon satellite configurations KL^i. The binomial distribution is adjusted at i=7.

1. J.P. Desclaux, Comput. Phys. Commun. 9, 31 (1975)
2. H.F. Beyer, K.-H. Schartner, F. Folkmann and P.H. Mokler, J. Phys. B11, L363
    (1978)

LAMB SHIFT MEASUREMENTS IN HYDROGENIC ION BEAMS
BY THE ANISOTROPY METHOD*

A. van Wijngaarden, S.P. Goldman and G.W.F. Drake

Department of Physics, University of Windsor,
Windsor, Ontario, Canada. N9B 3P4

The purpose of this paper is to describe the development over the past few years of an alternative method for measuring the Lamb shift in hydrogenic ions, and to present new results for He^+.   The method is based on the observation that when a hydrogenic ion beam in the metastable $2s_{1/2}$ state is subjected to an electric field, the induced Ly-α radiation intensity possesses an anisotropy in its angular distribution which is roughly proportional to the Lamb shift.   The ratio $I_{||}/I_{\perp}$ of the intensities emitted parallel and perpendicular to the applied electric field direction is measured.   The Lamb shift is derived from the value of the corresponding anisotropy defined by

$$R = \frac{I_{||} - I_{\perp}}{I_{||} + I_{\perp}}$$

Percentage uncertainties in theoretical calculations of the Lamb shift increase roughly as Z^2 along the isoelectronic sequence.   A theoretically significant measurement of the Lamb shift therefore need be less accurate at high Z than low Z.   Unfortunately, experimental difficulties increase at about the same rate so that ratios of uncertainties between theory and experiment remain about constant.

We have shown in previous work[1] that the Lamb shift of deuterium can be determined by the anisotropy method to an accuracy of at least $\pm$ 150 ppm.   We have now extended this work to He^+ with an accuracy of $\pm$ 200 ppm.   Our value of the Lamb shift is 14039.3 $\pm$ 2.9 MHz.   The accuracy of both measurements can be substantially improved with better photon counting statistics.   The relatively small loss in accuracy in going from D to He^+ suggests that a similar measurement for a somewhat heavier hydrogenic ion would yield a theoretically significant value of the Lamb shift - a goal which has not yet been clearly achieved by other methods.

1 A. van Wijngaarden and G.W.F. Drake, Phys. Rev. A 17, 1366 (1978).

* Research supported by the Natural Sciences and Engineering Research Council of Canada.

X-RAY TRANSITIONS IN SUPERHEAVY QUASI-MOLECULES[*]

W. Wölfli, E. Morenzoni, Ch. Stoller, G. Bonani and M. Stöckli

Laboratorium für Kernphysik, Swiss Federal Institute of Technology,
8093 Zürich, Switzerland

Molecular orbital (MO) X-rays emitted in heavy ion collisions exhibit a photon energy dependent anisotropy which is peaked near the transition energies of the united atom with combined atomic number $Z_u = Z_P + Z_T$, where Z_P and Z_T are the atomic numbers of the projectile and target atom, respectively. This effect was used to identify transitions into the minima of the $1s\sigma$ and $2p\sigma$ orbitals formed transiently during the collision time of a number of low Z_u-systems.[1-3]

We have investigated the anisotropy effect in the case of 20 superheavy systems with combined atomic numbers Z_u as high as 184. In each case a structure with well defined peaks was found. It is shown that the energy of these peaks reflects transitions into the minima of some of the M and L MO-orbitals of the corresponding superheavy quasi-molecules.

The experiments were performed at the ETH EN-tandem accelerator with heavy-ion beams of I, La, Pr, Sm, Ho, Ta, Au, Bi and U at energies between 13 and 60 MeV. Either self-supporting thin foils of high purity, thick enough to stop the beam, or thin films evaporated on a high purity aluminium stopper foils were used as targets. The following systems were investigated: I-Sb (104), I-I (106), I-Cs (108), I-La (110), I-Pr (112), La-La (114), Pr-Pr (118), Sm-Sm (124), Ho-Sm (129), Ho-Tb (132), Ho-Ho (134), Ho-Yb (137), Ta-Ta (146), Ta-Au (152), Au-Au (158), Au-Pb (161), Pb-Pb (164), Bi-Pb (165), U-Pb (174) and U-U (184). Normally the X-ray spectra were taken alternatively at 90° and 0° with a 80 mm^2 Si(Li)-detector or - for the heavier systems - with a 500 mm^2 HP Ge-detector. The anisotropy of the MO X-ray bands observed above the characteristic SA L-lines was determined from the 90° and 0° spectra according to the formula $A(E_x) = N(E_x, \Delta E_x, 90^{\circ})/N(E_x, \Delta E_x, 0^{\circ})-1$, where the number of counts N was determined from variable windows ΔE_x between 0.3 and 1 keV wide, depending on the statistics of the accumulated spectra. Prior to these evaluations the 0° spectra were corrected for the Doppler shift due to the centre-of-mass motion of the colliding system.

Fig. 1 gives an example of an anisotropy spectrum. In all other cases similar structures were observed which shift towards higher energies as the total nuclear charge of the colliding system is increased. Up to 5 different maxima are visible in each case, whose energies are plotted against Z_u in fig. 2. The comparison with the predicted UA neutral atom values (solid lines in fig. 2) of the lowest lying L and the M MO's suggest that all 5 peaks are correlated with the $3d_{3/2}$, $3p_{3/2}$

Fig.1. MO anisotropy spectrum obtained from the normalized 90° and 0° continua of the system Sm-Sm ($Z_u = 124$) at 42 MeV beam energy. At this low projectile energy only the region between the characteristic $L_{\gamma 1}$ and $K_{\alpha 1}$ X-ray lines of Sm can be investigated.

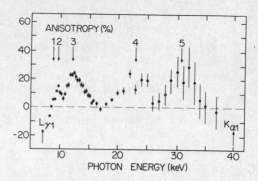

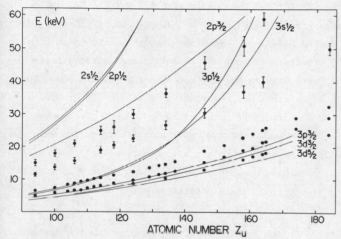

Fig.2. Plot of the anisotropy peak energies against Z_u as indicated in fig.1. For comparison the predicted L and M neutral united atom binding energies (solid lines) are shown.

and possibly the $2p_{3/2}$ but definitely not with the $3p_{1/2}$ and $3s_{1/2}$ orbitals. The fact that the energies of peak 3-4 exceed the UA-limit may indicate transitions into minima of the $3d\sigma$ and $3d\pi$ orbitals, which similar to the case of the $2p\sigma$ orbital, are reached not at the distance of closest approach but at considerably larger internuclear distances. Unfortunately a more quantitative comparison cannot be made at present, because the correlation diagrams of the higher lying MO's are only known with sufficient accuracy for systems with $Z_u \le 108$.[5]

---

* Supported by the Swiss National Science Foundation

1. Ch. Stoller, W. Wölfli, G. Bonani, M. Stöckli and M. Suter, J. Phys. B: Atom. Molec. Phys. 10, L347 (1977).

2. Ch. Stoller, W. Wölfli, G. Bonani, E. Morenzoni and M. Stöckli, Z. Physik A287, 33 (1978).

3. W. Wölfli, E. Morenzoni, Ch. Stoller, G. Bonani and M. Stöckli, Phys. Lett. 68A, 217 (1978).

4. W. Wölfli, Ch. Stoller, G. Bonani, M. Suter and M. Stöckli, Lett. Nuovo Cim. 14, 577 (1975).

5. J. Eichler, U. Wille, B. Fastrup and K. Taulbjerg, Phys. Rev. A14, 707 (1976).

MO X-RAY ANGULAR DISTRIBUTIONS FROM 1 GeV ^{208}Pb + ^{208}Pb AND ^{209}Bi + ^{209}Bi COLLISIONS [*]

Ch. Stoller, E. Morenzoni and W. Wölfli
Laboratorium für Kernphysik, Swiss Federal Institute of Technology,
8093 Zürich, Switzerland

W.E. Meyerhof
Department of Physics, Stanford University, Stanford CA 94305, USA

F. Folkmann, P. Vincent, P.H. Mokler and P. Armbruster
Gesellschaft für Schwerionenforschung, Postfach 110541, 6100 Darmstadt

The shape and the angular distribution of the molecular orbital (MO) X-rays emitted in ^{208}Pb + ^{208}Pb and ^{209}Bi + ^{209}Bi collisions have been measured. The experiments were performed at the UNILAC, GSI Darmstadt, with 4,7 MeV/N ^{208}Pb and 4,8 MeV/N ^{209}Bi beams using enriched ^{208}Pb (99%) and 99,9% pure Bi targets. The targets, oriented at 45° to the beam axis, were thick enough (40-60 mg/cm^2) to stop the beams. Two Ge(Li) detectors (86 cm^3 and 76 cm^3) placed alternatively at 90° and 0° to the beam axis were used to measure the MO X-ray spectra above the characteristic Pb and Bi K X-ray lines and absorbers of 2 or 3 mm Sn or Cd and $\sim$ 1 mm Cu or Al were used to keep counting rates below $\sim$ 4000 cps during beam pulses. A Si(Li) detector mounted above the beam axis at backward angles was used as a monitor to normalize the spectra to the same number of K X-rays. Calibrations and determinations of absorption and detector efficiencies were done by means of calibrated γ-sources placed in the scattering chamber at the target position.

In order to derive the pure photon spectra from the measured one the ambient background measured between the beam pulses and the spurious lines observed at 511 keV (positron annihilation), 570 keV, and 803 keV (Coulomb excitation in ^{207}Pb and ^{206}Pb respectively) or at 900 keV (^{209}Bi) as well as the Compton distribution of the MO continuum itself were all subtracted from the data. For the latter correction a simple method of rectangular Compton spectrum representation was used. Corrections for absorption and detector photopeak efficiency were then applied. Fig. 1 shows the resulting absolute thick target photon yields for Pb + Pb and Bi + Bi at 4,7 and 4,8 MeV/N. Above 400 keV the shape and magnitude agree well with the predictions of Kirsch et al.[1] for the Pb - Pb 1sσ-MO radiation. Contributions from transitions into higher lying MO's may be responsible for the deviation below 400 keV.

The directional anisotropy of the continuum radiation in its centre of mass frame was then calculated according to the formula
$A(E_x) = N(E_x, \Delta E_x, 90^\circ)/N(E_x, \Delta E_x, 0^\circ) - 1$, where the numbers of counts N were obtained from variable energy windows ΔE_x between 10 and 30 keV wide. The results of these calculations are displayed in fig. 2. In both the Bi and Pb cases, a distinct peak at 140 keV is seen which most probably can be explained by transitions

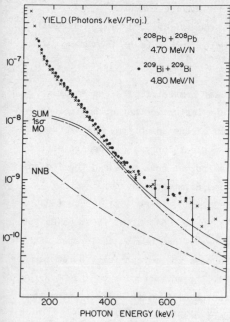

Fig.1. Absolute yield of continuum
X-rays from ^{208}Pb + ^{208}Pb (•) and
^{209}Bi + ^{209}Bi (×) collisions. The
curves show theoretical predictions
of Kirsch et al.[1] for 1sσ MO-radia-
tion and nucleus-nucleus bremsstrahlung (NNB).

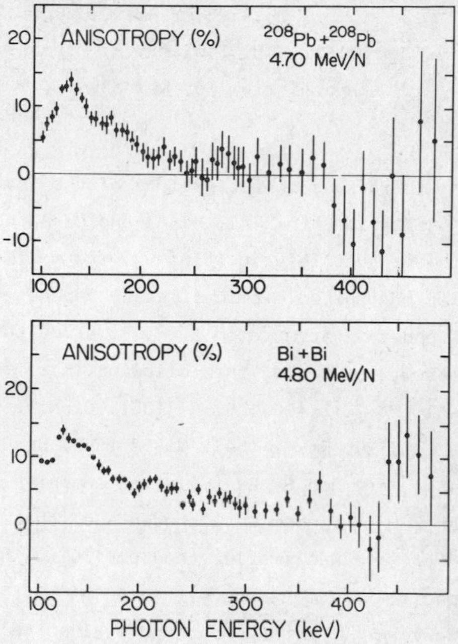

Fig.2. MO anisotropy spectra obtained from the normalized 90°
and 0° X-ray continua of the
systems ^{208}Pb + ^{208}Pb (upper part)
and ^{210}Bi + ^{210}Bi (lower part).

into the minima of one of the 2p orbitals formed not at the distance of closest
approach but at some larger internuclear distance. On the basis of these data the
possible existence of a peak associated with transitions into the united atomic
limit of the $2p_{1/2}\sigma$ shell at 400 keV could not be established due to large statistical errors, and the presence of backgrounds. For this reason the measurements have
been recently repeated using a lower beam energy (4.2 MeV/N), improved room background shielding, as well as an enriched ^{208}Pb ion source, and specially prepared
^{208}Pb target (≥ 99,96% ^{208}Pb). The results of these measurements will be presented.

*   Supported by the Swiss National Foundation, the U.S. National Science Foundation
     and the Danish Natural Science Research Council.

  1. J. Kirsch, W. Betz, J. Reinhardt, G. Soff, B. Müller and W. Greiner,
      Phys. Lett. 72B (1978) 298,
      and J. Kirsch, private communication

MO K X-RAY ANISOTROPIES AT LOW PROJECTILE ENERGIES[*]

<u>W. Wölfli</u>, Ch. Stoller, E. Morenzoni, M. Stöckli, P. Bürgy and G. Bonani

Laboratorium für Kernphysik, Swiss Federal Institute of Technology,
8093 Zürich, Switzerland

Previous investigations of the $1s\sigma$ molecular orbital (MO) X-ray angular distributions in F-Al, Al-Al and Cl-Al collisions indicated that at sufficiently slow projectile velocities v_p, the maximum value of the anisotropy peaks observed near the united atomic limit E_u depends on the nuclear charges of the projectile Z_p and the target atom Z_T [1]. To study this behaviour we have measured the $1s\sigma$ anisotropy spectra of the following 15 symmetric and asymmetric systems: F-Al ($Z_u = Z_p + Z_T = 26$), Cl-Al (30), Cl-Ni (45), Ti-Cu (51), Fe-Fe (52), Cr-Cu (53), Cu-Cr (53), Fe-Ni (54), Ni-Fe (54), Fe-Cu (55), Cu-Fe (55), Ni-Ni (56), Fe-Ge (58), Ge-Fe (58) and Ge-Ge (64). The energies of the heavy ions beams accelerated with the ETH EN-tandem were chosen such that in each case the adiabaticity parameter $a = v_p^2/v_e^2$ was smaller than 0.0175 ($v_e^2 = E_u/m_e$). The anisotropies of the MO X-ray spectra were measured with a 80 mm^2 Si(Li) detector of 5 mm thickness, using the experimental arrangement and evaluation procedure described in ref.[1].

The observed anisotropy peak maxima A_{max} versus Z_p/Z_T are displayed in fig. 1 for a constant adiabaticity of $a = 0.0069$. Clearly three different regions can be

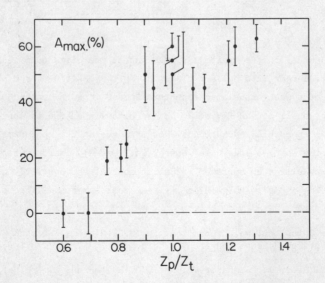

Fig.1

distinguished. A_{max} reaches a value of about 60% for all systems independently of Z_u, provided $Z_p \geq Z_T$. For asymmetric systems with $Z_p < Z_T$ the effect decreases rapidly and becomes negligibly small for $Z_p/Z_T \leq 0.7$. This behaviour can be understood if it is assumed that the anisotropy of the MO K X-ray transitions is the result of an alignment in the $2p\sigma$ and $2p\pi$ orbitals produced in a two collision process. The existence of such an effect has been predicted by Gross et al.[2] and Briggs et al.[3]. It should be noted, however, that the anisotropy shows a completely different behaviour if the projectile velocity is increased (see ref.[1]). This indicates that in the high velocity range ($a \geq 0.08$) a different mechanism may be responsible for the observed anisotropy of the MO K X-ray emission.

---

* Supported by the Swiss National Science Foundation.

1. W. Wölfli, Ch. Stoller, G. Bonani, M. Stöckli, M. Suter and W. Däppen, Z. Phys. A286 (1978) 249

2. M. Gros, P.T. Greenland and W. Greiner, Z. Phys. A280 (1977) 31

3. J.S. Briggs and K. Dettmann, J. Phys. B10 (1977) 1113

LINEAR POLARIZATION MEASUREMENT FOR QUASIMOLECULAR K RADIATION

P.H. Mokler[+], W.N. Lennard, and I.V. Mitchell

Chalk River Nucl. Labs., Canada; [+]GSI Darmstadt, Germany

Quasimolecular (MO-) x-ray radiation may be emitted during heavy ion-atom collisions. The corresponding emission patterns show non isotropic distributions. Several attempts have been tried to explain this fact. In order to shed more light on the excitation and emission mechanism for MO radiation the linear polarization of the K-MO radiation was determined for 1.3 MeV Mg → Mg and 1.7 MeV P → Si collisions at the Chalk River 2 MV Mass Separator using a 45° Bragg reflection polarimeter. X rays emitted perpendicular to beam direction were investigated, see Fig. 1. For such a 90° x-ray scattering with interchangeable diffracting

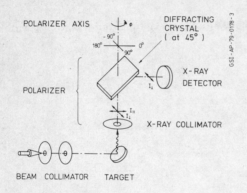

Fig. 1.

Sketch of experimental set up.

crystals only x rays having a polarization component (directions of the electric field vector) perpendicular to the scattering plane can be found at the Bragg-reflex. The x-ray intensity in this reflex was monotored by a Si(Li) detector. Rotating the whole assembly around the x-ray emission axis coinciding with the polarizer axis the linear polarization can be determined: $P = (I_\parallel - I_\perp)/(I_\parallel + I_\perp)$. $I_\parallel$ and $I_\perp$ are the intensities of x rays having linear polarization parallel or perpendicular to the original beam direction, respectively. $I_\parallel$ and $I_\perp$ are normalized via beam current integration. In the Table the found polarization values are given for the used crystals. The number in brackets at the collision

crystal x-ray energy	Ge 111 2.70 keV	LiF 200 4.36 keV	LiF 220 6.17 keV	
Mg → Mg (0.07)	8.2 ± 2	19 ± 2	40 ± 13	Tab. 1.
P → Si (0.06)	14 ± 2	8.3 ± 3	25 ± 8	Measured polarization values in percent.

system are the adiabaticity parameters determined by the ratio of impact velocity to K-orbital velocity in the united atom (u.a.) system, v_{imp}/u_K^{ua}. For the same adiabaticity parameter there exist calculations for linear polarization of the 1sσ radiation for the N-N collision system.[1] Scaling the various x-ray spectra

to the united-atom K radiation, $E_{rel} = 4\ E_x/E\text{-}K_\alpha^{ua}$, the results for the various
collision systems can be compared, see Fig. 2. First of all, we find for such a

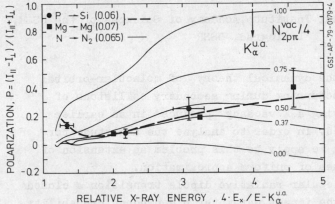

Fig. 2.

Measured and
calculated linear-
polarization.

representation that the experimental polarization values for both collision
systems coincide to one common curve. The parameters given for the calculated
curves are the probabilities of having $2p\pi$ vacancies at the beginning of the MO-
producing collision. For $2 \lesssim E_{rel} \lesssim 3.5$, the experimental values coincide about
with the theoretical curve calculated with $N_{2p\pi}^{vac}/4 = 0.4$. That means, that the
L shell of the projectile is ionized at a 80% level at the beginning of the
collision of interest. Looking on cross sections and double collision mechanism
active for our collision systems such a high ionization level seems not to be
unreasonable. The deviations to higher polarization values for higher x-ray
energies ($E_{rel} \sim 4.5$) may be caused by an increase in the $2p\pi$ ionization at small
internuclear distances due to direct excitation. The deviation at small x-ray
energies ($E_{rel} \sim 1.4$) is caused by transitions to the $2p\sigma$ level. This can be shown
by converting the polarization values into anisotropies. Assuming only E1
radiation a conversion gives the anisotropy values shown in Fig. 3. These values
coincide about with anisotropies given in the literature and measured for the same
adiabaticity parameters.

/1/ J.S. Briggs, J.H. Macek, K. Taulbjerg; AERE-Harwell-Report TP 734 (1978)

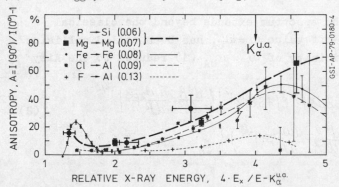

Fig. 3.

Anisotropies and con-
verted polarization
values.

THE ANISOTROPY OF THE X-RADIATION FROM TRANSIENT QUASI-MOLECULES

V.K.Nikulin

Ioffe Physico-Technical Institute,Academy of Sciences of the USSR,
Leningrad, USSR

In this report the dynamical theory of molecular-orbital (MO) x-ray emission occurring during secondary collisions of heavy-ion systems having a K vacancy produced in an earlier collision is discussed. In order to analyze the amplitude for emission of MO x-rays we apply to this problem an extension of the standard techniques of uniform approximation.

For a single molecular radiative dipole transition a closed form expression for the impact parameter b dependent probability $dP(b)/d\omega \, d\Omega$ of photon emission with the energy $\hbar\omega$ (coincidense spectrum) is derived. We take into account the time dependence of the dipole matrix elements and of the orientation of the molecular axis. The isotropic contribution of this spectrum for $2p\sigma{-}1s\sigma$ transition may be written in the form

$$dP(b)/d\omega = \frac{16\pi\omega^3}{3c^3}\left\{\left|<2p\sigma|\vec{z}\cdot\vec{\varepsilon}|1s\sigma>\right|^2\cdot\left|\frac{d\omega_{2p\sigma}}{dR}\cdot\frac{dR}{dt}\right|^{-1}\right\}_{t=t_\omega}$$

$$\times\left[\xi^{1/2}\cos^2\phi(t_\omega)\,Ai^2(\xi) + \xi^{-1/2}\sin^2\phi(t_\omega)\,Ai'^2(\xi)\right] \qquad (1)$$

Where $\hbar\omega_{2p\sigma}$ is the time-dependent energy difference between the $2p\sigma$ and $1s\sigma$ states at internuclear separation R(t)(t=0 is the time at the distance of closest approach); $\pm t_\omega$ are the two points of stationary phase; $\phi(t_\omega)$ is the angle between the directions of the internuclear axis at times $t=t_\omega$ and t=0; $\xi^{3/2}$ is the phase difference between the two points of stationary phase; Ai is the Airy function.

The fact that the spectrum extends beyond the classical united atom (UA) cut-off value $\omega = \omega_{UA}$ has been called collision broadening. In the vicinity of $\omega = \omega_{UA}$ (1) reduces to the Airy approximation

$$dP(b)/d\omega = \frac{8\pi\omega^3}{3c^3}\left\{\left|<2p\sigma|\vec{z}\cdot\vec{\varepsilon}|1s\sigma>\right|^2\cdot\left|\frac{1}{2}\frac{d^2R}{dt^2}\cdot\frac{d\omega_{2p\sigma}}{dR}\right|^{-2/3}\right.$$

$$\left.\times Ai^2\left((\omega-\omega_{2p\sigma})\middle/\left|\frac{1}{2}\frac{d^2R}{dt^2}\cdot\frac{d\omega_{2p\sigma}}{dR}\right|^{1/3}\right)\right\}_{t=0}. \qquad (2)$$

This approximation gives a good account of the emission spectrum in the tail of the photon energy distribution contrary to the quasi-static approximation. An estimate[1] of broadening Γ in this tail region for impact parameter b=0 gives $\Gamma \approx \frac{1}{4}\left(\frac{v^2}{D}\frac{d\omega}{dR}\right)^{1/3}$ (here v is the projectile velocity, D is the distance of closest approach at b=0, the quantity $d\omega/dR$ being evaluated at R = D). The last result is at variance with the arguments put forward in [2-4].

The integrated cross sections (singles spectra)and anisotropies were calculated for various radiative processes. Their photon energy dependence is investigated. An explanation is given to the measured [5] ratio between the x-ray energy at the inflection point of positive slope in the anisotropy peak and the united atom K_α transition energy.

[1] V.K.Nikulin, Abstracts of the Sixth International Conference on Atomic Physics, edited by E.Anderson, E.Kraulinya and R.Peterkop (Riga,1978) p.379.

[2] J.H.Macek and J.S.Briggs, J.Phys.B:AtomMolec.Phys. 7,1312(1974)

[3] B.Müller, The Physics of Electronic and Atomic Collisions IX, ed.by J.S.Risley and R.R.Geballe (Seattle, 1975), p.481.

[4] W.Fritsch and U.Wille, in Ref.1, p.316.

[5] C.Stoller, W.Wölfli, G.Bonani, M.Stöckli,and M.Suter,J.Phys. B: Atom.Molec.Phys. 10, L347 (1977).

A systematic study of the impact-parameter dependence of

quasimolecular radiation[*]

H.Schmidt-Böcking, K.Bethge, W.Lichtenberg, G.Nolte[+],R.Schuch[+],
H.J.Specht[+], K.E.Stiebing

Institut für Kernphysik der Universität Frankfurt,D-6000 Frankfurt/M
+ Physikalisches Institut der Universität Heidelberg,D-6900 Heidelberg

For all systems investigated so far the total cross sections of
quasimolecular K-radiation (K-MOR) show only structureless exponentially decaying slopes. According to different theoretical
approaches, however, impact-parameter dependent spectra should
show characteristic features of the K-MOR, e.g. "shoulder" near
E_{ua} (K_α-transition energy of the united atom) or interference
of transition amplitudes of incoming and outgoing part of the
collision. The existence of these structures has been investigated
by the impact-parameter dependence of K-MOR for the following
collision systems:

Si^{11+}	on Al	($4\mu g/cm^2$ /C-backing)	28 MeV
Si^{13+}	on Al	(" ")	28 MeV
S^{11+}	on NaCl	($20\mu g/cm^2$ ")	32 MeV
S^{15+}	on NaCl	(" ")	32 MeV
Ar	on NaCl	($30\mu g/cm^2$ ")	35 MeV
Ni^{58}	on Ni^{58}	($50\mu g/cm^2$)	90 MeV[+]
Pb^{208}	on Pb^{208}	($1500\mu g/cm^2$)	978 MeV[++]

For transition energies $E_x \approx E_{ua}$ the measured emission probabilities $dP(b,E_x)/dE_x$ show a strong impact-parameter dependence,e.g.
for Ni on Ni between b = 3000 fm and 300 fm an increase by more
than two orders of magnitude (see fig. 1). With increasing
nuclear charge the b dependence becomes even steeper. The
slope of the spectra for $E_x \gtrsim E_{ua}$ has been found b dependent too.
The spectra for hydrogenlike projectiles (e.g. Si^{13+} on Al) show
at large b-values the same shape as for Si^{11+} on Al and show not
the expected oscillations produced by the interference of decay
amplitudes between incoming and outgoing trajectory. At small b-
values oscillation amplitudes of the order of 30% peak to valley cannot
be excluded.

[*] Supported by BMFT

+   in cooperation with R. Anholt and P.Vincent, GSI-Darmstadt
++   in cooperation with D.Liesen, P.Mokler and P.Armbruster,
      GSI-Darmstadt, W-Germany

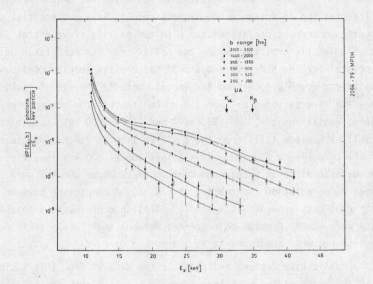

SELECTIVE OBSERVATION OF CONTINUUM RADIATION FROM THE Pb+Pb QUASIMOLECULE

P. Vincent, D. Schwalm, H. Bokemeyer, H. Emling, E. Grosse, GSI, Darmstadt, W-Germany

and J.S. Greenberg, Yale University, New Haven, Conn., USA

A coincidence experiment between continuum quasimolecular and characteristic K X-ray radiation from ^{208}Pb + ^{208}Pb collisions at 4.8 MeV/u has been carried out. The data indicate that the coincidence requirement results in a preferential observation of continuum transitions associated with the filling of vacancies in highly bound quasimolecular orbitals during the collision. Data were taken using a 3"x1 cm NaI crystal for the K X-rays and a 3x3" NaI crystal for the continuum X-rays both positioned roughly 3 cm from the target. Despite the use of isotopically enriched ^{208}Pb targets(.5 mg/cm^2 and 1.8 mg/cm^2 thick), the presence of lines from Coulomb excitation of ^{207}Pb (570 keV) and ^{206}Pb (800 keV) target contaminants, as well as Compton tails from the 3^- ^{208}Pb line at 2.6 MeV precluded observation of the coincidence continuum transitions above ~500 keV (see fig. 1). For the singles data, additional background contributions above 500 keV were caused by ambient room radiation (subtracted in fig. 1). A comparison between the thin and thick target data showed that multiple collision contributions to the coincidence data were small. Compton coincidences between the closely positioned detectors were also measured and found to be small.

The principle qualitative feature reflected in the data of fig. 1 is a significant change in the shape of the coincidence spectrum relative to the singles for photon energies below ~250 keV implying that large amounts of low energy continuum radiation are eliminated by imposing the coincidence requirement. As is illustrated in fig. 2, this observation can be qualitatively understood within the context of the molecular orbital picture since, in lowest order, only transitions between the most deeply bound $2p_{1/2}\sigma$ and $1s\sigma$ quasimolecular orbitals (high energy transitions) directly result in the presence of a vacancy in the separated atom K shell after the collision. Low energy transitions among the less tightly bound orbitals of the quasimolecule lead most diretly to the presence of separated atom L and M vacancies and are therefore discriminated against by the coincidence requirement.

Above 250 keV, the shapes of the singles and coincidence spectra are very similar. This observation in addition to considerations involving the relative magnitudes of the coincidence and singles yields suggests that either the shapes of both the singles and coincidence spectra at high photon energies are dominated by collision broadening effects or that processes other than $2p_{1/2}\sigma \rightarrow 1s\sigma$ transitions alone may be contributing to this part of the coincidence spectrum. The possible importance of these latter contributions depends most sensitively on the impact parameter dependence of the continuum radiation which has up to this time not been measured. However, despite these remaining questions involving quantitative inter-

pretation of the data, the main qualitative features of the results suggest that
the continuum radiation observed in these collisions is of quasimolecular origin
with low energy X-rays originating from loosely bound and high energy from tightly
bound orbitals.

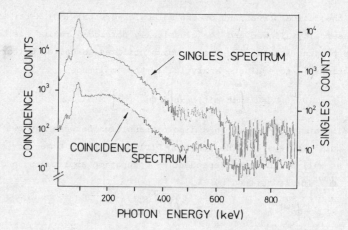

Fig. 1

Continuum singles (corrected for room background) and true coincidence spectra
from 4.8 MeV/u ^{208}Pb+^{208}Pb collisions. A 2.5 mm Sn and 1 mm Cu absorber has
been used to suppress copious K X-ray yields.

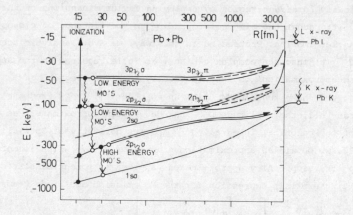

Fig. 2

Adiabatic molecular orbitals in the Pb+Pb quasimolecule as a function of internuclear distance R in fermis. Various molecular X-ray decay processes directly
leading to the production of separated atom K and L X-rays are illustrated.

ANALYTIC EXPRESSIONS FOR THE MOLECULAR-ORBITAL X-RAY SPECTRUM
IN THE CLASSICALLY FORBIDDEN REGION

W. Fritsch and U. Wille

Hahn-Meitner-Institut für Kernforschung Berlin GmbH
and Freie Universität Berlin, D-1000 Berlin 39, West Germany

A unified theoretical treatment of the molecular-orbital (MO) X-ray emission
in both the classically *allowed* and the classically *forbidden* region has been given
recently by the present authors[1,2]. The approach utilizes so-called uniform asymptotic approximations[3,4] to evaluate analytically the amplitude

$$D^{(\omega)} = \int_{-\infty}^{+\infty} dt\; D(t)\; \exp\left[i\; \phi^{(\omega)}(t)\right] \tag{1}$$

for X-ray emission at frequency ω in a dipole transition between any two MO of a
quasimolecular collision system. The function $D(t)$ comprises a time-varying dipole
matrix element as well as the time-dependent MO occupation amplitudes, and the
phase function $\phi^{(\omega)}(t)$ is defined by

$$\phi^{(\omega)}(t) = \omega t - \int_{0}^{t} dt'\; \Delta(R(t')) , \tag{2}$$

where the MO energy difference $\Delta(R)$ depends on time through the time dependence
of the internuclear distance $R = R(t)$. The uniform approximations systematically
generalize the simple stationary-phase approximation, which in the evaluation of
$D^{(\omega)}$ is applicable only in the classically *allowed* region[5].

In the present contribution, we study the behavior of the MO emission spectrum
in the classically *forbidden* region by employing Taylor expansions of the functions
$D(t)$ and $\phi^{(\omega)}(t)$ about the time corresponding to the distance of closest approach
of the internuclear motion. Proceeding in this way, we avoid analytic continuation
of $D(t)$ and $\phi^{(\omega)}(t)$ into the complex t-plane, as it is required in the application
of the uniform approximations in the classically forbidden region.

Expanding the phase function $\phi^{(\omega)}(t)$ up to order n+1 (n $\geq$ 2) and the function
$D(t)$ up to order n-1, the amplitude $D^{(\omega)}$ can be written approximately as a linear
combination of the canonical integral[4] $U^{(n)}$ and its derivatives. Specializing to
the case n = 2, we obtain an approximation scheme for $D^{(\omega)}$, which is mathematically
equivalent to the simple Airy approximation[6] applied in potential scattering theory. The resulting explicit expression for the MO emission amplitude reads

$$D^{(\omega)} = 2\pi\, (\dddot{\phi}_0/2)^{-1/3} \left\{ D_0\, \mathrm{Ai}\left[\dot{\phi}_0^{(\omega)}\, (\dddot{\phi}_0/2)^{-1/3}\right] \right.$$
$$\left. - i\, \dot{D}_0\, (\dddot{\phi}_0/2)^{-1/3}\, \mathrm{Ai}'\left[\dot{\phi}_0^{(\omega)}\, (\dddot{\phi}_0/2)^{-1/3}\right] \right\} \tag{3}$$

where quantities labelled by "o" refer to the distance of closest approach R_0. The
Taylor coefficients $\dot{\phi}_0^{(\omega)}$ and $\dddot{\phi}_0$ are given by

$$\dot{\phi}_0^{(\omega)} = \omega - \Delta_0 , \quad \dddot{\phi}_0 = -\Delta_0'\, \ddot{R}_0 \tag{4}$$

Note that $\ddot{\phi}_o$ vanishes due to the condition $\dot{R}_o = 0$. Assuming $\Delta(R)$ to be a monotonically decreasing function of R, we have $\Delta'_o < 0$ and hence $\ddot{\phi}_o > 0$; the classically forbidden region is then defined by the condition $\omega > \Delta_o$. The dynamics of the internuclear motion enters eq.(3) only via the *radial acceleration* $\ddot{R}_o$.

The expression (3) is formally valid for all ω-values. In the classically allowed region $\omega \lesssim \Delta_o$, however, the uniform Airy approximation is easily applicable[1,2] and will generally give a better approximation to $D^{(\omega)}$ than does the simple Airy approximation. In the classically forbidden region, the (standard) uniform approximations tend to break down if a complex saddle point of $\phi^{(\omega)}(t)$ approaches one of the complex singularities of $D(t)$. In these cases, the expression (3) still provides a meaningful approximation which should be particularly accurate for frequencies close to the classical threshold Δ_o.

As compared with the approximations leading to eq.(3), the approach of Macek and Briggs[5] relies on an expansion of $\phi^{(\omega)}(t)$ up to *second* order about some point off the distance of closest approach and assumes that the radial velocity $\dot{R}$ at this point is close to the (asymptotic) collision velocity. Therefore, the treatment of the MO emission amplitude by means of the simple Airy approximation is not a generalization of the Macek-Briggs theory, but rests on different physical and mathematical assumptions.

In the asymptotic region $\dot{\phi}_o^{(\omega)} (\dddot{\phi}_o/2)^{-1/3} \gg 1$ (simple estimates show that the latter condition is not well fulfilled for most of the cases investigated so far experimentally), the X-ray spectrum derived from eq.(3) is characterized, for fixed impact parameter b and collision velocity v, by a fall-off according to $\exp\left[- \text{const.}\ (\omega - \Delta_o)^{3/2}\right]$. The uniform Airy approximation gives[1,2] a behavior proportional to $\exp(- \text{const.} \omega)$, whereas the Macek-Briggs treatment[5] results in a fall-off according to $(\omega - \Delta_o)^{-6}$. For the half-width of the frequency broadening beyond the classical threshold Δ_o, one obtains from the asymptotic form of eq.(3) the expression $\Gamma_{1/2} = 0.513\ (|\Delta'_o| \ddot{R}_o)^{1/3}$. The velocity dependence of this width can be shown to follow, for arbitrary impact parameters, approximately a $v^{2/3}$ law. This result is intermediate between the result of Macek and Briggs[5] and that derived by means of the uniform Airy approximation[1,2].

Detailed model studies based on the expression (3) as well as on the generalized expressions obtained by extending the expansions of $\phi^{(\omega)}(t)$ and $D(t)$ to higher orders are in preparation.

1. W. Fritsch and U. Wille, Proc. 6th Int. Conf. on Atomic Physics (Riga, 1978), Abstracts, p.316.

2. W. Fritsch and U. Wille, Jap. J. Appl. Phys. Suppl., in press.

3. C. Chester et al., Proc. Cambridge Phil. Soc. 53, 599 (1957).

4. J.N.L. Connor, Molec. Phys. 27, 853 (1974).

5. J.H. Macek and J.S. Briggs, J. Phys. B7, 1312 (1974) [Corrigendum: J.Phys. B8, 156 (1975)].

6. M.V. Berry, Proc. Phys. Soc. 89, 479 (1966).

SEARCH FOR BONDING EFFECTS ON REC AND MO X-RAYS
IN HEAVY ION-ATOM COLLISIONS

H. Endo, M. Uda, Y. Sasa, Y. Terasaka,
K. Maeda, and M. Kobayashi

The Institute of Physical and Chemical Research,
Wako-shi, Saitama 351, Japan

In the X-ray emission accompanied by the passage of stripped heavy ions through solids, four types of radiation are expected:

1) Characteristic X-ray radiations;

2) A continuum X-ray radiation due to nuclear and electronic bremsstrahlung;

3) A broad X-ray band due to radiative electron capture (REC) which is a transition from the bound electron of the target to the K shell-hole of the projectile;

4) Radiative electronic transitions between temporarily formed quasi-molecular orbitals (MO's) made up of energy levels of the target atom and the incident heavy ion.

Processes 1) and 2) are, in general, less sensitive to the change in the chemical environment of ionized atom in target material. The REC cross section and its spectral shape are, however, directly related to the Compton profile[1] and then these may be sensitive to electronic momentum distributions of weakly bound electrons, i. e., valence electrons in a target system. The MO X-ray is arised from the radiative decay of a vacancy in the projectile, which has been transfered to an quasimolecular orbital through crossing of many levels including outer shells[2]. Then the bonding structure of target atom should be reflected in the cross section and spectral profile of MO radiation.

We have investigated the bonding effect on REC and MO radiations from various chemical compounds with different bonding characters. Significant differences were found in REC profiles obtained from 120-MeV nitrogen-ion impact on C, polypropylene, mylar, collodion, CAB, and teflon. Fig.1 shows spectra of MO radiations emitted from Si, SiO_2, Al and AlF_3 on 180 KeV Ar^+ bombardment. For metals and their chemical compounds extreme differences can be found in relative cross sections of characteristic and MO X-rays. The quantitative

39. *Inner-shell ionization: Continuum X-ray and electron emission. I*

739

discussion on cross sections and spectral profiles of the REC and MO radiations
will be given.

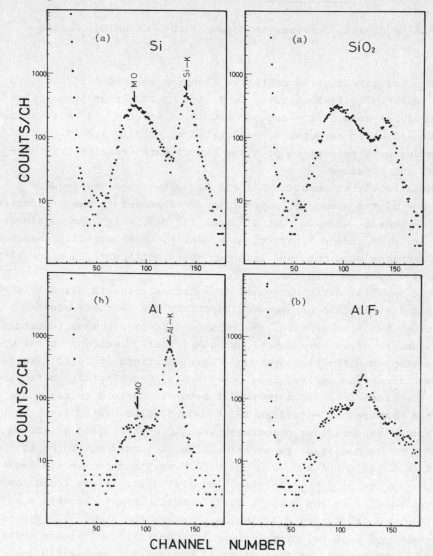

Fig.1: (a) 180-KeV Ar$^+$ on thick Si and SiO$_2$. (b) 180-KeV Ar$^+$ on thick Al
and AlF$_3$.

1) H. W. Schnopper, H. D. Betz, J. P. Delvaille, K. Kalata, and A. R. Sohval,
Phys. Rev. Lett. 29, 898 (1972).
2) F. W. Saris, W. F. Weg, H. Tawara, and R. Laubert, Phys. Rev. Lett. 28, 717
(1972).

RADIATIVE ELECTRON CAPTURE IN FAST HEAVY ION-ATOM COLLISIONS

E. Spindler, H.-D. Betz, F. Bell

Sektion Physik, Universität München, 8046 Garching, Germany

We have investigated radiative electron capture (REC) in fast heavy ion-atom collisions using O, S, Ar, Cu and Br as projectiles with energies between 20- and 360 MeV ($0.03 \leqslant v/c \leqslant .14$) and various gaseous and solid targets. We have tried to clarify some discrepancies with respect to previous experimental results and theoretical descriptions.

Measurement of absolute K-shell REC cross sections require knowledge of the number of appropriate K-vacancies in the projectile. For this reason, we used fast O^{8+} ions (97 MeV) which remain almost fully stripped inside a target. As a result, experimentally obtained cross sections were obtained which do not significantly deviate from theoretical values (Fig. 1).

The spectral distribution of REC-photons reflects directly the momentum distribution of captured electrons due to their binding in the target prior to capture. If one uses appropriate wave functions (i. e. Hartree-Fock wave functions both for all electrons in gaseous target atoms and for tightly bound inner electrons in solid targets; and wave functions derived from experimental Comptonprofiles for the outer electrons in solid targets) it becomes possible to reproduce well the measured REC-profiles in gases and solids (Fig. 2.).

Former expectations concerning angular distribution of REC-photons had to be modified: retardation effects turned out to be of significant influence and lead to large deviations from a $\sin^2\theta$-dependence in the projectile system. In particular, it was found that retardation effects and Doppler transformation behave in such a way that observed laboratory distributions retain the simple $\sin^2\theta$-form independent of beam velocity (except for quadratic and higher terms in v/c). Furthermore, we find at small observation angles (10°) relatively large REC-intensities which are enhanced by a factor of ~ 2.5 compared with a $\sin^2\theta$-dependence. This can be understood quantitatively by taking into account transverse momenta of strongly bound electrons.

On the basis of the above and other findings not communicated here we believe that the REC-process in heavy ion-atom collisions is reasonably well understood. REC-measurements could now be used to extract Compton profiles. Furthermore, one can use REC-measurements to extract mean numbers of vacancies in specific shells of projectile ions transversing solid targets. In case of 140-MeV Br on C, the number of L-vacancies turns out to be 100 times larger compared with vacancy numbers deduced from charge state measurements behind the foil.

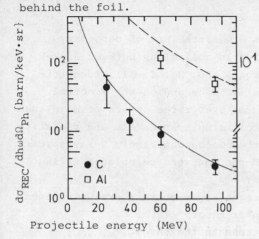

Fig. 1: Measured and calculated REC-cross sections per K-hole (in the maximum of the profile) for C- and Al-targets, as a function of oxygen projectile energy.

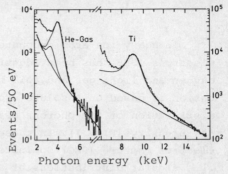

Fig. 2: REC profiles in He gas (97 MeV O) and Ti (346 MeV Ar); experiment (histogramm) and theory (smooth curve).

BREMSSTRAHLUNG OF SECONDARY ELECTRONS IN FAST ION-ATOM COLLISIONS

E. Spindler, H.-D. Betz, F. Bell

Sektion Physik, Universität München, 8046 Garching, Germany

In heavy ion-atom encounters Bremsstrahlung of secondary electrons (SEB) has been identified in collisions between 95-MeV oxygen and light gas and foil targets (He, Ne, C, Al). Identification is based on absolute cross sections and on the spectral distribution of SEB-photons measured over three orders of magnitude in intensity (Fig. 1). In these collision systems SEB and radiative electron capture (REC) dominate the noncharacteristic X-ray spectra.

Angular distributions of SEB-photons were calculated taking into account the following points:

1. Energy and emission angle of secondary electrons are calculated in the frame of "binary encounter theory" (BEA).
2. Energy loss of secondary electrons in the target.
3. Retardation in the angular distribution of Bremsstrahlung.
4. Polarisation of Bremsstrahlung as a function of photon energy.
5. SEB by projectile electrons, when present, is included.

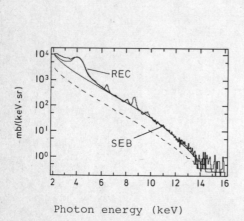

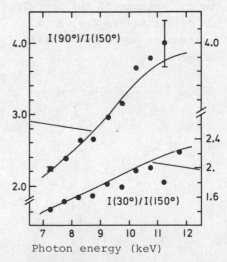

Fig.1: Measured photon spectrum for 97-MeV O→C (histogramm). Calculated distributions: REC and SEB (smooth curve), SEB from C-K-electrons (broken curve).

Fig.2: Intensity ratios for specified observation angles (93-MeV O→ Al). Measurements (full points) are compared with calculations, multiplied by .65 (smooth curve).

The experimental spectral distribution of SEB-photons at different observation angles is reproduced by our calculations (Fig. 2). Particularly the lower curve of Fig. 2 shows that retardation leads to forward-backward asymmetries which increase with energy. The measured angular distribution at fixed photon energies is not as pronounced as the calculated one. This may indicate that one should also account for the angular straggling of secondary electrons in the target foil.

TARGET THICKNESS ANALYSIS OF PROJECTILE K X-RAYS

AND REC FOR 40-80 MeV Cl on C

J. A. Tanis[+], S. M. Shafroth

University of North Carolina, Chapel Hill, and

Triangle Universities Nuclear Laboratory, Durham

and

J. R. MOWAT, North Carolina State University, Raleigh

A systematic investigation of projectile K x-rays and REC production cross sections has been undertaken for Cl^{q+} ($q \leq 10$) ions incident on thin (10-$100\mu g/cm^2$) carbon foils, at 40, 60 and 80 MeV incident energy. Data were parameterized according to the model of Betz et al.[1] in which the fraction[2] of ions with a K vacancy at a depth x in the foil is given by $Y(x) = (\sigma_v/\sigma)(1 - e^{-\sigma x})$. Where $\sigma = \sigma_v + \sigma_c + \sigma_\tau$ and σ_v is the K vacancy production cross section for the projectile in the foil, σ_c is the cross section for capture of a C electron to the projectile K shell, and σ_τ is the cross section for Cl K x-ray or Auger decay. Furthermore the projectile K x-ray production cross section $\sigma_x^P(T)$ for a foil of thickness T is given by[3,4]:

$$\sigma_x^P(T) = \frac{\lambda_x \sigma_v}{\sigma} + \left[\sigma_{xo}^P - \frac{\lambda_x \sigma_v}{\sigma}\right]\left(\frac{1 - e^{-\sigma T}}{\sigma T}\right)$$

where λ_x is the radiative decay probability per unit path length and σ_{xo}^P is the zero thickness projectile K x-ray production cross section.

Also[5] $\dfrac{d\bar{\sigma}_{REC}}{d\Omega}(T) = \dfrac{d\sigma^\circ_{REC}}{d\Omega}\left(\dfrac{\sigma_v}{\sigma}\left[1 - \dfrac{1}{\sigma T}(1 - e^{-\sigma T})\right]\right)$ where $\dfrac{d\sigma^\circ_{REC}}{d\Omega}$ is the zero thickness REC cross sections per K vacancy. Table I summarizes results of a least squares analysis of the target thickness study.

We find that Cl K vacancy production in C targets is about half that observed for Cu targets.[3] REC cross sections in C are about 2-3 times smaller than for Cu which is consistent with Bethe-Salpeter theory if it is assumed that each electron contributes equally to REC.[5] We acknowledge support of the UNC Research Council and the D.O.E. Division of Chemical Sciences Office of Basic Energy Sciences Atomic Physics Program.

1. H. D. Betz, F. Bell, H. Panke, G. Kalkoffen, M. Welz and D. Evers, Phys. Rev. Lett. 33, 807 (1974).

2. T. J. Gray, P. Richard, K. A. Jamison and J. M. Hall, Phys. Rev. A14, 1333 (1976).

3. J. A. Tanis and S. M. Shafroth IEE Transactions on Nuclear Science NS-26, 1068 (Feb. 1979) and Phys. Letts. 67A, 124 (1978).

4. K. O. Groeneveld, B. Kolb, J. Schader and K. D. Sevier, Z. Physik A277, 13 (1976).

5. J. A. Tanis and S. M. Shafroth, Phys. Rev. Letts 40, 1174 (1978).

[+]Present address: Lawrence Berkeley Lab, Univ. of California

Table I. Results of Target Thickness Analysis of
Projectile K X-ray Cross Section Data[*]

E_{Cl}	40 MeV	60 MeV	80 MeV[*]
σ_{xo} (kb)	35.2 ± 1.8	97.5 ± 2.6	157 ± 5
$\lambda_x \sigma_v$ (kb)^2	$44,100 \pm 8,000$	$59,400 \pm 12,000$	$21,500 \pm 4,300$
σ (kb)	$2,760 \pm 650$	$1,270 \pm 410$	620 ± 190
$\dfrac{d\sigma_{REC}^o}{d\Omega}\sigma_v\left(\dfrac{b}{sr}\right)$ (kb)	$43,900 \pm 810$	$44,900 \pm 790$	$35,700 \pm 500$

	INFERRED PARAMETERS		
ω (from Cl$\rightarrow$Cu)^a	0.30	0.42	0.64
$\sigma_v = \sigma_{xo}/\omega$ (kb)	120 ± 6	230 ± 6	250 ± 12
$\dfrac{d\sigma_{REC}^o}{d\Omega}\left(\dfrac{b}{sr}\right)$ Expt.	370 ± 60	190 ± 30	145 ± 20
Theory^b	460	280	190
$\sigma_c = \sigma - \sigma_v - \sigma_\tau$ (kb)	1400	420	240
$\sigma_{REC} = \dfrac{8\pi}{3}\dfrac{d\sigma_{REC}^\Omega}{d\Omega}$ (kb)	3.1	1.6	1.2
$\omega_{REC} = \dfrac{\sigma_{REC}}{\sigma_c}$	2.3×10^{-3}	4.8×10^{-3}	5.1×10^{-3}
λ_x (kb)	380	260	88
$\sigma_\tau = \dfrac{\lambda_x}{\omega}$ (kb)	1250	608	140
τ_x (10^{-14} sec) Expt.^{c}	1.8	2.2	5.4
Single K vacancy (10^{-14} sec) Theory^d	1.1	1.1	1.1

[*]Analysis was done assuming only single K vacancy production. The K_α and K_β hypersatellites were not included.

^{a}Ref. 3.

^{b} $6 \dfrac{d\sigma_{REC}^o}{d\Omega}$ (Bethe-Salpeter)

^{c}Calculated from $\tau_x = 1/nv\lambda_x$ where n = atomic density (atoms/cm^3) and v = incident velocity.

^{d} J. H. Scofield, Phys. Rev. $\underline{A9}$, 1041 (1974).

CONTINUOUS ELECTRON SPECTRA PRODUCED IN Kr^{n+} - Kr COLLISIONS

Yu.S. Gordeev[*], P.H. Woerlee, H. de Waard and F.W. Saris

FOM-Institute for Atomic and Molecular Physics
Kruislaan 407, Amsterdam, The Netherlands

Cross sections for the production of secondary electrons as function of the projectile charge state have been measured. Krypton beams with charge states from 2+ to 5+ and projectile energies between 50 and 1000 keV have been used. Electrons with energies between 80 and 1000 eV and emission angles between 45 and 135 degrees have been measured.

A typical spectrum for 200 keV Kr^{2+} - Kr ($\theta = 90^{\circ}$) is shown in fig. 1.

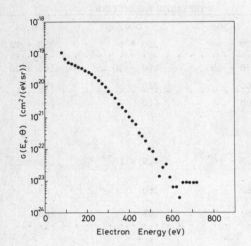

Fig.1.

Electron energy spectrum arising from 200 keV Kr^{2+} collisions on Kr measured at an electron emission angle of $\theta = 90^{\circ}$ with respect to the beam direction.

In this figure it is seen that the dominant part has a band structure and lies between 100 and 300 eV. This part of the spectrum was attributed by Afrosimov et al. [1] to a molecular autoionisation of the $4p\pi$ MO during the collision. In fact they could obtain details about the shape and the energy of this MO from the high energy limit of this band but were limited by rather low projectile energies. We have extended these measurements to higher projectile energies and measured also the angular distributions and charge state dependence. The MO obtained from the experimental spectra using the procedure similar to that used in [1] is shown in fig. 2. In our experiment we could achieve small internuclear distances $R \approx 0.02$ Å and in this region the experimental MO is close to the 4p level of the united atom. This confirms the interpretation of the experimental MO as the $4p\pi$ orbital of the Kr_2 system.

We found only a weak dependence on the projectile charge state which indicates that the $4p\pi$ MO has already a high degree of ionisation. Also the angular distribution was, after correction for kinematical effects, found to be almost

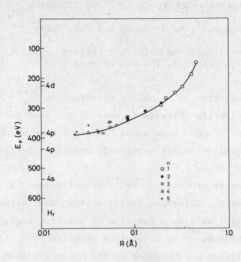

Fig.2.
MO obtained from the ex-
perimental Kr^{n+}-Kr data
(n = 2,3,4,5) using the
procedure similar to
that used in [1].

isotropic. The measured spectra are in reasonable agreement with simple model calculations. However at higher projectile energies an exponential tail for electrons
with energies above 300 eV starts to dominate the spectrum. Possible mechanisms
that can be responsible for this tail are studied in [2].

[1]   V.V. Afrosimov, Yu.S. Gordeev, A.N. Zinoviev, A.A. Korotov, A.P.
        Skergin, INT. Conf. Phys. Elec. Atom. Collisions, pp 924 (1977)
[2]   P.H. Woerlee, Yu.S. Gordeev, H. de Waard en F.W. Saris
        this conference.

*On leave from A.F. Ioffe Physical Technical Institute, Leningrad K-21, USSR.

CONTINUOUS ELECTRON SPECTRA PRODUCED IN Ne^{n+} - Ne COLLISIONS

P.H. Woerlee, Yu.S. Gordeev[*], H. de Waard and F.W. Saris

FOM-Institute for Atomic and Molecular Physics
Kruislaan 407, Amsterdam, The Netherlands

Experimental results for production of secondary electrons in Ne^{n+} - Ne collisions will be presented. Projectile energies between 25 and 1100 keV and projectile charge states from 1 to 4+ have been used. Electrons with energies between 16 and 500 eV and with emission angles between 45 and 135 degrees have been studied.

Measurements of electron spectra produced in Kr^{n+} - Kr collisions [1] showed that the spectra consist of two different parts: a broad band attributed to MO Auger decay and an exponential tail as a function of electron energy. Measurements of electron spectra for Ne^{n+} - Ne collisions show (see fig. 1) that in this case the exponential distribution dominates in the whole electron energy range higher than 20 eV.

Fig. 1.

Electron energy spectrum arising from 200 keV Ne^{2+} collisions on Ne measured at an electron emission angle of $\theta = 90^{\circ}$ with respect to the beam direction.

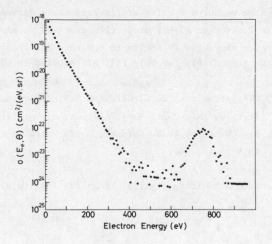

Similar results have been obtained before in several experiments (see for instance Cacak et al. [2]) and this behaviour seems to be a general feature of electron spectra for high energy heavy ion-atom collisions. The cross sections in the region of the exponential distribution decrease when the projectile charge state is increased in the Kr^{n+} - Kr case, for Ne^{n+}-Ne collisions this decrease is even stronger. The angular dependence of this part of the spectra is more anisotropic than for MO Auger electrons. Therefore we think that another mechanism than the Auger decay in the quasi-molecule will be responsible for the observed electrons. The charge state dependence points to a molecular origin of the electron production, instead of impact ionisation. If this is true the measured laboratory cross sections must be corrected for kinematical effects in the centre of mass system, which results in a symmetric angular distribution around 90 degrees. When we plot differential cross sections for 90 degrees (i.e. kinematic corrections are small) on a log-linear scale as a function of $1/v$ (inverse projectile velocity) and the electron energy as a parameter we obtain straight lines with increasing slope as the electron energy increases. This indicates that a direct radial coupling between MO's and the continuum may be important. We also find that the slope of the lines is linearly dependent on the electron energy i.e.

$$S = (^1/\alpha) \cdot (E_e - \delta), \alpha \text{ and } \delta \text{ are constants.}$$

As a result the cross sections can be written as

$$\sigma(E_e) \approx C \exp - \frac{(E_e - \delta)}{\alpha v}$$

Probably highly promoted MO's like the $4f\sigma$ are involved. These types of MO's can have a strong coupling with the continuum because they are promoted very rapidly in a very short range of internuclear distances. In this case we can convert cross sections to probabilities since

$$\sigma(E_e) = 2\pi \int_o^{b_o} P(b, E_e) b \, db = \pi b_o^2 P(E_e)$$

Empirically we find that

$$P(E_e) - C_o \exp - \frac{(E_e - \delta)}{\alpha v}$$

We will try to explain this empirically found dependence with a simple model which is based on the generalized exponential model from Nikitin [3]. From this simple model we will extract the parameters b_o, δ and α and we shall discuss the physical meaning of these parameters. This procedure is justified by a more formal theoretical treatment which will also be presented at this conference [4].

[1] Yu.S. Gordeev, P.H. Woerlee, H. de Waard and F.W. Saris this conference.
[2] R.K. Cacak and T. Jorgenson, Phys. Rev. A2, 1322 (1970)
[3] E.E. Nikitin, Adv. Quantum Chem. 5, 135 (1970)
[4] T. Watanabe, P.H. Woerlee and Yu.S. Gordeev, this conference.

*On leave from A.F. Ioffe Physical Technical Institute, Leningrad K-21, USSR.

CHARGE NUMBER AND SCATTERING ANGLE DEPENDENCE OF THE POSITRON PRODUCTION IN VERY HEAVY ION ATOM COLLISIONS

C. Kozhuharov, P. Kienle, E. Berdermann, Phys. Dep. Techn. Univ. München, W-Germany

H. Bokemeyer, J.S. Greenberg, Y. Nakayama, P. Vincent, GSI, Darmstadt, W-Germany

H. Backe, L. Handschug, E. Kankeleit, Inst. für Kernphysik, TH Darmstadt, W-Germany

At small distances of closest approach the superimposed Coulomb field for the heaviest available collision systems becomes large enough that the binding energy of the lowest electron state may come close to or even exceed $2mc^2$. In such a heavy-ion atom collision the time-varying Coulomb field creates a $1s\sigma$-vacancy which may decay, if imbedded in the Dirac sea, by emission of a positron. Moreover, this field can produce a pair by a transfer of energy either directly or by a two step process via an induced decay of an inner shell vacancy. In a continuation of experiments on atomic positron production in HI collisions[1] we report here on first measurements[2] of the dependence of the positron yield on the combined charge of the collision system and on the scattering angle.

An iron free 'orange'-type-β-spectrometer has been used to focus positrons onto a plastic scintillator coaxially surrounding a cylindrical NaI(Tl) crystal for detection of the 511 keV annihilation radiation γ-rays. For these investigations a positron energy range between 0.44 and 0.55 MeV was selected by the spectrometer. Scattered ions were detected in coincidence with positrons using an annular parallel plate avalanche counter with concentric anode rings covering scattering angles between 13.5° and 32.3°. γ-ray spectra related to positrons from the internal pair decay of nuclear excitations were measured in coincidence with scattered particles with a NaI(Tl) detector and were used to define the contribution of positrons from nuclear origin to the total cross-section measured.

Fig. 1 displays the nuclear background corrected differential positron production probability as a function of half the distance of closest approach R_{min} for the systems Pb-Pb, U-Pb, and U-U. The most striking feature of the data is, when compared under similar kinematic conditions, i.e. at equal R_{min}/a, that the positron yield increases by a factor of 2.6 when Z_1+Z_2 varies from 164 to 174 and by about the same factor for a variation between 174 and 184. This strong Z-dependence, which argues for the extension of the measurements for higher Z-systems using transuranic elements, is also reproduced in quantitative calculations performed by Reinhardt et al[3] taking into account the coherent direct and two step continuum excitation via inner shell vacancies (see fig. 1). Although the binding energy of the lowest electron quasiatomic state should exceed $2mc^2$ for the closest U + U collision measured, no remarkable change in the yield due to spontaneous e^+-production has yet been observed as a deviation from the smooth dependence of the yield on R_{min} (fig. 1), further suggesting that atomic positron production is dominated by dynamic effects for the relative velocities and projectile and target Z-values studied.

1. H. Backe, L. Handschug, F. Heßberger, E. Kankeleit, L. Richter, F. Weik,
   R. Willwater, H. Bokemeyer, P. Vincent, and J.S. Greenberg, Phys. Rev. Lett.
   40 (1978) 1443;
   H. Backe, E. Berdermann, H. Bokemeyer, J.S. Greenberg, E. Kankeleit, P. Kienle,
   C. Kozhuharov, L. Handschug, Y. Nakayama, L. Richter, H. Stettmeier, F. Weik,
   R. Willwater, X. ICPEAC, Paris (1977)162

2. C. Kozhuharov, P. Kienle, E. Berdermann, H. Bokemeyer, J.S. Greenberg,
   Y. Nakayama, P. Vincent, H. Backe, L. Handschug, E. Kankeleit,
   Phys. Rev. Lett. 78B (1978) 183

3. J. Reinhardt, V. Oberacker, B. Müller, W. Greiner, G. Soff, Phys. Lett. 78B
   (1978) 183

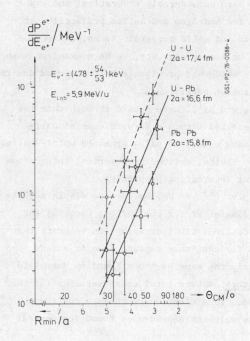

Fig. 1

Double differential positron production probability per scattered particle as a function of R_{min}/a (a = half the distance of closest approach in a head-on collision). For the calculation of θ_{CM} we assumed that the projectile-like particle has been observed. Solid and dashed lines are theoretical calculations from Reinhardt et al.[3]

TARGET DEPENDENCES FOR CONTINUUM CAPTURE
PROCESSES IN ION-ATOM COLLISIONS*

C. R. Vane, I. A. Sellin, M. Suter, S. B. Elston, G. D. Alton, and R. S. Thoe

The University of Tennessee, Knoxville, TN 37916 and
Oak Ridge National Laboratory, Oak Ridge, TN 37830

and

R. Laubert

East Carolina University, Greeneville, NC

Energy spectra of continuum electrons ejected in ion-atom collisions exhibit a cusp-shaped peak (the continuum capture cusp) centered at very nearly the projectile ion velocity vector. There has been considerable theoretical and experimental investigation of this phenomenon for hydrogen and helium projectiles at energies of 0.1 - 1.0 MeV incident on gas and solid targets[1]. By using bare and few-electron ions of higher charge, Z_1, on heavier targets, we have examined some fundamental aspects of continuum capture which had previously been obscured due to limitations imposed by high direct ionization backgrounds[2].

Beams of 1.6 - 3.9 MeV/u C^{6+}, O^{8+}, and Si^{14+} were passed through thin targets of He, Ne, and Ar. The electrons ejected within a forward cone of half-angle $\sim 1.8^{\circ}$ were energy analyzed with data collected using standard multi-scaling techniques as described in Reference 2. Yields, defined by numerical integration over suitably scaled limits, show several interesting properties.

As shown in Figure 1, where yields for O^{8+} + He, Ne, Ar are displayed, the velocity dependences of the yields are dissimilar for the various targets; the heavier gases resulting in much slower decline with increasing ion velocity than for He. The velocity dependences found for continuum capture from Ar and He ($\sim v_i^{-4}$ and v_i^{-8}, respectively) are nearly the same as those found by Macdonald and Martin[3] for single electron bound state capture total cross sections for the same collision systems and energy region. Thus electron capture to continuum states mimics bound state capture in the velocity dependences found for several targets.

A related feature which has been examined here is variation of the shape of the continuum capture peak as a function of incident ion velocity. Most theories predict a symmetric peak shape with half-width-at-half-maximum given by HWHM = $3/4\ v_i\ \theta_0$, where θ_0 is the analyzer acceptance half-angle and v_i is the ion velocity.

Cusp shapes, parameterized in terms of half-widths on the higher and lower energy sides of the cusp (Γ_r and Γ_L, respectively), exhibit definite asymmetry depending strongly on target as exemplified in Figure 2. The widths shown here have been corrected by 10 - 20% for distortions of the true peak shapes due to finite analyzer resolution. The peaks are highly skewed toward the low energy

side. Γ_r is almost entirely velocity and target independent while Γ_L is
strongly target dependent, showing a rapid increase at $v_i \simeq 10$ au for Ne alone.
This is apparently a target shell effect since the Ne K-shell orbital velocity is
~8 au. This also implies that Ne K-shell electrons contribute significantly to
the continuum cusp for ion velocities greater than about 9 au. While the observed
asymmetry is highly target dependent, it appears that it is projectile independent
as comparisons of half-widths for C^{6+}, O^{8+}, and Si^{14+} show little or no variation
with Z_1.

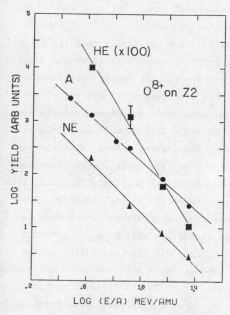

Fig. 1. Continuum capture yields proportional to cross sections for O^{8+} on
Ar, Ne, He under single collision conditions.

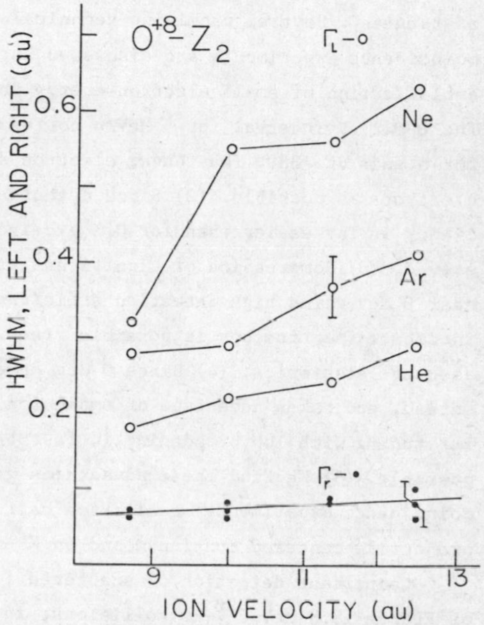

Fig. 2. HWHM for the lower (Γ_L) and
higher (Γ_r) energy sides of the continuum capture peaks for O^{8+} on Ar, Ne, He.

*Work supported in part by NSF; ONR; and by DOE under contract W-7405-eng-26
with Union Carbide Corporation

1.   W. Meckbach, K. C. R. Chiu, H. H. Brongersma, and J. Wm. McGowan, J. Phys.
     B 10, 3255 (1977), and references therein.
2.   C. R. Vane, I. A. Sellin, M. Suter, G. D. Alton, S. B. Elston, P. M.
     Griffin, and R. S. Thoe, Phys. Rev. Lett. 40, 1020 (1978); M. Suter,
     C. R. Vane, I. A. Sellin, S. B. Elston, G. D. Alton, R. S. Thoe, and
     R. Laubert, Phys. Rev. Lett. 41, 399 (1978) and 712 (1978).
3.   J. R. Macdonald and F. W. Martin, Phys. Rev. A 4, 1965 (1971).

COINCIDENCE EXPERIMENTS CONCERNING FORWARD ELECTRON EJECTION*

I. A. Sellin, M. Suter, C. R. Vane, S. B. Elston, R. S. Thoe, and G. D. Alton

The University of Tennessee and Oak Ridge National Laboratory
Knoxville, TN 37916, and Oak Ridge, TN 37830, USA

Pioneering work[1] on the forward peak (cusp) in electron emission from p, He impact on atoms and solids has recently been extended by us to a much enlarged range of faster, heavier, bare, and highly ionized projectiels in a greater variety of targets[2]. Several promising technical advantages of particular importance for coincidence experiments are discussed here. These advantages are: (1) A high gain amplification of small electron energy intervals in the projectile rest frame (prf). The 0-0.1 eV interval for 5 MeV/u corresponds to the range 2743-2776 eV (at 0 deg) for a gain of ~330. Thus Auger electron spectroscopy for low energy (~1eV) Auger electrons is possible. (2) Since detection of keV electrons with near unity efficiency is far easier than for 0.1 eV electrons, formidable detection problems are solved. (3) Compression of significant prf solid angle into a small cone (~1deg) near 0 deg gains high detection efficiency. Thus ion-induced K Auger electron coincidence spectroscopy is possible[3] (see companion paper), using sub-pA beams and adequate statistics. (4) Since 0 deg observation maximizes Doppler shift, minimizes spread, and takes advantage of small ion scattering angles at high velocity, Doppler tuning with low broadening in fast beam electron spectroscopy experiments is possible. (5) We find these advantages greatly facilitate efficient and powerful coincidence experiments on electron capture (ECC) and electron loss (ELC) to the projectile-centered continuum and on K Auger production in ion-atom/solid collisions.

Coincident detection of scattered ion charge state has facilitated our study of ELC in 18.8 MeV C^{2+}-Ar collisions, in which~2-20 eV Auger transitions from double projectile L-shell excitation and C K Auger transitions were both observed. Energy selected Auger electrons produce start pulses in one electron multiplier (CEM) while charge selected ions produce stop pulses in another. Individual electron spectra in coincidence with charge selected scattered ions are simultaneously recorded. We have also generated direct single collision cross section comparisons of ECC events with ECC accompanied by 1, 2, and 3 coincidnet bound state capture events[3]. Suppression of direct ionization background by the coincidence requirement[3] is yet another decided advantage. Figure 1 provides a schematic diagram of the apparatus. Because the standard TAC coincidence arrangement shown requires little discussion, we concentrate on numerical performance evaluation. Overall cross section normalization is provided by digitized Faraday cup charge (corrections from losses as each final charge state is tuned through a 6mm aperture collimating the ion CEM is usually ≲1%) Ion CEM rates up to 100 kHz required small (≲3%) dead time corrections. Moderately fast timing amplifiers (ORTEC 454) and timing discriminators (ORTEC 453) produced 10 nsec FWHM CEM pulses at the TAC stop/start inputs. The TAC spectrum was characterized by a Gaussian peak (FWHM~5 nsec) superposed on a very low randoms background -- reals/randoms ratios were often observed to be $\gtrsim$100:1. The 5m separation of the electron analyzer from the ion CEM gave rise to a $\sim$300 nsec delay which was easily matched to TAC requirements using delay lines. A memory routing interface designed by M. Suter permitted simultaneous storage of non-coincident, coincident, and random coincident events in separate sections of a MCS (MCA) unit. Routing of electron counts and windowed TAC outputs of equivalent width to corresponding memory blocks was accomplished with the aid of SCA's. Digitized ion charge served as a clock to step analyzer voltage for equal numbers of collected ions per step. Typical ion currents were $\sim$ 1-10 ppA. A typical K-Auger coincidence spectrum is shown in a companion paper (Ref. 3, this volume).

   A good test of the coincidence registration efficiency of the entire system was provided by study of 1-, 2-, and 3-electron loss contributions to ELC for 18.8 MeV C^{2+} ions in Ar. Of the electrons contributing to the loss cusp within a velocity interval within $\pm$ 10 % of the ion velocity, preliminary analysis of the raw data shows that $\sim$72% are observed to be coincident with C^{3+} ions, $\sim$17% with $C^{4!}$ ions, and $\sim$3% with C^{5+}, representing $\sim$92% of the possibly observable events, and thereby setting a lower limit of $\gtrsim$92% on ion detection efficiency, which will rise when an appropriate allowance for ECC contributions to the cusp are made.

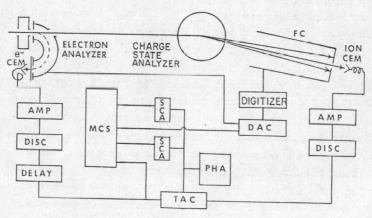

Fig. 1. Schematic diagram of the coincidence arrangement.

*Work supported in part by NSF; ONR; and by DOE under contract W-7405-eng-26 with Union Carbide Corporation

1. G. Crooks and M. E. Rudd, Phys. Rev. Lett. 25,1599 (1970); K. G. Harrison and M. W. Lucas, Phys. Lett. 33A, 142 (1970) and 35A, 402 (1971).

2. C. R. Vane, I. A. Sellin, M. Suter, G. D. Alton, S. B. Elston, P. M. Griffin, and R. S. Thoe, Phys. Rev. Lett. 40, 1020 (1978); M. Suter, C. R. Vane, I. A. Sellin, S. B. Elston, G. D. Alton, R. S. Thoe, and R. Laubert, Phys. Rev. Lett. 41, 399(1978) and 712 (1978); M. Suter, C. R. Vane, S. B. Elston, G. D. Alton, P. M. Griffin, R. S. Thoe, L. Williams, and I. A. Sellin, Z. Phys. A 289, 433 (1979).

3. Present authors, companion paper, this volume; M. Suter, C. R. Vane, S. B. Elston. G. D. Alton, P. M. Griffin, R. S. Thoe, L. Williams, and I. A. Sellin, Bull. Am. Phys. Soc. 24, 582 (1979), and 581 (1979); to be published.

Electron Capture from Silicon by Protons

Chau-Chin Wei

Department of Physics, National Tsing Hua University
Hsinchu, Taiwan, China

We investigate the following process:

$$p^+ + Si(2p^6) \longrightarrow H(1s, 2s \text{ or } 2p) + Si^+(2p^5) \qquad (1).$$

The differential cross sections for the capture of 2p electrons from silicon foils by protons of energy between 100 keV and 6 MeV into 1s, 2s and 2p hydrogen states have been calculated in the Born approximation. The significance of the results is discussed. Specifically, we estimate the energy dependence of the differential cross s section as E^{-6} (E in units of 100 keV). The possible Auger electron contribution to the electron capture is discussed.

For convenience we write $d\sigma_{1s}^{Si}(100 \text{ keV})$ (say) for the electron capture differential cross section by 100 keV incident protons into the silicon target to form the 1s hydrogen state.

In figs. 1, 2, 3 and 4, we show the calculated results of the process (1). The dip which is indicated by D in fig. 2, for example, is considered as an artificial product of Born approximation. The peak P in fig. 2 and its corresponding one in other figures is considered as the contribution from Auger electrons. Namely in proton-silicon collision, the Auger electrons are produced and those Auger electrons travel loosely with the incident protons. Those Auger electrons surfing together with protons contribute effectively to 1the capture process (1) and form the peak P. The facts that there is no peak P in proton-carbon collision and that characteristically the peak P becomes higher as proton energy increases in the present energy range, may be considered as the justifications of our explanation.

This work is supported by National Science Council of China under the grant number of NSC-68M-0201-03(0308).

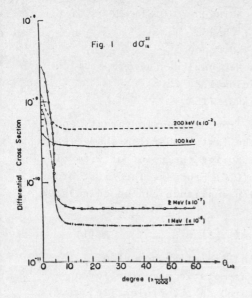

Fig. 1 $d\sigma_{1s}^{Si}$

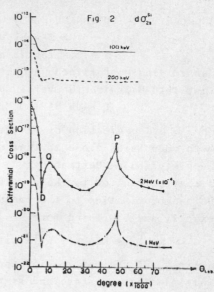

Fig. 2 $d\sigma_{2s}^{Si}$

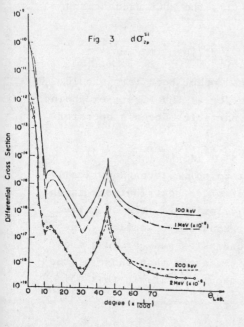

Fig. 3 $d\sigma_{2p}^{Si}$

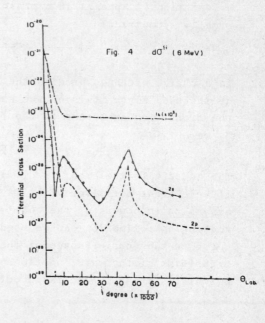

Fig. 4 $d\sigma^{Si}$ (6 MeV)

ANGULAR DISTRIBUTION OF ELECTRONS CAPTURED TO CONTINUUM STATES
OF A FAST HEAVY CHARGE

J.E.Miraglia and V.H.Ponce
Centro Atómico Bariloche (Comisión Nacional de Energía Atómica)
Instituto Balseiro (Universidad Nacional de Cuyo)
8400 BARILOCHE - ARGENTINA

The ejection of electrons from hydrogenic targets and
with velocities close to that of the fast bombarding charge has
been studied by Dettmann et al[1], assuming the point of view of
a charge transfer to the continuum(CTC) process. The first order
Born approximation to the transition amplitude can be calculated
exactly and in closed form

$$T_1^{BK} = \langle \vec{K}_f', \vec{k}' | \ w' | \vec{K}_i, i \rangle = \langle \vec{K}_f', \vec{k}' | \ w | \vec{K}_i, i \rangle \ , \qquad (1)$$

where $\vec{K}_i, \vec{K}_f'$ are the initial and final relative momentum, $\underline{i}$ the
initial electron state and $\vec{k}'$ the asymptotic momentum for an
electron in a continuum state centered on the projectile; $w(w')$
is the Coulomb potential between the electron and the charge $Z(Z')$
of the target(projectile). Since we leave aside the internuclear
potential, the above transition amplitude is of the Brinkman-
Kramers(BK) type. The doubly differential cross section(DDCS) is
obtained after integration of $|T_1^{BK}|^2$ over the final directions
of the scattered projectile; since the only dependence on the
orientation $\hat{k}'$ appears in a phase in (1), the DDCS will be spherically symmetrical

$$\sigma_1^{BK} = \frac{2\pi Z'}{k'} \ \frac{2^{15} Z^5 Z'^2}{5\pi} \ \frac{v_i^8}{(v_i^2 + Z^2)^{10}} \qquad . \qquad (2)$$

In a charge exchange process the second order Born term should
be included since it is of the same order as the first; expanding
the transition amplitude in the free particles Green's operator
G_o we obtain

$$T_2^{BK} = T_1^{BK} + \langle \vec{K}_f', \vec{k}' | w G_o w' | \vec{K}_i, i \rangle \qquad . \qquad (3)$$

The added matrix element is difficult to solve, even numerically;
if we content ourselves with its lower order contributions in an
expansion in powers of the collision velocity v_i, the so called
peaking approximation can be used: it consists essentially in
going to the Fourier space of the coordinates and, because the
transforms of the wave functions vanish faster than those of the
potentials these can be taken out of the integral. In this way

the contributions of order v_i^{-11} and v_i^{-12} to the DDCS are obtained; higher order contributions coming from the peaking approximation are not reliable since this procedure has neglected terms of such orders. The v_i^{-11} term is very small for high but non-relativistic velocities, while the important contribution v_i^{-12} is spherically symmetric. Shakeshaft and Spruch[2] obtain an appreciable $\hat{k}'$ dependence on σ_2^{BK} that should come from contributions from the peaking approximation of higher order than v_i^{-12}: this may be confirmed by the fact that any asymmetry in the electron distribution arises from CTC processes to electron orbitals with non-zero orbital angular momentum l, and it can be shown that the asymptotic behavior of the DDCS is then of order v_i^{-12-21}.

To obtain the $\hat{k}'$ dependence of σ_2^{BK} we have abandoned the peaking approximation and made a numerical integration of the second order matrix element in (3). For the range of velocities $3<v_i<20$ there is an appreciable asymmetry in the electron distribution that we represent by

$$A = \sigma_2^{BK}(\theta'=\pi)/\sigma_2^{BK}(\theta'=0) \quad , \text{ where } \cos\theta'=\hat{k}'\cdot\hat{K}_i.$$

v_i =	3	5	7	10	20
A =	1.51	1.46	1.37	1.26	1.03

To get a complete picture of the CTC process the role of the internuclear potential should be considered since, even though the first and second order Born terms coming from this potential cancel asymptotically, there may be an important contribution to the CTC process for the range of velocities studied, as is the case for charge transfer to a discrete state.[3]

1. K.Dettmann, K.G.Harrison and M.W.Lucas, J.Phys.B7, 269(1974)

2. R.Shakeshaft and L.Spruch, Phys.Rev.Lett.,41,1037 (1978)

3. P.J.Kramer, Phys.Rev.A6,2125(1972)

PROJECTILE CHARGE STATE DEPENDENCE OF K X-RAY PRODUCTION
IN HEAVY ION-ATOM SINGLE COLLISIONS

W.N. Lennard, I.V. Mitchell, P. Mokler* and G.C. Ball

Atomic Energy of Canada Limited
Chalk River Nuclear Laboratories
Chalk River, Ontario, Canada

The projectile charge state dependence of K X-ray cross sections has been measured for ~1 MeV/amu Cu and Br ion beams incident on Kr (gas) and Zn (vapour) targets. Pure charge state beams were selected magnetically downstream of a post acceleration carbon stripper foil. Gas cell pressure was varied to establish conditions free of charge state quenching. Ionization cross sections were made absolute through the use of proton excited target K X-ray yields and neutral atom fluorescence yields and are believed accurate to 20%.

Typical results are shown in Fig. 1 for the case of 88.2 MeV Cu^{q+} incident on Kr. The general features are similar to those observed previously by Warczak[1] and Schiebel[2].   Two regimes are recognizable. In the first, $q \leq 19$, the Cu 2p-shell is full (for ground state configurations) and there is very little variation in the cross section. The mechanism for K-shell ionization in this regime is not understood at present, but nevertheless the ionization systematics have been mapped extensively for many single collision systems[3].

For $q \geq 20$, the Cu 2p-shell is open and the K X-ray cross section is seen to increase dramatically, with approximately equal increments for each additional 2p-vacancy. This is consistent with a picture of a radial coupling[4] of the Cu 2p-vacancy from the 3dπ into the 2pπ MO followed by rotational coupling[5] into the 2pσ MO. Quantitative accord between experiment and theory is good, as may be judged from the solid line shown in Fig. 1. The small increase in cross section at q=19 is attributed to the presence of Ne-like metastables (e.g. $1s^2 2s^2 2p^5 3p$) in the incoming beam. Good agreement between experiment and theory is likewise found in a comparison of data for 55 MeV and 88.2 MeV Cu^{q+} bombardment of Kr, based on the expected $v^{2/3}$ dependence of the rotational coupling cross section[5]. The data for $Cu^{q+} \to Zn$ (vapour), $Br^{q+} \to Kr$ and $Br^{q+} \to Zn$ (vapour) are all explained satisfactorily by the same simple picture outlined above.

*Permanent address: GSI, Darmstadt, W. Germany

1. A. Warczak, K. Liesen, J.R. Macdonald and P. Mokler, Zeit. für Physik A 285, 235 (1978).

2. U. Schiebel and B. Doyle, Zeit. für Physik A 285, 241 (1978).

3. W.N. Lennard, I.V. Mitchell and J.S. Forster, Phys. Rev. A 18, 1949 (1978).

4. W. Lennard, I.V. Mitchell, J.S. Forster and D. Phillips, J. Phys. B. 10, 2199 (1977).

5. K. Taulbjerg, J.S. Briggs and J. Vaaben, J. Phys. B 9, 135 (1976).

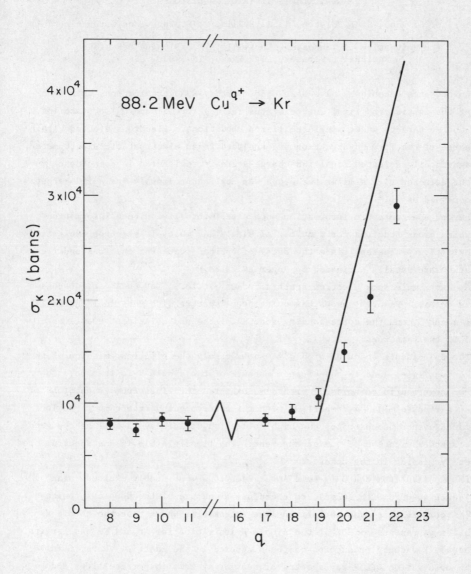

Figure 1

K-ionization cross section for 88.2 MeV Cu^{q+}→Kr as a
function of projectile charge state, q. The 2p-shell
is opened for q≥20. The solid line is constructed by
assuming σ_K is a constant for q≤19 and, for q>19, by
adding the 2pπ-2pσ rotational coupling contribution.

K-AUGER ELECTRONS OBSERVED IN COINCIDENCE WITH FINAL PROJECTILE CHARGE STATE IN ION-ATOM COLLISIONS*

M. Suter, C. R. Vane, S. B. Elston, I. A. Sellin, R. S. Thoe, and G. D. Alton

The University of Tennessee, Knoxville, TN 37916 and Oak Ridge
National Laboratory, Oak Ridge, TN 37830, USA

Coincidence techniques have been used to study K-Auger electrons as a function of the initial and final charge states (q, q') for C^{q+} and O^{q+} projectiles in Ar and Ne targets under single collision conditions. Electrons ejected within $\sim$1 degree of the forward direction are analyzed in an electrostatic spectrometer, and magnetically selected final ion charge state is registered in coincidence in a second detector[1]. A similar technique was applied previously for solid targets by Groeneveld et al.[2].

Beyond spectroscopic information such experiments give direct information concerning cross sections for a number of single and multiple electron excitation and ionization processes, since the decay of excited states of the ions under consideration are usually dominated by Auger emission.

As an example some electron spectra for C^{2+} at 18.75 MeV on Ar are discussed in more detail. Figure 1 shows the coincidence spectra with the final charge states 4 and 5, and the corresponding spectra of the non-coincident events observed in the same runs.

The coincidence spectrum with $q'=4$ shows mainly the electron emission of the Li-like ions $(q'-1)$ and is therefore a measure of the single K-ionization. The spectrum observed in coincidence with $q'=5$ exhibits the lines from transitions of He-like carbon $(q'-1)$. A comparison with the corresponding spectrum of the ion coincident events demonstrates the high collection efficiency as well as the good charge state-separation of our arrangement: The lines visible in one spectrum are completely missing in the other.

The He-like ions can only emit Auger electrons when doubly excited. The coincidence spectra with $(q'=5)$ are therefore a measure of the double K ionization. A comparison of the normalized line intensities shows that the double K-ionization represents $\sim$ 20% of the single K-ionization for Ar and Ne gas targets.

Double K-vacancy production has been studied in the last few years, mainly through observation of x-ray spectra of heavier systems (hypersatellites and two-electron-one-photon transitions). Most of these earlier measurements are done in a velocity regime, where molecular collision and vacancy sharing models can be applied, in contrast to these experiments where the projectile velocity is on the order of the velocity of the K-shell electrons. This fact may explain the high relative fraction of double K-vacancy production in our experiment compared to other data.

In a more detailed cross-section analysis the optical decay channel must also by taken into account along with drift of metastable components outside the viewing region and anisotropic electron emission.

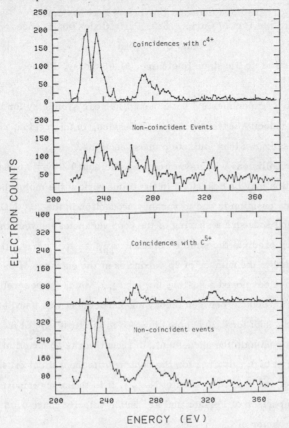

Fig. 1. Projectile K-Auger spectra for C^{2+} at 18.75 MeV on Ar. The uppermost spectrum observed in coincidence with C^{4+} exhibits the Auger lines of the Li-like ions. The spectrum composed of all electrons non-coincident with C^{4+} ions is shown directly below. Similar spectra are shown for final charge state $q' = 5$. The abscissa displays the projectile frame electron energies.

*Work supported in part by NSF; ORN; and by DOE under contract W-7405-eng-26 with Union Carbide Corporation.

1. I. A. Sellin, C. R. Vane, M. Suter, S. B. Elston, R. S. Thoe, and G. D. Alton, companion papers, this volume.

2. K. O. Groeneveld, G. Nolte, S. Schumann, and K. D. Sevier, Phys. Lett. 56A, 29 (1976); S. Schumann, K. O. Groneveld, G. Nolte, and B. Fricke Z. Physik A 289, 245 (1979).

K VACANCY AND CAPTURE CROSS SECTIONS
FOR NEAR SYMMETRIC COLLISIONS OF 300 MeV Kr IONS[*]

A. Chetioui, J.P. Rozet, J.P. Briand

Institut Curie and Université P et M Curie
11, rue P et M Curie, 75231 Paris Cedex 05, France

and C. Stephan

Institut de Physique Nucléaire, 91405 Orsay, France

Very few collision experiments [1] have been done near symmetry for impact velocity relative to K orbital velocity between 0.2 and 1. Besides, in this region, capture cross sections are even less known than ionization cross sections.

For 300 MeV Kr collisions with asymmetry coefficients $0.6 < \frac{Z_H}{Z_L} < 1$ and velocity ratios $v_1/v_K \sim 0.4$, ionization may be described in the framework of the molecular model [2]. In this model, K vacancy creation is due to vacancy production in the $2p\sigma$ MO by $2p\sigma - 2p\pi$ rotational coupling and subsequent sharing of the $2p\sigma$ vacancies between the $2p\sigma$ and the $1s\sigma$ MO [3]. The theory predicts the simple relation $\sigma_{2p\sigma} = \sigma_K(H) + \sigma_K(L) = N_{2p\pi}\,\sigma_{rot}$ where $N_{2p\pi}$ is related to the number of 2p vacancies at the entrance of the collision. Taulbjerg and al [4] have developed a scaling law for σ_{rot} which agrees well with ab initio calculations. A good agreement between theory and experiment was found at low energy but at higher energies, additional $2p\pi$ holes created in the first part of the collision were postulated in order to maintain the agreement. In recent works no quantitative test of the theory has been done at high velocity ; (on the contrary the theoretical cross section is assumed to be correct and is used to extract $N_{2p\pi}$). It is thus very important to test this theory. A recent comparison of Fortner and al [5] in the velocity range 0.06–0.2 shows discrepancies up to a factor of 2.

We have used solid targets (2 to $200\,\mu g/cm^2$ thickness) and developed [6] an original method to extract precise ionization and capture cross sections from K X-ray yield variations with target thickness. This method takes into account the variation of the mean L ionization with thickness and the resultant variation of K ionization, K radiative and Auger cross sections and K fluorescence yields. All cross sections are given for projectiles in which L equilibrium is reached.

The method allows us to determine approximately the mean number of $2p\pi$ vacancies in the middle of the collision. It has been shown by Lennard and al [7] that if a projectile carries 2p vacancies in a collision, these vacancies are shared between the $2p\pi$ and $3d\pi$ MO in a ratio analogous to the one in (3). Our data gave evidence of $2p\pi$ vacancies even in the first collision where no initial 2p vacancy exists, showing that we have to take into account coupling of the $2p\pi$ and $3d\pi$ MO with other higher lying vacant states [6].

[*]Work performed at the Variable Energy Cyclotron of Orsay, France.

In Fig. 1 one can see a comparison between $\sigma_K(H) + \sigma_K(L)$ and $\overline{N_{2p\pi}}\ \sigma_{rot}$ showing agreement for the tendancy of variation but discrepancy for the absolute value up to a factor of 3.

In Fig. 2 are compared experimental and theoretical [3] K vacancy sharing showing a rather good agreement.

K-K capture cross sections are given in table 1. The method leads to errors of the order of 50%. No calculations for K-K capture cross section exist in the framework of the molecular model. However, within experimental errors, measured values agree with calculated ones in the TSAE method [8] (C.D. Lin, private communication).

Table 1. K-K capture cross sections

target	Ni	Cu	Zr
$\sigma_{KK} (cm^2)$	4.10^{-19}	5.10^{-19}	6.10^{-19}

In conclusion, these data seem to support the validity of a molecular model in spite of some discrepancies the origin of which is not clear. The consideration of direct $2p\sigma$ ionization would increase the disagreement.

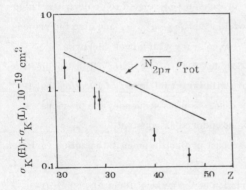

Fig. 1. Summed K vacancy cross sections as a function of target atomic number.

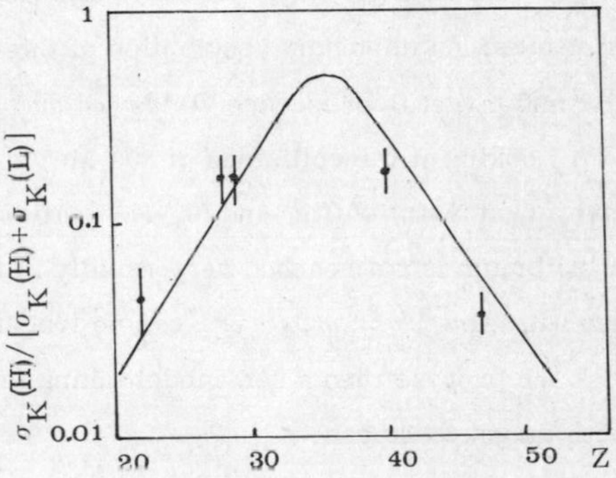

Fig. 2. K vacancy sharing as a function of target atomic number.

1. W.E. Meyerhof, R. Anholt and T.K. Saylor, Phys. Rev. A16 169 (1977).

2. W. Lichten, Phys. Rev. 164 131 (1967) ; M. Barat and W. Lichten, Phys. Rev. A6 211 (1972).

3. W.E. Meyerhof, Phys. Rev. Lett. 31 1341 (1973).

4. K. Taulbjerg, J.S. Briggs and J. Waaber, J. Phys. B9 1351 (1976).

5. R.J. Fortner, P.H. Woerlee, S. Doorn, Th. P. Hoogkamer and F.W. Saris, Phys. Rev. Lett. 39 1322 (1977).

6. J.P. Rozet and A. Chetioui, communication at this conference.

7. W.N. Lennard and I.V. Mitchell, J. Phys. B9 L317 (1976).

8. C.D. Lin, J. Phys. B11 L185 (1978).

INFLUENCE OF L IONIZATION VARIATION WITH TARGET THICKNESS ON K X RAY YIELDS INDUCED BY FAST PROJECTILES IN SOLID TARGETS

J.P. Rozet and A. Chetioui

Institut Curie and Université P et M Curie
11, rue P et M Curie, 75231 Paris Cedex 05, France

We have observed that in collisions of 300 MeV and 500 MeV Kr ions on various solid targets of Ti, Mn, Ni, Cu, Zr and Ag, L ionization equilibrium is not reached before target thickness of about 50 $\mu g/cm^2$. We have then modified the Betz's equations used to extract K ionization cross sections [1] by taking into account L ionization variation with target thickness.

Usually, non linear dependence of K X ray yield is mainly due to the variation with target thickness of the fraction of K ionized projectiles and to the occurence of K hole transfer processes from the projectile to K or outer shells of the target. A model [1] has been developed, allowing to extract from measured target and projectile K X ray yield variations, the cross sections of the various processes involved during the collisions : projectile (σ_V) and target (σ^*_V) K ionization , K-K transfer (σ_t) and capture to outer shells of the target (σ_c), radiative and Auger processes (σ) related to projectile K holes lifetimes. An important assumption of this model is that σ_V, σ^*_V, σ and also the projectile and target fluorescence yields ω and ω^* do not vary with target thickness.

Looking at the collisions of 300 MeV and 500 MeV Kr ions we observed that projectile and target X-ray shifts, and K_α/K_β ratios vary with target thickness, indicating that L equilibrium is not reached very rapidly in this case. As a consequence, the previous quantities σ_V, σ^*_V, σ , ω , ω^* can no longer be considered as constant.

We propose then a new model taking into account projectile mean L ionization variation with target thickness.

We have assumed a mean L ionization variation of the general form : $n_L(x) = \bar{n}_L (1-\lambda e^{-\beta x})$.

Parameter λ allows us to take into account possible direct 2p ionization in the first part of the first collision leading to K ionization. We have then corrected the previous equations [1], with the following assumptions :

i) σ, ω and ω^* vary with n_L as predicted by the statistical model [2]

ii) σ_V and σ^*_V are proportional to n_L. Within the M.O. model, this means that ionization in the 2pπx orbital and mean L ionization have similar variations. Numerical tests indicate that extracted results are not too much sensitive to this assumption.

In Fig. (1) is shown the result of a fit of our formulas to experimental data of Kr 300 MeV on Cu. For comparison, we have added the curves corresponding to $\lambda=0$ and $\lambda=1$ cases. We found also that $\lambda=0$ value (no mean L ionization variation as in Betz's case) would give negative value for the σ_c capture cross section. Table 1 summarizes the results obtained for 300 MeV Kr on Cu. We found that all the values of λ give the same value for $\sigma_V + \sigma^*_V$, but with the usual procedure ($\lambda=0$ case) one can get erroneous values by more than a factor of 2 for K vacancy sharing, K hole lifetimes (σ) and transfer and capture cross sections. Moreover, extracted value of λ gives original information about direct $2p\pi$ ionization during collisions.

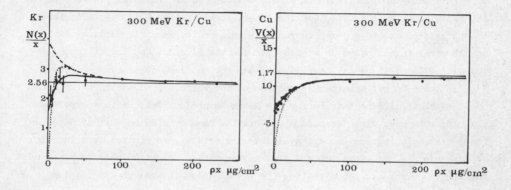

Fig. 1 : Projectile and target K X-ray yield versus target thickness (arbitrary units) :
dashed line : $\lambda=0$ (no L mean ionization variation)
dotted line : $\lambda=1$ (mean L ionization variation, no direct $2p\pi$ ionization)
full line : $\lambda=0,41$ (best fit).

σ_V	$(1.3 \pm 0.3)10^{-20}$ cm^2
σ^*_V	$(6.3 \pm 1.5)10^{-20}$ cm^2
σ	(2 ± 1) 10^{-18} cm^2
$\sigma_t (+ \sigma_c)$	~ 5 10^{-19} cm^2
λ	0.4 ± 0.02
α	1.5 ± 1
β	6.4 ± 0.6

Table 1 : Parameters and cross sections extracted from Fig. 1. Also given for comparison with β : $\alpha = n \sigma_T$ ($\sigma_T = \sigma_V + \sigma + \sigma_c + \sigma_t$).

1. H.D. Betz, F. Bell, H. Panke, G. Kalkoffen, M. Weltz, and D. Evers, Phys. Rev. Lett. **33** 807 (1974).

2. F.P. Larkins, J. Phys. **B4** L29 (1971).

PROJECTILE L-SUBSHELL DIFFERENTIATION
IN 1.4 MeV/U PB → Z_2 COLLISIONS

W.A. Schönfeldt and P.H. Mokler

GSI, Gesellschaft für Schwerionenforschung
6100 Darmstadt, Fed. Rep. of Germany

For Iodine projectiles Datz et al.[1] discovered fluctuations in the $\frac{L\beta}{L\alpha}$ x-ray intensity ratio as a function of the target atomic number Z_2. Especially for level matching there exists a steep increase in this ratio. Recently Hagmann et al.[2] and Meyerhof et al.[3] gave an explanation for the fluctuations investigating the dynamics of special radial couplings within the quasimolecule.

In order to get a better separation of the various L-subshells we studied the L-subshell differentiation for 1.4 MeV/u Pb projectiles. In this experiment the emitted x rays were detected at 90° to the beam by a 80-mm^2 Si(Li) detector. The $\frac{L\beta}{L\alpha}$ intensity ratios for all available projectiles are plotted as a function of Z_2/Z_1 in Fig. 1a. For such a Z_2/Z_1 representation we get an unified picture for the fluctuations, demonstrating the MO-origin of the relevant mechanism. For a $Z_2 + Z_1$ representation we find no unified picture. In contrast to the measurement with low-Z_1 projectiles we are able to get additionally separated ratios for subshells:

$$\frac{L_2}{L_3} \left(\frac{\eta}{l}\right) \, , \quad \frac{L_1}{L_2} \left(\frac{\gamma_{2,3}}{\gamma_1}\right) \, , \quad \frac{L_1}{L_3} \left(\frac{\gamma_4}{\beta_5}\right) \, , \quad \text{see Fig. 1b.}$$

The separability of the Pb-L subshells is caused by i) the higher atomic number Z_1 and ii) the collision induced line shifts. The shifts for various lines are given in Fig. 2.

A line shift analysis in connection with DFS calculation yields the true ionization ratios. The results can be interpreted within a two-state radial-coupling model by setting the interaction matrix element as

$$H_{12}(R) = A \cdot e^{-\lambda R} (\Delta H(R) - \Delta\varepsilon\infty), \quad \text{with A, } \lambda \text{ constants,}$$

R the internuclear distance, $\Delta H(R)$ the difference of the diabatic energies, and $\Delta\varepsilon\infty$ the difference of ionization energies for separated atoms. This Ansatz includes as special cases the models of Landau-Zener[4], Demkov[5], and Nikitin[6]. With our model we can explain the following features of the fluctuations: i) A slow decrease (with increasing Z_2) in the $\frac{L_2}{L_3}$ ionization ratio is caused by a slow approach of the target K- or L-shell to the projectile L-shell (a slow transition from a Demkov- to a Landau-Zener type coupling); ii) a step rise is caused by K-L or L-L level matching(variation of the coupling strength of a pure Landau-Zener type transition).

1. S. Datz et al., Phys. Rev. Lett. 27 (1971) 363

2. S. Hagmann et al., Z. Phys. A 290 (1979) 25
3. W. Meyerhof, A. Rüetschi et al., Preprint, to be published
4. L. Landau, Phys. Z. Sowjet 2 (1932) 40
   C. Zener, Proc. Roy. Soc. Ser. A 137 (1932) 696
5. Yu.N. Demkov, Sov. Phys. JETP 18 (1964) 138
6. E.E. Nikitin, Opt. Spektrosk. (USSR) 13 (1962) 431

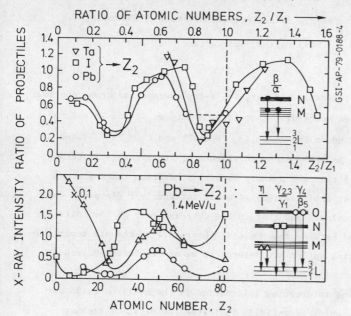

Fig. 1.

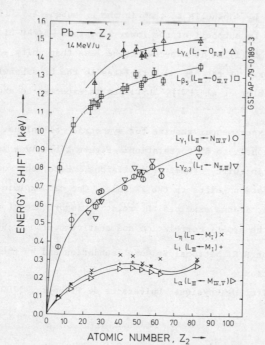

Fig. 2.

L-VACANCY PRODUCTION IN NEAR-SYMMETRIC HEAVY-ION COLLISIONS (Z$\gtrsim$35)[*]

W. E. Meyerhof, A. Rüetschi,[**] Ch. Stoller, M. Stöckli, and W. Wölfli

Department of Physics, Stanford University, California 94305, USA and

Nuclear Physics Laboratory, Swiss Federal Institute of Technology,

8093 Zurich, Switzerland

We have measured projectile and target L x-ray spectra and cross sections
for 41-MeV Ta projectiles bombarding thin targets between Ag and Th and for
17-60-MeV collisions of Ho on Ho, Au on Au, Pb on Pb and U on Th.[1] These
cross sections, as well as those measured elsewhere, are examined in terms
of a model which assumes that the primary vacancy production takes place in
the $4f\sigma$ and $3d\sigma$ molecular orbitals (MO) at small internuclear distances (by
a process not yet ascertained) and that on the outgoing part of the collision
the vacancies are shared between the MOs which correlate to the six separated-
atom L subshells. Sharing ratios are assumed to be of the Demkov-Meyerhof
type.[2]

A quantity providing interesting information is the $L\beta(1)/L\alpha$ ratio for
each collision partner, which essentially indicates the ratio of vacancy
production in the L_1 and L_2 subshells to that in the L_3 subshell.[3] If the
$4f\sigma$ MO correlates to the L_3 subshell of the lower-Z partner [Barat-Lichten
(BL) correlation rule],[4] $L\beta(1)/L\alpha$ is expected to be less than unity according
to our model calculations. If the $4f\sigma$ MO correlates to the L_1 subshell
[correlation rule of Eichler et al (EW)],[5] $L\beta(1)/L\alpha$ is expected to exceed
unity.

Figure 1(a) gives experimental results for symmetric collisions. Here,
the model points unambiguously to BL correlation. Figure 1(b) gives results
for the lower-Z partner in quite asymmetric collisions. Here, the model
suggests that the correlation shifts to the EW rule. One can explain the
shift in the correlation, if one examines the relative importance of electron
screening which favors the $4f\sigma$-L_3 correlation and that of Coulombic Stark

*Supported in part by the U.S. National Science Foundation and by the Swiss
National Science Foundation.
**Present address: Institut de Physique, Universite de Fribourg, 1700
Fribourg, Switzerland.

splitting which favors the 4fσ-L₁ correlation.[4,5] For symmetric collisions the Stark splitting is weak, so that the 4fσ-L₃ (BL) correlation occurs. With increasing collision asymmetry the Stark splitting increases rapidly, shifting the correlation to 4fσ-L₁ (EW).

[1] A. Rüetschi, Diplom thesis, Swiss Federal Institute of Technology, Zurich, 1977.

[2] W. E. Meyerhof, Phys. Rev. Lett. 31, 1341 (1973).

[3] W. E. Meyerhof et al, Phys. Rev. A 17, 108 (1978).

[4] M. Barat and W. Lichten, Phys. Rev. A 6, 211 (1972).

[5] J. Eichler et al, Phys. Rev. A 14, 707 (1976).

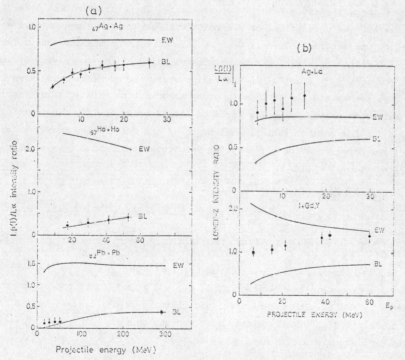

Fig. 1. Lβ(1)/Lα intensity ratio (a) for symmetric collisions, (b) for lower-Z partner in asymmetric collisions. Solid lines are model calculations, assuming a 4fσ-L₃ (BL) or 4fσ-L₁ (EW) correlation, as well as vacancy sharing between the MOs leading to the L subshells. Coster-Kronig transitions have also been taken into account. Experimental points from our and other work (G. Presser, S. Hagmann, P. Mokler, and A. Schönfeldt, Private communications).

RELATIVISTIC TREATMENT OF $2p_{1/2}$ - $2p_{3/2}$ TRANSITIONS IN ION-ATOM COLLISIONS WITHIN THE SMALL-R EXPANSION METHOD

D.H. Jakubassa and K. Taulbjerg

Institute of Physics, University of Aarhus, Denmark

K-shell vacancy production due to Coriolis coupling in ion-atom collisions is well accounted for in the non-relativistic case by a scaling procedure in combination with accurate *ab initio* calculations.[1,2] The scaling procedure was derived[1] by retaining only leading terms in the expansion of the elements of the coupling matrix in powers of the internuclear distance R.

The extension of this method to include spin-orbit coupling has been considered by Anholt et al.[3] The correction factor to the excitation cross section due to spin-orbit coupling was found to be very appreciable when the spin-orbit splitting in the united-atom L shell becomes large. The evaluation was done under the very simplifying assumptions of non-relativistic wave functions as well as straight-line trajectories. Then it was possible to express the correction factor in terms of a single universal parameter. The validity of the underlying assumptions is, however, very doubtful in the region where the correction is large.

We have reexamined the problem by using a consistent relativistic description and deflected paths. Retaining terms of lowest order in R we find the following expressions for the non-vanishing elements of the Hamiltonian matrix in a molecule-fixed representation given by the relativistic L_{II} and L_{III} wave functions of the united atom $(Z = Z_1 + Z_2)$:

$$E_{\frac{1}{2}m}(R) - E^0_{2p\frac{1}{2}} = f \cdot (R/a)^{2\gamma} \xrightarrow{\text{non-rel.}} 0$$

$$E_{\frac{3}{2}m}(R) - E^0_{2p\frac{3}{2}} = (-1)^{\frac{1}{2} + |m|} d \cdot (R/a)^2 \xrightarrow{\text{non-rel.}} (-1)^{\frac{1}{2} + |m|} \frac{Z_1 Z_2}{30} (R/a)^2$$

$$V = <\tfrac{3}{2}\tfrac{1}{2}|H(R)|\tfrac{1}{2}\tfrac{1}{2}> = g_1 \cdot (R/a)^2 + g_2 \cdot (R/a)^{\gamma_1 + \gamma} \xrightarrow{\text{non-rel.}} \sqrt{2}\, \frac{Z_1 Z_2}{30} (R/a)^2,$$

where $a = 2a_o/Z = 2\hbar/me^2Z$ is the L-shell radius, $\gamma = (1-Z^2\alpha^2)^{\frac{1}{2}}$ and $\gamma_1 = (4-Z^2\alpha^2)^{\frac{1}{2}}$ with $\alpha = e^2/\hbar c$. The expansion coefficients f, d, g_1, and g_2 are functions of the nuclear charges Z_1 and Z_2. The non-relativistic limiting values used in Ref. 3 are given to the right of the full-relativistic expressions.

The Schrödinger equation may now be written

$$i\hbar \frac{d}{dt} \underline{C} = \underline{\underline{M}} \cdot \underline{C} \quad ,$$

where $\underline{C}$ is a column vector containing the six amplitudes of the expansion of the time-dependent wave function in a basis consisting of co-rotating united-atom $|2p\ jm>$ relativistic wave functions. In addition to the Hamiltonian matrix $\underline{\underline{H}}(R)$, the coupling matrix $\underline{\underline{M}}$ includes the non-vanishing elements of the dynamical operator, $-i\hbar \frac{\partial}{\partial t}\Big|_r$. In the present representation these elements are given by the Coriolis terms $-\dot{\theta}<jm|\hat{J}_y|j\ m\pm 1>$ where $\dot{\theta}$ is the angular velocity of the internuclear vector and $\hat{J}_y$ is a component of the total angular momentum perpendicular to the scattering plane.

In order to incorporate appropriate boundary conditions it is useful to pre-diagonalise $\underline{H}$, i.e. to solve the Schrödinger equation in the adiabatic representation. This transformation induces radial coupling elements in $\underline{M}$ in place of the off-diagonal elements of the Hamiltonian matrix. The adiabatic potential-energy curves for the I + I system (Z = 106) are presented in Fig. 1 in the full-relativistic case (full drawn curves) and in the weak-relativistic approximation (dashed) used by Anholt et al.[3] It is obvious from Fig. 1 that a full-relativistic treatment is essential for a proper description of such high-Z systems.

In order to obtain the probability P(b) of K-shell excitation it is assumed that the upper two diabatic levels in Fig. 1 correlate to the 2p subshells of the separated atoms while the lower level correlates to the K shell. We then integrate the coupled equations subject to boundary conditions that corresponds to a collision with an initial unpolarized 2p vacancy on the projectile. The total K-excitation cross section per incident 2p vacancy is obtained by integration over impact parameter b and is shown in Fig. 2. The experimental data points are from Ref. 3.

The significance of a fully relativistic description will be further illustrated by a comparison with results based on the weak-relativistic assumption.[3]

1. K. Taulbjerg, J.S. Briggs and J. Vaaben, J.Phys. B <u>9</u>, 1351 (1976).
2. K. Taulbjerg, Proc.Sec.Int.Conf. Inner Shell Ionization Phenomena, Freiburg 1976, p. 130.
3. R. Anholt, W.E. Meyerhof, and A. Salin, Phys.Rev. A <u>16</u>, 951 (1977).

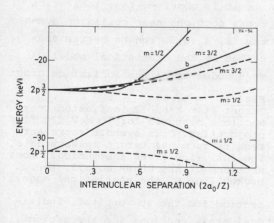

Fig. 1

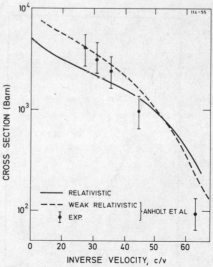

Fig. 2

INNER-SHELL IONIZATION PRODUCED BY MEV
FLUORINE AND SILICON PROJECTILES

G.Presser, E.Scherer and J.Stähler

Institut für Physik, Universität Dortmund
D 4600 Dortmund 50, Germany

The production of inner-shell vacancies was investigated by
measurement of X-ray emission cross sections with a Si(Li) detector
and a proportional counter. The experiments were performed with
1 to 25 MeV F and Si beams from the Dynamitron Tandem at Bochum,
Germany. Absolute cross sections were measured with gas targets under single collision conditions and with thin solid targets (thickness: 10 - 100 µg/cm^2). For almost symmetric collisions ($Z_1/Z_2 > 0.5$)
significant differences were observed between gas- and solid-target
results, that can be attributed to solid state effects.[1]

In Fig.1 is shown a comparison of experimental ionization cross
sections for 10 MeV fluorine ion impact and theoretical predictions.
The CPSS-model calculations[2] including relativistic corrections[3]
are in good agreement with data for asymmetry parameters $Z_1/Z_2 < 0.5$.[4]
Significant deviations are found for the more symmetric collisions
systems.

It is observed that ionization
cross sections near collision symmetry ($Z_1/Z_2 > 0.5$) can be better described by the statistical model.[5]
This model gives the ionization cross

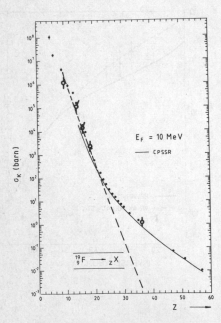

Fig.1:
Target atom K-shell ionization cross
sections measured for 10 MeV fluorine
projectiles. Open symbols represent
results from gas target measurements.
The full line gives theoretical cross
sections of the CPSSR modell, the
broken line of the statistical model.

section for the 2pσ orbital. Individual cross sections for the projectile
and target atom were calculated by
assuming 1sσ - 2pσ vacancy sharing[6]
The diffusion constant[5] for the statistical model calculations has been
taken as $D_K = ((Z_1 + Z_2)/C)^2 \hbar/m$, with the

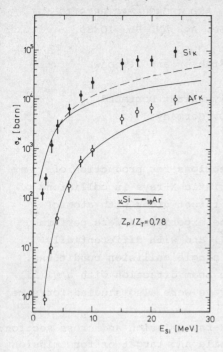

Fig.2:
K-shell X-ray cross sections of projectile (Si) and target (Ar) atoms. The curves represent theoretical cross sections of the statistical model, including vacancy sharing.

parameter C = 12.

The projectile energy dependence of X-ray production cross sections for projectile and target atom is given in Fig.2 for the collision system Si + Ar. Theoretical cross sections from statistical model calculations are shown for comparison.

1. H.Tawara et al., Phys.Rev. A18, 1373 (1978)

2. G.Basbas, W.Brandt and R.Laubert, Phys.Rev. A17, 1655 (1978)

3. P.A.Amundsen, L.Kocbach and J.M.Hansteen, J.Phys.B9, L 203 (1976)

4. B.Knaf, G.Presser and J.Stähler, Z.Physik A289, 131 (1979)

5. W.Brandt and K.W.Jones, Phys.Lett.57A, 35 (1976)

6. W.E.Meyerhof, Phys.Rev.Lett.31, 1341 (1973)

EMISSION OF CHARACTERISTIC AND NONCHARACTERISTIC
X-RAYS INDUCED BY Cu, Se, Ag AND Sb IONS

G.Presser, E.Scherer, J.Stähler and T.Thouw

Institut für Physik, Universität Dortmund
D 4600 Dortmund-50, Germany

We have measured absolute cross sections for production of
characteristic (K, L) and noncharacteristic X-rays in collisions of
1 - 30 MeV Cu, Se, Ag and Sb ions and target atoms with atomic
numbers in the range Z_2 = 18 to 63. The experiments were performed
with thin solid targets (10-100 $\mu g/cm^2$) and with differentially
pumped gas targets (Ar, Kr, Xe) under single collision conditions.
The X-rays were measured at 90° to the beam direction with a Si(Li)
detector. Angular distributions of X-rays were also studied for some
collision systems.

Cross sections of characteristic X-ray emission and cross section
ratios for X-ray emission from projectile and target or for emission
from different subshells in the case of L X-rays are compared with
theoretical predictions. In Fig.1 experimental K-shell cross sections
of the Cu-Kr collision system are shown together with statistical
model calculations.[1]

Intensity ratios of characteristic L X-rays emitted in heavy ion-
atom collisions can be used to get information on the coupling of
molecular orbitals and seperated atom levels.[2] A comparison between
experimental data and calculations of a vacancy sharing model[2] for

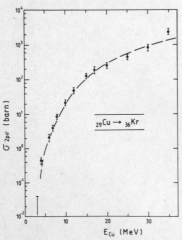

the Sb+Xe system is given in Fig.2. Evidently a $4f\sigma$-L_3 correlation is favoured
by the experimental results.

Fig.1:
Comparison of experimental cross sections
for $2p\sigma$ ionization and statistical model
calculations. A diffusion constant
$D_K = ((Z_1 + Z_2)/13)^2 \hbar/m$ was used.

Doppler shift measurements of noncharacteristic X-rays indicate that X-rays
observed in the energy interval between
characteristic L and K X-rays are preferentially emitted from the united system.
The shape of the NC X-ray spectra from the

$\sigma_{2p\sigma}$ (barn)

E_{Cu} (MeV)

$_{29}Cu \rightarrow {}_{36}Kr$

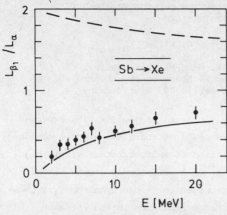

Fig.2:
Intensity ratio of $L\beta_{1,3}$ and $L_{\alpha 1,2}$ of X-rays of Sb[1],[3] for the almost symmetric collision system Sb+Xe, measured with a Xe gas target. The thick line represents calculations for a $4f\sigma-L_3$, the broken line for a $4f\sigma-L_1$ coupling.

Ag+Xe (gas target) and Ag+Cs (solid target) collision systems is in fair agreement with calculations.[3] The projectile energy dependence of the X-ray anisotropy was studied for Ag-Ag collisions at energies from 2 to 30 MeV. Significant changes in the anisotropy pattern were observed at lower (<10 MeV) bombarding energies.

1. W.Brandt and K.W.Jones, Phys.Lett.57A, 35 (1976)
2. W.E.Meyerhof et al., Preprint (1978) and private communication
3. T.Morović et al., Phys.Lett.63A, 12 (1977)

MOLECULAR–ORBITAL APPROACH TO ION–ATOM COLLISIONS WITH
MULTIPLY CHARGED PROJECTILES

J. Eichler, W. Fritsch and U. Wille

Bereich Kern- und Strahlenphysik, Hahn-Meitner-Institut für
Kernforschung Berlin GmbH, and Fachbereich Physik, Freie
Universität Berlin, D-1000 Berlin 39, West Germany

In slow ion-atom collisions with multiply charged projectiles the experimentally prepared initial state is an *excited* state of the quasimolecule composed of the target and the projectile. The definition of selfconsistent single-electron states, however, demands the construction of a variational *ground* state. In an earlier paper[1], it has, therefore, been proposed to impose upon the variational problem a constraint which enforces the charge imbalance in the entrance channel. One then obtains a new type of correlation diagram exhibiting curve crossings of levels with like symmetry.

This variational procedure will be numerically quite cumbersome to carry out. In the present work, we make use of the fact that the constraint can be interpreted as an auxiliary electric field $\mathcal{F}(R)$ (R internuclear distance) in the direction of the internuclear line (z-axis), which maintains the charge imbalance in a prescribed manner. We therefore simulate the results of a constrained variational procedure by introducing a modified effective Hamiltonian

$$H'_{eff} (R) = H_{eff} (R) - \mathcal{F}(R) \frac{z}{R/2}$$

where H_{eff} is provided by the variable-screening model[2]. The auxiliary field is adjusted at $R = \infty$ to the asymptotic energy difference of the experimental single-particle energies of the weakest-bound electrons. For $R < \infty$, $\mathcal{F}(R)$ reflects the charge equilibration during the collision and hence drops from its maximum value $\mathcal{F}(\infty)$ to $\mathcal{F}(0) = 0$. This behavior is phenomenologically represented by a Fermi function involving a characteristic charge equilibration radius R_c. Once $\mathcal{F}(R)$ is known, the Hamiltonian $H'_{eff}(R)$ can be diagonalized[2]. The single-electron energies can then be obtained as expectation values of $H_{eff}(R)$.

In Figs. 1 and 2 we present molecular correlation diagrams for the resulting "constrained physical energies". The systems N^{2+}+O and Ne^{4+}+Ne are shown as examples for a heteronuclear and homonuclear system, respectively.

Crossings between energy curves of like symmetry are indicated by arrows. The existence of these crossings is no violation of the noncrossing rule because the curves represent expectation values and not eigenenergies[1].

In both cases the correlation diagrams are consistent with the experimental results of Fortner et al.[3] who have measured the cross section for K-shell vacancy production in ion-atom collisions for various target-projectile combinations as a function of the charge state of the projectile. Both in the experiments and in our calculated diagrams the correlations turn out to be the same as for

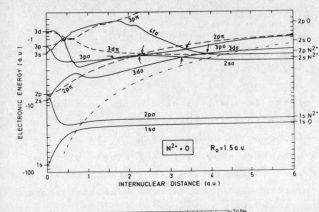

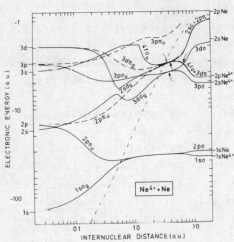

Fig. 1.
Correlation diagram for
the system N^{2+}+O. The
charge equilibration radius
is R_0= 1.5 a.u. The dash-
dot curve indicates the
height of the barrier
separating the two potential wells.

Fig. 2.
Correlation diagram for the system
Ne^{4+}+Ne. The charge equilibration
radius is R_0= 11 a.u. .

charge-balanced (or neutral) systems.

In conclusion it should be emphasized that our method to treat charge imbalance is relevant also for current experiments in which ion beams with very high
charge state are used.

1. J. Eichler, Phys. Rev. Lett. 40, 1560 (1978).
2. J. Eichler, U. Wille, Phys. Rev. A11, 1973 (1975)
3. R.J. Fortner, P.H. Woerlee, S. Doorn, Th.P. Hoogkamer, F.W. Saris,
   Phys. Rev. Lett. 39, 1322 (1977)

ION IMPACT IONIZATION OF BOTH 2s-ELECTRONS OF NEON

H.F. Beyer*, K.-H. Schartner, and R. Hippler**

I. Physikalisches Institut, Universität Giessen
Heinrich-Buff-Ring 16, D 6300 Giessen, W. Germany

Ion impact ionization of the 2s-shell of neon gains continuous interest (e.g. [1]). From the theoretical viewpoint this is due to the stronger binding of the 2s-electrons in comparison with the 2p-electrons, which supports a tentative application of single electron molecular orbitals commonly used in ionization processes of inner shells at sufficiently low impact velocities. At the same time these models are tested at the limits of their validity[2].

The experimental interest is apart from provision of data for comparison with calculated values due to the still existing experimental difficulties in determining accurate cross sections. They are caused by the spectral range of about 40 nm to 50 nm wherein the transitions filling 2s-vacancies of neon are observed[3].

In the course of studies related to this problem we have measured the ion impact ionization of both 2s-electrons of the neon L-shell. The transition $2s^o2p^6(^1S_o)-2s2p^5(^1P_1)$ can be observed at 52,82 nm[4]. H^+, He^+, and Ne^+-ions have been used as projectiles with energies between 50 keV and 1000 keV. In the case of Ne^+-ions, also He served as target gas. For the symmetric collision system Ne^++Ne, target and projectile radiation were seperated by the Doppler effect.

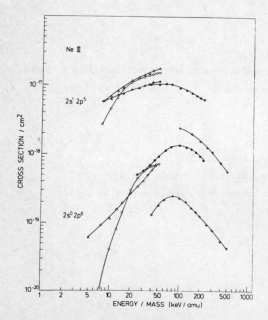

Fig. 1
Cross sections for production of the $2s2p^5$- and $2s^o2p^6$ configurations of neon.

+++ H^++Ne

●●● He^++Ne

ooo Ne^++He

▲▲▲
      Ne^++Ne
ΔΔΔ

Fig. 1 presents the measured cross sections as function of projectile energy divided by its atomic mass number. The full data points
indicate ionization of the target, the open ones ionization of the
projectile. For Ne^++Ne collisions, target and projectile cross sections are the same. In the upper part of fig. 1 cross sections
which we have measured for production of the $2s2p^5$ configuration
consisting of the summed cross sections for the ^1P- and the ^3P-
states are shown for comparison.

The presented data cover collision systems and energy ranges
where different excitation mechanism are expected to work. For the
impact velocities of the Ne^+-ions molecular excitation may dominate.

It can explain cross sections being equal for projectile and
target in Ne^++Ne collisions. Also the small cross sections at the
low velocities in the Ne^++He collisions can be understood qualitatively by the separation of the molecular orbital, leading the 2s-
electrons, from higher orbitals. At the higher impact velocities of
the H^+- and He^+-projectiles Coulomb ionization is expected to work
demonstrated by the maximum and the decrease of the cross sections.
A strong increase of the cross sections when going from H^+ to He^1
is observed (factor of 6). Classical models of double ionization[5]
processes predict a Z_{eff}^4 dependence resulting in $Z_{eff} \approx 1.6$ which
is quite reasonable.

The cross sections for production of the $2s^o2p^6(^1S_o)$ state are
necessary for cascade corrections of the cross sections for production of the $2s2p^5(^1P_1)$ state.

*   Permanent address: Gesellschaft für Schwerionenforschung,
                         D-6100 Darmstadt, W. Germany
** Permanent address: Fakultät für Physik, Universität Bielefeld,
                         D-4800 Bielefeld, W. Germany

1.   E. Bloemen, H. Winter, F.J. de Heer, R. Fortner, A. Salop,
     J. Phys. B 11, 4207 (1978)

2.   W. Fritsch, U. Wille, J. Phys. B 11, 4019 (1978)

3.   H.F. Beyer, R. Hippler, K.-H. Schartner, and R. Albat,
     Z. Physik A 289, 239 (1979)

4.   H.F. Beyer, M. Gros, R. Hippler, and K.-H. Schartner,
     Phys. Letters, 68A, 215 (1978)

5.   M. Gryzinski, Phys. Rev. 138, A336 (1965)

AUGER SPECTROSCOPY OF DEMOTING MO IN Kr$^+$-Kr QUASIMOLECULE

V.V.Afrosimov, G.G.Meskhi, N.N.Tsarev, A.P.Shergin

A.F.Ioffe Physical-Technical Institute,
USSR Academy of Sciences, Leningrad, USSR

Auger transitions in quasimolecule formed in Kr$^+$-Kr collisions at 50 keV are investigated by the coincidence "electron -
scattered ion" technique which enables us to measure the electron
energy spectra for definite impact parameters. Due to the impact
parameter definition $E_e(R)$ - the energy gap between the MO's involved in the Auger transition, and $W_A(R)$ - the vacancy decay probability, as a function of internuclear distance R can be derived
from the electron energy spectra much easier than in [1].

Fig.I shows the electron spectra measured at several impact
parameters. An intensive part of the spectra at E_e<I00 eV is connected primarily with 3d-vacancy decay in Kr ions after collision,
a wide distribution distinctly seen at E_e>I00 eV is due to Auger
transitions in quasimolecule. It is clearly seen in Fig.I that the
high energy side of MO distribution shifts to higher energies with
the impact parameter decrease. It indicates that the MO level energy gap increases as R decreases.

The dependence of $E_e(R)$ can be found from the MO electron
energy at the turning point R_o. In MO spectrum $d^2\sigma/dE_e dp$ the peak
abruptly cut off from the high energy side must exist at E_e corresponding to R_o. In real conditions there are several reasons leading to broadening the peak. To a large extent the broadening is
caused by the existence of the wide spectrum of upper electron levels populated in collisions. Even in the case when the vacancies
(3d-vacancies, for example) decay in separated atoms after collision the width of the Auger electron energy distribution has to be
as high as 40 eV [1]. The Doppler broadening caused by kinematic effects gives ~I0 eV. The dynamic effects [2] can also be a reason
for broadening.

Fig.2 shows $E_e(R)$ obtained after the correction of the experimental cross sections for the known broadening components.
$E_e(R)$ from [1] is also shown with dashed line. The accuracy of $E_e(R)$
determination in this experiment is more than 3 times higher than
in [1]. Specification of the collision trajectory makes it possible
also to determine $W_A(R)$ more accurately and principally easier
than in [1]. As shown in [3], Auger decay probability can be analytically expressed by measured cross section $d^2\sigma/dE_e dp$ and parameters

of the MO. Fig.2 shows $W_A(R)$ obtained in assumption of one initial vacancy in the MO. It is seen that $W_A(R)$ increases as R decreases and is approximately equal to $\sim 10^{16}$ sec^{-1}, i.e. the proper autoionization width of the MO level is ~ 10 eV.

I. V.V. Afrosimov, Yu.S.Gordeev, A.N.Zinoviev, D.H.Rasulov, A.P.Shergin. Pisma Zh.E.T.F., 24, 33 (1976), V.V.Afrosimov, Yu.S.Gordeev, A.N.Zinoviev, A.A.Korotkov, A.P.Shergin. Abstr. X ICPEAC, Paris, 1977, p.924.

2. G.Gerber and A.Niehaus. J.Phys.B, 9, 123 (1976).

3. V.V.Afrosimov, G.G.Meskhi, N.N.Tsarev, A.P.Shergin. Abstr. VI ICAP, Riga, 1978, p.398.

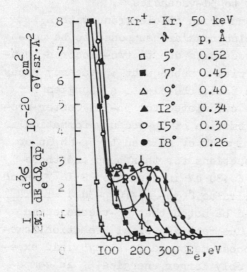

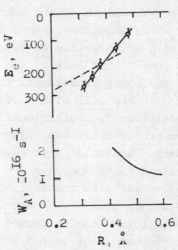

Fig. I. Energy spectra of electrons ejected in Kr^+- Kr collisions at 50 keV and at specified impact parameters p.

Fig. 2. Electron energy $E_e(R)$ and Auger decay probability of vacancy in demoting MO $W_A(R)$ as a function of internuclear distance R in Kr^+- Kr quasi-molecule. (—o— present experiment, ---- exp.[1])

DISCRETE STRUCTURE IN ENERGY SPECTRA OF ELECTRONS PRODUCED IN CLOSE Kr$^+$- Kr COLLISIONS

V.V.AFROSIMOV, YU.S.GORDEEV, A.P.SHERGIN,A.N.ZINOVIEV

A.F.Ioffe Physical-Technical Institute
USSR Academy of Sciences, Leningrad, USSR

In [1] the energy spectra of electrons produced in Kr$^+$-Kr collisions in the initial energy range E_o= 5÷50 keV have been measured. Fig.I shows the electron spectra for E_o= 5, 7.5 and I0 keV. Two groups of peaks with markedly distinguished cross-sections are seen. The first group is situated at the energies E_e= 20÷60 eV and connected with Auger transitions to 3d-vacancies [1].

Here the origin of the second group of electrons with E_e = = 60÷80 eV is discussed. These electrons are supposed to be connected with the creation of 3p-vacancies due to two-electron transitions (6h6^{-2}- 5f6^{-I}nlλ^{-I}) and with a subsequent 3p-vacancy decay via Coster-Kronig transition. In fact, the electron energies (60÷80 eV) agree well with those calculated for 3p-3dN Coster-Kronig transitions [2]. Another confirmation of 3p-vacancy formation is the presence of small bump with $E_e \approx$ I40 eV related to 3p-NN Auger transition. The ratio of cross-sections for this bump and those for electrons with energies E_e= 60÷80 eV is equal to ~2·I0^{-2} which is in agreement with theoretical value Γ(3p-NN)/Γ(3p-3dN) =I5·I0^{-2} for 3p-vacancy decay [3]. It should be noted that 3p-vacancies in Kr$^+$-Kr collisions can be formed due to 5f6-orbital promotion.However, the threshold of such a process measured in X-ray yield experiment [4] is situated at considerably larger energies E_o in comparison with energies in our case. Moreover remarkably, the cross-section for the emission of electrons with E_e= 60÷80 eV 6 has the threshold at the same E_o as the two 3d-vacancy production cross-section 6 (3d^{-2}) [5].

It is known [5] that in Kr$^+$-Kr collisions at the internuclear distances less than ~0.5 Å two 6h6-vacancies are formed with probability equal to I. Quasimolecular levels 6h6^{-2} and 5f6^{-I}nlλ^{-I} seem to be close to one another at large internuclear distances because in Kr ions the energies of states with two 3d-vacancies and with one 3p-vacancy are close to each other and even can coincide at some degree of outer shell excitation and ionization [2]. Outer shell excitation and ionization being rather strong in our case [5], the exact coincidence of energies can occur in the part of cases and such states prove to be strongly coupled due to two-

electron transitions in outgoing part of the collision. The obtained ratio of $\sigma/\sigma(3d^{-2})$ is indeed equal to 0.10 ± 0.03.

In [6] the two-electron transitions resulting in K-ionization
of N atom due to energy level crossing in N^{+}- Ar quasimolecule were studied. The transition probability was $2\div3\cdot10^{-3}$. In the present case 3p-vacancies are formed due to transitions between close
energy states. For this reason the two-electron probability turns
out to be considerably higher and practically does not depend on
collision velocity.

I. V.V.Afrosimov,Yu.S.Gordeev,A.N.Zinoviev,D.H.Rasulov,
    A.P.Shergin. Pisma ZhETF 24, 33 (1976).
2. F.P.Larkins. J.Phys.B 6, 2450 (1973).
3. E.J.McGuire. Phys.Rev. A5, 1043 (1972).
4. H.Tawara,C.Foster,F.J.de Heer. Phys.Lett.43A,266 (1973).
5. V.V.Afrosimov,Yu.S.Gordeev,A.M.Polansky,A.P.Shergin.
    Zh.Techn.Fiz. 41, 134 (1972).
6. V.V.Afrosimov,Yu.S.Gordeev,A.N.Zinoviev,D.H.Rasulov,
    A.P.Shergin. Abstracts IX ICPEAC, Seattle, 1975, p.1066.

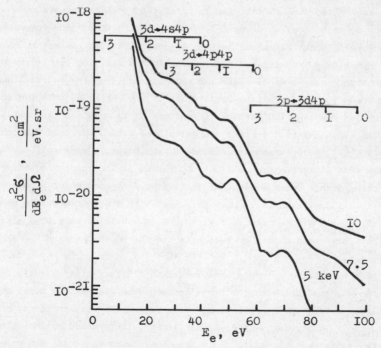

Fig. I. Energy spectra of electrons ejected in Kr^{+}- Kr collisions at 5, 7.5 and 10 keV. Electron energies calculated in [2]
for different degree of outer shell ionization are shown.

THEORETICAL INVESTIGATION OF K-L VACANCY SHARING IN SLOW NE+KR COLLISIONS

W. Fritsch and U. Wille

Bereich Kern- und Strahlenphysik, Hahn-Meitner-Institut für Kernforschung Berlin,
and Fachbereich Physik, Freie Universität Berlin, D-1000 Berlin 39, West Germany

While there is increasing experimental information on K-L vacancy-sharing
processes in strongly asymmetric collision systems such as B+Ar and Ne+Kr, no con-
clusive theoretical analysis has been performed on these data as yet. The theoretical interpretation on the basis of the molecular-orbital (MO) picture generally
starts from the assumption that during the collision process vacancies are created
in the diabatic $3d\sigma$ orbital near the united-atom limit. In the outgoing part of
the collision these vacancies are assumed to be shared due to dynamical couplings
between the adiabatic 4σ orbital and the 3σ, 2σ and 1π orbitals which correlate,
respectively, to the K shell of the lighter and to the L shell of the heavier
collision partner. The K-L sharing ratio is then commonly calculated from the
closed-form Nikitin formula which is based on the following assumptions: (i) the
sharing results from the coupling of two orbitals only, in the present case from
4σ-3σ coupling; (ii) the MO energies are given by diagonalization of the Hamiltonian in the space of two atomic orbitals; (iii) the potential-coupling matrix elements depend exponentially on the internuclear separation, the parameters being
fixed by a fit of the Nikitin energies to otherwise known MO spectra.

In this contribution, we study K-L vacancy sharing within the framework of
the coupled-state impact-parameter method. We concentrate on the Ne+Kr collision
system which has been investigated experimentally and analysed within the Nikitin
model by Woerlee et al.[1]. Single-particle energies and coupling matrix elements
are constructed from the effective Hamiltonian of the variable-screening model[2]
(VSM), which has been applied earlier in studies[3] of K- and L-shell excitation
processes. Internuclear trajectories are calculated from a screened Coulomb potential; only those trajectories are considered which result in a sufficiently
small distance of closest approach R_o ($R_o \leq 0.15$ a.u.). The coupled equations are
solved starting from R_o with a constant initial vacancy occupation probability in
the 4σ orbital. Calculations have been performed with the four orbitals mentioned
above as well as with two orbitals, i.e. 4σ and 3σ orbitals, only. Two potential
parameter sets have been chosen corresponding to the Ne$^+$+Kr and the Ne^{4+}+Kr system, respectively.

Fig. 1 shows sharing ratios of the two-state and four-state calculations for
the system Ne$^+$+Kr together with the curve derived from the Nikitin model as well
as experimental data[1]. In the following, we summarize the results of our study.

(i) In the velocity range under investigation, the sharing ratios of the full
dynamical two-state and four-state calculations are very close to each other al-
though, e.g., the 4σ-3σ and the 4σ-2σ coupling matrix elements are of roughly equal magnitude[4]. This finding can be attributed to the decisive rôle which is played
by the energy phases in the coupled equations and which is reflected in the rough-

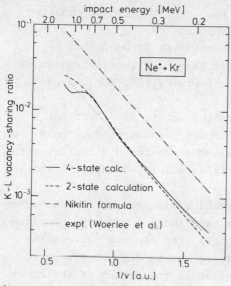

Fig. 1.

K-L vacancy sharing ratio for the Ne[+]+Kr system vs. the inverse collision velocity 1/v. The experimental curve shows X-ray data of Woerlee et al. on the system Ne[2+]+Kr, multiplied with the ratio of fluorescence yields[5] for single-hole atoms.

ly exponential dependence of the sharing ratio on 1/v. For the same reason an exponential dependence of the sharing ratio on the magnitude of the MO energy differences is expected and, therefore, the coupling of the 2σ to the 4σ orbital is negligible. We note that coupling of more than two orbitals can be important in cases where energy phases are less dominant, i.e. for higher collision velocities or for less asymmetric collision systems.

   (ii) The slope of the Nikitin curve is nearly identical to that of the coupled state results, mainly because the MO energies of the VSM enter directly[1] into the Nikitin formalism.

   (iii) The Nikitin formula overestimates the results of the full dynamical calculations by a factor of about four. It appears that the Nikitin coupling matrix element deviates largely from that calculated from VSM wave functions.

   (iv) Using the ratio of fluorescence yields[5] of single-hole atoms, the experimental data[1] for the system Ne[2+]+Kr is very close to the curves representing the coupled-state results. This agreement, however, may be fortuitous. Assuming that the ratio of fluorescence yields is independent of the projectile charge state, the experimental data[1] shows vacancy-sharing ratios decreasing with increasing charge state, while in our calculation the sharing ratio for the system Ne[4+]+Kr is larger than that for Ne[+]+Kr by a factor varying between 1.3 and 1.6. Measurements observing both X-ray and Auger transitions are called for.

   1.   P.H. Woerlee, R.J. Fortner, S. Doorn, Th.P. Hoogkamer, F.W. Saris, J. Phys. B 11, L425 (1978).

   2.   J. Eichler, U. Wille, Phys. Rev. A 11, 1973 (1975).

   3.   W. Fritsch, U. Wille, J. Phys. B 10, L165 (1977); ibid. 11, 4019 (1978).

   4.   W. Fritsch, U. Wille, Proc.5th Conf.Use of Small Accelerators,Denton 1978

   5.   M.O. Krause, J. Phys. Chem. Ref. Data, in print.

AN IMPROVED CALCULATION OF THE $2p_\pi$ - $2p_\sigma$ ROTATIONAL COUPLING
IN HEAVY ION COLLISION

B. Fricke, W.-D. Sepp, T. Morovič and A. Rosén[§]

Department of Physics, University of Kassel, D35 Kassel, Germany
[§] Department of Physics, Chalmers University, Göteborg, Sweden

The theoretical interpretation by Taulbjerg et. al.[1,2] of the K
X-ray cross section as function of impact parameter after heavy ion
bombardementhas been very successful. The predicted structure with
a kinematic and an adiabatic peak[3] is especially good for light and
nearly symmetric systems.[2,4]
For heavier colliding atoms an increasing discrepancy between experiment and theory is observed.[4] The experimental adiabatic maximum
is located at smaller impact parameters, the minimum between the
adiabatic and kinematic peak usually is not so deep as predicted
and a very strong experimental increase in the region of the kinematic peak is observed. There may be various reasons for these discrepancies. In most cases a scaled theoretical curve is used.[2] The
influence of the greater number of electrons in the system becomes
larger and no relativistic influence has ever been discussed. In
addition to this the direct ionization will be larger for heavier
systems and high impact energies. This effect should be subtracted
accurately which is not yet possible.
To check all these possible influences in some detail we have tried
to calculate the heavy system Ar-Cl as an example as accurate as
possible.This system (Ar-Ar) has also been measured.[5] As a first
step we have calculated a self-consistent adiabatic relativistic
correlation diagram. As one of the results of these calculations we
get realistic energetic distances between the 1π and 2σ levels as
function of the internuclear distance. Due to spin-orbit splitting
we get additional (pseudo-)crossings in the relativistic treatment
near 0.02 au. Also rotational coupling between σ levels (relativis-
tically Ω=1/2) has to be considered.
We do not only discussin detail the influence of these effects for
the special system Ar-Cl but also give general trends which result
from these more specific considerations.

1. K. Taulbjerg and J.S. Briggs, J. Phys. B8, 1895 (1975) ;
   J.S. Briggs and K. Taulbjerg, J. Phys. B8, 1909 (1975)
2. K. Taulbjerg, J.S. Briggs and J. Vaaben, J.Phys. B9, 1351 (1976)
3. J.S. Briggs and J. Macek, J. Phys. B5, 579 (1972)
4. H.O. Lutz, N. Luz, S. Sackmann, W. Jitschin and R. Hippler,
   Proc. Int. Workshop on Coherence and Correl. Phen. in Atomic
   Coll. London Sept. 1978
5. H.O. Lutz et. al. , Phys. Rev. Lett. 40, 1133 (1978)

V. Ion (Atom)-Molecule and Molecule-Molecule Collisions

H-D$_2$ AND H-Ne TOTAL SCATTERING CROSS SECTIONS AT THERMAL ENERGY

N. Hishinuma

Institute of Physics, College of General Education,
University of Tokyo, Komaba 3-8-1, Meguro-ku, Tokyo153, Japan

Absolute total scattering cross sections for the system H-D$_2$ and H-Ne are measured in the range of hydrogen atom velocities from 0.6 to 8Km/sec.

The primary beam produced by a rf-discharge source is velocity analyzed with a mechanical selector (FWHM9%). Hydrogen atoms are detected using a ZnO single crystal whose electric conductivity shows specific sensitivity to the atoms. The detector is completely insensitive to the undissociated hydrogen molecules in the primary beam. Velocity dependences of the effective cross sections are measured using a scattering chamber kept at the temperature 94.5K. The constant pressure in the scattering chamber is maintained using a fixed gas leak at a controlled temperature and keeping the reservoir pressure constant. Measurements of absolute effective cross sections at the primary beam velocity 4Km/sec and at target gas temperature 292K are made replacing the scattering chamber with another one which is specially designed for the accurate determination of the density of target gases by a dynamic expansion method.

Fig. 1 shows the comparison of our results with previous ones.[1,2,3] The calibration of our data is made by correcting the measured absolute effective cross sections (45.4 $\overset{\circ}{A}^2$ for H-D$_2$ and 42.7$\overset{\circ}{A}^2$ for H-Ne with accuracy of about 1%) for target gas temperature. As is shown in Fig.1 our results for H-D$_2$ are in good agreement with the previous results in the velocity dependence, but have smaller absolute values which suggest a little smaller distance parameters for the interaction potential. For H-Ne collision there exist rather large discrepancy between the two results in the velocity dependence. From our results it is clearly seen that the H-Ne repulsive potential is harder than the H-D$_2$ repulsive potential. Our H-Ne results also indicate a shallower well depth of the potential than the value obtained by the previous work.[3]

The H-Ne potential is considered to have a very close well depth to the well depth of H-H$_2$ potential from the concept of combination rule. The determination of the well depth is relatively easier for H-Ne case, because the hardness of repulsive potential and smaller thermal velocities of target Ne make it easy to observe the increase of cross section by the weak attractive potential. So, we think our measurements give useful imformation for more reliable determination of the H-H$_2$ potential. A Detailed analysis will be presented at the Conference.

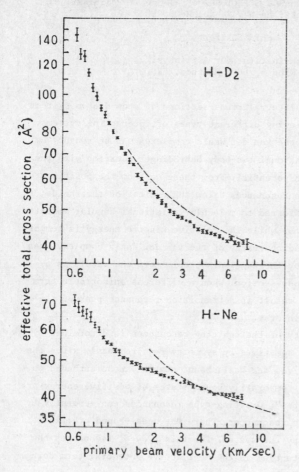

Fig. 1 The measured absolute
effective cross sections
plotted as a function of primary beam velocity. The target
temperature is 94.5K. Error
bars represent ± one standard
deviation of the mean cross
section. The broken line for
H–D₂ collision is taken from
ref.2 in which the velocity
dependence of cross section
obtained in the work of ref.1
(secondary beam at 77K) is
calibrated using the absolute
cross sections measured by the
authors of ref. 2. The broken
line for H–Ne collision is tak-
en from ref.3 (secondary beam
at 77K).

1. W. Bauer, R. W. Bickes, Jr., B. Lantzsch, J.P. Toennies and K. Walaschewski,
    Chem. Phys. Letters 31, 12 (1975).

2. R. Gengenbach, Ch. Hahn and J.P. Toennies, J. Chem. Phys. 62, 3620 (1975).

3. R.W. Bickes, Jr., B. Lantzsch, J.P. Toennies and K. Walaschewski,
    Disc. Farady Soc. 55, 167 (1973).

A DISCUSSION OF THE RESONANCE STRUCTURES OF ATOM-DIATOM SYSTEMS.
EXAMPLES: He-H$_2$, Xe-HD, H-CO

Joachim Schäfer

Max-Planck-Institut für Astrophysik,
Föhringer Ring 6, 8000 München, FRG.

The resonance structures of integral cross sections of atom-diatom systems will be discussed briefly by reviewing different types of interacting systems.

The bound state energies of the van der Waals complexes can be roughly determined by solving the 1-dimensional two-body Schrödinger equation with the isotropic atom-diatom interaction potential. From these we know the positions of the sharply peaking Feshbach-type resonances below the excitation thresholds: orbital angular momentum is transferred to molecular rotational angular momentum by the anisotropic potential terms, while the relative kinetic energy is temporarily lowered to the negative binding energy of the van der Waals complex. When the backward transition is done by the same anisotropic term the result is a resonance peak of the elastic cross section. When a different anisotropic term does the backward transition the result is a transition resonance peak of the inelastic cross section and its inverse.

The positions and the variety of the orbiting resonances is determined by the isotropic potential as well (and sometimes by symmetry requirements), since the vibrational-rotational series of van der Waals bound states can be extended to positive energies. Usually these temporarily bound states of positive energy are called "quasi-bound orbiting states". Orbiting-type resonances can generally be considered as quasi-Feshbach-type resonances. There the quasi-bound orbiting states are temporarily occupied by the system. For this type of resonances the leading isotropic interaction potential is the most active potential term doing the tunneling through the centrifugal barriers.

The findings extracted from the systems presented can be summarized as follows:

1) Resonance structure can be neglected when van der Walls bound state complexes are missing: The representative system showing this is He-H$_2$. The interaction potential used for calculations of cross sections of this system is pure ab initio and has been provided by W. Meyer et al.[1].

2) We can expect a significant orbiting resonance structure of the cross sections when there are several vibrational and orbiting rotational series of van der Waals bound states. The representative system showing this is Xe-HD. The interaction potential used for this system is a Tang-Toennies-type potential provided by J. P. Toennies and co-workers[2].

3) Significant Feshbach-type resonance structure can be expected when the molecular rotational excitation energies are of the same order of magnitude as the binding energies of the van der Waals complexes, and when the aniso-

tropies are at least medium sized. The system showing this type of resonance structure is H-CO. The interaction potential used for the calculations
has been published previously by S. Green and P. Thaddeus[3].

4) The lifetimes of the quasi-bound van der Waals complexes formed by the atoms
and rotationally excited molecules do not generally and monotonously decrease
for increasing relative kinetic energy, but roughly they do. Larger anisotropies in the range of the attractive well cause smaller lifetimes (or
larger peak widths).

5) In some cases sharp peaks of the partial integral cross sections do not show
up in the cross section for several reasons: There can be a different partial
wave having a negative peak at the same energy, or there can be many other
partial waves contributing as much or even more to the integral cross section.
The latter can be expected generally when the excitation energies of the
molecule are too large. Thus resonance structure can only show up in measured
integral cross sections for low relative kinetic energy collisions (up to
about 10 meV)

6) The resonance structures of inelastic cross sections (orders of magnitude
smaller) are generally much sharper than those of the elastic cross sections.
This in fact is just another confirmation of the well-known effect that
smaller cross sections are more sensitive than larger ones. For H-CO and
comparable systems even the rate coefficients should for this reason be
significantly dependent upon the resonance structure of the cross sections
at low temperatures.

1. W. Meyer and W. Kutzelnigg, private communication.
2. J.P. Toennies and K. Müller, private communication.
3. S. Green and P. Thaddeus, Astrophys. J. 205, 766 (1976).

A NEW H-H$_2$ SPHERICAL POTENTIAL FROM HIGH RESOLUTION
MOLECULAR BEAM EXPERIMENTS*

M.G. Dondi and F. Torello

Istituto di Scienze Fisiche dell'Università di Genova - Italy

High resolution elastic differential cross section measurements are reported for D-H$_2$ over an extended angular interval (up
to 100° in the CM system) with the interference structure fully resolved.[1] The quality of the data is greatly improved in comparison
to previous experiments on similar systems[2] due to a better geometry and to a careful minimization of the detector noise. The experimental apparatus is essentially the same of ref. 2. A velocity
selected (10% FWHM) atomic beam crosses the multichannel secondary
beam (temperature 20°K) at right angles and is detected by a bolo-
meter. The most probable relative collision energy (35.8 meV) is
below the threshold for rotational excitation.

Differential cross sections are calculated by direct numerical
integration of the Schrödinger equation, converted into the laboratory system and averaged over the experimental conditions. Trial
calculations performed with several spherical potential forms and
recent theoretical results suggest the following modified Born-
-Mayer-Dispersion potential:

$$V(r) = A \exp(-br-cr^2) - (\frac{C_6}{r^6} + \frac{C_8}{r^8} + \frac{C_{10}}{r^{10}}) F(r)$$

The repulsive term accounts for the Hartree-Fock energy and the
intra-atomic correlation correction to it. The expanded dispersion
terms are multiplied by a damping function F(r) which accounts for
charge-overlap and dispersion-exchange effect. For F(r) we assume
the function proposed in ref. 3 and for the coefficients C_6, C_8,
C_{10} the recent values of Meyer[4] were taken (8.813, 163.87, 4023.2
a.u.). The three free parameters are determined with standard trial-
-and-error methods (A = 29.5 eV, b = 2.3145 Å^{-1}, c = 0.1004 Å^{-2});
the resulting well depth is 1.83 meV at 3.46 Å and the distance at
which the potential is zero is 2.99 Å. This potential accounts for
our differential cross section experiment and for the integral cross
section measurements at low velocities of ref.5 with great accuracy.

A complete discussion and analysis of the present experiment with several empirical, semiempirical and theoretical potential surfaces will be reported at the Conference.

Work on other H(D)-molecule systems is in progress.

* Work supported by the Italian National Research Council through the "Gruppo Nazionale di Struttura della Materia".

1) F. Torello and M.G. Dondi – J. Chem. Phys. 70, 1564 (1979)

2) D. Bassi, M.G. Dondi, F. Tommasini, F. Torello and U. Valbusa – Phys. Rev. 13A, 584 (1976)

3) R. Ahlrichs, R. Penco and G. Scoles – Chem. Phys. 19, 119 (1977)

4) W. Meyer – private communication 1978

5) W. Welz – Dissertation, Bonn 1976. Max-Planck-Institut für Strömungsforschung, Göttingen. Ber. 20/1976; J.P. Toennies, W. Welz and G. Wolf – to be published.

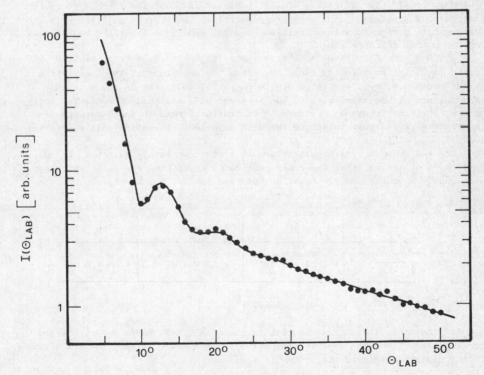

Fig. 1. Experimental points (●). Effective differential cross section calculated with the potential described in the text (——), versus the laboratory angle.

ABSOLUTE TOTAL CROSS SECTIONS FOR COLLISION IN $O-O_2$, O_2-O_2, $O-N_2$, O_2-N_2 SYSTEMS.

B.Brunetti, G.Liuti, E.Luzzatti, F.Pirani, and F.Vecchiocattivi.
Dipartimento di Chimica dell'Università di Perugia
06100 Perugia, Italy.

The absolute total cross sections for $O-O_2$, $O-N_2$, O_2-O_2, O_2-N_2 collisions have been measured as a function of velocity in a range between 0.7 and 2.2 Km/s. A beam containing O atoms and O_2 molecules from a microwave discharge in pure O_2 at 800 K° yielding up to 30% dissociation, is velocity selected by a slotted disk selector with ± 3% resolution and is scattered by N_2 or O_2 kept in a scat= tering box cooled to liquid nitrogen temperature. Detection is performed by a quadrupole mass spectrometer and measurement of O signal and of the O_2 signal can be made under the same experimental conditions of the whole apparatus/1/.

In figure 1 the absolute total cross sections for the systems studied are reported plotted as $Qv^{2/5}$ vs. 1/v. Deconvolution of the experimental cross sec= tions has not been performed since, even at liquid nitrogen temperature, the velocity spread of the target gases is comparable to the spacing of the observed oscillations.

The O_2-O_2 and O_2-N_2 systems show a glory structure of equal amplitude and frequency. Also this structure is very similar to the oscillations observed for O_2-Ar system /2/. In addition a similar behavior is found for these systems for gas phase IR spectra/3/ and transport properties. Therefore a multiproperty ana= lysis can be performed using flexible potential models to describe the interac= tion in a wide distance range.

The $O-N_2$ cross section is also very similar to the O-Ar cross section /1/ in the investigated velocity range. Here too the amplitude of the oscillation is not reproduced by a realistic single potential model. As in the O-Ar case such failure can be attributed to the presence of a manifold of potential energy curves. The same treatment of the data as that performed in the O-rare gases experiments is underway to obtain the most detailed information on the interac= tion.

For $O-O_2$ the oscillatory structure is almost completely quenched. In addi= tion the absolute value of the cross section is lower than the value which can be aspected from the similar behavior observed for Ar, N_2, and O_2.

X	Ar	N_2	O_2
$\dfrac{Q(O_2-X)}{Q(O-X)}$	1.24 ± 0.01	1.23 ± 0.01	1.30 ± 0.01

TABLE I

In the table I the cross section ratios O_2-X / O-X, where X= Ar, N_2, and O_2, are reported. Since the experimental error in this ratio is very small a signi= ficant deviation is evident for $O-O_2$.

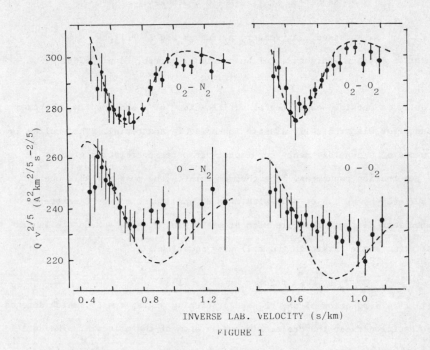

INVERSE LAB. VELOCITY (s/km)

FIGURE 1

The almost complete quenching of the glory oscillation indicates the existen= ce of several potential curves which are separated in the investigated region. Calculations by Hay and Dunning /4/ on the O_3 molecular states formed from ground O and O_2 states show the presence of moderately repulsive triplet states and strongly repulsive quintet states in addition to bound singlet states correspon= ding to the ground state of the O_3 molecules. The cross section value smaller that can be expected from the analogy with $O-N_2$ and O-Ar, can be explained con= sidering that these potential curves are not negligibly in the distance region probed by the experiments (6-7 Å). This effect can be taken as evidence of a re= sidual valence interaction at large distances. Calculations are being performed to evaluate the extend of such splitting. This observation has a strong bearing on the $O-O_2$ chemistry since it could indicate that the reactive path to O_3 forma= tion is strongly affected already at these distances.

REFERENCES

/1/ V.Aquilanti, G.Liuti, F.Pirani, F.Vecchiocattivi, and G.G.Volpi, J.Chem.Phys. 65, 4751 (1976).

/2/ E.Luzzatti, F.Pirani, and F.Vecchiocattivi, Mol.Phys. 34, 1279 (1977).

/3/ G.E.Ewing, Acc.Chem.Res. 8, 185 (1975).

/4/ P.J.Hay and T.H.Dunning, J.Chem.Phys. 67, 2290 (1977).

CHARGE-STATE EFFECT FOR QUASI-ELASTIC

Ne/Ne$^+$+D$_2$ SCATTERING, 0.5-3.5 keV[*]

N. Andersen[+], M. Vedder, A. Russek and E. Pollack

Department of Physics, University of Connecticut, Storrs, Conn. 06268, U.S.A.

Recently we obtained experimental verification[1] of a scaling law, proposed by Sigmund,[2] for electronically elastic ion-molecule scattering. The scaling is a consequence of a general theory for impact-parameter correlation effects in particle penetration phenomena. The theorem relates the most probable energy loss T_o suffered by an ion or atom with mass M_p and impact energy E scattered by a homonuclear diatomic molecule with atomic masses $M_1 = M_2 = M$ to the laboratory scattering angle θ through the following equation

$$T_o = \frac{M_p}{M} E\theta^2 f(E\theta). \qquad (1)$$

In eq. (1) f is a function of the reduced scattering angle, $\tau = E\theta$, which depends on the potential between the projectile and an atom of the molecule. The derivation was based on the following assumptions (i) the collision energy is sufficiently high to justify neglect of vibrational and rotational motion during the collision, (ii) small laboratory scattering angles θ, and (iii) the molecular scattering potential can be approximated by a sum of two spherically symmetric atomic potentials centered on the atoms.

Our previous experiments[1] showed the validity of the scaling law for 1.5-3.5 keV Ne$^+$+D$_2$ collisions. We have extended our measurements to include also the neutral Ne+D$_2$ system. For this collision the energy losses T_o have been measured by time-of-flight techniques. The results are shown in Fig. 1 and compared with some Ne$^+$+D$_2$ data from Ref. 1. The quantity $f(\tau) = T_o M/M_p E\theta^2$ is plotted versus τ. A value of $f(\tau) = 0.5$ is expected for elastic scattering by the molecule as a whole, while $f(\tau) = 1.0$ if the scattering is from just one of the atoms of the molecule, the other atom acting as spectator. These two values are the small and large angle limits, respectively. It appears from Fig. 1 that the scaling law also holds for the Ne+D$_2$ collision in this energy range. The f-function for

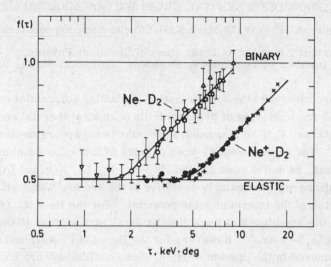

Fig. 1.   The function $f(\tau)$ for (∇) 0.5 keV, (o) 1.0 keV, ($\square$) 1.5 keV and (Δ) 2.0

keV Ne-D_2 collisions; (+) 1.5 keV, ($\bullet$) 2.5 keV and (x) 3.5 keV Ne$^+$-D_2 collisions.

Ne+D_2 scattering is, however, surprisingly different from the Ne$^+$-D_2 curve.   An

analysis of possible reasons for this large difference will be presented at the

conference.

*Supported by the Army Research Office-Durham and the University of Connecticut
 Research Foundation.
+Permanent Address: Physics Laboratory II, H.C. Ørsted Institute, DK-2100
                        Copenhagen, Denmark
1. N. Andersen, M. Vedder, A. Russek and E. Pollack, J. Phys. B11, L493 (1978).
2. P. Sigmund, J. Phys. B11, L145 (1978).

ANISOTROPIC INTERMOLECULAR POTENTIALS FOR He + CO_2, N_2O,
AND C_2N_2 FROM DIFFERENTIAL CROSS SECTION MEASUREMENTS*

Gregory A. Parker,** Mark Keil,*** and Aron Kuppermann

Arthur Amos Noyes Laboratory of Chemical Physics,
California Institute of Technology, Pasadena, California 91125, U.S.A.

We have measured the total (elastic + inelastic) differential cross
sections (DCS) for scattering of hypersonic He beams, at thermal energies,
from CO_2, N_2O, and C_2N_2 in a crossed molecular beam apparatus described
previously.[1a] The angular dependences of these DCS display quantum diffrac-
tion oscillations, as do the ones for the He + Ar, N_2, O_2, NO, and CO systems.
These oscillations are particularly sensitive to the van der Waals attractive
minimum region of the intermolecular potential. For the He + N_2, O_2, NO, and
CO systems, the amplitudes of these oscillations[1b] are similar to the corresponding ones in He + Ar.[1a] However, for the He + CO_2,[2] N_2O, and C_2N_2
systems considered in the present studies, these oscillations are considerably
dampened. This behavior is strongly indicative of the presence of large anisotropies in the intermolecular potential in the latter systems in the region of the
van der Waals minimum.[3-6]

In order to obtain quantitative information about these anisotropies from
the observed DCS, it is necessary to have an efficient method to calculate such
DCS from assumed forms of the intermolecular potential V as a function of the
distance r along the line connecting the centers of mass of the colliding species
and the angle γ between that line and the molecular target. Because of the
highly quantum nature of these He + molecule systems, semi-classical
methods[3-4] are not appropriate. A full quantum treatment, even in a rigid
rotor approximation,[7] leads to coupled channel equations whose solutions would
require excessive amounts of computer time for an iterative fit of the potential
to the data to be practicable. On the other hand, the infinite order sudden (IOS)
approximation[5] leads to sets of uncoupled radial equations. The resulting
computational algorithm for obtaining $V(r,\gamma)$ from a fit to the measured DCS
requires an amount of computer time of the same order as that for the analysis
of central field data. The conditions for the validity of the IOS approximation
are that the rotational energy level spacing and differences in the centrifugal
potentials for adjacent angular momentum channels be small with respect to the
incident relative kinetic energy. These conditions are satisfied for the experiments considered here.

Different mathematical forms were assumed for the $V(r,\gamma)$ potential in
the fitting procedure. In one of them, it was expressed as $\epsilon(\gamma)f[\rho(r,\gamma)]$, where
$\rho(r,\gamma) = r/r_m(\gamma)$. For an arbitrary γ, $r_m(\gamma)$ is the value of r for the potential
minimum and $-\epsilon(\gamma)$ is the corresponding potential energy. For the reduced
potential energy function $f(\rho)$ we used the MSV form.[8] The resulting V involved

five fitting parameters, two of which describe the anisotropy; when they vanish, V becomes a central field MSV function. In other assumed forms for V, this function was taken as a sum of central field potentials with different origins appropriately modified to exhibit the correct long-range behavior. No more than five parameters were varied in the iterative fitting of these potential forms to the observed data, since model central field sensitivity studies have shown that that is the maximum number of statistically independent parameters appropriate for these highly quantum systems.[9]

The potential functions obtained from these procedures will be described and discussed.

* This work was supported in part by a Contract (No. EY-76-S-03-767) from the United States Department of Energy.
** Present address: The James Franck Institute, University of Chicago, 5640 Ellis Avenue, Chicago, Illinois 60637, U. S. A.
*** Present address: Lash Miller Chemical Laboratories, University of Toronto, 80 St. George Street, Toronto, Ontario, Canada M5S 1A1.

1.   M. Keil, J. T. Slankas, and A. Kuppermann, J. Chem. Phys. (a) 70, 482 (1979); (b) 70, 541 (1979).

2.   M. Keil, G. A. Parker, and A. Kuppermann, Chem. Phys. Lett. 59, 443 (1978).

3.   R. E. Olson and R. B. Bernstein, J. Chem. Phys. 49, 162 (1968).

4.   R. J. Cross, J. Chem. Phys. 52, 5703 (1970).

5.   G. A. Parker and R. T Pack, J. Chem. Phys. 68, 1585 (1978).

6.   R. T Pack, Chem. Phys. Lett. 55, 197 (1978).

7.   A. M. Arthurs and A. Dalgarno, Proc. R. Soc. London, Ser. A: 256, 540 (1960).

8.   J. M. Parson and Y. T. Lee, Entropie 42, 146 (1971).

9.   M. Keil and A. Kuppermann, J. Chem. Phys. 69, 3917 (1978).

ROTATIONAL TRANSITIONS AND RATE COEFFICIENTS OF THE H+H$_2$ SYSTEM*

B. H. CHOI AND ROBERT T. POE
Department of Physics, University of California
Riverside, California 92521, U.S.A.

K. T. TANG
Department of Physics, Pacific Lutheran University
Tacoma, Washington 98447, U.S.A.

Rotational close-coupling calculations have been carried out for H+H$_2$ collisions from threshold to 1 eV. Integral and differential cross sections for rotational transitions $\Delta j = 0,2,4,6$ are obtained. The interaction potentials employed in the present calculation are believed to be more accurate than potentials previously used in the rotational excitation calculations. In one set of calculations, we adopted the isotropic part, V_0, of the potential from the work of Gegenbach, Hahn and Toennies[1] and for the anisotropic part, V_2, of the potential, the one proposed by Tang[2] and modified to be consistent with the ab initio calculation[3] was used. The V_2 is of the form: $V_2 = 47.31 \exp(-1.87R)$ $-11.54 \exp(-0.26 R^2-0.61R)$ in eV with the relative distance R in a_0. The calculational procedure used here has been well documented.[4] The sample results of rotational transition cross sections in a_0^2 are as follows

$J_i \rightarrow J_f$	E(eV) 0.3094	0.5	0.75
$0 \rightarrow 2$	1.140	8.67×10^{-1}	5.69×10^{-1}
$0 \rightarrow 4$	1.4×10^{-3}	1.67×10^{-3}	1.11×10^{-3}
$0 \rightarrow 6$	9.8×10^{-10}	4.15×10^{-7}	7.5×10^{-7}
$2 \rightarrow 0$	2.65×10^{-1}	1.91×10^{-1}	1.21×10^{-1}

The differential cross sections obtained from this potential generally have forward peaks. Since this V_2 does not have the appropriate asymptotic form, an improved potential was employed in another set of calculations. The results are similar to the above cross sections. But the present cross sections are quite

different from those obtained from other potentials.[5,6] Rate coefficients for individual transitions were also calculated. They
are order of magnitude smaller than all previous estimates.

*Work supported in part by the National Science Foundation,
 U.S.A.

1. R. Gegenbach, Ch. Hahn and J. P. Toennies, J. Chem. Phys.
   62, 3620 (1975).

2. K. T. Tang, Phys. Rev. 187, 122 (1969).

3. J. M. Norbeck and P. R. Certain, J. Chem. Phys. 63, 4127
   (1975).

4. B. H. Choi and K. T. Tang, J. Chem. Phys. 63, 1775, 1783
   (1975); B. H. Choi, R. T. Poe and K. T. Tang, Chem. Phys.
   Lett. 48, 237 (1977).

5. R. N. Porter and M. Karplus, J. Chem. Phys. 40, 1105 (1964).

6. A. Dalgarno, R. J. W. Henry and C. S. Roberts, Proc. Phys.
   Soc., Lond. 88, 611 (1966).

VIBRATIONAL AND ROTATIONAL EXCITATION OF n-H$_2$ AND H$_2$O BY Li$^+$ IMPACT ABOVE 100 eV

Y. Itoh, N. Kobayashi, and Y. Kaneko

Department of Physics, Faculty of Science,
Tokyo Metropolitan University, Tokyo 158, Japan

Vibrational and rotational excitation of n-H$_2$ and H$_2$O molecules by Li$^+$ impact was studied with the ion energy-loss spectrometer reported earlier.[1] The resolution better than 20 meV (F.W.H.M.) is routinely achieved.

A typical energy-loss spectrum of 207 eV Li$^+$ ion incident on n-H$_2$ is shown in Fig.1. The tails of the primary peak without target gas are shown by the dashed lines. The target gas, n-H$_2$, was kept at room temperature. The energy-losses corresponding to some rotational excitation are shown by the vertical lines. In this spectrum, pure rotational excitation, rotational de-excitation, and vibro-rotational excitation are observed. For pure rotational excitation, the transition with $\Delta J=2$ apperers dominant, i.e. $J=1\rightarrow3$, $J=2\rightarrow4$ and so on. The rotational de-excitation $J=3\rightarrow1$ is also observed. The vibrational excitation without change of the rotational quantum number is dominant.

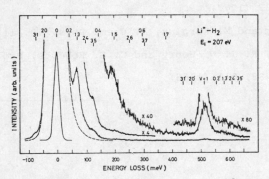

Fig.1.   Energy-loss spectrum of 207 eV Li$^+$ ion incident on n-H$_2$.

Above 150 eV, the apparent angular distribution of the scattered ions corresponding to the excitation $J=1\rightarrow3$ is nearly the same as that of the primary beam without target gas. Therefore, the integral cross section of the excitation $J=1\rightarrow3$ can be obtained from the peak height ratio of $J=1\rightarrow3$ to the primary beam, assuming that the ratio of the initial rotational distribution of $J=1$ state is 65.6%. The cross section obtained is shown in Fig.2. It is 2.5×10^{-16} cm^2 at 155 eV, which is much larger than that of vibrational excitation reported earlier.[2]

Since H$_2$O molecule has large dipole moment (1.84 D), a large cross section for rotational excitation by Li$^+$ impact is expected. Typical energy-loss spectra of 210 eV and 1010 eV Li$^+$ ion incident on H$_2$O are shown in Fig.3 and Fig.4, respectively. The dashed line indicates the primary beam with a higher sensitivity. When the target gas is introduced, the primary beam is broadened considerable extent. This is a sharp contrast to the case of H_2, and must be due to the rotational excitation. In Fig.3, no peak is observed on the spectrum, while in Fig.4, remarkable peaks are seen around 200 meV and 450 meV. The first peak corresponds to the vibrational excitation (010). The second peak corresponds to (100) and (001). Because the pressure of target H_2O gas is not measured accurately, absolute cross section have not been determined yet. At least, however, it is certain that the energy dependence of the rotational excitation is much different from that of vibrational excitation.

The spectrometer used in this work was constructed by the Grant-in-Aid from the Mitsubishi Foundation. This work was supported in part by the Grant-in-Aid from the Ministry of Education, Science, and Culture.

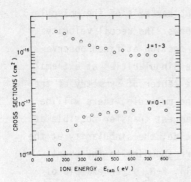

Fig.2.
Integral cross section of the rotational excitation J=1→3 of n-H_2 by Li^+ impact. Vibrational excitation cross section reported earlier is also shown.

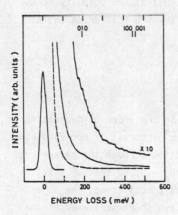

Fig.3. Energy-loss spectrum of 210 eV Li^+ ion incident on H_2O.

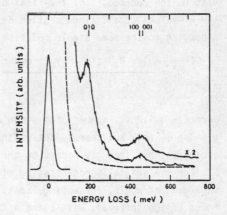

Fig.4. Energy-loss spectrum of 1010 eV Li^+ ion incident on H_2O.

1-2. N. Kobayashi, Y. Itoh, and Y. Kaneko: J. Phys. Soc. Jpn. 45, 617 (1978); ibid. 46, 208 (1979).

Classical Scattering From a Rigid Anisotropic
Potential Shell of Rotation Symmetry.
The Bulge Effect.

D. Beck, U. Ross and W. Schepper
Faculty of Physics, University of Bielefeld, Germany

The dominating features of "rotationally inelastic, repulsive K-N$_2$ and
CO scattering at 1 eV energies" (s.corresponding abstract of this conference) can be understood on the basis of classical scattering from
a rigid, ellipsoidal, initially non-rotating potential shell the figure axis of which coincides with the internuclear axis of the molecule.
This problem is analytically tractable. It shows: The recoil velocity
dependence of the orientation averaged cross section at fixed observation angle will exhibit classical, integrable singularities at extremal
amounts of rotational energy transfer. If the center of symmetry of the
shell coincides with the center of mass of the molecule, there will be
two such extremal transfers, $\Delta E = 0$ and a largest transfer possible at
the chosen angle. If the centers do not coincide, the singularity at the
largest transfer will split into two, one corresponding to the short,
the other to the long "lever arm" of the shell. K-N$_2$ is an example of
the centrical, K-CO of the excentrical case.
With u* the reduced, i.e. the final over the initial, CMS velocity of K,
the u* values of all singularities depend on the CMS scattering angle
according to the same simple relation

$$u_i^* = \frac{\sqrt{1 - B_i^2 \sin^2 \vartheta} + B_i \cos \vartheta}{1 + B_i}$$

Here i = 0,1,2 ... numbers the singularities in the order of decreasing
u*. The u_i^* (ϑ), and thereby the width of the u* interval of non-vanishing
cross section, strongly depend on the interaction through the parameters
B_i. For the initially non-rotating ellipsoid $B_0 = 0$, so that $u_0^* = 1$, independent of angle, for a singularity at elastic scattering, the upper
bound of the interval. With c and a the long and short semi-axes of the
ellipsoid and X$_0$ the distance between the molecular center of mass and
the center of symmetry of the ellipsoid as measured along its figure axis,

one has

$$B_1 = (\mu/I)(c - a)^2$$

I: Moment of inertia of the molecule

μ: Reduced mass of system

for the only inelastic singularity at the lower bound of the interval, if $X_o = 0$, i.e. for a homonuclear molecule, e.g. N_2. For $X_o = 0$, i.e. the heteronuclear case of

$$B_{1,2} = (\mu/I)(c - a \mp \frac{X_o}{\sqrt{1 + a/c}})^2$$

for two inelastic singularities, i = 2 appearing at the lower bound of the interval, thus determining its width. The latter result is an approximation valid for $X_o \ll 4(c - a)(1 + a/c)$ and good to better than 2% in the parameter range of interest. For shells of other than ellipsoidal geometry there may be more than three singularities.

In the figure the observed cross section for K-N_2 at $\vartheta = 150°$, E = 1.24 eV is compared with the model prediction at that angle, folded with the independently known experimental resolving power, and assuming (c - a) = 0.28 Å. As the experimental result is given in arbitrary intensity units the model curve has been normalised to roughly equal height.

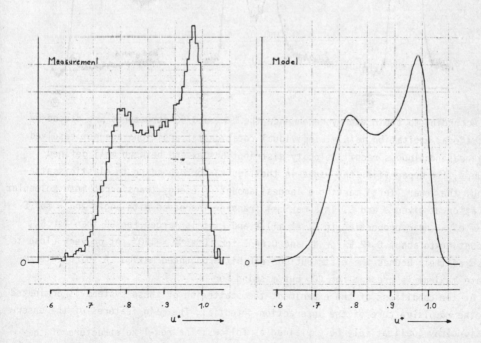

Rotationally Inelastic, Repulsive Scattering of
K-N_2, CO, O_2 at 1 eV Energies
The Bulge Effect.

D. Beck, U. Ross and W. Schepper
Faculty of Physics, University of Bielefeld, Germany

Structure is observed in recoil velocity distributions of potassium atoms scattered inelastically from N_2, CO and O_2 molecules at CMS angles $\vartheta > \pi/2$, collision
energies $0.34 \leq E \leq 1.24$ eV, and distributed, but slow initial molecular rotation
with average $\bar{j} = 2.5 \pm 1$ [1,2]. Typical primary data are shown in Fig. 1 representing the flux of K atoms into the detector which is scattered from the respective
target gases at constant LS velocity as a function of the LS angle Θ. Due to the
kinematics of these collisions this corresponds to scanning the scattering at a
stationary, i.e. nearly constant CMS deflection angle ϑ ($\sim 150^\circ$) as a function of
the CMS recoil velocity.

Fig. 1

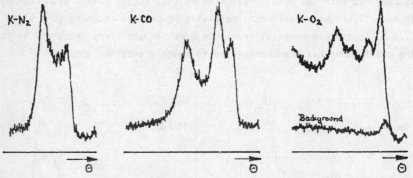

According to their energy dependence the K-N_2 and CO structures are caused by
rotational excitation mainly. Individual rotational transitions are not resolved.
The quasicontinuous recoil velocity distributions extend between well defined
bounds, the upper (i.e. the right in the figure) corresponding to elastic scattering, the lower (left) marking a largest amount of energy transferred into molecular
rotation at given ϑ and E. This maximal transfer increased with angle and - for E >
0.64 eV - near proportion to E. At all ϑ and E it is larger for CO than for N_2,
amounting to about 0.42 E for N_2 and 0.64 E for CO at $\vartheta = 150^\circ$. At or very close to
each of their bounds the distributions exhibit pronounced maxima. A third intermediate maximum is present for CO, but missing for N_2.

At the conditions of the experiment the scattering of these systems is dominated
by the repulsive core of the interaction potential. The main features of the observations may qualitatively be explained as follows: The rod-like structure of the

essentially rigid molecule exposes two lever arms of equal (N_2) or unequal lengths
(CO) to the incoming atom. Therefore, depending on impact parameter and molecular
orientation, a single or two different maximal amounts of angular momentum and rotation energy may be transferred in the collision. If the intermolecular potential
acted literally like a rigid bar, the maximal amounts (at each angle) would be
transferred by hitting its ends; the energy transfer dependence would simply break
off at a maximum. Actually the repulsive potential core has a bulge; as compared
to a bar it will be better approximated by ellipsoidal, egg or 8 shaped equipoten-
tials. The bulge provides a coupling of the length of the equivalent lever arm
with the direction of the impulse which is virtually independent of the direction
of incidence. Due to this coupling the extremal amounts of transferred angular
momentum and energy will not only be approached as a function of impact parameter
and molecular orientation, but will be passed through, thus giving rise to an
(orientational) rainbow phenomenon, the "bulge maxima", in the recoil velocity
dependence of the cross section.

With this cause it is intuitively obvious that the width as well as the shape of
the recoil velocity distributions will be a sensitive and very direct probe to the
anisotropy of the (repulsive) intermolecular potential. More details are explained
in a separate contribution to this Conference.

The $K-O_2$ distribution is more complicated. A preliminary explanation will be
given which is based on   (1) the fact that $K-O_2$ scattering proceeds on an
(essentially covalent) quartet and a covalent-ionic doublet potential which very
likely has a deep (1-2 eV) well; (2) the expectation that the former will produce
the two peak bulge structure of equal lever arms, while the latter largely destroys such structure, but generates noticeable vibrational excitation of O_2.

[1]   W. Schepper, U. Ross and D. Beck, Z. Physik A 290 (1979), 131.
[2]   D. Beck, U. Ross, and W. Schepper, to be published in Phys.Rev. A,
      June 1979.

A GENERAL RULE FOR THE CROSS SECTIONS FOR
ROTATIONAL TRANSITIONS IN COLLISIONS

Isao Shimamura

Institute of Space and Aeronautical Science
University of Tokyo, Meguro-Ku, Tokyo 153, Japan

Molecules may make transitions to different vibronic (α) and rotational (Γ) states in collisions with other particles, such as electrons, positrons, atoms, molecules, and atomic and molecular ions. This paper shows that, for nonreactive collisions, the differential cross section (DCS) for transition $(\alpha_f \Gamma_f) \leftarrow (\alpha_i \Gamma_i)$ is expressed as a linear combination of the DCS for transitions $(\alpha_f \Gamma) \leftarrow (\alpha_i 0)$ from the ground rotational state. In the case of molecule-molecule collisions, the DCS for simultaneous transition $(\alpha_{1f} \Gamma_{1f} \alpha_{2f} \Gamma_{2f}) \leftarrow (\alpha_{1i} \Gamma_{1i} \alpha_{2i} \Gamma_{2i})$ is similarly written in terms of those for $(\alpha_{1f} \Gamma_1 \alpha_{2f} \Gamma_2) \leftarrow (\alpha_{1i} 0 \alpha_{2i} 0)$.

The following assumptions are made. First, the wavefunctions of the initial and final molecular states are well approximated by the products of rotational and vibronic wavefunctions. Second, the initial and final rotational wavefunctions are represented by eigenfunctions of the Hamiltonians for symmetric-top rotators. Thus, Γ may be represented by J, M, and K which denote quantum numbers specifying the molecular angular momentum, its projection onto the quantization axis, and the angular momentum about the body-fixed symmetry axis. As special cases, spherical tops and linear rotators are included. Third, the collision process is well de-scribed by the rotationally adiabatic approximation in the sense of Chase.[1]

When the molecule makes a transition $(\alpha_f \Gamma_f) \leftarrow (\alpha_i \Gamma_i)$, the other collision part-ner may change its internal state, if any, from β_i to β_f. Let the initial and final relative motions at a large separation be represented by wave vectors $\underset{\sim}{k}_i$ and $\underset{\sim}{k}_f$. The DCS for this process, summed over the final M_f and averaged over the initial M_i, is expressed in terms of Clebsch-Gordan coefficients and the DCS for $J_i = K_i = 0$ as

$$\frac{d\sigma}{d\omega}(\beta_f \alpha_f J_f K_f \underset{\sim}{k}_f \leftarrow \beta_i \alpha_i J_i K_i \underset{\sim}{k}_i) = (\frac{k_f}{k_i}) \sum_J \{C(J_i JJ_f; K_i KK_f)\}^2 (\frac{k_0}{k_{JK}}) \frac{d\sigma}{d\omega}(\beta_f \alpha_f JKk \underset{\sim}{k}_{JK} \leftarrow \beta_i \alpha_i 00 \underset{\sim}{k}_0), \quad (1)$$

where the wave vectors $\underset{\sim}{k}_0$ and $\underset{\sim}{k}_{JK}$ satisfy $\underset{\sim}{k}_0 - \underset{\sim}{k}_{JK} = \underset{\sim}{k}_i - \underset{\sim}{k}_f$ and $\hbar^2 k_0^2/2\mu = \hbar^2 k_i^2/2\mu + E(J_i, K_i)$, where μ is the reduced mass and $E(J_i, K_i)$ is the rotational energy of the initial state.

For a spherical top, $E(J, K)$ and k_{JK} are independent of K and may be denoted by $E(J)$ and k_J. The DCS may be averaged over K_i and summed over K_f. Then,

$$\frac{d\sigma}{d\omega}(\beta_f \alpha_f J_f \underset{\sim}{k}_f \leftarrow \beta_i \alpha_i J_i \underset{\sim}{k}_i) = (\frac{k_f}{k_i})(\frac{2J_f + 1}{2J_i + 1}) \sum_{J=|J_i - J_f|}^{J_i + J_f} (2J+1)^{-1} (\frac{k_0}{k_J}) \frac{d\sigma}{d\omega}(\beta_f \alpha_f J \underset{\sim}{k}_J \leftarrow \beta_i \alpha_i 0 \underset{\sim}{k}_0). \quad (2)$$

For a linear rigid rotator, K_i, K_f, and K vanish, and we have

$$\frac{d\sigma}{d\omega}(\beta_f\alpha_f J_f k_f \leftarrow \beta_i\alpha_i J_i k_i) = (\frac{k_f}{k_i})\sum_J \{C(J_i JJ_f;000)\}^2 (\frac{k_0}{k_J})\frac{d\sigma}{d\omega}(\beta_f\alpha_f Jk_J \leftarrow \beta_i\alpha_i 0k_0). \tag{3}$$

When the collision partner is also a molecule, it follows that

$$\frac{d\sigma}{d\omega}(J_{1f}K_{1f}J_{2f}K_{2f}k_f \leftarrow J_{1i}K_{1i}J_{2i}K_{2i}k_i) = (\frac{k_f}{k_i})\sum_{J_1 J_2} \{C(J_{1i}J_1 J_{1f};K_{1i}K_1 K_{1f})$$

$$\times C(J_{2i}J_2 J_{2f};K_{2i}K_2 K_{2f})\}^2 (\frac{k_0}{k_{J_1 K_1 J_2 K_2}})\frac{d\sigma}{d\omega}(J_1 K_1 J_2 K_2 k_{J_1 K_1 J_2 K_2} \leftarrow 0000k_0). \tag{4}$$

The subscripts 1 and 2 refer to the colliding molecules. Quantum numbers specifying vibronic states have been suppressed. If both molecules are linear rigid rotators, the quantum numbers K_{si}, K_s, and K_{sf} (s=1,2) in the Clebsch-Gordan coefficients should be zero, and those specifying the DCS and wave number should be omitted. For collisions between spherical top molecules, it follows, after summation over K_{sf} and averaging over K_{si}, that

$$\frac{d\sigma}{d\omega}(J_{1f}J_{2f}k_f \leftarrow J_{1i}J_{2i}k_i) = (\frac{k_f}{k_i})\{\frac{(2J_{1f}+1)(2J_{2f}+1)}{(2J_{1i}+1)(2J_{2i}+1)}\} \sum_{J_1 J_2} \{(2J_1+1)(2J_2+1)\}^{-1}$$

$$\times (\frac{k_0}{k_{J_1 J_2}})\frac{d\sigma}{d\omega}(J_1 J_2 k_{J_1 J_2} \leftarrow 00k_0), \tag{5}$$

where J_s (s=1,2) in the summation runs from $|J_{si}-J_{sf}|$ to $J_{si}+J_{sf}$.

The results of the present paper are useful for many kinds of applications, when the adiabatic approximation is valid for the rotational motion. Because the number of processes having independent cross sections is drastically reduced, compact data compilation is possible. From the computational point of view, one has only to deal with transitions from the ground rotational state(s); from the knowledge of such processes, other transitions are easily studied. If the molecules of interest are initially distributed among many rotational states, the effective cross section for this system may be easily calculated. Different sets of experimental and theoretical cross sections which do not seem to permit comparison may now be compared by reducing them to the cross sections for transitions from the ground rotational state(s). Analysis of experimental data may be often greatly simplified. For example, rotational structures in electron or ion energy-loss spectra may be analyzed using a small number of unknown parameters. Especially, when the incident particle is an electron, there are usually only a few independent cross sections that are appreciable. Thus, ambiguities in line shape analysis are often reduced.

A preliminary account of this work is found in reference 2.

1. D. M. Chase, Phys. Rev. 104, 838 (1956).
2. I. Shimamura, ISAS Research Note No.79, Inst. of Space and Aeronaut. Sci., Univ. of Tokyo (1979).

TRANSFER OF POPULATION AND ALIGNMENT IN THE ROTATIONAL EXCITATION OF CO

BY H_2 AT THERMAL ENERGIES .

J.M.LAUNAY - Daphe - Observatoire de Meudon - 92190 - Meudon - FRANCE

Recent infra-red infra-red double resonance experiments using polarised
laser beams yield information about the depopulation and desalignment rates
of rotationally excited CO molecules by CO perturbers (1) or H_2 perturbers
(2) at room and liquid nitrogen temperature .

We have   computed the corresponding CO-H_2 cross-sections using an
ab-initio potential energy surface (3,4) and a body-fixed close-coupling
method (5) for the collision problem . We employed the multipole components
of the S-matrix formalism (6).

Results will be presented for the $\sigma^{(k)}(jj;j'j')$ and for the cross-sections
between Zeeman sublevels $\sigma(jm;j'm')$; they show a tendancy to conservation
of the initial orientation of the angular momentum.

The contribution of the interference term in pressure-broadening cross-
sections $\sigma^{(1)}(jj';jj')$ has also been considered and contributes less than
10% of the inelastic value , in reasonable agreement with erlier semi-clas-
-sical results for the CO-He system (7) .

A comparison has also been performed with the relations derived from the
IOS approximation relations (8,9).

In addition , inelastic rates have been computed for temperatures and
levels of astrophysical interest (j_{in}=0-11,T=10K-300K for para-H_2 ; j_{in}=0,6,
T=10K-100K for ortho-H_2) (10).

(1) Brechignac P.,Picard-Bersellini A.,Charneau R.,1979,Physics Letters, to be published .

(2) Brechignac P.,Picard-Bersellini A.,Charneau R.,1979,to be published .

(3) Prissette J.,Kochanski E.,Flower D.R.,1978,Chem.Phys.,27,373.

(4) Flower D.R.,Launay J.M.,Prissette J.,Kochanski E.,1979,Chem.Phys., in press.

(5) Launay J.M.,1977,J.Phys.B,10,3665.

(6) Omont A.,1977,Progress in Quantum Electronics,5,69.

(7) Smith E.W.,Giraud M.,Cooper J.,1976,J.Chem.Phys.,65,1256.

(8) Coldflam R.,Green S.,Kouri D.J.,1977,J.Chem.Phys.,67,5661.

(9) Varshalovich P.A.,Khersonski V.K.,1977,Astrophysical Letters,18,167.

(10) Launay J.M.,1979,to be published.

ADIABATIC NUCLEI THEORY OF HEAVY - PARTICLE SCATTERING

E. Ficocelli Varracchio

Istituto di Chimica Generale,
Università di Bari,
Via Amendola 173, 70126 Bari, ITALY

The adiabatic (or fixed) nuclei approximation to scattering is well established for e^-- molecule collisions[1-3]. Some efforts have recently been devoted to test the applicability of this same approximation to heavy-particle scattering[4-5]. On account of this renewed interest, we shall briefly sketch a derivation of such approximation, in a field-theoretic description of the process. For the sake of simplicity, we shall consider explicitly collisions involving a "bare" atomic nucleus, impinging on a diatomic species. The S-matrix of such a process can be written as[6]

$$S_{f\alpha_f k_f ; i\alpha_i k_i} \overset{\sim}{=} \langle f; f\alpha_f | T\left[\psi(r;\vec{R})\psi^\dagger(r';\vec{R})\right] | i; i\alpha_i \rangle = X^{i\alpha_i}_{f\alpha_f}(r,r';\vec{R}) \tag{1}$$

with the proportionality sign taking care of time limits and spatial integrations. ψ ($\psi^\dagger$) is the destruction (creation) field-operator for the bare nucleus, which depends parametrically on the position ($\vec{R}$) of the (diatomic) molecule in space. Finally, $|j;j\alpha_n\rangle$ labels the j-th electronic state and its related α_n-th vibro-rotational level. In the spirit of the Born-Oppenheimer (B.O.) approximation for bound molecular states, e.g.

$$|j;j\alpha_n\rangle \overset{\text{B.O.}}{\sim} |j\rangle|j\alpha_n\rangle \tag{2}$$

eq. (1) can be rewritten as

$$X^{i\alpha_i}_{f\alpha_f}(r,r';\vec{R}) \overset{\text{B.O.}}{\sim} \langle f\alpha_f| X^i_f(r,r';\vec{R})| i\alpha_i \rangle = \int d\vec{R} \langle f\alpha_f|\vec{R}\rangle X^i_f(r,r';\vec{R})\langle\vec{R}|i\alpha_i\rangle \tag{3}$$

where the following "electronic" only amplitude has been defined

$$X^i_f(r,r';\vec{R}) = \langle f|T\left[\psi(r;\vec{R})\psi^\dagger(r';\vec{R})\right]|i\rangle \tag{4}$$

Equation (3) represents the generalization of the fixed nuclei approximation to processes involving electronic excitation. If, in particular, we are simply interested in vibro-rotational transitions on one single electronic surface, eq. (3) reduces to

$$X^{i\alpha_i}_{i\alpha_f}(r,r';R) \overset{\text{B.O.}}{\sim} \int d\vec{R}\langle i\alpha_f|\vec{R}\rangle iG^i(r,r';\vec{R})\langle\vec{R}|i\alpha_i\rangle \tag{5}$$

which is the field-theoretic restatement of the fixed nuclei approximation for the process of interest. G^i in (5) is the one-particle Green's function, describing the motion of the bare nucleus. To obtain computationally useful relations, an equation of motion for G^i must be determined. This task can be most easily performed and it will be discussed at the Conference.

1. D. M. Chase, Phys. Rev. 104, 838 (1956).
2. A. Temkin and K. Vasavada, Phys. Rev. 160, 109 (1967).
3. E. Ficocelli Varracchio, Lett. Nuovo Cimento (in press).
4. S. I. Chu and A. Dalgarno, Proc. Roy. Soc. A342, 191 (1975).
5. G. Bergeron, C. Leforestier and J. M. Launay, Chem. Phys. Letts. 59, 129 (1978).
6. E. Ficocelli Varracchio, J. Phys. B 10, 503 (1977).

A STUDY OF VIBRATIONAL RELAXATION

C.S. Lin

Department of Chemistry
University of Windsor
Windscr, Ontario, Canada

A detailed theoretical study of rotational-vibrational transitions in the scattering of He by para-H_2 at the total energy E < 1.62 eV has now been completed. The method used is the Secrest-Eastes algorithm[1] which is based on the total angular momentum formalism of Arthurs and Dalgarno.[2] Since one of the purposes is to provide accurate close-coupling (CC) results to enable an unambiguous and wide-ranging assessment of various approximation methods a well-defined model, a non-rigid rotating harmonic oscillator, is used to describe the molecule and the ab initio interaction potential of Gordon and Secrest[3] is used. The molecular basis sets $\{\psi(v)\chi(j)\}$ include up to $j \leqslant 6$, and $\nu \leqslant 4$, where j and ν respectively stand for the rotational and vibrational quantum numbers. Calculation of the vibrational relaxation rate constants from these cross sections is now underway.

Some main features of the work are the following:
1) Extensive study of convergence. From the analyses it emerges that one need not include states with $j \geqslant 8$ in the molecular basis set for transitions to states with $j \leqslant 4$. Since the number of channels increases more rapidly with higher j, this observation is useful in the construction of the basis sets.

For the excitations to the $\nu = 1$ manifold a 3-v basis set, i.e. $\nu \leqslant 2$, in general leads to cross sections well within 10% of full convergence while a 4-v set is required for a convergence to within 1%.[4,5]

For all transitions ending up in the $\nu = 2$ manifold, convergence comes with more difficulty. For these processes a 4-v set is still quite inadequate and a 5-v set is needed for cross sections that re within 10% of full convergence.[6]

Adequacy of a basis set is shown to vary with energy. In the energy range where several closely-spaced rotational leveis are opening up, interference among these levels has been unambiguously demonstrated to adversely affect the adequacy of a basis set.[7]

2) Threshold behavior of the cross sections   The existence of the resonance structures in the cross sections near the threshold energies, first noticed by McGuire and Toennies,[8] has been confirmed and its detailed structure clarified.[9] Transitions to the state $\nu = 1$, $j = 2$ are found to have larger cross sections than that of $\nu = 1$, $j = 0$ in a small energy range immediately after $j = 2$ state becomes open, a possibility of a population inversion.

The same, albeit less pronounced, is observed for the excitations to the $\nu = 2$ manifold.

3) Vibrational relaxation rate constants. Several papers on this topic have been published.[8,10-12] Common to these studies is a continued accelerating decline of the rate constants toward very low temperature where experimental results show a tapering of the rate of decline.

It is shown[5] that approximation methods such as CS, EP, etc. are reliable at high energy but do badly near the thresholds: they tend to grossly under-estimate the cross sections for inelastic processes. It is obvious that this underestimation of cross sections causes the discrepancy. Results from the present study should remove this problem.

References

1. W. Eastes and D. Secrest, J. Chem. Phys. 56, 640 (1972).

2. A.M. Arthurs and A. Dalgarno, Proc. Roy. Soc. (London) A256, 540 (1960).

3. M.D. Gordon and D. Secrest, J. Chem. Phys. 52, 120 (1970).

4. C.S. Lin, Chem. Phys. Lett. 57, 186 (1978).

5. C.S. Lin and D. Secrest, J. Chem. Phys. 70, 199 (1979).

6. C.S. Lin, to be published.

7. C.S. Lin, to be published.

8. P. McGuire and J.P. Toennies, J. Chem. Phys. 62, 4623 (1975).

9. C.S. Lin, J. Chem. Phys. 70, 1791 (1979).

10. A.W. Raczkowski et al, J. Chem. Phys. 69, 2692 (1978).

11. H. Rabitz et al, J. Chem. Phys. 68, 647 (1978).

12. M.H. Alexander, J. Chem. Phys. 66, 4608 (1977).

INELASTIC CROSS-SECTIONS FOR ATOM-MOLECULE COLLISIONS

R. D. SHARMA

Air Force Geophysics Laboratory, Hanscom AFB, MA 01731

A formulation capable of calculating differential and total cross-section for rotational-vibrational inelastic prosesses during atom-molecule collisions is derived. The scattering matrix is approximated by the first term in the Magnus expansion[1]. This approximation becomes exact when the time development operator commutes with the matrix elements of the interaction potential. Since the Classical and Semi-Classical theories assume this commutation, the present formulation has intrinsically the same accuracy. The formulation is further developed for situations involving collisions with high relative transitional energy and molecules with small rotational constants. This situation involves many states and is therefore difficult to handle by close-coupling methods. The present formulation treats this by evaluating the integrals for relative translational motion using classical or quantum-mechanical distorted wave approximation[2]. Conditions for the validity of these approximations will be described. Numerical results obtained by the present calculation will be compared with those obtained by close-coupling method.

1. R. D. Levine, Quantum Mechanics of Molecular Rate Processes,
    Oxford University Press, London (1969).

2. R. D. Sharma and R. R. Hart, J. Chem. Phys. 63, 5383 (1975).

ISOTOPE AND TIME EFFECTS IN VIBRATIONALLY INELASTIC
$H^+(D^+)$-CO_2 COLLISIONS AT LOW ENERGIES

G. Bischof, V. Hermann, J. Krutein and F. Linder

Fachbereich Physik, Universität Kaiserslautern

6750 Kaiserslautern, West Germany

Vibrational excitation of CO_2 by H^+ and D^+ impact has been investigated with a crossed-beam apparatus[1] in the energy range 15 to 110 eV. With an energy resolution of typically $\Delta E = 30$ meV (FWHM) excitation of the various modes of CO_2 can be clearly resolved. Both the small-angle region and the rainbow region have been investigated which are sensitive to different parts of the interaction potential. As shown in previous work[1] one observes a very strong inelasticity with highly selective excitation of different modes in the two angular regimes.

In the present work, we have studied the energy dependence of vibrationally inelastic scattering in the forward direction. Interesting effects can be expected from the fact that the collision energy of the H^+ and D^+ projectiles is varied over a range where the collision time becomes comparable with the vibrational periods of the different normal modes of CO_2.

Fig. 1 shows one example of the measured energy-loss spectra. At small angles the excitation of the infrared active modes 010 and 001 is dominant, but excitation of higher harmonics and intercombination modes is also present.

The intensity ratio of the two dominant modes 010 and 001 is plotted in Fig. 2 a and b as a function of collision energy and velocity, respectively. The results show a clear isotope effect for vibrational excitation which is readily understood in a time-dependent picture. The strong increase of the ratio I_{010}/I_{001} towards low energies can be explained by time effects: the collision time comes into resonance with the vibrational period of the 010 mode which produces an enhanced excitation of this mode.

More results of the $H^+(D^+)$-CO_2 measurements will be presented at the conference. Other proton-molecule systems will be discussed for comparison.

1.) J. Krutein and F. Linder
        J. Phys. B $\underline{10}$, 1363 (1977)

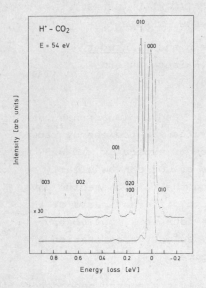
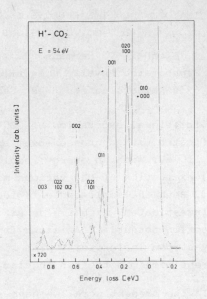

Fig. 1:

(a) Energy-loss spectrum for H^+-CO_2 scattering at $E_{lab} = 54$ eV and $\vartheta_{lab} = 0^o$.

(b) The same spectrum magnified by a factor of 720.

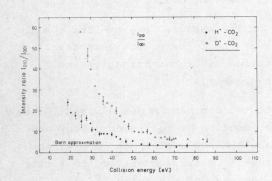

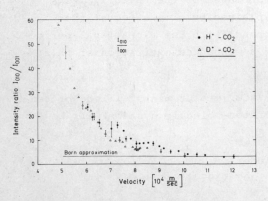

Fig. 2:

The intensity ratio I_{010}/I_{001} for H^+-CO_2 and D^+-CO_2 scattering at $\vartheta_{lab} = 0^o$

(a) as a function of collision energy,

(b) as a function of ion velocity.

OBSERVATION OF MODE SELECTIVE VIBRATIONAL EXCITATION OF SF_6 IN COLLISIONS WITH Li^+ IONS AT E_{CM} = 4.40 eV

A. Ellenbroek, J.P. Toennies and M. Wilde

Max-Planck-Institut für Strömungsforschung
Böttingerstr. 4-8, D-3400 Göttingen, Federal Republic of Germany

Previously we have reported time of flight measurements of vibrationally in-elastic scattering of Li^+ ions with center of mass energies, $0.6 \lesssim E_{CM} \lesssim 10$ eV over a wide range of angles from the molecular targets H_2[1], N_2[1], CO[1], CO_2[2], N_2O[2] and CH_4[3]. In CO_2 and N_2O the observed preferential excitation of the bending mode could be explained by a simple electrostatic model in which the Li^+ ion interacts with the charges on the individual atoms in the CO_2 (and N_2O) molecules which are compatib-le with the known quadrupole (and dipole) moments. In CH_4 the spectra showed ma-xima corresponding to the excitation of groups of vibrational states. It was not possible, however, to resolve individual transitions corresponding to a specific vibrational mode. The average energy transfer was found to be significantly larger than for CO_2. This observation could be explained by a simple statistical model, which predicts that the average energy transfer depends on the number of internal degrees of freedom of the molecule.[4] To test this theory further we have studied Li^+-SF_6 at E_{CM} = 4.39, 6.37, 9.75 and 12.29 eV at scattering angles $6 \lesssim \vartheta_{CM} \lesssim 30°$. The apparatus is nearly identical to that described previously[2,3]. Li^+ ions are energy selected ($\Delta E \simeq 40$ meV) and electrostatically pulsed ($\Delta t \simeq 0.2 \mu sec$, E_{lab} = 5 eV), before being scattered from an internally cold nozzle beam target. In the present apparatus time of flight spectra are measured simultaneously by five multipliers $2°$ apart at 163 cm from the target beam.

Fig. 1 shows spectra measured at E_{lab} = 4.60 eV (E_{CM} = 4.39 eV) at 6 dif-ferent angles smaller than the rainbow angle. As found in CH_4 the spectra change drastically with scattering angle. Since the density of vibrational states is much larger in SF_6 than in CH_4 and nearly uniform with energy it is surprising to find structure in the spectra. The observed peaks are best explained by the as-sumption that they are due to selective excitation of only the ν_4 vibrational mode (the F-S-F atoms along the symmetry axis move in a direction opposite to that of the 4 equatorial F atoms), each peak corresponding to a specific vibrati-onal quantum number n with no rotational excitation. At higher energies, the re-solution was not good enough to assign a specific mode but the results are compa-tible with this explanation. The time of flight spectra have also been analyzed in terms of the average energy transfer $\langle \Delta E \rangle = \sum_f P^{o \to f} \Delta E (o \to f)$, where $P^{o \to f}$ is the transition probability, $\Delta E^{(o \to f)}$ the spectroscopic energy diffe-rence and the sum is over all final vibrational states. Using the method descri-bed in Ref. 3 $\langle \Delta E \rangle$ is obtained directly from the spectra without determining $P^{o \to f}$ so that resolved spectra are not needed. The results are plotted in Fig. 2 in units, which satisfactorily correlated all the previous data[4]. Two important differences to CH_4 are found. $\langle \Delta E \rangle / E$ rises less steeply at small $E \cdot \vartheta_{CM}$ and bends off at values just beyond the value corresponding to the rainbow (RB). In terms of our statistical model this result suggests that not all vibrational degrees of freedom are involved in the energy transfer at $E \cdot \vartheta_{CM}$ less than the rainbow value and that the number of active degrees of freedom at higher energies becomes even less depending on the collision energy. Possibly this can be explained by the fact that in SF_6 the vibrations have periods comparable to the collision time whereas in CH_4 they are shorter than the collision time. Experiments on CF_4 and with H^+ and D^+ are in progress.

1. M. Faubel and J.P. Toennies, Adv.At.Mol.Phys. 13, 229 (1977)

2. W. Eastes, U. Ross and J.P. Toennies, J.Chem.Phys. 66, 1919 (1977)

3. W. Eastes, U. Ross and J.P. Toennies, J.Chem.Phys. 70, 1652 (1979)

4. W. Eastes and J.P. Toennies, J.Chem.Phys. 70, 1645 (1979)

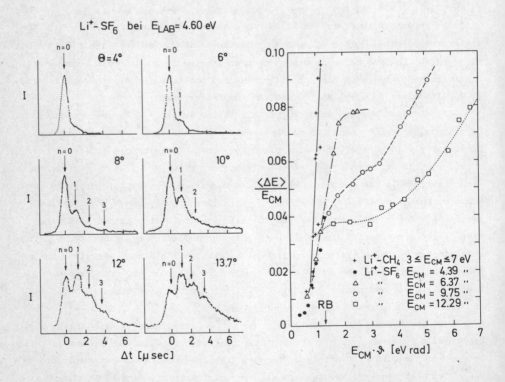

Fig. 1   Fig. 2

COLLISIONAL RELAXATION OF ELECTRONICALLY EXCITED URANIUM ATOMS IN GASES*

Hao-Lin Chen and C. Borzileri

Lawrence Livermore Laboratory
Livermore, California 94550, USA

In an effort to gain some understanding of the mechanisms whereby electronically excited levels of heavy atoms are collisionally deactivated in gases, we
have measured the rates for electronic relaxation for excited uranium atoms (low
lying metastables and highly excited states) via the method of laser induced
fluorescence.

We use a modified small angle scattering experiment which measures the
apparent attenuation cross sections of the ground and electronically metastable
uranium atoms in a scattering chamber. The particle densities of each electronic
state are individually monitored by a sensitive laser induced fluorescence detection
system. From such measurements we will show that relaxation of the lowest lying
metastable electronic states of uranium ($^5K_5^o$ and $^5L_7^o$ states) in hydrogen and methane
appears to proceed by near resonant electronic-to-rotation or electronic-to-
vibration/rotation energy transfer process. We have also measured the rates for
electronic relaxation for highly excited uranium atoms in gases. In general, the
level density of uranium in the region near 2 eV and above is considerably greater
than that near the low lying metastables. We will demonstrate that relaxation of
these high lying electronic states by foreign gases appears to proceed by an inter-
state-mixing process where the excited uranium atoms transfer their excitation to
their neighboring levels by collisions. For a given collision partner, quenching
cross sections or probabilities are also found to increase with increasing energy
of excitation.

In principle, the experimental technique presented here can be applied to
determine the rates for electronic relaxation of other refractory elements where
gas phase relaxation measurements using conventional spectroscopic and kinetic-
methods might be exceedingly difficult.

*Work performed under the auspices of the U.S. Department of Energy by the
Lawrence Livermore Laboratory under contract No. W-7405-ENG-48.

CHARGE TRANSFER IN PROTON-HYDROGEN MOLECULE COLLISIONS

PRITAM PRASAD RAY

Department of Physics, Visva-Bharati University
Santiniketan, W.B. 731235, INDIA

AND

B C SAHA

Department of Theoretical Physics, Indian
Association for the Cultivation of Science,
Calcutta 700 032, INDIA.

For purposes of charge transfer a hydrogen molecule has been considered as two hydrogen atoms at least at high energies of impact. That this assumption is quite unphysical has been supported by the experiment of Wittkower, Ryding and Gilbody[1] who showed that the molecular charge exchange cross section σ_M is 2.4 ± 0.15 times the atomic cross section σ_A in the energy range 110 - 250 keV. This contradicts the conclusions of the theoretical work of Tuan and Gerjuoy[2] for E < 400 keV. Recent calculations of Ray and Saha[3] on the ground state capture of electron from molecular hydrogen shows that $\sigma_M = 2\sigma_A$ at no energy and calculated σ_M is in close agreement with the experiment[1].

The purpose of this investigation is to study the nature of the charge exchange cross sections for capture into any excited state of the formed hydrogen atom in the frame work of first Born approximation (FBA).

$$H^+ + H_2 \longrightarrow H(n\ell m) + H_2^+ \qquad (1)$$

Using a contour integral representation of the hydrogenic wave function[3], the molecular Brinkman-Kramers (MBK) amplitude has been expressed in a closed form, while the molecular Jackson-Schiff (MJS) amplitude involving proton-proton interactions has been reduced to a one-dimensional integral over the real variables. The MBK amplitude for capture into ns state is given by (in the notation of Ref.3)

$$I_{MBK} = 16\pi \sqrt{z_m^5/n^3} \left[(\alpha^2 + z_m^2)^2 \beta \right]^{-1} \sin(n\,\theta) , \tag{2}$$

where $\tan \theta = -2\beta/n \left[\beta^2 - n^{-2} \right]^{-1}$

The MJS amplitude can be expressed as

$$I_{MJS} = I_{MBK} - 16\pi \, (z_m^3/n)^{1/2} \, \frac{\partial}{\partial z_m} \int_0^\infty dy \, B^{-1} \, Im(A) , \tag{3}$$

where $A = (Z+1)^{n-1} / (Z-1)^{n+1}$; $B = (GE - F^2)^{1/2}$; $Z = (-F+iB)/E$;

$D = \alpha^2 + z_m^2$; $E = n^{-2} (Dy^2 + 2z_m y + 1)$; $F = n^{-1} \left[Dy(z_m y+1) \right]$;

$G = Dy^2 \left[(\vec{\alpha} - \vec{\beta})^2 + z_m^2 \right] + \beta^2 (2z_m y + 1)$

We have calculated charge exchange cross sections for arbitrary ns state of the formed atom for both gerade and ungearde transitions of the molecular ion. Table I shows some of our results at 500 keV. It is found that $1/n^3$ law for the total cross section is satisfied asymptotically (i.e. $n \to \infty$) for both gearde and ungearde transitions.

Work on other higher angular momentum states is in progress and will be reported in the conference.

Table I : n-cubed charge transfer cross sections[+] (πa_0^2) at 500 keV.

	n	2	6	10	16	∞
I	MBK	8.209-4	8.670-4	8.709-4	8.722-4	8.724-4
	MJS	2.579-4	2.696-4	2.705-4	2.709-4	2.709-4
II	MBK	6.181-5	6.413-5	6.432-5	6.439-5	6.440-5
	MJS	1.845-5	1.893-5	1.897-5	1.898-5	1.898-5

I : Gerade transition
II : Ungerade transition
+ : $(a-b) = a. \, 10^{-b}$

REFERENCES :

[1] A.B. Wittkower, G. Ryding and H.B.Gilbody, Proc. Phys. Soc. **89**, 541 (1966)

[2] T. F. Tuan and E. Gerjuoy, Phys. Rev. **117**, 756 (1960).

[3] P. P. Ray and B. C. Saha, submitted to Phys. Lett. (1979).

CHARGE EXCHANGE IN D^+ + H_2 COLLISIONS[*]

R. S. Peterson, M. Vedder, and E. Pollack

Department of Physics, University of Connecticut
Storrs, Connecticut 06268, USA

A detailed study of the "quasi-elastic", inelastic, and charge-exchange scattering in the D^+ + H_2 collision system at low keV energies is currently in progress. This abstract reports on the small angle charge-exchange scattering.

The basic apparatus has been described elsewhere.[1,2] For the present measurements the angular distribution of D^O, from D^+ + $H_2 \rightarrow D^O$ + H_2^+, is obtained. Figure 1 shows a typical result at a beam energy E = 2.6 keV. The product $I\theta^2$ (scattered intensity x laboratory scattering angle squared) is plotted as a function of $E\theta$. The results show that the dominant charge-exchange process occurs in forward scattering. In addition there is some small structure for $E\theta$ values near 1.6 keV deg., suggesting the presence of additional charge exchange channels.

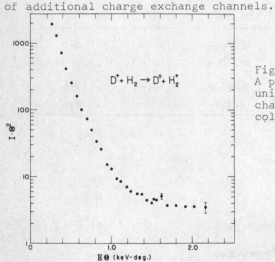

Fig. 1.
A plot of $I\theta^2$ (in arbitrary units) vs. $E\theta$ for charge exchange in 2.6 keV D^+ + H_2 collisions.

On the basis of a recently proposed[2] charge-exchange model, forward charge exchange is expected in D^+ + H_2, since the elastic channel lies close in energy to a charge-exchange channel. In He^+ + H_2 collisions a quasi-resonant channel is not available and

charge exchange is absent in forward scattering.[2] This model
attributes the structure near $E\theta = 1.6$ keV deg. (in Fig. 1) to a
coupling between the direct inelastic ($Q \sim 13$ eV) and close lying
charge-exchange channels. A similar result was found for the
dominant charge exchange process in $He^+ + H_2$.[2]

*Supported by the U. S. Army Research Office - Durham and The
University of Connecticut Research Foundation.

1.   A. V. Bray, D. S. Newman, and E. Pollack, Phys. Rev. <u>A15</u>,
       2261 (1977).

2.   W. L. Hodge, Jr., A. L. Goldberger, M. Vedder, and
       E. Pollack, Phys. Rev. <u>A16</u>, 2360 (1977).

DIFFERENTIAL CROSS SECTION MEASUREMENTS FOR He$^+$ + O$_2$ CHARGE-TRANSFER[*]

Keith T. Gillen

Molecular Physics Laboratory, SRI International, Menlo Park, CA 94025 U.S.A.

Aart W. Kleyn

FOM-Institute for Atomic and Molecular Physics, Amsterdam, The Netherlands

At center-of-mass collision energies near 100 eV, we have measured the differential cross section $\frac{d\sigma}{d\Omega}$ for fast neutral He production in the charge transfer of a fast He$^+$ beam in O$_2$ target gas. We have also determined the product energy distributions with time-of flight (TOF) techniques at various scattering angles.

The angular distribution peaks strongly at 0° and drops monotonically with increasing scattering angle. At small scattering angles, TOF measurements show that the only important charge transfer channel is essentially thermoneutral. The mechanism undoubtedly is a near-resonant one, He$^+$ + O$_2$ → He + O$_2^+$(c$^4\Sigma_u^-$). As the scattering angle increases, other energy loss features, both exothermic and endothermic, become significant.

Integration over scattering angle of the double-differential cross sections for the various observed processes confirms that the near-resonant channel is the major component of the total charge transfer cross section. The dominance of this channel was not apparent in a study[1] of collisional emission in this system, since predissociation[2] of the c$^4\Sigma_u^-$ O$_2^+$ state strongly attenuated the Hopfield bands. The importance of the near-resonant channel was however inferred earlier by Stebbings et al,[3] from the magnitude and energy dependence of absolute total dissociative charge transfer cross sections.

Another important "dark" channel, appearing in our work but not in the emission measurements, involves population of O$_2^+$ excited states approximately 3 eV above the c$^4\Sigma_u^-$ state. States in this region are suggested by photoelectron spectra[4] and could also be strongly predissociated.[2]

[*] KTG acknowledges the National Science Foundation for support of this research under grant PHY 78-09647 and for sponsoring the visit of AWK to SRI where the experiments were performed.

1. H. H. Harris, M. G. Crowley, and J. J. Leventhal, Chem. Phys. Lett. <u>29</u>, 540 (1974).

2. N.H.F. Beebe, E. W. Thulstrup, and A. Andersen, J. Chem. Phys. <u>64</u>, 2080 (1976).

3. R. F. Stebbings, A.C.H. Smith, and H. Ehrhardt, J. Chem. Phys. <u>39</u>, 968 (1963).

4. O. Edqvist, E. Lindholm, L. E. Selin, and L. Åsbrink, Phys. Scripta <u>1</u>, 25 (1970).

CROSSED-BEAM MEASUREMENTS OF CHARGE TRANSFER REACTIONS
FOR He^+ - N_2 AND He^+ - O_2 IN THE 2-10 eV ENERGY RANGE

H. Schmidt[*], M. Konrad, F. Linder

Fachbereich Physik, Universität Kaiserslautern

675 Kaiserslautern, West-Germany

In a crossed beam experiment [1] with high energy and angular resolution including mass-selection we have studied charge transfer reactions in He^+-N_2 and
He^+-O_2 scattering. In first investigations we have measured energy spectra of N_2^+
and N^+ for the He^+-N_2 collision process. The energy range varied from E_{Lab} = 2 eV
to 10 eV and the angular range from ϑ_{Lab} = 0° to ϑ_{Lab} = 90°. Fig. 1 shows a
series of energy spectra for N_2^+ taken at E_{Lab} = 4.3 eV and several scattering
angles. The spectra have been taken under nearly the same conditions, so the intensity from spectrum to spectrum gives an estimate of the angular distribution.
The instrumental energy resolution is measured in the elastic He^+-N_2 scattering.
The arrows indicate the energy positions for the energy resonant (ΔE_{CM} = 0 eV),
superelastic (ΔE_{CM} = +2.6 eV, 5.9 eV, 9 eV), and inelastic (ΔE_{CM} = -3 eV) processes, respectively. One sees, that not the energy resonant process, He^+ + N_2 →
He + N_2^+ ($C^2\Sigma_u^+$, v = 4), is the most probable one at these energies. The gain of
translation energy of the N_2^+ is ΔE_{CM} = 2 eV - 4 eV, corresponding to N_2^+ in the
$B^2\Sigma_u^+$ (v = 7-19) state. This shows, that the He^+-N_2 collision system in this energy
range is an example for a charge transfer reaction, where a considerable repartit-
ion of internal and translational energy takes place, rather than a simple electron jump.

Detailed experimental data will be presented at the conference.

1   H. Schmidt, V. Hermann, and F. Linder
     Journal of Chemical Physics 69, 2734 (1978)

     V. Hermann, H. Schmidt, and F. Linder
     Journal of Physics B 11, 493 (1978)

*   permanent address: Fachbereich Physik,
                        Freie Universität Berlin
                        1000 Berlin 33, West-Germany

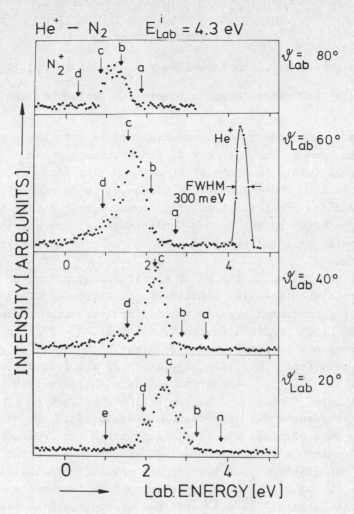

Fig. 1: Energy spectra of N_2^+ formed in $He^+ - N_2$ charge transfer reactions at $E_{Lab}^i = 4.3$ eV

a) $\Delta E_{CM} = +9$ eV   b) $\Delta E_{CM} = +5.9$ eV   c) $\Delta E_{CM} = +2.6$ eV
d) $\Delta E_{CM} = 0$ eV   e) $\Delta E_{CM} = -3$ eV

(+) superelastic   (-) inelastic

VIBRATIONAL EXCITATION OF MOLECULES IN COLLISION PROCESSES.
ROLE OF INTERMEDIATE STATES.

V.M.Lavrov, M.R.Gochitashvili, V.A.Ankudinov, B.I.Kikiani

A.F.Ioffe Physico-Technical Institute,Leningrad,USSR

The present paper has been aimed at studying the applicability of the Franck-Condon theory to the processes of excitation of vibrational levels in transitions between electronic states of molecules in slow ion-molecule collisions.It is known that in such collisions the populations of vibrational levels depart from the values predicted by the Franck-Condon model.At present there is no generally accepted point of view on the reasons for this disagreement.

To clarify the influence of electronic structure of the incident particle on the distribution of population of vibrational levels,we have measured cross sections for excitation of the bands of the N_2^+ First Negative system(transition $B^2\Sigma_u^+ - X^2\Sigma_g^+$) in collisions between N_2 molecule and 0.2-12 kev $H^+, H_2^+, He^+, N^+, O^+, Ne^+, Ar^+$ ions.As seen from Fig.I, the population of the I-st vibrational level of the $B^2\Sigma_u^+$ N_2^+ electronic state with respect to that for the 0-th level depends on the projectile structure and in most cases it increases with decreasing ion velocity.

The data obtained are considered within the framework of the quasimolecular multichannel model of vibrational excitation including exchange interaction between the colliding particles being developed by us.As shown in [I],the concept of long-range polarization interaction [2] is not confirmed by experimental results. Within the model suggested,the short-range exchange interaction is taken into account.It is as a result of exchange interaction between the approaching ion or atom and a molecule that the wave-function of the molecule is distorted and transitions between quasimolecular electronic states take place.

Another feature of the model is its multichannel character. The transition from consideration of interaction between only two potential energy surfaces[3]to that between a number of surfaces is essential since an additional mechanism appears in this case for electronic and,therefore,for vibrational excitation of the final state,connected with transition from the initial potential

surface to one or more intermediate surfaces with subsequent transition to the surface for the final state.

It is with the multichannel character of population of electronic states and,in particular,with the role of intermediate quasimolecular states corresponding to charge exchange and those corresponding to the ionic bond that we associate the discrepancy between
the experimental data on the population of vibrational levels and
the Franck-Condon calculations for electronic transitions. It follows from experiment(Fig.I) that,in $He^+- N_2$ collisions,the popula-
tion of the level $v\stackrel{!}{=}I$ with respect to the level $v'=0$ of the $N_2^+(B^2\Sigma_u^+)$
state is more probable than in $Ar^+- N_2$ collisions. This result can
be easily explained using the schematic diagrams of potential energy curves(Fig.2) from which it is seen that the intermediate quasimolecular state $He(Is^2)-N_2^+(C^2\Sigma_u^+)$ plays an important role in vibrational excitation in He^+ ion impact. On the other hand,in the case
of $Ar^+- N_2$ the contribution of the intermediate state $Ar(3p^6)$ -
- $N_2^+(X^2\Sigma_g^+)$ is seen to be small.

I.J.H.Birely, Phys.Rev.,IO,550,(I974)
2.M.Lipeles, J.Chem.Phys.,5I,I252,(I969)
3.J.D.Kelly,C.H.Bearman, H.H.Harris, J.J.Leventhal,
  J.Chem.Phys.,68,3345,(I978)

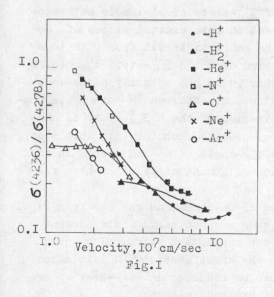

Fig.I

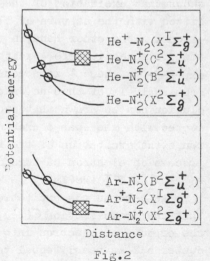

Fig.2

EXCITATION OF He-ATOMS AND N_2^+-IONS IN SLOW He$^+$-N_2 COLLISIONS

M.R.Gochitashvili,V.A.Ankudinov,V.M.Lavrov,B.I.Kikiani

A.F.Ioffe Physico-Technical Institute,
Academy of Sciences of the USSR,Leningrad,USSR.

In the present work,a systematic investigation of inelastic processes leading to the formation of excited He-atoms and
N_2^+-ions in He$^+$- N_2collisions has been carried out in the energy range from O.2 to IOkev.

In Fig.I we show some results of our measurements including
the cross sections $\sigma(B^2\Sigma_u^+)$for the excitation of the $B^2\Sigma_u^+$-state
of N_2^+-ion obtained taking into account the excitation cross sections for the O-th and I-st vibrational level only, the cross
sections $\sigma(He^*)$for the capture of one electron into excited states of He-atoms with principal quantum numbers n=3 and 4,the
emission cross sections $\sigma(3914\overset{\circ}{A})$for the band(0,0) $\lambda=3914\overset{\circ}{A}$,and the
total cross sections $\sigma(N_2^+)$for the formation of N_2^+-ions from pa-
pers[1,2].

As is clear from Fig.I,at energies about IOkev a conside-
rable part of N_2^+-ions is in the excited $B^2\Sigma_u^+$-state.A comparison
of the energy dependence of the cross sections $\sigma(He^*)$and $\sigma(B^2\Sigma_u^+)$
shows that excitation of the $B^2\Sigma_u^+$-state of N_2^+-ion is not associated with the capture of electron into excited states of He-
-atoms.On the other hand,in the energy interval from 3 to IOkev
the cross sections for excitation of the $B^2\Sigma_u^+$-state changes as
$\exp\{-\frac{A}{v}\}$,where A is a constant,v is the velocity of He$^+$-ion.
From analysis of this dependence,also obtained in paper[3],a conclusion can be drawn that excitation of the $B^2\Sigma_u^+$-state is connected with the charge exchange process.Therefore, in this energy
range,the excitation of the $B^2\Sigma_u^+$-state of N_2^+-ion occurs in the
process of electron capture into a ground state of He-atom :He$^+$+
+N_2 - $N_2^+(B^2\Sigma_u^+)$+He($1s^2$).

As regards the excitation of He-atoms,one can see from Fig.I
that the cross section $\sigma(He^*)$,even without taking into account
the capture of electron into the state with principal quantum
number n=2,is nearly equal to the cross section $\sigma(N_2^+)$.It means
that dissociative charge exchange processes He$^+$+N_2—He*+N$^+$+N are
important for the formation of excited He-atoms.

It should be noted that the energy dependence of the emis-

sion cross section for the (0,0) band $\lambda=3914\text{Å}$ changes its shape
when we pass on to small energies. Apparently, an additional mechanism of population of the $B^2\Sigma_u^+$-state appears at these energies.
It can be associated with interaction of potential energy surfa-
ces for states $N_2^+(B^2\Sigma_u^+)$+He and $N_2^+(C^2\Sigma_u^+)$+He in the region of their
pseudocrossing. Excitation of the last state occurs in near-reso-
nance processes due to exchange interaction between the particles.

The emission cross sections for He-spectral lines $\lambda=4472$ Å
($4^3D - 2^3P$) and $\lambda=4922$ Å ($4^1D - 2^1P$) as functions of energy have
a weakly pronounced oscillation structure (Fig.2). Positions of
cross section maxima as a function of inverse velocity of He^+ -
ions are practically equidistant. It can be interpreted as a result of interference of quasimolecular states of the system$(HeN_2)^+$.

I.R.F.Stebbings, J.A.Rutherford and B.R.Turner, Planet Space Sci.
13 ,II25 (I965).
2.R.Browning, C.J.Latimer, H.B.Gilbody, J.Phys.B,2,534(I969)
3.P.J.Wehrenberg, Phys.Rev.A,I5,843 (I977)

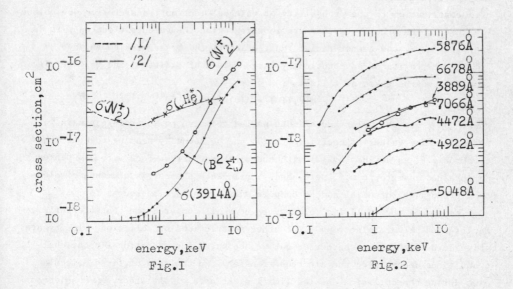

Fig.I

Fig.2

ASYMPTOTIC THEORY OF MOLECULAR RESONANT CHARGE TRANSFER BETWEEN

DIATOMICS

A.V.Evseev, A.A.Radzig, B.M.Smirnov

I.V.Kurchatov Institute of Atomic Energy, Moscow, USSR

In this paper the cross-sections for symmetric molecular charge transfer
reactions between diatomics

$$AB^+ + AB \longrightarrow AB + AB^+ \tag{1}$$

have been calculated in the broad range of collision energy where the values of
cross-sections much exceeded the area of molecular species.

On the contrary to paper[1], in which the electronic exchange potential for
H_2^+ - H_2 have been determined by using the exact variational wavefunction (w.f.)
of valence electron, and series of papers[2], in which the above potential for
more complex diatomics have been approximated by empirical formula, in the present
study we base our treatment on asymptotic theory of resonance charge transfer and
use in succession the small parameter of this theory: $1/R_0\gamma \ll 1$, where $\sigma \sim R_0^2$
is the cross-section of the reaction, $1/\gamma$ is the characteristic size of valence
electron orbit. In this case the region of electron coordinates removed from the
centers of colliding particles and placed near the internuclear axis gives the
main contribution to the probability of valence electron transfer from one molecular rest to the other. Furthermore in this region the valence electron w.f. is
approximated by one-center radial function corrected by angular dependence.

In the region of asymptotically large values of radius r the valence electron w.f. may be taken as follows

$$\psi(r,\theta,\phi) = A(\theta)r^{1/\gamma - 1}e^{-r\gamma}e^{im\phi} \tag{2}$$

where θ, ϕ are the polar and azimuth angles relative to internuclear axis in
molecule. The values of coefficient $A(\theta)$ can be found by seaming together the
electron w.f. as defined by (2) with one-electron Hartree-Fock w.f. (see tables[3]).
So obtained asymptotic w.f. were used to calculate the matrix elements of electronic exchange potential and to compute the cross-section sought for.

We assume the collision velocity to be small compared the characteristic velocities of valence electrons. The other restrictions on collision velocity are
stipulated by the fact whether or not we accounted for vibrational-rotational
transitions accompanied the electron transfer. In the case of _fixed_ molecular
axes during the collision the two limiting variants of the theory are considered:
1) - the collision time is assumed to be small compared the characteristic time of
vibrational transitions; 2) - the inverse relation between times is realized. In
the case of _small_ collision velocities compared the characteristic vibrational

velocities of nuclei also the two limiting cases have been considered: 1) – the molecular axes have no time to turn during the electron transfer; 2) – the inverse relation between times is realized. The discrepancy between the values of cross-sections found in above mentioned cases is in the range of (10-30)% and is near the accuracy of introduced asymptotic theory if the uncertainties in parameters are taken into account. In fig.1 we plot some calculated results for H_2^+-H_2, N_2^+-N_2, O_2^+-O_2 and CO^+-CO collisions and compare them with experiments.

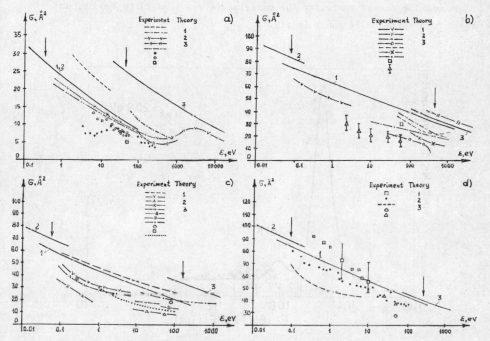

Fig.1. Comparison of theoretical and experimental cross-sections for reaction (1): a) H_2^+-H_2; b) N_2^+-N_2; c) O_2^+-O_2; d) CO^+-CO.

[1] D.R.Bates, R.H.Reid, Proc. Roy. Soc. A310, 1 (1969).

[2] M.R.Flannery, P.C.Cosby, T.F.Moran, J. Chem. Phys. 59, 5494 (1973); 61, 1259 (1974); 61, 1261 (1974).

[3] P.E.Cade, W.Huo, A.C.Wahl, At. Data Nucl. Data Tables 12, 415 (1973); 13, 339 (1974); 15, 1 (1975).

VIBRONIC EXCITATION IN ATOM-MOLECULE COLLISIONS

J. Los, A.W. Kleyn and E.A. Gislason[*]

FOM-Institute for Atomic and Molecular Physics, Amsterdam, The Netherlands

Excitation in collisions between potassium atoms and the diatomic molecules Br_2, O_2 and N_2 leading to neutral products has been studied using time of flight techniques. The energy range for the experiments was from 20 to 100 eV. An example of a spectrum is shown in fig. 1.

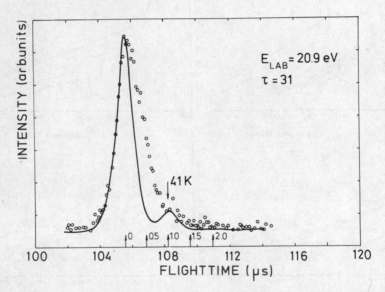

Fig. 1: time of flight spectrum for neutral scattering in K + Br_2 collisions. The full line shows the TOF spectrum of the main beam (note the [41]K isotope). The open circles show scattered signal at a reduced scattering angle of 31 eV*degree. On the lower time axis, an energy loss scale (in eV) is shown.

The experimental results for Br_2 show only vibrational excitation, which is peaked at small scattering angles. In case of O_2 and N_2 vibronic excitation is observed; for N_2 simultaneous electronic excitation of the projectile and vibrational excitation of the target is observed. The excitation probability increases with scattering angle. For O_2 electronic excitation of K and O_2 together with vibrational excitation of O_2 is observed. In this case the excitation is confined to reduced scattering angles smaller than 200 eV*degree. Moreover pure vibrational excitation can be seen for O_2 and N_2.

In all of these interactions the collision proceeds along an intermediate ionic state [1]. The three molecular systems have been selected, because they can be considered as prototypes of vibronic excitation.

In K + Br_2 collisions the vibrational excitation is mainly caused by a third crossing along the covalent scattering path. A short stay on the ionic surfaces takes care for vibrational excitation of Br_2 and attractive scattering over small angles. In K + N_2 collisions the ionic intermediate couples the groundstate to the K^* + N_2 state. During the stay on the ionic intermediate the N_2 gets vibrationally excited. Since all collisions are essentially repulsive, excitation is found at large scattering angles. In K + O_2 the excitation is mainly caused by (attractive) scattering along the ionic path.

The results will be discussed on the basis of a simple model which elucidates the molecular dynamics of these processes. Also the relation with the inverse process, quenching of electronically excited alkali atoms by molecules [2] will be pointed out.

[*] FOM visiting scientist 1977-1978 from the University of Illinois at Chicago Circle, department of chemistry, box 4348, Chicago, Ill. 60680, USA

[1] J. Los and A.W. Kleyn in: the alkali halide vapors, eds. P. Davidovits and D.R. McFadden, Academic Press, New York 1978.
[2] I.V. Hertell in: Adv. Chem. Phys. ed. J.Wm McGowan, to be published.

EXCITATION AND QUENCHING OF O $6s\,^5S_2^0$ IN COLLISIONS
OF 4 to 20 keV OXYGEN ATOMS WITH N_2*

J. R. Sheridan and J. A. Enzweiler

Geophysical Institute of University of Alaska
Fairbanks, Alaska 99701

Excitation and quenching cross sections for the $6s\,^5S_2^0$ states of atomic oxygen in collisions of oxygen atoms with N_2 have been measured in the energy range 4 to 20 keV. The measurements are accomplished by fitting the parameters in the theoretical equation for growth of excited states in the beam to measured values of the intensity of 5436 Å emission ($2p^3 3p$ - $2p^3 6s$ transition) from the beam as a function of pressure.

The basic method used has been described in earlier papers.[1,2] It can be shown that, for pressures sufficiently low that excitation processes involving two or more collisions can be neglected, the ratio of optical signal (photons per second) to the incident flux of atoms is given by:

$$\frac{\text{Signal}}{\text{Beam Flux}} = \frac{\varepsilon A_{ij} L \sigma^* n_t}{v\,(\alpha - \gamma)}\ (e^{-\gamma x} - e^{-\alpha x}) \tag{1}$$

where $\alpha \equiv \sigma_d n_t$, $\gamma \equiv \sigma_L n_t$, σ_d is the quenching cross section, σ_L is the cross section for loss of atoms from the beam, n_t is target gas number density, ε is overall detector efficiency. A_{ij} is the transition probability for the observed emission, L is the length of beam observed, v is beam velocity, σ^* is the excitation cross section and x is the pathlength of the beam through the target. The two unknown parameters in the equation are σ^* and σ_d. They can both be determined by a computer fit of equation (1) to measured values of Signal/Beam Flux as a function of pressure.

The results for σ^* and σ_d are displayed in Figures 1 and 2, respectively.

*Supported in part by NSF grant #ATM74-14428 AOI

1. J. R. Sheridan, T. Merlo and J. Enzweiler, Abstracts of Papers X ICPEAC (Paris, 1977), p. 290.
2. J. R. Sheridan, T. A. Merlo and J. Enzweiler, J. Chem. Phys. 68, 4343 (1978).

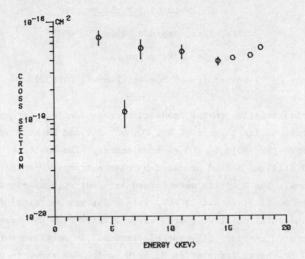

Figure 1.   Excitation of the $6s\,^5S^0_2$ state of oxygen
in collisions of oxygen atoms with N_2.

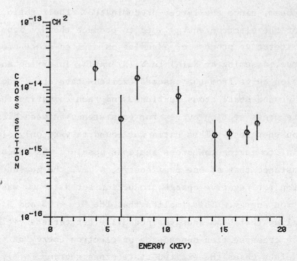

Figure 2.   Deactivation of the $6s\,^5S^0_2$ state of oxygen
in collisions with N_2.

LOW ENERGY IONIZING COLLISIONS BETWEEN EXCITED NITROGEN BEAM
MOLECULES AND N_2, CO, NO, O_2, AND Ar TARGET MOLECULES

Nyle G. Utterback

TRW, Inc., Redondo Beach, CA 90278

Bert Van Zyl

University of Denver, Denver, CO 80210

Absolute total negative charge production cross sections for excited nitrogen
molecules ($A^3\Sigma_u^+$) impacting targets of N_2, CO, NO, O_2, and Ar have been measured
from a few eV above threshold to 200 eV beam energy. The basic method has been
described[1,2] and utilized a beam produced by charge transfer neutralization of
N_2^+ molecular ions. The N_2^+ ions were formed by electron bombardment of N_2 at
electron energies of 17.5, 19 and 22 eV. Target gas was contained in a separate
target chamber and total negative charge was collected from the beam-target interaction region between guarded collector electrodes. In previous work[2] N_2^+ ions
were neutralized by charge transfer in N_2 or H_2 which was shown to produce ground
electronic-state beam molecules. In the present work N_2^+ ions were neutralized
in NO gas through the reactions $N_2^+ + NO \rightarrow N_2(A) + NO^+(X)$ and $N_2^+ + NO \rightarrow N_2(X) +$
$NO^+(a)$, both of which are almost energy resonant. (Both $N_2^+(X)$ and $N_2^+(A)$ ions
were involved, and both lead to production of $N_2(A)$ molecules, the latter through
decay of $N_2(B)$.) A major difficulty was determining the relative amounts of $N_2(A)$
and $N_2(X)$ in the beam, since the latter predominated. Their ratio, which was a
strong function of the electron energy used to produce the N_2^+ ions, was determined through an iterative process of assuming an excited-state cross section
versus energy curve, assuming an $N_2(A)$ to $N_2(X)$ ratio, inferring an expected composite cross section curve from the assumed excited-state cross sections and previously measured ground-state cross sections, and then comparing the expected and
measured composite cross section curves for consistency between different target
gases and electron energies. (This ratio was found to vary only slowly with beam
energy.) Essential to making the cross sections absolute was discovering the
fortuitous circumstance that at one beam energy, 47 eV, the measured composite
total cross section for negative charge production for $N_2^* + CO$ was not a function
of ionizing electron energy. This implies that the $N_2^* + CO$ and $N_2 + CO$ cross
sections are equal at that beam energy since all other targets yielded a strong
measured composite cross section dependence on electron energy at 47 eV beam
energy. (In all other cases the excited-state cross section, $\sigma(*)$, was found to
be much greater than the ground-state cross section, $\sigma(X)$, at 47 eV beam; the
large peak in the $N_2 + CO$ $\sigma(X)$ versus energy curve attributed[2] to $N_2 + CO \rightarrow NO^+ +$
CN^- occurs at 47 eV beam energy, carrying $\sigma(X)$ almost up to $\sigma(*)$ at that energy.)
At beam energies low enough that $\sigma(*)$ greatly exceeded $\sigma(X)$ it was possible to
directly determine the relative amounts of $N_2(A)$ as a function of electron energy.

Beam fractions of $N_2(A)$ at 47 eV beam energy were 0.15, 0.10, and 0.06 at electron energies of 22, 19, and 17.5 eV, respectively.

In all cases at all beam energies, $\sigma(*)$ values were considerably larger than the corresponding $\sigma(X)$ values (excepting the $N_2^* + CO$ case noted above at 47 eV). At 200 eV beam energy $\sigma(*)$ was from 4 to 5 times $\sigma(X)$ for the five target gases. At beam energies 1 eV above threshold for $\sigma(X)$ in the center of mass system, the values for the ratio $\sigma(*)/\sigma(X)$ were 20, 300, 200, 300, and 1000 for targets CO, NO, O_2, N_2, and Ar, respectively.

The most striking aspect of the results is the lack of structure in the curves of $\sigma(*)$ versus energy. This contrasts with the $\sigma(X)$ curves, all of which exhibit clear structure which was attributed[2] to positive ion-negative ion production processes such as $N_2 + CO \rightarrow NO^+ + CN^-$ and $N_2 + O_2 \rightarrow NO^+ + NO^{(-)}$. While one cannot conclude that such processes do not occur with $N_2(A)$ beam molecules on these targets (i.e. the $\sigma(*)$ case), it appears likely that other processes which do not show curve structure are relatively much more important for the $\sigma(*)$ cases than for the corresponding $\sigma(X)$.

1. N. G. Utterback and G. H. Miller, Rev. Sci. Instrum. <u>32</u>, 1101 (1961).
2. N. G. Utterback and B. Van Zyl, J. Chem. Phys. <u>68</u>, 2742 (1978).

ENERGY LOSS STUDIES ON ION-PAIR FORMATION REACTIONS
FOR THE K + SF$_6$ AND NO SYSTEMS

S. Okada and K. Kodera*

Department of Chemistry, Kyoto University
Kyoto, Japan

Energy loss spectra for the product K$^+$ ions scattered to zero angle in fast
potassium atom - molecule (SF$_6$ and NO) collisions, for example

$$K + SF_6 \longrightarrow K^+ + SF_6^-$$

are reported for collision energies between 15 and 40 eV.
From these measurements, it is possible to get information about the excitation
energy of the products and on the dynamics of the collisions.

The fast potassium atomic beam is generated by charge-transfer method.[1]
The beam with an energy spread of $\sim$0.2 eV FWHM enters the collision chamber in
which SF$_6$ or NO molecules are introduced at a constant pressure. Experiments
are carried out in the pressure range of $\sim$10^{-5} Torr which satisfies the
condition of a single collision. The energy of the K$^+$ ions produced by the
electron-transfer processes between the fast potassium atoms and SF$_6$ or NO
molecules is determined with a 127°-cylindrical electrostatic energy analyzer.

The technique which is employed permits the determination of energy losses
with an accuracy of about 0.2 eV, and permits to measure excitations to
different exit channels.

The energy loss spectra of the product K$^+$ ions scattered to zero angle for
the K + SF$_6$ and NO systems are shown in Figures 1 and 2, respectively.
In the case of SF$_6$, due to a vertical electron transfer from the bottom of the
SF$_6$ potential to the ground-state SF$_6^-$ potential, the formed SF$_6^-$ ions exceed
the dissociation limit ($\sim$1.0$\pm$0.1 eV) of SF$_6^-$. The SF$_6^-$ ions are on the
repulsive part of the potential and the bond of SF$_6^-$ will be rapidly stretched
forming SF$_5^-$ ions which correspond to the loss peaks at 5.0 and 5.4 eV.
The peak at about 5.6 eV closely corresponds to the value of 5.5$\pm$0.6 eV
measured by Hubers and Los[2] for F$_2^-$ production to K + SF$_6$ collisions at room
temperature.

In the attachment of low-energy electrons to SF$_6$ and the ion-pair formation
in collisions between fast alkali atoms and SF$_6$ molecules, the product negative
ions are mainly SF$_6^-$, SF$_5^-$, F$^-$, and F$_2^-$ ions. It is considered that, from the
magnitude of crossing radius R$_c$, the channel leading to the formation of F$_2^-$
ions can be observed and the channel leading to the formation of F$^-$ ions cannot
be observed in forward scattering.

But in the case of NO, the formed NO$^-$ ions do not exceed the dissociation
limit of NO$^-$. The NO$^-$ ions are populated in the ground state of NO$^-$.
The distribution of vibrational states might be governed by a law similar to
the Franck-Condon principle.

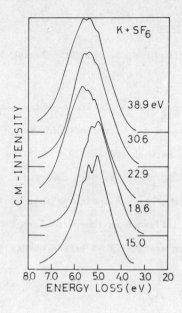 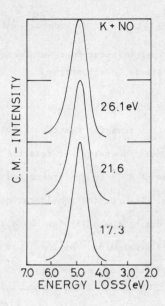

Fig. 1. Fig. 2.

Fig. 1. Intensity of K^+ ($d^2\sigma/d\Omega dE$) product ions for the $K + SF_6$ systems, normalized to the maximum ion intensity in each energy loss spectrum, as a function of loss energy for different collision energies in the direction of the incoming fast potassium atomic beam. (all values in the center-of-mass system)

Fig. 2. Intensity of product K^+ ions for the K + NO system as a function of loss energy.

*Professor Emeritus
1. S. Okada, J. Phys. D : Applied Physics 12, (1979) in press.
2. M.M. Hubers and J. Los, Chem. Phys. 10, 235 (1975).

DOUBLY DIFFERENTIAL CROSS SECTIONS OF THE REACTION

$$K + NO_2 \dashrightarrow K^+ + NO_2^-$$

M. Kimura[*] and K. Lacmann

Hahn-Meitner-Institut fuer Kernforschung Berlin GmbH, Bereich Strahlenchemie, 1000 Berlin 39, West-Germany

Doubly differential cross section, in energy and angle, are reported for the electron transfer reaction between potassium and nitrogendioxide in   a crossed beam apparatus[1] at relative energies between 2.7 and 30.8 eV. The formation of NO_2^- in its ground and excited $^3B_1$ state has been observed (Fig. 1). Theoretical consideration of these processes indicates that bond bending during the collision has a stronger influence on ion-pair formation than bond stretching. At the lower collision energies most excess energy is converted into internal energy of NO_2^-.

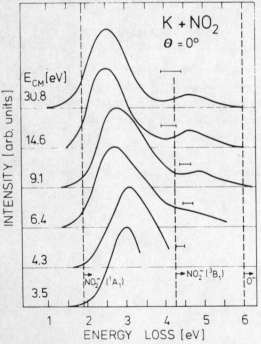

Fig. 1.

Normalized relative intensity of K^+ ions ($d^2\sigma/dE\,d\Omega$) in the direction of the incoming   K beam ($\theta = 0^\circ$) versus the trans-lational energy loss for different collision energies $E_{c.m.}$ (all values in c.m. system). Minimum energy loss values for NO_2^- ($^1A_1$) and ($^3B_1$) state and for O^- formation are indicated by broken lines. The final energy resolu-tion is shown by error bars.

* Present address:Faculty of Science, Osaka University,Toyonata,Osaka,Japan

1. M. Kimura and K. Lacmann, J. Chem. Phys. 69, 4938 (1978).

THE EXISTENCE OF THE NEGATIVE ION OF CH_2

B. Hird and S. P. Ali

Physics Department, University of Ottawa, Ottawa, K1N 6N5, Ontario, Canada

The recent development to use tandem accelerators for radiocarbon dating[1] makes use of negative ions to select ^{14}C from other elements. The existence of N^- from gas-phase collisions is unlikely[2] so that it is important to identify other mass-14 negative ions which may be a source of background.

We have measured the negative ion production cross section from a magnetically analysed 126 keV CH_2^+ beam in a krypton target about $4 \times 10^{14} cm^{-2}$ thick using a $\pi/\sqrt{2}$ electrostatic deflector. The measured ratio of channeltron counting rates with the electric field reversed periodically, was corrected for background by also measuring the rate with the deflector field set 1 keV either side of the beam energy.

Successive runs were added statistically to obtain a CH_2^- production cross section of $(1.25 \pm 0.14) \times 10^{-21} cm^2$. The negative ions were probably produced in single collision two electron transfer σ_{+-} processes, but there may also be a contribution from double collisions involving $(\sigma_{+0}\sigma_{0-})$.

The ions were detected 1μs after their creation so that they have a life-time at least comparable to the transit time to the stripper of a tandem accelerator. CH_2 may therefore be a source of background in methods of radiocarbon dating which use negative ions.

1. K. H. Pusser, R. B. Liebert, A. E. Litherland, R. P. Beukens, H. E. Gove, C. L. Bennett, M. R. Clover and W. E. Sondheim, Proceedings of the Second International Conference on Electrostatic Accelerators, Strasbourg, France, 24-27 May 1977.
2. B. Hird and S. P. Ali, Phys. Rev. Lett. 41, 540 (1978).

MECHANISM FOR PENNING IONIZATION OF Na BY VIBRATIONALLY EXCITED N_2

George F. Zahr

Chemistry Department, University of Jordan

Amman, Jordan

For a normal collisional ionization reaction of the sort ($A^* + M \longrightarrow A^+ + M + e$) to occur, the potential energy curve of ($A^* + M$) is required to be higher in energy than that of ($A + M^+$). It was found experimentally[1] that Na could be ionized by vibrationally excited N_2^+ (v $\geqslant$21).

$$Na + N_2^+ \text{ (v } \geqslant 21) \longrightarrow Na^+ + N_2 + e$$

The potential energy surface of N_2 + Na (S1) and that of N_2 + Na^+ (S2) were calculated by the SCF method. S1 turned out to be lower in energy than S2 all over the space studied. (See Fig. 1.) Thus, the accepted mechanism of the penning ionization does not explain the problem. A third potential energy surface (S3) for Na^+ + N_2^- was calculated and turned out to cross both S1 and S2.

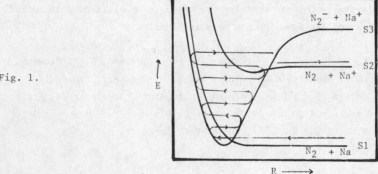

Fig. 1.

The mechanism proposed for the penning ionization in this case includes a transition from S1 to S3 at the crossing seam with the formation of $Na^+ \text{---} N_2^-$ complex; with internal energy transfere the complex could reach the part of S3 higher in energy than S2 where leakage to the continuum ionic surfaces S2's is possible. (See Fig. 1.)

1. R.Wang, G. Pappenecker, and C. Schmidt, Chem. Phys. 5, 255(1974).

Penningionisation of NO_2 by He(2^3S)

W. Goy, V. Kohls and H. Morgner

Fakultät für Physik der Universität Freiburg, West Germany

We investigate the Penningionisation of NO_2 by metastable helium He(2^3S). We measure the electron energy distribution and find similar results as Cermák[1]. In addition we run energy spectra of those electrons that are coincident with one of the produced ions NO_2^+, NO^+ or O^+. These latter results allow us to develop a complete picture of the process which differs substantially from the interpretation by Cermák[1]:

He(2^3S) and $NO_2(^2A_1)$ form doublet and quartet states when approaching each other. The quartet potential curve is repulsive. Ionisation that occurs out of this entrance channel leads (at our thermal collision energies) to narrow peaks in the electron energy distribution, similar to what one gets in photoionisation[2]. However, only the triplet states of NO_2^+ can be reached in this way. The singlet states of NO_2^+ can be formed only from the doublet entrance channel. The corresponding potential curve is strongly attractive ($D_o \gtrsim 4.5$ eV!) due to an avoided crossing with the $He^+(^2S)$-$NO_2^-(^1A_1)$ state. Therefore the electron energy distribution that arises from ionisation into the singlet NO_2^+ states is very broad. Accordingly the peaks of the singlet NO_2^+ states known in photoionisation[2] are missing in the Penning spectrum.

Our results can be viewed as a most direct proof that the spin conservation rule of Wigner and Wittner holds in Penningionisation of molecules since He-NO_2^+ singlet states are clearly not populated from a quartet entrance state.

1. V. Cermák, J.Electr.Spectr.Rel.Phen. 9 (1976) 419 - 439

2. C.R. Brundle, D. Neumann, W.C. Price, D. Evans, A.W. Potts and D.G. Streets, J.Chem.Phys. 53 (1970) 705 - 715

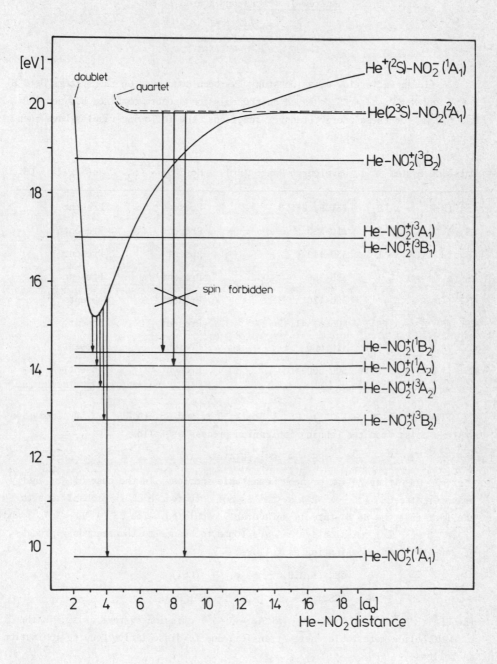

He-NO$_2$ distance

ENERGY TRANSFER PROCESSES IN REACTIONS OF He(2^3S) AND Ne($^3P_{0,2}$) WITH CS_2

Andrew J. Yencha and Konrad T. Wu

Department of Physics
State University of New York at Albany
Albany, New York 12222 U.S.A.

A flowing afterglow emission study has been conducted on the systems He(2^3S) + CS_2 and Ne($^3P_{0,2}$) + CS_2. Based on the emission spectra obtained between 200 and 600 nm for these energy transfer reactions, the following results have been found.

Emission System	Wavelength Range (nm)	He(2^3S) + CS_2	Ne($^3P_{0,2}$) + CS_2
CS_2^+ ($\tilde{B}\ ^2\Sigma_u^+ \to \tilde{X}\ ^2\Pi_g$)	281.9, 285.5	Present	Present
CS (A $^1\Pi \to$ X $^1\Sigma^+$)	210-330	Present	Present
CS_2 ($\tilde{a}\ ^3A_2 \to \tilde{X}\ ^1\Sigma_g^+$)	330-440	Absent	Present
CS (a $^3\Pi \to$ X $^1\Sigma^+$)	335-380	Present	Present
CS_2^+ ($^4\Pi \to \tilde{X}\ ^2\Pi_g$)	380-420	Present	Absent
CS^+ (B $^2\Sigma^+ \to$ A $^2\Pi_i$)	406.6, 411.5	Present	Absent
CS_2^+ ($\tilde{A}\ ^2\Pi_u \to \tilde{X}\ ^2\Pi_g$)	410-600	Present	Present
CS^+ (A $^2\Pi_i \to$ X $^2\Sigma^+$)	500-600	Present	Absent

The CS_2^+ ($\tilde{B}\ ^2\Sigma_u^+ \to \tilde{X}\ ^2\Pi_g$), CS_2^+ ($^4\Pi \to \tilde{X}\ ^2\Pi_g$), and CS_2^+ ($\tilde{A}\ ^2\Pi_u \to \tilde{X}\ ^2\Pi_g$) emission systems arise from the Penning ionization process as follows:

$$X^* + CS_2 \to CS_2^+ (\tilde{B}, \tilde{A}) + X + e^-$$

where X^* is either helium or neon metastable species. In the case of Ne* energy transfer, the CS_2^+ ($^4\Pi \to \tilde{X}\ ^2\Pi_g$) system is not detected which is probably due to the fact that the $\tilde{B}\ ^4\Pi$ state is unfavorably populated. The CS (A $^1\Pi \to$ X $^1\Sigma^+$) and CS (a $^3\Pi \to$ X $^1\Sigma^+$) emission systems are found to be due to the secondary process of ion-electron recombination as follows:

$$CS_2^+ (\tilde{X}, \tilde{A}, \tilde{B}, \tilde{C}) + e^- \to (CS_2)^*$$

$$(CS_2)^* \to CS (A,a) + S (^3P_2)$$

The CS^+ (B $^2\Sigma^+ \to$ A $^2\Pi_i$) and CS^+ (A $^2\Pi_i \to$ X $^2\Sigma^+$) emission systems arise, in the case of helium metastable energy transfer, due to dissociative Penning ionization as follows:

$$He(2^3S) + CS_2 \to He(1^1S) + CS^+(B,A) + S(^3P_2) + e^-$$

These emission systems are not detected in the neon energy transfer reaction because energetically neither the A $^2\Pi_i$ nor B $^2\Sigma^+$ states of CS^+ can be populated. The identification of the CS_2^+ ($^4\Pi \rightarrow \tilde{X} \, ^2\Pi_g$) and CS^+ (B $^2\Sigma^+ \rightarrow$ A $^2\Pi_i$) transitions, although observed previously in a similar study of He(2^3S) + CS_2 but not assigned,[1] is based on direct and indirect spectroscopic evidence and will be discussed in detail.

These results indicate that Penning ionization and dissociative Penning ionization are the two most important reaction pathways in energy transfer between helium and neon metastables and carbon disulfide. The secondary process of ion-electron recombination is an important post-ionization process due to the flowing afterglow technique used here.

Reference:

1. J. A. Coxon, P. J. Marcoux, and D. W. Setser, Chem. Phys. <u>17</u>, 403 (1976).

ENERGY DISTRIBUTION OF DRIFTING IONS

J.B. Hasted[‡] P.P. Ong[†] M.H. Khatri[*] and D. Mathur[‡]

[+]Department of Physics, Birkbeck College, Malet Street, London WC1E 7HX

[*]Department of Physics and Astronomy, University College London,
Gower Street, London WC1E 6BT

The variable length injected ion drift tube[1,2] is now fitted with a low
energy (~10 eV) ion injection facility (Figure 1) and retardation analysis
extraction system (Figure 2)[3] by means of which on-axis ion energy distribution
functions are measured, for comparision with theory and unfolding ion-molecule
rate functions. O^+He, Ar energy distribution functions are in course of being
obtained; an example of preliminary data at high reduced field is shown in
Figure 3.

1. Y. Kaneko, L.R. Megill and J.B. Hasted, Chem. Phys. 45 (1966) 3741.

2. R.G. Kosmider and J.B. Hasted, J. Phys. B 8 (1975) 273.

3. K. Naveed-Ullah, D. Mathur and J.B. Hasted, Int. J. of Mass Spectrometry
   and Ion Physics, 26 (1978) 91.

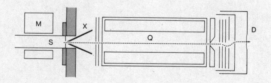

Figure 1

Ion injection facility for drift tube.
M. Microwave cavity   S. Ion source   X. Extraction electrode
Q. Quadrupole mass selector.   D. Drift tube.

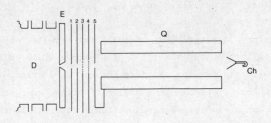

Figure 2

Retardation analysis extraction system

D. Drift tube.   E. exit plate. 1-5, electrodes.   Q. Quadrupole mass selector

Ch. Channel multiplier.   Potentials: E,1   0 V
                                               2 -10 V
                                               3 Linear ramp + 5 to -20 V
                                               4 -40 V
                                               5 -50 V

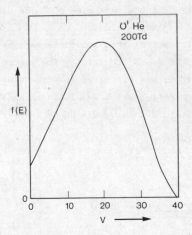

Figure 3

On-axis energy distrubution of O^+ ions in helium at $\frac{E}{P}$ = 200 Td

IONIZATION OF CO_2 BY METASTABLE HELIUM ATOMS AND THERMAL HELIUM IONS

Masaharu Tsuji, Hiroshi Obase, Mamoru Matsuo and Yukio Nishimura

Research Institute of Industrial Science, Kyushu University,
Hakozaki, Fukuoka 812, Japan

In our laboratory, a program has recently initiated to study reactions of triatomic molecules in a helium afterglow by UV and visible emission spectrometry. This paper deals with the results obtained for carbon dioxide.

Although main active species in a helium afterglow are metastable $He(2^3S)$ atoms, a small amount of ionic species inevitably involved in the helium flow takes part in the production of some excited species. Then, it is necessary to determine responsible active species for the detail study of excitation mechanism. For the purpose of reaction identification, ion-collector electrodes were added to the helium flow line. By use of ion-collector grid and synchronous photon counting equipment, Penning ionization and charge-transfer ionization can be separated.

Figure 1 displays schematically the flowing afterglow apparatus employed to monitor fluorescence resulting from thermal ion-molecule reactions. A pulse modulation system shown in Fig. 2 was used to distingush fluorescence from ion-molecule reactions from that from Penning ionization. The flux of ionic species in the helium flow was modulated on and off by pulsing the potential applied to the grid. Photons were alternatively counted up and down after an appropriate delay time t_D during a gate time t_G. The difference signal of interest was accumulated and registered.

A satisfactory efficiency of this apparatus was checked by observing $N_2^+(B-X)$ emission resulting from the He^+/N_2 reaction. The concentration of ionic species relative to metastable atoms was estimated from the vibrational population of the $N_2^+(B)$ state. The maximum ratio, which was found to be about 1/10, is larger than other reported values obtained in a dc discharge system.

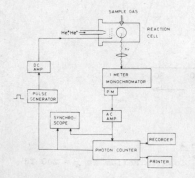

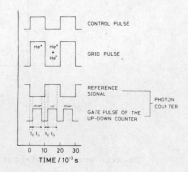

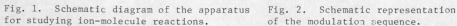

Fig. 1. Schematic diagram of the apparatus for studying ion-molecule reactions.

Fig. 2. Schematic representation of the modulation sequence.

When CO_2 was added to the helium afterglow, intense $CO_2^+(A-X,B-X)$ emission and weak $CO^+(A-X)$ emission were identified in the 280-500 nm region. The energy level diagram for CO_2^+ and $CO^+(A,B)$ from CO_2 is shown in Fig. 3. Based on the energetics, He^+ is only possible active species for the formation of $CO^+(A)$ from CO_2, whereas $CO_2^+(A,B)$ ions can be produced through both Penning ionization and charge-transfer ionization. For the determination of responsible active species, spectral variation by application of dc or ac potential to the ion-collector grid was monitored.

A typical emission spectra of CO_2 in the 350-440 nm region are shown in Fig. 4. Although both He* and He^+ are possible active species in the spectrum (a), only He* or He^+ is responsible for the production of emitting excited species in the spectra (b) and (c). In the spectrum (a), weak $CO^+(A-X)$ emission is superimposed on the intense $CO_2^+(A-X)$ emission bands. In the spectrum (b), $CO^+(A-X)$ emission is absent. On the contrary, only $CO^+(A-X)$ emission is observed in the spectrum (c). These spectral observation and a similar experiment for the $CO_2^+(B-X)$ emission lead us to conclude that $CO_2^+(A,B)$ and $CO^+(A)$ are produced through the following reactions.

$$He(2^3S) + CO_2 \longrightarrow CO_2^+(A,B) + He + e^- \qquad \text{Penning ionization}$$

$$He^+ + CO_2 \longrightarrow CO^+(A) + O + He \qquad \text{Charge-transfer ionization}$$

From the present study, it was found that dominant emissive product for the He^+/CO_2 reaction is $CO^+(A)$ and charge-transfer ionization leading to $CO_2^+(A,B)$ is inefficient. Our results are consistent with those of Anicich et al.[1] obtained in the ICR experiment. They reported that CO^+ is the major ion product in the He^+/CO_2 reaction and no CO_2^+ ions are detected.

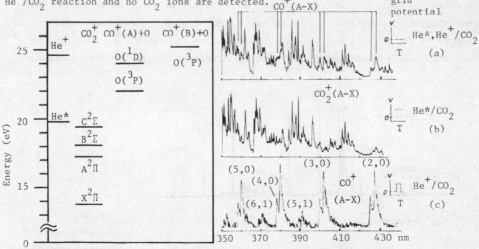

Fig. 3.   Energy-level diagram.   Fig. 4.   Spectra of CO_2 in a helium afterglow.

1.   V.G. Anicich, J.B. Laudenslager, W.T. Huntress, Jr. and J.H. Futrell, J. Chem. Phys., 67, 4340 (1977).

DISSOCIATIVE EXCITATION OF CYANIDES IN RARE GAS
FLOWING AFTERGLOW I. VISIBLE EMISSION IN THE
REACTION OF He^M AND Ar^M WITH HCN, DCN AND BrCN

Y.Ozaki, Y.Fukuda, T.Kondow and K.Kuchitsu

Department of Chemistry, Faculty of Science,
The University of Tokyo, Hongo, Bunkyo-ku, Tokyo 113, Japan

Dissociative excitation of HCN, DCN and BrCN by the impact of metastable helium (He^M) and argon (Ar^M) atoms were studied by a flowing afterglow technique. It was found from the visible emission spectra that $CN(B^2\Sigma)$, $CN(A^2\Pi)$, $CH(A^2\Delta)$ and H(n=2-15) were produced in the reaction of He^M + HCN, while CN(B), CN(A) and $CN(^4\Sigma)$ were produced in Ar^M + HCN. The CN(B-X) band spectra resulting from different metastables and targets showed markedly different features. The partitioning of the vibrational and rotational energies of the CN(B) produced from HCN, DCN and BrCN by Ar^M impact was also very different from those produced by the impact of VUV photons and electrons.

A flow of rare gas was discharged by 2450 MHz microwave, and the sample gas was mixed about 15 cm downstream. The pressures of Ar and He were typically 0.55 and 0.9 Torr, respectively. The sample pressures were on the order of 10^{-2} Torr, where the CN(B) can be regarded as essentially collision-free. The effects of charged particles produced concurrently were negligible, as confirmed by using two grid electrodes and using SF_6 as a quencher. The emission was analyzed by a 1-m spectrometer (Spex 1704) and detected by photon counting.

Figure 1 shows emission spectra in the reaction of He^M and Ar^M with HCN in the region of 340 - 460 nm. In the reaction of Ar^M with HCN, only the CN(B-X) emission was observed, whereas CH(A-X) and H-Balmer emission as well as CN(B-X) were observed in the reaction of He^M with HCN. Figure 2 shows high resolution spectra of the CN(B-X) 0-0 sequence produced from the reactions of He^M and Ar^M with HCN. As demonstrated in the spectra, levels of large vibrational quantum

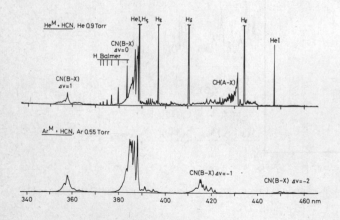

Fig. 1.
Observed emission
spectra from the
reaction of He^M
and Ar^M with HCN.

numbers v' of CN(B) are more heavily populated in the reaction of Ar^M than in that of He^M, even though He^M (19.8 eV) has much higher excitation energy than Ar^M (11.55 and 11.72 eV). A plausible interpretation is that, with He^M excitation, CN(B) is mainly produced via the reaction

$$He^M + HCN \longrightarrow CN(B^2\Sigma) + H(n=2),$$

because no CN(B-X) emission with $v' \geq 10$ was detected, as expected from the energetics. On the other hand, with Ar^M excitation the reaction

$$Ar^M + HCN \longrightarrow CN(B^2\Sigma) + H(n=1)$$

is the only possibility for the production of CN(B).

The dissociative excitation of HCN by Ar^M impact produces CN(B) with such a vibrational distribution that the populations decrease with v' extending to v'=14, and those for higher vibrational levels are greater than the corresponding populations given by photoexcitation (Lyman-α)[1] and electron impact excitations[2]. A marked isotope effect was observed in this reaction. The vibrational and rotational excitations in the CN(B) produced from DCN was found to be higher than those produced from HCN. A similar trend in the isotope effect was observed in the He^M impact. Photoexcitation and electron impact excitation also gave similar isotope effects. In the reaction of Ar^M + BrCN, the vibrational populations of CN(B) extend to v'=20 with anomalous enhancements at v'=12 and 14.

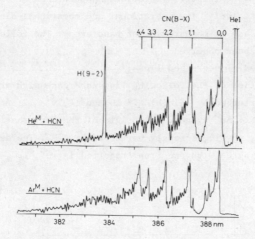

Fig. 2. CN($B^2\Sigma$-$X^2\Sigma$) emission spectra from the reaction of He^M and Ar^M with HCN.

1. S.Tatematsu and K.Kuchitsu, Bull.Chem.Soc.Jap. 50, 2896 (1977)
2. I.Nishiyama, T.Kondow and K.Kuchitsu, Chem.Phys.Lett. in press

DISSOCIATIVE EXCITATION OF CYANIDES IN RARE GAS FLOWING AFTERGLOW II.
ANOMALOUS VIBRATIONAL AND ROTATIONAL POPULATIONS OF CN($B^2\Sigma$)
PRODUCED FROM Ar^M PLUS BrCN AND THEIR COLLISIONAL RELAXATIONS.

Andrew J. Yencha

Department of Physics, State University of New York at Albany
Albany, New York 12222 U.S.A.

Yasushi Ozaki, Tamotsu Kondow, and Kozo Kuchitsu

Department of Chemistry, Faculty of Science, The
University of Tokyo, Hongo, Bunkyo-ku, Tokyo 113, Japan

When metastable argon atoms (Ar^M) react with BrCN, CN radicals are produced
in the $B^2\Sigma$ and $A^2\Pi_i$ states.[1-3] The violet $B^2\Sigma$-$X^2\Sigma$ emission exhibits pronounced
anomalies in the vibrational and rotational structures: Some vibrational levels
(v'= 12, 14, etc.) have larger populations than others, and some rotational lines
have intensity anomalies due to the rotational perturbations between the $B^2\Sigma$ and
$A^2\Pi_i$ or $^4\Sigma$ atates. In an attempt to understand the origin of the anomalies, the
B-X band system has been studied using the flowing afterglow technique. The Ar^M
atoms were produced in the microwave discharge (2450 MHz) of an argon flow. The
pressure of BrCN was about 0.01 Torr. The emission was observed by a Spex 1704
spectrometer and photon counting.

A typical spectrum and relative vibrational populations of CN($B^2\Sigma$) are shown
in Figs. 1 and 2, respectively. The vibrational and rotational distributions were
obtained by simulation and by measurement of band areas. The following dependences
on argon pressure have been observed:

(1) Intensity anomalies of perturbed lines:

The relative intensities of the following lines decrease with argon pressure.
(a) N'= 20, v'= 11, perturbed by $^4\Sigma$. (b) N'= 10 and 14, v'= 12; According to our
recent study of the HCN + Ar^M system, the origin of the perturbation seems to be
$A^2\Pi_i$. (c) N'= 7 and 10, v'= 14, strongly perturbed by $A^2\Pi_i$. The dependences observed for (a) and (c) agree with the trend reported in ref. 1.

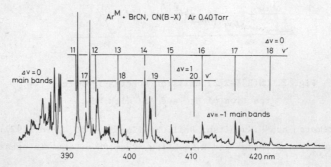

Fig. 1. Observed CN($B^2\Sigma$-$X^2\Sigma$) emission spectrum from the
reaction of Ar^M with BrCN.

(2) Vibrational populations:

(a) <u>v'= 11</u>: The relative vibrational population depends on argon pressure; the origin is reported to be a rotational relaxation from $^4\Sigma$ to $B^2\Sigma$ through rotationally perturbed levels.[1] Since the anomaly seems to disappear in the limit of low argon pressure (Figs. 2 and 3), the population at the low pressure limit seems to be the result of a direct formation in $B^2\Sigma$.

(b) <u>v'= 12 and 14</u>: The vibrational distributions have practically no pressure dependence (Fig. 3). Even when the argon pressure is extrapolated to 0 Torr, the populations still show anomalies.

Therefore, the pressure dependence of the relative vibrational populations and the intensity anomalies of rotationally perturbed lines for v'= 12 and 14 bands are due to different origins from those for v'= 11. The anomalies in the relative vibrational populations seem to occur via the direct energy-transfer process instead of the relaxation from $A^2\Pi_i$ to $B^2\Sigma$.

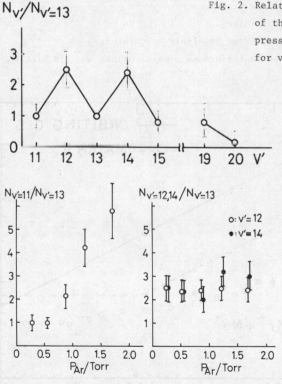

Fig. 2. Relative vibrational populations of the produced $CN(B^2\Sigma)$ at argon pressure 0.28 Torr. The population for v'= 13 is taken as a reference.

Fig. 3. Argon pressure dependences of the relative vibrational populations for $CN(B^2\Sigma)$ v'= 11, 12 and 14.

1. W. H. Duewer, J. A. Coxon, and D. W. Setser, J. Chem. Phys. <u>56</u>, 4355 (1972).
2. J. A. Coxon, D. W. Setser, and W. H. Duewer, J. Chem. Phys. <u>58</u>, 2244 (1973).
3. T. Urisu and K. Kuchitsu, J. Photochem. <u>2</u>, 409 (1973/74).

DRIFT TUBE STUDY OF CHARGE TRANSFER BETWEEN Kr^{++} AND Ne

T. Koizumi, K. Okuno and Y. Kaneko

Department of Physics, Faculty of Science,
Tokyo Metropolitan University, Setagaya-ku, Tokyo 158, Japan

Although a number of studies have been made on charge transfer reactions involving multiply charged ions above 100 eV, relatively few work has been reported on such reactions below a few eV. Recently, Okuno et al. reported a drift tube study of symmetric resonance double charge transfer in Kr^{++} + Kr, and Xe^{++} + Xe systems.[1] Here, we report the results of cross-section measurement of reaction

$$Kr^{++} + Ne \longrightarrow Kr^+ + Ne^+ + 3.0 \text{ eV}. \quad (1)$$

The energy range studied is from 15 meV to 3 eV. The reaction (1) is interesting from the following view points;

1) No molecular species are involved.
2) The potential crossing point can be simply calculated.
3) The products ions must be in the ground states, unless Kr^{++} is highly excited.

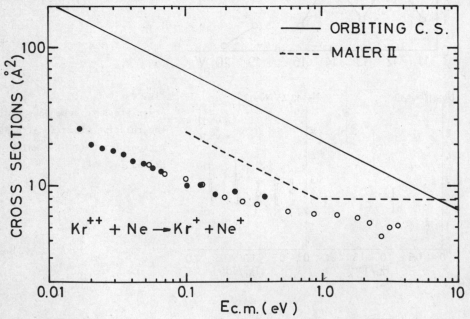

Fig.1. Charge transfer cross sections of the reaction (1). The cross sections measured at 82 K and 300 K are represented by (●) and (○), respectively.

The injected-ion drift tube apparatus used in this experiment is the same one used in the previous studies[2,3] except for an improvement of the drift tube to be cooled with liquid nitrogen. The doubly charged ions produced in a conventional ion source of electron impact type are mass analyzed and decelerated down to 20 eV before getting into the drift tube. The drift tube is filled with about 0.3 Torr of He gas that is used as a buffer gas. A small amount of Ne gas is mixed with the He gas. The ions getting out the drift tube are mass-analyzed again. From the second mass spectra, reaction cross sections are determined. The average collision energy is calculated by means of Wannier's formula[4] using the drift velocity of ions, which was measured in this experiment. The drift tube is made of copper, and cooled with liquid nitrogen flowing through the copper pipe coiling round it. The gas temperature was measured as 82 K. Owing to this improvement, the lower bound of the energy was extended to 15 meV. Besides, the effect of impurity in the buffer gas was reduced. In fact no impurity peaks were observed in the secondary ion mass-spectra.

The drift velocity of Kr^{++} ions in He gas at 82 K was measured as a function of E/N. The difference between the mobility curves at 82 K and 300 K provides a very interesting problem, but it is not the present subject and will be discussed elsewhere.

The result obtained is shown in Fig. 1. The agreement between the cross sections measured at 82 K and 300 K is fairly good. The charge transfer cross section appeares to be divided into two parts. The low energy part of the cross section has an energy dependence as almost $E^{-1/2}$. The solid line in Fig. 1 indicates the orbiting cross section assuming the polarization force. The high energy part of the cross section is less dependent of the energy. The dashed curve indicates the cross section curve measured by Maier II using a tandem mass spectrometer technique.[5] Qualitatively, they agree rather well with each other though the transient energy is shifted some extent.

1. K. Okuno, T. Koizumi and Y. kaneko, phys.rev. Lett. <u>40</u>, 1708 (1978).
2. Y. Kaneko, N. Kobayashi and I. Kanomata, J. Phys. Soc. Jpn. <u>27</u>, 992 (1969).
3. Y. Kaneko, N. Kobayashi and I. Kanomata, Mass spectrosopy <u>18</u>, 920 (1970).
4. G. H. Wannier, Bell. Syst. Tech. J. <u>32</u>, 170 (1953).
5. W. B. Maier II, J. Chem. Phys. <u>60</u>, 3588 (1974).

MEASUREMENTS OF SINGLE-ELECTRON CHARGE TRANSFER BETWEEN DOUBLY CHARGED
IONS AND ATOMS OR MOLECULES AT THERMAL ENERGIES[*]

Rainer Johnsen and Manfred A. Biondi

Dept. of Physics and Astronomy, University of Pittsburgh
Pittsburgh, PA 15260, U. S. A.

A drift tube - mass spectrometer apparatus has been used to determine the
rates of single-electron transfer at 300 K in reactions of the types $X^{++} + Y \rightarrow$
$X^+ + Y^+ + h\nu$ (radiative charge transfer), $X^{++} + Y \rightarrow X^+ + Y^{+*}$ (non-radiative
charge transfer) and $X^{++} + Y \rightarrow X^+ + Y^{++} + e^-$ (transfer ionization). The systems
studied include rare gas ions/atoms, $R_a^{++} + R_b$, where R = He, Ne, Ar, Kr or
Xe, as well as $O^{++} + N_2$ and O_2. The reaction rates have been determined by
the additional residence time technique. For the rare gases, it has been
possible to distinguish between ions in a low-lying, metastable excited state
(^1S or ^1D) and in the ground state (^3P) on the basis of their differing mobilities and reactivities.

Representative examples of the measured rate coefficients (or average
cross sections) for ordinary charge transfer and for transfer ionization are
given in Table I. It will be seen that the single-electron transfer rates

Table I.   Measured charge transfer and transfer ionization rates at 300 K

reaction	$k\,(cm^3/sec)$	$\bar{\sigma}\,(cm^2)$
$He^{++} + He \rightarrow He^+ + He^+$	$(4.8 \pm 0.5) \times 10^{-14}$	2.5×10^{-19}
$He^{++} + Ne \rightarrow He^+ + Ne^{+*}$	$(8.4 \pm 2.0) \times 10^{-10}$	5.6×10^{-15}
$He^{++} + Kr \rightarrow He^+ + Kr^{++} + e^-$	$(3.9 \pm 0.6) \times 10^{-9}$	2.8×10^{-14}
$Ne^{++} + He \rightarrow Ne^+ + He^+$	$(5.5 \pm 1) \times 10^{-15}$	3.7×10^{-20}
$Ne^{++}(^3P) + Ar \rightarrow Ne^+ + Ar^+$	$(5.3 \pm 1) \times 10^{-10}$	7.2×10^{-15}
$Ne^{++}(^1S) + Xe \rightarrow Ne^+ + Xe^{++} + e^-$	$(2.0 \pm 0.4) \times 10^{-9}$	3.1×10^{-14}
$Ar^{++}(^3P)$	$(7 \pm 2) \times 10^{-11}$	4.9×10^{-16}
$Ar^{++}(^1D) \Big\} + He \rightarrow Ar^+ + He^+$	$\sim 1.4 \times 10^{-10}$	$\sim 1 \times 10^{-15}$
$Ar^{++}(^1S)$	$\lesssim 2 \times 10^{-14}$	$\lesssim 1.4 \times 10^{-19}$
$O^{++} + N_2 \rightarrow O^+ + \ldots$	$(1.3 \pm 0.3) \times 10^{-9}$	1.5×10^{-14}

range from very fast, approaching the limiting Langevin rate, to the very slow, radiative charge transfer values. In some systems, e.g. Ar^{++} + He, large differences in reactivity are found for ions in different excited states.

A correlation of the observed rates with the initial and final energy states for the collision partners indicates that, for the atomic systems, an exoergicity $\Delta E \sim 4$ eV generally leads to fast reactions at thermal energies, while for $\Delta E < 2$ eV and > 7 eV the electron transfer rate drops off dramatically. This empirical finding can often be understood with the aid of model potential curves and energy level diagrams for the systems studied. A comparison will be made with other experimental results obtained at thermal energies (flowing afterglows or drift tubes) and above (beam experiments).

*This research was supported, in part, by the Army Research Officer under Contracts No. DAAG-29-77G-0079 and DAAG-29-78G-0044 (Defense Nuclear Agency).

1. R. Johnsen and M. A. Biondi, Phys. Rev. A 18, 989 (1978).

CHARGE TRANSFER VERSUS MOLECULE DISPLACEMENT IN INTERACTION OF CO_2
DIMER IONS WITH NEUTRAL MOLECULES

A.B. Rakshit and P.Warneck

Max-Planck-Institut f.Chemie (Otto-Hahn-Institut), Saarstr.23, POB 3060
D-6500 Mainz, Germany (FRG)

We have determined rate coefficients and product channels for reactions
of the $CO_2 \cdot CO_2^+$ Cluster ion with several neutral molecules using the drift
chamber technique described previously.[1] CO_2 was the main chamber constituent. CO_2^+ ions were produced from N_2^+ injected into the chamber via an orifice. At 0.8 torr pressure $CO_2 \cdot CO_2^+$ forms rapidly near the orifice from
CO_2^+ via third body attachment. The residence time of $CO_2 \cdot CO_2^+$ in the
chamber was measured using the double-pulse gating technique.[1] The reduced
ion mobility found, $\mu(CO_2 \cdot CO_2^+) = 1.19 \ cm^2/V$ sec, is in very good agreement with a previous measurement.[2] The loss of $CO_2 \cdot CO_2^+$ ion intensity and
the gain of product ion intensity in the presence of added constituents was
measured by mass spectrometry after the ions escaped through an orifice in
the rear plate of the chamber. Results are summarized in Table 1 below:

Reactant (Ion.Pot.) (ev)	$k_{expt.}$ $cm^3 s^{-1}$	k_L or k_{ADO} $cm^3 s^{-1}$	Product ions (%)
CO (14.01)	2.8 (−10)	7.1 (−10)	$CO \cdot CO_2^+$ (100)
N_2O (12.89)	1.0 (−9)	7.4 (−10)	$CO_2 \cdot N_2O^+$ (74); N_2O^+ (26)
CH_4 (12.70)	6.8 (−10)	1.03 (−9)	$CO_2 \cdot CO_2H^+$ (95) ; $CO_2 \cdot CH_4^+$ (5)
SO_2 (12.34)	1.3 (−9)	1.26 (−9)	$CO_2 \cdot SO_2^+$ (70) ; SO_2^+ (30)
O_2 (12.06)	1.9 (−10)	6.0 (−10)	$CO_2 \cdot O_2^+$ (42) ; O_2^+ (58)
COS (11.17)	1.1 (−9)	1.04 (−9)	$CO_2 \cdot COS^+$ (10) ; COS^+ (90)
C_2H_4 (10.45)	1.4 (−9)	1.05 (−9)	$C_2H_4^+$ (100)
NH_3 (10.17)	$\leqslant$ 5. (−13)	1.72 (−9)	−
C_3H_6 (9.74)	2.1 (−9)	1.08 (−9)	$C_3H_6^+$ (52) ; $C_3H_5^+$ (40) ; $C_3H_4^+$ (8)
NO (9.25)	4.5 (−12)	6.45 (−10)	$CO_2 \cdot NO^+$ (60) ; NO^+ (40)
CH_3NH_2 (8.97)	$\leqslant$ 5 (−13)	1.42 (−9)	−

Charge transfer and molecular displacement (switching) products are both prominent in most reactions suggesting that charge transfer as a long range interaction process is supplemented by intimate collision interaction leading to molecular re-arrangement at the nearly thermal energies prevailing in the experiments. The rate coefficients for reactions with CO, N_2O, CH_4 and O_2 agree approximately with those found by Sieck.[3] Most surprising is the lack of reactive behavior for the polar gases NH_3 and CH_3NH_2. Follow-on reactions of the products are displayed in several cases. Figure 1 gives an example for SO_2. The solid lines were calculated using the rate coefficient in Table 1 and: $k = 8 \cdot 10^{-10}$ $cm^3 s^{-1}$ for the reaction $CO_2 \cdot SO_2^+ + SO_2 \rightarrow (SO_2)_2^+$ and $k \approx 7 \cdot 10^{-10}$ $cm^3 s^{-1}$ for the reaction $SO_2^+ + SO_2 \rightarrow (SO_2)_2^+$, respectively.

References: 1) V.Nestler, B.Betz and P.Warneck, Ber.Bunsenges.Phys.Chem.81, 13 (1977);   2) G.P.Smith, P.C. Cosby and J.T. Moseley, J.Chem.Phys. 67, 3818 (1977);   3) L.W. Sieck, Int.J. Chem.Kinet.10, 335 (1978)

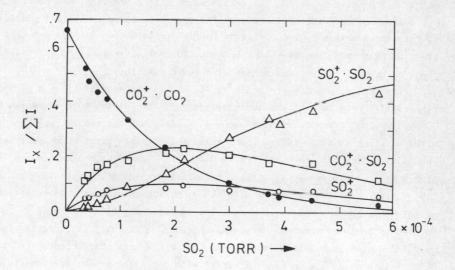

Fig.1: Relative ion intensities observed as a function of SO_2 partial pressure in CO_2 at 0.8 torr total pressure.

MEASURMENT OF THE FORWARD AND BACKWARD RATE COEFFICIENTS OF THE CLUSTERING
REACTIONS Li^+ ION WITH NOBLE GASES AND NITROGEN GAS IN DRIFT TUBE

M. Takebe, Y. Satoh, K. Iinuma, and K. Seto

Dept. of Nuclear Eng., Faculty of Eng., Tohoku University
Aramaki, Sendai, Japan 980

Clustering reaction rate coefficients have been measured by drift tube mass
spectrometer. The method, however, is hardly extended to higher pressure range
where clustering reactions play more important role, because sampling effects
more serious and has not been successful in direct determination of backward rate
coefficient.

We used a drift tube with movable ion source and paid much attention to the
experimental conditions, mobilities, diffusion coefficients, pressure dependence
and so on, instead of identifing by mass spectrometer. A simple technique is also
introduced. The technique provide absolute measurement of transport coefficients
for cluster ions. As can be seen in Fig. 1-a, a pair of spectra is obtained at
high E/N (B) and low E/N (A) in the pre-region of ion source under the identical
experimental conditions. Subtracting the spectrum (B) from (A), we have the same
spectrum (C) as an isolated cluster ion swarm drifts. Forward rate coefficients
are determined from the ratio of area (E) to non-reacting analytical profile (D)
at three or four ion source positions by difference method in Fig. 1-b. When spectrum (C) is raised from base line between two peaks, the backward rate coefficient is deduced in the same manner of forward reaction.

Experimental results are shown in Fig. 2. in the case of $Li^+ + N_2$. Backward
rate coefficients have strong dependence on E/N in contrast to forward reaction.
Comparing with Gatland's results[1], our data are about one and half and one tenth
times as large as their values for forward and backward reaction respectively.
In helium buffer gas, resonable value 8.0×10^{-31} cm^6/s at thermal energy is published by K. G. Spears et al[2]. Since no mobility shift of cluster ion is observed,
fast formation of 2nd cluster ion, $Li^+(N_2)_2$ may be unrealistic. We applied the
technique to krypton and argon gases. The backward reaction, $Li^+ + Ar$ is too fast
to find an isolated cluster ion spectrum in our drift tube. The arrival time spectrum calculated from Gatland's equation[3] using the rate coefficients reported by
G. E. Keller et al[4] is in poor agreement with our experimental spectrum in Fig.3.
Parameter fitting by computor shows that the similar deviations in rate coefficients are exist. It is concluded that the backward rate coefficients have strong
E/N dependence and disagreements between results by drift tube and drift tube
mass spectrometer are responsible for sampling region.

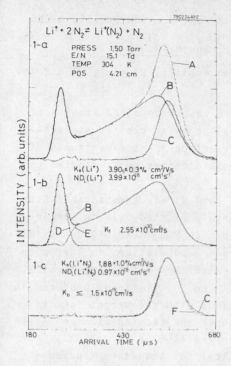

Fig. 1. Arrival time spectra for Li+ ions in nitrogen and analysed by the technique presented in this report.

A: One of the pair spectra, having higher contents of initial cluster ion.

B: The other spectrum, having negligible contents of initial cluster ion.

C: Spectrum for isolated cluster ion. Since the experimental spectrum closely fits non-reacting analytical profile (F) in Fig. 1-c, no detectable backward reaction occres.

D: Non-reacting analytical profile for Li+ ion in nitrogen.

E: A difference spectrum obtained by subtracting the spectrum (B) from the spectrum (D).

F: Non-reacting analytical profile for cluster ion in nitrogen.

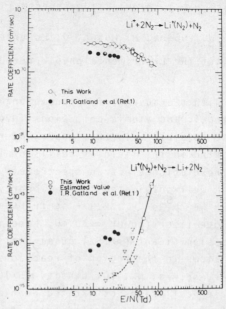

Fig. 2. Our experimental results of the forward and backward rate coefficients in the reaction $Li^+ + N_2$ and comparison with Gatland's data. The estimated value deduced from minimum detectable amounts.

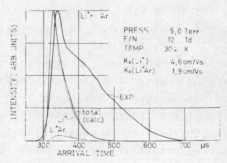

Fig. 3. Comparison of our experimental spectrum with an analytical profile calcualated by Gatland's equation on the basis of Keller's data.

1. I. R. Gatland, L. M. Colonna-Romano, and G. E. Keller, Phys. Rev. A 12, 1885 (1975).

2. K. G. Spears and E. E. Ferguson, J. Chem. Phys. 59, 4174 (1973).

3. I. R. Gatland, *Case Studies in Atomic Collision Physics IV* (*North-Holland, 1975*), p.371.

4. G. E. Keller, R. A. Beyer, and L. M. Colonna-Romano, Phys. Rev. A 8, 1446 (1973).

COLLISIONAL AUTOIONIZATION PROCESSES INVOLVING LASER-EXCITED ATOMS

W. Bußert, H. Hotop, J. Lorenzen, and M.-W. Ruf

Institut für Experimentalphysik der Universität, 23 Kiel, FR Germany

With the advent of intense tunable lasers detailed studies of
electronic and atomic collisions involving laser-excited atoms have
become possible[1]. In this paper, we report on first experiments of
this kind in the field of collisional autoionization as studied by
high resolution electron spectrometry.

A well-collimated thermal energy (400 K) mixed metastable Neon
beam - $Ne(2p^5 3s\ ^3P_2, ^3P_0)$ - is transversely excited by a cw single-
mode dye laser (power ≈ 30 mW, bandwidth 10 MHz) near 640.2 nm,yield-
ing a significant ($\approx 15\%$) quasi-stationary population of $^{20}Ne(2p^5 3p$
$^3D_3$) atoms in the region of reactions with the static target gas X
(X= Ar, Kr, Xe; N_2, CO; density $\approx 5\cdot 10^{12}$ cm^{-3}). Electrons produced in
ionizing collisions of excited Neon atoms with the target species
are energy-analyzed perpendicular to both the excited-atom and laser
beam with a 127° cylindrical condensor (resolution 20 meV).

FIG. 1 shows - as an example typical for the atoms studied -
the spectra obtained for X=Kr with three different polarizations of
the laser. In FIG. 1a, the electric vector of the linearly-polarized
laser is perpendicular to the metastable atom velocity ($\pi_\perp$), in
FIG. 1b it is parallel ($\pi_\parallel$), and in FIG. 1c, circularly-polarized
light (σ^+) was used (σ^- light gave the same result as σ^+). The
electron energy distributions depend on the type of polarization
used; the shapes of the peaks change as well as the relative populations of the two final-state fine-structure components 3/2 and 1/2.
This behaviour can be qualitatively understood on the basis of the
expected potential energy curves for Ne(3p)+R and Ne+R$^+$(3/2,1/2)
(R=rare gas). In the entrance channel, one has two substantially
different curves of Σ- and Π- character, where the latter, more
attractive curve is responsible for the low-energy part of the
distributions. Changes in the polarization of the pumping light
lead to varying contributions from the two different entrance
channels ($E_0 :=$ excitation energy minus ionization potential,resp.).

Interesting vibrational structure is observed for X=N_2. The
spectrum for $Ne(^3P_{2,0})+N_2$ (right and lower left part of FIG. 2)
shows enhanced vibrational population in $N_2^+(X;v')$ for $v' \geqslant 1$ as
compared with the $N_2^+(X;v') \leftarrow N_2(X;0)$ Franck-Condon factors. For
$Ne(^3D_3)+N_2$, anomalous vibrational structure is seen; it is attribu-

ted to the occurrence of excitation transfer processes involving several N_2 Rydberg states (associated with the $N_2^+(B)$-state,effective quantum numbers $n^* = 5-9$) with subsequent autoionization to the final $N_2^+(X;v')$-states.

1. I.V. Hertel and W. Stoll, Adv.At.Mol.Phys. <u>13</u>,113 (1978)

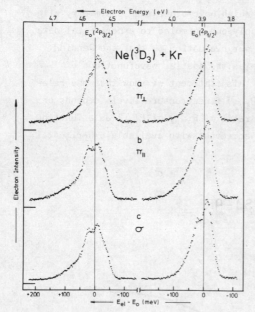

Support by the Deutsche Forschungsgemeinschaft is gratefully acknowledged.

FIG. 1 (left): Energy spectra of electrons released in $Ne(^3D_3)$+Kr collisions for three different laser polarizations (see text).

FIG. 2 (below):Energy spectra of electrons produced in $Ne(^3P_{2,0})$+ N_2 and $Ne(^3D_3)$+N_2 collisions, resp.(see text).

The spectra shown in FIG. 1,2 have not been corrected for the energy dependence of the electron analyzer transmission.

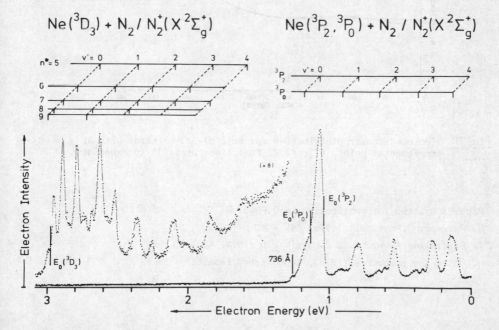

Interpretation of the Angular Distribution of Electrons
Emitted in Penningionisation of Argon by Metastable Helium [†]
V. Hoffmann and H. Morgner
Fakultät für Physik der Universität Freiburg, West Germany

We extend an existing theory[1] on the angular distribution of Penning-
electrons to the emission of electrons which have other than σ symmetry with
respect to the internuclear axis. We apply our formulae to experimental data[2]
for He(2^1S,2^3S)-Ar. The main result of our evaluation is that the Penning
process leads exclusively to He-Ar$^+$-states the spatial wavefunctions of
which have Σ symmetry. On the basis of this statement we show that the relative population of the two Ar$^+$(^{2}P$_{3/2}$,^{2}P$_{1/2}$) finestructure levels depends on
the collision energy. We calculate the ratio σ(^{2}P$_{3/2}$)/σ(^{2}P$_{1/2}$) as a function
of collision energy and find excellent agreement with available experimental
data.[3]

HE(2SING.S)-AR

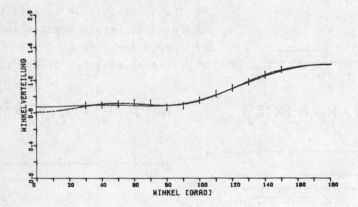

Fig. 1. Electron angular distribution for He(2^1S)-Ar. | : Error bars of
experimental points of ref. 2. Full line: best fit to experiment.

[†]Paper submitted for publication in J.Phys. B.
[1]H. Morgner, J.Phys. B11 (1978) 269 - 80
[2]T. Ebding and A. Niehaus, Z.Physik 270 (1974) 43 - 50
[3]H. Hotop and coworkers (1978), unpublished results

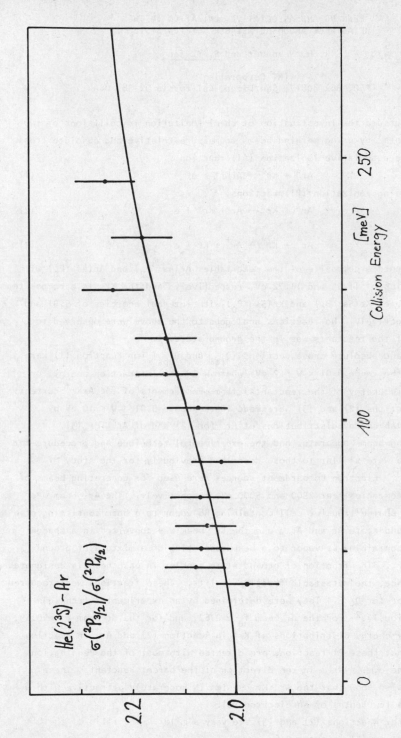

Fig. 2: Full line: calculated cross section ratio $\sigma(^2P_{3/2})/\sigma(^2P_{1/2})$ for He(2^3S)-Ar. Data points from ref. 3

PENNING AND ASSOCIATIVE IONIZATION IN THE
METASTABLE ARGON-METASTABLE KRYPTON SYSTEM*

R. H. Neynaber and S. Y. Tang

IRT Corporation
P.O. Box 80817, San Diego, California 92138, USA

We have pursued the investigation of chemi-ionization in collisions of two
excited reactants[1] by using merging beams to measure relative and absolute cross
sections of the associative-ionization (AI) reaction

$$Ar^* + Kr^* \rightarrow ArKr^+ + e \qquad\qquad (1)$$

and of the Penning-ionization (PI) reactions

$$Ar^* + Kr^* \rightarrow Ar + Kr^+ + e \qquad\qquad (2)$$

and

$$Ar^* + Kr^* \rightarrow Ar^+ + Kr + e \ . \qquad\qquad (3)$$

The Ar^* represents a composite of the metastables $Ar(4s\ ^3P_2)$ and $Ar(4s\ ^3P_0)$ with
internal energies of 11.55 and 11.72 eV, respectively; and the Kr^* is a composite
of the metastables $Kr(5s\ ^3P_2)$ and $Kr(5s\ ^3P_0)$ with internal energies of 9.91 and
10.56 eV, respectively. No reactions analogous to the above were observed to
occur if one of the reactants was in the ground state.

Relative and absolute cross sections (Q_{rel} and Q_{abs}) for Reaction (1) were
obtained over the range $0.01 \leq W \leq 2$ eV (where W is the interaction energy, or
relative kinetic energy of the reactants) from measurements of the $ArKr^+$ current.
Studies of Reactions (2) and (3) were made in the range $0.01 \leq W \leq 10$ eV by
measuring the lab-energy distributions of Kr^+ for (2) and of Ar^+ for (3).

The merging-beams apparatus and the experimental technique and procedure for
extracting data were similar to those described previously for the study of
He^*-Ne^*.[1(a),(b)] Electron bombardment sources were used for generating beams of
Ar^+ and Kr^+ at energies near 2500 and 5000 eV, respectively. The Ar^+ beam was
converted in a charge-transfer cell containing Rb vapor to a beam consisting of a
mixture of ground-state Ar and Ar^*, and the Kr^+ beam was converted in a charge-
transfer cell containing Cs vapor to a beam consisting of a mixture of ground-
state Kr and Kr^*. The fraction of ground-state species in each beam is designated
as f_g, and, hence, the metastable fraction is $1-f_g$. These fractions were required
for Q_{abs} but not for Q_{rel}. They were determined by an experimental technique
described previously.[2] For the Ar beam $f_g \approx 0.62$, and for the Kr beam $f_g \approx 0.69$.

Laboratory-energy distributions of Kr^+ in Reaction (2) and Ar^+ in Reaction
(3) indicate that these PI reactions are directed with most of the Penning ions
scattered in the c.m. system in the direction of the parent reactant. These
distributions also show that the Ar^*-Kr^* system is moderately attractive with a
well depth of a few tenths of an electron volt.

The Q_{rel} for Reactions (2) and (3) are very similar. The ratio of the Q's
for Reaction (2) to (3) is about 0.6.

Over the range $0.01 \leq W \lesssim 0.7$ eV the shape of the Q_{AI} (associative ionization cross section) curve for Ar^*-Kr^* is much like that of the Q_{AI} curve for He^*-He^*, which has also been found to be an attractive system.[1(c)] However, the Q_{AI} for Ar^*-Kr^* falls off rapidly for $W > 0.7$ eV, whereas the Q_{AI} for He^*-He^* does not show such a decline until $W \approx 2$ eV. Experimental evidence indicates that the formation of quasimolecules of $ArKr^+$ with lifetimes short compared to about 5 μsec is not an important process for the Ar^*-Kr^* system.

The fraction of AI to total ionization (AI plus PI) is only a few percent or less. Cross sections for total ionization Q_T vary as $W^{-0.41}$ for $W < 0.1$ eV. This is similar to Q_T for He^*-He^*. At $W = 0.033$ eV the $Q_T = 2.6 \times 10^{-14}$ cm^2. Such a relatively large Q_T appears to be characteristic of collisions between two metastable rare gases.

*Research sponsored by the Air Force Office of Scientific Research (AFSC), U.S. Air Force under contract F49620-78-C-0015 and by the Office of Naval Research.

1. Our previous studies of chemi-ionization of two excited reactants include (a) R. H. Neynaber and G. D. Magnuson, Phys. Rev. A12, 891 (1975); (b) R. H. Neynaber and S. Y. Tang, J. Chem. Phys. 67, 5619 (1977); (c) R. H. Neynaber, G. D. Magnuson, and S. Y. Tang, J. Chem. Phys. 68, 5112 (1978).

2. R. H. Neynaber and G. D. Magnuson, J. Chem. Phys. 65, 5239 (1976).

ASSOCIATIVE IONISATION IN H⁺-H⁻ AND D⁺-D⁻ COLLISIONS.

G. Poulaert, F. Brouillard, W. Claeys, P. Defrance and
J.W. Mc Gowan.

Institut de Physique Corpusculaire, Université Catholique de Louvain
B - 1348   LOUVAIN-LA-NEUVE   -   BELGIUM.

The associative ionisation reactions :   (1) $H^+ + H^- \rightarrow H_2^+ + e$

(2) $D^+ + D^- \rightarrow D_2^+ + e$,

have been measured through the energy interval 0.001-3 eV, using merged beams.
The experimental method has been described earlier[1]   together with the results obtained for reaction. Figure 1 shows the results for reaction (2).
Both reactions appear to have practically the same cross-section, although
reaction (2) becomes somewhat less efficient than reaction (1) at low energy.
The energy resolution of the experiment is 0.6×10^{-3} eV and mainly arises
from the angular spread of the beams. The energy dependence of the cross
section, below 1 eV, is as E^{-n}.   From the data given in Figure 1, n is
very close to 0.9. However, when taking into account the distortion produced at low energy, by the finite energy resolution, it is found that the
experimental data are better fitted by a E^{-1} law.

Our results unfortunately cannot be compared with theoretical predictions
as these are not available. The energy dependence however can easily be
explained with the following model :
- the ions H^+ and H^- are supposed to move along classical trajectories
  governed by the molecular potentials.
- The system is in the ionic state at nuclear separation R larger than 11a.u.
  and adiabatically becomes, at smaller distances, a mixture of the $B''\overline{B}^1\Sigma_u$
  and $H\overline{H}^1\Sigma_g$ states, the energies of which have been recently calculated [2,3].
- The associative ionisation is regarded as an autoionisation of the $B''\overline{B}$ or
  $H\overline{H}$ states, unlikely to occur below a threshold value R^* of R and proceeding
  with a characteristic autoionisation time τ when $R < R^*$.

The cross section for associative ionisation is then :

$$\sigma = 2\pi \int \frac{t(b)}{\tau} b \ db = \frac{2\pi}{\tau} I$$

where b is the impact parameter and t is the time spent by the ions at
a distance smaller than R^*.

The integral I has been calculated in the ungerade case and assuming
$R^* = 5.5$ a.u. The result, shown in Figure 2, gives an energy dependence
as E^{-1}, in agreement with Wigner's theoretical consideration[4]   .

For absolute agreement with the experimental data, the autoionisation time τ must be taken equal to 4 x 10^{-13} sec.

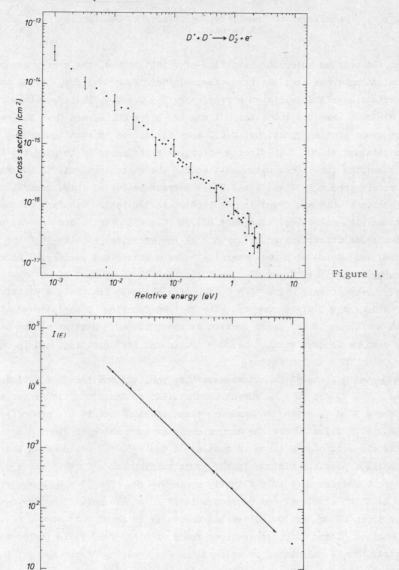

Figure 1.

Figure 2.

1. G. POULAERT, F. BROUILLARD, W. CLAEYS, J. Mc GOWAN and G. VAN WASSENHOVE J. Phys. B, 11, n° 2, L671, (1978).

2. W. KOLOS, J. Mol. Spect. 62, 429, (1976).

3. L. WOLNIEWICZ and K. DRESSLER, J. Mol. Spect. 67, 416, (1977).

4. E. WIGNER, Phys. Rev. 73, 1002, (1948).

ENERGY DEPENDENCE FOR IONIZATION OF HCL, CO, N_2 AND O_2 BY HE(2^1S) AND HE(2^3S) ATOMS*

T. P. PARR, D. HANSON-PARR and R. M. MARTIN

Department of Chemistry, University of California
Santa Barbara, CA 93106

Using the crossed molecular beam time-of-flight method[1] the energy dependences of the ionization cross sections for metastable He(2^1S, 2^3S) + HCl, CO, N_2 and O_2 were determined over the collision energy range 5-500 meV. The temperature of the effusive diatomic beam was 160°K for HCl and 120°K for CO, N_2 and O_2. The relative ionization cross section functions, $\sigma(E)$, were normalized to total quenching rate constants obtained at 300°K in flowing afterglow experiments[2,3] to give the absolute cross section functions, assuming that all the quenching leads to ionization.

The results shown in Figs. 1 and 2 are representative of three general types of $\sigma(E)$ functions that are found for excited state ionization and excitation transfer reactions with molecules. The He + HCl functions in Fig. 1 are inverse power or negative types characterized by $\sigma \sim E^{-m}$ at low energies, usually shifting to a more gradual dependence at higher energies. The m values and corresponding experimental energy ranges for ^{1}S and ^{3}S with HCl were 0.67 (8-63 meV) and 0.58 (5-334 meV), respectively. The ^{1}S + CO function shown in Fig. 2 is a positive type characterized by $\sigma \sim E$ at low energy. The ^{3}S + CO function is an intermediate type, with a minimum in the cross section at about 10 meV. Similar minima have been seen both by Woodard et al.[4] in ^{3}S + Ar, Kr and Xe ionization, and in our laboratory with ^{3}S + Kr ionization.

With N_2 and O_2, the ^{1}S functions were also positive and the ^{3}S functions intermediate. The ^{1}S and ^{3}S + N_2 curves were similar to those of Illenberger and Niehaus[5] above 30 meV, rising to maximum values of 21 A^2 and 12 A^2, respectively, at about 0.2 eV. Below 30 meV the curves converge to a value of about 2 A^2 at 5 meV. The slope of the ^{3}S curve is smaller in the 5-30 meV region than above 30 meV indicating a possible minimum in the cross section below 5 meV. Above 0.2 eV the cross sections decrease only slightly up to 0.4 eV. The ^{1}S + O_2 curve rises to a maximum of 51 A^2 at 20 meV and decreases to 17 A^2 at 440 meV. The ^{3}S + O_2 cross section is about 17 A^2 from 5-140 meV and decreases to about 8 A^2 at 440 meV.

The maximum ^{1}S and ^{3}S cross sections found with all four diatomics correspond approximately to the calculated cross sections for crossing of the neutral potentials with the ion-pair potentials, suggesting that ionization takes place predominately via the ionic potentials. The temperature dependence of the ionization rate constants calculated from the $\sigma(E)$ function for the ^{3}S + N_2 and O_2 systems was weaker than the quenching rate constant temperature dependence determined in flowing afterglow systems,[6] indicating either that ionization does not account for all the quenching or that the cross sections depend significantly on the diatomic internal state distributions.

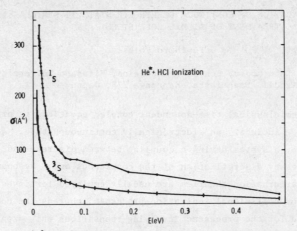

Fig.1. He$(2^1S, 2^3S)$ + HCl ionization cross section functions normalized to the rate constants of reference 2.

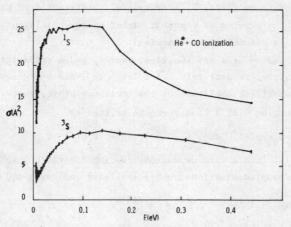

Fig.2. He$(2^1S, 2^3S)$ + CO ionization cross section functions normalized to the rate constants of reference 3.

*Supported by the National Science Foundation, Grant CHE77-08621

1. W. Lee and R. M. Martin, J. Chem. Phys. 63, 962 (1975).

2. Y. A. Bush, M. McFarland, D. L. Albritton and A. L. Schmeltekopf, J. Chem. Phys. 58, 4020 (1973).

3. A. L. Schmeltekopf and F. C. Fehsenfeld, J. Chem. Phys. 53, 3175 (1970).

4. M. R. Woodard, R. C. Sharp, M. Seely, and E. E. Muschlitz, Jr., J. Chem. Phys. 69, 2978 (1978).

5. E. Illenberger and A. Niehaus, Z. Physik B 20, 33 (1975).

6. W. Lindinger, A. L. Schmeltekopf and F. C. Fehsenfeld, J. Chem. Phys. 61, 2890 (1974).

DISCRETIZATION OF CONTINUUM ELECTRONIC STATE IN SEMICLASSICAL
TREATMENT OF ATOMIC COLLISIONS

Fumihiro Koike

Physics Laboratory, School of Medicine, Kitasato University,
1, Asamizodai, Sagamihara, Kanagawa 228, Japan

A set of semiclassical time-dependent coupled-equations is proposed for a
system that includes an electronically continuous state. A unified treatment is tried for a system having a coupling between discrete and continuum
electronic states by discretization of the continuous one. Resonant state
formalisms or perturbation theories are usually employed for investigations of
autoionization or collisional ionization processes, whereas the coupled equations
are often solved for the processes involving transitions only among the discrete
states. Bellum and Micha[1] have already tried such a discretization in a framework of a full-quantum-mechanical treatment. They have applied their theory to
Penning ionization in $He^*(1s2s, {}^3S) + Ar$ system. Different from their work, we
focus our aim to the problem of somewhat higher energy collisions. Nuclear
relative motion is assumed to be classical.

Let ϕ_n, ε_n, and a_n be a wavefunction, energy, and a probability amplitude
of the discrete state, respectively. And let ψ_γ, ε_γ, and b_δ be a wavefunction,
energy, and a probability amplitude of the continuum state, respectively.
The Total wavefunction Ψ at a time t can be written as

$$\Psi = \sum_n a_n \phi_n \exp(-i\int^t \varepsilon_n dt') + \int d\gamma b_\gamma \psi_\gamma \exp(-i\int^t \varepsilon_\gamma dt') \quad . \tag{1}$$

Substituting eq.(1) into a time dependent Sroedinger equation, we obtain a
following set of coupled equations, using auxiliary indices m and δ;

$$\dot{a} = -\sum_{m\neq n} <\phi_n|V|\phi_m> \exp[-i\int(\varepsilon_m-\varepsilon_n)dt']a_m$$

$$-\int d\delta <\phi_n|V|\psi_\gamma> \exp[-i\int(\varepsilon_\delta-\varepsilon_n)dt']b_\delta \quad , \tag{2a}$$

$$\dot{b} = -\sum_m <\psi_\gamma|V|\phi_m> \exp[-i\int(\varepsilon_m-\varepsilon_\gamma)dt']a_m$$

$$-\int d\delta <\psi_\gamma|V|\psi_\delta> \exp[-i\int(\varepsilon_\delta-\varepsilon_\gamma)dt']b_\delta \quad , \tag{2b}$$

where V is an interaction operator and is either of ones for radial, rotational,
and potential couplings. The continuous index γ is discretized by introducing
a discretized index γ_j and a discretization interval Γ_j of which definitions are
illustrated in the following:

The probability amplitude $\tilde{b}_{\gamma_j}$ and the wavefunction $\tilde{\psi}_{\gamma_j}$ associated to γ_j are difined as

$$\tilde{b}_{\gamma_j} = \frac{1}{\sqrt{\Gamma_j}} \int_{\gamma_j - \Gamma_j/2}^{\gamma_j + \Gamma_j/2} b_\gamma d\gamma, \qquad \tilde{\psi}_{\gamma_j} = \sqrt{\Gamma_j} \psi_{\gamma_j} \quad . \tag{3}$$

Equation (2a) and (2b) are transformed into a discretized form as

$$\dot{\tilde{b}}_{\gamma_j} = - \sum_n \langle \tilde{\psi}_{\gamma_k} | V | \phi_n \rangle \exp[-i \int (\varepsilon_n - \varepsilon_{\gamma_k}) dt'] a_n$$
$$- \sum_{j \neq k} \langle \tilde{\psi}_{\gamma_k} | V | \tilde{\psi}_{\gamma_j} \rangle \exp[-i \int (\varepsilon_n - \varepsilon_{\gamma_k}) dt'] \tilde{b}_{\gamma_j}, \tag{4a}$$

$$\dot{a}_m = - \sum_{n \neq m} \langle \phi_m | V | \phi_n \rangle \exp[-i \int (\varepsilon_n - \varepsilon_m) dt'] a_n$$
$$- \sum_j \langle \phi_m | V | \tilde{\psi}_{\gamma_j} \rangle \exp[-i \int (\varepsilon_{\gamma_j} - \varepsilon_m) dt'] \tilde{b}_{\gamma_j} \quad . \tag{4b}$$

The probability of the discretized state γ_j can be expressed as

$$\tilde{b}^*_{\gamma_j} \tilde{b}_{\gamma_j} = \int_{\gamma_j - \Gamma_j/2}^{\gamma_j + \Gamma_j/2} b^*_\gamma b_\gamma d\gamma \quad . \tag{5}$$

Then, we can treat a continuum state as a set of discrete ones.

The criterion for the determination of the discretization-interval Γ_j is obtained from the condition that the phase of b_γ must be the same in the interval. Let T be the duration time of the interaction. The product of Γ_j and T must be sufficiently small compared with the plank constant $\hbar$.

Reference

1. John C. Bellum and David A. Micha: Phys. Rev. <u>A18</u>, 1435 (1978)

DE-EXCITATION RATE CONSTANTS OF He(2^3S) AND Ne($^3P_2$, $^3P_0$ and $^3P_1$) BY ATOMS AND MOLECULES USING TIME-RESOLVED OPTICAL EMISSION AND ABSORPTION SPECTROSCOPY.

A. Yokoyama, T. Ueno, S. Takao and Y. Hatano

Department of Chemistry, Tokyo Institute of Technology,
Meguro-ku, Tokyo 152, Japan

There have been increased interests in the de-excitation processes of rare-gas excited atoms. The rate constants or the cross sections of these processes have been measured using a flowing afterglow technique, a crossed molecular beam method, a pulse discharge method, etc.

Our group has recently presented the first attempt of the application of a pulse-radiolysis technique, time-resolved spectroscopy combined with pulsed ionizing radiation, to the determination of a Penning ionization rate constant.[1] The time resolved optical emission of $N_2^+(B^2\Sigma_u^+ \rightarrow X^2\Sigma_g^+)$ induced by Penning ionization of N_2 by He(2^3S) has been measured upon the irradiation of He-N_2 mixtures by a nsec pulse of 600 keV electrons from a Febetron 706. The emission decay rate varies as a function of He or N_2 pressures, which gives the rate constant of

$$He(2^3S) + N_2 \longrightarrow He + N_2^+(B^2\Sigma_u^+) + e^- \qquad (1)$$

being $(6.8 + 0.4) \times 10^{-11} cm^3 s^{-1}$. The time resolved optical absorption of He(2^3S, 2^1S and 2^1P) has been also measured using the apparatus which is shown in Fig.1, where a new analysis procedure for absorption profile has been applied to the determination of the number density of helium excited atoms. Since atomic absorption experiments do not generally obey the well-known Beer-Lambert law, we have numerically calculated the density of the excited atoms from the values of transmittance obtained experimentally. The result, which is in good agreement with that obtained by emission spectroscopy, has been compared with those measured by other techniques. The addition of other atoms or molecules to He-N_2 mixtures changes the decay rate of the optical emission of $N_2^+(B^2\Sigma_u^+ \rightarrow X^2\Sigma_g^+)$, which gives the rate constants for He(2^3S) de-excitation by various atoms or molecules (Table 1).[2] The de-excitation cross section, σ, calculated by dividing the measured rate constant, k, by the relative velocity of the reacting particles in thermal equilibrium has been correlated with some physical constants for these atoms or molecules. The change in the values of k or σ with target atoms or molecules has been discussed from the viewpoint of a gas-kinetic collision model. It may be concluded that the larger the maximum energy of Penning electron ejected is, the larger the de-excitation probability becomes.

Since there are few investigations of the de-excitation processes of excited neon atoms in comparison with those of other rare-gas atoms, we have measured the de-excitation rate constants of Ne($^3P_2$, $^3P_0$ and $^3P_1$) individually by Ar, H_2, N_2, SF_6 etc, in a way similar to that for He(2^3S) de-excitation. The results are summarized in Table 2.

Table 1. He(2^3S) de-excitation rate constants and cross sections.

M	k ($10^{-11} cm^3 s^{-1}$)	σ (A^2)
Ar	8.9 $\pm$ 0.5	6.8
Kr	10.0 $\pm$ 0.5	7.8
Xe	17 $\pm$ 1	14
H_2	4.2 $\pm$ 0.6	1.9
D_2	3.7 $\pm$ 0.3	2.1
N_2	6.8 $\pm$ 0.4	5.1
O_2	23 $\pm$ 2	17
NO	21 $\pm$ 4	16
CO	9.2 $\pm$ 1.0	6.9
N_2O	50 $\pm$ 4	38
CO_2	60 $\pm$ 4	45
SO_2	122 $\pm$ 20	94
NH_3	50 $\pm$ 12	36
SF_6	46 $\pm$ 5	36
CH_4	19 $\pm$ 2	14
CCl_4	126 $\pm$ 11	99
CCl_2F_2	44 $\pm$ 7	34
H_2O	30 $\pm$ 6	22

Table 2. Ne* de-excitation rate constants and cross sections.

M	Ne*	k ($10^{-11} cm^3 s^{-1}$)	σ (A^2)
Ar	$^3P_2$	9.7 $\pm$ 0.5	14
	$^3P_0$	11 $\pm$ 1	16
	$^3P_1$	16 $\pm$ 1	24
H_2	$^3P_2$	6.5 $\pm$ 0.8	3.5
	$^3P_0$	6.5 $\pm$ 0.5	3.5
	$^3P_1$	7.4 $\pm$ 1.5	4.0
N_2	$^3P_2$	6.5 $\pm$ 0.5	8.6
	$^3P_0$	6.7 $\pm$ 0.9	8.9
	$^3P_1$	8.1 $\pm$ 0.6	11
SF_6	$^3P_2$	23 $\pm$ 2	38
	$^3P_0$	31 $\pm$ 2	52
	$^3P_1$	42 $\pm$ 3	70

Fig. 1. Experimental apparatus for optical absorption spectroscopy. (1) electron gun, (2) gas cell, (3) flash lamp, (4) power supply, (5) trigger generator, (6) delay trigger amp, (7) power supply, (8) monochromator, (9) photomultiplier, (10) power supply, (11) oscilloscope.

1) T. Ueno and Y. Hatano, Chem. Phys. Lett., 40, 283 (1976).
2) T. Ueno, A. Yokoyama, S. Takao, and Y. Hatano, Chem. Phys., to be published.

AN EMPIRICAL RELATION BETWEEN QUENCHING CROSS SECTIONS OF

METASTABLE RARE GAS ATOMS AND DIAMETER OF QUENCHERS

Yukio Nishimura, Kazuhiro Matsubara, Yoshitsugu Oono and Shoich Kai*

Research Institute of Industrial Science, Kyushu University, Fukuoka, Japan

*Department of Electronics, Kyushu University, Fukuoka, Japan.

So far many workers have studied the quenching cross-sections σ_Q, esp. for metastable argon, and also discussed the quenching mechanism. However, there seems to be no definite conclusion as to it. All the theoretical approaches are also unsuccessful. Therefore, what we should do first is to investigate the existing data[1-4] closely and search for accurate empirical laws.

An example of this empirical law is given; for polyatomic quenchers not containing fluorin atoms there is a fairly accurate linear relation between $\sigma_Q^{1/2}$ and the effective radius r of the quencher for metastable Ar, Kr and Xe (Fig. 1).

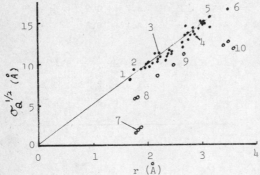

Fig. 1. The relation between r and $\sigma_Q^{1/2}$ for Ar(^3P_o). The line denotes $\sigma_Q^{1/2} = 4.80r$. • are with polyatomic and o with diatomic quenchers. 1: water, 2: ammonia, 3: ethane, 4: benzaldehyde. 5: 1-naphthol, 6: iodomethane, 7: nitrogen, 8:nitrogen monoxide, 9: bromine, 10: iodine monochloride.

As can be seen from Fig. 1, diatomic quenchers do not obey this empirical linear law.

Thus there is some qualitative difference between polyatomic and diatomic quenchers. It may seem quite curious that the number of nuclei is relevant. There is a possibility that the relevance is explained by the relation between the stochasticity of the motion of a nonlinear oscillators and its degrees of freedom. The stochasticity of the internal motion of the quencher enhances its quenching ability. Diatomic quenchers never exhibit stochastic internal motion, so that the quenching cross-section is smaller than would be expected from the empirical law for polyatomic quenchers.

1) L.G. Piper, J.E. Velazco and D.W. Setser, J. Chem. Phys. 59, 3323 (1973).

2) J.E. Velazco, J.H. Koltz and D.W. Setser, J. Chem. Phys. 65, 3468 (1976).

3) M. Bourène and J. LeCalvé, J. Chem. Phys. 58, 1452 (1973).

4) H.J. de Jong, Chem. Phys. Lett. 25, 129 (1974).

CORRELATION BETWEEN THE INTENSITY OF PENNING ELECTRON
SPECTRA AND THE NATURE OF MOLECULAR ORBITALS

Toshiaki Munakata, Yoshiya Harada[*] and Kozo Kuchitsu

Department of Chemistry, Faculty of Science, The University of Tokyo
     Hongo, Bunkyo-ku, Tokyo 113 Japan
[*]Department of Chemistry, College of General Education, The University of
     Tokyo, Komaba, Meguro-ku,Tokyo 153 Japan

In a number of recent studies of Penning ionization electron spectroscpy,
appreciable differences have been observed between the relative electronic
transition probabilities for Penning ionization and those for photoionization.
This difference is expected from that in the transition matrix elements between
the ground states of molecule and the states of molecular ion in the two cases.
However, very little work has yet been made to derive useful information on the
collision processes from observed changes in the populations of the ionic states.

In the present study the Ne ($^3P_2$) Penning electron spectra and Ne I photoelectron spectra of polyatomic molecules were measured under the same experimental
conditions. The purpouse of the work is to investigate whether a measureable
systematic trend exists between the band intensities of Penning electrons and
the nature of the molecular orbitals from which the electrons are removed.
Particular attention has been paid to the difference between the π and σ orbitals
of hydrocarbons and heterocyclic molecules containing conjugated double bonds.

Neon ($^3P_2$) metastable atoms were produced by the impact of 80 eV electrons.
Ne I photons were obtained by d. c. capillary discharge lamp.(Fig. 1) Penning
or photoelectrons produced in the interaction region were analyzed by a 127°
electrostatic energy analyzer at 90° to the metastable atom and the photon beams.

In Fig. 2 the spectra of benzene ionized
by $^3P_2$ neon atoms (16.62 eV) (below) and the
neon resonance lines (16.85 eV and 16.67 eV)
(above) are shown. In the photoelectron
spectrum of benzene the lowest four ionization
bands have been assigned as indicated in
Fig. 2. Comparing the photoelectron and the
Penning electron spectra, we find that the
intensities of the first and third bands in
the photoelectron spectrum are comparable with
those of the other bands, whereas in the
Penning spectrum their intensities are much
stronger than those of the other bands. Thus,
the Penning electron spectrum shows clear
enhancement of the π bands relative to the
σ bands.

Similar enhancements of the π bands were

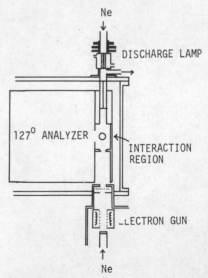

Fig. 1 Apparatus

also observed in the Penning electron spectra of ethylene, 1,3-butadiene and
styrene. These enhancements may be justified qualitatively if one assumes that
the transition probability depends on the degree of overlapping of the unfilled
2p (Ne*) shell with the electron distribution of the particular orbital of the
target molecule to be ionized. The cross sections for the σ orbitals are expected
to be smaller than those of the π electrons because the σ orbitals are spacially
limited and shielded by the π orbitals.

Systematic enhancements of the π bands were also observed for heterocyclic
aromatic molecules, thiophene and pyridine. (Fig. 3) However, the innermost π
band in pyrrole ( ) and furan ( ) were not enhanced significantly. This
discrepancy may be interpreted in terms of the electron distribution of the innermost π orbitals in the latter molecules. Because of the large electronegativities
of the N and O atoms the electron distributions are localized at the positions
of the heteroatoms and hence the σ electrons may not be shielded effectively.

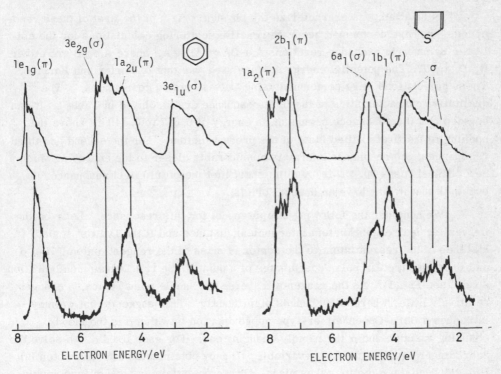

Fig. 2   Spectra for Benzene   Fig. 3   Spectra for Thiophene

Electron spectra measured by Ne* ($^3P_2$) (below) and Ne I photon (above) are
shown. The shifts of the vertical lines, 0.23 eV, correspond to the difference
in the excitation energies [16.85 eV (Ne I) - 16.62 eV (Ne* $^3P_2$)].

A SIMPLE MODEL OF DYNAMIC RESONANCES
IN COLLINEAR REACTIVE SCATTERING*

Aron Kuppermann and John P. Dwyer

Arthur Amos Noyes Laboratory of Chemical Physics,
California Institute of Technology, Pasadena, California 91125, U.S.A.

Dynamic Feshbach resonances have been detected in quantum collinear reactive scattering calculations for several atom-diatom systems.[1] Their presence is manifested by an oscillatory behavior of the reaction probability as a function of collision energy. For the $H + H_2 \rightarrow H_2 + H$ reaction, a lifetime analysis[1a] has shown that such oscillations are due to the interference between a direct and a compound state mechanism. The lifetimes of the first two resonances in that system are approximately 2 and 10 symmetric stretch vibrational periods of H_3 at the saddle point configuration.

In an attempt to characterize the physical origin of the first of these resonances, we have performed accurate reactive scattering calculations for the collinear symmetric exchange reactions $A + BA \rightarrow AB + A$, where A or B are either H, D, or T. The potential energy surface used was that of Porter and Karplus.[2] These calculations were performed using Delves' scaled coordinates.[3] The qualitative characteristics of the first resonance are displayed in Table I. It can be seen that the resonance occurs at an energy of 0.077 to 0.140 eV above the opening of the first excited state of the product diatom. For the second and third resonances, the resonance energy is considerably closer to the energy at which a new channel opens up. This, and the short lifetime of this first resonance, suggests that it may have an unusual origin.

We consider the following simple model for this resonance. Let r be the Delves' scaled reagent diatom internuclear distance and R the Delves' scaled distance of the reagent atom to the center of mass of the reagent diatom. Let ρ and α be the circular polar coordinates of a point in the r, R Delves' configuration space (see Fig. 1). As the reagents traverse the saddle point region, ρ changes relatively little, whereas α changes significantly. This suggests that we may introduce a Born-Oppenheimer-type approximation in which ρ is the slowly changing variable and α the rapidly changing one. For each fixed ρ, we solve the Schrödinger equation for the α variable, thereby obtaining an effective potential $U(\rho)$ in which the ρ motion takes place. These potentials, as $\rho \rightarrow \infty$, are doubly degenerate, corresponding to symmetric and antisymmetric wavefunctions, and can be labelled $U_v^S(\rho)$ and $U_v^a(\rho)$, respectively, where v designates the vibrational quantum number of the $\rho \rightarrow \infty$ diatom level. The $U_v^a(\rho)$ curves decrease monotonically, whereas the $U_v^S(\rho)$ ones, for $v \geqslant 1$, have a minimum with a depth of about 0.1 eV. The $U_2^S(\rho)$ curves support one bound state, which correlates with the second resonances. For $H + H_2$ this is a relatively long-lived resonance, as mentioned above. On the other hand, the $U_I^S(\rho)$ curves do not support bound states. They do, however, support a virtual state, whose location can be obtained from the position of the maximum in each of the $d\delta_I^S/dE$ versus E curves, where δ_I^S is the phase shift for a Delves' mass particle scattering off the one-dimensional $U_I^S(\rho)$ potential. These values are listed as model resonance energies in Table I and their positions correlate approximately with the exact one. The strengths of the exact resonances also show a qualitative correlation with the lifetimes $\hbar(d\delta_i^S/dE)$ calculated from this model. This leads us to associate these Feshbach resonances with virtual (rather than bound) states of the "internal" $U_I^S(\rho)$ potentials produced by the rapid α motion in which the system "bounces" back and forth between the skew axes. For large skew angles (but equivalent λ), this effect is too weak to produce strong resonances, as Table I indicates.

TABLE I. Characteristics of lowest resonance for A + BA → AB + A reaction.

Reaction	Delves[a] mass	Delves λ (Å)[b]	Delves skew angle θ (°)	ΔE^{reag} (eV)[c]	Resonance strength	Exact resonance energy (eV)	Model resonance energy (eV)	Error (eV)
$H + H_2 \to H_2 + H$	0.58	0.49	60.0	0.521	strong	0.598	0.544	-0.054
$D + HD \to DH + D$	0.89	0.42	48.2	0.451	strong	0.534	0.504	-0.030
$T + HT \to TH + T$	1.13	0.38	41.4	0.425	strong	0.510	0.491	-0.019
$H + DH \to HD + H$	0.71	0.45	70.5	0.451	weak	0.582	0.502	-0.080
$D + D_2 \to D_2 + D$	1.15	0.37	60.0	0.368	weak	0.508	0.452	-0.056
$H + TH \to HT + H$	0.71		75.5	0.425	none	none	none	--

[a] In units of the hydrogen atom mass.
[b] Delves' de Broglie wavelength at the resonance energy.
[c] Spacing between ground and first excited vibrational energy of the reagent diatom.

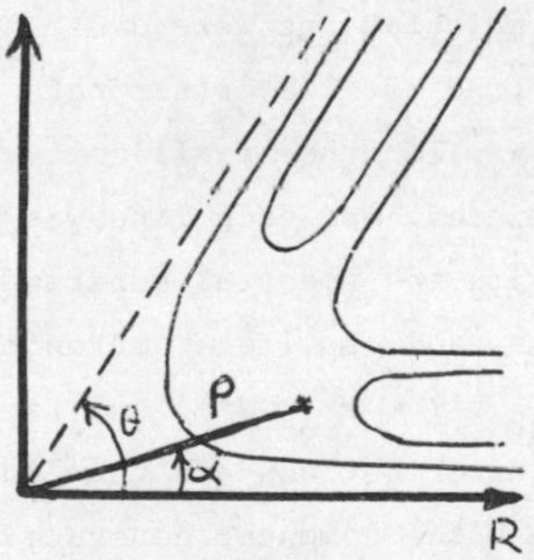

Fig. 1. Coordinates for resonance model.

* This work was supported in part by a grant (No. AFOSR-77-3394) from the United States Air Force Office of Scientific Research.

1. (a) G. C. Schatz and A. Kuppermann, J. Chem. Phys. 59, 964 (1973); (b) 63, 674, 685 (1975); (c) G. C. Schatz and A. Kuppermann, Phys. Rev. Lett. 35, 1266 (1975); (d) A. Persky and M. Baer, J. Chem. Phys. 60, 133 (1974).
2. R. N. Porter and M. Karplus, J. Chem. Phys. 40, 1105 (1964).
3. L. M. Delves, Nucl. Phys. 9, 391 (1959); ibid. 20, 275 (1960).

CHEMILUMINESCENT ION-MOLECULE REACTIONS: ROTATIONAL-VIBRATIONAL STATE
DISTRIBUTIONS OF $CH^+(A'\pi)$ and $CD^+(A'\pi)$ FROM $C^+ + H_2$ AND $C^+ + D_2$ COLLISIONS

I. Kusunoki

Research Institute for Scientific Measurements, Tohoku University, Sendai, Japan

Ch. Ottinger

Max-Planck-Institut für Strömungsforschung, Göttingen, Germany

The reaction of $C^+ + H_2$ may be the primary step in the formation of interstellar molecules. Radiative association involving excited electronic states of
this system has been proposed as a mechanism[1], and the study of $C^+ + H_2$ collisions
by spectroscopic means is therefore of great interest. Optical emission of electronically excited products has been reported earlier[2,3]. Most of the emission
observed in the low-energy collisions (3-8 eV) is due to $(A'\pi \rightarrow X'\Sigma^+)$ transitions
of CH^+. The present results are an extension of our earlier work[3] and include
CD^+ from $C^+ + D_2$ collisions.

Our apparatus has been described previously[4]. It permits the study of lumi-
nescent ion-molecule reactions in a beam-gas arrangement at ion energies in the
eV range. A typical spectrum is shown in Fig. 1. Similar high resolution spectra
were obtained at 3, 4, 6, 7, and 8 eV with $C^+ + H_2$ and at 4 and 5 eV with $C^+ + D_2$.
Low resolution spectra covering the range 3000 - 5000 Å with 20 Å FWHM were also
taken.

These results were analyzed by computer simulation. Taking into account ab
initio calculations of the strong dependence of the electronic transition moment
on the internuclear distance[5], relative transition probabilities $f_{v'v''}(J)$ were
calculated. They were found to depend strongly on the rotational quantum number
J. These calculations were done using the R-centroid approximation as well as
the exact band oscillator strength formula. In order to generate a synthetic
spectrum, wavelengths of all contributing rotational lines in a number of bands
were calculated, and each line was broadened with the apparatus resolution profile,
weighted with the spectral apparatus response, the London-Hönl factor and the
J-dependent band oscillator strength $f^{RC}_{v'v''}$, the vibrational and rotational population $P_{vib}(v') \cdot P_{rot}(J')$, and finally all these line profiles were summed. The
intensity distributions are then adjusted until a match is obtained between the
observed and the computer generated spectra. A very satisfactory simulation is
shown in Fig. 1, right-hand side, as an axample.

The vibrational and rotational population distributions obtained are given
in Figs. 2 and 3. Similar distributions were obtained for the $C^+ + D_2$ case. The
distributions $P(v')$ and $P(J')$ are strongly dependent on the collision energy.
Interestingly the rotational distributions are the same in the $v' = 0$ and 1 vibrational levels of CH^+, $CD^+(A'\pi)$. The rotational distributions $P(J')$ of CD^+ peak
at much higher J' than those of CH^+, but plotted versus the rotational energy

instead of versus J', the two sets of distributions coincide. A simple model is
proposed which explains the isotope effect on the rotational distributions and
gives directly the distribution of impact parameters leading to reaction.

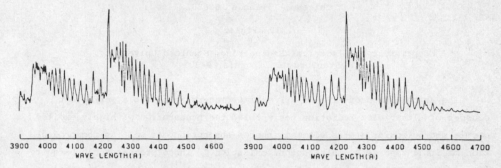

Fig. 1. Experimental (left) and computer simulated (right) optical spectra from C^+ + H_2 collisions at 5 eV, resolution 6 Å FWHM.

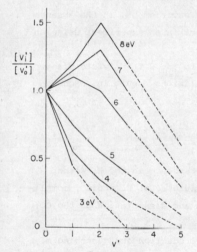

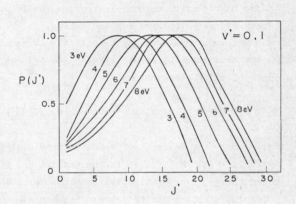

Fig. 2. Relative vibrational
level population of $CH^+(A^1\pi)$ as
used in the simulations of the
spectra. Note the inverted population at v' = 1 and 2 for E>6 eV$_{CM}$

Fig. 3. Relative rotational level
population of $CH^+(A^1\pi)$ as used in the
simulation of the spectra, for six
collision energies as indicated.

1. E. Herbst, J.G. Schubert, and P.R. Certain, Astrophys. J. 213, (1977),696.

2. H.H. Harris, M.G. Crowley, and J.J. Leventhal, Phys.Rev.Lett. 34, (1975), 67.

3. J. Appell, D. Brandt, and Ch. Ottinger, Chem.Phys.Lett. 33, (1975), 131.

4. Ch. Ottinger and J. Simonis, Chem.Phys. 28, (1978), 97.

5. M. Yoshimine, S. Green, and P. Thaddeus, Astrophys. J. 183, (1973), 899.

COLLISIONAL PROPERTIES OF NEUTRAL AND IONIC SPECIES
EXCITED BY MULTIPHOTON ULTRAVIOLET PROCESSES†

J. Bokor*, R. T. Hawkins, C. K. Rhodes

Department of Physics, University of Illinois at Chicago Circle,
Chicago, Illinois 60680

D. J. Kligler

Department of Electrical Engineering, Stanford University,
Stanford, California 94305

The introduction of ArF and KrF excimer lasers as reliable, efficient sources of ultraviolet radiation has enabled the preparation of highly excited atomic and molecular states via multiphoton absorption, as well as the production of ionic species by multiphoton ionization.[1] These processes can be quite efficient, leading to substantial excited state densities. The collisional properties of the excited species with each other, as well as with a variety of other collisional partners, can then be investigated. Note that these studies take place in a carefully controlled, laser-excited environment, in the absence of the high density of hot electrons normally present in an experiment using an e-beam or fast discharge for excitation.

Molecular hydrogen may be selectively excited to the $E,F\ ^1\Sigma_g^+$ state via two-photon excitation by an ArF laser.[2] Subsequent collisions result in resonant intramolecular energy transfer,

$$H_2\ (E,F\ ^1\Sigma_g^+) + H_2\ (X\ ^1\Sigma_g^+) \rightarrow H_2\ (C\ ^1\Pi_u) + H_2\ (X\ ^1\Sigma_g^+), \tag{1}$$

followed by the emission of vacuum ultraviolet fluorescence in the H_2 Werner system ($C\ ^1\Pi_u - X\ ^1\Sigma_g^+$) at 122 nm and 126 nm. In mixtures of H_2 and CO, complicated energy transfer kinetics result in excitation and dissociation of the CO molecule, yielding excited atomic fragments.

In other experiments, the kinetics of excimer production and quenching may be studied following excitation of rare gas species by the multiphoton processes,

$$Xe + 2\gamma(193\ nm) \rightarrow Xe^+ + e^- \tag{2}$$
$$Xe + 2\gamma(248\ nm) \rightarrow Xe^*\ (5p^5 6p) \tag{3}$$
$$Kr + 2\gamma(193\ nm) \rightarrow Kr^*\ (4p^5 6p) \tag{4}$$
$$Ar + 3\gamma(248\ nm) \rightarrow Ar^*\ (3p^5 4d). \tag{5}$$

These excited rare-gas species then react with ground-state rare-gas atoms to produce rare-gas excimers, or with various halogen donors to form rare-gas halide dimer and trimer excimer molecules. Collisional quenching processes involving the product excimers, as well as the formation and decay of triatomic species such as Rg_2X, may then be investigated.

As an example, in mixtures of Xe and Cl_2, the formation of XeCl* in both the B and C states from primarily ionic (reaction 4) or neutral (reaction 5) precursors can be observed. Figure 1 shows a typical emission spectrum of Xe/ Cl_2 mixtures upon optical excitation at 193 nm. Shown are the broad Xe_2Cl emission centered at 470 nm, the XeCl* (C-A) emission centered at 340 nm, and the XeCl* (B-X) emission at 308 nm. In mixtures of Xe and F_2, very different spectra are obtained. As expected, no Xe_2F emission is observed[3], and the C-A emission at 460 nm dominates[4] over the B-X emission at 351 nm.

These data indicate that while the B and C states in XeCl* are very nearly degenerate (within approximately 100 cm^{-1}), the C state in XeF* lies approximately 700 cm^{-1} below the XeF* B state.[4]

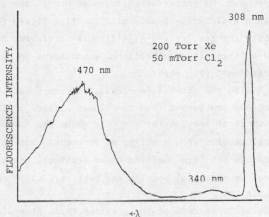

Fig. 1. XeCl and Xe_2Cl emission spectrum

†Supported by the Department of Energy under Agreement No. ED-70-3-00-1603 and the National Science Foundation under Grant PHY78-27610.
*Supported by the Fannie and John K. Hertz Foundation.

1. W. K. Bischel, J. Bokor, D. J. Kligler, and C. K. Rhodes, "Nonlinear Optical Processes in Atoms and Molecules Using Rare-Gas-Halide Lasers", IEEE J. Quantum Electron. (to be published).

2. Daniel J. Kligler and Charles K. Rhodes, Phys. Rev. Lett. **40**, 309 (1978).

3. D. C. Lorents, D. L. Huestis, M. V. McCusker, H. H. Nakano, and R. M. Hill, J. Chem. Phys. **68**, 4657 (1978).

4. D. J. Kligler, H. H. Nakano, D. L. Huestis, W. K. Bischel, R. M. Hill, and C. K. Rhodes, Appl. Phys. Lett. **33**, 39 (1978).

THREE-DIMENSIONAL QUANTUM MECHANICAL STUDIES
OF He + H_2^+ → HeH^+ + H REACTIVE SCATTERING*

K. T. Tang and Y. Y. Yung

Department of Physics, Pacific Lutheran University
Tacoma, Washington 98447

and

B. H. Choi and R. T. Poe
Department of Physics, University of California
Riverside, California

Three dimensional quantum mechanical calculations are carried out for the endothermic reaction He + H_2^+ (ν = 0,1,2) → HeH^+ + H with the Distorted Wave Born Approximation, where ν indicates the vibrational quantum number of the initial molecule. We have used the potential surfaces of Kuntz[1] and of Kuntz and Whitton[2] (KW), both are diatomic-in-molecules function fitted to Brown-Hayes ab initio data[3]. While the results are significantly different from each other, both results show no significant vibrational enhancement in reaction cross sections, in disagreement with experiment[4].

In comparison with the three dimensional trajectory calculations, our present quantum cross sections are larger than the classical ones[2]. In the threshold region, our quantum cross section for ν = 0 is about the same as that for ν = 1, while the classical results show a slight enhancement. But in terms of the amount of enhancement and the absolute reaction cross sections, the present quantum results and the previous classical results are both very different from the experimental results.

We have essentially reproduced the previous three dimensional quantum results of Zuhrt et. al.[5] for ground rotational state to ground rotational state transitions. However, after we include the higher rotational states, the reaction cross section becomes much too large as compared with experiment.

The potential surfaces are fitted to the ab initio points only in the linear configuration, for nonlinear geometries, they are more or less arbitrarily determined by the analytical representations. In an effort to promote the interplay between theory and experiment, we modified the Kuntz-Whitton surface by adding a short range repulsion term

$$V_{Mod} = V_{KW} + A \exp (-\alpha R) [1-P_2(\cos \theta)] \qquad (1)$$

where R is the distance between He and the center of mass of H_2^+, θ is the angle between R and the molecular axis, and $P_2 (\cos \theta)$ is the second order Legendre polynomial. By choosing A = 1.0 x 10^3 eV and α = 8 a.u.$^{-1}$, we are able to bring our quantum cross sections to good agreement with experiment.

The modified surface leaves the potential in the linear configuration exactly the same as before. For non-linear configurations, the differences between the modified and KW surfaces are not noticeable in the "reaction region" for

$0 \leqslant \gamma < 150°$ where γ is the angle between the axes of the initial and the product molecules. The modification in the two body potential in the entrance channel is small, but the modified two body potential is considerably more repulsive in the exit channel. This is the main reason for our quantum results to show a pronounced vibrational enhancement. Some of our results are shown in Table I, even the absolute cross sections are in semi-quantatitive agreement with experiment.

Table I.   Reactive Cross Section of $He + H_2^+ \rightarrow HeH^+ + H$ in a.u.^{2} as a function of the initial vibrational state ν and the total energy E_t.

$\nu \backslash^{E_t}$	1.0 eV		1.2 eV	
	Theory[a]	Experiment[b]	Theory[a]	Experiment[b]
0	0.162	0.21	0.387	0.27
1	1.141	1.75	3.431	2.10
2	5.054	6.96	7.375	9.82

a. Present calculation with KW potential modified as given by Eq. (1).
b. Estimate from experimental curves in ref. 4.

*Supported by grants from the National Science Foundation and the Petroleum Research Fund.

1. P. J. Kuntz, Chem. Phys. Lett. 16, 581 (1972).
2. W. N. Whitton and P. J. Kuntz, J. Chem. Phys. 64, 3624 (1976).
3. P. J. Brown and E. F. Hayes, J. Chem. Phys. 55, 922 (1971).
4. W. A. Chupka, J. Berkwitz, and M. E. Russell, Six International Conference on the Physics of Electronic and Atomic Collisions (M.I.T. Press, Cambridge, 1969), p. 71.
5. Ch. Zuhrt, F. Schneider and L. Zülike, Chem. Phys. Lett. 43, 571 (1976).

THE $H^+ + CH_4 \rightarrow H_2^+ + CH_3$ PROCESS IN THE DOUBLE SCATTERING MODEL

Robin Shakeshaft[*] and Larry Spruch[**]

[*]Physics Department, Texas A. and M. University
College Station, Texas, USA

[**]Physics Department, New York University
4 Washington Place, New York, New York, USA

The classical double-scattering model for the capture of electrons from atoms by fast ions[1] yields a cross section which dominates over the single scattering contribution for sufficiently fast ions. The magnitude of the classical double scattering model differs, however, from its quantum mechanical (second Born) analogue by an order of magnitude. Further, a "fast ion" means an ion of some MeV, and at those energies the cross sections are very low. On the other hand, the double scattering cross section for the capture of atoms from molecules by fast ions dominates over the single scattering contribution for incident ions of very much lower energy[2]; roughly, one must have the velocity of the incident projectile much larger than a characteristic internal velocity of the particles in the target. For the reaction

$$H^+ + CH_4 \rightarrow H_2^+ + CH_3 \tag{1}$$

with incident proton energies of 70 to 150 eV, the peak in the angular distribution as determined experimentally[3] is at almost precisely the value predicted by the classical model, but the theoretical total cross section is about 30 times too large. Using a quantum version[4] of the classical model, which involves the same kinematics and therefore preserves the agreement with the angular distribution, preliminary calculations suggest somewhat better agreement with the experimental total cross section, by a factor of about 5. (To obtain really good agreement, one may have to perform a really accurate calculation of large-angle elastic scattering of protons by CH_4.) In the center of mass frame, the first of the two scatterings involves the scattering of H^+ by H through an angle of close to 90°, and it follows that the nuclei of the emergent H_2^+ ion will almost all be in the singlet state.

Research supported by the National Science Foundation, Grant Nos. PHY77-07406 and PHY77-10131, and by the Office of Naval Research, Contract No. N00014-76-C-0317.

1. L.H. Thomas, Proc. Roy. Soc. 114, 561 (1927).

2. D.R. Bates, C.J. Cook, and F.J. Smith, Proc. Phys. Soc. 83, 49 (1964).

3. C.J. Cook, N.R.A. Smyth, and O. Heinz, J. Chem. Phys. 63, 1218 (1975).

4. See R. Shakeshaft and L. Spruch, Rev. Mod. Phys. 51,...(1979)(April issue).

ION-MOLECULE REACTION OF UO$^+$ WITH MOLECULAR OXYGEN

H. H. Lo* and W. L. Fite

Department of Physics and Astronomy, University of Pittsburgh
Pittsburgh, Pennsylvania 15260, USA

When uranium atoms are released in the upper atmosphere where atomic and molecular oxygen are present, the associative ionization reactions

$$U + O \longrightarrow UO^+ + e + 2.1 \text{ eV} \tag{1}$$

and

$$U + O_2 \longrightarrow UO_2^+ + e + 4.1 \text{ eV} \tag{2}$$

occur. The plasma produced by these reactions cannot be neutralized by the normal dissociative recombination reactions because of the endoergicity of the reactions inverse to Reactions (1) and (2), and hence a long-lived plasma can be produced.

It is of interest to determine the rate at which the reaction

$$UO^+ + O_2 \longrightarrow UO_2^+ + O + 2.0 \text{ eV} \tag{3}$$

proceeds. Where there are both O and O_2 present in the atmosphere this reaction can reduce the UO$^+$ spectrum with time and enhance the UO_2^+ spectrum.

The rate coefficient for the ion-molecule reaction of Reaction (3) at thermal energies was measured in the present experiment using a magnetic bottle apparatus.[1] Within the vacuum system are coils which produce a magnetic field bounded by two magnetic mirrors, the field strength being 1500 G at the center and 2500 G at the mirrors. A beam of uranium atoms crosses the magnetic field at the center of the bottle and the primary ions, UO$^+$ and UO_2^+, are formed along the atomic beam's length by associative ionization reactions,

$$U + N_2O \longrightarrow UO^+ + N_2 + e + 0.4 \text{ eV}, \tag{4}$$

and Reaction (2), where N_2O and O_2 are gases admitted into the vacuum system. The secondary ions, UO_2^+, are produced by ion-molecule reactions of Reaction (3) and

$$UO^+ + N_2O \longrightarrow UO_2^+ + N_2 + 5.4 \text{ eV}. \tag{5}$$

The primary and secondary ions escaping from the bottle are both mass analyzed by a quadrupole mass spectrometer, which is placed outside one of the mirrors, and detected by a venetian-blind electron multiplier. In the experiments curves of UO_2^+ and UO$^+$ ion currents vs. O_2 pressure are obtained on a X-Y recorder for a fixed N_2O pressure. The pressure of N_2O is typically 3×10^{-5} Torr while the pressure of O_2 is ranged from 0 to 1.5×10^{-4} Torr. The method used to analyze data will be described.

The rate coefficient for the ion-molecule reaction of UO^+ with O_2 was found to be $2.03 \pm 0.44 \times 10^{-9}$ cm^3/sec. It appears that at thermal energies Reaction (3) proceeds almost one order of magnitude faster than Reaction (5). The rate coefficient of the latter has been previously measured by the authors to be 2.73×10^{-10} cm^3/sec.

*Present address: Extranuclear Laboratories, Inc., Pittsburgh, PA 15238.

[1]H.H. Lo, L. M. Clendenning and W. L. Fite, J. Chem. Phys. 66, 947 (1977).

REACTIONS OF U ATOMS WITH INORGANIC OXIDES, ALCOHOLS AND HALOGENATED METHANES*

Richard C. Stern and Neil C. Lang

Lawrence Livermore Laboratory
Livermore, California 94550, USA

We have used the crossed molecular beams technique to identify neutral products, measure product angular distributions and estimate total cross sections for the reaction of uranium atoms with O_2, NO, SO_2, NO_2, H_2O, CH_3OH, C_2H_5OH, CH_3COCH_3, CCl_4, CF_3Br and CH_3I. A thermal beam of U atoms at 2500 to 2600°K is crossed with a gas beam effusing from a capillary array.

Reactions with all the oxygen containing compounds yield UO as the sole product. This result is particularly surprising for the case of CH_3COCH_3. The UO product angular distribution is narrow and peaked near the center of mass in all cases, indicating that little of the reaction exothermicity appears in product translation. This result has been verified for the U + O_2 system by time of flight analysis of the product UO.

Product angular distributions from U + halomethanes show more variety. The UI from U + CH_3I is clearly backward peaked for example. In general the pattern of angular distributions and relative total cross sections is very similar to that observed in barium.[1,2]

*Work performed under the auspices of the U.S. Department of Energy by the Lawrence Livermore Laboratory under contract No. W-7405-ENG-48.

1. S.-M. Lin, C.A. Mims and R.R. Herm, J. Phys. Chem. 77, 569 (1973).
2. R.W. Solarz and S.A. Johnson, J. Chem. Phys. 70, 3592 (1979).

DYNAMICS OF THE REACTION OF N_2O^+ WITH D_2 AND H_2

Akira Johgo and Yoshitada Murata*

Department of Chemistry, Faculty of Science, Gakushuin University
Mejiro, Toshima-ku, Tokyo 171, Japan
*The Institute for Solid State Physics, The University of Tokyo
Roppongi, Minato-ku, Tokyo 106, Japan

The ion-molecule reaction between N_2O^+ and D_2 (H_2) was studied by using the beam-collision chamber method with energy analysis of products. The relative collision energy between the primary ion and the molecule was over the range E = 2.3 ~ 6.3 eV.

A N_2O^+-D_2 (H_2) system was chosen due to an expectation that several kinds of ionic reaction products might be produced with large cross sections by different reaction mechanisms. A useful information for the study of an elementary process of the chemical reaction is given from the collision energy dependence of the reaction cross sections and the velocity distribution of the product ions. The results for the ions produced through different channels may have different features each other.

A schematic diagram of the apparatus used in the present experiment is shown in Fig. 1. Detection angle was fixed at 0°. Ion beam was produced by impact of 40 eV electrons of N_2O molecules and selecting N_2O^+ through a quadrupole mass filter. The velocity distribution of scattered ions was observed by an energy analyzer of the double-hemispherical type.

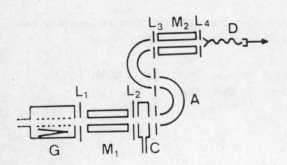

Fig. 1.
Schematic diagram of the apparatus. G: ion gun; L_1, L_2, L_3, L_4: lens; M_1, M_2: mass filter; C: collision chamber; A: energy analyzer; D: detector (channeltron).

Three ionic reaction products, N_2OD^+ (N_2OH^+), N_2D^+ (N_2H^+) and OD^+ (OH^+), were observed. The collision energy dependence of the cross sections of these product ions is shown in Fig. 2. The energy dependence of N_2OD^+ (N_2OH^+) shows a similar dependence to the Langevin cross section. On the other hand, N_2D^+ (N_2H^+) and OD^+ (OH^+) may have threshold energies, which are almost an equal value. In the formation of N_2OD^+, since the reaction is exothermic, i.e., the heat of reaction $\Delta E = -0.5$ eV, the experimental result is reasonable and N_2OD^+ must be produced by the same mechanism as those of the formation of ArH^+, COH^+, N_2H^+ and CO_2H^+ by the hydrogen abstraction reaction. In the formation of N_2D^+ (N_2H^+) and OD^+ (OH^+), the experimental result suggests that these ions are produced by the endothermic reaction with the same heat of reaction. Hence, the dissociation of the N-O bond in the incident ion may be a dominant process in the reaction, which may occur as follows;

$$N_2O^+ + D_2 \rightarrow N_2D^+ + O + D$$
$$\rightarrow OD^+ + N_2 + D.$$

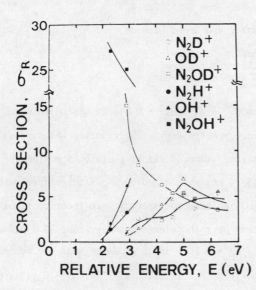

Fig. 2.
Collision energy dependence of reaction cross sections. Ordinate is shown in arbitrary units.

These conclusions are supported by the result of measurement of the energy distribution of product ions. All of the product ions were scattered forward, that is, the relative velocity of these ions was greater in the laboratory system than that of the center of mass. Therefore, the reaction proceeds by a direct short-lived interaction rather than by a long-lived collision complex. N_2OD^+ (N_2OH^+) and N_2D^+ (N_2H^+) were observed around the velocity predicted from the spectator-stripping model for the reaction and the velocity of OD^+ (OH^+) was almost the same as that of the incident ion, N_2O^+, over the whole range of the collision energy. The width in the velocity distribution of N_2D^+ (N_2H^+) and OD^+ (OH^+) was broader than that of N_2OD^+ (N_2OH^+).

The isotope effect in the formation of N_2D^+ (N_2H^+) and OD^+ (OH^+) was observed as seen in Fig. 2, while it has not been observed in the hydrogen abstraction reaction such as $Ar^+ + H_2 \rightarrow ArH^+$ and $N_2^+ + H_2 \rightarrow N_2H^+$.

STATE SELECTED ION-MOLECULE REACTION STUDIES
BY ELECTRON-ION COINCIDENCE SPECTROSCOPY:
I. $H_2^{+\dagger}(H_2,H)H_3^+$

Andrew J. Yencha

Department of Physics
State University of New York at Albany
Albany, New York 12222 U.S.A.

Adolf Münzer and Arend Niehaus

Faculty for Physics
The University of Freiburg
7800 Freiburg, Germany

The simple exothermic reaction $H_2^+ + H_2 \rightarrow H_3^+ + H$ has been studied using the technique of electron-ion coincidence spectroscopy. The reaction was carried out within a retarding field photoelectron - time of flight photoion spectrometer using helium I resonance radiation (58.4 nm) with a hydrogen gas target pressure of 8×10^{-4} Torr. The $e^- \text{-} H_2^+$ and $e^- \text{-} H_3^+$ coincidence spectra were recorded simultaneously on two multichannel analyzers over the electron energy range 3.4-6.4 eV. The electron intensity ratio $I_{H_3^+} / I_{H_2^+} + I_{H_3^+}$ in coincidence with the respective ions, as a function of internal energy of H_2^+ [= 21.22 eV - $IP(H_2) - E_e$], gives directly the relative cross section (v=0) for the reaction,

$$H_2^+(v) + H_2(v'=0) \rightarrow H_3^+(v'') + H.$$

Such a plot is shown in the figure. Also shown in this figure is the relative cross section results of Chupka, et al.[1] using a photoionization mass spectrometer and the recent results of Tanaka and Koyano[2] using the threshold electron-secondary ion coincidence technique for the same reaction. All three results indicate that the relative cross section decreases with increasing internal energy. The more rapid decline found here, from v=0 to v=3, is thought to be due to a difference in the average collision energies. Chupka, et al.[1] interpreted the decrease in the relative cross section as a function of internal energy to mean that a collision complex is formed in this reaction. However, more recently both experimental[3] and theoretical[3,4] results suggest that the formation of H_3^+ proceeds by a direct mechanism. Since this study was carried out at thermal collision energies, where the formation of a collision complex would be most favored, it was hoped that some evidence for its existence might be found. The increase in the reaction cross section from v=3 to v=4, as well as from v=8 to v=9, in the figure is believed to be real and is thought to arise due to the near resonant vibrational energy transfer process,

$$H_2^+(v=4,9) + H_2(v'=0) \leftrightarrow H_2^+(v=0) + H_2(v'=2,4).$$

There would seem to be two plausible explanations for the observed increase in the relative reaction cross section. The first is that the cross section for the reaction of $H_2^+(v) + H_2(v'=0)$ is different from the cross section for the reaction of $H_2^+(v=0) + H_2(v')$. The second possibility is that, due to the near resonant processes, an exchange interaction results which enhances the reaction cross section. The implications of these hypotheses shall be discussed in terms of the reaction mechanism.

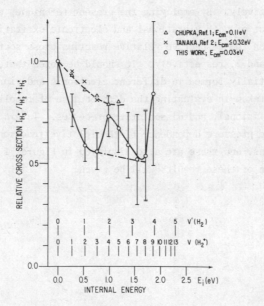

Figure: Relative cross section for the reaction $H_2^+(v) + H_2 \rightarrow H_3^+ + H$ as a function of vibrational internal energy of H_2^+.

References:

1. W. A. Chupka, M. E. Russell, and K. Refaey, J. Chem. Phys. 48, 1518 (1968).
2. K. Tanaka and I. Koyano, J. Chem. Phys. 69, 3422 (1978).
3. J. R. Krenos, K. K. Lehmann, J. C. Tully, P. M. Hierl, and G. P. Smith, Chem. Phys. 16, 109 (1976).
4. J. R. Stine and J. T. Muckerman, J. Chem. Phys. 68, 185 (1978).

STATE SELECTED ION-MOLECULE REACTION STUDIES
BY ELECTRON-ION COINCIDENCE SPECTROSCOPY:

II. $H_2O^{++}(H_2O,OH)H_3O^+$ AND $H_2S^{++}(H_2S,HS)H_3S^+$

Andrew J. Yencha

Department of Physics
State University of New York at Albany
Albany, New York 12222 U.S.A.

Adolf Minzer and Arend Niehaus

Faculty for Physics
The University of Freiburg
7800 Freiburg, Germany

We have investigated the ion-molecule reactions $H_2O^+ + H_2O \rightarrow H_3O^+ + OH$ and $H_2S^+ + H_2S \rightarrow H_3S^+ + HS$ using the technique of electron-ion coincidence spectroscopy. The studies were conducted within a retarding field photoelectron - time of flight photoion spectrometer employing helium I resonance radiation (58.4 nm) at varying pressures of target gas. The $e^--H_2O^+/e^--H_3O^+$ and $e^--H_2S^+/e^--H_3S^+$ coincidence spectra were recorded over the electron energy range 0.4-10.4 eV and 0.4-12.4 eV, respectively. By employing the present technique, we have been able to observe the effect of both vibrational and electronic excitation of the H_2O^+ and H_2S^+ reactants on the respective relative reaction cross sections. These are shown in Figures 1 and 2, respectively. It should be noted that, although the reactant ions are initially formed in different electronic and vibrational states, great care must be taken in evaluating the data because of complications arising from radiative, collisional, and dissociative processes. To aid in this regard, we have obtained the pressure dependence of the relative reaction cross sections for the two reactions, and these are also displayed in Figures 1 and 2. A complete interpretation of these results will be given.

Figure 1: Relative cross section for the reaction $H_2O^{++} + H_2O \rightarrow H_3O^+ + OH$ as a function of vibrational and electronic energy of H_2O^+.

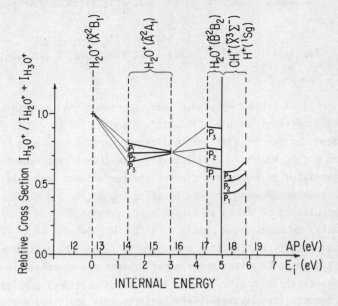

Figure 2: Relative cross section for the reaction $H_2S^{++} + H_2S \rightarrow H_3S^+ + HS$ as a function of vibrational and electronic energy of H_2S^+.

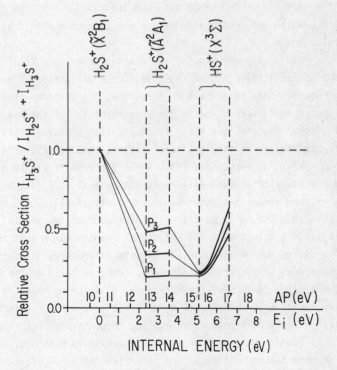

TRANSLATIONAL AND VIBRATIONAL ACTIVATION OF CHEMICAL REACTIONS.[*]

F. Heismann and H.J. Loesch
Fakultät für Physik, Universität Bielefeld, D 4800 Bielefeld 1, Germany

In a crossed molecular beam experiment the integral cross sections $Q(E)$ for the reactions $K + HCl \rightarrow KCl + H$ and $K + HF$ (v = 0,1) $\rightarrow KF + H$ have been measured for translational collision energies E ranging from threshold up to 35 and 50 kcal/mole, respectively. The thermal and superthermal energies were generated by the application of the seeded beam technique to the K-beam, the energy range being covered by using Kr, Ar, He and H_2 as carrier gases. The population of the first vibrational state of HF (v = 1) was controlled thermally by heating the nozzle oven to temperatures up to 2200 K. This provides a concentration of excited molecules up to 6%. The rotational temperature is considered to be always substantially lower due to relaxation collisions during the expansion of the beam[1]. The flux of scattered particles consists of two components, the elastically and inelastically scattered K-atoms and the product molecules, and both are detected with approximately 100% efficiency by a heated Pt-W-ribbon. The two components are separated via a time-of-flight analysis since atoms and products appear in the LAB-frame with drastically different velocities.

Preliminary results for the reaction $K + HCl \rightarrow KCl + H$ are shown in Fig.1. The steep increase of the cross section with increasing energy is typical for a reaction with an activation threshold. The position of the threshold E_{th} appears to be very close to the endothermicity of the reaction (1.5 kcal/mole)[2]. At higher energies the cross section passes through a flat maximum around 25 kcal/mole. The simple line-of-centers model gives, with E_{th} = 1.5 and 2.5 kcal/mole, reasonable fits, while the centrifugal barrier model[3] with its early maximum followed by a rapid decrease of $Q(E)$ (dotted line in Fig. 1) is in strong contrast to the results. Microscopically, $Q(E)$ consists of a sum of cross sections fully specified with respect to the initial (v,j,m) and final (v',j',m') vibrational and rotational quantum numbers of the relevant molecule. The energy dependence of $Q(E)$ reflects, therefore, in addition to that of the individual cross sections also the strong increase of the number of final quantum states accessible with increasing E. Assuming that the simple parameterized expression $Q_0[E-(E_{th}+E_{vib}+E_{rot})]^n/E^p$ (E_{vib} and E_{rot} = vibrational and rotational energy of the product molecules, respectively) describes each individual cross section (v=j=m=o) which is energetically possible, neglecting any angular momentum restrictions, the parameter set n = 0,67, p = 2,85 and E_{th} = 1.5 kcal/mole provides a reasonable fit of the data including the faint maximum at medium energies (solid line in Fig. 1).

First results of the K + HF reaction indicate that there is also an activation threshold near the endothermicity of 16.9 kcal/mole. Furthermore, as
in the case of HCl [4], the translational energy is very inefficient in promoting the reaction while the vibrational energy enhances the process substantially. At a collision energy of 24 kcal/mole the reactive yield would increase by approximately three orders of magnitude if all ground state molecules
were excited to the v = 1 level. Detailed results will be presented at the
conference.

* Work supported by the Deutsche Forschungsgemeinschaft

1. A.M.G. Ding and J.C. Polanyi, Chem.Phys. <u>10</u>, 39 (1975)

2. J.G. Pruett, F.R. Grabiner and P.R. Brooks, J.Chem.Phys. <u>63</u>, 1173
   (1975)

3. R.D. Levine and R.B. Bernstein, J.Chem.Phys. <u>56</u>, 2281 (1972)

4. T.J. Odiorne, P.R. Brooks and J.V.V. Kasper, J.Chem.Phys. <u>55</u>, 1980
   (1971)

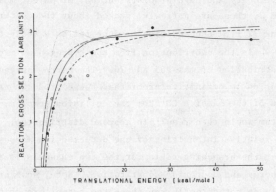

Fig. 1. The energy dependence of the integral cross section for the reaction K + HCl → KCl + H. Open and filled circles refer to the results of
Brooks et al.[2] and to the present results, respectively. The cross section
is given in Å^2 if the absolute scale of [2] is assumed. The various lines refer
to the following functions: $Q(E) = 3.158 (1 - 1.5/E)$ -.-; $3.158 (1 - 2.5/E)$
---; and $7.695 (E - 2.5)^{2/3}/E$ ....; for the solid line see text.

A CROSSED MOLECULAR BEAM STUDY OF THE REACTIONS OF $O(^3P)$ + C_6H_6, C_6D_6

Tomohiko Hirooka, Richard J. Buss, Piergiorgio Casavecchia,
Steven J. Sibener and Yuan T. Lee

Materials and Molecular Research Division, Lawrence Berkeley Laboratory and
Department of Chemistry, University of California, Berkeley, CA 94720 U.S.A.

The study of oxygen atom reactions with hydrocarbons under single collision conditions with crossed molecular beams can provide unambiguous product identification and detailed microscopic information essential to understanding combustion processes. We report here the results of our investigation of the reaction of ground state oxygen atoms with C_6H_6 and C_6D_6 in which we detect product angular and velocity distribution from two reactive channels. Supersonic beams of $O(^3P)$ produced in an RF-discharge[1] and C_6H_6 or C_6D_6 were crossed at two relative collision energies, 2.7 and 6.5 kcal mol^{-1}. Product was observed at the masses corresponding to simple addition to form C_6H_6O and C_6D_6O, and also at the lower masses from the hydrogen elimination channel to give C_6H_5O and C_6D_5O. The daughter fragment ions resulting from CO elimination during the electron bombardment ionization were the major fragment ions for all product species, and were used to monitor the velocity and angular distribution of parent molecules. As shown in Figs. 1 and 2, these are narrowly peaked about the center of mass direction; mass 66 and 72 from the addition product follow exactly the distribution of the centroid while the contribution from the hydrogen elimination channel has broadened the distribution of mass 65 and 70. The narrow spread of the product angular distribution is definitive proof that these products are not the result of elimination of the massive CO from the collision complex, as conservation of linear momentum would then result in a broad distribution.

In Table 1, the relative intensities of the detected ion masses are given and it is evident that the branching ratio for the two channels is affected by both the collision energy and deuterium substitution. Note, however, that these relative signal levels do not directly represent the actual branching ratios, as the signals at masses 65 and 70 contain contributions from fragmentation of both the adduct and elimination channels. The relative yield of the addition compound is increased by raising the collision energy as well as by substituting deuterium for hydrogen. The $O(^3P)$ approaches benzene on a triplet surface which has a moderate well, about 15 kcal mol^{-1}. Our results are consistent with the formation of a triplet complex which has two principal reactive channels, elimination of a hydrogen atom or radiationless transition to the singlet surface to produce the very stable ground state phenol.

1. S. J. Sibener, R. J. Buss and Y. T. Lee, Rarefied Gas Dynamics Proceedings, 1978, in press.

Acknowledgement. This work was supported by the Division of Chemical
Sciences, Office of Basic Energy Sciences, U.S. Department of Energy under
contract No. W-7405-Eng-48.

Table 1. Relative Intensity of Detected Ion Masses.

| | Mass | Species | Collision Energy | |
			6.5 kcal/mole	2.7 kcal/mol
	94	C_6H_5OH	0.01	< 0.005
$O + C_6H_6$	93	C_6H_5O	0.08	0.01
	66	C_5H_6	0.21	0.08
	65	C_5H_5	1.00	1.00
	100	C_6D_5OD	0.04	< 0.005
$O + C_6D_6$	98	C_6D_5O	0.04	< 0.005
	72	C_5D_6	1.05	0.18
	70	C_5D_5	1.00	1.00

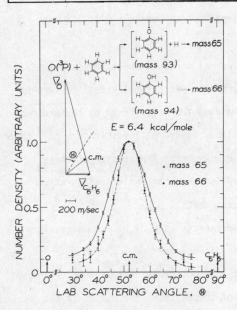

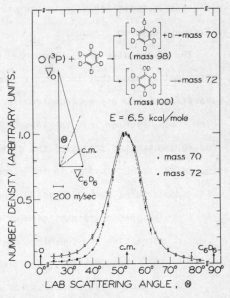

Fig. 1. Angular distributions from
the reaction $O + C_6H_6$. The primary
reaction products found were C_6H_5O
and C_6H_5OH, which subsequently fragmented in the ionizer.

Fig. 2. Angular distributions from
the reaction of $O + C_6D_6$. The primary
reaction products were C_6D_5O and
C_6D_5OD which subsequently fragmented
in the ionizer.

POSSIBLE ISOTOPE EFFECT IN DISSOCIATIVE COLLISIONS OF HD_2^+ IN H_2*

I. Alvarez and C. Cisneros
Instituto de Fisica, UNAM, Mexico, D.F.

J. A. Ray and C. F. Barnett
Oak Ridge National Laboratory, Oak Ridge, Tennessee 37830

and

A. Russek
University of Connecticut, Storrs, Connecticut 06268

Cross sections have been measured for the formation of H^+ and D^+ from dissociation of 50-500-keV HD_2^+ in H_2 gas. The dissociative fractions of H^+ and D^+ increased rapidly as the incident HD_2^+ energy increased, whereas the molecular fragments HD^+ and D_2^+ were nearly constant in this energy range. The D^+ formation cross section was found to be approximately a factor of six greater than that for H^+ formation. Any difference in D^+, H^+ production cross section (beyond the factor of two reflecting the relative abundance in HD_2^+) must arise from the different isotopic behavior in the vibrational motion due solely to the mass difference between D and H.

The eigenstates of the two symmetric normal modes in the harmonic potential approximation show that for HD_2^+ in the symmetric vibrational modes the largest separation of any one nucleus from the remaining two is achieved by the proton, which, being lighter, has the largest amplitude. Several investigators[1,2,3] have studied the excited states of the similar H_3^+ system. Application of these studies to the HD_2^+ system in the elongated isosceles triangle configuration with a deuteron at each base vertex indicates that:

1. The ground state is singlet and separates as $H^+ + D_2$. However, it is attractive and therefore does not dissociate.

2. Four excited states, two singlet and two triplet, are repulsive and dissociate as $H + D_2^+$. For two of these states the D_2^+ is in the ground state, and for the other pair D_2^+ is in a repulsive state, which further dissociates as $D^+ + D$.

These facts account for the experimental data rather well. Few dissociation fragments of H^+ would be expected but many of D^+ and D_2^+.

More definitive conclusions as to the collisional processes involved require a knowledge of all the electronic states over a wider range of geometries, as well as an understanding of which electronic states are preferentially excited in the collision process. Nevertheless, it is evident that the mass difference affects the relative populations of collision fragments via the internuclear configuration at the time of the collision, which is sensitive to the isotopic mass differences.

*The experimental work was supported by the Office of Fusion Energy. U. S. Department of Energy, under contract W-7405-eng-26 with the Union Carbide Corporation. The theory and analysis were supported by a joint grant from the Latin American Co-operative program of NSF (USA) and CONACYT (Mexico): NSF-PNCB-CONACYT #1367.

1. H. Conroy, J. Chem. Phys. 40, 603 (1964).

2. L. J. Schaad and W. V. Hicks, J. Chem. Phys. 61, 1934 (1974).

3. C. W. Bauschlicher, Jr., S. V. O'Neil, R. K. Preston, H. F. Schaefer III, and C. F. Bender, J. Chem. Phys. 59, 1286 (1973).

KINETIC STUDIES OF PROTON-EXCITED GAS MIXTURES*

C. H. Chen, J. P. Judish, and M. G. Payne

Oak Ridge National Laboratory, Oak Ridge, Tennessee 37830, USA

Pulses of 2-MeV protons were used to excite various gas mixtures producing ion pairs and excited states. The intensity of protons was controlled to vary the ion density from 10^5 to 10^{11} per cm^3. The emitted vuv (500 Å to 2000 Å) and uv-visible (2000 Å to $\sim$ 7000 Å) photons passing through separate monochromators were detected by using single photon counting techniques. Time-resolved and time-integrated fluorescence spectroscopies were used to study mechanisms for excitation, energy transfer, Penning ionization, charge transfer, and ion-ion combination. The energy precursors of various excited species in a number of gas mixtures were identified and the quenching rates of excited atoms and ions by numerous small molecules (such as O_2, CO, CO_2, NO, NO_2, etc.) were measured.

Rare gas atoms in resonance excited states can be monitored by vuv radiation; from time-resolved vuv spectra, the quenching rates of excited atoms [such as $Ar(^3P_1)$, $Ar(^1P_1)$, $He(2^1P)$, etc.] by various molecules can be determined. Although $He(2^1S)$ is a metastable state, the radiation at 601 Å can occur by collision-induced emission. Thus, the quenching rates or Penning ionization cross sections of $He(2^1S)$ by various molecules can also be measured.

It is well known that He^+, He_2^+, and Ne_2^+ can produce $N_2^+(B)_{v=0}$ by charge transfer processes. Thus, the time histories of He^+, He_2^+, and Ne_2^+ can be monitored by time-resolved fluorescence spectra of $N_2^+(B)_{v=0}$. The two-body and three-body quenching rates of He^+, He_2^+, and Ne_2^+ were measured. We also proved the existence of He_3^+ and Ne_3^+. Since He^+, He_2^+, and Ne_2^+ can be monitored by $N_2^+(B)_{v=0}$ for $He-N_2$ or $Ne-N_2$ mixtures, the charge transfer rates of He^+ and He_2^+ with CO, CO_2, N_2, and H_2S have been determined.

From time-resolved fluorescence spectra, it was discovered that $Ar(^3P_1)$ is the precursor of $ArCl^*$ in $Ar-Cl_2$ mixtures. It has also been concluded that $Ar(^3P_2)$ is the precursor of $N_2(C^3\Pi_u)_{v=0}$, and $Ar(^1P_1)$ contributes to the emission of $N_2(C^3\Pi_u)_{v=0}$ for proton-excited $Ar-N_2$ mixtures.

The radiative lifetimes of excited molecules and the quenching rates of excited molecules by foreign gases can be determined by time-resolved spectra. The lifetimes of $N_2(C^3\Pi_u)_{v=0,1,2,3}$, ArF^*, and Ar_2F^* were measured. The quenching rates of ArF^* and Ar_2F^* by F_2 have also been determined.

*Research sponsored by the Office of Health and Environmental Research, U.S. Department of Energy, under contract W-7405-eng-26 with the Union Carbide Corp.

VI.   Special Topics

PHOTOIONIZATION NEAR THRESHOLD IN THE PRESENCE OF EXTERNAL FIELDS

A. R. P. Rau

Department of Physics, Louisiana State University
Baton Rouge, Louisiana 70803, U.S.A.

Several recent experiments on the photoabsorption of atoms from the ground
state to high Rydberg states in the presence of external electric and magnetic
fields have observed a characteristic set of equally-spaced resonances near the
ionization threshold. Most interestingly, this pattern stretches out on either
side of the ionization limit and several of its features, such as the energy
spacing between the resonances, are independent of the specific atom under
study. Such a pattern can be understood[1] as a general physical feature to be
found near zero energy whenever two or more fields exert equally strong influences on the motion of a particle. In the atomic example, the external magnetic
or electric field can become equally as important as the Coulomb field for the
motion of a near-zero-energy electron, leading thereby to such a characteristic
spectrum.

All the different situations pertaining to atoms or negative ions in the
presence of electric or magnetic fields or combinations of both can be capsuled
in terms of two simple WKB expressions.[1] In some coordinate x, with a range of
variation from 0 to ∞, the potential $V(x)$ seen by the electron has the form of
being initially negative from x = 0 to some value $x = x_0$, beyond which it becomes positive and rises to infinity. For an atom in an electric field, this is
the form of the potential for m = 0 states in the parabolic coordinate $\xi(= r + z)$.
For an atom in a magnetic field, the combined Coulomb and diamagnetic terms give
$-e^2/r + \frac{1}{8} \mu\omega^2\rho^2$, where ω is the cyclotron frequency and the other symbols have
their usual meaning; once again, along the direction z = 0, this potential has
the requisite form. Given such a potential $V(x)$, it supports bound states at all
energies. In particular, around $E \simeq 0$, one can obtain from the WKB quantisation
condition:

$$2(2\mu)^{1/2} \int_0^{x_0} [E-V(x)]^{1/2}dx = (n + \frac{1}{2})\, h, \qquad (1)$$

an effective quantum number n for the states near zero energy. If this quantum
number is large compared to unity, so that the change in going from one state to
the next is small in comparison, then the energy difference between successive
states is approximately constant and is given by differentiating (1) and setting
E = 0:

$$\frac{dE}{dn} = \frac{h}{(2\mu)^{1/2}} \left[\int_0^{x_0} dx\,[-V(x)]^{1/2} \right]^{-1}. \qquad (2)$$

Thus, equally-spaced states around zero energy are always to be expected with
such a $V(x)$, provided the effective quantum number given by (1) is reasonably
large. So long as there is one direction x with such a $V(x)$, it is sufficient to
establish such a pattern of states. If there are, simultaneously, other direc-

tions of motion along which the electron is free to escape, the states will not be strictly bound but will show up as resonances, with decay widths expressing the probability of escape. For an atom in a magnetic field, one finds from (1) that $n \simeq 42[B/50,000G]^{-1/3}$ and, from (2), that $dE/dn = \frac{3}{2}\hbar\omega$. These are in agreement with the many experiments[2] that have observed such resonances. For an atom in an electric field, one has $n \simeq 18[\varepsilon/5000v/cm]^{-1/4}$ and $dE/dn \simeq 25cm^{-1}[\varepsilon/5000v/cm]^{3/4}$. A recent photoabsorption experiment[3] has, in fact, observed such equally-spaced resonances.

Similar results are to be expected in the case of photodetachment of a negative ion in an external field. Now, in place of the Coulomb attraction in the region from 0 to x_0, we have the short range attractive field that binds the extra electron. However, since this attraction is weak and not capable of supporting many states below $E = 0$ (usually it only supports one bound state) the criterion that the effective quantum number be large is not satisfied. For this reason the resonances seen in photodetachment just above threshold are simply the cyclotron (or Landau) pattern with a spacing of $\hbar\omega$. This is to be contrasted with photoionization of a neutral atom where one first has the $\frac{3}{2}\hbar\omega$-spaced resonances which gradually merge only higher up in energy into the Landau $\hbar\omega$ pattern. A recent photodetachment experiment[4] has, in fact, seen such Landau resonances just above threshold [The short range attraction should reduce the $\hbar\omega$ separation by about .2%]. They have also observed and accounted for another interesting effect of the external field, this time on the threshold law. The usual Wigner threshold law for s-wave photodetachment, $\sigma \propto E^{1/2}$, is modified in the presence of an external magnetic field to $\sigma \propto E^{-1/2}$. We note that were we to ask a similar question for the threshold law for photoionization of a neutral atom, no such change takes place. With or without a magnetic field, the cross-section has a finite value at threshold.

The experiments on neutral atoms in external fields have all so far been photoabsorption studies. The near-zero-energy equally spaced resonances should also show up, of course, in collision cross-sections of very low energy electrons with positive ions in the presence of external fields and in angular distributions of photoelectrons. These remain to be explored.

This work has been supported by NSF Grants PHY76-05721 and PHY78-08432 and by the Alfred P. Sloan Foundation. The work was carried out during a stay at Yale University. I thank the members of the Physics Department for their hospitality.

1. A.R.P. Rau, J. Phys. B Letter, to appear (1979).

2. K.T. Lu, F.S. Tomkins and W.R.S. Garton, Proc. R. Soc. Lond. A362, 421 (1978) and references therein.

3. R.R. Freeman, N.P. Economou, G.C. Bjorklund and K.T. Lu, Phys. Rev. Lett. 41, 1463 (1978).

4. W.A.M. Blumberg, W.M. Itano and D.J. Larson, Phys. Rev. A19, 139 (1979).

ELECTRON-HYDROGEN COLLISION IN THE PRESENCE OF CIRCULARLY POLARIZED COHERENT RADIATION

H.G.P. LINS DE BARROS

Centro Brasileiro de Pesquisas Físicas, Rio de Janeiro, RJ, Brasil

and

H.S. BRANDI

Departamento de Física, Pontifícia Universidade Católica
Rio de Janeiro, RJ, Brasil

In this work we consider electron-hydrogen atom collision in the presence of a circularly polarized laser field and compare our present results with those obtained for the case of linearly polarized light[1].

Under an appropriate space-translation transformation[1] the Hamiltonian of the system e-H for circular polarization is ($\hbar = c = 1$):

$$H = H_o + \frac{p_1^2}{2m} - \frac{e^2}{|\vec{r}_1 + \vec{\alpha}(t)|} + \frac{e^2}{r_{12}}$$

with $\quad H_o = \frac{p_2^2}{2m} - \frac{e^2}{|\vec{r}_2 + \vec{\alpha}(t)|} \quad$ and $\quad \vec{\alpha}(t) = - \frac{e\,\vec{E}(t)}{m\,\omega^2}$

ω is the frequency and $\vec{E}(t)$ is the electromagnetic field, i.e.:

$$\vec{E}(t) = E_o(\hat{x}\cos\omega t + \hat{y}\,\text{sen}\,\omega t)$$

We assume the dipole approximation for the laser field.

Treating $\vec{\alpha}(t)$ as a perturbation parameter, the bound wave function for the hydrogen atom is given, in first-order time-dependent perturbation theory, by:

$$\phi^{(1)}(\vec{r}_2,t) = \phi_n^{(o)}(\vec{r}_2,t)\,e^{i\rho_n(\cos\omega t + \text{sen}\,\omega t)}$$

For the first excited state of hydrogen (n=2) $\rho_2 = e^3 E_o / 2m\,\omega^3$.

The scattering amplitude (S.A.) in the Born-Oppenheimer approximation (B.O.A.) is obtained using Green's function formalism[1,2]. If we neglect the contribution of the one-particle potential in the exchange part of the S.A. we obtain a modified B.O.A., similar to that obtained by Ochkur[3].

For the case of excitation of the n hydrogen state from the ground state with absorption (or emission) of $|\nu|$ photons the ratio between the differential (or total) cross section for circularly and linearly polarized field is:

$$R = J_\nu^2 \ (\sqrt{2} \ \rho_n)/J_\nu^2 \ (\rho_n) \tag{1}$$

Figure 1 shows R as a function of $\rho_2(=e^3 E_o/2m \ \omega^3)$. For high frequencies or low intensities of the laser field, $R \approx 2^{|\nu|}$. These results show that excitation from the ground state to the first excited state of hydrogen by electron impact with absorption (or emission) of $|\nu|$ photons are more probable for the case of circularly polarized laser fields.

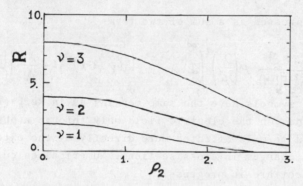

Figure 1: Ratio R defined by eq.(1) as a function of ρ_2 for some values of ν.

1 - Brandi, H.S., Koiller, B, Lins de Barros, H.G.P., to be published in the Phys. Rev. A.

2 - Brandi, H.S., Koiller, B., Lins de Barros, H.G.P., Miranda, L.C. and Castro, J.J. -1978, Phys. Rev. A17, 1900-1906.

3 - Ochkur, V.I. - 1966, Soviet. Phys. JETP 18, 503-508.

ELASTIC ELECTRON-HYDROGEN COLLISIONS IN ELECTRIC FIELD IN EIKONAL APPROXIMATION

C. Foglia

Sezione Teorica, Istituto di Fisica dell'Università e
Gruppo Nazionale Struttura della Materia del C.N.R.
43100 Parma- Italy

Elastic collisions of electrons by hydrogen atoms in a weak electric field are studied in eikonal approximation.

The scattering amplitude[1]

$$T_{f,i} = - \frac{m}{2\pi \hbar^2} \int e^{i \vec{q} \cdot \vec{R}} \, V(R, R', E) \, \Gamma(R, E) \, u_f^*(\vec{r}) \, u_i(\vec{r}) \, d\vec{r} \, d\vec{R}$$

can be expressed as a sum of two terms

$$T_{f,i} = - \frac{2mce^2}{\pi \hbar^2 \, \Gamma(i\eta)} \, \mu \left(\frac{\partial}{\partial \mu^2} \right)^2 \int_0^\infty d\lambda \, \lambda^{-i\eta-1} \int_0^1 d\chi \, (1-\chi)^{-1} \left\{ 1 - \frac{\lambda \chi}{\Lambda} \right\} \left\{ I^{(1)} + I^{(2)} \right\}$$

where the symbols have the same meaning as in Ref. (1). The first term depends on the electric field only through a phase factor. The second term is affected more directly by the external field and bears changes in cross sections. Numerical calculations on this subject are in progress.

1. C. Foglia, Phys.Lett. 65A (1978) 99.

ABSOLUTE MEASUREMENTS OF THE ION YIELD FROM LASER-INDUCED COLLISIONS
IN Na VAPOR AT RESONANCE

F.ROUSSEL, P.BREGER, G. SPIESS, C. MANUS
Service de Physique Atomique
Centre d'Etudes Nucléaires de Saclay
B.P. n°2- 91190 Gif-sur-Yvette,France

Anomalous ionization effects have been recently observed when a laser irradiates an alkali vapor at resonance /1-5/ Lucatorto and McIlrath /1/ have reported almost complete ionization of dense Na and Li vapors ($n \sim 10^{16}$ cm^{-3}) with a 1 MW/cm^2 pulsed laser.

We have also observed intense ionization and we have studied the variation of the ion yield of Na in the density range $10^{12} - 10^{15}$ cm^{-3} when the vapor, contained in a cell 10cm long, is irradiated by a Chromatix CM X-4 dye laser working with Rhodamin 6 G at $\lambda = 5890$ Å ($3P_{3/2}$ resonant line). The light pulses are $\sim 1 \mu s$ long. The laser light (spectral width : 70 GHz) is focussed in the cell to a 0.2 mm^2 cross-section where the full laser line intensity is $I_M = 3 \times 10^5$ W/cm^2. Neutral density filters can be used to reduce I down to 10^2 W/cm^2. The ions are not mass analysed and are detected with a 9V bias voltage applied between two plates 4mm apart in the cell. For $n > 10^{14}$ cm^{-3} the ion yield is sufficient to produce a deviation on a Keithley 602 electrometer. Typically 10^{12} ions per light pulse are collected for $n = 3.1 \times 10^{14}$ cm^{-3}, $I = I_M$. The effective illuminated vapor volume is estimated to be 5×10^{-3} cm^3. Trapping of radiation is observed in the vicinity of the light beam path. Tuning the laser to the $3P_{1/2}$ resonance does not change significantly the ion yield, showing that mixing of the sublevels of Na (3p) occurs. For $I = I_M$ the ion yield exhibits a quadratic dependence with n up to 10^{13} cm^{-3}. Thus there is evidence of a seeding collisional ionization process we discuss later on. For $n > 10^{13} cm^{-3}$ a steeper dependence ($\sim$ power 4 law) is observed while the electron temperature of the created plasma, measured with a Langmuir probe, increases by a factor 2.5, suggesting we are in presence of superelastic collision effects e-Na (3p) predicted by Measures /6/. At still higher n ($n \sim 10^{15} cm^{-3}$) the ion yield saturates due to the strong absorption of the laser light before reaching the zone of detection. The I dependence of the low density ion yield is found to be linear down to 4×10^4 W/cm^2 and quadratic at lower I. A piezo electric Perot-Fabry etalon was used to investigate the absorption profile of the laser light by the Na vapor. At $n = 10^{12}$ cm^{-3} significative absorption occurs only in a 3 GHz spectral width corresponding to the Doppler broadened line of the transition Na (3s)-(3p). The measured

absorption coefficient in the center of this line is found to be 3 orders
of magnitude lower than the low intensity theoretical value, showing high
transmission of the vapor and probable associated saturation effects in the
studied I range. Einstein coefficients considerations predict saturation
for $I > 200$ W/cm^2. When n increases an absorption of the whole of the laser
light is superimposed to the narrow atomic absorption line, prooving that
photon absorption from Na (3p) occurs with at least a 70 GHz spectral width.
We conclude that a non resonant laser induced collisional process is mainly
responsible for the ion yield at $n < 10^{13}$ cm^{-3}. The laser induced process
studied by Geltman /7/

$$Na\ (3p) + Na\ (3p) + h\nu \rightarrow Na^+ + Na + e$$

interprets correctly our n dependence and the high intensity I dependence,
but the calculated cross-section is several orders of magnitude too low to
explain the present ion yield, even when is taken into account the correction due to the spectral width of our laser. The associative ionization
process suggested by Hellfeld et al /5/.

$$Na\ (3p) + Na\ (3p) \longrightarrow Na_2^+ + e$$

with an estimated cross-section of 10^{-17} cm^2 could explain our high ion
yield by taking into account the volume where trapping of radiation occurs,
but it is not in agreement with our observed I dependence. The sum of our
data is rather consistent with a two photon ionization process between
colliding atoms. The formation of a resonant pseudo-molecular intermediate
state Na_2^* at a radiative crossing point, followed by photoionization, is
suggested as a competitive ionization channel. Analysis of the data is
presently pursued in this line and will be available at the Conference time.

/1/ - T.B. LUCATORTO and T.J. McILRATH
      Phys. Rev. Let., 37, 428 (1976)

/2/ - G.H. BEARMAN and J.J. LEVENTHAL
      Phys. Rev. Let., 41, 1227 (1978)

/3/ - M. ALLEGRINI,T.G. ALZETTA, A.C. KOPYSTYNSKA, L. MOI and G. ORRIOLS
      Opt. Commun., 19, 96 (1976)

/4/ - T.J. McILRATH and T.B. LUCATORTO
      Phys. Rev. Let., 38, 1390 (1977)

/5/ - A.V. HELLFELD, J. CADDICK and J. WEINER
      Phys. Rev. Let., 40, 1369 (1978)

/6/ - R.M. MEASURES
      J. of Appl. Phys., 48, 2673 (1977)

/7/ - S. GELTMAN
      J. Phys. B, Atom. Molec. Phys. 10, 3057 (1977)

THE SCATTERING OF LIGHT BY COLLISIONALLY INTERACTING PAIRS OF ATOMS.[*]

<u>Lothar Frommhold</u> and Michael H. Proffitt
Physics Department and Electronics Research Center,
University of Texas at Austin, Texas, 78712

Two helium (or neon, argon,..etc.) atoms acquire during a collisional encounter certain new, "molecular" properties, which contain much information about their interaction that can be obtained by measurement. Collisional pairs ("diatoms") feature, for example, a polarizability, which is very different from the sum of the atomic polarizabilities. The invariants of this diatom polarizability tensor can be measured by rather conventional Raman spectroscopy: the polarized spectrum is directly related to the trace (i.e. the spherically symmetric part of the diatom polarizability), and the depolarized spectrum is similarly given by its anisotropy. Whereas the collision-induced depolarized spectra of Ar, Kr, Xe etc. diatoms have been known for some time[1], measurements of polarized spectra of the He and Ne diatom are reported for the first time, along with measurements of their depolarized spectra[2]. These new results are of interest especially for helium, since efforts are being made elsewhere to compute the diatom properties from first principles. Measurements of this kind provide a most desirable test of such ab initio computations, which apparently are rather involved.

Typically, the Raman spectra are obtained in the conventional 90°-scattering geometry, and with double monochromators with holographic gratings. Gas pressures are $\approx$ atmospheric. With the help of a half-wave plate, the electric vector of the linearly polarized incident beam (≈ 1 Watt at usually 4880 or 5145 Å) is oriented either parallel or perpendicular to the direction of observation, which gives rise to signals $S_{\parallel}(\omega)$ and $S_{\perp}(\omega)$, respectively. These are nearly exponential continua, whose intensities at all shifts ω vary as the square of the gas density, owing to their diatomic origin. Absolute intensities are determined relative to certain Raman nitrogen lines of known intensities. From these signals, the polarized and depolarized spectra of helium and neon are obtained on an absolute scale. (In the case of the heavier rare gases, the depolarized spectra are too weak to be recorded.)

For comparison, spectra were also computed with the help of a rigorous wave-mechanical formalism[1]. Collision-induced scattering can be understood as the Raman scattering process of diatoms. Trace and anisotropy of the diatom polarizability, which are functions of the internuclear separation, give rise to certain nonvanishing matrix elements (Raman transitions), with the usual selection rules for diatomic molecules: $J \rightarrow J$ for the polarized, and $J \rightarrow J$, $J\pm2$ for the depolarized spectrum. Nuclear wavefunctions of the free atoms are obtained by numerical integration of the Schrödinger equation, using the best semi-empirical interatomic potential functions known as input; the wavefunctions are energy-density normalized. Matrix elements can then be computed, if a "model" of the trace or anisotropy function is available (say: from ab initio calculations). Upon summation over all partial waves, energies etc., the resulting theoretical spectra can directly be compared with the shape and intensity of the observed spectral distribution functions. In this way, the theoretical diatom models are tested by experiment.

At the time of this writing, preparations are being made to also measure the two collision-induced spectra of ^{3}He, the rare isotope of helium, for comparison with the fundamental theory. Due to its half-integer spin, the light scattering properties are largely determined by the partial waves with odd angular momentum, whereas for the common isotope pair only the even angular momenta are allowed. It is hoped that this work can be fully discussed at the meeting, along with the complete overview of the collision-induced rare gas spectra.

*The support of the Robert A. Welch Foundation, and of the Joint Services, Electronics Program, is gratefully acknowledged.

1. L. Frommhold, K.H. Hong, M.H. Proffitt, Molec. Physics 35, 665 (1978);

2. L. Frommhold, M.H. Proffitt, J. Chem. Phys., May 15, 1979.

LASER-ASSISTED REARRANGEMENT COLLISIONS[o]

G. Ferrante[+], E. Fiordilino[+] and C. Leone[++]

[+]Istituto di Fisica dell'Università
Via Archirafi 36, 90123 Palermo Italy
[++]Istituto di Fisica della Facoltà di Ingegneria
Parco d'Orleans, 90125 Palermo Italy

A treatment of rearrangement collisions in the presence of a laser radiation field based on the first order time dependent perturbation theory (First Born Approximation) is presented. The case is considered when a structureless projectile collides with a one electron target atom, and as a result the atomic electron is captured into a bound state around the projectile. The laser radiation field is taken in the dipole approximation as $\underline{A}(t)=\underline{A}_o\cos\omega t$. As the perturbation causing the rearrangement are taken the projectile-target atom coulomb interaction. Thus the initial and final unperturbed states are those of the relative motion and of the atom, both embedded in the laser field. Choosing the wavefunction of the atomic electron in the laser field as proposed by Kowarski and Perelman[1] in the case of l-degenerate states, or as proposed by Keldish[2], when degeneracy is absent or neglect, for the unperturbed states we write

$$|\alpha\rangle = \exp(i\underline{K}_\alpha\cdot\underline{R}_\alpha)\,\varphi_\alpha(\underline{r}_\alpha)\,\exp\left[-\frac{i}{\hbar}\widetilde{E}_\alpha t + i\lambda_\alpha\sin\omega t - i\rho_\alpha\cos\omega t\right], \qquad (1)$$

$$(\alpha=i,f),\quad \lambda_\alpha = Q_\alpha(\underline{K}_\alpha\cdot\underline{A}_o)/M_\alpha c\omega;\quad \widetilde{E}_\alpha = E_\alpha + \frac{\hbar^2 K_\alpha^2}{2M_\alpha}.$$

In Eq. (1) ρ_α is the coefficient of the phase factor modulating the bound electron[1,2]; Q_α and M_α are the reduced charge and mass related to the relative motion before ($\alpha = i$) and after the collision ($\alpha = f$). The other simbols have the meaning usual in the field-free rearrangement collision theory[3].

Using Eq. (1), expanding the phase factor containing $\sin\omega t$ and $\cos\omega t$ into an infinite series of Bessel functions, performing the required time integration, the first order S-matrix element is obtained as

$$\langle f|S^{(1)}|i\rangle = -(2\pi i)\sum_{N=-\infty}^{\infty}(-1)^N \exp(-iN\eta)\,J_N(-\beta)\,\delta(\tilde{E}_f-\tilde{E}_i-N\hbar\omega)\,V_{fi}\,, \quad (2)$$

where $\beta = [(\lambda_f-\lambda_i)^2+(\ell_f-\ell_i)^2]^{1/2}$, $tg\,\eta = (\ell_f-\ell_i)/(\lambda_f-\lambda_i)$,
V_{fi} is the Born Approximation spatial matrix element[3], with K_f gi-
ven by the energy conserving delta function, and J_n is the Bessel
function.

Continuing in the usual way, for the total cross section the
following expression is arrived at

$$\sigma_{if} = \sum_{N=-\infty}^{\infty}\frac{M_f M_i}{(2\pi\hbar^2)^2}\left(\frac{K_f}{K_i}\right)\int_{\Omega}J_N^2(-\beta)\,|V_{fi}|^2\,d\Omega \qquad (3)$$

From the energy conserving delta function, Eq. (2), it is easy
to see that an interesting consequence of the presence of a laser
radiation field is that the field may act to change a non resonant
process into a resonant one. This feature may be of help in obtaining
population inversions in the appropriate physical situations. From
β , on the other hand, it may be concluded that in collisions
involving heavy projectiles, the laser field assists the collision
essentially by modifying the bound energy levels.

°Partially supported by GNSM-CNR and CRRNSM.

1. V.A. Kovarski and F. Perelman, Sov. Phys. Jetp 34,
    738 (1972).

2. L.V. Keldish, Sov. Phys. JETP 20, 1307 (1965).

3. A.S. Davydov, Quantum Mechanics (Pergamon Press,
    Oxford, 1976).

CHARGED PARTICLE SCATTERING IN THE PRESENCE OF
A MAGNETIC AND A LASER FIELD[+]

G. Ferrante, S. Nuzzo and M. Zarcone

Istituto di Fisica dell'Università
Via Archirafi, 36, 90123 Palermo, Italy

Charged particle scattering by a potential $V(r)$ and assisted
by a quantizing magnetic field and a laser field, both directed a-
long the z axis is studied in the first-order time-dependent perturbation theory. The magnetic field is chosen to be homogeneous and
constant, while the laser field is taken in the dipole approxima-
tion as $\underline{A}_L(t) = \underline{A}_0 \cos \omega_0 t$. As the static potential $V(r)$ is taken as the
only perturbation causing the transition, the unperturbed states
of the charged particle undergoing the scattering are those of a
free particle embedded in a magnetic and in a laser field.

The wavefunctions corresponding to the unperturbed states are
exactly known, and are given by products of two wavefunctions, one
corresponding to the motion of a free particle moving in the z direction and embedded in a laser field, the other corresponding to
a two dimensional harmonic oscillator in the xy plane and accounting
for the spiralling motion of the free particle induced by the quantum numbers n and S, n identifying the n-th Landau level[1].

Starting from the first-order S-matrix element the total transition probability and the total cross section from a particular
initial state with quantum numbers $(m_i k_i)$ and S_i unspecified to all
the allowed final states are obtained as

$$P_{TOT} = \frac{m}{\hbar^3 k_f} \sum_{S_i m_f S_f} \sum_{\ell=-\infty}^{\infty} J_\ell^2 (\lambda_{fi}) |\langle m_f S_f k_f | V | m_i S_i k_i \rangle|^2 \tag{1}$$

and

$$\sigma_{TOT} = \frac{m^2}{\hbar^4 k_i k_f} \sum_{S_i m_f S_f} \sum_{\ell=-\infty}^{\infty} J_\ell^2 (\lambda_{fi}) |\langle m_f S_f k_f | V | m_i S_i k_i \rangle|^2 \tag{2}$$

with K_f given by

$$K_f = \pm \left[K_i^2 + \frac{2m}{\hbar^2} (m_i - m_f) \hbar \omega_c + \frac{2m}{\hbar^2} \ell \hbar \omega_0 \right]^{1/2}, \tag{3}$$

the positive values corresponding to transmission while the negative ones to reflection. In Eq.s (1)-(3) J_ℓ are Bessel functions, $\lambda_{fi} = -e(K_f - K_i) A_0 / m c \omega_0$; $\langle m_f s_f K_f | V | m_i s_i K_i \rangle$ is the laser field-free spatial matrix element, and it is exactly calculated for screened coulombic, pure coulombic and exponential potentials[2,3]; ω_c is the cyclotron frequency. From Eq. (3) it is seen that at the zeros of K_f, P_{TOT} and σ_{TOT} exhibit resonant behavior, and that the simultaneous presence of a laser and a magnetic field give rise to a rich variety of cases, which may do K_f to vanish. On the other hand, multiphoton inverse bremsstrahlung is also possible, even accompanied by excitation of Landau levels.

[+]Partially supported by GNSM-CNR and CRRNSM

1. A.A. Sokolov and I.M. Ternov, Synchrotron Radiation (Pergamon, New York, 1968).

2. J. Ventura, Phys. Rev. A9, 3021 (1973).

3. G. Ferrante, S. Nuzzo, M. Zarcone and S. Bivona: "S-matrix formulation of charged particle scattering in the presence of a quantizing magnetic field" Submitted to J. Phys. B.

COLLISIONS OF HIGH RYDBERG ATOMS WITH
NEUTRAL ATOMS OR MOLECULES.

E. de PRUNELE and J. PASCALE

Service de Physique Atomique, Centre d'Etudes Nucléaires de Saclay
B.P. N° 2, 91190 GIF-sur-YVETTE (France).

A semiclassical model is proposed[1] for the calculation of the total (elastic + inelastic) cross section for collisions of high Rydberg atoms with neutral perturbers. It is based on the assumption that the electron perturber interaction is of very short range compared with the mean radius of the Rydberg atom. It uses data on total cross sections for the scattering of a free electron by the perturber to express the quasi-free behaviour of the Rydberg electron, in the atomic core field, with respect to the perturber. The originality of the model is, for a given impact parameter b, to relate directly the collision probability to the spatial probability density of the Rydberg electron. The two cases (a) $\langle \mathcal{V}_e \rangle_{nl} \gg 1$ and (b) $\langle \mathcal{V}_e \rangle_{nl} \ll 1$ have been considered; $\langle \mathcal{V}_e \rangle_{nl}$ is the quantal mean value of the velocity of the Rydberg electron in the state n, l, m and V the velocity of the perturber relative to the atomic core. In case (a) which corresponds to usual cell-type experiment conditions, a compact expression has been obtained for the total cross section. It involves a dimensionless parameter chosen equal to unity; this choice is justified a posteriori by comparison with experimental data. In order to avoid a rather costly numerical average of the cross section over all orientations of the collision plane relative to a space-fixed coordinate frame, upper and lower limits of the cross section have been derived:

$$Q_{nl}^{upper}(V) = 2\pi \int_c^\infty b \left\{ 1 - \exp\left[-\frac{4}{V} \langle \mathcal{V}_e \rangle_{nl} \langle \overline{\sigma_e} \rangle_{nl} \frac{1}{4\pi} \int_{-\infty}^{+\infty} \mathcal{R}_{nl}^2(\sqrt{b^2+s^2})\,ds \right] \right\} db$$

$$Q_{nl}^{lower}(V) = 2\pi \int_c^\infty \frac{b}{2l+1} \left\{ 1 - \exp\left[-\frac{4}{V} \langle \mathcal{V}_e \rangle_{nl} \langle \overline{\sigma_e} \rangle_{nl} \frac{2l+1}{4\pi} \int_{-\infty}^{+\infty} \mathcal{R}_{nl}^2(\sqrt{b^2+s^2})\,ds \right] \right\} db$$

$\langle \overline{\sigma_e} \rangle_{nl}$ is the cross section for the electron-perturber scattering averaged over the quantal distribution of velocities of the Rydberg electron; and $\mathcal{R}_{nl}$ is the normalized radial wavefunction.

The model has been applied to the calculation of cross sections for collisions of quasi-hydrogenic (nl) levels of alkali atoms by rare gas atoms or N_2 molecule. In order to compare with experimental data on the quenching of n^2D levels of Na[2] and n^2F levels of Rb[3] a statistical estimation of the elastic collisions has been done. The results are in satisfactory agreement with all the experimental results for about $n \gtrsim 10$ [1]. Table 1 shows some results for Rb (nf) colliding with He, Ar and Xe. Details of the theoretical model and comparisons to experimental and other theoretical works will be presented and discussed at the conference.

REFERENCES

1   E. de Prunelé and J. Pascale, J. Phys.B: Atom Molec Phys 1979 (to appear).

2   T.F. Gallagher, S.A. Edelstein and R.M. Hill, Phys. Rev. A15 1945 (1977).

3.   M. Hugon, F. Gounand, P.R. Fournier and J. Berlande, J. Phys. B: Atom Molec. Phys. 1979 (to appear); see also abstract to this conference.

Table I. Quenching cross sections (in $10^{-13} cm^2$) for Rb (nf) colliding with He, Ar and Xe. T present work (upper and lower limits); E experiment[3].

n		9	13	17	21
rare gas					
He	T	1.82–1.35	1.32–1.21	0.977–0.959	0.777–0.774
	E	$0.87^{\pm}0.175$	$1.00^{\pm}0.20$	$0.56^{\pm}0.14$	$0.44^{\pm}0.13$
Ar	T	3.00–1.87	3.19–2.80	2.90–2.80	2.60–2.57
	E	$1.30^{+}0.30$	$3.50^{\pm}0.70$	$2.80^{\pm}0.70$	$2.20^{\pm}0.70$
Xe	T	20.3–3.75	49.5–15.5	59.3–32.1	57.0–43.4
	E	$4.6^{\pm}1.40$	$13.0^{\pm}4.0$	$31.0^{\pm}11.0$	$53.0^{\pm}21.0$

DEPOPULATION OF RYDBERG S and D STATES OF RUBIDIUM

IN COLLISION WITH GROUND-STATE RUBIDIUM ATOMS

F.GOUNAND, P.R. FOURNIER and M.HUGON

C.E.N. Saclay, Service de Physique Atomique, BP N° 2, 91190 Gif-sur-Yvette
(France).

The collisional properties of alkali Rydberg states are currently of
large interest, but only few experiments deal with alkali-alkali collisions[1,2]
The knowledge of the corresponding cross-sections is of interest for experi-
mentalists because such collisions are always present in cell-type experiments.
Moreover these collisions provide a good test for the interaction between a
quasi-free electron (the outer electron of the Rydberg atom) and a highly polarizable perturber (ground-state alkali atom). We report here results con-
cerning the quenching of nS ($12 \leqslant n \leqslant 18$) and nD ($9 \leqslant n \leqslant 18$) states of Rb.
The values of the cross-sections are deduced from the measurements of the
effective lifetimes of the corresponding levels as a function of the density
of the ground-state Rb atoms. The nS or nD states are prepared by classical
stepwise excitation. Experiments are performed at T = 520 K. The experimental
set-up is described in ref 3.

Level	Q_{Rb}^{q} (nS)	Q_G
12S	$(1.4 \pm 0.4) \, 10^{-12}$	$1.35 \, 10^{-12}$
14S	$(2.1 \pm 0.5) \, 10^{-12}$	$3.00 \, 10^{-12}$
16S	$(3.9 \pm 1.0) \, 10^{-12}$	$6.00 \, 10^{-12}$
18S	$(7.0 \pm 1.4) \, 10^{-12}$	$1.05 \, 10^{-11}$

Table I: Quenching cross-sections
of nS states of Rb by Rb (5S) atoms.
Q_G values are the geometrical cross-
sections. All values are in cm ^{2}.

Using different pumping shemes and an
appropriate model we have been able to
determine separately (in the case of
D states) both the fine structure
changing cross-section Q_{Rb}^{fs} (nD) (i.e.
$D_{3/2} \rightarrow D_{5/2}$) and the quenching cross-
sections Q_{Rb}^{q} (nD) of the nD state as a
whole. The results are reported in
Tables I and II. It is interesting

to note that the geometrical cross-sections (i.e. $\pi \langle r^2 \rangle$ where the brackets
denote the quantum mechanical average corresponding to the considered state)
give a good order of magnitude of both Q_{Rb}^{q} (nS) and Q_{Rb}^{fs} (nD). This was observed by Deech et al. in the cesium case[1]. The same conclusion holds also for
the Q_{Rb}^{q} (nF) values, which are reported in an other abstract[4]. The Q_{Rb}^{fs} (nD)
values always increase in the investigated range of n, which is not the
case when the perturber is helium[5]. Similar variations of both Q_{Rb}^{fs} (nD) and
Q_{Rb}^{q} (nD) values as a function of n have been observed for lower D states of
cesium[6]. It has been shown that all these results reflects the high polarisa-
bility of the alkali ground-state atom which therefore possesses a large interaction range with Rydberg atom. More detailed comparisons with available
theoretical works will be made at the conference.

Level	Q_{Rb}^{fs} (nD)	Q_{Rb}^{q} (nD)	Q_G
9D	$(7.0\pm3.0)10^{-13}$	$(8.0\pm3.0)10^{-14}$	$7.0\ 10^{-13}$
10D	$(1.0\pm0.2)10^{-12}$	$(2.5\pm1.0)10^{-13}$	$1.2\ 10^{-12}$
11D	$(2.0\pm0.6)10^{-12}$	$(6.0\pm2.0)10^{-13}$	$1.8\ 10^{-12}$
12D	$(2.4\pm0.6)10^{-12}$	$(7.0\pm3.0)10^{-13}$	$2.7\ 10^{-12}$
13D	$(2.9\pm0.5)10^{-12}$	$(7.0\pm3.0)10^{-13}$	$3.9\ 10^{-12}$
15D		$(3.6\pm0.7)10^{-12}$	$7.6\ 10^{-12}$
18D		$(7.1\pm1.4)10^{-12}$	$1.7\ 10^{-11}$

Table II: Collisional cross-sections of Rydberg D states of Rb
by ground-state Rb atoms. All values are in cm^2. Q_G , Q_{Rb}^{fs} and Q_{Rb}^{q}
are defined in the text.

REFERENCES

1/ J.S. DEECH, R. LUYPAERT, L.R. PENDRILL and G.W. SERIES, J. Phys. B 10,
L137 (1977).

2/ F. GOUNAND, P.R. FOURNIER and J. BERLANDE, Phys. Rev. A15, 2212 (1977).

3/ M. HUGON, F. GOUNAND, P.R. FOURNIER and J. BERLANDE, J. Phys.B, to
appear (1979).

4/ M. HUGON, F. GOUNAND, P.R. FOURNIER and J. BERLANDE, Abstract of XI
ICPEAC KYOTO (1979).

5/ M. HUGON, P.R. FOURNIER and F. GOUNAND, Abstract of XI ICPEAC KYOTO (1979).

6/ A.C. TAM, T. YABUZAKI, S.M. CURRY, M. HOU and W. HAPPER, Phys. Rev. A17,
1862(1978).

COLLISIONAL DEPOPULATION OF NON HYDROGENIC S and D

RYDBERG STATES OF RUBIDIUM BY HELIUM

M. HUGON, P.R. FOURNIER and F. COUNAND

CEN/SACLAY, Service de Physique Atomique, B.P. N°2 - 91190 Gif-sur-Yvette (France).

L-mixing processes for quasi-hydrogenic Rydberg levels of alkali atoms in collision with rare gas atoms have been studied by two groups[1,2], while collisions of non-hydrogenic Rydberg states have been the subject of only one study[3]. These levels are well isolated from the others and their quenching cross sections Q^q have been found very small. To reach a better understanding of the quenching process, we have performed extensive measurements of the cross sections Q_{He}^q $(n\ell)$ of highly excited nS $(12 \leqslant n \leqslant 18)$ and nD $(9 \leqslant n \leqslant 15)$ states of rubidium by helium. Besides we have been able to measure the fine structure changing cross sections Q_{He}^{fs} (nD) corresponding to the transitions $nD_{3/2} \rightarrow nD_{5/2}$. The experimental method is reported in ref.4. Our results are shown in tables 1 and 2.

level	Q_{He}^q (nS) (cm^2)
12S	$(1.10 \pm 0.20) \, 10^{-14}$
14S	$(2.05 \pm 0.50) \, 10^{-14}$
16S	$(1.45 \pm 0.40) \, 10^{-14}$
18S	$(3.25 \pm 0.65) \, 10^{-14}$

level	Q_{He}^q (nD) (cm^2)	Q_{He}^{fs} (nD) (cm^2)
9D	$(1.05 \pm 0.20) 10^{-15}$	$(4.70 \pm 1.00) \, 10^{-14}$
10D	$(1.50 \pm 0.50) 10^{-15}$	$(4.00 \pm 1.00) 10^{-14}$
11D	$(2.75 \pm 0.50) 10^{-15}$	$(2.30 \pm 0.50) 10^{-14}$
12D	$(4.50 \pm 1.00) 10^{-15}$	$(1.65 \pm 0.50) 10^{-14}$
13D	$(5.50 \pm 1.00) 10^{-15}$	$(1.30 \pm 0.50) 10^{-14}$
15D	$(1.30 \pm 0.40) 10^{-14}$	

Table 1   Table 2

Both Q_{He}^q (nS) and Q_{He}^q (nD) values are increasing with n, because the final states accessible for the quenching process become closer, when n increases. It should be noticed that the closest final states accessible for the quenching of the nS levels are the degenerate states (n-3)F, G, H,..., while for the nD levels the closest neighbours are the non degenerate (n+2)S levels. Therefore the Q_{He}^q (nS) values are observed larger than the Q_{He}^q (nD) ones, pointing out that the quenching cross section is directly related to the multiplicity of the final accessible states. This is confirmed theoretically using the first Born approximation and the Fermi pseudo-potential : it shows that the nS levels are mainly depopulated to the states (n-3) F,G,H,.... The Q_{He}^{fs}(nD) values are continuously decreasing with n just as the Q_{He}^q (nF) values[5], which is in agreement with the quasi-elastic nature of both ℓ-mixing and fine structure changing processes. It has been also shown that the Q_{He}^{fs} (nD) values are in fair agreement with those derived from the elastic cross sections of the nD levels calculated using the approximation mentioned above. In contrast with a recent suggestion[6] made for the quenching of the lowest nS states of sodium ($6 \leqslant n \leqslant 11$) by He, Ar and Xe (i.e. this process proceeds via the interaction of the Na^+ core with the rare gas atom), all collision processes between He and Rydberg Rb atoms (whatever they involve S, D or F states) proceed via the interaction of the valence electron with the helium atom in the range of n we have investigated ($9 \leqslant n \leqslant 21$).

REFERENCES

1/ T.F. GALLAGHER, S.A. EDELSTEIN and R.M. HILL, Phys. Rev. A15, 1945 (1977).

2/ M. HUGON, F.GOUNAND, P.R. FOURNIER and J. BERLANDE, J. Phys. B, to appear (1979).

3/ F. GOUNAND, P.R. FOURNIER and J. BERLANDE, Phys. Rev. A15, 2212 (1977).

4/ F. GOUNAND, P.R. FOURNIER and M. HUGON, Abstract of XI ICPEAC KYOTO (1979).

5/ M. HUGON, F. GOUNAND, P.R. FOURNIER and J. BERLANDE, Abstract of XI ICPEAC KYOTO (1979).

6/ T.F. GALLAGHER and W.E. COOKE, Bull. Am. Phys. Soc. 23, 1102 (1978).

COLLISIONAL DEPOPULATION OF RYDBERG F STATES OF RUBIDIUM AT THERMAL ENERGIES

M.HUGON, F. GOUNAND, P.R. FOURNIER and J. BERLANDE

C.E.N.SACLAY - Service de Physique Atomique , BP N° 2, 91190 Gif-sur-Yvette (France).

Collisional quenching of Rydberg levels has been measured for the first time over a wide range of principal quantum numbers ($9 \leqslant n \leqslant 21$) and for a wide variety of more or less polarizable perturbers (He, Ar, Xe and Rb ground-state atoms; $\alpha_{He} \sim 5.10^{-3} \alpha_{Rb}$); this has allowed a better understanding of the main parameters leading to the quenching of quasi-hydrogenic levels as well as detailed comparisons with theoretical approaches. We have chosen for this study to consider the highly excited F levels of rubidium. The values of the Q_G (nF) cross-sections (G being the perturber) are deduced from the measurements of the effective lifetimes of the nF level as a function of the density of the perturbing atom. The rubidium atoms are prepared in the nF state by using an original method based on the superradiant properties of Rydberg levels[1]. The experimental set-up is described in ref. 2. All the experiments are performed at T = 520K. We have demonstrated that the main process responsible for the quenching of the (n; l=3) levels is the collisional angular momentum mixing[3] with the neighbouring (n; l > 3) levels. Figs 1 and 2 show the results. The magnitude of the $Q_G(nF)$ values, as well as its variation as a function of n reflects the essential influence of the interaction between the quasi-free outer electron of the Rydberg atom and the perturber. This is clearly demonstrated for the first time for a wide variety of interactions and experimental situations.

In particular the continuous increase observed for both the Q_{Xe}(nF) and Q_{Rb}(nF) values, while Q_{He}(nF) and Q_{Ar}(nF) decrease for n > 10, is well explained by the fact that the (e⁻-Xe) and (e⁻-Rb) interactions are much stronger than the corresponding ones for He and Ar. A new theoretical model developed by de Prunelé and Pascale[4] provides satisfactory agreement with all the results presented here . Besides in the helium case it has been shown that the first Born approximation gives close agreement with the experimental results. More extensive discussions with other available theories will be presented at the conference.

REFERENCES

1/   F.GOUNAND, M.HUGON, P.R.FOURNIER and J.BERLANDE, J.Phys.B12, 547 (1979).

2/   M.HUGON, F. GOUNAND, P.R.FOURNIER and J. BERLANDE,J.Phys.B,to appear (1979).

3/   T.F. GALLAGHER, S.A. EDELSTEIN and R.M.HILL, Phys. Rev. A15, 1945 (1977).

4/   E de PRUNELE and J. PASCALE, J. Phys. B, to appear (1979).

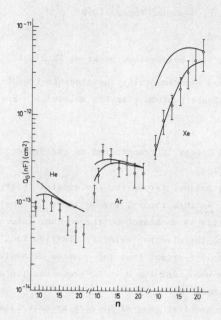

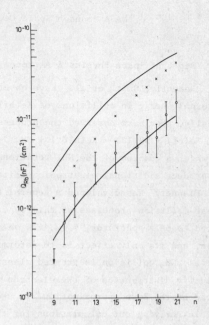

Fig.1- Quenching cross-sections of
rubidium nF levels by He, Ar and
Xe. Solid lines are the upper and
lower limits derived from the theoretical model of ref. 4.

Fig.2- Quenching cross-sections of
rubidium nF levels by ground-state Rb
atoms. Crosses are the geometrical
cross-sections (i.e. $\pi \langle r^2 \rangle$). Solid
lines as in Fig.1.

EXCITATION OF RYDBERG ATOMS BY NH_3 MOLECULES: SEMIQUANTAL THEORY

R. D. Rundel

NASA Johnson Space Center, Houston, Texas 77058

and

Dept. of Space Physics & Astronomy, Rice University, Houston, TX 77001

Recently, Smith et al.[1] have observed experimentally the discrete transfer of internal energy in collisions of Xe(nf) Rydberg atoms with NH_3 molecules. Specifically, they have observed the process

$$Xe(nf) + NH_3(J) \rightarrow Xe(n'\ell') + NH_3(J-1)$$

in which a quantum of the NH_3 rotational energy is transferred to the Rydberg atom to produce additional electronic excitation.

Flannery[2] has developed a general technique, termed the semiquantal theory, to treat collision processes of this type. In this theory, the Xe^+ core is considered to be a spectator, i.e., its velocity is unchanged by the e − NH_3 interaction, and its only effect is to determine the electron velocity distribution. The e − NH_3 collision is treated classically, except that the quantum mechanical velocity distribution of the electron is used, and the e − NH_3 cross section calculated by the Born approximation[3] is assumed.

In carrying out calculations for the specific case of Rydberg atoms colliding with NH_3, careful attention must be paid to the details of the NH_3 rotational levels and their statistical weights. NH_3 is a symmetric top molecule belonging to the point group C_{3v}, and is characterized by an unusually large inversion doubling of the rotational energy levels of 0.66 cm^{-1}.[4] The rotational energies are given by

$$E(J,K) = BJ(J+1) + (A-B)K^2 \pm \Delta/2$$

where J is the total angular momentum, K its projection along the figure axis, Δ is the inversion splitting, and A and B are molecular constants. Selection rules for dipole transitions are $\Delta J = \pm 1$, $\Delta K = 0$, plus symmetry considerations, leading to an energy change ΔE of

$\Delta E = 2BJ - 2\Delta$ K = 0, J odd $\rightarrow$ J even

$\Delta E = 2BJ + 2\Delta$ K = 0, J even $\rightarrow$ J odd

$\Delta E = 2BJ \pm 2\Delta$ K > 0

In addition, rotational levels for which K mod 3 = 0 have twice the statistical weight.

Results for collisions of Xe (31f) Rydberg atoms with NH_3 are presented in Figure 1. In order to provide direct comparison with experiment, the results are presented as reaction rates at 300°K. For the J = 4 $\rightarrow$ 3 and J = 5 $\rightarrow$ 4 transitions, the effects of the inversion doubling are clearly seen. Table 1 presents total rates, i.e., integrated over all final n levels.

Table 1

Reaction Rates for $Xe(31f) + NH_3$ (J) $\to$ Xe (nℓ) + NH_3 (J-1)

J	K
1	4.23×10^{-9}
2	1.02×10^{-7}
3	1.66×10^{-7}
4	1.62×10^{-7}
5	1.37×10^{-7}
Total	$5.61 \quad 10^{-7}$

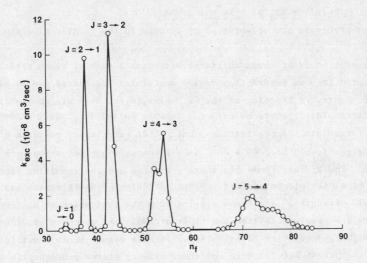

Figure 1.   Reaction rate for $Xe(31f) + NH_3$ (J) $\to$ Xe(nℓ) + NH_3(J-1) as a function of
n.

1.   K.A. Smith, F.G. Kellert, R.D. Rundel, F.B. Dunning and R.F. Stebbings, Phys.
Rev. Lett. 40, 1362 (1978).

2.   M.R. Flannery, Ann. Phys. 79, 480 (1973).

3.   O. H. Crawford, J. Chem. Phys. 47, 1100 (1967).

4.   G. Herzberg, Molecular Spectra and Molecular Structure, Vol. 2, Van Nostrand
Publishing Co. (1966).

COLLISIONS OF Xe (nf) RYDBERG ATOMS WITH AMMONIA†

F.G. Kellert, G.W. Foltz, K.A. Smith, R.D. Rundel,

F.B. Dunning, R.F. Stebbings

Department of Space Physics and Astronomy
Rice University, Houston, TX 77001

In collisions with ammonia three distinct processes[1] lead to the depopulation of a laser excited Xe (nf) state,

ℓ changing collisions

$$Xe(nf) + NH_3 \rightarrow Xe(n\ell') + NH_3$$

n changing collisions

$$Xe(nf) + NH_3(J) \rightarrow Xe(n'\ell') + NH_3(J')$$

and collisional ionization

$$Xe(nf) + NH_3(J) \rightarrow Xe^+ + e^- + NH_3(J')$$

The two latter processes are accompanied by changes in the rotational state of the ammonia.

In the present study of these collision processes a beam of xenon metastable atoms is directed into an interaction region containing NH_3 target gas at pressure of $1 \rightarrow 6 \times 10^{-6}$ torr. A fraction of the $^3P_0$ atoms in the beam are photoexcited to a single, selected Xe(nf) state by use of a tunable pulsed dye laser and then interact with the target gas. Approximately 5 µsec after each laser pulse an electric field, which rises from 0 to 2000 V cm^{-1} in ~ 1 µsec, is applied across its interaction region. The Rydberg atoms are thereby ionized and the resulting electrons are detected by a particle multiplier. Since different Rydberg states ionize at different field strengths,[1] electrons arising from the ionization of different Rydberg states are resolved in time and their arrival time spectrum provides a measure of the Rydberg population distribution. In this manner it is possible to identify both the parent Xe(nf) state and those Rydberg states subsequently populated by collision.

Using this state selective ionization technique we have accurately determined collisional depopulation rates for Xe(nf), $22 \leq n \leq 40$, by measuring the populations of these states as a function of time following laser excitation. Fig. 1 shows the measured rate constants and these are very large, being of the order of 2×10^{-6} cm^3 sec^{-1}.

The rate constants for collisional ionization of Xe(nf) atoms determined by use of a technique described in detail elsewhere[2] are also included in Fig. 1 together with the results of a recent semi-quantal calculation by Rundel.[3] The calculated values are in good agreement with the present data.

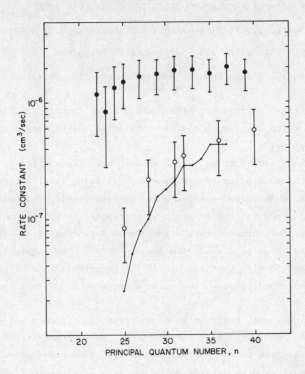

Figure 1: Rate constants for collisional depopulation and collisional ionization
of Xe(nf) atoms.

● collisional depopulation;   Φ collisional ionization;   ———————— calculated
collisional ionization rates.

1. K.A. Smith, F.G. Kellert, R.D. Rundel, F.B. Dunning, and R. F. Stebbings,
    Phys. Rev. Lett. 40, 1362 (1978).

2. G.F. Hildebrandt, F.G. Kellert, F.B. Dunning, K.A. Smith, and R.F. Stebbings,
    J. Chem. Phys. 68, 1349 (1978).

3. R.D.Rundel, private communication.

†Research supported by the Robert A. Welch Foundation, and the National Science
Foundation under contract number PHY 78-09860.

EFFECTS OF BACKGROUND RADIATION ON RYDBERG ATOMS*

E.J. Beiting, G.F. Hildebrandt, F.G. Kellert, G.W. Foltz,

K.A. Smith, F.B. Dunning, R.F. Stebbings

Department of Space Physics and Astronomy, Rice University
Houston, TX 77001

In recent experiments involving high Rydberg atoms in this laboratory, effects have been observed which are due to the interaction of the Rydberg atoms with 300 K background radiation.[1]

In one experiment sodium atoms in a beam were stepwise excited to ns or nd levels by two synchronously pumped dye lasers. Following laser excitation, an ion signal was observed whose time dependence was characteristic of a collision process but whose magnitude was too large to be attributed to collisional ionization by background gas. Furthermore, this signal was independent of the vacuum chamber pressure in the range of 2×10^{-7} to 2×10^{-8} torr. The magnitude of this ion signal, however, agreed with that calculated for photoionization of the Rydberg state by a 300 K blackbody photon flux using a cross section predicted by quantum defect theory.[2]

In a second experiment, designed to study transitions from a well-defined Rydberg state to adjacent levels, a similar effect was observed. Here, $Xe(^3P_0)$ atoms were laser- excited to the 23f state. As discussed previously,[3] the Rydberg population distributions were determined by applying an electric field, which increased from zero to ~ 1000 V/cm in 1 μsec, across the production volume. As the field strength increases, Rydberg atoms in states of successively lower energy are ionized producing an electron arrival time spectrum which is a measure of the excited state distribution. Data of this type, taken 9 μsec after laser fire and at background pressure $\sim 10^{-8}$ torr, are shown in Figure 1. Clearly this spectrum shows significant populations in many levels other than the laser-excited 23f level. Variation of the background gas pressure by an order of magnitude had no observable effect on this signal. The production of these additional states is interpreted as resulting from the photoexcitation of the Xe(23f) atoms by background radiation. A simple model based on atomic hydrogen oscillator strengths and the 300 K blackbody photon number density produces a time-dependent population distribution in good agreement with the experimental data.

The studies of effects due to background radiation are now being extended by shielding the interaction volume with a cold box which permits direct control of the background radiation density. The implications of these measurements will be discussed.

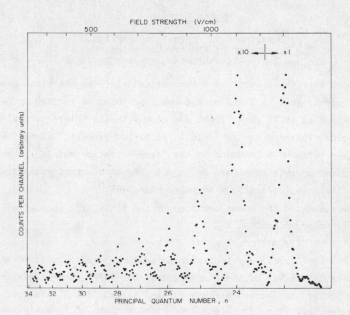

Figure 1: Field ionization spectrum of Xe high Rydberg atoms taken 9 μsec after laser fire. The peak on the right corresponds to the ionization of the laser excited 23f state and those to its left to levels subsequently populated by background radiation. Xenon nf states field ionize at the positions indicated at the bottom of the figure.

1. E.J. Beiting, G.F. Hildebrandt, F.G. Kellert, G.W. Foltz, K.A. Smith, F.B. Dunning, and R.F. Stebbings, J. Chem. Phys., (in press).

2. G. Peach, Mem. R. Astron. Soc. 71, 13 (1967).

3. K.A. Smith, F.G. Kellert, R.D. Rundel, F.B. Dunning, and R.F. Stebbings, Phys. Rev. Lett. 40, 1362.

*Research supported by the Robert A. Welch Foundation, and the National Science Foundation under contract number PHY 78-09680.

STATE-CHANGING COLLISIONS OF HIGH-RYDBERG ATOMS
WITH NEUTRAL SPECIES

Michio Matsuzawa

Department of Engineering Physics,
The University of Electro-Communications,
Chofugaoka 1-5-1, Chofu-shi, Tokyo 182, Japan

We report here the results of a theoretical study on the title processes at thermal energies. This is based on the model in which an excited-Rydberg electron behaves as if it were "free" and slow with its interaction with the neutral species playing a central role in collision process. (Hereafter, for simplicity, we refer to this model as the "free" electron model.) Theoretical results[1,2] based on this model are in good accord with experimental findings, for example, collisional ionization with polar molecules.[3]

We have evaluated the cross sections of the title processes with I) rare-gas atoms and II) polar molecules, ie,

$$A^{**}(n,\ell)+B(\beta) \to A^{**}(n',\ell')+B(\beta'). \tag{1}$$

Here $n(n')$ and $\ell(\ell')$ are the principal quantum number and angular momentum of the initial (final) state of the high-Rydberg atom (A^{**}) repectively and $\beta(\beta')$ specify the set of the quantum numbers of the initial (final) state of the neutral species (B). The "free" electron model enables us to write scattering amplitude f for process (1) in terms of that f_e for scattering of a slow electron by the neutral species (B), ie,

$$e+B(\beta) \to e+B(\beta'). \tag{2}$$

For collisions with the rare-gas atoms, there is no internal degree of freedom, which a thermal electron can excite. Thus we can specify process (2) as elastic scattering. The results calculated for the rare-gas atoms indicate that the cross sections decrease drastically as energy defect $|\Delta E|$ for process (2) increases. Thus, usually, the cross sections for n- (and -ℓ) changing collisions are negligibly small compared with those for ℓ-changing collisions except for accidental resonance. For collisions with $\Delta n = 0$ and $\Delta \ell = 0$, the cross sections are proportional to the ratio of the cross section of elastic scattering for process (2) at zero velocity to the geometrical cross section of A^{**}, ie, proportional to n^{-4}. The ℓ-changing collisions decreases monotonically as n increases. Table I shows the typical results for the ℓ-changing collisions of $Rb^{**}(nf)$ with He and Ar.

For collisions with the polar molecules, we assume the previously proposed mechanism[1,2] for the title processes, ie, energy transfer from the molecular rotation to the Rydberg electron because the polar molecule is in a rotationally excited state at therml energies. Thus process (2) is specified as rotational transition of the polar molecule by the slow electron impact. We have evaluated the cross sections of the title processes with various types of the polar molecules. The calculated results again show that the cross sections decrease

Table I Cross sections for the title processes

Collisions processes	T(K)	$\sigma(cm^2)$
I) $Rb^{**}(21f)+He \rightarrow Rb^{**}(21g)+He$	520	2.92×10^{-15}
$Rb^{**}(21f)+Ar \rightarrow Rb^{**}(21g)+Ar$	520	1.42×10^{-14}
II) $Xe^{**}(27f)+HCl(6) \rightarrow Xe^{**}(68)+HCl(5)$	300	1.14×10^{-12}
$Xe^{**}(27f)+HCl(6) \rightarrow Xe^{**}(71)+HCl(5)$	300	8.80×10^{-14}

Relative velocities are adopted to be $V = (8KT/\pi\mu)^{\frac{1}{2}}$.

drastically as $|\Delta E|$ increases. This has been already shown for the ℓ-changing
collisions with the asymmetric-top molecules.[4] However, in contrast to the
collisions with the rare-gas atoms the cross sections of the n- (and ℓ-)
changing collisions are comparable with those of the ℓ-changing collisions
because process (1) can become resonant due to the energy transfer from the
internal degree of freedom of the molecule, ie, the molecular rotation.[5] Thus
linear and symmetric-top polar molecules with large rotational constants can
cause large n change for $A^{**}(n)$ and selectively excite it into higher excited
states with n'. Table I also shows the typical results for the n- (and ℓ-)
changing collisions of $Xe^{**}(nf)$ with HCl corresponding to the rotational transi-
tion from J = 6 to J = 5. The cross sections attains maximum for $|\Delta E| \approx 0$, ie,
n' $\approx$ 68 for the example given in Table I and decreases drastically as $|\Delta E|$
increases. For example, we have $|\Delta E| = 2.1$ cm^{-1} for n' = 71. De-excitation of
$Xe^{**}(nf)$ is very unlikely due to its low state density at low n which inevitably
leads to the large $|\Delta E|$ for process (1). These results[5] are in agreement with
recent experimental finding.[6]

Details of the present study and its comparison with experiment will be
presented at the Conference.

1. M. Matsuzawa, J. Chem. Phys. 55 2685 (1971), ibid 58 2674 (1973).
2. M. Matsuzawa, J. Electron Spectrosc. Relat. Phenom. 4 1 (1974).
3. R.F. Stebbings, Proc. X ICPEAC ed. by G. Watel (North Holland 1977)
    p 549.
4. M. Matsuzawa, Phys. Rev. A 18 1396 (1978).
5. M. Matsuzawa, Phys. Rev. A in press.
6. K.A. Smith, F.G. Kellert, R.D. Rundel, F.B. Dunning and R.F. Stebbings,
    Phys. Rev. Letters 40 1362 (1978).

DE-EXCITATION OF HIGHLY EXCITED He$(n^{1,3}S)$ BY COLLISIONS WITH RARE GASES

A. Hitachi and T. Doke

Science and Engineering Research Laboratry, Waseda University
Shinjuku-ku, Tokyo 162, Japan

S. Kubota

Department of Physics, Rikkyo University, Nisi-Ikebukuro, Tokyo 171, Japan

C. Davies and T. A. King

Physics Department, University of Manchester, Manchester M13 9PL, U.K.

The total quenching cross sections for He$(n^{1,3}S)$ $(n \leqslant 11)$ states by thermal collisions $(600^{+200}_{-100}K)$ with He, Ne, Ar, Kr, and Xe have been measured. The main quenching mechanism of highly excited states is attributed to the angular momentum transfer,

$$He(nS) + X \rightarrow He(n\ell) + X \qquad (\ell \neq 0) \tag{1}$$

A semiclassical model[1] with a Breit-Fermi pseudopotential has been applied to the calculation of the angular momentum transfer from an ns state to all $n\ell$ states with $\ell \neq 0$ by collisions with rare gases.

The experimental method is similar to that described before.[2] Helium atoms were excited by pulsed electrons of energy close to the energy of ns states and the decays of $nS \rightarrow 2P$ emissions were monitored by single photon counting techniques. The decay rate was obtained as a function of pressure of a perturber X at constant helium pressure, then the quenching cross sections were obtained.

The results are shown in table 1. Those values are of the same order of magnitude as those obtained by Freund et al.[3] for S $\rightarrow$ D transitions. Gallagher et al.[4] have measured cross sections for Na(nD) + X $\rightarrow$ Na(nℓ) + X (2). Their values are of the order of 10^{-13} cm^2 and increase in proportion to the geometrical cross section $(\sim n^4)$ for $5 \leqslant n \leqslant 10$. The values reported here are much smaller than those for process (2) and do not increase in proportion to n^4. The cross sections for the singlet states increase smoothly with n except for the case of Ne, while those for the triplet states have a minimum at n=4~5 for Ar, Kr, and Xe. The cross sections for Ne tend to decrease with n although those for the singlet states begin to increase at n=8. The cross sections for the singlet states are larger than those for the triplet states of the same n (n>5) for X except Ne. The cross sections for n>5 increase in the same order as the magnitude of the scattering length a of the electron, i.e., $a_{Xe} > a_{Kr} > a_{AR} > a_{Ne}$.

The results can be explained as follows. The main quenching mechanism is Penning ionization when $n \leqslant 4$ as the process (1) is expected to be small. For the larger values of n, the Penning ionization cross section will decrease with n increase. Because, in Penning ionization, three particles, He$^+$, e$^-$, and the perturber X have to interact simultaneously, such a process unlikely occurs when

Table 1. The quenching cross sections of $He(n^{1,3}S)$ (in 10^{-16} cm^2)

	Experiment[b]										Theory		
	Singlet					Triplet					Singlet		Triplet
n	He	Ne	Ar	Kr	Xe	He	Ne	Ar	Kr	Xe	He	Ne	He
3	1.3	21[a]	14[a]	16[a]	61[a]	0.1	24[a]	23[a]	24[a]	49[a]			
4	13	10		31	73	15		13	25	84			
5	19	11	29		67	20	11	9	18	59			
6	35	9		67	96	22	11	19	34	64	56		6
7						29	7	20	49	79			23
8	80	20	50	130	170	36	11			100	240	9	35
9						39		70	120				48
10		40			220	48		140				12	59
11						70							

[a] Reference 2.
[b] The typical statistical errors are ±3~8% for n=4 and ±10~20% for n=8. Systematic errors of +15% -8% due to the uncertainty in the determination of the temperature shoud be added.

the electron is far from its nucleus[5] such as a highly excited atom. So, angular momentum transfer should be responsible to the quenching of higher n states. A relatively large energy spread ΔE between ns and $n\ell$ states reduces the cross section significantly. As the spread is narrower in the singlet states, the cross sections for the singlet states are larger than those for the triplet states.

Calculations have been carried out by keeping ΔE as a variable parameter. The calculated values are also shown in table 1. The calculation shows that the contribution from lower values of ℓ is dominant for small values of n (i.e., large ΔE), for the larger n, contributions from higher values of ℓ becomes comparable. The agreement between the theory and the experiment is fairly good for the triplet states, but the theory tends to give larger values than the experimental values by a factor of 2~3 for the singlet states excet for Ne. Further theoretical analysis is needed to fully explain the experimental results.

1. J.I. Gersten, Phys. Rev. A14, 1354 (1976).

2. S. Kubota, C. Davies, and T.A. King, J. Phys. B8, 1220 (1975).

3. R.S. Freund, T.A. Miller, B.R. Zegarski, R. Jost, M. Lombardi, and A. Dorelon, Chem. Phys. Lett. 51, 18 (1977).

4. T.F. Gallagher, S.A. Edelstein, and R.M. Hill, Phys. Rev. Lett. 35, 644 (1975).

5. M. Matsuzawa, private communication.

RELAXATION OF RYDBERG S AND D STATES IN ATOMIC SODIUM PERTURBED BY He, Ne, Ar, Kr, OR Xe*

R. Kachru, T.W. Mossberg, and S.R. Hartmann
Department of Physics, Columbia U., New York, NY   10027

We have performed extensive noble-gas-induced broadening measurements of S-S and $S-D_{3/2}$ two-photon transitions in atomic sodium vapor.[1] Transitions from the 3S ground state to most upper S and D states with principal quantum number n ranging from 4 to 40 have been studied. The collision cross sections are obtained by monitoring the simple exponential decay of the tri-level echo[2] as a function of noble-gas pressure. The Doppler-free character of the tri-level echo technique allows the broadening cross sections to be obtained at low (< 1 Torr) noble-gas pressures. Our measurements, which have been performed with all five noble gases, constitute the first comprehensive survey of the broadening of transitions to high-lying (Rydberg) states which have the same parity as the ground state.

In our experiments the tri-level echo is produced by three collinear (but not parallel) excitation pulses. The first excites the $3S - 3P_{1/2}$ transition, while the second and third excite a particular $3P_{1/2} - nS$ or $3P_{1/2} - nD_{3/2}$ transition. Assume that the times and wavevectors of the excitation pulses and the echo are given by t_i and $\vec{k}_i$, respectively, where i = 1, 2, 3, and e. Assume also that $\vec{k}_2 \| \vec{k}_3$, and that $\vec{k}_1$ and $\vec{k}_2$ are anti-parallel. Then the echo occurs on the $3S - 3P_{1/2}$ transition at the time $t_e = t_1 + (t_3 - t_2)k_2/k_1$ and $\vec{k}_e \| \vec{k}_1$. The echo occurs only if $t_e \geq t_3$, i.e. we must have $(t_3 - t_2) \geq (t_3 - t_1)k_1/k_2$. In our experiments $t_1 \cong t_2$; thus it is necessary that $\vec{k}_2 \geq \vec{k}_1$. The excitation pulses have the following relative linear polarizations: 1(↑), 2(↑), and 3(→). The polarization of the echo depends in general on the angular momenta of the three levels involved, but it usually has a component along (→). The echo can then be detected while using only a Glan-prism polarizer to prevent detector saturation (the Glan-prism blocks the only excitation pulse copropagating with the echo). For fixed t_i, a simple model predicts that the tri-level echo intensity varies with foreign gas pressure P according to[1]

$$I_e(P) = I_o \exp(-\beta P)$$

where

$$\beta = [9.65 \times 10^{18} \, ^\circ K/(cm^3 - Torr)]\frac{2v_r}{T}[\ \sigma_{20} + \sigma_{10}(k_2-k_1)/k_1]\ (t_3 - t_2)$$

Here k_b is Boltzman's constant, $v_r = (8k_bT/\pi\mu)^{1/2}$, T is the absolute temperature, μ is the Na - noble gas reduced mass, and σ_{20} (σ_{10}) is the broadening cross section for the 3S-nS or $3S-nD_{3/2}$ ($3S-3P_{1/2}$) transition.

The values of σ_{20} obtained from our experiments[3] (T = 400 ± 15 K) are shown in Fig. 1 We plot σ_{20} (Å^2) versus the principal quantum number. The most pronounced feature of the data is the fact that σ_{20} reaches a peak and subsequently declines to a lower asymptotic value. Qualitative explanations of this behavior, which has been previously observed in broadening studies of the principal series transitions, have been given. Detailed predictions,[4] however, have only been made for high n where the outer electron and the atomic core can be considered to scatter the noble-gas atom "separately." We will discuss the existing theories in light of our data. The $3S-nD_{3/2}$ broadening cross sections are generally larger than those for the 3S-nS transitions. We attribute this at least partially to the large collisional transfer cross sections between the $nD_{3/2}$ states and the nearly degenerate states of the same n but higher ℓ.[5] The broadening cross sections of Ar, Kr, and Xe start out approximately equal at low n, and they remain so until one by one the broadening cross section due to each gas ceases its increase with n and begins to decrease. In the case of the 3S-nS transitions, in the region where the broadening cross sections of each of Ar, Kr, and Xe are increasing, they are nearly equal to the geometric cross section of the excited Na atom. The small polarizabilities of He and Ne are seen to lead to qualitatively different behavior.

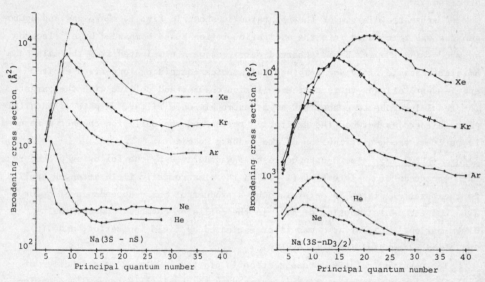

Figure 1

* This work supported by Joint Services Electronics Program under Contract No. DAAG29-77-C-0019 and by the Office of Naval Research under Contract No. N00014-78-C-0517.

1. A. Flusberg, R. Kachru, T. Mossberg, and S.R. Hartmann, Phys. Rev. A 4/79 to be published.

2. T. Mossberg, A. Flusberg, R. Kachru, and S.R. Hartmann, Phys. Rev. Lett. **39**, 1523 (1977).

3. The quantity σ_{10} in the expression for β is independently determined by photon echo measurements. See refs. 1 and 2 for details.

4. A. Omont, J. Phys. (Paris) **38**, 1343 (1977); V. A. Alekseev and I. I. Sobel'man, Zh. Eksp. Teor. Fiz. **49**, 1274 (1965) [Sov. Phys. JETP **22**, 882 (1966)].

5. T.F. Gallagher, S.A. Edelstein, and R.M. Hill, Phys. Rev. A **15**, 1945 (1977).

REACTION OF RARE GAS ATOMS AND HYDROGEN MOLECULES
IN HIGHLY EXCITED RYDBERG STATES. I. COLLISIONAL IONIZATION

H. Hiraishi, M. Uematsu, T. Kondow, T. Fukuyama and K. Kuchitsu

Department of Chemistry, Faculty of Science,
The University of Tokyo, Hongo, Bunkyo-ku, Tokyo 113, Japan

Collisional ionizations of highly excited rare gas atoms (A^{**}) and hydrogen molecules (H_2^{**}) by a polar molecule (H_2O) and SF_6, which has high efficiency for thermal-electron attachment, were investigated. For $Ar^{**} + H_2O$, SF_6 systems the dependence of the ionization cross section σ on the principal quantum number n was obtained, while for $H_2^{**} + H_2O$, SF_6 systems the absolute cross sections were estimated. These data provided information on the mechanism of the ionization processes.

A schematic diagram of the apparatus is shown in Fig. 1. Rare gas and hydrogen gas was introduced into the excitation region E and bombarded by an electron beam crossing the gas beam. Charged particles were eliminated from the main beam by electrostatic field and only neutral species containing long-lived excited species were allowed to reach the collision chamber and collide with the target. The resulting ions were analyzed by a quadrupole mass filter. A pair of parallel-plate electrodes between the excitation region and the collision chamber were used to estimate the n-distribution of the Rydberg species.

1) $Ar^{**} + H_2O$, SF_6— The n-dependence of σ was derived by the following procedure. The dependence of Ar^+ intensity (I_{Ar^+}) on the electrostatic field strength applied to the parallel plates is determined by a product of the n-dependence of σ for Ar^{**} and the n-distribution of Ar^{**} in the collision chamber. Hence, the n-distribution, f(n), of Ar^{**} was first estimated by field ionization, and $\sigma(n)$ was obtained by dividing I_{Ar^+} by f(n).

The observed relative cross section is plotted in Fig. 2 as a function of n together with the cross section calculated on the basis of Matsuzawa's equation.[1] This calculation is based on the mechanism that the Rydberg electron is liberated by rotational deexcitation of the target molecule. The observed cross sections, normalized at n=29 to the calculated values, agree with the latter; this agreement supports Matsuzawa's model.

The same experimental procedure was applied to the SF_6 target, and a relative cross section was obtained for each n. In this case the intensities of both Ar^+ and SF_6^- were analyzed. The dependences of $\sigma(n)$ derived from Ar^+ and SF_6^- were consistent and were weaker than those obtained for the H_2O target. This trend is in line with the model that the Rydberg electron behaves like a free thermal electron and that the ionization by SF_6 is similar to the thermal electron attach-ment to SF_6.

2) Collisional Ionization of H_2^{**}— The intensities of H_2^+ produced by the H_2O target are plotted in Fig. 3 as a function of the electron energy.[2] The threshold energy was determined to be 15.4±0.3 eV. Since the ionization potential of H_2 molecule

is 15.43 eV, the precursor of the observed H_2^+ ions can be ascribed to H_2^{**}. A TOF measurement resulted in the same conclusion.

The cross sections of H_2^{**} and He^{**} in collision with H_2O were determined on a relative basis from the target-pressure dependence. Their absolute cross sections were estimated to be of the same order of magnitude. By use of the known cross section for the process $He^{**} + H_2O \longrightarrow He^+ + H_2O + e$, $(2.9\pm0.5) \times 10^{-13}$ cm^2,[3] the absolute value for H_2^{**} was estimated to be $(3.8\pm1.0) \times 10^{-13}$ cm^2. The cross section for ionization of H_2^{**} by the SF_6 target was also found to be of the same order of magnitude. All the present observations suggest that the ionization processes of H_2^{**} are similar to those of rare gas atoms in high Rydberg states.

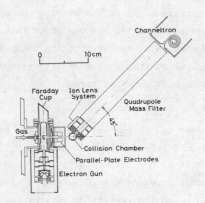

Fig. 1. Apparatus

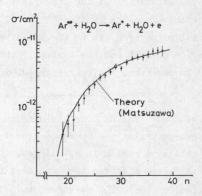

Fig. 2. Experimental and theoretical cross sections for collisional ionization of Ar^{**} with H_2O plotted as a function of n. The observed cross section is normalized at n=29 by use of Matsuzawa's theoretical value.

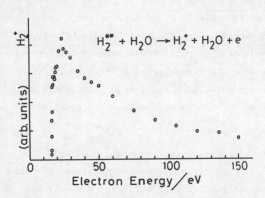

Fig. 3. Excitation function for H_2^{**}

[References]
1) M. Matsuzawa: J. Electron Spectrosc. 4, 1 (1974).
2) H. Hiraishi, T. Kondow, T. Fukuyama and K. Kuchitsu: J. Phys. Soc. Jpn. 46, 1628 (1979).
3) H. Hotop and A. Niehaus: J. Chem. Phys. 47, 2506 (1967).

REACTION OF RARE GAS ATOMS AND HYDROGEN MOLECULES IN HIGHLY EXCITED RYDBERG STATES. II.   REARRANGEMENT IONIZATION

T. Kondow, H. Hiraishi, M. Uematsu, T. Fukuyama, and K. Kuchitsu

Department of Chemistry, Faculty of Science,
The University of Tokyo, Hongo, Bunkyo-ku, Tokyo 113, Japan

Highly excited Rydberg states of argon atoms (Ar^{**}) were produced by electron impact, and the relative cross sections for rearrangement ionization,

$$Ar^{**} + H_2 \longrightarrow ArH^+ + H + e, \quad \cdots \cdots \quad (1)$$

were measured by mass spectroscopy as a function of the principal quantum number n. The dependence of the cross sections for process (1) on the kinetic energy was determined from the profile of the (TOF) spectrum of Ar^{**}. It was shown that this ionization process can be viewed as being dominated by the interaction between the core ion of Ar^{**} and the target if the principal quantum number of Ar^{**} exceeds 25. In addition, the rearrangement ionization with rare gas targets (A)

$$H_2^{**} + A \longrightarrow AH^+ + H + e \quad \cdots \cdots \quad (2)$$

was studied. The AH^+ ion was detected for A=Ar and Kr but not for A=He and Ne. The energetics of the corresponding ion-molecule reaction showed that the H_2^{**} in the collision region is not vibrationally excited.

A pulsed electron beam was used to produce a pulsed beam of high Rydberg species for their TOF measurements. The width and the repetition rate of the pulse were so chosen as to provide a TOF spectrum of necessary time resolution, typical values being 2 μs and 2.9 KHz, respectively. Further experimental details[1] are given in part I.

Figure 1 shows the relative cross sections for process (1) as a function of n. The cross sections increase with the increase in n and tend to level off around n=25. On the other hand, cross sections for collisional ionization by a polar target (see part I), where the Rydberg electrons play a major role, increase indefinitely with n. The cross section for state-unselected Ar^{**} in collision with H_2 estimated in the present study was about 10^{-14} cm^2, being comparable with the cross section (6×15^{-15} cm^2) for the corresponding ion-molecule reaction,

$$Ar^+ + H_2 \longrightarrow ArH^+ + H \quad \cdots \cdots \quad (3)$$

This finding indicates that for n > 25 the rearrangement ionization of Ar^{**} for the production of ArH^+ is essentially governed by the interaction between the core ion of Ar^{**} and the target molecule whereas the influence of Rydberg electrons is significant for lower n.

The TOF spectrum of Ar^{**} was observed by detecting the ArH^+ ions produced in process (1) in order to estimate the dependence of the rearrangement cross sections on the velocity of Ar^{**}. The TOF spectrum thus obtained is shown in Fig. 2, where the broken curve is calculated under the assumption 1) that the velocity of Ar** follows a modified Maxwell-Boltzman distribution at 330K and 2) that the cross section is inversely proportional to the velocity. A calculated spectrum for the Maxwell-Boltzman distribution at 330K is also shown by a solid curve. The TOF measurements support that the cross sections for process (1) is inversely proportional to the velocity of Ar**. This velocity dependence was also suggested by the TOF profile for process (1); it was nearly identical with that for the collisional ionization by a polar target, where Matsuzawa's theory predicts v^{-1} dependence.

The H_2** (or D_2**) produced by electron impact was allowed to collide with He, Ne, Ar and Kr. Ions of the AH^+ and A^+ types were observed clearly when A=Ar or Kr was admitted in the chamber. The AH^+ ions were produced via process (2), while the A^+ ions appeared to be produced via a charge transfer process between the core ion and the target atom, being similar to that in the corresponding ion-molecular reaction. The excitation functions for the production of the A^+ and AH^+ ions confirmed that H_2** was the precursor of these reactions.

No ion signals were detected when He or Ne was used as a target. Since the binding energy of the Rydberg electrons is less than thermal energy, the energies of process (2) can be regarded as essentially that of the corresponding ion-molecular reactions,

$$H_2^+ + He \longrightarrow HeH^+ + H \qquad (v \geq 3)$$
$$H_2^+ + Ne \longrightarrow NeH^+ + H \qquad (v \geq 2) \qquad \cdots\cdots \quad (4)$$
$$H_2^+ + A \longrightarrow AH^+ + H \qquad (v \geq 0) \quad \cdots\cdots \quad (5)$$
$$(A = Ar, Kr)$$

Reactions (4) are reported to be endothermic unless H_2^+ is vibrationally excited, whereas reactions (5) are always exothermic. Therefore, production of HeH^+ or NeH^+ needs vibrational excitation of H_2**. Accordingly, it is likely that only H_2**(v=0) can reach the collision chamber even though nascent H_2** contains vibrationally excited components. This inference is consistent with our present observations.

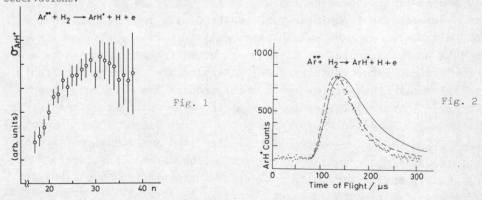

Fig. 1

Fig. 2

1. H. Hiraishi, T. Kondow, T. Fukuyama, and K. Kuchitus, J. Phys. Soc. Japan <u>46</u>, 1628 (1979).

TEMPERATURE DEPENDENCE OF DEPOPULATION RATES IN TRANSITIONS BETWEEN RYDBERG LEVELS OF HELIUM INDUCED BY ELECTRON COLLISIONS

G.Baran,J.Boulmer,F.Devos,and J-C Gauthier

Institut d'Electronique Fondamentale
Universite Paris XI,91405 ORSAY (France)

Recently,we have reported [1,2] measurements of electron-induced collisional transfer rates between Rydberg levels using time-resolved fluorescence spectroscopy.With this method we have been able to study very precisely the variations of the depopulation rate coefficient k_p and the transfer rate coefficient k_{pq} for principal quantum numbers p and q over the range $8 \leq p,q \leq 17$.Similarly,results of k_p for p=10 at electron temperatures varying from $390 \leq T_e \leq 2000°K$ have been obtained. Below 1500°K,experimental values were found in satisfactory agreement (within 35%-see Fig.1)with the Monte-Carlo calculations of Mansbach and Keck [3] and the semi-empirical results of Johnson [4],based on a quantum treatment within the impact-parameter approximation.At higher temperatures,fluorescence signals were extremely weak and the depopulation rate seems to saturate at a value of $1.5 \ 10^{-4} \ cm^3 s^{-1}$,close to the classical result [3] neglecting collisional ionization.

In this paper,we report on an extension of the measurements at much higher electron temperatures with an experimental sensitivity increased by a factor of about four.This work was stimulated by the fact that most of the stepwise excitation and deexcitation processes which form an essential part of collisional-radiative recombination in gas discharges occur at electron energies around or below 1 eV.

The experimental system has been described in detail elsewhere [2]. Briefly,the 10^3P sublevel is reached by direct photoexcitation from the $He(2^3S)$metastable atoms present in sufficient concentration($\approx 10^{11} cm^{-3}$) in a high-purity,room temperature helium afterglow at 2.6 Torr.Electron density and temperature are independently measured and changed by suitable microwave pulses[2].Rate coefficients are obtained from a data analysis procedure already described in Ref.2.Systematic errors are not expected to exceed 30%.Results are shown on Fig.1(dots) together with the earlier results obtained at low electron temperatures [1,2](circles).Theoretical predictions are also exhibited in Fig. 1:the curve labelled MK(for Mansbach and Keck[3])and JOH(for Johnson [4]) correspond to the summation of the calculated individual rates over all levels $j \neq 10$,including the continuum.The dashed line corresponds to the classical MK results neglecting ionization(the contribution of ionization to Johnson rates is negligible over this energy range).

Conclusions are twofold.First,the present results confirm the

detailed analysis made in Refs.1 and 2.They clearly show that no saturation occurs on the depopulation rate above 1500°K(this temperature corresponds exactly to the 10^3P ionization threshold energy).
Second,the experimental data reproduce equally well the functional
dependence of MK and JOH rates on the extended electron temperature
range investigated here.The present results may be useful for the
evaluation of the recombination coefficient and line intensities in
non-equilibrium plasmas sincethey verify and extend the range of validity of standard semi-empirical formulas of electron-induced transfer rates in highly excited atoms.

1.J-F Delpech,J.Boulmerand F.Devos,Phys.Rev.Letters 39,1400(1977)
2.F.Devos,J.Boulmer and J-F Delpech,J.Physique 40,215(1979).
3.P.Mansbach and J.C.Keck,Phys.Rev.181,275(1969).
4.L.C.Johnson,Astrophys.J.,174,227(1972).

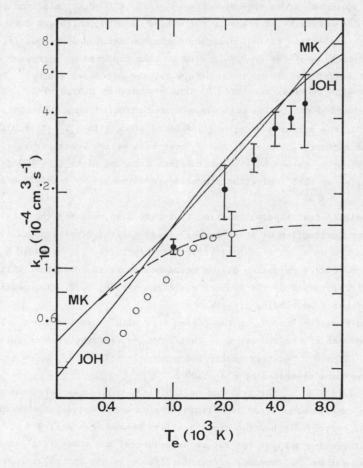

Fig.1 Measured and calculated 10^3P depopulation rate

ELECTRON SCATTERING RESONANCES IN FAST D(HIGH n) COLLISIONS WITH N_2*

Peter M. Koch

Gibbs Laboratory, Physics Dept., Yale University
New Haven, CT 06520 USA

For a highly excited atom X(n>>1) in a fast beam, the ratio of its translational velocity v_T to its most probable orbital velocity v_0 can be v_T/v_0>>1.
Butler and May[1] first predicted that in this limit, the Rydberg electron ionization
cross section σ_I in X(n)-Y collisions at velocity v_T should be n-independent and be
equal to the total scattering cross section σ_e for free electrons with the same
velocity v_T colliding with Y. Matsuzawa[2] and Smirnov[3] have further developed the
theory of X(n)-Y collisions.

To test directly the above prediction, I have measured σ_I for D(high n)+N_2 →
D^++e^-+N_2 (Σ) collisions, where $N_2(\Sigma)$ refers to all possible final states of N_2.
The 6-11 keV D(high n) atoms were produced by D^+-Xe or D^+-C_8F_{16} electron transfer
collisions. The intensity of atoms in the n-band 36≲n≲50, which was defined by a
modulated static electric field ionization technique developed previously,[4] was
measured by detection of the energy-labeled D^+ ions produced by microwave multiphoton ionization of the n-band in a voltage-labeled microwave cavity.[5] The intensity of the energy-labeled, scattered D^+ ions produced by D(high n)-N_2 collisions
in a voltage-labeled scattering cell was measured with the same apparatus.

In Fig. 1, the measured σ_I values are shown along with σ_e.[6] There is obviously reasonable agreement between σ_I and σ_e over most of the energy range. That the
resonance bump in σ_e caused by the intermediate compound state $N_2^-(^2\Pi_g)$ is also
present in σ_I shows that ionization proceeds predominantly by quasi-free e^--
scattering.

In a separate transmission experiment, I have also measured the total cross
section σ_d for destruction of Stark-tuned,[7] laser excited D(n=46) atoms by N_2. The
energy dependence of σ_d in Fig. 1 is strikingly similar to σ_e, although $\sigma_d > \sigma_e$
always. The partial suppression of the resonance peaks is consistent with the
calculated energy spread of the Rydberg e^-, $\Delta E/E \simeq 4v_0/v_T \approx 0.12$. The peaks may be
shifted to higher E by binding effects.

Electron transfer from N_2 to the D^+ ion core with cross section σ_{10}~11$\overset{o}{A}^2$ will
lead to detachment of the Rydberg e^-. That $\sigma_e + \sigma_{10} \approx \sigma_d$ for the present data is
evidence both D^+ and e^- scatter nearly independently off the N_2, which is reasonable since they are separated by $n^2 a_0$~1100 $\overset{o}{A}$.

At E_D = 7.75 keV, σ_d for n=46 and n=71 D(n)-N_2 collisions were measured to be
equal within experimental error, confirming the expected n-independence of σ_d
when v_T/v_0>>1. Precisely how the cross sections behave when n>>1 and v_T/v_0~1
is a very interesting subject for future experimental and theoretical study. One
also wonders whether the Ramsauer effect for free e^--noble gas collisions will

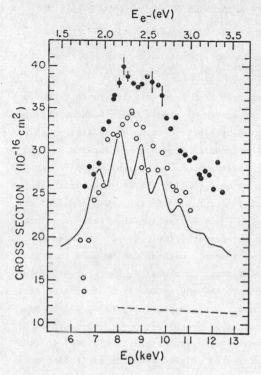

Fig. 1. Present data: open circles, σ_I for $D(35 \lesssim n \lesssim 50)+N_2$; closed circles, σ_d for $D(n=46)+N_2$. Some typical relative error bars are shown. v_T/v_0 ranges from 26 to 36. The N_2 target thickness was measured in each case by using the value for σ_{10} for H^+-N_2 collisions presented in Ref. 8 and shown here as a dashed line. The estimated error in the present absolute cross section scale is <20%. Full line, σ_e for e^-+N_2, Ref. 6.

show up as a minimum in σ_I for fast X(high n)-noble gas collisions.

*Research supported by NSF and A.P. Sloan Foundation.

1. S.T. Butler and R.M. May, Phys. Rev. 137, A10 (1965).

2. M. Matsuzawa, J. Phys. B 10, 1543 (1977).

3. B.M. Smirnov, invited paper IX ICPEAC (Univ. of Wash., 1975), pp. 701-711.

4. J.E. Bayfield and P.M. Koch, Phys. Rev. Lett. 33, 258 (1974).

5. J.E. Bayfield, L.D. Gardner, and P.M. Koch, Phys. Rev. Lett. 39, 76 (1977).

6. D. Mathur and J.B. Hasted, J. Phys. B 10, L265 (1977).

7. P.M. Koch, Phys. Rev. Lett. 41, 99 (1978).

8. P.M. Stier and C.F. Barnett, Phys. Rev. 103, 896 (1956).

DOUBLE-RESONANCE STARK SPECTROSCOPY AS A PROBE OF FAST ATOMIC COLLISIONS*

Peter M. Koch, James B. Bowlin, and David Mariani

Gibbs Laboratory, Physics Dept., Yale University
New Haven, CT 06520 USA

We have very recently developed new fast beam laser-spectroscopic techniques
for production and precise study of Stark states of simple atoms such as hydrogen.[1]
A beam of protons is partially neutralized by electron-transfer collisions in a
gas scattering target. The resultant fast neutral atomic beam contains excited
atoms which may be further excited with laser photons. Externally-applied static,[1]
dynamic,[2] or mixed electric fields F can be used to lift the F=0 degeneracy of the
excited states for improved state definition or to modify the level populations.

Our initial studies have concentrated on understanding the field-atom interactions themselves, particularly in the non-perturbative regime.[1] It is quite
clear, however, that these new laser-spectroscopic methods can be used to measure
relative populations of various excited states. In a weak F, Rayleigh-Schrodinger
perturbation theory can be used to calculate the energy spectrum of excited states,
matrix elements, and rates for transitions. What is possible, then, is the development of a precise tool for the measurement of cross sections for production of
a wide variety of individual Stark substates of hydrogen(or other atoms) in fast
ion-atom electron transfer collsions, atom-atom or electron-atom excitation collisions, or molecular dissociation collisions.

We report the first steps toward the development of this new tool for collision studies. We have developed a laser double-resonance technique to resolve
individual Stark states of H with parabolic quantum numbers $(n, n_1, n_2, |m|)$ that were
produced by 7.51 keV H^+-Xe collisions in F=0. $^{12}C^{16}O_2$ laser 10μ-band R-22 photons
were directed colinear with the atomic beam and were used to drive 1-photon transitions between particular n=7 and n=10 Stark states Stark-tuned into resonance in a
first electric field F_q ~tens of kV/cm and then between n=10 and n=31 Stark states
Stark-tuned into resonance in a second electric field F_p ~hundreds of V/cm. The
laser-produced n=31 atoms were detected by microwave multiphoton ionization.[2]
For example, we have cleanly resolved the transition (7,2,4,0)-(10,1,8,0) at $F_q =$
42.56 kV/cm from the nearly degenerate transition (7,1,3,2)-(10,0,7,2) at $F_q =$
42.62 kV/cm. It will also be possible to resolve $|m|>2$ states if they are produ-
ced in the collision.

For unambiguous cross section determination, it will be necessary to have the
collisions take place in F≠0 and to prevent non-adiabatic transitions between substates. The very exciting possibility exists to study the target specie-, energy-,
and F-dependences of these cross sections, perhaps even in the large-F non-perturbative regime in which calculation of wavefunctions is an unsolved problem. These
and other possibilities will be discussed at the conference.

*Research supported by NSF and A.P. Sloan Foundation

1.   P.M. Koch, Phys. Rev. Lett. <u>41</u>, 99 (1978).

2.   J.E. Bayfield, L.D. Gardner, and P.M. Koch, Phys. Rev. Lett. <u>39</u>, 76 (1977).

CHARGE TRANSFER PROCESSES INVOLVING HIGHLY EXCITED HYDROGEN ATOMS

Nobuyuki Toshima

Institute of Space and Aeronautical Science, University of Tokyo
Komaba, Meguro-ku, Tokyo 153, Japan

We have studied the following charge transfer processes,

$$p + H(n\ell m) \rightarrow H(n'\ell'm') + p, \tag{1}$$

where $(n\ell m)$ denote the usual quantum numbers of the hydrogen atom. We have applied the Born approximation in the high energy region where the incident proton velocity v_p is greater than the orbital electron velocity v_e. Hitherto, several papers have been published which deal with the processes (1) by means of the Born approximation or other versions of the first-order perturbation theory.[1-4] However, they treated only the limited case in which the primary hydrogen atom is in its ground state. May[5] has treated the case in which both the initial and the final hydrogen atoms are highly excited, but he has neglected the internuclear interaction. (i.e. the Brinkman-Kramers approximation.[6])

We have obtained the Born cross sections in closed forms for s-s and s-p transfers.[7,8] In the calculation of the transition matrix elements, we have made use of the sum rules of the atomic wave functions in the momentum space. The calculated cross sections for 8s-3s and 8s-8p transfers are presented in Figs. 1 and 2 together with the Brinkman-Kramers cross sections. The cross sections show oscillatory structures at low energies, which have relation to the nodes of the atomic wave functions in the momentum space. The oscillations of the full Born cross sections are more remarkable than those of the Brinkman-Kramers cross sections. We have also obtained an approximate expression for the cross section averaged over the initial azimuthal and magnetic quantum numbers and summed over the final ones. The averaged cross section does not show oscillatory structures and satisfies a scaling law in the resonant case, that is, $\sigma(n \rightarrow n;E) = n^4 \sigma(1s \rightarrow 1s; n^2 E)$.

In the low energy region $(v_p < v_e)$, we have applied the PSS (Perturbed Stationary State) method to the resonant transfer.[9] Some approximations are employed; the two-state approximation, the classical trajectory with a constant velocity for the relative motion, and the neglect of the overlap integrals. However, we have included the momentum transfer effect of the electron. This effect is found to play a dominant role on the energy dependence of the cross sections in the case of the highly excited states.

Koch and Bayfield[10] have measured the charge transfer cross section for $n \approx 47$. Comparison with the present results is made in Fig. 3. The measured cross section is greater than the calculated cross sections by about a factor of five. This discrepancy comes partly from the contribution of the non-resonant transfer processes which is included in the experimental cross section and partly from the uncertainty of the experimental data.

1. R. Mapleton, Phys. Rev. 126, 1477 (1962).

2. S.T. Butler and I.D.S. Johnston, Nuclear Fusion 4, 196 (1964); R.M. May, ibid. 4, 207 (1964).

3. Y.B. Band, Phys. Rev. A8, 2857,2866 (1973).

4. K. Omidvar, Phys. Rev. A12, 911 (1975).

5. R.M. May, Phys. Rev. 136, A669 (1964).

6. H.C. Brinkman and H.A. Kramers, Proc. Acad. Sci. Amsterdam 33, 973 (1930).

7. N. Toshima, J. Phys. Soc. Japan 46, 927 (1979).

8. N. Toshima, J. Phys. Soc. Japan 46, 1295 (1979).

9. N. Toshima, J. Phys. Soc. Japan (to be published).

10. P.M. Koch and J.E. Bayfield, Phys. Rev. Lett. 34, 448 (1975).

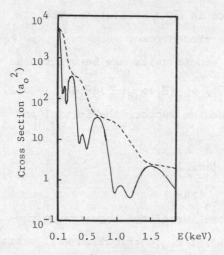

Fig. 1. The Brinkman-Kramers (---) and the Born (——) cross sections for 8s-8s transfer.

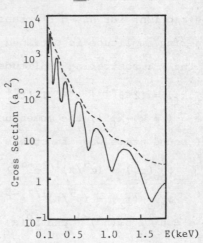

Fig. 2. The same as Fig. 1 but for 8s-8p transfer.

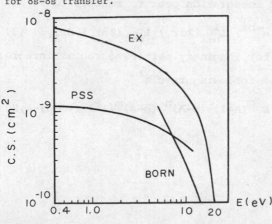

Fig. 3. The charge transfer cross sections for n=47. EX denotes the experimental data (ref. 10). PSS and BORN denote the theoretical cross sections of the resonant process (n=n'=47) by the perturbed stationary state method and the Born approximation, respectively.

TRANSITION OF ATOMIC HYDROGEN BETWEEN HIGHLY EXCITED STATES [*]

N C SIL AND B C SAHA

Department of Theoretical Physics,
Indian Association for the Cultivation of Science,
Jadavpur, Calcutta 700 032, INDIA.

The investigation of atomic transition processes which involve highly excited initial and final states has wide application in many fields. Sophisticated quantum mechanical treatment of such problems is enormously complicated. Even the calculation in the first Born approximation (FBA) is rather difficult. As a first attempt we have used the FBA to calculate the arbitrary excitation cross sections for $ns \rightarrow n's'$ transition in $\bar{e}$ -H collisions. The scattering amplitude is obtained in a closed form.

The FBA scattering amplitude in atomic units may be written as

$$f^D(\hat{k}_i \cdot \hat{k}_f) = (2\pi)^{-1} \int e^{i\vec{q} \cdot \vec{r}_1} (r_{12}^{-1} - r_1^{-1}) \, \Phi_{ns}(\vec{r}_2) \Phi_{n's'}(\vec{r}_2) d\vec{r}_1 d\vec{r}_2 \quad , \qquad (1)$$

where $\vec{q}$ ($= \vec{k}_i - \vec{k}_f$), the momentum transfer vector, the initial and final bound state wave functions are

$$\Phi_{ns}(r_2) = (\alpha^5/\pi)^{1/2} e^{-\alpha r_2} \, L_{n-1}^1(2\alpha r_2) \tag{2}$$

and $\qquad \Phi_{n's'}(r_2) = (\beta^5/\pi)^{1/2} e^{-\beta r_2} \, L_{n'-1}^1(2\beta r_2)$

with $\alpha = n^{-1}$, $\beta = (n')^{-1}$ and $L_a^b(x)$ is the associated Laguerre polynomial[1]. As Φ_{ns} and $\Phi_{n's'}$ are orthogonal, $1/r_1$ contribution will vanish. Substituting (2) in (1) the integration over r_1 can easily be carried out. Eq.(1) after the angular integration over $\hat{r}_2$ reduces to

$$f^D(\hat{k}_i \cdot \hat{k}_f) = 8q^{-3}(\alpha\beta)^{5/2} \, \text{Im} \int_0^\infty r_2 e^{-br_2} \, L_{n-1}^1(2\alpha r_2) \, L_{n'-1}^1(2\beta r_2) \, dr_2, \qquad (3)$$

for $b = \alpha + \beta + iq$ and Im stands for imaginary part. The radial integral over r_2 is evaluated using the following result[2]

$$\int e^{-bx} x^\alpha \, L_n^\alpha(\lambda x) \, L_m^\alpha(\mu x) \, dx = E \, \Gamma(A+1) \, (b-\lambda)^n \, (b-\mu)^m \, {}_2F_1 \, (-m-n; -A, Z)$$

when $A = m+n+\alpha$, $z=b(b-\lambda-\mu)/\left[(B-\lambda)(b-\mu)\right]$, $E = 1/(m_!n_!b^{A+1})$ and $_2F_1$ is the usual hypergeometric function.

Inclusion of the exchange effect by Ochkur approximation[3] leads to the following expression for the exchange scattering amplitudes : $\quad g^E(\hat{k}_i \cdot \hat{k}_f) = (q/k_i)^2\, f^D\, (\hat{k}_i \cdot \hat{k}_f)$

Present computed FBA results are in good agreement with available results of Vainshtein[4]. Table I represents some of our preliminary results for the excitation cross sections at $E = 4.8$ (in threshold units).

The details of results for transitions involving highly excited states will be presented at the conference.

Table I : Excitation cross sections[+] (πa_o^2) in e^- - H scattering.

	PRESENT		Vainshtein[4]
	FBA	Ochkur	
$2s \rightarrow 7s$	.2014(-1)	.1986(-1)	.201(-1)
$6s \rightarrow 7s$	.1841(+4)	.1768(+4)	.181(+4)

+ $a(x) = a.10^x$

*Supported by the University Grants Commission, INDIA.

[1] Higher transendental Functions, Ed. A. Erdelyi (McGraw-Hill book Co., Inc., 1953) Vol. 2, p 189.

[2] Tables of Integrals, Series and Products, I.S.Gradshteyn and I.W.Ryzhim (Acad. Press, Lond., 1965) p 844

[3] V. I. Ochkur, Sovt. Phys. JETP 18, 503 (1964)

[4] L. A. Vainshtein, Opt. Spectr. USSR 18, 538 (1965).

n-SCALING OF ELECTRON-LOSS CROSS SECTIONS FOR FAST $H(n)^0$ + N^{3+} COLLISIONS*

H. J. Kim and F. W. Meyer

Oak Ridge National Laboratory, Oak Ridge, Tennessee 37830, USA

Using an ion-atom crossed-beams apparatus,[1] we measured the yield of protons resulting from electron-loss collisions between a fast atomic-hydrogen beam and a slower N^{3+} beam at 40-keV/amu relative collision energy (collision velocity $v \simeq$ 1.3 v_0 where the Bohr velocity, v_0, is 2.2 x 10^8 cm/s). Because the atomic beam, obtained by passing energy-analyzed protons through a charge-capture cell, contained a distribution of excited states, the observed proton yield is $\sum_{n=1}^{N} P_n \sigma_n$, where P_n and σ_n are, respectively, the population and electron-loss cross section of atomic hydrogen in the nth excited state and N is the largest value of n. An auxiliary experiment[2] confirmed that the population P_n was proportional to n^{-3}, which agrees with previous experiments. The values of N, ranging from 9 to 20, were varied by changing the strength of the static transverse electric (or magnetic) field in which the excited hydrogen atoms with n > N were field ionized and attenuated from the beam. This population relates the proton yield Y_N to σ_n by the expression $Y_N = C \sum_{n=1}^{N} (\sigma_n/n^3)$, where C is an experimentally observed constant.[2]

The experimentally observed N dependence of Y_N is shown in Fig. 1. Because the de Broglie wavelength for the collisions under consideration is much smaller than the corresponding collision diameter, we expect the collisions to be adequately described by classical dynamics, but not by first-order quantal theories such as the Born approximation. Also shown in Fig. 1 are predicted yields based on two different classical theories. Bohr's theory,[3] which predicts $\sigma_n \propto n^3$ for the present cases, leads to $Y_N = CN$, whereas the theory of Garcia et al.,[4] which predicts $\sigma_n \propto n^2$, leads to $Y_N = C \sum_{n=1}^{N} (\frac{1}{n})$. The extra n factor in Bohr's theory arises from the special consideration he gives to those collisions with impact

*Research sponsored by the Office of Fusion Energy, U. S. Department of Energy, under contract W-7405-eng-26 with the Union Carbide Corporation.

parameters near the "adiabatic" radius by letting the impulsive force (which causes the electron loss) to act for the entire duration of time required for the projectile to traverse the whole atom. A similar consideration was not included by the theory of Garcia et al.

From Fig. 1 it is apparent that Bohr's theory, which considers not only such traditional dynamical variables as velocity and energy but also the duration of collision, gives a better description of collisions involving large atoms.

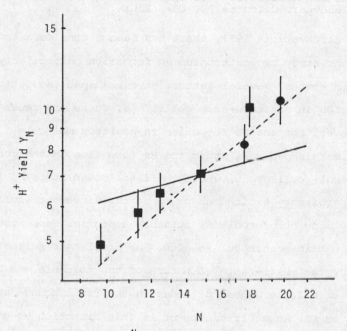

Fig. 1. Proton yields $Y_N = C \sum_{n=1}^{N} \sigma_n/n^3$ in arbitrary units vs. N. The error bars shown are relative errors only. The square data points were obtained with electrostatic field-ionization and the circular points with magnetic field ionization. The theoretical yields based on n^2-scaling are represented by the solid line, and n^3-scaling is represented by the dashed line. Calculated yields were normalized to the data point N = 14.

1. H. J. Kim and F. W. Meyer, Bull. Am. Phys. Soc. 23, 1095 (1978).
2. F. W. Meyer and H. J. Kim, "Measurement of H Atomc Rydberg State Population by a Transmission Method," abstract submitted to this Conference.
3. N. Bohr, Det. K. Dan. Vidensk. Selsk., Mat.-Fys. Medd. 18 (1948).
4. J. D. Garcia, E. Gerjuoy, and J. E. Walker, Phys. Rev. 165, 66 (1968).

POSITRONIUM FORMATION IN e^+ - H_2 COLLISIONS

APARNA RAY AND <u>PRITAM PRASAD RAY</u>

Department of Physics, Visva-Bharati University
Santiniketan, W. B. 731235, INDIA

AND

B C SAHA

Department of Theoretical Physics,
Indian Association for the Cultivation of Science,
Jadavpur, Calcutta 700 032, INDIA.

Since its discovery in 1951, there has been a considerable
interest in the study of positronium Ps formation particularly
in the excited states[1] Several authors have examined theoretically
the Ps formation in positron-atom collisions. There are fewer
studies, however, for the Ps formation in positron molecule
collisions. In this paper we study the Ps formation in the positron-
hydrogen molecule collisions, where the final bound state Ps is
formed in an arbitrary excited ns or np state. Since such collisions
are basically many body problems, suitable approximations must be
developed to obtain meaningful results. The problem is further
complicated by the multi-centered nature of the molecule and by
the presence of a large number of nodes in the final bound state
wavefunction of Ps. As a first attempt in this direction we employ
the first Born approximation (FBA) to study the behaviour of Ps
formation cross section in highly excited states.

The differential cross section in FBA for the Ps formation,
averaged over all orientations of H_2 may be written as (in
atomic units)

$$\frac{d\sigma}{d\Omega} = (4\pi)^{-3}(k_f/k_i)\int \left| \langle \Psi_f | V_i | \Psi_i \rangle \right|^2 \ d\Omega_f \qquad (1)$$

where $\langle \Psi_f | V_i | \Psi_i \rangle = \exp(-i\,\vec{\alpha}.\vec{\rho}/2)\,\int\,\exp\,(i\vec{\beta}.\vec{r}_1' - i\vec{\alpha}.\vec{r}_1)\,\Phi_I^*(\vec{r}_2,\vec{\rho})$

$$U_{n\ell m}^*\,(\vec{r}_1')\,V_i\,\Phi_m(\vec{r}_1,\vec{r}_2,\vec{\rho})\,d\vec{r}_1\,d\vec{r}_2\,d\vec{r}_1' \qquad (2)$$

Here V_i is the prior interaction potential. $\vec{k}_i$ and $\vec{k}_f$ are the initial and final momenta. Φ_I and Φ_m are the wave functions for the molecular ion and molecule respectively. For the final bound state wavefunction $U_{n\ell m}$ of the Ps atom we have used a contour integral representation[2].

Analogous to atomic case the molecular Brinkman Kramers (MBK) and molecular Jackson-Schiff (MJS) amplitudes for the charge exchange cross sections have been evaluated. The MBK amplitude can easily be calculated in closed form while the MJS amplitude can be expressed as a one-dimensional integral which has been carried out numerically.

Detailed numerical results will be presented in the conference.

REFERENCES :

[1] A.P.Mills, S.Berko and K.F.Canter, Phys. Rev. Lett. <u>34</u>, 1541 (1975).

[2] P.P.Ray and B.C.Saha, submitted to Phys. Lett. (1979).

POSITRONIUM FORMATION IN MULTIELECTRON ATOMS C, N, O, Ne

SUNANDA GUHA   AND   PUSPAJIT MANDAL

Indian Association for the Cultivation of Science
Jadavpur, Calcutta 700 032, India

A variety of first-order theories - the first Born approximation (FBA), the first-order e xchange approximation (FOEA) and the modified Born approximation (MBA) - is considered for positronium (Ps) formation by the K-shell electron capture from the many-electron atoms C, N, O and Ne in the incident energy range 1 - 1000 keV. The primary objective of doing such a calculation on this rearrangement collision process which has been found to be of great importance in many areas of physics is two-fold. First, we wish to make an estimate of the Ps formation cross section in order to find the possibility of the inner-shell vacancy production as a two-step process as is known to exist for ion-atom collisions where there is greater possibility of such a reaction due to the heavier mass of the projectile. Second, it might be of interest to see the applicability of the first order theories for those collision processes in which the effective charge of the target is far greater than unity.

Let the incident positron collide with the target atom with effective charge Z_A and finally capture the active K-shell electron to form the ground state Ps atom in the exit channel. In describing the many-electron target system, the simplest single-particle approximation is employed and the effect of the passive electrons is completely neglected. Different forms of the Ps formation scattering amplitude in the prior form of FBA, FOEA and MBA may now be written starting from the two-state approximation[1]. In this calculation, the effective charge Z_A for the target is taken to be $Z_A = Z-5/16$, where Z is the charge for the bare target nucleus. For the binding energy of the initial bound state of the atom, we use the experimental K-shell ionisation energy and for that of the Ps, the exact value 0.25 (a.u.).

Results for the total Ps formation cross section are shown in

Table I at incident energies 2 and 10 keV. From these results it may
be concluded that the probability for an energetic positron to capture an atomic K-shell electron from C, N, O and Ne is very small. We
may however contend ourselves with the fact that the class of first
order theories that we consider here predict cross sections which
are consistent in merit with our earlier findings for the H atom.

Table I : Total cross section (πa_o^2) for Ps formation at 2 and 10 keV.

E(keV)		C	N	O	Ne
2	FBA	1.35-5	1.08-5	7.01-6	3.44-6
	FOEA	1.27-5	9.57-6	5.19-6	7.62-7
	MBA	3.64-5	3.43-5	2.56-5	7.35-6
10	FBA	9.58-9	1.76-8	2.78-8	5.02-8
	FOEA	1.19-8	2.11-8	3.25-8	5.56-8
	MBA	1.52-8	2.84-8	4.59-8	8.72-8

1. P. Mandal and S. Guha, J. Phys. B12, in press (1979).

MODEL POTENTIAL APPROACH FOR POSITRON ALKALI-ATOM COLLISIONS

PUSPAJIT MANDAL AND SUNANDA GUHA

Indian Association for the Cultivation of Science
Jadavpur, Calcutta 700 032, India

We study the ground state positronium (Ps) formation in positron scattering from the alkali atoms Na, K, Rb and Cs by using a pseudo-potential formalism in the distorted-wave approximation (DWA) . The complexity of working with the multielectron atom is circumvented by visualising it as an one-electron atomic species. The lone valence electron of the atom is assumed to move in the field of a model potential. We thus consider essentially a three-body rearrangement collision in which the positron is incident on a bound system of an alkali atom (electron + alkali ion) in the ground state and in the final exit channel, the positron and the electron form a bound pair (Ps) in its normal state, while the alkali ion is left free. It is assumed here at the outset that the incident positron captures the 'active' valence electron while the core electrons remain mere spectators.

In DWA[1] the scattering equations may be obtained from the two-state approximation by simply neglecting the back-coupling term arising from the Ps-alkali ion interaction in the incident positron channel. In addition we also neglect the self-coupling Ps-Ps interaction in the final rearrangement channel. It may however be noted that this interaction for positron-hydrogen and positron-helium atom collisions vanishes due to the coincidence of the centre of mass and centre of charge of the Ps. In this calculation we solve the DWA scattering equations considering both the post and the prior forms of interaction and try to show how the Ps formation cross sections are influenced as such.

We have computed results for the total and differential cross sections at several incident energies in the range 0.5 - 20 eV for each of the atoms Na, K, Rb and Cs. The formation differential cross sections in DWA for these atoms shows the general structure of reaching a minimum at some scattering angle, while in FBA it becomes zero at an angle depending upon the positron energy. This general pattern is displayed by the differential cross section in both the post and prior forms of interaction. The values however differ by appreciable amounts in these cases.

In Table I we show the total formation cross section for only two incident positron energies 1 and 10 eV. From this table we may see that at an energy the FBA formation cross section becomes large in magnitude with the increase of the number of core electrons in the alkali atom. This may be due to the fact that with the increase of the core electrons, the binding energy of the outermost valence electron becomes smaller and as a result, incident positron has a greater chance of capturing this electron to form the Ps atom in the final channel. We may also find that the DWA cross sections are much smaller than the corresponding FBA values for each of the atoms. It is however not possible at this stage to say anything for certain about the relative merit of retaining either the post or the prior form of the interaction potential in the calculation unless experimental data on the cross section are available.

Table I : Total Ps formation cross section (πa_0^2) for Na, K, Rb, Cs atoms.

E(eV)			Na	K	Rb	Cs
1	FBA	a	1.98+2	4.29+2	1.07+3	2.26+3
		b	1.77+2	4.12+2	1.06+3	2.32+3
	DWA	a	3.37+1	1.92+1	1.91+1	2.07+1
		b	6.90+1	2.75+1	2.24+1	1.87+1
10	FBA	a	1.13+1	2.50+1	7.87+1	1.75+2
		b	1.52+1	2.83+1	8.32+1	1.83+2
	DWA	a	4.32	3.88	4.33	4.87
		b	7.09	4.90	4.86	5.02

a Prior interaction
b Post interaction

1. P. Mandal, S. Guha and N. C. Sil, J. Phys. **B12**, in press (1979)

POSITRONIUM FORMATION IN ARBITRARY EXCITED ns STATES IN ALKALI ATOMS

SUNANDA GUHA AND PUSPAJIT MANDAL

Indian Association for the Cultivation of Science
Jadavpur, Calcutta 700 032, India

Positronium (Ps) formation in positron scattering from alkali atoms is practically possible for all positron energies. In other words, the incident positron can capture the outermost electron from these atoms with an energy of even zero eV or more. In a recent study, the distorted-wave approximation and the first Born approximation (FBA) are applied for Ps formation in 1s state in the alkali series of atoms Na, K, Rb and Cs within the framework of the model potential theory[1]. We have in the present work extended this calculation to Ps formation in arbitrary excited ns states where we however make use of only the simplest FBA. This we do in view of the fact that it is rather difficult to obtain a close form of the scattering amplitude where the final bound state wavefunction may involve arbitrarily large principal quantum numbers. The present values of n-cube times the FBA total formation cross section with the post form of interaction potential are displayed in a table for only a single incident energy 10 eV. The cross sections are found to be fairly large. We also see that the Ps formation cross section satisfies the inverse n^3 law and n-cube multiplied by the total cross section practically attains its asymptotic limit when $n \to \infty$ beyond the excited state 20s.

Table : n-cube times the total cross section for Ps formation in excited ns states (πa_o^2) in alkali atoms Na, K, Rb and Cs at 10 eV.

	σ_{1s}	$2^3\sigma_{2s}$	$4^3\sigma_{4s}$	$20^3\sigma_{20s}$	$n^3\sigma_{ns}$
Na	4.92+1	2.31+1	9.55+1	4.57+1	4.59+1
K	2.83+1	3.66+1	3.73+1	4.12+1	4.14+1
Rb	8.32+1	9.75+1	6.62+1	5.77+1	5.75+1
Cs	8.83+2	2.34+2	1.56+2	1.22+2	1.20+2

1. S. Guha and P. Mandal, to be communicated shortly (1979).

TOTAL CROSS SECTIONS OF e^+ - He COLLISION IN A MODIFIED GLAUBER METHOD*

T.T. Gien

Department of Physics, Memorial University of
Newfoundland, St. John's, Newfoundland, Canada A1C 5S7

A modified Glauber amplitude [1] in which, the eikonal approximation is only considered from the third order of scattering up (rather than for all orders of scattering as in the conventional Glauber method) is applied to analyze the elastic scattering of helium atom by positron and especially, to obtain the total cross sections of e^+ - He collision. Since the first-order eikonal term of the Glauber amplitude is identical to the first Born term, in practice, to evaluate the modified Glauber amplitude, the following expression is used,

$$f_{GM} = f_G - f_{G2} + f_{B2}$$

where f_G, f_{G2} and f_{B2} are the conventional Glauber amplitude, the second-order eikonal term and the second-Born term respectively. The non-consideration of the eikonal approximation for the second-order scattering term is mainly to avoid a very serious deficiency inflicted by such an approximation on it (violation of conservation of probability in quantum mechanics).

In the case of positron elastic scattering by helium, the Glauber amplitude can, in principle, be calculated by a method initiated by Thomas and Chan [2]. Within the method, f_G is shown to be composed of two parts: one, corresponding to the single-particle scattering, can be evaluated with a closed form and, the other, to the double-particle scattering, is evaluated with the one-dimensional integral involving the modified Lommel function. However, here in the modified Glauber method, since the essential idea is to eliminate the divergence of the scattering amplitude in the forward direction, the closed-form terms in f_G (which is the source of the divergence) must be calculated simultanously with a similarly divergent term in f_{G2} by a two-dimensional integral form. This is, in fact, the key point of the technique of calculating the modified Glauber amplitude. By this procedure, one can obtain the imaginary part of the modified Glauber amplitude in the forward direction and hence, derive the total cross sections of e^+ - He. The total cross sections (in a_0^2 units) (some of them are shown below) are found to agree very well with experimental data at intermediate energies [3].

It should be noted that although the basis for adopting the method of approximation as well as the techniques of calculating the amplitude in the modified Glauber theory are different from those of the eikonal-Born-series (EBS) method [4], but in case if one is interested in comparing the two amplitudes term-by-term, one sees that the two differ from each other by an _infinite_ number of eikonal terms implicitly contained in f_G. These terms depress the values of the scattering amplitude and hence, make the modified Glauber method yield the total cross sections in better agreement with experimental data. The differential cross sections in the case of e^+ - He are also found to be drastically different at all angles for the two methods of approximation.

Total cross sections of e^+ - He collision						
Energy in eV	EBS	Modified Glauber	Experimental data			
			Brenton et al.	Twomey et al.	Jaduszliwer et al.	Stein et al.
100	4.68	3.430	3.267	3.36(9)	3.49	3.204
200	2.92	2.571	2.576	2.29(9)	2.48	2.199
300	2.15	1.990	2.042	1.69(9)	1.93	1.696
400	1.71	1.626	1.665	1.38(9)	–	1.426
500	–	1.379	1.319	1.38(9)	–	1.206
600	–	1.099	1.288	1.10(6)	–	–
800	–	0.878	0.880	0.94(6)	–	–
1000	–	0.735	0.754	0.31(3)	–	–

*Work supported by the Natural Sciences and Engineering Research Council Canada (Operating Grant A-3962).

1. T.T. Gien, Books of Abstracts, X ICPEAC (CEA, Paris,1977) pp. 398; J. Phys. B 9, 3203 (1976); Phys. Lett. 61A, 299 (1977); Phys. Rev. A 16, 123 (1977); ibid, 1736, 1793 (1977); Phys. Lett. 65A, 201 (1978); Phys. Lett. 68A, 33 (1978).

2. B.K. Thomas and F.T. Chan, Phys. Rev. A 8, 252 (1973).

3. A.G. Brenton et al., J. Phys. B 10, 2699 (1977). T.R. Twomey et al., Books of Abstracts, X ICPEAC (CEA, Paris, 1977) pp. 808-9 and private communication. T.S. Stein et al., ibid, pp. 802-3 and private communication. B. Jaduszliwer et al., Can. J. Phys. 53, 962 (1975).

4. C.J. Joachain et al., J. Phys. B 10, 207 (1977).

On Coulomb Distortion Effects in K-Shell Ionizations
by Electrons and Positrons

G. Hock

Institute of Nuclear Research, Hungarian Academy of Sciences,
H-4001 Debrecen, Pf. 51, Hungary

In the last years Tawara[1] suggested to describe the electron to positron ionization cross section ratios, σ^-/σ^+ by making use of the Møller and Bhabha cross sections[2] within the Kolbenstvedt theory[3] corrected classically for the distortion of the projectiles by the nucleus, which seems to be in agreement with the high energy σ^-/σ^+ measurements[4]. Recently, Ito et al.[5] carried out a low energy experiment on this ratio of the K-shell ionization of Ag (see fig.) where the Coulomb distortion was to be expected much more pronounced. Mukoyama[6] applied a Coulomb deflection correction to the close collision ingredient, similar to that as in ref. 4, based on an ionization probability ratio of the classical hyperbolic path to the straight-line path particles for both kinds of projectiles, in order to explain the strongly reversed cross section ratio σ^-/σ^+ compared to the uncorrected prediction (see fig.) . The uncorrected case corresponds to the modification of the Kolbenstvedt approximation, the results of which were published earlier[7]. This modification is concerned, among others, with the symmetrization of energy transfer in the close collision according to refs.[8,9].

In this work it was attempted to correct the close collisions (Møller and Bhabha) themselves for the initial and final state Coulomb interactions, at least in the low energy region. To the ejected electron – nucleus distortion the ratio of the nonrelativistic Coulomb wave atomic matrix element to that for plane wave, differential in energy transfer can be used[10]. On integration of the differential close collision cross sections multiplied by this factor one obtains reasonable agreement with the plane wave-projectile ionization theories. For the projectile–nucleus Coulomb distortion the nonrelativistic Coulomb wave bremsstrahlung cross sections[2] (Sommerfeld) , different for electrons and positrons, normalized by the common plane wave one (Born approximation) was used, both differential in photon energy. This ratio is approached by the well-known[11] Elwert factor. On the other hand a shift in the photon energy compared to the projectile – electron energy transfer of the order of the K-shell binding energy should be taken into account owing to the different laboratory frames. Finally, the two kinds of the Coulomb distortion factors multiplied by the corresponding close collision differential cross sections give rise after integration to the ratio σ^-/σ^+ seen in the figure.

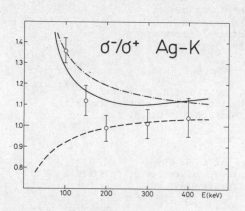

Fig. σ^-/σ^+ ratio for Ag K-shell ionization by electrons and positrons. Experiment :   Ito et al.[5] ; solid line :   quantum mechanical corrections ; dashed-dotted line : classical correction[6] ; broken line : uncorrected. (See text)

References

1.   H. Tawara, Proc. X. ICPEAC, Paris 1977 , Invited Papers and Progress Reports, Ed. G. Watel, N-Holl. Publ. Co., p. 311

2.   For example, V.B. Berestetskii, E.M. Lifshitz and L.P. Pitaevskii, 1971, Relativistic Quantum Theory, Pergamon P. Chapters 82 and 90

3.   H. Kolbenstvedt, J. Appl. Phys. 38 (1967) 4785 and 46 (1975) 2771

4.   U. Schiebel, E. Bentz, A. Müller, E. Salzborn and H. Tawara, Phys. Lett. 59 A (1974) 274

5.   S. Ito, K. Kubota and S. Shimizu, Int. Conf. X-Ray and XUV Spectroscopy, Sendai 1978, Program and Abstracts, p. 14

6.   T. Mukoyama, unpublished

7.   D. Berényi and G. Hock, Proc. Int. Conf. X-ray and XUV Spectroscopy, Sendai 1978, Japanese J. Appl. Phys. Vol. 17, 1978 Suppl. 17-2

8.   A. Burgess and I.C. Percival, Adv. Atom. Mol. Phys. Vol. 4, 1968, p. 109

9.   V.I. Ochkur, in " Atomic Collision Problems " , Vol. 1., 1975, Ed. by Yu. N. Demkov, Leningrad State University, in Russian

10.   J.W. Cooper and H. Kolbenstvedt, Phys. Rev. A5 (1972) 677

11.   R.H. Pratt and H.K. Tseng, Phys. Rev. A11 (1975) 1797

COHERENT RADIATION FROM CORRELATED COLLISIONS OF POSITRONS WITH Si*

S. Datz and J. H. Barrett

Oak Ridge National Laboratory
P. O. Box X, Oak Ridge, Tennessee 37830, U.S.A.

and

M. J. Alguard, R. L. Swent, and R. H. Pantell
Department of Electrical Engineering, Stanford University
Stanford, California 94305, U.S.A.

and

B. L. Berman and S. D. Bloom
Lawrence Livermore Laboratory, University of California
Livermore, California 94550, U.S.A.

Charged particles moving through crystals at small angles with respect to atomic rows and planes undergo correlated collisions which constrain their motion to well defined trajectories ("channeling"). One possible consequence of the correlated collision sequence is coherence in the radiation which accompanies changes in the acceleration of the particle from each single collision.

We report here the observation of such radiation from 56 MeV positrons confined to motion in the (110), (111), and (100) planes and to directions close to the <110> axis of Si[1] together with the results of theoretical models based upon Monte-Carlo calculations of correlated single collision scattering from Si atoms (Molliere potential) and from a continuum potential model for pure planar channeling.

An example of the radiation spectrum observed in the forward direction when a 56 MeV e⁺ beam (with divergence of 4 × 9 mr) was passed through an 18 μm Si crystal in a (110) planar direction is shown in Fig. 1. Here we show the ratio of the photon intensity per incident positron for incidence in a channeling direction divided by the yield in a random direction. A peak in intensity appears at 42.5 ± 0.5 keV with a line width of 24% FWHM. A Monte Carlo calculation of the spectrum anticipated under these experimental conditions including thermal vibrations is in reasonable agreement with the result; however, the removal of beam divergence in the calculation leads to an enhancement of a factor of ∿100 (rather than ∿2.5) with a linewidth of ∿10%.

For pure planar channeling an alternative treatment involves the averaging of the individual atomic potentials into a symmetric planar potential V_p and the radiation can be viewed as arising from transitions between states bound in this potential. Calculations based on these potentials[2] also agree well with the observed spectra. In the harmonic approximation, the anticipated maximum frequency of the radiation in the forward direction is $\omega_M \simeq 2\gamma^{3/2} (k/m_0)^{1/2}$ where k is the force constant ($= V_p''(0)$). The resultant radiation is variable

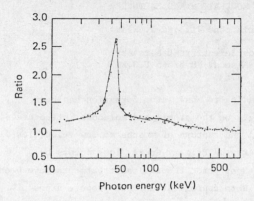

Fig. 1.
Ratio of spectrum observed from
positrons channeled in the (110)
plane of Si to the spectrum
obtained in random incidence.

in frequency, linearly polarized, and highly directional. Experimental tests
of the γ and k dependence and evidence for other forms of coherent radiation
(e.g., "coherent bremsstrahlung") will be discussed.

*Research supported by the U. S. Department of Energy under contract numbers
W-7405-eng-26, EY-76-5-0326, and W-7405-eng-48.

1. M. J. Alguard, R. L. Swent, R. H. Pantell, B. L. Berman, S. D. Bloom,
   and S. Datz, Phys. Rev. Lett. (in press).
2. R. H. Pantell and M. J. Alguard, J. Appl. Phys. 34, 798 (1979).

A NEW MODEL FOR NEGATIVE MESON MODERATION AND CAPTURE*

James S. Cohen, Richard L. Martin, and Willard R. Wadt

Theoretical Division, Los Alamos Scientific Laboratory,
University of California, Los Alamos, NM 87545 U.S.A.

The capture of negative mesons leading to mesic atom formation has been found experimentally to depend strikingly on the atomic and molecular structure of the stopping medium. The scattering and capture of mesons at low velocities ($v \lesssim 1$ a.u. $= \alpha c$) is of particular interest. Primary energy loss occurs by ionization of the target's electrons. Most prior theoretical treatments have been carried out quasiclassically or in the Born approximation. We propose a new model which describes the scattering by a complex potential with a real part given by a diabatic interaction potential and an imaginary part given by the ionization width of the diabatic state embedded in the electronic continuum.

Application has been made to negative muon (μ^-) and antiproton (p^-) collisions with the H, He, Li, and Be atoms. The diabatic interaction potentials for hydrogen-negative meson interactions, obtained with and without allowance for charge polarization, are compared to the adiabatic interaction potential in Fig. 1 (the $1/R$ meson-nucleus Coulomb potential has been subtracted out). The diabatic crossing into the electronic continuum also occurs for systems like He + μ^- where the adiabatic state is bound in the "united-atom" limit. The imaginary part (width) of the complex potentials has been obtained by approximating the continuum orbital as a plane wave in the golden-rule expression and, more rigorously, by using recent developments in Stieltjes moment analyses.[1]

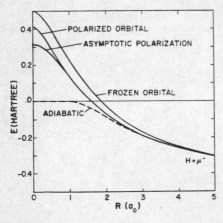

FIG. 1.   Electronic energy curves curves for H+μ^-.

Differential energy loss and total ionization cross sections are obtained with a quasiclassical treatment of the heavy-particle trajectories. These cross sections and corresponding stopping powers are large. Most meson captures are found to occur at collision energies near the ionization potential. The capture cross sections for muons by hydrogen are largest for muonic orbitals with $15 \lesssim n \lesssim 30$.

*Work done under the auspices of the U.S. Department of Energy.

   1.   A. U. Hazi, J. Phys. B: Atom Molec. Phys. <u>11</u>, L259(1978).

PRIMARY LEVEL POPULATION IN HELIUM MESONIC ATOMS

G. Ya. Korenman

Institute of Nuclear Physics, Moscow State University;
Moscow 117234; USSR

S.I. Rogovaya

Institute of Terrestrial Magnetism, Ionosphere and Radio-Wave
Propagation, the USSR Academy of Sciences, MOSCOW-Region
U S S R

We have calculated the primary populations of the levels of
μ^-, π^-, K^- and $\bar{p}$-atoms of helium

$$C_{n\ell} = \int_0^{E_c} dE \ w(E) \ \sigma_{n\ell}(E) / \sigma_c(E) \tag{1}$$

Here $w(E)$ is the energy distribution of the probability for the atomic
capture of mesons, $\sigma_{n\ell}$ the cross section for capture of a meson
into a level with the quantum numbers n, ℓ ; σ_c the total capture
cross section. The cross sections have been calculated in the plane
wave Born approximation with the dipole operator $V_1 = (\vec{r}_\mu \sum_i \vec{r}_i / r_i^3$).
For hydrogen, this operator yields the capture cross sections differing
from those calculated using the total operator by not more than several
per cent at $E_\mu > 40$ eV.[1]

The function $w(E)$ have been obtained by solving the kinetic equation in the continuous energy-loss approximation [2]. The stopping
power of He for mesons was expressed in terms of a similar quantity
of hydrogen[3] at the same velocities: $\mathcal{H}_{He}(v) = 2 \, Z_1 \, \mathcal{H}_H \, (v / Z_2)$,
where $Z_1 = 1.8$, $Z_2 = 27/16$. The maxima of the function $w(E)$ for
μ^-, π^-, K^- -mesons and antiprotons lie at energies of 80 eV, 85 eV,
110 eV, and 180 eV, respectively.

The distributions of the various particles over the principal quantum
number $C_n = \sum_\ell C_{n\ell}$ are shown in fig.1. The distributions of muons over
the orbital angular momentum at different n are presented in fig. 2. For
the heavier mesons, the overall picture of distribution in ℓ is analogous.

REFERENCES

1. G. Ya. Korenman, S.I. Rogovaya. Primary level population in hydrogen
   mesic atoms. Preprint of IZMIRAN, No.22(221) (1978).

2. G. Ya. Korenman, S.I. Rogovaya. Yad.Fiz.,22,754 (1975).

3. L. Rosenberg, Phil. Magazine, 40, 759 (1949).

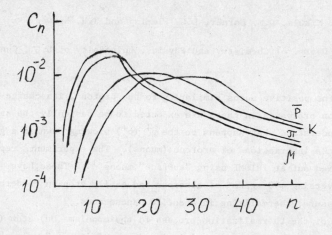

Fig.1

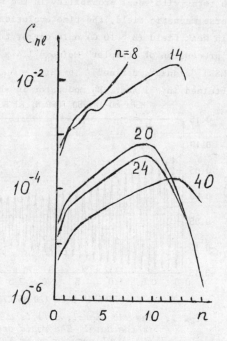

Fig. 2

μ^+ CHARGE EXCHANGE AND MUONIUM FORMATION IN LOW PRESSURE GASES

R.J. Mikula, D.M. Garner, D.G. Fleming and J.H. Brewer

TRIUMF and Depts. of Chemistry and Physics, University of B.C., Canada

In view of the positive muons similarity to the proton[1], its charge-changing and thermalization processes in gases are expected to be basically the same. Thus we can hope to understand what happens to the μ^+ (p^+) slowing down in a gas from measurements of the interactions of protons (muons). The experiments reported herein were carried out at TRIUMF using "surface" muons [1]. These have ~ 2 MeV energy after traversing ~ 90 mg/cm^2 of absorber and easily stop in "moderator" gases at ~ 1 atm pressure, thermalizing in about 20 nanoseconds.

One product of the thermalization process is the muonium (Mu) atom ($\mu^+\bar{e}$), which can be monitored via the parity violating decay of its μ^+ "nucleus", $\mu^+ \rightarrow e^+ \nu_e \bar{\nu}_\mu$, in which the positron exists preferentially along the μ^+ spin direction[1]. Since the μ^+ is polarized, Mu forms with equal probability in two spin states, $|\alpha_\mu \alpha_e\rangle$ and $|\alpha_\mu \beta_e\rangle$; in transverse magnetic field, the time evolution of the μ^+ involves four frequencies but in weak field (B $\leq$ 10 G) only one of these can be observed, the classical Larmor precession of "triplet" Mu($\omega_{Mu}= 1.4 \times 10^6 \times$ B(G)). A typical Mu spin rotation (MSR) "signal", defined [1] by $S(t) = A_{Mu}e^{-\lambda t}\cos(\omega_{Mu}t + \phi_{Mu}) + A_\mu \cos(\omega_\mu t - \phi_\mu)$ and obtained in $\sim$ 1 atm. N$_2$ moderator is shown in Fig. 1:

A_{Mu}, ϕ_{Mu} and A_μ, ϕ_μ are the measured amplitudes and phases of Mu and "free" μ^+ precession, respectively, while λ is the transverse relaxation rate.

The Table below shows the fraction of muons thermalizing as Mu (f_{Mu}) and as μ^+ (f_μ) in various gases. These are simply defined by $f_{Mu}=2A_{Mu}/A_o$ ("singlet" Mu does not precess) and $f_\mu=A_\mu/A_o$; where A_o is the

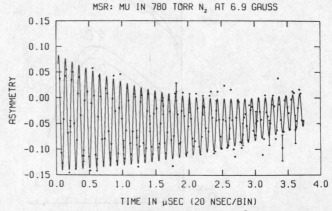

MSR: MU IN 780 TORR N$_2$ AT 6.9 GAUSS

TIME IN μSEC (20 NSEC/BIN)

Fig. 1: The MSR signal, S(t) is a χ^2-minimum fit to the data. The rapid oscillations are due to μ^+ precession in Mu, while the slowly curving drift is due to "free" μ^+ precession.

maximum asymmetry. The present TRIUMF results (T) generally agree well with those obtained at other laboratories using much higher energy μ^+ beams and hence generally much higher stopping pressures[2,3]. Any interpretation though of f_μ as being due to "free" μ^+ is not unambiguous, since those μ^+ in any diamagnetic environment will precess in the magnetic field essentially as free.

TARGET GAS	PRESSURE (ATM.)	f_μ	f_{Mu}	REFERENCE
He	50	99(5)	1(5)	2
He+150ppm Xe	50	83(15)		2
He+900ppm Xe	50	25(9)	75(9)	2
He	1.2	96(9)	4(9)	T
He+290ppm Xe	1.2	46(11)	54(11)	T
He+570ppm Xe	1.2	28(9)	72(9)	T
He+1300ppm Xe	1.2	29(8)	71(8)	T
Ne	26	100(2)	0(2)	2
Ne+1500ppm Xe	26	19(3)	81(3)	2
Ne	1.2	94(6)	6(6)	T
Ne+115ppm Xe	1.2	50(5)	50(5)	T
Ne+230ppm Xe	1.2	42(7)	58(7)	T
Ne+460ppm Xe	1.2	23(7)	77(7)	T
Ne+920ppm Xe	1.2	22(9)	78(9)	T
Ar	30	35(5)	65(5)	2
Ar	3		85(9)	3
Ar	1.7		64(16)	3
Ar	~ .9	37(7)	63(7)	T
N_2	~1	20(4)	80(4)	T
Xe	4.4	10(5)	100	2
NH_3	~1	20(8)	80(8)	T
CH_4	~1	20(8)	80(8)	T

In order to further elucidate the nature of the charge exchange process trace amounts of Xe, Ar and CH_4 impurities have been added to Ne (and He) moderators. The effect on the initial amplitude of the Mu and μ^+ signals is shown in the Table. The observed loss in amplitude of the μ^+ signal, mirrored by a corresponding increase in the Mu signal, provides confirmation of the epithermal nature of the charge exchange process since any thermal reaction would not lead to coherent precession. The thermal relaxation of the diamagnetic muon signal is shown in Fig. 2 as a function of impurity concentration I(I=Xe, CH_4, and Ar). The slopes yield the bimolecular rate constant for the process "μ^+" + I → Mu + I^+: K = (1.7 $\pm$ 0.3) x 10^{-11}cc/atom-sec with Xe, (5.6 $\pm$ 2.2) x 10^{-12}cc/atom-sec with CH_4 and zero in Ar. These rates correlate well with the difference in ionization potential between Mu and the impurity I and are much smaller than the diffusion controlled spin exchange rates for Mu + O_2 and Mu + NO, k_{Mu}=(2.8$\pm$0.2) x10^{-10}cc/atom-sec, strongly suggesting the involvement of (Neμ^+) molecular ions.

Fig. 2: Thermal relaxation of the μ^+ signal due to Mu formation in "impurity" gases.

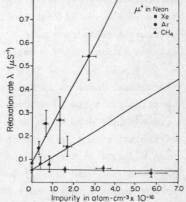

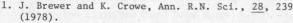

1. J. Brewer and K. Crowe, Ann. R.N. Sci., **28**, 239 (1978).
2. R.D. Stambaugh et al, Phys. Rev. Lett., **33**, 568 (1974).
3. B.A. Barnett et al, Phys. Rev., **A11**, 39 (1975)

MUONIUM SPIN EXCHANGE IN LOW PRESSURE GASES: Mu + O_2, Mu + NO

Donald G. Fleming, Randy J. Mikula and David M. Garner

Department of Chemistry and TRIUMF, University of B.C., Canada

The physical-chemical interactions of the muonium atom ($\mu^+ e^-$) can be monitored via the parity violating decay $\mu^+ \to e^+ \nu_e \bar{\nu}_\mu$, in which the positron exits preferentially along the μ^+ spin direction. Previous studies in gases of the interaction of muonium (Mu) with the paramagnetic molecules NO and O_2 by Mobley et al[1] were carried out at moderator pressures $\sim$40 atm, necessitated by the use of "conventional" μ^+ beams of high momentum. The interpretation of these data in terms of spin-exchange cross sections, however, is not unequivocal due to the large anticipated effects at such pressures of "3-body" chemical reactions[2]. At TRIUMF, we have been using a low momentum (29 Mev/c) "surface" μ^+ beam[3,4] which easily stops in low pressure ($\sim$1 atm.) gases to re-investigate these basic spin-exchange reactions, Mu + O_2 and Mu + NO.

Since the μ^+ is polarized, the Mu atom forms in the moderator gas in two spin states with equal probability, $|\alpha_\mu \alpha_e\rangle$ and $|\alpha_\mu \beta_e\rangle$; in transverse magnetic field, the time evolution of the μ^+ involves four frequencies but in weak fields ($B \leq 10$ G) only one of these can be observed, the classical Larmor precession of "triplet" Mu($\omega_{Mu} = 1.4 \times 10^6 \times B(G)$), giving rise to the muonium spin rotation (MSR) "signal" S(t), essentially defined[4] by S(t) $\sim A_{Mu} e^{-\lambda t} \cos(\omega_{Mu} t + \phi_{Mu})$ where A_{Mu} and ϕ_{Mu} represent the measured amplitude and phase of Mu precession while λ is the overall transverse (pseudo-first order) relaxation rate. The magnitude of $\lambda = \lambda_o + \lambda_c + \lambda_D$, where λ_o is "background" relaxation, λ_c is due to the loss of polarized Mu by chemical reactions[4] and λ_D is due to the actual spin depolarization of otherwise unaffected Mu atoms.

In its collision with an O_2 or NO molecule (X), there are two potentially important reactions of the Mu atom: Mu + X $\xrightarrow{M}$ MuX and Mu($\uparrow$) + X($\downarrow$) $\to$ Mu($\downarrow$) + X($\uparrow$). The first reaction requires a third body (M) and is characterized as "chemical" although it may produce a free radical which can subsequently cause μ^+ depolarization. The second reaction represents electron spin exchange. At 1 atm. pressure a relaxation rate $\lambda_c \lesssim 2.5 \times 10^4 s^{-1}$ is predicted for the termolecular process forming MuX - a factor of $\sim$20 lower even than the measured value of λ_o ($\lesssim 4 \times 10^5 s^{-1}$). It is unlikely that further "dynamic" isotope effects of the nature discussed in Ref. 4 could markedly increase this value. We conclude therefore that the Mu + NO and Mu + O_2 reactions in $\sim$1 atm. moderator must be predominantly ones of Mu spin depolarization (λ_D) by electron spin exchange. On the other hand, one cannot ignore the possibility that what has actually been measured in the previous work of Mobley et al.[1] at $\sim$40 atms. moderator pressure is λ_c and not λ_D; indeed calculations yield $\lambda_c \sim 3.0 \times 10^6 s^{-1}$, comparable to the measured values over the concentration range of that experiment.

Since the overall reaction is first order, $\lambda = \lambda_o + k_D[X]$ where k_D is a bimolecular (depolarization) rate constant. The predicted linear dependence of λ on the reagent partial pressure is verified in the present experiment, as can be seen in the Figure, which shows λ for Mu + O_2 and Mu + NO (in N_2) at 295 K: preliminary analysis yields $k_D(Mu + O_2) = (2.65\pm 0.18) \times 10^{-10}$ and $k_D(Mu + NO) = (2.85\pm 0.50) \times 10^{-10} cm^3 sec^{-1}$ at 1 atmosphere. Additional runs at 2.5 atm pressure (also on the Figure) yielded $k_D = (2.83\pm0.25)$ and $(3.41\pm0.31) \times 10^{-10} cm^3 sec^{-1}$ for Mu + O_2 and Mu + NO, respectively. The bimolecular rate constant k_D can be related to a

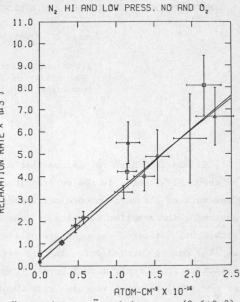

corresponding "depolarization cross section", σ_D, $k_D = \sigma_D \bar{v}$, giving $\sigma_D = (3.6\pm0.3) \times 10^{-16} cm^2$ for Mu + O_2 and $\sigma_D = (4.2\pm0.4) \times 10^{-16} cm^2$ for Mu + NO, independent of low moderator pressures.

These measured cross section σ_D can in turn be related to the "spin-exchange" cross sections of interest, σ_{SE}. In transverse magnetic field[5], $\sigma_{SE} = 2\sigma_D$ for Mu + NO and 9/8 x $2\sigma_D$ for Mu + O_2: at 295 K and ~1 atm. pressure, $\sigma_{SE}(Mu + O_2) = (8.1\pm0.7) \times 10^{-16} cm^2$ and $\sigma_{SE}(Mu + NO) = (8.4\pm0.8) \times 10^{-16} cm^2$. In view of the above mentioned uncertainties, these numbers are in surprisingly good agreement with those reported by Mobley et al: $\sigma_{SE} = (5.9\pm0.6)$ and $(7.1\pm1.0) \times 10^{-16} cm^2$ for Mu + O_2 and Mu + NO, respectively. There is unfortunately considerable uncertainty in the corresponding H atom numbers: eg., Berg[5] reports "spin-flip" cross sections for H + O_2 and H + NO of 21 and 25 x $10^{-16} cm^2$, respectively, whereas Brown[6] reports $\sigma_{SE}(H+O_2) = (8.0\pm2.5) \times 10^{-16} cm^2$. The latter value in particular is essentially the same as reported herein for σ_{SE} (Mu + O_2). A largely mass independent σ_{SE} would be expected if the "random phase" approximation to the difference between singlet and triplet phase shifts is valid.

1.   R.M. Mobley, Ph.D. Thesis, Yale University, 1967; R.M. Mobley et al., J. Chem. Phys. 47, 3074 (1967).
2.   K. Oka et al., J. Chem. Phys. 67, 4681 (1977); S.W. Benson et al., Int'l. J. Chem. Kinetics, Vol. VII, Supplement, 1975.
3.   A.E. Pifer, T. Bowen and K.R. Kendall, Nucl. Inst. and Methods 135, 39(1976).
4.   D.G. Fleming et al., A.C.S. Advances in Chemistry Series, 1979 (in press).
5.   H.C. Berg, Phys. Rev. 137A (1965) 1621.
6.   R.L. Brown, J. of Research, N.B.S., 76A, 103 (1972).

MUONIUM REACTION DYNAMICS AND HYDROGEN ISOTOPE EFFECTS: Mu + X$_2$, Mu + HX

Donald G. Fleming and David M. Garner

TRIUMF and Department of Chemistry
University of British Columbia
Vancouver, B.C., CANADA, V6T 1W5

It has long been recognized that one of the most useful inputs in the study of chemical kinetics is the determination of isotopic reaction rates. Within the framework of the Born-Oppenheimer approximation, the potential energy "surface" governing the reaction dynamics is independent of isotopic substitution so that rather sophisticated calculations of the ratios of reaction rate constants (e.g. k_{Mu}/k_H) can be carried out. In this regard, it is vital to have available a wide variation in isotopic mass in order to provide the capability of critical tests of the predictions of reaction rate theory; in particular, the quantum mechanical effects of zero-point motion (affecting the effective activation energy) and tunneling (determining barrier penetrability). Both of these effects are particularly sensitive to the motion of light atoms and in the recent past have been studied by comparisons of the reaction rates of H, D and T, which differ at most by only a factor of three in mass. Muonium (Mu) is the atom (μ^+e^-) formed by an electron bound to a positive muon "nucleus" (charge:1, spin:1/2, lifetime:2.2μs). Since the muon is 207 times as massive as the electron, the Mu reduced mass is 0.996 that of the hydrogen atom and the Bohr radii and ionization potentials of Mu and H are essentially the same. Therefore, the chemical behavior of the Mu atom is that of a very light H isotope ($m_{Mu}=1/9m_H$). Clearly, a systematic comparison between experiment and theory of the reaction rates of Mu and H, D or T, which differ by up to a factor of 27 in mass, is bound to be of major importance in furthering our understanding of chemical reaction dynamics.

Muonium is formed during the slowing down process of the muon in certain moderator gases; its existence can be followed via the parity violating decay, $\mu^+ \rightarrow e^+ \nu_e\bar{\nu}_\mu$, in which the positron exits preferentially along the μ^+ spin direction. In weak transverse fields (B $\lesssim$ 10 G) the classical Larmor precession of triplet Mu is seen (the "MSR signal") along with a (slow) μ^+ precession signal. The experimental data are fitted then to an amplitude $S(t) = A_{Mu}e^{-\lambda t}(\cos(\omega_{Mu}t + \phi_{Mu})) + A_\mu\cos(\omega_\mu t - \phi_\mu)$. The important quantity determined experimentally is the relaxation rate λ. In pure Ar and N$_2$ moderator this is ~0.3 μsec^{-1}, defining a background relaxation λ_o. The effect of added reagent is to cause further relaxation in the signal, as shown in the Figure for Mu + HI. The overall relaxation rate is given by $\lambda = \lambda_o + k$ [c] where k is the bimolecular rate constant and [c] is the concentration of added reagent. A typical run consists of a million events and usually 5 or 6 runs are made at different reagent concentrations; a plot of λ vs [c] yields the rate constant k[1,2].

Only thermally averaged experimental rate data are presently available on the reactions of Mu since state selected rate measurements involving this transient atom are not yet feasible. The table compares the gas phase Mu reaction rate data obtained at TRIUMF with that for the analogous H atom reactions. Since thermally averaged rate constants are proportional to $\mu^{-1/2}$, where μ is the reduced mass of the reactants, H isotope rate constant ratios are expected to display the trivial temperature independent isotope effect ratios 2.9:1:0.72:0. 59 for Mu:H:D:T. Deviations from these trivial ratios provide clues to the reaction dynamics[1,2,3].

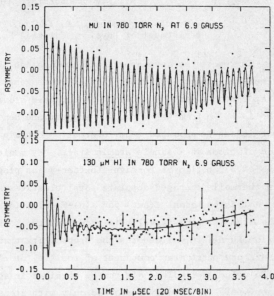

The effect of chemical reaction on the relaxation rate of the MSR signal. In inert gas (N_2) $\lambda=0.3$ μs^{-1}; in the presence of HI $\lambda=3.8$ μs^{-1}.

Table I. Reaction Rate Parameters for Mu and H in the Gas Phase[a]

Reactant	Reaction Type	k_{Mu}[b]	$E_a(Mu)$[c]	k_H[b]	$E_a(H)$[c]	k_{Mu}/k_H
F_2	X abstraction	1.4 ± 0.1	$.92\pm.23$	$.20\pm.05$	2.4 ± 0.2	5.2-10
				$.09\pm.01$	2.2 ± 0.1	13-19
				1.7 ± 0.6	1.8 ± 0.3	2.1-4.8
Cl_2	"	5.1 ± 0.2	1.4 ± 0.2	$.41\pm.04$	1.4 ± 0.2	11-14
				1.2 ± 0.2	1.2 ± 0.1	3.8-5.3
Br_2	"	24 ± 3		2.2 ± 1.5	1.0 ± 0.5	5.7-38
HCl	H abstraction exchange	$<3.4\times10^{-5}$		$(4.2\pm0.4)\times10^{-3}$ $\sim1.8\times10^{-5}$	3.1 ± 0.3 ≥ 4.0	$(6.5-10)\times10^{-3}$ ~2
HBr	H abstraction exchange	0.9 ± 0.1		$.21\pm.02$ $\leq2.3\times10^{-3}$	2.6 ± 0.1 $5-6$	3.5-5.3 350-440
HI	H abstraction	2.5 ± 0.1		0.9 ± 0.4	1.2 ± 0.4	1.9-5.7

a) details in Ref. 1   b) $k\times10^{10}\ell M^{-1}s^{-1}$ c) Ea in kcals/mole

1. D.M. Garner, Ph.D. Thesis, University of British Columbia, 1979.
2. D.M. Garner, D.G. Fleming and J.H. Brewer, Chem. Phys. Lett. **55**, 163 (1978).
3. J.N.L. Connor, et al, Chem. Phys. Lett. **45**, 265 (1977); Chem. Phys. **28**, 219 (1978); Mol. Phys. (in press).

STIMULATED PHOTON ECHO MEASUREMENTS OF ATOM-ATOM ELASTIC SCATTERING IN BUFFERED ATOMIC VAPORS*

T. W. Mossberg, R. Kachru, and S. R. Hartmann
Department of Physics, Columbia U., New York, NY 10027

We report the development and application of a technique,[1] employing the stimulated photon (SP) echo, that is quite generally applicable to the study of atom-atom elastic scattering in buffered atomic vapors. Although the SP echo is known from NMR work,[2] we suggest and demonstrate for the first time that it can be produced from information contained in the velocity <u>distribution</u> of atoms in a <u>single atomic state</u>. By monitoring the decay of the SP echo as a function of foreign- (buffer-) gas pressure, one can determine both the thermally averaged absolute total elastic scattering cross section σ and the collision kernal $f(\Delta v_i)$ for A(n)-F collisions, where A(n) [F] denotes the echo atom in energy level n [a ground-state   foreign-gas atom]. The collision kernel $f(\Delta v_i)$ denotes the probability that a single collision will change one particular component of the A(n) atom's thermal velocity by Δv_i. While velocity-resolved σ's can be obtained in atomic-beam experiments, such experiments are readily performed only with atoms in ground or metastable energy levels. The SP echo technique, however, can be easily applied to levels with short ($\approx$ 10 nsec) lifetimes, and thermally averaged <u>absolute</u> elastic cross sections can be obtained. Other techniques[3] using photon echoes and saturated absorption have been used to study collisions in gases, but for various reasons they cannot be used to determine absolute total scattering cross sections and/or they are applicable only in special cases.

The SP echo is generated by three excitation pulses at times t_i. Assume that pulses 1 and 2 are resonant with the $|0\rangle$ - $|1\rangle$ transition, where $|0\rangle$ ($|1\rangle$) is an initially populated (unpopulated) state, and that $\vec{k}_1 \| \vec{k}_2 \| \hat{z}$, where $\vec{k}_i$ is the wavevector of the ith pulse. After pulse 2, levels $|0\rangle$ and $|1\rangle$ are populated as

$$n'(v_z) = c_o \exp(-mv_z^2/2k_bT) \, f(k_1 v_z t_{21}/2) \qquad (1)$$

where $t_{ij} \equiv t_i - t_j$, $f \equiv \sin^2$ ($f \equiv \cos^2$) for state $|0\rangle$ ($|1\rangle$), $v_z \equiv$ the z-component of velocity, k_b is Boltzman's constant, and T is the absolute temperature. The third pulse ($\vec{k}_3 \| \pm\hat{z}$) can excite the same transition or any other allowed transition of the form $|i\rangle$ - $|2\rangle$, where i $\equiv$ 0 or 1 and $|2\rangle$ is a third level. The echo, which propagates $\|\vec{k}_3$, occurs at a time $k_1 t_{21}/k_3$ after and at the same frequency as pulse 3. If a transition such as $|i\rangle$ - $|2\rangle$ is excited by pulse 3, then, neglecting inelastic scattering, during t_{32} only collisions which thermalize the velocity distribution in level $|i\rangle$ (Eq. 1) will contribute to echo decay. In this case the echo intensity decays as a function of foreign-gas pressure P according to

$$I_e(P) = I_o \exp\{-[2n_o v_r t_{32}/P_o]\sigma_{eff} P\} \exp\{-\beta P\} \tag{2}$$

where

$$\sigma_{eff} = \sigma[1 - \int_{-\infty}^{\infty} \exp(-ik_e \Delta v_i t_{e3}) f(\Delta v_i) d(\Delta v_i)],$$

n_o denotes the foreign-gas density at pressure P_o, $v_r \equiv (8k_b T/\pi\mu)^{\frac{1}{2}}$, and μ is the A - F reduced mass. The exp $[-\beta P]$ factor, which represents the effect of colli-sions during the intervals t_{21} and t_{e3}, can be determined and removed by auxiliary experiments (e.g. setting $t_{32} = 0$). In general there are two unknowns in Eq. 2, i.e. σ and $f(\Delta v_i)$. However, for long t_{e3} the integral involving $f(\Delta v_i)$ vanishes; thus $\sigma_{eff} \rightarrow \sigma$ and the absolute scattering cross section can be unambiguously de-termined. Given σ, SP echo measurements for short t_{e3} can be used to determine $f(\Delta v_i)$.

We have applied the SP echo technique to the study of Na(3S) - He and Na(3P$_{\frac{1}{2}}$) - He elastic scattering.[1] (Note that the lifetime of the 3P$_{\frac{1}{2}}$ state is 16 nsec.) Fig. 1 shows the behavior of σ_{eff}[Na(3S)-He] as a function of $t_{e3} = t_{21}$. The solid (dashed) curve was plotted using Eq. 2 while assuming a Lorentzian (Gaussian) form of $f(\Delta v_i)$. Contrary to general assumption, the Lorenztian kernel provides the better fit. It is found that the average Δv_i is approximately 1 % of the rms v_z. The $\sigma \cong 176$ Å^2 measured for Na(3S) - He scattering agrees with atomic-beam results. We also find that σ[Na(3P$_{\frac{1}{2}}$)-He] $\simeq 2.5\sigma$[Na(3S)-He]. Preliminary Na(3S) scattering experiments have also been performed with F = Ne, Ar, and CO.

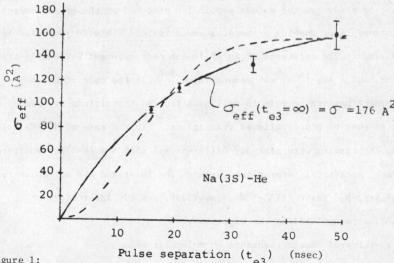

Figure 1:

* Supported by Joint Services Electronics Program under Contract No. DAAG29-77-C-0019 and by the Office of Naval Research under Contract No. N00014-78-C-0517.

1. T. Mossberg, A. Flusberg, R. Kachru, and S.R. Hartmann (to be published).

2. E. L. Hahn, Phys. Rev. 80, 580 (1950); W.B. Mims, K. Nassau, and J.D. McGee, Phys. Rev. 123, 2059 (1961).

3. See Review by: P.R. Berman, Adv. At. Mol. Phys. 13, 57 (1978).

Molecular Collisions Studied by Novel Spectroscopic Methods

T. Shimizu, S. Kano, N. Konishi, N. Morita, T. Kasuga,
F. Matsushima, H. Sasada, and H. Kuze

Department of Physics, Faculty of Science, University of Tokyo
Bunkyo-ku, Tokyo 113, Japan

Collision-induced relaxations among vibrational and rotational molecular levels have been studied with strong coherent radiations from infrared lasers and microwave klystrons. Generally the spectroscopic methods give us detailed informations on the molecular level which participates in collision processes. In the double resonance experiment both initial and final levels involved in the collisional "relaxation" can be indicated. The coherent transient spectroscopy provides a variety of switching techniques which cause free induction decay, transient nutation, photon echo, rotary echo, and so on. We may isolate an individual type of relaxation such as T_1 or T_2 process from the collective analyses of the various transient phenomena.

(1) Infrared-microwave double resonance

Since NH_3 molecule has many inversion transitions at microwave frequencies, it is convenient to study how the excess population produced on the proper energy level with strong laser pumping propagates among various vibration-rotation levels due to collisions. The existence of an efficient near resonant V-V energy transfer in $^{14}NH_3-^{14}NH_3$ and $^{14}NH_3-^{15}NH_3$ was demonstrated.[1-4] In the case of NH_3-NH_3 collision the dominant preference rule in collision induced transitions has been revealed to be that of dipole allowed transitions.[5] In the case of NH_3-He collision, however, the results were markedly different and $\Delta J \gtrless 2$ and $\Delta K = \pm 3n$ transitions were observed.[4] Accidental coincidences between the laser and the molecular transition frequencies, N_2O laser $P(13)-^{14}NH_3\nu_2asQ(8,7)$, and CO_2 laser $R(42)-^{15}NH_3\nu_2R(2,0)$, were utilized in the experiment.[1,4]

(2) Infrared-infrared double resonance on molecular beam

In a molecular beam we can apply two independent tuning stark fields on the molecule. It is not necessary to search for the accidental frequency coincidence between the laser line and the molecular transition. Along the stream the molecule is first tuned to the pumping laser radiation, and then travels in the field free region where collisions occur, and finally is tuned again to the probe laser radiation. The achieved sensitivity of the system is good enough to detect 0.01% change in the probed infrared intensity caused by collision induced transitions[6]. It is found that the rate of excitation energy transfer is closely related to the molecular energy level structure.

(3) Infrared transient spectroscopy

The longitudinal (population difference) and the transverse (polarization) relaxation constants of NH_3 were separately obtained by comprehensive experiments of delayed nutation, photon echo, and free induction methods. The populational decay constants of the vibrational excited states were also determined. Non-empirical calculations of decay constants in NH_3-NH_3 collisions gave us the consistent results with those of observations.

(4) Microwave transient spectroscopy

The relaxation phenomena on the $6_{16} \leftarrow 5_{23}$ microwave transion of H_2O attract our special interests because of its maser action in an interstellar space. T_1-relaxation constant first determined by the frequency modulated transient spectroscopy. T_2-relaxation constants for various perturbers such as He, H_2, N_2 and CO were also determined[7].

1.   S. Kano, T. Amano, and T. Shimizu, J. Chem. Phys. <u>64</u> 4711 (1975)

2.   S. Kano, N. Morita, T. Amano, and T. Shimizu, J. Chem. Phys. <u>68</u> 2020 (1978)

3.   N. Morita, S. Kano, and T. Shimizu, J. Chem. Phys. <u>69</u> 277 (1978)

4.   N. Morita, S. Kano, Y. Ueda, and T. Shimizu, J. Chem. Phys. <u>66</u> 2226 (1977)

5.   N. Morita, S. Kano, and T. Shimizu, J. Chem. Phys. <u>68</u> 3897 (1978)

6.   F. Matsushima, N. Morita, S. Kano, and T. Shimizu, J. Chem. Phys. to be published, May (1979)

7.   T. Kasuga, H. Kuze, and T. Shimizu, J. Chem. Phys. <u>69</u> 5195 (1978)

EFFECTIVE PATH LENGTH CORRECTIONS IN BEAM-BEAM EXPERIMENTS[*]

S. Trajmar and R. T. Brinkmann[**]

California Institute of Technology, Jet
Propulsion Laboratory, Pasadena, CA 91103 USA

The scattering signal intensities measured in a beam/beam scattering experiment are related to the cross sections by a rather complicated expression involving geometrical and instrumental functions. Although experimental arrangement can be made such that the proportionality factor relating the scattered signal intensity to the corresponding cross section is independent of scattering angle and impact energy, in practice this is seldom feasible. One, therefore, has to determine the angular (and energy) dependence of this factor, or at least assess it's importance, in order to be able to obtain accurate cross sections.

In the present treatment of the problem we consider electron and atomic (or molecular) beams with realistic flux and density distributions intersecting at right angles, and a detection view cone defined by two coaxial circular apertures. Each volume element within the view cone serves as a source of scattered signal. In integrating over the scattering volume, to compute the overall detected signal, the volume elements are weighted for atom beam density, electron beam flux, solid angle extended by the volume element at the detector and the average cross section associated with the position of the volume element. The result of this integration is an effective scattering path length as a function of nominal scattering angle (for each impact energy). The flow equations for tubes and capillary arrays were those of Olander and Kruger[1] which takes into account the influence of intermolecular collisions and nonzero densities at the tube exit. Although the effective path length correction value could serve to generate absolute cross sections, in practice it is a much more reliable procedure to generate only relative cross sections and carry out the normalization to the absolute scale by other means.

Figure 1 shows examples of effective path length correction factors (normalized to unity at $90°$) for detector and electron beam geometries listed in Table I and commonly used in our laboratory in combination with static targets, thin orifice, tube capillary array (CA), collimated capillary array (CCA) and jet sources. For purposes of comparison the frequently used $\sin \theta$ correction factor is also shown. In all these cases the differential cross section was assumed to decrease as $10^{-0.32 \, \theta'}$ over the range of actual scattering angle (θ' in degrees) which contribute at a nominal scattering angle (θ). The aspect ratio (γ), target species, tube back pressure and beam collimation are also indicated in Table I. The gas kinetic collision cross sections for He and Ba were taken as 2.18 and 100 $\mathring{A}^2$ re-

[*] Work supported by the National Aeronautics and Space Administration, Contract No. NAS7-100.
[**] Present address, Hughes Aircraft Co., Culver City, CA 92030, USA.

spectively. ϑ and ρ are the target beam divergence angle and density. The geometrical parameters indicated as SE, SB and SV are the distances of the electron beam source, target beam source and detector first aperture from the scattering center respectively. D1, D2 and D12 are the first and second view cone defining aperture diameters and their separation respectively. The values of the correction factor span an order of magnitude at low scattering angles, but with carefully designed geometry and small, well defined targets it can be made nearly unity over the whole angular range.

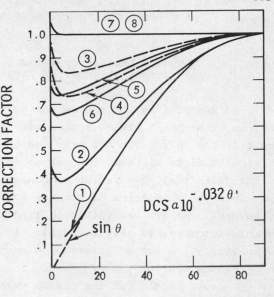

More detailed discussion of the various scattering geometries, effects of energy distribution of the electron beam, energy dependence of the detector efficiency, explicit considerations concerning the energy and angular dependence of the cross section, and comparison with experiment will be presented.

Fig. 1. Typical effective path length correction factors as the function of scattering angle. See text and Table I for detailed explanation. The effect of gas kinetic collision cross section is shown by curves 3 and 4 and the influence of capillary back pressure is indicated by curves 5 and 6.

Target type	SE	SB	SV	D1	D2	D12
	(cm)					
1. Static; ρ = const; He	50	--	1.27	0.076	0.076	1.27
2. Orifice; $\rho \propto \cos\vartheta$; He	"	0.50	"	0.152	0.100	"
3. Tube; γ = 0.120; He; 1 Torr	"	0.25	"	"	"	"
4. ·Tube; γ = 0.120; Ba; 1 Torr	"	"	"	"	"	"
5. CA: γ = 0.010; He; 0.1 Torr	"	"	3.81	0.092	0.050	2.54
6. CA: γ = 0.010; He; 760 Torr	"	"	"	"	"	"
7. CCA: γ = 0.010; He; 760 Tor; $\vartheta = \pm 12°$	"	"	"	"	"	"
8. Jet, ρ = const; ϑ = 0°	"	"	"	"	"	"

1. D. R. Olander and V. Kruger, J. Appl. Phys. **41**, 2769 (1970).

A SIMPLE DUAL FUNCTION SOURCE FOR HEAVY IONS

E. Veje

Physics Laboratory II, H.C. Ørsted Institute
Universitetsparken 5, DK-2100 Copenhagen Ø, Denmark

We describe an ion source which with a slight modification, can be run either as a plasma source with a filament or as a cold arc sputter ion source. It has been designed for outer-shell atomic collision studies. The beam current necessary for such experiments is often quite small (a few nA), consequently no big effort has been put into the production of intense ion beams, which may be needed elsewhere. The aim was rather to find a construction which runs stable for days, is easy to repair, and can ionize (singly as well as multiply) a large variety of elements.

Plasma Source:

A cross section of the plasma version of the source is shown in Fig. 1. The filament is at a negative potential of approximately 100 V compared to the exit aperture, sustaining an arc between the two. The filament-to-anode distance is approximately 5 cm and the diameter of the exit aperture 1 mm. The arc is connected in series with a resistor of 20 ohms which makes it burn in a self-stabilizing mode with an arc current of approximately 1 A.

If a piece of a solid is placed inside the glass tube below the filament, it will evaporate gradually into the discharge, and in this way ions from solid elements may be obtained. As examples, the following mass analyzed beam currents have been obtained (without adding any gas to the source): 5 µA Mg^+, 2 µA Ca^+, 8 µA Zn^+. Generally the beam current of doubly and triply charged ions are approximately 10% and 3% of that of singly charged ions, respectively, and in some cases four times ionized ions (e.g. Ar^{4+}) have been detected (a few nA). No current was obtained for some elements, e.g. B and Al.

Sputter Source:

A cross section of the sputter version of the source is shown in Fig. 2. The cylindrical electrode forming the exit aperture is made of the element of interest.

A potential drop of approximately 800 V between the back flange and the exit aperture results in a plasma discharge with a current of approximately 0.3 A. The glow of the discharge is located mainly inside the exit aperture cylinder. Introduction of a gas (e.g. Ar) into the source is necessary to ignite the discharge. As an example. 0.5 µA Al^+ ions has been obtained. The production of multiply charged ions is considerably smaller in the sputter source than in the plasma source.

The high tension transformer of the power supply for the sputter source has a small air gap in the iron yoke. This limits the discharge current and prevents short circuits.

For both ion source versions the housing is a 150 mm long standard pyrex glass tube of 50 mm diameter with a wall thickness of 3 mm. In this way the back flange, carrying either the filament or the positive sputter electrode, is insulated electrically from the exit aperture flange which serves as anode in the plasma source or as cathode in the sputter source.

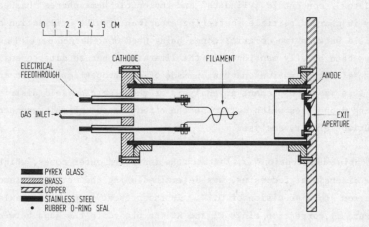

Fig. 1. Cross section of the plasma source.

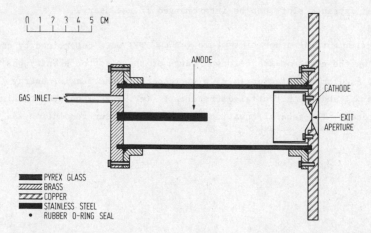

Fig. 2. Cross section of the cold cathode sputter source.

CO-AXIAL ELECTROSTATIC VELOCITY ANALYSER

W.R. NEWELL, D.F.C. BREWER[*] AND A.C.H. SMITH

Department of Physics and Astronomy, University
College London

[*]Present Address : Scicon Consultancy Ltd, 49-57
Berners Street London W1P 4AQ.

Velocity analysis of charged particles by the electric fields established between parallel plates[1], concentric cylinders[2] and concentric hemispheres[3] has been used extensively in charged particle scattering experiments. The utilisation of the electric field between two co-axial cones being used as a charged particle velocity analyser has been briefly mentioned in the literature[4] but to date no analytical or experimental determinations have been made of the properties of such an analyser. In this paper we present an analysis of the electric field distribution and focussing properties which determine the effectiveness of this geometry as a high resolution velocity analyser.

The potential distribution $V(r,z)$ between the inner and outer cones, which produces three dimensional focussing, was determined using the method of successive over relaxation[5] to a precision of 0.1%. In the present truncated co-axial cone system (figure 1) correction rings R1 and R2 are placed in the gaps between the inner and outer cones and are maintained at a potential which produces the minimum distortion of the electric field. Charged particles enter the analysing field through a slot (r_0, z_0, $\phi(= 0-2\pi)$) in the inner cone and leave, after analysis through another slot at (r',z') in a direction parallel to the z-axis. The exit and entrance slots can be interchanged if necessary.

The electron optical properties of the core analyser were determined by computing the effect on the electron trajectory range of the electron's entry position (r_0, z_0, ϕ_0), angular orientation (α, β) with respect to the r axis, energy (E_0), energy loss (E) and the potential difference V_s ($= V_{ic} - V_{oc}$) between the inner and outer cones. The general equation giving the analyser resolution was found to be

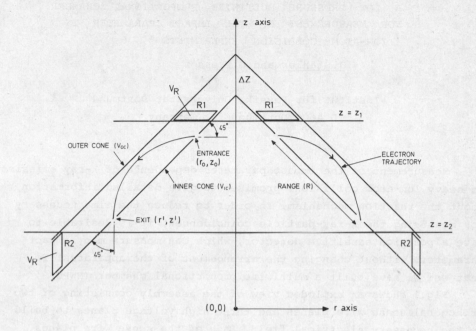

FIGURE (1)

$$\frac{\Delta E}{V_{ic}} = \frac{\Delta R}{D} + \frac{R_0}{D} (0.0234\alpha^2 + a\beta^2)$$

Where D is the dispersion of the instrument, R_0 is the trajectory of the central path and a is equal to 0.43 or 1.08 depending on the direction of the electron beam through the cone analyser.

A comparison of the operational characeristics of the co-axial cone analyser with the parallel plate and hemispherical analysers has been made. Further details of the instrument and its applicability to high resolution electron scattering experiments with measurements of electron differential cross sections and resonance profiles in helium, will be presented.

1. Harrower G.A., 1955 Rev. Sci. Instr. **26**, 850-54.
2. Purcell F.M., 1938 Phys. Rev. **54**, 818-26.
3. Hughes A.L. and Rojansky V., 1929 Phys. Rev. **34**, 284-90.
4. Kuyatt C.E., 1968 Methods of Experimental Physics Vol. 7A. ed.B. Bedersen and W.L. Fite (Academic Press).
5. Carré B.A., 1961 Computer J. **4**, 73-78.

A LOW PRESSURE MULTIWIRE PROPORTIONAL CHAMBER
FOR MEASUREMENT OF THE IMPACT PARAMETER IN
ION-ATOM COLLISION EXPERIMENTS *

J.Stähler and G.Presser

Institut für Physik, Universität Dortmund
D 4600 Dortmund 50, Germany

Measurement of the impact parameter dependence of X-ray emission
in heavy ion-atom collisions promises to give detailed information
about the reaction mechanism. In order to reduce the time necessary
for measuring the X-ray-particle coincidences, it is desirable to
have a position sensitive detector, which can measure many impact
parameters without changing the arrangement of the apparatus. To
that end we have built a multiwire proportional chamber (MWPC).[1,2]
Fig.1 shows an exploded view of the assembly consisting of two
orthogonal sense wire planes and three high voltage planes to build
up the necessary electrical field. Each of the sense wire planes
consists of 96 parallel tungsten wires, 20 µm in diameter with a

signal planes

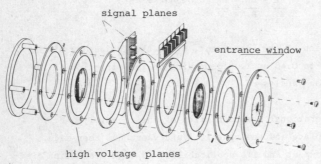

entrance window

high voltage planes

Fig.1:
Exploded view of the
low pressure MWPC.
The active area of the
chamber is 300 cm[2].

spacing of 2mm. Each of the high voltage planes consists of
approximately 200 wires with 50 µm diam. and separated by 1 mm.
As counting gas we use isobutane at pressures from about 10 mbar
up to 100 mbar depending on the energy loss of the ions to be detected.
The efficiency of the chamber reaches always more than 98%
for heavy ions as well as for α-particles. The fast time resolution
of low pressure MWPC's, compared to chambers operating at normal
pressures, has been ascribed to the high mobility of electrons due
to the high values of the reduced electric field (E/p).[3] We have
measured a time resolution (FWHM) better than 10 ns at gas

pressures of about 50 mbar, which is compatible with published
values[3] taking into account the different geometric arrangements.

The readout system of the chamber (Fig.2) consists of an amplifier plus discriminator for each wire, mounted directly on the
chamber and a CAMAC module for each signal plane. The CAMAC module
receives the discriminated wire signals, stores them in latches and
computes wire addresses before they are sent to an on-line computer
where the events are stored on magnetic tape.

First results, taken at scattering angles from 3° up to 40°,
will be discussed.

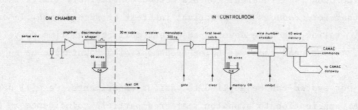

Fig.2:
Readout electronics sketched for one wire only. The different
delays and memories allow to decide whether an event shall be
accepted or not by fast trigger electronics.

*Work supported in part by Land Nordrhein Westfalen

1. For a general description of the properties of MWPC's see,
   for example, F.Sauli, CERN report 77-09, (1977)

2. J.Stähler, G.Hemmer and G.Presser, Nucl.Instr.Meth., in print

3. A.Dreskin, Nucl.Instr.Meth. 141, 505 (1979)

A FAST MULTICHANNEL TIME CORRELATOR

J.C. Brenot, J. Fayeton, J.C. Houver

L.C.A.M. Bât. 351 – Univ. Paris-Sud 91405 ORSAY Cedex FRANCE

Large improvement in the detailed understanding of collision phenomena has been achieved by using various coincidence techniques. The main drawback is obviously that such experiment is usually very time consuming . The development of multi-channel plates detector (MCP) opens a new area in this field allowing in particular a multiparameter data acquisition such as the simultaneous detection of particles in several scattering angles[1]. The next step is the extension of this technique to, for exemple, multiangle photon-scattered particules coincidences. In this res-pect, the conventional method using a time-to-amplitude converter could be applied. However, the large dead-time inherent to this method considerably limits the usable count-rate and therefore reduces the practical interest of such device. In order to overcome such limitation, we have developped a fast multichannel time correlator (3ns resolution, 400 ns dead time) allowing treatment of a count-rate up to about $5 \ 10^5$ c/s.

Although our system can be applied to various experiments, we will describe here a particular application to a photon scattered particle coincidence in a con-ventional beam target experiment. Scattered particles are detected by 2 MCP assembly. The out.put pulses colected on 64 concentric collectors are individually amplified and discriminated from background by 32 double hybrid circuits (as developped multiwire spark chamber application). A MECL 64 line priority encoder delivers simultaneously a single timing signal (t_1) and a 6 bit position code (M). The pulses issued from the photon detectors are treated in the same way (t_2, N). The multichannel correlator determines the significant time t_1-t_2 which associated with the M,N detector position codes forms a "binary word" containing all infor-mation. These words are then temporarily stored in a 32 K memory waiting for the treatment by a PDP 11 computer (figure 1).

In order to test our system we have measured differential cross sections (DCS) for both He metastable and He(2^1P) excitation in He-He collisions where expe-rimental[2] (energy loss technique) and theoretical[3] data are available. In Fig. 2 typical coincidence spectra show UV photons (A) and recoil metastables (B) for several scattering angles. The He(2^1P) DCS is compared in figure 3 with theory.

[1] R.W. Wingneandts van Resandt, H.C. den Harink and J. Los (1976) J.Phys.E : Sci. Instr. 9, 503

[2] J.C. Brenot, D. Dhuicq, J.P. Gauyacq, J. Pommier, V. Sidis, M. Barat, E. Pollack (1975) Phys.Rev.A 11, 1245

[3] J.P. Gauyacq (1976) J. of Phys. B 9, 2289

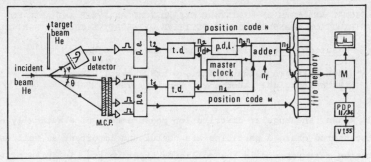

Fig. 1. Schematic diagram of the multichannel correlator :
P.e. : priority encoder, t.d : time digitizer, p.d.l. : programmed delay line,
M. : 32 K x 16 bit memory.

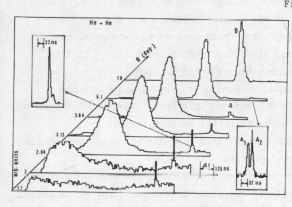

Fig. 2 : Typical spectra at E=1 keV and various scattering angles for coïncidence between scattered particle and :

A) U.V. photon emited after the following reactions :

$He(1s^2)+He(1s^2) \rightarrow$
$He(1s^2)+He(2^1P)$ A_1
$He(2^1P)+He(2^1P)$ A_2

B) Recoil metastable particles comming from the reactions :

$He(1s^2)+He(1s^2) \rightarrow$
$He(1s^2)+He(2^1S)$
$He(2^{3,1}S) + He(2^{3,1}S)$

the increasing width of the B peak is due to the thermal motion of the target.

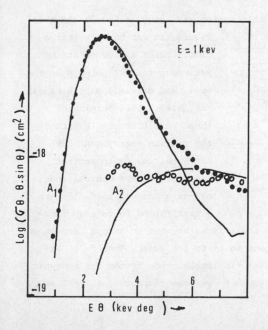

Fig. 3 : Differential cross sections for reaction A_1 and A_2 above.

•••, ∘∘∘ experiment
——— theory (3)

COMPUTATIONAL ANALYSES OF MINIATURE CYLINDRICAL ANALYZER SUITABLE FOR
ANGULAR DISTRIBUTION MEASUREMENTS OF POSITIVE OR NEGATIVE CHARGED PARTICLES

Masatoshi Tate*, Isao H. Suzuki and Kogoro Maeda

*Nihon Software Kaihatsu Inc., Ginza, Tokyo, JAPAN
Electrotechnical Laboratory, Tanashi, Tokyo, JAPAN

As is well known, the angular distribution measurements of elastically or
inelastically scattered charged particles are useful and important as well as the
energy distribution measurements in the collision experiments. In spite of this
situation, almost no appropriate analyzer has appeared or published yet for this
purpose. Some research workers turn the conventional types of hemispherical or
parallel plate analyzers and sometimes they had to pay some extra efforts to keep
the exact geometry of the electrode configurations, and construct a large vacuum
housing for the rotation of the analyzer. At least from the stand points of
design and construction, and further of the present purpose, the so-called non-
dispersive type is somewhat more appropriate. This type of the analyzer, however,
has only poor resolution generally, and almost no spacial resolution. If this
type has a good energy and spacial resolution, it would be much better for the
present purpose. We, therefore, intended to examine a very simple electrode
system, an analyzer composed of a cylinder and two aperture plates at the two ends
of the cylinder. The end plates are grounded to the earth potential and a
negative or positive voltage is applied to the inner cylinder to retard the incoming charged particles through the first aperture.

    In order to examine the system to be suitable or not for the present purpose,
the potential distribution of this cylinder electrode system was first calculated,
according to the most usual procedures.

    The obtained equipotential lines in this system are shown in Fig.1. In this

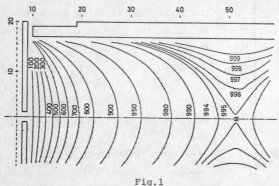

figure, it can be seen that a
saddle point is formed at the
maximum potential point M on the
axis, and off-axis particles can
not pass if the energies of
these particles are less than
the maximum energy. At the
entrance, the equipotential
lines are always convex, and
off-axis charged particles are
always forced to go away from

Fig.1

the axis. Furthermore, the curvatures of these lines are not so strong, and these
particles would have less experience to back again to the axis. Therefore, it
would be possible to expect that the present simple electrode system has somewhat
good space resolving character. To confirm this, we have to proceed to next step,

the trajectory calculations in this field over many charged particles having various energies and starting positions.

In the present study, basically the method proposed by Hechtel was used in which the so-called normalized time step is used to prevent the partices from divergence of velocity and obtain the reasonable results of the trajectories[1].

According to the procedures, the extensive computations were made over many, many electrode configurations and applied voltages.

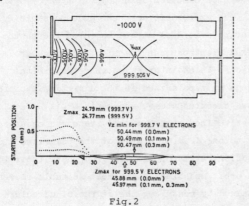

Fig.2

Only one example of the results, however, is shown in Fig.2 to show how the present electrode system has good spacial and energy resolution in spite of it simple geometry. Total length of the system was 10 cm and inner diameter was 2.2 cm. The maximum potential on the axis was 999.505 V. With this small dimension, two particles having 999.5 eV and 999.7 eV can be separated as shown in lower part of the figure, but the two particles starting at 0.5 mm both cannot pass the field, being forced to get back again. This means the present electrode system has some spacial resolution.

On this basis of the results, some other calculations were made for the case of more practical geometries, as shown in Fig.3. For this configuration, double precision calculations were made over 15 particles from 0.0 ~ 0.5 mm at 10 Voltages from 999.95 V to 1000.05 V. It could be seen that the particles having 999.99 eV and exactly 1000.00 eV can be separated. This means that the present system has a good energy resolution about $10^{-4} \sim 10^{-5}$ in spite of its small dimensions, and is very advantageous for the angular distribution measurements, although still many things to be tested remain. With this simple system, we would be able to measure directly the energy distribution as well as the spacial angular distribution, without any kind of retardation that is now practically used

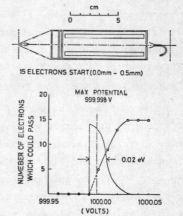

Fig.3

in every kind of analyzer, especially in the X-ray photoelectron spectroscopy.

Some other caluclations are now in progress for the influence of magnetic fields on the performance of the present miniature analyzer.

1. J.R. Hechtel, Trans. Inst. Radio Engrs. ED-9, 62 (1962).

OPTICAL MEASUREMENT OF ELECTRON SPIN POLARIZATION
AND DEVELOPMENT OF THE ACTIVATED GALLIUM ARSENIDE SOURCE

M. EMINYAN and G. LAMPEL

Laboratoire de Physique de la Matière Condensée,
Ecole Polytechnique, 91128 Palaiseau, France

We report here the first measurement of electron spin polarization by optical means [1,2] in a crossed beam experiment. The experiment has been made possible by the development of a very intense source of polarized electrons based on the photo-emission of activated GaAs. [3,4] Polarized electrons can transfer spin angular momentum to atoms by inelastic collisions. In an interaction where no orbital momentum is transfered, the atoms become spin polarized in the direction Z of the spin of the incident electrons. For two electron atoms, when spin orbit effect can be neglected, the excitation of a ^3S state from the ^1S ground state can occur only by <u>exchange</u>. The light from the decay to the $^3P_{0,1,2}$ states of the polarized atoms is circularly polarized in the Z direction. Atoms of the IIB group have their lower $^3P_{0,1,2}$ states well separated by spin orbit and Zinc is the most suitable element. The electron polarization is then obtained by measuring the degree of circular polarization $\mathscr{P}$ of the light ($I_{\sigma\pm}$) propagating along the Z direction. For the most intense line $5s\ ^3S_1 - 4p\ ^3P_2$ ($\lambda = 481.19$ nm) :

$$P_e = -\ \kappa\ \frac{\mathscr{P}}{2} \qquad (1) \qquad \text{with} \qquad \mathscr{P} = \frac{I_+ - I_-}{I_+ + I_-} \qquad (2)$$

and κ a numerical factor very close to unity. The light polarization $\mathscr{P}$ should be constant and P_e given by (1) as long as the $5s\ ^3S$ state is populated only by electron impact. The optical method renders results sensitive to depolarization due to cascades from higher excited states thus reducing $\mathscr{P}$ at high energies. For Zinc atoms the $5s\ ^3S$ threshold is at 6.65 eV and the first levels able to cascade are about 1 eV above.

The most important part of the experiment is the polarized electron source. It is a p-doped GaAs sample activated to negative electron affinity (N.E.A.) and kept under ultra high vacuum. The sample at room temperature is irradiated with circularly polarized light at an energy h =1.55 eV slightly higher than the band gap E_g=1.40 eV. The spin polarized electrons created in the conduction band can escape into vacuum because of N.E.A. The spin polarization can be easily modulated by rotating the quarter wave plate of the circular polarizer. GaAs photocathodes have a different behaviour than ordinary cathodes : Exposure to residual gas may alter the activated surface. This "aging" of the surface reduces the N.E.A. and consequently the kinetic energy of the electron beam is slightly decreased. For each run the correct electron kinetic energy was established by the onset of light emission from the $5s\ ^3S - 4p\ ^3P_2$ transition.

Figure 1 shows the experimental setup which includes the preparation chamber, electron optics lenses, the collision chamber with the Zinc oven and the optics for analyzing the emitted light.

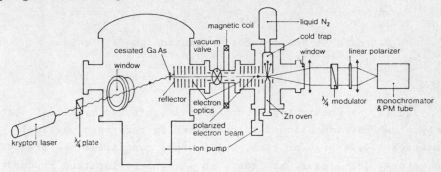

Fig. 1 : Schematic diagram of the apparatus (not to scale).

The electron polarization given by (1) from the light circular polarization measurements is presented in Fig. 2. At high energy, light depolarization due to cascades alters significantly the measurements of P_e which remains valid only in a range of ~ 1 eV above threshold. Experimental points below the apparent threshold may be due to electrons leaving the GaAs sample with kinetic energy and a larger polarization.

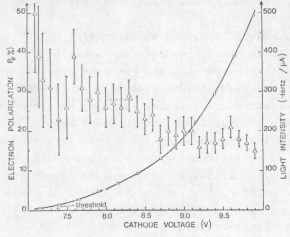

Fig. 2 : Electron polarization measured by the optical method and plot of the radiation intensity versus the cathode voltage.

Although the GaAs source needs ultra high vacuum techniques it gives a very intense beam of polarized electrons (typically 4 µA at 8 eV with $P_e = 28 \pm 5\%$ at room temperature). Optical measurement of spin polarization is less sensitive than the Mott detection, however in the optical method, electron polarization is deduced by the angular momentum properties of the atoms involved, thus it does not require any calibration. It is also independent of the spin direction and is well adapted to low energy electrons.

1. J.S. Wykes, J. Phys. B Atom. Molec. Phys. 4 L 91 (1971)
2. P.S. Farago and J.S. Wykes, J. Phys. B Atom. Molec. Phys. 2, 747 (1969).
3. G. Lampel and C. Weisbuch, Solid State Commun. 16, 877 (1975).
4. D.T. Pierce and F. Meier, Phys. Rev. B 13, 5484 (1976).

USE OF A MICROPROCESSOR IN SCATTERING EXPERIMENTS

Gérard Joyez

Groupe de Spectroscopie Electronique et Ionique
L.P.O.C., Tour 12, E.5, 4,Place Jussieu
Université Pierre et Marie Curie
75230 Paris-Cédex 05 - France

Usually, a scattering experiment is monitored by a multichannel analyser whose each channel is dedicated to a certain physical quantity, i.e. energy or time, while other quantities are treated as parameters. This leads, at least, to several calibration procedures in which errors are accumulated. Also, when scanning an energy range, it is rather a tedious task to run an experiment otherwise than with a constant energy step and constant dwell time. For instance, to get a line spectrum most of the time is wasted accumulating data in uninteresting zones.

By using a microprocessor, it is possible to program all the variations of these parameters, improving the accuracy of the cali-bration because it is done once and for all, and this considerably reduces the time of data storage.

A Z-80 microprocessor, mounted on a SDB 80 board from MOSTEK with 16 K bytes of Random Access Memory has been connected to a conventionnal electron impact spectrometer, and has made possible an excitation threshold study, reported elsewhere at this conference.

This equipment provides all the facilities for easy programming, including Text Editor, Assembler, Relocating boarder and Debug facilities. It has also many interfaces which allow real time experi-ments, such as three modes of maskable interrupt with impending hierarchy, counter timer, 8 bits peripheral ports and an asynchronous serial receiver transmitter which allows communications with a tele-type or a display terminal. In addition, programs and data can be saved on a minifloppy disk(LEANORD PICODISC).

Four digital-to-analog converters have been added to monitor the experiment. Computationnal facilities are possible to do data treat-ment such as smoothing, extrapolation, Fourier's transformation, etc..

As an exemple Figure 1 shows the energy scanning which was the first use of this equipment.

In conclusion, for a low cost, less than a cheap multichannel analyser, and a man year of work, it is possible to develop a very powerful and versatile data handling system, which can be used by adding some evolved language such as BASIC, as a table minicomputer.

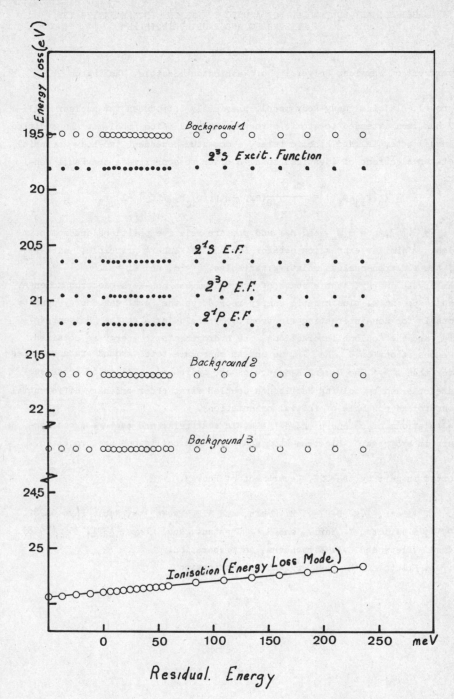

Residual. Energy

A CLASSICAL MANY-BODY MODEL FOR ATOMIC COLLISIONS INCORPORATING THE HEISENBERG AND PAULI PRINCIPLES*

Lawrence Wilets

Department of Physics, University of Washington, Seattle, Washington 98195

A novel, classical many-body model, previously introduced for nuclear collisions,[1] has been extended to atomic structure and collision problems. In addition to the usual potential and kinetic terms, a momentum-dependent two-body potential acts between electrons of identical spin in order to approximate the Pauli constraint:[1]

$$V_p(r_{ij}, p_{ij}) = \frac{\hbar^2 \xi_p}{10 \mu r_{ij}^2} \exp\{-2.5[(p_{ij} r_{ij}/\hbar\xi_p)^4 - 1]\} \quad ,$$

where[2] $\xi_p = 2.767$, $\mu = \frac{1}{2} m_e$, and r_{ij} and p_{ij} are relative positions and momentum variables. A similar expression obtains for the Heisenberg principle,[2] with r_{ij} and p_{ij} the electron-nucleus relative variables, $\mu \simeq m$, and $\xi_H = 1$.

The lowest energy, static state of the system has non-zero electron momenta. The "Pauli" potential plus kinetic energy reproduces the Fermi gas energy-density relationship for non-interacting electrons. By including also the "Heisenberg" potential and the Coulomb interactions, the hydrogen atomic energy is obtained. Static calculations on H^-, He, Li, Ne and Ar reproduce total ground state energies to better than 10%. The H_2^- and H_2 molecules are overbound. Collision cross sections are obtained by solving Hamilton's coupled first order ordinary differential equations for an ensemble of initial orientations.

Calculations of μ^- and p on Ne inelastic scattering and capture cross sections are in progress.[3] Electron-atom and atom-atom collisions are projected.

*Supported in part by the U.S. Department of Energy.

1. L. Wilets, E.M. Henley, M. Kraft, and A.D. MacKellar, Nucl. Phys. A282, 341 (1977); L. Wilets, Y. Yariv, and R.P. Chestnut, Nucl. Phys. A301, 359 (1978).

2. L. Wilets and C.L. Kirschbaum, in preparation.

3. L. Wilets and M. Basu, private communication.

DETERMINATION OF THE POTENTIAL FROM EXPERIMENTAL DATA
ON ENERGIES AND WIDTHS OF QUASISTATIONARY LEVELS

Nanny Fröman and Per Olof Fröman

Institute of Theoretical Physics, University of Uppsala,
Thunbergsvägen 3, S-752 38 Uppsala, Sweden

The problem concerning the decay of a quasi-stationary state for a quantal particle moving in a spherically symmetric potential has recently been
treated by G. Drukarev, N. Fröman and P.O. Fröman.[1] Using, in the first-order
approximation, the phase-integral method developed by N. Fröman and P.O. Fröman,[2-7] these authors treated in detail the case when the angular momentum quantum number l is equal to zero, and they indicated the generalization to the
case when l may be different from zero and when phase-integral approximations
of arbitrary order may be used. Formulas for the energies and widths of the
quasi-stationary levels, valid also close to the top of the potential barrier,
were given.

In the present paper the inversion problem is treated on the basis of the
formulas given in ref. 1. The potential is explicitly expressed in terms of experimental data on the energies and widths of the quasi-stationary states. The
treatment is closely related to a previous treatment by Wheeler,[8] which, in
turn, is closely related to the Rydberg-Klein-Rees method.

1.   G. Drukarev, N. Fröman and P.O. Fröman, J. Phys. A12, 171-186 (1979).

2.   N. Fröman and P.O. Fröman, 1965, JWKB-Approximation, Contributions to
     the Theory. North-Holland Publishing Company, Amsterdam, 1965.

3.   N. Fröman, Ark. Fys 32, 541-548 (1966).

4.   N. Fröman, Ann. Phys. (N.Y.) 61, 451-464 (1970).

5.   N. Fröman and P.O. Fröman, Nucl. Phys. A147, 606-626 (1970).

6.   N. Fröman and P.O. Fröman, Ann. Phys. (N.Y.) 83, 103-107 (1974).

7.   N. Fröman and P.O. Fröman, Nuovo Cimento 20B, 121-132 (1974).

8.   J.A. Wheeler, published as a chapter (pp. 351-422) in Lieb, E.H.,
     Simon, B., and Wightman, A.S., eds., Studies in Mathematical Physics:
     Essays in Honor of Valentine Bargmann, Princeton University Press
     1976.

PHASE-INTEGRAL CALCULATION OF QUANTAL MATRIX ELEMENTS BETWEEN UNBOUND STATES,
WITHOUT THE USE OF WAVE FUNCTIONS*

N. Fröman, P.O. Fröman and F. Karlsson

Institute of Theoretical Physics, University of Uppsala,
Thunbergsvägen 3, S-752 38 Uppsala, Sweden

Starting from a radial Schrödinger equation, we consider the case that the
effective potential, i.e. the potential with the centrifugal barrier included,
is real and that there exists only one generalized classical turning point. On
the basis of a phase-integral method developed by N. Fröman and P.O. Fröman we
derive a general formula for the calculation of quantal matrix elements between
unbound states without the use of wave functions. Our treatment is also based on
a general phase-integral formula for matrix elements between bound states published by N. Fröman and P.O. Fröman.[1] For details on the phase-integral method
used, see ref. 1 and references given therein. For phase-integral approximations
of order $2N+1$ the resulting formula is

$$\langle 1,k|f(r)|1',k'\rangle = \frac{1}{4} (k\,k')^{\frac{1}{2}} \int_{\Gamma} f(r) \frac{\exp\{i\,[w_{1,k}(r) - w_{1',k'}(r)]\}}{q^{\frac{1}{2}}_{1,k}(r)\,q^{\frac{1}{2}}_{1',k'}(r)} \, dr$$

where

$$q_{1,k}(r) = Q_{mod}(r) \sum_{n=0}^{N} Y_{2n}$$

and

$$w_{1,k}(r) = \frac{1}{2} \int_{\Gamma(r)} q_{1,k}(r) \, dr \, .$$

The functions Y_{2n} are terms in an asymptotic series, and the integration contours Γ and $\Gamma(r)$ are non-closed loops encircling in the generalized classical turning points r_0 and r_0' as shown in Fig. 1.

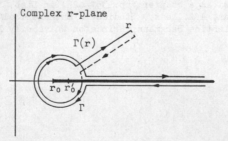

Complex r-plane

Fig. 1.
The integration contours
Γ and $\Gamma(r)$. The generalized classical turn-
ing points are r_0 and
r_0' .

While conventional methods present difficulties when the wave functions
oscillate rapidly in space, this phase-integral formula, in which the wave func-

*To appear in Molecular Physics

tions do not appear, is more accurate the more rapidly oscillating the wave functions are. The formula is tested numerically for a Lennard-Jones (12,6) potential, describing the interaction between two colliding ^{129}Xe atoms (Cf refs. 2 and 3), and is found to yield extremely accurate results. The accuracy of the formula is judged by means of certain generalized Wronskian relations. Some of the relations involve asymptotic scattering phase shifts, which are also calculated by means of a phase-integral formula.

When specialized to the first-order approximation, our formula goes over into a formula derived previously by other authors (see, e.g., eq. (13) in ref. 4). They derived the formula by introducing the first-order JWKB approximation for the wave functions in the integral defining the matrix element and simplifying the resulting expression by using simple qualitative arguments. The remarkably good accuracy of this first-order formula has puzzled previous authors. So has also the fact that attempts to improve it, by including quantities neglected on the basis of the previously mentioned simple qualitative arguments, and by using Airy functions or uniform approximations for the wave functions through the turning points, have failed. Our derivation throws light on the question of the accuracy to be expected, and it explains why already the first-order formula is remarkably accurate and why no improvement is gained in the above-mentioned attempts to improve it.

1. N. Fröman and P.O. Fröman, J. Math. Phys. <u>18</u>, 903-906 (1977).
2. B. Shizgal, Chem. Phys. Lett. <u>24</u>, 369-372 (1974).
3. A.S. Dickinson and B. Shizgal, Mol. Phys. <u>30</u>, 1221-1228 (1975).
4. R.T. Pack and J.S. Dahler, J. Chem. Phys. <u>50</u>, 2397-2403 (1969).

SETTLING THE QUESTION OF THE HIGH-ENERGY BEHAVIOUR OF PHASE SHIFTS
PRODUCED BY REPULSIVE, STRONGLY SINGULAR, INVERSE-POWER POTENTIALS*

Nanny Fröman and Karl-Erik Thylwe

Institute of Theoretical Physics, University of Uppsala,
Thunbergsvägen 3, S-752 38 Uppsala, Sweden

The high-energy limit of the non-relativistic scattering phase shift produced by strongly singular potentials has been studied analytically by several
authors. For a general review, the reader is referred to the extensive article
by Frank et al. .[1] While there is agreement as to the form of the energy dependence of the leading term, the expressions for the coefficient of this term, obtained by different methods, do not agree, though they give similar numerical
values (see Table I in ref. 1). Thus, for pure inverse-power potentials, i.e.,
for $V(r)$, in units of $\hbar^2/(2m)$, given by

$$V(r) = g^2 r^{-n} , \qquad n > 2 , \tag{1}$$

where g^2 is a coupling constant, various authors[2-5] agree that

$$\delta_l(k) \underset{k \to \infty}{\sim} - A_{n,0} \chi , \tag{2}$$

where

$$\chi = k \left(g^2/k^2\right)^{1/n} = g^{2/n} k^{(n-2)/n} \to \infty , \quad \text{when } k \to \infty , \tag{3}$$

but for the constant $A_{n,0}$ the following differing expressions are given,

$$A_{n,0} = \frac{2^{1-2/n} \pi/n}{\sin(\pi/n) \ \Gamma(3-2/n)} . \qquad \text{Calogero,}[2] \tag{4}$$

$$A_{n,0} = \frac{\sqrt{\pi}}{2} \frac{\Gamma(1-1/n)}{\Gamma(3/2-1/n)} , \qquad \begin{array}{l}\text{Bertocchi et al.}[3]\\ \text{Paliov and Rosendorff,}[4]\end{array} \tag{5}$$

$$A_{n,0} = \frac{1 - 1/(2n)}{1 - 1/n} , \qquad \text{Jabbur.}[5] \tag{6}$$

Calogero obtained his result by a variable-phase calculation, Bertocchi et al.
as well as Paliov and Rosendorff used the JWKB-method, and Jabbur worked with
Volterra integral equations, matching solutions valid for small and large r
at the classical turning point. In a more recent work, suggested by Calogero,
Dolinszky[6] has numerically investigated the problem for a potential proportional
to $1/r^4$. His results support, for that particular potential, the asymptotic
exactness of the result (5) obtained by means of the JWKB-approximation. However, a decisive and general proof, valid for all $n > 2$, is lacking hitherto.

    In a recently completed work we have rigorously shown that the JWKB-expres-
sion for the phase shift, produced by the class of potentials (1), tends to ex-

*To appear in J. Math. Phys. Aug. or Sept. 1979

actness in the high-energy limit. Our proof is based on the theory for mastering connection problems developed in ref. 7. We use an exact formula for the phase shift derived in ref. 7, which is shown to apply to the case of strongly singular potentials. Thus we have

$$\delta_l(k) = [\delta_l(k)]_{JWKB} - \arg F_{11}(+0,+\infty) . \tag{7}$$

This exact formula gives the phase shift as the JWKB-expression minus the correction term $\arg F_{11}(+0,+\infty)$, where $F_{11}(+0,+\infty)$ is defined by a convergent series for which an upper bound is obtainable. We show, by rigorous estimates, that the correction term tends to zero at least as fast as χ^{-1} (see eq. (3)), when the energy tends to infinity. The correct high-energy expansion yielded by the JWKB-approximation thus reads:

$$\delta_l(k) \underset{k \to \infty}{=} - A_{n,0} \chi + (1+\tfrac{1}{2})\pi/2 + O(\chi^{-1}) , \tag{8}$$

where $A_{n,0}$ and χ are given by (5) and (3), respectively. According to our analysis, also the constant term $(1+\tfrac{1}{2})\pi/2$ in (8) is significant.

Our treatment can easily be generalized to apply to a class of inverse--power potentials with an energy dependent coupling constant. In fact, if we replace g^2 in (1) by $g^2 = g'^2 k^\alpha$, where $-(n-2) < \alpha \le 2 < n$, the expansion (8), with χ replaced by $\chi' = k (g'^2/k^{2-\alpha})^{1/n}$, still applies also for the class of energy dependent potentials in question.

1. W.M. Frank, D.J. Land and R.M. Spector, Rev. Mod. Phys. 43, 36 (1971).

2. F. Calogero, Phys. Rev. B135, 693 (1964).

3. L. Bertocchi, S. Fubini and G. Furlan, Nuovo Cimento 35, 633 (1965).

4. A. Paliov and S. Rosendorff, J. Math. Phys. 8, 1829 (1967).

5. R.J. Jabbur, Phys. Rev. B138, 1525 (1965).

6. T. Dolinszky, Nuovo Cimento 22A, 578 (1974).

7. N. Fröman and P.O. Fröman, JWKB-Approximation, Contributions to the Theory, North-Holland Publishing Company, Amsterdam 1965.
   Russian translation: MIR, Moscow 1967.

BOUNDS ON MEAN EXCITATION ENERGIES IN TERMS OF OSCILLATOR-STRENGTH MOMENTS

Isao Shimamura

Institute of Space and Aeronautical Science
University of Tokyo, Tokyo 153, Japan

and

Mitio Inokuti[*]
Argonne National Laboratory, Argonne, Illinois 60439, USA

Consider the moment of the μth order

$$S(\mu) = \int (df/dE)\, E^{\mu} dE \tag{1}$$

of the oscillator-strength density df/dE as a function of the excitation energy E of any atom or molecule. The integral is taken over all continua and also includes the summation over discrete spectra. Further, we define

$$L(\mu) = dS(\mu)/d\mu = \int (df/dE)\, E^{\mu} \ln E\, dE \ , \tag{2}$$

and the mean excitation energy with weight $(df/dE)E^{\mu}$ by

$$\ln I(\mu) = L(\mu)/S(\mu) \ . \tag{3}$$

The quantities $I(\mu)$ or $L(\mu)$ are crucial to many properties of the atom or molecule,[1] e.g., the total inelastic-scattering cross section ($\mu = -1$), the stopping power ($\mu = 0$), and the straggling ($\mu = 1$), all for fast charged particles; and the Lamb shift of energy levels ($\mu = 2$).

Precise calculation of $L(\mu)$ is straightforward if df/dE is completely known over the entire spectrum. Unfortunately, this is rarely the case. In contrast, $S(\mu)$ values for $\mu = 2, 1, 0, -1, -2, -4, \cdots$ are either calculable as ground-state expectation values by virtue of sum rules,[1] or are often deducible from experiments. Therefore, it is useful to relate[2-5] $L(\mu)$ with $S(\mu)$ and thereby to estimate $L(\mu)$ without recourse to the full knowledge of df/dE.

It is the purpose of the present paper to make two major points that will be useful in many applications: 1. the meaning of a set of elementary inequalities that bound $L(\mu)$ from above and below, and 2. variational bounds that are tighter and yet are nearly as easy to apply as the elementary inequalities.

It is easy to show that $d^2 \ln S(\mu)/d\mu^2 \geq 0$ for any atom or molecule initially in the ground state. Thus, the curve showing $\ln S(\mu)$ against μ is always concave upwards, as exemplified in Fig. 1 based on data of Zeiss et al.[6] As an elementary consequence, one sees that

$$\ln [S(\mu)/S(\mu-1)] \leq L(\mu)/S(\mu) \leq \ln [S(\mu+1)/S(\mu)] \ . \tag{4}$$

The inequalities give a tight set of bounds on $I(\mu)$ when the curvature of the

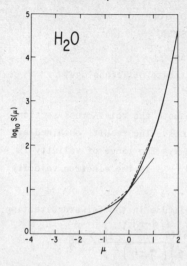

FIG. 1. The quantity $\log S(\mu) = 0.434 \ln S(\mu)$ for H_2O. The thin straight line is the tangent of the curve at $\mu = 0$, giving $I(0)$. The broken straight lines are chords passing the point $0, 1$; clearly the slopes of the chords bound the slope of the tangent—the meaning of relation (4). The Rydberg unit, 13.605 eV, is used in the definition of the $S(\mu)$ values used here.

$\ln S(\mu) - \mu$ curve is small.

Most often one knows the oscillator strength f_n and the excitation energies E_n for several lower excitations $n = 1, 2, \cdots, N$. This knowledge is useful for sharpening the bounds. To this end we have developed a variational method,[7] in which trial functions are so chosen that the resulting bounds on $I(\mu)$ are calculable from several $S(\mu)$ and (f_n, E_n) for $n = 1, 2, \cdots, N$.

The evaluation of the bounds involves matrix algebra including diagonalization. We have also established relations of the variational method to the construction of discrete pseudo-spectra.

*Work performed under the auspices of the U.S. Department of Energy.

1. M. Inokuti, Rev. Mod. Phys. 43, 297 (1971). Section 3.3.

2. C. L. Pekeris, Phys. Rev. 115, 1216 (1959).

3. A. Dalgarno, Proc. Phys. Soc., London 76, 422 (1960).

4. R. P. Futrelle and D. A. McQuarrie, J. Phys. B 2, 640 (1969).

5. P. W. Langhoff and A. C. Yates, J. Phys. B 5, 1071 (1972).

6. G. D. Zeiss, W. J. Meath, J.C.F. MacDonald, and D. J. Dawson, Radiat. Res. 63, 64 (1975).

7. I. Shimamura and T. Watanabe, J. Phys. Soc. Japan 34, 483 (1973).

CALCULATION OF TOTAL CROSS-SECTION AND STOPPING-POWER

FOR PARTICLE-HYDROGEN SCATTERING

S. Rosendorff and A. Birman

Department of Physics, Technion-Israel Institute of Technology,
Haifa, Israel

A new technique has been developed to calculate both the total cross-section and the stopping power for particle-hydrogen collisions. The results obtained are an exact expansion in inverse powers of the momentum k. The range of validity is $v \gg v_0$ where v is the velocity of the particle and v_0 is the electron velocity in the first Bohr orbit.

We start with the second-order elastic Born amplitude in the forward direction

$$f_{ii}^{(2)} = \left(\frac{2Me^2}{\hbar^2}\right)^2 \frac{1}{2\pi^2} \sum_n \int \frac{\langle i|e^{i(\underline{k}-\underline{q})\cdot\underline{r}} - 1|n\rangle \langle n|e^{i(\underline{q}-\underline{k})\cdot\underline{r}} - 1|i\rangle}{(\underline{k}-\underline{q})^2 \left(q^2 - k_n^2 - i\varepsilon\right)\left(\underline{q}-\underline{k}\right)^2} d\underline{q} \tag{1}$$

We put

$$k_n^2 = p^2 - 2ME_n \tag{2}$$

where

$$p^2 = k^2 - 2M|E_0| \tag{3}$$

M being the mass of the particle and $|E_0|$ the ionization energy of the atom. p is thus the momentum of the outgoing particle when the energy of the atom is raised by one Ry. The propagator is now expanded in powers of $(2 M E_n)$, thus the imaginary part of the amplitude becomes

$$\mathcal{I}m\, f_{ii}^{(2)} = \left(\frac{Me^2}{\hbar^2}\right)^2 \frac{1}{\pi} \sum_{j,n} \frac{1}{j!} \left(\frac{\partial}{\partial p^2}\right)^j P \int \frac{d\Omega_p}{(\underline{k}-\underline{p})^4}$$

$$\cdot \langle i|e^{i(\underline{k}-\underline{p})\cdot\underline{r}} - 1|n\rangle (-2ME_n)^j \langle n|e^{i(\underline{p}-\underline{k})\cdot\underline{r}} - 1|i\rangle \tag{4}$$

The leading terms in energy are now easily projected out and the evaluation of the summations over j and n is straightforward. Making use of the optical theorem the Bethe-Born formula of Kim and Inokuti[1] for the total cross-section is obtained. Additional terms of order k^{-6} and higher can easily be evaluated. The calculation of the contribution of the third-order Born amplitude $f_{ii}^{(3)}$ to the total cross-section by the same technique is now in progress. Its leading term is of order k^{-4}, the same as the last term of the Kim-Inokuti expression. The fourth-order Born amplitude $f_{ii}^{(4)}$ also contributes to the same term. It is easily calculated by making use of the analytic expression[2] of the Glauber amplitude.

The evaluation of the stopping power from $f_{ii}^{(2)}$ has been made along similar lines. The calculation of the contribution of $f_{ii}^{(3)}$ and $f_{ii}^{(4)}$ to it is also now in progress.

1. Y.K. Kim and M. Inokuti, Phys. Rev. A3, 665 (1971).
2. B.K. Thomas and E. Gerjuoy, J. Math. Phys. 12, 1567 (1971).

A VARIATIONAL PRINCIPLE ON THE ENERGY FOR ELECTRON-ATOM SCATTERING

M. Klapisch and E. Gal

Racah Institute of Physics, Hebrew University

Jerusalem, Israel

We show that the total energy of the system: atom and electron in the continuum, satisfies a variational principle, as in the case where all the electrons are bound. This follows from the connection between variational principles and minimization of distances in the Hilbert space of wavefunctions, when these distances are defined in terms of semi-norms, based on semi definite positive operators[1]. The conditions of validity are then found: (i) definition of a norm for continuum wavefunctions--this can be achieved with the wave packet formalism, (ii) orthogonality of the wavefunctions to eigenfunctions of lower energies (including all possible bound states). This is achieved to a good approximation by employing the parametric potential method[2]. We write for an N electron-atom (ion)

$$H = H_0 + H_1 \; ; \; H_0 = \sum_{i=1}^{N+1} -\tfrac{1}{2}\nabla_i^2 + u(r_i) \; ; \; H_1 = \sum_{i=1}^{N=1} -u(r_i) - \frac{Z}{r_i} + \sum_{i<j}^{N+1} \frac{1}{|r_i - r_j|}$$

$u(r) = u(\alpha_1, .., \alpha_n, r)$ is a potential described by an analytic function depending on a set of parameters $(\alpha_1, .., \alpha_n)$ and is the same for all (N+1) electrons. The trial wavefunctions are then constructed from linear combinations of eigenfunctions of H_0, which are all orthogonal. We then look for the minimum of $(\psi|H_0 + H_1|\psi)$ as a function of the parameters $(\alpha_1, .., \alpha_n)$. It is worth noting that there is no pole in this function.

We show in figure 1 numerical results for $He^+ 1sk\ell$, ($\ell = 0, 1, 2$) and $He^+ 2pkp$ for $k^2 = 5$ Rydbergs. These wavefunctions may be used for the calculation of cross sections in a variety of approximations that will be described and compared with standard methods.

[1] S.G. Mikhlin - <u>Numerical performance of variational methods</u> Wolters-Noordhooft, (Holland) 1971.

[2] M. Klapisch, Ph.D. Thesis, Orsay (France) 1969, and Comput. Phys. Comm. <u>2</u>, 239 (1971).

Figure 1: total energy of some states of $He^+ + e^-$ as a function of the potential parameter α. Here $u(\alpha, r) = -\frac{1}{r}[1 + e^{-\alpha r}(1 + \frac{\alpha r}{2})]$

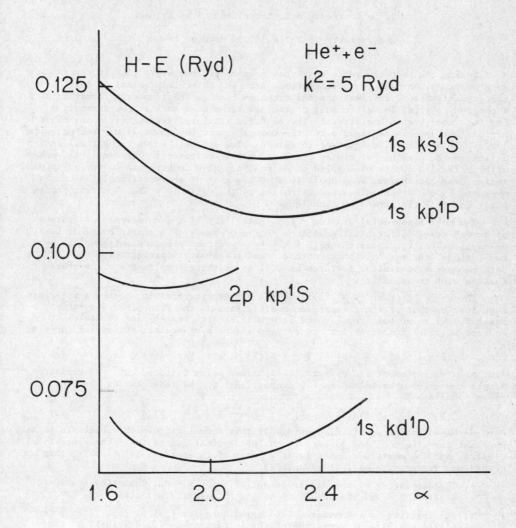

COMPARATIVE MERITS OF NEW METHODS FOR SOLVING LOCAL COUPLED SCATTERING EQUATIONS.
THE VARIABLE PHASE, R-MATRIX PROPAGATOR, GAILITIS EXPANSION METHODS

M. Le Dourneuf, B.I. Schneider and Vo Ky Lan

Observatoire de Paris, 92190 Meudon, France

During the last few years there has been considerable progress in the develop
ment of new techniques to solve electron atom and molecule problems at small distances where strong interactions and exchange lead to the temporary formation of
a compound system. The efficiency of the new techniques such as the R-matrix method
for the inner region has stressed the need for similar developments in the outer
region. Exchange is negligible but the number of coupled channels may become quite
large. The difficulties inherent to this problem are well known ; numerical instability in the presence of closed channels, rapid increases in computational work
with increasing number of coupled equations, and slow convergence to the asymptotic
regime near thresholds. We propose to show how most of these difficulties can be
overcome by one or an adequate combination of the variable phase, R-matrix propagator and Gailitis expansion techniques.

The most fundamental problem – the instability of the numerical integration
of second order differential equations in the presence of strongly coupled, locally
or asymptotically, closed channels – has been overcome almost simultaneously by
two methods, the variable phase method [1] and the R-matrix propagator method [2,3].
Both methods have similar features as well as distinct complementary advantages
that we wish to emphasize.

A)   The variable phase (VPM) replaces the direct determination of the scattering
functions by that of their expansion coefficients on the decoupled asymptotic
basis $\underline{J}, \underline{N}$ of solutions (regular and irregular Ricatti Bessel/Ricatti Hankel or
Coulomb/Whitaker functions for open/closed channels of neutral or ionized targets)

$$\underline{F} = \underline{J}\,\underline{A}(r) - \underline{N}\,\underline{B}(r) = \{\,\underline{J} - \underline{N}\,\underline{K}(r)\,\}\,\underline{A}(r) \quad ; \quad \underline{K}(r) = \underline{B}(r)\,\underline{A}^{-1}(r) \qquad (1)$$

The known variation of the asymptotic solutions being factored out, the variation
of the new unknown becomes directly proportional to the strengths of the long
range couplings $\underline{V}$

$$\underline{K}' = -\,(\underline{J} - \underline{N}\,\underline{K})\,2\underline{V}(\underline{J} - \underline{K}\,\underline{N}) \quad ; \quad \underline{A}' = -\,\underline{N}\,\underline{V}(\underline{J} - \underline{N}\,\underline{K})\,\underline{A} \qquad (2)$$

Beyond the essential specific advantage of this formulation which visualizes point
by point the effect of the potentials on the physical quantities – the generalized
K-matrix and the amplitude A-matrix of a basis of independent solutions –, this
method has important numerical advantages :

1. The decoupling of the equations satisfied by $\underline{K}$ – only quantity needed for
   scattering – and the stability of its outwards integration

2. The rapidity of the numerical integration – for typical long range potentials, the rate of variation of the integrants in (2) are small so that
   large step sizes can be used

3. Part of the numerical work involved (calculation of the $\underline{J}, \underline{N}$ basis)
   increases only linearly with the number of channels.

4. If the wavefunctions are needed for further applications (photodetachment,
   free free transitions...) they are easily calculated and stored (a few
   values of the slowly varying expansion coefficients)

B)   The R-matrix propagator similarly avoids the instability of the numerical
integration by propagating another quantity

$$\underline{R}(r) = \underline{F}(r)\,\underline{F}'^{-1}(r) \qquad (3a)$$

from the left boundary (r_1) to the right one (r_r) of a cell i

$$\underline{R}^i = -\,\{\,\underline{G}^i(r_r|r_r) + \underline{G}^i(r_r|r_1)\left[\underline{R}^{i-1} - \underline{G}^i(r_1|r_1)\right]^{-1}\underline{G}^i(r_1|r_r)\,\} \qquad (3b)$$

Variants of the method are based on alternative techniques to calculate the Green's function G^1 inside each cell.

a) The first variant [2] defines cells sufficiently small to assume the couplings to be constant inside. The potential matrix is diagonalized by a transformation independent of the scattering energy. The remaining energy dependent step is the analytic evaluation of the Green's function in the free particle basis (sin, cos, exp)

b) A extension of this has been recently developed for ionized targets. The effect of the Coulomb potential, strong and rapidly varying, but scalar is incorporated by replacing the free particle Green's function by the Coulomb Green's function in each cell

c) Another variant [3] using a basis set expansion in each cell allows the use of reasonably large cells in the case of strong potentials.

Further developments are necessary to extend the R-matrix propagator to the determination of scattering wavefunctions. When only scattering information ($\underline{K}$ or $\underline{R}$) is needed, the R-matrix propagator has advantages complementary to the VPM :

1. The integration is stable

2. The size of the integration cells is determined by the characteristics of the potentials and is independent of the wave number

3. For strong couplings, variant (c) is probably the most powerful of all the above mentioned techniques

4. Part of the numerical work is independent of energy, making the technique particularly efficient when a large number of scattering energies are required

In both approaches the efficiency can still be increased by reducing the range of the numerical integration. This is particularly important near thresholds or with strongly coupled nearly degenerate channels in which case the asymptotic forms are approached quite slowly. The key idea is to account for the largest part of the diagonal potential using asymptotic expansions in terms of the $\underline{J},\underline{N}$ basis. These expansions lead to recurrence relationships which determine the expansion coefficients. The expansions, first derived formally by Gailitis [4] have been implemented in the program.

Specific numerical examples will be presented at the poster session to illustrate and elaborate on the above discussion.

1. M. Le Dourneuf and Vo Ky Lan, J. Phys. B10,L35 (1977); Proc. CECAM workshop on electron molecule scattering. Meudon (France) 1977; Electron and Photon Molecule Collisions, ed. by Rescigno, McKoy and Schneider (NY. Plenium Press 1979)
2. J.C. Light and R.B. Walker, J. Chem. Phys. 65, 4272 (1976)
3. B.I. Schneider and R.B. Walker, in press J. Chem. Phys. (1979)
4. M. Gailitis, J. Phys. B9, 843 (1976)

CATASTROPHES IN SCATTERING BY SPHEROIDAL POTENTIAL

I.V.Komarov, A.P.Shcherbakov

Leningrad State University, Institute of Physics,

Leningrad, USSR

The peculiarities of quasiclassical scattering amplitude are investigated for potentials

$$V(\xi,\eta) = -\frac{2}{R^2}\frac{a(\xi)+b(\eta)}{\xi^2-\eta^2} \tag{1}$$

(R is intercentre distance) , allowing separation of variables in Schrödingen equation in prolate spheroidal coordinates ξ and η . Those potentials well approximate the interaction between a diatomic molecule and atom or ion.

The partial waves analysis for spheroidal potentials[1] is applied to the quasiclassical evaluation of scattering amplitude and gives

$$f(\vec{n},\vec{n_c}) = \frac{1}{4\pi i K}\int_{\lambda_{min}}^{\infty}d\lambda\int_{-m_{max}}^{m_{max}}dm\,\frac{e^{i\Phi_1(\vec{n},\vec{n_o},\lambda,m)}+e^{i\Phi_2(\vec{n},\vec{n_o},\lambda,m)}}{[(1-\eta^2)p(\eta)(1-\eta_o^2)p(-\eta_o)]^{1/2}} \tag{2}$$

Here $\vec{n_o}$ and $\vec{n}$ are directions of incident and scattered waves with polar angles ($\theta_c=\arccos\eta_c$, φ_o) and ($\theta = \arccos\eta$, φ) respectively; $\Phi_i = S_i - S_c$, where S_o is the free "action function", $S_{1,2}$ are the "action functions" along the trajectories with the same azimuthal quantum number m , but with different impact parameters; λ is the constant of separation in prolate spheroidal coordinates; $p(\eta)$ is the quasi-momentum in angular equation; K is the wave number.

According to catastrophe theory[2,3], the asymptotic behaviour of the integral with fast oscillating integrand such as in Eq.(2) is closely connected with the number and arrangement of the stationary phase points. When two or more stationary phase points coalesce, the Hessian of Φ_i equals to zero

$$H(\Phi_i) = \frac{\partial^2\Phi_i}{\partial\lambda^2}\frac{\partial^2\Phi_i}{\partial m^2} - \left(\frac{\partial^2\Phi_i}{\partial\lambda\,\partial m}\right)^2 = 0 \tag{3}$$

and classical differential cross section become infinite (a rainbow singularity).

The potential of two equal screened charges ($a(\xi) = A\xi e^{-\gamma \xi^2}$, $\ell(\eta) = 0$) the unfolding of singularity provides

$$\Phi_i = \Phi_0 + u x + v y + w(x^2 + y^2) + \frac{x^3}{3} - x y^2 ,$$

where u, v, w are new parameters, depending on the polar scattering angles (α, β), x and y are new integration variables. At the rainbow points (α_r, β_r) one has $u = v = 0, w \neq 0$. Thus according to Thom's classification[3] it is the elliptic umbilic catastrophe. Variation of α and β leads to motion on a surface in the space of parameters u, v, w, crossing caustic at some distance from the elliptic umbilic point. When $\gamma = 0$, one has $u = v = w = 0$ in the rainbow points, and this surface crosses caustic in the elliptic umbilic point.

For scattering by potential of two charges Z_1 and Z_2 of the same sign Eq.(3) can be resolved explicitly in the small angles scattering limit   to give

$$\alpha_r = \frac{2 |Z_1 + Z_2|}{k^2 R \sin \theta_0} , \qquad \beta_r^{(1,2)} = \begin{cases} \psi_r^{(1,2)}, & Z_1 + Z_2 < 0 \\ \pi + \psi_r^{(1,2)}, & Z_1 + Z_2 > 0 \end{cases}$$

where $\psi_r^{(1)} = \arcsin \left((Z_2 - Z_1) / (Z_2 + Z_1) \right)$, $\psi_r^{(2)} = \pi - \psi_r^{(1)}$. The point (α_r, β_r) corresponds to a coalescence of four stationary phase points in Eq.(2). Two points are real and two are imaginary. Variation of α and β corresponds to motion on the surface that crosses caustic for this catastrophe in the single elliptic umbilic point.

1.   D.I.Abramov, I.V.Komarov, Teoret. Matemat.Fiz. 22, 253 (1975);

2.   V.I.Arnol'd, Funkt.Anal.Ego Pril. 6, 61 (1972);

3.   Th.Bröcker, L.Lander. Differentiable Germs and Catastrophes, Cambridge University Press, 1975.

NEW NUMERICAL METHODS IN THREE-BODY SCATTERING PROBLEM.

S.P.Merkuriev and S.A.Pozdneev

Leningrad State University, Leningrad, USSR

The progress in numerical solution of the three-body problem for the case of short-range interaction has been achieved by means of Faddeev equation [1] both in integral and differential forms [2,3].

But the equations obtained in [1-3] cannot be applied directly to the problems with charged particles. In the work [4] the modificated Faddeev equations was proposed obtained by the renormalisation procedure. These equations have a compact kernels below the threshould. The renormalisation procedure developped in [4] was used recently for p-d calculations in the quasi-particle formalism [5].

In the work [6] the modificated Faddeev equations was formulated in configuration space. These equations are proved to be compact below and above the threshold. The equivalent boundary-value problems are obtained for the Coulomb wave functions [6].

In the present contribution the differential formulation of the scattering problem is used for the scattering dates calculations.

Firstly the model of three charged identical particles is considered interecting in s-state only. The phase shifts of elastic scattering and breakup amplitude is calculated. The results are shown in tables 1,2. Such calculations may prove useful for investigation of reactions with charged particles at low energies.

Table 1. Phase shifts for three identical particles

E, Mev	without coulomb deg,interaction	deg, with coulomb interaction
4	−12	−89
10	−34	−38
20	−57	−58

Table 2. Modulus squared of the physical breakup amplitude as a function Θ at $E^{lab} = 14.4$ MeV

Θ, deg	5	10	20	30	40	50	60	70	80
$|A_d(\Theta)|^2$	0.020	0.05	0.13	0.25	0.35	0.45	0.43	0.35	0.20

Our second example is dealing with the $H/^2S/ + H_2/^1\Sigma_g^+/$ exchange and breakup scattering in the three-body model where the interaction potential is given by a sum of pair potentials [7]. The results are presented on the fig. 1,2.

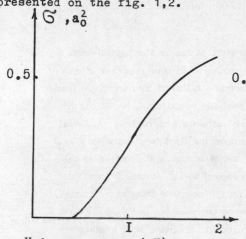

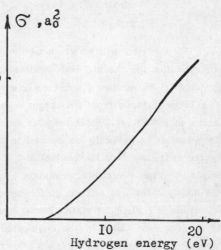

Fig.1. Cross section for
$H + H_2 \rightarrow H + H_2$ reaction
process.

Fig.2. Dissociation cross
section for $H + H_2 \rightarrow H+H+H$
reaction.

R E F E R E N C E S

1. L.D.Faddeev. Trudy Matem. Tn-ta AN SSSR, 69, (1963)
2. R.Tamagaki, Y.Fujiwara. Progr.Theor.Phys. Suppl.,61 , (1977)
3. S.P.Merkuriev, A.Laverne, C.Gignoux.Ann.Phys., 99, 30, (1976)
4. A.M.Vesselova. Teor.Mat.Fiz.,35, 180, (1978), 8, 326, (1970)
5. E.O.Alt, W.Sandhas, H.Ziegelmann. Phys.Rev.Lett.,37, 1537, (1976)
6. S.P.Merkuriev.Yad.Fiz., 24, 289, (1976); Proc. of 1977 Europ. Symp. on few- particle problem., Potsdam, 94, (1977)
7. G.E.Kellerhals, N.Sathyamurthy, L.M.Raff. J.Chem.Phys., 64,818(1976)

THE S-MATRIX STATES IN ELECTRON-ATOM AND ELECTRON-
MOLECULE COLLISIONS

Erling Holøien

Institute of Physics , University of Oslo , NORWAY

A review will be given on the S-matrix states in the partial-wave representation for the two-body scattering problem . In this representation , if the potential in question (spherically symmetric) falls off more rapidly than r^{-2} at large distance from the target , the analyticity and unitarity of the S-matrix have been well established in several textbooks and reviews (1, 2, 3, 4). The S-matrix is generally expressed in terms of the Jost function with a real angular momentum for the projectile . The zeros of the Jost function in the complex k-plane (vanishing S-matrix) correspond to the states . Thus the true bound states are defined by the zeros on the negative imaginary k-axis , the antibound (virtual) states by the zeros on the positive imaginary k-axis , and the resonant states by the conjugated zeros in the upper half k-plane (decaying and capture states) . The zeros in the lower half k-plane are the poles of the S-matrix in the upper half k-plane , or contrary . It is more convenient to define the states as the poles of the S-matrix , i. e. the bound states as poles on the positive imaginary k-axis , the antibound states as poles on the negative imaginary axis , and the resonant states as conjugated poles in the lower half k-plane . Mapped onto the complex energy plane , the upper half k-plane becomes the first Riemann sheet , commonly called the physical sheet , whereas the lower half k-plane becomes the second Riemann sheet , commonly called the unphysical sheet (a terminology being today somewhat misleading) .

A discussion will be given concerning the existence of the different S-matrix states for multi-channel scattering systems such as the electron-atom and the electron-molecule collisions . The situation is not so clear concerning the analytic properties of the multi-channel S-matrix as for the one-channel case , but it is generally believed that the existence of the compound states of the total sytems still are associated with poles of eventual S-matrix elements . It is extremely interesting to examine in very low energy electron-atom scattering the existence of antibound (virtual) states associated with poles lying close to origin on the negative real axis of the second sheet of the complex energy plane. The existence of resonaces originated from compound states of the total system associated with poles lying above the second bisector in the lower half k-plane , or in the right lower half of the second sheet of the complex energy plane with postive real part of the energy , in low energy multi-channel scattering , has been weel established since the 1960's , both theoratically and experimetally .

In the Feshbach projection-oper.ator formalism the resonaces are referred to as which channel they belong , an open or a closed channel (5) . The compound states (Feshbach states) of closed-channel resonances are associated with poles close to the real axis with lifetimes of about 10^{-5}ns . On the other hand , the compund states of open-channel resonances (shape resonances or single particle resonances) are associated with poles fare from the real energy axis , i. e. close to above the second bisector in the lower half k-plane and have much shorter lifetimes . In electron-molecule collisions the existence of resonace compound states are associated with the transient molecular negative ions in general .

The compound states of resonances associated with poles of the S-matrix lying below the second bisector in the lower half k-plane , or in the left lower half of the second sheet of the the complex energy plane with negative real part of the energy , have no clear interpretation and physical meaning in particle collisions so far (1) .

1. P. Roman , Advanced Quantum Theory , Addison-Wesley Publishing Company , Inc. , Reading , Masschusetts , 1965

2. N. F. Mott and H. S. Massey , The Theory of Atomic Collisions , The Clarendon Press , Oxford , 1965

3. S. Geltman , Topics in Atomic Collision Theory , Academic Press , New York and London , 1969

4. J. C. Y. Chen , Theory of Transient Negative Ions of Simple Molecules , Published by John Wiley and Sons , Inc. , 1969

5. H. Feshbach , A Unified Theory of Nuclear Reactions , Annals of Physics 19 , 287-313 , 1962

ON THE DYNAMICAL ORIGIN OF THE QUANTUM DEFECT

Dipankar Chattarji and Partha Ghose*

Department of Physics, Visva-Bharati University
Santiniketan, West Bengal, India

Quantum defect theory (QDT) provides the atomic physicist with a useful tool which relates spectroscopy to scattering phenomena. Using Rydberg units, the quantum defect $\mu_{n,\ell}$ for the atomic state (n, ℓ) is defined by writing the binding energy of the electron in the form

$$\varepsilon_{n,\ell} = -Z^2/(n - \mu_{n,\ell})^2 = -Z^2/\gamma_{n,\ell}^2 \quad , \qquad (1)$$

Z being the nuclear charge. Seaton[1] showed that near the ionization threshold the phase shift δ_ℓ of a continuum state in electron-ion scattering is equal to $\pi\mu_{n,\ell}$ extrapolated as a function of energy. To get this result, one writes the asymptotic value of the atomic wave function in the form

$$\psi(\gamma, r) \sim \exp(Zr/\gamma) \, S^{-1} - \exp(-Zr/\gamma) \quad , \qquad (2)$$

where the scattering operator $S = (T - K)/(T + K)$, $K = \tan \pi\mu$. For $E > 0$, $T = i$ and $S = \exp(2i\delta)$, where $\delta = \pi\mu$. For $E < 0$, we get $T = \tan \pi\gamma$. In this case, $\psi(\gamma, r)$ satisfies the boundary condition for a bound state only if $S^{-1} = 0$, i.e.

$$\left| \tan \pi\gamma + \tan \pi\mu \right| = 0 \quad , \qquad (3)$$

giving $\gamma = n - \mu$, where n is an integer. Essentially, therefore, one is using here the slow variation of μ as a function of energy to make an analytic continuation across the ionization threshold. However, the approach is basically phenomenological and the dynamical origin of the quantum defect is not quite clear.

In the present work, we propose to use Jost function theory to investigate the origin of the quantum defect. The Jost function contains full information about the analyticity properties of the scattering amplitude and the phase shift. For a short-range potential, its zeros correspond to bound states and its phase gives the phase shift experienced by a partial wave of given angular momentum[2]. In a many-electron atom, such a potential, as seen by an electron in a particular state, is generated by the screening of the nuclear Coulomb potential by the other electrons. Thus, for an atomic system, Jost function theory provides us with a custom-made tool for studying the relation between the scattering amplitude and the properties of bound states.

From Thomas-Fermi theory, we know that the short-range potential within a many-electron atom can be represented effectively by a superposition of Yukawa potentials $\int \exp(-\alpha r) \, \rho(\alpha) \, d\alpha$ where α^{-1}, the screening distance, is typically much smaller than the inter-electronic separation[3]. By considering the Jost function for such a potential embedded in a Coulomb background, we shall show that for an electron-ion system, the phase shift δ_ℓ relative to this background is that given by the quantum defect theory.

* Present address: British Council Division, 5 Shakespeare Sarani, Calcutta-700071.

1. M.J. Seaton, Compt. Rend. <u>240</u>, 1317 (1955); Monthly Notices Roy. Astron. Soc. <u>118</u>, 504 (1958).

2. R.G. Newton, <u>Scattering Theory of Waves and Particles</u> (McGraw-Hill, New York 1966).

3. N.F. Mott, Proc. Camb. Phil. Soc. Math. Phys. Sci. <u>32</u>, 281 (1936).

AUTHOR INDEX